The Collected Letters of Charlotte Smith

THE COLLECTED LETTERS OF CHARLOTTE SMITH

Judith Phillips Stanton

Indiana University Press
Bloomington & Indianapolis

Publication of this book is made possible in part with the assistance of a Challenge Grant from the National Endowment for the Humanities, a federal agency that supports research, education, and public programming in the humanities.

This book is a publication of

Indiana University Press
601 North Morton Street
Bloomington, IN 47404-3797 USA

http://iupress.indiana.edu

Telephone orders 800-842-6796
Fax orders 812-855-7931
Orders by e-mail iuporder@indiana.edu

The paper used in this publication meets the minimum requirements of American National Standard for Information Sciences—Permanence of Paper for Printed Library Materials, ANSI Z39.48-1984.

Manufactured in the United States of America

Library of Congress Cataloging-in-Publication Data

Smith, Charlotte Turner, 1749–1806.
[Correspondence.]
The collected letters of Charlotte Smith / [edited by] Judith Phillips Stanton.
p. cm.
Includes bibliographical references (p.) and index.
ISBN 0-253-34012-8 (cloth : alk. paper)
1. Smith, Charlotte Turner, 1749–1806—Correspondence. 2. Authors, English—18th century—Correspondence. I. Stanton, Judith Phillips, date II. Title.
PR3688.S4 Z48 2003
823'.6—dc21

2002007966

1 2 3 4 5 08 07 06 05 04 03

To Albrecht B. Strauss,
a sterling model of the scholarly life
and the kindest mentor

CONTENTS

Acknowledgments

A work of this scope depends on the generosity of many collections and collectors, public and private. For permission to publish the three largest groups of letters, I am particularly grateful to the Beinecke Rare Book and Manuscript Library at Yale University, the Huntington Library and Art Gallery, and the Right Honorable the Lord Egremont, owner of the letters preserved in the Petworth House Archives, West Sussex Record Office, Chichester. Permissions were also graciously extended by the Bodleian Library; the British Library; the Liverpool Libraries and Information Services; the Trustees of the National Library of Scotland; Pierpont Morgan Library; Department of Special Collections, University Research Library, UCLA; the Houghton Library, Harvard University; Princeton University Library; the Charles Roberts Autograph Letters Collection, Haverford College Library; the University of Iowa Libraries (Iowa City, Iowa); and the Archbishop of Westminster, the Westminster Diocesan Archives.

Additional permissions were granted by the Syndics of the Fitzwilliam Museum, by the trustees of the Cowper and Newton Museum, and by courtesy of the Trustees of the Boston Public Library/Rare Books Department. The William Ready Division of Archives and Research Collections, at McMaster University Library, Hamilton, Canada, supplied three letters. Both the Pennsylvania State University Libraries and the Walter H. and Leonore Annenberg Rare Book and Manuscript Library, Van Pelt–Dietrich Library, the University of Pennsylvania, contributed one. Three separate collections within the New York Public Library, named individually at the end of the respective letters, gave permission to publish their holdings by Smith.

Private collectors granting permission to publish their letters were Lucy Magruder; the Duke and Duchess of Devonshire; and the heirs of the late John Robert Geoffrey Comyn for their Collection of Burney Family Papers.

To the many archivists, research librarians, and assistants at each of these facilities whose assistance was quick, expert, and courteous, my heartfelt thanks.

A grant from the National Endowment for the Humanities funded one summer's research in England, and grants from the College of Liberal Arts at Clemson University partially funded two summers' work. The University of Wisconsin at Eau Claire and Clemson provided graduate assistants at early stages.

Indiana University Press signed on to this project early on. I thank Joan Catapano, sponsoring editor, for standing by it as it doubled, and then tripled, in size and for keeping it alive despite cutbacks and budgetary restrictions. Her successors, Michael Lundell, sponsoring editor, and Jane Lyle, managing editor, ably took over the project; they enthusiastically greeted the last-minute discovery of more than 100 additional letters by Charlotte and Benjamin Smith and without protest delayed the publication process so that I could incorporate the new find. Finally, four very early letters found very late were included in an appendix.

Over the years, in a solitary adventure such as this edition, the student becomes a scholar, and the lone traveler not only explores distant byroads but also cements old friendships and discovers new ones. Albrecht Strauss, Isobel Grundy, Betty Rizzo, Ruth Perry, and Paul Korshin encouraged my work on Charlotte Smith and answered questions and gave timely advice. Loraine Fletcher, Diana Bowstead, Edward Copeland and Margaret Mathias, Anthony and Yvonne Hand, Matthew Hand, Rosalyn and Van Hartmann, and Lillyan Smith all helped me stretch grant money by inviting me into their homes when research took me to London, New York, New Haven, and Pasadena.

Ann B. Shteir directed me to Charlotte Smith's letter to James Edward Smith, and Paula Feldman put me in touch with Smith relatives in the United States. Dr. Peter Curtis advised me about Smith's various health complaints. Richard Wenger first pointed me to the Smith letters in the Petworth House Archives and shared not only much pertinent Turner family history from his research into the history of Stoke House but also a wonderful day exploring Petworth House and grounds.

Matthew Bray, Diana Bowstead, Stuart Curran, Henry Fulton, Loraine Fletcher, and Ellen Nugent Harris read the manuscript in part or whole, filling in many gaps and pushing me to fill in others. I am especially grateful to Loraine and Diana for passionate and enlightening conversations about Smith's challenging character and difficult life. Felicia Sturzer and Nora M. Armstrong helped me puzzle over Charlotte Smith's irregular French.

Alison McCann, archivist of the Petworth House Archives at the West Sussex Record Office, discovered the new letters, which brought a wondrous upheaval to a project all but ready for the press. She promptly provided information about key local figures from her own research and the WSRO while Loraine Fletcher proofread my transcription against originals. Alice Falk brought her erudition, keen eye, passion for consistency, and endless patience to both phases of the final copyedit. For hers and everyone's help in making this edition more accurate and illuminating, I am deeply grateful. Errors and oversights that remain are mine.

My largest debt I owe to my husband Peter Harkins. He has lived with and tirelessly moved boxes of copies and stacks of notes and drafts, almost forever, and put up with weeks at home alone caring for cats and horses while I gallivanted all over this country, England, and Canada. Just as important, before personal computers could handle such a large document, he urged me to put the letters onto a mainframe text processing system. He then helped translate files from mainframe to mainframe as I changed universities, and to word processing systems at home. There he saw to it that the project and its editor always had a working computer and a room of their own. I never forgot for a minute how badly Charlotte Smith had needed such a champion. He would have been her hero too.

Introduction to Charlotte Smith's Letters

Charlotte Smith is gaining increasing recognition for her contribution to the novel, sonnet, and children's books in the late eighteenth century. One of her early publishers, Thomas Cadell, Sr., believed that her reputation would rest on her novels. And until very recently, it has done so. Yet late in her life, Smith asserted that "it is on the Poetry I have written that I trust for the little reputation I may hereafter have & know that it is not the least likely among the works of modern Poets to reach another period" (18 Aug. 1805). This has not been the case. Up until recently, with new editions of four of her novels and seven reprinted since 1969, Cadell's prediction has proved more correct. But her poetry is now included in anthologies of women writers, and, at last, her poetry has been collected into a single volume.[1]

Even so, the relative obscurity of her works throughout the nineteenth century and much of the twentieth has been complemented by scant information about her life. A few months after Smith died, William Hayley wrote to John Hawkins, who had purchased the Turner family estate at Bignor Park, that plans were afoot to publish Smith's memoirs and letters:

> The difficulties she had to struggle with, & the spirit with which she surmounted many such Troubles as would have annihilated the Talents of a weaker mind, are hardly credible; & many of these Troubles are more fit perhaps to be sunk in friendly oblivion, than to be blazoned in circumstantial description. Yet, I trust, the bright Qualities of a woman, so singularly admirable, will be justly & delicately recorded by a living Charlotte Smith, the eldest daughter of the deceased, who inherits the excellent understanding of her Mother, & has promised to undertake the arduous Task of commemorating the merits of her literary parent with the pen of filial affection. Her Life and Letters composed & selected by such an Editor, will form, I hope, a publication universally interesting, & beneficial to some desolate branches of her Family.[2]

Perhaps Charlotte Mary's precarious health intervened, or the raw material proved too personal and painful to too many people. Smith may also have contributed to her own neglect as a writer when she had her unpublished material destroyed. For, as Catherine Ann Dorset reported in her sister's biography, "Mrs Smith left no *posthumous* works whatsoever. The sweepings of her closet were, without exception, committed to the flames."[3] This loss of manuscripts and, doubtless, family records and letters has thus obscured a life rich with creativity, endeavor, and achievement, as well as plagued with suffering, poverty, and grief.

The present volume of letters supplies what escaped the flames—nearly all of the almost 500 surviving letters that Smith wrote to publishers, patrons, solicitors, relatives, and friends. These letters shed light on her significance as a literary figure and woman of her time in several ways. First, they provide a detailed record of one woman writer's relations with booksellers, and they thereby shed light on women and patronage in the late eighteenth century. Covering her entire publishing career from 1784 to 1806, they contain letters to all but two of her publishers and details about the publication of all but two of her twenty-two titles. The letters reveal her usual practices in composing, in dealing with publishers, and in exploring with them new ideas for marketable books. The letters also show her relationship with patrons, whether literary, such as William Hayley, or aristocratic, such as the duchess of Devonshire.

Second, the letters provide the history of an extraordinary woman challenged by the need to provide for a large family with little help or support beyond her own wits and perseverance. The letters contain a wealth of substantive new information about Charlotte Smith's miserable failed marriage; her twelve children's lives, marriages, and deaths; her own poor health; and her many changes of residence. They also tell a story of loss, loneliness, and isolation. Often she faced all of this with great courage and resolve; sometimes she complained bitterly about her fate and the men who she believed withheld their true inheritance from her and her family.

For the letters also finally illumine one woman's life in a world of limited rights for women and her children's lives in a world of no rights for children at all. Born the daughter of a gentleman, she was urged into marriage just before turning sixteen, and her fortunes followed those of her husband. He was in debt; she was in debt. He squandered away his father's estate and was sent to jail; she went to jail with him. He fled creditors; she fled with him, children in tow. Even after she began to live apart from him, she was bound to him legally and financially. She devoted her life to settling her father-in-law's will from which her children stood to benefit greatly. It would have provided university educations for her sons and spared them military service; it would also have provided legacies for her daughters that might have attracted more eligible suitors.

But this was not to be. In the legal terminology of her day, she was a *femme covert,* a single legal entity with her husband, her very being subsumed in his. When she wrote volumes of lucrative fiction to provide for their children, those earnings belonged to him. Despite the threat of creditors, he crept back into England once or twice a year from his Scottish hideaway to claim money she had on hand or money her publishers held for her. And she churned out hundreds of letters, tirelessly pursuing a final settlement of her father-in-law's will. Yet time after time, the interim settlements brought about by her initiative were awarded to her husband: even though Benjamin Smith lived in exile to escape creditors, much of the estate's interest belonged to him, not to his wife or to their children whom she labored to support. He took advantage of that fact; she never accepted it, never failed to deride her country's laws and its solicitors.

Charlotte Smith's letters add much to our understanding of her life and work,[4] while at the same time adding hundreds of new facts about her life. Moreover, they raise many questions about her professional life and her character, questions never before raised and not easily answered. These must intrigue and perplex the reader. How, for example, did Smith regard her own works? Was she engaged in her tremendous literary effort only for money, or was there an underlying seriousness about the artistic value of what she wrote? Why did she quarrel with so many different persons—publishers, patrons, relatives, friends; who was at fault? Was she simply difficult, too demanding, too importunate in her attempts to provide for and defend her family? Or did men quarrel with her because she constantly overstepped the boundaries of women's proper place in mastering fine points of business and law, and in trying to force the legal system to award her what it ought, rather than what it had to? And what of her own character? Had she adopted Benjamin Smith's extravagant spending after twenty years of living with him, as Joseph Johnson once hinted (CS to Sarah Rose, Aug. 1805)? Was she the charming woman some described, or was she the woman we sometimes glimpse in the letters, concerned to align herself with persons of rank, obsessed with the inheritance, ever ready to insult the trustees to the estate, sinking into despair or, less acceptably, self-pity over her lot in life? Or given her lot in life—"[c]hained to her desk like a slave to his oars," as William Cowper observed[5]—was she courageous, tenacious, self-sacrificing? Let us look a little more closely at some of the conflicting readings that the letters yield.

CHARLOTTE SMITH AS AN AUTHOR

The Charlotte Smith we meet in the letters is more caught up in the details of the publishing process than in the creative act. We learn how she contracted for work, assessed and responded to the book market, and came up with ideas for new publications. She struggled to meet deadlines, mailing out each finished volume as soon as she had fair copy in order to meet her contractual obligations for advance payments. She was able to persuade most of her publishers to give her advances, and indeed, most kept running accounts for her. Thomas Cadell, Sr., and later Cadell, Jr., and William Davies allowed her to write drafts on these accounts to pay for food, lodging, and expenses for her children. She haggled with various booksellers over copyright, a printer's competence, or the quality of an engraving for an illustration. She would argue that the time was ripe for a second edition of a novel.

Against these ordinary and often irritating details, the letters show the dark side of Smith's publication experience. Early on she wrote to Dr. Shirly that she was unsuited for the life she was forced to live:

> [D]uty rather than inclination has for many years compelled me to live in a way for which I am very ill calculated. It has often been so bitter to me that nothing but my tenderness for the children could have carried me thro it—— (22 Aug. 1789)

This theme continued, sometimes almost self-pityingly, as she complained to Cadell, Jr., and Davies after they refused her a second advance:

> When a person is fallen as I am from quite another rank of life to the necessity of writing for her daily bread, it is fit she should submit to any terms on which it can be earned & be thankful that it is to be had at all. (15 Sept. 1794)

She probably did not exaggerate the difficulty of her work. She suffered from rheumatism from the beginning, complaining as early as 1788 that "I write with extreme difficulty having lost the use of my right hand" (winter–spring 1788). In the winter of 1794, one of her most prolific years, she wrote that "I have kept my bed frequently this winter from having lost the use of my limbs with the Rhumatism, and because a constant pain in my side gave me no respite" (20 Jan. 1794). She thought herself stricken by gout, which ran in her family. Two months later she was "entirely crippled, so as not to be able to walk across the room . . ." (25 Mar. 1794), and decided to go to Bath, which she could ill afford, for the waters. The treatments helped her hands, but not her legs. At least, she went on, she could write.

Her physical miseries must have been exacerbated by endless difficulties with publishers. She demanded that they be gentlemen and then expected gentlemanly treatment from them. At times, she expected them to live up to her exacting standards for her sentimental heroes—young men generous with a crown or guinea, even their last, to one less fortunate. Thomas Cadell, Sr., suited her; she considered it "an advantage to have a connection with a Publisher so highly respected as Mr Cadell's house" (10 Sept. 1794). From 1787 to 1793, he gave her advances, handled her mail in London, and trusted her to fulfill her contracts with him. Her relationship with this firm turned sour when Cadell, Sr., retired and Cadell, Jr., and William Davies took over. They complained that she overdrew the money they held on her account, as indeed she did. Her heavy expenses during her daughter Augusta's dangerous pregnancy and subsequent illness did not move them to special consideration for her. Distressed by this quarrel, she wrote to them:

> [I]f the mistrust of your House is so great that you cannot take my word for what I assert and promise . . . , if you, really, or if Mr Davies understand me so little as to suppose me capable of deceiving you, It is far better that our dealings should cease for ever. (10 Sept. 1794)

She clung to her own sense of herself as a gentlewoman of integrity and to her hope that a publisher who was truly a gentleman would not question that integrity.

Sampson Low, who is mentioned in these letters, became Smith's next publisher-champion after Cadell, Sr., providing advances, handling her mail in London, and fostering new publications. At first reluctant to turn to him because of his shop's undesirable location, she had realized his value to her by the time he died in 1801. Along with favors, he came to her rescue when Joseph Bell, who published *The Old Manor House,* had her arrested—probably because *The Wanderings of Warwick* was late and one volume short.

Publishers other than Bell disappointed her too. Longman, who took over *Letters of a Solitary Wanderer* after Low's death, printed the final three volumes in an edition she found embarrassingly cheap. Joseph Johnson, a gentleman of great integrity who usually was kind to Smith, treated her with "strange neglect mingled with so much bonhommie [*sic*] that I cannot complain" (2 July 1805), but his slowness to respond had to be a drawback to one so in need. Richard Phillips, near bankruptcy himself, embittered the last years of her life: "He now once in three or four months writes to me in a threatening & very rude manner" about adding more to her *History of England . . . to a young lady at school* (2 July 1805). In one of her very last letters, she still struggled to end his harassment: "I trust that, as I solemnly protested from the very beginning against having any thing to do with the reign of the present King . . . , that you will spare me the needless expence of postage at 3^s a week . . ." (29 Apr. 1806). She encountered, in short, as much trouble as aid from her booksellers.

FRIENDSHIPS

For such a prolific and popular writer, Smith was sadly isolated from other writers and literary friends. Befriended by William Hayley at the beginning of her career, Smith depended on him to correct her work, to teach her the ways of the booksellers' world, and to introduce her to other writers. In fact, Hayley arranged for her to meet the like-minded William Cowper on their well-documented visit to Eartham in August 1792. Cowper subsequently read Smith's blank verse poem *The Emigrants* (1794), presumably with a critical eye, before its publication, and she dedicated it to him. Her melancholy work touched him, as his did her. Sadly for her, he soon slipped into madness, far away from the gentlemanly literary friendship he promised and she clearly yearned for. Two letters from about that time, filled with revolutionary sentiment, show a similar hope for a friendship with Joel and Ruth Barlow, soon dashed by their move to France. In contrast, her letters to Dr. Charles Burney about Augusta's marriage to a French émigré, a situation so similar to Fanny Burney's, betray her knowledge of her social limits; she never mentions meeting him, but her letters are filled with due respect and gratitude for his attention.

Unhappily and unaccountably for Smith, Hayley withdrew his support from her in 1794 and corresponded with her infrequently after that. It was the most painful breach with a friend in a life of many breaches, and she refers to her loss of Hayley's friendship dozens of times. As mediocre as his poetry has proved to be, it is worth remembering that he was well enough regarded in their time to have been offered the laureateship upon the death of Thomas Warton. He was liked, respected, influential. Several events probably led him to withdraw from this association. He defended her to Cadell, Sr., after she borrowed £50 while at Brighton to avoid being evicted for back rent.[6] She had no agreement for a work in progress at that moment, and both men felt that she had violated their trust. At the same time, Hayley had just met William Blake and was consumed with this new friendship. As the years went on, Hayley may have been unwilling to realign himself with a woman so bold as to deride the trustees in prefaces to her works—what she called her "public floggings" of the men who withheld her children's inheritance. Finally, a letter of Hayley's to John Hawkins, the purchaser of Bignor Park, suggests a darker reason: marked as "private and confidential," written not long after her death, and signed only "Hermit," Hayley alludes to her questionable mental state.[7]

Only three people provided Smith with genuine and sustained friendships: Henrietta O'Neill, the Reverend Joseph Cooper Walker, and Sarah Rose. No letters to O'Neill survive, but Smith mentions her often in early letters to others. O'Neill, who had married into a great Irish house, provided Smith with a poetic, sympathetic friendship and with literary connections. Smith stayed with O'Neill in London on at least two occasions, and the two women planned trips to the O'Neill family seat in Ireland. "I should be able to get off the thorns for a little while & begin a New Novel at Shanes Castle," Smith wrote to Dr. Shirly (22 Aug. 1789). Much as she needed the distraction, the trips were never realized. The time spent at O'Neill's home in London, however, briefly gave Smith entry into a fashionable, literary world to which she otherwise had little access; here she almost certainly met Dr. Moore (author of *A View of Society and Manners in Italy* and *Zeluco*) and Lady Londonderry, among others. O'Neill died in 1793, within weeks of the time one of Smith's sons was seriously wounded on the Continent. Smith was devastated almost equally by both events:

> To me, who have been too long suffering the bitter blasts of adversity and have of course not many friends to spare, it [her death] is one of the most cruel blows I could sustain. (9 Oct. 1793)

With the Reverend Joseph Cooper Walker, Smith shared her longest and most gratifying correspondence. An antiquarian and writer of Dublin, Walker handled her dealings with John Rice, who published Dublin editions of many of her works. She confided openly in Walker about literary and familial matters, for she felt that he was "one of the few people who seem to be truly interested in my behalf" (20 Jan. 1794). Indeed he invited her confessions about "[d]omestic duties & domestic troubles, of which you shall know more when I write again (because you desire me to do so)" (6 Feb. 1793). The twenty surviving letters to Walker are filled with literary observations, family history, and the business of the trust. From the very first, her letters to him were spontaneous and personal: "I have no other time to write this than what I snatch while my maid is dressing my hair, an operation that I very seldom undergo. Will you forgive my writing so very vilely[?]" In a postscript, written large, she goes on to complain about "the cruelty of my Childrens tyrannical Aristocratic relations," who have contributed to her current lack of money (16 Dec. 1792). And this confiding tone continues in letters ten years later.

From Tunbridge Wells, for example, in 1801, Smith summarized an entire year of calamities in her longest and most gripping letter. She had been completing *Letters of a Solitary Wanderer* against the backdrop of her children's troubles. Lucy, the next youngest daughter, who had married against Smith's wishes, had two children and was at the mercy of her husband, and so she turned to her mother for help. Charles, the injured son, and Charlotte Mary, the eldest daughter, who had been living away, returned home to news that Lionel, now a soldier, had received a perilous assignment. The year before, Harriet, the youngest daughter, had sailed to India with William, the eldest son, in hopes of making a suitable marriage. He wrote that he was shipping her back home. She had contracted malaria, which would only have worsened in that climate, and she might not survive the voyage home. Soon Harriet returned, recovering, and Smith's concern turned to Charles, still in the military, who had set sail for Barbados, like India a climate of deadly diseases. There had been no news of Lionel for months. Suddenly, he returned, just in time to attend to Lucy's dying husband. Now Smith had to provide for not only Harriet but also Lucy with two children and a third on the way. Benjamin Smith, hiding still in Scotland, "positively refuses to let me have even the small share of interest from my fortune which he formerly allow'd me, & because in consequence of my Mother-in-law's death there is more to have, he will let me have none." She explains to Walker that she had not written during this "procession of troubles" because of her fears for Lionel's safety: "hardly daring to look steadily at my fears, I could not bear to put them upon paper——" She goes on to news of Hayley, the death of her publisher Low, Mrs. Piozzi's newest book, Mrs. West, and the Lee sisters. Finally, she asks whether there is "any hope of seeing you in England?" (14 Apr. 1801). Evidently, there was not. It is one of the saddest of Smith's many sadnesses that she never met this friend, whose kind concern gave her much comfort.

Neither did she meet her other most reliable correspondent, Sarah Rose, to whom she wrote twenty-three letters in the last three years of her life. As with the letters to Walker, these are searchingly personal, though often more playful and entertaining. These letters are the best corroboration that Charlotte Smith was a cheerful woman, for any expression of cheerfulness in her last years of grim poverty and failing health was indeed remarkable. Describing her condition, Smith was capable of this humorous self-portrait:

> Nor indeed is it likely I shall now ever be able to do more than vegetate, for my few remaining years or months in this or some other solitude. It is literally vegetating, for I have very little locomotive powers beyond those that appertain to a cauliflower. (5 Mar. 1804)

Or in another mood, thinking about a new work she might undertake, she describes herself as a "good old body of an Authoress" who does not need to "fear being accused of twaddling I trow, if Miss Seward escapes" (18 Apr. 1804). As Sarah Rose continues to respond to Smith's desire for an epistolary friendship, Smith becomes freer in expressing her feelings and remembering the past to her than in letters to anyone else. Much as the loss of Hayley's friendship hurt her, she can banter about missing his corrections to her latest publication, *Conversations Introducing Poetry:*

> However we so little kn[ow] ourselves in any thing that when I fancy I have made a very pretty book, it is possible I may have written a very absurd one, and I have not now, as in other days, a friend who certainly could judge better of the works of others than of his own. I remember he once told me (Alas! it was some fourteen or fifteen years ago) that he wish'd I was old and ugly, for then he could shew the very great friendship he felt for me without hazarding many inconveniencies that arise from the malignant disposition of the World. I am now as old & as ugly, God wot, as his heart can desire, & I suspect he would mentally (as the cant of novels goes) say, "I liked thee better as thou wert before—" (4 July 1804)

Nevertheless, particularly because Sarah's husband Samuel was a solicitor involved in an arbitration of the trust, Smith wrote at length to her friend about trust business as well as about her writing, her children, and her husband. After Samuel Rose's death, Smith sympathized with Sarah's loss as best she could, having never known a loving husband:

> [E]ven if you should . . . learn from sad experience that there is little good among Men, still your solicitudes are for the children of a Man you loved, and every exertion of your fortitude will be scanctified [*sic*] & sweeten'd, While I have labourd for the children of one who lived only to disgrace them & insult me, while he render'd those labours abortive & made me every day & every hour ashamed that I had ever been sold the victim of a ~~Man~~ being, human only in form. (14 Feb. 1805)

SMITH'S HUSBAND AND CHILDREN IN THE LETTERS

It was Smith's marriage that set the course of her life as a mother, writer, and, for all practical purposes, an exile from polite society. Without a doubt, the portrait of Benjamin Smith that emerges in Charlotte's letters is biased, but it is also full and difficult to refute. His fifty recently discovered letters complicate but do not erase her picture of a self-centered and self-indulgent man. Written from 1799 until shortly before his final imprisonment for debt in 1805, his letters to Egremont are courteous and articulate, and show a passing familiarity with Shakespeare and Latin. He claims to act in honor and as a gentleman, and presents himself as eager for a fair and amicable settlement of the trust. Initially deferential, he shows an appropriate gratitude to his family's benefactor; and yet, like his beset wife, he often needs advances to pay expenses. It is only in his two sarcastic and bitter letters to Charlotte that we get a glimpse of the man she claimed he was.

A violent, capricious spendthrift, the Benjamin Smith of Charlotte's letters is a much more thoroughgoing scoundrel than Smith ever created in the wayward, thinly autobiographical husbands of some of her novels. It seems a shame that she was ever taken to task for criticizing him through her characters. Their antics pale when compared to the real havoc he wrought in the lives of so many. Even so, he had his defenders. The earl of Egremont, sickened of dealing with Charlotte, finally met Benjamin at Petworth and called him "the best of the Bunch," an epithet which did not leave Charlotte at a loss for words. "If it be indeed so," she wrote to Mrs. Rose, "As this British legislator opines, I must have . . . been touchd by some Circean wand which has transformed me into a creature compounded of Hyena, Sow, & Wolf" (5 Mar. 1804). Still, she understood that her husband had charm and could wield it precisely as needed to influence an earl; it failed him only with his creditors, the sheriffs who arrested him, and the judges who sentenced him to jail.

Owing money as he did to so many, he had lived in exile in Scotland since the late 1780s, but he regularly slipped back into England under an alias to collect his share of the interest payments on Charlotte's marriage settlements. These July and January interest payments represented to her his continuing oppression of his own family: legally his, she steadfastly claimed they were rightfully hers and the children's. Early letters also show her trying to protect what she had already earned: she warned Cadell to secure money that he kept for her in special accounts because her husband was in England. Benjamin could claim it only if he could find it. In late 1787, after their separation, she ventured to meet with him; he asked to see his "dear Wife and children" before he fled to Barbados. She met him at an inn both to show him that she had "no malice against him" and "to conceal his journey from his numerous creditors in Hampshire and Sussex." He followed her home and soon "took possession" of her study and began to treat her "with more than his usual brutality." Before leaving, a "new fit of frenzy" seized him. He broke into her drawers, destroyed "foul copies" of works in progress, took signed receipts for her subscription edition of the sonnets, and left. Little wonder she announced at the end of this letter to the elder Cadell that she "firmly resolved never again on any pretence whatever to see him & [had] no longer the least wish to keep terms with him" (14 Jan. 1788).

As years passed, she showed more and more disgust with Benjamin Smith, at first refusing to call him by name, and then inventing epithets for him: that "wretched man," the "wretch," that "voracious, unfeeling monster," "Mr. Monstroso," "this infamous brute." She refused finally to call him a man, using whatever circumlocution came to mind, from "being" to "biped." Bit by bit, in letters to friends such as Walker and Sarah Rose, she revealed the extent of his misdeeds.

> Tho infidelity, and with the most despicable objects, had renderd my continuing to live with him extremely wretched long before his debts compelld him to leave England, I could have been contented to have resided in the same house with him, had not his temper been so capricious and often so cruel that my life was not safe. (6 Oct. 1793)

It is never clear whether his abuse was continual or sporadic, although the episode above suggests periods of calm. Once she complained of his exploits with the kitchen help and even more darkly hinted of behavior in front of his daughters that she would not tolerate. Only after his death eight months before her own did she allow herself to break down the thin veil of respectability she had barely maintained, and tell the worst she knew. This she confided to Sarah Rose:

> I will not pollute my paper by relating the dreadful instances of atrocity & vice, that have (& some of them very lately) come to my knowledge of that wretched being to whom I was so inhumanly sacrificed. They are beyond any thing I could have beleived possible, who had every reason to think as ill as I could well think of any body. . . . [H]ad I died, [he] projected & even promis'd to marry a Girl of 18, the niece of his old Concubine, with both of whom he lived in common!—& by the former, he has left a child which he desires his family to protect & bring up! (26 Apr. 1806)

In several late letters, she wrote of being sacrificed while still a child, forced into a state worse than slavery to this man whose daily life mocked her own moral standards and her sentimental ideals.

Indeed, to arrive at a sense of her horror at her unending association with Benjamin, it is useful to compare his sins to the virtues and vices of her fictional heroes and villains. All of her young heroes go about cultivating their own notions of justice, kindness, pity, and right. They are born with a natural rectitude and unaffected tenderness. They see the injustice in war, slavery, and primogeniture (all a direct critique of patriarchy); they rise above nationalism, above vice, above desire. In *Emmeline* (1788), Godolphin can see goodness in his rival, the wild, ungovernable Delamere, even as Delamere lies dying from his excesses. In *The Old Manor House* (1793), Orlando sees nobility in the savage who saves his life even while he is repulsed by the Indians' ignorance, brutality, and pleasure in scalpings and torture. In his chaste love for Monimia, Orlando teaches her to read to free her from ignorance and superstition, which her aunt has used to control her. For her, he is willing to sacrifice a vast inheritance and live peacefully on a farm. D'Alonville in *The Banished Man* (1794) is receptive to learning about the essential goodness of people across national boundaries; an émigré during the French Revolution, he travels through Germany, Poland, and England, forced to confront the prejudices of those of other nations but also seeing through those prejudices to identify sympathetic individuals.

The villains are bad enough, but their vices could be presented to the public, as Benjamin Smith's could not. Charlotte Smith was first taken to task for depicting her husband in Mr. Stafford, the wayward husband of Emmeline's friend and advisor. Mr. Stafford is a sanitized version of Benjamin Smith: only imprisonment and the kitchen help are left out.

> Tho' married very early, and tho' father of a numerous family, he had thrown away the time and money, which should have been provided for them, in collecting baubles, which he had repeatedly possessed and discarded, 'till having exhausted every source that that species of idle folly offered, he had been driven, by the same inability to pursue proper objects, into vices yet more fatal to the repose of his wife, and schemes yet more destructive to his family. . . . [P]ossessed of every reasonable means of happiness, he dissipated that property, which ought to have secured it's [*sic*] continuance, in vague and absurd projects which he neither loved or understood; and his temper growing more irritable in proportion as his difficulties encreased, he sometimes treated his wife with great harshness; and did not seem to think it necessary, even by apparent kindness and attention, to excuse or soften to her his general ill conduct, or his "battening on the moor" of low and degrading debauchery.[8]

The letters show how much worse Benjamin Smith really was. Still, the vividness of profligate characters in this and other novels suggests how powerfully Benjamin's life operated on Charlotte's imagination. In *Emmeline* the apparent hero, Delamere, is rash and impetuous to the point of being brutal. A minor character, Trelawny, like Stafford, sacrifices his wife to his gambling. Among many others, surely Philip Somerive in *The Old Manor House* echoes Benjamin Smith as he runs off with Betty Richards, a maid at Rayland Hall, and gambles away his family's inheritance while his parents, brother, and three sisters still at home can only watch.

Living under her husband's shadow, Charlotte Smith was all the more passionately devoted to her children (see Biographical Notes for details on each one's life). It was her goal to launch them in life into the landed gentry, a station appropriate to her own birth and equal to the promise of their inheritance. As a mother she tirelessly and aggressively pursued for them a short-term income through her own writing and long-term security through the hoped-for settlement of Richard Smith's will.

As a history of a diverse and able family at the beginning of England's expansion into an empire, Charlotte Smith's letters document a range of possibilities for achievement, disaster, and defeat. Her two oldest sons were successful civil servants in India. William Towers Smith worked his way up to a judgeship and retired to England a wealthy man. Nicholas Hankey Smith became a resident (a type of governor) and was a respected translator, aide, and diplomat until he broke the rules for civil servants by participating in a military action, and was sent home.

Smith's three other sons were soldiers. Lionel, whose rise through the ranks of officers Smith had been at great pains to support, rewarded her pride and confidence in him by achieving some of his success while she was alive. He was finally knighted, long after she had died. But her two other sons met with sad ends. Charles Dyer survived the loss of a leg at the Siege of Dunkirk in 1793 only to die of yellow fever in Barbados in 1801 while on business for the trust. George Augustus Frederick, Smith's youngest child—who she felt was *tout à moi,* all her own, because he had just turned two when she separated from his father—died of malaria in Surinam shortly before her own death. She died still believing that she had launched this youngest son on a promising career.

The four daughters' lives were all unfortunate. Charlotte Mary, the eldest, often served as her mother's amanuensis, but she was subject to periods of despondence. She stood to inherit the most from the trust, finally gaining it when matters were settled in 1813, thirty-seven years after her grandfather died. By then she was long past marriageable age. Anna Augusta, the second daughter, married a French emigrant, Alexandre de Foville, with her mother's blessings. Her death from consumption, nine months after the death of her newborn only child, broke her mother's heart. Smith's love and grief for Augusta were the subject of a dozen poems in her *Elegiac Sonnets* and set the elegiac tone of *Marchmont.* And the letters as well make clear that Smith never recovered from this loss: "Eleven years on Wednesday have dragg'd their sad length along since that time—yet my misery has never abated" (26 Apr. 1806).

In contrast, Lucy Eleanor's life rankled her mother. Marrying an older medical student, Thomas Newhouse, against Smith's wishes, Lucy found herself abused, poor, and often pregnant. When Newhouse died of an infection, Lucy turned to her mother to support her two children; a third was about to be born. Harriet Amelia's young life was nearly ended by malaria when she traveled to India with William to look for a husband. At home again in England, she was subject to fits of fevers and delirium for many years. These put her mother to great expense for medical advice. Harriet did become engaged to a fine but poor man, William Geary, a young cripple. They married only after Smith's death released part of Harriet's inheritance and provided the couple with a competence.

Bits and pieces of these individual stories are woven into Smith's letters, which come alive with her tenderness and concern for each child. To close friends Smith expressed pride in various children's accomplishments and generosity to her. She adored William and Nicholas, who loyally sent her money from India. She was always waiting for India ships to arrive with a packet containing the £100 or £200 that William sent each year. Nicholas sent similar amounts after he rose in the ranks of the East India Company; he also sent valuable Persian shawls—some as gifts, others to sell. Charles's injury devastated her, but she tried to comfort herself that he was cited for bravery in the action that cost him his leg. Later she recounts his advancements to the rank of lieutenant, apparently in charge of invalids, and then to paymaster of his regiment. Lionel's rapid rise thrilled her even while she was hard put to it to come up with the money needed to purchase each new rank. Lionel was all the more a favorite for his manly handling of difficult family problems. Before he was sixteen, he was the one sent to bring home his wounded brother Charles; at twenty-three, he was the one who tended to his dying brother-in-law Newhouse.

Smith took pride in helping her sons in return, not so much with money early in their careers as with influence later on. At various times, she sent copies of the sonnets or sets of the children's books or of novels to their commanding officers, who had asked for them on discovering who their young officers' mother was. She intervened with the earl of Egremont and wrote letters directly to commanding officers.

Her daughters also were a source of pride. Augusta may have been Smith's favorite child, although this preference is stated only after her death. Still, it is clear that her mother was deeply pleased when Augusta, who was beautiful and adored by all, married for love. And Smith herself was enamored of de Foville, Augusta's young émigré, who loved country retirement, undertook to translate one of Smith's children's books into French, and proposed to do the drawings for it. Harriet, too, touched her heart. It was one of the last efforts of Smith's life to free up some money so that Harriet could marry William Geary, whom she had met shortly after her return from India. Both families approved of the match but delayed the marriage for five years until the couple had means.

While William, Nicholas, and Lionel provided strength and support from abroad, Charlotte Mary did so at home. Her mother's dependable amanuensis, she could also be entrusted to handle legal business in London or to care for Nicholas's children sent home from India. Of all the children, Charlotte Mary is the only one to whom a letter from Charlotte Smith survives. Its warmth, directness, and confidence in her daughter are what we would expect to see in her dealings with all the children.[9]

Yet there were many sorrows and much anxiety. Smith's constant complaint is the difficulty of knowing whether one son or another is safe and well in India, France, the West Indies, Gibraltar, Canada, or South America. In Bombay, Nicholas, a diplomat and translator to the Persian ambassador, was standing near him when the ambassador was assassinated; in England, Smith read of the assassination in magazines, which failed to report that her son was safe. Charles's trip to Barbados on trust business filled his mother with an overwhelming dread of that climate's diseases; her fears proved justified when he died of yellow fever. For several months in 1801, the family lost touch with Lionel, who was on a hazardous mission in Sierra Leone. They knew he was safe only when he walked through the door, weeks past the latest time they had hoped to see him alive. Each of the daughters suffered long, costly illnesses that sapped their mother's strength as well as her purse.

Moreover, Smith's loyalty and devotion to her children were often tested when their behavior came up short. After his injury, Charles threw her into debt by staying on at her house in Storrington when she could ill afford to support two houses. Lionel and de Foville embarrassed Smith by involving themselves in a duel with Thomas Dyer, a relative associated with the trust. But much worse, when William returned to England in 1798, his gambling and other behaviors similar to his father's sickened her. She quarreled with him irreconcilably, probably over this; as she wrote later to Sarah Rose, "Bengal ships, tho my eldest Son is there, never bring me even letters" (10 Sept. 1804). After his visit to England, she never writes about his successes or his support. Lucy's marriage and subsequent destitution similarly alienated Smith from her daughter, for Smith rarely mentions Lucy after settling her in a cottage (at considerable expense).

THE BUSINESS OF RICHARD SMITH'S WILL

While the desire to ensure her children's success and social standing motivated Smith to write, it also fueled her tenacious occupation with her father-in-law's estate. To describe a complex situation briefly: these troubles were brought about by her father-in-law Richard Smith's intended generosity to Benjamin and Charlotte's children. Old Smith's elder son Richard was settled in the family's living, the perpetual advowson of Islington, and was well provided for. Both his daughter Mary Smith and his stepdaughter Mary Crow had married well. Therefore, Smith, who knew his second son's spendthrift ways only too well, meant for the will to benefit Benjamin's children most. He wrote out a detailed document and updated it with four different codicils, all without benefit of counsel. Having made a fortune in the East India Company, he had a great deal of stock to spread around three children and their children. Benjamin, along with Charlotte and Richard's wife Lucy, was executor to the will. In the seven years following Richard's death in 1776, the value of the estate was reduced from £36,000 to about £20,000 with Benjamin as its executor.[10] Collateral branches of the family who were heirs sued him on a writ of devastavit, which Benjamin later declared unjust. Many of his creditors called in outstanding debts he could not pay, forcing him to spend seven months in King's Bench Prison. Though free to come and go, Charlotte spent much of the time with him and made her first sale—of *Elegiac Sonnets*—to help pay his debts.

A new board of trustees—including Sir John Dyer and old Smith's son-in-law, John Robinson—was formed to administer the trust. This pair did not sympathize with Charlotte's needs, perhaps because she was associated with Benjamin despite the couple's separation, perhaps because they were more closely related to other branches of the family. When they subsequently denied her many requests for interest payments, she came actively to despise them:

> I, who am fete'[d] eternally by the most eminent literary Men and told that I am in the first order of beings, can have but little delight in exposing myself to the supercilious and purse proud insolence of Robinson Or the mean insulting contention of that detestable cream colourd Dyer. (8 Dec. 1791)

In 1793 and 1794, Smith feared that their agent was embezzling profits from the sugar plantations that Benjamin had purchased for the trust in 1781. In 1794, a significant preliminary settlement was brought about by the earl of Egremont and duchess of Devonshire, who sponsored legal counsel; Egremont separately contributed several thousand pounds to pay off a debt that was holding up further settlement.

By 1798, Smith still had had no satisfaction from the trustees and was deeply alienated from them. Confident of Egremont because of his past generosity, his past praise of her unceasing pursuit of settlement, and the kind support of his estate agent William Upton Tripp, Smith persuaded Egremont and her brother Nicholas Turner to replace Dyer and Robinson. In an unexpected reversal of her hopes, the new trustees were soon embroiled in matters against her. Their good intentions were no doubt aggravated rather than aided by her many, lengthy letters explaining fine points of the will, the law, and the history of the trust.

Smith and Egremont's steward, William Tyler, actively disliked each other as well. With twenty-two years more experience in trust matters than Tyler, Smith argued with him point by point on every decision he tried to make, and she was offended by what she took to be his high-handed treatment of her. Tyler almost certainly had no kind words about her for his employer, as he was by nature not a good-humored man. He was wildly unpopular in Petworth. Moreover, her brother acted against her, possibly because she stood up to him in a lawsuit he had against their sister, Catherine Dorset, and possibly because he despised Frenchmen, and Smith argued for her French son-in-law's right to Augusta's share of the estate.

Expecting the new trustees to settle the estate rapidly, Smith had slackened her publishing efforts. By 1802, Egremont and Tyler were withholding the modest interest payments she had previously received. By the spring of 1803, she was penniless, distraught over being forced to sell her treasured library, and on the road to yet a cheaper and more humbling lodging. From December 1802 to March 1803, almost daily letters document the anguish with which she finally faced actual poverty:

> [A]s I am now wholly divested of every power, of every voice, & of every shilling, I had in the World; As I am an houseless beggar & likely to die in an hospital, I hoped there would be an end at least of all talk of Chancery. I have been made to look like a fool[.] (31 Jan. 1803)

After two decades of involvement with the trust, she found being silenced unbearably humiliating:

> [A]ll my former trouble has ended in my being told I must be treated like a child, that I knew nothing of the matter & was to have no voice even in things which are absolutely a part of the will. (15 Jan. 1803)

Distressed and too poor to heat her house, by February she was a cripple again, unable to walk and barely able to scribble. In March, Egremont forbade her to write to him or to have any say in the affairs. Despite the sale of her books, he would not lend her £20—for lack of which she expected to be sent to the county jail. By the end of the month, she had moved to Elsted, to her cheapest lodgings yet.

In 1803, her friend Sarah Rose's husband Samuel was called in to arbitrate an interim settlement, dividing the award between Charlotte and Benjamin. Each one cried foul. In 1804, Smith resumed writing to ensure her own support. Benjamin Smith died in February 1806, eight months before Charlotte. Some income then reverted to her, but she never achieved the settlement for which she fought for thirty years. When the trust was finally settled, in 1813, her children received their shares, but they were nowhere near what her father-in-law had originally left them. In a case that Loraine Fletcher sees as a source for Jarndyce v. Jarndyce in Charles Dickens's *Bleak House,*[11] decades of delay and litigation had reduced the estate's value to about £4,000.

CHARLOTTE SMITH'S CHARACTER

Charlotte Smith's complex character is not easily summarized. In his epitaph for her, William Hayley called her "Lady of signal sorrows, signal woes." But while this is certainly true, she was also a woman of signal achievement, energy, ambition, devotion, and sacrifice. Her children and her literary career evoked from her her best efforts, and did so in about equal measure. Sons and daughters, novels and poems gave her the few pleasures she found in life. Yet even with them, the letters show her repeatedly torn and divided: her children supported her and required her support; she took great pride and great pains with her books. And over against these two generally positive areas of her life stand its perpetual miseries—her husband, her failing health, and her battles with the trustees. Her life, indeed her character, as seen in the letters is illuminated by her beliefs as a writer, for here too she was divided between real and ideal worlds.

Smith's works place her squarely in the cult of sensibility: she believed in the virtue of kindness, in generosity to those less fortunate, and in the cultivation of the finer feelings of sympathy and tenderness for those who suffered needlessly. Her letters show that she acted on these beliefs when she could, opening her doors to French émigrés and writing a subscription narrative to benefit the widow of a shipwrecked sailor. More often, however, she herself needed the support of people of such beliefs, which did not often come her way. She faced a grim reality with great energy and determination. She ruined her health working to support her children and encountered little of the sort of aid or fortune with which she was able to award her female and male heroes. And yet she continued as a writer for two decades.

Her character thus was forged in the conflicts she endured: she could imagine and create a more rational, sympathetic, and equitable world than the one she lived in. On the other hand, she had also discovered that her pen had the power not only to create ideal worlds but also to redress wrongs in the real world. Modern readers may find some of her letters nagging, haranguing, even self-pitying. Others may seem assertive in ways that are still not acceptable for women. In the absence, by and large, of letters by her correspondents that would give the other side of the story, it is difficult to know how provoked she was.

It seems to me critical to realize, however, that one of her most persistent complaints was true. She had no lasting champion. No husband or brother stepped up to her defense. Booksellers retired, died, went bankrupt. The trustees, who could have made her life easier, delayed the settlement of the will for so long that her sons—who clearly would have defended her—were scattered around the world pursuing the only respectable careers they could afford. Thus left to her own defenses in a world where women's rights were negligible, she had long since discovered that her insistent, complaining, abrasive letters yielded results. To write, whether fiction, poems, or letters, was her one resource.

CHARLOTTE SMITH'S ACHIEVEMENT

The letters finally take on their particular significance when seen against Smith's achievement as a writer. One of the most popular poets in her own time, Charlotte Smith revived the sonnet form in England, influencing Wordsworth and Keats. Author of ten novels, Smith wrote in answer to the tastes of her day. Her novels cut across many popular genres: Gothic, epistolary, educational, revolutionary, but always the novel of sensibility. She and Ann Radcliffe read each other's novels and influenced several of each other's works. Moreover, Jane Austen—though she ridiculed Smith's novels—actually borrowed plot, character, and incident from them. Even for her children's books, which have received no critical attention today, Smith was well regarded in her time. She aimed at the same readership for which Mrs. Barbauld and the Edgeworths wrote, and here, too, found an audience and helped shape a genre. Now her letters will enlarge our sense of her achievement, for they show the private world of determination, anger, spirit, and sorrow in which she wrote.

NOTES

1. Charlotte Smith, *The Young Philosopher,* ed. Elizabeth Kraft (Lexington: University Press of Kentucky, 1999); *Desmond,* ed. Janet Todd and Antje Blank (Peterborough, Ont.: Broadview Press, 2001; London: Pickering and Chatto, 1997); *The Old Manor House,* ed. Anne Henry Ehrenpreis (Oxford: Oxford University Press, 1969); ed. Gina Luria (New York: Garland, 1974); ed. Judith Phillips Stanton (Oxford: Oxford University Press, 1989); ed. Janet Todd (London: Pandora, 1989); and *Emmeline, the Orphan of the Castle,* intro. Zoe Fairbairns (London: Pandora, 1987); ed. Anne Henry Ehrenpreis (Oxford: Oxford University Press, 1971).

There have been seven facsimile editions: *Letters of a Solitary Wanderer* (Oxford, N.Y.: Woodstock Books, 1995); *The Wanderings of Warwick,* intro. Carolyn Franklin (London: Routledge/Thoemmes Press, 1992); *Montalbert. A novel* and *Marchmont: a novel,* both edited by Mary Anne Schofield (Delmar, N.Y.: Scholar's Facsimile Press, 1989); and *Desmond. A novel, The Old Manor House,* and *The Young Philosopher: a novel,* all edited by Gina Luria (New York: Garland, 1974). Selections from the preface to *Desmond* and from the novel *The Banished Man* appeared in *Before Their Time: Six Women Writers of the Eighteenth Century,* ed. Katharine M. Rogers (New York: Frederick Ungar, 1979), pp. 76–94.

Stuart Curran has recently edited *The Poems of Charlotte Smith* (Oxford: Oxford University Press, 1993). Smith's poems have also appeared in *The New Oxford Book of*

Eighteenth Century Verse, ed. Roger Lonsdale (Oxford: Oxford University Press, 1989), p. 756; *Eighteenth-Century Women Poets,* ed. Roger Lonsdale (Oxford: Oxford University Press, 1989), pp. 365–73; and *The Norton Anthology of Literature by Women: The Traditions in English,* ed. Sandra M. Gilbert and Susan Gubar, 2nd ed. (New York: W. W. Norton, 1996), pp. 234–41.

2. Letter from "Hermit" to John Hawkins, 7 Feb. 1807, Hawkins papers, vol. 2, part 2, no. 328, West Sussex Record Office, Chichester, Sussex.

3. Catherine Ann Dorset, "Charlotte Smith," in *The Miscellaneous Prose Works of Sir Walter Scott, Bart.,* by Sir Walter Scott, vol. 4 (Edinburgh: Robert Cadell, 1834), p. 57.

4. The first full-length modern biography of Smith, completed by F. M. A. Hilbish in 1939 (*Charlotte Smith, Poet and Novelist (1749–1806)* [Philadelphia: University of Pennsylvania Press, 1941]), was written without reference to any letters. The letters themselves confirm the accuracy of most of Hilbish's conclusions. Two new biographies of Smith have recently appeared. Loraine Fletcher's *Charlotte Smith: A Critical Biography* (Basingstoke: Macmillan; New York: St. Martin's, 1998) makes extensive use of this edition of the letters and adds many new facts and insights. Carroll Fry's *Charlotte Smith* (New York: Twayne, 1996) also refers to the letters.

5. William Cowper, *The Letters and Prose Writings of William Cowper,* ed. James King and Charles Ryskamp, vol. 4 (Oxford: Clarendon, 1979), p. 218.

6. Letter from William Hayley to Thomas Cadell, 12 Apr. 1973, Cowper and Newton Museum, Olney, Buckinghamshire.

7. Letter from "Hermit" to Sir John Hawkins, 7 Feb. 1807.

8. Smith, *Emmeline,* p. 177.

9. Charlotte Mary, Lionel, Lucy, and Charles wrote a number of business letters to Egremont, which are now in the Petworth House Archives. Notably, they state their business firmly and admit nothing derogatory about their mother in the face of Egremont's and Tyler's complaints against her. Letters to Cadell and Davies at Yale include notes by Charlotte Mary, Lionel, and Lucy.

10. In her biography, Dorset claims that the estate was greatly reduced, by £20,000, because a sum was lent to a distressed baronet on a mortgage and then lost ("Charlotte Smith," pp. 36–37). It is not clear whether that sum is related to the amount, variously given as £16,000 and £17,000, that CS accuses BS of losing.

11. Fletcher, *Charlotte Smith,* pp. 251–52, 338.

Sources of Charlotte Smith's Letters

For the purpose of studying Smith's literary career, the largest significant collections of her letters are the 140 letters at the Beinecke Rare Book and Manuscript Library at Yale University and the 50 letters at the Huntington Library, San Marino, Calif. Most of the Yale letters are addressed to Thomas Cadell, Sr. and Jr., and to William Davies, who published a number of her works. The Huntington collection includes letters to friends, particularly the Reverend Joseph Cooper Walker and Sarah Rose. Most of the remaining letters are to be found in groups of a dozen or fewer, and they help round out the picture of Smith's life.

In Great Britain, letters are located at the Bodleian, Oxford; the Fitzwilliam Museum, Cambridge; the British Library, London; the Cowper and Newton Museum, Olney, Buckinghamshire; the Liverpool Libraries and Information Services; and the Westminster Diocesan Archives. The National Library of Scotland, Edinburgh, has one note. In Canada, Mills Memorial Library of McMaster University, Hamilton, Ont., has three letters. In the United States there are letters at the Houghton Library, Harvard University; Pennsylvania State University Libraries; Princeton University Library; the New York Public Library; Boston Public Library; J. Pierpont Morgan Library, New York City; Magill Library, Haverford College Library, Haverford, Pa.; Charles E. Young Research Library, UCLA; the Walter H. and Leonore Annenberg Rare Book and Manuscript Library of the University of Pennsylvania; and the University of Iowa Libraries (Iowa City, Iowa). Finally, there are letters in the private collections of the duke and duchess of Devonshire and the Comyn Collection of Burney Family Papers in England, and of Lucy Magruder in California.

For a more intimate look at Smith's personal life and financial difficulties, there is an important body of letters in the Petworth House Archives, administered by the West Sussex Record Office, Chichester, England. Originally, their collection was thought to consist of 250 letters Smith wrote from 1799 to 1806 to her onetime patron and trustee to Richard Smith's estate, George O'Brien Wyndham, the third earl of Egremont. These shed new light on the maneuvering and litigation surrounding the Smith trust from its beginnings as well as Smith's slow, humiliating slide into poverty at the end of her life. The present collection includes all of her letters to Egremont but only the most informative of many long, repetitious business letters to Tyler.

In the spring of 2001, just as this edition was being readied for the press, two new groups of letters were discovered in an old tin muniments chest as the Petworth House Archives was moving into its new quarters. First are fifty-six letters Smith wrote from 1790 to 1795 to James Upton Tripp, estate agent to Egremont. Along with several written to others, they add enormously to our picture of her early years of success.

The second includes fifty remarkable lost letters by Smith's reviled husband Benjamin, written from 1799 until his imprisonment for debt in 1805. The only two known letters he wrote to her are given in full in footnotes, as are passages he cites from her letters to him. Substantial passages from his remaining letters to Egremont and Tyler are also cited in footnotes to fill in the picture of this difficult man and his bitter relationship with his estranged wife.

In the winter of 2003, four additional notes to Tripp were found concerning Egremont's purchase of Benjamin's horse. They show earlier dealings with Egremont than previously known and continued business with Benjamin after the separation. These letters are in the appendix.

Textual Principles

HOLOGRAPH LETTERS

Holograph letters constitute the vast majority of Charlotte Smith's surviving correspondence. They are almost uniformly clear and readable with few errors, corrections, or emendations. Smith, who was observed to write rapidly and correctly while composing *The Old Manor House* at Eartham, wrote letters rapidly as well. A literal transcription of each holograph would preserve her actual writing practices, but it would be difficult to read. Her punctuation in particular creates the greatest barrier to readability. Consequently, I have modernized punctuation along the following lines. Commas and dashes used only for emphasis are eliminated. Most other dashes are changed to periods or commas as appropriate. Smith rarely used semicolons as we do today, so they are converted to periods or commas as sense dictates. She rarely used commas to set off nonrestrictive and other parenthetical elements; when she did, she usually supplied only one, at the end of the phrase or clause. I supplied one or both as needed. When the nonrestrictive element is very long, I set it off with dashes as a means of preserving the sense of her hasty use of dashes elsewhere. I preserved all of her more emphatic dashes: — —, ——, and ———.

The longer one of Smith's letters is, the less likely it is to have paragraphs. Because lack of paragraphing makes for tedious reading, I have added paragraphs in most of the letters. Frequently, a long dash or interjection (such as *My dear Madam*) marks the beginning of a new sequence of thought, and thus is a reliable clue for paragraphing. Where there are no clues, I indent for paragraphs when the subject changes.

Strikeovers and corrections are few, and they are included. Her rare grammatical errors are included as well as her consistently and frequently idiosyncratic spellings, such as *awkard, ballance, beleive, burthen, generousity, inconveniencies, Brighthelmstone, Josepth, obligd, proffit, schawls, seperate, Teusday, underserved,* and others; [*sic*] marks only those spellings or constructions that are likely to create confusion or to appear implausible. I have also left words written as two that we now spell as one word: *any body, copy right, where ever, whom ever, worth while.* She often used contractions for the past tense of verbs: *called* became *calld* or *call'd.* These spellings are retained, as are her ampersands and abbreviations, as they suggest the speed of her writing. She generally abbreviated dates, months, honorifics (D^{ss} for duchess, L^{dsp} for Lordship), and words in complimentary closes to letters. All these are retained; however, where the abbreviations require explanation, such as re^{d} for *received,* py^{t} for *payment,* and ad^{v} for *advertisement,* they are spelled out: for example, *re[ceive]*^{d}.

Smith's punctuation consisted mainly of dashes, and their length varies. The longer the dash, the more likely it reveals her haste, irritation, or emphasis. I changed all but long emphatic dashes to appropriate modern punctuation. She often ended paragraphs with no punctuation; there I supplied periods and indented the next paragraph.

I have not modernized punctuation in her few letters from printed sources or in footnotes where I cite passages from others' holograph letters. The postal addresses given at the end of each letter are not modernized.

Editorial information is supplied in brackets [ ]. Blank spaces, usually where the page has been torn away by breaking the seal or where the edge of a page has been destroyed, are also shown by square brackets, containing an ellipsis. The few questionable readings are presented in angle brackets <>. The infrequent strikeovers show the words or phrases that Smith crossed out.

COPIES AND PRINTED SOURCES

The few letters from printed sources are transcribed directly as found. Mrs. Dorset's biography contains one complete letter and four excerpts from other letters (one of those copied from Richard Phillips's *Public Characters*), and James Edward Smith's *Memoirs* contains one letter from Smith; all of these were much modified for print. Hayley's copies of two Smith letters appear to have been somewhat corrected from her original, but are made much more readable by being modernized. The letter to John Nichols appears to be a literal transcription, and I have modernized it.

HEADINGS AND POSTSCRIPTS TO LETTERS

Each letter is headed by the name of its recipient. The date of the letter then appears between the recipient's name and the body of the letter. If the original letter is dated at the end, or a missing date is inferred, the date is given at the beginning in brackets for the reader's convenience.

At the end of each letter is given the source of the copy-text; the complete address, if any, in Smith's hand; and any postmark, including date and place.

ANNOTATION

Brief biographies of the letters' recipients are given in an appendix (which also contains biographies of Smith's children). These biographies show the subjects' position and achievements in life—especially as they may have appeared to Smith, who took careful note of status in choosing friends and business associates. I then review their involvement in Smith's life and career.

I have attempted to keep the annotations for each letter concise, even while providing a background to the world in which Smith lived and wrote. I have identified persons, titles, places, and obscure terms and have also commented on inconsistencies from one letter to another. Keeping track of Smith's large family is a challenge, and I have provided two aids for the reader of the letters. First, each year or period begins with an overview summarizing publications in progress and completed, the children's activities, and the state of the trust. Second, when possible, annotations provide names where sons, daughters, and other relatives are alluded to.

Finally, some annotations cite portions of unpublished letters related to the letter at hand. For example, among the 127 letters at Yale University's Beinecke Rare Book and Manuscript Library are about three dozen replies from Cadell and Davies, several letters by Smith's children, and about two dozen receipts for loans. The publishers' replies shed light on her difficult relationships with them, while the children's letters suggest how much they helped her in her work. The receipts permit us to verify amounts borrowed and spent.

Similarly, the Petworth House Archives contain letters that the earl of Egremont, as trustee, and his steward William Tyler wrote to Smith after 1799. Letters by Smith's children from this collection show how they worked to help settle the trust. From the archives, I also cite relevant passages from wills, depositions, account books to the trust, and Tyler's letterbooks, as well as the important extracts from Benjamin Smith's letters.

Chronology of Charlotte Smith's Life

1748	Jan.	Nicholas Turner and Anna Towers married.
1749	4 May	Charlotte born in London, eldest child of Nicholas and Anna Towers Turner.
	12 June	Charlotte baptized at Stoke Park, the family seat, near Guildford in Sussex.
1752		Charlotte's mother dies; her father travels abroad, leaving his three children in the care of their aunt, Lucy Towers.
ca. 1755		Charlotte already reading, possibly already writing verse.
ca. 1756–57		Charlotte in school in Chichester; drawing lessons from George Smith.
1757		Nicholas Turner returns from abroad, places children in school, possibly at Kensington. Charlotte excels in reading, composition, drawing, and acting.
1759–60		Charlotte's family regularly resides at Bignor Park; Stoke Manor sold.
1761		Charlotte taken out of school and given expensive private lessons in music, drawing, dancing, and French; also introduced into society.
1764	30 Aug.	Nicholas Turner marries Miss Henrietta Meriton of Chelsea for a settlement of £20,000.
1765	23 Feb.	Charlotte marries Benjamin Smith. The couple lives for a few months with Benjamin's sister Mary Berney, then moves to Cheapside in London with his parents.

1766		CS's first son born in spring, name and exact date unknown. Her demanding mother-in-law dies, and her friendship with her father-in-law grows.
1767		Richard Smith marries CS's aunt, Lucy Towers, on or about Mar. 15.
	30 Apr.	Second child, Benjamin Berney, christened; first child dies during her pregnancy.
		Richard Smith provides BS and CS with a small house in Southgate, a village near London, but their children born there were christened at St. Faith under St. Paul's.
		Catherine Ann Turner, CS's sister, marries Capt. Michael Dorset.
1768		Third child, William Towers, born; exact date unknown.
1769	10 Apr.	Fourth child and first daughter, Charlotte Mary, born; christened 2 May at St. Faith.
1770	19 July	Fifth child, Brathwaite, christened at St. Faith.
1771		Smiths move to a larger residence in Tottenham, 5 miles from London.
	4 Nov.	Sixth child, Nicholas Hankey, christened at All Hallows Church, Tottenham.
1773	27 Feb.	Seventh child, Charles Dyer, christened at All Hallows.
1774	18 June	Eighth child, Anna Augusta, christened at All Hallows.
		Smiths move to Lys Farm, Hampshire (with seven children), where they live for the next nine years; Richard Smith resumes management of the West Indian business.
1776	17 Apr.	Ninth child, Lucy Eleanor, christened at Hinton Ampner.
	13 Oct.	Richard Smith, CS's father-in-law, dies, leaving estate worth about £36,000.
1777	1 June	Eldest child, Benjamin Berney, age 11, dies of consumption at Hinton Ampner.
	9 Oct.	Tenth child, Lionel, born; christened 11 Nov. at Hinton Ampner.
1781		Benjamin Smith appointed sheriff of Southampton (Hampshire).
1782	Apr.	Eleventh child, Harriet Amelia, born; place uncertain.
1783	Dec.	Benjamin Smith imprisoned for debt until July 1784; CS spends some of this time in jail with him.
1783–84		Lys Farm sold.

1784	June	*Elegiac Sonnets, and Other Poems* printed by James Dodsley at CS's expense, first and second editions; preface 10 May, Bignor Park.
	2 July	CS leaves prison with Benjamin; goes to Bignor Park where her brother Nicholas has kept her children.
	Oct.	CS goes to Dieppe for a day to settle BS there; he is again in debt.
1784–85		CS and all the children spend winter with BS in Normandy near Dieppe.
1785	Feb.	Twelfth child, George Augustus Frederick, born in Normandy.
	spring	Smiths return to England and settle at Woolbeding, Sussex, by October.
	winter	CS begins translating *Manon Lescaut.*
1786	Feb.	*Elegiac Sonnets,* Dodsley, third and fourth editions; preface dated Woolbeding, 22 Mar.
	18 June	Brathwaite, age 16, dies after a 36-hour illness.
	ca. Sept.	CS publishes and withdraws translation of *Manon Lescaut.*
1787		*The Romance of Real Life* (translated from *Les cause célèbres* by Gayot de Pitaval) published by Cadell.
	15 Apr.	CS separates from BS.
	summer	CS and children living at Wyhe (now called Wyke), near Guilford.
1788	10 Feb.	CS at Norton St., Portland Place, London.
	Apr.	*Emmeline, the Orphan of the Castle* published by Thomas Cadell, Sr. Revised second edition by end of year.
		William Towers leaves for India as a writer.
1789		*Ethelinde, or the Recluse of the Lake,* Cadell.
		Elegiac Sonnets, fifth subscription edition, Cadell; *Emmeline,* third edition, Cadell.
	3 Feb.	CS in London.
	18 June	CS living mainly at Brighton until Feb. 1793.
1790		*Elegiac Sonnets,* Dublin edition; *Emmeline oder die Wayse des Schlosses,* German translation; *Ethelinde,* second edition, Cadell.
	19 Feb.	CS in London.
	26 Mar.	CS at Graffham near Petworth.
	Sept.	Nicholas Hankey, appointed writer in 1788, arrives in India.
1791		*Celestina. A novel,* first and second edition, Cadell.
1791	8 June	CS in London.

	Dec.	CS in London at Henrietta St. all month with Henrietta O'Neill.
1792	10 Apr.	Charles joins 14th (Bedfordshire) Regiment of Foot.
	Apr.	CS in London.
		Elegiac Sonnets, sixth edition; preface dated 14 May.
		Desmond. A novel, George Robinson; preface dated 20 June.
	Aug.–Sept.	CS at William Hayley's Eartham, where she meets William Cowper and George Romney, finishing first volume of *The Old Manor House.* Interrupts her stay with a visit to Brighton.
1793	Mar.	*The Old Manor House,* Joseph Bell.
	Apr.	CS in serious financial difficulties in Brighton.
	30 Apr.	Lionel takes over Charles's ensigncy in 14th Regiment.
		The Emigrants, a poem, in two books, Cadell; preface dated May 10, Brighton.
	July	Augusta marries Alexandre Mark Constant de Foville, a Catholic émigré.
	13 Aug.	CS and family are settled at Storrington, Sussex.
	6 Sept.	Charles is wounded at Siege of Dunkirk; his leg is amputated.
	10 Sept.	Henrietta O'Neill dies in Spain.
1794	Jan.	*The Wanderings of Warwick,* Bell.
	31 Mar.	CS has just moved to Pultenay St., Bath, with only her daughter Harriet.
	23 July	Augusta is confined; her son dies three days after birth.
	Aug.	*The Banished Man. A novel,* Thomas Cadell, Jr., and William Davies.
		Desmond, second edition, Robinson; *The Old Manor House,* second edition, Bell, and first Dublin edition, Rice.
		CS has recently moved to Seymour St., Bath.
1795	20 Jan.	CS makes a short trip to London on family business, staying at Osborne Hotel, Adelphi.
		The Banished Man, second edition, Cadell and Davies; *Elegiac Sonnets,* seventh edition, Cadell and Davies; first and second U.S. editions.
	23 Apr.	Augusta, CS's favorite child, dies at Bristol of consumption.
	12 June	CS has just arrived in Exmouth, Devon, where Miss Peckham has been keeping her children, and plans a short stay.
	? June	*Montalbert. A novel,* Sampson Low; Dublin edition, P. Wogan, P. Bryne, et al. (first reviewed July 1795).
	1 Sept.	Charles stationed at Gibraltar until 1798.

		Rural Walks: in dialogues: intended for the use of young persons, Cadell and Davies, preface dated 19 Nov. [1794]; Dublin edition, P. Wogan, P. Byrne, et al.
1796	7 Feb.	CS has finally moved to Weymouth, 7 Esplanade.
		A Narrative of the loss of the Catharine, Venus and Piedmont transports, etc. (an account of the wreck of seven ships near Weymouth, to aid a widow of one of the sailors, by subscription).
	26 Apr.	CS moves to Belle Vue 1, Weymouth.
	Aug.	*Rambles Farther. A continuation of Rural Walks,* Cadell and Davies. Dedicated to Lady Georgiana Cavendish, the duchess of Devonshire's daughter; Dublin edition.
		Marchmont. A novel, Low.
	16 Nov.	CS living in Headington near Oxford for at least one month.
	23 Dec.	CS moves to High Street in Oxford opposite University College.
1797		*Elegiac Sonnets,* vol. 2, subscription edition, Cadell and Davies; preface dated 15 May. Vol. 1 in eighth edition.
	22 June	CS at Charlotte St., London, through July.
	1 Aug.	CS returns to Headington through Nov.
	30 Dec.	CS at Charlotte St., London, briefly.
1798	3 Jan.	CS takes rooms at Duke St., London.
	23 Feb.	Charles stationed at Berwick-upon-Tweed, as lieutenant of invalids.
	June	*Minor Morals, interspersed with sketches of natural history, historical anecdotes, and original stories,* Low. Dedicated to Lady Caroline Ponsonby, daughter of the countess of Bessborough (the duchess of Devonshire's sister).
		The Young Philosopher. A novel, Cadell and Davies, preface dated June 6, 1798.
	12 June	Lucy marries Thomas Postlewaite Newhouse at Holbourn against CS's advice.
	9 Nov.	CS has moved to Upper Baker St., London.
1799		CS living in London; Charlotte Mary has three severe bouts of illness. William visiting from India.
	2 Apr.	Harriet sails from England for India with William.
	25 May	Lucy Newhouse's first child, Thomas Henry, christened.
		Minor Morals, Dublin edition; *Romance of Real Life,* second American edition.

1799	27 Aug.	The earl of Egremont and Nicholas Turner, Jr., assume trusteeship of Richard Smith's estate.
	28 Aug.	CS visits sister, Catherine Dorset, at Bignor Park and returns to London.
	Sept.	William and Harriet arrive in Madras.
1800–1802		*The Letters of a Solitary Wanderer: containing narratives of various description,* vols. 1–3, published by Low; vols. 4–5 published by Longman's in 1802 after Low's death.
1800	15 Mar.	William marries Catherine Maria Morris.
	29 Apr.	Lucy's second child, William Charles, christened.
	18 May	CS living in Hastings with George and Lucy's older child.
	4-9 Aug.	CS at "Mount Misery," Tunbridge Wells.
	Aug.–Sept.	CS and Charlotte Mary at Bignor with Mrs. Dorset.
	Oct.	Harriet returns from India very ill; she is subject to fevers and delirium for the next four years.
	23 Oct.	Charles made paymaster of 47th Regiment, sails for Barbados in early Dec.; Charlotte Mary lived with him at Berwick for some time up until August.
		Elegiac Sonnets i, ninth edition, and *ii,* second edition, Cadell and Davies; *Rambles Farther,* second edition, Cadell and Davies; *Minor Morals,* Dublin edition.
1801	4 Feb.	CS at Hartridge, Tunbridge Wells, for a month.
	28 Mar.	Lucy's husband, Thomas, dies in London.
	21 Apr.	CS in London briefly.
	after June	Charles, age 28, dies of yellow fever in Barbados on trust business.
	24 July	CS at Frant through August.
	27 Sept.	George joins the army.
	30 Sept.	CS in London briefly.
	6 Oct.	CS at Bignor Park with Mrs. Dorset until Oct. 20, then at the Half Moon, Petworth, on 21 Oct. on her way to London.
	7 Oct.	Charlotte Susan, Lucy's third child, overdue, expected immediately.
	26 Oct.	CS in London at 35 Rathbone Place until at least 4 Nov.
	15 Nov.	CS moves to Frant, her primary residence until Mar. 1803.
		Emmeline, American edition.
1802	17 Jan.	CS at Buckingham St. in London on business until early April.
	2 July	CS at Half Moon, Petworth.
	13 July	CS at Bignor Park.

1803	3 Mar.	CS, out of money and abandoned by the trustees and her family, stays at Wightons, Tunbridge Wells.
	10 Mar.	CS moves to Elsted near Godalming, Sussex.
	7 May	CS at The Swan, Petworth, to see Lord Egremont.
	27 Sept.	Samuel Rose's arbitration award divides monies between CS and BS.
1804		*Conversations Introducing Poetry: chiefly on subjects of natural history. For the use of children and young persons,* Joseph Johnson, preface dated 28 July.
		Nicholas has sent his daughter, Luzena, age 5, to CS to care for; she lives mostly with Charlotte Mary. *Conversations* is for her.
		Lionel marries Ellen Marianne Galway (d. 1814), an Irish Catholic.
	27 Oct.	CS visits Bignor Park for several days.
1805	14 May	CS visits Bignor Park for several days.
	18 Aug.	CS at Bignor Park until Aug. 27, when she goes to Brighton for her health.
	20 Oct.	CS living at Tilford near Farnham, her last residence.
1806	26 Feb.	Benjamin Smith dies in debtor's prison at Berwick-upon-Tweed, freeing up CS's marriage settlements to be awarded to the younger children.
		CS has the care of Luzena and a boy, possibly Nicholas's son, William Hankey, born ca. 1800–1802.
		History of England, from the earliest records, to the Peace of Amiens, in a series of letters to a young lady at school, Richard Phillips (vols. 1 and 2 of three are by CS).
		Elegiac Sonnets ii, third edition.
	16 Sept.	George, age 22, dies of yellow fever at Surinam.
	28 Oct.	CS dies at Tilford, near Farnham, Surrey. Buried at Stoke Church, near Guildford.
1807	20 Jan.	Harriet marries William Geary at Farnham.
		Beachy Head: with other poems, Johnson.
		The Natural History of Birds, intended chiefly for young persons, Johnson.
1813	22 Apr.	Final settlement of Richard Smith's estate.

The legatees of Richard Smith's estate: his children and grandchildren

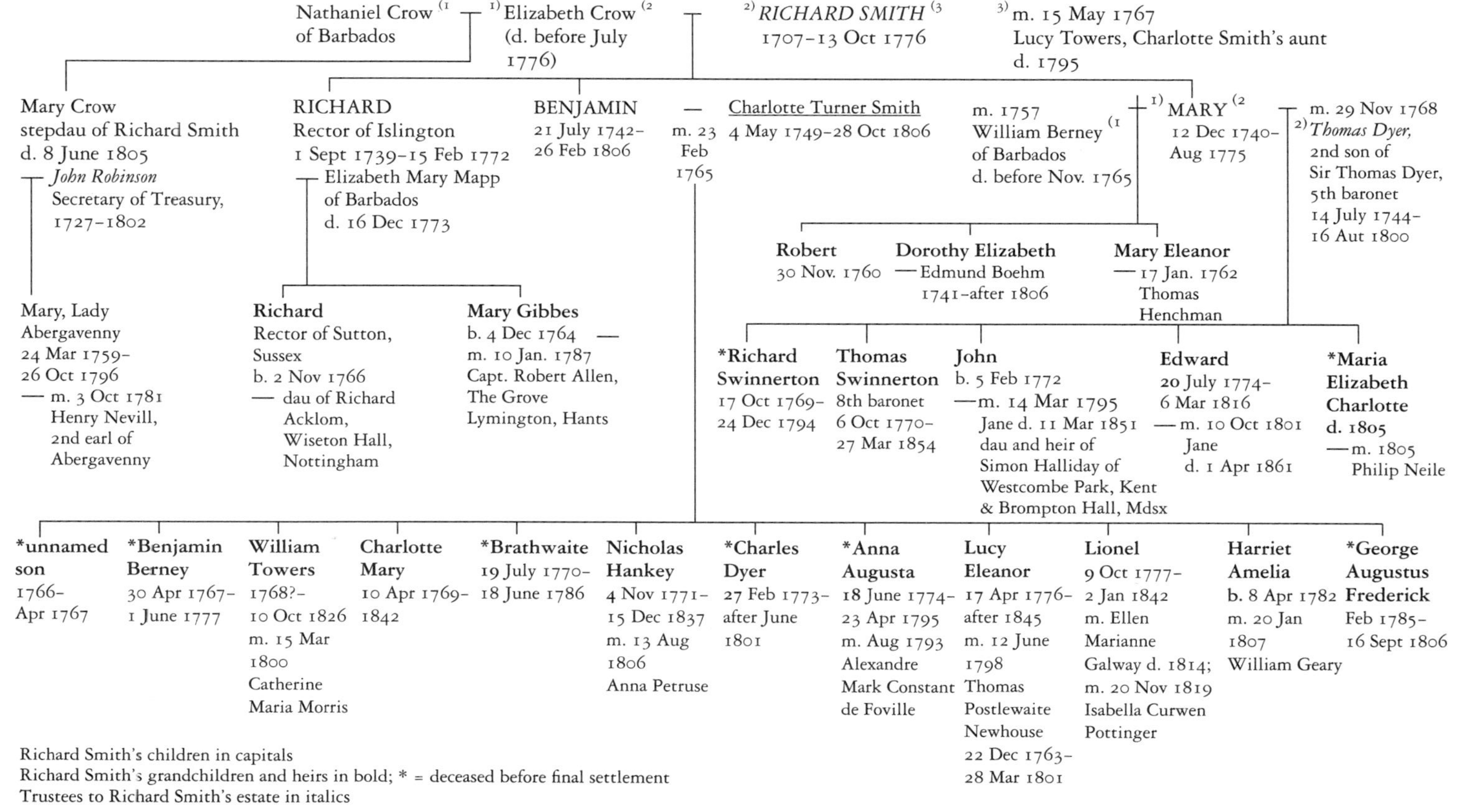

Richard Smith's children in capitals
Richard Smith's grandchildren and heirs in bold; * = deceased before final settlement
Trustees to Richard Smith's estate in italics

The Collected Letters of Charlotte Smith

1765-83
"THE HORROR OF THE ABYSS"

—1768

Young Charlotte Turner seemed destined for a happier and more prosperous life than the one she lived, for she was born in the elegant St. James Square in London and christened near her family's seat, Stoke Manor, at Guilford. When Charlotte was three, her mother, Anna Towers Turner, died. Her grieving father, Nicholas, left Charlotte and two younger siblings with Anna's sister, Lucy Towers, while he traveled in Europe. Charlotte was placed in a private school in Chichester before she was eight and later enrolled in a fashionable school in Kensington. There she was known as a brilliant student, especially in acting and writing.

When her father returned home in financial difficulty, he married a wealthy spinster to repair his fortune; but Miss Henrietta Meriton despised her elder step-daughter and insisted on marrying her off. Introduced to society at thirteen, Charlotte, at fourteen, was placed before Benjamin Smith, a high-spirited son of a wealthy London merchant. Under pressure, she agreed to marry him. Neither her father nor her aunt inquired seriously into the young man's character, taste, or real prospects, though an uncle discouraged the match.

The two surviving fragments of letters from Charlotte Smith's first twenty years of marriage speak volumes of this disastrous match. From the beginning she had to live in London, an uncongenial environment for her health, with both a husband and relatives who lacked social refinement or intellectual sophistication. She had been educated to read, write, draw, and dance, but her mother-in-law chastised her for her ignorance of housekeeping. Her husband brought home rough acquaintances and abused her. For the first decade of her marriage, Charlotte and her father-in-law were in some measure able to contain Benjamin's spending, but she was still subjected to a careless and indifferent companion. Her daily life became an endless round of caring for their growing family—she gave birth to twelve children between 1766 and 1785. Three had died by the time she began to write. The first, whose name is not known, died just as the second, Benjamin Berney, was born; young Benjamin and her fifth child, Brathwaite, died in adolescence.

To an Early Friend

[ca. 1765–66]

I pass almost every day with the poor sick old lady,[1] with whom, however, I am no great favourite; somebody has told her I have not been notably brought up, (which I am afraid is true enough,) and she asks me questions which, to say the truth, I am not very well able to answer. There are no women, she says, so well qualified for mistresses of families as the ladies of Barbadoes, whose knowledge of housewifery she is perpetually contrasting with my ignorance, and, very unfortunately, those subjects on which I am informed, give me little credit with her; on the contrary, are rather a disadvantage to me; yet I have not seen any of their paragons whom I am at all disposed to envy.

Dorset, "Charlotte Smith," p. 40.

NOTE

1. Mrs. Elizabeth Crow Smith, widow of Nicholas Crow of Barbados, Richard Smith's second wife and BS's stepmother. For a few months after CS and BS married on 23 Feb. 1765, they lived with his sister, Mary Berney; they then moved in with his parents in Cheapside. Neither the place nor the company was congenial for CS at 16, a brilliant, educated girl raised for a life in society.

To an Unnamed Recipient

[ca. 1768–70]

No disadvantage could equal those I sustained; the more my mind expanded, the more I became sensible of personal slavery; the more I improved and cultivated my understanding, the farther I was removed from those with whom I was condemned to pass my life; and the more clearly I saw by these newly-acquired lights the horror of the abyss into which I had unconsciously plunged.[1]

Dorset, "Charlotte Smith," pp. 32–33.

NOTE

1. The letter containing this passage could have been written somewhat later than I suggest, as it is clearly a reminiscence; but it does refer to the early years of CS's marriage. During this time, her father-in-law RS had settled his son's growing family in a small house in Southgate outside London. Left to herself, CS read freely, but reading only served to point up the inadequacies of her married life.

1784-90
"TO LIVE ONLY TO WRITE & WRITE ONLY TO LIVE"

—22 AUGUST 1789

Charlotte Smith began to write professionally under humiliating circumstances. Her husband, Benjamin, long a ne'er-do-well, was imprisoned for debt in December 1783. She spent most of his seven-month term with him in King's Bench Prison. Profits from her first publication, Elegiac Sonnets *(1784), helped obtain his release. William Hayley, a neighbor and himself a poet, presented her work to James Dodsley, her first publisher. Letters are scarce in the years that follow, a troubled time during her marriage. After following Benjamin to Normandy to escape his creditors in October 1784, she separated from him, fearing, she admitted years later, for her life and her children's safety.*

Burdened by the need to support them, she took up writing full-time. Hayley, John Sargent, and the Reverend Charles Dunster read her early work. Her second effort, a translation of Manon Lescaut, *was considered scandalous, and its publisher, Thomas Cadell, Sr., withdrew it from publication. Her next work for Cadell,* The Romance of Real Life, *another translation, met with more success. The experience of retelling bizarre real-life legal cases, along with the narrative of* Manon, *gave her confidence to undertake a fiction of her own. Her first novel,* Emmeline, the Orphan of the Castle *(1788), was an immediate success. A misunderstanding with Cadell over advance money led her to offer* Ethelinde, or the Recluse of the Lake *secretly to G. G. and J. Robinson, but in the end Cadell published it in 1789. It, too, was well received. Her poetry continued to be very successful. After Dodsley published four editions, Cadell took over the volume and offered the expanded* Elegiac Sonnets and Other Poems *in a subscription edition in 1789. By 1790, Smith's third novel,* Celestina, *was under way.*

The younger children for whom Smith labored lived at home during these years, wherever home was. In 1784 they lived at Bignor Park, the Turner family seat; in 1785 in Normandy; in 1787 in Woolbeding and London; and in 1788 in Wyke and London again. In 1789 and 1790, Smith made several moves between London and Brighton with most of the children in tow. Her eldest son, William Towers Smith, achieved his rank as a writer with the East India Company in 1783 and was established in Bengal by 1788. Nicholas Hankey Smith earned his rank as a writer in 1788, arriving in Bombay in 1790. Charles Dyer and Lionel attended school at Winchester. The four daughters—Charlotte Mary, Anna Augusta, Lucy Eleanor, and Harriet Amelia—and the youngest son, George, stayed at home. Behind the scenes, Smith worked for a proper settlement of her father-in-law's estate; her legal cause attracted the support of the earl of Egremont and his estate agent, James Upton Tripp.

To James Dodsley[1]

Bignor Park,[2] May 4th 1784,
nr Petworth, Sussex
Sir,

I am this evening favor'd with yr Letter. I am so totally a novice in the business in question that I must beg yr excuse if I do not answer the querys you put to me by this post. A recent loss in a family, through whom some of the pieces you have of mine have been seen & approv'd by Mr Hayley, has made an application to him through them improper, till a few days ago.[3]

To night I am inform'd that a copy of the whole will be transmitted to him immediately, & I shall probably hear from him in the course of a few days, & I have reason to beleive I shall have his permission to dedicate them to him: with such other assistance as he can give me towards publishing them to advantage. Tho we are near Neighbours, I have not courage to address myself directly to him & have therefore been oblig'd to wait till his friend, Mr Sarjent,[4] could undertake to prefer my request—— I apprehend you may nevertheless go on with printing the manuscript. Mr Smith has a particular reason for wishing them to be advertis'd once at least in the morning papers <u>before</u> they are published. His motive relates to a matter I cannot explain to you, but you may be assur'd that whatever is the expence, if it should exceed what ye[5] sale of the Verses produce, you shall be punctually reimburs'd.

In regard to accounting, I dare say we shall have no difficulty, & You shall have as little trouble as possible. All I meant by a copy was that I wish'd to see one before publication as there are, I suppose, always some errors of the press, however carefully conducted, & even the manuscript you have got may have errors in it—As I wrote it out in great haste & had nobody at hand, judge enough of such matters, to correct it.

In a few days, you shall have further, & final, information on this business from, Sir,

Your very Obedient Ser[t],
Charlotte Smith

Huntington MS (HM10800). Address: Mr Dodsley/ Pall Mall/ London. Postmark: PETWORTH; 6/MA.

NOTES

1. See Biographical Notes.

2. After Nicholas Turner, Sr., sold Stoke Manor in 1761, Bignor Park became the Turner family seat. CS's younger sister, Catherine Ann Dorset, lived at Bignor Park most of CS's life and provided her sister with refuge and a business address. On Dorset, see CS to William Davies, 11 Nov. 1795, n. 1.

This letter is dated concurrently with BS's seven-month term of incarceration at King's Bench Prison for debt. Wives and children were permitted but not required to live with convicted husbands. Although it was reported that CS shared all of BS's prison term, this letter and the next show that she spent time away from prison trying to raise money for his release. The preface to the second edition of *Elegiac Sonnets* is dated 10 May from Bignor Park.

3. From her earliest efforts at publication, CS was aided by the poet and friend of poets William Hayley of Eartham. About three miles from Bignor Park, Eartham was near many of CS's later Sussex addresses. Hayley apparently suggested minor improvements and read proofs for printing errors. CS obtained his permission to dedicate these fourteen sonnets to him.

4. John Sargent of Lavington, who later built Woollavington House, was member of Parliament for Seaford in 1790 and chief clerk of the ordnance in 1793. He published *The Mine: A Dramatic Poem* with Thomas Cadell, Sr., in 1788.

5. CS frequently gave the old-fashioned spelling of "the," using the thorn symbol.

To an Unnamed Recipient

[ca. July 1784]

It was on the 2d day of July that we commenced our journey. For more than a month I had shared the restraint of my husband in prison, amidst scenes of misery, of vice, and even of terror. Two attempts had, since my last residence among them, been made by the prisoners to procure their liberation, by blowing up the walls of the house. Throughout the night appointed for this enterprise, I remained dressed, watching at the window, and expecting every moment to witness contention and bloodshed, or perhaps be overwhelmed by the projected explosion. After such scenes and such apprehensions, how deliciously soothing to my wearied spirits was the soft pure air of the summer's morning, breathing over the dewy grass, as (having slept one night on the road) we passed over the heaths of Surrey. My native hills at length burst upon my view. I beheld once more the fields where I had passed my happiest days, and, amidst the perfumed turf with which one of those fields was strewn, perceived with delight the beloved group from whom I had been so long divided, and for whose fate my affections were ever anxious. The transports of this meeting were too much for my exhausted spirits. After all my sufferings, I began to hope I might taste content, or experience at least a respite from calamity.

Dorset, "Charlotte Smith," p. 40.

To an Unnamed Friend

[after spring 1785]

My voyage[1] was without accident; but of my subsequent journey, in a dark night of October through the dismal hollows and almost impassable chasms of a Norman cross-road, I could give a most tremendous account. My children, fatigued almost to death, harassed by sea-sickness, and astonished at the strange noises of the French postillions, whose language they did not understand, crept close to me, while I carefully suppressed the doubts I entertained whether it were possible for us to reach, without some fatal accident, the place of our destination. In the situation I then was, it was little short of a miracle that my constitution resisted,[2] not merely the fatigues of the journey, with so many little beings clinging about me (the youngest,[3] whom I bore in my arms, scarce two years old), but the inconveniences that awaited my arrival at our new abode, in which no accommodation was prepared for my weary charges.

Copy from Hays, "Mrs. Charlotte Smith," in British Public Characters, *3:56. Also quoted in Hilbish,* Charlotte Smith, Poet and Novelist, *p. 113.*

NOTES

1. In Oct. 1784, CS took her eight children to Dieppe to join her husband. The eldest son William was appointed writer with the East India Company in 1783 but did not leave England for India until 1788. Whether he made the ninth child in this entourage is not known. Already afoul of creditors after his recent imprisonment for debt, BS had rented a castle from a Scottish nobleman for his family. Here they stayed through a severe winter into the spring. CS's youngest child, George, was born here that winter and stolen from her (presumably by Catholic priests) to be baptized in the local parish church.

2. Pregnant, CS was concerned about her health during the voyage. Later she feared the birth would be fatal to her.

3. Harriet.

To an Unnamed Recipient

[Woolbeding, Sussex, ca. Sept. 1785]

To Miss ———.[1]

When I found, from your first communication of Mr. ———'s critique,[2] that he greatly disapproved this humble story, which I hardly imagined he would think it worth his while to read, I hoped that what he could not praise he would at least forbear to blame; but, it seems, even if I had been under the circumstances which he says could alone justify, or rather palliate, the dispensation of such literary poison, it is evident such a plea would not have softened the asperity of his criticism, or slacken his invincible zeal for public justice, in detecting what he terms a literary fraud, which seems to me a term rather harsh; for I really see no fraud in a person endeavouring to make a better translation of a work already translated.[3] A fraud means a thing which the imposer hopes to make pass for what it is not. This, surely, could not be the case with the book in question. I never pretended it was otherwise than a translation; and whether it was the first or the second, I was as perfectly ignorant as I believe most of my readers were; and had I been as well informed as Monsr Scourge himself,[4] I should have thought it very immaterial, for I am persuaded the former translations are very little known, and have probably been out of print for years. I will venture to say, they are not to be found in any catalogue of the circulating libraries; and perhaps are only known to those who would take the pains to seek after such trumpery; and I leave to your suggestion whether any one is so likely to take the trouble as your friend, or so likely to succeed if he did. Do not imagine, however, I mean to bounce and fly in the * * *[5] style about this said letter; I only wish it had not happened, and that he had given the book a more gentle damnation, and at least have suffered it to have lived its day, which is all I expected. As it is, I shall withdraw the book rather than let Cadell suffer.

I have the pleasure to add, that the last edition of the Sonnets is, as Jacques[6] informs me, so nearly all sold, that it is high time to consider of another edition, which, however, I shall not do hastily, as I intend they shall appear in a very different form as to size and correctness, and I think I shall be able to add considerably to the bulk of the volume.[7]

Dorset, "Charlotte Smith," p. 46.

NOTES

1. CS's only known unmarried female friend at this time, Charlotte Collins (b. 1747) of Graffham, Midhurst, was along on 28 Sept. 1784 when CS fell ill while riding and was taken in by William Hayley (see Hayley's *Memoirs of the Life and Writings of William Hayley,* 1:432). Charlotte Collins was well acquainted with George Steevens (see n. 2, below), who left her £500 on his death.

2. CS had sent a copy of *Manon Lescaut* to the critic and Shakespearean commenta-

tor George Steevens (1736–1800). As he had already purchased it, he returned her copy to Thomas Cadell, Sr., to spare her the expense. Steevens's sharp, thorough criticism of the novel on moral grounds is preserved in a letter in Dorset's biography of CS ("Charlotte Smith," pp. 43–44). Presumably he made the public objection to the work as a literary fraud. See n. 4, below.

3. Abbé Prevost's *Histoire du Chevalier Des Grieux et de Manon Lescaut,* first published in 1731, was indeed translated into English more than once. Erskine's translation was published by T. Cooper: *The Memoirs and Adventures of the Marquis de Bretagne, and Duc d'Harcourt . . . . to Which Is Added, The History of the Chevalier de Grieu {sic} and Moll Lescaut, an Extravagant Love-Adventure* (1743). It appeared in a second edition in Dublin (1770). A two-volume translation appeared in 1767 titled *The History of the Chevalier des Grieux.*

4. CS felt obligated to Cadell to withdraw the novel after a short notice by "Scourge" appeared in the *Public Advertiser,* complaining that it was a "literary fraud" as it had been twice before translated, "once annexed to the Marquis de Bretagne, and once by itself, under the title of the Chevalier de Grieux" (Dorset, "Charlotte Smith," p. 45). Dorset claimed that Scourge—that is, George Steevens—was the one who had attacked Garrick and Hayley (p. 47). While the 1785 edition was suppressed, an anonymous edition was printed in 1786 with an unsigned preface dated Normandy, winter 1784–85, the date CS returned to Normandy with BS and their children.

5. Dorset's asterisks.

6. Dennett Jacques (1758–1837), a printer of Chichester from 1783 to 1788, printed several of CS's earlier works. He is named as the printer of Dodsley's second edition of *Elegiac Sonnets* (1784) only. In the early days, when CS was moving among Bignor Park, Woolbeding, London, and later Brighton, Chichester was a central location. In 1794, Jacques moved his printing business to Lower Sloane Street, Chelsea, London.

7. Dodsley had printed the third and fourth editions of *Elegiac Sonnets* after March 1786, but published no more. CS's plan for a larger edition was realized in the expanded fifth edition, published by Cadell in 1789.

To John Robinson[1]

Bignor. Septr 19th 1785
My Dear Sir,

I enclose the schedule of papers del[ivere]^d^ in July 1784 to The Attorney Rickman,[2] which together with what I gave myself in July 1783 to Sir John Dyer[3] & for which I have his receipt (copy of which schedule and receipt you have had) contain all the papers that I could find at Islington in the Boxes where Mr Richard Smith[4] always kept his papers, and all that were any where to be met with, which we thought the Trustees had a right to. I trust this schedule will convince you we withheld nothing material to which the trustees had a claim and that Mr Boehm,[5] to conceal his blundering ignorance or to make a parade of his ridiculous assiduity, has not scrupled (as indeed he never does when he has a point to carry) to say that which was not.[6]

Whatever he found (if he found anything) was a duplicate, or duplicates, and put away among papers of inferior consequence for ye Tin Boxes I absolutely emptied entirely except of a few loose papers that related to buying Lottery tickets, shares of ships & such affairs for Barbados correspondents thirty or forty years ago—— And so far was I from meaning to give too little that I (in the terror I was under) lost my recollection and gave too much. Otherwise I should not now [*sic*] to put to inconvenience and trouble to recover one of the copys of the declaration of Trust.

In regard to the deeds that relate to Sir John Gibbons's M[or]tgage,[7] Mr Smith desires me to say that the purchasers of the Stanwell Lands[8] will give up ye Original bonds, but not ye M[or]t[ga]ge deeds. Therefore if they must be had, it must be by attested Copys, and if it be your pleasure to have it done, he begs you will send him a written order to that effect, signifying that ye trust direct such copys to be taken and will pay ye expense.

As you were so very good as to inform me that some effects were sent from Gays,[9] I hope you will not think me intrusive if I request your attention to ye payment of the interest that is due to me (it will be two years in February of which I have received fifty pounds)——I shall really be so extremely distress'd without some part of this arrear that I shall not know what to do for the actual exigences of my family. I am now near a quarter behind hand with my Butcher & Grocer, besides Williams Schooling,[10] the Boys Taylor (the House rent & taxes ~~besides~~ much more), all of which must be paid in the course of this & next month) for if I do not pay what I owe now, I shall not get credit for the quarter to come; & until January I have not a shilling to reckon upon.

As to the other Moneys promis'd will I apprehend more than reimburse Mr Boehm & pay Mrs Lucy Smith.[11] I flatter myself you will have the goodness to direct that I may receive at least some part if not ye whole of what is due to me as soon as the Sugars are sold. Otherwise I shall be in a dreadfull situation. As it is, I am obliged to see my children languishing in the whooping Cough, which only change of air will remove, because I cannot afford to send them out for that benefit. I should not, my dear Sir, be so pressing on this subject had I any other resource than this little pittance to support us all; but if we do not receive it, we must actually want necessarys. Therefore it is not in my power to make it so easy to ye Trustees as I shd wish to do was I not so very much straightend.

Permit us to offer our condolences for the late loss in your family.[12] We shall be truly happy to hear You and Mrs Robinson, Lord & Lady Abergavenny,[13] & the children are well.

I have the honor to be
Dear Sir
your Obedient & most Oblig'd Sert
Charlotte Smith

Petworth House Archives MS. No address or postmark.

NOTES

1. See Biographical Notes.

2. Gawler Griffith Rickman, a London attorney of Tooke's Court, Cursitor Street, represented the collateral branches of the family whose suit sent BS to jail in Dec. 1783.

3. Sir John Swinnerton Dyer, sixth baronet (1738–1801) of Swinnerton Lodge, Dartmouth, was an army colonel and Groom of the Bedchamber to the Prince of Wales. The older brother of Thomas Dyer, he was appointed trustee to Richard Smith's estate from 2 July 1784 with John Robinson, Edmund Boehm, and Richard Atkinson. He requested to be released and was discharged on 29 July 1788. Anthony Parkin replaced him.

4. CS's father-in-law, of Barbados and Islington (1707–13 Oct. 1776), merchant and plantation owner. His first marriage to the widow of Nathaniel Crow of Barbados brought him a stepdaughter Mary Crow and produced three children, Richard, Benjamin, and another Mary. (See Genealogical Chart.) His second marriage was to Lucy Towers, Charlotte's maternal aunt, whom he evidently met when she worked to arrange Charlotte's marriage to BS. When dividing his considerable estate to his children and stepchildren according to their needs rather than equally, he wrote his own will and set the stage for decades of legal wrangling.

5. Edmund Boehm (1741–d. after 1806), a director of the South Sea Company and the Russia Company, of Ottershaw Park in Chertsey, Surrey. He was involved in trust affairs by virtue of having married Richard Smith's granddaughter Dorothy Elizabeth Berney, second child of William Berney and Mary Smith Berney (later Dyer). Although Boehm was on cordial social terms with his wife's cousin, Charlotte Mary Smith, who often visited them, CS herself did not trust him.

6. In Jonathan Swift's *Gulliver's Travels* (1726), part 4, chapter 4, the Houyhnhnms—talking horses—explain that they cannot lie or "say the thing which is not," for that defeats the ends of speech, which are understanding each other and receiving information. CS often uses this phrase.

7. This transaction would have preceded Sir John's death on 9 July 1776.

8. Location not identified.

9. Gay's plantation was one of the trust's holdings in Barbados.

10. See Biographical Note on William Towers Smith. He had received his rank as writer in the East India Company on 7 Aug. 1783, but CS would not have been completely relieved of his support until he was actually called into service. He arrived in Calcutta on 7 Aug. 1788. Her other sons, Nicholas, Charles, Lionel, and George, were still at home.

11. Lucy Towers Smith (d. 1795), CS's maternal aunt who raised CS and her siblings and helped arrange for young Charlotte to marry BS. Lucy then married CS's father-in-law, Richard Smith, on 15 May 1767.

12. It is not known who died.

13. In 1781, Robinson's daughter Mary (d. 1796) married Henry Neville, second earl of Abergavenny (1755–1843).

To Thomas Cadell, Sr.[1]

[Woolbeding, 3 June 1787]
Sir,

Many of my friends and several persons of high fashion have express'd a wish that the Edition of Sonnets which I have some time meditated may be publish'd with plates by subscription.[2] And indeed I find the expence of good plates (and with no other should I be satisfied) is so great that I cannot otherwise engage in such a work without hazarding the profit of the Edition which at present I am so circumstanced as to be unable to do—— With such illustrious Patronage[3] as has (unsolicited) been offer'd me, it would perhaps be a failure of my duty to my family and yielding to the suggestions of ill-placed pride if I refusd to take advantage of the offers of my friends and the good opinion of the public. I wrote to Mr Sargent while he was in Town on this business and requested the favor of him to see you upon it, Which I beleive he did, but tho I have seen him once since his return into Sussex, we were so entirely occupied by the relation of other business which he was so good as to negociate for me that he did not tell me whether he had had any conversation with you and wether it would be agreeable to you to take in the subscriptions if the scheme is carried into execution.

I purpose to add other Sonnets and two or three longer poems, the whole forming a pocket volume, printed on fine paper with four or six plates At half a Guineau.[4]

Mr Gardner,[5] who is known particularly to some of my friends, I mean also to engage to open a book for the subscription unless You object to any second place being named for that purpose.

As I intend keeping the subscription open till after Christmas, it will give time for the plates to be well executed and for the yet unprinted poems to appear in as correct a state as possible And will also give my friends opportunity to exert themselves for me with effect.

I shall be greatly oblig'd to you to let me know wether you will allow me to name your house as the first where the subscriptions are to be paid. And any information you will give me as to the proper manner of conducting this matter will extremely oblige me.

By the time I have your answer, I hope to have seen Mr Hayley, without whose concurrence and assistance I do not mean finally to conclude on it. But a variety of untoward circumstances have prevented my reaching Eartham since his return.

I am, Sir,
your obt & oblig'd Sert,
Charlotte Smith

Woolbeding, June 3rd 1787

I beg to know whether a Manuscript[6] which I wish to submit to your perusal in the course of a fortnight or three weeks should be forwarded to London? The first volume waits only the Transcriber and by that you will, I apprehend, be able to judge wether you will purchase the copy.

University of Pennsylvania MS. Address: Mr Cadell/ Strand/ London. Postmark: Place not clear; JU 5 87.

NOTES

1. See Biographical Notes. See Appendix for four additional letters written to James Upton Tripp in September 1787.

2. This correspondence resulted in a subscription edition, *Elegiac Sonnets, by Charlotte Smith. The Fifth Edition, with Additional Sonnets and Other Poems* (1789). CS's first illustrated work, it contained five engraved plates, three drawn by Richard Corbould and two by the better known Thomas Stothard. They were engraved by John Milton, James Neagle, Thornthwaite, and James Heath.

3. Among the persons of fashion who subscribed to this edition was the duchess of Cumberland, who put herself down for ten copies. A good number of nobility subscribed to this edition.

4. Dodsley's fourth edition contained thirty-six sonnets but no other poems or engravings. Along with engravings, twelve sonnets and four other poems were added to the fifth edition.

5. Henry-Lasher Gardner (d. 1808), bookseller, opposite St. Clement's Church, the Strand.

6. In her letter of 10 Feb. 1788, CS states that she had not begun to write *Emmeline* until Sept. Thus this manuscript was *The Romance of Real Life* (1787), which she translated from *Causes célèbres et intéressantes, avec les jugemens que les ont décidées* (Paris, 1735–45) by the lawyer François Gayot de Pitaval. CS shortened its thirteen volumes to three, and its seventy-four cases to fifteen. Though she complains in the preface of the original's obscure style, repetition, and lack of focus, her journeywork with these extraordinary and often bizarre narratives must have sharpened her own plotting.

To Thomas Cadell, Sr.

Wyhe——14th Jany 1788
Sir,

The reluctance I ever feel to give you farther trouble—who have already had so much and who have voluntarily undertaken so much on my account—has prevented me mentioning my renew'd apprehensions abt Mr Smith's taking the residue of what may be in your hands on my ~~account~~ behalf. But now it becomes necessary for me to inform you that abt a month since, he wrote to me to say that, as he had taken his passage for Barbados, he beg'd to see his children before he went.

As I could not doubt an assertion so positive and as many of our joint friends to whom he had represented his sorrow at being parted from his "dear Wife and children" thought I ought to comply with this request, I not only assented to it, but instead of sending his children to meet him at the Inn as he suppos'd I should, I hired a post chaise and met him myself at Godalming, desirous not only to convince him I had no malice against him, but to conceal his journey from his numerous creditors in Hampshire and Sussex—concluding he would only stay a day or two and then return to sail for the West Indies.

But I soon found reason to repent my credulous folly. Tho my house is so small & I have eight children at home[1] & am therefore forced to put a tent bed up in my little Book room, he took possession of it & treated me with more than his usual brutality—threatening to sell the furniture, the Books, and every necessary which I have twice saved from the rapacity of his Creditors. This is the situation I have been in for three weeks; yet I have borne it with patience in hopes of obtaining what I at length got him to do, a deed providing out of my fortune for his three Younger children born since the death of their Grandfather, who has given to the rest some provision.[2] But within these two or three days a new fit of frenzy has seizd him: he has broke open all my drawers where my papers were, taken away several sign'd receipts for the Sonnets (Of which Heaven knows what use he may make) and foul copies of many things I am writing, all of which he has taken {away} with him; and he openly declared a resolution of demanding of you the money You hold of mine.

To day he is gone—to London, & there is reason to suppose may make immediate application to you. I now beleive him capable of <u>any</u> thing and therefore, relying entirely on you, beg the favor of you if you have any apprehensions of his having the <u>power</u> to take the money that you will be so good as to pay it into the hands of your own Banker or any confidential friend; and on your informing me that you have done so, I will instantly forward to you a receipt in full of all demands. And I am informed that on your producing Such receipt to Mr Smith he can have no power to molest or trouble you[3]—— I shall be extremely uneasy till I hear from you or Mr Davis[4] on this matter As he appears careless of every thing & totally regardless of the infamy that must attend such an action. ~~And~~ From his own account he is connected with persons in Town, who are engaged in the desperation of gaming houses, and I know not what—& from such a Man so acquainted, I and my family have every thing to fear.

Conscious of having done for him more than any other person on Earth would have done and in this last instance shewn a foolish reliance on his word which I knew was worth nothing, I am now firmly resolved never again on any pretence whatever to see him & have no longer the least wish to keep terms with him, & I beg that if he calls at your shop as I find he has already done, you will give him no information whatever As to the Sonnets or any thing else.

Mr Duer, whom I have seen only for a moment, informs me that no receipts have been sent to Bull at Bath where during his (Mr Duers) stay he could have been of great use.[5] He has however interested some friends there for me, and if you will be so good as to let some receipts be sent to Bull, much may yet be done for me.

I hope to hear from you by an early post and Am, Sir,

y^r^ oblig'd & ob^t^ hble Ser^t^,
Charlotte Smith

General Manuscripts, Manuscripts Division, Department of Rare Books and Special Collections, Princeton University Library. No address or postmark.

NOTES

1. Charlotte Mary (age 18), Nicholas Hankey (16), Charles Dyer (13), Anna Augusta (14), Lucy Eleanor (11), Lionel (10), Harriet Amelia (5), and George Frederick Augustus (2).

2. When Richard Smith, BS's father, died in 1776, he settled a great deal of his fortune of £36,000 on the six living children to protect them from BS's already apparent profligacy. Lionel, Harriet, and George, born after his death, were not covered. CS never succeeded in persuading BS to settle her much smaller fortune of £7,000 on them but did so herself before she died.

3. As husband, BS had the right, under law, to any of his wife's money, including her earnings by her own enterprise.

4. That is, William Davies; see Biographical Notes.

5. Bull was a bookseller at Bath with whom CS had other dealings. Duer is not identified.

To an Unnamed Recipient[1]

36 Norton Street, Portland Place [London]
Feby 10th [?1788]
Sir,

You have very little reason to fear that if the Comedy should be matured, You would be deprived of "your darling priveledges of curtailing, altering, hinting"—— So far from it that, had I not been encouraged to beleive you would condescend to take such trouble, I had never ventured to think of an undertaking to which I still fear my talents are unequal——

You have reason to smile at the <u>two</u> Lessons I have taken since I have been in Town. I have learned however from them how I should <u>not</u> write, & I have also learned what strange compositions are by the courtesy of the Town, call'd <u>Comedies</u>!——

Your objections I admit to be just.[2] Arbitrary runs ill off the tongue, & I did not like it myself when I put it down merely for want of being able to find~~ing~~ another that express'd the character I meant to draw & knowing that it might easily be changed. Fanfarron[3] is exceptionable as being

French; otherwise the word expresses that for which we have no synonyme in English. But I am by no means partial to it & will look for another.

You are very good to give me a reproof for writing bad English. I consider it as a very flattering testimony of real kindness & good opinion, as it shews me that you beleive I have sense enough to hear of any errors. Had I not learned to receive & value friendly correction, the Novel of which you speak with so much partiality[4] would not perhaps so well have deserved your approbation or that of the public, for M[r] Hayley had the goodness to be my critic, & I think that in no one instance I had occasion to doubt the excellence of his judgement or to prefer my own. The event has proved that I was right in adhering to his decisions.

The scenes I have written I will not trouble you with till they are more worthy of being attended too [*sic*]. I have only to say that possibly you may beleive I shall be much circumscribed in point of time, as a Comedy of three acts is no light undertaking. I am trying by removing to a quieter lodging (& to a cheaper) to obtain more tranquillity, & my eldest Girl[5] becomes my copyist so that—tho I have a Novel absolutely pawned to Cadell of three Volumes[6] & am not yet half thro it, & tho I have a very large family ca et la[7] to all of whom I must attend—Yet I do hope that I may manage it in the time, Seeing that Emmeline was only begun in September & in the press the middle of January following——

Your Letter is so very friendly & good humoured that I have written with as much freedom, as if I had the [. . .][8]
how very few of our modern writers do I feel any inclination to be acquainted with—— If the future is to be foreseen from the present, I think a winter or two more will eradicate the very last remains of real & rational comedy. And that farce, inferior even to pantomime & buffoonery (at which I own I cannot laugh), will wholly usurp the Stage, & play going people will speak of the day of Garrick & Colman as we talk of those of good Queen Bess. At thirty eight (I am afraid almost thirty nine), this signifies little to me as the time is approaching when plays will delight not me nor "Opera" "neither!"——

You was not aware perhaps, when you so obligingly ans[d] my Letter, that you made yourself liable to the trouble of reading another & a yet longer one & may possibly exclaim with a slight alteration of Hudibras—

> "I think quoth Thomas Womens pens
> Of [Aspen leaves are made?"][9]

Osborn Collection, Yale University MS. No address or postmark.

NOTES

1. The recipient may well be George Colman the elder, a London publisher. On 8 Feb. 1795, CS wrote to the duchess of Devonshire that Colman had urged her to write a

comedy for him "about five years ago, & immediately after the publication of *Emmeline.*" The earliest date for this letter would be 1788, the latest (and less likely) 1790.

John Sargent, CS's and Hayley's neighbor, is also a possible recipient. No correspondence with him has survived, though he is mentioned in Maida Butler's article describing some early letters now lost, "Mrs. Smith and Mr. Cadell." Hayley is discussed in the letter, and CS had not yet met Cowper, a later critic, nor did she write to him so informally.

Brian Edwards, author of *The History of the British Colonies in the West Indies* (1793–1801) and some poems, was among the first to encourage her to publish her sonnets. In the 1790s, CS submitted her work to the rector of Petworth—the Reverend Charles Dunster, a Milton scholar—before sending it to the press, but this letter is probably not to him. It is much chattier than her sedate, respectful letter to Dunster (see 16 July 1794).

2. Later in the letter it is clear that CS has submitted a scene from a comedy for perusal; here she is responding to suggestions for revisions. She has recently published *Emmeline,* her first novel, and has contracted with Cadell to write *Ethelinde* for advance money. CS mentions attempting a play only twice; here and in the letter described in n. 1. The play long attributed to her, *What Is She?* was not published until 1799. She never named it in her letters.

3. That is, *fanfaron,* "bragging, blustering."

4. *Emmeline.*

5. Charlotte Mary (see Biographical Notes).

6. *Ethelinde, or the Recluse of the Lake* (Cadell, 1789) was five volumes long, and the fifth volume was the longest. CS sent the first volume to press a year later (3 Feb. 1789).

7. Here and there.

8. The rest of this page is cut away. The text continues on the back of the page. The end of the letter, which includes the signature, is also missing.

9. The second line is mutilated where the page is cut away. *Hudibras* has no similar line. CS often cited lines from memory and her quotations are often inexact.

To Thomas Cadell, Sr.

[London, winter-spring 1788][1]
Dr Sir,

I write with extreme difficulty having lost the use of my right hand. Will you be so good as to send to day time enough for ye Post a Guinea to Fry, Robinson,[2] & Cs to supply my Son[3] at Portsmouth with his weekly allowance.

I am, d^{r} Sir,
your humble Ser^{t},
C Smith

Norton St [London]
Saturday Morn[4]

Bodleian (MS Montagu d. 10). No address or postmark.

NOTES

1. The Bodleian dates this letter as 1787, but the only other letter from Norton Street was written on 10 Feb. 1788, making winter-spring 1788 a more likely date. CS had been in Wyke on 14 Jan. 1788.

2. Fry and Robinson are not listed in Kent's *London Directory* and similar sources.

3. At 16, Nicholas Hankey Smith was appointed a writer, a clerk in the East India Company, in 1788; but he did not arrive in India until Sept. 1790 and thus might still have been in England. See Biographical Notes.

4. A note written at the bottom of the page in another hand shows that this was paid: "Paid one Guinea/ Mess[rs] Fry and Robinson/ Mildred Court."

To William Hayley

[London, late 1788–89][1]

Copy of a letter from C. S.

Friday Evening

As I know you love a dialogue,[2] here follows one that passed this morning:

Scene. The poor Novelist at her desk just about a chapter of ~~Ethelinde~~. Enter her Servant.

Ser. "a Gentleman wants you Ma'am below."

"A gentleman! who is it? anybody of this place?" for I had seen from the window a vulgar fat Man & heard a consequential rap.

"I don't know Ma'am, but I believe it is a stranger."

"Ask his name & business."

Exit Servant. Enter again. "Ma'am, he says he can't leave his name or business but must speak with you."

I now concluded it was some dun on account of T.[3] with w[hic][h] I have been so repeatedly plagued & harassed, & submitting to the interruption as patiently as I could, I went down with sad civility & an acking heart.

Scene the parlor. A consequential red-faced pert looking Man Solus. Enter to him the unfortunate Novelist.

Man. "Madam! your obedient—my name is Lane—I hear you are writing a novel."

"Well, Sir, sit down, sir. M[r] Lane the Bookseller?"[4]

"At your service Madam. Novels are—as perhaps you know—quite my forte &, understanding you are about one, I called to know if you are disposed to deal for it!"

Novelist. "Whatever may be my intention Sir, as to disposing of it, I am and have long been engaged to M[r] Cadell"——

"I assure you Madam that—no disparagement to Mr Cadell—you w^{ld} not be hurt by giving him up for me. I will venture to say that where he will give you one hundred pounds, I will give you 2."

"I have no reason Sir at present to complain of Mr Cadell, nor any intention of leaving him."

"Well, Ma'am, but the thing is this. Mr Cadell has made a great fortune. Now I have a fortune to make & for that there is no reason d'ye see, I would give you twice as much as he will; by reason that a novel of yours just now would be worth any money to me."

"I cannot listen Sir to any proposals for that in question, it is already disposed of."

"I am very sorry to hear it. I hoped I might have got the preference—what you have enter'd into an agreement with Mr Cadell? I hope you have made a good bargain. Why I am told now that he gave you but £60 for the Orphan of the Castle."

"You have been misinformed, Sir. The Copyright of that is my own."

After a few more very impertinent enquires & professions on his part, & what I thought necessary hauteur on mine, he departed, but in about half an hour, a servant in a fine laced livery came with a letter thus—

> Madam—
>
> Understanding the Copyright of the Orphan of the Castle is yours, wish to treat for 100 Copies of same, as in consequence of my extensive dealings & supplying all the libraries, can put them into extensive circulation & will deal on such terms as you will find advantageous & wait on you immediately as I leave the place at four ^{o}Clock. Any future production in the novel way, flatter to be remembered, which will oblige
>
> your humble sev^{nt} Willm Lane—

Answer

> Sir,
>
> The copyright of Emmeline is mine. But I leave to Mr Cadell the sale & all trouble & expense. On applying to him, you may I apprehend have any quantity of the 3rd Edition when it is published. I have at present not the least intention to change my publisher, having found Mr Cadell hitherto equally liberal & respectable. I am, Sir, Y^{r} ob Sr C. S.

There is something highly in character in this dealer in wit. He would make a glorious figure in the farce we were talking of. But I am such a proud fool that I feel humbled & hurt at being supposed liable to his negociations & felt then all in a tremble about it. Somebody I apprehend has told him how cruelly I want money, & he thought my poverty w^{ld} make me Eagerly grasp at his offers, & finding the first fail, thought I c^{ld} not resist 40 or 50£ for 100 Copies of Emmeline, by w^{t} means he c^{d} get a sort of hold on me. But I think

I have done right in repulsing forever his pert advances. Alas! how unfit I am for the common intercourse of common life, & how very unfit for all I am forced to encounter.

The Fitzwilliam Museum, Cambridge. Copy by Hayley. No address or postmark.

NOTES

1. CS spent most of 1788 and part of 1789 writing *Ethelinde,* the one factual clue in dating this letter. Late 1788 seems a likely time for it. The second edition of *Emmeline* came out in 1788, giving William Lane time at the end of the year to try to obtain this popular work.

2. CS's use of stage directions and dialogue in this letter is unique. On 10 Feb. 1788, she refers to undertaking a comedy in three acts. Perhaps she had just tried her hand at comedy, and so this letter's dramatic form would come naturally.

3. "T." is not identified.

4. William Lane (1738–1814) of Leadenhall Street helped establish circulating libraries while publishing at his Minerva Press (1790–1820) many of the cheaply produced volumes that supplied them. CS wanted scrupulously to avoid any connection with "Lanes trumpery Novels" (CS to Thomas Cadell, Jr., and William Davies, 5 Jan. 1796).

To Thomas Cadell, Sr.

{London} Feby 3rd 1789
Sir,

I troubled you last night with a draft, ab^t^ which I hardly knew what I wrote as I was at the moment much hurried. My Son[1] waits upon you with this, but if it is unpleasant or inconvenient to you to give me Cash for the Ballance of the draught, I will send it to a Bankers who negociate matters for the Chichester Bank & repay you the five G^s^. This however will be attended with some trouble, & therefore if you can oblige me, I conclude you will.

The first Volume of Ethelinde will in a week be transcribed for the Press. Do you wish to have it sent to the Printers before the whole is deliverd? & do you mean Jacques should have it? He desired me to ask it of you, saying, that if you was so kind as to favour him with the business, he w^d^ execute it as to money & time of payment on the same terms as any other Printer. I told him I would mention it, but should not make myself a party in the matter ab^t^ which you will decide as best pleases you.

I am, Sir, your most ob^t^ & oblig'd Ser^t^,
Charlotte Smith

Huntington MS (HM10802). Address: To/ Mr Cadell/ Strand/ Opposite the end of Catharine Street. No postmark.

NOTE

1. Possibly Nicholas, who had not yet left for India.

To George Robinson[1]

[Brighton, 18 June 1789]
Sir,

In consequence of a conversation I had yesterday with Mr Hayley at Eartham, and of some difficulties likely to arise between me and Mr Cadell, I give you this trouble. I mean not to complain of Mr Cadell who has hitherto conducted himself towards me with a liberality which is from the account of others sometimes unusual with him.[2] But, as he has made a very considerable profit by the Novel of Emmeline and has in his hands a certain security for a small advance (vis, near fifty pounds to be paid him in the course of Trade by a Bookseller on the Sonnet account), I think myself hardly used in having a draft for fifteen G^s returned, which I had not made payable till the last Volume of the work I am about should be in the hands of the Printer. A work which it is beleived by good Judges will equal in success, as in merit they think it exceeds, Emmeline.[3]

It is very disagreeable to me and quite out of my way to have any disagreement on the subject of money. And as I always find accounts irksome & frequently not very clear as to the Authors profit, I will sell the copy right of the Novel I am on the point of finishing. It will be in five volumes of which two are actually printed; the third in the Printers hands; the fourth ready & the fifth in such forwardness that it will be very soon perfectly prepared for the press.[4]

The price Miss Burney obtain'd, & the fix'd price for works whose Authors are known, is fifty pounds a volume, & this price Mr Cadell would have given me & will still give. He has advanced ab^t seventy pounds on account of this Novel.[5] The profit he allow'd for two thirds of Emmeline, first Edition (for of the others I had only half) was one hundred and thirty pounds, I think (but I have not the sketch of the account by me, & a regular statement has never been render'd). Of course I thought I had still money coming to me on it the new one, & that he would not, knowing how I am situated as to my private fortune, have refus'd a small accommodation (tho I know it is not usual to pay Authors till a month after publication), & all circumstances consider'd I do think he has not acted with kindness which, as he could not have lost by it in any way, I must think dissolves all obligations on my side to continue with him——

Let me know therefore whether it will be agreeable to you to purchase the five Volumes on the above terms, Paying to Mr Cadell the Money with in[tere]s[t] he has advanced, and half the rest, on delivery of the whole work, The remainder at a month after publication——

Emmeline, the copy right of which is mine, is now reprinted in a third edition, & M[r] Cadell reserved it I beleive to re-publish with the present Novel. Two thousand copies of that work have been sold within little more than a Twelvemonth, & I will venture to say that the demand for the present work will be very great as soon as it is publish'd——even at this late season——— I will own to you that I had various solicitations while I was in London from Persons in the Trade, but there are names which No profit should induce me to accept as my publishers. M[r] Cadells respectability cannot be denied, & if I am compelled to change, it must be only for a Gentleman of equal respectability.[6] For which reason I apply Sir to you, and beg the favour of an answer by the return of the Post which will oblige, Sir,

your obed[t] humble Ser[t],
Charlotte Smith

Brighthelmston, June 18th 1789

I need not name to you I am persuaded the necessity of secrecy, that in these cases being always understood.

Henry W. and Albert A. Berg Collection of English and American Literature, The New York Public Library, Astor, Lenox and Tilden Foundations MS. Address: To/ M[r] Robinson/ PaterNosterrow/ London. Postmark: BRIGHTHELMSTONE; JU 19 89.

NOTES

1. CS settled her present quarrel with Cadell but turned to Robinson again after Cadell rejected *Desmond* (1793) on account of its revolutionary sentiments. G. G. J. and J. Robinson published the controversial work, but nothing else by CS.

2. Neither the records of Cadell and Davies in the Longman Archives at the University of Reading nor Theodore Besterman's *Publishing Firm of Cadell and Davis* offer much evidence that Cadell was generous toward authors in advance of publication.

3. *Ethelinde, or the Recluse of the Lake,* published by Cadell in 1789, was nearly as successful as *Emmeline, the Orphan of the Castle* (1788). It is a quieter, more sustained portrait of characters caught in a sentimental situation of tender love and anguishing separations.

4. CS finished revising the second through the fifth volumes of this long novel between 3 Feb. and 18 June 1789.

5. In 1782, Fanny Burney received £250 for her five-volume *Cecelia.* Although usual, the price cannot be called "fixed." In 1794, Ann Radcliffe was paid £500 for the four-volume *Mysteries of Udolpho.* Cadell often gave CS considerable advances on work in progress. Authors were usually paid, as she goes on to say, one month after a work was published.

6. Known for hospitality at his Streatham villa as well as for politically liberal views, Robinson was very much the sort of gentleman bookseller whom CS sought to publish her works.

To Dr. Thomas Shirley[1]

[Brighton, 22 August 1789]
Dear Sir,

When first Charlotte came hither, her Grand Mother talk'd much of coming down to Brighton under the idea that the sea air would be of great use to her & that she might be able to use the hot baths.[2]

Of this I now hear no more, tho the marriage of Miss Berney and their intentions of passing some time here would, I suppose, be a very strong additional motive to my Aunt—— Now I am going to tell you why I wish she may again think of & execute this project. I have a friend in Ireland[3] whom I love extremely who is very desirous of my going over to her for a few weeks and returning with her to England in December. She is in a rank of life which enables her to be of great use to my family, & policy as well as pleasure urge me to oblige her if I could. If my Aunt would come down and inhabit my house, I should leave my Girls without being uneasy; she would have a comfortable house without any expence, and I should be able to get off the thorns for a little while & begin a New Novel at Shanes Castle—

I need not say to you that duty rather than inclination has for many years compelled me to live in a way for which I am very ill calculated. It has often been so bitter to me that nothing but my tenderness for the children could have carried me thro it—— When I can escape from it without injury to them, it is a duty which I think I owe myself; I owe it indeed to them also, for on my health & power of writing depends their support, and I need not tell you that neither are promoted by incessant anxiety & sameness of scene. The two little ones[4] will be at day school, & the old Lady will have no trouble with them; The elder Girls will be I suppose rather pleasant to her, & she will have a spacious dining room and a bed chamber adjoining within two hundred yards of the Sea. An easy stair case & a Sedan chair may always be had to carry her down to ye sea So that consulting her own health only perhaps she could not do better. And when her dear Boehms & dear Miss Berney,[5] now made dearer by being on the point of marrying a Man who keeps three carriages, are here also, what can be wanting to her felicity? Unless one could transport Mrs Scrivener and the Sieur Davison also[6]——

Will you, if you think that change of air &c may really be useful to her, promote her coming if she names it to you? I shall write to her on Monday about it, & you will doubtless be consulted When you will Of course say what you think right without adverting to <u>secret</u> influence. I am so strongly tempted on one hand & so weary of the labour of Sysyphus on the other that I am afraid I shall not hold out unless some little change renews my powers of perseverence. Virtue of all sorts is a mighty perishable commodity. Mine has held out miraculously for the space of four & twenty years, & tis not worth while to let it fail in my fortieth year.

But really it is almost too much for me, having the power to live so much otherwise, to be compelled to live only to write & write only to live. While every body seems to think (I mean of the family) that I am bound to do it, forgetting that I was a mere child when they talk'd me into bonds, which I have found most insupportably heavy, & that to provide for them I promis'd what it is wonderful that I have perform'd in any part. But there is a time when the soul rebels against fetters so unjustly imposed and when, if they are not a little lighten'd, they must be wholly thrown off. I say all this to you knowing that, with great liberality of mind, you are perfectly aware of my situation.

Charlottes face is much better, & I have receiv'd much benefit from the remedy you prescribed for me.

Nobody knows of my writing to you; you will of course let it remain a secret & beleive me, with great regard,

Dear Sir,
your oblig'd & ob[t] Ser[t],
Charlotte Smith

Aug[st] 22nd 1789

University of California at Los Angeles MS. Address: To/ M[r] Shirly/ at/ Islington/ {London}. Postmark illegible.

NOTES

1. Probably the Islington surgeon Thomas Shirley (b. 1729), although the last record of him in P. J. and R. V. Wallis's *Eighteenth Century Medics* is 1781.

2. Charlotte Mary, the oldest child at home, now 20. This grandmother was CS's mother-in-law, Mrs. Lucy Towers Smith. She had an unusual double relationship to CS and her children. Before becoming Richard Smith's third wife, she was Lucy Towers, the maternal aunt who had raised CS and her siblings after their mother Anna Towers Turner died—hence the reference to "my Aunt" in the next sentence. Richard Smith's only daughter Mary married William Berney of Barbados in 1757. (Hilbish called him Walter {*Charlotte Smith, Poet and Novelist,* p. 54}, but CS's use of "William" seems authoritative {see CS to William Tyler, 9 Aug. 1801}.) Mary had three children by him. The Miss Berney mentioned in the following sentence is the youngest, Mary Eleanor, who later married Thomas Henchman. (See Genealogical Chart.)

3. The Honorable Henrietta Boyle O'Neill (1758–1793), with whom CS stayed when in London at Norton Street, Portland Place. There is no evidence that CS was able to make this much-needed trip away from her work and troubles. She hoped that Mrs. O'Neill's rank in life would benefit her family. Henrietta was the only daughter and heiress of Charles Boyle, Viscount Dungarvon, eldest son of John, fifth earl of Cork and Orrery. Her husband, John O'Neill, belonged to the great dynastic house of O'Neill, the oldest family lineage in Europe, traceable to 360 C.E.; they had been kings of Ireland until the thirteenth century and of northern Ireland until 1603. With

John, Henrietta created a private theater at the family seat, Shanes Castle, Co. Antrim, Ireland. He was created viscount in 1795, after her death.

4. CS's two youngest were Harriet (7) and George (4). The elder girls were Charlotte Mary, Augusta (15), and Lucy (13).

5. Richard Smith's granddaughter (Mary Berney Dyer's older daughter) Dorothy Elizabeth had married Edmund Boehm. (See Genealogical Chart.) Compared to the other legatees, the Boehms were on relatively good terms with CS and were close friends with her daughter Charlotte Mary throughout her life.

6. Not identified as either real people or pet names of family members.

To George Robinson

Middle Street Brighthelmston
Sep[tr] 28th 1789
Sir,

Having now completed my last engagement with M[r] Cadell & finding much of scruple and hesitation abt him which is irksome to me, I wish to know whether I may consider you as being willing to treat with me for a work I purpose immediately to begin Of tales in the way of Marmontel.[1] I am told there is no such book well done in English & that three small volumes w[d] probably be successful. I sh[d] perhaps want some advance before the delivery of the book, which may & probably will be in April, But certainly none, till the Books were in considerable forwardness & approved by the first literary Judges———

Your early an[swe][r] will much oblige, Sir,
your very humble Ser[t]
Charlotte Smith

John Wild Autograph Collection, Manuscripts Division, Rare Books and Special Collections, Princeton University Library. Address: Mr Robinson/ Pater Noster Row/ London. Postmark: BRIGHTHELMSTONE/ { / / }89.

NOTE

1. Jean-François Marmontel (1728–1799), French moralist, philosopher, man of letters, and playwright. His *Contes moraux* (1761), or moral tales, were widely influential. They may have been the impetus for CS's longer *Letters of a Solitary Wanderer* (1800–1802), not undertaken for another ten years, or for her shorter, more explicitly moral tales for children, beginning with *Rural Walks* (1795). For the time being, she continued to write long fiction.

To Benjamin Smith[1]

[London, 19 February 1790][2]

I enclose you the order necessary for y[e] Emancipation of y[e] papers in the hands of yr friend, the Sieur Browne,[3] and I advise you to pursue the matter, as I think he must refund. If you sign your name above mine & send the order to M[r] Bicknell,[4] I apprehend ~~you~~ he would do the needful.

[Unsigned]

Petworth House Archives MS. No address or postmark.

NOTES

1. See Biographical Notes. This first of CS's four surviving communications to her husband is the shortest and most business-like. It is one-third of the usual page of stationery, and a fragment of the original address can be seen: "To . . . / B . . ."

2. The name of the recipient and date of the note are given on the back in another hand.

3. It seems unlikely that BS's friend Browne was related to John W. Browne from whom CS rented the troublesome house at Storrington in 1793 that she kept through 1794 for her son Charles's sake.

4. Charles Bicknell, Esq., of 41 Norfolk St., Strand, was CS's solicitor until her death. By 1802 he is in the Law Lists as solicitor to the Admiralty and Navy and deputy bailiff of the City and liberty of Westminster. CS relied upon him heavily for advice as well as for copies of legal documents from earlier years. Ultimately she felt him unsuited for trust business, for, as she wrote to the earl of Egremont, he "is an honest, humane, conscientious & good Man, & [so] . . . unfit for the defence of a cause where there has already been great dishonesty & prevarication & falsehood on the part of the assailants" (12 Oct. 1803).

To William Davies

[London, 19 February 1790]

Sir,

I forgot to day to take the two Sonnets & therefore must trouble you to send them to the Excise Office——directed for Miss S—— and Miss M—— Ekins at Chelmsford:[1] to the care of the Hon[ble] John Olmius Excise Office.[2] When Miss Williams's books[3] come out pray let me have a copy, & I should be glad to have Zeluco[4] also & M[rs] Piozzi's last publication.[5]

I am y[r] obed[t] Ser[t],
Ch Smith

London, Feb[y] 19th 1790

Bodleian MS Montagu d. 2, fol. 160–61. (Address: M[r] Davies/ at M[r] Cadells/ Strand. Postmark: <Paid/Penny/Post.>

NOTES

1. CS may have known the Ekins for some time. Both Mrs. Ekins and Miss Ekins subscribed to the 1796 *Narrative of the loss of the Catharine, Venus and Piedmont transports.*

2. The Honorable John Luttrell Olmius (ca. 1742–1829), commissioner of excise since 1784. His wife, Elizabeth Olmius (1742–1797), later befriended CS while gathering subscriptions for *Elegiac Sonnets ii;* they each subscribed for two copies.

3. In 1790, Helen Maria Williams (1762–1827) had published two works, her novel *Julia* and *Letters Written in France in the Summer of 1790.*

4. Dr. John Moore (1729–1802), a native of Scotland, wrote the successful novel *Zeluco: Various Views of Human Nature Taken from Life and Manners, Foreign and Domestic* (1789). He was trained in Glasgow and practiced medicine and surgery there for twenty years. After six years abroad as companion and physician to the young duke of Hamilton, he quit regular practice and moved his family to London to advance his sons' careers and write for the popular market. His best-known works were *A View of Society and Manners in France, Switzerland, and Germany* (1779), *A View of Society and Manners in Italy* (1781), and his novel *Zeluco* (1789). Among Moore's political friends were the Foxite Whigs the duke and duchess of Devonshire (whose involvement in CS's affairs might have been due to Moore) and the controversial earl of Lauderdale. His literary friends were Sir Joshua Reynolds, Samuel Rogers, Mrs. Piozzi, Helen Maria Williams, Tom Paine, and Mrs. Barbauld—predominantly sympathizers, like himself, of the revolution in France.

5. Hester Lynch Thrale Piozzi (1741–1821) had recently published *Observations and Reflections Made in the Course of a Journey through France, Italy, and Germany* (1789).

To {James Upton Tripp}[1]

Graffham[2] March 26th
1790
Sir,

I take the liberty of <u>sending to you</u> the two Volumes Lord Egremont was so very obliging as to lend me. And request the favor of you to give directions for their being immediately replaced in the Library: from which, if it be not intruding too much, I would beg to borrow "Original Letters publish'd by Sir John Fenn."[3] I want to refer to Le Dictionnaire de Bayle,[4] which is a very voluminous book. I am afraid too much so to make my having it convenient. It is a large Volumes {*sic*} or more, originally French in which Language it will most probably be found in his Ldships Library; and if it can be had without any hazard of hurting the Books by their weight, I should be very much oblig'd to you to let me have them sometime before the 3rd of April when I return to Brighthelmstone——Bayle gives the history of Eminent Men. There is an English Translation, but I should prefer the Original.

I trust you will pardon this trouble from, Sir,
your oblig'd humble Ser[t]
Charlotte Smith

Petworth House Archives MS. No address or postmark.

NOTES

1. See Biographical Notes. See Appendix for four additional letters written to James Upton Tripp in September 1787 concerning CS's relationship with Egremont.

2. This is her only known sojourn at Graffham, a village south of Petworth.

3. *Original Letters, Written During the Reigns of Henry VI, Edward IV, and Richard III,* 5 vols. (1787–1825).

4. Pierre Bayle's *An Historical and Critical Dictionary* was published in 4 folio volumes in its first English edition (1710) and 5 folio volumes in its second (1734–38).

To Thomas Cadell, Sr.

Brighthelmstone
Aug[st] 22nd
1790
Dear Sir,

Some circumstances have lately occurred, which make me think it better and more secure for you to enter into such an agreement in regard to the new Novel[1] as was drawn up (but I think never sign'd) in regard to Ethelinde. The Work will be comprised in four Volumes which, when completed, will do more I hope than get me out of debt to you. But I do hope also that (as you will certainly be on the whole a considerable gainer by our transactions and as my writing is just now so much in fashion) you will agree to make a further pay[t] of ten pounds a volume on the publication of the second edition.

This is indeed but a poor compensation for the loss I must inevitably sustain in selling the copy right. I am very ready to do justice to your liberality in general, & do believe that you had rather not buy it because I must so lose. But Alas!— it is my poverty and not my will that has forced me to do it, & while M[r] Smiths circumstances remain as they are, I do not know whether it is not better to sell intirely all my literary property—— Which, when once bought and paid for, no claimant against him can, as I am well informed, affect—— Whereas I am much afraid that there are circumstances wherein every thing really mine w[d] be given up during his life to the use of M[r] Smiths Creditors. This information & some talk from M[r] Halliday[2] of a very discomforting nature has revived a wish to sell entirely the Copy right of Celestina & that of Emmeline and the Sonnets for whatever they may be worth. A purchaser for the latter I could easily find as I apprehend you do not think them objects. But I have ever cautiously avoided any step which could be construed into a wish to loosen or break a connection with you which I have reason to speak so well of.

In regard to Celestina I cd wish that when the agreement is drawn up, the purchase of a £50 a volume might be compleated & the draft I gave you on Mr Dyer[3] & Turner[4] returned——I shall then know what I work for; & tho the Balance, if any, will be but small, it will be of service to me now, as I am straining every nerve to keep up appearances to my daughters establishment with a Man of fortune who has been some months attach'd to her is secured. For this, as it is worth every thing to me & my other children, I would spare no exertion; & indeed it is well worth every effort; as the ~~only~~ one of few things that wd give a new colour to my hitherto dark & sad destiny———

I wish to have your early answer on this, or rather on these subjects & Mr Bicknell may if you please draw up the agreement. The four Volumes to be delivered between this period & the 1st of January—I name a longer date than we at first talked of because I am compelled to be much more in company on account of my daughter than I was last year & of course work more slowly—besides that, an increasing reputation I am of course very unwilling to risk, & I think it better, & so I am sure will you, to be a few weeks later than to send an hurried or incorrect performance abroad. Mr Hayleys absence in France[5] deprived me at present of a corrector, & I am by no means secure enough of my own powers, flattered as I daily am, to hazard the press without the opinion & correction of a literary friend.

In all these reasons, I am persuaded you will not object to giving me the farther latitude from November to January. It may perhaps be not unpleasant to you to hear that my literary acquaintance & of course my fashion is daily increasing. I have been introduced among others to Mr Sheridan[6] who complimented me very highly on both the Novels—& indeed I have reason enough to be proud of ye attention I daily receive. While I cannot but lament that from the peculiar circumstances of my family, the money I might earn for their future provision is all consumed by their support & their Grandfathers property likely, I fear, to be wasted in Law.

Pray let me hear from you as soon as you can, and believe me with all wishes for yr health & pleasant recess at Broadstairs,

Dear Sir
your most obedt Sert
Charlotte Smith

Robert H. Taylor Collection, Manuscripts Division, Department of Rare Books and Special Collections, Princeton University Library. Address: To/ Thomas Cadell Esqre/ Broad Stairs/ near/ Margate/ Kent. Postmark: BRIGHTHELMSTONE. AU 23 90.

NOTES

1. *Celestina* (1791), CS's third novel with Cadell.

2. Probably Simon Halliday, a friend and advisor of BS in England who acted as liaison between CS and BS once he was in exile.

3. Thomas Dyer (1744–1800) of Kensington, second brother of Sir John Swinnerton Dyer and second husband of Richard Smith's daughter Mary Berney. (See Genealogical Chart.) They had one daughter, Maria Elizabeth Charlotte (d. 1805), and four sons: Richard Swinnerton (1769–1794), Thomas Swinnerton (1770–1854), John (1772–1816), and Edward (1774–1816). Thomas Swinnerton succeeded his uncle as eighth baronet.

Sir John, the sixth baronet, was a trustee to the Smith estate until discharged from that duty on 29 July 1788 (he was replaced by Anthony Parkin).

4. CS's younger and only brother, the Reverend Nicholas Turner (1750–1819). See Biographical Notes.

5. Hayley was in France from 3 Aug. 1792 until the end of the month.

6. The dramatist Richard Brinsley Sheridan (1751–1816).

To Thomas Cadell, Sr.

Brighthelmstone, Sep^t 8th 1790
Dear Sir,

I should have been glad to have had your idea's of the value of the copy right of the Sonnets & the future edit^ns of Emmeline after the third As it is not to be suppos'd I can appreciate them & a thousand reasons deter me from enquiring their value of any other of the Trade.

I am extremely sick of my trade and very anxious to leave it off. When ever my Childrens affairs are settled, I shall not need it for them & have at all events an independence for myself.[1] Therefore I had rather sell the copy right of the Sonnets & of Emmeline for less than their value than keep them—at some hazard perhaps of their becoming at some time or other the property of Mr Smiths Creditors if the right remains in me.

You need not be solicitous now for the Paper I named from him because I have a general power of Attorney from him to transact every sort of business, relative to his affairs, mine, or the Childrens, which I am assur'd very fully authenticates & secures any pecuniary transaction either in regard to you or others.

Having done the Poetry for Celestina[2] and having no doubt of putting the whole upon paper (since it is already settled in my head) by the time named, I have been strongly tempted to overlook the Translation of a very curious and interesting book just procured from France Which w^d^ probably have a very rapid sale and w^d^, as it is mere play, be ready in about six weeks. There are two volumes of ab^t^ 450 pages, the two——of french—which w^d^ make nearly the same in English & as it relates to the present crisis, w^d^ probably be read with great avidity. It should be twenty five pounds a volume, & I w^d^ publish it with my name. Let me know your opinion & whether if it were done you w^d^ engage for it. You may be assured it shall not prejudice the progress of Celestina. Celerity however in such a matter is everything; favor me therefore with a speedy answer[3]——

As to the other matter, I will sell the copy right of the Sonnets for Forty, and of Emmeline for twenty pounds[4] & at this Sum, I am sure you must be a considerable gainer.

I have drawn on you at ten days for five G^s^ the ballance of what for Celestina will be payable, according to your statement, for Messrs the Trustees return'd two Bills of mine after promising to pay them & till by the intervention of Mr Hardinge,[5] I can get them paid, I am literally pennyless —————— Certainly This trifle will make no difference between us. As soon as I get the agreement which Mr Bicknell is drawing up, I will sign & send it you——Jacques has printed all I have yet seen of Celestina (ie—the greater part of the first volume) very neatly and correctly.

I am, Sir, in hopes of an early an^r^,
your most obed^t^ & oblig'd Ser^t^,
Charlotte Smith

Houghton Library Autograph File MS, Harvard University. No address or postmark.

NOTES

1. This is probably not the case, though CS always asserted that some money belonged to her. None of the three settlements made on her at and after marriage provided for her if she separated from BS. She discusses these settlements in later letters in detail but describes no settlement or legacy that would have provided her with an independent income.

2. *Celestina. A Novel* (1791) contained five sonnets and one lyric poem, "The Peasant of the Alps."

3. CS never translated such a work nor mentioned it again.

4. Inserted above the word "pounds" is "G +" for Guineas. According to Butler in "Mrs. Smith and Mr. Cadell," CS had already received £60 for the third edition of *Emmeline.*

5. CS had a small income from the trust to Richard Smith's unsettled estate, controlled by the trustees. Mr. Hardinge may be George Hardinge (1743–1816), member of Parliament, senior justice of the counties of Brecon, Glamorgan, and Radnor. An author and poet, he was known for benevolence and wit. He was slightly connected with CS from 1790 to 1792 (see CS to George Robinson, 20 Jan. 1792, and CS to Cadell, Sr., Apr. 1792).

To James Upton Tripp

Brighthelmstone
Octr 1st 1790
Sir,

You have ever been so obligingly attentive to every request I have taken the liberty to trouble you with that I hesitate the less to trouble you now. A very particular circumstance makes me desirous of obliging a family here to one branch of which I have been indebted for several brace of Partridges. This Country produces no Pheasants, & I should be very glad to send them a Leash[1] or four, which, as I know are likely to be in great plenty in your Country, and that I may beg them from Lord Egremonts Manors, without hazard of being very intrusive, I venture to request the favor of you to oblige me with them as early as you can do it without prejudice to the claims of those who have a better right to your kindness. If they are sent to the Norfolk arms at Arundel p^{r} Petworth diligence[2] On a Monday, Wednesday, or Friday evening, they will reach me the next day by the Coach that comes from thence to this place, on Tuesdays, thursdays & Saturdays. I will not ask you to pardon this freedom, persuaded as I am of your good nature. I am, Sir,

your obedient & Oblig'd Ser^{t}
Charlotte Smith

Petworth House Archives MS. Address: James Tripp Esqre/ Petworth/ by London. Postmark: BRIGHTHELMSTONE; OC/ 2/ 90.

NOTES

1. A sporting term meaning three.
2. A public stagecoach.

1791–92
"HOPE LONG DELAY'D"

—31 AUGUST 1791

After seven years of productive authorship, Charlotte Smith began to chafe under the strain of writing to support her children. She had embarked on her career to earn money while waiting for the settlement of her father-in-law's will, worth £36,000 when he died in 1776. Complex and ambiguously written, the will settled the bulk of Richard Smith's fortune on Charlotte and Benjamin's children. Fifteen years after his death, Benjamin's mismanagement had reduced the value of the estate by at least £16,000. No real settlement was in sight. Thomas and Mary Smith Berney Dyer, Richard Smith's only daughter, interpreted the will to award more to their children than Charlotte Smith would agree to. Moreover, two sugar plantations in Barbados still supplied the trust with earnings that were often subject to shipping delays. The January 1792 meeting of the families in Chatham Place, London, resolved nothing.

Seven of her children depended on her for support during this time. The expense of educating Charles and Lionel at Winchester College may have contributed to her lack of money as Christmas 1791 approached. Smith was prolific, publishing Celestina *in 1791 and* Desmond *and the sixth edition of* Elegiac Sonnets *in 1792; she also began several works that were finished in 1793. Charlotte Mary, her oldest daughter, sometimes stayed with relatives in London, leaving Augusta, Lucy, Harriet, and George at home. Smith had some comfort and support during these years from her London friend Henrietta O'Neill, a fellow poet. She had a cordial, almost literary relationship with the earl of Egremont's estate agent, James Upton Tripp, who loaned her books from the Petworth library and sent her pheasants shot in its fields.*

To [James Upton Tripp]

Brighthelmstone Jany 17
1791
Sir,

I receiv'd about a fortnight since four volumes of Bayle in French,[1] which I understood from a short note of my Brothers,[2] Lord Egremont had been so very good as to send for from London in consequence of my application for them last year. I am extremely sorry I was the occasion of giving his Ldship so much trouble & cannot sufficiently express my gratitude.

The Books are so large that they are bad travellers, and I am much afraid have been a little rubbed in their Journey hither, tho they appear'd to have been very carefully pack'd. This renders me uneasy about their return to Petworth, & I fully intended bringing them with me as far as Graffham towards the end of this week, & to have left them a day or two afterwards at some safe place at Petworth in my way thro it as I intended to have gone that way to London.

But Letters I have received to day compell me to relinquish this plan, and to go from hence on Teusday. I have however given strict orders ab^t the Books, and if my stay is very long, they shall be sent back, sewn in soft cloth to prevent their receiving any injury, which would vex me extremely.

Allow me to take this opportunity of thanking you for the Pheasants which unluckily never reach'd their destination but for which I am equally oblig'd to you. And I must always acknowledge myself for many civilities, Sir,

your most obedient
& much oblig'd Ser^t
Charlotte Smith——

Petworth House Archives MS. No address or postmark.

NOTES

1. CS requested Bayle's dictionary on 26 Mar. 1790.
2. Nicholas Turner. See Biographical Notes.

To Thomas Cadell, Sr.

[Brighton, 8 May 1791]
Sir

I shall be oblig'd to you to send me down Lorenzo,[1] & if it is in Print, Dr Darwins Lover of the Plants[2] as soon as possible, as the latter, indeed Both, I particularly want. Also Mr Hardinges Letter to Burke.[3]

——————— I am in haste.

Sir, y^{r} obed^{t} humble Ser^{t},
Charlotte Smith

Brighton
May 8th 1791

Boston Public Library/Rare Books Department MS Ch.H.3.20. No address or postmark. {"Strand/ London" appears on the back of this sheet, which appears to have been mailed with something else. It is on a scrap of paper the size of a receipt, 3" by 7". Few such hasty notes have survived.}

NOTES

1. William Roscoe (1753–1831) published his popular *Life of Lorenzo De' Medici, Calld the Magnificent* in 1795. CS here refers to the earlier version of the work, which he had privately printed in 1791.

2. *The Loves of Plants. With Philosophical Notes* is part 2 of *The Botanic Garden; A Poem, in Two Parts* (1791) by the naturalist Erasmus Darwin (1731–1802). *The Loves of Plants* was first issued alone in 1789.

3. George Hardinge (see CS to Cadell, Sr., 8 Sept. 1790, n. 5) wrote "A Series of Letters to the Rt. Hon. Burke [as to] the Constitutional Existence of an Impeachment against Mr. Hastings" in 1791.

To William Davies

[London, 8 June 1791]
Sir,

At the end of Lorenzo, there are Poems advertis'd said to have been publish'd in the Oracle by Mr Merry & others, particularly one call'd the Interview.[1] Will you be so good as to get me this book this evening?

I expected Mr Jacques[2] to have brought a proof here to day or two, but I have seen nothing of him. If he calls tomorrow, do be so good as to send him hither as early as possible as I shall be out on business all day & wish to avoid all delays now in correcting the press. Since the work is finish'd.[3]

I am, Sir,
your oblig'd hble Ser^{t},
Charlotte Smith

June 8th 1791
Have you got Stewarts travels to ascertain Moral Motion?[4] If you have, I w^{d} borrow for I shall not buy them till I am sure they are worth it.

Send me Miss Williams's farewell to England[5] by the bearer and the above mention'd Poems if you have them.

Yale University MS. Address: Mr. Davies/ at Mr Cadells/ Opposite the end of/ Surry Street/ Strand. No postmark.

NOTES

1. "The Interview" documents the "meeting" between Della Crusca (Robert Merry) and Anna Maria (Hannah Cowley) following their long newspaper flirtation in verse. When they discover each other to be middle-aged, they determine to continue as friends. *The Oracle, Bell's New World* was a daily published in London from 1789 to 1794, when it merged with the *London Daily Post.*

2. On the printer Jacques, see CS to an unnamed recipient, ca. Sept. 1785, n. 6.

3. Possibly *Celestina* (1791).

4. John Stewart (1749–1822), the "walking Stewart," had served in India and traveled, usually walking, through much of the Near East, North Africa, and Europe. Highly eccentric, he wrote a number of odd philosophical works, including *Travels over the Most Interesting Parts of the Globe, to Discover the Source of Moral Motion* (?1789).

5. Rather early in her productive career, Helen Maria Williams wrote *A Farewell for Two Years to England; A Poem* (1791). A poet and novelist, she is most remembered for her *Letters from France* (1794, 1796) and for later works chronicling the events of the French Revolution and its aftermath. She held on to her liberal views through the worst of times; she is not known to have returned to England after 1792.

To Joseph Warton[1]

Brighthelmstone, Aug^st 31st [1791]
Dear Sir,

When Your very obliging Letter reach'd this place, I was in London, or I should not so long have delay'd my acknowledgements. The information you have the goodness to give me about Lionel[2] gives me some concern, but if his slow progress is solely oweing to inattention and not to a defect of ability, I trust that as he acquires more reason, this neglect will no longer exist. In better hands he cannot be, and I own I have fondly flatterd myself that one of my Boys at least would be found to answer the kind wishes my partial friends have express'd for them, merely because they were mine. Lionel has a very good heart and is really I believe solicitous to gratify me in this hope, for, when on my taking leave of him on Wednesday, I represented to him the complaint which you and Mr Goddard[3] had made of his want of proper exertion, he defended himself some time on the ground that he was sometimes put upon a task utterly beyond his powers: I told him that he should consider that as a compliment from his Masters, & that instead of shrinking from such a task because it was difficult, he should exert his powers to conquer it & justify the opinion of his capacity which from their assigning him difficulties to execute, it was evident they entertain'd———

At length he burst into tears & said, "Good God, Mama, what a worthless fellow you must think me, if you beleive that I do not do all I can at my Books, when I know that you have so much uneasiness and trouble for us all and that you pay so much money for me." There was heart in this which pleased me very much, and I am persuaded that my Son will finally be a comfort to me & no discredit to those who are so good as to be interested in his education.

I am afraid your partial opinion in regard to the powers I possess has received no additional strength from the entire perusal of Celestina, for many parts of it are weak, and none, except perhaps the close, of equal strength to the former Novels. I wrote it indeed under much oppression of Spirit from the long and frequently hopeless difficulties in which my childrens affairs continue to be involved—Difficulties that my time & perseverance as well as the generous interposition of many friends of superior abilities in the Law have been vainly applied to conquer. For two three or four years, the burthen of so large a family whose support depends entirely upon me (while I have not even the interest of my own fortune to do it with) might be undertaken in the hope that at the end of that period their property might be restored to them.

But when above seven years have pass'd in such circumstances, that sickness of the Soul which arises from Hope long delay'd will inevitably be felt. The worn out pen falls from the tired hand, and the real calamities of life press too heavily to allow of the power of evading them by fictitious detail——— Another year however is coming when I must by the same motives be compelled to a renewal of the same sort of task—— A Tragedy would most undoubtedly be more honourable and more profitable. But it still appears to me an effort in which I should fail. And it is a very discouraging circumstance that the taste of the Modern World is not for Tragedy———

I cannot however but be highly flatterd by having in my favor an opinion to which I must ever pay the highest deference. And should I be able to obtain, what indeed I have little reason to expect, an interval of quiet & peace of mind this Winter, I will make an attempt such as your encouragement should urge me to make——

I am, Dear Sir, with great esteem,
your most oblig'd, and obed[t] Ser[t],
Charlotte Smith

My Friend M[rs] ONiell of Shanes Castle in Ireland is coming over in October to place her two sons at a Public School. They have been educated under Private Tutors. And she represents the eldest who is about fourteen as a very good Scholar. So good indeed that it is rather to introduce him into the World than to carry him forward in learning that M[r] ONiell intends to put him to one of the great English seminaries. He is himself much dispos'd to fix on Winchester. M[rs] ONiell rather prefers Eaton, but they have with their usual partial opinion of my judgement referred the matter to my decision, whose wishes and best opinion certainly must be for Winton. My Friend, who was a Boyle,[4] & whose talents are very extraordinary, is willing to beleive that her eldest Son inherits all the splendid Abilities of her family. He is Heir to a very Princely fortune, & these two Boys are the only descendants in a direct line from Shan ONiell.

Of course the debates where to place them are long and frequent. In her last Letter which I received the moment I had concluded this, she desires me to let her know what Young Men of rank are at Winchester and whether there are any objections made by the Masters to a private Tutor & a private boarding House? I could wish to be able to answer these questions from the best Authority. Yet do not mean to give you the trouble of writing about them. Only, as I have not at this moment the draft for Lionels bills ready for M[r] Goddard, nor time to write, I take the liberty of mentioning it here, And as my answer to Ireland is immediately required, w[d] entreat you to commission some person to furnish me by the Posts return with this information. Here is a Postscript longer than any Letter———

British Library Add. MS 42561 fol. 230. No address or postmark.

NOTES

1. The Reverend Joseph Warton, D.D., was headmaster of Winchester College (see Biographical Notes). The importance CS attached to Lionel's excellent academic placement at Winchester is underlined by the unusually fine quality of paper she chose for this letter.

2. See Biographical Notes. Lionel, 14 at this time, left Winchester in Apr. 1793 because of his role in what came to be known as "the rebellion of 1793." Initially the schoolboys meant to protest the punishment of the whole school for the misdeeds of one boy, a punishment that they had been assured would not be exacted. The boys and the staff exchanged demands and counterdemands. The boys eventually seized the keys to the college and prepared for a regular siege with swords, guns, and bludgeons as well as provisions taken from shops. The participants might still have been reconciled with the school authorities, but Dr. Budd, a physician, gave his son the choice of surrendering to the warden or resigning. When young Budd resigned, the remaining boys, Lionel included, resigned in support of him, and the warden accepted their resignations. Thirty-five boys were thus forced to step down—at considerable cost to the college, which had no new admissions in 1794. Many blamed the beloved Dr. Warton and his notoriously lax discipline for this debacle (Adams, *Wykehamica,* pp. 143–52).

A family version of this story was passed down to Lionel's great-grandson Sir Lionel Eldred Pottinger Smith-Gordon, who recalled that Lionel "headed a schoolboy rebellion at Winchester so successfully that troops had to be called out, to whom he surrendered with full military honours and on being sent home he told his mother not to worry as the only difference it made was he would have to become a general instead of a bishop" (Hilbish, *Charlotte Smith, Poet and Novelist,* p. 227).

3. The Reverend William Stanley Goddard (1757–1845), headmaster of Winches-

ter College, 1796–1809. From 1784 to 1796 he was *hostiarius,* or second master. Known for sound educational principles that were said to have influenced Thomas Arnold, he strove to counteract Warton's lax discipline but without full success. His house was broken into during the 1793 rebellion described above. When he presented himself to the school during the uprising, the boys, who were armed with clubs, at one point hissed and shouted him down; some of the young students pelted him with marbles (Adams, *Wykehamica,* p. 146).

4. On the family background of Henrietta O'Neill, see CS to Dr. Shirly, 22 Aug. 1789, n. 3. The eldest son, Charles Henry St. John (1779–1841), first Earl O'Neill, and his brother, John Bruce Richard (1780–1855), both attended Eton in the end.

To Lucy Hill Lowes[1]

[Brighton, 27 November 1791][2]
Madam,

I intended to have done myself the honor of waiting on you yesterday, but Augusta[3] told me at one period of the morning you were out, and I was afterwards detain'd by M[r] Wordsworth[4] (whom I could not take leave of, till he embark'd) till it was too late to have the pleasure I intended. This morning I am summoned to London & thus deprived of an opportunity of paying my respects to you here, but if you will allow me to wait on you in Town where I am likely to be a fortnight, I will avail myself of that permission with great pleasure. My abode during that time is at "The Hon[ble] Mrs. ONiells, Henrietta Street, Cavendish Square" where, if you favor me with intelligence of your being at your London residence, I will take the earliest opportunity of assuring you personally that I am

Madam
your most obed[t] & oblig Ser[t]
Charlotte Smith

Sunday morning[5]

J. Pierpont Morgan MS. Address: M[rs] Lowes. No postmark.

NOTES

1. Probably an error for Lowe (see Biographical Notes).

2. The year and date of this letter can be ascertained from William Wordsworth's movements in Nov. 1791, when he visited CS in Brighton and received from her letters of introduction to Helen Maria Williams in France and possibly to Brissot, a member of the National Assembly. Mark Reed's chronology puts this visit between 23 and 26 Nov. As CS wrote this note on Sunday morning, the exact date must have been Saturday the 26th (Reed, *Wordsworth,* pp. 123, 126–27).

3. On Anna Augusta Smith de Foville, see Biographical Notes.

4. It is likely that Wordsworth knew of CS not only as a respected poet but also as a troublesome in-law. He was distantly related to her by marriage. John Robinson (see Biographical Notes), a trustee to the Smith estate, was married to BS's stepsister, Mary Crow. Robinson was Wordsworth's second cousin once removed (Robinson's aunt on his father's side of the family was married to Wordsworth's grandfather).

5. At the end of this note, handwritten remarks apparently by Thomas Lowe attest to the damage done to CS's reputation by her interest in politics:

> I saw a great deal of Charlotte Smith one Autumn at Brighthelmstone & bating a democratic twist (which I think detestable in a woman). I liked her well enough for some time, but she disgusted me completely, on the acct arriving of the Massacre of the Swiss Guards at the Tuileries by saying that they richly deserved it: I observed that they did merely their duty, & if they had not done what they did they w[d] have been guilty of Treason & that I thought they deserved the pity of every person who reasoned & felt properly. After this I never w[d] see Charlotte, but she & M[rs] L sometimes met. Not long after this Augusta (mentioned in the note) married an emigrant French nobleman, & I understand that her style both in her conversation & novels altered considerably.
>
> —TL

As the Swiss Guards were massacred on 10 Aug. 1792, Mr. Lowe and his wife must have seen a great deal of CS during the fall of 1791, and he would have turned away from her the next year.

To an Unnamed Recipient[1]

Henrietta Street {London}—Decr 8[th][2]
1791

I obey you, dear Sir, in writing to day tho I have only to repeat that I hope nothing will prevent my seeing you before I leave this place. Tomorrow morning we seem likely to be obsedé[3] 'till one or two o clock when it is probable we shall go out, not to return till five to dinner. Miss Moncton and Frank North[4] dine here. But there is always a fire for me in the breakfast parlour so that if the Evening of tomorrow should suit you, I could there have the honor of having five minutes conversation with you, as far as relates to business, and if you will fav[r] me & my friend with longer time, we can afterwards join the witty party above, for you know you are as witty as they are. On Saturday I conclude you go to Twickenham, & on Monday or Teusday I go from hence. Tomorrow Evening therefore seems the only time when I hope to be so fortunate as to see you.

It seems to me very strange that a Meeting should not be thought necessary now, when the debts are on all hands acknoledged to be paid, & when M[r] Robinson[5] himself has dwelt upon the necessity of a general meeting in repeated Letters. When I assure you that Mr Sayler[6] has repeatedly said the sugars from Gays are all sold at 82s[hillings], Where can the difficulty remain? The fact is that no farther debt remaining against the Estate of Richard Smith, The Trust rests in possession of the ~~a certain~~ remaining assets—& must now decide whether they will pay such residue back to the Exors[7] or divide it, as appears to them to be the meaning of the Will & according to the powers invested in them by the trust. If the former of these is their choice—a la bonne heure—<____>[8] voila ready to receive their resignation as Mr Smiths Attorney. If the latter mode be their election, surely it cannot be too soon to carry it into execution at the end of eight years.

Mr Robinson himself will do me the justice to say that, in obedience to his advise, I have exercised my admirable talents as long as I have strength to do it, & more successfully than could have been expected. I have gone over this ground till my very soul is sick of the subject, & tho I continue to look sleek & smug (by candlelight) & to walk about & talk some nonsense and write more, yet upon my honor my health is such as renders it utterly impossible for me to continue another Year the fatigue of spirit to which the necessity of supporting such a family subjects me—— It is impossible I well know to communicate to another any notion of the suffering I have gone thro on this subject nor that sickness of the soul which arises from hope long delay'd. Whenever business seems coming to any point, when I flatter myself my wretched Anxieties are to be ended & some provision ascertain'd for my poor children, I no sooner grasp the phantom than it vanishes, & I am told, "Not yet—nothing can be done Yet—there is no necessity for any thing yet—"

Surely nobody can suppose that I seek this meeting as a matter of pleasure. I, who am fete'[d] eternally by the most eminent literary Men and told that I am in the first order of beings, can have but little delight in exposing myself to the supercilious and purse proud insolence of Robinson Or the mean insulting contention of that detestable cream colourd Dyer.[9] Yet this precious interview is put off from time to time & made a favor of, As if it was to be a festival to me.

I am interrupted & will only add that I entreat you to consider what is to become of my family. I must go home to seven of them[10] without money to pay their Christmas Bills & consequently with[ou]t credit to carry them On.

I this moment receive your note saying you cannot favr me with a moment any part of tomorrow. Let it then be Saturday, either Morning or Evening,

I hope I shall not be disappointed again,

I am, dear Sir,
your most oblig'd Sert,
Charlotte Smith

I have just added Dr Moore to the list of my literary friends. Are you an admirer of Zeluco?[11]

M^rs^ ONiell does not know Lady Londonderry[12] but has always wishd to know her from the report of her talents & manners.

I wish you knew M^rs^ ONiell. All the Men of reading who have been here to see me since I have been with her are absolutely frantic.[13]

Osborn Collection MS, Yale University. No address or postmark.

NOTES

1. This letter has no outside address; the original from which the copy was transcribed was taken from a letter book. It is not certain with whom CS would have been on such cordial social terms. Joel Barlow was in England during this time and visited Twickenham; another possibility is John Sargent. The most likely candidate is George Hardinge, who lived at Ragman's Castle, a small house near Twickenham. In a postscript, CS casually alludes to Lady Londonderry, who was Hardinge's friend (see n. 12 below). Hardinge is named again in letters of 20 Jan. 1792 and Apr. 1792, but the extent of CS's relationship with him is not known.

2. CS was staying with Henrietta O'Neill.

3. Beset.

4. This meeting would have been something of a literary coup for CS, as the Honorable Frances North (1761–1817), son of Frederick North, second earl of Guilford, had had his dramatic piece *The Kentish Baron* presented at Haymarket in June and then published. Frances succeeded his brother, George Augustus North the third earl, as fourth earl of Guildford in 1802. Miss Monckton was probably the writer Charlotte Monckton-Arundell (d. 1806).

5. John Robinson (see Biographical Notes).

6. Mr. Sayler is also connected to Richard Smith's estate, which included a sugar plantation in Barbados. Here CS is concerned with the sale of hogsheads of sugar from it.

7. The executors of Richard Smith's will.

8. The sense of this passage is "If they choose the former, so be it; as for me, I'm ready for them to resign."

9. Thomas Dyer (see CS to Thomas Cadell, Sr., 22 Aug. 1790, n. 3). He was a trustee with Robinson to a £2,000 marriage settlement due to CS upon her stepmother's death. But worse, he always advocated for his children to get a larger share of Richard Smith's estate than CS, and others, thought the will allowed.

10. Nicholas Hankey Smith, the second eldest son, had been in India as a civil servant or writer since Sept. 1790, leaving CS with seven dependent children.

11. CS had asked William Davies to send her a copy of Dr. John Moore's *Zeluco* in a letter of 19 Feb. 1790. She almost certainly met Moore through Henrietta O'Neill or the duchess of Devonshire.

12. Frances (1787–1822), eldest daughter of Earl Camden. George Hardinge inscribed an ode to her "as an affectionate admirer of her Genius and Virtues, who takes pride in recording their Friendship as a title of honor to his name" (Nichols, *Literary History,* 3:30).

13. Little can be deduced about CS's friendship with Henrietta (Dungarvon) O'Neill (1758–93) from the letters. See letter to Joseph Cooper Walker of 9 Oct. 1793, n. 1. Walker's friend Mr. Kirwen met O'Neill at Shanes Castle in Co. Antrim and "was charmed with her," as Walker wrote to Bishop Percy on 21 Aug. 1791 (Nichols, *Literary History,* 7:717).

To John Nichols[1]

[London] Decr 28th 1791

I certainly ought, after so many years of our conversation to know what you mean, Dear Sir, by the question you ask me, but in truth I do not. If you will have the goodness to <trust> it to my Capacity, I will say any thing to M^{rs} O'Neill that I should say, and I am sure that I can answer for her as for myself in whatever depends on secrecy or any other virtue of the Heart. Favour me therefore with your commands by return of the Post.

My Situation is extremely terrible, for I have no means whatever of supporting my children during the Holidays, nor of paying their Bills when they return to School: & I am so harrassd with Duns that I cannot write with any hope of getting any thing done by that time. I know not where I find resolution to go on from day to day Especially under the idea of Mr Smith's being in London, liable every hour to imprisonment.[2] Were it not for M^{rs} O'Neill & two or three other friends who soften to me the horrors of my destiny, I cannot answer for what I should do. Thus it was last Christmas, & thus for ought I can see it may be next if I so long live. Even when the present Accounts with the Grocers are settled, you heard M^{r} <Herman> say that the Accounts c^{d} not be closed as Berney[3] has omitted to send from Barbadoes an Account of what he had received & that there would still be something due to the Trustees. Reasons enough to be sure to keep my unhappy children starving and destitute. But would the Chancellor think so. Charlotte talks of appealing to him, which I shall not oppose.

Whatever any of us were to do would have its excuse if a narrative were published of all the infamous treatment we have received.

You did not return Robinson's last letter; if it be not too much trouble be so good as to send it to my Daughter with this address.

Miss Smith
Upper Street near the Church
Islington

Be kind enough also to let your servant put the others into the Post.

I am, Dear Sir,
Your ever oblidg'd & obed^{t} Servt,
Charlotte Smith[4]

Bodleian MS Eng. Lett. c. 365, fol. 50. *Address: Nichols, Red Lion Passage, Fleet St.*

NOTES

1. A printer and publisher; see Biographical Notes.

2. Though in danger of arrest, BS often returned to London when Jan. and June interest payments were made on the trust.

3. William Berney, who married Richard Smith's daughter, Mary. (See Genealogical Chart.)

4. This letter is not in CS's handwriting, but the copier uses many of her usual abbreviations and thus may have copied carefully.

To George Robinson

Brighthelmstone Jany 20th
1792
Sir,

By this time I imagine you have received 131 pages of MMS.[1] My friend[2] who was to deliver them to you yesterday afternoon has pointed out two trifling inaccuracies, which I shall wish to remedy in the MMS. But as I have to day received advice that ~~a meeting of~~ my Childrens Trustees and all the parties concerned in the Will of their Grandfather are to meet in Chatham Place on the 28th instant, I find it will be absolutely necessary for me to be in London on the 26th. I shall therefore be again at M^rs^ ONiells in Henrietta Street Cavendish Square & beg the favor of you when the first sheet ~~copy~~ is printed to send it to me there.

It would be much more agreeable to me and conducive to the rapid progress of the Work, could I remain in Town. Whether I shall be able or no depends on the settlement made in regard to my childrens affairs on the 28th: but if it should happen that no money will be immediately coming to them from their Grandfathers property, which is in the Island of Barbados, and that they must still wait for the interest of their Legacies till the arrival of the next crops from that Island, I shall be extremely distress'd for money for their actual support; and w^d^ in that case venture to enquire whether it would be inconvenient or disagreeable to you to Accept a bill at three months for fifty or sixty pounds—assuring you that the whole work will be deliverd before that time and that therefore the accommodation will be a very great one to me without, I trust, any injury to you. But if you should feel any apprehensions or repugnance, I would by no means desire you to do it but will try to find some other means to prevent the excessive inconveniencies to which I shall be exposed by the delay that I fear from long mismanagement of the Estate and the many disadvantages attending West India property may yet happen in the affairs——

After this year they cannot occur again, as the debts on the Estate are now all clear'd, & it will come into other management. Therefore if I can weather this storm (I mean the inconveniencies that attend the want of money for them when I have their School bills & bills for necessaries to pay, which are expected at this season), I shall do very well—— The favor of your answer will very much oblige,

Sir, your most obed[t] humble Ser[t],
Charlotte Smith

I send this under cover to M[r] Hardinge. But as he may be out of Town on Sat[y] afternoon would rather have y[r] answer in the Common course of the post.

Huntington MS (HM10803). Address: M[r] Robinson/ Pater Noster Row. {There is no postmark, as this letter was taken to London from Brighton by a friend.}

NOTES

1. *Desmond. A novel* (1792), her only work published by the firm of G. G. J. and J. Robinson.

2. Not identified.

To Thomas Cadell, Sr.

{London, April 1792}[1]
Sir,

I return the Sonnets alter'd. And a short preface you shall receive some time in the course of tomorrow. I have reason to believe these will have a very rapid sale & wish to know (merely as {a} matter of curiosity) the price you intend to affix to them.

I certainly mis-understood you, when you first wrote to me about them. Your expression was that, if I had any new Sonnets & chose to send them to you, I should receive a Compliment. Yet on my enquiring what you propos'd, you inform'd me you were much surpris'd. The fact was that, with these additional Sonnets and the Poems that have not till now been printed & some others, I did mean in a few months to have formed ~~a certain~~ another Volume, & I could not, as you well know, <u>afford</u> to sacrifice any part of that plan without some consideration. You fix'd the price, after expressing your surprise that I should expect any, at ten Guineas, on the supposition that there would be twenty pages of new matter——I thought it necessary to say in answer that there w[d] be twenty pages, <u>inclusive</u> of the 5 Sonnets, and little Lyric Poem in Celestina, already your property.[2] And I therefore drew for only five Guineas Tho I will honestly confess I think the advantage you will obtain from the new Poetry will amply indemnify You for the whole price.

I beg to know what you propose doing in that respect, as I promis'd the five Guineas if I get them to my daughters for some trifles they want. I think it necessary to say that in the preface I mean to touch on the hardship of my situation:[3] Who after waiting nine years while the Estate of Richard Smith the Grandfather was at <th . . . ?>, now that all his debts are confessedly clear'd & Effects arriving every day, am no better off than before because Mr Dyer, whose children have an 8th share (& that partly conditional, in the property), opposes any division till his youngest child is of age, who is abt Seventeen, tho he has not the shadow of pretence for it. I am driven almost to despair by these circumstances And the conduct of Mr Smith who lives upon the interest of my fortune with a Woman he keeps, leaving me to support as well as I can his seven Children who are in England.[4]

I should not, Sir, trouble you with this history, but to account not only for steps ~~I have~~ it has & must still be compell'd ~~me~~ to take, but to shew you that I cannot afford to lose the smallest profit that may arise from my exertions which, but for these difficulties, I should never make.

Mr. Hardinge informed me as long ago as the Novel of Celestina was begun, that you had spoken to every body of my distress & of my having borrow'd fifty pounds of you. I disregarded this information then because, as every body knows that I have brot no part of my inconveniencies upon myself, I was not ashamd [of] borrowing fifty pounds which I know I should honestly earn. In the same reason, I am not ashamed of stating to you my situation now, nor shall I be deterred from explaining it to the World. But perhaps you may object to the mention of these circumstances wherefore I tell you what I propose my preface to be—A short sketch of my long-subsisting reasons for writing.

I shall direct my Messenger who leaves this to deliver also the preface tomorrow, and await your Answer to, Sir,

your obed humble
Sert,
Charlotte Smith

I should be glad to see a proof of the new Sonnets before they are worked off.

Neilson Campbell Hannay Collection of William Cowper, Manuscripts Division, Department of Rare Books and Special Collections, Princeton University Library. Address: Mr Cadell/ Strand/ Opposite the end of Catharine/ Street. No postmark.

NOTES

1. Date provided in another hand at the top of the letter. The preface to the sonnets mentioned in the first and last sentences as being ready "tomorrow" suggests a date in late Apr. at the earliest. The preface itself is dated 14 May 1792, however, which may be closer to the date of the letter. The preface was not printed off and corrected until 21 Oct. 1792.

2. The sixth edition of *Elegiac Sonnets* was published three years after the fifth (the subscription edition of 1789). In all CS added eleven new sonnets and four new lyrics.

Sonnets 49–53 and the lyric "The Peasant of the Alps," along with the other sonnets and lyrics, added 22 pages to the new edition. CS did not publish "another Volume" until 1797, when *Elegiac Sonnets ii* came out. *Elegiac Sonnets i* went into seven more editions, with no new poems added.

3. In the short preface, CS complained of "'the Honorable Men' who *nine years ago,* undertook to see that my family obtained the provision their grandfather designed for them[.]" In fact, the trustees Sir John Dyer, Esq., and John Robinson were considered by others to be honorable men (see CS to Cadell, Sr., 22 Aug. 1790, n. 3, and Biographical Notes). She felt condemned "Still to receive—not a repetition of promises indeed—*but of scorn and insult,* when I apply to those gentlemen, who, though they acknowledge that all impediments to a division of the estate they have undertaken to manage, are done away—will neither tell me when they will proceed to divide it; or, *whether they will ever do so at all*" (*Elegiac Sonnets i,* p. xi). CS's use of her prefaces to pressure the trustees and family members into settling the will drew much criticism and injured her reputation.

4. By Apr. 1792, the third to the eldest son, Charles Dyer Smith (19), had not yet joined the 14th Regiment. Here CS first mentions the woman she elsewhere called BS's "concubine," who seems to have been his cook or housekeeper. CS called her "Maistress Mellar" in a letter to Charlotte Mary, 2 Feb. 1803, perhaps a mocking spelling of Mrs. Miller.

To George Robinson

[London, 4 July 1792]

Sir,

I shall be oblig'd to you to send down 6 Copies of Desmond[1] for my own family at Brightelmstone directed to Miss Smith, West Street, Brighton, & They may go by the Waggon.

I shall leave London in a few days for Herefordshire and shall be oblig'd to you to forbear giving any person who may apply to you a direction to me as I am harrass'd to death for debts not my own & my Spirits are so much injured by such applications that I suffer extremely in my health without benefitting anyone.

If you have any necessary intelligence to favour me with within this for-night, my address will be at Mrs Clyffords, Perrystone, Ross.[2]

I am, Sir,

your obed^t^ humble Ser^t^,
Charlotte Smith

July 4th 1792

Comyn Collection of Burney Family Papers. Address: To/ Mr Robinson/ Pater Noster Row. Postmark: {illegible}.

NOTES

1. *Desmond* had just been published; its preface, written last, was dated 20 June 1792.

2. Apart from this one visit, nothing is known of CS's relationship with Eliza Maria Clifford, eldest daughter of Richard Lewis of Llantillio. In 1775, she married William Morgan Clifford of Perristone near Ross on Wye. How CS knew Mrs. Clifford, whether she actually visited her, how long she stayed, whether her family joined her, and even whether she was hiding from creditors are matters for conjecture. The setting of the early chapters of *Emmeline* suggests earlier visits here as well.

To James Upton Tripp

Eartham[1] 29th Augst 1792
Sir,

This waits upon you with two Books[2] from Lord Egremonts Library which I have detain'd very long but which will now I hope be safely return'd——

May I take the liberty to inquire if there is in the Petworth Library "Lavater on Physiognomy"[3] either in English or the Original French, either with or without the Engravings. If There is either that work or his "Aphorisms on Man," and they are not very finely bound so as to make their travelling hither hazardous to their binding (for one of them is I think a very large book), I would intrude upon Lord Egremont for the loan of them for a few days, & if you will have the goodness to prefer my request & it can be granted, they may be sent with ease to Arundel by the Coach from whence I can either have them hither (as they are not in this library) should they arrive within this week; or take them with me at the end of that time on my return to Brighthelmstone——

As they are somewhat recent & very remarkable publications, I imagine they are not so much in the midst of the Catalogue as to give you the trouble in enquiring for them that I fear some of my requests may have given. I trust you will pardon me for taking the liberty to apply to you, and I am,

Sir,
your oblig'd & obedt Sert
Charlotte Smith

I am not sure that I am correct in the title, but the name of Lavater is I believe enough to point out the work——

Petworth House Archives MS. No address or postmark.

NOTES

1. William Hayley's home. He invited CS to a writers' retreat that introduced her to William Cowper and George Romney; the event was surely the apex of her reception into literary and artistic circles. We can only speculate whether she requested the books solely for her own use on *The Old Manor House* or shared them with her fellow artists.

2. She asked for *Le Dictionnaire de Bayle* and *Original Letters* of Sir John Fenn in March 1790 and received the Bayle in January 1791.

3. The Reverend Johann Caspar Lavater's *Essays on Physiognomy; For the Promotion of the Knowledge and the Love of Mankind,* originally in German, had been translated into English by Thomas Holcroft with 360 engravings for Robinson (3 vols., 1789). H. Hunter had translated an edition from the French with more than 800 engravings (3 vols., 1789–98). Lavater's *Aphorisms on Man* (1787) is a handsome, slender volume containing 643 thoughtful aphorisms.

To William Davies

[?Brighton, 21 October 1792]

Sir,

The preface is perfectly right. Save only an S. to be added to the word Rossignols in the second page as it is there us'd in the plural. This however was I beleive not the fault of y^r Printer but mine. The repetition of toujours Rossignols I have eras'd & wish it omitted.[1]

I trust Mr Cadell will soon send this Edition into the World. I am tormented to death about its appearance. He will of course give me a few copies for my Children abroad & at home.

I am, Sir,
your oblig'd humble Ser^t,
Charlotte Smith

Octr 21st 1792

I think effect & cause, which I have scored, should be in Italics.

Osborn Collection MS, Yale University. No address or postmark.

NOTE

1. Each of these corrections to the preface of *Elegiac Sonnets,* 6th ed., was made.

To Joel Barlow[1]

Brighthelmstone Novr 3rd 1792

I am extremely flatterd, Dear Sir, by your early and very obliging attention to my Letter & indeed have great reason to quarrel with Dr Warner[2] for neglecting an appointment which would have been the means of introducing me to your acquaintance. I read with great satisfaction the "Advice to the Priveledged Orders" and have been, as well as some of my most judicious and reasoning friends here, very highly gratified by the lesser tract, Your Letter to the National Convention[3] Which cannot I think fail of having great effect not only where it is address'd, but on those who at present consider themselves as less immediately interested in the questions it discusses. I really pity the advocates for despotism.

They are so terribly mortified at the late events in France, and as they had never any thing to say that had even the semblance of reason and now are evidently on the wrong side of the question both in Theory and Practice, it is really pitiable to hear the childish shifts and miserable evasions to which they are reduced.

I am however sensibly hurt at the hideous picture which a friend of mine, himself one of the most determined Democrates I know, has given of the situation of the Emigrants. He has follow'd the progress of the retreating Army in their retrog[r]ade motion, and describes the condition of the French exiles as being more deplorable even than their crimes seem to deserve. The magnitude of the Revolution is such as ought to make it embrace every great principle of Morals, & even in a Political light (with which I am afraid Morals have but little to do), it seems to me wrong for the Nation entirely to exile and abandon these Unhappy Men.[4] How truly great would it be, could the Convention bring about a reconciliation. They should suffer the loss of a very great part of their property & all their power. But they should still be considerd as Men & Frenchmen, and tho I would not kill the fatted Calf, They should still have a plate of Bouille at home if they will take it & not be turnd out indiscriminately to perish in foreign Countries and to carry every where the impression of the injustice and ferocity of the French republic—— That glorious Government will soon be so firmly establish'd that five and twenty thousand emigrants or three times the number cannot affect its stability. The people will soon feel the value of what they have gain'd and will not be shaken by their efforts in arms from without, or their intrigues within (even if they were to intrigue), & many of them have probably sufferd enough to be glad of returning on almost any terms. Their exile includes too that of a very great number of Women and Children who must be eventually not only a national loss but on whom, if the Sins of the Father are visited, it will be more consonant to the doctrine of scripture than of reason.

I not only wish that an amnesty was pass'd for these ill advisd Men, but that their wretched victim Louis Capet[5] was to be dismiss'd with his family and an ample settlement made upon him & his posterity so long as they do not disturb the peace of the Republic. I do not understand of what use it can be to bring to trial an Officer for whom the whole nation determines it has no farther occasion. To punish him for the past seems as needless [as] to make him an example for the future, for, if no more Kings are suffer'd, it will avail nothing to shew the ill consequence of being a bad one by personal punishment inflicted on the unfortunate Man who could not help being born the Grandson of Louis 15th—— Surely it would be great to shew the world that, when a people are determind to dismiss their King, he becomes indeed a phantom & cannot be an object of fear, & I am persuaded there are on all sides much stronger reasons for dismissing than for destroying him. On this occasion, the Republic should perhaps imitate the magnaminity of Uncle Toby, "Go poor devil! why should we hurt thee? There is surely room enough in the World for Us and thee!"[6] It is making this unhappy individual of too much consequence to suppose that his life Can be demanded for the good of people. And when he was reduced to the condition of an affluent private Gentleman, & even that affluence depending on the Nation, I cannot conceive that he would do any harm, but wd sink into total insignificance & live a memento of the dependence of Kings, not on hereditary and divine right, but on the will of the people——

Will you have the goodness to send the Poem by Mr Fingal to Bells,[7] Bookseller Opposite the end of Bond Street in Oxford Street, who will on Teusday or Wednesday forward to me a pacquet of Books—— I will carefully return it when I have done with it by the same conveyance. I am afraid I shall not be in Town this Winter as my friend with whom I staid last year in Henrietta Street is gone to Lisbon.[8] But if I should see London for a short time it will give me infinite pleasure to wait on Mrs Barlow[9] by whose favorable opinion I am much flatter'd as well as to have an opportunity of assuring you personally of the esteem with which I am,

Sir,
your most oblig'd & obedt Sert,
Charlotte Smith

Huntington MS (BN404). No address or postmark.

NOTES

1. See Biographical Notes.

2. Dr. John Warner (1736–1800), chaplain to the British ambassador in Paris, Lord Gower. Warner would have returned to England when Lord Gower was recalled to London in Oct. after the Sept. massacres. CS knew of Warner and may have met him through Hayley, whose friendship with Warner began in 1786. In 1789 Warner stayed for a time at Eartham in the gardener's quarters, reading and writing ten hours a day. A wit and an excellent scholar, he was very sympathetic to revolutionary ideals.

3. *Advice to the Privileged Orders, in the Several States of Europe, Resulting from the Necessity and Propriety of a General Revolution in the Principle of Government,* by Joel Barlow, part 1 (London: Joseph Johnson, 1792). The first part of *Advice to the Privileged Orders*

was published by Johnson on 4 Feb., just before the second part of Thomas Paine's *Rights of Man.* Its four chapters covered the feudal system, the church, the military system, and the administration of justice. The second part, printed in France in Sept. 1793, discussed only revenue and expenditure. In Sept. 1792, Johnson had published Barlow's *A Letter to the National Convention of France on the Defects in the Constitution of 1791, and the Extent of the Amendments Which Ought to Be Applied.*

4. After the king's murder, the plight of the ousted aristocrats turned the tide of liberal English opinion against the Revolution. CS would soon give her blessings to her most beloved child, Augusta, to marry a French émigré, the chevalier de Foville. Two of CS's works explored the emigrants' trials: a long blank verse poem, *The Emigrants* (1793), and her fifth novel, *The Banished Man* (1794), which in part describes de Foville and Augusta. Its working title was *The Exiles.*

5. "Louis Capet" was the *citoyen* name of Louis XVI.

6. Tristram Shandy's Uncle Toby would not kill a fly, but instead said: "Go poor devil, get thee gone, why should I hurt thee?—— This world surely is wide enough to hold both thee and me." Laurence Sterne, *The Life and Opinions of Tristram Shandy, Gentleman* (1759-67), vols. 1-3 of *The Florida Edition of the Works of Laurence Sterne,* ed. Melvyn New and Joan New ([Gainesville]: University Presses of Florida, 1978), 1:131.

7. CS probably meant John Trumbull's *M'Fingal,* completed in 1782 and recently reissued in London (1792). Since Barlow and Trumbull had collaborated on *The Anarchiad* (1786-87) with the other "Connecticut Wits," Barlow would be an appropriate person to ask for the work. Joseph Bell, whose shop was at 148 Oxford Street from 1792 to 1820, had engaged to publish *The Old Manor House* and may have briefly handled matters like this for her.

8. Henrietta O'Neill.

9. Ruth Barlow had joined her husband in London, where she mainly resided while he traveled back and forth to France, in the spring of 1790. During his absences she became friendly with Mary Wollstonecraft (Woodress, *A Yankee's Odyssey,* pp. 99-141). CS, who had her "favorable opinion," probably never met her.

To Joel Barlow

Brighthelmstone. Novr 18th [1792]
Dear Sir

Will you pardon my intruding upon you once more & in a very hasty way? It is to enquire if it be true that you are going or gone to Paris?[1] If you are not gone, will you allow me to trouble you with a Private Letter to Francais de Nants?[2] if you are, will you write to me from thence, simply to say that I may trouble you with a trifling enquiry to be made for me there who am trying to go over in March or April, an enquiry which is to assist in this plan on which my rebellious heart is set.[3]

Hayley said in a Letter to me a few days since (about ten I believe) that he had hopes of seeing you & Mrs Barlow at Christmas before you went to America & that I should meet you at Eartham. How is this to be? I shall lose the post if I ad[d] more than an entreaty to you to pardon my thus <troubling> you, & I conclude as does a Letter I have to day received from Paris.

Permettes, Citoyen, qu'en ecartent les formules de l'ancien esclavage, je me borne à vous assurer de mon respectueuse attachement[4]—Charlotte Smith

If you see Dr Warner (est il encore docteur?), fail not to remind him of me.

18th Novr 1792

Brighthelmstone

Huntington MS (BN405). Address: Joel Barlow Esqre/ In the care of/ Mr Johnsons St Pauls /Churchyard/ London./ To be forwarded. Postmark: BRIGHTHELMSTONE; NO/ 19/ 92.

NOTES

1. Barlow had left England in the middle of Nov. with John Frost and was in Paris preparing to speak for the Constitution Society to the French Convention by 22 Nov. (Woodress, *A Yankee's Odyssey,* pp. 130–31).

2. Antoine François de Nantes (1756–1836), deputy of Lower Loire in the Legislative Assembly, an expert on tariffs. Having survived the Terror, he became a member of the legislature of the Five Hundred during the Directory. Mentioned by Dr. John Moore in his *Journal during a Residence in France* (1793), he was possibly introduced to Moore by CS.

3. That is, CS's plan to go to France in the coming year, mentioned in the preface to *Desmond*. The letters shed no light on such a trip.

4. "Allow me, Citizen, while eschewing expressions of former oppression, I content myself with assuring you of my respectful attachment." That is, without signing the conventional "obedient humble servant," she merely offers her attachment or affection.

To Joseph Cooper Walker[1]

[Brighton] December 16th 1792

Dear Sir,

I cannot express how much I am oblig'd to you for the very warm interest you take in regard to the sale of my Books. I have now sent the remainder of the first Volume[2] and great part of the second—which I received only last night from my Bookseller who by some accident has omitted to send two sheets of it, i e the 2nd Vol which however I will send for to night and hope to forward to you in a very few days. On recollection, I beleive it will be best to forward part of the third volume too. Thus, of the ~~three~~ five pacquets which accompanies this, the first contains the last sheet of Vol 1st & three of Volume 2nd; the 2nd packet 3 sheets of the 2nd; the 3rd two sheets of D[itt]o & this letter.

The 4th packet 4 of ye 3rd; the 5th Do. Of the fourth I have a MSS making out that it may be sent to Ireland while I write it, wch will enable Mr Rice[3] to print it at the same time it is printed here, & it may even be publish'd the day before it is publishd here, & sooner I am sure you will agree with me that I could not, whatever advantage might accrue to myself, wish to have it out in Ireland without injury to Mr Josepth Bell, the Bookseller who has purchas'd the Copy right.

I will have the honor of sending you a set of the new Sonnets if you will be so good as to accept them & will write to Mr Cadell to day to forward them to Ireland. This is a very Poor acknowledgement of my great obligations to you. I think within a fortnight I shall send over the whole of the "Old Manor House." Would Mr Rice make any agreement for the copy right in Ireland of a Poem in two Books—which I am writing—about 1000 verses I think[4] & which will be sold here in Quarto at 4s and then printed in a small Edition to make a second volume to the Sonnets and other poems already publish'd.[5] I hope to have this finishd in the Course of the Month of February. I do not beleive I shall sell the copy right here.

I know Mr Hayley receiv'd Your Adamo,[6] & he express'd himself extremely indebted to you for sending it, as it is a very scarce book. He told me when I last saw him that he should write to you &, in the mean time if I had that pleasure, desird me to mention it.

I am so extremely harrass'd to day—for "Sunday shines no sabbath day to me"—that I have no other time to write this than what I snatch while my maid is dressing my hair, an operation that I very seldom undergo. Will you forgive my writing so very vilely & thus abruptly assuring you

that I am, Dear Sir,
your most oblig'd Sert,
Charlotte Smith

Mrs ONeills address is thus:

Honble Mrs ONeill
To the care of ——— Sill Esqre
at Lisbon.

She will be very happy to hear from you.

I have been ill & perplex'd with the cruelty of my Childrens tyrannical Aristocratic relations, who will not allow me a shilling for them or even tell me what they have done with their property, & these torments, which often affect my spirits & drive me almost to despair, have prevented my going on with the Novel so rapidly as I hoped to have done. It will hardly be publishd here sooner than the 20th of January or perhaps beginning of February tho my agreement was for the 5th of this Month that it might be out by Christmas.

Huntington MS (HM10804). No address or postmark {because this letter was enclosed in the third packet of the manuscript of The Old Manor House sent for Rice's Dublin edition}.

NOTES

1. See Biographical Notes.
2. Of *The Old Manor House* (1793).
3. John Rice, 111 Grafton Street, Dublin, printer.
4. Thomas Cadell published the 1793 English edition and Rice the 1793 Irish edition of *The Emigrants.* The final version of this poem was 823 lines long. The preface to Cadell's edition is dated 10 May, Brighthelmstone.
5. Up until now, the sonnets and other poems had been contained in a single volume, which grew fuller and fuller from the fourteen sonnets and two other poems in the first edition to the sixty-four sonnets and other poems in the sixth edition in 1792. With the seventh edition in 1797, a second volume was put forward. It did not contain *The Emigrants.*
6. William Hayley's son Thomas was working with Thomas Sockett to translate Giovanni Battista Andreini's *Adamo* (1613).

To Thomas Cadell, Sr.[1]

[?Brighton, ca. 16 December 1792][2]
Sir,

I shall be much oblig'd to you to trust me so much farther as will suffice for a Copy of the new Edition of Sonnets,[3] neatly very neatly bound with a Cypher in Gilt Letters on the cover which I should wish to have Graven J. C. W. —— & on the other side, "From the Author." It is for M[r] Walker of Dublin, Author of Irish Antiquities &c &c, a Gentleman to whom I am much oblig'd & to whom I wish to make this small acknowledgement. You will therefore increase the favor I ask of you If you will be so good as to forward it to Ireland, directed to Josepth Cowper Walker, Esq[re], Eccles Street, Dublin.

If I had not been so effectually repulsed by your answer to D[r] Moore,[4] I should offer you a poem in blank verse which will be finish'd in about a Month, and will be corrected by the very first of our present Poets, Cowper. I can assuredly make a very considerable proffit of it if I print it on my own account, first in Quarto, & then in a small volume to make a companion to the Sonnets with a portrait. But as I shall go to France as soon as I have fulfilld my present engagement with Bell[5] and shall withdraw everything from England which can give me any trouble for three or four years, should I so long live, I would sell it, if I could do so to reasonable advantage. It will consist of about twelve hundred verses of which near half are done.

As I know you decline all farther dealing with me, I only mention this to beg the favor of you to let me know what you think may be the value of such a work, of which I am not a judge since it is quite unlike in its nature any I have printed & is, tho not on politics,[6] on a very popular & interesting subject mingled with descriptive & characteristic excursions in the way of the Task, only of course inferior to it. Yet of what is done my friends with their usual partiality think very highly — —

Your answer at your leisure will very much oblige

Sir
your obed[t] humble Ser[t]
Charlotte Smith

I thank you for the 6 sets of Sonnets, which Bell informs me he has rc[d].

General Manuscripts, Manuscripts Division, Department of Rare Books and Special Collections, Princeton University Library. No address or postmark.

NOTES

1. The manuscript at Princeton identifies this letter as being to James Dodsley, but there is ample evidence that it was written to Thomas Cadell, Sr. CS's letter to Joseph Cooper Walker of 16 Dec. 1792 proposes to "have the honor of sending you a set of the new Sonnets if you will be so good as to accept them & will write to M[r] Cadell to day to forward them to Ireland."

2. The date of this letter is further confirmed as being in 1792 by CS's reference to her poem in blank verse of about 1,200 lines. *The Emigrants* was read by Cowper and published in May 1793.

3. *Elegiac Sonnets i,* published in May 1792.

4. This exchange has not survived.

5. Joseph Bell published *The Old Manor House* in Mar. 1793.

6. *The Emigrants* is surely political in painting a sympathetic picture of women, children, priests, nobility, and military men who were exiled from France during the Revolution. As Cadell published it in the end, he must not have found it as politically offensive as *Desmond,* which he refused to publish.

1793
"A NEW COURSE OF SUFFERING"

—9 OCTOBER 1793

During this year, Charlotte Smith completed and published The Old Manor House, *now considered her best novel, and her long blank verse poem* The Emigrants. *Both show her anti-war stance. Her previous novel,* Desmond, *had been attacked for supporting the democratic ideals of the early French Revolution, attacks that were the fiercer because the book's author was a woman.* The Old Manor House, *partly set in America during the revolt against British rule, offers a safer protest against a war that is distant in time and place.* The Emigrants, *however, confronts the local and current turmoil of the French Revolution, which had by 1793 evolved into the Reign of Terror; many English liberals who had supported the revolution now recanted. In her new poem, Smith describes the miseries of the displaced with great empathy:*

> *. . . They, like me,*
> *From fairer hopes and happier prospects driven,*
> *Shrink from the future, and regret the past.*

The Revolution did indeed touch Smith's life—in terrible as well as wonderful ways. During 1793, Smith's own home became a refuge to some of the very clerical and aristocratic refugees whose fate her poem laments. To her great satisfaction one young chevalier, Alexandre de Foville, fell in love with her favorite daughter, Augusta. Smith was busying herself about ensuring a proper Catholic wedding for them when disaster struck—twice. Her third-to-the-oldest son, Charles, described as idling at home early in the year, had obtained an ensigncy in one of the new regiments sent to the Continent to fight. In September, he was severely wounded and sent home, a cripple for life. His condition burdened his mother emotionally as much as financially. Sadly, too, in this year, Smith's friend Henrietta O'Neill died while in Spain. O'Neill had provided Smith not only with lodging in London on business trips but also, and more important, with literary companionship. Against a darkening financial landscape, CS turned more and more to James Upton Tripp, the earl of Egremont's estate agent, for loans of books and ever-needed money.

To Joseph Cooper Walker

[Brighton, 1 January 1793]

Dear Sir,

I enclose 5 letter press sheets of Volume the third and, in another cover, 2 chapters of MMS of Volume 4th.[1] I hope the former packets have been received safe. The missing chapters of Vol. 2nd I have not yet got from my Printer as, on Account of the Holydays, the Men will not work. I rather hope to have them and the remains of Vol. 3rd to night but would no longer delay forwarding all I could. Should there be any mistake of omission in the series of Chapters, except those I have already mention'd (which are not yet deliver'd to me), I shall be infinitely oblig'd to you to give me the earliest notice of it tho I am in truth ashamed of giving you so much trouble & shock'd that I intrude upon you with Letters so uninteresting as this.

I am, Dear Sir,
in great haste—your most obedt & oblig'd Sert
Charlotte Smith

1st Jany 1793

Huntington MS (HM10805). No address or postmark.

NOTE

1. Walker acted as liaison for CS with the Dublin printer and bookseller John Rice. His intervention enabled her to earn some money on the Irish edition, as the advance letterpress permitted Rice to publish the books before they were pirated. The novel in question is *The Old Manor House,* published in England by Joseph Bell.

To James Upton Tripp

[?Brighton, 17 January 1793]

Dear Sir,

My Son[1] is so good as to undertake to convey this to Petworth for me & to beg the favr of your answer. I am shock'd to trouble you, but I have to day the most urgent Letter from my Landlord Mr Browne[2] for his £25, and the next summons I have will probably be an Execution in my House. As I had hoped from what Mr Turner said that the business you have been so kindly engag'd in would be completed so as to enable me to pay this last week, I ventured to promise it & am reproached with not being as good as my word——

I am very sensible, dear Sir, that I have not the least right to intrude on your kindness in this matter; but situated as I have been, It has been impossible to make any provision for this, and indeed I know not how I shall go on 'till the time when My Brother says the whole will be settled to your satisfaction.

May I request of you to have the goodness to let me know by Charles whether you can assist me, & that if you can oblige me with the draft for the 25£, you will be so very good as to send it up at any date by to days post, as any draft from you will satisfy my clamourous Landlord who is I believe really distrest.

I entreat you to forgive my taking this liberty with you & to believe me in all events, always,

your most oblig'd Ser[t]
Charlotte Smith

January 17th 1793
M[r] Brownes Address is no. 14 Thornhaugh Street
Bedford Square

Petworth House Archives MS. No address or postmark.

NOTES

1. Charles, her oldest son at home, about to turn 20 and enter the army (see Charles Dyer Smith in Biographical Notes).

2. John W. Browne (d. before 1826), probably of the Browne family formerly of Steyning, owned a house in Storrington until 1795. In 1796, he lived at Store Street, Middlesex. Her semiannual payment for rent was £25. As her situation with Mrs. Browne and her son worsened, CS described them as "a troublesome & not too honest family with whom I have to do" (see CS to Cadell and Davies, 24 Dec. 1794; see also CS to BS, 19 Feb. 1790, for a possible early mention of Browne).

To {William Tyler}[1]

[?Brighton, ?January 1793]
Sir,

As I find it will be impossible for me to get the matter of the Annuity, on which M[r] Turner has spoken to you, settled in time to enable me to pay my rent, I am under the necessity of troubling M[r] Tripp with an inquiry relative to the 35£ which I made over to him (on his being so good as to advance me that Sum)——which will be due to me on the 2nd January; & if it is paid, as I believe it will be, I have reason to hope M[r] Tripp will oblige me, on my securing it by the next half years payment, with as much as will release me from the difficulties that may attend my paying my rent——

For this reason I trouble you, if M[r] Tripp is not return'd, to forward to him in London or whereever he may be, the enclosed Letter, which will greatly oblige, Sir, your obed^{t} & most humble Ser^{t}

Charlotte Smith

Petworth House Archives MS. No address or postmark.

NOTE

1. See Biographical Notes. Although the recipient is not named, it is likely to be James Upton Tripp's assistant and eventual successor, William Tyler. The tone of this letter, so much more reserved than CS's letters to Tripp, suggest an early difference with Tyler, if not an outright rift.

To Joseph Cooper Walker

[Brighton] 6th Feby 1793

Dear Sir,

I am extremely oblig'd to you for your favor of the 30th January—— The inconvenience I put Mr Corry[1] to in sending him such heavy packets, and as it seems so many more than he expected, has extremely vexd me. I stopped so indiscreet a mode of conveyance as soon as I knew how deeply I had trespass'd, and in pursuance of your Brother's direction, I sent up on Monday by one of my French friends who was going to London a packet containing 100 pages of MMS being the continuance of the 4th Volume for Mr Rice. It has been long since compleat, and I should send the whole up this evening, but the Printer in London from whom I last night received the residue of the 2nd & third Volumes has from some very senseless blunder left out all [of] a sheet towards the end of the latter. I have written to day for it, and hope to have it down on Friday, & by Monday's Coach to send the whole for Ireland. I am sorry to put Mr Rice to the expence of receiving this work in three packets, but I think it better to forward what I have immediately, least the press sh^{d} stop. I shall therefore send up by tomorrow's Coach the remains of the 2nd and 3rd ~~& part of the 4th Vol~~ Volumes, reserving the residue of the MMS of the 4th & the whole of the 3rd till the last packet which will leave London ab^{t} the middle of next week. I apprehend that from several causes the work will not appear here till the 1st March.

I am impatient for the French Sonnet. But I will not now detain you longer, either with my impatience for this pleasure or my gratitude for all the kindness you exert towards me, because I much fear being too late for the post of to day & propose writing fully by the conveyance which will put Mr Rice into possession of the whole work. I therefore detain you only to repeat the assurance of the regard & esteem with which I ever remain,

Dear Sir, your most oblig'd Ser^{t},
Charlotte Smith

Domestic duties & domestic troubles, of which you shall know more when I write again (because you desire to do so), have prevented my seeing Mr Hayley for above ten weeks & will I fear still prevent my having that pleasure for some time to come. But we have frequent communication by Letter as he is my literary Cynosure, & I shall, by the stage of tomorrow, send your last obliging favor for his perusal since I know it will give him pleasure.

Should Mr Rice object to ye expence of conveyance, I must share it or take it upon myself when the account is settled if these perverse accidents do not prevent me from having any accounts to settle————

Huntington MS (HM10806). Addressed: Josepth Cooper Walker Esqre/ Eccles Street/ Dublin. Postmarked: {BRI}GHT{HEL}MSTONE; FE/ 7/ 93;FE/14.

NOTE

1. Isaac Corry, Esq., subscribed for two copies of *Elegiac Sonnets i.*

To Joseph Cooper Walker

Brighthelmstone 12th Feb^y^
1793
Dear Sir,

I now send for Mr Rice the whole of the Old Manor House & am compelled to ask you a very great favor which is that you would have the goodness to direct, & very particularly to request, that some intelligent person may look over the manuscript. It has been copied by a very careless or ignorant person, & it is very true that I might have corrected it in all the time that it has been lying by me, but Occupied & harrassd as I always am, I have neglected it from time to time, & now there is not a moment to lose as I find Mr Bell proposes publishing in ten days or thereabouts. However, Mr Rice will have the whole so much before any other Booksellers can have it that I hope it will answer his purpose. Will you forgive me, Dear Sir, for this short and incoherent letter, but I am writing in company & in embarrassments inconceivable of new & strange natures, out of which Heaven knows how I shall escape[1]——I go tomorrow to Eartham for a few days, & this makes my dispatching this last parcel to night more necessary. Adieu! Dear Sir, I will have the pleasure of writing to you more fully & of expressing the gratitude & regard with which I am, Dear Sir,

your much oblig'd Ser^t^,
Charlotte Smith

Huntington MS (HM10807). Addressed: Josepth Cooper Walker Esqre/ Eccles Street/ Dublin/ To be delivered/ immediately. No postmarks. This sealed letter was apparently mailed in the packet with the manuscript.

NOTE

1. Her "company" were emigrants living with her. The embarrassments were almost certainly the seizure of her books and furniture for failure to pay her rent (see CS to James Upton Tripp, 20 Dec. 1793). On 12 Apr. 1793, Hayley responded to a letter from Thomas Cadell in which Cadell complained that CS had written two drafts on her apparently empty account with him—"immediately after your liberal aid." Cadell is "hurt" by her doing so, and Hayley "chagrined." He goes on: "Humanity will lead us both to reflect, that the Necessities of this wretched sufferer have been extreme.—She must have literally wanted Bread, had I not obtained from your generosity, & that of a few other Friends, some occasional Relief" (Cowper and Newton Museum MS).

To Joseph Cooper Walker

Brighthelmstone. Feb. 20th 1793
Dear Sir,

My stay at Eartham<s> was so short—and so much was I occupied during that short time in engaging Mr Hayley's humanity on behalf of some French friends of mine who were likely to be compelld to leave this place & knew not where to find refuge within the distance mark'd by the order of Council—that I was not able to find as much as would suffice to offer you our joint thanks. He assured me that it was his intention to write to you himself in a few days after my departure on Monday last.

I Sent the last packet of MMS and a sheet of Letter press that was missing in the 3rd Volume on Monday last from London. I trust Mr Rice will receive it so soon as to preclude all possibility of the other Booksellers overtaking him—— I troubled you with a short Letter in the packet & shall be greatly oblig'd to you to Let me hear if it was received safe. I am yet more impatient for the French Sonnet. The Old Manor House is not yet publishd here. It has however been advertis'd as being speedily to be publishd, but it will be probably quite the end of the month first so that, as Mr Rice wd be undoubtedly a fortnight or three weeks before the other Booksellers, I imagine your most obliging wishes in my favor will not be baffled. Whatever advantage may accrue in consequence of your friendly interposition, I shall be still more obliged to you if you will receive for me & remit to Mr Thomas Walkinson, No. 10 Water Street, Blackfriars, who is so good as to befriend me in the little money matters I have, & indeed without very great kindness from my friends, I know not what would have become of me & my Children this Winter.

The Poem which I am about is in Blank verse & is to be entitled "The Emigrants." Mr Cowper is to correct it under the auspices of Mr Hayley who thinks many parts of the first book, which is nearly done, very capital.[1] But indeed I always fear the partiality of his friendship—— The Book is to consist of two parts—about a thousand or twelve hundred lines—and will be publish'd here, if I can get peace to finish it, about the beginning of May. It is not a party book but a conciliatory book,[2] & M[r] Hayley thinks there is some very good drawing in it——

Will you forgive this short and incoherent Letter? My Son Charles goes to London tomorrow to see if he can prevail on the Trustees to let him have three hundred pounds to purchase an Ensigncy in some of the new raisd companies[3] as nothing can be more distressing to him & to me than his being at home with[t] any plan of Life. I send up by him several letters on business—which I must write in company as the Emigrants who are yet here, some of whom are very agreeable Men, find some consolation in the society my small book room affords them of an evening. The confusion of tongue therefore that I have around me prevents my adding more at this instant than a repetition of that gratitude & regard with which I must ever be, Dear Sir,

your much oblig'd and most obed Ser[t],
Charlotte Smith

Huntington MS (HM10808). Addressed: Josepth Cooper Walker Esq[re]/ Eccles Street/ Dublin. Postmarked: FE/22/93; MR/2.

NOTES

1. *The Emigrants,* published later in 1793, is dedicated to William Cowper in a preface dated from "Brighthelmstone, May 10, 1793" (p. ix). CS regards him, she writes, "with pride, as one of the few, who at the present period, rescue her from the imputation of having degenerated in Poetical talents . . ." (p. vi). In a letter of 19 Mar. to Hayley, Cowper wrote of receiving three days ago a "swingeing pacquet by the post . . . Mrs. Smith's poems" (Cowper, *Letters and Prose Writings,* 4:308).

2. That is, CS does not mean for the book to favor one or the other side of the French Revolution. Book I is concerned with victims—clergymen of all ranks, a mother fleeing with her children, a shepherd. Book II describes the ravages of war. Most notable throughout is her personal identification with the emigrants, whose loss of "fairer hopes and happier prospects" (p. 39) reminds her of her own losses. The comparison intensifies from book I, which takes place in November, to book II, in April.

3. A Charles Smith had obtained the rank of ensign as of 10 Apr. 1793 (*Army List* [1794], p. 90). It is difficult to imagine anyone other than Egremont laying out such a considerable sum.

To James Upton Tripp

[Brighton, 21 March 1793]
Dear Sir,

As my hard fate compells me still to write however weary and however unable, I am again engag'd in a work in doing which I have occasion to refer to the History of Jamaica[1]——I mean the natural History. I am told there is one in quarto of three volumes by Long, which is the best—— If it should be in Lord Egremonts library, I shall be very much oblig'd to you to ask his Lordships permission to send it to me. If not, I request that you will not name it, as I cannot bear to give Lord Egremont the trouble he has already had the goodness once or twice to take on my account in regard to Books.

I trust you will excuse my taking this liberty with you; & if chance throws M[r] Turner in your way, pray be so obliging as to say to him that the 27th instant is the latest time obtaind by his friend M[r] Walker[2] before the dismission of the suit against Lady Gibbons[3] will take place; and that I find all our expense is likely to be thrown away and our trouble baffled, but that I wish to hear from him————

On second thoughts, I must write to him myself and therefore will not intrude upon You for the delivery of this message. But I am so hurried & so unwell that I cannot write my Letter over again, which you will I hope forgive———I am, Sir,

your oblig'd & obed[t] humble Ser[t]
Charlotte Smith

Brighthelmstone
March 21st 1793

Petworth House Archives MS. No address or postmark.

NOTES

1. CS probably confused Edward Long's *The History of Jamaica: Or, General Survey of the Antient and Modern State of That Island: With Reflections on Its Situation, Settlements, Inhabitants,* 3 vols. (1774), with Patrick Browne's *The Civil and Natural History of Jamaica* (1789). The latter had Linnaean indexes and a map of the island.

2. Probably not Joseph Cooper Walker's brother (see CS to Walker, 6 Feb. 1793).

3. Rebecca (d. 1811), daughter of Vice Admiral Watson, married William Gibbons in 1771. He was created baronet on his father Sir John's death in 1776. Neither the nature of the suit against her nor its plaintiff is known, but the Smith family had long disputed a Barbadian property with her husband and father-in-law.

To Bishop Douglass[1]

Storrington near Petworth
Sussex, 30th July 1793
Sir,

You will not I trust be surprised at being address'd by a perfect stranger when the (to me) important occasion of my giving this trouble is explained which I will do as briefly as possible. I have a daughter, the object of my ~~fondest~~ fondest solicitude who is on the point of being married to a native of France—An Emigrant officer and, of course, of the Roman Catholic Religion of whom, after an acquaintance of eight months, I have every reason to beleive he deserves the attachment she has to him. All her family, however, as well as her Fathers side as on mine are averse to this marriage & have endeavourd as much as they can to prevent it. But as she is determined upon it, & I am well persuaded her happiness is in question, I am not moved by their reasons, most of which are in my opinion illiberal and unworthy of people calling themselves Christians——

But as it is ~~already~~ double incumbent on me thus circumstanced to take care, I think it necessary to attend to the information they have lately given me; which is, that a marriage contracted here with a Protestant will not be binding in France, That a Catholic cannot marry a Protestant, & ~~is~~ in short that he may return to his own Country &, leaving my Daughter, marry again without any danger of committing a crime in the eye of the French law.

Tho I have the most perfect reliance on his probity, yet I certainly should leave nothing to chance; & therefore by the advice of a Clergyman of the Catholic religion in this neighborhood, I take the liberty of addressing you Sir, & entreat you to inform me by what means a Gentleman professing himself a Catholic, & disclaiming any obedience to the present French Government, can be <xxxxxxxx> legally married here to a Protestant, and if you would have the goodness to give me, either ~~by~~ address'd to myself, or to Mr Pierpoint[2] at Burton, such instructions as you may deem necessary, it will confer on me a very great favour. I propos'd after the ceremony was performed here by Banns in the Parish Church to have it re-performed ~~her~~ after the rites of the Catholic religion by a French Minister[3] resident not far off. But upon my applying to him, I find it is impossible—at least he beleives so. Yet certainly instances daily occur in which such marriages are made.

As Monday is the day fix'd, I must entreat the favor of your early answer, and that you will pardon this trouble from, Sir,

your most humble & obed Sert,
Charlotte Smith

Westminster Diocesan Archives vol. A. 45, AAW 4S, p. 177. No address or postmark.

NOTES

1. See Biographical Notes.

2. William Pierpoint (d. 1828), Catholic priest at Burton Park near Petworth in Sussex (1784–1810). Burton Park was the family seat of John Biddulph, Esq. (d. 1835), a Catholic then living in Italy. See CS to Dr. Burney, 21 Aug. 1793.

3. Mr. Fortier. See CS to Dr. Burney, 21 Aug. 1793, n. 2.

To Dr. Charles Burney[1]

Storrington near Petworth
Sussex
August 13th 1793
Sir,

An address, and of the nature of that I am about to make, from a perfect stranger will probably surprise you, but without availing myself of the priveledge which one literary person sometimes presumes upon in addressing another, I beg leave to apologize for taking so great a liberty as the present and as briefly as possible to state the occasion of it.

I saw some few days since in the papers an account of the marriage of Miss Burney to Mr D'Arblay[2] and observed that the Ceremony was a second time performed at the chapel of the Sardinian Embassador. As my second daughter[3] was then within three days to give her hand to Mr De Foville,[4] I had taken the precaution to address myself Near a week before to Mr Douglas, the Catholic Bishop in London, to beg his directions how the marriage of my daughter might be made binding according to the Laws of France, by its being a second time performed by a Catholic Minister. A Gentleman of that description, who usually resides in this nieghbourhood being then in Town,[5] Mr Douglas answer'd that he had given him proper directions and that on his coming down He would satisfy my mind. I sent to him therefore on the day Mr Douglas had named for his return, informing him that as the following Monday was fix'd for the ceremony to be perform'd at the Parish church here, we would afterwards, or before, attend him at the Chapel in the House where he resides or at any other within ten miles (& there are two or three) which he should appoint.

He answered by informing me that he would be here at eight Oclock on Monday Morning. I concluded that he then meant to perform the Ceremony, but was unpleasantly undeceived when on his arrival he made an infinite number of trifling objections, such as his uncertainty how lately Chevalier de Foville had been at Confession, His doubts whether he was thirty years of age, & others of which I comprehend nothing. But after Mr de Foville had in a private conversation with him obviated most of these, he ownd that Mr Douglas had given him a sort of dispensation to enable Mr Fortier, an Emigrant Priest, at Petworth to perform the Ceremony who we were then directed to meet in the Chapel at Burton. Instead however of meeting Mr Fortier, we received a note from him with an Excuse that he was busy!

The parties being met from a considerable distance in the morning, it was quite impossible to put off the ceremony in the Parish Church here even if it had not been perform'd previous to this unexpected refusal. But that it was perform'd & the marriage completed is now one of the reasons given for the Catholic Priests declining to perform the Ceremony according to the rites of the Gallican Church. I am under peculiar circumstances with regard to the disapprobation of all my child's family for no other reason but because she has chosen a French Man, for individually his character is irreproachable, and they chuse (tho my poor Girl is not under the least obligation to any of them) to tieze me with prognostics and reproaches. They tell me that if my daughter should have Children, they will not inherit the Estate M^r^ De Foville has at present lost or that which remains in possession of his Mother[6] unless the Marriage is performed according to the Laws of France. What the Laws of France now are I beleive nobody knows. Nor can it be guessed, I fear, what they will be. What they were however can be ascertain'd, & to these M^r^ De Foville and his Wife are willing and desirous to appeal in repeating the Ceremony of their marriage as those laws direct with regard to those persons who consider them still in force.

Not having the honor to be acquainted with you Sir, or with your daughter, tho I have the highest esteem for the private, & admiration of the literary, characters of both, I know not what I have to plead in excuse for thus intruding upon you unless it be my conviction that you will both feel for my situation from the general goodness of your hearts. If then you, Sir, can give me any information how I may now proceed to put an end to the cavils of persons who seem to have a malignant pleasure in encreasing the number of thorns which infest my pillow, I am persuaded you will. Perhaps the Chaplain of the Sardanian or the Chaplain of the Spanish Ambassador may be known to you, & by their means the difficulty, whether real or imaginary, may be got over. I have within these two days been advis'd to apply to the Archbishop of Rouen, but I beleive De La Mechefaucauld,[7] who was Archbishop at the Revolution, is dead, & has never been replaced by an Archbishop whom M^r^ De Foville would acknowledge. From another person, I have heard that it is necessary to apply to the Bishop of St Polde de Leon.[8]

But being myself doubtful which advice to follow, I have thought it best to trouble you with this enquiry, not doubting Your obliging readiness to give me any information & supposing from the marriage of Miss Burney with a Gentleman under the same circumstances as M^r^ De Foville (at least I apprehend so) that to afford me such information may be in your power, which will be received with infinite gratitude by, Sir,

your most obed^t^ humble Ser^t^,
Charlotte Smith

Osborn Collection MS, Yale University. No address or postmark.

NOTES

1. See Biographical Notes. The three letters to Dr. Burney concerning her daughter's marriage suggest that he acted to help CS solve the problems incurred in marrying a Catholic émigré.

2. Fanny Burney married Alexandre d'Arblay on 31 July 1793 and remarried the next day at the chapel of the Sardinian ambassador.

3. A copy of the marriage settlement between Augusta and Alexandre de Foville, dated 1 Aug. 1792 [*sic*], survives (PHA #8222).

4. Alexandre Mark Constant de Foville (PHA #8222).

5. William Pierpoint, priest at Burton Park.

6. De Foville's estates were in Normandy, in the possession of his mother, Marie Charlotte Le Carvier de Foville.

7. Not identified.

8. On 14 Mar. 1793, inhabitants of Saint-Pol-de-Léon, chief town of the district of the arrondissement of Morlaix, had revolted against the Convention's attempt to draft 300,000 men. They were led by their bishop, a former captain in the cavalry.

To James Upton Tripp[1]

[Storrington, 16 August 1793]

Dear Sir,

If Monday next is fine, Miss Bridger[2] will have the goodness to meet my little George[3] at Petworth to take him to School, where M[r] Parsons[4] has again desired to receive him, notwithstanding it is not in my power to discharge his arrears. The Chevalier de Foville & my daughter intend to convey the little Boy to Petworth in a whiskey,[5] which is to be hired in this Village, & the former wishes to take the opportunity of seeing Petworth House, Stables &c. I know I may take the liberty if you should be at home, to recommend him to your Courtesy, both as a foreigner and a relation of mine. With your permission therefore, M[r] & M[rs] De Foville will have the pleasure of attending your commands at the Swan at about half past one on that day, & should you be engag'd, you will have the goodness to let them know. I am, Sir, your much oblig'd Ser[t]

Charlotte Smith

16th Aug[st] Storrington——1793

Petworth House Archives MS. No address or postmark.

NOTES

1. A note at the end of the letter in William Tyler's difficult handwriting gives his reply:

> Mr Tripp is at present in Somersetshire, and will therefore be deprived of the Pleasure (which I am sure, if he had been at Petworth, he would have

courted) in accompanying the Chevalier and Mrs de Foville about Lord Egrmont's Premises; to which, however, access may be had by that Gent & Lady without any difficulty, notwithstanding Mr Tripp's absence. I am, WT.

The Tripps were a Somerset family originally and were connected with Petworth through their involvement with the Wyndham family on the latter's Somerset estates, centered on Orchard Wyndham.

2. Of Easebourn near Midhurst. CS gave her a set of *The Banished Man* as soon as it was published (see CS to Cadell, Jr., 29 Aug. 1794).

3. George Augustus Frederick Smith (8) was CS's youngest child. See Biographical Notes.

4. Charles Parsons was master of Midhurst Grammar School from 1788 to 1795. The school still exists, but no records survive of pupils at this period.

5. A light two-wheeled carriage drawn by one horse.

To Dr. Charles Burney

Storrington by Petworth, August 21th 1793
Sir,

I am extremely honour'd and oblig'd by your Letter, which I receiv'd yesterday, enclosing that of Monsieur Jamart.[1] Allow me to express my acknowledgements for both, and to say that after the refusal of Mr Fortier,[2] which was undoubtedly in consequence of the conduct of Mr Pierrepoint (who is English or Irish and resides at Burton, the Seat of Mr Biddulph,[3] a Catholic of an ancient and respectable family in this County who is himself in Italy), it would be with reluctance that I should again apply to Monr Fortier or ask of Mr Pierrepoint the use of Burton Chapel, which is the nearest to the Chevalier de Foville and my daughter (who reside with me here). But at Midhurst or rather at Easebourn, the adjoining Village, there is a chapel formerly belonging to the Viscounts Montague[4] where there is a very large congregation of Catholics; and resident at Midhurst and now employ'd as Instructor in the French language at the School where my youngest boy is placed is a Mr Bougaie,[5] who is extremely respected by that neighbourhood and appears to be a very worthy Man.

If Monr Jamart would have the goodness to obtain from Monsieur L'Abbe Osmont, grand Vicaire of Rouen, the dispensation requisite and which shall authorise Monr Bougaie to celebrate according to the rites of the Gallican Church, a marriage between Alexandre Marc-Constant de Foville and Anna Augusta Smith at any time, it would be considerd by me as a very great obligation, and equally so by the Chevalier de Foville who—being of opinion (in which I entirely agree with him) that an honest Man cannot change his religion and that he ought to conform as far as is in his power to its rules—is very desirous of having the Ceremony repeated by a Catholic Priest as well to satisfy his own ideas of duty, as to obviate as far as possible any scruples that may hereafter give pain to his Mother, whose attachment to her Religion is such that his marrying a protestant will perhaps give her some concern which his affection for her will induce him to alleviate as much as possible by not appearing to slight, in neglecting its forms, the persuasion to which she is so warmly devoted.

He is however thirty years of age, & as it was impossible for him to ask his Mother's consent, he trusts that the circumstances he was in and the character of my daughter will reconcile her to the step he has taken. I am myself perfectly easy about it, as I am sure the simplicity of Augusta's mind & her affection for him (with the advantage of a person reckon'd very beautiful) will not only plead with Madame de Foville the pardon of her Son, but interest her in favor of his choice. In regard to going to confession, the Chevalier de Foville has not the least objection to complying with any rules that may be perscribed him, and the reason why I wish the permission to be made for any time is that Mr Bougaie may himself name any interval he thinks requisite for these preliminary forms.

And now, Sir, having thus far availd myself of the very obliging offers of service you have made me, for which I cannot sufficiently express my gratitude, allow me to go still farther in presuming upon that disposition to which I am already so much indebted and to ask if your Friends, natives of that unhappy Country, can any of them put M^r De Foville in a way of conveying a Letter to his Mother in France from whom he has never heard since the communication ceas'd and relative to whom he is under great inquietude. She is probably yet more unhappy about him, as she cannot know that his oeconomy has made her last remittance supply him till now, and is probably in pain for his subsistence. He promis'd that he never would again enter the Army till there was a prospect of entering France to restore Monarchy, but Madame de Foville, who extorted this promise from him at the close of the last unfortunate Campaign, cannot be sure that it has been in his power to keep it. The Chevalier is persuaded that, as his Mother is a most excellent Parent and lives only for him, she waits only for the means to send him another remittance, which on the occasion of his marriage would very certainly be acceptable, but he would not for a thousands worlds venture an application for it unless very sure that such application could be made without subjecting her to danger from the horrid conduct of the Men who dare to violate under pretence of Republicanism every law of God & Man.

I have been trying by means of some of my friends who are travelling thro Germany to Italy to get a Letter put into the post on their route, but one of them, after promising to try, excus'd himself, and the other, Lady Bolingbroke,[6] inform'd me on Sunday that the Person she has hired as Courier declares he cannot undertake the Journey with any Letters about the Carriage directed to France. I cannot therefore press it farther either on her or my dear and respectable friend her father. I have since been trying what could be done with certain Countrymen of mine who deal (I am afraid not according to Law) on the other side of the Water, & whose traffic, if I may judge of it by their nightly convoys, is not at all impeded by the War or by the Anathemas of the Conventionists against Englishmen (I conclude honest Englishmen only are proscribed), but these Men, besides that they are not much to be trusted, say that they now go to Ostend instead of Fescamp[7] tho there is one of them who for ten Guineas seems dispos'd to tempt putting in a Letter at Fescamp into the Post. I hardly dare trust him, and the Sum is very great, unless paid on better assurance than one can have on the conduct of such a person. So that upon the whole, we have determin'd not to confide in him till we are more assur'd that we may do so in safety and, in the mean time, to enquire among those equally interested, if any way has yet been found to get over the cruel impediments which exist between the Emigrants & their friends.

I am sure I may rely on your kindness in this instance, and I must again repeat my thanks for that which I have experienced in the instance wherein you have already taken so much trouble. I know that, to a mind like yours, it will be a gratification to learn that your Letter has been extremely consolatory to an heart torn with too many other sorrows to bear without (perhaps too much) impatience the reproaches of my relations & the sneers & sarcasms of soi disant friends, for that I have dared to consult my own judgement and the happiness (as I firmly beleive) of my child, rather than those illiberal and absurd prejudices which they entertain and which lead them to condemn a most amiable Man, merely because he is of another Country— for as to Religion surely we have the same God! I am, Sir, with the greatest esteem & gratitude, your most oblig'd Ser[t],

Charlotte Smith

As I cannot procure a frank to day and am unwilling to lengthen my letter, I make an awkward Corner here[8] to beg the favor of you to present my Comp[limen]ts with those of M[r] de Foville to Monsieur Jamart with our very sincere thanks for the trouble he is so obliging as to offer to undertake.

Osborn Collection MS, Yale University. Address: D[r] Burney/ Chelsea College/ near—/London. Postmark: PETWORTH; AU/22/93.

NOTES

1. As Jamart and Bougaie, mentioned below, are not identified in Bellenger, *French Exiled Clergy*, it can be assumed that they were not exiled French clergy.

2. Jean Nicolas Fortier, a parish priest from Rouen. Bellenger gives no dates or further information for him.

3. See CS to Bishop Douglass, 30 July 1793, n. 2.

4. Anthony Joseph Browne (1728–1787), seventh Viscount Montagu, who returned to his Catholic faith on his deathbed. In 1793 the Montagu mansion at Cowdray burned. Egremont bought the borough of Midhurst from Montagu's executors for £50,000.

5. Not identified.

6. Charlotte Collins, daughter of the Reverend Thomas Collins of Winchester. Her father served as tutor to George Richard St. John, third Viscount Bolingbroke and fourth Viscount Saint John (1761–1824). She married him in 1783 and was ultimately separated from him. CS may have corresponded with her fairly often and mentions her in two later letters to Thomas Cadell, Jr., and William Davies, 22 Sept. 1796 and 16 Feb. 1797.

7. Or Fecamp, a military encampment; now a marshy plain no longer identified on maps.

8. CS drew a rectangle in the upper left-hand corner of the first page of this long letter and squeezed in this "postscript" upside down in a tiny hand.

To James Upton Tripp[1]

Storrington 1st September
1793
Dear Sir,

It is with infinite reluctance I am troublesome to you, but I have causes enough to offer, which, with one so very good natured as you are, will I know be sufficient. As after long solicitation & a thousand falsehoods & evasions between the Men who call themselves Trustees, I find I am to have no present money for the support of my family (tho my Solicitor Mr Morgan[2] offer'd to advance it himself on the promise of being repaid by them when they were in Cash).

I must raise what I have the most pressing and immediate occasion for, on the Sum of 35£ which they are oblig'd to pay me half yearly out of the small remains of my own fortune, which Mr Smith spares me and his family. It is due the 2nd of January 94. Of course the draft drawn for it will have four months to run. The Gentn have deign'd to say to Mr Morgan that they will pay when due tho they will not accept it- —Could you, Sir, without inconvenience discount it for me so that I might receive the amount (allowing ~~of course~~ the discount) in the course or rather in the early part of this week As I am getting deep into debt here without the power of helping it; having been buoy'd up with hopes of receiving 200£ which Mr Morgan seem'd convincd I should receive from the Trustees in consequence of the accounts he saw of the produce of the Estates———

I troubled Mr Johnson[3] with this request a few days ago, who assured me he would have complied with my request had it been in his power, which I really believe. It possibly may not be in yours; but if it is, I am persuaded you will oblige me——and that in addition to many other civilities you will at all events pardon this trouble from, Dear Sir,

your oblig'd & obedt Sert
Charlotte Smith

I meant to have sent this by the post tomorrow, but as I must send a Servant on another occasion, I have orderd him to leave it, & shall be much indebted for an early answer——

Petworth House Archives MS. No address or postmark.

NOTES

1. A note at the end of the letter records William Tyler's reply. "Madam, Mr Tripp is not yet returned from Somersetshire; But I expect his Return on Monday or Tuesday, and I will then communicate to him the Contents of your Letter. I am &c WT."

2. Jonathan Morgan of Lincoln's Inn, witness to Augusta and De Foville's marriage articles in 1793 (PHA #8222) and lawyer for BS in 1802 (see CS to William Tyler, 16 Sept. 1802).

3. Not identified.

To James Upton Tripp[1]

[Storrington, 4 September 1793]
Dear Sir,

I am very sorry that I troubled you with a Letter & a request when a melancholy event in Mrs Tripp's family might render attention to either inconvenient to you. Will you however excuse my requesting an answer by the post of Friday; as I have the most pressing occasion for the amount of the small draft I named to you in order to discharge a Servant & for other purposes which cannot be delay'd without extreme inconvenience to me. If therefore you cannot oblige me, I wd lose as little time as possible in attempting to procure the accommodation elsewhere. I beg your Pardon for being thus troublesome. I am, dear Sir,

your oblig'd Sert
Charlotte Smith

Storrington Septr 4th

Petworth House Archives MS. No address or postmark.

NOTE

1. William Tyler had written on CS's letter to Tripp sent Sunday, 1 Sept., that he would communicate the contents of her letter to Tripp when he returned on Monday or Tuesday. Here, not yet hearing from Tripp and perhaps not trusting Tyler, she writes to Tripp on Wednesday for money needed on Friday.

To James Upton Tripp

[Storrington] Septr 15th 1793
Dear Sir,

From a message received by Lionel,[1] I hoped to have heard from you to day, what mistake I had made in the note that I might have alterd it. It grieves me most truly to be so troublesome to you———

But the miserable accident[2] that has happen'd to my poor Boy redoubles my want of money at this moment; as I must send his Brother to him, & I have in vain applied to the inhuman Trustees for a few guineas for the use of my dear cripple. They take no notice of my application tho to their infamous conduct it is oweing that he has taken up from necessity, & because a young Man cannot be idle, this trade of Death, which at twenty years old has made him a mutilated cripple for life.

Forgive me if I cannot command my temper, & if you are at home when the bearer brings this, have the goodness to inform me in which way I can settle the note of 35£ to your satisfaction; as I propose to send Lionel off to-morrow if I can get money, which the small remains of this, and a trifling pay^{t} made from another quarter, will enable me to do———

I am, dear Sir,
your oblig'd humble Ser^{t}
Charlotte Smith

Dear Sir,

Mr Naish[3] has just been here to say he has no news of the note ab^{t} which I have been compelld to give you so much trouble. I cannot get an horse to send a servant over & therefore am oblig'd to write by the post.[4]

Petworth House Archives MS. No address or postmark.

NOTES

1. Lionel, the oldest son still at home, having been sent down from Winchester School after participating in the rebellion of 1793 (see CS to Joseph Warton, 31 Aug. 1791, n. 2). He turned 16 on 9 Oct. CS was about to send Lionel to France to bring home his injured brother.

2. The 14th (Bedfordshire) Regiment of Foot had been extremely active since Charles signed up in Apr. 1793. In May, at the opening of the campaign, it stormed

Famars playing a French tune, the "Ça Ira." On 23 July 1793, the 14th "furnished a detachment for the storming of the Mons hornwork." And, almost fatally for Charles, the 14th participated in the Siege of Dunkirk, fighting "at the head of the Column that repulsed the sortie, and in one fire from the enemy, when the regiment had not more than three hundred men in the field, about fifty-six men were brought down, and not withstanding, the 14th continued and made a gallant charge" (O'Donnell, *Historical Records of the Fourteenth Regiment,* pp. 58–59).

3. Michael Nash (d. 1808) of Storrington, mercer of Guildford, married to Mary Upton of Petworth.

4. CS wrote this postscript upside down on the fourth page of the letter. The rest of the page, including any address, is torn away.

To James Upton Tripp

[Storrington, 16 September 1793]

Dear Sir,

I am very much oblig'd to you for the draft you have sent me & will take the earliest opportunity of repaying you the 10£ which you are so very obliging as to let remain till I can get something done, for which purpose I fear I must go to London. I am so unwell that I write from my bed, tho I must attempt going to Mrs Dorsets[1] to day to settle with her the departure of Lionel for Ostende. I am, dear Sir,

your much oblig'd Ser^t
Charlotte Smith

16th Septr 1793

Petworth House Archives MS. No address or postmark.

NOTE

1. Catherine Ann (or Anna) Turner Dorset (chr. 17 Jan. 1753, d. 1834), CS's younger sister, who lived nearby at Bignor Park, the family seat. Catherine married Captain Michael Dorset, son of the Reverend Michael Dorset, an eccentric local vicar. Catherine supported both CS and their brother Nicholas in their times of need, but she also quarreled with them and was estranged from them. She and CS collaborated on *Conversations Introducing Poetry* (1804), and Catherine went on to author her own children's books, beginning with *The Peacock at Home and Other Poems* (1809). In later life she lived happily in Brighton and died quite old in Chichester.

Her middle name is sometimes given as Anne, but legal documents almost always give it as Ann or Anna (WSRO, Hawkins papers ## 77, 78, 79, 86, 92, 93). One witnessed signature is Anna. Their mother's name was Anna, a name continued in the family with CS's daughter Anna Augusta.

To James Upton Tripp

[Petworth, 18 September 1793]
Dear Sir,

Lord Egremonts goodness has enabled me to return you the ten pounds with which you had the ~~goodness~~ kindness to accommodate me; but as I want present money to send to Ostend, I have done it in the form of the draft on Sir William Gibbons[1] who, conscious that his family owe my children 17,000£ and upwards, has desir'd me to draw on him for twenty Guineas at fourteen days. You will I know have the goodness to send it to your Bankers in London; & when it is paid to take what I am indebted to you & send me the rest in any form convenient to you. I am, dear Sir,

with many thanks
your oblig'd Ser[t]
Charlotte Smith

Petworth. 18th Sept[r] 1793
I write at M[r] Palmer's[2] half distracted by the variety of things I have to think of, & I believe I have written sad nonsense.

Petworth House Archives MS. No address or postmark.

NOTES

1. Sir William (1751–1814) was also a lawyer. His father Sir John had a mortgage on the Stanwell lands which were subsequently sold, perhaps accounting for CS's claim of £17,000 lost. For more on the disputed property, see CS to John Robinson, 19 Sept. 1785 and n. 7.
2. Robert Rice Palmer, mercer and draper, the only Palmer in Petworth at this time.

To James Upton Tripp

Storrington, Oct[r] 5th [17]93
Dear Sir,

May I trouble you to be so good as to let any of the books mention'd on the within paper be look'd out for me in the Library at Petworth if they happen to be there—— I am employ'd on something in which I have particularly occasion for Youngs tour to the North and that in France.[1]

I am also going to solicit another favor of you. As I have a short lease of this old place, and there is a long wall in the Garden without a single fruit tree, I may as well plant a few. The soil being a warm sand is particularly calculated for Grapes which I am piggishly fond of, tho in England they are generally sour to me for It is rare to taste them.[2] If you would be so good as to make interest with Lord Egremonts gardener for a vine or two of good sorts from his nursery, but such as will ripen in this cold climate without an hot house, I shall be very much oblig'd to you. I believe this is the time of year to plant them. The old Gardener here tells me that there are a great many seedling Cypresses at Petworth or young ones of two or three years growth of which if you would beg me two or three, I shall be also greatly oblig'd to you and any other evergreen or other shrubs of which there may happen to be plenty of young plants——

I am sure you will be glad to hear that my poor Charles is doing well, and Lionel in his last Letter informs me the Surgeons think that he may very soon venture to England——

If Sir William Gibbons has paid the draft with which I troubled you, I shall be very much oblig'd to you if, after deducting the Sum you were so very good as to accommodate me with, you will pay to M[r] William Upton, Junior,[3] Six pounds seven Shillings.

I beg a thousand pardons for taking this liberty with you and am, Dear Sir,

your most obed[t] Ser[t]
Charlotte Smith

I have at present of Lord Egremonts La vie de Turenne.[4] 2 Vol.

Petworth House Archives MS. No address or postmark. Photograph by Michael Moore, by permission of the Right Honorable the Lord Egremont, Petworth House Archives, West Sussex Record Office.

NOTES

1. Arthur Young's *A Six Months Tour through the North of England. Containing an Account of the Present State of Agriculture, Manufactures and Population, in Several Counties of This Kingdom* (1770). As secretary to the Board of Agriculture, Young wrote about French politics, farming, and resources, his current work being *Travels during the Years 1787, 1788, and 1789. Undertaken More Particularly with a View of Ascertaining the Cultivation, Wealth, Resources, and National Prosperity of the Kingdom of France,* 2 vols. (1792–94).

2. She may mean that she loves real grapes, but the grapes she usually has in England are sour ones, that is, the fruits of rancor.

3. The Uptons were ubiquitous in Petworth and there were several Williams.

4. *La Vie du Vicomte du Turenne* by Du Buisson, pseud. (Gatien de Courtilz de Sandras), 2nd ed. (1687). See CS to Tripp, 31 Oct. 1793, for a fuller picture of this course of reading in French political history.

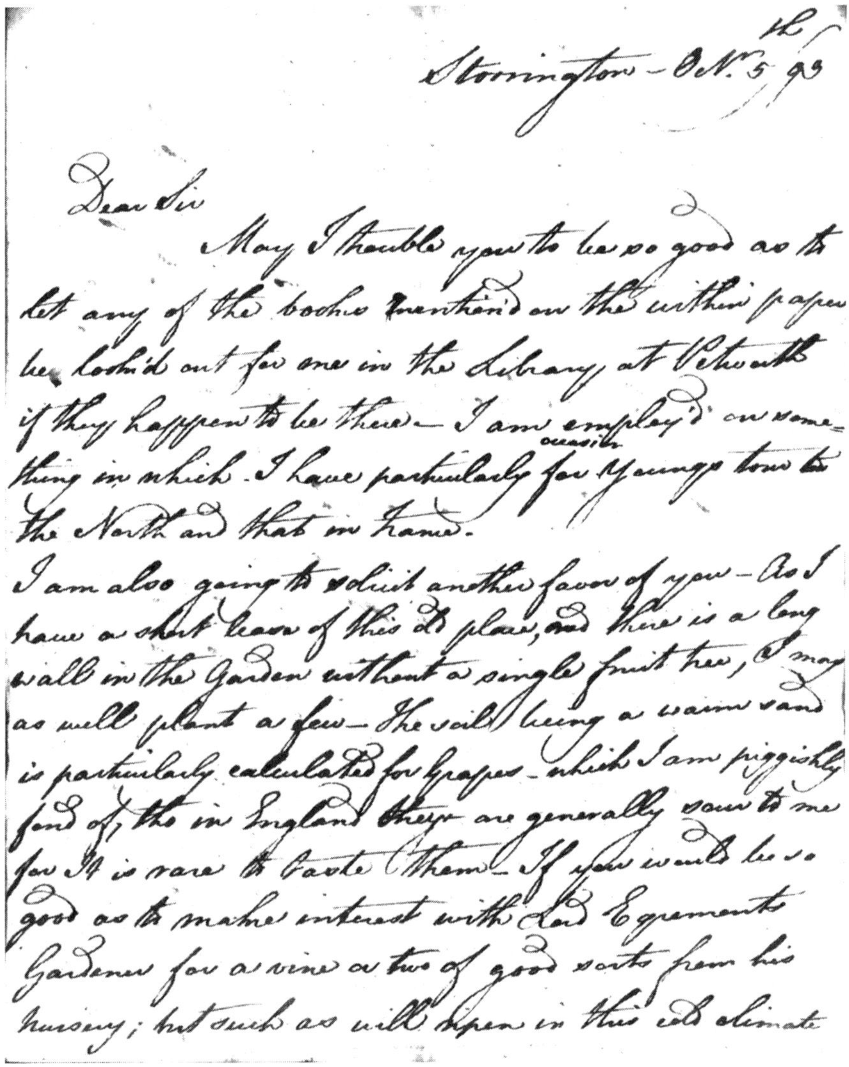

Storrington – Oct. 5th 93

Dear Sir

May I trouble you to be so good as to let any of the books mention'd on the within paper be look'd out for me in the Library at Petworth if they happen to be there – I am employ'd on something in which I have particularly occasion for Youngs tour to the North and that in France.

I am also going to solicit another favor of you – As I have a short lease of this old place, and there is a long wall in the Garden without a single fruit tree, I may as well plant a few – The soil being a warm sand is particularly calculated for Grapes – which I am piggishly fond of, tho in England they are generally sour to me for It is rare to taste them – If you would be so good as to make interest with Lord Egremonts Gardener for a vine or two of good sorts from his nursery; but such as will ripen in this cold climate

Figure 1. Letter to James Upton Tripp, 5 Oct. 1793.

To Joseph Cooper Walker

[Storrington, 9 October 1793]

I have perhaps appear'd negligent in that I have left your last very obliging Letter so long unanswerd. Alas! Dear Sir, if you have not overlook'd in the papers two paragraphs that have lately appear'd there, my apology is already made. Every year of my unhappy life seems destin'd to a new course of suffering. The year 1793 and the month of September has been productive of unusual sorrow. My gallant Boy lost his leg on the 6th before Dunkirk, & the retreat, which was immediately and rapidly made, compelld them to remove the wounded at the utmost risk of their lives. My poor Charles was remov'd only two hours after his leg had been amputated and not only sufferd extremely in consequence of it but has had the cure much retarded. I received this cruel intelligence on the 11th, and it was a shock almost too severe for me. A few days afterwards I heard from Lisbon of the death of my amiable and invaluable friend Mrs ONeill.[1] Yet I must bear these and probably many other evils—

> "We must endure"
> "Our going hence, even as our coming hither"[2]—

——My poor invalid, to whom I have sent his next brother, is at Ostend; he has now left his bed and thinks he shall be at home in about three weeks. Nothing can be more dreadful to my imagination than to figure to myself his appearance; a fine active young Man, twenty years old, thus mutilated for life, must appear an afflicting object to a stranger—but to me! I really know not, ardently as I wish to have him at home, how I shall support the sight.

You who have heard much of the perfections of my belov'd friend, tho I think you were not personally acquainted with her, will easily imagine how irreperable her loss must be to all her friends. To me, who have been too long suffering the bitter blasts of adversity and have of course not many friends to spare, it is one of the most cruel blows I could sustain. But let me not dwell too long, dear Sir, on subjects so mournful.

I own that the suffering and injury received by my brave young Soldier appear the more afflicting because his going into the Army was entirely in consequence of the cruel conduct of the Men who call themselves Trustees to his Grandfather's property. There is a considerable living[3] in the family which Mr Smith's Father gave by his Will to any Son of mine who should take orders. As the eldest and the second preferred rather to go to India, Charles was destined for the Church. But when these Men got possession of the property And Mr Smith took the interest of my fortune to live upon, I was unable to keep him at School. I was therefore under the hard necessity of suffering him to remain unemploy'd at home for three years, continually imploring Mr Robinson[4] to allow me wherewithal to place him at a University—or only a part of what would have been necessary: & from year to year hopes were given me that this would be done, but latterly Mr Robinson has not given me any hopes, but on the contrary, tho there is enough to pay all the legacies told me by his Son in Law Lord Abergavenny,[5] that there was for me neither present assistance or future prospect. My literary labour (and yet it has till very lately been incessant) was quite inadequate to the purpose of supporting a young Man at even a Scottish College, but my entreaties and representations were vain, and my poor Charles, being of a spirited and active disposition, at length grew weary of lingering at home in hopeless inaction and told me he would go for a Volunteer unless I could get him a Commission.

I succeeded, Alas! but too well, and tho he has acquired the most flattering character, nothing can make him amends for being thus crippled. I am told that all Government allows is about sixty pounds a year—on which he is to live like a Gentleman if he can; God knows, if this be the case, how I shall manage to procure for him the few indulgencies requisite to soften his sufferings. I must keep him a Servant and a low chair in which he may drive himself. The only consolation I can now feel will be in rendering his life as comfortable as I can; and this consideration has set me to work again on a Novel,[6] which as fast as I write I get my daughters to copy. Perhaps as the MMS will be ready at the same time (in the Month of April if my health is spared), I may be more fortunate in attempting to sell it in Ireland. But I have really given you, dear Sir, so much trouble that I am unwilling to ask your interposition again. Favor me however with your opinion on the subject, and I will write myself to the Bookseller if you think it worth while. I beleive I shall print here on my own account and not sell it to any Bookseller & shall print it at Bath.

You are very good to interest yrself so much in my unfortunate situation in regard to Mr Smith. Tho infidelity, and with the most despicable objects, had renderd my continuing to live with him extremely wretched long before his debts compelld him to leave England, I could have been contented to have resided in the same house with him, had not his temper been so capricious and often so cruel that my life was not safe.[7] Not withstanding all I sufferd, which is much too sad a story to relate (for I was seven months with him in The Kings Bench Prison where he was confin'd by his own relations),[8] I still continued to do all that was in my power for him; I paid out of my book money many debts that distress'd him & supplied him from time to time with small sums so long as he gave me leave, but it is now above seventeen months since I have heard from him, and the few people who know (which I beleive are his Sister Mrs Robinson and one of his friends) have received his instructions not to let me know where he is; I beleive he has another family by a Cook who liv'd with him, and has hid himself in Scotland by another name;[9] so that if I were disposed to commence any process against him to compell him to allow me my own income for his children's support, I know not where to find him.

But I have no such design. My marriage articles, in which there are two flaws that deprive me of any jointure in case of his death, make no provision for a seperation. I was not quite fifteen when my father married me to Mr Smith and too childish to know the dismal fate that was preparing for me. Every thing my Father gave me then (3000£) was settled on him for his life; and £2000 more, which comes to me after the death of my Fathers Widow, a Woman of near 70 years old, is dispos'd in the same manner,[10] So that for me I see no other prospect than being the slave of the Booksellers as long as my health or fancy hold out. Alas! continual anxiety & especially what I have sufferd lately have very much impair'd both: and this precarious resource is very likely to be exhausted.

A Miss Bartar near Derry has requested me to correct a Novel she has written.[11] I own to you that this task is not a pleasant one, for I love Novels "no more than a Grocer does figs," but if I can do any little service to the young Lady in question, I will conquer my repugnance—— As she seems to be in haste, I shall be much oblig'd to you to send me the pacquet address'd to Cadells as soon as she forwards it.

I have at present every reason to be happy in the marriage of my belov'd Augusta. The Chevalier de Foville is still in my opinion worthy of her, which is saying every thing. But so strong are the prejudices against his Country that not one of her Father's family, and but one of mine can forgive me for consenting to let my daughter make herself happy her own way. This troubles me but little———

Adieu, dear Sir, let me have the pleasure of hearing from you soon, and allow me to remain with sincere regard,

your most obedient and oblig'd Ser^t^,
Charlotte Smith

My present residence is in an obscure village

Storrington, near Petworth, Sussex—

October 9th 1793—

Huntington MS (HM10809). Addressed: Josepth Cooper Walker Esqre/ Eccles Street/ Dublin. Postmarked: PETWORTH; OC/10/93; OC/13.

NOTES

1. Henrietta O'Neill died on 3 Sept. while with her husband, John, on a diplomatic mission to Spain. CS was devastated by the loss of this supportive friend. In the winter of 1791 and in the spring of 1792, O'Neill provided lodgings for CS when she traveled to London on trust business and a room where she could write. (See CS to an unnamed recipient on 8 Dec. 1791 and to George Robinson on 20 Jan. 1792.) While staying at Henrietta Street, CS met literary figures otherwise outside her social circles. In memory of her friend, CS published two of her poems in the first edition of *Elegiac Sonnets ii* (1797).

2. A slight misquotation of *King Lear* 2.5.9–10.

3. The perpetual advowson of the parish of St. Mary Islington. Richard Smith, BS's father, purchased this living from Thomas Brigstock on 22 July 1771 (PHA #7372) and bequeathed it to "which so ever of the Sons of my Son Benj[n] Smith that shall take upon him the profession of the Church of England the Eldest to take before the younger." Richard Smith further noted that his "late Son Richard Smith [i.e., BS's brother] always in his life time declared that his son should not be bred to the Church." The will also set aside £5,000 in trust to educate BS's five sons (including the first son, Benjamin Berney, and third, Brathwaite, both of whom died after their grandfather) (Hilbish, *Charlotte Smith, Poet and Novelist,* pp. 566, 570); this legacy was never used, because the estate was not settled. With William and Nicholas already in India, Charles would have been next in line for the living.

In 1808 Richard Smith, the grandson, made an arrangement about the advowson, described in a letter by the Smith children's solicitor, Anthony Spedding, to the earl of Egremont's solicitor, William Tyler (28 May 1808; PHA #7367). Interestingly, the grandson had been ordained and apparently recovered this living from its incumbent, Dr. Strahan (letters of 11 May 1810 from Charlotte Mary Smith to Egremont and to Rev. Nicholas Turner; 24 Sept. 1810 from Rev. Richard Smith to Egremont; and deeds and writings conveyed on 25 Feb. 1811 from Egremont through Rev. Nicholas Turner to Rev. Richard Smith [PHA #7372]).

4. That is, John Robinson, trustee to the Smith estate. CS thought, probably wrongly, that he could allocate money for her sons' education before the will, which provided for their education, was settled.

5. Henry Nevill, earl of Abergavenny, was married to Mary, Robinson's only daughter.

6. *The Banished Man* (1794).

7. This comment is one of several alluding to physical violence in the marriage. In one incident, BS threw a four-pound loaf of bread at her head (see CS to Egremont, 25 Jan. 1804).

8. For mismanaging funds connected with the trust to his father's will. As a result, the unyielding, unhelpful trustees were established. Perhaps this early offence of BS made them more unwilling to aid CS and her children.

9. The obituary for BS in *Gentleman's Magazine* for 22 Mar. 1806 names him as "Thomas Smith, Esq., husband of the justly celebrated Mrs. Charlotte Smith." The alias he used at the end of his life was Brian or Bryan Simmonds/Symmonds (see CS to William Tyler, 13 June 1802, and to Egremont, 14 and 15 Oct. 1803).

10. This transaction puts CS's father, Nicholas Turner, Esq., in a rather bad light. Ten years after his first wife's death, he become engaged to a Miss Meriton, a 40-year-old spinster who brought with her to the marriage £20,000 and a strong dislike of her future stepdaughter. For this reason, CS was hurriedly married off to BS, with little inquiry into his character and with all of her small fortune settled on him to his permanent advantage.

11. The *English Short Title Catalogue, British Library Catalogue, National Union Catalog,* and *The English Novel 1770–1829,* vol. 1, *1770–1799,* do not list a novel by Miss Barter.

To James Upton Tripp

[Storrington, 10 October 1793]
Dear Sir,

As Mr Boehm generously threatens to send back a bill he gave my poor Charles leave to draw upon him from Ostende for 10 G^s^ unless I pay the money here, & and as there is no post from hence to day, and I did not know of this New kindness of Mr Boehms till last night, I am so fearful of his being brute enough to send back the Bill & thereby distress my dear Invalid (for whose support Government has yet allow'd nothing during his cruel confinement) that I am oblig'd to send Lucy[1] over to get a credit convey'd to London the quickest way possible.

I trouble you therefore by her to say that the boy will bring any books you may have had the goodness to have look'd out for me. I am much oblig'd to you for the Cover to Mr Mowatt[2] frank'd by Mr Sargent[3] which I receiv'd this morning by some unknown hand, but as I was under the necessity of writing to Mr Mowatt by yesterdays post, it was of no use. However I am equally indebted to you for your obliging intention, & have many apologies to make for the frequent trouble I have given you—— I am, Dear Sir,

your most obed^t^ Ser^t^
Charlotte Smith

10th Oct^r^ [17]93

Petworth House Archives MS. No address or postmark.

NOTES

1. Lucy Eleanor Smith, CS's third youngest daughter, was 17. See Biographical Notes.
2. Not identified.
3. CS met John Sargent (d. 1831), member of Parliament for Seaford in 1790 and author of *The Mine* (1793), through Hayley.

To James Upton Tripp

[Storrington, 11 October 1793]
Dear Sir,

I am extremely oblig'd to you for the precaution you have been so friendly as to take to prevent my poor Boys draught from being return'd. Mr Geo Dorset[1] has I hope prevented the necessity of your being troubled with it; but at all events as this is uncertain, I am under very great obligations to you for your readiness to releive my mind from this anxiety and I am,

Dear Sir,
your much oblig'd Ser[t]
Charlotte Smith

11th Oct[r] [17]93

Petworth House Archives MS. Address: James Upton Tripp Esq[re]/ Petworth. No postmark.

NOTE

1. Possibly an in-law of CS's sister Catherine Dorset (see CS to William Davies, 11 Nov. 1795, n. 1).

To Dr. Charles Burney

Storrington. 15th October 1793
Dear Sir—

Your last most obliging and friendly Letter, as well as every other with which you have favour'd me, demanded my earliest acknowledgements, but I have been in a state of mind that disqualified me for every thing. The Calamity which on the 6th of last month befell my poor Charles almost overwhelm'd spirits which have been contending too long against misfortune of a different nature, and tho anxiety for him has since almost absorbed every other sentiment, I find that a mind so much fatigued as mine has been, has very little fortitude to resist the impression of an evil, which, tho it might be expected as probable, is not the less <severe>.

My Boy has however acquitted himself with so much honor that if I had much of the Spartan or the Roman about me might make me proud rather than miserable. Very few young Men in their first campaign have had equal opportunities of acquitting themselves so much to the satisfaction of their commanding Officers. I have had from Colonel Doyle[1] the most flattering character of my invalid, as well as from almost every other Officer in the Regiment, and they tell me that he will be provided for, tho he has not yet received the usual promotion. For active service as a Soldier he is disqualified for life, as his leg is taken off a little below the Knee. He was moved only three hours after the amputation at the imminent risk of his Life, but the retreat was so rapid that there was no alternative between removing him in that dismal condition and leaving him to the mercy of the soi disant Patriotes, which, if their conduct towards their Prisoner resembles their conduct in other respects, would have been less eligible than leaving him to the humanity of Iroquois or Natches——

The removal however has greatly retarded his cure & lengthen'd his sufferings, and tho he has left his bed, he is still so extremely weak and liable to such continual fits of faintness that my hopes of seeing him in England in three weeks are I am afraid too sanguine. His Brother, whom I sent over to him as soon as I could after he reach'd Ostende, remains with him there to accompany him home. Much as I wish to have him under my humble roof, that we may all contribute as much as we can to render his life as chearful as under such circumstances it can be, yet I know not how I shall support the sight of him at first.

The anxiety we have all been under and my frequent indispositions since have prevented the Chevalier de Foville from attending on the Abbe Fortier at Petworth, which is, it is understood, necessary before the second marriage can take place. But as we are now out of doubt about the life of our dear Charles, the Chevalier and my daughter are gone to stay a few days in the Neighbourhood of Petworth, where he will make a point of settling with Monsieur Fortier who resides there the preliminaries dictated by Mon^r^ Osmont in order that the marriage may be repeated according to the rites of the Catholic Church at Midhurst.

I ought to apologize for troubling you with so long a Letter—"and all about myself"—but the obliging and friendly interest you take for me and the garrulity of sorrow have together betray'd me into it. Allow me to repeat my thanks for your very great kindness of which I shall ever retain the most pleasing recollection & rejoice in being allow'd to remain,

Dear Sir,

your most oblig'd & faithful Ser^t^,

Charlotte Smith

Pray let your Servant put this into the penny post.

Osborn Collection MS, Yale University. No address or postmark.

NOTE

1. Colonel Welbore Ellis Doyle of the 14th (Bedfordshire) Regiment of Foot.

To James Upton Tripp

[Storrington] 31st Oct^r^ [17]93

Dear Sir,

I return Young[1] with a round frock on, for fear his fine coat should suffer from his journey. I hope you will receive this large book & the 4 others

(Tour to the North) in good condition, and I beg the favour of you to cause them to be put into the Library, a trouble I would not give you if I had any chance of getting to Petworth, as I am much asham'd of being so frequently troublesome.

At your leisure I must farther importune you on behalf of the Chevalier de Foville for Orlando Furioso[2] in French——that is to say, a French Ariosto ——La Vie de Cardinal de Retz[3]——& l'Histoire de la Fronde—— Any of these that are in the library, the Chevalier will take the Liberty of borrowing in pursuance of Lord Egremonts obliging permission when he had the honor of seeing his Ldship at Petworth.

We have still belonging to Ld Egremont La Vie de Turenne which being a piece de resistance, we have not quite finish'd———

Pray don't forget the Vine Cuttings & a Cypress or two if the Gardener can spare such———

I am very uneasy least Charles should be by this time hunted[4] from Ostende. The Surgeon did not think him in a condition to travel by land, but he thought he must go on the 25th. Nothing has been yet done for him in the way of provision, nor has he even had a support from Government, but I suppose it will come in time. I am, Dear Sir,

your much obed^{t} Ser^{t}
Charlotte Smith

31st Oct^{r} [17]93

Petworth House Archives MS. No address or postmark.

NOTES

1. This was an unusually quick return of Lord Egremont's books requested only on 5 Oct. A round frock was an overall worn by children to keep their clothes clean underneath. Here, a cloth would protect the book's binding from the rigors of travel.

2. CS appears to be borrowing books for her new French émigré son-in-law, as she wants the Italian Ludovico Ariosto's 1516 romantic epic in his native language.

3. The life of Turenne, the memoirs of Cardinal de Retz, and the history of the Fronde suggest that CS and her new son-in-law had embarked on a course of revolutionary readings—perhaps debate—that doubtless pleased CS immensely. The Fronde was a series of uprisings in France from 1648 to 1653 in which the parliament stood up to the Crown's increasing power and the people protested the financial excesses of Richelieu and Mazarin. Jean François Paul de Gondi, Cardinal de Retz (1613–1679), a leader in the Fronde and enemy of Mazarin, left popular memoirs published posthumously in 1717 and translated into English in 1723.

4. Either because the French are threatening Ostend or CS is angry with the inhumanity of the British army toward its fallen men.

To James Upton Tripp

[Storrington, between 31 October and 7 November 1793]
Dear Sir,

I am very much ashamed of being so troublesome to you. But by the failure of Mr Morgans promises, who engag'd to accept a Bill for me to procure the money of the Trustees & then left Town without doing either the one or the other at the moment I want it most, I have been compelld to get into debt to Mr Naish who is impatient for his money, & I am harass'd to death, being so unwell as to write this from my bed——

If you will have the goodness to pay this Bill for me, I will in case Lord Egremont should condescend to think of it himself, return the whole amou[nt imm]ediately.[1] If not, the enclos'd will be your secur[ity on] repayment on the 2nd January. I am very m[uch] obliged to you for the accommodation you fav[ored me] with on Monday ev[enin]^g^——

But I am unwilling you should name the matter again to Lord Egremont, as I have not any pretense to trouble him & have already been so much oblig'd to him that I am ashamd of any thing that sh^d^ look like importunity from me. I can hardly make my writing legible. I am,

Dear Sir, your much oblig'd Ser^t^
Charlotte Smith

If you will be so good as to pay the 25£ to Mr Naish, he will bring me what remains after his acc^t^ is settled.

Petworth House Archives MS. No address or postmark.

NOTE

1. Words supplied in brackets are missing where the seal was torn away.

To James Upton Tripp

[Storrington, 7 November 1793]
Dear Sir,

Without meaning to tieze you ab^t^ the Books for which I am in no haste, the bearer has orders to call merely to know if you have any commands for me, & he can bring two or three volumes in case you have had an opportunity to procure them for me better than the Post.

My wounded Soldier is I hope in London, & I send the Boy over [in ho]pes of getting Letters from him. I am, dear Sir,

your most oblig'd Ser^t^
Charlotte Smith

7th Novr [17]93

Petworth House Archives MS. No address or postmark.

To [William Davies]

[Storrington, 13 November 1793]

Sir

My Son Charles has occasion for a Set of Emmeline, one of Ethelinde, & one of Celestina, also a copy of "the Emigrants" bound, and a Copy of the last Edition of the Sonnets. These are for a present to the Surgeon who has attended him since the loss of his leg before Dunkirk with great assiduity and kindness, and who prefers this present to the Money he must otherwise have been complimented with. Indebted as I am to you, I know not whether I ought to request your farther indulgence for the amount of these books, but as My Son has yet receivd no compensation from Government (tho I conclude he will) his misfortune has been an additional expence to me, ~~& in~~ and a great addition to the misery it has pleas'd God to have inflicted upon me. I am now however writing again & hope still to get thro my difficulties & to acquit myself to you. ~~M~~ In regard to a plan on which I sometime since applied to you,[1] A friend of mine has promis'd to see you upon it in his way thro London, & I have a frank for Sunday's post in which I mean to trouble you upon it farther.

I have no doubt but that from your general liberality you will oblige my Son Charles in the present request, & I Am Sir

your much oblig'd & obedt Sert

Charlotte Smith

Storrington, Novr 13th [17]93

Bodleian MS Montagu d. 10, fol. 68. No address or postmark.

NOTE

1. Perhaps an early proposal for a children's book.

To Thomas Cadell, Sr.

Storrington, 16th Decr [17]93

Petworth

Sir,

I forbore to trouble you at the time I propos'd doing so because I heard from Mr Hayley, not only that you seem'd to be disinclined to engage in any purchase with me, but that you were then under very uneasy apprehensions for the health of your daughter, which I most sincerely hope are long since entirely removed. As I am now remov'd to a part of the Country where I have no opportunity of reaching the Neighbourhood of Mr Hayley, I have not seen him since his return into Sussex & therefore have not perhaps heard, in regard to your determination what might prevent you the trouble of reading this. I cannot, however, take a resolution to offer the work I am employ'd on[1] to any other person or to arrange matters for printing it on my own account (to which I have been strongly advised) till I enquire whether you are disposed to receive it, either on the terms on which you publish'd Emmeline or on those you agreed to give for Celestina. The first Volume is so nearly compleat that I should be able to deliver the MMS in the course of the month of January. Indeed 3 parts are not ready for the press. I am perfectly aware that the inconvenience of any advance is what you will not subject yourself to, & therefore have no intention to propose it but imagine that your liberality would induce you to agree to pay for each volume on delivery if I should need it.

The truth is that my expences are very considerably encreas'd by the return of my poor Charles, for whom I am under the necessity of keeping a ManServant; & Government has yet done nothing for him, nor has he any prospect at present, but of an Ensign's pay, on which he could not exist unless he lived with me. I am inform'd by the Medical Men that the contraction of the poor remains of his leg—which is now drawn up close to the ham (& prevents his having an artificial Leg either of wood or cork)—might be removed & his misfortune greatly alleviated if he could have the benefit of the Bath Waters. I have been desired to go thither myself for my own health but cannot afford it, as all I receive from my own labour is not sufficient for the common purposes of my family, & from Mr Robinson and the other Men who have so long detain'd my unfortunate Children's property, I now receive nothing, nor can I obtain any remedy against their injustice and oppression. If I could sell the Book I am writing for a certain Sum to be paid for on the delivery of each volume, I might possibly continue to pay for a lodging there for a month or six weeks, which is all the difference between living there & at home. I have no right to expect however that you will break thro any resolution you may have formed to oblige me. But merely propose it to satisfy myself that I have endeavour'd to do for the best.

The work in question is to be call'd "The Exile" and is a story partly founded in Truth, & as I beleive myself will be particularly interesting & somewhat on a new plan, for it will be partly narrative and partly Letters.[2] It is some satisfaction to me to possess twenty volumes of my own writing (without reckoning the Sonnets) all of which are in the second and one in the third Edition.[3] As to the work I sold to Messrs Robinson, it has been in a second Edition a long time tho they never advertis'd it, & of "The Old Manor House" a new edition was call'd for in two months, tho Mr Bell for some reasons or strange management of his own never got it ready till lately. I do not like for many reasons to continue my dealings with Mr Bell with whom I have now compleated my whole engagement.[4] And should you adhere to your resolution of withdrawing your property from the purchase of Copy right, and either for that or any other cause decline this proposal, I shall either endeavour to print the work at my own expence or seek some purchas[er][5] or publisher who is in a more respectable line of business than it seems to me Mr Bell adheres to (who has lately I see publishd trials & other very discreditable works) and one too who may know a little more how to treat me, for by Mr Bell I seem to be conside[rd] as a miserable Author under the necessity of writing so many sheets a day. This is but too true, but I have not yet learned to endure contempt <& I> very naturally wish to return where I have always received the treatment of a Gentlewoman. If however your mind is made up, I have only [to] beg you would not name what I have herein mention'd to any perso[n] in the trade, as it might prevent my success elsewhere, & I beg for the reaso[n] I have given to be favour'd with your early answer. I am, Sir,

your oblig'd & obed Sert, Charlotte Smith

The Pennsylvania State University Libraries MS. No address or postmark.

NOTES

1. *The Banished Man,* under the working title *The Exile.*

2. The elder Cadell, to whom this letter is addressed, retired during 1793, but his longtime partner, William Davies, and his son, Thomas Cadell, Jr., published *The Banished Man* in Aug. 1794. Its later volumes do indeed rely on occasional long letters to advance the story.

3. *Emmeline* was in its third edition; *Celestina, Ethelinde, Desmond,* and *The Old Manor House* were all in second editions.

4. Apparently Bell did not agree. In Jan. 1794, he complained in the preface to *The Wanderings of Warwick,* a sequel to *The Old Manor House,* that CS was late and one volume short of the two she had promised.

5. Because this letter was bound in a letter book, some lines are truncated at their end. I have supplied the likely obscured letters in brackets.

To James Upton Tripp

Storrington Decr 20th 1793
Dear Sir,

The time now approaches very near when the Bill of thirty five pounds which you had the goodness to discount for me will become payable. As notwithstanding this is my own money, being part of the interest of the poor remains of my own little fortune, which Mr Smith allows for his numerous family, the Men who are in possession of the Estate on which this money was lent, have sometimes cavild and sometimes attempted to evade paying it, I have been very solicitous that no such Cavil or difficulty or delay of any kind should arise now, when you have been so very good as to advance the money when I was in such distress.

And I have therefore written to them to know on what day they will pay it, that I might save you all the trouble possible (having more than once gone after the half yearly payment ten times before I could get it), but they have given me no answer, either to that question or to another which I thought I had a right to make viz——Whether they had sent over orders to remove the Estate so evidently plunderd into the hands of some other person who shall deal more honestly by the proprietors; but to this they also deny me an answer. Nor will they tell me what they have done with the small crop that was this year received.

As I can obtain no satisfaction, I request the favor of you to let your Agent in London take the Bill to them for acceptance if it is not already done——As it will be a means of satisfying me as well as acquitting my debt to you————

Oblig'd to you as I consider myself, and particularly for your readiness to assist my wounded Son when Mr Boehm was ab^{t} so brutally to return his draft, I ought not again to trouble you, nor should I have done so, but that all my provision for my rent is baffled by the expenses I have been put to for him, & he has yet receivd nothing of Government, not even his expenses at Ostende while under cure, tho they are promisd him. The difference that this has occasion'd to me, I had hoped to have made up by writing, & by this time to have had a claim on my Bookseller for fifty or sixty pounds; but ill health & despair have arrested My weary hands so frequently that I have not been able to accomplish this.

If therefore this Bill of 35£ which you now hold should be duly paid, as I hope and beleive it will, might I in that case (but not otherwise) request so great a favor of you as to advance me a week or ten days afterwards twenty five pounds on the next half yearly payment, due ye 2nd July 1794 to enable me to pay my rent, which will be due early in January & which I will make payable to you as before (I mean the half yearly payment due in July).[1]

I suffered such misery at Brighthelmstone by having my books and furniture seiz'd,[2] and my present Landlord has such a character that I should tremble to be an hour in his power, & have therefore endeavourd to reserve this Sum out of the assistance I obtaind some months since, but the furniture & other things indispensably necessary for my unfortunate poor boy & other heavy demands upon me which in a family so numerous cannot be avoided, have renderd this impossible; and I now fear that unless M[r] Turner can sell for me the remains of a small annuity (the greater part of which I have already been compelled to dispose of during my sad pilgrimage in adversity), which I fear he will not accomplish; that I shall be in some risk of failing to pay my rent at the time it is due unless you will once more have the goodness to assist me on the security of my summer pay[t] of £35———

I have no apology to offer for taking this liberty with you unless it be that of necessity & a persuasion of your good nature. Favor me with an answer as early as may be convenient to you, that, should my request be unreasonable & not to be granted, I may have time to look about me and endeavour to get over this difficulty by getting the Bill discounted at 6 months: tho the Sum is such as hardly bears the discount, & as the Trustees will never promise to pay it tho they know they must, it is very difficult to procure it unless by means of a friend who like you have no purpose but to oblige & assist me———

I do not know that I have clearly explain'd myself, being half crippled in my hands and half distracted in my head by the Rhumatism—— You will however believe me in all events, Dear Sir,

your oblig'd Ser[t]
Charlotte Smith

Petworth House Archives MS. No address or postmark.

NOTES

1. In other words, two weeks before her January interest payment of £35 will be paid her, enabling her to pay off a previous loan from Tripp, CS attempts to borrow against her next semiannual payment due in July.

2. See CS to Joseph Cooper Walker, 12 Feb. 1793, where CS writes of "embarrassments inconceivable of new & strange natures, out of which Heaven knows how I shall escape," and n. 1. Her last letter from Brighton was dated 21 Mar. 1793. There is then a gap in surviving letters until CS to Bishop Douglas, Storrington, 30 July 1793, shedding no more light on the situation. Presumably, in a desperate grasp for money to pay her rent in Brighton, she had drawn on Hayley and Cadell without their permission, then moved to cheaper lodgings in Storrington, all the while struggling in ill health to complete *The Emigrants,* which was published in May.

To James Upton Tripp

[Storrington, 29 December 1793]
Dear Sir,

I shall be extremely oblig'd to you if, with your first Leisure, you will favor me with an answer to my former Letter——As the time draws very near when I must either pay my rent or be expos'd to difficulties from my Landlord. Mr Turner informs me he is in hopes of getting the sale of the Annuity completed, but it cannot be done in time to enable me to pay my rent, which I have promisd for the 5th Jan^{y} & which ought to have been paid on the 26th of the present month. Pardon this trouble in consideration of my comfortless situation & believe me ever, Dear Sir,

your most oblig'd Ser^{t}
Charlotte Smith

Decr 29th 1793

Petworth House Archives MS. No address or postmark.

1794
"A STATE OF ANXIETY"

—22 JUNE 1794

One of Charlotte Smith's more prolific years, 1794 nonetheless found her plagued by poor health, pressed for money, and tormented with family concerns. Early in the new year, she had revenue from The Wanderings of Warwick, *completed late and shorter than agreed on for Joseph Bell. In about eight months she had finished the four-volume novel* The Banished Man, *published at the height of her financial need in July; she complained of the quality of the first edition. Smith immediately embarked on her first children's book,* Rural Walks, *also for Cadell and Davies. But they turned down her seventh novel,* Rosalie, *later retitled* Montalbert *and published by a bookseller new to her, Sampson Low. Second editions of* Desmond *and* The Old Manor House *also provided some income. Surviving receipts verify what the letters tell us: Smith borrowed small sums throughout the year against any work contracted for the press.*

All this necessary labor barely covered expenses. Her old rheumatic complaints settled in her hands and forced an expensive move to Bath for treatment. Once there, Augusta showed signs of having a difficult pregnancy, and her mother was wracked with anxiety for the life of this beloved child. Expensive doctors attended Augusta several times a week as her time grew near, during a difficult confinement and the loss of her newborn son, and frequently during her decline in the fall. A costly move to the coast failed to improve her health. Also to Smith's dismay, Lionel was idling at home while she tried to raise money to send him to Oxford. Worse yet, he entertained the notion of taking over Charles's commission as ensign in the army. Support for her children remaining at home was jeopardized when a substantial income from the Barbados plantations was embezzled, delaying the release of her twice-yearly interest money. Smith's sole relief was in money sent by her two oldest sons in India, a source of support first mentioned in this year's letters, and in advances from the earl of Egremont's estate agent, James Upton Tripp.

To Joseph Cooper Walker

Storrington, January 20th 1794

It was <with> extreme concern, dear Sir, that I yesterday receiv'd your Letter. I am very sorry you have been ill and very sorry that at such a time I should have troubled you with my unlucky concerns. Your Letter has been three weeks on its way, for it is dated the 26th Decr and did not reach me 'till the 19th Jany. I hope that long before this time you are quite recover'd of your fever or rather of the effects of it, & I beg you will not think of troubling yrself about my literary Affairs till you are. The first Volume of the Novel calld "the Exile"[1] is finish'd and two thirds of it transcribed, for the Irish Market if you can make one for me, But I rather wish that even its name may not be known 'till it is nearly ready for publication, as it seems mine is thought useful enough to tempt people to forge it. Very certainly I never wrote a line of the Novel you name call'd D'Arcy,[2] or ever saw or heard of it.

Miss Barter,[3] who afterwards troubled you I beleive with the MMS, wrote to me some months since requesting of me to correct a Novel for her & to let her publish it or sell it in my name. The latter request which was accompanied with an offer of sharing any Sum the work might under such a name produce, I imputed to the youth & ignorance of Miss Bartar, but she represented herself as attempting these literary exertions for the support of an aged Father—A motive so amiable, that it interested me in her favor and tho I told her I certainly could never put my name (inconsequential as I beleived it to a good work) to any that I did not write, yet, that I would readily correct her Novel & do the best I could to ~~sell it~~ for her in England in regard to its sale.

She sent it over, & it happen'd to arrive just as I received News of the accident that had befallen my third Son at the ill starr'd Seige of Dunkirk. However as soon as I was able to rally my wretched spirits to their usual tasks, I look'd at the MMS, and it really was a something—for I cannot call it a narrative so devoid of connection, costume, sense, & even English (for it was throughout spelt ill)—that it was ~~really~~ totally impossible even if I had had the time to give to it that I could have made any thing of it. Nor could I without a violation of truth, have recommended it to sale, for it was not saleable—& had I so calld it to any Bookseller, I must have committed myself.

Still however, perhaps from "seeing feelingly"[4] the fondness of an Author (and a Young Author) for A work of fancy, I did not like to shock Miss Barters amour propre with saying in plain terms that her work was worth nothing, but I desir'd My daughter de Foville to write to her to inform her that the anxiety and concern I had sufferd about My Son Charles and the recent death of my ever lamented Harriet (M[rs] ONeill) had so much affected my health that there was little probability that I should be able to attend to the correction or disposal of the work in question—& that as it was uncertain how long it might be before I could be of any use to her, I thought it best not to attempt it, as it would be perhaps to her prejudice from the delay. Wherefore I entreated of her to let me know to whom I c[d] send it—— She desir'd it might go to Lanes.[5] Thither I sent it & I have heard nothing more of it since, but that he receivd it. How far this attempt of mine to be of what little use I could to a Stranger has expos'd me to the inconvenience of having my name us'd, I know not, but I own it is very disagreeable [to] me on more accounts than I will now enumerate, and should it be in your power, dear Sir, either by an advertisement or in any other way that you may judge advisable, to signify publickly that it is not mine, I shall be very much oblig'd to you——

It is quite enough Heaven knows, to answer for the nonsense one writes oneself, & there are a thousand reasons why to answer for more (tho among it was prose like Gibbons and Poetry like Grays) would be particularly disagreeable to me. Perhaps it may not be improper to insert in the Dublin Paper most read an Advertisement to this Effect: "We are authoris'd to say that the Novel calld —————— said to be by Charlotte Smith, is not written by M[rs] Charlotte Smith, Authoress of the Elegiac Sonnets, Emmeline, Ethelinde, Celestina, Desmond, the Old Manor House, and the Wanderings of Warwick." Perhaps this D'Arcy may have been written by a Charlotte Smith, for one of that name was divorced not long since, and another hang'd. If I were to indulge a jeu de mots,[6] I should say that I am neither so fortunate or so unfortunate as to be either of those Ladies.

But to confine myself to mere matter of fact. You are so good as to feel much concernd for the state of health of which my last letter spoke. It is not materially mended. Chagrin of many sorts & vexations, which tho I am unable to contend with I cannot escape from, continually counteract my endeavours to be well. I have kept my bed frequently this winter from having lost the use of my limbs with the Rhumatism, and because a constant pain in my side gave me no respite.[7] I have been repeatedly orderd to Bath, but I cannot afford to go tho if my novel is finish'd in any time, and I can make any little addition to its English price by selling it in Ireland, I will try. I live here in a very obscure village and in a very inconvenient part of the Country, and I fix'd here purely because I thought it would be a cheap residence and be near the friends I most wish'd to see. But it so happens that I never see these friends and that my domestic expences are nearly double

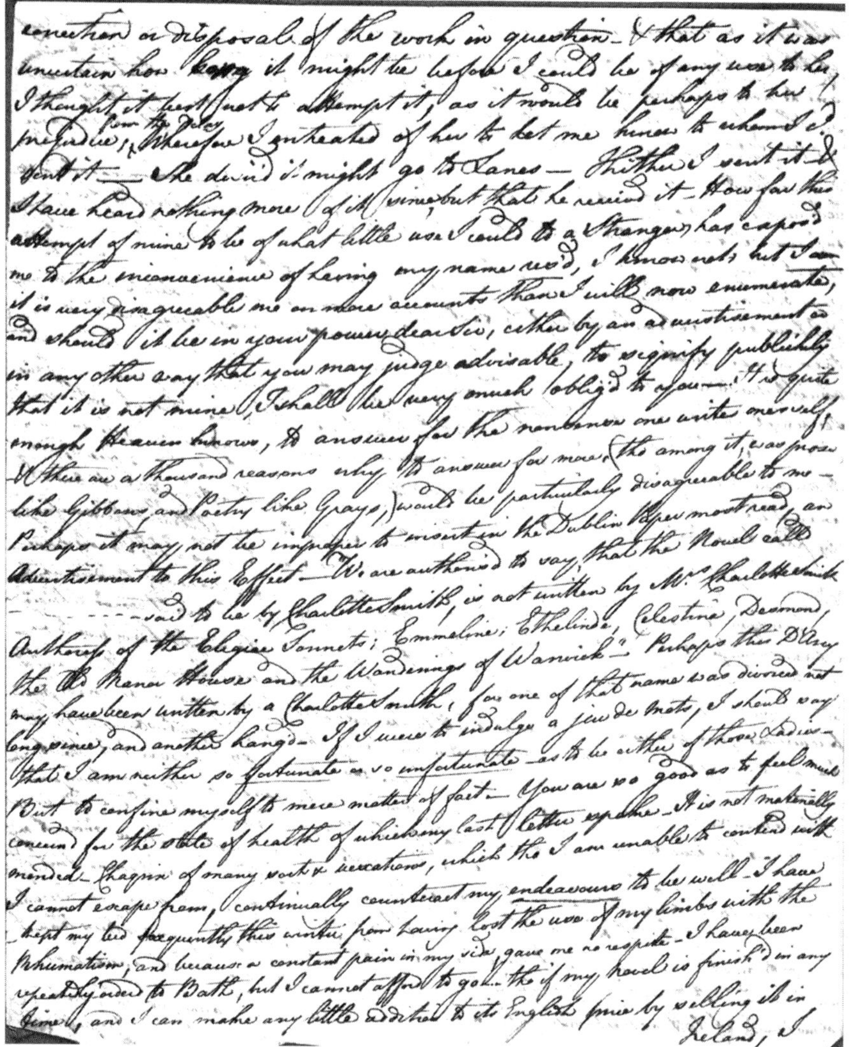

connection or disposal of the work in question—& that as it was
uncertain how long it might be before I could be of any use to her,
I thought it best not to attempt it, as it would be perhaps to her
prejudice; & Wherefore I intreated of her to let me know to whom I
sent it— She desired it might go to Lanes— Thither I sent it &
I have heard nothing more of it since but that he receiv'd it— How far this
attempt of mine to be of what little use I could to a Stranger has expos'd
me to the inconvenience of having my name used, I know not; but I am
it is very disagreeable me on more accounts than I will now enumerate,
and should it be in your power dear Sir, either by an advertisement or
in any other way that you may judge advisable, to signify publickly
that it is not mine, I shall be very much oblig'd to you— It is quite
enough Heaven knows, to answer for the nonsense one writes oneself,
& there are a thousand reasons why to answer for more (tho among it, was prose
like Gibbons and Poetry like Grays,) would be particularly disagreeable to me—
Perhaps it may not be improper to insert in the Dublin Paper most read, an
Advertisement to this Effect— We are authoris'd to say, that the Novel call'd
- - - - said to be by Charlotte Smith, is not written by Mrs Charlotte Smith
Authoress of the Elegiac Sonnets; Emmeline; Ethelinde, Celestina, Desmond,
the Old Manor House and the Wanderings of Warwick— Perhaps this D'Arcy
may have been written by a Charlotte Smith, for one of that name was divorced not
long since, and another hang'd— If I were to indulge a jeu de mots, I should say
that I am neither so fortunate or so unfortunate as to be either of those Ladies—
But to confine myself to mere matter of fact— You are so good as to feel much
concern for the state of health of which my last letter spoke— It is not materially
mended— Chagrin of many sorts & vexations, which tho I am unable to contend with
I cannot escape from, continually counteract my endeavours to be well— I have
kept my bed frequently this winter from having lost the use of my limbs with the
Rheumatism, and because a constant pain in my side gave me no respite— I have been
repeatedly order'd to Bath, but I cannot afford to go— tho if my Novel is finish'd in any
time, and I can make any little addition to its English price by selling it in
Ireland, I

Figure 2. Letter to Joseph Cooper Walker, 20 Jan. 1794.

what they were at Brighthelmstone, tho the necessaries of life are not to be had at any price such as Butter, Milk &c &c. Everything daily encreases in price in England, & I do beleive there is no Country in the World where one pays so much for accommodations so inferior.

I dont love England to tell you the truth, & have always meditated flying away from it if my fetters or any part of them should fall off—— Some late circumstances, some bites and scratches I have had from the empoison'd teeth and talons of ingratitude (& I have a skin extremely subject to fester) have occasion'd me to meditate more seriously than ever on quitting it. France is now shut to me & my most belov'd child & her amiable husband, who is indeed jeune homme il n'y en a peu,[8] but I do not see why I should not go to Switzerland.

In regard to my childrens pecuniary affairs, I do not see that my presence is of the least use. The time that it costs me to pursue them, I could employ much better in earning money, & I struggle in vain against the Men who have by cunning possess'd themselves of all the effects and by fraud keep that possession. I am weary and worn out with attempting it, and at the end of near eleven years, during which I have supported my Children from infancy till all but two are grown up, it is surely excusable if I wish to go where I may have such enjoyment as peace can afford me & contemplate the fine scenes of Nature while I have mental & bodily strength to enjoy them and "before the night comes wherein no Man can work."[9]

I have now some friends abroad[10] who might be of use to me in determining my future progress, but I wish you who have lately been in that Country to give me your opinion as to what would be the expence if managed in the most frugal manner of conveying myself with My second daughter, her husband, my daughter Lucy of 17, & Harriet of 11, and my Youngest Boy of 8 with one maid & one Man servant to the banks of "the Leman Lake"—& for what sum such a family could reside in Italy or Switzerland p^r Ann[um]. I beleive could make with the Booksellers an agreement that would very much assist my project, & very certainly I could educate my younger children more to my mind there than here.

In a word the more I think of this, the more I become fond of the Scheme. My health has no other chance of being re-establish'd, & many considerations unite to make my executing it desirable. I shall never be freer from fetters than I am now, and I think that within these three or four months, I shall have an opportunity of letting this House with a short lease of which I have foolishly embarrassed myself. I am asham'd, Dear Sir, of giving you the trouble of reading so long a Letter & a Letter all about myself, but you are one of the few people who seem to be truly interested in my behalf—— Allow me then to repeat my acknowledgements for all the trouble I have given you, and to assure you of the regard & esteem with which I must ever remain,

Dear Sir,
your most oblig'd Ser^t,
Charlotte Smith

I have written to day to Mr Cadell to desire he would send me Hermann d'Unna;[11] I will peruse & carefully return it as you desire. I conclude it is in

French, as if it is German you know I could not read & still less translate it. When I write to M[r] Hayley, I will not fail to mention the unfortunate cause of your silence—— But I now never see him & very seldom hear from him, oweing probably to his having other engagements. Let me hope to have the pleasure of hearing from you soon, & I trust you will be able to tell me you are perfectly recover'd——

If you can find the French Sonnet, pray recollect that you promis'd me a copy of it.

Huntington MS (HM10811). Address: Josepth Cooper Walker Esq[re]/ Eccles Street/ J. Olmius[12] Dublin. Postmark: PAID/ JA/ 22/ 94; JA/ 30. Photograph reproduced by permission of The Huntington Library, San Marino, California, from HM10811.

NOTES

1. Published as *The Banished Man* by Thomas Cadell, Jr., and William Davies in late Aug. of this year.

2. *D'Arcy* was long ascribed to CS, but here she definitively denies having written it.

3. First mentioned in CS to Walker, 9 Oct. 1793, as Miss Bartar.

4. *King Lear* 4.6.149, Gloucester to Lear: "I see it feelingly."

5. William Lane published cheap sentimental novels at the Minerva Press.

6. Pun. This is an unusually wry passage.

7. The pain in her side at this time is not explained. On her rheumatism, see CS to Walker, 25 Mar. 1794, and n. 1.

8. A young man like few others.

9. John 9.4: "I must work the works of him that sent me, while it is day: the night cometh, when no man can work."

10. CS had no known friends in Switzerland, nor is it known when Walker was there.

11. By Benedicte Naubert. One of several popular and influential German romances, this novel appeared as *Herman of Unna* in 1794 in a translation ascribed to Professor Cramer and reviewed in the *Monthly Review* in Sept. Its scene of a girl imprisoned in a mountaintop convent may have influenced Ann Radcliffe in *The Italian* (1797) (Tompkins, *The Popular Novel in England, 1770–1800,* pp. 281, 376).

12. John Luttrell Olmius, an excise officer, had franked this letter. See CS to William Davies, 19 Feb. 1790, n. 2.

To James Upton Tripp

[?Storrington, 12 March 1794]
Dear Sir,

M[r] Turner has sent me M[r] Tylers account for the expenses of the Annuitys being made over, which I wish very much to discharge, but my fund is already reduced so low that I cannot do it unless I can get a bill on Cadell for five & twenty, or fifty pounds discounted. This Sum of 50£ is my due, or will be so about the twentieth of April,[1] but I have engaged not to ask for it (the whole sum) till a stipulated time & to receive 25£ at a time a certain period after the Books I have sold him are deliverd. He is in possession of as much as is to be paid for after the rate of 100£ (& I have had five & twenty).

On Monday I send up more so that I have no doubt——unless illness should prevent me & this vile Rhumatism arrest my hands——of being very punctual: at all events he has wherewithal to answer this demand. But if I could get the Bill discounted, or half of it, it would be a great accommodation to me, & enable me to discharge this little account with Mr Tyler & to obtain some relief for this miserable complaint which renders my life an absolute burthen to me.

I have been advised to try change of air & scene & should leave home for a few weeks if I could manage ab^t money, so as to go & yet provide for my family here, but otherwise I cannot do it.

You have been so very obliging repeatedly that I cannot think of troubling you to ask this favor of you, but I mention it to assure you that if I can get it done, I will immediately quit myself of my debt to Mr Tyler.

I return your books with many thanks. I want Cicero's Letters in Latin[2] for a referrence; I am pretty sure I saw them in my Lords library. If you could get at them without much trouble, I should be very much oblig'd to you. But if they are finely bound or very large books, I would not venture them by the post. If I am fortunate enough to get out for a little health, I shall carefully return this & three other Books I have of Lord Egremonts before I go, which if I accomplish it at all, must be early in next week. As I must be in the way to settle about Lionels going to Oxford by the 12th of April[3]—— Another difficult & uneasy business which rests entirely upon me, & God knows how I shall get thro it—— This variable weather so completely cripples me that I cannot write without difficulty from contraction in my hands. I am ever, Dear Sir, your oblig'd Ser^t

Charlotte Smith

March 12th 1794

Petworth House Archives MS. No address or postmark.

NOTES

1. CS apparently contracted to complete *The Exile,* issued later this year as *The Banished Man,* on a deadline. By this date, the first and second volumes were in the press (see CS to Joseph Cooper Walker, 25 Mar. 1794). The third volume was sent on May 9 (see CS to William Davies on that date). Here, she is borrowing against money she does not yet have.

2. The edition of Cicero's letters in the Petworth library is not known. There were several new editions throughout the seventeenth and eighteenth centuries.

3. CS was still trying to qualify one of her sons to be the perpetual advowson of Islington, a living held by the family. In his will, Richard Smith had conferred this liv-

ing upon any one of her sons who obtained a university education (see CS to Joseph Cooper Walker, 9 Oct. 1793, n. 3). Her April effort to enroll Lionel failed.

To James Upton Tripp

[?Storrington, ca. 22–24 March 1794][1]

Dear Sir,

On setting out, I find so many petty demands on me & so many & so much to provide for that I can hardly do for less than thirty pounds divided among us. For my family have no dependence but on me, & while I go on life & death, for it is really nearly come to that, I must continue for them to live in the mean time.

I have therefore, presuming on your kindness, given Mr Naish[2] a draft for eighteen Guineas at 3 days, & beg the favour of You to send my family as much as makes up thirty pounds, for which I enclose a draft at a month on Cadell.

To settle with Mr Tyler,[3] I trouble you with another draft at 6 weeks for twenty pounds (making together fifty), & I Entreat the fav^r^ of You to let my family have the rest when it is more nearly due (I do not mean to trouble you for it now) if I should not come home before this day month. I know not whether you will forgive me for giving you all this trouble & taking such liberties with you. But you are very good, & my situation is singularly distressing. I leave my Servant at Petworth with this who will return with your draft or cash for the remainder of the 30£ as I have left my family without money.

I am, dear Sir,
your most oblig'd Ser^t^
C Smith

I mean only to have the 2nd draft paid when it shall be more nearly due, & not to trespass too much on you. I do not know whether I have explain'd myself. They must manage the money they have as well as they can. Have the kindness to direct it to M^rs^ De Foville by the bearer.

Monday morn^g^

Petworth House Archives MS. No address or postmark.

NOTES

1. This undated letter was written as CS was traveling from Storrington to Bath for a month of treatment at the waters. In CS to Tripp, 24 Mar. 1794, she apologizes for the obscurity of this letter and explains "I took the liberty of sending my servant in my

way thro Petworth" with this hastily written note "to request" the loan. As her last letter from Storrington to Joseph Cooper Walker was postmarked 21 Mar. and her first letter from Bath to Tripp was postmarked 24 Mar., she must have been traveling on 22–23 Mar. Her stay lasted several months owing to Augusta's serious illness during pregnancy and after delivery.

2. Michael Nash (see CS to Tripp, 15 Sept. 1793, n. 3).

3. That is, William Tyler, Tripp's assistant and eventual successor (see Biographical Notes).

To James Upton Tripp

10 Pulteney Street Bath
March 24th [17]94
Dear Sir,

I was so extremely ill the day I left home that I am much afraid I gave you a great deal of trouble by the obscurity of my Letter. When I said I should get Mr Nash to let me have the Money Which you were so very good as to say you w^{d} advance for me on a bill ~~of~~ on Cadell, I imagined he Could have furnishd me with the whole, but he had no more by him than eighteen pounds or Guineas for which I gave him a draft on you, & taking As much of that as I was not oblig'd to pay away, for my journey, I took the liberty of sending my servant in my way thro Petworth to request you would be so very good as to furnish my family with the remainder to the amount of thirty as I found five and twenty inadequate to ~~my~~ the demands upon me, & I knew it would make no difference to you, & I sent you a draft on Cadell for thirty & for twenty at a longer date of which I wish'd to have Mr Tylers Bill deducted.

I really do not know in what form of words to couch my apology for taking with you such liberties. But you are so very good natur'd & know so much of my singularly unfortunate situation that I rest on those circumstances my hopes that you will pardon me. To find from week to week subsistence for so large family, & struggling under ill health, is too much for me, & I assure you the certainty that I should sink under it was the only reason that drove me hither—— Where I am already better by having obtain'd what I so greatly needed, a few days of quiet.

But to day all my anxiety & uneasiness is return'd on the receipt of M^{rs} De Fovilles Letter in which she says that she has not had the good fortune to hear from you, so that the family are without money, & my Neighbours are not much dispos'd to trust—— I am willing to flatter myself this is only oweing to your absence, and not to your being wearied out with my troublesome requests—— As I am now going on fast to earn more of Cadell than I have drawn for, I trust I shall give you no other trouble ab^{t} those bills than the advance, or than I have already done——

Augusta says in her Letter that the Chevalier de Foville has had a Letter from Mr Hayley in which he mentions having written to Lord Egremont ab^{t} the old Woman[1] who was a candidate for the Hospital & whom his Lordship has had the goodness to place there as he has been so good as to inform me. I now seldom hear from Mr Hayley & do not often ~~hear from~~ write to him, & I have lately been so ill & so much out of spirits that I have neglected much that I ought to have done; otherwise I ought to have inform'd Mr Hayley that Lord Egremont with his usual goodness had attended to my request & that any application farther to him was needless. My omitting to do this was not from the want of a proper sense of his Ldships goodness but merely from the inattention of languor & sickness. I am afraid it has given Lord Egremont & Mr Hayley trouble, but however I cannot intrude upon the former with a Letter about it, & wish that if a proper opportunity offers, you would make my apology.

I intended to have gone into Essex thro London & to have seen the Trustees: but I was so ill & so unequal to any such undertaking, that by the advice——indeed the peremptory opinion——of Farquhar,[2] I determined to come hither. The warm bath has already operated like a charm, for a few days since I could not move my right hand, & if I could obtain only a month of repose, I believe I should be well. This however I do not expect. God help me! Nor is it to be had for me but in the Grave.

If you have not already been so good as to furnish my family with the requisite supply, may I take the liberty of requesting you to do so. Or should anything should [*sic*] have happen'd to prevent your doing so, let me I entreat you have a Letter that they may not be distrest, for I must in that case apply some other remedy. I am, dear Sir, at all events

your oblig'd & obed^{t} Ser^{t}
Charlotte Smith

I beg a thousand pardons for putting you to one & three pence expense, but I know no Soul here to give me a frank, wishing to remain as little known as possible; & I dare not take the liberty unless permitted to enclose it to Lord Egremont.

Petworth House Archives MS. Address: James Upton Tripp Esqre/ Petworth/ Sussex. Postmark: BATH; MR/25/94.

NOTES

1. Possibly an ironic reference to herself, the "hospital" being Bath.
2. As Sir Walter Farquhar (1738–1819) practiced in London, it is not clear that she

actually saw him. Trained in Edinburgh and Paris, he settled in London in the 1790s, finished his medical degree from Aberdeen, and was created baronet in 1796 before being appointed physician-in-ordinary to the Prince of Wales.

To Joseph Cooper Walker

Storrington, March 25th [17]94
Dear Sir,

Illness and dejection, together with some expectation of hearing from you again, were the reasons of my delaying to answer your most kind letter on the 4th of February—I have been a martyr to the Rhumatism, the gout, or something, ever since & now am entirely crippled, so as not to be able to walk across the room; I have reason to fear it is an ill form'd gout (my family being extremely afflicted with that complaint) which, brought on by anxiety, my constitution has not strength to throw out.[1] And as my life is so necessary to my family, tho Heaven knows how little desirable to myself, I have at length determined to follow the advice of my Physicians and go to Bath for a Month or six weeks. But as I could not take my family without incurring an expence I can ill afford, I shall only be accompanied by my Maid & my youngest Girl,[2] About twelve years old whose education will suffer if I leave her behind and who will be some sort of companion to me. I suppose I may go to a lodging House & yet be retired enough to write, at least such is my plan. But I wish to avoid every kind of society whatever, having too large an acquaintance there just now, to enter into any without being compelled to engage in more than my circumstances or occupation will allow——

Having thus far indulged my Egotism, let me thank you for the very friendly zeal you have so incessantly exerted in my service. I am really ashamed of all the trouble You have taken, & whatever may be the event of it, I shall ever consider myself as equally oblig'd to you. My expectations have never been very sanguine, but I thought it better on many accounts to have a copy made of the work I am now engaged in, which my Nephew & a Writing Master of the Village have done of the two first Volumes with little expence, as the latter does his part cheap.[3] The Work is in the English Press &, if the partiality of the Author does not deceive me is the best I have yet done. At least it costs me more time and trouble than I have yet given to any thing. I own I do think it hard that The Irish Booksellers should derive so much profit from a very successful English work, injure the sale to the English Proprietor, and be at no expence whatever but the printing & paper. The great London Booksellers, a powerful because a rich body, have had several consultations about this, & one of them assured me not long since that many years would not elapse before some remedy was again attempted, for what they reckon so crying an evil. It might therefore be worth while for the Irish Booksellers to be more liberal, least they should lose entirely what they now possess in this respect. This of course is between ourselves, for I would not offend Messieurs the Booksellers of Dublin upon any account.

Some time since it was propos'd to me to publish a second Volume of Poems with Plates of the same size as the first V[olume] (the property of which is Cadells to whom I was compelld to sell it) with a portrait, & it was suppos'd that those I have being nearly enough, a few additions and good engravings might make the Scheme answer extremely well as to profit. But ~~I have~~ there is no portrait of me but one in Crayons in possession of a Friend who does not like either to have it copied in his house or to part with it for that purpose.[4] And the events of these last eighteen months & the extreme vexation I have undergone & the ill health it has brought on has so very much changed my appearance that nobody w^{d} know me who had not seen me for two years to be the same person. Some remains of female Vanity which it is high time to have done with would have deterred me, had I been otherwise in a situation to have done it, from going of late to London to accept Romneys offer, who painted the former picture, and who would do one in oil without any expence to me—But should I pursue this plan of another publication, & as I beleive it is wronging my children not to do so, I must get over this, & if My friend will not part with the Portrait which was done about two years since (& was a very good likeness neither flatterd nor otherwise), I must be content to be represented as hideous as I am now. I beleive I shall in the course of a few days send up to Cadell, who has engaged to manage the matter for me, an advertisement to run thus:

In the course of twelve months[5] will be publishd a second Volume of Poems by Charlotte Smith. With plates, and a portrait of the Author. Subscriptions at half a Guinea will be receiv'd by Mr Cadell. Only half the money to be paid on Subscribing to defray the expense of the Engravings, ~~which will with~~ the drawings for which will ~~to~~ be made ~~xxxxxxxxx~~ under the direction of the Author—The Portrait from a Picture painted by Romney."

If you beleive, dear Sir, that advantage may be obtain'd from publishing this proposal at Dublin with reference to a Bookseller there, I put it entirely into your hands, requesting you to do the best you can for me & at what ever time seems most likely to Give it success. For the money, I would not receive any till the plates were paid for, which are very expensive. Of the rest, a little fund might be made for my Children who, from the present appearance of their Grandfathers affairs, seem likely to be robb'd of everything. I could give you a detail of all of this that would amaze you, but I have neither the time nor the conscience to trouble you with it——

Perhaps I may be compelled to tell my story somewhat at length un de ces beaux jours—Nous Verrons; Cependent,[6] I assure you that I have neither naturally nor artificially the least partiality for my native Country, which has not protected my property by its boasted Laws, & where, if the Laws are not good, I know nothing that is, for the climate does not agree with me, who am another creature in France, & where one leads a melancholy insulated life at about four times the expence that one might live for, upon the Continent in well-informed society. Therefore if Death or Justice or any other decisive personification, should happen to interfere on my poor childrens behalf, so as that I could get their property out of the tenacious talons of the worthy Gentlemen who keep it "All for their good," I w[d] not hesitate a moment (that is if I am able to move) to bid to "the Isle Land that from her pushes all the rest" a long & last Adieu! Any intelligence therefore that you can procure for me of the sweet house you describe on the banks of the Leman Lake or any other as to terms of living in Switzerland or Italy will very much oblige me.[7] I do not mind dying, but I want to see the Alps & Vesuvius first, & I feel somehow as if I ought to make haste. I have no tragic powers I fear, nor if I had do I beleive they would succeed. We are grown so childish in England that even what us'd to be call'd a good Comedy, we cannot now see to an end, but make our entertainments out of three ridiculous farces, or two & a pantomime——John has in somethings changed character with the ci devant Louis (For what, he that was Louis is now, nobody can guess I think)——

If you should succeed in your most kind endeavours to serve me, The first & second Volumes of the Novel[8] are ready in MMS & shall be sent by any conveyance you name at my expence. I am much oblig'd to you for the perusal of Hermann d'Unna which you have probably seen by the papers is already translated. I sent it up this day to M[r] Cadells where it waits the orders of your friend—— I am, Dear Sir,

your most obed[t] & ever oblig'd Ser[t],
Charlotte Smith

I am not much in habits of making apologies but it seems necessary to do so for this Letter, which I have written not only in bodily pain, but with people talking near me.[9]

If I am so happy as to hear from you, be so good as to direct hither under cover to the Hon[ble] J Olmius,[10] Excise Office, London.

Huntington MS (HM10812). Address: Josepth Cooper Walker Esq[re]/ Eccles Street/ J. Olmius Dublin. Postmark: Post/ MR/ 21/ PAID; MR/ 25.

NOTES

1. CS's overriding health problem at this time was probably rheumatoid arthritis, not gout. Gout is unusual in the hands and would not prevent her from walking. Rheumatoid arthritis can lead to weight loss and the facial changes she describes later in this letter. Her depression could have increased her pain and the frequency of flare-ups.

2. Harriet.

3. CS's brother's son Nicholas matriculated at Oxford the next month, but would have been living with his parents at Fittleworth about four and a half miles distant.

The writing master is not identified; the work in progress is *The Banished Man.*

4. George Romney painted this portrait in Aug. 1792 during CS's ten-day stay at Eartham. She and Romney, along with William Cowper, were Hayley's guests. It is not clear whether Hayley is the friend who does not want to release the portrait.

5. *Elegiac Sonnets ii* was not published until 1797.

6. One of these fine days—Let us hope; however . . .

7. CS's highly autobiographical novel, *The Banished Man,* was half completed at this time. In it, she allowed her alter ego, the novelist Mrs. Denzil, to move permanently to Italy. Mrs. Denzil's new son-in-law d'Alonville, an émigré, and her beloved daughter Angelina—a pair that closely parallels de Foville and Augusta—move with her.

8. *The Banished Man.*

9. This letter has more insertions and strikeovers than usual, but the handwriting is large, clear, and vigorous.

10. John Luttrell Olmius, a commissioner in the office of Revenue, Excise Office, Old Broad Street.

To Thomas Cadell, Jr.

Bath. March 31st {17}94
Dr Sir,

By the Coach of tomorrow, April 1st, I send the remaining part of the 2nd Volume.[1] There appears to me to be a great deal of it. Yet it is twenty five pages short of my agreement not because I shrink from that engagement, for I fear I shall have rather too much than too little matter, But because I observe in the two sheets I receiv'd that the printing makes in each sheet 4 pages more than the MMS, & of course 288 pages of the latter would have swelld the volume to another sheet. As the point at which it now closes is convenient to the narrative, I thought it better to end there, but if it is insufficient, The Printer will take the 1st ~~Volume~~ chapter of the next volume which will be ready (the greater part) in abt 10 days. I have made some strange blunder in numbering these pages, which I have endeavourd in vain to rectify entirely, but the sense will guide the printer. If any quantity or all the first Volume is ~~done~~ printed, I should be Very glad to be oblig'd with it. I have done as well as I could without the latin Book,[2] not being able to get it. I am, Sir, your obed^{t} & oblig'd Ser^{t},

Charlotte Smith

General Manuscripts, Manuscripts Division, Department of Rare Books and Special Collections, Princeton University Library. Address: Mr Cadell. No postmark.

NOTES

1. Of *The Banished Man.*
2. Not identified.

To James Upton Tripp

[Bath, 4 April 1794]
Dear Sir,

I have found that tho I have shut myself up since I have been here, & have not even sent for a Physician on account my inability to pay a Guinea a day, that I cannot live for nothing. I have no resource but my own labour which this cruel disorder, especially when it attacks my hands as it does to day, sadly impedes——

However I have now deliverd to the Sieur Cadell to the value of 100£ & therefore have no scruple in regard to the money. I hope as I work whether able or no, & sometimes in extreme torture, to finish the other two Volumes in a month & have venturd to draw on you in fav^{r} of Mr Dunster,[1] who has been so good as to let me have the Money, for 10 Guineas——for tho I meant to have left the ballance of the 20£ ~~for~~ which I took the liberty of ~~drawing up~~ entreating you to discount (after pay^{g} Mr Tyler) for my family, I find my illness so expensive as to oblige me to take part of it. The small ballance will do little for them, but I am in hopes of procuring them a supply before what they have is gone, either by getting the £35 due to me on the 2nd July discounted, or by finishing my work, when I shall have £100.

I do not know whether you will accept my apology for taking such liberties with you; & I wish I had any means better than by a repetition of words, to assure you that I am truly sensible of the friendly part you have acted on my behalf, who had no manner of claim to your kindness.

I write in such pain to day from my right hand being swelled that you will hardly read this. Yesterday I could write as well as ever I could in my life, & so I perhaps shall tomorrow. I am, dear Sir,

your most obed^{t} & oblig'd Ser^{t}
Charlotte Smith

Bath. April 4th 1794

Petworth House Archives MS. No address or postmark.

NOTE

1. The Reverend Charles Dunster; see Biographical Notes.

To William Davies

[Bath, 4 April 1794]
Sir,

I see there is a Ship from India. If my Letters are sent to your House, I beseech you to send them down by the Stage immediately directed to me at No. 10 Pultenay Street, As I am particularly impatient to hear from my two Sons.[1] I should have been oblig'd to Mr Cadell had he found time to write relative to the 2nd Volume of Poems — — Hope to hear from him, or some other Gentleman in the House, soon. Also that the MMS completing the 2nd Vol of the new Novel is received. I am, Sir,

your obed^t & oblig'd Ser^t,
Charlotte Smith

10 Pultenay St Bath
4th April [17]94

General Manuscripts, Manuscripts Division, Department of Rare Books and Special Collections, Princeton University Library. Address: Mr Davies/ Mr Cadells/ Strand/ London. Postmark: BATH/ AP/ 5/ 94.

NOTE

1. During this period, both William's and Nicholas's careers with the East India Company were flourishing, and they regularly sent CS remittances of £100 or more by way of East India merchant ships. CS depended on Cadell and Davies to receive her sons' packets and forward them to her.

To James Upton Tripp

[Bath, 22 April 1794]
Dear Sir,

I have but a moment to thank you for your repeated kindness & civility & to say that instead of the 20£ for which I gave you a draft on Cadell, I have made another arrangement, which will be more convenient to me & will make no difference, I trust, to you. I was not aware of Mr Dunsters writing to day & therefore have not either my Letter or a draft ready which will account for the liberty I have taken in drawing for ten G^s which if you will be so good as to honor, I will send another draft to you by tomorrows post & beg you will be so good as to not to [*sic*] send up the 20£ to Cadell till then—— I am, dear Sir,

your ever oblig'd & obed^t
Ser^t
Charlotte Smith

April 22nd [17]94[1]

Petworth House Archives MS. No address or postmark.

NOTE

1. A note at the bottom of this note in William Tyler's hand reads "Pray return this."

To James Upton Tripp

[Bath, 24 April 1794]
Dear Sir,

I fear you were surpris'd at the scrambling Letter I wrote to you on Teusday, but Mr Dunster was in an hurry to close his packet & I had not time to explain myself. I have at length received a Letter from Mr Robinson[1] in which he promises that he will pay the 35£ due to me in July (on the 2nd). This being ascertain'd, I take the liberty of sending you a draft for it from the 2nd of May.

I do not immediately want the money. If you will have the goodness to credit Mr Dunsters account as before for 10 G^s and send five to Storrington, I will not trouble you for the rest till some time hence when I must provide for my daughters lying in. My cruel illness which has prevented my going on rapidly with my work, which I ought to have finish'd by this time,[2] has made Mr Cadell in a fidget least he should not receive the MMS had by the time the 2nd draft becomes due, which you were so very friendly as to discount for me. I have been so much better this last week that I was in hopes I should have completed my 3rd Volume, but being thrown so much behind hand, I have only been able to do 2 3^rds of it which go up to Cadells tomorrow evening. We have compromis'd the matter, & instead of twenty payable on Monday next, he has agreed to let me have 40 at 3 weeks from tomorrow. Our accounts will then stand thus:

In fav^{r} of James Tripp Esqre	25£
In fav^{r} of Mich^{l} Naish	25£
In fav^{r} of James Tripp Esqre	30£
D^{o} due in May	40£
	120
4 volumes at 50£ vol.	200 (In case of a 2nd Ed^{n} 50£ more)
The Ballance to me on Finishing my work	80

This being arrang'd, I am persuaded you will have the goodness to cancel the draft for 20£ due on Monday next & in place of it receive that for 40£ which I enclose. The Money remaining I do not want till it is due, as I cannot think of intruding upon you more—— Nor should I have done it now had I not been so harrassd with illness & the expenses attending upon it that I have been render'd more helpless and distress'd than ever & have no resource but in the assistance my friends will give to such feeble endeavours as I can yet make to help myself.

I consulted Mr Dunster whether I could in conscience take all these liberties with you, & told him how much I had already troubled you & how very good natured you had been on many occasions & that I was ashamed of seeming to ask more because you had already taken so much trouble & been so friendly. He told me he thought there was no doubt of your being still so good as to allow me to ask your assistance in these negotiations.

So if I have gone too far, I shall have an excuse in following his opinion. I own to you that it is very distressing & expensive to me to be under the necessity of keeping House at Storrington during my absence; M^{r} & M^{rs} De Foville have had an invitation to pass the next six or seven weeks till her confinement at the House of a friend, & they wish as much to accept it as my daughter Lucy does to come here (tho Heaven knows she could not go out if she did for I am unable to go into company).

But Mr Charles Smith, tho this place has been order'd for him, does not like to come. His recruiting he says prevents him, having made his head quarters at Storrington & his Sisters cannot leave him. And as I wish—— poor dear Boy!——to do all I can for him while I am able, I must submit, tho God alone knows how I shall pay the expenses of keeping House there & living here too (This is infinitely the cheapest of the two), & should I return ~~South~~ now, the expense I have been at will be thrown away, as my Physician,[3] whom Mr Dunster has brought to me & who takes no fee, recommends perseverance as the only chance I have of getting quite well. I thought I was getting on fast, but to day I am very much a cripple in both my hands, & have a return of the lurking fever which would bring on gout if I had strength enough———

Were it not for the expenses I am condem'd to, I sh^d do pretty well, for as soon as ~~my~~ Dr Falconer dismisses me, I meant to have gone into Herefordshire to Mrs Clyffords[4] for a few weeks till it becomes necessary for me to attend M^rs De Foville, & there I should have been at no expense either for myself or such of my family as were with me———While the time would be coming round when I may expect (if my eldest Son's health & life continues)[5] his annual remittance for me & his Sisters.

Mr Turner does not write to me ab^t the Gibbons's,[6] so I suppose even the 1300£ must be given up, hardly the 17th part of what is due to us, & which undoubtedly might be recoverd because in 1786 they offerd it, & little as it is, it is better than nothing.

I rejoice extremely that My Brother has been able to place his Sons name on the Books at Oxford.[7] I beg your pardon, dear Sir, for giving you the trouble of reading this long Letter, & am ever your much oblig'd & obed^t humble Ser^t Charlotte Smith
10 Pultenay Street Bath April 24th 1794

Petworth House Archives MS. No address or postmark.

NOTES

1. John Robinson, trustee to Richard Smith's estate since 1783, now with Anthony Parkin. The estate owed CS and her children £35 interest biannually on 2 Jan. and 2 July. A half year rarely passed when CS did not try to draw against it from someone else beforehand, and the trustees adamantly refused any early payments, no matter how straitened or desperate she reported her circumstances to be.

2. She contracted to deliver the novel complete on 20 Apr.

3. William Falconer, M.D., FRS (1744–1824). Dr. Falconer was elected physician to the Bath General Hospital in 1784 and served there until 1819. His two dozen medical and other writings include an essay on the French revolution praised by Burke and "An Account of the Use, Application, and Success of the Bath Waters in Rheumatic Cases," both aligned with CS's interests and needs. In 1800, Rev. Dunster inscribed his *Considerations on Milton's Early Readings* to Falconer.

4. CS had previously visited Eliza Maria Clifford in Perrystone, Ross (see CS to George Robinson, 4 July 1792 and n. 2).

5. At times, weather delayed the ships that brought William's money, but his health was never an issue.

6. The property in Barbados of Sir William Gibbons, which was the subject of a lengthy dispute (see, e.g., CS to James Upton Tripp, 18 Sept. 1793 and n. 1).

7. A "Turner, Nicholas, cler. fil." matriculated at Worcester College, Oxford, 11 Apr. 1794. He did not complete a course of study. *Cler. fil.* indicates "son of a clergyman."

To Joseph Cooper Walker

10 Pulteney Street, Bath, April 30th 1794
Dear Sir,

Yesterday I dispatch'd a Letter to you with a copy of the proposals printed here, as I was not aware that you would have the goodness to undertake that part of the troublesome business which you have with so much friendly zeal engaged in on my behalf. But your copy is so perfectly what it ought to be that I had certainly no occasion to trouble you with any other. I am extremely oblig'd to you for the exertions you have already made for me & most sincerely wish I may have an opportunity of thanking you in Person. As these Waters have been recommended to you, I hope you will be induced to try them. It would be highly gratifying to me to see you here. For my own part I am likely to stay some time, for I have found the waters of very great service to me in removing that excessive lowness and depression which render'd me unfit for every thing, & is perhaps the most distressing of all evils to a person situated as I am—who must live to write & write to live——

My daughters approaching confinement renders me so anxious that I really destroy myself.[1] I have determined to have her come hither as being the place where the best advice is to be had, tho it will add to my expence, it will be such a releif to my mind that I cannot help indulging myself in it. As this will keep me here till the middle of August, I trust it will give me an opportunity of seeing you. After that period, if all goes well, I shall go into Herefordshire for six or eight weeks & return hither possibly for the Winter if I can let or otherwise dispose of the house with which an unfortunate combination of circumstances induced me to encumber myself ~~with~~ in Sussex. I cannot say perhaps that a Poet like a Prophet has no honnour in his or her own Country, for I have found many friends there, but there are circumstances of family uneasiness[2] which have render'd it uncomfortable to me, and I should be easier any where else. I was going to say happier——but for me to talk of happiness is an abuse of terms. I fear however I am chain'd to the dwelling & shall not be able to disengage myself. One great charm that Sussex once had was the society and friendship of Mr Hayley——— That I have lost,[3] and the nearer I am to the possibility of being restor'd to it, the more I regret that it cannot be restored. But enough of this. If you will have the goodness to remit the Sum you have collected to Harris, & Co., Bankers at Bath, in any form that may be most agreeable to you, it will be rather more convenient to me than having it sent to London.

I have a new subject of heartache; my poor wounded boy has been persuaded to take orders & to give his Commission of Ensign in the 14th [I]nfantry to his Brother Lionel.[4] It is entirely agai[nst my][5] inclination, &

I have said so. But as it is very true that a young Man of six feet high & upwards ought to do something for his support, and as I am denied the means of keeping him at Oxford to be qualified for orders for which he was always intended, I do not know that I ought to oppose his inclinations, tho certain that in suffering him to follow them, I must be condemned to such misery & anxiety as I endured for Charles, perhaps to be follow'd by a Catastrophe as shocking. It is very difficult for a Mother to know how to act with Boys when there is no Father or near relation who has authority over them, & it would be unreasonable were I to expect that all my Sons should be what the eldest is. He is indeed jeun homme comme il y'en a peu—— But I shall probably never see him again—

Adieu Dear Sir, it is more than time to finish this <croaking> Letter, or you will not beleive that the Bath Waters have been of the service I have been boasting of. My hands, thank God, are for the present restor'd to me, but I am not able to walk just now, but that is a much less inconvenience to me than not being able to write——

I am, dear Sir,
with great regard your most oblig'd Ser[t],
Charlotte Smith

Huntington MS (HM10813). Address: To/ Josepth Cooper Walker Esq[re]/ Eccles Street/ Dublin. Postmark: BATH; MY/ 4/ {94}.

NOTES

1. Augusta Smith de Foville was in the seventh month of a pregnancy rendered dangerous by her consumption.

2. Her sister Catherine Ann Dorset's undue influence on Charles was an unexpected turn of events, adding to CS's maternal and financial worries (see CS to James Upton Tripp, 16 May 1794 and n. 1).

3. This is CS's first mention of the rift with Hayley.

4. In the end, although Charles's taking orders would have suited CS's inclination, he resisted and stayed in the 14th Regiment. Lionel never served in the 14th. When he signed up on 28 Oct. 1795, he was attached to the 24th Regiment as a lieutenant.

5. Covered by seal.

To James Upton Tripp

{Bath, 1 May 1794}
Dear Sir,

I was never more hurt in my life than to find that Cadell had sent back unpaid the draft for 30£, for not only I have earn'd the money, but he told me before I drew for it that he would pay it. I wrote to him to give him notice when it would be due, and he never even hinted that it wd not be accepted. I therefore cannot but think it is oweing to his being so much absent from the ~~compting~~ Shop. I sent it up to him by yesterdays post as soon as I re[eive]d it and begg'd of him to send you down a Bank note for the amount as you had already been so good as ~~as~~ to let me have the Money. I enclose you what Robinson says; it is a thousand to one if he will accept the draft tho he has promis'd to pay it.

I am so vex'd that your good nature to me should be attended with so much trouble to you that I shall fret myself as ill as ever. Indeed all my attempts to get restor'd to any degree of health are vain while my mind is torn to pieces as it is. It wd be much better for me to be dead. I will send you the other drafts as soon as possible, for as to Cadell, I shall soon have earned the whole 200£.

I am so ill & in such pain in my hands that I can hardly write. I most sincerely rejoice in dear Nic's[1] good fortune, which I suppose is oweing to the good offices of Lord E. for I know no other person who ever does us any good.

I am, dear Sir,
ever your oblig'd Sert
Charlotte Smith

1st May 1794
Return me Robinsons Letter when opportunity offers.

Petworth House Archives MS. No address or postmark.

NOTE

1. Nicholas Turner's only son, CS's only living nephew. Egremont probably helped him matriculate at Oxford (see CS to Tripp, 24 April 1794 and n. 7). This is not CS's son Nicholas. He was doing very well on his own about this time in India, and CS never called him Nic. *Nicholas* had been the eldest Turner son's name for several generations.

To James Upton Tripp

[Bath, 4 May 1794]
Dear Sir,

Your letter which Mr Dunster sent me yesterday is every thing that is kind and friendly. I am more oblig'd to you than I Can express for the repeated instances of kindness you have shewn me—— I expected to day to have received accepted, a draft at 3 weeks I sent up to Cadell for £50 in order to replace the thirty & leave a ballance of twenty. But he has not sent it.

In less than three weeks the money will be my own As I to day send up the 3rd & part of the 4th Volume. Therefore I have no doubt of his doing it. But as he is getting entirely out of business, he is now much engaged as Chairman of Charitable association &c &c that there is no getting at him. However I have sent a friend to him to day who will not be easily put off and shall probably have the Bill in the day or two. In the mean time, I trust there is no doubt in your mind about the £35.

And my poor Girl writes to inform me that the Butcher at Storrington behaves with great insolence & has refus'd them credit, so she is oblig'd to pay for whatever they can get, which is merely the refuse meat, and it gives her a great deal of vexation. It is hard in her situation and with her feelings to be expos'd to this & still harder, as she has staid at Storrington entirely on account of Charles, whose recruiting it seems will not allow him to go from thence——tho God knows I can ill afford to keep house entirely on that account which he does not seem to consider. My daughter has also a servant to discharge, & therefore if you w^{d} have the goodness to send her ten or twelve Guineas, it will put an end to my uneasiness which is extreme, least her precious health should suffer from being expos'd to all these inconveniencies.

Why the Butcher is insolent, I know not, as I never owed the Man five pounds at a time in my life. It is very sad to be insulted by such people, & Augusta's Letter of yesterday has vex'd me so, that I have never clos'd my Eyes during the night, & tho I was I thought getting quite well, I am to day almost as ill as I have been at all.

I return the Draft on Robinson, which he return'd to me unaccepted but ~~but~~ with assurances as before that it shall in all events be paid. What his reasons are for not accepting a bill he declares he will pay, I cannot guess, & it w^{d} answer no purpose to enquire for he is just like an old Mule; & the less reason he has for any resolution he takes, the more obstinately he adheres to it.

However after the Letter you saw and after what he has since repeated, there can be no doubt ab^{t} the matter, & what I must trouble you, Dear Sir, to do will be to send the Bill up to the old Rat catcher a few days before it is due; & he will return it accepted and payable at Drummonds[1] so that the Bankers to whom you send it will have no trouble about it, for I know that Bankers Clerks will not be plagued with dancing after folks, nor with Bills drawn on persons in the Country.

I am going into Herefordshire as soon as I can get these money matters settled, & Lucy to come to me [*sic*] which she will do by the Stage from Chichester to Southampton & hither. M^{r} & M^{rs} De Foville will go as soon afterwards as they can, as she must soon be where she is to lye in—— But till I know what Charles & Lionel determine upon,[2] I am utterly a loss to know what to do, & all I know certainly is that I am driven into expenses that deprive me of the necessaries of life & will soon of life itself———

Pray send this scrap of paper to M[r] Turner. I am unable to write more to him. I wish, dear Sir, I could express as warmly as I feel, the gratitude I owe you for the kindness you have exerted towards me. I am ever

y[r] much oblig'd Ser[t]
C Smith

4th May [17]94

Petworth House Archives MS. No address or postmark.

NOTES

1. Drummond and Co., Charing Cross, London, under Robert Drummond (1775–1804), who was the private banker to George III.

2. That is, whether Charles would take orders and Lionel take over his commission as ensign in the 14th. Charles was serving as recruiting officer, based in Storrington. Though not signed up for the army or for Oxford, Lionel appears to have been keeping his brother company.

To James Upton Tripp

[Bath, 4 May 1794]
Dear Sir,

I find the refusal of the 30£ draft was oweing to a blunder, partly mine who was half dead when I drew those two drafts, & partly to M[r] Cadell's being never in the Way, being about to quit business next month[1] so that it is impossible for other people as well as myself to get the regular attention we used to have.

I hope & beleive it will be all put to rights in the course of this week, & I shall send you an accepted draft for the 50£ for I am so near finishing my whole work, having labourd at it incessantly since my health has permitted, that I shall almost immediately have that Sum due to me <u>without a favor</u>. The misery is, that my expenses at Storrington run away with my whole earnings faster than I can work for them, do what I will.

M[rs] De Foville has a Servant to discharge & will I fear want six or 8 Guineas, & M[r] Dunster has furnish'd me with 6 more for myself. All this is sheer intrusion upon you till I send you Cadells accepted Bill, & I am but too conscious of the liberty I am taking with you. As to the £35, you see by Robinsons Letter that it will be discharged. I have sent him the draft, but it may be some time before I get his answer. I am however very easy about it, knowing that he must pay it, & indeed cannot evade it after what he has said. I am also sure that unless I die within this fortnight which is very improbable I trust, that my draft on Cadell will be as good as the Bank.

All that grieves me is to have given you so much trouble & to have been intruding thus on your great good nature.

Towards the end of the week I will write again with the Bills, & I request till then your Patience & that you will Allow me to remain your greatly oblig'd Ser[t]

C T Smith

4th May [17]94
You see I have the use of my hands again.

Petworth House Archives MS. No address or postmark.

NOTE

1. The elder Thomas Cadell's retirement this summer was especially unfortunate in light of CS's family's health and her ensuing financial troubles. She wrote her last letter to him on 30 July, and then wrote to Davies, to Cadell, Jr., and to both men, floundering to replace her former champion. They rejected her next book proposal, *Rosalie,* which Sampson Low published as *Montalbert* (1795), but they did purchase *Rural Walks* (1795); the payment it provided was much more modest but sorely needed.

To James Upton Tripp

[Bath, 9 May 1794]
Dear Sir,

I have not yet heard from M[r] Cadell which is extremely strange on his part, as he now actually owes me the money for the Bill he returnd & I have his engage[t] to pay it. But M[r] Dunster assures me it is merely oweing to his business at this time of the year, & tho it distresses me beyond all expression, I must endure it. As I shall very certainly have one hundred and twenty five pounds due to me (your 30£ not be first paid) or 95£ (if it is paid) due to me in three weeks, because I shall then have deliverd my whole work.[1] I make no scruple of send[g] you again the draft for 30£ which I know will be paid & if you will <u>then</u> only have the goodness to send it up p[r] post to Cadell, who will return it accepted & prevent any difficulty to your Bankers Clerks, & then I have no doubt but that you will be so good as to let my family have the ballance of the 35£ on Robinson which I reckon at about 14£ if they have not re[ceive][d] it since I last heard from them or even four or five G[s] more should they want it, which I assure you I will most punctually settle with you the instant I get my Money.

But there is no telling how the difficulties I am under distract me. My daughter, whose health & life are the most precious things I have left, has been so teized & vex'd by being insulted by the Brutes at Storrington (& such brutes I believe never did exist any where) that M[r] De Foville is in an agony about her & entreats me to let her ~~come~~ go immediately where she proposes to lye in.

As I cannot make Charles come to any determination, I must leave a person in the House who will do what he wants. It is very hard upon me; but nothing seems to lessen my expense or trouble.

I have had the kindest the most humane the most considerate Letter ~~imaginat~~ imaginable from Lord Egremont. He is going again to Parkin & Lambert[2] on our behalf. Who upon Earth is there but him, who w[d] interest themselves so long & so generously. Perhaps in the humour Robinson seems to be in at Present, this timely interposition may do much. But Alas all this while the estate remains in possession of Prettyjohn[3] & we shall not receive a sous I fear. While the Grass grows, the Steeds will starve[4]——for my family will have nothing to support them but from the Labour of my weak hands———

If you do not approve of this draft to replace the 30£ you have with so much good nature advanced, I will send it in any other form, or again apply for Cadells acceptance [of i]t, which cannot now be call'd a favor; but suddenly rich Men are hard to deal with, & poor Authors <u>must</u> bear with rich booksellers.

I was not born to all this drudgery & mortification tho I have now been in it ~~two~~ ten long long Years![5] & Cadell seems to think it a matter of course. I could bear it still but that my poor Children should be expos'd to want & insult is very very hard to bear.

Dear Sir, I beg you many pardons for being so very troublesome a correspondent—— I shall never have it in my power to express how much I am oblig'd to you, but the consciousness of a good natured action has I know its value with you. I entreat the fav[r] of you to let M[rs] De Foville hear from you on Sunday, & should the post be gone, if you send over a Man on purpose, she will pay him. I am so excessively uneasy at her being so situated that I am really half killed by it. But were it not for this continual anxiety, my health w[d] be soon re-establishd, for I have brought the Gout into my left hand where it remains with no other inconvenience but making my third finger look like a great toe. There was a time when this would have been a mortification to my vanity, but I have now too many real miseries to care if all my fingers were like dead radishes. I beg the fav^{r} of hearing from you & am, dear Sir, your most truly oblig'd Ser^{t}

Charlotte Smith

May 9th 1794

Petworth House Archives MS. Address: James Upton Tripp Esqre/ Petworth. No postmark.

NOTES

1. That is, in three weeks after she delivers her work to Cadell, he would send her either £125 if he hadn't discounted Tripp's £30, or 95£ if he had discounted it.

2. Not identified.

3. William Prettyjohn had been agent for Gay's plantation from 1784 or 1785 to 1798 and for Mapp's from 1784 or 1785 to 1800 (PHA #7371).

4. CS repeated this proverb with feeling in several letters, perhaps thinking that while the Barbadian plantations produced sugars at a profit, she and her children were starving. Versions of the proverb survive in writers as various as John Carpave, John Heywood, and John Taylor, the water poet. But she may have been reminded of it in one of her favorite plays when Hamlet says dismissively, "'While the grass grows'—The proverb is something musty" (*Hamlet* 3.2.343–44).

5. CS dated the dedication to the first edition of her *Elegiac Sonnets* 10 May 1784, making this month the tenth anniversary of her first publication.

To William Davies

[Bath, 9 May 1794]
Sir

Have the goodness to let the porter who brings this, take the Basket back to the White Horse, Fetter Lane, as it is something my daughter[1] wishes for, & I fear its not getting to her in time or while it is good. Whatever is the difference of expence, I will pay. I now send the 3rd Vol of the Banish'd Man, all but the few last pages which will be up with part of ye 4th in about five or six days. I wish I could have more of the Letter press, & I wish to hear from Mr Cadell if he w^{d} be so good.

I am, Sir,
y^{r} obed^{t} humble Ser^{t},
Charlotte Smith

Bath May 9th

Huntington MS (HM10814). Address: Mr Davies/ at Mr Cadells/ to be open'd immediately. No postmark.

NOTE

1. Probably Charlotte Mary, who often stayed in London with relatives. The White Horse was an inn and posting house in London.

To James Upton Tripp

[Bath, 16 May 1794]

Dear Sir,

At length I have settled with Mr Cadell but not quite to my mind as to the time of his accepting the Bill. However this I shall adjust in a day or two, & then my debt to you in regard to the 30£ will be finally settled, but never will the obligation I owe you for your friendly good nature be eras'd from my mind——

I am still tormented by the uncertainty I am in, in regard to my family. I had directed Lionel & Lucy to come to me as soon as they had money by the Southhampton Stage & expected them to day: but somebody or other has made them change their mind who is I conclude wiser than I am.[1] This is extremely inconvenient to me as I meant to have gone into Wales as soon as by their coming I could have got rid of the intolerable expense of keeping house at Storrington, being order'd by my Physician to omit the Water for a little while and return to it again.

The impossibility of pleasing so large family when I am, tho compelled to support them all, they all (except M^{r} & M^{rs} De Foville) seem to think I do not do enough, is really a most afflicting circumstance; & tho I have nobody to assist me, There are people enough who seem to delight in adding to my troubles. At the head of whom is Mrs Dorset, who has so entirely estranged my Son Charles from me, that I have not the least influence over him, & indeed hardly receive common civility from him which is a cruel return I think for all I have done & endeavour'd to do for him. I have now kept House at Storrington entirely on his account more than six weeks, & even now I do not know what he intends to do. I wrote him repeatedly to know, but I received no answer. I then wrote to Mrs Dorset to beg, as I had no power even to obtain an answer from him, she w^{d} use her influence to get him to come to some determination——

<u>She sent my Letter back unopen'd</u> after keeping it a fortnight—— Conduct so brutal & extraordinary that it is hardly credible. I own I have fretted myself sick about these <boys>. My fate altogether appears too bitter to be borne—— ~~I do not m~~ I beg pardon however for being so troublesome to you, but my heart is too much pain'd to allow me to govern my pen———

I do not know whether I have miscalculated about the 35£ but I believe the account stands thus:

Self by M[r] Dunster	10.10
M[rs] De Foville	5.5
Self by M[r] Dunster	6.6
M[rs] De Foville	10.10
	32.11

If this acc[t] is right, there is a small ballance of £2.9 remaining, which, tho I am really shocked at being so troublesome to you, I will trouble you (if I am right) to send over by Sundays post; for tho I have sent besides a small supply of money, I fear these long delays And the necessity they are under of paying for every thing, will prevent My daughters having enough for her journey, & I cannot bear that she should be made unhappy in her present situation, for she deserves nothing but good & ought to have the World at her feet, instead of being harrass'd & treated with insult because she has married the man she liked & whom I approved of.

Pray forgive me, Dear Sir, for the infinite plague I have been to you. I will get the business of the now accepted draught settled immediately with M[r] Cadell & send it to you accepted in which case, that you have may be cancelld—— I am, Dear Sir,

with repeated thanks,
your most oblig'd Ser[t]
Charlotte Smith

Bath 16th May 1794

Petworth House Archives MS. No address or postmark.

NOTE

1. Probably an ironic reference to the interference of her sister, Catherine Dorset, who also complicated CS's relationship with her invalid son Charles (see next paragraph).

To James Upton Tripp

[Bath, 18 May 1794]
Dear Sir,

Nothing but the inconveniencies I am expos'd to can for a moment apologise for my taking such liberties as I do with you——— I am not however going to tieze you for any farther pecuniary trouble as I have received a small supply from Ireland & have sent Mrs De Foville half of it for her journey, but she writes to me in great terror & uneasiness, least the people at Storrington to whom there cannot be thirty pounds due, and to whom I have paid so much money weekly & regularly during the whole year, should stop their coming on Wednesday, as they seem to threaten. To stop them legally I know to be impossible, for they cannot owe anything; but as the Chevalier de Foville is a foreigner & her situation is such as will make him do any thing rather than have her terrified, I think the people very likely to make some attempt to extort the money from them with which I have supplied them for their journey.

I am persuaded such an attempt would be attended with the most fatal consequences to my daughter. The very apprehension of it seems to have shaken her spirits dreadfully & has thrown me into an agony of apprehension—— I will pay the Storrington people most certainly, but I cannot do it till I can close my account with Cadell, for the draft he has agreed to accept forthwith is destin'd to settle with you & will wait on you by Mr Dunster. If they were not the most unprincipled harpies existing, such an idea as distressing Mrs De Foville would never enter their heads. But such a set I never saw———

This recruiting service has brought me into this scrape; not content with doing nothing for Charles, Government has contrived to load me with additional expenses, for my whole family wd have been gone from Storrington five weeks since, and I should have been in Herefordshire now if Charles had known his own mind. What I have gone thro ever since I have been here is not to be described or imagined about him & Lionel——

Dear Sir, what I wd entreat the favor of you is, to send a Servant or somebody over on Wednesday when I have appointed a Chaise to go for them, Who may if it is necessary prevent any attempt from these people to alarm my daughter by convincing them they cannot legally stop any part of my family from going where they please. Nothing that I know of will do this, but your having the goodness to interfere for me——not in the way of answering for the money; that is not my meaning, but to prevent any insolence which they ~~are~~ are very capable of, & which might kill Augusta, whose spirits are never very equal to difficulties[1]——

Your humanity & good nature I know are such as will induce you to save me from the misery I shall suffer if any thing evil should befall her—— Such is my reliance on the generous Sympathy of the excellent ~~Lord~~ Man whose business you transact that I should in this new exigence have besought his interposition, but that it looks so like begging which is not at all my meaning—— I would not have given you this trouble had I know [*sic*] what else to have done to have saved myself from the possibility, nay probability, of having my child destroy'd—— These are thy works & triumphs Oh Robinson & Rickman![2]——— I am, dear Sir, in agitation of Spirits that there is no describing, your much oblig'd

Ser[t] C Smith——

18th May 1794

Petworth House Archives MS. Address: James Tripp Esq[re]/ Petworth/ Sussex. Postmark: BATH; {M}A/19/94.

NOTES

1. Augusta's journey may have been delayed. In any event, CS's brother Nicholas Turner had a different take on the matters of Augusta's debt and illness. He wrote to Tripp:

> . . . I fancy Mad de Foville has fretted herself because she could not discharge every body at Storrington and my wife writes me she is too ill to set off tomorrow but if she was in health I cannot see any reason for the alarm my sister expresses—tho I am sure they are both very much obliged for your kind offer. (Nicholas Turner to James Upton Tripp, n.d., unpub. letter in PHA #0.15/10q).

2. Gawler Griffith Rickman, a London attorney. He had represented the collateral branches of the family whose suit sent BS to jail in Dec. 1783.

To James Upton Tripp

[Bath, 20 May 1794]
Dear Sir,

I have but a moment to answer your obliging favor. In regard to M[r] Robinsons note, there seems to me to be as in all he does a desire to puzzle and confound. He has engaged himself to pay the £35 due to me on the 2nd July whether remittances come or no. Therefore there can be no doubt, I am persuaded, of the Bills being paid, & without having obtain'd a certainty of that, I would not, cruel as my situation is, have intruded upon your good nature for it.

In regard to the Affairs being moved out of his hands, I wish there was any ~~opportunity~~ probability of it, but he knows there is not. I cannot get Parkin to put in his Answer to the Bill I have fyled, and I suppose he may take three terms——God knows there is no chance of getting any settlement before ye 2nd July—— I will do however any thing you wish me to do & will write to him a civil Letter praying him to accept it if that will be more satisfactory to you than letting it remain as it does. Certainly I ought to make every exertion to serve you, to whom I am oblig'd for so many instances of friendship from being in the least plagued to receive the repayment of money advanced to my necessities——

Good God! how much trouble I have given you. By to days post, You receive another troublesome Letter from me. My poor Augusta is in extreme terror least she should be stopped, as if any body had a right to stop her: but in her situation such an alarm may be her death, & it is impossible to imagine the anxiety I am under about her. If I once get her where I am, never will I expose her to such inconveniencies again. I know not what to do but to write to you, knowing you are humane & good natured enough not only to forgive it, but to prevent any such attempt from the troop of savages at Storrington.

It is more than probable that I have misreckon'd, for I have been so tormented by the Boys who, without meaning it, have contrived to distract me as well as expose me to needless expense ever since I have been here, that I really have not known what I am about. I know however that out of 200£ that I have now nearly earn'd, I have received 100£ & that whatever I am Minus in y^{r} obliging account, I will give you a draft for which must be paid when the work is deliver'd and which Cadell has agreed to accept.

Mr Dunster[1] to whom I am very greatly oblig'd has the goodness to overlook the last volume which is now in considerable forwardness. I hope to touch the money for ye 2nd edit^{n} very soon after the publishing of the first. I beg you will have the goodness to let me know any debt to you, & you may rely on my send^{g} you a draft which shall be good, to its full amount with a thousand & a thousand thanks for all your kindness: which indeed demands more than I am able to say in acknowledg^{t}. I keep the draft on Robinson till your orders. Luckily it is not now above five weeks before it will be paid. I fear Mr Dunster will go before there will be time for me to hear from you as he talks of Wednesday or Thursday. But whenever I receive your directions, you shall have an ans[we]^{r} with the drafts p^{r} posts return. I am,

d^{r} Sir, y^{r} obligd Ser^{t} CS.

Petworth House Archives MS. No address or postmark.

NOTE

1. Here and in the next letter to Tripp, 1 June 1794, CS identifies the "literary friend" who reads her works before she sends her final copy to her booksellers. The Reverend Charles Dunster (see Biographical Notes) edited several of Milton's works, including *Poems on Several Occasions* (1785) and *Paradise Regained* (1795). CS was surely flattered that such a serious scholar noticed her works. He also lent her money.

To James Upton Tripp

[Bath] 1st June 1794
Dear Sir,

I have every day expected to hear whether I should return Mr Robinsons note (I mean my draft on him) which will be paid the 2nd next Month, or apply to him again for acceptance of it—— I fear from my not having had the pleasure of your instructions on this subject (also information whether it is thirty or forty pounds for which I must draw on Cadell to repay all I owe you) that I was not explicit in what I wrote or that I have been some how or other remiss.

But I assure you I meant to do what was right as far as was in my power, & if I faild of explaining myself, I entreat of you to impute it to the confusion & anguish of mind I was in about my daughter, which had nearly killd me & quite disabled me from writing by Mr Dunster. I have been a great deal better, but uneasiness abt her & abt Charles together with the impossibility of getting any thing done by the Trustees & the probability there is that my family will be starved, have of late so harass'd my constitution already over fatigued, that all my complaints threaten to return & I write with the greatest difficulty & pain.

I beg, dear Sir, to hear from you soon & assure you that by the return of the Post, you shall have the drafts for the money due to you in any way you desire. Perhaps you can put me into a way of sending them free. I have no franking acquaintance here. I beg you to be so good as to give my best respects to Mr Dunster. My propos'd work,[1] which is nearly finish'd, will suffer greatly ~~for~~ by his departure as he was so good as to look over it for me——

I am your
much oblig'd
& obedt Sert
Charlotte Smith

Petworth House Archives MS. No address or postmark.

NOTE

1. *The Banished Man.*

To James Upton Tripp

Bath June 6th [17]94
Dear Sir,

An accident prevented my receiving your obliging Letter to day so soon as usual here, so that I answer it in extreme haste.[1] I enclose the draft on Robinson which it is very certain will be paid. I believe you are mistaken as to havg return'd the last draft on Cadell, as in yr last Letter you merely say you will cancel it whenever I please. I forbear to renew it now; not because it is a matter of any consequence whether it remains uncancelled in yr hands; but because I do not know whether it is thirty or forty pounds I owe you. If you will be so good as to let me know, I will settle it accordingly. Should you have time, there are two or three kindnesses I wd ask of you while you are in town, nothing however that would be very troublesome. I am so overwhelm'd between anxiety for Mrs De Foville & personal suffering that I am unable, did not time press, to write more now, but will trouble you with a Letter on Sunday, post, & also take the liberty of enclosing one for My good friend Mr Dunster. I am, dear Sir,

your ever oblig'd Sert
Charlotte Smith

Petworth House Archives MS. No address or postmark.

NOTE

1. The faint scrawl of this letter suggests CS's haste and poor health.

To Thomas Cadell, Sr.

[Bath] June 11th [17]94
Dear Sir,

Tho my daughter de Foville bore her journey extremely well, she was taken dangerously ill three days afterwards, & from the reasoning of the Medical Man[1] who attended her, I have been under the most terrible apprehensions which alone has occasion'd me to neglect sending up the proofs Mr Stafford[2] sent me, which I meant to have done some days ago, for there are several such mistakes as I fear can hardly pass. As my terror is for the moment appeas'd, I will send up these proofs by tomorrows Coach correctd with a parcel of MMS. I should have sent it all up before now, but this illness of my Angel child has distracted me, & the winding up of a story ought to be so well done that It requires every attention. I think in three or four days if Augusta has not a relapse it will be complete prefaces & all—— In the mean time as I cannot get a sixpence from the Trustees & my expences run so high, you will I am persuaded accept the two drafts of 12 & 6 Guineas I have drawn in fav^r of Mr Pickwick, as before they will be due I trust & am indeed assur'd that I shall have compleated my engagement——

I think of undertaking for the rest of the summer (as I can only do Poetry occasionally) a work such as you once recommended. A sort of School book, calculated not for mere children, but for young persons from twelve to sixteen, intended to form their taste for Poetry, drawing & natural History, or rather to give them, without the alloy of romance, a relish for the beauties of Landscape &c. To be call'd "Rural Walks"[3]—— Would Your Successours like to engage for such a work? In that case I w^d get it printed here & superintend the Press. There is time enough to think of this. Excuse the haste in which I write & believe me, dear Sir,

y^r much oblig'd Ser^t,
C S

Yale University MS. Address: Thomas Cadell Esqre/ Strand/ London. Postmark: BATH; JU/ 12/ 94.

NOTES

1. Dr. Thomas Denman (1733–1815), a distinguished London obstetrician who wrote several tracts on pregnancy and labor and textbooks on the subject that were used into the nineteenth century. After 1791, he lived in semi-retirement in Felpham, near Hounslow, but took on consultations. Nearer the time of delivery and again in the fall, he attended Augusta in consultation with Dr. Caleb Hillier Parry (see CS to Cadell, Sr., 22 July 1794, n. 2); Parry had served his residency with Dr. Denman in his London years.

2. George Stafford, printer, Crane Court, Fleet Street, from 1790 to 1796. These June and July letters are the most detailed surviving record of how CS prepared copy for the printer.

3. *Rural Walks* (1795), published by Thomas Cadell, Jr., and William Davies. Cadell, Sr., had retired from the firm in 1793—hence "Your Successours" in the next sentence—but he continued to deal with some authors.

To Thomas Cadell, Sr.

[Bath, 22 June 1794]
Dear Sir,

The relapse my daughter had, & the apprehensions Dr Denman as well as the Medical people here had & still seem to have of the event, has kept me in such a state of anxiety, as I will not attempt to explain to you, who are I know a most tender and affectionate Parent. Within these few days, thank God, My dear Augusta has suffer'd less, & I think gains strength So that I have more hope than I had that the event will be favourable. I have at intervals continued my work & have now finish'd it all but the two last Chapters, which I wish, like the last line of a Sonnet to have forcible and correct. They will I hope be concluded so in the course of this week. By the mail of this evening I send up a quantity of MMS—— But I fear delay (which for particular reasons will be very inimical to my interest) may arise from the following circumstance——

The second Volume from I know not what cause, for I did not intend to spare my labour, prints in only nine sheets; that is, there are but 212 pages of Letter press instead of 280. The MMS I think ran to 289 or thereabouts, & I could not foresee it would print so little as, of the first parcel I sent up, the Letter press made near twenty pages more than the MMS (and one of Mr Bells[1] complaints against me was that I made my Volumes too big).

However I believe the present deficiency is partly oweing to Mr Stafford having printed this work closer than mine have usually been & that each page contains 15 lines instead of 14, which makes in the whole a very considerable difference—— But be it from whatever cause it may, I would most willingly apply a remedy as Mr Stafford recommends by adding 40 or 50 pages more to close the second Volume. But on examining how far it will be possible, without adding an incongruous episode, I have reason to fear it will be greatly more difficult than to write almost any thing else, & of course to eke out this volume tolerably will take me as many days as to write half another. Still I will do it if you desire it & as expeditiously as possible. But I thought it better to state the circumstances to you, & I beg your opinion upon it, if not too much trouble, by the return of the Post that I may set about it immediately.

Mr Andrews[2] informs me that he has procured several names of Subscribers, but I conclude the whole are not many, as you have yet had only 30 receipts—— I should be glad to hear from Mr Davies how it goes on, as I do not mean to trouble you about it——— I wish however to hear from you relative to this unfortunate thinness of the 2nd Volume of the Novel. The Third is also thinner than I intended and from the same cause. If one is en-

larged the other must undergo the same operation. But I am not so solicitous to escape the trouble of doing this, because I know I ought to fulfill my engagement, as anxious not to have delays arise in the publication at this late season of the year, & when the appearance of the work is from particular circumstances so material to my interest. Perhaps you may recollect that I mention'd to you When I sent up these volumes, that if the Printer found them deficient in Quantity, I desired he w^d take one or more chapters from the subsequent Volumes As I did not mind my labour. This I repeated more than once to Mr Stafford; I trust therefore you will not impute to me as an omission of punctuality, the deficiency in quantity, or the delay that the remedy must cause——
Bath, June 22nd [17]94

I am, Dear Sir,
with great esteem,
your most humble & oblig'd Ser^t,
Charlotte Smith

Yale University MS. Address: Thomas Cadell Esqre/ Strand/ London. Postmark: BATH; JU/ 23/ 94.

NOTES

1. Joseph Bell, bookseller at Oxford Street from 1792 to 1824, had published CS's most recent works, *The Old Manor House* (1793) and *The Wanderings of Warwick* (1794).
2. James Andrews, printer, at 10 Little Eastcheap, London, from 1784 to 1799.

To James Upton Tripp

[Bath, 23 June 1794]
Dear Sir,

I should have taken the liberty to have written to you while you were in London, but I was so ill that I had it not in my power. I shall now in about a week finally close with Cadell. My noble[1] is reduced to a ninepence, but I have reserved enough to settle my obligation to you whether it be thirty or forty pounds, which I wish to know with your first leisure——

I have been applying to Mr Robinson for him to let me have thirty five pounds advanced between the 2nd July next (<u>after</u> your obliging advance is repaid) and the 2nd of January, for the purpose of paying Lionels fees & sending him to Oxford,[2] but He will do nothing, & as I have absolutely no other resource than my own labour for the maintenance of the whole family, it is impossible that I can do it by mere dint of Bookmaking. I wish Mr Turner could be prevaild upon to write to Robinson representing the ruin of the

Boy if kept at home and my total inability to support him——I do not know that this w^{d} do any good, but I think of every thing——

I am, dear Sir, with unceasing gratitude for your kindness

y^{r} much oblig'd Ser^{t}
Charlotte Smith

Bath June 23rd 1794
M^{rs} De Foville is tolerably well, but I am still in extreme dread of the event after what Denman has said about her.

Petworth House Archives MS. Address: James Upton Tripp Esqre. No postmark.

NOTES

1. A gold coin in Edward III's reign, the noble was now worth only a few shillings. "Noble into ninepence" was a popular saying denoting wasteful spending.

2. CS had failed to raise Lionel's Oxford money from Robinson through Tripp in April, even while Egremont sponsored her nephew Nicholas Turner's enrollment.

To William Davies

[Bath, 25 June 1794]
Sir,

Imagining that Mr Cadell may be out of Town I write to you to say that as I shall complete the 4th Volume on Saturday (my daughter being thank God much recoverd in health & strength within these few days), I will proceed immediately after to enlarge the 2nd & if requisite the 3rd Volume in the best manner I can. I trust Mr Cadell, seeing how I am circumstanced, will not refuse me the fav^{r} of accepting a bill[1] for 10 G^{s} which I drew for yesterday at ten days in fa[vo]^{r} of Mr Barratt.[2] And that should I want the rest on account of my daughter, whose confinement I now expect every day, I am persuaded he will not refuse it, even if it should happen to be before the additional pages are deliver'd.

By the Coach of Thursday evening, or the Mail of friday, I shall send up a considerable quantity of MMS. Indeed all but the closing chapter & the prefaces, which will follow I trust about Monday so that the work will be complete save only the unforseen additions, in the course of next week——

The work I propose setting about as soon as this Novel is out of my hands is design'd for the use of Young people, who being too young to read novels or romances, are yet superior to the usual run of books offer'd to children. Walks in The Country, which shall give an opportunity of discoursing on Landscape on the simple parts of botany, and natural history, with short stories of suppositious persons (whose houses may be seen in the distance, or may be brought to recollection) such as may be at once interesting and moral, A Work less desultory than Mrs Barbaulds "Evenings at home" (which have had & still have an amazing sale)[3] & calculated for young persons three or four years older. Such is my plan, & I have a sketch of the first volume, which I think would work up into about 200 pages—Tho I am persuaded that, from the universal complaint that there is no such book, ~~that~~ any tolerable performance would have a great and continued sale (and a French Translation w^{d} be highly advantageous) And that therefore I might venture to print it myself, yet As I have not exactly the talents necessary to make bargains with printers & should probably be plagued about it, I had rather agree with Mr Cadell Junr & you—At a certain Sum on the delivery of the first volume, conditional advantages in proportion to the sale. I apprehend such a work might be usefully extended to three if not 4 [volumes] & a Volume at a time might be publish'd,[4] since [it] would not be like a novel, the chain of which cannot be broken by publishing at different times. Should we agree & I sh^{d} continue here, I apprehend you w^{d} employ Cruttwell[5] or some Bath Printer, in which case I would superintend the press. When you have consulted Mr Cadell & considerd the matter, I should be oblig'd to you to let me know M^{r} T Cadells & your sentiments as to the terms.

I am, Sir,
your most obed Ser^{t},
Charlotte Smith

Bath, 25th June 1794
Pray tell Mr Stafford that I much doubt whether I have quoted the passage right in the last parcel of MMS:

"There be some sports are painful" & &c

I did it only from Memory having no good Edition of Shakespeare here. It seems to me to be nonsense as I have remember'd it. I beg he will look; it is in the Tempest. A speech of Ferdinands.[6]

Osborn Collection MS, Yale University. Address: Mr Davies/ (Thos Cadells Esqre)/ Strand/ London. Postmark: BATH; JU/ 27/ {94}.

NOTES

1. CS habitually borrowed money from merchants and bankers against the sum that Thomas Cadell, Sr., or Cadell, Jr., and Davies would owe her for the completed work. Many of these receipts survive with the Cadell and Davies letters at the Beinecke Rare Book and Manuscript Library, Yale University, but not those for this transaction. Among the receipts is a tally sheet, undated but noting "Payments to Mrs. S." on 29 Aug. and 17 Sept. She rarely saw her earnings directly, but drew against Cadell and

Davies as if they were a bank. She had earned £200 for *The Banished Man* and £50 for *Rural Walks i.* They also handled £100 of an "India Bill," money from one of her sons.

2. Joseph Barratt, a bookseller at Bath.

3. Anna Laetitia (Aiken) Barbauld (1743–1825) contributed essays to her brother John Aiken's *Evenings at Home* (1792), a successful instructional book for younger children.

4. Instead of publishing this work as CS proposed, Cadell and Davies put forward *Rural Walks* in two volumes in 1795 and *Rambles Farther* in two volumes in 1796.

5. Richard Cruttwell, printer, bookseller, and publisher in Bath from 1773 until his death in 1799. Among other titles, he had printed *The Strangers Assistant and Guide* to the city of Bath, and he owned and edited *The Bath Chronicle.*

6. *The Tempest* 3.1.1. When her sources were in short supply, CS cited passages from memory. Here, despite her doubts, she is correct.

To Thomas Cadell, Jr., and William Davies

[Bath] 8th July [1794]

Mrs Smith, being much fatigued to night with getting ready the close of the Book of which about 30 pages more remain to be sent up in two days, cannot write to night fully to Mr Davies ~~to night~~ but will endeavour to do so tomorrow &, in the mean time, begs the bills she has drawn to the amount of 22 pounds:

in 12—Mayo
5 ——Williams
5 ——Barrett.[1]

At ten & fifteen days may be honourd it, being as she beleives nearly the whole 200£. She wishes at his Leisure to have the names of the subscribers & his resolution as to her new work, as this is now so very nearly out of hand. She wishes if agreeable to [Mr Cade]ll that it may now be advertised as being in the press—Which will be of use to her in particular view of her own—— But she also begs that should any body apply for her address, it may be said that it is not exactly known at Mr Cadell's shop.

Osborn Collection MS, Yale University. No address or postmark.

NOTE

1. Receipts dated later survive for the amounts drawn against Barratt, but there are none against Mayo. A receipt survives for five guineas drawn against Mr. Williams, Bath, 30 June 1794, and payable in fifteen days. Thomas Cadell, Esq., paid £5.5 on 28 July. All were probably Bath tradesmen. John Mayo and Co. were linen drapers in Market Place. Several Williamses were in various trades, including George, a draper, and Roger, a woolen draper, both in Abby-yard.

To the Reverend Charles Dunster[1]

[Bath] 16th July 1794

Dear Sir,

I am inexpressibly oblig'd to you for your kind Letter and kinder solicitude in regard to my health. I am persuaded Dr Falconer would with his usual goodness & humanity give me his advice, but I really make a conscience of troubling him when I am well convinced that unless he could "minister to the minds disease,"[2] it is merely being troublesome. The weight I have on my spirits is too heavy. My daughter is this morning taken ill again with symptoms that make me suppose the event I so much dread, yet wish for, is at hand. But these symptoms are far from being favourable.

I have been up all night and should really sink under fatigue and apprehension, if I was not resolved on her account to struggle as long as I can. Till this matter is decided, it were vain for me to hope for any relief from the most skillful advice, and when it is over, I have still so many difficulties to encounter that I believe attempts to recover my health will be very bootless——

I am very much oblig'd to you for speaking to Mr Tripp on my troublesome business. Every day I have intended writing to him, but I was afraid of being more troublesome than was necessary, and that I should hear from Cadell how the account stood. Cadell however is gone out of Town, and I have not a word from any of the people in the Shop. In the mean time, I have been under the necessity of overdrawing him I fear, for my Landladies here have been in want of Money, and my poor Girl who has been supported only by ice creams by order of Dr Denman, has of course required many little indulgences that have considerably added to my expense.

Besides which I have been disappointed in the Sum I hoped to raise among his Fathers relations (all of whom are people rolling in money)[3] in order to place Lionel at Oxford before the long vacation. And after humbling myself to beg as for an alms, I have obtain'd only fifteen Guineas. Mr Robinson (who suffer'd us to be robbed last year of 650£)[4] gives me ten Guineas, and Mr Boehm, who has been one principal cause of our calamities, who is immensely rich & has no family, most magnificently adds five, and even this they have not sent.

The Sum necessary is thirty five, and I have been compelled to send Lionel off to day with drafts of my own to Oxford, where a friend of mine waited on purpose to enter his name, pay the caution money[5] &c &c—— But I should not trouble you, Dear Sir, with this detail of wretchedness, were it not to beg the favour of you to represent my situation in regard to Cadell to Mr Tripp, and to beg the favor of him on my behalf ~~to~~ that if he has not sent in the draft to Cadell, to permit me in consideration of my distress'd situation to replace it with another at a longer date (as I am in treaty with Cadell & Davies for another work)[6] or to accept the payment from the proffits of the second Edition,[7] which I trust are as sure as the first in a fortnight after publication ——or finally to accept as security my next half years dividend. I know the ~~Sum~~ waiting will be of no consequence to him, but I fear in the present agitation of my mind being unable to explain to Mr Tripp the history of transactions with booksellers so as to clear up my meaning.

If he has sent the Bill in and received the Money, I shall then have overdrawn Cadell so considerably that perhaps he will return my draughts and I shall be pennyless, but in that case I would entreat him, Mr T., to have the goodness to give me a credit for thirty or forty pounds in any way he wd chuse till I can turn myself about and get over the present almost insupportable moment.

Perhaps my subscription may turn out better than I expect (at present it has produced hardly any thing) & if my Son should send me a remittance, it will enable me to stem the tide a little longer, but it is very uncertain & when I do get it, never arrives till September. At all events if I can work, I shall be able to repay Mr Tripp any indulgence he will shew me.

A thousand thanks to you for your attempts to relieve me from the house at Storrington. I have been dunned for the half years rent by Mr Browne,[8] who will without any scruple put in an Execution if it is not paid, & this is what I expect to hear & must submit to. I shall get some friend or other to save my books which are the only things of any value in the house. I was in hopes from the prospects my Lawyers have held out to me that The Chancery suit which I am driven into would by this time be in such a state that I might petition for maintenance & for the removal of Prettyjohn, the Man whom Mr Robinson suffers yearly to plunder us with impunity. But to day, by way of a cordial to my spirits, the Attorney in London[9] informs me that nothing can be done till November. He is not sure it can then & is surprised at my impatience when I ought to know the tediousness of a Chancery suit! God help me!

Alas, dear Sir, I shall tire you out as I have done other of my friends I fear,[10] & I am sure I have not the least right to intrude upon you with all this because you allow me to address you on literary matters. But I know you have feeling & humanity enough not only to forgive me but to serve me in what I have ask'd with Mr Tripp, & I entreat an early answer as my uncertainty about money matters makes me so uneasy that it disables me from bearing my other terrors. Allow me to offer my respects to Mrs Dunster & to remain, Dear Sir,

your most oblig'd Sert
Charlotte Smith

I rejoice to hear that you are now so well. I begin to envy those ev[________s]hades[11] & green downs. All is burnt up, & [________ere]—but local circumstances have lost their effect on me.

Petworth House Archives MS. Address: The Revd Charles Dunster/ Petworth/ Sussex. Postmark: BATH JY/{16}/94.

NOTES

1. See Biographical Notes.

2. *Macbeth* 5.3.40.

3. The wealthiest, Edmund Boehm, married to BS's niece Dorothy Elizabeth Berney, was a director of the East India Company (1784) and the South Sea Company (1793). Thomas Dyer, the second husband of BS's sister Mary, and BS's nephew Richard Smith were financially secure. (See Genealogical Chart.)

4. That is, earnings from the trust holdings in Barbados, Mapp's and Gay's plantations. Mapp's earned £626.8.2½ in 1791 and £686.19.11½ in 1797 (see CS to Egremont, 18 Nov. 1802). CS was persuaded that a similar amount of money was kept back for other purposes in 1793 that should have been used to pay off the debt on Gay's (see CS to Egremont, 21 July 1803), but by then she sometimes confused the years, mentioning 1792 in subsequent letters to Egremont (e.g., 12 Oct. 1803).

5. A security deposit, especially for a student entering college or an Inn of Court. Having failed to enroll Lionel in Oxford in April, this time CS secured the money by drawing on her account with Thomas Cadell, Sr. (see CS to Cadell, Sr., 18 July 1794). Unfortunately, Cadell was in the process of retiring. His successors—Thomas Cadell, Jr., and William Davies—did not appreciate her taking this latitude.

University records show that Lionel matriculated at Oxford on 16 July 1794. The duration of his stay is not known.

6. In Sept. Cadell, Jr., and Davies refused *Rosalie,* published in 1795 by Sampson Low as *Montalbert.* They must have accepted *Rural Walks* (1795) about this time.

7. Of *The Banished Man.*

8. On John W. Browne, see CS to James Upton Tripp, 17 Jan. 1793, n. 1. CS attempted to raise £25, her semiannual rent, from Tripp in Dec. 1793. She may have failed and then talked Browne into another arrangement, for she writes of paying Browne "so much money weekly & regularly during the whole year" (see CS to Tripp, 18 May 1794).

9. Probably Charles Bicknell, CS's own lawyer for many years.

10. Such as William Hayley. In the spring of 1793, CS apparently drew money on him before clearly obtaining his permission to do so.

11. The seal is torn away and the words in the postscript and the date in the postmark are lost.

To Thomas Cadell, Sr.

[Bath, 18 July 1794]
Dear Sir

I yesterday sent up the close of the 4th Volume which will arrive in Town this afternoon. I have now therefore completed my engagement, save only the additional pages necessary to the quantity of the 2nd Volume, in which (as there is only one piece of Poetry in the other three volumes) I wish'd to have inserted another ~~one~~ & still hope to do it if my belov'd Augusta, whose precarious situation seems now very near its crisis, does well. But my fears for her & the fatigue I undergo as I am with her night and day greatly affects me in my present state of health so lately restored by the Bath Waters.

I find that my Account with Mr Tripp is settled another way & therefore that there remain'd a Ballance to me of 27 or 30£ on the two hundred. This, as It was absolutely necessary for me to send my Son to be enter'd at St Johns Oxon before the long vacation, I have drawn for, for his kind relations & honest Trustees wd do nothing; & if it happens that I have exceeded my due, I must apply the little that the subscription may have produced to answer it, as I trust that Mr De Foville and I shall make the drawings together (as he draws delightfully and it will be a great saving), and I have directed some money arising from the same source in Ireland to be paid into your hands, besides which I expect some on the same account from other quarters—— I hope & beleive I have a considerable remittance on its way from Bengal,[1] but except that, I have no resource but my own application, as Mr Robinson persists in refusing me the least support for my family whose property he has now held eleven years.[2] You may imagine what a task I have & what must often be my situation.

Messrs Cadell & Davies offer me 50£ pr Vol. for the Work I propos'd, which certainly is a fair price as to the labour because it is less labourious than a Novel, but I am persuaded the proffits will be more. However, if it should answer to them the sanguine expectations that have been entertain'd of such an undertaking, I have no doubt but that I might place the same confidence in their generousity as I have done on yours. I therefore accept the terms & will set about the work as soon as the prefaces, &ct, to "the Banishd Man" are sent up, which I hope to dispatch to day if my daughter[3] continues thro it as she is now. In regard to the Printing, all I meant by naming its being printed here was that I could correct the press myself, & I thought your house might have a connection with some Bookseller here who has a press. It is not at all an object to me, as even my stay here is very uncertain. I am, Dear Sir,

your most obedt & oblig'd Sert
Charlotte Smith

Bath 18th July [17]94

Mrs Smith is much oblig'd to Mr Davies for the care he took of her Letters to India and requests the favour of him to forward instantly any that may be sent to Mr Cadell's late House in the Strand, & by the most expeditious conveyance.

Osborn Collection MS, Yale University. Address: Thomas Cadell Esqre/ Strand/ London/ In his absence to Messrs Cadell & Davies. Postmark: BATH; JY/ 19/ 94.

NOTES

1. At least £100 from her eldest son William, a Bengal civil servant in India.
2. John Robinson, with Anthony Parkin, was appointed trustee to the estate in 1783, when BS was dismissed as executor of the will because he had mismanaged the funds.
3. Lucy, CS's second daughter, was with her in Bath and took over Charlotte Mary's job of writing out fair copy of her mother's works for the printer.

To Thomas Cadell, Sr.

[Bath, 22 July 1794]
Dear Sir,

Before I re[ceive]d your account & on a loose reckoning of my own, I had drawn for 33£: vis. Bull—£15.15; Pickwick—£10; Barratt—£7.7,[1] when I had in fact only £24.3. This leaves me near nine pounds in your debt. I cannot now withdraw the Bills, nor can I replace ~~them~~ the Sum till I receive the Money I expect from Ireland, or from a friend who is endeavouring to farther my interest. I beg the favor of you not to return the Bills but to give me credit for the difference till I can make it up.

My mind is at present in such a state that I really know not what I say or do—— Mrs De Foville continues still in so dangerous a way, and the event is so very uncertain in the opinion of Mr Perry[2] who attends her, as well as in that of Dr Denman, that nothing but the necessity of my keeping up an appearance of courage on her account could induce me to ~~keep~~ struggle with the terror that overwhelms me. I have no consolation but that of having procured for her every assistance & every comfort possible, for ill as I can afford it, considerd in a general light, Every thing I can do will be cheap if I can but save her—for should I lose her—It is presumptuous to say I could not bear it, for perhaps I must, but I do not know <wether> it would not put a final end to all my troubles. I am always so unfortunate that I think I have not, for some reason or other, any thing but misery to expect. This would indeed compleat the bitterness of my destiny, for tho I have so many other Children, this dear Child is the most precious. Nor do I reproach myself with this partiality as a crime, for the others have never found it make any difference to them, & I think it is not caprice as <u>they</u> all equally love her—& her Uncle,[3] his Wife, & even many unconnected persons idolize her, which must be the effect of her disposition. As to her husband, he worships the ground she treads upon & is in a state of suffering equald only by mine. God Almighty knows how long we shall be in this suspence. It cannot be very long as she is at her full time.

If I get an hour's respite this afternoon, I will copy the preface &c which I have finish'd & will send them up by the post tomorrow. In the mean time, I send you a receipt for the money for the copy right of "the Banish'd Man," which I suppose will be necessary, tho there is no longer any thing to fear from poor Mr Smith who contents himself with taking my fortune, or considerably more than <u>half</u> of it, & desires me to do with the children as well as I can. There are but three things that can releive me—Chancery, where I have at length a suit in some forwardness;[4] the death of my (own) Father's Widow, which will be some encrease to my fortune;[5] & remittances from India. But these last are not only uncertain, but I receive them with pain as the price of my dearest William's banishment & as kindness which will lengthen that banishment, for so high is the interest he cd make of money in India that <u>we</u> ought to have sent him his Grandfather's Legacy long since instead of receiving Money from him.

Have the goodness to desire Mr Davies add to the list of subscribers[6] the following names sent from a friend

Captain Mackelean—Royal Engineers ——— 3 Copies
Captain Burn—Marines ——————— 1
Mr Fowler, Princes Street, Hanover Square —— 1
Mrs Fenn. Clapton—1
Miss Aldersey, Seward Street
Mrs Carey—Woburn 1
Rev'd T. <Choxton>. 1
Miss Gutteridge, Luton 1
Miss Humberstone Ampthill
Revd F. Festing, Lethbury, Bucks
Revd S. Greatheed 5 copies
Mrs Greatheed 2 copies

I am, dear Sir, with a perfect sense of your kindness,

your much oblig'd Sevt,
Charlotte Smith

Bath 22nd July 1794

Yale University MS. Address: Thomas Cadell Esqre/ Strand/ London. Postmark: BATH; July/ 24/ 94.

NOTES

1. Receipts survive for two amounts drawn on 16 July: seven guineas on Barratt

payable in seven days, which Cadell, Sr., repaid as £7.7 on 28 July, and £10 on Pickwick payable in ten days, which Cadell, Sr., repaid on 5 Aug. There is no receipt for the amount to Bull. Like Joseph Barratt, Lewis Bull, Old Rooms, was a bookseller at Bath. Eleazer Pickwick owned the White Hart, a popular, luxurious inn at Bath (Barbeau, *Life and Letters at Bath,* p. 52; Peach, *Historic Houses in Bath*), but the Pickwick bill might have been to Thomas Hulbert Pickwick for clothing.

2. Caleb Hillier Parry, M.D., was a prominent physician at Bath for more than forty years (1755–1822). He ordered four copies of *Rambles Farther* in 1796. CS's *Elegiac Sonnets ii* includes "Sonnet LXV. To Dr. Parry of Bath, with Some Botanic Drawings which had been made some years."

3. Augusta was a favorite of CS's brother Nicholas Turner and with her husband was often a guest of Turner and his wife Sarah.

4. The earl of Egremont and duchess of Devonshire, sometime patrons of CS, sponsored this suit. See CS to Cadell, Jr., and Davies, 6 Nov. 1794.

5. Of the £7,000 settled on Charlotte Turner before and after her marriage, £2,000 were to come to her on the death of her father's widow, the wealthy Miss Henrietta Meriton. Mrs. Turner's dislike of her new stepdaughter led CS's father Nicholas Turner, Sr., and her aunt Lucy Towers to arrange for Charlotte's ill-considered marriage to BS. After Turner's death his widow married Mr. Chafys and lived on for many years. CS describes the fortune of £7,000 in CS to Egremont, 12 Jan. 1802.

6. Possibly owing to the delay in publishing *Elegiac Sonnets ii,* only two from this list, the Reverend and Mrs. Samuel Greatheed (see Biographical Notes), are listed as subscribers.

To the Reverend Samuel Greatheed

[Bath, 23 July 1794]
Sir,

Nothing but the dreadful anxiety I have been in about my daughter, who has been in a most precarious & alarming state, should so long have prevented my acknowleging your most polite & friendly Letter with the enclosure of a ten pound bank post Bill.[1] Accept my very sincere, tho hasty, acknowledgements for the trouble you have had the goodness to take, & allow me to avail myself of some future day to express more fully the sense I have of your unmerited attention. My poor Girl is not yet in her bed, & tho the symptoms which have for some days terrified me almost to frenzy are abated, I fear her sufferings will be long and severe.

I cannot but express, hurried as I am, my concern to hear that the admirable mind of so invaluable a Man as Mr Cowper is still in a state so very distressing to his friends & so injurious to the moral interest of mankind—— From Mr Hayley, I hardly ever hear as I used to do, & he never said more to me than naming, at first, the unhappy circumstance and his own solicitude &, since, that our excellent friend continued still in a state of mental indisposition, but that there were hopes of his speedy restoration as his bodily health was restored.[2]

As amidst many & very heavy troubles of my own, I cannot but feel the liveliest interest in what relates to the restoration of a mind so superior, you will oblige me greatly, dear Sir, if you will favor me with some intelligence on this sad subject of general regret, should I be so fortunate as to hear from you again. I beg my Compliments to M[rs] Greatheed & shall esteem myself happy to have the pleasure of forming an acquaintance at some future period, which an unlucky accident deprived me of at Brighthelmston.

I am, Sir,
your most obed[t] and oblig'd Ser[t],
Charlotte Smith

10 Pulteney Street, Bath, (Wednesday) 23rd July [17]94

Neilson Campbell Hannay Collection, Manuscripts Division, Department of Rare Books and Special Collections, Princeton University Library. Address: <Ans?> 17 Nov/ The Rev[d] S. Greatheed/ Newport Pagnel/ Bucks. Postmark: BATH: JY/ 24/ 94.

NOTES

1. Greatheed and his wife each subscribed to *Elegiac Sonnets ii.* The bank post bill for £10 would not, however, have covered the cost of his five copies and her two (see CS to Thomas Cadell, Sr., 22 July 1794). This money may have been an outright gift. CS often mentioned the generosity of friends, and her language here—especially "unmerited attention"—is not that of author to subscriber.

2. In Jan. 1794, William Cowper sank into a depression that never fully abated. Hayley had last visited Cowper in May 1794, and knew that he was not improving (King, *William Cowper,* p. 264). It is a clear sign of Hayley's estrangement from CS (first mentioned in CS to Joseph Cooper Walker, 30 Apr. 1794) that he had not yet told her.

To James Upton Tripp

[Bath, 27 July 1794]
Dear Sir,

I am afraid by my not hearing from you that all your friendly solicitude on my behalf cannot prevent your thinking me a most troublesome & intrusive correspond[t]. My dear Unhappy girl, after being attended by two of the most emminent Accoucheurs[1] here & being 70 hours in the greatest peril & in most excruciating tortures, was deliver'd on thursday night of a very fine boy,[2] but it was so much bruised & injurd that it lingerd till this morning & then died in my arms—A victim I think of what happend at Storrington & another victim of the Trustees.

She is so weak that we keep from her the death of the infant. What the effect will be when she must know it, I tremble to think of. Perhaps I shall lose her too. I have not been in bed since this day sennight & do not very well know why or what I write, but I believe it is to request the favor of you, if Browne should put in an Execution into the House at Storrington for 25£ as I conclude he will do, to purchase at least my books till I can redeem them.

The great expenses to which this unfortunate illness will ~~reduce~~ expose me, as I cannot give the two Surgeons for such an attendance less than seven guineas a piece, will reduce me to dreadful straits, & I am out of all heart &

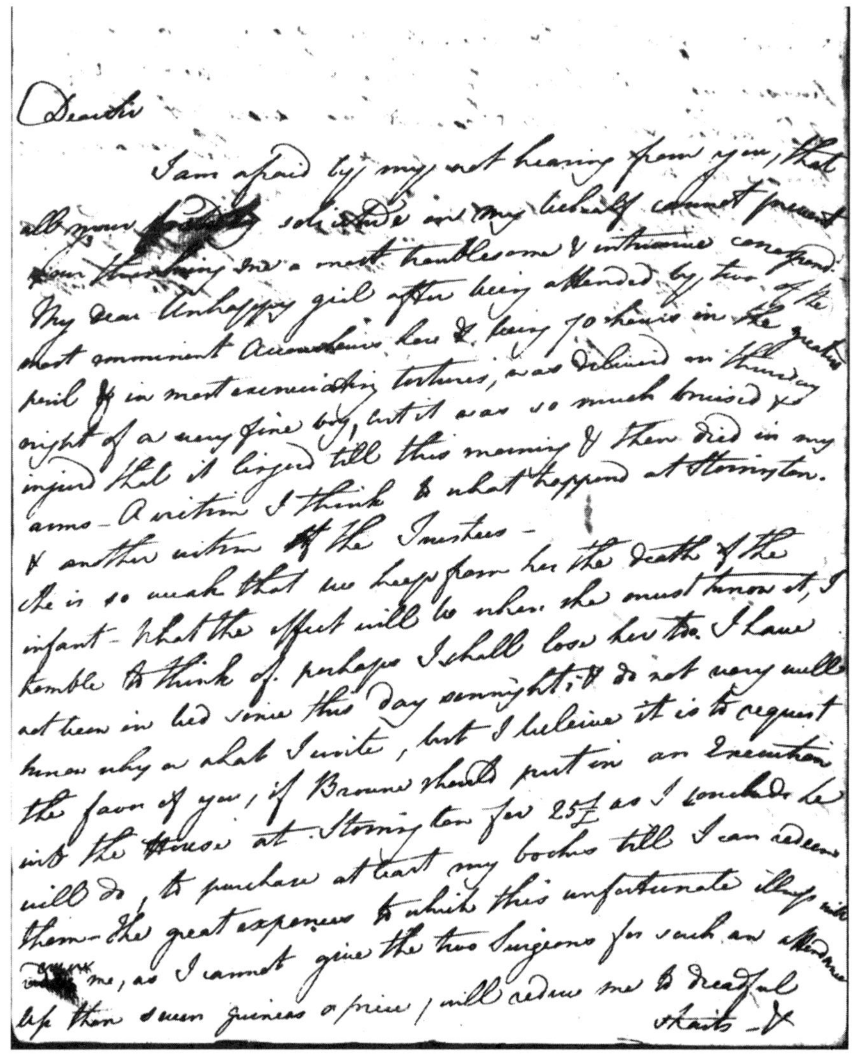

Dear Sir

I am afraid by my not hearing from you, that all your ~~[illegible]~~ solicitude in my behalf cannot prevent ~~[illegible]~~ in a most troublesome & inhuman [illegible]. My dear Unhappy girl after being attended by two of the most eminent Accoucheurs here & being 70 hours in the greatest peril & in most excruciating tortures, was delivered on thursday night of a very fine boy, but it was so much bruised & injured that it lingered till this morning & then died in my arms — A victim I think to what happened at Storrington. & another victim of the Trustees — She is so weak that we keep from her the death of the infant — What the effect will be when she must know it, I tremble to think of. perhaps I shall lose her too. I have not been in bed since this day sennight & do not very well know why or what I write, but I believe it is to request the favor of you, if Browne should put in an Execution into the House at Storrington for 25£ as I conclude he will do, to purchase at least my books till I can redeem them — The great expenses to which this unfortunate illness will ~~[illegible]~~ me, as I cannot give the two Surgeons for such an attendance less than seven guineas a piece, will reduce me to dreadful straits — &

Figure 3. Letter to James Upton Tripp, 27 July 1794.

hope. Misery never ceases to pursue me. But poverty alone I could bear. My head aches so much I cannot do more but beg to know in what way I shall send you the repayment of the Money that Cadell did not pay.

I am, Dear Sir,
your most oblig'd Ser^{t}
Charlotte Smith

July 27th [17]94
Pray send the enclos'd.

Petworth House Archives MS. No address or postmark. Photograph by Michael Moore, by permission of the Right Honorable the Lord Egremont, Petworth House Archives, West Sussex Record Office.

NOTES

1. Attendants at a birth; obstetricians (Thomas Denman and Caleb Hillier Parry).
2. Augusta's son was born Thursday, 24 July, and died Sunday morning, 27 July.

To Thomas Cadell, Sr.

[Bath, 30 July 1794]
Dr Sir,

I beg you will accept my sincere thanks for y^{r} Letter which I received yesterday. My belov'd Augusta is pronounced out of danger unless any thing happens very unexpectedly. She was inform'd last night of the death of her Child which expired a few moments after I seal'd my Letter to you. She bore the intelligence with more fortitude than we expected & is this morning calm & reasonable——

The Letter I had the comfort of receiving from Bengal, forwarded from your house, containd an excellent account of both my Sons and a Bill of 100£ from the eldest of which I have received only the 3rd part, as it is triplicate. I am ignorant enough not to know whether I can get this discounted or whether I must wait for the other two. Here follows a copy of it, & I shall be very much oblig'd to Mr Davies to enquire for me if your Banker or any other will discount it for me, as my expences are such as compell me to get it done speedily.

> 3^{d} Exchange for £100. St^{g}——.
> Calcutta the 14th Jany. 1794[1]
> Six months after sight of this my Third bill of Exchange (the first & second of the same tener[2] and date not being paid) please to pay to

Mrs Charlotte Smith on order the sum of one hundred Pounds Sterling, for value re[ceive]d—& place the same to account as p^r advice from

Gent^n
y^rs &c
I. B. Esteve

To
Messrs Richard Muilman & Co[3]
London

If ~~your~~ Mr Davies can get it done for me, I will send the Bill up immediately & request your house in the mean time to pay five or ten pounds for me if I should want it (as I fear I shall) to be deducted from this.[4] I have 20 Guineas to pay the two Accoucheurs in consequence of the extraordinary difficulty of the Case and the length of their attendance, & it is a matter I cannot put off longer than the 9th or 10th day.

My mind is now so much easier that I shall be able to send up the prefaces &c immediately, & I hope to be soon after alive enough to begin arranging the materials I have for my "Rural Walks"—— This supply is a great releif to me, but not enough to allow me, circumstanced as I am, to be idle. I am, Dr Sir,

with many thanks for your kindness,
your oblig'd Ser^t,
Charlotte Smith

30th July 1794

Yale University MS. Address: Thomas Cadell Esqre/ Strand/ London. Postmark: BATH; July 31, 94.

NOTES

1. From William Towers Smith, assistant judge at Ramghyr, 200 miles from Calcutta, in 1794.
2. Obsolete form of *tenor,* the stated value of a bill or banknote.
3. Merchants at 46 Old Broad Street, London.
4. Cadell and Davies's reply was copied at the bottom of this letter:

> In Answer to your Letter of Wednesday last, addressed to Mr Cadell, we take the earliest opportunity of acquainting you that if you will be pleased to send us the Bill on the Muilmans we will ourselves immediately on its being accepted discount it, but must request that no Bills may be drawn upon us in the mean Time.

To Thomas Cadell, Jr., and William Davies

[Bath, 3 August 1794]
Gent^{n}

I enclose you the India Bill, & thank you for your readiness to ~~accept~~ discount it. I will draw no bills which shall be payable before such acceptance after which you will have of course no objection to pay them, but I must entreat the fav^{r} of you to keep this account seperate from every other, as part of this money belongs to Miss Smith by desire of her Brother,[1] & whatever Bills more than my due Mr Cadell has paid for me, I will replace within a fortnight by the Volume I am to furnish you with. It would be want of integrity in me to apply this Sum otherwise than as my Son directs, as it is in fact Trust money.[2] I am in great haste (& begging early notice of the acceptance of the Bill),

Gent^{n}, your most obed^{t} & oblig'd Ser^{t},
Charlotte Smith

Bath. 3rd August 1794
My packet for Mr Stafford cannot be up before Teusday on account of the multiplicity of business I have to day in writing Letters.

Huntington MS (HM10815). Address: Messrs Cadell & Davies/ Strand/ London. Postmark: BATH; AU/ 4/ 94.

NOTES

1. William sent the money. Charlotte Mary was on good terms with both brothers throughout their lives.
2. It is not clear how this amount was trust money.

To William Davies

[Bath, 20 August 1794]

To Mr Davies

Sir,

I received with some surprize the account you sent me In which I observe that, contrary to what I said to your House when I ask'd if you could get the Bill on Muilman's &c discounted, you have mingled it in a general account. I then inform'd you that if you could oblige me, it must not be mingled with any other Account, as part of the money belong'd to Miss Smith. This entirely cancels the fav^{r} I owed Mr Cadell when, in consideration of my very greatly distress'd situation, he promis'd he w^{d} not return the Bills which I knew not that I had overdrawn, as I could not foresee that every charge w[d] be set against the Sum I had earned by the Copy right of the Banish'd Man & that M[r] Elmsley[1] &c were to be paid with[ou]t [3.19.0][2] any question made to me.

You will allow me also to remark that the Sum charged for A set of my works publish'd by Cadell—Vis. Emmeline, Ethelinde, & Celestina in thirteen Volumes, & one book of Sonnets bound the same—is a mischarge, for M[r] Cadell, as I can immediately convince him when I get his Letters which I have sent for from home, made me a present of them. M[r] Hayley will recollect my telling him what an obliging present I re[ceive][d] from M[r] Cadell, & I wrote in each of the Books the date & a memorandum that he had given them me, which I really thought did him honor. This charge [2.14.6][2] therefore you will be so good as to expunge.

I imagined that I was working to clear my debt thus unconsciously incurred with y[r] House & have almost done half the new work,[3] hoping that I should shift on the remains of what was left of my Son's remittance, till it could be done entirely. If, however, the account is so changed, I must, notwithstanding my very earnest wish to continue with y[r] House in preferrence to every other, endeavour to make some other bargain elsewhere which may be more immediately productive—& I have no doubt of procuring the acceptance of fifty pounds, at a Month or six weeks, even from the Booksellers here, when I can produce so large a portion of the work done, & know, that for such a work there is a demand so great in this place that it w[d] answer to me even to print it on my own account. I proposed making, with the Assistance of the Chevalier de Foville, a French Translation of this work[4] as it went on, & was this day about to write to you to request you would enquire for me of M[r] Elmsley whether he w[d] purchase when done a French Work of this sort for which, I will answer for it, there will be a yet greater demand for than the English. Would to God I had money & time to publish both on my own account. I am very well convinced I should make twice the money I shall do in selling it, however advantageously I may dispose of it.

But cruelly circumstanced as I am, I must submit to such terms as I can make for present accommodation. My daughter has had so long & so dangerous an illness that my expenses have greatly exceeded every calculate I made, & the application of my Son's draft thus made cannot but extremely distress me, As I know not when the second hundred he is <to> send me will arrive. You will be so good as to send me by the return of the Post a list of the names of such Subscribers as have enter'd them at y[r] Shop to y[e] second Volume of Sonnets. I ask'd for it before, but imagined it escaped your recollection—— You will be pleas'd also to give me an answer to the question I make relative to "Rural walks" that, as I am reduced to four or five pounds,

I may take immediate measures accordingly before famine stares me in the face. I am, Sir,

your most obed[t] humble Ser[t],
Charlotte Smith

The enclos'd is the whole of the Banish'd Man, which sh[d] [have][5] been sent sooner, but verses are not always ready at hand in con[fusion &] distress like mine—— I have received some o[rders] to be sent to your shop for the New Novel, but I imagine it will be time enough to give you the list when the day of publication is announced—— —— From The number allow'd me, you will be so good as to deduct a set for Miss Smith, Islington.[6]

Yale University MS. Address: M[r] Davies—/ Mess[rs] Cadell Jun[r] & Davies/ Opposite the end of/ Catharine Street/ Strand/ London. Postmark: BATH; AU/ 20/ 94.

NOTES

1. Bookseller in the Strand, specializing in French books. Later in this letter, CS explains a plan to propose a translation of *Rural Walks* to him.

2. These sums were written in lightly under the words they follow here.

3. *Rural Walks.* By this time, she had begun *Rosalie,* published as *Montalbert.*

4. De Foville probably did not complete this. A French translation of *Rural Walks* and *Rambles Farther* combined appeared in 1798 while he was still in England: *Les Promenades Champêtres: Dialogues à l'usage des jeunes personnes; Traduit de l'Anglais de Charlotte Smith* (Paris: chez Maradan, Libraire, rue du Cimetière André-des-Arts No. 9, an VII [1798]). No translator is given.

5. The edge of the page was torn away here and where words are supplied in subsequent lines. "Confusion & distress" might be construed as "constant distress" or "continual distress."

6. Charlotte Mary often stayed with her cousin, the Reverend Richard Smith, at Islington; he held the living at St. Mary Islington where CS hoped to place one of her sons.

To William Davies

Bath. Aug[t] 25th, 1794
Sir,

I have drawn in favour of M[r] Barrett for ten Guineas more than the fifteen which you inform'd me was due to me.[1] I expect £100 in a few days, but its arrival is uncertain. If it comes as I rather think this week, I will close my account entirely with you, but otherwise I must beg the fav[r] of you to let it remain open till the 1st Volume of Rural Walks is done, which will be [done][2] shortly. If I should overdraw you, all that can [be d]one is to send my Bills back again, but from my present expectations, I flatter myself that will not be the case. At present, you are indemnified by the Money in yr hands on account of the Subscription, & I do assure you that, before I ~~drew~~ receiv'd the 100£ Bill from Bengal, Mr Cadell[3] had agreed to let the 27£ (I think) that I had unconsciously overdrawn go to the account of the intended publication. I will look out his Letter if you doubt it.

I am very sorry to be compelled to ask all these favours of any Bookseller, but I know not only that it is not unusual for the miserable race of Authors to have these accommodations, but that Your House will never lose one shilling by granting me such small advances as I may want: I should not now have wanted any, but that my own and my daughter's illness has put me to such immense expences. She is now order'd to Bristol hot wells, having all the symptoms of a decline, & I send her thither tomorrow without being able to attend her because I cannot immediately settle for my lodgings & other things due here. All this time, and while I am expos'd to such dreadful inconveniencies, my Children's estate, on which I have a Mortgage of 3000£, is making seven or nine hundred pounds, not one farthing of which we receive, not even the interest of my money. Nor can I obtain any answer from Mr Robinson and Mr Parkin when any money is likely to come or what they mean to do to recover from their agent 750£ which they know he embezzled last year, while I and my children absolutely wanted the necessaries of life & had no resource but my writing, & while my Son Charles had no home but my House to receive him (& a Servant) Lamed & maimed as he was & in a state that doubled my expences. All this is certainly nothing to my Bookseller, but I mention it to shew you how difficult it is for me to act otherwise than I have done & that I have no design to take any undue advantage of the liberal &, I must say, friendly disposition that Mr Cadell has always shewn towards me.

As the new publication is in its form unlike any other of mine inasmuch as it is in Dialogues for the most part, and as I imagine Your Printers are now much at leisure, I should be glad, if it suited you, to send up what is done in a few days in order to have a proof sent me before I go from hence, as it is possible when I am able to get away, & if my poor Girl should get better, that we may cross the Severn and go into Wales for a few weeks in which case I could not so conveniently see such a specimen. The first Volume will consist of seven dialogues—or Chapters; 5 of these are done and, I believe, correct enough to be printed immediately off.

With them, if you please, I will send a considerable part of another Work, A Novel in two Volumes[4] about the size of the Vicar of Wakefield. I have been in treaty with Mr Cruttwell for Printing it here, having an inclination to try the experiment of printing a work on my own account. But I find there are difficulties as to credit for the paper & other things which would tieze me, especially if I should be at any distance, I own I should like much to print it here, but that, all things consider'd, I had rather sell it. I have reason to beleive Mr Dilly[5] w^d^ purchase it, but I should certainly prefer your House. My terms would be these. The Copy right for 80 G^s^ if I had any money advanced; for 100, if I produce the MSS finish'd, & these I know I can get. I mention sending the MMS that you may see, not only the forwardness it is in with[ou]^t^ having interfered with the other, but be assured that it is of my writing, of which there were some doubts when the Banish'd Man was first in question between me and Mr Cadell, & indeed it is difficult to beleive that, surrounded as I am with troubles, I can write as I do. Favor me with your answer. I am, Sir,

y^r^ oblig'd & obed^t^ Ser^t^ Charlotte Smith

People here are distracted for the New Novel,[6] & I am worried to death. Pray send mine down early.

Yale University MS. Address: Mr Davies/ Messrs Cadell & Davies/ Strand/ London. Postmark: BATH; AUG/ 26/ 94.

NOTES

1. No receipt against Barratt for this amount survives.

2. In this line and the next, the letter's seal obscures a word.

3. Presumably, Thomas Cadell, Sr., to whom she had been writing. Though retired, he kept a hand in the business; Cadell, Jr., was not involved in it at first. The £100 mentioned earlier was from William at Ramghyr, several hundred miles from Calcutta in Bengal. CS never names Ramghyr; she writes instead of Bengal and Calcutta when referring to William.

4. *Rosalie,* later *Montalbert,* was three volumes long and purchased by Sampson Low (see CS to Cadell, Jr., and Davies, 6 Nov. 1794).

5. Charles Dilly, bookseller and publisher (1739–1807), in partnership with his brother Edward (1732–1779). Their house was a meeting place for literary men in London. Charles Dilly published Boswell's *Life of Johnson* (1791) and became master of the Stationers' Company in 1803. He published none of CS's works.

6. *The Banished Man.*

To Thomas Cadell, Jr.

[Bath] 29th Aug^t^ [17]94
Sir

By tomorrow's or at farthest by Monday's Coach, I will send up a quantity of the work Call'd Rural Walks, and would have done it by the Coach of this evening but that My daughter being gone to Bristol, Hot Wells,[1] the

Chevalier de Foville, who is making a French Translation[2] of the work, took with him the greatest part of it—— I must go over there to day, as she still continues so ill that he has sent for me: & I will dispatch it from thence, if I am under the necessity of staying longer than till tomorrow—— I will also send 70 or 80 pages of my new novel intended to be in two volumes, which are all I have corrected, but which will enable you to judge how far it may be agreeable to you to engage for it——

I receiv'd the 6 copies of the Banish'd Man in due course. I observe with extreme vexation such numerous errors of the press as I never observed before in any work. It is very certain that Mr Stafford's compositor cannot read my hand, Almost universally mistaking a's for o's, or o's for a's, but it is astonishing that the corrector of the press did not detect this & that he has suffer'd many words to pass which are not ~~any~~ English or any other language under Heaven—Now tho I may have written very ill (& indeed I inform'd Mr Stafford that from having the Rhumatism in my hand I could not write as I usd to do), yet as I never could have meant to have written words that do not exist, the corrector should most certainly have changed these. The Stopping is in many places so sadly managed as totally to alter the meaning and sense of many sentences. And as to the French, Italian, and Latin sentences, they are made sadly incorrect, & of that perhaps the discredit will fall on me——

One of the copies you sent me down is imperfect from being bound wrong. This I shall keep to correct, in the hope and belief that the book will not be very long before it will be in a second Edition. I shall therefore send you up this set & beg to have it replaced by another, which I request the favour of you to send to Dublin by the most immediate convenience directed thus—"To the Honourable Mrs St Leger,[3] Park Street, Dublin— & write in it "From the Author"—— Also a set to Joseph Cooper Walker Esqre, Eccles Street, Dublin, with the same memorandum. Of the 3 sets that will then remain, I beg you will be so good as to send one to Miss Bridger,[4] Easebourn near Midhurst, Sussex, by the Midhurst and Petworth Coach, & the other by the same conveyance & in the same parcel directed to Mr Nicholas Turner, Fittleworth, Petworth, Sussex. There will then remain one set which you will be so good as to keep till I want it. I have two or three orders for other sets to purchase to be sent, but I have mislaid the Letters, & indeed this lingering illness of my daughter's distracts me, for as soon as I think her a little better she has constantly relapsed, & I know not what I shall do for her, no advice, tho I have had the best that could be procured, having yet done her any good.

From a Letter I receiv'd last week, I had reason to believe that in the course of this I should receive an hundred pounds (not from the Trustees).

I still think I shall have it in the course of ten days, when I shall send up fifty to you to answer any bills that may be sent in before the final delivery of the Volume on which You have advanced me £12—— & till I either make that delivery or send up the cash, I ~~only~~ beg you will only decline accepting such, but saying that you will pay them when due, if you are in cash. This will afford me the accommodation I want, without any risk or inconvenience to you. I do not know whether I have explain'd myself clearly, as I am so vex'd and hurried & must now set out for the hot wells. I am, Sir,

your obed^t humble Ser^t Charlotte Smith

Yale University MS. Address: Mr Cadell Junr/ Strand/ London. Postmark: BATH; AU/ 30/ 94.

NOTES

1. Augusta and de Foville had gone to Clifton, Hot Wells, a known retreat for consumptives, for her health.

2. Never published; see CS to William Davies, 20 Aug. 1794, n. 4.

3. The Honorable Mrs. St. Leger (CS also spelled her name "Sentleger") lived at Park Street, Dublin, and at Donnerayle (also CS's spelling). She may be Anne (d. 1809), daughter of Charles Blakeney and wife of Richard St. Leger (1756–1840), a colonel in the army and younger brother of Hayes St. Leger, second Viscount Doneraile. CS may have met her through Henrietta O'Neill; on 24 Sept. 1794 (letter to Cadell, Jr., and Davies) CS describes writing to Mrs. Sentleger for a copy of O'Neill's poem to be printed in *Rural Walks.*

4. A friend who once took George to Mr. Parsons' school (see CS to James Upton Tripp, 16 Aug. 1793, and n. 2).

To Thomas Cadell, Jr.

[Bath, 5 September 1794]
Sir,

I enclose you a draft for thirty five pounds which will be due to me <u>and must be paid</u> on the 2nd of January <u>[17]95</u>. This is to secure you the pay^t of the money drawn on you[1] <u>if</u> (which will not happen) ~~it~~ Bills should become due before I send you the rural walks, entire. I sent up two Chapters from Bristol yesterday morning which I hope you received—— In regard to the ~~rest~~ new Novel, my proposal was to take 80 Gs for two Volumes if I had money advanced, <u>100</u>, if I deliver'd each Volume entire. You now probably know whether you will accept the work on these terms. I have only to say, not by way of influencing, but of <u>hastening</u> your determination, that I can sell it immediately on those Terms; therefore, if they are not agreeable to you, you have only to return the MSS, which I entreat you do by the earliest stage, as the Gentleman[2] who will deal with me is hourly expected in Bath & will accept Bills to the Amount of 40£ on my delivering him the MMS as far as it goes.

If, on the contrary, you chuse to keep it on these terms, I must have bills to the amount of 40£ at 6 weeks or two 2 months accepted immediately. The Rural Walks are a seperate account, & I have every reason to be assured I could have sold them for more money. I have sent you 44 Pages. There are about the same number ready except some corrections. You will be so good as to favor me with your answer by the return of the Post, & be very exact in what you will or will not do. On the supposition that Mr Stafford is your Printer, I send to him the note on the other side. I am, Sir, begging an immediate Answer,

your most obed Sevt,
Charlotte Smith

To the Printer employed by Mr Cadell & Davies to Print "Rural Walks"——

The name of the plant omitted in 31, or 32, is Pile wort——

Mrs Smith entreats that, if the Printer sees any word which he cannot read, that He wd write to Mrs S. for an explanation. She had rather pay any postage than have

Calamites printed for Calamities
Dinging, for dingy—&c &c &c &c &c &c &c &c &c

And other words that exist in no language & that a very small portion of attention or intelligence wd convince a compositor cd never have been meant by an Author not qualified for Bedlam.

To Mr Cadell, Junr

I will send a corrected copy of the Banish'd Man up abt Monday with more of "Rural Walks." I rely so much upon ~~Mr C~~ the honor of Mr Cadell's house & name that I have no doubt of receiving ten pds a volume in case of a second Edition, as for Celestina from Mr Cadell, & for Desmond from Mr G. G. & I. Robinson's P. N. R. (only they left me minus five Guineas), & from Mr Josepth Bell for the Old Manor House. Mr Cadell never positively answer'd this, but I have as much reliance on his integrity as if he had.

5th Septr 1794
10 Pulteney Street

Yale University MS. Address: Mr Cadell Junr/ Strand/ London. Postmark: BATH; Sept/ 6/ 94.

NOTES

1. Here CS answers a curt, troubling letter from Cadell, Jr. (Davies being out of town). She was desperately writing drafts on presumed advances for *Rural Walks*, having submitted the first short chapters. Cadell, Jr., deferring to Davies, had already accepted bills totaling £18.15.0 when two further bills arrived. Davies had not authorized him to accept them.

> [G]reat was my Astonishment at having a Bill drawn on us for 21£ presented for Acceptance last Monday and immediately after another for 10£. Situated as I was Mr Davies being absent I was under the disagreable Necessity of refusing acceptance to the above two Bills, had I (as you requested in your Letter) declined accepting such Bills as you thought proper to draw on us at the same time saying that we would pay them when due provided we were in Cash, had I done this, I should have thought myself equally answerable with respect to the Payment had I absolutely promised to take them up at the time they were due—— I send you the above Statement in order to save you the trouble of drawing any more on us untill the whole of the first Volume of Rural Walks is delivered and myself the unpleasant office of returning the Bills unpaid.

This misunderstanding marks the beginning of the demise of CS's relationship with Cadell and Davies. Cadell, Sr., and possibly Davies may have accepted such actions by CS, but Cadell, Jr., too young to be much involved in the business, was cautious.

2. Sampson Low, printer at 7 Berwick Street, Soho, from 1794 until his death in about 1800. He published *Montalbert* (1795), *Marchmont* (1796), *Minor Morals* (1798), and the first three volumes of *Letters of a Solitary Wanderer* (1800).

To Thomas Cadell, Jr., and William Davies

[?Bath, 5 Sept. ?1794][1]

Gentlemen,

Not having yet received the pacquet I expected from London, I fear there is some mistake. Pray let me know.

I am, Sirs,
y^r^ oblig'd Ser^t^
Charlotte Smith

Septr 5th [?1794]

Yale University MS. No address or postmark.

NOTE

1. Probably an inquiry about the return of the manuscript *Rosalie.* A clerk's note at the end of CS's letter of 6 Sept. states that Cadell and Davies placed *Rosalie* in the mails on that date.

To Thomas Cadell, Jr., and William Davies

{Bath, 6 September 1794}

I began writing this {note} in a book but find it inconvenient & shall not continue it. At page 37, there is the name of a flower omitted which I must send up, but have not got my own books here, & there are no books to be had at Bath but very trumpery ones. I apprehend these 44 pages will make at least 2 sheets of Letter press, But should be glad to see a sheet when work'd off. The next two dialogues will be ready immediately.[1]

Yale University MS. No address or postmark.

NOTE

1. Another hand on this one-page sheet notes: "The MSS called Rosalie was returned to Mrs Smith Septr 6, 1794. by Bath Coach——."

To Thomas Cadell, Jr.

{Bath, 9 September 1794}

Sir,

I receiv'd yesterday morning the MMS of the New Novel which you return'd. I wish you had been so good as to have written a line either in the packet or by the Post, as I should have been glad to have heard that you received the draft for 35£[1] & will accept it as security for what I may draw till the Book you have purchas'd of me is finish'd, Because, should it not be agreeable to you, I will get Mr Tripp to discount it for me as he did the last half year. Your immediate answer therefore is requested. As to the Novel, I have only to conclude you decline the purchase, and I shall act accordingly. Very hard indeed is my situation and almost insupportable. My daughter, who has now been at Clifton a fortnight but has receiv'd little or no benefit, is orderd by Dr Denman to the Sea, but I have not the means of sending her thither.

However, Sir, I send up by this evening's Coach 60 pages more of ~~Evening~~ "Rural Walks" which, with 44 you have received, make upwards of 100. As I do not mean to make the work exceed 140 or 150 Pages (I mean the first Volume), I shall send the whole within three days, Wherefore I imagine you will not think it necessary to return drafts not exceeding the amount of 50£ (with what you have already advanced) should they be presented but not be due, before the receipt of this. The remainder would have accompanied this, but that it contains an Original Sonnet applicable to the subject; It was written many years since & the only friend[2] who has a Copy of it is in Sussex. I have written to her for it, as I cannot correctly remember it, & expect her answer by tomorrow's post.

If I have time, I will enclose in the packet the two first Volumes of the Banish'd Man corrected. As I understand by a sentence in your Letter that there will be a speedy demand for a second Edition (which is a matter that I apprehend you can now calculate to a certainty), I shall be much oblig'd to your Father with whom my bargain was made in this matter to let me know <u>whether</u> it is his meaning to make me the same allowance as he formerly made for Celestina on a second Edition & which I have invariably had since for each of my works. If it be (as the liberality and integrity of Mr Cadell leaves me no room to doubt), He will very much oblige me by informing me immediately at what ~~time~~ date he will accept drafts to the amount of £40 & at whatever distance this shall happen, it will be equally an accommodation to me, who am at this moment under the most cruel exigencies for money, not being able to obtain a shilling from the Trustees for any one of my family, & not knowing when the farther supply from my Son William will arrive, of which he gives me notice in his last Letters, but does not say by what Ship or even what Fleet his agent will send the money; & to him he is compelled to refer the time & mode of conveyance, as he is himself more that [*sic*] four hundred miles from Calcutta. If, therefore, Mr Cadell means to make this farther allowance and will permit me to draw on him even at 6 weeks or 2 months for two twenties, It will greatly accommodate me as well as the Young persons[3] in whose house I have apartments and who are distress'd for money to pay their rent, now nearly due. I shall only remark that both Robinsons & Bell suffer'd me to receive this profit before the 1st Edition of the respective books sold to them ~~xxxxx xxxxx~~ were sold, & I am well persuaded that Mr Cadell's liberality will not be question'd in regard to what I now ask. However, it is absolutely necessary for me to be at a certainty—Also whether you mean to become the purchasers of another ~~Edition~~ volume of Rural walks. I am ~~Gen~~, Sir,

your obed Sert,
Charlotte Smith

I request the favor of an immediate answer.

Yale University MS. Address: Mr Cadell Junr/ Strand/ London. Postmark: BATH; SE/ 9/ 94.

NOTES

1. *Rosalie* was returned to CS on 6 Sept., and she received it on 8 Sept. Cadell, Jr., still acting in Davies's absence, wrote her a letter dated 9 Sept. which would have crossed this one in the mails. In it, he acknowledged receiving the draft for £35 and re-

turning the manuscript, because as she assured them that she had another publisher, they did not want to publish it. Early sales of *The Banished Man* did not yet warrant a second edition, but should they do one, they would pay her the £40 she has been pressing for. Cadell, Jr., did not seem to be aware that a second volume of *Rural Walks* had been mentioned. Worst of all, CS's draft of £35 (which she tried to draw from the trust against next Jan.'s interest money) had not been accepted. Her letter of 10 Sept. to Cadell, Jr., seems to accuse him of approaching the trustee John Robinson with the bill, even though she had clearly stated it would not be paid until Jan.

2. Not identified, but possibly Charlotte Collins of Midhurst or Mrs. John Sargent of Woollavington.

3. Not identified.

To Thomas Cadell, Jr.

[Bath, 10 September 1794]

Sir,

By the mail yesterday, I sent up a considerable Quantity of your recent purchase, & the whole will be finish'd tomorrow and sent off on the evening of Friday So that I hope you will be so good as to accept the Bills I have drawn to the amount of 46£ 18 shillings (including the Eighteen pounds which you advanced on this work) & that you will also be kind enough to recollect that in the account stated there was the price of a whole set of Books, Viz. Emmeline, Ethelinde, Celestina and the Sonnets, charged to me, Which your Father very politely gave me as appears by his Letters. This makes therefore a ballance remaining of six pounds eleven, Admitting that we close our account here. For this I shall draw at 14 days and apprehend, that, as my bargain will be compleat before this is due, there will be no difficulty in regard to this matter, but, if the mistrust of your House is so great that you cannot take my word for what I assert and promise (tho very certainly in my long dealing with M[r] Cadell I never deceived him, or has he ever I think lost by me), if you, really, or if M[r] Davies understand me so little as to suppose me capable of deceiving you, It is far better that our dealings should cease for ever. This I own w[d] be a subject of regret to me, as I know it is an advantage to have a connection with a Publisher so highly respected as M[r] Cadell's house, but it is so humiliating to me to be suspected of an intention to cheat that, if I must write on, I must try to do it on my own account.

In regard to the Bill of £35, I beleive I never said M[r] Robinson (for the Lawyers are merely his stalking Horses) w[d] accept it, but it must be paid; being part of the interest of my own fortune, it is as perfectly secure as if it was accepted. And as security only I intended it. If, however, you do not chuse to accept it as such, you will have the goodness to cancel or return it. My Lord Egremont's Steward M[r] Tripp will do it for me, as I beleive I mention'd to you in my Letter.

There is no time to be lost in regard to your Answer to my Question whether you will go any farther in purchasing "Rural Walks," For I have not the least doubt of a purchaser, Nor, if I could wait a return, of being a very considerable gainer myself. So well am I convinced, that defective as this work may be, any work of that kind is so much wanted that it cannot fail of success. I am sorry you were too sanguine as to A 2nd Edition of the Banish'd Man. But I am not at all surpris'd at it, for it is really so mangled not merely in regard to mistakes, but as to faintness of impression, all the copies that I have being in many places not legible (especially in the mottos) that persons among my friends who know my works go usually into a second Edition have declined purchasing this set of books till that appears—because this is so imperfect. I have a Letter to day out of Essex exactly to this purpose & have heard the same from other quarters. I am very sorry for myself & very sorry for M[r] Stafford, who certainly can print better & who has always behav'd with so much civility and consideration towards me ~~th~~ during my late distress'd situation that I account the circumstance particularly unfortunate. As you say there is no hurry ab[t] a 2nd Edition, I shall not send up the corrected Copy until you want it. I have heard nothing from M[r] Strahan's office & am under the necessity of going this evening to Clifton, where my daughter still continues very ill, but if I stay there longer than till tomorrow, I shall direct any parcel to be sent to me. As I shall any Letters from hence. I am, Sir, requesting the fav[r] of an immediate answer, your most obed Sev[t],

Charlotte Smith

As I especially named Mrs. Barbauld['s] evenings at home as the size I propos'd, I beleive we shall have no difficulty in settling the matter even if I had not a proof sent down. They consist of 144 pages or ab[t] 6 sheets each——
Bath
Sept[r] 10th, 1794

Yale University MS. Address: To Mess[rs] Cadell & Davies—/ Strand/ London. Postmark: BATH; SE 11 94.

To James Upton Tripp

[Bath] 10 Pulteney S^{t}—Septr 12th 1794
Dear Sir,

I have acquitted myself so ill in regard to punctuality towards you that nothing but a conviction of your friendly wishes to serve me & an internal evidence that I mean by every exertion in my power to acquit myself finally, could give me courage to address you again to ask new fav^{rs} of you. All the amount of the price of the new Novel, & fifty pounds that I have earned since,[1] have hardly afforded me & my family a subsistence, M^{rs} De Fovilles illness only having already cost me more than an hundred pounds (& much is not yet paid). She lives however and is mending, tho slowly. A week or ten days since, I despair'd of ever seeing her restor'd, & it was only on my going over to see her yesterday that my dreadful apprehensions began to subside——

As she is now mending & has lost the cough and fever which prevented her taking the bark[2] and has no longer those other symptoms of a decline that have kept me so long in Torment, She wishes to leave Clifton, which is extremely expensive, and to come to a very small lodging I have found for her near Bath where I am myself compelld to stay, not only because I cannot at this moment discharge my arrears of lodging in Pulteney S^{t}, but because I have no other remedy but the pump & warm bath against the spasms which at times contract my hands & entirely deprive me of the use of them.

Mr Cadell,[3] tho he owns that the new Novel will speedily be in a New Edition, positively refuses to pay me the 40£ that will then be due to me till the 2nd Edition is publish'd. He is got into one of his fits of close-handed caprice, which makes him often think he shall die in an Hospital——tho worth 70000£——& he will not buy another novel I offer'd him "for fear I should overwrite myself and he should lose by it"; tho I offer'd it at 20 p^{d} less than I had ever sold one before because I wanted the Money partly advanced. Here then is an end of all hopes from him.

My dear William spoke of money he propos'd sending me, but I have letters by these last Ships dated the 21st of March, in which he not only makes no mention of it but tells me (which I am sure he w^{d} not do if it were a slight affair) that After many months of disagreement with the resident at Chittea,[4] whose first assistant he is, they have had so serious a difference that he is determin'd at all events to quit the station. He is already appeald to the Governor General, but the event was not known when the ships came away. But from the Character the resident bears, which is that of being a great brute, & the vif[5] & determin'd Spirit of my Son, who was famous at College for being the best temperd fellow in his class, but the most violent &

persevering when once rous'd, I am in terror such as cannot be described, least some personal rencontre should affect my Son who is the greatest blessing I have left, & on whom I depend for the protection & support of his Sisters when I am harrass'd to death which I think must soon happen———

Not however to detain you longer with my complicated Miseries, I will only add that, tho in consequence of Ld Egremonts most generous & unwearied efforts to serve me, together with my luckily seizing an opportunity of telling that old Hog Robinson a great piece of my mind (which he found rather more hard of digestion than Venison), there are hopes of a final settlement in some months of my childrens affairs——

Yet I have been deceived so often that I dare not rely on this. Or if I did——You know "while the Grass Grows, the Steed starves"——& they have sufferd the Widow's annuity to remain unpaid till the arrears due to her (which must be first paid after my 70£ p^{r} Annum) will prevent my children's receiving a shilling even if Prettyjohn will send any effects over (which I do not expect) to more than the amount of 100 or 150.

Now as I know not which way to turn myself for money to pay my poor Girls expenses at Clifton, which she must leave on Teusday or they will fall still heavier, Could you, dear Sir, continue to accept for me bills at 3 & 6/ 9 months ~~which~~ on the 35£ due half yearly, in the 2nd Jan^{y} & 2nd July 1795 and which must be paid by Robinson & Parkin on whom I will give you Bills to that amount.

I am well aware, Dr Sir, what a great liberty I take with you in asking such a thing, indebted as I am to you already. But after thinking of every thing, the necessity there is for my speedily doing something compels me to what is perhaps absurd & unreasonable—— If you feel it to be so, be assur'd that your refusal will in no degree diminish the sense I have of all your past kindness & good nature——

I do not know whether I have ~~explained~~ explain'd myself, for my head is sadly confus'd. But my meaning is, that if I might draw on you for £35 at 3 months from the 2nd Octr and 6 months from d^{o}—for £35 each Bill, I could get Cash for one or ~~xxxxx~~ both to supply my present pressing necessities, and you need not be in advance (further than ~~I~~ you are at present).

But however I am aware that this expedient may be utterly disagreeable to you, I beseech you in that case not to give it a second thought. On the 10th of October, Lionel must go to Oxford, & I fear it will be impossible for me otherwise to raise the money necessary for his furniture &c &c——which keeps me in a fever for the future, while I really know not how to provide for the passing day. Say nothing to my Brother of this, as the disagreeable business ab^{t} William will vex him, and it is useless to make friends uneasy who cannot help us——

May I beg, dear Sir, an an[swe]^{r} by the Posts return and to be believed, in all events, your much obliged Ser^{t}

Charlotte Smith

Is it possible I might hear from you by the Post of Teusday?

I fear it is asking too much——but if you can do———

Petworth House Archives MS. No address or postmark.

NOTES

1. That is, £200 on the completion of *The Banished Man* and £50 for *Rural Walks.* Drs. Denman and Parry each charged a guinea a day for attending her dangerously ill daughter's lying-in and convalescence.

2. Bark, or quinine, was commonly prescribed for malaria. Augusta's coughs and fevers were more likely to be consumption, especially as she was treated at Clifton, Hot Wells, a known retreat for consumptives.

3. Though now retired, the elder Cadell was still involved in the company's affairs. But his last letter to CS was dated 30 July. Afterward there was confusion about who was her primary bookseller—after a few letters from Cadell, Jr., he and Davies wrote her jointly, with occasional letters involving money or details of the press from Davies alone.

4. The event and the name of the resident William served under are not part of the East India Company's official record of his service.

5. Lively, energetic (French).

To Thomas Cadell, Jr., and William Davies

[Bath, 14 September 1794]

Messrs Cadell & Davies

Gent^{n}

Be pleas'd to pay to Mr Moore of Leadenhall Street the Sum of £34.19.6 specified as the ballance due to me on the first Volume of "Rural Walks," Whose receipt shall suffice, & you will be pleas'd to refer to Mr Moore, when he has receivd this money, the Bills you decline pay^{g} for me, vis.:

Mr Barratt ——	£5.5 referred to Mr M. Septr 16th
Mr Mays ——	£5.5
Mr Bull ——	6.6
Mr Pickwick ——	8.8 referred to Mr M. the 20th Inst.
25.4[1]	

I am, Gent^{n}, your obed^{t} Ser^{t},

Charlotte Smith

Septr 14th, 1794

Yale University MS. No address or postmark.

NOTE

1. On 17 Sept., Cadell, Jr., responded that he has sent CS the first proofs for *Rural Walks;* he has paid the £34.19.6 to William Moore, stationer and bookseller of 8 Leadenhall Street; and he will "strictly observe [her] Directions" about the four bills to be referred to Mr. Moore. He concludes that "The Acct therefore between us is for the present clearly settled——."

To Thomas Cadell, Jr., and William Davies

Bath. 15th Septr 1794
Messrs Cadell & Davies.
Gentlemen,

I was favour'd with M^{r} T Cadell's Letter yesterday And am concerned that I have misunderstood your meaning till now. It would have saved me not only a great deal of vexation and mortification, but near a Guinea for the expences of protesting the Bills & postage if they are return'd, as two of them have been already. By this evening's mail, I send up thirty MMS pages of "Rural Walks" & entreat you to give me credit for the seven and twenty Pages that remain to compleat the Volume—only till Teusday's Mail or Coach, when I will send them, and you will then have my acquittal for the 50£.

I should have sent them to day, but that I cannot get any books here that I want; I had the prose & original part of what I now send finish'd the middle of last Week, but it is as strange as true, that, having occasion to quote those lines of Pope's which begin "Where is the North?"[1] I could not procure at Mr Bull's or Mr Barratt's, the Volume of Pope in which they are &, after losing some days, was under the necessity of altering the sentence & omitting the lines. The last Chapter is in exactly the same predicament. But I have sent to borrow the books I want of a Physician here who has a good library & hope to get them tomorrow. But even if I should not, & it should be a day later before I deliver the ~~deliv~~ whole Volume, I trust that for a difference of 27 pages, which you are certain of receiving, you will not refuse to pay the ballance specified of 34£19. S. 6 d[2] to Mr Moore, Bookseller, of Leadenhall Street, who, at the desire of his Correspondent Mr Barratt, will take the trouble to pay the Bills I have drawn to the amount of £35. 10^{s} in all, to prevent my having the expence & humiliation of having the Bills returned, and to him they must be referred. Taking it for granted, that should Mr Moore call on Teusday for s[ai]^{d} Sum, Even tho you should not have receiv'd the 27 pages before mention'd, that you will not so scrupulously adhere to your resolution, as to refuse me this favor.

The necessity I have been under of going continually to Bristol Hot wells to see My daughter & the misery I have gone thro on account of ~~my~~ her illness has made me, together with the want of my books, twice as long about this work as I should otherwise have been. And they were circumstances that I was weak enough to imagine would have been consider'd, but when a person is fallen as I am from quite another rank of life to the necessity of writing for ~~their~~ her daily bread, it is fit ~~they~~ she should submit to any terms on which it can be earned & be thankful that it is to be had at all. The 2nd Volume, since you are pleas'd to buy it when finish'd, I will set about, & perhaps by dint of sitting up half the nights, I may get thro it in a fortnight, as Mrs De Foville is coming to a small lodging near Bath, being still too ill to allow me to think of going as I intended a scene hunting into Wales, which I am therefore forced to give up.

I have not yet received any specimen of the new work from Mr Strahan. In regard to the present of Books which Mr Cadell Senr thinks was included in some previous transaction, I have only to say that I never had but two sets of them—of which the last was sent to Mr William Smith and is included in the account, and the first, which is what I have at Storrington in my Study, I re[ceive]d from Mr Cadell as a present & have so mark'd them with the very date, as they now stand charged, in the account. If this explanation is not satisfactory, I will appeal to Mr Hayley, tho unwilling to trouble him on such a matter, as it happen'd that he particularly knew of my having them as a present. But I am persuaded Mr Cadell himself will recollect it on farther consideration.

I have received some Letters lately with complimentary verses from persons to whom I am very much oblig'd for their intended kindness, but it is so very expensive, & I am so poor, even in thanks as well as time, that I wish to decline these Compliments & therefore entreat you not to give up my address to any person whatever, But to say that I am not at Storrington, for that is worse & makes double postage, but travelling in the West for health—I am, Gentn,

yr obed humble Sert,
Charlotte Smith

Boston Public Library/Rare Books Department MS Ch.H.3.18. Address: Mr Cadell & Davies/ Strand/ London. Postmark: BATH; SE/ <17/94>.

NOTES

1. The passage from the discussion on vice in *Essay on Man* (1734), 2.222:

> Ask where's the North? at York, 'tis on the Tweed;
> In Scotland, at the Orcades; and there,
> At Greenland, Zembla, or the Lord knows where:
> No creature owns it in the first degree,
> But thinks his neighbour farther gone than he.

2. CS seems to be responding to a very firm, undated note from Cadell, Jr. It reads in part:

> I am truly sorry that we totally misunderstand each other—the above is the exact state of your Acct & the ballance of 34.19.6 I will immediately pay on receiving the remainder of the copy. . . . I truly lament that we are under the necessity of declining further dealings upon the present plans—we are ready to pay for the second Volume of the Rural walks when deliverd, but must decline accepting any more Bills on in [*sic*] part of payment as by doing this the acct may run into confusion, and is besides a subject of continual altercation. Your connection is highly respectable, but no profit will answer the continual complaints on one side, vexations and trouble on the other.

To Thomas Cadell, Jr., and William Davies

[Bath, 16 September 1794]
Gent^{n},

By the Coach of this evening from the White Lion, you will receive the remaining pages of your purchase. I cannot get it ready [*sic*] time enough for the Mail. But I trust that this instance of my punctuality will convince you that neither the difficulties of my situation or the fatigue I have been oblig'd to undergo have prevented me from acquitting myself towards you. This being deliverd, our accounts I suppose are clear. I beleive, from the little judgement I have, that the work will answer the purpose I intended. At the same time I certainly could have made it more perfect had I been allow'd more time. The same thing will occur in the subsequent Volume, but of that you must be aware.

By the generous interposition of Lord Egremont & the public flogging[1] I have given the Villainous Men who have for so many years reduced me to a state of mendicity (or what is as bad, to the necessity of writing for bread) and by their fears, which are well founded, that what I have said is only an antepast of what I will say, I am now in more hopes than I have hitherto been that My children's Estate will be forced out of their hands; & then I trust I shall never again have occasion to solicit advances—nor to write a line. I shall be in Town about the middle of next month on my way into Essex, where I shall stay till the Court of Chancery opens. I beleive by that time the 2nd volume of Rural Walks will be ready——I know not whether it adds any thing to the value of these little Books that, in the first, there is an original Sonnet of mine and, in the other, will be an address to her two Children written by M^{rs} ONeill, which has never been printed & is extremely beautiful[2] (with perhaps another little piece fit for such a work)—

I am, Gentlemen,
your most obed[t] humble Ser[t],
Charlotte Smith

Sept 16th, 1794

Boston Public Library/Rare Books Collection MS Ch.H.3.21. Address: To/ Mess[rs] Cadell & Davies/ Strand/ London. Postmark: BATH; {date illegible.}

NOTES

1. CS had depicted lawyers as corrupt and wealthy relatives as unfeeling, especially in *Emmeline* and *The Banished Man*. She attacked the trustees Robinson and Parkin even more directly in prefaces to *Elegiac Sonnets i* and *ii* and in *Desmond* and *The Banished Man*. In the preface to *Elegiac Sonnets i*, 6th ed. (1792), she wrote:

> Still to receive—not a repetition of promises indeed—*but of scorn and insult*, when I apply to those gentlemen, who, though they acknowledge that all impediments to a division of the estate they have undertaken to manage, are done away—will neither tell me *when* they will proceed to divide it; or, *whether they will ever do so at all*. (p. xi)

2. Henrietta O'Neill's address to her two children, "Written by the Same Lady on Seeing Her Two Sons at Play," and her "Ode to the Poppy" appeared in CS's *Elegiac Sonnets ii* (pp. 76–81). The ode first appeared in vol. 3 of *Desmond*.

To Robert Tayler[1]

[Bath, 19 September 1794]
D[r] Sir,

I am so much hurried by the necessary attendance on my daughter who is still very ill that I can only enclose the draft which I beg the fav[r] of you to send to M[r] Tripp for acceptance under Cover thus:

Earl of Egremont
Petworth

Date the place from whence & day when sent. Which is the mark by which M[r] Tripp knows when the Letters are for him & opens them without waiting for Lord E——

I w[d] not have taken this liberty with you, but it is impossible to get a Bill sent from hence beyond London.

I am, Sir,
your oblig'd hble Ser[t]
Charlotte Smith

Bath 19th Sept [17]94

Petworth House Archives MS. No address or postmark.

NOTE

1. For Robert Tayler, merchant and friend of BS, see Biographical Notes.

To Joseph Cooper Walker

[Bath, before 24 September 1794]
. . . in[1] search of ideas for the Poetry I must make to compleat the intended Volumes; But I do not imagine I shall accomplish this, nor indeed do I at all know what is to become of me. I cannot get my house in Sussex off my hands, & therefore I am afraid I must return thither tho the place disagrees with me so much that to return there for the winter is to return to disease & perhaps to death. On the other hand, being unsettled entirely is on some accounts disadvantageous, for I am compell'd to be without books which I cannot move with me. I have now little or no communication with Mr Hayley, whose present mode of life & pursuits are I beleive incompatible with the trouble he formerly took in correcting my writing & in other friendly Offices.

If I could do as I would, I w^d^ take Apartments here by the year for myself and my younger children & place the Chevalier and Augusta in some small retired house within a few miles, for he, unlike the generality of his Countrymen, is fond of country retirement; & my daughter is never happy & indeed never well in a great Town. These are indeed Chateaux en Espagne, and it is more likely that we must all go into a Garrett together, but whether I "hear soft zephers thro a broken pane"[2] or am able to sit at a large sash Window as I do now and look at the magnificent lodgings of Lady Inniskilling,[3] I am in every event, dear Sir, your most oblig'd Ser^t^,

Charlotte Smith

Huntington MS (HM10828). Address: Joseph Cooper Walker Esqr / Eccles Street/ Dublin. {Not in CS's handwriting.} Not postmarked.

NOTES

1. The first pages of this undated letter are missing. CS wrote it before her letter of 24 Sept. 1794 in which she writes of taking a cottage for Augusta within a mile of Bath.

2. Pope, "An Epistle to Dr. Arbuthnot" (1735), l. 42.

3. Ann, Lady Enniskillen (1742–1802), wife of William Willoughby Cole, created earl of Enniskillen in 1789.

To Thomas Cadell, Jr., and William Davies

[Bath, 24 September 1794]
Sirs,

By the Mail of Friday, you will receive about two thirds of the second volume of Rural Walks; The last part I keep back merely to procure a perfect copy of the little Poem I mention'd to you written by M^rs^ ONeill, for which I have been oblig'd to write to Ireland, for tho I have a copy of it, it is lock'd up at Storrington, and I cannot very conveniently send my keys thither. However, as I wrote to Mrs Sentleger ten days ago, this cannot occasion any delay beyond the middle of next week. I wish to conclude the little Volume with something original of my own, which I have to think so far done that I can venture to assure you, you will receive it all by this day sennight—— This being the case, I make no doubt but that you will be so good as to pay a draught of ten or fifteen pounds for me, should I have occasion to draw for it at 10 days, which is the only trouble I will give you & which I think you will not refuse[1] when I tell you that my daughter, for whom I have taken a Cottage within a mile of Bath, is still so ill that she is attended by Dr Parry every other day, which has already cost me a great deal of money. My family's property is arrived—Sugars to the amount of 900£,[2] but their Grandfather's Widow,[3] who has recieved nothing these three years, must first be paid, & when insurance & other charges are deducted, I doubt whether there will be much left for them So that I must continue to struggle for them as well as I can.

My friend, Mr Walker of Ireland, is at Buxton for his health. He has ten or eleven Guineas (I know not which) in his hands of mine, which he will remit to you in a few days & which when it comes you will be so good as to pay to my order. I should be much oblig'd to you to procure for me the concordance of Shakespeare I mention'd to you as soon as convenient, & I am, Gentlemen,

your most obed^t^ Ser^t^,
Charlotte Smith

Bath
Septr 24th 1794

Huntington MS (HM1842). Address: Messrs Cadell Junr & Davies/ Strand/ London. Postmark: BATH; SE/ 25/ 94.

NOTES

1. They did refuse. They copied their reply on the third page of this letter. In it, Davies replies firmly that "we cannot possibly accept any Bills whatever till I receive

the Mss of the second vol. of Rural Walks quite compleat." Moreover, they are surprised at receiving her second volume so soon, especially as she had originally proposed publishing the two volumes separately. Davies expressed further concern that "the Volume now printing has not received the Revisal from its Author which would undoubtedly given it that decided Superiority over similar Works . . . which alone could have led us to offer so very handsome a Sum for a Volume of that size."

2. Gay's and Mapp's plantations in Barbados still belonged to the trust; their sugar crops provided income for the estate.

3. Lucy Towers Smith, CS's maternal aunt and her father-in-law's wife.

To Thomas Cadell, Jr., and William Davies

[Bath, 30 September 1794]
Gentlemen—

By the mail of Friday, I shall send up the whole of the second Volume of Rural Walks. I trust you recieved the 1st part on Saturday; by a mistake of my Maid's, it was not sent by the Mail but by a later Coach.

I shall give an order to Mr Moore to receive on Monday the Sum of forty one pound twelve shillings, being the ballance of fifty pounds. As I gave Mr Pickwick a draft for Eight Guineas.

I have had a Letter to day from Mrs Sentleger, who complains that when she left Dublin on the 15th her Books had not arrived. She is now at Donerayle, & her Papers being at Dublin, she could not send me the Verses I wrote for. But I find a Lady[1] who is now at Teingmouth in Devonshire has got a copy of them. I write to her by to day's post & hope I shall get an answer before ~~Saturday~~ Friday, but if not, I shall send the Book without it, as they will easily be placed where I intend them.

I shall have materials enough for a third Volume[2] sh^{d} you be disposed to engage for it when you have tried the success of these. I am, Gent^{n},

your obed^{t} Ser^{t},
Charlotte Smith

Septr 30th 1794

Yale University MS. Address: Messrs Cadell & Davies/ Strand/ London. Postmark: BATH; OC/ 1/ 94.

NOTES

1. Not identified.

2. A sequel, also in two volumes, was published by Cadell and Davies in 1796 as *Rambles Farther.*

To Thomas Cadell, Jr., and William Davies

[Bath] 2nd October 1794
Gentn

I really do not know why you express apprehensions that I have not properly revis'd the work which you seem'd eager to purchase of me.[1] I can only say that if I could have done it better I would, & that any part of it which strikes you as incomplete I will revise if you are pleas'd to send it to me. I really did not know that your resolutions in regard to printing a second volume varied so much, & therefore I work'd at it instead of going on with any other work. I gave you what I thought very satisfactory reasons for detaining the MMS remaining a day or two longer, for the whole is actually finish'd and I was about to send up as far as page 135 by this evenings Coach. I am ignorant how to act now & am beyond measure vex'd at the contents of your Letter, but indeed I am so enured to mortifications that I expect nothing else.

I really am not conscious of having faild in my engagement, nor do I know what you expected in a work of this kind. I believe my proposals were to form a book that should be somewhat above those intended for the use of mere children, and yet not have the tendency of novels, and that I would select such pieces of poetry as seem'd likely to form the taste, & add if possible something original of my own, connecting the whole by domestic scenes. I may have fail'd in this, but If I have, it has not been for want of endeavouring to succeed. However, Gentlemen, if such is really your opinion, I recommend it to you to stop the press, and to have the work revised, which I will do to the best of my power. More I believe it is useless to say. I really did flatter myself that—As I have not in any one instance fail'd of fulfilling my engagements And as You are so well acquainted with my situation—that I should have received more kindness from you than I have in this instance experienced.

Tomorrow I shall send up the work by the evening stage, & if it is not after all what you supposed it to be & if I have deceived you, You must I believe return it. You will recollect however as to the price that it was your offer, not my demand, and that the second volume you agreed to take without my pressing the matter or naming any time (& I think, after you had seen the first or a specimen of it). In regard to the <u>size</u> of the volume, I always named Mrs Barbaulds "Evenings at home" as the size I intended, & indeed the idea of writing such a work occurred to me from the extreme difficulty of finding any such books as were fit for my youngest daughter, a child of twelve years old.[2]

Perhaps I named to Mr Cadell some intention of inserting some easy lessons on botany, but on setting about it, I found it could not be done without engravings, & that to nineteen persons in twenty, it w^d^ have been wholly uninteresting.

I repeat my wish of having any part sent to me which may appear to want revisal; & am, Gent^n^, your obed^t^ Ser^t^, Charlotte Smith

Yale University MS. Address: Messrs Cadell & Davies/ Strand/ London. Postmark: BATH: OC/ 3/ 94.

NOTES

1. See CS to Cadell, Jr., and Davies, 24 Sept. 1794, n. 1.

2. Harriet Amelia. This paragraph accurately reviews details of the original agreement. CS's many misunderstandings with Cadell and Davies occurred as management changed from Cadell, Sr., to Davies, and as Davies was out of town at crucial times.

To Thomas Cadell, Jr., and William Davies

[Bath, 8 October 1794]
Gent^n^

Not having heard to the contrary as I expected to have done from the <u>unexpected</u> tenor of your last Letter, I shall by a stage this evening send up 106 pages which completes the 2nd volume of rural walks; You will have the goodness to pay the ballance of my account to Mr Moor when he, <u>after</u> you have rec[eive]d this, calls for it—deducting whatever I may owe you.

I have to day received a Letter from Lady Crofton[1] informing me that "the banish'd Man" had not on the 27th of September reach'd Dublin & desiring I w^d^ immediately order her over a set & a copy of the Emigrants which she has never seen—— I shall be oblig'd to you therefore to send these books as early as you can & to address them to your Bookseller in Dublin, requesting him to forward them to Lady Crofton, who is a Woman of fashion and of course much known. Her letter is dated from ~~Dub~~ Backwesten a Villa not far from Dublin, but she is going very soon into the North of Ireland. You will be kind enough therefore to expedite this matter as much as possible, as she is impatient to have the books to take with her—The Money for which she will pay to your Bookseller or who so ever else you please to appoint.

I am, Gent^n^, your most obed^t^ humble Ser^t^,

Charlotte Smith

Bath, October 8th 1794

I had almost forgot to add that a set of "the banish'd Man" must be sent immediately to Mrs R Allen,[2] Robert Allen, Lymington, Hants, for which she will either send you the money or pay it me, & in that case it may be deducted from my account.

From the complaints I have from several people that they cannot get this Novel, it seems to have met with some impediment in its circulation.

The intended publication of the Sonnets also seems very little known,[3] and many of my distant friends have never even heard of it. I propose being in London early in November if my daughter continues to amend, to settle the engravings[4] &c&c&c——at the same time that I attend my childrens law business.

Yale University MS. No address or postmark. {The portion of the page where the address would have been is cut away.}

NOTES

1. Armida/Anne, Baroness Crofton of Mote (d. 1817), only daughter and heiress of Thomas Croker, Esq., of Backweston, Co. Kildare, and wife of Sir Edward Crofton, Bart., Co. Roscommon. She also subscribed to *Elegiac Sonnets ii.*

2. Mary Gibbes Smith Allen (b. 4 Dec. 1764), only daughter of Rev. Richard Smith, BS's older brother. She married Capt. Robert Allen in 1787 and lived at the Grove, Lymington. (See Genealogical Chart.)

3. That is, of the subscription edition of *Elegiac Sonnets ii.* It was delayed until 1797.

4. Engravings, some to be executed by Lady Bessborough, sister of the duchess of Devonshire (see Biographical Notes), were planned for the new subscription edition of the sonnets.

To James Upton Tripp

{Bath, 16 October 1794}
Dear Sir,

My daughter has inform'd me of Mr Brownes[1] proceedings & that you were kind enough to go over to Storrington. I am really so very much worried ——so much distracted beyond what any fortitude will bear, that I cannot express myself as I ought to do. But I mean to say that it would be doing me a very great kindness if you would take the Books which I will get Mrs Turner carefully to pack, & let them be put any where, in any out house or other place at Petworth till I can determine what to do with them, & till I have somewhere or other an home where they may not be seized. Good God, what a destiny is mine—— How very hard to bear!

I will send you the draft on Robinson for the 35£ which I have not forgot or neglected, but really have been so persecuted that I have not known what to do or whither to turn me——I shall be very much oblig'd to you to write to me. The Letter M[rs] Tripp sent did not reach me till about a fortnight ago——

I am, Dear Sir,
your most obed[t] & oblig'd Ser[t]
Charlotte Smith

Bath Oct[r] 16th 1794

Petworth House Archives MS. No address or postmark.

NOTES

1. A note from Browne, dated Storrington, 29 Sept. 1794, survives:

Mr. John Browne presents his Compts to Mrs. Smith and assures her his Mother is realy distressed for Money, being so long disappointed of her Rent from Mrs. Smith. B. is sorry to add that unless the last half years Rent is Paid to him at Storrington on or before the 10th of October next B. will be under the necessity of taking disagreeable steps in order to save his Mother from the same predicament who certainly will be distrained unless Her Rent is Paid by the 12th of October in London.

A second note to Tripp dated Gray's Inn, October 18th, 1794, followed:

Sir, Herewith you will receive the Charge in Mrs. Smith's distress which Mr. Johnson thinks I am entitled to as it is little more than my Money out of Pocket, Yours, J W Browne.

Notices of distress	0.13.4
Paid two Men in Possession 4 Days	1.0.0
Paid Trower for their Board 4 Days	1.0.8
Paid Letters from Mrs Smith	0.1.0
Paid John Stator of Storrington	
Auctioneer for taking Inventory—— Drawing notices of Sale and for Clerks Fees of different Parishes Crying same	0.5.0
	£3.0.0

Mr. Brownes Comp[limen]ts to Mr Trip and will trouble him to pay the amount to Mr Falconer of Petworth whose Receipt shall be a Discharge. Mr T will observe there is no charge made for orders——

John Trower kept the White Horse Inn at Storrington, and the two men sent down to take possession of the goods were evidently fed by him and possibly stayed at the inn.

To Joseph Cooper Walker

[Bath, 16 October 1794]

Dear Sir,

I much fear that I said something in my last Letter improper or, what is worse, that you are ill, as I wrote to you sometime since & have had no answer. I am apprehensive that you might think it wrong that I requested the favor of you to pay the Sum you have been so good as to collect for me in London, but I am harrass'd really to death, and tho I often sit up all night to write, I cannot obtain wherewithal to support my family. There is now an Execution in my house at Storrington for 25£, & My books, the only things I had been able to reserve, are seized for rent & will be sold. This is so cruel a blow to me that, added to the inconveniencies I suffer here for want of Money, I am unable to support my courage. My children have a thousand pounds worth of Sugars[1] come this year, but I cannot obtain a farthing for them. Nor can I send my Son Lionel to Oxford tho his future welfare depends upon it and tho ~~xx xxxxxx~~ it is impossible for me to support him at home.[2]

Such has been the conduct of the Trustees that they have now robbed me of every thing. I beg a thousand pardons for giving you this sad detail, but my spirits are quite worn down with vexation, and I am in absolute despair.

Let me entreat the favour of hearing from you soon if you still continue to me that friendship to which I have already been so much oblig'd, & beleive me,

Dear Sir,
your faithful & obed[t] Ser[t],
Charlotte Smith

Bath
Oct[r] 16th 1794

Huntington MS (HM10816). Address: Josepth Cooper Walker Esq[re]/ Buxton/ Derbyshire. Postmark: BATH; OC/ 17/ 94.

NOTES

1. See CS to Cadell, Jr., and Davies, 24 Sept. 1794, where CS notes that sugars worth £900 have arrived.

2. Evidently CS was unable to raise the additional money needed to establish Lionel at Oxford, her dream for his future safety and security. His whereabouts before joining the army in the fall of 1794 are not known.

To James Upton Tripp

[Bath, 24 October 1794]
Dear Sir,

I should not so long have delay'd writing to you, but I expected to have heard again from Miss Smith, and that before I thank'd you, I might know the whole extent of my obligation. I have only to say I am infinitely oblig'd to you. How much it would be difficult to say, & therefore I will not attempt it. I will send you the draft for the thirty five pounds dated the 2nd of November at two (2) months, & if I receive any tolerable Sum from the Sugars (which however I do not expect since there is 500£ due to the Widow and so many hungry claimants on the residue that there will be little or nothing left for me). I will endeavor farther to acquit myself of my great obligations to you.

I have been so sadly harrassd within this last fortnight that It has made me quite ill, but a little repose and having recourse again to these waters would restore me. My daughter, tho better in her general health, cannot yet walk and is still attended by a Physician. I am almost in despair of her every [*sic*] enjoying perfect health again, which added to so many other troubles, is almost too much for me—— Indeed I do not know how I have got thro the Summer & am much amaz'd at finding myself yet alive——

There will be no doubt now of the payment to the £35 due Jany 2nd. And if it be any satisfaction to you to have a draft for that payable in July 1795, you shall certainly have it till I can do better. Be so good as to send the enclos'd to Fittleworth & Easebourne[1] & to believe me, Dear Sir,

your most oblig'd & obedt Sert
Charlotte Smith

No 10 Pulteney St 24th Octr 1794
I believe I have written Nonsense more than usual, for I am half dead with head ache.

Petworth House Archives MS. No address or postmark.

NOTE

1. It is not clear what was enclosed. CS's brother Nicholas Turner held the living at Fittleworth, and Augusta and her husband De Foville spent part of this autumn with him. Miss Bridger, who took CS's youngest son George to Midhurst Grammar School, was at Easebourne.

To James Upton Tripp

[Bath, 28 October 1794]

Dear Sir,

I have just received the enclosd from Mr R Smith,[1] but I own I am not very clear as to what he means. I suppose that he will pay the rent to this October if I will pay it to Christmas in case I wish to preserve my furniture. As I do not know what is to become of me, I am unwilling to part with my furniture till I do. But I cannot answer for it that I shall be able to pay the money, or indeed what I shall do to exist. My own labour, tho exerted to the ruin of my health & never allowing myself a moments respite, is quite ~~xxxxxxxx~~ inadequate to the weight I have to sustain. I do not know very well what I ought to do about the House, but my daughter inform'd me that Mr Browne said he would release me intirely if I would pay the next half year.[2] I ~~do~~ have nothing to offer as security for any farther kindness on your part, nor have I any right to ask it: but if I could find the means to get rid of the House, I am in hopes I could find friends who would be my security for such a Sum as twelve pound ten shillings.

I therefore trouble you to know what Mr Browne said to you, and in general what you advise me to do. I wd have sent you the draft in this inclosure for the 35£ due at Christmas to replace the Bill you have discounted, but I write this at Lark Hall, a cottage I have hired for my daughter at some distance from Bath where illness, the effect of fatigue and vexation, and the weather, have conspired to keep me these two days, and I cannot get a proper stamp. But I will have the pleasure of sending it to you immediately on my being settled in other lodgings whither I am going as soon as I can pay my old ones. I ~~xxxxx~~ direct therefore to be left at the post office & believe me, Dear Sir,

your ever oblig'd Sert
Charlotte Smith

Bath
Oct 28th 1794

Petworth House Archives MS. No address or postmark.

NOTES

1. The Reverend Richard Smith, BS's nephew. (See Genealogical Chart.) Evidently, at least one of BS's rich relatives to whom CS applied for aid in July delivered a sum of money (see CS to Charles Dunster, 16 July 1794).

2. That is, £25.

To Thomas Cadell, Jr., and William Davies

6 Seymour Street Bath. Novr 6th [17]94
Thursday eve^{n}
Gent^{n}

I receiv'd your favor,[1] and in the course of a very few days, you shall receive the preface you desire in a packet which I shall have occasion to send up. I never dreamed but that it was <u>understood</u> that my name was to be put to the work; I cannot assuredly have the least objection to it.

I shall be glad to have the advertisement of the new Volume of Poems publish'd as soon as possible as I hope it will now go on, & I think I shall be ready to meet it in April, but the illness of my family & my own severe distresses, which have been dreadful, have prevented my application. I have reason to believe that certain Ladies of High rank[2] would interest themselves on my behalf were they properly appriz'd of the publication, which I must endeavour to do if the advertisements are not likely to reach them——

I imagine that few or no subscriptions have been received since the account you gave me when you thought there was not more than enough to pay the expenses already incurred. But if there is & it is possible for you to spare me a note of five pounds, it would be doing me the greatest favor in the World, as it is impossible to describe how cruelly my daughters very long illness—who is still attended constantly by a Physician twice or thrice a week—and my being oblig'd to have her at a seperate lodging out of the Town has distress'd & harrass'd me. Messieurs the Trustees have received a very considerable quantity of sugar from the plantation this year and have already sold to the amount of 4 or 500£ of it. But after writing a circular Letter to all the parties concern'd, to know how the surplus (after paying the arrear due to the Widow) should be dispos'd of, they have received the only answer that can be given, viz—That it must be dispos'd of according to the meaning of the Will (which they knew before) & now sit down very quietly & keep the money themselves, while I and my family literally want the necessaries of life: for tho I have finish'd the first Volume of the Novel I had begun and have received the money for it £50 from a Bookseller in Soho,[3] it is quite impossible that the most incessant labor on my part can entirely support a family of seven persons[4] in the requisites of existence, & my daughters four months illness, & five Medical Men, who have continually attended her have really reduced me to more cruel exigencies than I have ever yet known, & in a place where not being near my own friends, I find it more than I can do to supply my family with the means of existence from one day to another. If you cannot conveniently do what I request but w^{d} write to Mr Bull to advance on my draft five Guineas should I have occasion for it, it might at this period be of more service to me than it can be at any other, for I trust I can hardly be so driven again, as Mr Erskine—at the request of the Duchess of Devonshire, Lord Egremont, Mr Sheridan, and Dr Fordyce[5]—has engagd to undertake the cause of my injur'd children against their infamous Trustees as soon as the pressure of public business is a little over. I have therefore once more hopes that the cruel exigencies and mortifications I am now expos'd to will cease. They have indeed nearly lasted long enough, having now for eleven years unceasingly oppress'd me with severity that has nearly destroy'd my intellects and entirely my health. If you can oblige me in what I should once have thought a trifling fav^r^ but which is now most material to me, be so good as to let me hear by the return of the post. I am, Gent^n^,

your most obed^t^ humble Ser^t^,
Charlotte Smith

If you have a copy left of the subscribed for Sonnets with the Name and could send it me, I sh^d^ be oblig'd to you.

Mrs Sentleger, now one of my Irish friends, had a very little time since received "the Banish'd Man."[6]

Yale University MS. Address: Messrs Cadell Junr & Davies/ Strand/ London. Postmark: BATH; NO/ 8/ 94.

NOTES

1. A note in another hand at the top of the letter may explain "your favor": "Bank Note £5—Octr 6, 94 No 7987."

2. The duchess of Devonshire collected subscription money for *Elegiac Sonnets ii* and permitted CS to dedicate *Rambles Farther* to her daughter, Lady Georgiana Cavendish. The duchess's sister, Lady Bessborough, contributed a drawing which appeared as an engraved plate in the new work.

3. Sampson Low (see CS to Cadell, Jr., 5 Sept. 1794, n. 2).

4. It is not clear which children constitute this seven. The younger children—Lucy, Harriet, and George—were of course at home. Augusta and de Foville, who was not employed, would make five. Lionel was apparently with his mother; he was not at Oxford and did not enlist in the army until 28 Oct. 1795. Either Charles or Charlotte Mary was still at home; CS to Cadell, Jr., and Davies, 7 Dec. 1794, suggests that Charlotte Mary is in London, where she often resided with Rev. Richard Smith at Islington. CS took responsibility for all eight named here when she could.

5. Whigs all, these five intercessors for CS shared political alliances, sponsorships, and friendships, and also worked for the kinds of liberal causes CS supported. Thomas Erskine (1750–1823), later the first Baron Erskine and lord chancellor, was actively defending a number of cases at this time involving freedom of speech and the press—including Thomas Paine's trial for the second part of the *Rights of Man,* which resulted in his being vilified by government newspapers and relieved from his post as attorney-general to the Prince of Wales (1792), and John Frost's trial for making seditious statements at Percy coffeehouse (Mar. 1793), which he lost.

Both the duchess and Egremont were active Whigs (see Biographical Notes). The duchess was a particular friend of the dramatist Richard Brinsley Sheridan, whom she supported by a letter in his 1780 election for Stafford. Erskine was a friend of Sheridan as well.

Dr. George Fordyce (1736–1802), a physician, may appear in this group in part through his membership in the Literary Club of which Sheridan was also a member.

6. CS had asked for the book two months earlier, on 29 Aug.

To James Upton Tripp

[Bath, 11 November 1794]

Dear Sir,

I beg you many pardons for not having sent the enclos'd before, but my poor Girl has been suddenly seizd with a fever which is of the epidemic kind, but it is now abated & Dr Parry tells me will be nothing. It has served however extremely to alarm me, & together with the eternal difficulties about money, has served to drive every thing out of my head. Even my punctuality, as far as is in my power. My obligation however to you, Dr Sir, escapes never from my memory.

I now send you a draft for thirty five pounds due the 2nd of January 1795——With a thousand thanks for the favor you did me in granting me such an accommodation. Allow me to request the favor of you to forward the enclos'd and to believe me, Dear Sir,

your ever oblig'd Ser^{t}
Charlotte Smith

6 Seymour Street Bath
Novr 11th 1794

Petworth House Archives MS. No address or postmark.

To Thomas Cadell, Jr., and William Davies

[Bath, 15 November 1794]

Gentlemen

Mr Walker of Dublin & some other friends, having informed me that they have paid or mean to do so in a few days some subscriptions into your hands & as I am particularly distress'd for money at this moment, I request the fav^{r} of you to accept a draft at 6 days which I have drawn in fav^{r} of Mr Barratt, & if there is not already money in your hand, there will be before it is due. I cannot explain myself farther being in extreme hast CS.

Yale University MS. Address: Mr Cadell & Davis/ Strand/ London. Postmark: BATH: NO/ 15/ 94.

To James Upton Tripp

{Bath, 20 November 1794}
Dear Sir,

I have but a moment with very crippled hands to tell you that, as a very great instance of their bounty (having above 1000£ of effects in their hands), Messieurs Robinson & Parkin do intend to pay me soon, that is within a fortnight, the capital Sum of 35£ due to me on the 2nd of January 1795. About a month or five weeks before the time they must pay it me, & this as a great favor and all I am to expect. They are in truth honest & pleasant fellows!

I shall send you the money of course when I receive it——But if you could without inconvenience lend me 35£ to be repaid in July 95, it would render me the most effectual service, & I hope without any risk to you, as this little income must at all events be paid regularly.

I am so sensible of all the debts I owe you that nothing but dire necessity c^{d} induce me to intrude farther upon you, but I am so utterly at a loss to know what to do with such a family & no resource but my own labour that I fear I shall sink under my troubles before Lord Egremonts kind interference on my behalf with Mr Erskine can releive me——

Favor me, Dear Sir, with an immediate~~ly~~ answer, & pardon the incoherence of the Letter written in pain of body and uneasiness of mind. My Daughter[1] requests the fav^{r} of you to forward her Letter to Mrs Turner. I am very anxious to know what had best be done about Storrington. I am, Dear Sir,

your much oblig'd Ser^{t}
Charlotte Smith

Novr 20th Seymour Street Bath. No. 6.
1794

Petworth House Archives MS. No address or postmark.

NOTE

1. Augusta and her husband had stayed at Fittleworth with her uncle Nicholas Turner and his wife Sarah and would have been on good terms with Sarah.

To Thomas Cadell, Jr., and William Davies

6 Seymour St Bath. 7th Decr 1794
Gent^{n}

I shall be oblig'd to you to send me down in the course of this week 50 of the printed receipts. Also a list of names of persons subscribing since y^{r}

last list on that subject in the month of July or August. I mean a list that shall include the whole for the purpose of my correcting some mistakes of which M[r] Greatheed has informed me & on other accounts.

I had on friday a Letter from Lady Crofton who appears to be very much vex'd and hurt at not having received the Banish'd Man & Emigrants which she order'd. She says that She is convinced that Mess[rs] Cadell & Davies do not like to sell books to Ireland & shall make no farther attempt, but says she has read the Novel in an Irish Edition so miserably disgraced that it was hardly to be read at all—— Very certainly when, to the stupid blunders which M[r] Stafford chose to make, are added the pleasant emendations of an Irish printer, the work must do great honor to all concerned in it——

Miss Smith has got a pacquet to send down to me, which I have desir'd her to forward to your house. And when it comes, I shall be oblig'd to you to enclose it with the receipts in a small parcel, & send it by the Stage as early as possible after you hear from Miss Smith[1]——

I must be in London abt the 19th or 20th January, when the plates &c &c may be put in hand—I am, Gent[n],

your obed[t] humble Ser[t],
Charlotte Smith

Yale University MS. Address: Mess[rs] Cadell Jun[r] and Davies/ Strand/ London. Postmark: BATH; DE/ 8/ 94.

NOTE

1. Enclosed with this letter on a separate sheet is a copy of Cadell and Davies's response to CS's several requests and observations. They immediately sent her the parcel from Charlotte Mary, fifty printed receipts, and a list of subscribers to date. They regret that Lady Crofton has not received her books but note that the books were sent to Mr. Archer, a Dublin bookseller who orders great volumes of books from them; they know he has already forwarded copies to Mrs. St. Leger and Mr. Walker. They go on to say that "The Demand for the Banished Man has been so very slow comparatively with that for Emmeline Ethelinde &c. &c. that we have had but little Hopes of printing a 2d Edition." They offer to print an edition of 500 copies, half the usual number, at half the price originally offered, £20 instead of £40. Given past disagreements and misunderstandings, they are careful to allow her to decline this offer if she thinks they "depart from the accustomed Dealing of our House." But in that case, they will "give up all idea of a 2d Edition."

To Thomas Cadell, Jr., and William Davies

[Bath, 16 December 1794]
Gentlemen

Lucy[1] forgot to say to you that the corrected copy of the banishd Man should be ready for you immediately. I have a copy reserved on purpose in which most of the errors are noted, but I am going over it again & about friday will send it up in a parcel I am sending to Mr Lows,[2] whither I will give you notice to send for it when I send up the long list of subscribers which I have not yet had time to look out.

I am, Gentlemen,
your obed^{t} Ser^{t},
CS ———

6 Seymour Street
Decr 16th 1794

Yale University MS. Address: Messrs/ Cadell and Davies/ Strand/ London. Postmark: BATH; DE/ 17/ 94.

NOTES

1. Lucy had written to Cadell and Davies on 12 Dec., "my mother being very much engaged." CS accepted their terms for a short edition of *The Banished Man* providing they would pay her the remaining £20 if another 500 copies were printed later. Lucy further describes difficulties in getting subscription money from the duchess of Devonshire, who was out of town. Lucy adds a postscript that CS will send her list of subscribers, but few have paid. Finally, CS advises them not to send another set of books to Lady Crofton, for she "thinks they cannot be lost but only delayd."

2. A copy of *Montalbert,* to her new publisher, Sampson Low.

To Thomas Cadell, Jr., and William Davies

[Bath, 24 December 1794]
Gentlemen—

It is true that I have had for many months a corrected copy of the Banish'd Man by me, but As I am every day beset with people who tell me of faults, I wish'd to go and have gone over it again. It will be in Town tomorrow evening, as I shall send it from hence to night by the Stage from the white Hart. I shall be oblig'd to you to send me down the number of copies you propose to allow me of ~~the Banishd Man~~ Rural Walks as soon as they are out & a parcel from Islington which I have desir'd Miss Smith to send in order to have it come down at the same time. You are certainly at liberty to make the deduction of twenty shillings, and I beg of you to do so Tho I did not imagine that—considering our agreement & that I trust entirely to your honor as to printing 500 or 1000 Copies—that such a trifle could be any object. If you had expressd yourselves clearly, that you would not accept or pay the Bill till you received the corrected copy, I should have acted accordingly, but on reference to your Letter, I find that in pursuance of the apparent meaning I could not act otherwise than as I did.[1]

I recommend it to you, if you have no objection of which I am not aware, to take 48 pages from Volume the 4th to add to Volume 3rd As one is too thick and the other too thin. The third Volume will then begin with the Chapter of which the Motto is

(Down many a weary steep &c—) at page 48.

Look at the printing of this sentence only and see if I complain without reason,

I am, Gentlemen,
your obed[t] humble Ser[t],
Charlotte Smith

Since writing the above, I have receiv'd a Letter ~~from~~ in consequence of which I have desir'd M[r] Richard Smith to pay into your hands twelve pounds ten shillings for his share of a ready furnish'd house for 7 months. The rest I shall have the pleasure of paying myself.[2] When you get the money, I must trouble you to pay it to my order to the Woman the House belongs to, a M[rs] Browne[3] of Thornhaugh Street, Bedford Square—— I do not know her exact direction & cannot therefore send the money immediately to her, or if I did know it, could I make the payments without a proper receipt, as it is a troublesome & not too honest family with whom I have to do. I am persuaded you will take this trouble for me.

Yale University MS. Address: Mess[rs] Cadell & Davies——— / Strand/ London. Postmark: BATH; DE/ 24/ 94.

NOTES

1. The sum of 20 s. was intended to cover shipping the parcel from Islington. Many surviving copies of letters from Cadell and Davies to CS are not dated, making it difficult to ascertain whether they had explicitly warned her of their plan.

2. Richard Smith, CS's nephew, agreed to pay half of her £25 half year's rent on the house at Storrington (see CS to James Upton Tripp, 28 October 1794, and n. 1).

3. John W. Browne's mother. Now part of the University of London campus, Thornhaugh Street is a side street off what is now Russell Square.

To Mr. Fordyce[1]

Seymour Street 27th Dec[r] 1794

Do not imagine, Dear Sir, that I have willfully neglected to prepare the papers which you have the goodness to undertake to send to M[r] Erskine for me. I wrote to M[r] Morgan[2] to send me the deed of 1784 which has been one cause of our calamity. Of which deed, M[r] Morgan has that Copy that belongs to me. I intended to have had it copied here by my Children to save expence & to have return'd it to M[r] Morgan, who has papers of mine in his hands of infinitely more consequence & who, as he undertook My business merely as a friend, would I hoped have trusted so far to my integrity as to have indulged me with a copy of this deed. But he has refused, & I am under the necessity of waiting for such documents as may supply to me the want of it.

This, dear Sir, is the only reason why I have not sent you the Case, but I am now occupied in writing it, & as I hope to receive tomorrow the few dates I want, I trust that I shall complete it on Monday. I hope Mrs Fordyce is quite recover'd & that you continue well. Our sincerest good wishes attend you both. I am, with great regard and respect,

Your most oblig'd Ser^t^,
Charlotte Smith

Huntington MS (HM10817). No address or postmark.

NOTES

1. See Biographical Notes.
2. Jonathan Morgan of Lincoln's Inn, later lawyer to BS.

To the Reverend Samuel Greatheed[1]

No. 6 Seymour Street, Bath
29th Decr 1794
Sir

I should not thus long have delay'd writing to thank you for your last obliging Letter with the corrections of the list of subscribers which your friendly endeavours have procured for me, but I have had so much writing to do, as well of Letters as on the unfortunate affairs of my family, and my health has been so precarious, that I can truly say I have hardly had time to speak to a belov'd friend who is in the same Street: and I have I fear appeard to neglect those whom I most esteem and to whom I am most oblig'd——

When you were so obliging as to send the first list, together with the Bank note of ten pounds, I was in such a state of misery and anxiety that I could only send the list up to Messrs Cadell and Davies. I shall be under the necessity of going to London towards the middle of next month and will then endeavour to rectify the errors that may have been occasion'd by my not writing for the second list. At all events, it shall be adjusted before any list is printed.

I do not often hear from Mr Hayley now, and his last letter being filld with an account of his wishes and endeavours to serve my family, he did not as he generally does mention Mr Cowper, from whence I fear I am to conclude he has no intelligence to give me which he knows it would give me pleasure to hear—— Hardly a day passes in which I do not hear some enquiry about Mr Cowpers health. It is indeed a national concern, while those who have ever been honourd with the slightest degree of friendship and attention from that excellent Man must doubly feel the cruel circumstance of his protracted illness. Should you have the goodness to write to me, a favor for which I should be truly grateful, I should be extremely glad to hear Your friend is recover'd or more likely to do so than when you wrote last.

I cannot conclude without entreating you to accept my thanks for the trouble you have taken for me and that you will allow me to remain, with Comp^{ts} to Mrs Greatheed, Sir, your most obed & oblig'd Ser^{t},

Charlotte Smith

Neilson Campbell Hannay Collection of William Cowper, Manuscripts Division, Department of Rare Books and Special Collections, Princeton University Library. No address or postmark.

NOTE

1. See Biographical Notes.

1795
"OVERWHELMD WITH SORROW"

—2 MAY 1795

Although Charlotte Smith embarked on new literary projects in 1795, Augusta's death in April shadowed her every accomplishment and every other concern. Smith's letters afford little information about this year's actual publications. Montalbert, *her only new work, was put out by Sampson Low late in the year. It marks her retreat from political themes to the safety of sentimental romance.* Rural Walks *and* Montalbert *appeared in Dublin for Wogan, Byrne, et al., and Cadell and Davies issued the seventh edition of* Elegiac Sonnets i. *Probably unknown to Smith, the sonnets were first published in America by two different presses. In Massachusetts, Isaiah Thomas based his first Worcester edition on Cadell and Davies's sixth, while William Spotswood based his edition on the seventh. At home, Cadell and Davies first rejected her proposal for a two-volume sequel to the successful* Rural Walks, *but later accepted it when the duchess of Devonshire intervened and allowed Smith to dedicate it to the duchess's elder daughter.*

Even while Augusta's illness and death dominated the year, the other children also presented problems. Lionel and de Foville were served with a warrant after sending a challenge to Thomas Dyer, a troublesome brother-in-law instrumental in delaying the settlement of the will. An early, unexpected summons nearly led to the forfeiture of bonds posted by two of her friends, Dr. Caleb Hillier Parry and Col. Frank North. Smith traveled to London to intercede. She had to extract an unnamed family member from an undesirable match. Her children were scattered: Harriet stayed at home, but the dying Augusta spent time with her uncle the Reverend Nicholas Turner at Fittleworth. Charlotte Mary visited relatives in Islington. The younger children, Lucy and George, were sent to live with a friend, Miss Peckham, at Exmouth. Late in the year, Lionel joined the army, starting as a lieutenant. In June, desolate over Augusta's death, Smith joined her children at Miss Peckham's to recover her health and spirits, only to find herself trapped there, lacking the money to move back to Sussex. The £100 that William sent in 1794 had not yet arrived, the trustees would not give Smith advances on her biannual interest money, and her lawyer was unable to obtain £500 of estate money held by merchants in London. Mail and parcel services to the countryside were infrequent and untrustworthy, possibly accounting for the fewer and shorter letters later in the year.

To William Davies

[Bath, 11 January 1795]
Sir,

I am under the disagreeable necessity of being in London on Teusday evening, My Son Lionel and the Chevalier de Foville, having been served with Cheif Justices warrants to appear for having sent each a challenge to Mr Dyer to whom the Trustees referr'd them for an answer, whether he would suffer 500£ which now lies dead in Mr Blackmans[1] hands to be divided between his children and mine in pursuance of the Will of their Grandfather.[2]

Rather than we should have the money, he refuses to let his children participate, so inveterate is his malice & so much greater his malignity even than his avarice. Tho I am persuaded the Letters written will not be construed into amounting to Challenges, yet it must unavoidably put us to great trouble & expence. As My Solicitor[3] lives in Norfolk Street, Strand, and my business lies ab^t^ that part of the Town, I must request of you to have the goodness to procure me a lodging in some street near that part of the Town. I must have two bed chambers one for myself & one for M^r^ & M^rs^ De Foville and a sitting room. It matters not how small if clean. There is a good and reasonable lodging at Mr Smiths, Surry Street, the same as I used to lodge with, who now inhabit, or at least did last Summer, opposite that large old house which is now pulled down. If disengaged, this would do. I shall call at your house to have a direction if you are so good as to take this trouble for me—— I hope to be in London by daylight on Teusday. I am, Sir,

your obed^t^ humble Ser^t^,
Charlotte Smith

Bath
January 11th 1795

Yale University MS. Address: [Cadell] & Davies's/ Strand/ London. Postmark: BATH. [One-fourth of the page with the address on it is torn away.]

NOTES

1. George Blackman, Esq., and Co., Chatham Place.

2. The outcome of the warrant is not known. Thomas Dyer, BS's brother-in-law, may have blocked distribution of this money, as CS claims.

3. Charles Bicknell acted as CS's solicitor from as early as 1790 until her death, after which he represented her family's interest until the estate was finally settled. By 20 Jan., CS was in London. By 20 Feb., Bicknell with Thomas Erskine's help had obtained a compromise settlement over the property. They did not settle the disputed £500 at Blackman's, however; on 28 July, CS wrote to Davies that the money was still being held.

To William Davies

[London, before 20 Jan. 1795][1]

Sir,

I must trouble you to send me ten Guineas, as I think you have more than that of mine in your hands, & I am disappointed in the Letter I have received to day from Bath in which I expected to have received fifteen from the bursar of St Johns College[2] who was to have sent it a fortnight since, but from some mistake of Mr Marlowe's, it is not come.

I am to meet Mr Erskine[3] to night &, till I have seen him, know not how long I shall be detain'd in Town. But at all events, I must quit these lodgings immediately, as they are so extremely inconvenient that I cannot bear them even for the short time I stay, & I must pay the <u>Lady</u> of the House this morning as well as the extravagant Tavern bill & therefore cannot wait for the remittance I expected.

In regard to your apprehensions of not having enough to pay the charges, apprehensions that I do not recollect Mr Cadell ever express'd on the publication of the former volume,[4] I believe you need not be alarmed on that subject, as There is now in the hands of different friends as much as will answer all those expences so that you will not be in advance. If I recollect aright, Mr Cadell thought the sale would answer that, but it is true that you are not to be expected to advance money. I wrote to Mr Hayley last night, foreseeing it was still possible that I might be disappointed in the money from Oxford & That you might have some scruple as to letting me have this, and I imagine he will call upon you to day.

I know nothing of the Man I send; therefore, you will be so good as to send me an immediate answer with the money. I am, Sir,

your oblig'd humble Ser^t^,
Charlotte Smith

Since writing the above, I find my Son calls with this,[5] but he is going farther, you will be so good as to send somebody down. ~~On farther reflexion Mr De Foville will bring the money~~

Yale University MS. Addressed: Mr Davies. No postmark.

NOTES

1. This letter is next to the 9 Sept. 1794 letter postmarked Bath in the Beinecke collection; while such proximity can be helpful in dating undated letters, it was obviously written during a London stay. CS did not go to London until Jan. 1794, visiting briefly between 11 Jan. and 20 Feb., by which time she had returned to Bath. Her letter of 20 Jan. 1795 to Davies, written from the Osborne Hotel Adelphi, takes up points mentioned in this letter, which led to a misunderstanding with Davies. In the undated letter, she asks for 10 guineas which she thought he had of hers; in the letter of 20 Jan., she continues that she thought he had "considerably more than 10 Gs" on account of subscription money collected by the duchess of Devonshire and Mrs. Olmius. In the undated letter, CS refers to the "former volume" providing enough money to pay charges, meaning the 1789 subscription edition of *Elegiac Sonnets.* The 20 Jan. letter discusses her responsibility for the cost of a *present* subscription volume, that is, the subscription edition of *Elegiac Sonnets ii.* Apparently CS moved to the Osborne Hotel after leaving the unsuitable lodging described here. Finally, in a letter written from Bath on 20 Feb., she mentions "Mr Erskines interference" in the trust business, which effected a compromise settlement.

2. Lionel, the next-youngest son, matriculated at Oxford 16 July 1794 but CS did not have adequate funds to set him up for the fall term. This £15 may have been the refund of the caution money paid in the summer.

3. The duchess of Devonshire and earl of Egremont sponsored Thomas Erskine's involvement in this preliminary settlement of the trust. On Erskine, see CS to Cadell, Jr., and Davies, 6 Nov. 1794, n. 5.

4. The 1789 subscription edition of *Elegiac Sonnets i.* The rest of this letter discusses the planned subscription edition of a new, second volume of sonnets. The duchess and Mrs. Olmius had begun collecting subscriptions, but the book was not published until 1797.

5. Lionel or Charles. George was only 9.

To Thomas Cadell, Jr., and William Davies

Osborne Hotel Adelphi[1] [London] 20th Jany 1795

Sir,

I have not time now to answer fully the purport of your Letter.[2] But I am sorry to see that we do not understand each other. After a transaction [*sic*] for so many years during which time I think I have—notwithstanding my heavy & bitter calamities—committed no act of dishonorable tendency towards your house, it it [*sic*] hard that I should now be suppos'd likely to do it. Very different I am conscious would be the treatment I should receive were I more fortunately situated. The friends who subscribe to the work (for which certainly I am answerable to the public) are the best judges what their intentions are in subscribing. To them only I am accountable for the money, for the expence of the publication I must answer, & I again repeat that, If you forsee any inconvenience likely to arise from being the publisher, I would not on any account wish you to continue your obliging endeavours to serve me—with which however I do not know that I ever testified any discontent, feeling on the contrary that I was oblig'd to you. I thought that, deducting the 15 Guineas I receiv'd of you at Bath, there was at this time considerably more than 10 g^s^ in your hands because I suppos'd that the Dutchess of Devonshire had paid what she has collected & that Mrs Olmius[3] & some other person had sent their money. This not having been done alters the case, but I by no means blame you for it, nor could mean it.

Have the goodness to send by the bearer any Letters that may be for me. I will endeavour to call upon you before I go out of Town & to settle any thing in my power for your future satisfaction. I am,

Sir, your obed^t^ Ser^t^,
Ch Smith

Yale University MS. Address: Mr Davies/ Messrs Cadell Junr & Davies/ Strand—— No postmark.

NOTES

1. Adelphi, a literary neighborhood whose inhabitants included David Garrick, was developed by two Scottish architects, the brothers Robert and James Adams. It had been called Osborne. The Adelphi Hotel at the corner of Adam and John Streets occupied 1–4 John Street.

2. Davies's letter does not survive. At issue here is money from subscribers to the forthcoming *Elegiac Sonnets ii.* Elizabeth Olmius and the duchess of Devonshire were among several friends who collected money from subscribers. Later, CS learned that the duchess had lost her list of subscribers. As the duchess's own financial affairs were usually in disarray, it is likely that she lost track of the money as well.

3. Elizabeth Olmius (see CS to William Davies, 19 Feb. 1794, n. 2).

To the duchess of Devonshire

Seymour Street, Bath. Feby 8th 1795
Madam,

I have to day received your Grace's most obliging Letter enclosing two drafts, one from you & the other from Lady Elizabeth Forster.[1] I beg permission to make my acknowledgements for both, but terms would be wanting were I to attempt saying all I feel of gratitude for the generous attention with which your Grace honours me.

I will not now intrude upon you to say more of the affairs Mr Erskine has so kindly endeavour'd to help us in. I had a Letter from him to day in which he obligingly answers one I troubled him with & seems to beleive that his interposition has effected (as it ought to have done) the accommodation we desire, for such it appeard to him by Mr Robinson's conduct[2] and Letter (which he sent me). But while they were thus dissimulating with my friends, Dyer and his Attorney,[3] taking advantage of some trick that the Law allows, have brought on the trial, for the Challenges—as it seems, unknown to Mr Erskine & my Solicitor Mr Bicknell—and summonses are come down for my Son Lionel and the Chevalier de Foville to attend on Wednesday next to receive Judgement of which neither Mr Erskine or my Solicitor seem to be inform'd. The Chevalier de Foville and my daughter are gone on a visit to my Brother who lives near Petworth in Sussex, and Lionel (as the trial was not by Mr Erskine's desire to come on till May) return'd to his Regiment, and is recruiting at Bedford, Newport Pagnell, and Northampton, and as the notices were sent down hither, I fear they will not receive them in time to attend in which case Col^l^ North & Dr Parry[4] will each forfeit 100£, and My Son & De Foville will be imprison'd till they can pay 200£ each.

I think I never was so very miserable as the dread of this makes me, & yet I thought I had experienced every degree almost of sufferings, from every kind of anxiety. I still feel myself however confident in Mr Erskine's protection, & think it impossible that the chicane of an infamous Grub Attorney can baffle his upright & enlighten'd mind. Talents so superior united to an heart so generous and manly. I have written to him & endeavor to make myself as easy as I can till Teusday when I hope to hear that the measures he has directed to be taken will deliver us from this impending ruin, for it would indeed be ruin.

How very good is your Grace to encourage me with <u>such</u> approbation of the little Book.[5] It has been so much liked that I intend with my first leisure to carry it on to two Volumes more, but tho it is unusually well spoken of, my Publisher looks very blank upon me, & says that so bad are the times that nothing sells, and that where they sold ten copies of a popular work two years since, they do not now sell one. He own'd however reluctantly that he had sold (within a month) 500 of the 1000 copies, which I thought by no means a bad sale. I am to have 20 £ on the publication of the 2nd Edition, and 20 £ is now become a great object to me. Therefore, tho I was compelld to sell the copy right, my friends serve me very materially in forwarding the circulation of the Book, not only as it will put that Sum more speedily in my pocket, but as it will greatly assist in my getting a good price for any future work of the same sort or a continuance of this.

Alas! I am talking of literary schemes as if I had health certainly to execute them which is so far from being the case that at this moment I cannot walk across the room, having again lost the use of my legs, nor can I rise from my seat without help. Fortunately my hands, which were affected a few days ago, are now restored to me, & as necessity is imperious & irrestible, I must continue to work. I have just now finish'd two Volumes of a Novel call'd "Montalbert," & am beginning with an heavy heart the third and last, which if I were not harrass'd by this persecution and compelled to provide from day to day for the time that is passing over me, I should finish in a fortnight. It is most flattering to know that your Grace condescends to honor with your approbation what I have been able to do in this way and to encourage me to continue, & still more gratifying must be your opinion that I might succeed in the higher walk of Comedy.

About five years ago, & immediately after the publication of Emmeline which made a great impression on his imagination, the elder Colman wrote to me desiring me to undertake a Comedy which he would correct & fit for the Stage.[6] I accordingly finish'd two acts which with the general outline he greatly approv'd of, but his mental derangement then overtook him, & I was discouraged from persevering on finding that other persons at the head of the department where he had Govern'd were by no means of the same opinion as to my abilities for that species of composition, & indeed when I saw such plays as <u>were</u> accepted, I was convinced that mine would have faild. I destroy'd what I had done and felt no temptation to try again.

Such encouragement however as your Grace deigns to give me would awaken these latent hopes in a disposition less sanguin than mine <u>has been</u>, and if I can weather the present Tempest & obtain this Spring either at some Welsh or Western bathing place a few months of repose with my two daughters, I will make one more attempt, submitting it however to your Grace, how far it may afterwards be worthy of the protection you so generously and humanely offer.

And in every event I must consider it as the highest honor to be allow'd to call myself,

Your Grace's most oblig'd Ser[t],
Charlotte Smith

Devonshire MS, Chatsworth: 5th Duke's Group no. 1277. No address or postmark.

NOTES

1. Second wife of William, fifth duke of Devonshire, who lived with him during

his marriage to Georgiana, his first wife (d. 1806). Lady Elizabeth Foster, widow of John Thomas Foster and daughter of the fourth earl of Bristol, married the duke in 1809 and died in 1824.

2. On the trustee John Robinson, the husband of Richard Smith's stepdaughter, Mary Crow, see Biographical Notes.

3. On Thomas Dyer, the second husband of Richard Smith's daughter, Mary Berney, see CS to Thomas Cadell, Sr., 22 Aug. 1790, n. 3. Dyer's attorney for this case is not identified.

4. On Dr. Caleb Hillier Parry, see CS to Thomas Cadell, Sr., 22 July 1794 and n. 2. On Col. Frank North, see CS to an unnamed recipient, 8 Dec. 1791, n. 4. As there is no mention or record of Lionel or de Foville being imprisoned, it appears that they met the summons and CS's friends Parry and North did not forfeit the bonds.

5. That is, *Rural Walks.*

6. CS mentions a comedy in progress in a letter to an unnamed recipient dated 10 Feb. [?1788]. The letter may be dated as late as 1790, and its recipient may be George Colman (see that letter [pp. 14–15], n. 1). See also CS to William Hayley, late 1788–89; this letter is the only one CS wrote in dramatic dialogue with stage directions. Her lighthearted use of dialogue suggests that she was writing a play about that time.

To Thomas Cadell, Jr., and William Davies

Bath, Feb 20th 1795

Gentlemen,

As I shall in the course of next week compleat my engagement with Mr Low of Berwick Street, who purchas'd of me at fifty pounds a Volume the 3 Volumes of a Novel, of which only about 100 pages remain to be deliver'd,[1] I shall almost immediately be at liberty to fill up the outline of a plan I have had some time sketch'd & begin two Volumes on the same plan as Rural walks, which either may or may not be a continuation of that work[2]——

Should it be agreeable to you to purchase these books on the same terms as the others to be paid for on delivery, I shall not offer them to any other person, but if not, I Can sell them at that price unless, which is probable, I should print them at Mr Cruttwells[3] press on my own account, as I am advis'd to do by many friends. Your immediate answer therefore will much oblige me. I have to day received a Letter from my Solicitor Mr Bicknell of Norfolk Street, informing me that the persons who have by litigation and chicane so long kept My children out of their property have, at length and in consequence of Mr Erskines interference for me, agreed to settle the whole business by compromise as Mr Erskine recommended. I hope therefore I shall no longer write for actual bread or appear in the mortifying character of a distrest Author. But, as, while the grass grows the steed starves, I am and shall be dreadfully inconvenienced in the time of this settlement which will take up at least three weeks or a month, & if you have five Guineas of mine in yr hands, I shall be much oblig'd to you to send it down[4] as I know not which way to turn myself for present money. As you do not consider yourself as accountable to the public & I shall take care not to commit myself with them, you need not I should apprehend have any scruples on this head. I am, Gent[n], Your obed humble Ser[t],

Charlotte Smith

There is a packet arrived at Cork from Bengal; should there be any Letters for me, they will be sent to y[r] House, & I entreat the favor of you not to lose a moment in sending them down pr post.

Yale University MS. Address: Mess[rs] Cadell Jun[r] & Davies/ Strand/ London. Postmark: BATH; Feb 21 95.

NOTES

1. Sampson Low had agreed to publish *Montalbert,* a novel CS had offered to Cadell and Davies in Sept. 1794 as *Rosalie.* Low published several subsequent works by CS.

2. *Rambles Farther: A Continuation of Rural Walks: in Dialogues. Intended for the Use of Young persons,* 2 vols. (Cadell and Davies, June 1796). They initially rejected it, however, as a note in Davies's hand at the end of the letter shows: "We beg Leave to decline the Purchase, upon the Terms proposed, of the new Work you obligingly offer us."

3. CS first mentions using Richard Cruttwell in CS to William Davies, 25 June 1794 (see n. 5).

4. Their note at the end of her letter shows that they sent a bank note for £5.

To Thomas Cadell, Jr., and William Davies

[Bath, 15 March 1795]
Gentlemen,

My daughter de Foville is dangerously ill at Fittleworth near Petworth & order'd immediately to Bristol as her only chance of life. I have not the means of having her sent, for the Bills to a considerable amount announced by my Sons Letters are not come to hand. If you have any money of mine in your hands, I beg you to send her an order for it by the first post that her journey may not be delay'd an hour for want of money. If you have not any, I have no right to ask any fav[r] of you. The direction is M[rs] De Foville ~~Fittleworth~~ at the Revd N. Turners. Fittleworth near Petworth, Sussex.[1] Even 5£ w[d] be of use should you have no more. I am half distracted & know not what I write. I am, Gent[n], y[r] obed[t] Ser[t],

Charlotte Smith

March 15th 1795

I am persuaded that Mr Cadell Senr would have the humanity to assist me with this trifle which shall be deducted out of the first money I can by any means procure.[2]

Yale University MS. Address: Messrs Cadell & Davies/ Strand/ London. Postmark: BATH; MR 16 96 {sic}.

NOTES

1. CS's younger brother, Nicholas Turner, was rector at Fittleworth until 1799, when he was removed to a lesser living at Burton cum Coates and Lurgashall, just west of Petworth.

2. A note at the end of this letter shows that a £5 bank note was remitted on "March—16—to Mrs De Foville at Fittleworth by Mrs. Smiths Desire———"

To James Upton Tripp

{Bath, 16 March 1795}
Dear Sir,

After the innumerable obligations I am under to you, only the direst necessity could make me thus intrude upon you. I have five & twenty pounds that will be paid as soon as I can deliver a certain Quantity of writing which I have just done to a Mr Low, a Bookseller in Berwick Street Soho. Two days will suffice to finish it as I have only ab^t^ 20 pages to write.

In the mean time I hear to day that my daughter at Fittleworth gets worse & worse, & M^r^ De Foville entreats that she may come to me while she is yet in a condition to be moved. I have not money to send her, nor can I obtain any. I have written repeatedly to implore even a trifle for this purpose of those cruel men who have destroy'd us all, but have been refus'd; & I have no resource for every thing but my labour from time to time. If you will have the goodness, Dear Sir, on the receipt of this to send my poor Girl ten Guineas to come hither, I will send you a draft for that Sum by Teusdays post, payable at sight in London as this money when due (I mean the 25£) will be paid at Mr Blackmans Merch^t^ in Chatham place who have paid me the rest that I have earned of this Mr Low.

Any thing but Augusta's illness at such a distance I could bear; I have 200 or 300 on its way to England from my Sons in India as their Letters inform me. But the Bills are not arrived, & I suppose are in some of the Indiamen that are waiting at St Helena for Convoy. If all those remittances come to my hands, my first purpose will be to repay you all I owe you. If I can get a stamp, however, I will send you the draft for this to day.

I know not what I write, tears blind me. I shall never see My Augusta again unless I can see her soon——I fear I do not make myself understood——My fortitude quite forsakes me——I suffer more than I can endure—— I have nobody to write for me——I am too miserable——& if in the excess of my suffering, I ask too much, pray forgive me——I am ~~always~~ almost ~~xxx~~ distracted—— I am ashamed of troubling you—— But which way can I turn me!

Your ever oblig'd Ser[t]
Charlotte Smith

Sunday 15th March——
I have sent out for a stamp but the shops are all shut——

Petworth House Archives MS. Address: James Tripp Esq[re] / Petworth/ Sussex. Postmark: BATH; MR/16/95.

To the Reverend Nicholas Turner[1]

[Bath], 5 April 1795
My Dear Brother,

Poor Foville received your Letter to day—— Augusta continuing to languish in the greatest danger, indeed with little or no hope, it becomes indifferent to him what he does. All I can say therefore on this subject is that M[r] Erskine has undertaken in a Letter I had from him yesterday to settle the matter by drawing up an [xxxx][2] which Foville will sign.

In such a situation as mine, with a darling child dying before my Eyes, & without a single shilling[3] in the World to buy for her the necessaries she has occasion for, I know not how I shall support myself. If I could save her there is nothing I would not do & endure, but such complicated misery must overwhelm me. I am Affectionately yours

CS

Sunday April 5th 1795——

Petworth House Archives MS. No address or postmark.

NOTES

1. See Biographical Notes.
2. The page is torn away at the seal.
3. This is one of only two surviving letters from CS to her brother. Turner sent the letter to Tripp to justify his request for a loan on Augusta's behalf:

> Dear Tripp——
>
> I have recd the inclosed which distresses me greatly, and tho I can by no means afford it yet I must send to Poor Augusta some assistance to enable

> her to go to Bristol. I wish to send her 10£ and Nich [Turner's son] will the same. I shall therefore be much obliged to you for a draft at 10 days for £20 to send by the Post this day in order to loose no time and as Jim Mitchel will bring Nich some Money on Friday he will repay you then. (unpub. letter of Nicholas Turner to James Upton Tripp, PHA # 015.10r)

To Thomas Cadell, Jr., and William Davies

[Bath, 2 May 1795]
Gentlemen,

On the other side you will find an advertisement which I beg you will insert in such Papers as you usually engage. That I might not commit you, I have not even named your house as that where application should be made for the restoration of the subscription money, for which my Sons will give me the means of ~~subscribe~~ providing. I trust you will approve of this precaution and oblige me with the immediate insertion of these lines, so as to diffuse the notice as generally as possible. The Trustees have refus'd me not only assistance for my daughter while she lived, but wherewithal to bury her.[1] However as I do not name any names, there is no libell in this I trust, & what I may do else will not affect ~~me~~ any person but myself. Your speedy answer will oblige, Sir,

your most humble Ser^t^,
Charlotte Smith

Advertisement.

The oppression and injustice under which I have labour'd for twelve years, having now involv'd in its consequences the most cruel & irreparable calamity that could befall me, I am too much overwhelmd with sorrow to be able to fulfill the engagement I had enter'd into with the public which was to have been completed this month[2]—— If I can recover ~~enough of~~ resolution to continue my efforts for the support of my family, whose property is wholly detain'd from them, I will forward the publication so as to deliver the Books subscribed for in the course of six months. If not, the money shall at the end of that period be return'd to all who demand it on producing their receipts at ~~the~~ a place of which due notice shall be given——Charlotte Smith

General Manuscripts, Manuscripts Division, Rare Books and Special Collections, Princeton University Library. Address: Messrs Cadell and Davies/ Strand/ London. Postmark: BATH; MA/ 2/ 95.

NOTES

1. Augusta died on 23 Apr. of consumption complicated by her pregnancy the previous summer. CS was despondent over this loss and at first curtailed her publishing ef-

forts. Though she mourned Augusta's death for the rest of her life, the letters CS wrote during this year do not show the full intensity of her early grief. A surviving excerpt from a lost letter printed in her biography by Mary Hays in *Public Characters* (1801), 3:62, shows how much this daughter, her fourth child to die in her lifetime, meant to her:

> How lovely and how beloved she was those only who knew her can tell. In the midst of perplexity and distress, till the loss of my child, which fell like the hand of death upon me, I could yet exert my faculties; and, in the consciousness of resource which they afforded to me, experience a sentiment not dissimilar to that of the Medea of Corneille, who replied to the enquiry of her confidant—"Where now are your resources?"—"In myself!" (quoted in Dorset, "Charlotte Smith," p. 51)

2. On Cadell and Davies's recommendation, this advertisement was not published, nor was the subscription money restored. *Elegiac Sonnets ii* was not published until 1797, and its subscription list was rather short.

To Thomas Cadell, Jr., and William Davies

6 Seymour Street, Bath—May 17th
1795
Gentlemen,

I have a Letter to day from the Dutchess of Devonshire in which her Grace mentions her intention of sending to desire to speak with one of you on the subject of two more volumes of "Rural walks" Which she has for some time (indeed ever since she received the two first) wish'd me to undertake & has had the goodness to write to me repeatedly upon that subject. My unhappy suspence during the long illness of my lamented child prevented my doing more in it than telling her Grace that my want of money had induced me to offer you the two Volumes at your own price, but (that tho I had received individual kindness from the elder Mr Cadell) you had declined (on Mr Hayleys application) any engagt for two other Volumes, alledging that you had lost by the first publication & had paid me too much for them.

I shall only observe that the price was offer'd, not asked, & that, after I had told you I propos'd the books to be of the same size as Mrs Barbaulds "Evenings at home."[1] However it is certain that after the 1st sheet or two was printed, you manifested discontent; I know not why, for I promis'd nothing that I did not to the utmost of my abilities perform, & if your house overrated those abilities, it was not my fault but the elder Mr Cadells who made the proposal to me for a work of this sort many years ago.

The times, however, may be reason sufficient for any failure of success. Yet this was a sort of book which some of my friends thought less likely to be affected by them than any other. I own I cannot yet see how that can be calld an unsuccessful publication of which (as M[r] Davies himself said) near 500 Copies had been sold in about 5 weeks (when I saw him in Town), but however that may be, I do not wish you to buy what I am now setting about if you are likely to lose by it. The Dutchess has desird these volumes may be dedicated to her eldest daughter, Lady Georgiana Cavendish, & proposes naming them to you as a work which Her Grace means to promote with all her interest. Nothing however engages you to buy them even on your own terms, which was what I mention'd to M[r] Hayley; All the difference it will make to me is (except that I had much rather engage with your House than any other) that instead of calling these volumes "Rural Walks," I must find some other name for them & offer them elsewhere where I trust I may yet have credit enough with the Dutchess's assistance to get them accepted.

But you will see Gentlemen the necessity of your obliging me with an early answer tho after M[r] Hayleys application I should not have given you th[e] trouble, had I not received the Letter in question from the Dutchess of Devonshire, her Grace having arrived in Town after a long absence of five months only on Friday last. I am Gentlemen requesting the favor of hearing from you,[2]

y[r] obed[t] & most humble Ser[t],
Charlotte Smith

I am going from hence in ab[t] a week to the House of a friend on the Western Sea coast[3] & wish to make what arrang[ts] I can as to my Summer employ[t] before I go; & while my mind has yet force to exert itself so as to engage me in something which becomes more necessary, as when I am not compelld to be occupied, I sink into despondence—— and Poetry will not always be at hand.

Yale University MS. Address: Mess[rs] Cadell and Davies/ Strand/ London. Postmark: BATH; MA 18 95.

NOTES

1. See CS to Davies, 25 June 1794, and n. 3.

2. Ten days later Cadell and Davies answered in a very conciliatory tone, suggesting that the duchess's interest had influenced them to accept the work they had just refused:

> Madam
> The day after we were favoured with your Letter of the 17th we received a Note from the Duchess of Devonshire desiring to know when she could see us on the Subject of two more Volumes of "Rural Walks" in answer to which we informed her Grace that we would wait upon her whenever she would be pleased to direct, the Expectation of receiving her Grace's Commands, which we have not as yet been honoured with, induced us to delay writing, or we should have immediately answered your Letter—We are surprised to find that some Misapprehension has led you to understand that we declined the Purchase of your new Volumes upon any Terms whereas the only Proposal ever made to us respecting them was in your Letter of the 20th of Feby

> wherein you offer them to us upon the same Terms as the two first and in Answer to which we wrote declining them upon those Terms, but we assigned no Cause for our so doing, nor did we then express the smallest Dissatisfaction at the Price that had been paid for the former Volumes—— It is certainly true that we had, by this time discover'd that £100 was considerably too great a Sum for a Work of this Description but the Offer had been our own & we were therefore silent on the Subject—Considering ourselves much obliged by your writing to us further respecting these Volumes we are ready to undertake if it meets with your Approbation to pay you fifty Pounds for the Copyright of them the Instant we receive the MSS compleat —but we strongly recommend that the Work have some other Title than "Rural Walks" (though professing itself to be in some Degree a Continuation of that Work) being convinced that a book calculated for Schools and young Persons should not be extended beyond two Volumes——

3. CS's first letter from Exmouth, where she retreated to stay with her friend Miss Peckham, is dated more than three weeks later on 12 June. Virtually nonexistent in Devon, the Peckhams were a numerous family in Sussex; Miss Peckham, who left no trail in Exmouth, may have been a family friend there for her own health.

To Thomas Cadell, Jr., and William Davies

[Bath, 3 June 1795]
Gentlemen.

After I wrote to you enclosing Mrs Olmius's list of persons who had paid, I recieved a Letter from the Dutchess of Devonshire recommending it to me to take the Sum of 50£ for two additional Vol. (under some other title) on condition however of yr ~~advanting~~ advancing me 30£ which her Grace will answer for in case of any deficiency on my part (as I understand). She had even the goodness to say she would see you again upon it, but considering the numberless engagements with which I know her to be overwhelm'd at this moment, I doubt whether it will be possible for her to carry this intention into execution at least in time to procure for me what I want—the Sum necessary to remove from hence before I enter on a longer time for my lodgings which will involve me in great & needless expence while my own health suffers extremely by my stay here. I have no great hope that these considerations will much influence you, therefore do not urge them on that account, but I beleive that you wd find your own interest promoted. I can never want the money so much as I do now because as soon as the East India ships come in, I shall be releived from my difficulties, and in July I have interest money due to me,[1] but to be confined here six weeks in pain & grief will be very sad. The late distressing event has exhausted the kindness of my friends, & indeed were it not for these circumstances I would not sell any work for 50£ for which if done I Am sure I could procure more. I shall be much oblig'd to you to favour me with your answer by the return of the post.

The Dutchess of Devonshire is so obliging as to offer to dispose of several receipts for me. If you have any number sign'd, you will be so good as to send them immediately, if not to let me know that I may send up the few I have—or rather be pleas'd to write by the Coach, and send me some down that I may return them as soon as possible to her Grace, who will probably not be long in Town after the Birthday,[2] but who during her stay there has the means of serving me so materially in this respect. I shall be much oblig'd to you however to favor me with yr answer in regard to the other matter as soon as possible——

I am, Gent^{n}, your obed^{t} humble Ser^{t},
Charlotte Smith

June 3rd 1795——
Should you see her Grace you need only say that you have accepted or rejected my proposal, & leave her to make any proposition afterwards that she may have the kindness to think of on my behalf with^{t} naming any thing I have said[3]——

I shall be oblig'd to you to send me 2 sets of the new Edit^{n} of the Banish'd Man, As I sacrificed both my own to the corrections, a trouble which I find no other person ever takes.[4] If however this is deem'd too much, I will allow for them——

Leave to draw at a month or six weeks w^{d} answer the same end, as I have a friend who w^{d} then give me the Cash immediately.[5]

Yale University MS. Address: Messrs Cadell & Davies/ Strand/ London. Postmark: BATH; JU/ 4/ 95.

NOTES

1. CS's sons in India, William and Nicholas, sent her remittances of at least £100, but often £200 or £300, each year. This year, however, their money did not arrive until the following Jan. Each year in Jan. and July, she received interest money amounting to £35 from the trust.

2. That is, George III's birthday: 4 June. Cadell and Davies's note on this letter shows that they also sent 100 receipts for subscribers for her to sign and asked her to return 50 to them.

3. On the third, blank page of this letter, Cadell and Davies recorded their response:

> we consider fifty Pounds as the full Value (in a commercial Point of View) of two Volumes of the extent of those which you now propose to write—Since we have had the Honour of being connected with you as your Booksellers, we have, we trust, manifested a Disposition to afford you every Accommodation you desired, and, in Order to meet your Wishes on the

> present Occasion, we request you will draw upon us at a Month for £30 on Account of the new Work, and we will take Care it shall be honoured, trusting that the Manuscript will be sent to us as soon as you shall have compleated it——

4. They sent two copies of *The Banished Man* by coach. When it had been first published in Aug. 1794, CS complained angrily about its many errors.

5. That is, if you will send me a check that I can cash in a month or six weeks, my friend will give me cash against it immediately. The friend was probably Mrs. Augusta Nott of Bath (see CS to William Hayley, 12 June 1795, n. 5). A surviving receipt shows that CS had already borrowed £7.7 from her on 30 May against her account with Cadell and Davies.

To William Hayley

Exmouth, June 12th 1795
Dear Sir,

I seize the first moment after a long and fatigueing journey and the painful circumstances that attend seeing my family (particularly one of them whom I have not met these fifteen months)[1] to thank you for your very kind Letter & to apologize for My indiscretion in having repeated my request about Cadell and Davies. You will I trust recollect that it was before I knew yr resolution on that hand, & I beg you will beleive I will not so intrude upon you again.[2] Mr De Foville desires me to say that he is very much oblig'd to you for all the trouble you have taken for him. There is but little probability of success, & he will go under the auspices of the Dutchess of Devonshire to Jersey when ever a descent is really made on the Coast of France. Not that I expect such a measure on the part of Government will ever take place—— We are both rather better for change of scene, but we seem to follow or to be follow'd by sickness and sorrow, for the kind young friend who with so much tenderness and affection received my children when I was unable myself to attend them[3] & who has shewn them so much kindness when their relations & my friends stood aloof is in so bad a state of health herself and I fear so decidedly in a decline, that I apprehend ~~fear~~ there are no hopes. To day she keeps her bed, & I find the Physical Men who attend her think extremely ill of her situation——

The situation of this place is charming to any one who cares about beauty, But to me all places are now alike—— I wish I could afford to take a small house here, but that I shall now hardly ever be able to do any where—— What is to become of me or where I am to drag on the few months or years my unhappy existence, I know not & to say the truth I do not much care———

If it should happen (which however I do not expect) that you have any commands for me, Lord Egremont will I doubt not be so good as to give you a frank Under which, if it be directed to Miss Smith,[4] I may have the pleasure of hearing from you. If the money you are so Good as to mention goes to Bath, My inestimable friend Mrs Nott[5] will open any of my Letters & dispose of the contents for me there; it was with very great difficulty I found the means of leaving Bath. I am very sorry to hear so sad an account of Cowper, Yet those who are awake to imaginary evils feel not the real, & I really think there are sorrows compared to which madness is preferable—

My family unite in every good wish with, Dear Sir,

your most oblig'd Ser^t^,
Charlotte Smith

I wish to have all Letters directed under cover to Miss Smith because I hope to escape being harrass'd as I have been by my place of residence being for at least a while unknown.

Liverpool Libraries and Information Services MS. Address: {William Hayley Esqre}/ London June thirteenth 1795/ W. Hayley Esq/ Eartham/ Chichester./ Egremont.[6] *Postmark: {no place}; JU/ 13/ 95.*

NOTES

1. It is difficult to determine which of her family she had not seen for so long a time. Augusta, de Foville, Lucy, Harriet, and George had all been with CS at Storrington on 20 Jan. 1794. On 25 Mar., CS was planning to move to Bath with only Harriet. Augusta came to Bath, ill and pregnant, early in June. Lucy was living with her mother and writing letters for her on 12 Dec. When CS went to London in Jan. to straighten out the warrant on him for sending a challenge to Dyer, Lionel was already recruiting with his regiment at Bedford, Newport Pagnell, and Northampton. Although it seems likely that George, the youngest, spent some of this time with her, he is not mentioned. Thus he may have been at Mr. Parsons' school at Midhurst and then moved to Miss Peckham's. It is more likely that CS had not seen Charlotte Mary or Charles. Charlotte Mary was living with relatives in Islington on 20 Aug. and was still there on 7 and 24 Dec. Charles, also not mentioned, had returned to military service and had been estranged from his mother since at least the spring of 1794, when he caused her undue expense by staying on in the house at Storrington.

2. Hayley must have refused to intervene further with her publishers. His trouble on de Foville's behalf is not explained.

3. Miss Peckham had kept several of CS's children, but no explanation is given of who stayed with her and how long they stayed. She recovered sufficiently from her illness for CS's family to stay with her until Jan.

4. That is, to Charlotte Mary at Miss Peckham's.

5. A near contemporary of CS, Augusta Hawkins (1746–1813) married Samuel Nott (1740–1793) in 1766. Her father, Pennell Hawkins, had served as sergeant-surgeon to the king and her husband as the king's chaplain.The Reverend Mr. Nott

and Mrs. Nott separately subscribed for two copies each of *Elegiac Sonnets i,* and one copy each of *Elegiac Sonnets ii.* Mrs. Nott occasionally lent CS money, and she helped gather subscriptions for the second volume of sonnets.

6. Addressed in another handwriting, this letter was probably franked.

To Thomas Cadell, Jr., and William Davies

[Exmouth, 29 June 1795]

Gentlemen,

I conclude you have before now receivd the sign'd receipts[1] & sent those to the Dutchess of Devonshire which were design'd for her Grace. The occasion of my troubling you now is to beg you w[d] send me a direction to M[r] Corbould the Engraver[2] if you know it And farther to request the favor of you to forward to me under cover to Miss Peckham, Exmouth (as I am not sure of being there myself) any Letters which may come from India. I hope the Ships will now almost immediately be in.

The first volume of the continuation of Rural Walks will very soon be done. Do you wish to have it sent up before the other?

I shall be glad also to know the progress of the subscription, as it is now many months since I had any list—— Your attention to these requests at your leisure[3] will oblige, Gentlemen, your most obed[t] humble Ser[t],

Charlotte Smith

Should any body enquire at your house for a direction to me, I entreat you not to give it, as my stay here will not only be very short, but as quiet is the only chance I have for regaining my health & pursuing my business. June 29th 1795——

Osborn Collection MS, Yale University. Address: M[r] Cadell & Davies/ Strand/ London. Postmark: {no place}; JY/ 2/ 95.

NOTES

1. On 3 June, Cadell and Davies had sent 100 subscription receipts for CS and asked her to sign and return 50 of them.

2. Richard Corbould (1757–1831) painted oil and watercolor portraits and landscapes and also did porcelains, miniatures on ivory, enamels, and, as here, book illustrations.

3. On 7 July, Cadell and Davies replied that the subscription receipts had come "safe to hand" and those for the duchess had been sent to her. They sent CS Corbould's address at John Street, Tottenham Court Road, and they agreed to put the first volume of *Rambles Farther* into the printer's hands as soon as they received it. They added that they had received "very few" new subscriptions since the last reported, the "whole amount received by us being 60.7.6."

To William Davies

[Exmouth, 9 July 1795]
Sir,

Having received a Letter to day from Mr Robinson in which he assents to the payment of 35£ at the House of I L Blackman, Son, and Co—which 35£ is but half a years interest of 3000£ (my own money) which Mr Smith is so very good as to allow me for the maintenance of myself and his children, I beg you will be so good as to permit me to draw for it payable to you, as I dare not draw in favor of any person here as I at first thought of because the post is so uncertain that I have lost two Packets of Letters directed to Sir Elijah Impey[1] within this month, wherefore it would be hazardous to send up an endorsed draft. When it is paid, I shall be much oblig'd to send it down in a cut bank note by two posts, or in any other way which is likely to be safe.[2] I suppose it will be paid as Messrs Blackman & Co have 394£ pounds [*sic*] in their hands & have had for many months. I shall esteem it as a favor if you will take the trouble to do this for me and also to let me hear from you as soon as may be convenient as I want the money. I am, Sir, your most obedt Sert,

Charlotte Smith

I have sent Messrs Blackman & Co notice of this draft & a copy of Mr Robinsons Letter. I shall not however be surprised if they find some excuse to evade the payment, but it is material to me to know as soon as possible. I also beg to hear at yr Leisure in answer to my last. You will of course charge the Postage &c——

Osborn Collection MS, Yale University. Address: Mr Davies/ Messrs Cadell & Davies's/ Opposite ——— ——Catharine Street/ Strand/ London. Postmark: [no place]; JY 9 95.

NOTES

1. First chief justice of India under Warren Hastings, from 1774 to 1789. In 1784, Sir Elijah (1732–1809) returned to England to face impeachment over his handling of Nand Kumar's trial but was acquitted, not resigning his post for another five years. In 1794, he settled at Newick Park, Sussex, near Uckfield, where CS would have been writing to him. The subject of her letters to him is not known. In 1789, Lady Impey had subscribed to *Elegiac Sonnets i,* as had her husband's natural and oldest son, Archibald Elijah Impey.

2. Davies added that the first halves of the notes were sent to CS at Miss Peckham's on 14 July and the second halves on 18 July.

To William Davies

[Exmouth, 16 July 1795]
Sir,

I received the 2 half bank bills this morning and am sorry that for want of precision in my date or direction I have given you more trouble than was necessary. I shall be much obliged to you to forward the other halves under the same address by the earliest post; if put in on Saturday night, they will reach me on Monday—— If not till Monday, they will not be hear [*sic*] before Wednesday as there is no post here on Teusdays. I am much obliged to you for the trouble you have taken. My friend being unable to remove from hence yet, my family part of whom reside with her will remain stationary here for some time; when therefore the India Letters arrive, I shall be much obliged to you to send them to the same address. I think they may now be expected every day. I am, Sir, with thanks,

your obed[t] humble Ser[t],
Charlotte Smith

Exmouth. July 16th 1795
Direction
"Miss Peckham; Exmouth, Exeter; Devon"

Yale University MS. Address: Mr Davies/ Mess[rs] Cadell & Davies's/ Strand/ London. Postmark: no place; JY 18 95.

To Thomas Cadell, Jr., and William Davies

[Exmouth, 22 July 1795]
Gent[n]

I received the two other halves of Banknotes to day and am much oblig'd to you for the trouble you have taken. I was and am so uncertain of my stay here (because our friend is so very unwell as to wait only for strength to go to Portugal) when or at least in Autumn I shall return to Bath that I have given nobody my address & wish if it is enquired after you would not give it, as I am unable to attend to matters of business, and postage is very expensive. In regard to the Book, I will send it up in the course of a fortnight or three weeks, but oweing to frequent weaknesses in my hands, I have written part of it so ill that my eldest daughter[1] is transcribing it for me which goes on slowly. However you will have it during the Leisure of the Printers—— —

There ~~are people~~ is here a person who keeps a circulating Library who wishes to lay out from eight to ten pounds in novels to encrease his small collection for which I understand he pays ready money. He applied to me to inform him of a bookseller in London who would supply him. I do not know whether it is any object to your House, or whether you deal in this way, but I told the Man that, having occasion to write to you to day, I would mention it, and that if your House undertook it, there was no doubt of his being treated with the greatest integrity. But that if it was out of your line of business, of which I was not sure, that I had no doubt but that you would put it into the hands of some Bookseller of reputation who was in habits of supplying Country dealers. I shall be oblig'd to you to let me know whether you can furnish these books, and how far the Sum above named will go in the purchase of the undermentiond Books—bound in strong bindings for circulation: The Recess, Errors of Innocence, Man of feeling, Man of the World, Fatal Obedience, Manon l'Escaut, Modern Wife, The Sylph, Ethelinde, Paul and Mary, Things as they are, Zeluco, Emily Montague, Arundel, Henry, The Sorrows of Werter, The Mirror, The Adventurer, The World, Florians new Tales,[2] & such other new books of <u>very</u> light reading as are most in request—— As this is the season when the Library is most frequented & I understand the Man's Money is ready, I shall be oblig'd to you for as early an answer to this article as possible.

Having occasion for some of my own books without which I cannot write, I have directed a box of them to be sent out of Sussex where I left them, & as some difficulties & delays might arise in their passing thro London, I have order'd them to be directed to be left at yr house p^{r} Waggon from Petworth. You will be so good as to put the carriage and porterage to my account & to let the Trunk or box remain in some corner of y^{r} Warehouse till you hear from me; as however I want the books, I am unwilling to have them sent {on} so long a journey till I know more than I do now whether I shall remain here or pass the rest of the Summer at some other place before my return to Bath. In doing this, you will very much oblige, Gentlemen, your most obed^{t} Ser^{t},

Charlotte Smith

Exmouth. 22nd July 1795

If I should remove from hence, I will give you immediate notice on account of the India Letters. Till then you will be so good as to direct for me as y^{r} last & sh^{d} those Letters come to forward them instantly.

Yale University MS. Address: Messrs Cadell and Davies/ Strand/ London. Postmark: {no place}; JY 24 95.

NOTES

1. Charlotte Mary, the eldest daughter, had joined the family at Exmouth to help out.

2. Circulating libraries abounded in London by the 1780s and were spreading into the provinces in the 1790s. Subscribers could pay quarterly or yearly (up to three pounds), or could rent books singly at two pence a volume. The demand to stock the shelves of these libraries is widely blamed for the decline of the novel's quality in CS's time, compared to its brilliant beginnings with Richardson, Fielding, Smollett, and Sterne. CS's list of novels shows her attempt to help a man later identified as Mr. Langsford start his new library with some current and some older works of good reputation.

Their full titles, dates, and authors are *The Recess* (1783–85), Sophia Lee; *Errors of Innocence* (1786), Harriet Lee; *The Man of Feeling* (1771) and *The Man of the World* (1773), Henry Mackenzie; *Fatal Obedience; or the History of Mr. Freeland* (1780?), introductory letter signed "T. Wilmot"; *The Modern Wife. A Novel* (1769), John Stevens; *The Sylph* (1779), Georgiana Cavendish, duchess of Devonshire; *Paul and Mary, An Indian Story* (1789), Jacques-Henri Bernadin de Saint-Pierre's *Paul et Virginie* (trans. Daniel Malthus); *Things As They Are; or, the Adventures of Caleb Williams* (1794), William Godwin; *Zeluco* (1789), Dr. John Moore; *The History of Emily Montague* (1769), Frances Brooke; *Arundel* (1789) and *Henry* (1795), Richard Cumberland; and *The Sorrows of Werther* (1779), attributed to Richard Graves or Daniel Malthus as translator (from a French translation). Presumably in requesting *Manon Lescaut,* she was referring to the anonymous 1786 translation with her preface (see CS to an unnamed recipient, ca. Sept. 1785). *New Tales, from the French* (1792) was by Jean Pierre Claris de Florian; no translator was named.

Three were journals, reprinted and available in book form: *The Mirror* (1779–80, nos. 1–110), 10th ed., published by A. Strahan and T. Cadell (1794); *The Adventurer* (1752–54, nos. 1–140), edited by John Hawksworth with 29 nos. by Samuel Johnson; and *The World* (1753–56, nos. 1–209), published by Robert Dodsley and edited by Edward Moore.

To William Davies

[Exmouth, 28 July 1795]

Sir,

Among the Letters you were so obliging as to forward to me from India (which however I hope are not all that will come for me when the whole shall be deliverd) was the within Bill from my second Son[1] for One hundred pounds; I have received the first, second & third by the Montrose, Raymond and Sir Edward Hughs, which makes me fear that my Son has not written by any of these Ships & gives me great concern, as I have now had no Letter whatever from him dated later than May, 1793. However his having given an order for this remittance gives me the comfort of knowing that he was alive & well in January 1795——As this Bill has twelvemonths after sight to run, I do not suppose I shall get it discounted but at a great loss.

However I must request the favor of you, if not too much trouble, to have it forthwith presented for acceptance, & then I must do as well as I can about it——I trust that by tomorrows post I shall receive other Letters from both, but particularly from my eldest Son who is now, as his Letter of the 25th Novr informs me, in possession of a place of great trust and advantage, & who in a former Letter told me he had sent me in May 1794 a considerable remittance, of which (probably supposing that it was already out of question) he makes no mention in this last Letter but which I have never received. The last amount was two hundred pounds, but I had reason to expect more. I trust you will excuse my taking the liberty to ask this favor of you, & if such trouble is inconvenient to you, to say so. As Messrs Blackman & Co., tho they hold near five hundred pounds of my childrens in their hands, decline parting with any of it tho Mr Robinson has written for that purpose an order to them, which they will not honor because Parkin the other Trustee will not join with him, I think their conduct so unfriendly that I do not wish to give them any trouble on my account, & indeed I feel some reluctance to put myself in any way in their power, for they have as much right to withhold this Bill as the money they have.[2] I mention this to account for my asking this favor of you when it seems more in the course of business to apply to them—& In expectation of your answer, I am,

Sir,
your most obedt humble Sert,
Charlotte Smith

Exmouth. July 28th 1795

Osborn Collection MS, Yale University. Address: Mr Davies/ at Messrs Cadell & Davies's/ Strand/ London. Postmark: {no place}; JY/ 30/ 95.

NOTES

1. Nicholas Hankey Smith (1771–1837), CS's second-oldest son. Like her oldest son William, he was with the East India Company, starting as a writer in 1788 and arriving in Bombay in 1790. From October 1792 to October 1798, he was resident at Bushire. His bill, dated Bombay, Jan. 1795, was to have been drawn by Rivet Wilkinson & Co. on Thomas Wilkinson, Esq., or in his absence by William Dent, Esq., at Garraway's Coffee House, and endorsed by CS. Davies added a note that Dent accepted it, and it was returned on 4 Aug. to CS at Miss Peckham's.

2. CS here acknowledges that because the bill was made out to her, Parkin and Robinson could have kept it on BS's account.

To Thomas Cadell, Jr., and William Davies

[Exmouth, 19 August 1795]

. . . you[1] entertaind, is likely to go into another Edition—If these written corrections do not answer your purpose, I will send you up the set I have here corrected, but I thought that if this answerd the same purpose, it w^{d} save you the carriage & me the necessity of parting from the books which I want. But if you apprehend the printer cannot work as well from written corrections, I will send you up these volumes with the 1st of the Sequel[2] which will be ready in ten days or a fortnight. I have not yet made up my mind about a name, & to find one is more difficult than I apprehended. I do not find that Mrs Barbauld has found the objection you stated to obtain: i.e. that no childrens books or those intended for young persons, should exceed 2 volumes, for I understand that she had publish'd a fourth volume of Evenings at home—tho the 3rd was very inferior to the two first, & tho her narrative being disjointed & desultory she had not the same reasons as I sh^{d} have for continuing the same title. However I must fix upon a title as well as I can if it is still your opinion that the same must not be continued.

Soon after I had written to you about the Books wanted by the Man who keeps a sort of circulating Library in this Village, he received from Mr Owen, his former correspondent (who had he thought much neglected him,) some of those he wanted, but the following he still wishes to have. Zeluco, The recess, Ethelinde, Sidney Biddulph, Things as they are, Fatal Obedience, The Man of feeling, A simple story, The last publication of D. Moore <Nat Natura?>[3]—I do not know what is the title. If you will be so good as to let me previously know the amount of these, most of which I think you publishd He will send up the money; I shall be oblig'd to you to send me Mr Hayleys Elegy on the death of Sir W Jones, and Mr Merrys Fenelon or the Nuns of Cambray[4]——

I have been much disappointed at not receiving any Letters from My eldest Son since the first with the 300£ remittances of which he speaks. As the Boddington, Eccho & Dart all arrived since the fleet have probably deliverd their Letters, I fear there are now no hopes but in the 2nd fleet. If any Letters however reach y^{r} hands, I entreat the fav^{r} of you to let me have them by the very earliest conveyance—— I am, Gent^{n}, y^{r} most obed Ser^{t},

Charlotte Smith

Exmouth. August 19th [17]95

64.4.4½
19.1.0

45.5.4½
57.18.10½
12.13.6

45.5 .4½[5]

Yale University MS. Address: Messrs Cadell Junr & Davies/ Strand/ London. Postmark: BATH; AU 21, 95.

NOTES

1. The first half of this letter is missing.

2. "These volumes" refers to the four volumes of *The Banished Man,* which CS had just corrected in hopes of a second edition. She is returning a corrected four-volume set, along with the first volume of the sequel to *Rural Walks,* which has not yet been named *Rambles Farther.*

3. To her original list sent on 22 July, she has added the following: *Memoirs of Miss Sidney Biddulph* (1761), by Frances Sheridan, and *A Simple Story* (1791), by Elizabeth Inchbald. Dr. John Moore's most recent novel was *Zeluco: Various Views of Human Nature* (1789); the word "nature," which she seems to be trying to write here, does not appear in the titles to his more recent philosophical tracts.

4. William Hayley's *An Elegy on the Death of the Honourable Sir William Jones [1746–1794], a Judge of the Supreme Court of Judicature in Bengal, & President of the Asiatic Society* (Cadell and Davies, 1795); *Fenelon or the Nuns of Cambray* (1795) is Robert Merry's adaptation of Marie Joseph Blaise de Chénier's play.

5. Written upside down at the end of the letter.

To Thomas Cadell, Jr., and William Davies

[Exmouth] Sep^{t} 3rd [17]95
Gentlemen,

I received the Elegy with y^{r} Letter on Teusday & sent the list of books to Langsford, who has desir'd me to receive from him the amount & remit it to you, which I will do in the pacquet with the first volume of the continuation of Rural Walks, if you have not as much as that in your hands of mine which I imagine you have. This you will inform me of, & I will act accordingly; and in the mean time, as the money is paid to me, the Man will consider himself oblig'd to you to send down the books (including fatal Obedience and Sidney Biddulph if you can get them, even at second hand) As soon as possible because the place is now full and the demand of his readers at this time greater than at any other.

Mr Walker[1] of the Treasury Chamber, Dublin, informs me that Mr Archer, Bookseller of Dublin, who is (as I recollect) your correspondent there, has or will call upon you with some names (and I conclude the money) for the new ~~Edition~~ Volume of Sonnets; I should be glad to know if you have seen him. Mr Walker promis'd to send me a Novel call'd (I have forgot what) but I beleive Darcy, publish'd in my name at Dublin with a dedication to the Duke of York — — The Maneuvre was even more impudent than the usual impudent attempts of Irish bookmakers & booksellers, & I had rather a curiosity to see what the worthy Author said to his RH[2] in my name. If therefore it is left with you, be so good as to send it down with Langsfords books; I am much afraid, as you do not mention its arrival, that the box of Books out of Sussex are not come which I account for by beleiving that Mr Turner's unhappiness ab^t^ his Son, who is order'd abroad, has prevented his attending to my request. I have written to him again about them & beg the favor of you to let me know when they arrive, as I cannot possibly finish what I am about without the books, & it is extremely discouraging to be delayd for want of them—— As to sending to the Libraries at Exeter, nothing can be so fruitless, for after being at great expence for carriage I get only mutilated books or sets so incomplete that what I want to refer to is not to be found.

My stay here I now beleive will be lengthen'd till the middle of next month, but least it should not, I w^d^ not have the books sent from London till I have notice. In expectation of hearing from you soon relative to Langsford if you prefer any other method to that I have propos'd, I am, Gent^n^,

y^r^ oblig'd & obed^t^ Ser^t^, in Great haste,
Charlotte Smith

MS Vault, Yale University. Address: Messrs Cadell & Davies/ Strand/ London. Postmark: {no place}; SE/ 5/ 95.

NOTES

1. Joseph Cooper Walker.
2. His Royal Highness, Frederick, the duke of York (1763–1827), second son of George III.

{To William Davies}

{Place and date uncertain}
. . . I[1] should however be glad to know how the matter really stands by an early post. I have also to beg you would add to the Subscription book the name of "the Revd Mr Carwardine" And that you would inform Mr Cadell

that in in [*sic*] course of next week I shall probably have occasion to draw for ten pounds which will exceed by two or three pounds only the Sum I named to Mr Hayley & which will I conclude make no difference to him—— I am, in expectation of an early answer, Sir, y^r ob^t Ser^t,

Charlotte Smith

Yale University MS. No address or postmark.

NOTE

1. This undated note appears just after the letter of 3 Sept. The top half of the page is cut away.

To Thomas Cadell, Jr., and William Davies

[Exmouth, 24 October 1795]
Gent^n

As I have every day reason to hope for Letters from India which I should have had to acknowledge and as I was every day expecting to hear you had received the MMS and to know whether you desired to have the rest up by the post,[1] I did not write to acknowledge the receipt of the Boxes which came perfectly safe, but not till the 16th of this month.

Excessive vexation about one of my family[2] has so occupied me in Letter writing & so worried my spirits that I have not had the heart to set about correcting and writing out fair such parts as may want it of the new publication, but now, as it is of no use to fret any more ab^t inevitable evils, I will apply myself to the MMS & send you up a considerable parcel in three or four days. I wish I may at the same time have an opportunty of acknowledging the receipt of Letters from My Son which I have so long expected. I will then let you know whither to direct when I quit this place. I am, Gent^n, Y^r most obed humble Ser^t,

Charlotte Smith

Exmouth. 24th Octr 1795

General Manuscripts, Manuscripts Division, Rare Books and Special Collections, Princeton University Library. Address: Messrs Cadell & Davies/ Strand/ London. Postmark: {no place}; OC/ 26/ 95.

NOTES

1. Some portion of *Rambles Farther.* A week later CS finds the whole of the first volume too heavy to send by post. See CS to Cadell and Davies, 2 Nov. 1795.

2. She explains this "vexation" more fully in CS to Cadell and Davies, 2 Nov. 1795.

To Thomas Cadell, Jr., and William Davies

Exmouth, 2nd Nov [17]95

Gentlemen,

By the Carrier tomorrow, I shall send off a parcel of the new publication for young persons which will be too heavy for the post, & you shall have the whole of the 1st Vol. immediately afterwards. The anxiety I have been in abt one of my family who was likely to form a connection utterly disagreeable to me[1] has kept my spirits in such a state of trouble that tho the Work has been long in a state to want only correcting & clearing for the press, I have been utterly unable to attend to that or any thing. My uneasiness is now at an end, & I hope to summon resolution enough to go on with my business since continually to labour while others remain possess'd of the property to which I have a right seems to be my unhappy lot——

I am cruelly disappointed at not receiving any Letters from India by these last Ships. Ever since the month of March, I have been in expectation of remittances to the amount of 300£ which my eldest Son, in Letters I received from him by the Sugar Cane Country ships & Nancy Packet, inform'd me he had partly sent & should send in the course of the year 94: but I have never had the least intelligence since of any such remittances, nor can I account for their detention as it never happen'd before. I have written to Muilmans House[2] on which his former draughts were usually given by my Sons agents at Calcutta—Messrs Barber and Palmer, but they have no advise of any such bills. I have also lost two very valuable Persian Shawls made on purpose at Thibet & worth at least 40 Guineas a piece. These were sent by order of my second Son from a Mr Church at Bombay, but they have never come to my hands.

Disappointed of every hope & not able to obtain any settlement from the Trustees tho they have never had less than 500£ of my Childrens money laying dead in their hands, I know not whither to turn me. It is impossible that I can support my family if I were to work at my desk from Sun rise to Sun set, & I am not able to make the exertions I have done, for since my last bitter misfortune my spirits are too much depressd.

On the 2nd of January, I shall have thirty five pounds due to me, part of the interest for half a year of such part of my own fortune as Mr Smith pleases to allow me for myself & my family. As there is in Mr Blackmans hands 285£ left of the produce of last year & twelve hgds[3] of Sugar received this, One wd think that I might be oblig'd with so very small a favor as only two months advance of this small Sum. I extremely want it, as I must remove from hence on Wednesday sennight at latest & cannot witht this money. Will you, Mr Davies, be so obliging as to see if you can get this bill which I enclose accepted for me, & possibly you may also get it discounted & be able to send me the money. I am very sorry to trouble you, but I really know not what to do or where to apply.

I have written to the Dutchess of Devonshire to try again what her Grace can do for us towards obtaining a settlement for us in which benevolent purpose she engaged with goodness all her own for many months last year, but I fear from the dreadful confusion which reigns in London[4] her Grace will not have so much of her time & kindness to give me as she has given. In the mean time, every article of life even at this distance from London so rapidly encreases in price that I now pay (& with a smaller family) sixteen shillings p[r] week for an article of absolute necessity which a little time since cost me only nine,[5] & I find it will be impossible for me to go on with[t] this my just right. I shall pay the carriage of the parcel as it is my fault that it is sent up in pieces. I am, Gent[n],

y[r] obed[t] & oblig'd Ser[t],
Charlotte Smith

You will charge me the postage of this &c As being solely on my business.

Yale University MS. Address: M[r] Davies/ Mess[rs] Cadell Jun[r] & Davies/ Strand/ London. Postmark: {no place}; NO/ 5/ 95.

NOTES

1. Discretion prevents CS from naming the wayward family member here or elsewhere. "He," as she later lets slip, could not have been one of her sons as all were either out of the country or too young. Charles had been stationed at Gibraltar since Sept. 1795. Lionel was stationed in Quebec, and on 29 May 1796, she wrote to Joseph Cooper Walker that she had last heard from him in Oct. 1795. George was only about 9 or 10 years old. With her sons accounted for, the family member might have been de Foville or one of the nephews.

2. Richard Muilman and Company, Merchants, 46 Old Broad Street, London.

3. Hogsheads are large casks or barrels, holding 63 to 140 gal. The volume of a hogshead of molasses was set at 100 gal. in 1749.

4. In Oct., crowds had stoned the state coach, shouting "Down with George!" and protesting inflation driven by war on the Continent; the king's growing unpopularity reflected a widespread dislike of the Prince of Wales's conduct.

5. Inflation had increased the prices of most basic commodities during the year. A measure of wheat alone, which had cost 7 s. in Jan., had risen to 13 s. 6 d. in Aug.; it dropped back down to 10 s. 5 d. only in Nov.

To William Davies

Exmouth, 11th Novr
[17]95
Sir,

I am very much oblig'd to you for the trouble you have taken abt the draft. As I have an agreement from the Wretches who call themselves Trustees, dated in 1787, to pay this small allowance always 6 months in advance, I was well authorisd in the request I made. The infamous refusal of Parkin will hasten the execution of a resolution I had before taken, and I have accordingly sent up an advertisement for which, if a person engaged in the printing business should call upon you for the payment, you will be so good as to satisfy him. It will be but a few shillings——

I hope you have before now received a parcel sent from hence on Saty last Some days later than I mention'd to you, but it was oweing to a blunder of the Carrier who goes from hence to Exeter & whose journies depend on the business he has to make them answer so that at this time of the year he has no regular days.

I am going on correcting the rest, & I hoped to have been by this time settled so much nearer London that I might without expence or trouble have seen the progress of this little work & have had all my books which are in Sussex about me, the want of which extremely protracts composition and correction, but the refusal of this trifling accommodation & the delay of that final arrangement which Mr Erskine, the Dtss of Devonshire, and Lord Egremont have taken so much pains to bring about—together with the failure of my expected remittances from India—at once detain me here & depress my spirits so much that I have hardly any heart to work at all.

My Sister Mrs Dorset[1] insists upon it that there must be letters lying for me at the India House or Post Office, but as Mr W[illiam]. T[owers]. Smith always used to direct your care & his Letters always came safe, I cannot imagine this to be the Case. Should you witht much trouble have an opportunity of making any enquiry, it would much oblige me tho it is rather to satisfy her than because I have any hope myself that there are any Letters whatever kept back—— I will give you due notice of the next parcel which will contain the whole of the 1st Volume. I believe I have found a name which will be proper, you will let me know if you want it when you begin to Print.

I am, Sir, your oblig'd humble Sert,
Charlotte Smith

Yale University MS. Address: Mr Davies/ Messrs Cadell Jun & Davies/ Strand/ London. Postmark: {no place}; NO/ 13/ 95.

NOTE

1. Catherine Turner Dorset, CS's younger sister, author of several children's volumes beginning with *The Peacock at Home and Other Poems* (1809).

To Thomas Cadell, Jr., and William Davies

[?Exmouth, 17 November 1795][1]
Sir,

Be so good as to put the within in the Penny post and charge the amount of postage up to me.

If you begin printing the new work, I shall be glad to see the 1st sheet. You shall receive the residue of the 1st volume in the course of the ensuing week—— I am, Sir, yr most obedt humble Sert,

Charlotte Smith

Yale University MS. Address: Mr Davies/ Messrs Cadell Junr & Davies's/ Strand/ London. Postmark: {no place}; NO/ 17/ <95>

NOTE

1. In Nov. 1795, CS was sending the first volume of *Rambles Farther* to Cadell and Davies in bits and pieces. Although undated, this note has a partially legible postmark, leaving both year and place unclear. The date stamp is the same as other letters sent from Exmouth, and like them, the place is not stamped.

To William Davies

[Exmouth, 22 November 1795]
Sir

I beg the favor of you to let a careful person go for me to the General post Office and pay the postage of the enclos'd, which is a Letter of consequence, to whatever port Letters to Germany are now sent from, charging it to me[1]—— I am persuaded you will pardon my giving you this trouble, as the people at the post Office here know not what to take or whither to send it—— I am in hopes of very material Letters from India—— pray send them immediately. I shall write with the MMS in a few days. I am, Sir,

yr oblig'd humble Sert,
Charlotte Smith

Exmouth, Novr 22nd 1795

Yale University MS. Address: Mr Davies/ at Messrs Cadell & Davies's/ Strand/ 22nd Novr/ London. Postmark: {no place}; NO/ 24/ 95.

NOTE

1. Cadell and Davies posted other letters to Germany for CS's son-in-law de Foville. See CS to Cadell, Jr., and Davies, 17 Mar. 1797 and 16 May 1797.

To [Robert] Bliss[1]

[Exmouth, 22 November 1795]
M^rs^. Smith requests Mr Bliss will be so good as to send her two or three more numbers of the British Critic, particularly that in which "Montalbert" is Review'd which is she thinks four or five months since. Perhaps more——
She wishes also to see a Novel call'd "the Ghost seer, A translation from the German"[2] if Mr Bliss has it or can get it——
Teusday 22nd Nov^r^

National Library of Scotland, Edinburgh, MS 844, f.50v. No address or postmark.

NOTES

1. Robert Bliss, bookseller, Oxford. Following a pattern set with booksellers in Bath while she was living there, CS regularly borrowed money from Bliss during the next two years while she lived at Headington, a village next to Oxford.

2. Johann Friedrich von Schiller's *The Ghost-Seer; or Apparitionist. An Interesting Fragment, Found among the Papers of Count O*****,* trans. Daniel Boileau (1795).

To Thomas Cadell, Jr., and William Davies

[Exmouth, 25 November 1795]
Gent^n^,

So tedious is the carriage to this place that I did not get the proof till Yesterday. I return it as soon as possible by the post as the only quick conveyance on which I can depend, & even that is of two days, & I fear will turnout very dear, but as I imagine it very possible that the press may stand still, I dare not trust to the Carrier who sometimes leaves parcels a day or two at Exeter before he brings them hither, & I suppose they often lie there as long as I had lately a small box from Bath ten days on its way. If I am so lucky as to have any Lttrs from India by these ships, I beg of you, however heavy they may be, not to send them by the Coach, for Poor as I am, I w^d^ rather pay any Sum for postage than wait in anxiety for News from Mr W. T. Smith or M^r^ N[icholas]. H[ankey] Smith. I have occasion to send up to my Solictor, Mr Bicknell, Norfolk S^t^, Strand, two deeds on my Childrens affairs, which I shall be much oblig'd to you to let y^r^ porter take to him as soon as they arrive. I propose sending them Off on the evening of tomorrow; When they will reach London, it is hard to say. The MMS of "Rambles farther" will accompany them.

As soon as I receive Money from India or from the Men who chuse to detain what belongs to me, I shall move from hence, and I beleive to the neighbourhood of London where I can more conveniently overlook any Letterpress you may wish to put into my hands for correction, but at present my hands are tied. I have compelld the wretched miscreants to pay me my 35£, but it is not yet come down, & I have waited for it so long that It will do but little towards my removal. I am, Gent^{n}, Y^{r} Oblig'd hble Ser^{t},

Charlotte Smith

Novr 25th [17]95

Yale University MS. Address: [Cade]ll Junr and Davies—/ Strand/ London [half of page cut away]. Postmark: [no place]; No/ 27/ 95.

1796
"A WANDERER UPON EARTH"

—29 MAY 1796

In the year after Augusta's death, Charlotte Smith did indeed wander from one to another residence, leaving Exmouth in January for Weymouth, where she had two different addresses, and moving on by November to Headington near Oxford. She had recovered enough from her grief to complete several projects begun the year before. Early in the year, Sampson Low and C. Law published her Narrative of the loss of the Catharine, Venus and Piedmont Transports, *a subscription edition for the benefit of a sailor's widow.* Marchmont, *published by Low, also came out in this year. Her letters are mainly concerned, however, with* Rambles Farther, *which Cadell and Davies first rejected and then agreed to publish under the sponsorship of the duchess of Devonshire. Smith struggled to make her dedication to the duchess's older daughter perfect. That work completed in early summer, Smith resumed work on her long-delayed second volume of* Elegiac Sonnets, *which was being published by subscription.*

Smith's children's lives were calm during this busy year. Only copying law papers and coping with the renewed threat of one child's bad marriage interrupted Smith's steady labor. William and Nicholas sent needed money from India, and Charles served under General Trigge in Gibraltar. Lionel was an ensign in the 24th regiment in Canada. The three daughters were well. Charlotte Mary stayed with her cousin Richard Smith in Islington, and Lucy visited Richard's sister, Mrs. Robert Allen, in Lymington. Harriet and George were living at home.

To Thomas Cadell, Jr., and William Davies

Exmouth, Jan[y] 5th 1796
Gentlemen,

I receiv'd yesterday y[r] obliging Letter. I had before heard the pacquet was safe, but the tediousness of every mode of conveyance from hence as well as the risk is extremely distressing. I am doing my utmost now to make up for the lost time that this & the generally untoward circumstances of this place [where it is impossible to get the least assistance from Books, which in such a work cannot be dispens'd with,][1] have occasion'd in the delivery of the small publication.[2] I am sensible of your indulgence in not having press'd for it & that it ought now to be in the press, But if it were possible for me to explain the troublesome & discouraging events which have perplexd me, you would be convinced that my inclination to be punctual has been as great as my Ability has been small. In a work of imagination merely, it is possible to trust to oneself to a certain degree, But where instruction is to be convey'd, it is impossible to do without books of referrence. I have sometimes waited a week to get a book from Exeter & at last have heard that, tho it was in the Catalogue, it was not in the Library, or I have received a mulilated [*sic*] Copy of no use. I am now writing out fair the two last dialogues of vol. 1st and hope to send them up at least in the course of this week, & the rest soon enough to be publish'd during the Recess.[3] If any thing could make me wish this more than my general desire to be just, it would be the inclination the Dtss of Devonshire & Lady Georgiana have shewn to encourage its success——

The books I want are

A Bengal Callender for 96
Memoirs de Madm De Polignac French } Both I beleive Debrett[4]

Baratti's Italian Library—(5 v)[5]
Appel a Limpartiale Posterite Fr Madme Roland[6] } either Johnson or
Aikens application of Natural History to Poetry[7] } Robinson
Bottarelli's dictionary—Italian French & English, 3 volumes[8]—

A book of Spanish Proverbs, Or a Spanish Grammar[9] in which there are proverbs. I know the former book Exists, & I think it very probable Mr Elmsley[10] may have it or know where to get it for me, & as I particularly wish to have it, I shall be very much oblig'd to you to get it for me or at least a Grammar. As to the Books I more immediately want for my present work, as I have them all of my own in Sussex, it is very disagreeable to be oblig'd to buy them again. Indeed I cannot afford it.

Mr Langsford, finding people complain of the miserable insufficiency of the Library here, which is filld almost entirely with Lanes trumpery Novels,[11] has desir'd me to tell him what he should do to make the Collection worth subscribing to by Gentlemen who now decline it as there is not one set of books fit for them but those Dr More &c you sent down.[12] I told him that I thought the most generally useful set of Books were the Annual Registers,[13] but I beleived them to be very expensive. He seems not to mind that, & I beleive is well able to lay out from fifteen to thirty pounds in books really readable. I therefore told him that tho it is out of y^{r} way to supply Country Customers, yet I imagined you w^{d} inform me how he could get these at the best hand [unless they are among your own publications].[14] And that you w^{d} also be so good as to tell me what books you have lately publish'd & can recommend from y^{r} own shop as being fit for readers who are not deeply scientific yet cannot read Novels such as those written for 5£ a set for Mr Lane &c. If I were to chuse, it should be the periodical publications from the Spectators to the Lounger & Observer.[15] But if you will be so good as to send a list & estimate, Mr Langsford will send back the order which I imagine, as far as relates to y^{r} own publications, you will not object to execute on the Condition, which I told him must be understood, that he should make prompt payment, for tho I believe him to be a responsible Man & in a considerable way of business as a Carpenter besides possessing some of the best Houses here which let at enormous rents, I do not mean to make myself in any way answerable for a considerable Sum.

I am, Gentlemen,
y^{r} obed^{t} & oblig'd Ser^{t},
Charlotte Smith

You will be so good as to let me hear from you directly & to name the price of a set of the New annual Register.

Yale University MS. Address: Messrs Cadell Junr & Davies/ Strand/ London. Postmark: EXMOUTH; JA 7 96.

NOTES

1. CS's brackets.
2. *Rambles Farther.*
3. Of Parliament.
4. *The Bengal Calendar and Register* listed the East India Company's employees in Bengal and other British subjects who lived in Calcutta and other parts of India. It was published irregularly, in 1787, 1790, 1792, and 1796. In the last year it was bound with the *London Calendar* for 1790 and 1796. J. Stockdale reprinted it in London; Debrett may have sold it.

Jones lists *Mémoires de M De Poligny* (1749) by Madame d * * *. A later edition, *Les Victimes de l'amour ou Mémoires de M. de Poligny,* was published in 1773 in Amsterdam. Jones also notes that "in spite of all our efforts we have not been able to trace this book which Raynal attributes to the Chevalier de Mouhy" (*A List of French Prose Fiction,* p. 100). Again, I have not found the connection with Debrett.

5. Probably *A Dictionary of the English and Italian Languages* (1760) by Guiseppe Marco Antonio Baretti (1719–89). A friend of Johnson, Thrale, Goldsmith, Burke, Boswell, and Reynolds, he had been teaching Italian in London in 1751.

6. *Appel à L'Impartiale Postérité, par la citoyenne Roland, femme du Ministre de l'Intérieur, ou Recueil des écrits qu'elle a rédigés, pendent sa détention, aux prisons de l'Abbaye et de Sainte-Pélagie; imprimé au profit de sa fille unique* (1795), by Madame Roland. This personal tract by an imprisoned minister's wife, written for the benefit of her only daughter, would naturally appeal to CS.

7. *An Essay on the Application of Natural History to Poetry* (1777), by J. Aiken, discusses how the accurate use of natural description can improve poetry.

8. *The New Italian, English, and French Pocket-Dictionary { . . . } Compiled from the Dictionaries of La Crusca, Dr. S. Johnson, The French Academy,* 3 vols., 3rd ed., corr. and improved (1795) by Ferdinando Bottarelli. Though primarily a translator of operas, Bottarelli had two successful works on language, the book CS ordered and *Exercises upon the Different Parts of Italian Speech* (1778).

9. *Proverbou Spagnol, troet e verzou brezonnec gant M.* * * * (?1760).

10. Bookseller in the Strand who specialized in French books.

11. William Lane's novels, many of which were cheap and ill-written, were a staple of circulating libraries. Some felt that they contributed to the decline of the novel's reputation. When Lane approached CS to buy the copyright of *Emmeline,* she felt "humbled & hurt" by his "pert advances" (CS to William Hayley, late 1788–89).

12. See CS to Cadell and Davies, 22 July and 19 Aug. 1795. It appears that she was still in touch with Dr. Moore (see CS to an unnamed recipient, 8 Dec. 1791, n. 11).

13. The *Annual Register* provides a detailed account of the year's political and financial events; a chronicle of interesting and unusual happenings to individuals; lists of important births, marriages, and deaths; and statistics about the year's deaths, prices, and weather.

14. CS's brackets.

15. Each of these literary magazines was available in bound volumes. The *Spectator* (1711–14) of Joseph Addison and Richard Steele was one of the earliest successful periodicals; Henry Mackenzie's *Lounger* (1785–87) and Richard Cumberland's *Observer* (1787–91) were recent.

To Thomas Cadell, Jr., and William Davies

{Exmouth, 7 January 1796}
Sirs,

I send up 14 pages of the new book because I fear as the Holy days are over, the press may stand still; I will send 14 others by the post of Saturday (Tomorrow there is none from hence). My daughter is now at Lymington,[1] & I have no person with me but my two younger children so that I Cannot obtain even the advantage of having my work read over but trust only to my own correction & being without necessary books, I cannot but write under great disadvantages. I beleive this MMS is tolerably correct, & I hope the printer will not find it difficult to decypher. Unless you find this way too expensive, I shall continue to send a paquet every other day. But even in this mode of conveyance, there is no security as to time, for I this day receivd a

Letter which tho of the utmost consequence to me has been ever since the 26th Decr coming from Guildford in Surry & since the 28th from London. & this has now happen'd so often that I am convinced there is some great fault in the post. I shall be much oblig'd to you if you would enquire of Mr Elmsley if he has or can procure for me the Works of "Le Chevalier de Bouffless."[2]

I am, Gentn, your oblig'd Hble Sert,
Charlotte Smith

Exmouth, Jany 7th 1795[3]

Yale University MS. Address: Messrs Cadell Junr & Davies/ Strand/ London. Postmark: EXMOUTH; {date illegible.}

NOTES

1. Lucy, CS's amanuensis when Charlotte Mary was away, was at Lymington with her cousin, Mrs. Robert Allen, a daughter of Rev. Richard Smith. With her husband, Capt. Allen of the 91st Highlanders, Mrs. Allen resided at the Grove, Lymington, Hampshire. CS's two youngest children were Harriet and George.

2. *Œuvres diverse en vers et en prose de M. le Chevalier de B * ** (1787), by Marquis Stanislas Jean de Boufflers.

3. Obviously an error for the new year, 1796. In Jan. 1795, CS was living at Bath and makes no mention of a brief journey to Exmouth, though she traveled to London. Nor did she have a "new book" for Cadell and Davies under way at that time.

To Thomas Cadell, Jr., and William Davies

{Exmouth, 17 January 1796}
Messrs Cadell & Davies
Gentlemen,

I shall be much oblig'd to you to let me know when you are so good as to send the Books for which I wrote, & if there is difficulty about any of them to send the Bengal Calender & such others as may be procured without difficulty as soon as possible. As abt that (the B Calender), I am particularly anxious, and I dread the length of time every pacquet is in coming to as well as going from hence—— On the 12th instant,[1] a parcel was sent to me containing some Law papers and two Books left for me as a present at the House of a friend; I have sent three times to Exeter for them, but can obtain no tydings of them, & perhaps shall at last be forced to go, as once happen'd in the summer, to get them myself from Exeter, for so sluggish & so stupid are the people of this Country that it is impossible for one to get any thing done by them. These Law papers are of the utmost consequence, but perhaps are carried on to Plymouth & will return hither a week hence—— I mention this as a reason why I must trouble you to be very particular in having the parcel book'd & letting me know when to send for it, & also as a reason why I take the pains to write the MMS. a second time & on long paper that it may go as at [*sic*] little expence as possible by the post, which is of ~~the~~ two bad conveyances the best. I now send in this & another single folio sheet, more than equal I think to ten of Letter press. This half sheet follows the 3 sides includ'd in No. 1, & the next half sheet or possibly three sides, as I cannot tell how much it will make, will conclude (with three original stanza's) the 1st Volume—— There is no post tomorrow from hence, but you will recive it by that of Teusday, with I hope part of the 2nd Volume, if I am not broken in upon in a morning which I cannot always avoid——

I fear that I am so unhappy as to be again disappointed of Letters & remittances from India—— If you have no Letters for me, pray be so good as to enquire when you write if those by the Lascelles and Royal Admiral are deliver'd. To know that, however mortifying the disappointment, would at least releive me from the misery of anxious & fruitless expectation—— I am, Gentn,

your most obed Sert,
Charlotte Smith

If I should have any Letters, pray send them directly by the post whatever may be their weight——

Yale University MS. Address: No. 2/ Messrs Cadell Junr & Davies./ Strand/ London./ Single Sheet/ Exmouth 17th Jany. Postmark: EXMOUTH; JA/ 19/ 96.

NOTE

1. That is, on the 12th of this month.

To Thomas Cadell, Jr., and William Davies

[Weymouth, 7 February 1796]
Gentn,

Some never ending law business naild me to the misery of answering & copying Law Papers for more than a week before I left Exmouth. I am now somewhat settled & will go on with yr small purchase as quickly as possible. I Was not quite certain that I cd get hither and therefore desired Lord Egremont and some other friends from whom I expect Letters on business to direct them to yr House; have the goodness if any such come to direct them down to <u>Mrs Smith</u> (Omitting my Christian name), <u>No. 7</u> Esplanade, Weymouth, & should any enquiry be made after me either by friends or Duns,

~~do not~~ do not give them any direction, for I have no time for the first or money for the last, & only quiet can enable me to find either hereafter——

I am, Gent[n], your oblig'd & obed[t] Ser[t],

Charlotte Smith

Weymouth, 7th Feb[y] 1796——

Miscellaneous Papers, Charlotte Smith, Manuscripts and Archives Division, The New York Public Library, Astor, Lenox and Tilden Foundations MS. No address or postmark.

To Thomas Cadell, Jr., and William Davies

[Weymouth, 23 March 1796]

Gentlemen

I shall in a few days send up the greater part, perhaps the whole, of the 2nd Volume of the small work you have purchas'd of me. Ill health and the difficulty of procuring books (which I have found not less here than at Exmouth) have prevented the completion of it sooner. I should have taken it kind if you had been so good as to have sent me down the small order for books which I sent to M[r] Johnson, as you might have been assur'd I should not have sent for them unless they had been necessary. The periodical work I knew to be out of your way and therefore did not trouble you for it.

I beg the favor of you to send me for my son George a School book which I observe is printed for you, "Entertaining and instructive exercises, with the rules of the french Syntax."[1] And I should be very glad to have Smiths Tour.[2] I have also to request the favor of you to send to a Mathematical Instrument maker, and procure for me a double convex lens of three inches diameter,[3] and also that you will be so good as to desire to know the price of a glass such as is us'd by miniature painters for diminishing objects. I wish to know the price mounted & unmounted[4] and trust you can procure me this article and this intelligence without giving you any particular trouble, as you have such shops very near you. Whatever I may owe you, You will be pleas'd to deduct from the money which may be due to me when the whole of the ~~landscap~~ manuscript is deliver'd—The rest you will then be pleas'd to pay Mess[rs] Sam[l] Smith & Sons, Aldermanbury.[5]

I shall be oblig'd to you to inform me whether M[r] Hayley is in London, as I have occasion to write to him on business relative to the publication of the Sonnets.

A severe inflammation in one of my Eyes[6] has been one reason why it has hardly been in my power to write more than a Letter for some weeks, & not that, without pain and difficulty. I now only keep the MMS in hopes of sending it before the end of the week, altogether, and tolerably correct in which I have nobody to assist me—

I am, Gent^{n},
your most obed^{t} Ser^{t},
Charlotte Smith

No. 7 Esplanade, Weymouth, March 23rd/ [17]96

Yale University MS. Address: Messrs Cadell Junr and Davies/ Strand/ London. Postmark: WEYMOUTH; MR/ 24/ 96.

NOTES

1. Jean Baptiste Perrin's *Entertaining and Instructive Exercises, with the Rules of the French Syntax* was in its seventh edition in 1796. Cadell and Davies's note to this letter says that Smith's *Tour* (see n. 2) and Chambaud's *Exercises* were ready to be sent to CS. But on 16 Apr., having received the package of books from them, CS writes that she wanted Perrin's *Exercises,* not Chambaud's. Even though she gave Perrin's title more precisely than usual for her, their confusion is understandable. Louis Chambaud's *Exercises to the Rules and Construction of French Speech* was in its 13th edition in 1792. To further confuse matters, Perrin had revised earlier works by Chambaud, including *Nouveau dictionnaire françois-anglois, & anglois-françois* for W. Strahan, T. Cadell, and P. Elmsley in 1778.

2. James Edward Smith, *A Sketch of a Tour on the Continent, in the Years 1786 and 1787,* 3 vols. (1793).

3. A note on this letter reads: "Cannot tell what sort of Convex Lens to send unless Mrs Smith can describe the focus or if she cannot do that—to mention what purpose it is intended for."

4. Another note says that there are "various sizes and prices of glasses for diminishing objects" and "a pretty good one" can be had for 10/6.

5. These merchants had been in business continuously at 12 Aldermanbury, London, but by 1796 they had become Samuel Smith, Sons, and Company and had moved to 73 Lombard Street, where they were last listed in business in 1799.

6. Possibly iritis, an inflammation associated with rheumatoid arthritis but not with gout.

To Thomas Cadell, Jr., and William Davies

[Weymouth, 7 April 1796]
Gentlemen,

I have waited for some time for an answer to the Letter I troubled you with; I imagined that during the Easter week it might be inconvenient to you to oblige me, but many days having since elapsed, I conclude that for some reason or other you find it inconsistent with your plans to take the trouble I thought from your obliging Letters while I was at Exmouth that I might venture to give you. The next civility would have been to have told me so that I might neither wait in suspense for what I really wanted or write to some friend in Town by which means (in case the delay was accidental) I might have two sets of books &c & double expence of carriage—— I cannot now conclude it to be accidental, but must impute it to the contemptuous sort of indifference which perhaps a necessitous author must be subject to but which I do not mean to subject myself to again.[1] I am very sorry to have given you the trouble ~~of~~ and have now only to inform you that I shall send up next week the sequel of the small publication, of which the whole w^{d} have been corrected before now, but that the friend at Bath[2] on whom I depended for its correction has been & is still engaged in the last attendance on her Mother, & I cannot trouble her, but shall send it without. I wishd to have ask'd some friendly offices of Mr Hayley had he been in town, but as I did not hear from you, I have now written to him at Eartham.

I shall be oblig'd to you when you receive the whole to let me know, as I have reason to doubt the safe arrival of parcels from hence, having heard to day that a parcel for Canada sent from this place to the care of a Merchant of London on the 17th of March has never been received.

I am, Gentlemen,
your obed^{t} humble Ser^{t},
Charlotte Smith

Weymouth, April 7th 1796

Yale University MS. Address: Messrs Cadell & Davies/ Strand/ Post paid——. London. Postmark: WEYMOUTH; PAID/ AP/ 9/ 1796

NOTES

1. They answered this letter on 13 Apr., apologizing that the "extreme Hurry of Business" of the last three or four weeks had prevented their answering earlier. Among other things, they have just published "several Works of great Consequence." They found the "Glasses used by Miniature Painters for diminishing Objects" at Dollonds for half a guinea, pointed out that they could not send a convex lens without knowing what it would be used for, and promised to send Smith's *Tour* and the French exercises by that day's coach.

2. Probably Augusta Nott.

To Thomas Cadell, Jr., and William Davies

[Weymouth, 13 April 1796]
Gentlemen,

I now send as much as ~~126~~ 122 pages of the small work. I have endeavour'd to correct the whole as well as I can without any assistance even of books; I have also endeavour'd to make the stops right & every where to prevent such mistakes as occur'd in the first two volumes. With what success I know not.

To the first of these volumes belongs a short preface ~~to the~~ and the dedication to Lady Georgiana Cavendish.[1] These, with the remains of the last Chapter of this, you shall receive in the course of the week by the post.

There is a mistake in the first Dialogue of this the 2nd volume. It is a mere trifle, but I recollect that I meant to have corrected it, but afterwards having an opportunity of sending the two dialogues in a parcel to Mr Bicknell,[2] it escaped my memory—— I shall be oblig'd to you whenever you print the sheet to let me see it that I may change the half doz^{n} words, or rather to send me the MMS which I will immediately return——

You possibly may wish to defer paying the money till the last eight or ten pages are deliver'd and the dedication; ~~but~~ about that you may do as you please. I do not mean to intrude upon you for any favor—— I wish to finish with a short piece of original Poetry which, not being able to make yet quite what I wish & having I hope some character to lose, I do not hastily send because it cannot be immediately wanted—and three or four days can make no difference.

When I propos'd some time since[3] to insert an advertisement in regard to the delay of the Sonnets, Mr Davies advis'd me against it. As ~~my~~ the severe calamities of last year, which I shall never recover, have so much affected my health that it has been equally impossible for me to be in Town or to have the portrait made where I have been obliged to remain; I have made another attempt to procure a copy of the only picture that ever was made of me, but have been positively refused the loan of it, nor have I any hopes given me of being allow'd to ~~send a~~ have a copy of it till August or September, as it does not till then suit the person in whose possession it is[4]—— As to my having a likeness taken now it is impossible, as I am in such a state of health as to appearance that it could not be known—I have given directions for drawings to be made for two plates, and the writing part is in such forwardness that the book might still be out in the Summer were it not for the portrait & plates. Thus circumstanced, I shall be oblig'd to you for your advice how to act. My own idea is to insert an advertisement. I shall be glad to hear from you immediately on this subject. Likewise to know when you are so obliging as to pay the 20£ I wish to subscribe to Madame D'Arblays Camilla[5] but do not venture to desire it, as I conclude you are not in cash for me even to that amount tho I imagine, when the person to whom the enclos'd is address'd sends a small pacquet to yr House, you will be so good as to pay the amount.

I am oblig'd to you for transmitting the ~~India~~ Letters; one I receiv'd to day from my Second Son,[6] & another from Brighthelmstone. If my two Sons live & do well, I shall have no farther occasion after this year to write for bread, tho my childrens & my own property should still be kept from us — — Of course I shall never again I trust be a troublesome correspondent.

As a parcel of cloaths sent from hence to Mincing Lane to be forwarded from thence to Quebec to my Son Lionel is totally lost, I shall be very desirous of hearing that this parcel (of which I also give you notice pr post) is duly received. I am, Gentn, your most obed Sert,

Charlotte Smith

7 Esplanade, Weymouth, April 13th Wednesday night
Whenever it is agreeable to you to pay the money, it is to be paid to Messrs Saml Smith & Son & Co, Aldermanbury, in my name on account of Sir Stafford Northcote,[7] Hennaway & Co, Exton Bank.

Yale University MS. Address: Messrs Cadell Junr and Davies—. No postmark.

NOTES

1. The duchess's elder daughter, Lady Georgiana Cavendish, born 11 July 1783; she was later Lady Morpeth and countess of Carlisle.

2. Charles Bicknell, her solicitor.

3. See CS to Cadell and Davies, 2 May 1795.

4. CS identifies the portrait's owner as William Hayley in a letter to Joseph Cooper Walker (29 May 1796). Hayley wanted to wait until George Romney's visit, planned for Aug. or Sept., before releasing it.

5. CS may have subscribed to *Camilla,* but the only name given is "Mrs. Smith." A "Miss Smith," perhaps Charlotte Mary, also subscribed to it.

6. Nicholas Hankey Smith.

7. Sir Stafford Henry Northcote (1762–1851), seventh baronet, of the Pynes, Upton Pyne, Exeter, was a new supporter who lent CS money during her stay in Exmouth.

To Thomas Cadell, Jr., and William Davies

[Weymouth] Saturday night, April 16th 1796
Gentn,

I am sorry to tell you that the pacquet[1] you mentiond in yr obliging Letter, which I receiv'd on Thursday, never has reachd me. There is but too much reason to fear it has shared the fate of my pacquet to my Son[2] on the

17th of last Month which it [*sic*] now certain I shall hear of no more—— It is excessively vexatious. Have the goodness to enquire abt it in London; if it was book'd, the people must ~~receive~~ pay the value of it. I hope my MMS has had better fortune, but it really makes me afraid of sending any thing—

I have lately received some particular kindnesses from two medical friends,[3] which as they will receive no other acknowledgement, I wish to say I thank them for by presenting each with a book of the last Edition of the Sonnets.[4] I also want one for myself, & if you are kind enough to send down the things I wrote for from London (ie from Newport Street), be so good as to add three of these books all bound, which you may charge to any account you best like between us. It was not Chambauds, but Perrins Exercises I wrote for, & beg to have with these.[5]

I am, Gentn, your oblig'd humble Sert,
Charlotte Smith

I shall send the remaining MMS in the Course of the ensuing week——

Yale University MS. Address: Messrs Cadell Junr & Davies/ Strand/ London. Postmark: WEYMOUTH; AP 18 96.

NOTES

1. Containing Smith's *Tour* and the French exercises.
2. A parcel of clothes sent to Lionel in Quebec from Weymouth by way of Mincing Lane had been lost (see CS to Cadell and Davies, 13 Apr. 1796).
3. Two doctors attached to regiments stationed in Weymouth. They were soon to leave (see CS to Cadell and Davies, 1 May 1796).
4. Seventh edition, 1795.
5. See CS to Cadell and Davies, 23 Mar. 1796, n. 1.

To Thomas Cadell, Jr., and William Davies

[Weymouth, 18 April 1796]
Gentlemen,

I lose no time in informing you that the parcel came this morning. I shall return Chambaud when I send any pacquet to London and beg to have Perrin when you send any thing down[1]——I am, Gentn, in great haste,

your most obedt Sert,
CS

April 18th Monday

Yale University MS. No address or postmark.

NOTE

1. Cadell and Davies replied to this brief note and the preceding letter one week later, on 26 Apr.:

> We have received very safe the different Packets of Mss you have sent us, and we believe the Printer has continued to proceed on the Work so closely that the Alterations you desire to be made can only, at present, be done by a List of Errata—Trusting that the little Volumes will be compleatly in the Printer's Hands in a few Days, we shall, tomorrow, pay the £20 still due to you thereon, into the Hands of Messrs Smith & Co. according to you—The small Balance due to us on the general Account may be settled hereafter ——With Regard to the further Delay in the Publication of the Sonnets, we are totally incapable of offering any Advice—but we will pay particular Attention to any Instructions you will give us on the Subject—The Printseller in Newport Street has not yet brought to us what you ordered from him, but the Instant we receive his Packet we will send with it a Copy of Perrin's Exercises and a Print left here by Mrs Berkeley—Should any Letters arrive from India, we will take Care to forward them instantly by Post——

To Thomas Cadell, Jr., and William Davies

[Weymouth, 26 April 1796]
Gentlemen,

I waited till after the post came in to day in hopes of hearing from you. I conclude you received the packet. Since I have got Smiths Tour, I find I have made some mistakes in regard to the names of the plants, which names I should be very sorry to print incorrectly. I cannot recollect the page, but I know I have somewhere written Rododendron Alpinum. It ought to be Rhododendrum Ferrugineum. In another place, the word Mesphilus should be Mespilus, and wherever the word, Rhododendron occurs it should be Rhododendrum. May I request that you will be so obliging as to let these corrections be made? I had not a book here of any sort and find it very vain to hope for them from any Library So that nothing can exceed the disadvantages I have labourd under since [I] have been at a distance from my own.

On the other side, I have re-written as much as four pages of Letter press. There ~~are~~ will not be above six more which, with the dedication, I will copy in the same manner and send up by Teusdays post as the way most expeditious and convenient. I shall be glad to have notice when these little Books are likely to be ready because I mean to have two sets of them very neatly bound in Green for the Lady Cavendishes and am painting a box which I shall send up to enclose them in, & a thing of that sort takes a good deal of time to varnish. As I conclude you look upon this work as deliver'd, I shall be oblig'd to you to pay to S Smith & Co., Aldermanbury, whatever may be due of the price you agreed for, as I have been disappointed to my great wonder about an order from India which I sent up to Messrs Muilman & Co. & on which I depended upon having the money this week, but have not heard about it & in consequence of that dependence, I shall be extremely distress'd unless you are so obliging as to accommodate me with the 20£ or what ever may remain after you have deducted whatever you may not have chosen to charge to my other account that you have expended for me. I trust you will be so good as to oblige me herein, as I shall be otherwise perhaps much inconvenienced, for tho I have thirty five pound due to me from Robinson & Parkin of my own Money,[1] & they have above 600£ in their hands, I can procure neither money nor answer. Perhaps I shall be so happy as to have Letters by the Nonsuch, & not unlikely remittances, for the last India Letter you sent me was from my Son Nicholas, who informs me he had sent 100£ more to his Brother at Bengal as the shortest conveyance to me. You will I am sure have the goodness to send me any India Letters that may arrive by the post with^t heeding their weight, for I dare not trust the delays or indeed the carelessness of the Mail Coach. Favor me, Gentlemen, with an immediate answer including y^r opinion about the Sonnets. I am,

Gentlemen, your most obed^t humble Ser^t,
Charlotte Smith

I have moved my Lodgings to a place call'd Belle Vue—No 1.

General Manuscripts, Manuscripts Division, Rare Books and Special Collections, Princeton University Library. Address: Messrs Cadell and Davies./ Strand/ London. Postmark: WEYMOUTH; AP/ 26/ 96.

NOTE

1. It is not clear whether Robinson and Parkin had withheld her usual Jan. payment or whether she is looking ahead to the payment she should receive in June.

To Thomas Cadell, Jr., and William Davies

[Weymouth, 28 April 1796]
Gent^n,

I now send you the Close of the last volume of the small work which I finish with an original Sonnet.[1] The Dedication, a matter always difficult to manage well, I have not yet been able to please myself in quite as I wish to make it in verse if I can get what I have to say into that form.[2] I know it will be the last thing you will want, and therefore am sure that nothing will be delay'd for want of it. I hope to hear from you to day & will not seal this till after post time which on Teusdays is never earlier than 4 o clock here.

½ past five

There is no letter or parcel.

I therefore conclude I shall not yet hear from you. Be so good as to let me know however that you have rec[d] the whole of "Rambles farther" & when it will be convenient to you to pay the money that may be due.

[Unsigned]

Yale University MS. Address: Mess[rs] Cadell Jun[r] & Davies/ Strand/ London. Postmark: WEYMOUTH; AP/ 28/ 96.

NOTES

1. That is, *Rambles Farther,* first named at the end of this letter; it ends with one of CS's own sonnets.

2. The printed dedication is in prose (see CS to Cadell and Davies, 18 May 1796, n. 1).

To Thomas Cadell, Jr., and William Davies

Weymouth, 1st May 1796

Gentlemen,

I am oblig'd to you for hav[g] paid the money to Smith & Co & for having sent me two Letters from India both of which arrived safe.

As my medical friends are going from hence with the Regiments to which they belong, I beleive I must trouble you to send the Books down before the Gilder[1] sends the things as I suspect that I sent the order wrong somehow. And as I shall soon make another move towards, if not to, Southampton in order to be nearer Sussex with[t] quite returning [to] a scene which I do not know that I could bear,[2] The materials for Gilding may as well remain till I am fix'd for the Summer as every thing adds to one's trouble in moving.

I shall be oblig'd to you to send me Perrin for George, tho I forgot to return Chambaud but will send it up in a few days wth another parcel that goes to a person in Town. I wish very much to see Miss Sewards poems (I know not what she calls her last publication but you know what I mean),[3] & pray put Miss Lee's Almeyda & Letter to Sheridan[4] into the packet which I shall be very glad to [*sic*] in the course of this week. I am, Gent[n], your oblig'd & obed[t] Ser[t],

CS

Pray let me know the latest time you can give for the dedication——as I cannot please myself.

Yale University MS. Address: Messrs Cadell & Davies/ Strand/ London. Postmark: WEYMOUTH; MA 3 96.

NOTES

1. The presentation copies for the duchess and her daughter were to be bound in green Morocco leather with gilt edges.

2. That is, towns in Sussex where Augusta had lived.

3. Anna Seward (1742–1809), a friend of Hayley, published *Llangollen Vale, with Other Poems* (1796). Seward's letters show nothing but disdain for CS's works.

4. Sophia Lee (1750–1824) wrote in many genres, sometimes with her sister Harriet (1757–1851), and they also ran a successful school for girls in Bath. They met many of the famous people who visited Bath, among them CS. *Almeyda, Queen of Grenada,* a five-act tragedy in verse, was not a success. Even with Sarah Siddons in the lead, it ran only four nights. CS explains to Joseph Cooper Walker on 29 May that Lee advertised the play again and printed a "very sharp letter to Sheridan," but publication of the play was stopped, and it was acted one last time.

To Thomas Cadell, Jr., and William Davies

Weymouth, 10th May 1796

Gent^n,

I flatter'd myself you would have oblig'd me before now with the information I requested relative to the time when the Dedication to Lady Georgiana Cavendish would be wanting & also with the books you were so obliging as to say you would send. I hope no accident has befallen them.

The advertisement for this small publication must run thus——

Dedicated by permission to the Right Honourable
Lady Georgiana Cavendish

—

Rambles Farther—
By Charlotte Smith
being the Sequel—to Rural Walks—

If you find any change necessary, you will make it acording to y^r own Judgement, but the beginning is what the Dtss of Devonshire has mention'd as proper——

The instant the work is out of the press, two sets must be most elegantly bound in Green morrocco & gilt edges ~~In which~~ I shall send up a small painted Box to enclose them in & must trouble you to place them in it & send a person with the box to Devonshire House. You shall have the dedication when ever you write for it by the return of the post.

I hardly know what has been done about the Subscription to the Sonnets such has been the State of my mind these last twelve months. Now that I look around me again, I am apt to suspect that great confusion will arise in the business. I know the Sum the Dutchess of Devonshire has sent me, but unless[1] About fifteen names which I beleive I sent you at different times, I know none of the rest, & her Grace I am afraid has kept no list. I find some persons, and some who have calld themselves my friends have murmerd extremely at the delay of the publication but as the principal of these M^{rs} O[lmius][2] has not paid above a third of the subscription of the persons whose names she sent me, I see no great right she has to complain. I am more solicitous about the opinion of the public, & therefore it was I wrote to ~~know~~ have your advice on the subject. I mean, when the advertisement for "Rambles Farther" is inserted to ~~send up~~ have an advertisement also in regard to this publication. In the mean time, I wish you w^{d} send me the list you have since the last, if any, & I will endeavour to get the Dutchess's.

An advertisement must also be sent to Ireland.

These names are to be added. I have not yet received any of the money for the 4 first, which you will note by some marks.

Dr Edward Jenner, M.D.FRS—(Berkely Glocestershire)
Mr Henry Jenner Surgeon—D^{o}[3]
Revd William Davies, MA. Marg Coll. Oxen
Leiut William Fisher Shrapnell, South Glocester Militia
[M^{r}]^{s} Willoughby
Honble Miss Elphinston
Mrs Blundel
John Archer, Esqre[4]

The money for the last four Has been receivd by a friend of mine at Bath.

Mr Barrett, Bookseller, Bath, desires to have 25 Sets of Rambles farther Which however must be placed to my account, as I owe him a bill which he has begged to have paid in this manner. Of the twelve sets which I suppose [you] will be so good as to send to me, I beg to have sent

4 to Dr Parry[5] Bath——which will go with Barretts
two for myself—where ever I may be & Hayley
1 Miss Smith[6]
1 Miss Lucy Smith
& 3 may be sent with Barretts, directed to Mrs Nott,[7] Seymour Street, Bath——

Pray Let me hear from you Gentlemen immediately.

I have reason to beleive my eldest Son[8] will come from India for two years. This expectation renders me so anxious that I dare not propose any scheme to myself; otherwise I mean, as soon as the Novel I am now about is out of hand (which I undertook for the immediate means of living, & sold volume by volume to Mr Low),[9] to begin a work of a quite different nature from any I have yet undertaken: & perhaps Your house may agree for it.[10] I mention this only as a means of settling <any> account between us should not other & more speedy occur. My two Sons[11] are so generously solicitous for my ease that I trust, if they do well, I shall not work under the disadvantages I have done from the necessity of asking advances. I am, Gent^{n}, y^{r} obed & oblig'd Ser^{t},

Charlotte Smith

Yale University MS. Address: Messrs Cadell Junr & Davies/ Strand/ London. Postmark: WEYMOUTH; MA 12 96.

NOTES

1. I.e., except for.

2. Elizabeth Olmius (see CS to Wiliam Davies, 19 Feb. 1790, n. 2).

3. "D^{o}" is CS's abbreviation for "ditto."

4. Of these eight intended subscribers, only a Lieut. Shrapnell is in the printed list in the new edition.

5. Dr. Caleb Hillier Parry had attended Augusta during her difficult pregnancy in Bath in July 1794 (see CS to Cadell, Sr., 22 July 1794, n. 2).

6. Charlotte Mary. By convention, the eldest unmarried daughter was addressed by her surname.

7. On Augusta Nott, see CS to William Hayley, 12 June 1795, n. 5.

8. William Towers Smith arrived in England in July 1798, was listed in *Bengal Civil Servants* as being "out of employ" during all of 1799, and resumed his post as judge and magistrate of Ramghyr on 31 Oct. 1800. CS may have been anxious over his undertaking the dangerous five-month voyage home or over some possible suspension of his regular payments to her.

9. Sampson Low published *Marchmont* in 1796.

10. In June 1798, CS published *The Young Philosopher,* a novel, with Cadell and Davies and *Minor Morals,* a children's book, with Low. Neither is "of a quite different nature" from her other works, but she considered the novel to be so.

11. That is, William and Nicholas. CS never mentions gifts from her other sons, who were in military rather than civil service and often needed money for outfits or advancement.

To Thomas Cadell, Jr., and William Davies

[Weymouth, 18 May 1796]
Gent^{n},

On the other side is the dedication.[1]

I have not yet received the parcel which you said you w^{d} be so obliging as to send by Saturday. This is very unfortunate, as the friend to whom I wish to give a set of Sonnets is gone. I hope to receive three Sets. If Miss Lees play does not come out, I had rather not wait for it.

I shall send up the Box for Lady Georgiana's books in a few days—wish to know exactly when it will be wanted. The Advertise[t] I will send when I have seen the list.

I am Gent[n],
your obed Ser[t],
CS

I have sent a Copy of the dedicat[n] to the Dutchess. If you hear nothing to the contrary from her by friday, you will print it as expeditiously as possible.

Yale University MS. Address: Mess[rs] Cadell & Davies/ Strand/ London. Postmark: WEY-MOUTH; MA 18 96.

NOTE

1. That draft did not survive. The printed dedication shows what CS had worked on so carefully; it is addressed as much to the duchess as to her daughter. CS did not cast it in verse as she had hoped:

> Madam,
>
> The favourable opinion expressed by the Duchess of Devonshire, of the little Work to which this is a Sequel, induced me to solicit permission to dedicate these Volumes to your Ladyship.
>
> While I recollect all the acts of kindness I have experienced from her Grace, I can find no terms to express my sense of them, that do not seem to border too much on those of the (frequently insincere) adulation used in common Dedications.
>
> But I certainly advance no more than I believe to be exactly true, when I say, that in enjoying that internal satisfaction which arises from the consciousness of good and benevolent deeds, the Duchess of Devonshire has also the happiness of seeing in her daughters those amiable qualities that have rendered her Grace so greatly beloved by her friends, as well as the boast and ornament of her country.
>
> May it be your felicity, Madam, to emulate and to reward the tenderness of such a mother!
>
> May 16, 1796

To Joseph Cooper Walker

Weymouth, May 29th 1796

Indeed, Dear Sir, you have great reason to beleive your kindness to me has been displaced, for I have appeard sadly negligent. I am sure however could I explain only half the causes that have combined to produce this effect, you w[d] be convinced that it has been my misfortune rather than my fault; I need name only one; which is, that when last Summer I went after my cruel loss to Exmouth for a little of that gloomy repose my broken heart demanded, One of my family who was with me got into an entanglement with a person, whom if he was to marry, he must be utterly undone, & this tho I warded it off for a time, has hung over me like a threatening ruin ever since; & now I am again tormented with the dread of it.[1]

As to my pecuniary affairs, I have never been able to obtain one shilling of all that is due to me & my family, tho the Trustees hold very considerable Sums of money & the friends who thought they could get the matter settled for me by arbitration have dropped off one by one, quite tired out by the unblushing chicane of the parties. I am now in anxious expectation of my eldest Son from India who on receiving an account from one of my friends of what had happen'd to his darling Sister[2] seems to have determined to come to England to see how far he can protect the rest.

All these circumstances, dear Sir, added to my sad state of health have render'd so much progress impossible as should have been made in the book to be publishd by subscription; another unconquerable impediment has been Mr Hayleys repeated refusal to let me have copied the only picture that I ever had made of me once when I was writing at Eartham. It is extremely like, & I wish'd for two copies of it, one for an Engraving & another for my Son. As I now look so very ill and am so very much alter'd that it would be mortifying to me to have a likeness of me taken now. However I am promis'd a Copy when Romney goes down to Eartham in Autumn,[3] & this, & because I cannot get the engravings done before, compells me to delay the publication 'till November when I shall go to Town on purpose to have it done properly. I send you a copy of the Advertisement which, as soon as Election papers will permit, Is to be inserted in the London papers. I leave it to your discretion to put it or not into an Irish paper if you will be so good as to take the trouble. But I beg the favor of [you] to deduct any expence attending on this &c from the Second pay^ts^ of subscriptions——

I never now see Mr Hayley & very seldom hear from him. Long absence & other friendships cannot but weaken that with which he so long honourd me & the loss of which I severely feel in my literary pursuits. I am afraid Miss Lees Tragedy did not answer her expectations.[4] She advertised it for sale with a very sharp letter to Sheridan annex'd, but I fancy they came to some compromise, as the pamphlet was stopped, Almeyda was acted once more, and I beleive it is not yet publish'd as Cadell & Davies were to send it down to me as soon as it came out of the press. I have subscribed to Madame D'Arblays Novel of which of course great expectations are formed.[5] The fashionable book was (for at this moment nobody reads any thing) the Life of Lorenzo de Medici by a Mr Something of Liverpool whose name I never heard before and cannot now recollect.[6] The book I beleive is a very pleasant one, but I, who am a wanderer upon Earth & can get near nothing but wretched circulating libraries where nothing circulates but the most wretched novels, am not likely very soon to see it.

I am writing (pour vivre) another Novel[7] which I hope will be the last. Indeed the present moment is very unfavorable to every species of literature. Just now a sort of <dum> election madness seems to pervade all sorts of people, & then the brouillerie of the illustrious pair, & the Grand-meretricious influence of Lady Jersey,[8] & the strange accident that has befallen Lord Charles Townsend who with his Brother seems to have made a party to run mad,[9] occupy every mind that has not some urgent troubles of ~~their~~ its own. I shall not leave myself room to send the advertisement unless I hasten to assure you that I am, Dear Sir,

with great Esteem, your most oblig'd & obed^{t} Ser^{t},
Charlotte Smith

Advertisement

M^{rs}. Charlotte Smith begs leave to acquaint the Subscribers to the ~~first~~ second Volume of Sonnets that very severe domestic afflictions and Other cruel consequences of a long series of ~~domestic affliction~~ Oppression have so greatly affected her health and to have render'd it impossible for her to be in London to forward the publication of the work in the manner she intended; she finds herself therefore under the painful necessity of delaying its appearance till Autumn, when she hopes the subscribers will find her engagement fulfilld in manner not unworthy of the favor to which she is so greatly indebted.

I shall be very glad, dear Sir, to hear from you & most sincerely hope I shall have an account of the perfect reestablishment of your health, the frequent want of which cannot fail to give y^{r} friends great pain. My poor Lionel was well in Canada in October last, but I have no later accounts. I am very sorry you had so much trouble ab^{t} Darcy.[10] Pray continue to direct to Cadells, as I am going soon into Hampshire I hardly know whither.[11]

Huntington MS (HM10818). Address: Joseph Cooper Walker Esqre——— / 15. Eccles Street/ Dublin. Postmark: WEYMOUTH; MA/ 31/ 96; JU/ 4/ 96.

NOTES

1. CS first mentions this problem on 2 Nov. 1795 (to Cadell, Jr., and Davies; see n. 1). We never discover which family member was so involved, but she never again mentions the situation, and so perhaps succeeded in averting the perceived evil.

2. Even though William contributed generously to his mother's and siblings' welfare, CS's shortage of money for medical care may have hastened Augusta's death.

3. In other words, Hayley had kept the portrait of CS that Romney had painted in Aug. 1792, and would not release it until Romney came on a visit. It is not clear why Hayley would not write to Romney for permission to copy the portrait.

4. Sophia Lee's *Almeyda, Queen of Grenada.*

5. *Camilla.*

6. William Roscoe, *The Life of Lorenzo De' Medici Called the Magnificent,* 2 vols. (1795).

7. *Marchmont,* for Sampson Low. "Pour vivre": to live.

8. The Prince of Wales, later George IV, had made a disastrous arranged marriage in Apr. 1795 to his cousin Princess Caroline of Brunswick. By May of 1796, the prince had asked the king to permit them a formal separation, but he refused it. By late May, several newspapers had ventured opinions favoring the princess. The "illustrious pair" could hardly be said to have had a *brouillerie*—a tiff, or passing misunderstanding—as CS writes, for they never reconciled. The prince had further offended his new bride by appointing his mistress, Lady Jersey, to be one of her Ladies of the Bedchamber. Frances, countess of Jersey, was the wife of George Bussy Villiers, fourth earl of Jersey, seventh Viscount Grandison, and the prince's Master of the Horse. Nine years older than the prince, Lady Jersey had two sons, seven daughters, and several grandchildren, hence CS's pun "grand-meretricious" (Hibbert, *George IV, Prince of Wales,* pp. 130–54).

9. The *Annual Register* for 1796 reports this incident of 17 May as a possible suicide. Lord Charles and Lord Frederick Townshend, sons of the Marquis Townshend, were returning from Great Yarmouth where Charles had been elected representative. On arriving in Oxford Street and asking directions to the bishop of Bristol's, Lord Frederick began to act insane; he stripped off his coat and shirt, and challenged a coachman who did not know the directions to fight. After the man refused and Lord Frederick walked away, others found Lord Charles dead in the carriage. Lord Frederick later calmed down, and he was able to report that he and his brother had been discussing a religious subject when Lord Charles took out a pistol and shot himself in the head. The coroner noted that there were two bullets, one through the head and one lodged in the mouth, with no sign of a struggle.

10. When this slim 167-page volume was published in London in 1793 by T. Dangerfield, the dedication to the duke of York was signed "E. Todd." When published in Dublin the same year by Brett Smith, the dedication was signed "C. Smith." It asserts that Sir Charles Asgill sought the duke's permission for her. The work is still erroneously attributed to her (see CS to Cadell, Jr., and Davies, 3 Sept. 1795). CS never mentions Asgill and had no known association with Smith.

11. The letters do not reveal that CS went to Hampshire; there is, however, a hiatus in letters from 22 Sept., when she was still in Weymouth, to 16 Nov., when she arrived in Headington near Oxford and sent Cadell and Davies her new address.

To Thomas Cadell, Jr., and William Davies

[Weymouth, 25 June 1796]

M[r] Davies is requested to be so obliging as to unpack the box himself (the key is within side) to place one set of the books in it—it will hardly hold two (the other therefore must go without in a paper)—and to send it by some very careful person; The packing box is so small that there is hardly any room to replace it; perhaps it may go as well in several folds of paper, if care be taken that it be neither scratched nor bruised—to both of which accidents it is from its manufacture extremely liable.[1]

Mr Hayley perhaps may have forgotten the order.[2] Should he not send it, Messrs Cadell & Davies are requested to trust Mrs Smith with a Copy for which, shd the Author forget it, she will pay, as she wishes to have her sets of "Rambles farther immediately——

[unsigned]

Weymouth, June 25th

Yale University MS. No address or postmark.

NOTES

1. These are instructions for mailing the presentation copy to Lady Georgiana Cavendish. One copy is to go in the "small painted box" that CS mentioned earlier. Both sets were liable to being scratched and bruised for they were "most elegantly bound in Green morrocco & gilt edges" (CS to Cadell and Davies, 10 May 1796).

2. It is not clear what order is meant.

To Thomas Cadell, Jr., and William Davies

[Weymouth, 1 July 1796]
Gentn,

The extreme carelessness with which the business of carriage is conducted between this place and London makes it necessary for me to inform you that the box for Lady G[eorgiana]. C[avendish]. was sent from hence on Sunday so that you ought to have receivd it by Monday—which I fear you did not, as I have seen no advertisement of the book——I wish it cd be settled before the Dss of Devonshires family Leave London or Chiswick for the Summer.

I am afraid that from the hurry of Your business, you may have forgotten that I wish to have Miss Lee's Tragedy sent down, & that I meant & hope I do stand as a subscriber[1] to Madme D'Arblays Camilla which, if publish'd, I hope to have with my own books & these above mention'd, which to receive immediately will much oblige, Gentn, your most obedt humble Sert,

Charlotte Smith

Weymouth
July 1st 1796

As I see some Poems by a certain "Eliza"[2] were publish'd by you dedicated to Lady Abergavenny, perhaps you can tell me if her Ladyship is or is not dead; tho my children are so nearly related to her, Such are the terms I am upon with her Father Mr Robinson on account of the unexampled cruelty & oppression with which he has contrived to ruin their fortunes that I have no communication with any of the gang. But I must write to the old wretch on the Sum of 544£ which he now holds unaccounted for of my childrens property, & tho he had no mercy on me, I would not intrude even upon his sorrow, brute as he is. Lady A-s death was contradicted in the Bath papers.[3] I only wish to know the fact, which if you can inform me I shall be oblig'd to you. I wrote to Mr Bicknell, but he forgot to mention it in his answer——

1st July 1796

Yale University MS. Address: Messrs Cadell Junr & Davies/ Strand/ London. Postmark: Weymouth; JY 2 96.

NOTES

1. See CS to Cadell and Davies, 13 Apr. 1796, n. 5.
2. *Poems, and Fugitive Pieces. By Eliza* was published in 1796.
3. Lady Abergavenny was Mary Robinson, the only daughter of John Robinson, hated trustee to the Smith estate. Married to Henry Neville, second earl of Abergavenny, she died 26 Oct. 1796 at the age of 36. (See Genealogical Chart.)

To Thomas Cadell, Jr., and William Davies

Weymouth. Septr 22nd [17]96

Gent^n^,

I understand Mr Walker of Dublin has sent a Book to y^r^ House for me. Lady Bolingbroke[1] will also send one in a few days. Whenever it arrives, have the goodness to send them to Mr Low, Printer, Berwick Street, who will have an opportunity of forwarding them without additional expence ——In about ten days, you will be troubled with a box of Books out of Sussex directed to Mr Barton of Heddington near Oxford:[2] they belong to me, & as yr house is so central, I have taken the liberty to desire you will let yr porters forward them to the Oxford Waggon, for all expences attending on which I will pay.

I hope Mr Corbauld[3] received the Letter I directed to him thro your hands & is going on with the drawings. It is really necessary to request you Gentlemen as being on the spot to hasten this as much as may be in your power, which will much oblig'd y^r^ most humble Ser^t^,

Charlotte Smith

J. Pierpont Morgan Library MS. Address: Messrs Cadell & Davies/ Strand/ London. Postmark: WEYMOUTH; SE 23 96.

NOTES

1. Charlotte Collins, Lady Bolingbroke, married George Richard, Viscount Bolingbroke in 1783 and died 11 Jan. 1803. She and CS had a literary friendship. In 1797, Lady Bolingbroke sent CS a manuscript of forty-seven sonnets and two other poems that she had translated from Italian. See CS to an unnamed recipient, ca. Sept. 1785, n. 1.

2. CS is about to move to Headington. Mr. Barton may be her new landlord.

3. Richard Corbould (see CS to Cadell and Davies, 29 June 1795, n. 2).

To Thomas Cadell, Jr., and William Davies

Heddington near Oxford, Nov[r] 16th 1796
direct to M[rs] Smith only.
Gentlemen,

Since I take the liberty to trouble you with my Letters, it is necessary to let you know of my arrival here. You will also be troubled with a box directed to y[r] care for M[rs] Turner[1] which pray have the goodness to send to the Petworth & Arundel Coach. Having had one such thing lost in changing Coaches in London, I was afraid to venturing it again & should not have intruded on your good nature. I shall be oblig'd to you to let me know what you are dispos'd to give for the Copy right of the second volume of Poetry? It will consist of nearly the same, probably some pages more of poetry than the last Edit[n] of the last, a portrait, & four engravings. I will if you wish it send up a list of the prices. (I do not mean to include the Emigrants as I once talk'd of.) There will be fewer sonnets & more of pieces in other measures & manners. Of course the numbers subscribed for & a certain number for myself must be allow'd. Your early answer will oblige me, & I trouble you to beg any letters left at y[r] House may be immediately forwarded to,

Gent[n], y[r] oblig'd Ser[t],
Charlotte Smith

6 Sheets N° 1000—@ 2.5.0 ———	13.10.0[2]
Paper 12 Reams @ S24/ n ———	14.8.0
Plates & Drawings ———	63.0.0
Working D°—& Paper ———	8.8.0
Adv[ts] & Incidents ———	20.14.0
	120.0.0
200 Author	
800 at 4/4 (Sale Price)———	173.6.8
Deduct Expences———	123.6.8
	50.0.0

6 Sheets N° 1500 @ 2.12.6 ——	15.15.0
Paper—18 Reams @ 24/ ——	21.12.0
Plates & Drawings—& Work^{g} & Paper	75.0.0
Adv^{ts} &c. ——	27.13.0
	140.0.0
200 Author	
1300 at 4/4 (Sale Price) ——	281.13.4
Deduct ——	141.13.4
	140.0.0

6 Sheets N° 2000 y @ £3 ——	18.0.0
24 R^{m} Paper @ 24/ ——	28.16.0
5 Plates Drawing & Engraving ——	63.5.0
Working D^{o}—& Paper ——	15.4.0
Adv^{ts} & Incidents ——	25.00.0
	150.0.0
750 to Author	
9 Stationer's Hall	
1241 Sold at 4/4 (Sale Price) ——	268.17.8
Deduct ——	158.17.8
Profit ——	110.0.0

---

200 Author		
1800 Sold at 4/4 ——	390.0.0	
Deduct Expences —	150.0.0	
2000		
		260.0.0
	240.0.0	8.17.8

British Library Add. MS 42561 folio 230. Address: Messrs Cadell Junr & Davies/ Strand/ London. Postmark: OXFORD/NO/ 17/ 96.

NOTES

1. CS's sister-in-law, Sarah Turner, wife of Rev. Nicholas Turner at Fittleworth.
2. These figures detailing the cost of publishing a book confirm CS's knowledge of bookmaking and bookselling.

To Thomas Cadell, Jr., and William Davies

Heddington. Novr 20th
1796
Gentlemen,

I am not certain by the date of your last Letter (the 14th) whether it was an answer to mine written from hence or whether it was meant as such merely to a former Letter from Weymouth enclosing the drawings and had been detain'd somewhere. To answer it however in my turn, I beg to be understood as not being by any means positive, relative to the price I mention'd as what had been paid for the drawings and plates in the first volume of the Sonnets. I had myself no other memorandum of the Transaction than what remain'd on my memory, for all my papers of every kind are in Sussex & I know not that I ever had or ask'd for any copy of the account that Mr Cadell Senr finally settled with me in the presence of Mr Bicknell (as I think) about the year 1790, for whatever Mr Cadell transacted for me I was sure was with perfect integrity & honor & the particulars made no impression on me that I can very safely rely on. Only I thought that 10 G^{s} each, 5 for the drawing and 5 for the engraving was what he paid, but this may be I apprehend ascertain'd, as it is doubtless easy for you if it answers any purpose to turn to the running account I had with Mr Cadell between the publication of Emmeline in the year 1788 and the close of every account in the Winter of 1790, which Mr Cadell thought necessary for his own security, inasmuch, as I was supposed to be then liable to Mr Smiths controul in regard to the proffits of my writing.

However all that can be said is, that if the price of Artists is rais'd in proportion to the prices of almost every thing else, there is nothing to be done but for the writer to have less proffit. There are no set of Men to whom I would so willingly pay money if I had it as Artists of merit; therefore, if you think Mr Neagle more likely to do justice to the drawing, I beg you will put it into his hands—for I own I am afraid of Mr Heaths <u>inequalities</u>,[1] & I should be more vex'd than would be perhaps worth while if the plates were to be done as coarsely as those in "the pleasures of Memory." As the whole Subscription money does not amount to above hundred & fifty pounds, this will be but a losing game for me. I mean if the expence of plates amount to ten Guineas each besides the drawings I am to pay for. However circumstances may arise which may make this no object to me, & if it be, I had rather gain less from a subscription I was never very anxious about than have the last book of the kind I shall ever publish[2] appear shabbily done and in a bad taste.

I have to day received a Letter from Lady Bessborough by which I have the satisfaction of finding that the Dtss of Devonshire is a great deal better,[3] & Lady B. is so good as to undertake the drawing, & Poggi[4] will probably do another; this I apprehend will be an advantage to the work, & no part of the Ornamental business now remains undecided upon, but the portrait about which I really know not what to do. That of M^r^ Le Hardi[5] is, in the opinion of all to whom I have ever shewn it, so very unlike that I might as well send a portrait of Mother Shipton[6] to the engraver. Mr Hayley informd me above 6 weeks ago that the Copy he had caus'd to be made of Mr Romneys drawing waited only for a glass before he should send it to me, but I have heard nothing since So that I fear something has occurred to prevent it. I should be very much oblig'd to you if you will take occasion when any of your Messengers go to that part of the Town to let him call at Lord Grandison's[7] with the enclos'd note & get the money if he can, as it is for a Packing case M^r^ De Foville paid for him, desiring that the Money might be sent to y^r^ Shop, which I imagine has not been done, & I have no notion of not dunning him for it, as M^r^ De F. paid it from his pocket & had a great deal of trouble besides. I shall be very much oblig'd to you to send down whatever Letters or parcels you have for me. I am, Gent^n^, Y^r^ most obed^t^ & oblig'd Ser^t^,

Charlotte Smith

Yale University MS. Address: Messrs Cadell Junr & Davies/ Strand/ London. Postmark: OXFORD; NO 22, 96.

NOTES

1. James Neagle (ca. 1760–1822) and James Heath (1757–1834), line engravers. Neagle contributed plates to John Boydell's *Shakespeare Gallery* (1793), and Heath was appointed engraver to the king in 1794. In the end, four drawings were engraved for *Elegiac Sonnets ii:* Corbould's drawings opposite pp. 11 and 74 were engraved by Heath; another Corbould drawing opposite p. 78 was engraved by Neagle; and the drawing by Lady Bessborough opposite p. 39 was engraved by Neagle.

2. It was not her last. A third collection of poetry, *Beachy Head,* was published posthumously.

3. Henrietta (Harriet) Frances, countess of Bessborough (1761–1821), younger sister of Georgiana, duchess of Devonshire; they were daughters of the first Earl Spencer. An artist rather than a writer like her sister, Lady Bessborough's drawings for the new volume are as effective as those by professionals. The duchess was recovering from an eye operation in July; by Oct. she was well enough to write letters. Lady Bessborough attended her constantly during her recuperation.

4. Anthony de Poggi, printseller, 91 New Bond Street.

5. A sarcastic reference to Thomas Hardy, engraver, 92 Norton Street, 1796–1802.

6. Legendary English prophet, thought to be daughter of Agatha Shipton and the devil, who supposedly wrote "Mother Shipton's Prophecies." Although dates are given for her (1488–1559), there is no evidence that she lived. Richard Head's *The Life and Death of Mother Shipton* (1684) was still being reissued in the 1800s.

7. George Child Villiers, eighth Viscount Grandison, son of the fourth earl of Jersey and Lady Jersey. The nature and contents of the case are unknown, but CS was still seeking de Foville's £18 four months later (see CS to Cadell and Davies, 17 Mar. 1797).

To Thomas Cadell, Jr., and William Davies

[Headington, 13 December 1796]
Gentlemen,

I flattered myself that I should e'er this have had the satisfaction of hearing that Mr Hayley had made such an arrangement in regard to the Copy right[1] that I might have known what farther present advantage I can derive from its sale. In all probability, if my eldest Son was living & well on the departure from India of the Ships now arrived, I have remittances come or orders on Muilman & Co that will answer the same end. But as I want ten Guineas for my daily use, I have drawn upon you for that Sum at 7 days;[2] If the negociation with Mr Hayley is not concluded, I imagine so small a Sum will make no present difference to you, and I will in that case replace it the instant I receive my remittances if it is not conformable to the agreement made or to be made—— I persuade myself you will be so good as to pay it — — Tho I can make no use whatever of M^r^ Le Hardi's portrait of me, I must not omit making him the acknowledgement I propos'd to him when he desird to draw it. I mention'd his acceptance of two or three sets of Books, whichever he preferred, & as It is probable he may prefer some of those of which you are proprietors, I in that case beg the favor of you to let him have them and charge them to my account.

My India Letters will as usual be sent to you. Have the goodness to forward them instantly by the post, as I am particularly anxious to hear from My Son & every moment seems an age——

I am Gent^n^,
your obed^t^ & Oblig'd Ser^t^,
Charlotte Smith

Heddington, Decr 13th 1796

Yale University MS. Address: Messrs Cadell & Davies/ Strand/ London. Postmark: OXFORD; DE 14 96.

NOTES

1. On this letter is a copy of an undated note to Mr. Rose—presumably the solicitor Samuel Rose (see Biographical Notes), acting in Hayley's stead—by Cadell and Davies, proposing terms for the copyright:

> They [Cadell and Davies] will supply Mrs Smith with 200 Copies in Boards free of Expence for her Subscribers and her own use—They will discharge her from her present Book Debt to them, which is between £20 and £25—They will pay Mrs Smith the Sum of £70—and, upon the Publication of a second Edition, a further Sum of £30. These Terms, which, altogether, may be estimated at 175, they trust Mr Rose will consider as handsome—especially when he recollects that they have, in Addition hereto, to defray the whole Expence of the Drawings, Plates, &c. &c——
>
> It is of Course to be understood that the £15 remitted to Mrs. Smith a few Days since, and the ten Guineas for which she has now drawn upon them are to be deducted from the first mentioned Sum of £70.

This note clears up the question of who finally paid for the drawings and engraved plates.

2. A receipt survives for ten guineas drawn on the Cadell and Davies account from the bookseller Robert Bliss of Oxford, 14 Dec. 1796.

To Thomas Cadell, Jr., and William Davies

Opposite University Coll, Oxen, 23rd Decr [17]96
Gentlemen,

In consequence of my Letters being taken to Heddington notwithstanding my directions to the contrary & there detain'd a day, I did not receive a Letter I have been favour'd with from Mr Hayley till a day after I ought to have had it. I lose no time in telling you that I think your proposal in regard to the Copy right very liberal, & I accept it as such with no other exception than the small one of entreating the favor of you to let me have ten Guineas now, instead of reserving the whole to be paid on delivery of the MSS—Which indeed I could do in a few days, if I did not think that by keeping the MMS till it is actually wanted for the press, I shall be able to make the poetry more perfect, for it is certain that by frequent trifling revisals at a short distance from each other, such compositions are considerably improved, & before the whole is deliver'd to the press, Mr Hayley, to whom thro your hands I shall send it, will correct the whole. As this little book will contain all I shall ever publish & I have even more reputation than I thought I had to lose, I shall certainly be solicitous on that account as well as in justice to you to send it fourth as compleat as may be in my power.

I had yesterday a Letter from Lady Bessborough who has done the drawing so as to have it nearly ready for the Engraver. I have written to her Ladyship to request that as Poggi has superintended the business, he will be so good as to undertake to get the engraving done. I have reason to beleive that this engraving will cost you nothing, but if it should turn out otherwise & the charge on account of any particular engraver should exceed what appears to you reasonable, I will make any allowance for the surplus charge that you think fair—

There now remains only one drawing, the last, which will be done by another friend.[1] Of course these two not being to be paid for (I mean the drawings) will be a saving of five or six Guineas. The engraving will I think be less expensive than the others because the drawing is very simple. I hope to send it up in a very short time. The following is the list of Poems with the plates:[2]

Sonnet—Dº,Dº,Dº,Dº,Dº to Dr Parry
Dº—the Gossamer/—Dº written on the Western Coast/Dº—— Dº—— /
Dº the Lunatic—With a plate——
Dº—— / Dº—— / Dº—— /
Epitaph on a faithful Servant, in the Churchyard at Boreham in Essex
Elegy—
Ode—with a plate—
Verses, near the Catholic Chapel of St Pedro di Sul in Portugal
Verses. written in Portugal—to CS.
These by
Mrs. ONeile[3]

Answer to the last—
Verses—
Ode
Lines
Elegy—with a plate——
Ode to the Morning Star
Verses
Occasional address for a Charitable purpose
Dº——
Elegy to the Southe~~rn~~ Downs, with a plate—& probably two other Short Poems, which are not yet in such a polishd state as authorises my inserting them.

I have complied as well with my own wishes as the earnest desire of my friends in inserting in the Collection the three pieces by Mrs ONeill. Not only because they are exquisitely beautiful, but because I am persuaded it will engage all her friends & connections to become purchasers & gratifies at once my taste & the tender affection I had for her. It may be stated in the advertisement that there are three pieces by a deceas'd friend if you should think that people may (if there be any so fastidious) say that they meant to buy my verses & not those of another——

I am afraid I have no more India Letters, but Mess[rs] Muilman & Co will make the advance directed by my Son I trust. So that it is only on account of my being press'd for time & the many trifling expences, even of this short removal, that I take any farther liberty with you, but it will be the last.

[Unsigned]

Yale University MS. Address: Mess[rs] Cadell Jun[r] and Davies/ Strand/ London. Postmark: OXFORD; DE 24 96.

NOTES

1. The other three drawings in *Elegiac Sonnets* are by Richard Corbould; her friend's drawing was not used.

2. The poems were printed with quite different titles. "D[o] the Lunatic" refers to "Sonnet LXX. On Being Cautioned Against Walking on an Headland Overlooking the Sea, Because It Was Frequented by a Lunatic." It faces a plate by Corbould and Neagle. "Ode—with a plate" refers to Henrietta O'Neill's "Ode to the Poppy," with a plate by Corbould and Neagle. "Elegy—with a plate" refers to "The Forest Boy," with a plate by Corbould and Heath showing Phoebe mourning her young lover lost in war. She does not name the poem "The Female Exile" that Lady Bessborough's drawing accompanied.

3. In the end only two of Henrietta O'Neill's poems were printed: "Ode to the Poppy" and "Verses Written by the Same Lady on Seeing Her Two Sons at Play." These were followed by CS's "answer to the last," which she titled "Verses, on the Death of the Same Lady, Written in September, 1794."

1797
"A NECESSITOUS AUTHOR"

—22 OCTOBER 1797

Charlotte Smith spent the early months of this year fearing arrest for sums owed here and there and writing letters to raise money, the trustees having failed her once again. While in London in June and July on estate business, she was ill nearly the entire time. It was a year of meager income and little literary productivity. In May, the eighth edition of Elegiac Sonnets *was published, the first to which she added no new poems, and in June the long-awaited second volume of sonnets, the subscription edition, was issued at last. But there were fewer than three hundred subscribers, whose fees had trickled in since 1794; and the expenses of publication would not have left her much remuneration. This year's letters show, nevertheless, her assiduous attention to the work's final content—to the notes, the illustrations, and of course the poems themselves. In October, Cadell and Davies agreed to publish* The Young Philosopher, *their first novel of hers since* The Banished Man. *Its publication signaled her financial need. But a bitter exchange of letters between author and bookseller over honesty and profit marks the end of this once successful business relationship.*

As in the previous year, the children's lives are in the background. In the spring, Lucy was seriously ill when her mother's finances were at their most desperate. And Thomas Newhouse, who later married Lucy, appeared on the scene as a friend to whom Smith entrusted errands in London. Charles returned home on leave from Gibraltar, and Smith still entertained hopes of educating George to enter the church.

To Thomas Cadell, Jr., and William Davies

Oxford, January 17th 1797
Gentlemen,

By tomorrow nights coach from the Mitre, I shall send up a book in which is written the Poetry I propose for publication. I am persuaded that it will not be less agreeable to you, than desireable to me, to have it pass under the friendly correction of M[r] Hayley; I have therefore directed it to him & shall be oblig'd to you to take the trouble of enquiring if he is, or is likely to be, very soon in Town; & if not, that you would be kind enough to send it, taking every precaution for its safety, to Eartham. The last Letter I had from M[r] Hayley, written ab[t] eight days since, mention'd that he was then leaving home for a short time, but he did not say whether it was to London or elsewhere that he was going.

Such alterations as M[r] Hayley may recommend he will mark on the blanks I have left, & should they be numerous or important enough to make transcription necessary, he will return it to me to transcribe again. If not, & the corrections can be put in without puzzling the Printer, I have desir'd him to send it immediately to you——— I have not yet receiv'd the last drawing I expected from my friend & begin to fear that he cannot satisfy himself. As there is now no time to lose, I have written about it again, & if I do not hear by the return of the post, I shall send up the subject to M[r] Corbould,[1] for it must not be delay'd longer——

Concluding that you will consider my engagement as in a great measure compleat & being assured that you have every disposition to oblige me where you can do it with propriety, I have drawn on you for 9£/one shilling in fav[r] of M[r] G W Syms, & 5 Guineas in fav[r] of M[r] Robert Bliss,[2] the 1st at 7, y[e] latter at 5 days—Which however I should not have done till the MMS was actually return'd to you ready for the printer, but that I have been served such an infamous trick by M[r] Robinson[3] as has thrown me into a more awkard & unpleasant situation than I was ever yet in (much as he has long made me suffer) & left me absolutely without the daily means of subsistence —— I have been worn to death with the writing this persecution brings upon me & have been prevented from finishing the verses so soon as I sh[d] otherwise have done——

As I am likely to remain here for some time on account of my Youngest boy (whom I hope to educate for the valuable living of Islington which must be his, should M[r] Strahan live till he is in orders, as I heartily hope he may & even longer),[4] I shall order up some more of my books & have no doubt but that you will be so good as to forward them, should I find it convenient to direct them to your house from Sussex—— I am, Gentlemen,

your obligd hble Ser[t],
Charlotte Smith

Opposite University Coll, Oxen., Jan 17th

Yale University MS. Address: Mess[rs] Cadell & Davies/ Strand/ London. Postmark: OXFORD: JA 18 97.

NOTES

1. In the end, Richard Corbould executed three drawings for *Elegiac Sonnets ii.* Lady Bessborough did the fourth.

2. Possibly George William Syms, wine merchant, of 16 Abchurch Lane, London. Robert Bliss, the Oxford bookseller, often lent CS money while she lived in Headington.

3. John Robinson, trustee to the Smith estate, controlled funds owed to CS. In addition to her semiannual interest payment of £35, she hoped for another £100, promised when she complained that £500 profit from the Barbados plantations had been held by George Blackman, Esq., and Co., since Jan. 1795. CS later told Cadell and Davies that the trustees were withholding £1,000 (17 Mar. 1797). Later still, she told William Hayley that they held £800 and that she had agreed to accept £100 for not contesting the larger amount (16 Apr. 1797). Robinson's "infamous trick" was to allow her to draw £10 of the £100, and then change his mind.

4. George, now almost 13, was never educated for the church (on the living at Islington, see CS to Joseph Cooper Walker, 9 Oct. 1793, n. 3); he joined the army in Sept. 1801. There is no evidence that CS could afford to place him in school as she had placed Charles and Lionel at Winchester and then Lionel briefly at Oxford.

To Thomas Cadell, Jr., and William Davies

[Oxford, 16 February 1797]
Gent[n],

I received the engraving & drawing in due course. To the neatness of the former, I have nothing to object. The style of the back ground is particularly pleasing, but Mr Neagle has certainly alterd the face of the female figure and given it quite another character. I imagine there is no question now of an engraver for Lady Bessboroughs drawing, as Mr Poggi has given it to Mr Heath. I think of Mr Rogers's plates & tremble![1]

I suppose Mr Condé has not done the portrait.[2] You will of course hasten him if you have reason to think him tardy. Mr Heath also might be reminded that he has had the drawing of the lunatic a long while in his hands. From Mr Corbould, I expect the last drawing every day.

Mr Hayley, in a few lines to my daughter, mentions having return'd you the MMS, as it wanted very little correction. M[rs] ONeills poetry & three original pieces of mine are not included in that book; they will travel under frank covers to M[r] Hayley in the course of next week, my everlastingly tormenting business having so wearied & distracted me that I have never been able to obtain quiet leisure enough to correct & write them out for the last time. When they are done, should an Opportunity occur I could wish to have the book return'd in which I have left some blanks on purpose; to put in as they are to be printed, what remains—As well as such a list of subscribers as can be made out.[3] Perhaps however I may be oblig'd to be in London before the book goes to press.

Lady Bolingbroke, in the small parcel you last sent, has oblig'd me with a MMS Copy of forty seven Sonnets & two poems of mine translated into Italian.[4] They are dedicated to her Ladyship & appear to be extremely well done. Some of my friends wish for copies, & perhaps it might answer to print about an hundred copies. Pray fav^r^ me with your opinion whether you think a sale likely for that or any other small number beyond those for my friends, & if you think it might be worth while, I w^d^ obtain Lady Bs permission to print them. It might give a sort of eclat to the new volume as well as add something to the reputation of the other——

I receivd the heavy Letter you sent me very safely; it was not however from India but from my Son Charles at Gibraltar;[5] from India I fear I shall not hear so soon as I had hoped, but should Letters come, beg to have them by the post. I am, Gent^n^, Your oblig'd & obed^t^ humble Ser^t^,

Charlotte Smith

Oxford, Feby 16th 1797

Yale University MS. Address: Messrs Cadell & Davies—/ Strand/ London. Postmark: OXFORD; FE 17 97.

NOTES

1. James Neagle and James Heath, both line engravers, each did two drawings for *Elegiac Sonnets ii* (see CS to Cadell and Davies, 20 Nov. 1796, n. 1). After some confusion in this and the next two letters about who would engrave Lady Bessborough's drawing, Neagle finally did it. His engraving for Henrietta O'Neill's "Ode to the Poppy" shows a woman seated with a book open in her lap while she gazes up toward the right corner of the frame with an oddly transfixed expression.

William Rogers was a copperplate printer, Craven Buildings, Drury Lane.

2. Possibly John Condé (fl. 1785–92) or his son Peter (fl. 1806–24). The elder was a miniaturist who worked in stipple and the younger an engraver. In either case, Condé was preparing a drawing of CS from George Romney's original done at Eartham in 1792.

3. The unclear syntax of this sentence prevented me from modernizing its punctuation.

4. Neither the author nor the volume of poems dedicated to Charlotte Collins, Lady Bolingbroke, is identified.

5. Charles was stationed at Gibraltar in the Royal Garrison Battalion as a lieutenant under General Trigge from Sept. 1795 until Feb. 1798.

To Thomas Cadell, Jr., and William Davies

[Oxford] Feby 26th 1797
Gentlemen,

I have to day been favourd with your Letter & lose no time in replying to its contents as well as the pacquet wch reach'd me about an hour after—— In regard to Lady Bessboroughs determination about the plate, I had a Letter from her Yesterday with these words:

"I hope you will not disapprove of my having persisted in Mr Heaths engraving the little drawing. He is named to me by several judges as next to Bartalozzi,[1] & he had already prepar'd the plate, when M^{r} C and D. sent. I hope too Messrs C. & D. will not be angry."

It seems by this as if, contrary to the purport of your Lttr, Lady Bessborough had decided & that there is some mistake in the business which wants explanation. I could not do otherwise than leave the choice of an engraver to Lady Bessborough after the trouble she had taken, and I naturally concluded you did not object to Mr Heath, the objection originating with me merely from a sight of the plates he had done for "the pleasures of Memory"[2]—— As you Gent^{n} have that book at hand, do look at the prints & see if my fault finding is merely fastidiousness. I do not think however that I ever saw any others so bad, & I believe the drawings for the Pleasures of Memory, notwithstanding the great names affixd to them, must have been defective. Very certainly the only plate he did for the first volume of my Poems is one of the best &, touchd up as it has been, is still to my idea one of the best engravings. Still however I do think Neagle a more pleasing engraver. Perhaps if Mr Davies would take the trouble of calling on Lady Bessborough who is very obliging & polite, a few minutes w^{d} settle the matter if it is not already done so that no farther delay would occur. Mr Heath, however, if he undertakes it, must have the goodness to complete it in less time than he has taken to do the Lunatic. The new drawing I will return under a frank—— That I conclude is intended to be in the hands of Mr Neagle. I shall write a few remarks on it for Mr Corboulds consideration which you will be so good as to shew him, & if he thinks as I do, he will give directions for a few trifling variations to the engraver——

Mr Hayley has this week as much more MMS (original Sonnets of mine) as A frank wd convey written in a small hand. Another frank goes Off to night & about Wednesday the last. I imagine that these MS will require very little correction or alteration so that I might almost have ventured to desire M^{r} H to return them to you as soon as he had look'd them over, but on reflection, it will be better & less liable to puzzle the Printer if I insert in the Book those I have left room for (it will not hold all by a good deal) & put the notes & preface & what remains in another book. In that case (if as in most cases the preface is last printed), that, & the names being the last necessary, may be reserved, & the printer may almost immediately proceed on the book you have return'd which I will send up as soon as fill'd & will obtain time for it tomorrow if no way, by shutting myself up in the garret, for I am worn to death by company from morning to the nigh[t]. I think Mr Condé has done all that could be done save only that my family say, what I do not venture to suggest myself, that there is a want of spirit in the Eyes. I see not any great cause myself to find fault with it. I only fear that it is done so delicately that it will not bear so many impressions as will be required for your sale. I have some three or four subscribers who have subscribed for 2 Copies who desire, instead of two copies of this last book, to be allow'd one of the first & one of the last. Of this it will be time enough to speak when the books are out, but I may name three of these now least I sh^d^ forget it. They are Mr Nott, Mrs Nott[3] & Lady Templeton.[4] You forgot to give any answer about the Italian Sonnets. I am &c CS.

I beleive I shall return the Miniature, as my family & some friends I have shewn it to insist upon a want of animation in the Eyes which I beleive a single touch of the Graver w^d^ remedy.

I will send back the drawing for the ode to the Poppy with the book & wish a slight alteration may be made.

What is to be done to make up the list the Dtss of Devonshire has forgot, I cannot guess.

Yale University MS. Address: Messrs Cadell and Davies—/ Strand/ London. Postmark: {place illegible}; FE/ 27/ 97.

NOTES

1. Francesco Bartolozzi (1727–1815), an Italian noted for stipple engravings and etchings, was summoned to England to be engraver to the king. He was a founding member of the Royal Academy.

2. By Samuel Rogers; published by Cadell and Davies in 1793 and 1795. For her objections, see CS to Cadell and Davies, 20 Nov. 1796.

3. The Reverend Samuel and Augusta Nott (see CS to William Hayley, 12 June 1795, n. 5).

4. Elizabeth Broughton Upton, Lady Templetown (d. 1823).

To Thomas Cadell, Jr., and William Davies

[Oxford, 5 March 1797]
Gentlemen,

On receiving back the last pacquet from Mr Hayley, I proceeded to complete the book you return'd to me, but without adverting to the Poems by Mrs ONeill, I find it insufficient for my own without confusion that may give trouble to the Printer. I have therefore with the assistance of my daughter enter'd the whole in a larger book which is to day completed except only the notes & preface. The ~~latter~~ former will take at least three days, As I will not be told as I was before (by Dr Darwin[1] & another judge) that I was deficient in correctness of natural History. In some very beautiful verses of my poor friends, there are some descriptive lines of the Scenery & natural productions about Lisbon which, for want of being accustomed to study such objects, are I am sure represented by wrong names & in other respects incorrect. Nothing is more easy to correct without injury to the Poetry or Spirit, but I have not been able to obtain any history of Portugal to enable me to do this, & I am afraid I must omit the Poem on that account. If you know of any such book as relates to the plants & trees of Portugal & could borrow & send it me, I could perhaps please myself in the alterations I wish, & it need not hinder my sending up the book of verses as it could follow long before it is wanted in the course of printing & would be placed without difficulty among the other pieces by the same Lady——

I beleive I shall be able to send off the books entirely ready for the press on Wednesday evening, but not to lose any more time about the last drawing, I return it herewith & beg the favr of you to say that I am charm'd with the landscape part which is the prettiest thing I ever saw in my life, but I think the figure of the Nymph too fat. It takes off all that pensive look which becomes such an ideal being & looks more like the plump damsel of the Dairy than a ~~Niaid~~ Naiad. Nor do I like the bracers; they look too modern & take off the classical Appearance which such a figure ought to have. A very little alteration wd do away all these objections, & I dare say Mr Corbould wd have the goodness to name to the engraver these little remarks, so as to have them (the changes) made without altering the drawing, which is so very pretty in point of scenery that it cannot be better. I hope the Engraver will take care of it for me. If instead of flowers round the head a reed like wreath, or what represents ~~such~~ aquatic plants, was substituted, I think it would be more charicaristic,[2] but that is not very material.

In regard to my picture, I do not return it because I very much doubt whether the faults that I see in the engraving can be alterd. The face is too long; that must remain so, I know. My family & such friends as I have shewn it to think there is a want of spirit in the eyes. If that can be amended it may, & I will send up the picture with the book. Under the portrait is to be this motto from Shakespeare which perhaps may be set about immediately:

> Oh! grief has changed me since you saw me last
> And sorrowing hours with times deforming hand
> Have written strange defeatures in my ~~fate~~ face[3]—

I am, Gentlemen, your obedient humble Ser^{t},
Charlotte Smith

March 5th 1797
I find Lady Bessborough has left to Mr Poggi & Mr Davies to settle about the engraving.

General Manuscripts, Manuscripts Division, Rare Books and Special Collections, Princeton University Library. No address or postmark.

NOTES

1. A lover of nature, CS admired the naturalist Erasmus Darwin, but no record of his criticism survives (see CS to Thomas Cadell, Sr., 8 May 1791, and to Cadell, Jr., and Davies, 28 Aug. 1799, and n. 2).
2. As published, the nymph is still a bit plump and the bracers plain and modern; but the landscape is appealing, and the nymph's headpiece appears to have been redrawn as a reed rather than flowers.
3. *Comedy of Errors* 5.1.298–300.

To Thomas Cadell, Jr., and William Davies

[Oxford, 9 March 1797]
Gentlemen.

Having waited under the utmost inconvenience in expectation of hearing from the Dutchess of Devonshire who not only has the goodness to have re^{d} a sum of money for me, but has sent Letters to the persons who possess nearly, if not quite, a thousand pounds in money belonging to me and my children, I have really staid till I was reduced to my last sixpence & have time after time written to Mr Bicknell in vain. I obtain no answer, & am wearied with conjectures & worn down by the petty inconveniencies I am thus needlessly Compelled to sustain. Two days since I sent up to Mr Low a draft for 20£ drawn in his favor, as I was unwilling to trouble you & I desird him to try if he could get the money for me. If he does not, he will be indebted to me exactly the same Sum in a week or ten days from a MMS he will ab[t] that time receive;[1] I am well aware that you can owe me nothing, but As M[r] Bliss, the only person who supplies me here, knows you & is not acquainted with M[r] Low, and as it is extremely difficult to get Money here at all for a draft on any body, I have taken the liberty to draw on you for five pounds as I really had not a shilling left, & the enclos'd draft on M[r] Low will replace it, if before the latter is due, M[r] Bicknell who is to receive the money from the Dutchess for me does not receive it, which ie if he does she shall repay ~~him~~ You in cash, & you will in that case cancel the note.[2]

Be assured I have no intention of intruding on you, nor would have done it now but on account of the unaccountable silence of those on whom I fully relied for releif from suspence so disagreeable & indeed dreadful where there is a large family to support & no credit even for a week. I have been so perplex'd that your book is not quite compleated. Three other Sonnets which I compos'd a few days ago—"To the Goddess of Botany," "To the Moon," & "an insect," which I beleive are on new idea's, I have sent to M[r] Hayley since I wrote last, as it is my wish & purpose to make the volume as large & as good as I can. I shall probably have these last return'd tomorrow, & almost all the rest is written but the notes—— I conclude that if it is in y[r] hands within a week, it will be printed before the engravings are done & be ready for delivery at or immediately after Easter——

I am Gent[n],
y[r] obed & Oblig'd Ser[t],
Charlotte Smith

Oxford, March 9th 1797

Yale University MS. Address: Mess[rs] Cadell & Davies/ Strand/ Post paid London. Postmark: OXFORD; PAID MR/ 10/ 1797.

NOTES

1. *Marchmont,* published by Sampson Low.

2. This unusually impenetrable run-on sentence seems to say that Bliss in Oxford would not advance money to CS because he did not know Low in London. Therefore CS wrote a check against Cadell and Davies, whom Bliss did know, even though they had no money on her account. She trusted that this would be all right because she "knew" that Low would soon owe her money for a volume of *Marchmont* and the duchess of Devonshire would soon be sending money to her through her lawyer, Charles Bicknell. No doubt Cadell and Davies found her presumption offensive.

To Thomas Cadell, Jr., and William Davies

[Oxford, 17 March 1797]
Gent^{n},

I have taken the liberty to send to your house a watch which is to go to Canada to my Son Lionel. It is to be deliver'd to Mr Black of Mincing Lane who will be so good as to call for it.

If you will be so obliging as to let me know by An early post whether you wish to print the preface & list of names with the first sheet of Letter press, I will insert both in the book & send it up immediately that it may be proceeded upon. The last poem only is not completed to my mind, & that may follow after the first sheets are put to press.

I do not to this hour know whether Mr Low will get the money for me or no. The Trustees, now possess'd of a thousand pound ready money & conscious they cannot legally keep it, know not what excuse to make & refer backwards & forwards to each other.[1] While more than half my time is passed in writing to the Dutchess of Devonshire and other persons who have been so good as to try to help me. It is impossible to express half the fatigue & distress of mind this subjects me to, nor how much it prevents my earning what the times would yet afford me by my pen.[2]

Give me leave to ask, whether you are likely to be dispos'd to purchase any book of entertainment. I do not know that I shall be able to produce one, but a literary Man has given me an idea on which I think something might be produced.

Be so good as to give me an answer as to the book, & you shall have it by the next stage.

I am, Gent^{n}, y^{r} oblig'd Ser^{t},
Charlotte Smith

Oxford, March 17th 1797
Mrs Nott of Bedford Street, Bedford Square, has several subscriptions or at least names to ~~pay,~~ send. The Money is of course yours. The names must be collected before the list is printed.

I suppose Lord Grandisons[3] people never condescended to pay the 18 <£?> Mr Foville paid at Weymouth. If any of y^{r} people sh^{d} go that way, pray dun them for it.

Mr Foville, being desirous to write to his particular friend in the Prince de Condé's Army, desires me to enclose the within to you, & I beg the favour of you to pay the Postage to the Port whence the Hamburgh mail sails from, & charge it to my account.

Pray be so obliging as to let it be done carefully.

Yale University MS. Address: Messrs Cadell & Davies/ Strand/ London. No postmark.

NOTES

1. See CS to Cadell and Davies, 17 Jan. 1797, n. 3.

2. The handwriting of this letter, and particularly this paragraph, is larger, hastier, and less regular than usual. The four added notes further indicate what she would have called her "distraction." The note about de Foville is upside down.

3. Nothing more is said about CS's or de Foville's connection with George Child Villiers, eighth Viscount Grandison (see CS to Cadell and Davies, 20 Nov. 1796 and n. 7).

To William Davies

[Oxford] 24 March 1797
Sir,

I yesterday heard from M[r] Blackman, the Merch[t] who holds the produce of my childrens Estate, that M[r] Dyer, the Man who has been one of their principal robbers and torments to them & me, has graciously been pleas'd to accept of my Offer of his taking an hundred pounds & my having the like Sum, tho the share due to my children & to his is in proportion of nine to five;[1] of course his is the advantage in taking even this small Sum on an equal footing. However as I may still, from past conduct, fear some equivocation or attempt at delay & know that you are not only remarkably punctual & exact in money dealings but beleive that you would oblige me when in your power, I have taken the liberty to draw upon M[r] Blackman for 68£ in your favour, & I shall be very much oblig'd to you if you would be so good as to send a trusty person with the draft. Receive the money in such paper as may be most current here for the common expenses of my House, and send it me the beginning of the week in some safe mode of conveyance. Deducting however if you Chuse it the amount of the small draft you were so good as to pay for me. If you have any new & not dear publications worth reading & buying, the Bills might be enclos'd with them.

I should not trouble you on this business but that M[r] Bicknell has so much to do that my affairs suffer continually from his delay, & I may write four or five Letters before I get an answer——

If Any thing occurs as to denial of the draft (notice of which I have given to M[r] Blackman in consequence of his Letter of yesterday), have the goodness to give me immediate notice that I may be upon my guard against the new villainy which may very probably be attempted.

I am, Sir, your obed[t] humble Ser[t],
Charlotte Smith

Yale University MS. Address: M[r] Davies at/ Mess[rs] Cadell & Davies's——/ Strand/ London. Postmark: OXFORD MR/ 25/ 97.

NOTE

1. See CS to Cadell and Davies, 17 Jan. 1797, n. 3. CS is playing fast and loose with these proportions. By this time she had eight living children, the three youngest of whom had been born after her father-in-law died and were thus excluded from the will. Her ninth child, Augusta, is dead, so she counts her son-in-law DeFoville as legal recipient of Augusta's portions. At the same time, Benjamin's sister Mary Smith Berney Dyer, wife of Thomas Dyer, had eight children in all, three by Berney and five by Thomas (four sons and a daughter). (See Genealogical Chart.) All were recognized by the will, as Richard Smith drew up separate provisions for the three Berney grandchildren and the five Dyer grandchildren.

To William Davies

[Oxford, 26 March 1797]
Sir,

I am extremely oblig'd to y^u for the trouble you were so kind as to take for me relative to the Bill. Of Mr Parkin's scoundrelism there is no end. He hopes to tire me quite out & to get his bill of 23£ paid because of my distress for money, but he will for once reckon upon pusilanimity that he will not find. I am determined rather to perish with the rest of my family than to submit to his impudent robbery, & such being my resolution, I have by the advice of one of my friends, taken such a measure as must produce something decisive. If it has the effect I expect from my knowledge of the parties, The Bill will be paid; be so good as to keep it therefore till after Wednesday when I expect to know the Issue & will write to you by Thursday's post. I make no apology as to the expence of Letters because you of course charge them, but I beg leave to repeat how much I consider myself as oblig'd to you. I am, Sir,

your most oblig'd & obed^t Ser^t,
Charlotte Smith

Oxford, March 26th 1797

Yale University MS. Address: Mr Davies./ Opposite the end of/ Catherine Street/ Strand/ London. Postmark: OXFORD: MR/ 27/ 97.

To William Hayley

Opposite University Coll., High Street, Oxford, April 16th 1797

I did not think after all the plague I have occasiond to you that I should ever again have had either occasion or courage to torment you for your assistance in pecuniary matters, but my Son has sent no remit since January 1796, and I have lost the resource he directed for me in Muilman's house by its Bankruptcy and the suicide of its' principal. On the other hand, the eight hundred pounds are in the hands of Blackman & Co., belonging, certainly the greatest part of it, to my children, I cannot obtain one shilling, & tho I was assured after long writing & imploring that I should have 100£ & ten of it was actually paid, yet before I could draw for the rest, the worthy Gentlemen had alter'd their minds,[1] and my Bills for the common necessaries of life to the amount of only 25£ were sent back; the consequence of which is that I am indebted 25£ to a Tradesman here who advanced the money & can very ill afford to wait even for a day,[2] & I have no resource now because I cannot procure money for a draught again, & of course Famine, which I have often seen very near, seems nearer than she has ever yet been— To add to my satisfaction. The Bankers who lent me 80£ to send to my two poor Lieutenants, Charles and Lionel, who were quite destitute (& for whom the Wretches who possess their property refused me the least assistance)—The Bankers who so obligingly accommodated me have written to me to say that if it is not immediately replaced, they must proceed to recover it; that is to say I shall be arrested & sent to Prison. To that I am however quite reconciled & had rather it should happen than not, if it would bring the business to an issue.

The most pressing necessity is for money to pay this civil Tradesman who will so extremely suffer if I do not immediately replace the 25£, & next to that for the loaf that is to feed my family. I have long been promisd 35£ by the Dtss who has not the money but, wishing to assist me, has sent me an assurance of it to make what use of I please. This I have to day sent to Davies Who is, on the publication of the volume of Poems, is to receive at least 18£ of unpaid subscriptions which he says belong to me. These two Sums seem to be no very inadequate security for 50£ which I have implored him to send down on Teusday—— Perhaps he will not, & then I do not know what I shall do unless I sell my time at a proportionable lower price for present help, & in this, indeed in the whole negociation, you could materially befriend me, & I know no other person that can——

Have the goodness to try what you can do, & I assure you that I never will voluntarily tieze you again on such a subject, nor should any thing but the last necessity urge me to it now. Davies seem'd dispos'd to purchase a work of entertainment. If you knew the extreme misery, I am subject to & which I must yet bear, for what can I do with my three daughters & a boy of twelve years old? You w^{d} wonder how, shatterd as my health is, I get on from one day to another. It is rather despair than fortitude that carries me on. I have so little to hope, I am so little sensible to the pleasure which they say there is even in existence that I seem habituated to suffering just as a wretch is ~~with~~ to his dungeon, & I do not beleive that any thing less than such misery as I am compelled to endure would make me feel at all. I am not yet I think at the very bottom of personal suffering, for I imagine I shall die in a prison. So am I rewarded for my wretched & laborious life—with the loss of all that is accounted good & with that of the one good which w^{d} have reconciled me to the deprivation of every other. Will y^{u} see if you can be of any use to me with Davies, and let me hear from you soon?

I wrote some time ago to Lord Egremont enclosing a Letter from Mr Graham, the Chancery Lawyer and friend to Mr Erskine who first engaged to direct the suit which must be instituted, but afterwards said, that nothing could be even begun in it without Money & that he thought Lord Egremont & the Dtss of Devonshire might contribute towards it as they had shewn so much kindness towards me. It was an idea I sh^{d} not have ventur'd upon, but as he did, I sent the Letter to Lord Egremont to be afterwards forwarded to the Dtss. From her Grace, I have had an answer, but as she neither spoke of Lord E. nor Have I had any notice from his Lordship, I imagine there is not the least likelihood of my being assisted in this by him of which I have no right in the World to complain. I shall always owe him as it is very great obligations——

Lucy has been so alarmingly ill with what appears to be the beginning of a decline that she has been attended by a Physician, and he has not yet taken leave of her tho she is rather better. She has never been well since her Sisters death & is subject to fits and depressions of spirits that are terrifying. I have represented how much this aggravates my sufferings, but I am disregarded & shall be till it is too late. After what happen'd this time two years, what infamy, what cruelty may I not expect & endure.[3] Pray let me hear from you as soon as you can, & forgive my putting you to the expence of a Ltter, but I am unwilling to trouble Ld E. & think it possible you may be in Town. Is it true, I hope not, that the Sargents[4] are almost undone? So I have heard from Quarters that I fear know too well to make it doubtful——— God bless you. Forgive my being so great a plague.

y^{rs} very truly, CS.

Cowper and Newton Museum MS. Address: William Hayley Esqre/ Eartham,/ near Chichester. {In the care of Messrs Cadell & Davies/ Strand/ London.} Postmark: OXFORD; AP/ 17/ 97.

NOTES

1. See CS to Cadell and Davies, 17 Jan. 1797, n. 3.
2. Identified as Robert Bliss, the bookseller, in her next letter.
3. Augusta died on 23 Apr. 1795.

4. John Sargent, author of *The Mine* (1784), and his wife, Charlotte, of Woollavington, were friends and neighbors of Hayley. Early in CS's career, they befriended her as well, Sargent having undertaken some business for her in 1787.

To William Davies

High Street, Oxford, April 16th 1797
Sir,

I have to day received the very distressing information that Bills to the amount of £25—which Mr Bliss Bookseller here was so good as to let me have the money for and for which I drew on the information of Mr Blackman himself (who inform'd me I was to have an hundred pounds of the 800£ that are in his hands)—have been not only return'd to the great distress and inconvenience of Mr Bliss, who has a large family & makes an hard struggle to provide for them, but any satisfaction relative to them refus'd to a particular friend of mind (fellow of a College here),[1] who having occasion to go to London was yesterday so good as to call on Mr Blackman and Mr Parkyn; the former is willing [as he says][2] to pay any Sum if Mr Parkyn will consent, Mr Robinson's consent being already obtain'd. Mr Parkyn has upon this taken new Ground & says he will not consent to my having any money unless all the parties named in the Will of Richd Smith, my childrens Grandfather, consent—which he knows to be utterly impossible, for there are legatees for trifling Sums named conditionally in the fourth or fifth division of the Estate, who never think of their legacies & know that they never will be had; yet to apply to these people will take up months or years & of course render useless any application for present assistance. Nothing is more evident than that this villainous monster is determined to perpetuate the miseries he has inflicted on me. His present answer is altogether unlike what he gave to the person you sent with the Bill I troubled you to try to get paid for me. I am utterly at a loss to know what I am to do. I still have those resources in my own endeavours which have already produced me near 3000£, but if I am incessantly to be tormented in this manner, it is impossible I can make the most of what I am able to do, for half my time is taken up in soliciting for what is actually my own & with held from me on the most infamous pretences.

The present exigence is beyond every other distressing to me. I have no other possible means of getting out of it than to ask a favour of Mr Cadell & you which I assure you I do very reluctantly. It is to advance on the note I enclose from the Dtss of Devonshire and on the Sums on the Subscriptions yet due to me, vis About 7 guineas from Ireland from Mr Walker, seven as I think from Mrs Olmius, & three or four from Mrs Nott, the Sum of 50£, which these Sums, when received (which I imagine will be immediately or very soon) will repay you, or if you consider that security as inadequate, I will enter into an engagement with you to furnish a Novel in three volumes in the course of next winter which you mention'd being dispos'd to buy when done.[3] I wish not however to deceive you about it; the plan is laid, & about 60 pages written but not more, & if you grant me the favor I ask, I know that it will be merely a favor. If you cannot, return to Mr Newhouse, the Gentleman who will call upon you on my behalf the Dutchess's note. She means to take it up this week as she assures me, but perhaps it may not be possible on account of public distress. My great trouble is for Mr Bliss whom I cannot bear to inconvenience & who will I know be extremely & seriously inconvenienced if I cannot replace on Tuesday the money he advanced on the faith of My Bills which I had not a doubt of Blackmans paying after what he wrote to me. Not only do I suffer extremely from the injury it will do him, but I really shall not know how to supply my family with necessaries the ensuing week. I trust I shall hear by Tuesdays post that Mr Cadell & you agree to oblige me. I received last night the 3rd proof of the Poems, which I shall return corrected tomorrow with more MMS. I should have sent it to night, but I shall be wearied with these endless & hopeless Letters on business, & I know nothing will be done by the Printers tomorrow. Surely the engravers are very tardy; Recollect that three of the engravings I have never seen.

I am, Sir, your oblig'd & obed^t^ Ser^t^, Charlotte Smith

I desir'd that old brute Robinson to send an an^r^ to you^r^ house to what I wrote to him. Do let it be forwarded inst[ead by][4] post if it comes.

I have directed a Lttr to Mr Hayley to yr Care thinking he may be in Town & that it will save time. If not, pray let it be forwarded direct.[5]

Yale University MS. Address: Mr Davies/ at Messrs Cadell & Davies's/ Strand/ London. Postmark: OXFORD; AP/ 17/ 97.

NOTES

1. See Lucy Eleanor Smith Newhouse in Biographical Notes. Thomas Postlethwaite Newhouse, the son of a Petworth attorney, was soon to marry Lucy, against CS's advice.
2. CS's brackets.
3. Cadell and Davies published *The Young Philosopher* in 1798.
4. Or perhaps "instantly."
5. Written vertically at the top left margin of the first page.

To Thomas Cadell, Jr., and William Davies

Oxford, April 20th [17]96 [*sic*]
Gent^{n},

I am much obliged to you for yr Letter & do you the justice to beleive you would have obliged me with what I asked if you could. To day I have heard again that there is a probability of the bills of 100£ being paid, as Mr Parkin on certain conditions (which conditions are already fulfilld) says to my friend who went to him that he has no objections to the 100£ being paid. Mr Davies already holds a bill of mine of 68£ which, with that for 7£ I now enclose & the 25£ I have drawn for to replace the money Mr Bliss was so good as to supply me with, makes the Sum of 100£. Will Mr Davies be so good as to go to Mr Blackman, Chatham Place, about twelve or one Oclock the morning after he receives this. I w^{d} not ask this if I did not know that it will be less easy to shrink from Mr Davies's application, if he will have the goodness to make it for me, than if the bills are sent, & as it is not far, I venture to trouble Mr Davies on a matter of the most material import to me. In consequence of Mr Bliss's bills being return'd, I cannot get a bill cash'd here & am without the actual daily supplies for my family. I have written to my solicitor, Mr Bicknell, Norfolk Street, who knows that there ought not to be any objection, & taken every precaution to prevent the excessive distress of another disappointment, & I am persuaded Mr Davies has good nature enough to give me half an hour of his time.

I sent up last night almost all the Poetry requisite to Vol 2nd, The last poem & names & notes being all now wanting which I propose send^{g} on Monday. I shall then have nothing to do, but to work at the Undertaking I mention'd to you, & wish I could know certainly what are y^{r} wishes in regard to it. When first I had dealings with Mr Cadell Senr, I was new to Bookselling transactions & left the terms to him <yet?> I had rather now receive than make proposals & therefore had rather y^{u} w^{d} adopt the same conduct. I am, Gent^{n}, y^{r} obed^{t} & oblig'd Ser^{t},

Charlotte Smith

Yale University MS. Address: Messrs Cadell & Davies/ Strand/ London. Postmark: OXFORD; AP/ 21/ 97.

To William Davies

[Oxford, 25 April 1797]

To M[r] Davies.

Sir,

I received the parcel last night but not till so late an hour that I could not do any thing to day more than writing the enclos'd to the Printer & sending this Copy of the list of Subscribers, which I beg the favor of you to correct by your own if any where deficient & then send to the Dutchess of Devonshire who is now at Chiswick—with a Note to this effect:

> "Mess[rs] Cadell & Davies respectfully acquaint the Dutchess of Devonshire that they have receiv'd from M[rs] Charlotte Smith the enclos'd list of Subscribers to the 2nd Vol of Sonnets &c who mentions that Grace [*sic*] has she beleives several names to add for most of which M[rs] CS. has received the Subscription money. As the Book will now in a few days be compleated, it is necessary to prepare the list for the press. Wherefore at M[rs] Smiths desire, Mess[rs] C. & D. take the liberty of begging of her Grace to do them the honor to add such names as are omitted, & it will be an additional obligation if her Grace will be pleased to send it as soon as may be convenient."

Unless this is done, I am afraid I shall never get the list completed, & tho I care very little about its being so much inferior both in rank & numbers to the first (the reason of which I know perfectly well & by no means am sorry for),[1] Yet there are some among the Dutchess's friends whom I very particularly wish to have, & whose names are in my opinion the first in this Country. Be so good as to give your attention to this as soon as possible. I should imagine a day might very soon be fix'd for the Publication—— I return the last proof to the Printer & propose sending up every thing but the preface by a conveyance that Offers on Thursday to M[r] Low, who is sending Copies of the book he publish'd for me to one of my absent sons by a Gentleman going to Canada, & I send a pacquet at the same time of Letters &c for Leiut Lionel Smith to the care of M[r] Lowe. Therefore the delay will not occasion you double expence, & I will write to Low to beg he will send you the pacquet, or You may send for it On Thursday after the arrival of the Oxford Coaches. The Preface I send to M[r] Hayley to correct who will return it to you——

I am now to speak of the proofs, & let me before I forget it say that I was disappointed at not having Lady Bessboroughs & the other two drawings sent down with the proofs. Pray let me have them with the next pacquet without fail. I cannot say (because I cannot say the thing that is not) that I am satisfied with either of Mr Heaths engravings. It seems to me that the expression of the Lunatic is quite changd & instead of a Madman the figure is that of a fool with a black Wig on, & his mantle looks like a piece of a ploughed field flying in the Air. It is of no use to complain now, for I know it cannot be alterd & if Mr Heath did it, as assuredly he did, to the best of his comprehension, I may perhaps be merely fastidious & fancy perfection which is not to be found in engraving on so small a scale, except with French Engravers, who certainly do execute small plates with an elegance & delicacy that we have not yet reached. I have two small plates done in France that have perhaps set my expectations too high. Do not therefore say any thing to Mr Heath for he will hate me, & it will be of no use.

As to the single female figure, Mr Corbould originally faild in comprehending my idea which perhaps was for want of my expressing myself clearly. But my notion which I meant to give him was that of a River Nymph—— The fat girl he first produced was any thing but such an ideal Sylphish representation. She is now a little subdued but still not a river Nymph, not the Naiad of a Stream or any thing like one, but the figure is now simple & pretty, and the Landscape, tho a little too dark, very much what it ought to be in general, & upon the whole I shall take the figure for the Pheobe of "the Forest Boy" instead of what I had intended it for—the closing Poem—As it will not badly represent her melancholy Musing—

By the brook where it winds thro' the Copse of Arbeal

But I wish that, if it can be done without much trouble, ~~that~~ a little more of sorrowful, mournful expression may be given to her Countenance ~~& I will add another~~ which may I beleive be done with a single stroke of the Graver about the mouth or perhaps brows.

Allow me also to remark that the Water wants effect: it is almost mingled with the rock near the ~~left~~ right margin, & the piece of ground on which her feet rest looks too much like a twelf cake, it is so extremely regular. The trees too on the left margin in the first distance are very shelly, not to say wiggy[2]—— A very little trouble only (as I suppose) is necessary to break the straitness of the fore ground & give a little more freedom to the Trees in the second distance. I do not mean those on the rock over her head. If there is any wish of spoiling the face, it is better to let it go as it is——

The Plate from Lady Bessborough's drawing is beautiful—& sweetly done, particularly the little Girl standing. But there is something odd in the face of the figure. It seems as if the nose was so long that the Lady was forced to go without either Mouth or chin. Can it be so in the Drawing?

This puts me in mind to beg you would add to the note to the Diss, as follows:

> Mess[rs] C. & D. beg the favor of being inform'd whether they may put Lady Bessboroughs name to the Plate of "the Female Exile," & if so, hope to be honourd with her Ladyships instructions how it is to be engraved at the bottom——"

I beleive from the fifth plates taken off up to the 30th or thereabouts are the best. You will I am persuaded reserve some of the best for the Dutchess, Lady B—& others of my immediate friends.

When a few have been taken off, the prints will lose something of the blackness they now have——

As I have no Letters to day on my money matters, I suppose I am not to have the money, at least not without going to Town for it.

I am, Sir, y[r] Obed & Oblig'd Ser[t], Charlotte Smith

Oxford, April 25th 1797
In answer to your Question whether I w[d] have my name at the bottom of the Portrait, I had rather not. There seems to be no occasion for it, & it will be no advantage. I hope You will take such precautions as are in your power to prevent its being exhibited in Magazines "with anecdotes of this admir'd Authoress" like M[rs] Mary Robinson[3] & other Mistresses whom I have no passion for being confounded with, & also that you will prevent the Poems getting into Newspapers or being printed "with beauties of Poetry, or elegant selections," which to my certain knowledge have done an infinite deal of harm to the first Vol as to its sale——

I beg the favor of you to buy for me & send down by the next pacquet Southeys Poems[4]——

I wish you would ask M[r] Hayley if any name sh[d] be put (to the portrait) of the Painter. M[r] Condé will of course put his if he thinks it worth while, but I am afraid of offending M[r] Romney if I do the other with[t] asking him, or let it go unask'd.

Yale University MS. Address: M[r] Davies—. No postmark.

NOTES

1. The subscription edition of *Elegiac Sonnets i* had 817 subscribers; *Elegiac Sonnets ii,* only 283. Several factors contributed to the decline, including a two-year delay before publication on account of Augusta's death, confusion about who had subscribed and whose money had actually been collected, and the duchess of Devonshire's lost list. CS's public protests against the trustees to the estate in prefaces to other works as well as her stands taken for and then against the French Revolution may also have affected her popularity.

2. CS's detailed critique of the engravings reminds us that she had studied with an artist as a child and drew for amusement as an adult. Her suggestions probably were not taken, for the water and rock are not well differentiated, and the water is still indi-

cated by a few straight lines. A twelf cake is a large frosted, decorated cake made for the twelfth night or twelfth-tide festivities. By *shelly,* CS means "shell-like" and by *wiggy,* like a curled wig.

3. Poet, novelist, actress, and dramatist, also known as "Perdita" (1758–1800), perhaps best remembered as the beloved of a young Prince of Wales. Apart from Robinson's scandalous liaisons, her marriage and her writings paralleled CS's closely enough that CS wished to avoid being compared to her. Like CS, Robinson began writing while in debtors' prison with her husband, and the duchess of Devonshire had been patroness of her first volume of poems in 1775. Robinson wrote to supplement pensions and support a daughter and mother. In the 1790s, she published several volumes of poetry: *The Beauties of Mrs. Robinson* (1791); *Poems,* 2 vols. (1791–93); *Sight, The Cavern of Woe, and Solitude* (1793); "Sappho and Phaon" (1796); and *Lyrical Tales* (1800). These volumes included sonnets and other verse forms. She also wrote novels, including *Vancenza; or, the Dangers of Credulity* (1792), *The Widow, or a Picture of Modern Times* (1794), *Angelina* (1795), *Hubert de Sevrac* and *The Wanderings of the Imagination* (1796), *Walsingham, or The Pupil of Nature* (1797), and *The False Friend* and *The Natural Daughter* (1799).

The sticking point for CS was Robinson's year as mistress of the Prince of Wales and her subsequent lifetime annuity from him. From 1783 to 1797, she was in a relationship with Col. Banastre Tarleton, who also later provided her with money. The dignity and respectability that CS struggled to maintain as a woman separated from her husband and writing for money was threatened by being in any way likened to such as "Perdita."

4. Southey's *Poems,* 2nd ed. (1797). CS needed this volume to verify claims she made in her forthcoming volume. Her note to "The Dead Beggar" observes that she had been attacked for asserting that funds should be dispensed to the poor more effectively. Not only does she dismiss the criticism, but she notes that "a circumstance exactly similar" is treated in the "Pauper's Funeral," in Southey's new volume of poems (*Elegiac Sonnets ii,* pp. 126–27). CS also draws attention to a stanza in her poem "The Forest Boy," which Southey "so happily imitated" in "poor Mary."

To Thomas Cadell, Jr., and William Davies

Oxford, April 28th 1797

Sir,

I should not have delay'd a moment sending up the remainder of the MMS, if I had not calculated that the Printer had enough for another sheet. I am sorry for the delay my mistake has occasion'd.

I now send by the Post a short poem (from which I have taken the passage I meant that the print should have alluded to—) And written out a fragment of a part that has been much applauded of the Poem publish by your House in 1793[1]—Not because I want it merely to fill up, but because I wish to make as much variety of verse in this book as possible—& have studiously varied the measure of the quatrains &c, & if you have no objection (&

I should think it would rather promote than injure the sale of the copies you have on hand of that Poem), I should be glad to have this piece of blank verse inserted. The closing Poem is about forty lines & shall follow tomorrow. It is an address to M[r] Romney on the sketch he made of a likeness, but to tell you the truth, he is so odd & capricious a Man that I do not know whether I can print it without his consent for which I have written to M[r] Hayley with the preface & hope you will have them both in a day or two; in the mean time, I shall send up the lines & notes, & if you do not hear to the contrary before, it may be printed.[2]

On reflection I have cross'd out the note written at the back of the Poem call'd April, least it should create any mistake. The notes will take up above sixteen pages I think. The preface will be about six. You forgot to mention whether M[r] Hayley is in Town. Pray do not forget Southebys [*sic*] Poems. I wish I c[d] see the General list of Subscribers before it is printed. I recollect that three or four names I sent up to you from Weymouth which I have totally forgotten are omitted in my list. I have had no money for those.

I am, Sir, y[r] obed[t] Ser[t], Charlotte Smith

Yale University MS. Address: Mess[rs] Cadell & Davies——/ Strand/ London. Postmark: OXFORD; AP/ 29/ 97.

NOTES

1. *The Emigrants.* She excerpted 49 lines and titled them "Fragment Descriptive of the miseries of war"; see *Elegiac Sonnets ii,* pp. 86–89. The fragment describes the fears of a female refugee fleeing with her child and a "feudal Chief" who returns to his castle to find his family murdered.

2. She did not obtain this permission, as she notes in her letter to Cadell and Davies of ca. 15 May.

To William Davies

[Oxford, 12 May 1797]
Sir,

I have expected the proof next due every day this week; I hope no accident on the way has detain'd it. Probably I may receive it this evening. I am very sorry to trouble you, but I am persuaded you will not think it much to send me down bank Paper for the enclos'd draft which I had to day notice from M[r] Bicknell w[d] be paid at 3 days sight & which I have obtain'd for my (now) second daughter's[1] journey to the Sea for an illness which D[r] Wall seems to think may terminate fatally if something is not immediately done for her. I therefore beg the fav[r] of you to send the within down as soon as you can obtain it in one twenty & one ten bank [*sic*], & for fear of accidents, perhaps it would be adviseable to cut them & send them at two days.

On the other side, I have written to M[r] Blackman to beg he would pay the money immediately, as my daughter's situation is such as admits of no delay.

All that remains of the notes, preface, &c, is ready to return with the next proof.

I am, Sir, your most obed[t] & oblig'd Ser[t],
Charlotte Smith

Will you be so obliging as to send to the Shop late Elmsley's to enquire & procure for me if it can be had a Novel calld Adele de Senanges?[2] It is French, but tho it has been much recommended to me, I cannot learn by whom it is publish'd, but for very particular reasons, am particularly anxious to have it & sh[d] be very much oblig'd to you if y[o] c[d] send it me in the next parcel.
Oxon, May 12th 1797

Yale University MS. Address: Messrs Cadell & Davies's/ Strand/ London. Postmark: OXFORD; {no date; franked}.

NOTES

1. Lucy.

2. *Adèle de Sénange ou lettres de Lord Sydenham* (1794) was a partly autobiographical novel by Adélaïde-Marie-Émilie Filleul, comtesse de Flahault, later the marquise de Souza. Her first husband, the comte de Flahault, was guillotined in 1793. She lived with a group of émigrés in Mickleham, Surrey.

Elmsley was a bookseller in the Strand who specialized in French books.

To Thomas Cadell, Jr., and William Davies

[Oxford, 14 May 1797]
Messrs C & D—— ——
Gent[n],

I received this morning the half of a ten & of a twenty pound bank note[1] received of you from Mr Blackman, & I am extremely oblig'd to you for the trouble you have taken for me. I believe what I now enclose concludes the whole that I have to do in the book of Poems. I assure you that, ill as the preface is written, it is the third time I have copied it, but I perpetually find some word to change when ever I copy my own writing. I beleive the printer will be able to make it out. But I wish to see it before publication together with the rest of the notes, & that I trust will be the only trouble more this work will give you. The delay of the last parcel I do not understand; you mention having sent it some days since; it was not deliverd here till late last night.

This delay must at the present period be doubly inconvenient, As I take it for granted You wish to get the book out by the 1st June at the latest. I wish to know as soon as it can be ascertain'd that I may write to my distant friends to send for their books.

Mr Walker of Dublin must be particularly attended to as nobody has so zealously promoted the subscriptions. He complains that he never received the books I last sent him; I have totally forgotten whether they pass'd thro y^{r} hands or whether I mention'd it before. I am, Gent^{n},

Your oblig'd humble Ser^{t},
CS

14th April [*sic*]
I rather expect ye names of Lord & Lady Oxford & perhaps of Lord Egremont;[2] keep the list therefore from being reprinted ~~'till~~ A day or two if it hinders nothing.

Yale University MS. No address or postmark.

NOTES

1. She received the rest on 17 May (see CS to Davies, where she also mentions the earl and countess of Oxford).

2. The earl of Oxford and countess of Oxford are each listed as subscribers to the sonnets, but Egremont is not.

To Thomas Cadell, Jr., and William Davies

[Oxford, ca. 15 May 1797][1]
Sirs——

I now return the last proof of the Letter Press in wch there is hardly an error. I also have written the Mottos for the plates (that which is to go under the portrait & the Italian Motto for the title page I think you have). As to the plates themselves, I beleive, except the slight alteration of giving an expression somewhat more melancholy to Pheobe (plate 3rd), it will be as well to let them remain as they are. If they are not exactly what I wish, It is some satisfaction to know that [they] are infinitely superior both in taste & execution to most of such plates in the books daily publish'd.

But there is one thing I do wish could be done, tho I fear it is now impossible. That is, as there are (from the structure of the verse) many considerable marginal vacancies, such as those in P. 67, 68, & 77, I could wish ~~a trophy~~ trophies (which if it had been thought of sooner I could have drawn appropriate to the subjects myself) Could be put to fill up such vacancies.[2] I am stupid enough not to know whether such things are printed with the sheet or how they are done, but I see them much in use that perhaps you might obtain plates of them or the Printer may have such, & Which, tho not so elegant as they might have been, will fill these awkard vacancies. If there was any possibility of getting them engraved, so as not to occasion delay (such as must not now be thought of), I c[d] send up drawings in a day's time. You will comprehend what I mean by the scratches I have made. I am afraid getting it done however in any way is quite out of the question. I would willingly allow any part of the expense. I send another short poem which I beleive must conclude the volume; I am trying however another, & if I can bring it to pass, you will receive it on Monday by the post which, if you do not, you may conclude I cannot finish it to my mind. The preface also you shall have by that post; I now send 16 pages of the notes & find on writing them out anew—which was more necessary than I was aware of—that 16 pages will not do much more than contain half. The rest will be sent with the next proof, w[ch] I conclude will be nearly the last.

Be so good as to add to the list

Sir Digby Mackworth Bart. . . . .

Lady Mackworth—

D[r] Wall—Oxford—2 copies, but desires to exchange one for a copy of the 1st vol.[3]

Pray let the small pacquet sent with this be deliverd to M[r] Low when he sends for it.

It was the names of Leiutenant Shrapnell & D[r] Jenner I think I forgot at Weymouth—Perhaps another or two. I have not re[d] any money for these nor the 4 above mention'd.

I must give up publishing the lines I had written (some years since) to Romney. However we shall not want them. If you have no more MMS by Monday's Post, you may direct the printer to proceed with the notes.

[Unsigned]

Yale University MS. Address: M[r] Davies. No postmark.

NOTES

1. This letter was written after 12 May (when the notes mentioned in the last paragraph were described as ready to be sent) and before 17 May (when they were returned to her). CS is adding names to the list of subscribers for the first edition of *Elegiac Sonnets ii*.

2. Trophies are emblems or designs that fill extra space left when the text ends well above the bottom margin of a page. None were added for this edition.

3. These were added, as well as Lieutenant Schrapnell and Dr. Jenner, named below.

To Thomas Cadell, Jr., and William Davies

[Oxford, 16 May 1797]

Gent[n],

As the letters M[r] De Foville has sent thro your hands have always got to Germany particularly quick & safe, he desires you will have the goodness to forward this for him in the same manner, charging the inland postage which must be paid to me as usual, & we are both much oblig'd to you for the trouble you have taken.

Were you kind enough to enquire for me about Adele de Senanges, a french book?[1]

I sent up all that remains of the Sonnets last night. CS——

Yale University MS. Address: Mess[rs] Cadell & Davies/ Strand/ London. Postmark: OXFORD; MA <16> 97.

NOTE

1. See CS to Davies, 12 May 1797, n. 2.

To William Davies

[Oxford, 17 May 1797]

Sir

I to day received the second parts of the notes & am very much oblig'd to you. You will be so good as to add the names of

The Earl of Oxford
The Countess of Oxford

to the list of subscribers.

I flatter'd myself that it was possible I might have Letters from India; should any reach your hands, pray be kind enough to send them by the Post whatever may be their weight. I am, Sir,

y[r] most obed[t] & oblig'd Ser[t],
Charlotte Smith

If Lady Oxford sh[d] send or call with it, be pleas'd to take the money, as I

have not received it. If she does not, it will of course stand over till the books are deliver'd.
May 17th 1797

Yale University MS. No address or postmark.

To William Davies

[Oxford, 18 May 1797]
Sir,

As I am extremely anxious that my Letters may go by the Ships now on the point of departure, I trouble you with them, tho I have nothing to send up; I was afraid of waiting till the second proof comes least I should miss the Ships. Pray be so obliging as to let these go to the India House or Post Office, ~~to~~ whichever may be most secure. The expence of this pacquet you will of course charge to me.

I hope the Sonnets will be ready to go by the next Ships, as I must send 6 copies to my eldest Son & three to his Brother. The former owes the greatest success he has had & the best friends he has found in India to the former Books publish'd by his Mother of which that Mother is with reason proud.

Trusting that you will pardon my giving you this trouble,

I am, Sir,
your most obedt Sert,
CS.

18th May 1797

Yale University MS. Address: Mr Davies. No postmark.

To William Davies

[London, spring 1797][1]

I imagine that not more than 3 verses quatrains or two of five lines can be printed in a page. But the printer will manage this according to the preceding part of the volume.

Mrs CS begs the favor of seeing the proofs.

[Unsigned]

36 Alsops Buildings, New Road

Yale University MS. No address or postmark.

NOTE

1. This letter would have been written in the spring of 1797, before the first edition of *Elegiac Sonnets ii* was published. It contains occasional poems whose quatrains are printed three to a page and five-line stanzas two to a page (pp. 90–97).

To William Davies

[Oxford, 21 May 1797]
Sir,

I now return the proof with some remarks to the printer & have to beg the favour of you to let the Lttr to Mrs Nott be put into the P[enny]. Post. I imagine Mrs Inchbald is well enough known to have hers reach her safely by the same means,[1] tho I do not know the number. Mr Bicknell's it will not be much trouble for one of your Porters to leave, and the other two are notes of thanks to the gentlemen who have been so obliging as to send me copies of their books.[2]

I imagine you can now nearly fix the day of publication. As soon as you can, I should be glad to know it. The French Novel[3] I conclude you could not get for me.

I am, Sir, y^r^ oblig'd Ser^t^, CS.

21st May 1797

Yale University MS. No address or no postmark.

NOTES

1. This is the only indication that CS corresponded with the novelist and dramatist Elizabeth Inchbald (1753–1821).

2. Not identified, but one might have been Southey, whose new volume of poems she had requested.

3. *Adèle de Sénange.*

To Thomas Cadell, Jr., and William Davies

[Oxford] May the 26th [17]97
Gent^n^,

Having various pacquets to send to London, I forward the last proof by the Coach rather than return it by the post. You may charge the carriage to me, as it is cheifly on my own account. Be pleas'd to forward the two Letters you will find herein by the P[enny]. Post & also the pacquet to Mr Lowe.

Finding new difficulties thrown in the way of a final settlement of my children's affairs, I am under the disagreeable necessity of being in Town & propose setting out on Sunday next.

I have desir'd Mr Bicknell—if I am denied the money I shall want for this purpose—to ask you to advance me 10 G^s on his faith that it shall be repaid if the Subscript[ions] (previous to my sale of the Copy right) which yet remain due do not reimburse you immediately on publication. I trust you will oblige me sh^d Mr B. find it necessary Which perhaps he will not. I am, Sir, y^r oblig'd hble Sert, Charlotte Smith

I observe, in returning the within proof, that the additions I wish'd to have made to the Notes on the Sonnet to the Goddess of Botany seem to have been left out. I wish they had been inserted as they had a direct & particular referrence to the subject & were a beautiful specimen of Elegant french.[1] Mrs Nott will send for her pacquet; so will Mr Lowe.

Yale University MS. Address: Mess {sic} Cadell Junr & Davies——. No postmark.

NOTE

1. These were reinstated. She cites several sentences from Rousseau's "Promenades," or *Les rêveries du promeneur solitaire* (1782), about turning to nature for consolation, which is the subject of the sonnet.

To Thomas Cadell, Jr., and William Davies

84 Charlotte Street, Rathbone Place {London}
June 22nd 1797
Gentlemen,

I have seen Mr Graham[1] (Kings Councel), a Man of the first eminence and fairness in his profession, & having shewn him the case, he is clearly of opinion that considering the conduct of the people I have to do with, there is nothing to be hoped for but from Chancery Which, while it is depending, will entirely prevent my receiving for the support of my family, one shilling, from their Grandfathers estate.

As my remittances from India are always so uncertain, this is a very gloomy prospect for me, & much as I have been accustomed to contemplate it, I own it is difficult for me to look at it with steadiness. I have no resource but in my pen or in going to service, & I should without hesitation prefer to do so if it was not so material an object to me to educate my youngest son for the Advowson of Islington which must be his (after Mr Strahan) if he is in orders, as I beleive you may have heard.

My friends encourage me to try what I can do, & promise me assistance which I am sure they mean to give, but to say the truth, I have more reliance on my very good friends the Booksellers——

It is no compliment to you to say that, tho I have found As much fair dealing & liberality from Mr Low as I could ask (indeed never ask'd him for money while I was writing for him without immediately receiving it), Yet I had rather deal with your House than with any other whatsoever. But you will see that the peculiarly hard situation I am in, which makes my writing a matter of necessity,[2] compels me also to sell my works before they are completed to who ever will, on that hazard, buy them of me. I beleive Mr Rose[3] saw you on this business some time ago, & I understood from Mr Hayley that you absolutely refus'd to purchase any Novel before it was complete. I had done about an hundred pages of one that I thought would be promising, but I laid it by from the despair I felt of being able to finish it as well as I wish'd in time to supply my family's wants because, from the nature of the plan, it will require books and leisure. I meant to have call'd it "The Young Philosopher," & I thought some of the idea's that occurd to me both of character & incident were likely to be work'd up into a composition of some novelty & of more solidity than the usual croud of Novels—— I must perforce resume this or some such work, & unfortunately I must sell it before hand, as I shall not be able to leave London without at least 40£ & see not (from Mr Parkins positive refusal to let me have one shilling of the 277£ still in Mr Blackmans hands and the absence of Mr Bicknell who could alone have press'd it for me), that I have any resourse on Earth but this.

Should it be agreeable to you, Gentlemen, to accept the work on these (I own) disagreeable terms, I will not propose it to any other persons. I beleive that with what I have done, I could finish the 1st volume in about five weeks So long you would have to risk the chance of my life, but you may be assur'd that, should any accident happen of that sort, the honor & feeling of my eldest son, to whom I have repeatedly written on that subject, would prevent your being ~~a~~ losers; I beleive the work would not exceed three volumes of twelve or fourteen sheets, at least the plan I have at present is not more extensive, but you know I am very apt to have a great deal to say just at last, so that it might exceed that number & swell to four. I beg the favor of your answer, Gentlemen, this evening, & assure you that should it be a refusal, it will make no difference in my wish to be on your list of Authors when ever more fortunate times may enable [me] to write when & for whom I will, nor in the esteem with which I am,

Gentlemen, your obligd Sert,
Charlotte Smith

If the weather is less intolerable, I must go into Mincing Lane this evening & will call as I go by for y^{r} answer & also for Mr Cowpers book of Sonnets,[4] if not yet deliver'd w^{ch} ~~are~~ is to go to Mr Johnson's St Pauls Church yard. Also for another which is to be left (1st & 2nd volume) for one of the Essex subscribers 2 copies (who I beleive has not paid nor do I see her name down) [*sic*] at an House in the <Poultry>.

I understand from Mr Low that he printed 1050 copies of Marchmont of which all are sold save 130 (or hardly so many fairly left, for he has sold 12 within these few days, but then he has 15 return'd from Ireland).

This surely is not a bad sale for the times, & considering that he cannot (I think) on account of the situation of his shop & want of a name sell a book so well as greater Booksellers, <setting> the Author out of the question.

Yale University MS. No address or postmark.

NOTES

1. Robert Graham (1744–1836), Lincoln's Inn, New Square, was appointed to the King's Counsel in 1794 and knighted in 1800. The *DNB* remarks that he was "an urbane but inefficient judge."
2. CS later inserted an ampersand here, which turns the sentence into a fragment.
3. Samuel Rose, a solicitor and friend of William Cowper and William Hayley (see Biographical Notes).
4. *Poems,* 6th ed. (1794).

To Thomas Cadell, Jr., and William Davies

[London] June 24th 1797
Gentlemen,

I am much oblig'd by your Letter. To be as explicit as you have a right to expect, I mean to sit down to the work in question immediately on my return home, & as I have a retir'd House at Heddington whither my family are now remov'd, I hope to get thro the first volume done in a very short time & the whole by or soon after Christmas. The price p^{r} volume I imagine you would not wish to lessen from what I have always had of you as well as every other person. Indeed for the last, I had 50 Guineas a volume & an engagement for 10 Guineas pr volume more in case of a second Edition—— If on these terms you are so obliging as to make the advance which my unfortunate circumstances render necessary, I would not wish to intrude upon you for the whole money for the first volume till its delivery & so on of the rest, the money to be paid on delivery of the volume.

Mrs Inchbald, to whom I was talking the other day of the sale of Novels, hinted to me that she had got more for hers which are very small books. I imagine that Mrs Radcliff has more, as I understood that Mr Robinson had given her for the Mysteries of Udolpho an hundred pounds a volume.[1] As to the merit of the work's, that is merely comparative or perhaps depending on taste—at least the sale certainly is—— For my own part, I know only that my judgement is not weaken'd by use, and that from habit, I write with more facility than ever, but at the same time under such disadvantages that I cannot reasonably expect to raise the price, & the accommodation I am under the necessity of asking puts any thing of that sort out of the question. On these terms, 50£ or Guineas therefore I shall be glad to agree with you, & as I have this moment a letter from Lord Egremont (who engages to support the suit at Law) desiring me to have it begun on Monday, I wish to leave London as soon afterwards as possible & therefore beg to have your final decision as soon as may be possible. I yesterday desir'd Mr Johnson to send for Mr Cowpers copy of Sonnets. Are Mr Hayleys gone? If not, I wish to have them sent p^r^ Coach & have a pacquet I sh^d^ be glad to send with them.

The bearer may wait y^r^ reply to, Gentlemen,

y^r^ oblig'd & obed^t^ Ser^t^, Charlotte Smith

Yale University MS. Address: Messrs Cadell & Davies/ Strand. No postmark.

NOTE

1. George Robinson published *The Mysteries of Udolpho* in 1794 for £500; he also paid Ann Radcliffe £900 for *The Italian* in 1797. Elizabeth Inchbald received £200 for *A Simple Story* in 1791 and £150 for *Nature and Art* in 1796, but improved her earnings greatly with an additional £600 that Robinson paid for the extended copyright on both novels (Tompkins, *The Popular Novel in England, 1770–1800,* p. 9). CS's remarks in these letters make clear that she received £50 a volume for each of her novels, neither more nor less, and that she earned another £10 per volume for each new edition, the only exception being the short run for the second edition of *The Banished Man.*

Nowhere else in the letters does CS mention meeting Inchbald.

To William Davies

[London, ca. 4 July 1797][1]

Sir

I shall be very much oblig'd to you to let my daughter have 10 g^s^ on my account. I had rather as she is alone that she sh^d^ take no more than I want today & will not trouble you for the remainder till I leave London. When that will be depends upon those ~~for~~ that have no mercy upon me. Will You be so good as to get 2 sets of Sonnets Strongly bound for My Son Nicholas; 4 for William—two bound 2 unbound; & one bound one unbound for Charles. I suppose India Ships will go soon. CS

Yale University MS. No address or postmark.[2]

NOTES

1. A receipt shows that Smith received a £40 advance from Cadell and Davies on 4 July, a likely date for this note. Of that, 10 guineas went to Charlotte Mary, the eldest daughter.

2. This note was written vertically on a sheet longer than the usual. A brief horizontal note in another hand states: "Received Ten Guineas/ C M Smith." CS's address is on the back of this page: "M[rs] Charlotte Smith/ No 84. Charlotte Street/ Rathbone Place."

To John Robinson

[before 29 July 1797][1]
Sir,

This Evening in consequence of a Proposal made on Saturday by Rickman,[2] He has on behalf of Dyer, & M[r] Bicknell has on my behalf signed an Agreement to this purpose.

That I will consent to M[r] Dyers receiving all the Money Assets of the late Richard Smith, my childrens Grandfather, now in the 3 pC[ts] [3] standing in the name of yourself and Parkin.

And I will agree and do agree to pay to Dyer the moment the Deed for this purpose is drawn up & signed the Sum of Two hundred Pounds. This he proposed taking in two Years from the produce of the Estate, but Lord Egremont (desirous to extricate my family from some of the blood suckers at least, directly) has lent me the money, and M[r] Bicknell will be in possession of it by a Draft on his Lordships Banker to be paid when ever the release is made & signed.

For, on condition of M[r] Dyer's receiving these Sums, that is to say the Money in the 3 pC[ts] before mention'd, and the 200£ he does for himself and his Children, renounce every claim what ever on the rest of the profits and produce or other assets of the Estate of Richard Smith deceased, & exonerate M[r] Benjamin Smith & myself from every claim whatever.

Sir, you have often declared that whenever the parties were agreed among themselves, you would relinquish your trust & I really think it high time. Behold, Sir, the Parties are agreed. The Estate is solely M[r] Smiths & mine as Mortgagees & our Childrens. I believe you will not say that you have any claims on us, & all that Mr Parkin so infamously made he has attempted to secure regardless of either decency or any human feeling.

Messrs Oddie & Foster[4] are at this moment drawing up a Bill against you & Mr Parkin acclaiming on my behalf my right to act as Executrix to the Will (which I proved in 1792) and calling for the Accounts & the Monies embezzled and unaccounted for by Prettyjohn and Firebrace[5] whom, contrary to my wishes so often repeated, you & your Colleague have now for thirteen years persisted in keeping on the Estate, tho you know that they have embezzled considerable Sums, & never have sent one account since they were entrusted with it.

I expect, Sir, or rather I demand, your instantly sending Directions to your Colleague to resign to me all power over the Estate called Gays and every other part of the Assets of Richard Smith, and that Mapps, so senselessly and unjustly withheld from its owners, may be relinquish'd to <u>them</u>. If this done directly, & Prettyjohns powers withdrawn by the very first Ship with orders to deliver the Plantation & Negros, and stores into such hands as I shall direct, I will when all this is done & not till then withdraw the Bill which, whenever it is brot to a hearing, must overwhelm you with disgrace &, as Mr Graham is clearly of Opinion, oblige you & your Cousin Parkin "to pay in your persons & properties for waste & malversation."[6]

Lord Egremont is determined to carry me thro' this, & I am persuaded were I to consult the Interest of my Children only, I should persevere, but I am weary of you, and of the harpy you have let loose upon us, & tho nothing can be so infamous as his receiving for doing worse than nothing more money than any of my Children have yet received from their Grandfathers property, tho your whole Conduct has been a tissue of wickedness fraud & folly, unexampled among men (even among such as you and he are), yet my earnest desire to deliver my Childrens property the little wreck of their property from Guardians so false, so stupid, so base, will induce me to sign a general release upon the terms I have named, but you must agree to them directly without Shuffle Evasion or lying of any kind. Indeed you will find it hard I think to evade my demand. If you do but for one unnecessary hour, nothing shall induce me to stop the Suit.

Your answer directed to Mr Bicknell Norfolk Street, will be expected by

Charlotte Smith

Petworth House Archives MS. No address or postmark.

NOTES

1. This undated clerk's copy of CS's letter to John Robinson, hated trustee to Richard Smith's estate, can be dated in July 1797 on two points. First, a deposition by John

Humbleby in the eventual Chancery suit (PHA #8010) confirms that Prettyjohn became agent for Gay's and Mapp's plantations in 1784 or 1785, thirteen years earlier. Robinson probably appointed him agent on assuming the trust in 1784. Second, 29 July 1797 is the date of an indenture of release by the Dyer grandchildren to CS and BS's children (PHA #7371).

2. Gawler Griffith Rickman, a London attorney who represented the collateral branches of the family.

3. The 3 percent consols, or consolidated annuities, were the government securities of Great Britain.

4. Not identified.

5. William Firebrace of Barbados. Embezzler or not, Firebrace was owed £254.2.11 on Gay's estate when William Prescod bought it in Sept. (see CS to William Tyler, 30 Sept. 1802).

6. The copyist represented this sentence with no punctuation. For clarity, I set off its complicated dependent clauses.

To Thomas Cadell, Jr., and William Davies

[Oxford, 1 August 1797]

Gentlemen,

I was so hurried & perplexed by repeated disappointments before I left London & so anxious to get away the moment the deed was sign'd that I did not find an opportunity of calling upon you as I intended——

I have now to request the favor of you to look out a good & early impression of the 2nd vol Sonnets for my Sister Mrs Dorset & one for another friend to whom she will convey it and send them to her, Mrs D, at the Lees near Guildford[1] with a parcel which Mr Low will leave at your Shop in the course of a day or two. Your being so good as to do this as soon as you receive this parcel will much oblige me.

Mrs Dorset, whose skill in botanical drawings is greater than that of almost any person I know, has a plan of our doing together a set of drawings, one to illustrate each of Linneas's orders—to be etched with a page of Letter press to each & the characters done with precision for the use of botanical students & those who cultivate this branch of drawing. I am sure the thing wd answer because the plan does not interfere either with Sowerbys or Curtis's[2] & would be the desirderata for those who wish to study the elements of botany without distracting themselves with the terms that are so alarming to beginners or going to the expence of buying elementary books, where there are seldom any thing more than very bad plates copied from the same models time out of mind. This work, as the writing would be but trifling & Dr James Edward Smith would correct it for me,[3] & as Mrs Dorset has already twelve or fifteen drawings that would answer extremely well, it would not at all interfere with the work I now steadily sit down to.

I have given up all society whatever, & as I cannot write all day, when I have done twenty or thirty pages, I sometimes go to drawing by way of relaxation when other's would walk, or converse, or play at cards. I do not know that such a sort of book would answer your purpose, as I understand there are two or three in the Trade who are almost enclusively engaged in the purchase & sale of objects of natural history, but I mention it to you because if we do it, & it is at all desirable to you, I always prefer your house to another.

At your leisure you will answer this. It will be many months of course before the thing will be ready, but we could put some of the plates to etch almost immediately. I am, Gentlemen,

your most obed[t] Ser[t],
Charlotte Smith

August 1st 1797
Be so good as to pay for a set of books I have orderd of ~~Johnson~~ Robinson. They are necessary for the work I am about, as I was & am afraid one of my characters will be thought an imitation wch I must avoid, & I want the books as there is thinking in them.

Yale University MS. Address: Mess[rs] Cadell & Davies/ Strand/ London. Postmark: OXFORD; AU/ 2/ 97.

NOTES

1. Several Lees subscribed to *Elegiac Sonnets i,* and one of them, Launcelot Lee, Esq., also subscribed to *Elegiac Sonnets ii;* all were associated with Winchester College.

2. James Sowerby, *English Botany; or, Coloured Figures of British Plants,* vol. 1 (1790); vol. 2 (1793); vol. 3 (1794); and with James Edward Smith, vol. 4 (1795); there were 36 volumes in all. Below, CS writes that Smith would correct her proposed book.

William Curtis's *The Botanical Magazine; or, Flower-Garden Displayed* was published first as a magazine, then reissued in 14 vols. from 1787 to 1800.

3. See CS to James Edward Smith, 15 Mar. 1798; on Smith, see Biographical Notes.

To George Robinson and Co.

[Headington, 1 August 1797]
Gentlemen,

I intended to have calld at your house for a set of "Caleb Williams"[1] but could not reach so far before I came away. I beg the favor of you to send them down in boards by the first Oxford Coach after the Receipt of this, & I shall also be much oblig'd to you to procure for me the satire call'd "the pursuits of Literature,"[2] all the parts (which are four I beleive) printed together & sold by some bookseller at the West end of Town, but I have forgot who.

If you will send to Mess[rs] Cadell and Davies, they will pay you for the above for, Gentlemen,

your obed humble Ser[t],
Charlotte Smith

Heddington near Oxford
Aug[st] 1st 1797

I have just discoverd that the Telamachus I have had sent me in a parcel of my own books from Sussex is an English one; I want a French one for my youngest Son. Pray send me the latest edition (without plates) strongly bound for a school book.[3]

Be so good as to include the Critical Review for July in the pacquet.[4]

Huntington MS (HM10819). Address: Mess[rs] Robinson——/ Pater Noster Row/ London. Postmark: {place illegible}; AU/ 2/ 97.

NOTES

1. William Godwin's *Things As They Are; or, the Adventures of Caleb Williams* (1794). This may be the novel CS requested at the end of the previous letter, reflecting concern that Delmont of *The Young Philosopher* might be thought to resemble Caleb.

2. CS had two strong reasons to ask for this book. It criticized the government's assistance to the French emigrant clergy as overly generous, and it referred to her disparagingly as the author of *Celestina,* a work representative of those of other "ingenious ladies, [who] yet are too frequently *whining* and *frisking* in novels, till our girls' heads turn wild with impossible adventures, and now and then are tainted with democracy" ([1797], part 1, p. 14).

More commentary than poem, all four parts of *The Pursuits of Literature, or What You Will: A Satirical Poem* had been issued in July 1797 in 2nd and 3rd eds., part 1 having first appeared in 1794 and parts 2 and 3 in 1796. Its author, Thomas James Mathias, a satirist of other pieces and a scholar of Italian, was not identified until 1812; by that time, the work had gone through sixteen editions.

3. Numerous editions of Fénelon's *Les aventures de Télémaque, fils d'Ulysse* (1699) appeared almost yearly in either French, English, or Spanish. Editions in French were published in London, Dublin, and Edinburgh as well as in Paris.

4. These brief paragraphs are written vertically across the back of the sheet. Below them, a note in another hand reads: "2 Copies of Sonnets Vol 2 boards sent to M[rs] Dorset at the Lees near Guildford with a parcel from M[r] Lowe."

To Thomas Cadell, Jr., and William Davies

[Headington, 15 August 1797]
Gentlemen,

I felt the fatigue I was subjected to in Town so much that I was quite ill for some time after my return, and particularly so when you were so obliging as to forward to me the 12£ re^{d} from Mr Daniel[1] Which came very safe[2] <tho I was not well enough to write the day it arrived.>[3]——& I am much oblig'd to you. It is past all description vexatious that I am still tormented about these omitted Subscriptions. I have to day a Letter of four pages about it which really worries me more than I can describe. I thought it certain that I should hear no more about it & that if the people had their books they would be satisfied. Instead of that, a Mr Sykes of Hull is among others extremely discomposed at not having his name [Nicholas Sykes][4] among the subscribers in the publish'd list, & as my friend sends me a list of 25 other names omitted, they desire me to advertise that such and such names are by mistake left out. What good this can do them I cannot guess, certainly none adequate to the trouble & expence it will put me to, but as it is so strenuously insisted upon, I do not know how I can very well escape from it. I suppose therefore it must be done.

Having lately had some MMS papers that have long lain by sent to me, I have recoverd some fragments of unfinishd Sonnets & other Poetical sketches of which I have finishd four or five very much to my mind. I am not certain that if my health should continue tolerable, I should not be able to put together enough for a third volume in the course of next year, not however to be publish'd by subscription, but in the common way with plates for ~~such~~ pieces as might be susceptible of such ornament (the drawings of which Lady Bessborough would produce for me). You recollect that I mention'd to you in London that the Dss of Devonshire told me that, if I would publish another Edition of the first volume, Lady B would make new drawings for it. I told her Grace that the Copy right of that vol. was the property of the elder Mr Cadell to whom I would cause it to be named. Perhaps it may have escaped your recollection, but if it has been named to him, be so good as to let me know his an[swe]^{r}. I wish to know how far it might be advantageous to me (waving the thoughts of a third vol.) to add the Poems I have finish'd and shall finish to the 1st Volume with new plates & what consideration Mr Cadell might think it worth his while to give me for such an addition. I know this must depend very much on the number of Copies yet in hand of the last Edit^{n} he printed. I shall be much oblig'd to you to let me hear from you soon on this.

M[rs] Dorset, who is at work on our projected botanical publication, is to write to me in a few days upon the size of the paper & price of the etchings &c of which, from former information she collected on this subject, she is a better judge than I am. You shall hear from us shortly.

M[r] Foville begs the fav[r] of you sh[d] any Letter come to your care directed to M[r] Alexandre that you will ~~honor~~ send them to him for some of his family have ever since his emigration directed to him by that name,[5] which he is apprehensive if not mentiond may occasion some mistake sh[d] such arrive.

I am, Gentlemen, with many thanks for your repeated kindness y[r] oblig'd Ser[t], Charlotte Smith

Heddington, Oxon., August 15th 1797

Yale University MS. Address: Mess[rs] Cadell & Davies/ Strand/ London. Postmark: {place illegible}; AU/ 17/ 97.

NOTES

1. Thomas Daniel, merchant, of 4 Mincing Lane. He often lent CS money during the rest of her life.

2. This sentence does not make sense, but CS seems to be saying that she had been ill when Cadell and Davies sent her the money she needed. Her illness and fatigue may have led to an untypical lack of clarity and other errors such as "dawings" for "drawings."

3. CS wrote the phrase in angle brackets above the line without indicating where to insert it.

4. CS's brackets. Six other Sykes were given by name, including Rev. Richard, John, Esq., and Mark, Esq. Such omissions made the list even shorter than feared.

5. Many emigrants had used aliases from the early days of the French Revolution because the government had drawn up lists of emigrants, used as bounty lists, for arrest. De Foville—who used his given name, Mr. Alexandre—had been on three such lists (see CS to the duchess of Devonshire, 23 Nov. 1800).

To Joseph Cooper Walker

Heddington near Oxford, August 23rd
1797

Dear Sir,

I receivd to day your Letter of the 8th August with concern & wonder, since it mentions your not having yet seen the Book of Poems, which, from your exertions on their behalf, you ought first to have been in possession of. They have been publish'd ever since the end of June (I beleive about the 20th). I was in Town at the time, & the directions I gave at M[r] Cadells, which M[r] Davies assured me repeatedly he had comply'd with, had I hoped prevented any possibility of what I since find has happen'd: Your not receiving your books &

your friends & the Irish Subscribers in general being in possession of their respective Copies as least as soon as was possible after the delivery of the books in England. By what chance it has happend that, on the 8th of August you were still without them, I cannot guess. But I will write by this days post to Messrs Cadell and Davies, the latter of whom assured me that he had forwarded a large parcel of the Sonnets (I beleive 40 copies) to Mr Archer at Dublin with directions to advertise in the Dublin papers that they were in his possession & that the subscribers were to send for them. This method Mr Davies assur'd me was the best he could devise, & I assented to it because I understood from your last Letter that you were usually at a purchase you had made in the Country, & I imagined that to send to you even the books design'd for your immediate friends might put to expence as well as trouble. I hope nothing has happen'd to the parcel & that Mr Archer has not neglected, or misused, or misunderstood his commission.

I had some apprehensions at the time of delay & inconvenience because I happen'd just then to have heard from another bookseller that Mr Archer had return'd to him all the copies that remain'd of many works of amusement which the London Bookseller had furnish'd him with within the last nine or ten months, assigning as a reason that, tho such return of bespoke books was contrary to the rules of the Trade, yet that he (Archer) thought it honester to give his English Correspondent a chance of disposing of his goods in London than by keeping them at Dublin to risk his never receiving any remuneration at all, which from the then & threatend state of Affairs in the Irish Capital, & the Kingdom in general, seem'd inevitable.[1] Indeed I understood that Archer had decided to shut up his Shop & come to England, & I told Davies what I had heard, who said that he hoped things were not yet come to that & that, tho Archer had also return'd some books to their house, he beleived there was no reason to suppose his business was totally at a stand.

I feel that I was very remiss in not writing to you, Dear Sir, at the time, but the truth was that I was hurried very unexpectedly to London on my childrens affairs, to which for above two months I was compelled to give my whole attention in a state of health very ill adapted to the fatigue, heat, and anxiety I was incessantly suffering. I did not take your direction to London with me, & as I expected every day to be released to the attention I owed to my literary friends and literary business, I continued to delay writing to announce to you the so long promisd publication of the little book whose success you had so greatly promoted; I did not leave London till the 29th of July &, on my return, was a good deal embarrassed about a family affair relative to the marriage of my daughter Lucy, which will soon (I suppose) take place with such prospects as are not very flattering, except as far as relates to the individual worth of the Gentleman she has chosen.[2]

This, as so much responsibility lays on me, wore my spirits a good deal, & other things perplexing me at the same time, I continued to become dangerously ill with a nervous fever, attended with other complaints, that have reduced me to the lowest state of weakness; insomuch that I write with great difficulty, & only my solicitude to account to you for this extraordinary and unpleasant failure as far as may be in my power would have enabled me to write so long a Letter, which after all is, I am conscious, confus'd and ill written.

I therefore will not lengthen it by adding to it any thing relative to your former Letter, which I will however do myself the pleasure of answering soon by which time I most earnestly hope to hear you have received the books, & that deficient as it may be of what I could have made it, it still bears evidence of my wish to make it not altogether unworthy of the zeal it excited in my friends. It is very well liked here.

You ask whether I am still at work. Alas! yes, when I am able; I have got my childrens affairs arrang'd for the future better than I dared hope, but at present we are very poor, which however I should not mind if I were not very sick, which makes it uncertain how long I may be able to do any thing worth doing while I creep about this troubled planet, beleive, Dear Sir, that I must always be y^{r} much obligd Ser^{t}, CS

Huntington MS (HM10820). Address: Josepth Cooper Walker Esqre/ Treasury/ Dublin. No postmark.

NOTES

1. Unrest in 1797 led to the bloody Irish Rebellion of 1798.

2. Lucy did not marry Thomas Newhouse until the following summer on 12 June at St. Marylebone, London. The nature of the embarrassing family affair is never made clear. Smith later revised her favorable estimate of Newhouse's personal merit.

To Thomas Cadell, Jr., and William Davies

[Headington] Aug 27, 1797
Gent^{n},

Be so good as to send the enclos'd to Mr Black[1] as directed, & when you receive a parcel from Mr Newman, Gerrard Street,[2] be pleased to send it down with the Catalogue of the Gibraltar Library[3] which is to be forwarded thro the hands of Messrs Egerton & Leigh. I wish also you w^{d} be so good as to send me a list of your recent publications, as I wish of course to take as many of them as appear likely to answer the purposes of the gentlemen who have commission'd me—— If you will take the trouble to let me know by a line when this parcel to me is forwarded, it will save the delays often occuring by these Stages & much obliged, Gentlemen,

your most obed[t] & oblig'd Ser,
Charlotte Smith

If you direct the parcel to be left at the White House, Etchington Ale house, at Heddington it will stop here instead of going on to Oxon. You will charge the present Letter of course——

Will you be so good as to let one of Your Porters take the enclosd & the parcel of books directed to My Son Lionel to M[r] Black Jun[r] at Sargent & Chamber's Mincing Lane?

Yale University MS. Address: Mess[rs] Cadell & Davies/ Strand/ London. Postmark: OXFORD; AU/ 28/ 97.

NOTES

1. Mr. Black, Jr., at Sargent and Chamber's, merchants, 38 Mincing Lane; he acted as agent for Lionel, who was stationed in Canada.

2. J. Newman, 17 Gerrard Street, Soho, "Colourman to Artists."

3. Stationed at Gibraltar since 1795, CS's son Charles returned home on leave and was staying with his mother when she wrote this letter. Apparently, he had offered her help in identifying and procuring works that the Gibraltar Library lacked. See the following letter of CS to Cadell and Davies, 22 Sept. 1797.

To Thomas Cadell, Jr., and William Davies

[Headington, 22 September 1797]
Gentlemen,

You will oblige me by sending to M[ess][rs] Egerton[1] & Leigh the following Books publish'd by you. The manner of their being bound I know not; I apprehend it might be proper to ask directions from M[r] Egerton on that point. Knowing however from my Son that the following books are not in the Gibraltar library, I order them without waiting for the Catalogue which I conclude is lost.

Private memoirs ~~of the life of~~ relative to the last year of the reign of Louis 16 &c 3 vol. by Bertrand de Molleville
The life of Milton in 3 parts. By W[m] Hayley
The life of Lorenzo de Medici
The works of Sir Joshua Reynolds. by Ed[d] Malone
Poems of various kinds by Ed[d] Hamley
English Lyrics[2]

Perhaps it may be better to have these sent as soon as An occasion offers, as I know not how to complete the order till I can procure a Catalogue.

I sent for a large box of my own books from Sussex and took the liberty to desire they might be sent to your House meaning to have them sent hither, but from some Letters I have re[d] within these few days, it seems very likely that my childrens affairs will make my removing to town for the whole winter absolutely necessary, & in that case as I shall remove thither early in November, it will not be worth while for me to have any more books sent hither, & I shall venture to beg you will give them room in one of your warehouses till I am determined.

I am Gent[n],
your oblig'd & obed[t] Ser[t],
Charlotte Smith

Headington
Sept[r] 22nd 1797

Yale University MS. Address: Messrs Cadell Junr & Davies/ Strand/ London. Postmark: OXFORD; SE/ 23/ 97.

NOTES

1. Thomas Egerton, bookseller, Charing Cross, from 1784 to 1809. No affiliation with Leigh is given in Maxted, *The London Book Trades: 1775–1800* (1977).

2. Antoine François Bertrand de Moleville, *Private Memoirs Relative to the Last Year of the Reign of Lewis the Sixteenth, Late King of France,* 3 vols. (1797); Hayley, *The Life of Milton,* prefixed to Boydell and Nicol's edition of Milton's works (1794), but printed separately by Cadell and Davies (1796); Edward Malone, *The Works of Sir Joshua Reynolds* (1797); Edward Hamley, *Poems of Various Kinds* (?1795)— all published and sold by Cadell and Davies. Two books she ordered were not theirs: William Roscoe, *The Life of Lorenzo De' Medici,* 2 vols. (Liverpool: J. M'Creery, 1795) and William Smith, *English Lyricks* (Liverpool: J. M'Creery, 1797).

The unusual accuracy of these titles, particularly the *Private Memoirs,* tempts one to conclude that these books were in CS's rather large personal library.

To Thomas Cadell, Jr., and William Davies

[Headington, 8 October 1797]
Gentlemen,

My Son, who is yet uncertain whether or no he returns to Gibraltar,[1] will settle with you as to what farther books it will be proper to send to the Library. I am recommended to purchase for it Townsons Travels, or tour, in Hungary,[2] which you will be so good as to get, & if the collecting the rest that I shall select will be of any advantage to you worth the trouble, I will send up the list as soon as I can make it up.

I have finish'd the first volume of "the Young Philosopher" and should have sent the MMS up by my Son, but that parting with it will be a considerable hindrance to me in the progress of the second volume & occasion mistakes for want of the former pages to refer to. The MMS consists of 267 pages, this sized paper & written about as closely as this Letter, which (as I intend a sort of prefaratory discourse on Novel writing to be annex'd to it)[3] is I believe a fully sufficient quantity for a Volume. As I conclude you have no intention of beginning to Print till the whole is in your hands & I wish my corrector to have more of the story before him at once than can be convey'd in the first volume, I should rather not send it to M[r] Hayley (who has kindly undertaken to correct it for me) till at least [a] great part of the second volume is done So that I hope & beleive you will trust to my word. If not, I will send the MMS up——

I beleive it was your intention to complete the pay[t] of 50£ when the volume was done & not to retain the ballance on any other outstanding account against me. If so, I shall be very much oblig'd to you to let my Son have 5 G[s] £ [*sic*] if he should want it & to send me down a 5£. He return'd in a most disagreeable situation in regard to money—& tho By Lord Egremonts having lent me a Sum of money, I have paid off & got rid for ever of the Dyer family, who by their Grandfathers will had so large a claim on the W[est]. I[ndian]. property belonging to my family & which has been for so many years a drawback & trouble to them—yet M[r] Robinson & Parkin, tho there are now no other claimants but us, refuse to give up the estate or transfer the money in the Stocks belonging to us till we & all the rest of the family, Whom they have been plundering for 14 years, will exonnerate them from being hereafter calld upon, which many of them (the family) will not do, particularly a Nephew & Niece of M[r] Smiths[4] of whose property they have embezzled 800£ st[g], a Sum that nobody can very quietly relinquish. They therefore (the Trustees) Continue to keep back every thing they can and to put us to all the expence possible for Lawyers and Law business, & after all the money they oblig'd me to expend in a ten weeks stay in London & the neglect of my literary business while I was waiting upon them, it may easily be suppos'd how much their conduct torments & distresses me. There are hopes I see that the E India Men[5] will arrive in a few days, & if so, I may be releived. I entreat the fav[r] of you to send the Letters down <u>by the post</u> if any reach you from India for me whatever may be their weight, and I am, Gent[n], your oblig'd & obed[t] Ser[t], Charlotte Smith

I beleive I shall take an house in London some time in November to pass the Winter.
Oct[r] 8th 1797

Yale University MS. Address: Messrs Cadell Junr & Davies/ Strand. No postmark.

NOTES

1. It is unlikely that Charles returned to Gibraltar; the *Army List* shows him to have a new appointment as lieutenant of invalids at Berwick on 23 Feb. 1798.

2. Robert Townson, *Travels in Hungary, with a Short Account of Vienna, in the Year 1793* (1797).

3. This was never published.

4. Probably the Reverend Richard Smith (b. 2 Nov. 1766), rector of Sutton, Sussex, and his sister, Mary Gibbes Smith Allen. (See Genealogical Chart.) They were the only children of BS's older brother Richard and were provided for differently from the three Berney grandchildren (a nephew and two nieces) and the four Dyer grandchildren (three nephews and a niece). A fourth Dyer nephew died in 1794.

5. That is, East Indiamen, or ships from India with remittances from William or Nicholas.

To Thomas Cadell, Jr., and William Davies

[Headington, 15 October 1797]
Gentlemen,

Not having heard how far it is agreeable to you to comply with my request sent to you by my Son, I am rather led to conclude it is not, but I wish much to know.

Since you seem to think a third volume of poems might not answer, I beleive I shall in two or three months print the Sonnets I have either finish'd, or which I know I can finish, in quarto. They are about 16, & I should add an half sheet of prose. Allow me to ask if I should execute this scheme whether you would chuse to be the publishers? I understand, indeed recollect, that the expence of such a book as to printing is but trifling.

I shall be very much oblig'd to you if you would put the following advertisement in the proper papers for me & send to any place convenient to you for the answers.

Wanted from the 1st December next at Clapham or in the immediate neighbourhood of that village a ready furnish'd House for six months or longer if approv'd of. Two sitting rooms & five bed rooms with garrats would be required. Any person having such an house to direct to S. C. [*sic*] at ———— describing the premises.

As I find (for Mr Parkin will now not give up his trust nor will he let us have one Guinea of the 200£ belonging to my children in the 3 pC.^{ts1} tho, the Dyers being paid, no other person has any claim to it) I must be in London to attend the business myself, for——Once more ~~therefore~~ we are compelled to apply for redress to Chancery, & as my health will not allow me to be in London, I must have recourse to some village near it & prefer Clapham on account of the air & its being in the road where my family & friends pass from Sussex & Surry. I wish however to have nothing said of my intention till it can be nearer execution &, trusting that with your usual good nature & politeness, you will do the best you can to assist my views, I am,

Gentlemen,
your humble & obligd Ser[r],
Charlotte Smith

Heddington, Oct[r] 15th 1797

Yale University MS. Address: Mess[rs] Cadell & Davies/ Strand/ London. Postmark: OX-FORD; OC/ 16/ 97.

NOTE

1. Her £3,000 marriage settlement was invested in 3 percent consolidated annuities. At this point, she was still allowed the interest on her marriage settlements. For a rundown of her three marriage settlements, totaling £7,000, see CS to Egremont, 12 Jan. 1802 and n. 2.

To Thomas Cadell, Jr., and William Davies

Headington, Oct[r] 20th
1797
Gentlemen,

I cannot help saying that I feel hurt at the intimation in your Letter last received that it would not be dealing quite fairly with you to publish so soon any other poems, and by the word withheld, you seem to intimate that a suspicion arises that I either kept back some verses I might have added to the Subscription volume (with a view to make a farther & unfair advantage of them) or should defraud of poetry that might figure there the new work on which you have made me an advance.[1]

I did not intend to publish the Sonnets till Spring, & very surely I not only did not withhold any from the Vol of which you purchas'd the Copy right but did my utmost to make it worthy of the former, of whose success, and the proffit that has arisen from it, I think M[r] Cadell Sen[r] has had no reason to complain. Perhaps my saying I had received some sketches among my books out of Sussex might have given rise to the idea you intimate, but nothing can be less correct, for so far from withholding I had forgotten (in the miseries I have gone thro since) what I had in some old memorandum books which were merely notes of subjects or half a doz^{n} unconnected lines. As to any verses whatever that I have compos'd since, surely neither the Subscribers nor the holders of the Copy right of the former volume have any right to complain of my making the most I can of them, nor can I see ~~how~~, if I publishd them tomorrow instead of four or five months hence, that any mortal would have cause to say I had injured ~~them~~ him. As well might a farmer who buys a crop of wheat of another complain that he the Seller look'd out for the sale of a crop of oats a year after. So it strikes me however.

As to my reserving verses for the Novel, perhaps it did not occur to you that not one of the 16 Sonnets I propos'd publishing in 4to might suit any of the characters & situations in the Novel, nor might you perhaps recollect that there are other species of small poems that, if any poetry can be introduced, do better for such a work because they are more the fashion at this moment. However it may be rememberd that in Ethelinde, the second standard of the perfection you expect, there is not a line of Poetry & that it is impossible to bargain for Poetry as for prose; Dryden indeed sold his works by the line of ten syllables, but Alas! I am not Dryden & assure you that Poetry, such as one can endure to risk, will not always come when it is call'd ~~I have~~ tho sometimes it will come when it is not call'd. I have been tormented by a want of sleep ever since I left Town & have taken all sorts of Soporifics in vain till I have at last left them off in despair & go for the most part without Sleep. In the stillness of the night, verses occur to me, & I hasten to put them down in the morning. And if I can make any thing by them, surely no one has a shadow of right to prevent it——

I am sensible Gentlemen, Alas! but too acutely sensible of the misery, the humiliation of being compelled, with so handsome a fortune of my own and such claims on behalf of my children, to be dependent on my writing for [. . .],[2] being distracted by business, by the cares of so large a family & yet doom'd from year to year to invent fables for the public & to take as a favor any price offerd me because I am necessitated to ask advances—— It would certainly add to this humiliation if I were therefore to be deprived of the liberty of printing any thing else while I was so engaged. But certainly you cannot mean this.

However I have written to Mr Hayley &, as he has frequently been Umpire between us, I have desird him to give me his Opinion, by which, whatever it may be, I shall conduct myself. But if he thinks I am at liberty to do as I will & you decline publishing, you will not take it amiss if I engage another publisher. I am very sensible of the value of your reputable names to a book as Publishers, but I also know that my books will under less advantageous circumstances sell enough at least to make it answer very well to purchase them, & Low w^{d} have given me <50> G^{s}[3] & have made the whole for the 1st Vol advance when I left London, for a Novel[4] he press'd me indeed very much to promise him something, but I evaded any answer because I had spoken of the Novel I had thought of to you & had some reasons to prefer the advantages yr name offer'd—— I do however beleive that, were you to repent, I could dispose of it & repay you the advance tho I repeat that I prefer your house to every other whatever.

As to the Gibraltar business, I had not the least wish to trouble myself about it, having much more than I can do of my own. I shall write to Genl Trigge[5] that it is done without me. I am, Gentn, yr obed & oblig'd Sert,

Charlotte Smith

Yale University MS. Address: Messrs Cadell and Davies/ Strand/ London. Postmark: OXFORD; OC/ 21/ 97.

NOTES

1. On 16 Oct., Cadell and Davies had answered her letter of 15 Oct. with courteous firmness. First, they had called on Egerton only to discover that he had already supplied the library at Gibraltar with most of the titles she mentioned and was the outpost's appointed bookseller. Second, although they have paid Charles 5 guineas, as she asked, they now list out her account: since Mar. she has borrowed £134.3.0. Deducting £120 (£70 for the sonnets and £50 for the first volume of the new novel), she still owes them £14.3.0, plus several smaller payments amounting to £10. Finally—the point that she is responding to here—they "trust you will excuse our observing" that when they agreed to do the second volume of sonnets, they "had not the smallest Conception that any were withheld" or that "you would have had an Idea of publishing more Poems so immediately." They conclude curtly that the "Sale of the 2d Vol. has been, hitherto, extremely confined."

2. This word is torn away at the seal, leaving part of a letter, possibly a "b." CS often wrote of writing for "bread."

3. It is not clear here whether she meant 50 or 60 as she wrote over the numeral; however, 50 is the amount repeated near the end of CS to Cadell and Davies, 22 Oct. 1797.

4. The phrase, "for a Novel," is inserted here awkwardly.

5. Charles's commanding officer at Gibraltar.

To Thomas Cadell, Jr., and William Davies

Headington. 22nd Octr 1797

Gentlemen,

I cannot refrain (however unwilling I am to break in on your time or my own) from expressing my astonishment at the angry terms in which your Lttr red to day is couched.[1] Nothing upon my honor was farther from my intention than to write "illiberally" or to give you any offence. But as I always suppos'd every Author had a right to make the most of any original composition, without adverting to their preceding works, & did certainly not perceive how <sellin> Publishing sixteen Sonnets in 4to in 98 could injure a volume, publish'd with plates & consisting of various poems in 1797, I did not imagine you w^{d} take so much amiss my explaining my idea's on this subject. More especially as I told you that Mr Hayley, having so frequently and as I beleive to both our satisfaction, settled business between us, I had mention'd the circumstance to him & should abide by his opinion. I shall probably hear from him in a few days, but since you seem so decidedly of opinion that I shall injure you materially, I shall give up the half form'd plan I had conceived of a publication, by which I did suppose I might have gain'd a few Guineas without injury to any human being. No, Gentlemen, it is not that you are at my mercy; the reverse is the fact: I am evidently at yours.

I have not been condemn'd in the character of a necessitous Author to deal with Booksellers for about nine years without understanding how much it is in the power of the most eminent of them to combine in crushing an Author who attempts to derive proffit, either by publishing for himself, or sells his works to less establishd Characters in the Trade. I am not ignorant that, beside the meetings held by Gentlemen of this description at which the proposals of Authors are canvassed, Reviews (on whatever principle they first set out) are now little else but vehicles under the command of Publishers to advertise their respective ~~works~~ purchases, & keep down those of others. And this is not all. When an Author of any name, from what ever cause, quits a bookseller of name or is dismiss'd by him (as the poor devils are not unfrequently), Enquiry is of course made of the great bookseller when the Authors next work comes out why the connection is dissolved, and the Answer probably determines the enquirer not to purchase: "We found the work in question inferior to the former" (tho peradventure the Bookseller read not a line of it) "we find M^{r} or Mrs Such a one goes off. There was no encouragement to us to publish for him or her"—— Certainly the customer changes his mind and buys something else: A ghost story in verse or prose instead of the Essay on the representation of real life that he meant to have purchas'd.

That I have always found you Gentlemen, the most liberal & the most respectable of all those with whom I have dealt, I have always & invariably acknowledged. Nor does the present difference between us alter my opinion because it is probable you have some rule on your side with which I am unacquainted. I own I should wish to know how long the prescription is to last because, circumstanced as it is my hard lot to be, if I can not make till, [*sic*] such a period any advantage of my literary labours, I must reckon accordingly. I certainly feel very much mortified to hear that by your various engagements with me you have not gain'd a single Guinea; Those dealings have (according to my present cursory recollection) been to the amount of about, or almost, 500£ paid to me besides expences (exclusive of the present advance made in 1797 for a Novel), & if on such a Sum you have gain'd nothing, you must undoubtedly have lost. As it is hardly possible you have merely saved y^{r}selves by even money & very surely if you have been losers of only a single Guinea, I am under much greater obligations to you than I was aware of—for only the most disinterested kindness, which I had not the least right to expect, could induce you to continue this losing game & especially while I avow'd to you that I continue under the pressure of pecuniary distress & of course under the same disadvantages as have always been against me but more particularly since 1793. There is no reason in the World why you should lose a shilling, & yet according to this calculate, you must have lost pounds.

I did not mean to give you Offence when I mention'd that I could have had 50 G^{s} of Mr Low. I merely meant to releive you from the fear of loss if the present work was not in your apprehension equal to Emmeline & Ethelinde (it is certainly intended to be very different from either & whether better or worse is after all an affair of taste), but I will tell you honestly that, tho I have always had the greatest reason to be satisfied with Low, who has occasionally been deeply in advance for me, yet the situation of his Shop is very much against the sale of my work; he is too apt to take anything that is offerd him & publishes for people among whom I have no ambition that my name should figure on his list—but a still stronger objection is my apprehension that he is connected with Bell[2] of Oxford Street by whom he was employ'd to buy Montalbert underhand, which I did not know till very long afterwards, & tho he protests that he has now no connection with that Man, I cannot say that I feel satisfied, for Bell is a person with whom <u>no distress should induce me to have any dealings directly or indirectly</u>. If however you really repent the engagement, I will try either by Low or another person to releive you from it. If not, I shall proceed in the best way I can to fulfill it.

I am, Gent^{n}, y^{r} obed Ser, CS.

I am much oblig'd to you for the enclosures & will write to the person whose house (if not too expensive) will suit me.[3]

I shall be glad to hear from you at y^{r} Leisure in an^{r} to the last lines of this.

You are requested to understand that I shall for the present give up any thoughts of publishing the Sonnets in question.

Yale University MS. Address: Messrs Cadell & Davies/ Strand/ London. Postmark: OXFORD; OC/ 23/ 97.

NOTES

1. Cadell and Davies answered her defensive letter of 20 Oct. immediately. It is worth quoting their bitter, hasty response in full, for this misunderstanding marked a change in their essentially tolerant, helpful attitude toward CS: after publishing *The Young Philosopher,* they undertook no more new titles. And the number of letters she wrote to them—which had been three or four dozen a year since 1794—dropped to half a dozen or fewer a year for the rest of her life.

> Madam
> We do not attempt, nor have we a Wish, to reply to you in the peculiar Stile of the Letter with which we are just favoured but We must beg Leave to repeat that had we had the smallest Conception that you intended so soon to publish any more Poems, except such as probably you might introduce in the new Novel in which you are at present engaged, we should most certainly have declined the Purchase of the second Volume—This Transaction we are convinced you will, on further Consideration, see clearly has not the smallest Analogy with the Farmer and his Crop of Oats. Had we looked merely to the Profit of such Copies as were likely to be sold within the first Twelvemonths, it would have been Madness to have undertaken even the Expenses of the Plates and other Charges of the Edition, independent of the very liberal Price we paid you for the Copyright—But, so many Copies of the first Volume having been sold, it appeared to us probable that in the Course of a few Years a Number of those who possessed the first would purchase the second Volume to compleat their Sets and consequently that we should be gradually remunerated the Monies we advanced, with the moderate Profits to which we were entitled—Whilst, now, before the Sale has repaid us a third Part of the Expences of the Edition merely, no further Collection is intended to be published, a Circumstance evidently calculated to affect most materially the Sale of a Work which has cost us so much Money—But we are wholly at your Mercy, Madam—We certainly made no Stipulation that you should not publish whatever you pleased and as soon as you pleased—
>
> With Regard to the new Work, the Novel—We have not the smallest Hesitation about relinquishing all our Claim to it to Mr Lowe or to any other person who will repay us the Monies &c we have advanced and we hereby most readily submit this Business to your own Decision—we have certainly felt a Degree of Pleasure in appearing as your Publishers, it has unfortunately happened that with unremitted Exertions on our Part to afford you Accommodations of every kind within our Power, we have failed to give you Satisfaction—And, considering the Connection in a commercial Light, we have nothing to regret in the Prospect of its being brought to an early Close, for to the present Moment, we can with Truth declare, we have not derived from it a single Guinea of advantage.

They ended on a brief business note, notifying CS that they are sending her three letters responding to her advertisement for a house to rent.

2. The bookseller Joseph Bell.

3. This and the two following last-minute thoughts were crowded into the margin at the top of the first page.

To Thomas Cadell, Jr., and William Davies

[Headington, 27 November 1797]

Gent^{n},

I am oblig'd to you for y^{r} compliance with my request as intimated in y^{r} Letter of yesterday. Not doubting your readiness to oblige me & having been (by an accident) disappointed of a small supply from the Merc^{ts} Messrs Daniel which I wanted to pay for some trifles on Saturday, I drew for <u>5 G^{s}</u> at 6 days on you—which, if it makes any difference, I will replace as I have now got the money from Mess Daniel. If it makes none, it ~~will~~ may remain, & I shall draw at two months from same day this week for forty five pounds, or 44.15^{s}.

Having ~~received~~ heard that I shall receive a side of Doe Venison out of Sussex, I have delay'd my Journey from Friday till Monday to give me an opportunity of seeing some of my friends on Saturday to eat it. But on Monday, we hope all to reach London.

Nevertheless should it happen that in the interim Letters sh^{d} arrive from India, at least till Saturday have the goodness to forward them by the Post, as it is so very long since I have heard from my eldest Son that I never was so impatient for Letters, & I understand that Ships are hourly expected.

After Sat^{y} sh^{d} any arrive, be so good as to send them to Charlotte Street. I do not know the number of the House taken for me, But at Mr Pattersons no. 84 where I lodged in the Summer, a direction may be had sh^{d} I not send one before you have occasion to direct thither. I am, Gent^{n},

your oblig'd humble Ser^{t},
Charlotte Smith

Novr 27th 1797

Yale University MS. Address: Messrs Cadell Junr & Davies/ Strand/ London. Postmark: OXFORD; NO/ 28/ 97.

To Thomas Cadell, Jr., and William Davies

[London, 30 December 1797][1]
Gentlemen,

I have procured at last an engagement from Mr Parkin to transfer to me on the opening of the books a nominal hundred pounds of the 3000£ in the 3 pCts belonging to me, which is about 49£ I suppose. But he has as usual delay'd this so long that It distresses me beyond description. I must remove my lodgings on Monday to an house I have taken for 6 months in Duke Street, Portland place, & as the transfer days are not before the 5th or 6th, there is no telling how it inconveniencies me. And the more so as Mr Daniel is out of Town who wd otherwise oblige me. If you wd do me the great friendship of lending me 20£ till the day of transfer, I will the moment I get the nominal hundred transferd repay you & I assure you it will be consider'd as a most essential favr. My India remittances not coming & so many difficulties every way surrounding me, I know not what I shall do unless you are so good for these few days to assist me. My Son will bring your answer which I trust will not be a refusal to, Gentn, your obed & oblig'd Sert,

Charlotte Smith

Saty Decr 30th [1797]

Osborn Collection MS, Yale University. Address: Messrs Cadell & Davies/ Strand. No postmark.

NOTE

1. CS moved into her new residence on Duke Street in Jan. 1798. This hand-carried note would have been written from a temporary London lodging. See CS to Davies, 3 Jan. 1798.

1798–1800 "Lord Egremonts extraordinary kindness"

—31 May 1799

By May 1799, the earl of Egremont had paid off all outstanding debts on Richard Smith's estate and agreed to become its trustee, replacing the troublesome John Robinson and Anthony Parkin. Expecting an imminent settlement, Charlotte Smith relaxed her publishing efforts for the first time since separating from her husband. From 1798 to 1800, her new works included one novel, one book for children, and three volumes of tales; in contrast, she had written a novel almost yearly during the previous decade. In June 1798, Cadell and Davies published the work that they and Smith had quarreled over, The Young Philosopher, *and Sampson Low published his first of her children's books,* Minor Morals. *It was dedicated to Lady Caroline Ponsonby, daughter of Lady Bessborough who had long befriended Smith and who provided a drawing that was engraved for this edition. In 1800, Low published the first three volumes of a five-volume collection of tales,* Letters of a Solitary Wanderer. *The number of new editions of Smith's published works also decreased. In 1799,* Emmeline, The Young Philosopher, Minor Morals, *and* The Romance of Real Life *were published in unremunerative foreign editions; in 1800,* Elegiac Sonnets i *went into its ninth edition and* Rambles Farther *into its second, both for Cadell and Davies. Smith's earnings plummeted.*

During these years, Smith lived in London, first on Duke Street and then Upper Baker Street, hoping by her presence and assiduous attention to the trust business to bring about its resolution. Her grown children were struggling to make their way in life. William was back in England for the first time since leaving in 1788. He returned to India in April 1799 with his youngest sister Harriet in the hope of finding her a husband. Illness forced her back, and she arrived at Deal in October 1800 near death from the fevers and delirium of malaria; in the following years, whenever these recurred, her mother would take on the burden of nursing her and paying for her medical treatment. Charles and Lionel were in the army. Charlotte Mary lived with Charles at Berwick-upon-Tweed until he was promoted and sent back to Gibraltar. Lionel was stationed in Quebec. George was at school, preparing for Oxford, his mother's old dream for all her sons. Lucy, Smith's least favorite daughter and perhaps least loved child, married Thomas Newhouse, an unsuitable, brutal, impecunious man. Smith lent the couple money during Newhouse's term as a medical student. When Newhouse died, she supported Lucy and her two young children. The third child, born after Newhouse's death, was an added expense.

To William Davies

[London, 3 January 1798]
Sir,

If not too much trouble, have the goodness to inform me whether you know from whence the verses came Post mark Liverpool, which you enclos'd to me some time ago. If they are from any person you know, or if you beleive such sort of things are of use in the sale of your purchase, I have no objection to their being sent as the Author said he intended—to the Monthly Magazine. Otherwise, it is a matter of great indifference to me, as there is very little praise that gives me much pleasure, & common place consolation rather gives me pain. I will send them back to you when I can find them, to be done with as you please.

I observe what you were pleas'd to say in answer to my Letter sent by Lieu^t^ Smith.[1] I have no sort of right to make any observation on the reason of y^r^ refusal, nor do I intend making any. In the course of ten days, I hope to send another volume of my work &, for the present, am accommodated without presuming to give you any farther trouble, but thus much I cannot help saying not from any late instance, but from general observations on your manner towards me: that if you are doubtful of the success of the work & really repent having engag'd for it, I would much rather seek another purchaser to repay you than that you should have hereafter any complaint against me. It is not pleasant to know that any such doubts exist; many things that have passed have not been pleasant to me, particularly your saying you have never got one penny by me. If so, I am sure I cannot feel easy in the idea of your continuing a losing game, & the less so, as there are people who are not afraid of losing by me, & who from their solicitude to purchase, certainly expect to gain.

I trust my openness will give you no offence which I do not mean—— My motive for preferring your house to any other was from its respectable

& establish'd character & not because it offer'd me any accommodation that I could not have obtain'd at another; If however you have lost by me, I am the more oblig'd to you for having afforded me any.

I troubled you in a former Letter with a request to borrow Edwards or Long on Jamaica.[2] Not having had an answer, I imagine you w[d] not oblige me. If you will be pleas'd to lend me "Walks in a Forrest,"[3] I will purchase it if I like it. If not, return it uninjur'd.

My second Son who is at Bushire in Persia has sent to me for several of my books printed for you, but I know Ethelinde is out of print,[4] & the only copy I had, I parted with to the Duchess of Devonshire. If you are willing to send M[r] Nicholas Smith such as are to be obtain'd to Bombay, you need not doubt his enabling me to repay you, & I will send you a list of what he wants.

I am, Gent[n],
your obed[t] humble Ser[t]
Charlotte Smith

Jan[y] 3rd 1798
No 3 Duke Street, 3 doors from Portland Chapel
I beg the fav[r] of an answer to this.

Osborn Collection MS, Yale University. Address: M[r] Davies/ at Mess[rs] Cadell & Davies's Strand/ London. Postmark: no place; 8 o'Clock/ 4. JA/ 98 MORN; {Portland}/ Unpaid/ Penny Post.

NOTES

1. Both Lionel and Charles were lieutenants at this time, Lionel in Canada with the 24th Regiment and Charles at home on leave from the Royal Garrison Battalion in Gibraltar.

2. Bryan Edwards's *The History, Civil and Commercial, of the British Colonies in the West Indies,* 2 vols. (1793) and Edward Long's *History of Jamaica,* 3 vols. (1774).

3. Thomas Gisborne's *Walks in a Forest: or, Poems Descriptive of Scenery and Incidents Characteristic of a Forest, at Different Seasons of the Year* was in its third edition for Cadell and Davies in 1797.

4. *Ethelinde* (1789), CS's second novel, was printed in Dublin and London (2nd ed.) in 1790 and after her death in 1814 and 1820. Except for editions arranged by Joseph Cooper Walker with John Rice in Dublin, there is no evidence CS earned anything from editions published outside London.

To Thomas Cadell, Jr., and William Davies

No 3 Duke Street
Portland Chapel {London}
5th Jany 1798

I am concern'd to see that we are not likely to understand each other. You seem to have misunderstood me. No matter. I have faild of explaining myself, but I cannot misunderstand that you think I have completely departed from my engagements. Allow me to ask in what? I did not ask you to oblige me with the Sum which Scoundrelism on the part of Parkin compelld me to solicit, as any advance on the work. It w^d have been replaced to day by a transfer of stock made to me. I do not therefore see wherein "the terms have been so utterly departed from"—— The imputation is unpleasant but must be endur'd. I shall be oblig'd to you when any of y^r people come this way to let them call for the 2 vol. Rural Walks, as what I wanted to borrow was "Gisbornes Walks in a Forest,[1] Which if I like I mean to purchase, having heard it highly spoken of. If the verses do not come from any one you know, I have no wish about them. I thought it might be Dr Curries or Mr Roscoes,[2] as the lines are rather above the common run of Magazine verses.

I cannot conclude this without saying that I made no continual mention of other booksellers wishing to purchase the work I am upon because certainly not one knows from me that I am at work on any. I told you what was true, that Mr Low solicited me to put some work into his hands, either a school book or a Novel, & he w^d have given me fifty guineas p^r vol & have advanced what money I wanted, but I beleive I also said that, tho his dealings with me had been remarkably liberal, I could not engage with him with any comfort to myself because of his connections with Bell—a Man who had treated me so infamously—& because his shop was so ill situated.[3] ~~As~~ I have seen him on some printing business for a friend since I have been here, but have never mentiond a syllable ab^t the work, but I know I could get a purchaser if you had wish'd it.

As to other booksellers of whom you once hinted in the way of reproach that I had had recourse to many, I must beg leave to observe that, if necessity compell'd me to that, it should rather have excited concern than sneer, And that till the elder Mr Cadell refus'd "Desmond" when I told him there were sketches of French affairs in it, I never thought of applying to another. Mr Hayley then advis'd me to go to Robinson to whom he had himself sold a book (tho not for the same reason); I did so & might still have been on his list of Authors had not M^rs ONeill thought he treated me Cavalierly ab^t a trifle (not ab^t money) & almost insisted on my going to Bell, a Man till then hardly known as a publisher.[4]

The Books my Son Nicholas wants are: Ethelinde, Celestina, the Banish'd Man, The old Manor House, Wanderings of Warwick, Montalbert & Marchmont. The last[5] are now on their way to him; If you have not Ethelinde & Celestina, I fear they are not to be got. He also wanted the Romance of real life. School books would of course be of no use to him, as he has no young friends where he is—— If you can get these, I shall be very glad to send them by the next ships. I am, Gen[t],

your obed[t] hble Ser[t],
Charlotte Smith

Osborn Collection MS, Yale University. Address: Mess Cadell & Davies/ Strand. Postmark: {London}; 8 o'Clock/ 6.JY/ 98 MORN; Portland/ Unpaid/ Penny Post.

NOTES

1. See CS to Davies, 3 Jan. 1798, n. 3.

2. Dr. James Currie (1756–1805) of Scotland settled in Liverpool, where he wrote primarily medical works, his best known on the use of cold water to manage fever. He belonged to a literary circle that included William Roscoe with whom he published essays opposing slavery. CS admired Roscoe's *Lorenzo,* a biography published in 1795, but Roscoe also published poems, including the successful *Wrongs of Africa,* in two parts (1787, 1788); "Ode to the People of France" (1789); and "The Life, Death, and Wonderful Atchievements of Edmund Burke. A New Ballad" (1791).

3. Sampson Low's address on Berwick Street was removed from more fashionable publishing and shopping areas. In CS to Cadell and Davies, 22 Oct. 1797, CS described Low's connection with Joseph Bell: Bell had once employed Low to buy *Montalbert* "underhand." Bell's "infamous" treatment of her surely refers to his acid preface to *The Wanderings of Warwick* (1794), placing full blame on Smith for the novel's being late and short one of the two volumes originally promised.

4. CS must have heeded Henrietta O'Neill's advice against using George Robinson again; he published only CS's novel *Desmond* in 1792. Joseph Bell published *The Old Manor House* (1793) and its sequel, *The Wanderings of Warwick* (1794).

5. That is, the last four titles, which CS has marked off with parentheses.

To Thomas Cadell, Jr., and William Davies

{London, 29 January 1798}
Gent[n],

I observe by the papers to day that the Exeter, Brunswick, Bombay Castle, & Earl House are all going immediately to Bombay. By one of which I beg the favor of you if possible to send my Son Nicholas's Books—pack'd as your usual packages to India are made and thus directed:

Nicholas Hankey Smith, Esq[re], Resident at Bushire[1]—To the care of Patrick Hadow, Esq[re], Bombay

---

And if you can ascertain what Ship the parcel goes by, I should be glad to know it that I may write to Mr Hadow; otherwise, these Books may share the fate of my poor schawls which, for want of knowing what ship they were sent by, I have lost.[2]

I have taken the liberty to name your house as one to which some Gentlemen in the City, who wish to know M^r^ De Fovilles character before they entrust him with the instruction of their Children, may refer. You may mention his relationship to me & very safely say that his character & conduct is unimpeachable. These Gentlemen preferred a reference to some respectable Commercial house to those he could have given to the Dss of Devonshire, Lady Bessborough, Lord Egremont &c &c &c which I hope will excuse my taking this liberty with you.

On making up my account with Messrs Daniels house Mincing Lane, there is a ballance of £18.13.2 coming to me, which I appropriate to Miss Smith who has the first claim on her G^d^fathers property. I have only so young a Messenger to send that, if it be not giving you too much trouble, I shall be very much oblig'd to you to let some trusty person go with the enclos'd order any time to day or tomorrow to receive this money, Mincing Lane being so very far from hence that I am not equal to the fatigue of fetching it, nor have I time. If you are kind enough to do this, be so good as to keep the money till Miss Smith calls or sends for it.

I shall this evening finish a parcel of MMS of 300 pages[3] which I hope to send tomorrow for Mr Hayley, & as the work is so far advanced, I submit it to you whether it w^d^ not be advisable, when Mr Hayley returns two entire volumes & the greater part of the third, & when I have made alterations & corrections which he advises (which however are he says very few), to put the work to press—— As I wish to see every sheet myself & now give up my whole time to the latter part of it, I think it will be done better if the printing is begun directly, than if it is hurried off directly before publication when it is possible I may be under the necessity of being more engaged in company, & even out of town for a day or two occasionally. Of this, you will judge, & when determind, let me know. Mr Hayley, on receiving the present pacquet, will I apprehend return the whole in a few days, as this completes the part he had unfinish'd, & a day or two after I get it back, 800 pages will be ready for the printer.

I am, Gentlemen,
your obed^t^ & oblig'd Ser^t^,
Charlotte Smith

3 Duke S^t^
Jan 29th 1798

Do you know anything of "Anecdotes of living Authors & criticisms on their works" printed for Faulder?[4] It is too dear to buy, yet I sh[d] like to see it.

J. Pierpont Morgan Library MS. No address or postmark.

NOTES

1. Residents were civil servants appointed to act as governors with the power only to advise local rulers. Bushire is a seaport in southwest Iran, in what was then Persia. Nicholas, who became fluent in Persian, was a successful and respected resident.

2. Two Persian shawls worth 40 guineas each had been specially made for her in Tibet (see CS to Cadell and Davies, 2 Nov. 1795).

3. CS's most recent novel, *The Young Philosopher,* which she and Cadell and Davies quarreled over during the fall of 1797. That William Hayley would still edit CS's manuscripts is surprising in view of her protests since 1794 that she had lost his friendship.

4. *Literary Memoirs of Living Authors of Great Britain . . . including a List of Their Works, with Occasional Opinions upon Their Literary Character* (London: R. Faulder, 1798).

To Thomas Cadell, Jr., and William Davies

[London, February 1798][1]
Gent[n],

I have just re[d] this from M[r] Henchman[2] which I hope will secure the safe delivery of the Box for My Son N.H.S. — —

I had a Letter from M[r] Hayley to day which gives me every encouragement as to the effect of my work. I have at this moment 296 pages of one & 40 of another volume before me in which I wish to complete a particular part & have only 20 pages to do, yet I have been hinder'd for three days—first by the necessity of drawing up memorials for Charles to present to the Duke of York,[3] then by the eternal Law business, & to day by a friend from the Country, but I do hope to send you the packet tomorrow & request the fav[r] of you to dispatch it to Eartham directly as M[r] H. is desirous of seeing so considerable a part before he returns the whole that he has, which he wishes to do speedily, thinking you mean to put it to press as soon afterwards as may be.

I am much oblig'd to you for the trouble you took ab[t] the money & did not mean to give you that of sending it.

Gent[n], I am y[r] Obligd humble Ser,
CS

Osborn Collection MS, Yale University. No address or postmark.

NOTES

1. This letter can be dated in early Feb. CS's letter of 29 Jan. to Cadell and Davies describes, first, a package of books sent to Nicholas in Persia by Cadell and Davies; second, a request that Cadell and Davies send "some trusty person" to Mincing Lane with a money order for her as she is not well enough to go; and third, a completed third volume of a work in hand being sent to Hayley for correction, leaving us to infer that he already has the first two that he writes about with encouragement.

2. Thomas Henchman, husband of Mary Eleanor Berney; she was Nicholas's cousin and one of the legatees to the Smith estate. (See Genealogical Chart.)

3. Since 1795, Frederick, duke of York, had been commander in chief of the army in Great Britain.

To Thomas Cadell, Jr., and William Davies

{London} Feby 26th 1798

Gentlemen,

This pacquet contains the 2nd Volume complete, save only a short poem of four stanza's at page 54 which, not being able to adjust quite to my mind, I kept back, but it shall be ready when ever the Printer sends for it.

The third volume, as Mr Hayley in his present distrest state of mind[1] cannot finish correcting it for me, I have sent (at least the latter part) to another friend, who will go over the uncorrected parts of it, & it will be ready in about ten days——

I beleive you recollect that there was 17£ left of the sum of 50£ which I told you I sh^d^ want on the first of March. You will no doubt have the goodness to ~~send~~ honor my Bill for that Sum when I shall send it in, payable to M^r^ G Symms.[2] And if you w^d^ for the last part of the account accept a Bill for 40£ at 2 months, it would be the greatest accommodation to me, & I trust would not engage you much in advance, as the Book will be finishd by that time—I hope much sooner. I sh^d^ however have been very glad not to have touch'd this money, but I can get none from Mr Parkin till all the deeds are ready & signd creating Lord Egremont & my Brother Trustees & dissolving the accursed Trust of Robinson & Parkin.[3] This I have gone after repeatedly to no purpose, & in the mean time my rent becomes due, and I have all the family to support.

Favor with y^r^ answer,

Gentlemen,
your oblig'd Ser^t^,
Charlotte Smith

M[r] Daniel will discount the bill if you w[d] have the goodness to assist me with it.

I return the Flora Scotica[4] with many thanks.

204.5.3
39.0.0

243.5.3
54

300[5]

Osborn Collection MS, Yale University. Address: Mess[rs] Cadell & Davies/ an an[sr] requested. No postmark.

NOTES

1. Hayley was distressed over the illness of his son Thomas Alphonso. In 1800, Thomas died of complications of a severe curvature of the spine.

2. George William Syms, wine merchant, 16 Abchurch Lane.

3. These appointments were not final until 27 Aug. 1799.

4. James Lightfoot, *Flora Scotica, or, A Systematic Arrangement, in the Linnæan Method, of the Native Plants of Scotland and the Hebrides* (1777).

5. Written on the address page.

To Thomas Cadell, Jr., and William Davies

[London, 27 February 1798]
Gent[n],

I am much oblig'd to you for yr compliance with my request to the extent or beyond what I have left of my anticipated earnings. I cannot but think my fate particularly hard, & the more so as I have lately learned how much more money has been given for Novels—even to those who had occasion for advances. I do not mean by this to murmur at any bargain between us, nor have I any reason to complain of your want of liberality, but I name it as a circumstance adding very heavily to the Opression I have labourd under from the Monsters calling themselves Trustees who, by their infamous conduct, have every way impoverish'd me & compelld me to be so wholly dependent on my labour. Lord Egremont came to Town yesterday &, by his desire, My Brother & M[r] Smiths Nephew who are parties in the dissolution of the Trust. Lord E. was in expectation of having the Deeds ready, & he now becomes a Trustee, but the deeds are not ready, & it will yet be a fortnight so that, as Parkin will not let my family have any money till then (if then he does not take it for another bill, which I suspect he intends to do), I am compell'd whether I will or no to supply my whole family as well as I can, & it is almost too much for my strength & will but little contribute to the spirit of the work I am about, which I wish'd & still wish to make as good as I can, Always in the hope that what I write will be the last I shall be forced to write——

I return the proof wch is very well printed & almost without an error. As the friend who overlooks the rest of the 3 vol & the 4th (a literary Man of considerable reputation)[1] says he cannot judge of the conduct & probability of the Story so well unless he has the preceding parts before him, I shall be much oblig'd to you to direct Mr Hugh's[2] people to send me every sheet of the corrected Letter press as fast as it is work'd off—with the proof sheet that follows which will be attended with but little trouble to them & will be convenient to me—& if you were to direct them (M^r H's Men) to say when a proof is left when they are to call for it, I w^d always take care to have it ready.

I enclose the bill I have drawn in fav^r of Daniel & sons with a Letter to them. I am afraid of sending the little Messenger for the Money, as they (the Messrs Daniels) will give an order on their Banker for it, & there will be risk of his making some mistake or of losing it. Therefore if between this time and tomorrow at one oclock you c^d oblige me so far as to send a safe person for it, some one or other of my family will call for it at y^r house tomorrow, for I have eight & twenty pounds to pay at 3 tomorrow for rent.

I am, Gentlemen,

Your oblig'd hble Ser^t,
Charlotte Smith

Duke Street, Feby 27th 1798

If you will have the goodness to accept the Bill, the Boy is to go on with it to Mr Daniel, & it may be left there——

You will be kind enough to put the L^ttr to Mr Daniel in a Cover with the Bill.[3]

Huntington MS (HM10821). Address: Messrs C & D. No postmark.

NOTES

1. Probably the Reverend Charles Dunster. Apparently Hayley had to abandon editing the work.

2. Henry Hughs (d. 1810), printer at 6 Great Turnstile, Lincoln's Inn Fields, from 1779 to 1800.

3. This note was written upside down, and added under "Messrs C & D" on the address.

To Thomas Cadell, Jr., and William Davies

[London, March 1798][1]
Gent^{n}

I intended waiting on you to day on my way to Threadneedle S^{t} and the India House, but the accursed affairs, all the fatigue of which is thrown upon me, & my endeavours to keep my engagement with you & to supply the press which I have now done to the entire close of Vol 3, have so much overcome me, together with some other unpleasant circumstances that I am not able to walk so far; I therefore write to beg you w^{d} be pleas'd to give me credit for 4 sets of Sonnets vol. 1st & 2nd—One for myself, for as usual I cannot keep one, & three for my Son Lionel at Quebec who informs me that they have been the means of introducing him to all the best society in Quebec & Montreal & have obtain'd for him friends in his profession who have been of great use to him & may be of more.

Amidst the many mortifications & very severe sufferings to which I am needlessly expos'd, it is some consolation to know that the talents I first exerted to procure bread for the infancy of my Children (Alas! it is now, fourteen years ago) have been the means of the success in life of those who are grown up: at least of my sons—for Mr William Smith was for that reason (after he had read my books) taken up by Sir John Shore in India;[2] Nicholas by the same means found friends in Bombay; Charles got his late appoint^{t} entirely by Lord Clanricarde[3] & Lady Bessborough, my particular friends. And Lionel has been greatly benefitted by them in Canada.

Mrs Nott begs me to ask you whether a M^{r} & Mrs Brooke, each Subscribers for a book of Sonnets 2nd vol., have sent for their copies & <u>paid you</u>. If not, the mony is due to me or you. Have the goodness to let me know. I should ask to borrow <6> Guineas if I thought you w^{d} oblige me, as I literally have but half a crown in the house. Mr Bicknell, to whom I to day applied to try Mr Parkin again for me (who has 13£ snug in his hands of mine) or to borrow 10 or 20 of Mr Daniel, wrote me word to day that money he had no hope of getting for me but that the difficulty he hoped was got over that stopped all our proceedings & that the writings now waited for Mr Winterbottom.[4] I am going to send to him, but as the mere engrossing will take up a week & Parkin will then perhaps find some new excuse, I am very much afraid I shall be starved in the mean time, as I have no longer credit, nor can I get any money; I do not however press it upon you, as y^{u} have already advanced so much more than you say is due. I am, Gent^{n},

your oblig'd hble Ser^{t},
Charlotte Smith

The boy will call for an an^{r} as he[5]

University of Iowa Libraries MS. Address: Messrs Cadell & Davies/ Strand/ An anr desir'd as the Sert returns from Threadneedle Street. No postmark.

NOTES

1. This letter can be dated by CS's references in letters of 26 and 27 Feb. 1798 to having sent the completed third volume of *The Young Philosopher* to a friend to read.

2. Shore (1751–1834) succeeded Cornwallis as governor-general of India from 1793 to 1798, a time of relative peace.

3. Henry de Burgh, earl of Clanricarde, died 8 Dec. 1797 and was succeeded by his brother John Thomas de Burgh, who took his seat in the House of Lords on 2 Mar. 1798 and was created earl of Clanricarde on 29 Dec. 1800. Charles had been appointed a lieutenant in the Royal Garrison Battalion under General Trigge in Gibraltar on 1 Sept. 1795 after he was wounded, an appointment that would have been made by the older brother. On 23 Feb. 1798, he was appointed lieutenant of invalids at Berwick; the younger brother would have been involved in making that appointment although he was not yet earl.

4. Abraham Winterbottom, 32 Threadneedle Street, solicitor to Richard Smith and Robert Allen, acting for his wife Mary Gibbes Smith Allen. Charles Bicknell was CS's solicitor.

5. The very last line of this letter is cut off because it is in a grangerized edition—a book of blank pages in which prints or manuscripts have been trimmed to fit the page to which they are attached.

To Thomas Cadell, Jr., and William Davies

[?London, ?March 1798][1]

Gentlemen,

I have receiv'd a Commission from my Son, Lieut Charles Smith; he desires I would send him two compleat sets of all my novels for which he will give an order on his agents.

I have told him that to obtain all is I apprehend impossible, But I beg the favr of you to send a set of each of those you have, plainly bound. I fear these are only Emmeline & the Banish'd Man. If more than one set of these is wanting I will send the <u>other</u> by some other opportunity. They go to Scotland tomorrow. I have been afraid there was some mistake between me & Your Printers, as I have had but 2 proofs this fortnight, & 4 sheets of Letter press sent to me for correction (the close of the 3rd volume) have lain ready above a week. To day they sent to enquire if I had any thing ready so that I am convinced there has been some blunder between us, which I only mention that you may not think me to blame. I hope the work will now be ready forthwith. I send MMS to night & give every moment to its completion that I can spare from the cruelty of the persons who keep from me the very means of existence from day to day — — Mr Dayrell[2] has been in Town a fortnight but has . . .

Osborn Collection MS, Yale University. No address or postmark.

NOTES

1. CS must have written this unfinished note early in 1798 while composing *The Young Philosopher,* since it refers to *The Banished Man* as completed (the only other novel that Cadell and Davies published for her). On 26 Feb. CS sent the completed second volume to them and had sent the third to an unnamed friend to correct, Hayley being too distressed to do so. On 27 Feb. she reported that her friend, probably the Reverend Charles Dunster, requested the first two volumes to help him "judge of the conduct & probability of the Story." Perhaps this delayed the proofs being sent her for correction. If the several mailings back and forth took at least ten days, and the letter press of the completed third volume had lain unread above a week, this letter would have been written in middle to late Mar. The novel was not published until June.

2. Edmund Dayrell, 10 Lincoln's Inn, Old Square, was a lawyer often consulted by CS as well as by Egremont and his steward, William Tyler.

To Dr. James Edward Smith[1]

March 15, 1798
Sir,

The freindly politeness with which you honoured me when I took the liberty of addressing you almost twelve months since, has made on my mind too flattering an impression to allow me to forget, that in the letter you then favoured me with, you mentioned that in the months of April and May you were usually in London. As I am now settled there, permit me to hope that I may be so fortunate as to be favoured with your personal acquaintance when you this year make your annual visit. Though after a long and successless struggle I am compelled to leave the country, my passion for plants rather increases as the power of gratification diminishes; and though I must henceforth, or at least till peace, or something equally conclusive, dismisses me to the continent, (whither I will go if I have strength whenever it is practicable,) botanize on annuals in garden pots out at a window, it will be a considerable consolation to have an opportunity of being known to the principal of that delightful and soothing study; and who is, as well in science as in benevolence of mind, an acquaintance so greatly to be desired.

I have not forgotten (being still compelled to write, that my family may live) your hint of introducing botany into a novel. The present rage for gigantic and impossible horrors, which I cannot but consider as a symptom of morbid and vitiated taste, makes me almost doubt whether the simple pleasures afforded by natural objects will not appear vapid to the admirers of spectre novels and cavern adventures. However I have ventured a little of it, and have at least a hope that it will not displease those whose approbation I most covet.

A domestic occurrence, very much unexpected and very unpleasant, has made my heart ache and my hand tremble; but they are used to it, and both should by this time know better. It would be a prettiness, though very true, to say that while either are in existence it is a pleasure to say how much

I am, dear Sir,
Your obliged Servant,
Charlotte Smith.

Copy in Memoir and Correspondence of the Late Sir James Edward Smith, M.D., *ed. Lady Pleasance Smith (London: Longman, 1832), 2:75–76.*

NOTE

1. See Biographical Notes.

To William Davies

[?London, 29 June ?1798][1]
Sir,

It was not till Friday I knew that the two last Bengal Ships of the Season And the Swallow packet are on the point of sailing. It is extremely material to me to write to my Son. If it be not too much trouble, I shall be very much oblig'd to you to have these three Letters deliver'd at the proper Office & if possible to go by the three different ships, but if this cannot be, then by the most speedy conveyance. They are so extremely material to me that I venture to ask you to attend to their being dispatch'd for me. The necessity of writing them has hinderd me from closing my work, but the only reason why I have sent only about 20 pages new is that there is a little piece of Poetry to follow page 220, which I have sent to Mr Hayley for correction, not daring to trust my own judgement. I hope to have it back corrected by the next post, & then the Pages that follow shall be immediately dispatch'd.

I am, Sir, y^r^ ob^t^ Ser^t^,
CS

29th June
[To] Mr Davies

Osborn Collection MS, Yale University. No address or postmark.

NOTE

1. Probably 1798, in reference to a poem added to the first edition of *The Young Philosopher.* Hayley had read its first volumes in manuscript for her in the winter of 1797–98.

To Thomas Cadell, Jr., and William Davies

5 Upper Baker Street [London]
Novr 9th at night [1798][1]
Gentlemen,

I receiv'd your account this evening, which I beleive to be perfectly correct. There is still money due to you I beleive, from Archer[2] at Dublin. I do not clearly comprehend whether it goes in part discharge of your account, but when Mr Walker sends what he says belongs to me & which he informs me he has paid to a friend coming to London, you will be pleas'd to take that as a small dimunition of the gross amount——

I not only continue to be kept out of my money by Mr Robinson, every thing being now finished but what depends on him, but I am under acceptances which become due in the course of this end of next month for my furniture in this house, & as I have done no literary work for many months & have given up the plan of Translating (on finding some translator by the sheet had undertaken the book I had begun), I shall be very poor I fear for the next three or four months, but as I shall hardly, I trust, be reduced again to the exigencies I have been in, I flatter myself I shall have it in my power to acquit myself towards you in the course of the next four or five months; if not at once, yet by degrees.

You will give me leave to assure you that I should feel very much concern'd not to beleive that you can say, altho our connection does not continue, that I have always conducted myself with honor towards you—And that Mr Bell of 148 in Oxford Street is the only Man with whom I have had literary dealings who will say otherwise. I beleive I have somewhere such an acknowledgement under the hand of Mr Davies, and perhaps as I am determined to go to trial with Mr Bell (because his bill is utterly unjust & dishonest & he arrested me in the street),[3] I may have occasion to call upon Mr Davies to speak to the conduct I have observed with your house in transactions at various times to the amount of near 3000£ and during the space of eleven to twelve years. Mr Low, who was so obliging as to be bail for me & to find another, is also ready to give this testimony in my favor, & I flatter myself it will not be beleived that I could deal with Mr Bell only in the manner he represents—which is that I promisd him two volumes of the Wanderings of Warwick, produced only one, & cheated him out of the money he had advanced for the other.

I happen now to have discoverd that he has desseminated this story among the Trade, which may perhaps have done me at first some prejudice, but if it has, it is blown over, for I had only yesterday an offer from one of the most eminent booksellers in this quarter of the Town to take any work

I was writing on my own terms—— As I cannot however leave those I am oblig'd to, it is out of the question, yet such things are satisfactory because they prove M[r] Bells impudent calumny has fallen harmless, & that to purchase my books is not a losing game. I beg leave, Gentlemen, to repeat that, as soon as I get possession of what is due to me from my family for whom I have lately recover'd 4000£ (accounted not worth two pence by their Trustees who gave it up as desperate),[4] I will begin to pay off whatever shall remain due to you, & with a due sense of many kindnesses received from you, I am,

Gentlemen, y[r] obed[t] & oblig'd ser[t],
Charlotte Smith

I have continually applications to know where Ethelinde & Celestina can be had. Surely it would answer to reprint a small number of them.

Yale University MS. No address or postmark.

NOTES

1. The gap in correspondence from June until Nov. 1798 is unexplained. As CS was still working on the last volume of *The Young Philosopher* when the letters abruptly stop, it seems likely that a folder of correspondence was lost from among those that ended up at Yale and its contents sold separately (as the single letters in this series [CS to Cadell and Davies, 29 Jan. 1798, at the J. Pierpont Morgan Library and Mar. 1798 at the University of Iowa Library] further suggest).

2. A bookseller.

3. There is no other mention of his bill, the arrest, or a trial.

4. Apparently CS succeeded in recovering debts owed the estate by pursuing various debtors, especially those in Barbados, through friends there. But she gained by it little more than earlier action in settling part of the trust and perhaps payment for her expenses.

To Thomas Cadell, Jr., and William Davies

[?London, after 11 Nov. 1798][1]
Gent[n],

I was equally surpris'd & concern'd to receive this Letter to day from a Gentleman whom I particularly wish'd to have attended to myself punctually. I had not an idea that you w[d] refer the Subscribers to me, as you must, I think, recollect that if a greater number of books were wanted than you allow'd me, you were to supply them at the Bookseller's prices, And you must know that I had none wherewith to furnish M[r] Greathead,[2] having dispersed & disposed of all allowd me Almost twelve months ago. If you will be so good as to send the quantity he desires, I must account to you as for others — — & as I now shall in a very few days finish with Mr Hugh's office, I hope to close the account by the assistance of East India remittances to your satisfaction. But as I have never seen it, not indeed since we settled for "the Banishd Man," you will be so good against the time when I can repay you to let it be made out.

I am very sorry you have had occasion to complain of inconceivable plague relative to this last work—Plague I know not that you have had, unless in obliging me with some advances, for otherwise certainly the press has never stood still for want of copy, but some times I have seen no proof for four or five days, which I imputed to the time necessary to work off the corrected sheets, & sh^d never have complaind of it or nam'd it, but that I was aware how much my uncomfortable situation & the embarrassments I have been subjected to all the winter were likely to give occasion to complaints of dilatoriness, while in fact I have sacrificed my health, my sleep, & my friends to an almost incredible exertion to prevent your having reason to say I deceived you or again that you have lost money by me.

There are many ways of doing a favor, Some of which redouble the obligation, others which almost cancel it. You w^d have oblig'd me infinitely more if you had taken my bill on Mr Walker than by sending me 5£ with such a Letter. If you did not know the particular circumstances I labour under & how little either from birth or education or connections I ought to turn beggar, there w^d be less unkindness in the manner of obliging me — — But I hope, Yes, I will still hope that any future difficulties will be done away. I return Sketches &c of the present State of France,[3] & I am, Gent^n,

your most obed^t & oblig'd Ser^t
Charlotte Smith

Osborn Collection MS, Yale University. Addressed: Messrs Cadell and Davies/ Strand — —. No postmark.

NOTES

1. This letter can be dated after her letter of 9 Nov. 1798, where she notes in the first paragraph that Joseph Cooper Walker is sending money owed to her by a friend coming to London. She asks them to credit that money to her account, and apparently they sent the money to her instead.

2. The Reverend Samuel Greatheed (see Biographical Notes).

3. Helen Maria Williams's *A Tour of Switzerland, or a View of the Present State of the Governments and Manners of Those Cantons, with Comparative Sketches of the Present State of Paris* (1798).

To Joseph Cooper Walker

No. 5 Upper Baker Street, Portman Square {London}
Jany 9th 1799
Dear Sir,

I have not indeed been quite so ungrateful as you must necessarily think me if I had not written for so long a time and in answer to so many obliging and friendly Letters. But the fact was I wrote a short Letter acknowledging that to my daughter which answer of mine it appears from your more recent favor, you never received. Since Mr Cadell Senr has relinquishd the business & no longer attends even to the general routine of the Shop, it is easy to see that every little commission is a trouble to those who are now in it, & that it is not worth their while to be very civil.[1] Your Letters have invariably lain some time with them, & when I did receive your last, I wrote twice to know if the six Guineas and an half had been paid, & at last (only a few days ago) received an answer that it had been receiv'd by them ever since the 2nd October. On making up the account for the last transactions between us, they were Creditors upon me, & therefore the money you were so obliging as to send went in part liquidation of that account. So also will the little remaining Sum for which I understand Mr Archer is accountable. I have mention'd to them the necessity of sending other books to Ireland in place of those taken by Mrs Evans,[2] but a prompt compliance with this requisition I have very little reason to expect. As we have now finally parted as Author and Publisher, I shall not again trouble them with any Letters of mine, & as I hope I shall be able to keep the small house I have taken in London, I beg favor of you to direct in future to me at No. 5 Upper Baker Street, Portman Square where, should you be in London, I shall be most happy to see you. I only hope that I shall be in a situation to reside in it; I hardly venture to beleive it, for my prospects are still dark and stormy. The roguery of the old Trustees on one hand & the folly I beleive might say madness of the unfortunate Man whom I must call my Husband have combined to undo all I have been labouring at,[3] & I am still destined to experience the fate of the Danaids when Alas! my health & hopes are gone.

My eldest Son arrived from India in July last in the intention undoubtedly of assisting his family. But he brought only 2000£ with him & was not aware of the expence a Man of pleasure soon gets into here,[4] & it has happend that, so far from his being of any use to his family, he has redoubled all my expences and brought upon me every creditor I had in the World who all imagined this was the time to get paid, Circumstances of which, strange as it is, he really has not the least comprehension. While on the other hand your friend Lionel has contrived in Canada to contract a debt of

300£, and he informs his family that if it is not paid, he must sell his commission and be entirely undone.

This, Alas! is not the worst, bad as it is; Lucy married much against my inclination a Man who, when he resign'd the fellowship he possess'd at New College Oxford, was not only entirely pennyless, but without any profession or means of procuring a guinea, for, instead of being able to earn a subsistence as a Physician, he is now studying for it without a shilling to pay for the very expensive courses of London lectures.[5] They have now a child & are literally destitute of daily existence except what I supply them with—which is a circumstance so distressing that I am afraid I shall not long be able to struggle with it. I cannot tell you a twentieth part of what I have to undergo, & indeed, so singularly unfortunate do I consider myself, that I feel a sort of humiliation in always troubling my friends with the history of my calamities. Yet it is necessary in more instances than one to account to them for my acting in so many cases so very differently from what I should do did not domestic misery drag me down to Earth & render my faculties useless and my acquaintance rather a burthen than a pleasure to my friends. Basta Basta!——

Yet I must still linger on the sorrowful subjects. You ask after Mr Hayley, & it is from the information of others, not from his own, that I am enabled to give you a sad account of him. His Son who has been in a declining state many months is now afflicted with an incurable curvature of the spine which bends him quite double, & he is oblig'd to be carried about in the arms of a Servant like a cradled infant. His limbs, I understand, are all contracted, & he is universally deform'd without the least hope, if he lives, of recovering any strength or power to help himself. A severer blow to a Father who had been nursing up this feeble plant for eighteen years, & fancying & flattering himself he would be something extraordinary, can hardly be conceived. But contrary to the manner of most Men who fly to their long approved friends for consolation, Mr Hayley has either found new ones to alleviate his afflictions or keeps them wholly to himself; for tho he was in London lately above two months & knew I was settled there, he never came near me till I wrote, supposing him gone out of Town to one of our mutual friends to enquire how his Son did, which brought him for five minutes, a silent formal visit when the only sensation of pleasure he express'd was when he jump'd into the Carriage that brought him as if he had escaped from plague pestilence and famine, & there I beleive ends as to any future communication a friendship of fifteen years. But whoever has lived as I have for forty & eight years must know how to appreciate all the good things of this World among which friendship is certainly one of the best.

I beleive literature never was at so low an ebb as at present. The booksellers complain they have no sale for any thing and look cold on Authors whom a few years since they were eager to engage with. I am not speaking of myself in this respect, for I understand my last work has been tolerably successful. I am very glad you like it notwithstanding the politics which I thought by no means thickly sewn or offensive, but it seems the mention of the Gracchi is very much disapproved, & the histories of Rome or of the Grecian Republic are soon likely to be among proscribed books. To this soreness on the score of politic's may be imputed the excessive stupidity of all our theatrical productions. But you must be dead sick of Politics, & my paper reminds me that it is time, with renew'd acknowledge[ts] for all your kindness & best wishes for your health, to assure you that I have great pleasure in being allow'd to remain, Dear Sir,

your most oblig'd Ser[t],
Charlotte Smith

Huntington MS (HM10822). Address: Josepth Cooper Walker Esq[re]/ Eccles Street/ Dublin. Postmark: {LONDON}; JA/ 9/ 99; JA/ {}2/ 99.

NOTES

1. Thomas Cadell, Sr., who had sponsored most of CS's earliest works, retired in 1793, leaving the business to his son Thomas Cadell, Jr., and William Davies. The new proprietors argued that CS's works for them did not show a profit, and they were not so willing to fulfill her many requests.

2. Not identified.

3. Even as the old trustees were on the way out, BS was already ingratiating himself with the future one (as of 27 Aug. 1799), requesting an interview and disparaging his estranged wife:

> The best apology I can make for troubling your Lordship on mine, and my Familys concerns, is to acknowledge your goodness, in the alacrity You have shewn to extricate us from poverty, and misery. I all along rejoiced that You were so Kind, and humane, as to offer to take them under your administration, and should never have thought of giving any delay to it, had it not been for the improper and indecorous treatment of M[rs] Smith, and Her intention to divest me of what I am entitled to both now, and in future, as Residuary Legatee to my late Father, & her cruel conduct in with-holding from me, the pecuniary assistance of One Hundred pounds to discharge my bills. (BS to Egremont, unpub. letter in PHA #0.11)

4. William Towers Smith had been a magistrate, a commissioner at Cooch Behar, and a senior merchant in the civil service when he returned in 1799 to England, where he spent the entire year "out of employ" (*Bengal Civil Servants*). He was back in India by Mar. 1800, when he married Catherine Maria Morris.

William left England persona non grata with both his parents. On 27 Feb. 1799, BS wrote from Hamilton, Scotland, to Egremont of having paid liquor bills for £28 and 8, and having £16 outstanding, because of visits from his sons: "my Sons, Whom I was happy to see, I gave every latitude to, and as I was ill in bed the greatest part of the time they were with me, I beg'd they would make the House their own, and it was seldom a day pass'd that they had not the Sussex Officers, and other Gentlemen with them, which with preparations for their reception, have greatly augmented my bills" (unpub. letter in PHA #0.11).

The other son must have been Charles, who was stationed at Berwick in 1798–99. The extent of William's financial difficulties is suggested by a surviving bond (IRO #200) in his name for £3,000 drawn on his relatives, Thomas Henchman and Edmund Boehm (his cousins' husbands), dated 1 Mar. 1799. It is incomplete, however.

5. Lucy married Newhouse on 12 June 1798 at St. Marylebone, London. Their first child was christened 25 May 1799 at St. Andrew, Holborn, Newhouse's parish at the time of the marriage.

To Thomas Cadell, Jr., and William Davies

[London, 16 April 1799]

Gent^t^,

I hoped before now to have liquidated at least part of y^r^ acc^t^ against me, but my furniture is not yet quite paid for. Such very heavy taxes as I have paid & am to pay and very severe disappointments from quarters whence I expected assistance have made it impossible. I know not whether after all I shall be able to continue in my house, but as at last we have releas'd & got rid of our fourteen years Trustees, tho the deeds were finished only on Sat^y^,[1] I do hope I shall have an assured income & be in a short time out of debt.

I have an opportunity of send^g^ to Canada & beleive my Son Lionel has never had "the young Philosopher." Be kind enough therefore to let the bearer have a set (for which he will pay) plainly & strongly bound and also the play of the Secret,[2] together with Mr Bowles's last Poem; I do not mean the Song of the Nile, but a descriptive poem the name of which I have forgotten.[3]

I am, Gent^n^, your obed^t^ Ser^t^,
Charlotte Smith

April 16th 1799

Yale University MS. No address or postmark.

NOTES

1. On 2 July 1784, the day Benjamin Smith was released from King's Bench Prison, his duties as trustee to the estate were taken over by John Robinson, Edmund Boehm, Richard Atkinson, and Sir John Swinnerton Dyer, elder brother of Thomas Dyer, the second husband of BS's sister Mary Smith Berney Dyer. (See Genealogical Chart.) Anthony Parkin replaced Sir John Dyer on 31 July 1788. Robinson and Parkin were replaced by George O'Brien, third earl of Egremont, and the Reverend Nicholas Turner, CS's younger brother. The bonds and deeds of release were dated 18 and 19

Mar. 1799, but were not signed by everyone until Saturday, 13 Apr. 1799. Thus only Robinson and Boehm had been involved in the trust the entire time, which was not fourteen but fifteen years. The Robinson and Parkin trusteeship was finally dissolved on 27 Aug. 1799 (see CS to Cadell and Davies, 28 Aug. 1799).

2. Edward Morris's very successful comedy. It had been performed sixteen times at Drury Lane since opening on 2 Mar.

3. William Lisle Bowles (1762–1850) is often credited, along with CS, for reestablishing the sonnet form in England. Like her, he wrote in other forms, including the poems named here. *Song of the Battle of the Nile* (1799) had just been published by Cadell and Davies with Charles Dilly. Two poems published by Dilly in 1798 featured places: *Coombe Ellen: A Poem, Written in Radnorshire, September, 1798,* and *St. Michael's Mount.* Perhaps she expected Cadell and Davies to send *Coombe Ellen,* which they co-published with Dilly.

To Thomas Cadell, Jr., and William Davies

[London, 14 May 1799]
Gent[n],

I am extremely sorry to be oblig'd to repeat to you in consequence of another Letter I have received from M[r] Walker that the Sonnets subscribed for in Ireland of which I spoke to you about two months since have never been received. Great blame attaches to me, & M[r] Walker seems much hurt at having taken so active a part in a business which has been so ill managed as to have occasion'd great discontent. I also feel myself much hurt as in cases of Subscription An Author is always consider'd as a kind of literary beggar & is open to all the invidious reflections of arrogant prosperity. To this sort of contumely, I trust in your known integrity & punctuality that I shall no longer be expos'd—— I am, Gentlemen, your obed humble Ser[t],

Charlotte Smith

May 14th 1799
Upper Baker S[t] No 5——

Yale University MS. No address or postmark.

To Thomas Cadell, Jr., and William Davies

[London, 31 May 1799]
Gent[n]—

On my return from Wansted on Teusday evening, I found a Letter from M[r] Walker dated the 10th ins[t] informing me that he had at length received the copies of the second volume of Sonnets due to the Irish subscribers and was satisfied. The fourth must undoubtedly have been with Mr Archer & will put you no doubt on your guard against such troublesome delay on any future occasion.

I took with me into the Country the MSS & sketches which have lain some time by me & find that (without reckoning the Poetry in the Young Philosopher wch has been much approv'd & is already y^{r} own) I shall have ten or fifteen pages of Original poetry fit for the work, & which is either finish'd or in such a state of forwardness that it may be ready when ever you are ready to go to press. I cannot however but observe that, as Mr Cadell Senr gave me 10 G^{s} for the few additional Sonnets put to the latest addition of the 1st Vol, your offer of cancelling the account & giving me some copies for myself & friends is hardly adequate to the value which I can make these small pieces of, if I add them to others of a different description to form a volume at some future period. Your account is—

	42.0.0	
against wch is		
to be set	30.0.0.	the agree^{t}. for a second addition
And	7.7.0.	Received from Ireland
	37.7.	

Ballance only 4.13.0—which is certainly an inadequate pay^{t}—— Besides which the half subscriptions to be received in Ireland which are either yours or mine, but I rather think mine, as y^{r} agreement was to supply all the Books to subscribers.

If so, you will not only be paid the whole of your debt, but the ballance would be in my favour.

I cannot therefore but think that, as Mr Cadell voluntarily offer'd me 10 G^{s} for 6 Sonnets—vis from Sonnet LIV to Sonnet LIX—that the same Sum cannot be too much for a larger & more varied addition to the present edition of a second vol.[1] If you are of this opinion, it would confer a singular obligation on me if you would send me the money to day, for strange to tell, yet unhappily it is true, I have never been more distress'd. Having been by my own exertions & Lord Egremonts extraordinary kindness enabled to pay off, or compound, for all the debts against my childrens Grandfathers estate so that it remain'd clear to them, & having prevaild on Lord Egremont to become their Trustee to preserve & divide what remains, The deeds for these purposes, which have cost me some years of solicitude to get made out, were sent down to Scotland for Mr Smith to sign. My Son Charles went himself with them. But his father—instead of thankfully agreeing to an arrangement which he had promis'd to join in & which would considerably have encreas'd his income & have settled with all his family—has refused his signature & is come to London, insisting on having 6500£ paid him to be at his own disposal before he will sign any thing.[2] Ever since October there has been 1000£, part of a recover'd debt which I got in, laying at Pybus's[3] in Lord Egremonts name, & next month we expect Sugars to the amount of twelve hundred pounds from Barbados. But I and the family remaining for whom I am oblig'd to provide cannot have a shilling while this Man acts in such a manner, & as I have struggled on from day to day, looking in full assurance for repayment after all my trouble and fatigue, I am now more exhausted & destitute than ever. We are going at last to Chancery to compel him to do his children justice, but what we are to do in the mean time unless Lord Egremont assists us, I know not.

His Lordship has been indefatigable in trying to save & serve us, but such folly & ingratitude are not to be borne.

I am, Gent^{n},
your oblig'd & obed^{t} Ser^{t},
Charlotte Smith

5 Upper Baker S^{t}, May 31st

General Manuscripts, Manuscripts Division, Rare Books and Special Collections, Princeton University Library. No address or postmark.

NOTES

1. For the second edition of *Elegiac Sonnets ii,* eight new sonnets and four new lyrics were added, three of the latter from *The Young Philosopher.*

2. BS tried to hold out for large sums at other times, but there is no indication that he received this much. Nor was the matter of the sugars, mentioned in the next sentence, quickly settled. In one of only two surviving letters to CS from her estranged husband, BS complained on 19 Sept. 1799 in ironic terms:

> Madam,
> I had the extreme felicity of receiving your letters, enclosing Two Hundred pounds in Bank bills, which I did myself the honor to acknowledge immediately on the arrival of the second part of the Notes but as Post Marks, and hand writings, are too apt to make discoverys, I thought it best to send my letter under Cover to my friend M^{r} R Tayler, and requested him to direct it to you. By this time I suppose you have received it, & from the same precaution I shall forward this in the like way. I have the honor to remain Madam your most Obed^{t} Hum^{ble} Servt BS
>
> I wish the Noble Descendant of Turnor would be so condescending as to procure Franks for her letters to me, as my Humble station of life, cannot afford such extravagant postage.

I understood both Rum, and Sugar, came to the Family last year from Gays for their private use, but though I was promised it, none of it found its way to me. If any arrives this year, I should be glad to have my share of it as both the articles are very high here, the first 18 s pr Gallon, and very indifferent soft Sugar 11 d pd. In short every article in life, is so much advanced that there is no encouragement for a second Generation, but if I die first, who Knows, you may try for little Lords, and Ladys & make them Poets & Poetess's. (unpub. letter in PHA #0.11)

For the rest of his life, BS requested mail be sent to him through his friend Robert Tayler in London in order to avoid discovery by his creditors. The £200 CS sent him was probably from the recovered £1,000, but the matter of the sugars was not settled by Sept.

BS's antipathy for his estranged wife shows in his allusion to the possible nobility of the Turner line, a belief of some members of the family that clearly annoyed BS and in the end did no one any good.

3. Pybus, Call, Grant, and Hale, 148 Old Bond Street, were Egremont's bankers; this firm handled much of the money that Egremont, as trustee, allowed CS to have.

To Joseph Cooper Walker

5 Upper Baker Street, Portman Square {London}
June 23rd 1799

If I had not, Dear Sir, too good reasons to assign for my apparent ingratitude, I should be ashamed of writing to you at all. I am now three Letters in your debt & know how little such a one as I can to day write will be capable of conveying to you my sense of my own omission or of your kindness——

I know not even whether I have ever written to you since the unexpected arrival of my eldest Son in England after an absence of thirteen years. I was unwilling to say to my friends, who naturally congratulated me on the return of one who was always particularly dear to me, that so greatly was he changed, & so totally was he become unlike the William my memory had cherish'd, that my pleasure was empoison'd by disappointment which I shall never conquer.[1] It is useless and painful to dwell upon it tho such is the effect it has had on my mind that I shall never recover it. Nor is that effect weaken'd by his having extorted my consent to take his youngest Sister, Harriet, to India with him. She was the only one of his family that appeared to interest or attach him. Some of the others nearer his own age and with whom he had been brought up seem'd to be even <u>hateful</u> to him, & Lucy (whose marriage has certainly been very unfortunate, very imprudent) appear'd to be a poor substitute for the Sister he had lost, who was indeed the darling of all her family even from her earliest infancy. Beauty has probably its influence even in the person of a Sister, & Harriet having an uncommon share of it (tho not in my mind by any means equal to what my adored & lamented Augusta possess'd) her Brother, who fitted her out with even a profusion of accommodations, imagines she will marry to advantage in Bengal which is certainly very probable. They saild from England on the 2nd April,[2] & we have since had intelligence that they were all well off Madeira twenty days afterwards. There were very respectable Ladies on board, two of them married Women going to their husbands; Harriet was accommodated with a very useful female Servant & indeed every thing that could make such a voyage tolerable. Still my heart reproaches me for having sent this young creature or rather sufferd her to go, for it was quite her own inclination, & tho I could hardly do otherwise circumstanced as I was, yet I shall be most miserably anxious till I know my child is safe, & then perhaps, sacrificed as I was to a chimera of fortune, she may live only to be miserable.

Ever since their departure, indeed long before, a gloom which I have vainly endeavourd to conquer has hung over me. A long series of calamities the most bitter seem to have corroded my heart, which is no longer alive to any sentiment of pleasure——Or if to any, to the single one of hoping all the Friends I esteem have not forgotten me, & even the sentiment is embitterd by the idea that, if they have really a regard for me, their affection must be a painful rather than a pleasurable sensation, & that has partly reconciled me to the loss of Mr Hayleys notice and correspondence. He has frequently been in Town, but I have neither seen nor heard from him since September; His own troubles, for his Son still continues a wretched cripple,[3] being [I] believe too heavy to allow him to feel as he used to do for the troubles of his friends, or at least of one, whose miseries are so interwoven with her destiny that it is impossible for even the most active friendship to be of much use.

I do not know, for my memory partakes of the torpidity of my faculties, whether I told you that these last two years have been pass'd by me principally in arranging the distracted affairs of Mr Smith & his Children, which have been in a Trust for fourteen years, a trust so ill managed that they every year became worse and more hopeless. By the assistance of Lord Egremont who gave me the money, I paid off a demand on the property equal to 6,000£. I recoverd a debt of four thousand more and compounded for almost nothing legacies to the amount of another thousand. The residue remaining to my family would be upwards of 20,000£ & who would imagine when Lord Egremont offerd to become Trustee for the proper distribution of that Sum, but that all my pecuniary difficulties were over——

Alas! no—Mr Smith himself is come from Scotland to oppose it. He wants to take not only my fortune but all that his Father left his Children to his own use. He desires me, hearing I have been in an ill state of health, to die as speedily as I can that he, at the Age of 58, may marry again & have a young family on whom he intends to bestow what belongs to me & my children—— The Man is mad, yet not enough so to be confined while he is quite enough so to complete the ruin of a family I have exhausted my life in attempting to save. What we are now to do I have no guess, & yet I cannot escape from the misery of being worried with it all, as I would most willingly do, while another Summer is wearing away, & my spirits & health daily declining.

Can you wonder, Dear Sir, that I have no courage to write to my friends while I am thus a persecuted victim of whose misery there seems no end? Sickness too in my family has been very hard upon me. My eldest daughter[4] has had three severe fits of illness almost immediately following each other, & I have been deprived by the necessity of attending her not only of all the literary society I expected to have had when I fixd in London, but of the advantage which my own languid health requires of a little quiet & occasional country air with my friends. She is now slowly recovering from a sore throat & fever, & the "time of flowers" is rapidly going by, a time which I may never live to see again.

Mr Caldwell,[5] for whose acquaintance I cannot be too grateful, had nearly been sent from my door after he had settled to fav^r^ me with his company at dinner, from this unfortunate illness, for it was announced to be infectious. However he had no fears & by his favouring me with his conversation at dinner, I pass'd on Wednesday last the only agreeable day I have long known. Our tastes are so much the same, & he is so pleasant company as well as appearing of so benevolent a disposition that I assure you I shall think the notice with which he honors me a great acquisition. Of literary News, I am as ignorant as the veriest badaud that ever drank tea at White Conduit[6] house "with china & gilt spoons." I enquired for your last publication[7] at Cadell and Davies's who informed me they did not print it & could not tell me who did, nor, as it has never been advertised, did I know 'till Mr Caldwell inform'd me. I shall now procure it & read it the moment I am releas'd from my present durance, if ever that may be——

Our friends the Lees have publishd a third volume of Canterbury tales in which that of the elder Sister is certainly not the best.[8] As a labourer in the same vineyard, I hold it best to "say nothing" but doubt whether the Sisters will acquire any great addition to their fame by this work. Mr Roscoe seems the favourite Poet of the day,[9] & Mrs West the favourite Novellist,[10] but my time has been so occupied that I have not read either the one or the other. Indeed it seems strangly perverse, but since I have been stationary & had an house of my own & a bookseller, I find I can neither read nor write, & I beleive I can only do either, as I <can> So that if the clouds of the present hour break away, I shall set out for the Sea & perhaps give up my house.

Allow me however to hope you will write to me here & soon—that you will tell me y° forgive me & that you suffer me still to be, Dear Sir, your most oblig'd & faithful humble Ser^t,

Charlotte Smith

Lionel is well and soon expected with his regiment from Quebec.[11]

Huntington MS (HM10823). Address: Josepth Cooper Walker Esqre/ Eccles Street/ Dublin. Postmark: JU/ 24/ 99; JU/ 28/ 99.

NOTES

1. See CS to Walker, 9 Jan. 1799 and n. 4. For many years, William had made generous contributions of £100 to 300 a year to his mother and siblings, but after he returned to India, CS never again mentions receiving money from him. Indeed, she later wrote that "Bengal ships, tho my eldest Son is there, never bring me even letters" (CS to Sarah Rose, 10 Sept. 1804).

2. William and Harriet boarded the *William Pitt* at Portsmouth 23 Mar. 1799. It sailed out on 4 Apr. with a large fleet of East Indiamen, including whalers. Of the twenty-four passengers, seven were women, including a Mrs. Wilson and Mrs. Staunton, bound like Harriet for Bengal. They disembarked at Diamond Harbor 1–2 Sept.

3. See CS to Walker, 9 Jan. 1799.

4. Charlotte Mary.

5. Andrew Caldwell (1733–1808), a wealthy Irish solicitor, was a patron and encourager of the arts. Along with an interest in architecture and the arts, he had a large library with many works on botany and natural history. Nichols's memoir in *Illustrations of Literary History* describes Caldwell as a "worthy and amiable" man with "gentle and pleasing" manners: "as his benevolence and other virtues made him generally respected through life, so his urbanity, various knowledge, and cultivated taste, extremely endeared him to the circle of his friends" (8:25). Caldwell's regard for CS is evident in his sympathetic remarks about her in letters cited in Nichol's memoir of him. In 1801, he observed that CS "is a woman full of sorrows, and I fear her misfortunes are scarcely to be mitigated" (8:35, Caldwell to Bishop Percy, 8 June). A few months after her death, he remembered, "I became acquainted with her in the year 1799, and she favoured me with three or four letters . . ." (8:65, Caldwell to Percy, 4 Mar. 1807). Caldwell's interests and character must have appealed to her very much.

6. An archaic spelling of *Conduct*. A *badaud* is a gaper or gawker.

7. *Historical Memoir on Italian Tragedy, from the Earliest Period to the Present Time* (1799).

8. The Lee sisters' *Canterbury Tales* (1797–1805) contained modern stories told by seven pilgrims on their way to Canterbury. Each sister contributed one story to vol. 3 (1799). Sophia's was "The Clergyman's Tale: Henry." On Sophia and Harriet Lee, see CS to Cadell and Davies, 1 May 1796, n. 4.

9. Not only was William Roscoe of Liverpool not the favorite poet of the day, but he has few admirers now. In addition to the poems mentioned above (see CS to Cadell and Davies, 5 Jan. 1798, n. 2), he had most recently published "The Nurse," a short pamphlet translated from Luigi Tansillo, urging mothers to breast-feed their children.

10. Jane West (1758–1852), like CS, was a poet, novelist, and author of children's books. Of her eight novels, West had published three by 1799: *The Advantages of Education* (1793), *A Gossip's Story* (1796), and *A Tale of the Times* (1799).

11. Written upside down in the top margin of the page.

To Benjamin Smith[1]

[London, 4 July 1799]

We are taking every measure possible to expedite the final signature of the Deeds. They are now gone to Lymington. Mr Parkin[2] holds about £130 Sterlg in the 3 pC^ts^ belonging to your Fathers Estate which was what Dyer[3] demanded & Lord Egremont supply'd[.] [T]his & whatever further is wanted to complete the first £200 to be paid you, We Will have ready as soon as the New Trustees[4] are competent to give discharges. The rest I imagine you will not object to receive at 4, 6, or 8 Months & within the year according to the agreement which your Son Charles[5] made on honor with you. But if there is any particular way in which this business wd most accommodate you, Name it, and while I do intervene at all, it will be my wish, and is I am sure the Trustees intention to do all that is right towards you. CS[6]

Petworth House Archives MS. No address or postmark.

NOTES

1. In a letter to Egremont (13 Oct. 1802), BS quoted part of this letter CS had written to him on 4 July 1799 (unpub. letter in PHA #0.11).

2. Along with John Robinson, the current hated trustees to Richard Smith's estate, soon to be replaced by Egremont and Turner.

3. Sir John Dyer was trustee to the estate before Parkin. His younger brother Thomas Dyer married BS's sister and was therefore concerned in the settlement of the estate. It is not clear which Dyer made this request or when.

4. The earl of Egremont and CS's brother Nicholas Turner.

5. Charles Dyer Smith, after the loss of a leg at Dunkirk in 1793, remained in the army. In Feb. 1798, he was lieutenant to the company of invalids at Berwick-upon-Tweed near his father's Scottish residence in Hamilton.

6. To this extract from CS's letter, BS added a related note from their son: "Major [Lionel] Smith's agreement relative to the £400 to be paid last year: 'The Agreement made with Mr Benjn Smith was Viz £200 on or before the 7th Octr 1801 & £200 in the course of the Three following Months.'"

To Thomas Cadell, Jr., and William Davies

{London, 19 July 1799}
Gentlemen,

I acknowledge myself extremely remiss in not having sent you the additional MMS before, but I have been extremely ill & not less harrass'd than usual, The support of all the family being still thrown upon me, while there is twelve hundred pounds now in hand belonging to them. The perplexities I have been involved in while attempting to get the signatures of all parties to the deeds that constitute Lord Egremont & My Brother Trustees have been not only very prejudicial to my health which has long been much shaken but to my pocket & devours every thing faster than I can collect it, while a mind so tiezed with perplexing business is ill fitted to write poetry or even prose or, what is more difficult, to give the finishing hand to productions of the former description where one has some reputation to lose.

Dr Reynolds[1] has order'd me into the Country, but it is impossible for me to go till these long depending deeds are quite completed. I beg leave however to assure you that I will do my utmost to get y^r work out of my hands immediately.

I thank you for hav^g transmitted two Letters from India with duplicates of a bill received as long since as last March from My Son Nicholas.

The death of a near & beloved relation[2] has prevented my noticing y^r Letter sooner.

I am, Gent^n, y^r most obed hble Ser^t,
Charlotte Smith

5 Upper Baker Street
July 19th 1799

Yale University MS. No address or postmark.

NOTES

1. Henry Revell Reynolds, M.D. (1745–1811), of London, recently appointed physician extraordinary to George III.
2. Not identified.

To Thomas Cadell, Jr., and William Davies

{Bignor Park, 27 August 1799}
Gentlemen,

A very few days after I wrote to you excusing myself for the delay which ill health had occasion'd in the completion of my engagement with you, I became so alarmingly ill that my family insisted on my again seeing Dr Reynolds, who pronounced my disorder to be undoubtedly dropsical oweing to extreme weakness from over fatigue & uneasiness of mind. He wished me to go immediately to the Sea side, but the affairs which oweing to Mr Robinson have so long perplex'd & impoverish'd my family and myself, being as I was once more taught to hope on the eve of being concluded, and the difficulty of finding proper accommodations on the Kentish Coast, added to my fear of expence while the business still remaind unsettled, were considerations that united to determine me on accepting the offer my Sister Mrs Dorset[1] made to lend me the house now hers, which has for many years been the habitation of my family. I have found very great benefit from this my native air, but many very disagreeable symptoms still remain. In looking over one of my favorite books, The Botanic Garden of Dr Darwin, I observe in a note that a pamphlet calld "Experiments on Musilagenous and purulent matter"[2] their is an account of the virtues of Digitalis in dropsics. It was printed for Mr Cadell in 1780. I shall be very much oblig'd to you to send it me from the White Horse, Fetter Lane, By Petworth & Arundel Stage, & also if you could send me any new Poetry which may be judged worth reading, & the two following works of Gilpin which I beleive will complete my set—"Picturesque remarks on the lakes of Cumberland and Westmoreland," D^o^ "on the Highlands of Scotland"[3]——

I have used every moment of my convalescence (save what the necessity of going out in a Park chair for exercise has robbed me of) in trying to finish in the best manner the little poems I owe you which I trust will not be worse done for being retouched in this beautiful & beloved spot. There are only two relative to which I have not been able to satisfy myself, but as my spirits & health are so much amended, I think I shall have power to give them the spirit they want in a very short time, & as this day, Teusday the 27th, is fix'd for the final dissolution of Mr Robinsons & Mr Parkins trust when Lord Egremont & My Brother will be invested with full power over the whole property belonging to my family, I hope if this does take place (tho I have been so often disappointed that I dare hardly say it will till I see it) that I shall receive pay^t^ of the great Sums I have expended for my family's support during their being under such infamous oppression, and of course be able to acquit myself of every obligation to those who have by loan or otherwise assisted me.

I am, Gentlemen, y^r^ oblig'd & obed^t^ Ser^t^, Charlotte Smith

If you are so obliging as to send the parcel, be pleas'd to direct it to me at the Revd N. Turners, Fittleworth near Petworth. The Petworth Coach goes by his door in its way to Arundel & will leave it there whereas, if it is left at Petworth, I seldom send thither & may not get it for some days. The coach comes down from the White Horse, Fetter Lane, Teusdays, Thursdays & Saturdays.

Yale University MS. Address: Messrs Cadell and Davies/ Strand/ London. Postmark: Fittleworth; F/ AUG28/ 99.

NOTES

1. Catherine Turner Dorset lived with her husband Capt. Michael Dorset at Bignor Park, the Turner family seat, where CS had lived from about the age of 3 until she was married at 15. In a letter to Sarah Rose (14 May 1805), CS explains that Bignor was made over to "Mr." Dorset when her brother Nicholas, often in financial difficulties, was unable to pay Catherine her annuity out of the estate. Rather than forgive the debt, Catherine sued for the estate and won. CS hoped that Bignor would stay with her sister, but Catherine's daughter's marriage necessitated selling it.

2. Erasmus Darwin's *Botanic Garden* (2 vols., 1789–92) is a poem in heroic couplets with extensive learned footnotes. The pamphlet, also by Darwin, is named in a long note in part II, "The Loves of the Plants." It describes symptoms of dropsy in detail; because CS is unusually interested in the pamphlet itself, it may describe her present physical condition. It reads in part: "The effect of this plant [foxglove] in that kind of Dropsy, which is termed anasarca, where the legs and thighs are much swelled, attended with great difficulty of breathing, is truly astonishing. In the ascites accompanied with anasarca of people past the meridian of life it will also sometimes succeed. The method of administering it requires some caution, as it is liable, in greater doses, to induce very violent and debilitating sickness, which continues one or two days, during which time the dropsical collection however disappears . . ." (2nd ed., p. 87).

3. William Gilpin (1724–1804) was a landscape draftsman who drew and engraved beautiful illustrations in a number of topographical works, including the two CS requested here, *Observations Relative Chiefly to Picturesque Beauty, Made in the Year 1772, On Several Parts of England; Particularly the Mountains, and Lakes of Cumberland and Westmoreland* (1786) and *Observations Relative Chiefly to Picturesque Beauty . . . of Great Britain; Particularly the High-lands of Scotland* (1789).

To Thomas Cadell, Jr., and William Davies

[London, 21 October 1799]
Gent^n,

I came to Town a few days since much recoverd in my health, yet still unable to encounter any fatigue. In consequence of the great expense of Housekeeping so continually encreas'd by taxes, I have quitted my house in Upper Baker Street for which, as my family are dispersed, I had no occasion & am for the present in lodgings, No 36 Alsops build^gs, new Road. Whither I have bro^t the Poetry I owe you finish'd all but a few notes & find my books are all pack'd in great boxes whence I cannot take out what I want without considerable trouble. Be so good therefore as to lend me Popes Homers

Odyssey from whence I must take the only note I cannot otherwise supply —& send me a copy of the Young Philosopher (which I will return) that I may correct a word or two of the poetry to be taken from thence. I am very sorry to have been so long in fulfilling this engagement, but I was for many weeks not only incapable of the least exertion, but afraid of attempting it, least I should never be able to fulfil my engagement at all.

I have the above books of my own, but it w^d^ take a whole day to look for them. I will return what I borrow with the MMS & hope not later than Wednesday or Thursday to do so in person. I am, Gent^n^, y^r^ obed^t^ Ser^t^,

Charlotte Smith

Monday, Octr 21st 1799

Private collection of Lucy Magruder. No address or postmark.

To Thomas Cadell, Jr., and William Davies

[London, 25 November 1799]

Mrs Smiths Comp^ts^ & thanks to Messrs Cadell and Davies for the perusal of the Novel she returns, which is better written than most she has lately met with, & has afforded her an agreeable amusement for an evening. M^rs^ CS. has received no proof from Mr Noble this week.[1]

25th Nov^r^ [17]99

Osborn Collection MS, Yale University. No address or postmark.

NOTE

1. That is, for the revised, enlarged second edition of *Elegiac Sonnets ii,* published in 1800, and printed by Richard Noble, 4 Great Shire Lane, Temple Bar.

To Thomas Cadell, Jr., and William Davies

[?London] Decr 19th [17]99

Gent^n^

I have been extremely distress'd by the unexpected death of a near relation[1] who came to Town from York on military business & died of a violent fever in a few days, for, as I was one of the only four relations he has in the world & no other was either in or near Town, the melancholy offices that follow'd fell to my lot as well as a very painful attendance on the poor Man who was delirious for many days. It has shook my uncertain health a good deal & must be my apology for not hav[g] call'd on you, as I have from day to day intended, to state to you why I was under the necessity of remaining so long in y[r] debt, which however I suppose you will not be supris'd or angry at when you recollect the state of W[est] I[ndies] property. We have 30 hgds[2] Sugar which have lain since August in M[r] Daniels warehouses, & our inconvenience has been extreme. Allow me to encrease the debt so much as will be done by the set plainly bound of "the Young Philosopher," As I have an opportunity of sending it to Bombay tomorrow, & I sh[d] take it as a fav[r] if you w[d] so pack them up as to enable me to forward them in as secure small a compass as possible to the person Who is so kind as to take charge of them. I am, Gent[n], y[r] most obed Ser[t], C Smith

Yale University MS. No address or postmark.

NOTES

1. Possibly her cousin, "the late Captain Towers," a son of her uncle William Towers, both of whom are named in CS to Egremont, 26 Oct. 1801. As their aunt Lucy Towers Smith had died in 1795, this cousin would have had few close relatives indeed.
2. Hogsheads, large casks or barrels, each containing 63 to 140 gallons of liquid.

To William Davies

[Place uncertain, before April 1800][1]
Sir,

I return the book of Sonnets with the few corrections necessary (which are not in the first post) imagining that as the whole is now ready (I was merely prevented from writing it all out fair yesterday & Wednesday by my daughter & her child coming to stay while they moved their furniture to other lodgings), you may like to put the first sheet to press. I imagine the Subscribers' names are to be taken out. After Sonnet 84th, the last in this book, will follow eight other Sonnets. And after the other poems, a small poem calld Lydia and the others from the Young Philosopher &c. Would you wish for a New Preface? I return The Young Philosopher & will send the other books back with the MMS as soon as the incessant interruptions from which I cannot escape will give me time to write them fair, I hope certainly on Monday. CS

Yale University MS. No address or postmark.

NOTE

1. Two clues help establish this letter's date between May 1799 and Apr. 1800. First, the reference to Lucy and her child places the note after 25 May 1799, the

christening of her first child, and before 29 Apr. 1800, the christening of her second. Second, *Elegiac Sonnets ii,* 2nd ed., omitted the list of subscribers to the first edition. To the second edition, CS added eight new sonnets after Sonnet 84 and four new lyrics, including "Lydia."

To Thomas Cadell, Jr., and William Davies

[?London, 6 March 1800]
Gent^n^

I send you a news paper in which one of my Sonnets in the book purchas'd by Mr Cadell in 88 is printed word for word as written by the Revd David Rivers.[1] Ab^t^ Six weeks ago, there was a series of five or six of them printed in the same way in one of the morning Papers, as some friends of mine inform'd me from Scotland. I have written to the Editor of the Morning Herald as this is rather too stupid & too impudent & own I wish it could be put an end to. I am much oblig'd to you for the loan of Mordaunt[2] which I will return in a few days. I imagine as I received no answer relative to the other books that it is not convenient to you to oblige me with them. I am, Gent^n^,

your oblig'd hble Ser^t^,
Charlotte Smith

March 6th 1800
Be so good as to send the N Paper by to nights post as directed.

Yale University MS. Address: Messrs Cadell & Davies/ Strand. No postmark.

NOTES

1. Rivers, a Dissenting divine, had published *The Beauties of Saurin* (1797) and was thought to have contributed to *Literary Memoirs of Living Authors* (1798) and the later *Biographical Dictionary of the Living Authors* (1816).

2. *Mordaunt. Sketches of Life, Characters, and Manners, in Various Countries* (1800), by Dr. John Moore. CS had earlier read his *Zeluco* and probably met him while at Henrietta O'Neill's (CS to unnamed recipient, 8 Dec. 1791 and n. 11).

To Thomas Cadell, Jr., and William Davies

[London, 19 March 1800]
Gentlemen,

I am applied to, to lend the Banish'd Man to Mrs Berkely,[1] the wife of the Admiral who is confined by hopeless illness & has no amusement but reading. But I had rather buy a set in boards to lend her, for I cannot refuse her, than send my own bound ones (which belong to my own set of books) into Sussex from whence they may never return, as nobody scruples keeping any books they get of me on the idea that I pay nothing for them myself. I have not seen the Banish'd Man advertis'd lately (tho Ethelinde was again advertis'd last week) but conclude you have plenty & beg you will be so good as to send me a set by the bearer in boards to be charged to my account. I sh^{d} have return'd with many thanks the 3 vol of Mordaunt, but my Servant is going to the City with an heavy parcel for Hackney School[2] & could hardly carry them. I am, Gent^{n}, y^{r} oblig'd Ser^{t},

Charlotte Smith

I wrote this yesterday but something happen'd that prevented my sending my servants thro the City & Strand. I must therefore trouble you to send the books. Did you forget "the Romance of real life" for me?——[3]

Yale University MS. Address: Messrs Cadell and Davies/ Strand/ P.P.p^{d}. Postmark: 7.O'clock PENNY POST PAID/ 19+MR/ 1800; Penny Post {illegible} paid.

NOTES

1. Emily Charlotte Berkeley, daughter of Lord George Lennox and wife of the Honorable George Cranfield Berkeley, rear admiral of the Blue in 1799.

2. CS's youngest son George may have been enrolled at this Dissenting school. That she sent him to school is clear from her remark in an unpublished letter to William Tyler (8 Sept. 1802) that she was still paying off his schooling.

3. Written upside down in top margin of the first page.

To Joseph Cooper Walker

Hastings, Sussex, May 18th 1800
Dear Sir,

I have on so many occasions experienced your kindness and regard that, altho I fear you have sometimes had reason to beleive me not sufficiently sensible of it, I venture once more to ask you if you can render one of my family a service which will be a considerable releif to me. I beleive you are one Letter in my debt, but, tho I imagined after the fortunate circumstance of Lord Egremonts taking the Trust of my childrens property, that I should enjoy some tranquillity and have time to avail myself of the obliging wishes of many distant friends that we might sometimes hear of each other, it has so happen'd that between illness and the affairs that are still left to me to settle & the sad situation of Lucy which has most distressfully engaged my attention, I never had so little time before, either for any literary employment or to dedicate to the friends I have so much reason to love and esteem.

That unfortunate young Woman, my poor Lucy, married, as I beleive you know, a Man who, tho he has very good talents, was absolutely without one shilling of fortune or any chance of ever having any and, what is worse, without any profession, having only since he married undertaken to pursue the study of physic,[1] for which her family have found the money (as it is in this Country attended with great expence), doubting whether his future success would ever answer their endeavours, and seeing with concern that Lucy must in the mean time suffer all the evils of indigence, all they could do being too little to support her & the persons now attached to her while her husband could contribute nothing. Whatever were my feelings at the beginning of this unfortunate connection, with which I had on many accounts very little reason to be pleas'd, I could not see my daughter circumstanced as she has been without forgetting every thing but that she was still my child & in distress. I have therefore very much inconvenienced myself to supply her necessities during two very dangerous lyings in, the last of which happend two months since, & had so nearly cost her her life that for some days she was given over.[2]

I was very unwell at the time, but being oblig'd to attend upon her night & day for almost a week, I caught a violent cold, which, added to fatigue and anxiety, has brought on the same or rather a greater degree of weakness than that I so slowly recover'd from last year. As my life, however valueless to myself, is absolutely necessary still to some parts of my family, I should have conform'd to the directions of my medical friends and have come sooner to the Sea side, but it was requisite that I should stay to arrange some business by which Lionel was to be releived from the pressure of debts unavoidably contracted since his being station'd in America (now five years) and a small supply obtain'd for Lucy which however debts almost immediately swallow'd up. As soon as this was done, I came hither with George my youngest Son & brought the eldest of Lucy's two infants with me as he has always been a weak and unhealthy child. She follow'd me with the new born child as soon as I was settled in an house, and I now must endeavour to support them as I can till Mr Newhouse can procure some means of at least assisting in it—— ——

It is now half a year since Mr Newhouse has been private Tutor to the Son of Lord Allen,[3] who is at Westminster School & is, I understand, a very promising young Man in point of talents. It appears that Mr Newhouse has given great satisfaction to Lord Allen. His terms are 100£ a year, which the Bishop of Killala[4] and his Lordship were at first dispos'd to think high, but from Letters I have lately seen, it seems as if they were now perfectly satisfied. Now, Dear Sir, I come to the point on which I wish to ask your assistance. I have no doubt but that you are acquainted with Lord Allen, and, in considering what can be done to releive the present exigence in which Mr Newhouse finds himself, it has occurred to me that you may perhaps be so good as to interest yourself, for me & for Lucy, by contriving to intimate to Lord Allen that, however small the Sum may appear, yet such is Mr Newhouses situation, that the half yearly payment of 50£ made now, will be of the greatest use to him, and consequently to me, who must otherwise support this family wholly myself, a task which ill health that I have now no hope of every [*sic*] conquering renders it almost impossible for me to do, and I own to you that the solicitude I feel for the living, added to the regret & anguish I have now felt five years for the loss of my loveliest and most deserving child,[5] is slowly undermining not only my frame but the few powers of mind I possess'd, and the fatigue and interruption of young children in a small lodging house, when I have so much need of repose, prevents my now having a chance of regaining strength either of mind or body. I know the favor I solicit, even if you are so good as to undertake & succeed in so delicate a commission, is only a temporary releif, but if it carries them on till July, I have hopes that I shall receive remittances from the Estate (if we are not so fortunate as to sell it) and that we may make some permanent provision for poor Lucy and her children & place them, after Mr Newhouses engagement with Mr Allen is over, in some Country town where he may obtain practice as a Physician.

Thus, dear Sir, I have troubled you once more with a detail of some of my present distresses—indeed the heaviest of them, & I know that if you can assist me you will; if not that you will tell me so with the candour & friendship I have ever found from you and which I assure you I highly value. I have hardly left myself room for any other topic, & unfortunately that nearest my heart after what I have written is also a melancholy one. I mean poor Hayleys unhappy situation. Yet however strange it may seem, after our long friendship, I perhaps know less of this than you do. The last intelligence I had about him was from Lord Egremont, who told me about three weeks since that his Son was at the last extremity; but as I have heard this so long, & when I saw Mr Hayley in Sussex in October, he seem'd not to entertain the slightest hopes, I imagine the unhappy young Man may still live tho his recovery is I suppose decidedly impossible. Notwithstanding this cruel misfortune—the greatest in my opinion that the human heart can sustain—our friend has had the resolution to finish an elaborate poem on Sculpture,[6] a subject which I should have imagined it very difficult to treat with spirit and calmness, as it was to that science he had devoted his suffering Son. I do not know whether the poem is publish'd, for of literary matters I know nothing, having been distracted with my domestic troubles & not having seen even a newspaper for some weeks. I am now, tho in the same County, almost seventy miles from Eartham or Felpham at which last place M[r] Hayley now resides almost entirely, & his Son may be dead for aught I shall know here.[7] He never writes to me now, & tho my regard & good wishes for him can never diminish, I content myself with feeling that my gratitude & regard for him is proof against even apparent unkindness & never importune him with expressions of friendship which can do him, certainly, no good & which he seems not to wish to hear. His friend, the admirable and unhappy Cowper, is I beleive dead.[8] I saw his death in a Magazine & imagine it to be true——

I expect Lionel home in a few months. I am sure you will be glad to hear he has an excellent character & is likely to rise fast in his profession—— It is a profession I do not love tho. You will learn the confusion London has been thrown into by attempts on the life of the King.[9] Our general situation from the high price of the most immediate necessaries of life is far from being pleasant. I am however only a lodger who consider my lodging in this changed & shatter'd form as very brief; while it continues, I cannot cease to be, Dear Sir,

your most oblig'd friend and Servant,
Charlotte Smith

Pray let me hear from you & direct to Cadell & Davies.

I beg y[r] pardon for not directing to y[r] Bro[r] as you desired, but I have not his address here & cannot recall it to my mind.[10]

Huntington MS (HM10824). Address: Josepth Cooper Walker Esq[re]/ S[t] Vallori near Dublin/ or Eccles Street/ Dublin. Postmark: HASTINGS; MAY 19/ {1800}; MY/ 22/ 1800.

NOTES

1. Certainly one of CS's objections to the marriage would have been Thomas Newhouse's late start on a career.

2. Lucy and Thomas Newhouse's second son, William Charles, was christened 29 Apr. 1800.

3. The Honorable Joshua William Allen (d. 1845), son of Joshua, Viscount Allen (1728–1816), entered Oxford the next year on 22 Oct. 1801 at age 18. According to Cokayne, the son went on to fight under Wellington in the Peninsular War and was known for his "dashing conduct." Money may well have been an issue: a note in Cokayne adds that Allen was "a penniless Lord and Irish Pensioner, well behaved, and not encumbered with too much principle" (*Complete Peerage,* 1:111).

4. Joseph Stock (1740–1813), Trinity College, Dublin; he served as bishop of Killala between 1798 and 1810.

5. Augusta de Foville, who died on 23 Apr. 1795 of consumption.

6. Hayley's *An Essay on Sculpture: In a Series of Epistles to John Flaxman, Esq., R.A.* (1800).

7. Thomas Alphonso Hayley died on 2 May 1800.

8. William Cowper died on 25 Apr. 1800.

9. This second attempt on the life of George III occurred at Drury Lane Theatre on 15 May 1800, as the king entered his box for a command performance of Colly Cibber's *She Would and She Would Not.* He was unharmed by the would-be assassin, James Hatfield, and calmly looked round the theater before taking his seat (Brooke, *King George III,* p. 315; Ayling, *George the Third,* p. 181).

10. Written upside down at the top edge of the final page in a tiny hand.

To Barabara Marsden Meyer[1]

Hastings, Sussex, June 9th 1800
My Dear Madam,

As I heard only a few days since from my Sister that our friend had at length sustain'd the loss he has so long apprehended (& she mention'd nothing more than that "Mr Hayleys Son was dead which she supposed I must know"), I cannot tell how much time has pass'd since this cruel event. Tho I now have no intercourse with Mr Hayley and know that what is usualy call'd condolance is the most useless and oppressive of all intended kindnesses & therefore would by no means write to him, yet I cannot be satisfied without hearing about him. You were so very good to me some months ago that I hesitate not to trouble you again tho rather doubting whether you may be at Kew.

Will you, dear Madam, have the kindness to let me hear how my ever valued friend bears this sad loss? Where he is? and how the unfortunate Mother of the lamented young Man has been able to sustain her misery, for I know her sufferings will deeply affect the spirits of Mr H.

I came hither as the quietest Sea place I could find, & in that respect it quite answers my expectations. The Country around it is various & beautiful, but as I am not able to walk & cannot afford a carriage, I am not much benefitted by that circumstance. All I regret however is that, tho in Sussex, I am so far from my few friends in the Western part of it that I know no more of them than if I were in Cumberland. This circumstance and my knowledge that you & Mr Meyer are always in correspondence with Mr Hayley will I hope excuse to you my requesting you to take the trouble of writing to me—— When you do so, direct to me only by the name of Mrs Smith, adding (as Smith is no name at all) at Mr Bredes, Hastings. I find it so very unpleasant & sometimes inconvenient to be known as a bookmaker at these places where there are always some idle folks who have nothing to do but to saunter about and ask questions that I sink as much as I can the luckless appellation of one, who is, dear Madam, with great esteem,

your faithful Ser^t^,
Charlotte Smith

I never saw Mr Cowpers death in the papers, but I was told in company he was certainly dead & afterwards read it in a Magazine so that I cannot doubt the truth of it. Alas! how many & severe are the losses our friend & I have suffer'd since we pass'd (at least I pass'd) so delightful a fortnight at Eartham in 92!

Boston Public Library MS.[2] *Address: Mrs Meyer./ Kew Green——{"Mrs Charlotte Smith" written between these two lines in another hand.} Postmark: {London}; 4 o'Clock/ JU 10/ 1800EV; {another stamp is illegible}.*

NOTES

1. See Biographical Notes.
2. This folder (Boston Pub RBR Ch. H. 3. 19) has a handsome engraving endorsed "Charlotte Smith/ from a Picture by [John] Opie in the possession of/ the late William Hayley Esq:/ London. Jan 1, 1824. Published by W. Walker, 5 Grays Inn Square Drawn by G. Clint ARA. Engraved by A. Duncan." But the picture was in fact by George Romney.

To the earl of Egremont

Hastings, July 9th 1800
My Lord,

I beg leave to enclose to your Lordship a copy of a Letter I have to day receiv'd from Mr Alleyne[1] written to him from a Mr Prescod with proposals for the sale of the Estate. As it is on this that my familys provision as well as any peace & competence I may hereafter obtain depends, I am persuaded your Lordship with your usual goodness will give the affair your early consideration. I am utterly unable to say how far the mode of payment for so considerable a Sum is safe. Messrs Daniel & Co. & Blackman & Co.[2] are undoubtedly very responsible Men. But I own, considering the fluctuation of West India property & the chances against any Mercantile houses in time of War, I should suppose it would be more prudent to ask a mortgage in the estate as security till the whole Sum is paid which (tho perhaps I do not express myself clearly) is, as I understand, sometimes done for better security in these cases, for I beleive it has sometimes happend that persons having paid only part of the purchase money have taken possession of an Estate & kept it without fulfilling the whole agreement. I should be the more cautious about this Mr Prescod because I beleive it is the same Man who in partnership with one ONeale owed us & still owes us a Sum of money which, oweing to some mistake in the presentation of the Bill, he evaded paying—which was rather a dishonest trick.[3]

I shall send a copy of this Letter to Charles and Charlotte but take no other steps till I have the honor of your Lordships commands. Whatever may then be necessary for me to do, I will set about immediately in regard to going to Town to meet Mr Alleyne &ct. It would releive me from inexpressible torments was this business once gone thro——

Such is my reliance on a continuation to me, of that kindness and beneficence to which I have been so much indebted, that I ventured to enclose in another cover a Letter I have received from Mr Brathwaite,[4] who with Mr Robinson & Mr Dyer are appointed Trustees in the settlement made on me of 2000£ now immediately payable in consequence of Mrs Chafys death[5] & to be divided share and share alike among the children of my marriage after the death of Mr Smith & of mine.

Mr Brathwaite is near eighty years old & on my application to him seems, however willing to act, to beleive that his doing so could not long be useful to me. The other two Trustees I have never applied to, but I said to Mr Brathwaite that Your Lordship was my best & almost my only friend, for that to you I owed every thing that will be saved from the wreck of Richard Smiths property, & the means of subsisting, while I contended for it. That as your Lordship had so generously undertaken a trust unavoidably attended with considerable trouble, I did hope you would at my request have the goodness to take this, in which there would be none. I presumed too much perhaps on your past kindness, yet I hope your Lordship would not deny me this request, which will make my mind easy as to the security of my children for this little property. Mr Robinson and Mr Dyer never having acted would not I imagine hesitate to give up the Trust to your Lordship & My Brother if you will condescend in this second instance to befriend me as Trustee. But should I appear too apt to intrude, beleive me, my Lord, the favours I have already received will never be lessen'd in my opinion, tho I expect too much in asking an encrease of them.

I believe the money Mr Prescod offers is exactly the Sum for which three freeholders valued the property last year. Mr Turner has the valuation. I think by his Prescods eagerness to give the same money tho there are seven Negroes lost (I cannot guess how) that the estate is worth more, but I submit it to your Lordships judgement whether, circumstanced as the parties selling are & under all the apprehensions that are at present entertaind for the West Indies, it would not be prudent to close with the offer if the payment of the money is secure.

As Mr Prescod seems to expect as one condition to have our answer in

September, I imagine no time is to be lost. I have therefore written by this post to my Brother, desiring him to wait on you as soon as your Lordship permits him with the valuation, & he will write to me immediately upon it as you shall direct.

I have a short Letter from Mr Alleyne saying he shall be in Town soon but giving me no information as to the produce this year. Mr Breme,[6] another of the Attornies, will be in England ab^t^ the 20th of August. The accounts are come to Mr Daniels, & I shall send for them down.

I trust that, as things are at present situated, your Lordship will not think me guilty of an impropriety if I solicit you to Authorize Messrs Daniels to pay M^r^ B Smiths half yearly payment of 40£ & to furnish me with a small supply for my present use, as I am a good deal distress'd—— In all likelihood, there will be effects enough come by the August fleet to support these demands. I request the favor of you to direct Mr Turner to give me an answer.

I have to day a Letter from Mrs Dorset which is <u>meant</u> to induce me to apply again to your Lordship for your interposition to induce Mr Turner to drop the suit.[7] She complains heavily of the injuries the property has received at Ashling. Her house has been broken open & the trees destroy'd. She says it will fall during the winter & that all this happens when no good can possibly accrue to Mr Turner by the dispute. I am myself afraid it will involve him in a great deal of trouble. But my endeavours to conciliate have been so unsuccessful that I hardly dare venture to try again & still less to ask you my Lord to give any more of your time where your benevolent meaning seem'd so little to be understood, Or valued, as it ought. I am y^r^ Lordships ever oblig'd Ser^t^, Charlotte Smith[8]

Petworth House Archives MS. No address or postmark.

NOTES

1. John Forster Alleyne (1762–1823), chief judge of the Court of Common Pleas, of Barbados, was involved in the sale of Gay's plantation to William Prescod (see Biographical Notes). Gay's was the single largest holding of the Smith trust in Barbados, and from it, the family regularly received income from hogsheads of sugar cane. Prescod offered £21,000 Barbados currency for the entire estate, which consisted of 257 acres of land with buildings, 171 "Negroes," and cattle, sheep, hogs, and one horse. Only 120 acres were under cultivation owing to the rockiness of the rest. A wealthy landowner with six estates and £50,000 to 80,000 in securities, Prescod bought the plantation for a large down payment of £10,000, then proposed paying off the remaining money with yearly payments of one-third, or £3,331. Over the next six years, receiving this money was critical to CS's finances, and she often mentions the difficulty of collecting it.

2. The estate had been dealing with Thomas Daniel and Sons, merchants, of Minc-

ing Lane, since 1797, and George Blackman, Esq., and Co., Chatham Place, since 1795. Daniel and Sons ended up with the Prescod account.

3. On O'Neale and the outstanding debt, see CS to William Prescod, 4 Aug. 1800.

4. John Brathwaite was a trustee on the first marriage settlement between BS and CS and co-signed their second marriage settlement of 18 Aug. 1773 (PHA #8204).

5. Mrs. Henrietta Meriton Turner Chafys, CS's stepmother. Miss Meriton's dislike of her prospective stepdaughter led Nicholas Turner and aunt Lucy Towers to arrange Charlotte's marriage to BS. Interestingly, this deed of settlement for £2,000 was drawn up between Nicholas Turner and BS on 24 and 25 Aug. 1764 (PHA #8204)—months in advance of Charlotte and BS's marriage on 23 Feb. 1765. This suggests a longer courtship than her biographers have reported.

6. Breme was acting as John Forster Alleyne's agent in the sale of Gay's.

7. CS's younger brother, Nicholas, was defendant in a suit in Chancery brought against him by their younger sister, Catherine Dorset, on unknown charges. In addition, he was in debt, had borrowed money from CS, and had sued his parishioners at Fittleworth, possibly for nonpayment of tithes. William Tyler's letterbooks suggest that the Turner v. Dorset case was under way as early as May 1800 (PHA #5482); it was still unsettled on 1 Feb. 1802 (PHA #5483), when Tyler wrote to Dorset that he had to prepare briefs because Dorset was advancing the cause. Tyler adds that Turner had tried early on for a "friendly adjustment of the objects of the Suit" and continued to hope for a referee so that the outcome would "fully establish his Honor as a gentleman & his Probity as a Clergyman."

Turner's case against his parishioners is first mentioned in the letterbooks on 17 June 1801 (PHA #5483). The settlement of the case of Turner v. Henry Chalwin is described by Tyler's 29 Jan. 1803 letter to Rev. Dunster: it was settled in Turner's favor, but he was not given costs (PHA #202). Several subsequent letters shed more light on this family feuding: see CS to Egremont, 18 July 1800, 9 Aug. 1800, and 7 Feb. 1803.

8. An enclosure in this letter reads:

Copy.

To the Honble John Forster Alleyne

April 7th 1800.

Dear Sir.

Agreeably to what pass'd betwixt you and myself some days ago, I send you a calculate &c, underneath of what I would give for Gay's plantation, supposing I could have an answer, and the time of taking it up to be about September next. It was apprais'd as pr inventory in June 1798. a time when perhaps Negroes and Cattle &c. were never in more demand or at so high a price in this Country. The land, buildings stock and Negroes as pr inventory are apprais'd—Vis.

171 Negroes	to £11260
257 Acres land & buildings ————	7710
1 Horse, Cattle, sheep and hogs.——	788.15.
	19, 758.15.

But notwithstanding there has been a decrease of seven Negroes since the appraisement, I am willing to give the amount of it say Nineteen thousand seven hundred and fifty eight pounds fifteen shillings Barbados Currency. & to pay for the young crops &c by appraisment at the time of taking up which at present affords but a very dreary prospect: however should it meet the wishes of the parties concern'd I will give 21,000£ Barbados Currency for the Estate & Crop &c as it may stand in the month of September next, notwithstanding I conceive the value of the crops will be very trifling from its appearance. I am induced to make this latter offer with a view of preventing any delay, as it is my earnest wish and intention to get to England as soon as possible, and this business can only be transacted while I am in this Island. It may perhaps strike any person not acquainted with that Estate, that 30£ p[r] Acre is a short price for land—It may not be amiss to hint, that only 120 Acres can be planted in canes, and that mostly very rocky—and a great deal of the land can hardly be said to be worth the Church dues.

The mode of payment I shall propose is at foot——I only beg leave to remind you that if the terms should meet with approbation it will be necessary to send over proper vouchers, with full power &c for making good the title. I am with much respect Dear Sir your most obed[t] humble Ser[t]

(Signd) William Prescod.

CS continues by way of explanation:

After paying down what money may be necessary in Barbados Bills will be given immediately on London, payable at 3, & 6 months for the Amount———save 10,000 Sterling for which bills will also be immediately given as follow.

⅓ payable in one year. A bill—for £3333.6.8. St[g]
with interest on 10,000£ St[g] at 5pC[t]. . . 500
£3833.6.8

⅓ payable in two years at D[o] for —— 3333.6.8 St[g]
with interest on 6666.13.4 a D[o]—— 333.6.8
£3666.13.4

⅓ payable in 3 years a D[o]——— 3333.6.8.
with in[ts] on 3333.6.8. at D[o]. 166.13.4
£3500

The above proposals are in consequence of supposing persons in England would be better satisfied with English security. I purpose to draw the above bills on the Houses of Mess[rs] Tho[s] Daniel & Co. & Mess[rs] Geo Blackman & Co—and I have no objection to their being consulted as to their acceptance if the parties have any doubts. The Exchange to be governed by the rate at the time of drawing.

To the earl of Egremont

Hastings July 18th 1800
My Lord

Since I last took the liberty of troubling you with a Letter, I have receiv'd one from Mrs Dorset (not in anr to my last but to a former one of conciliation) which convinces me I ought not to think of going to Bignor, as it is not only impossible for me to hear with patience such ungrateful reflections on my best friends & the real benefactor of her family (so that we should quarrel in half an hour), but I hate hypocrisy & cant & cannot keep my temper when a Woman talks of trying her interest with the Bishop for her Brother while she refuses him an hundred pounds & involves him in a Lawsuit. I was really unwilling to beleive all that narrowness of heart existed in my Mothers daughter which now forces itself upon me too Strongly. She desires me "to make haste if I do come because she shall take advantage of the "Beau saison" (which, only she despises the French language too much to be correct, is usually I beleive written belle saison[1]) "to go into the East of Sussex (on a visit to Dear Chancellor Hollist[2] of course)" which is as much as to say, dont come at all—— She is besides "afraid of the expence of Georges Horse (who has no horse)" & she is so far from being able to keep an horse that Mr Bishop[3] cheats her, & she is going to sell her Cow"——

No—I will write ballads to be sung in St Pauls church yard or hung against Whitehall Wall at a penny a couplet, Rather than George shall owe her a blade of grass or an oat—— She, poor Woman, is oppress'd by every body & has no protector but him who is the husband of the Widow & father of the fatherless! Such cant makes me so cross that I have written her a Letter she will not like, which however I would not have done while there remaind the least hope of what I did flatter myself she intended I should try at—a reconciliation with her Brother. In my last Letter I even offerd to try to raise a part of the money (tho I never was poorer than I am now) to settle this matter with her Brother, & relieve him from the distress which threatens him with a jail. I shall only have an insulting answer, & what I cannot bear is her going out of her way to say what she thinks—exceedingly bitter things of every one for whom she beleives I have any affection or friendship and of those to whom she knows I have such very great obligations. If she was with the Laird of Raith[4] again, I would gladly go to Bignor where I paid for every thing I had last year—either for myself, Son or Servants, even to the milk of her Cow——

But as it is I cannot ~~send I~~ beleive that it will be necessary, my Lord, to send out our determination by the August Packet, as Mr Prescod seems to make a point, indeed a condition, of the purchase, that the plantation shall be made over to him in September. I have written to every person likely to inform me how far his proposals are such as can be safely accepted and to all the parties concern'd, & I hope to have their answers in the course of a week. I wish <to> know & have enquird if M[r] Prescod has any agent here with whom the agreement can be closed (as I rather fear his retreating), and as soon as I have collected every particular necessary, I shall hope to have your Lordships commands as to whom I am to apply to, to have the proper papers prepared, imagining that it must be done by some eminent conveyancer. There is so little time that I take the liberty of requesting you, my Lord, to enable me by your Letter to M[r] Daniel ab[t] the advance) to leave this place whenever the business may be in a state of forwardness so as to make my going to, or being near Town, requisite. It is my family's little all, & on the sale & payment, depends whether I shall, however late, have a small certain income to die upon (for I have not much hope of living upon it) & enabling my poor George to live after me.

My poor Brother is so tardy that I {am} compelled to give your Lordship more trouble than I would otherwise do. Charles and Charlotte consent willingly to the sale & will come up whenever their signatures are necessary. I have such an inflammation in my eyes that I write in pain & I fear illegibly. My situation is the only excuse for my so often intruding on your time. Pardon it, as you have already done much importunity from

y[r] Lordships truly oblig'd Ser[t], Charlotte Smith

Petworth House Archives MS. No address or postmark.

NOTES

1. CS is correct, but her own French is not without error.

2. Richard Hollist, Esq., an equity draftsman at Pump-Court, Middle Temple, is elsewhere named as a lawyer and family advisor on several pending cases. He signed as executor to Catherine Dorset's will on 5 Sept. 1794 (WSRO, Hawkins papers E76).

3. Later letters name the Honorable William Bishop as involved in the sale of Gay's plantation. Henry Bishop of Spring Hall, Barbados, represented the family there, but it is not clear which one, if either of these, would have cheated Mrs. Dorset.

4. William Berry came to the surname and arms of Ferguson and the estate of Raith, Kirkaldy, Fifeshire, when his uncle Robert Ferguson died in 1782. His father, David Berry, was a wealthy merchant, and William Berry, or Sir Ronald C. Ferguson, died worth £300,000. As Sir Ronald had had to change his name to obtain the estate, CS is sarcastic. Sir Ronald was uncle to Mary and Agnes Berry. Their correspondence, *The Berry Papers,* does not suggest that the sisters knew Catherine Dorset, however.

To Mary Hays

Hastings, July 26th 1800

I cannot, my dear Madam, look at the date of your last obliging Letter without doubts whether you can forgive my apparent negligence in leaving it so long unanswered. Apologies are generally feeble or false. I will make none, but relate the simple truth that the friend whom I wish'd to have commissiond to have looked out the books and who has the Key of my book room has been so ill that, as he lives in a village on the Essex road at a great distance from the quarter of the town where my lodgings are, I could not ask him to undertake, indeed he could not have undertaken, even so slight a journey.

I have myself been harrass'd with sufferings both of the mind and body with an account of which, however, I will not intrude upon your patience, but tho amid this delicious weather & on this very pleasant coast, I have been for many weeks almost entirely confin'd to my lodgings, I have been so much occupied with some very troublesome family business which it falls to my lot to transact that I have been equally prevented from continuing my labour for the press or writing to my friends, for having seldom written less than five and often seven or eight Letters a day, I was so fatigued by the time of dinner that it was impossible for me to write another line — — — —

If I could not at times have been a little amused with the study of botany, which by sending out into the fields & hedges I could indulge here, I should have hardly sustain'd my fatigued spirits at all, for of even tolerable Novels or books of any kind of amusement, the wretched collection in what they call a library here ~~does not~~ contains not a single specimen & still less of books of science. I marvel at the people who read such stuff or who find a wretched resource in lingering in a public room call'd a library, & I am afraid that the necessity my shatter'd health imposes upon me to frequent these places increases my extreme dislike to general society, while the impossibility, situated as I am, of enjoying that which is select makes me wholly a recluse—or rather would make me so if I was not about to be engaged again in a larger family, my eldest daughter coming from Scotland with one of her Brothers with whom she has resided this last year[1] & my Son Lionel being soon expected from Quebec where he has been five years. I shall then be surrounded by those who, without having the same tastes, have a right I believe to my time, and it is very seldom I can have the indulgence of literary society — — — — for which, & quiet alone, my heart languishes.

What you describe, however, in what are call'd literary meetings, I have more than once felt, & have wonder'd how it happens that when several persons of reputed talents are collected, the conversation is often so little pleasant. I was heretofore admitted, being then a mere novice & much in favor, to the celebrated conversations at Mrs Montagues,[2] & I found that the greatest difficulty I had was to resist a violent inclination to yawn tho I suppose every body talk'd their very best. Since, I have been at other assemblies of literati when I own I have been equally disappointed tho not quite in the same way.

Of several new acquaintance, I know none for whom I am more interested than Mrs Fenwick.[3] She always appears to me to be not only a Woman of talents but of great sweetness of temper & an excellent heart, & it grieves me when I hear she is not as fortunate as I am sure she deserves to be. I have really felt afraid of knowing more of her because I am sure I should love her enough to feel an additional source of concern in knowing so excellent a woman to be unhappy from causes which might be releived without having the power to remove those causes. I have known so much of pecuniary distress myself & feel so acutely what it is to have children for whose future fate the mothers heart is always oppressed, while their immediate wants claim every hour of the passing day, that it makes me feel acutely for our friend in whose pleasing countenance I imagine I see all those sensations. I wish I had the house & the income I ought to have; less for any other reason (for I am become indifferent to almost all the World calls good) than because I could then sometimes receive my friends & sometimes ask proofs of their friendship, but I am——married——! & tho released by my own resolution from the insufferable misery I endured from the age of fifteen (tho then like a child, I was half unconscious of it) till my thirty-seventh year, yet I am still in reality a slave & liable to have my bondage renew'd <tho> I am now well content to purchase a remission by giving up far the greater part of the interest of my own fortune & obtaining my own & much of my children's support by my labour.

Circumstances are lately becoming rather more favourable thro my indefatigable toil in the affairs of my childrens Grandfather and the friendship of a Nobleman, who saw the difficulties I was struggling with & did what only a Man of his property could do, & by one act of generousity set me free—— My family have now a clear estate worth nearly twenty thousand pounds in the West Indies, & this I am this year about to sell. But this you will perhaps hardly beleive that, tho I have rescued this & about seven thousand pounds more for them, I have been opposed & thwarted in every thing I have done by their father & now have from day to day to contend with him when any step is to be taken for the benefit & security of his own children, more than half of whose patrimony he wasted, & then to save himself from the consequences of that folly gave up the rest to be plunder'd by his own relations from whose clutches I have, after incredible difficulties, rescued it.

Do not imagine all this egotism means nothing but to tell you of my own feats. I have another purpose. It is to ask you what I can do or ought to do in regard to the request Mr Phillips made me to send him or allow him to collect materials for an account of me to be inserted in his "Public characters" of this year.[4] I promis'd him I would put the sad narrative, for sad I assure you it is, into the hands of a friend to compose it for the press, but an heavy domestic affliction has made that request to him impossible.[5] It is very difficult to speak of oneself, & I find it would be very difficult to speak of the very unhappy Man whose name I bear without injuring myself by withholding too much truth or my children by telling it. I wish Mr Phillips would leave me for his necrology. My internal notices greatly deceive me if this will require much patience on his part. Advise me, & assist me if you can. I should not be pleased, tho it would not hurt me much, to be attack'd by some of those reptiles who have the audacity to call themselves critics. I am extremely disliked by them, & nothing is more likely than that if they insult me one of my sons would personally resent it. Something of that sort has already happen'd,[6] & such disagreeable contention I am not now in a state of health to support. As Mr Phillips informs me he goes to press the first of August, I wish to have your immediate opinion upon it.

I am afraid I must go to town about this sale, & as I am weary of being here because I cannot walk and have not one acquaintance here nor any books, I shall go tomorrow to Tunbridge Wells which is half way between this place & London. The Season there I beleive is nearly over, & I shall find only a few Invalids, and perhaps the very prolific & profound Mr Cumberland,[7] who lives there, but he has so great an antipathy from [*sic*] Lady Authors & so perfect a contempt for female talents that I shall not venture to approach so aweful a personage—— From Tunbridge I can be in London at any time & at short notice when the conveyancers want me. At all events my daughter will after friday be in Clipstone Street, & I will desire her to bring the books which I am ashamed of having delayed so long.

Forgive me for paying for this Letter. It is worth nothing, & I cannot get a frank here. If I am so fortunate as to hear from you, be so good as to direct to me at Tunbridge Wells—where my Christian name must distinguish me from the numbers of Mrs Smiths of all ranks and conditions that are to be found at all such places & indeed in all places.

When you see Mrs Fenwick, assure her of my affectionate wishes, & tell her I am impatient for the Novel promis'd in the papers.[8] I trust you will yourself beleive me.

Dear Madam, your most oblig'd friend & Servant,
Charlotte Smith

Carl H. Pforzheimer Collection of Shelley and His Circle, The New York Public Library, Astor, Lenox and Tilden Foundations. Address: Miss Hayes/ Hatton Garden/ London/ Post paid/ No. 22. Postmark: F/ PAID/ JUL 28/ 1800.

NOTES

1. Charlotte Mary stayed with Charles on some of his military posts.

2. Elizabeth Robinson Montagu (1720–1800), bluestocking, writer of letters, patron, and critic. Her salons, modeled on the French, included such guests as Frances Boscawen, Mary Delany, Elizabeth Carter, Hester Mulso Chapone, and Hester Thrale.

3. Eliza Fenwick (1766–1840), anonymous author of *Secresy, or the Ruin on the Rock* (1795), had claims to CS's interest in her similar life story. After her alcoholic husband was arrested for debt in 1799, she left him with her two children in 1800. A friend of liberals in the Godwin and Wollstonecraft circle, she was present when Wollstonecraft died, and she had a long correspondence with Mary Hays. After 1800, she supported herself and her family by writing children's works and teaching in Ireland and America.

4. *Public Characters of 1800–1801* (London, 1801), pp. 42–64. Hays wrote the biography of CS.

5. Possibly Hayley, still mourning his son Thomas Alphonso, who died in May 1800.

6. That is, the challenge issued by Lionel and her son-in-law de Foville to Thomas Dyer (see CS to William Davies, 11 Jan. 1795).

7. Richard Cumberland (1732–1811), playwright and novelist.

8. Fenwick did not publish another novel.

To William Prescod[1]

[London, 4 August 1800]
Sir,

Mr Alleyne soon after his arrival in England forwarded to me your proposal for the purchase of the Plantation calls Gays; the Property of the Legatees of the late Richd Smith Merch^t^ & held in trust for them & to the uses of his, Richd Smiths, Will by the Earl of Egremont and the Revd Nicholas Turner.

As soon as I could collect the sentiments of the Persons concerned and had received Lord Egremont's opinion on the propriety of selling the Estate, I applied, as you seem'd to wish I should, to Messrs Daniel & Sons; and to a Gentleman in the House of George Blackman &c. Their answers, as to the acceptance of Bills to be drawn on them by you, are satisfactory.

I therefore write by the most immediate conveyance to inform you that it appears to be the intention of the Trustees, the Earl of Egremont and the Rev^d^ N Turner, by and with the consent of the Legatees, as well specific as residuary, to accept of your proposal for the purchase of the said Plantation.

The Title Deeds (of the nature of which you are undoubtedly well acquainted, or may at any time satisfy yourself, as there are Copies, & they are registered in the Courts of Law in Barbadoes) are in the Possession of Lord Egremont. I am informed the proper method is to have an attested Copy or Copies sent from hence with power to two Gentleman who are to be (as I have agreed with Mr Alleyne) the Honble Willm Bishop, and Mr Phillips, to transfer the Estate to you, and receive the Bills you propose drawing. This transaction seems to be simple & will not be attended with any great expense. The expense is I understand to be shared between the Purchaser and the Seller according to the Custom of the Island.

The original of the Deeds, which it is proper to retain in case of accident by Sea or otherwise, will of course be given up to you when the Purchase is complete.

Mr Alleyne, appearing to think that you require an answer before the forms can be gone thro', I send this with the approbation of the Trustees, & at the same time assure you that no time shall be lost in completing whatever is necessary on our parts.

Thus much being premised, give me leave to state to you my hopes and expectations that you will consider the heavy Losses my Family have sustained, and from your opulence and the little difference it will make to you in comparison of what they will suffer, agree to make the whole payment at 25£ Exchange, whatever the Exchange may be.[2] The valuation last year was £22,048.15.0. Your present Proposal is near 1,000£ less. It is true the value of the Negroes is by death lessen'd; but only three of considerable value have died: a Man worth (as pr valuation of 1798) 70£ called Kit James, a young Woman called Catharina, stated to be worth £100, and a Woman called Sarah or Sareey worth £80. The three other Girls or Women were of inferior value, and one Slave named Bennah, tho stated in the Managers Account to be a Man, was a very old Woman worth nothing; her death therefore & that of the old Men is rather a relief than a disadvantage to the Estate.

While on the other hand I am informed there are Men on the Estate now worth two hundred Pounds, and two hundred & fifty Pounds Sterling & might be sold for that money at any time. The highest valued in the Estimate of 1798 put on any Male Slave is £130 Currency & there are but four so valued. This being the case, and the land according to your own remark being at a low price at 30£ an acre (which low price was rather owing to its having been so cruelly neglected than from any original sterility), I do hope and believe you will not think my proposal unreasonable that the exchange shall be settled at 25; any difference that may happen notwithstanding.

At that exchange the Amount will be little more than 17,000 Stg. I was assured that could I last Year have got the new trust created in time to have sold about October or November last, I might have obtained £20,000 St[g] and upwards. I may also without impropriety remind you, that my Family have lost the Sum of 219£ by a Bill of yours for a debt to the late Richard Smith, under the firm of Prescod & O'Neale; and tho I now perfectly acquiesce in the assurance I have received, that as you had paid the Money but the Person who was to have paid it to R. Smith broke, before his house claim'd it (by some neglect of the people who transacted the concerns of that house for R.S.) that therefore no blame attaches to you.

Yet, Sir, I cannot but flatter myself you will reflect on this additional loss, & on the various deductions that have been made from the wreck of M[r] R. Smith's Property to the diminution of my Children's little fortunes, and agree that the final price of the Plantation shall, since we make no other Condition, not depend on the fluctuation of the Exchange. It was at first suggested to me that I should ask to have the Estate remain on Mortgage till the Instalments were paid, but since I have convers'd with M[r] Alleyne & am better informed than I was on first reading the Proposals, I think the Trustees will not judge it necessary to make any such requisition. I am, Sir, Your most obedient humble Serv[t]

Charlotte Smith

London——
August 4th 1800

Petworth House Archives MS. No address or postmark.

NOTES

1. Copy of CS's letter in a clerk's hand. On Prescod, see Biographical Notes.

2. Commerce with Barbados was complicated by different currencies and rates of exchange. Although the legal coinage was British silver and law required accounts to be kept in pounds, shillings, and pence, the silver dollar was the standard of value and the law was widely ignored. In addition to the different values of coinage, exchange rates were applied to bank notes used in trade (Schomburgk, *The History of Barbados,* pp. 160–72).

To the earl of Egremont

Mount Misery Tunbridge Wells
August 4th 1800
My Lord

As M[r] Prescod makes a sort of condition that he shall have an answer immediately, M[r] Alleyne advis'd me to write to him by the Jamaica packet which is going out in a few days. I am asham'd to have yielded so far to the fatigue of my terribly hot journey on Thursday & to some increase of illness in consequences of it, as to have omitted till to day to prepare this Letter. I hope however if your Lordship approves of it, it will still be in time. There was I thought no harm in trying to fix the payment at 25£ exchange; otherwise if any disagreeable event should happen so as to lower it considerably, it may make 2000£ difference in the value, & certain it is (to make use of a vulgarism that The Devil never sleeps when I or my poor folks are in question); therefore I dare say something or other will happen to reduce the exchange to the minimum of 40: the maximum is 25——I last year got the sum ~~offer'd reduced to~~ the estate was valued at made out in English Money, & I subjoin the same, as only persons accustomed to mercantile dealings can make such calculates. 22,048£ the money at which, Barbados Currency, the Plantation was valued in the year 1798 brought into St^{g} Money, according to the variations of exchange—

£22048, at 40pC^{t} exchange is ——St^{g}——	15,749.2.4
D^{o}————at 35 D^{o} ————————	16,332.8.1
D^{o}———. . . at 30 D^{o} ————————	16,960.11.6½
D^{o}———at 25.D^{o} ————————	17,639.0.0

Your Lordship will from hence perceive that if chance should be against us, and I never recollect its being for us save when Mr Dyer took 400£ for his share (for yr kindness in giving it to me was not a matter of chance), we may perhaps obtain only 15,700£ or thereabouts for the plantation which will be indeed a sad falling off from 20,000£ St^{g} & which we might have had last year & probably should have had if Mr Benjn Smiths unexampled folly had not delay'd the transfer of the Trust till it was too late.

I have fully inform'd myself of Mr Prescods property: he has six estates in Barbados & about fifty thousand pounds (or as it is beleived by some 80,000) in the Government securities of this Country. Mr Alleyne assures me he has not the least doubt of the payments being made as stipulated, but if, from any very improbable event, they should not, we have always a resource in going upon the Estate. He, Mr Alleyne, bought a considerable estate not long since, the pay^{ts} for which were made in this way—— And he says he would sell on the same terms had he occasion to sell knowing it perfectly secure.

The way in which it is to be done is thus: Attested Copies of the Title deeds in your Lordships possession must be sent—With full powers to the two persons I have, on Mr Alleynes advice fix'd upon, to transfer the Estate and ~~send~~ receive the bills. These persons are the Honble William Bishop and ________[1] Phillips, Esqre, Agent to Mr Alleyne, & Mr Breme (whose Christian name I will obtain). The expence to us will not exceed 40£ in Barbados where it is customary for each party to bear a share. Here I understand the Purchaser pays the expences. Mr Prescod therefore ought to pay for the expence of the Copies &c &c.

May I request, on the supposition of your Lordships approving of what I have written, that you will be so good as to Frank this Letter enclos'd to Mr Daniel to send to Mr Prescod by the Jamaica packet & as soon as possible to give your authority in writing to Mr Bicknell to receive from you & prepare copies of the title deeds to be attested, to send out directly, with power under the City Seal, to sell this Land in particular, & every other piece & parcel of Land belonging to the Estate of the late Richard Smith in Barbados. I have settled all this with Mr Bicknell (under reserve of your Lordships orders), & he has promis'd me to lose no time in getting all done to go by an early packet, & I will take care it shall be done correctly & right.

I have other business on which to trouble you, but this being the most momentous, I will reserve the rest to another Letter. I am ever your Lordships most oblig'd Ser^t^,

Charlotte Smith

Petworth House Archives MS. No address or postmark.

NOTE

1. CS's blank. Apparently, she planned to send full powers of attorney to Bishop and Phillips. Phillips was a solicitor and agent for John Forster Alleyne in Barbados on the sale of Gay's as well as uncle and partner of Thomas Went, Esq., who later sent an account of Charles Smith's death in Barbados in 1801 (see CS to Egremont, 15 Feb. 1802 and n. 1).

To the earl of Egremont

Mount Misery. Tunbridge Wells
Aug^st^ 9 1800
My Lord

Not having had the honor of hearing from y^r^ Lordship before I left Hastings (which I did as soon as I had the means) & finding there was a necessity for my seeing Mr Alleyne, who inform'd me he return'd to Bristol on friday, Knowing that I could not on account of my Landlord stay long in London even if my health would have allow'd it, I took here (which is on my way from Hastings) a very small & retird lodging. But still not hearing from my

Brother, to whom I had written to say what I meant to do, to whom I stated the necessity of dispatch, & knowing that yr Lordship is often absent from Petworth at this season of the year & therefore might not have received my Letters, I thought it best, on receiving a second Letter from Mr Alleyne to go to Town on Thursday, & meet him at Mr Bicknells—— I return'd here directly so extremely fatigued as to be unable before to thank your Lordship for your kind Lettr of the 27th which (contrary to my orders) my person who has the care of my apartment sent to Hastings——

I have now obtain'd from Mr Alleyne every necessary information, & I find the business is equally simple & secure. As I have a great deal more to trouble your Lordship upon relative to this important business than I am able clearly to write to day, I only take that liberty now that you may not think I neglect any thing I have undertaken or am unmindful of your generous purpose to assist me by giving if possible an whole day to the affairs. I cannot sufficiently thank you for that & all your other kindness without which it would be impossible for me to contend with the difficulties which I am expos'd to from all quarters. Of my unhappy Brother I have heard not a word. God knows what will become of him———

I am very sorry I did wrong in send^{g} the case to Mrs Dorset, but I thought your Lordship meant that I should. If I said more than was proper to her ab^{t} poor Turners misconduct & its consequences, it was in the hope of convincing her that her unkindness when he has so acted as to have lost your Lordships good opinion might add to the confusion of his mind, & (knowing his temper as she does) I hoped she might reflect on the consequence of irritating & driving him to despair. I am miserable to find he has acted so extremely wrong & know but one excuse that can be made for it, which however I will not now urge. Ungrateful to your Lordship I do beleive he never was, but I have seen him so excessively afraid of offending you, in matters where I knew you were too generous to be offended, that I have often blamed him & said to him that it was want of judgement & of confidence to feel that abject apprehension when you were the judge of his conduct, who I was sure liked manly & plain dealing ~~better~~ & would be disgusted but not deceived by any other.

As I imagine yr Lordship will be engaged at Lewes & Brighthelmston this week, I will give the next two days to writing the Letters to Barbados & other things to which y^{r} Lordships approval will be necessary, & await your command; as soon afterwards as you can honor me with them, the Letters sh^{d} go by the Jamaica packet. I am, My Lord, your ever oblig'd Ser^{t}, Charlotte Smith

Petworth House Archives MS. No address or postmark.

To the earl of Egremont

Bignor Park
Septr 25th 1800
My Lord.

As my poor sick Girl is, if she is yet alive, arrived at Deal[1] where to days paper announces the Lord Hawkesbury to be, My eldest daughter will go to Town this tomorrow morning Where she probably is by this time, and I shall wait here only till I know the state of her health and where it will be necessary for her to be either for advice or air — — I am so doubtful of her being alive that I dare not decide on any plan till I hear. I take it for granted Charles is gone to Deal & that I shall hear from him tomorrow. As I must pay Mrs Dorset for my stay here & shall have to provide for my journey & Georges removal to Mr Coppers,[2] on which subject I took the liberty of addressing your Lordship Yesterday, I should be extremely oblig'd to you to give me authority to draw for 50£ on Messrs Daniel, Those Gentlemen declining to let me have any money from the present advance, saying I have already had my share, & tho I am authoris'd to receive the parts appropriated to My elder Sons, Willm & Nicholas, I have in vain representd <u>that</u> to Messrs Daniels & in consequence of their refusal have been under the necessity of borrowing 20£ of my Publisher to whom I was before in debt———

I am ready and indeed desirous of laying before the Trustees an account of all the money I have had—& of the disposal of it—but I really had not courage when I saw your Lordship to trouble you with accounts, & it w^d have been useless to have address'd myself to my Brother. <u>I</u> have been the greatest sufferer in being never able to say what my income was or which of my family I had to support so that it has been impossible for me to do otherwise till lately than struggle on from day to day, & write for the support of those who had long very little other support but who now <u>perhaps</u> may think I take more than I ought. My only ambition now is, as it has long been, to have a cottage any where, I am really indifferent in what place, where I may pursue while I am yet able the business which, while it detaches my mind from its miseries, may contribute to the support of my younger children & prevent my being too burthensome to the elder.

Forgive me, my Lord, with your usual goodness for this additional trouble. It is to that goodness I have long learn'd to appeal, certain of your consideration towards one who is not thus importunate thro any fault of her own. I am y^r Lordship's obed^t & oblig'd Ser^t,

Charlotte Smith

Petworth House Archives MS. No address or postmark.

NOTES

1. Harriet sailed from England for India on 2 Apr. 1799 with her eldest brother William, who sent her home the next year after she contracted malaria. The fleet was expected to land at Portsmouth but landed instead at Deal, where Charles went to meet Harriet. Charlotte Mary met them both in London, and they joined their mother in mid-Oct., with Harriet somewhat recovered. Nevertheless, CS's attendance on Harriet's illness may account for the scarcity of letters for the rest of this year (see CS to Joseph Cooper Walker, 14 Apr. 1801).

2. Not identified, but he probably ran a Dissenting school at Hackney.

To the duchess of Devonshire

[Tunbridge Wells, 23 November 1800]

Your Grace's early and kind attention to the requests with which, thro dear Lady Bessborough, I presumed to trouble you demands my liveliest gratitude. You will indeed do me a most essential favor if you will have the goodness to write to Lord Wellesly.[1] Since I took the liberty of writing to your Grace, I have had an overland Letter from my poor William, filld with expressions of anxiety for his Sister's safety & saying that he had unavoidably embarrass'd himself on her account (she cost him upwards of twelve hundred pounds as I now understand) which however he should not regret if she was once restored to her health and my protection, but the uncertainty he was in on her account was almost insupportable. He adds that Lord Wellesley had not yet given him a situation, which could not fail to be a distressing circumstance; his Lordship gave him hopes, but that nothing would so certainly determine him as another Letter from your Grace to whose recommendation he pays more regard than to that of any other person in England, even the Directors. If therefore, dearest Madam, you will once more indulge my importunity, and write <u>(so as that the Lttr might go by the most immediate conveyance) such a request in favor of William Towers Smith, as you judge proper</u>, be assured that you will confer another and most serious obligation on a family who are most sensible of the value of Your friendship & protection. I believe no particular post must be specified.

My Son has been fourteen years in the Service & is of course qualified in point of rank to hold any that Lord W. sees good to entrust him with. He is now married,[2] & the Father of his Wife, a Man of a certain age & who has been long in India, will by his influence counteract the faults of poor William as a Man of business, which were merely indolence & a love of hunting rather than writing. The latter has cured itself in a great degree, and as he will probably have a family to provide for, he will no longer indulge the former. In point of integrity & unimpeachable honesty, I know he is unusually strict & might have been now very rich if he could have forgotten the romantic lessons which his Mother gave him when he went out at seventeen, the protegeé [*sic*] of John Robinson, for which he has been laughed at as well as that luckless Mother. I believe it is hardly necessary to add another word on this subject.

Your Grace is so good as to enquire after poor Foville. He has now been two years establish'd, if it may be so call'd, as French & drawing Master to a boarding School of considerable reputation at Wansted to attend which he lives in a small lodging at Mile end. By this employment and a few private scholars, added to very great oeconomy, he has continued to live, rather pleas'd than murmurring at the necessity of fatigueing work, because it allowd him no time to brood over his miseries. They are indeed severe. His only sister, whose first Husband Monsr de Trevé[3] became an emigrant at the beginning of the revolution, divorced herself from de Trevé by whom she never had any children that she might, as she said, preserve her Mother's & her Brother's property. But instead of doing so, she married very soon afterwards a republican of Rouen, who has left her a widow with two children; those children have made her so entirely forget her Brother, to whom she used to be so attach'd, that she not only avoids all communication with him, but prevents his letters reaching his Mother, who is old, infirm, & wholly in the power of Madame <D'Hangarde>.[4]

Foville has long been extremely desirous of returning to France, and now he is become more so Since it will hardly be in his Sister's power to prevent his seeing his Mother if she is still living as he beleives. But till he can obtain a part of the little that is allow'd to be due to him of my lost love's little fortune (which he very handsomely offers to compromise for any consideration I shall name, leaving it wholly to me), he cannot throw himself out of bread here on so uncertain a prospect as he has there because he fears he should not be able to return if he found himself, as might happen, totally destitute in France. His name is three times on the Emigrant list—once in the departement, ci devant, of <Caux?>; once at Rouen; & once at <Balbec?>[5] where he had a relation with whom he often resided for several months at a time when he was not with his regiment. He has however not borne arms against France since 1792, and I had determined to have written to Bonaparte on his behalf, if the late regulation in regard to Emigrants had not made me hope that he would be now received without difficulty so that I am now trying to obtain the means of his going over without exposing him to actual beggary, for I suppose his Sister to be fully in possession of his property.

I am not without hope that Lord Egremont (tho I fear his Lordship has conceived some prejudice against him) would, on a fair representation of the case, allow me to ~~get~~ raise the money on his future claims, but Lord E. has taken such an infinite deal of trouble on other of our affairs lately that I cannot collect courage to address him yet on this, tho I own it is very near my heart.

On Friday I took leave of Charles who goes to day to Portsmouth, Lord Spencer[6] having most obligingly directed, at Lord Egremont's request, that he shall ~~xxx~~ have his passage to Barbados on board the Andromeda frigate. (Your Grace will observe how greatly I and mine are indebted to every one of your family.) The advantage this gives to my Son is incalculable, both as to accommodation & security, & it softens to me & his Sisters the solicitudes of parting. Pray do not forget me in regard to St Gothard.[7] Let me offer to Lady Bessborough my truest thanks. I cannot vary them because your Graces & her Ladyship's goodness to me is invariable. I have been sadly troublesome to you both.

Charles took the Schawl to town, & his Servant was to leave it at Devonshire house to day. On examining it when I put it up, I see that there are two trifling blemishes in it which I impute either to his Persian highness having taken it from his royal person to present to Nicholas, or to the difficulty with which the mate of the Indiaman got it on shore, which very probably oblig'd him to wrap it round his humbler person & exposed it to two or three spots of sea water. I suppose all the schawls made in Persia are woven without borders which are afterwards sewn on, for in ~~to~~ an inferior one that my Son sent me two years since, that has been done, as well as to this, tho the border to mine is slight. It detracts considerably from their beauty and value.

I do not know whether the Solitary wanderer will be worth your Grace's reading. The second volume is the best, I think. I am now going on with three others.[8] And tho it is not very pleasant to know one must work "when youth and health are flown," yet I am subdued to my fortune, & tho I do not suffer less, I cease to complain—

"Je remplis mon destin, je suis neé pour souffrir"[9]—

Allow me, dearest Madam, such alleviation as arises from the hope of enjoying some share of the esteem of those whose esteem is best worth having, & permit me to remain

your Grace's most faithful
and oblig'd Sert,
Charlotte Smith

Tunbridge Wells
Novr 23rd, 1800

Harriet has recovered her health in a greater degree than I expected since she has been here, But my eldest daughter is now confined to her bed by one of those Quinsy's which she has always been liable to.

Devonshire MS, Chatsworth: 5th Duke's Group no. 1536. No address or postmark.

NOTES

1. Richard Colley Wellesley, Marquess Wellesley (1760–1842), governor-general of Bengal from 1797 to 1805, elder brother of the (later) duke of Wellington.

2. William married Catherine Maria Morris on 15 Mar. 1800, about the time Harriet became ill and was sent home. The couple had at least two children: Catharine Augusta, christened on 8 Oct. 1810, and Seton Lionel, born in 1817.

3. Not identified.

4. Not identified.

5. I have not located Caux or Balbec.

6. The duchess's brother.

7. The duchess's poem "The Passage of Mount St. Gothard."

8. *The Letters of a Solitary Wanderer,* vols. 1 and 2 (Sampson Low, 1800). Low also published vol. 3 late in 1800 (dated 1801); CS would still have been working on it when she wrote this letter. Vols. 4 and 5 were published by T. N. Longman and O. Rees in 1802.

9. I fulfill my destiny; I am born to suffer.

1801
"DOMESTIC MISERIES"

— 14 APRIL 1801

The year 1801, the first since 1787 in which Charlotte Smith had no new publications and no new editions of older works, marked a turning point for her in authorship, motherhood, and the trust business. Confident that the earl of Egremont as new trustee to the Smith estate would uphold her children's interests, she quit writing to support her family. Her first letters to Egremont in this year display not merely confidence in him but also admiration for him. In early letters to his steward, William Tyler, too, she presumes that Egremont will rely on her knowledge of the trust, taking her advice about it and supporting her needs. Their withdrawal of support can be felt in the tone of her letters later in the year: those to Egremont are apologetic, while those to Tyler become more direct, businesslike, and argumentative.

Misery and disaster attended her children. In the winter Lionel did not arrive home for Christmas as expected, and the family feared him lost or dead. Miraculously, he turned up later and attended the death of Lucy's husband in March. Lucy was left with two toddlers, a third child on the way, and no support but what little money her mother could spare. In September, Smith's youngest son George joined the army, and she was forced to give up her hope of educating him at Oxford. Meanwhile, Charles was reassigned to a post in the West Indies. He took it in part to see to trust business in Barbados. By October, Smith had learned the worst news: Charles, age 28, had died there of yellow fever. She blamed the trustees, lawyers, and litigants—everyone who had delayed and complicated the trust settlement—for Charles's death. From July through October, Benjamin Smith was in London, attempting to arrange an interview with the earl of Egremont. When that failed, he pled his cause to the earl in letters.

To Richard Phillips[1]

[Tunbridge Wells, 4 February 1801]
Sir,

As sending down any thing by Mr Serrange or Mr Knight is extremely uncertain thro the medium of their booksellers, I shall be much oblig'd to you to send the books for which I troubled you, with the Monthly Magazine, by the [stage][2]—— At the same time, I wish to know what [. . .] ~~your~~ the works at present projected for your press [. . .] in which any department I could fill is at liberty. I wish to undertake some work of greater permanency than Novels (tho Mr Cadell himself is of opinion my Novels will live), & now look towards the time when without any injury to Mrs Low, I could enter on such an engagement.[3]

I am, Sir, you obedt humble Sert,
Charlotte Smith

Feby 4th 1801

University of California at Los Angeles MS. Address: Mr Philips/ St Pauls Church Yard/ London. POSTMARKED: F FEB 5 1801.

NOTES

1. English publisher; see Biographical Notes.
2. The bracketed words and ellipses indicate where the paper was torn away by breaking the seal.
3. Sampson Low died between 25 Sept. 1800, when CS last mentioned him, and the date of this letter. His wife, Mary Ann Low, registered the press at 7 Berwick Street in 1801, presumably taking over the business herself.

To Robin Allen[1]

[Hartridges, Tunbridge Wells, 20 February 1801]
Sir,

As my health makes my remaining at this place necessary, it will not for some time be in my power to call upon you for the books I intended to take at your repository in lieu of those I sent to you last, for which I have certainly not had any thing like the value, as there was Ld Chesterfields Letters, Littletons Heny 2nd in Qto in very good condition & many others as by my account, for which I have had Anatomy of Melancholy, & two or 3 old books of Jeremy Taylors which are not what I meant.[2] I shall esteem myself oblig'd to you if you would let me know by an early post how the account stands (Hayleys life of Milton was sent at the same time to be bound),[3] as I have other books I wish to exchange & shall be glad to have your last catalogue & to arrange my little collection before I remove to the house I shall take in this place.

Your early answer therefore will oblige,

Sir, your obedt hble Sert,
Charlotte Smith

Hartridges Tunbridge Wells
Feby 20th 1801

Bodleian MS Montagu d. 2, fol. 163–64. Address: Mr Allen/ Messrs Lackington & Allen/ Finsbury Square/ London. Postmark: TUNBRIDGE WELLS; F/ FEB 21/ 1801. Also in another hand: "Ch^e Smith / 1801 '20 {Febry}.

NOTES

1. See Biographical Notes.

2. Apparently Allen and his partner, George Lackington, had traded her *Letters Written by the Late Right Honourable Phillip Dormer Stanhope, Earl of Chesterfield, to His Son* (11th ed. by P. Dodsley, 1797), and George Baron Lyttelton's *History of the Life of King Henry the Second* (4 vols., 2nd ed. by W. Sandy and J. Dodsley, 1767) for inferior copies of older works: Robert Burton's *Anatomy of Melancholy* (1676) and one of Jeremy Taylor's works of piety, such as *Holy Living* or *Holy Dying.* In any case, these writers' works were not typical reading fare or reference material for CS.

3. William Hayley's *Life of Milton* was first published with Boydell and Nichol's 1794 edition of Milton's work, then separately by Cadell and Davies in 1796.

To Mrs. Sherwill

{Place uncertain, after spring 1801}[1]
Madam — —

Ann Walker lived with me about three years & left me with an intention of being married. She is a very good natured person but weak & easily misled, & if she does not entirely break off all connection with the family of the Man whom she was to have married, I will not, & I have told her so, answer for her, for tho she is herself honest and well meaning, such people will entirely ruin & render her unfit for a respectable service. If they are still at Tunbridge Wells where she unfortunately became acquainted with them, she will do very well, as she is a very tolerable cook & can send up a dinner very well. As I keep little company & live in a plain way, I have had no great occasion to try her in extraordinary cookery, & when I had, my other Servant who is an excellent Cook assisted. The Woman has the good qualities of civility & good nature & is herself honest & worthy of trust, but if she will not determine to divest herself of the influence of those people, she will never be the good servant she might otherwise make herself — —

I am, Madam,
your obed Ser^t,
Charlotte Smith

Osborn Collection MS, Yale University. Addressed: Mrs Sherwill/ Sloane Street. No postmark.

NOTE

1. CS resided in Tunbridge Wells, where Ann Walker would have met her husband-to-be and his family, from Feb. till Apr. 1801, suggesting a date later in that year for this letter of reference. Mrs. Sherwill is not identified.

To the earl of Egremont

[Frant, 5 April 1801]
. . . about[1] the papers which there was an evident design to withhold—— Mr Boehm,[2] I remember, not being able or willing to give me an answer, said that, If I would apply to Mr Berney[3] as a Gentleman, he would give me an answer about the money paid in Barbados. I replied that it was the business of Robinson and Parkin[4] to make that enquiry, and I certainly did say that I could not apply to Mr Berney as a Gentleman because he had so behaved that I did not consider him as such——

Really, my Lord, it is too much that your Lordship shd be liable to applications from these stultified branches of the old Merchant. I am asham'd of the trouble it must give. Perhaps to prevent a repetition on the part of Mr R Berney, the best way would be to direct that an official kind of Letter be written to him with the enclos'd extract (perhaps copied in another hand might be better as he [about four lines cut away]

your Lordship as Creditor & the interest due on the first legacies paid. That being done, it is not only extremely doubtful but very improbable that any thing will remain for the remote contingencies which he claims. But whenever the prior demands are settled, a statement of the whole will be made out. Of that, however, there can be no prospect for three years, as it will be so long before the payments are made for the property which is to be dispos'd of in the West Indies—— I do by no means intend to dictate to yr Lordships superior judgement, but knowing the facts and the Man, I wish, without my appearing in it, which I apprehend you would not approve, to save all the trouble I can to the Gentleman whom yr Lordship may direct to ansr Berneys Letter which I return [about four lines cut away]

I submit it to your Lordship whether another sentence might not be added—— "That Mr Berney must perceive that whatever intelligence he can give as to Sums received or outstanding in Barbados will facilitate this conclusion and possible save the expences of an enquiry which the present Trustees may otherwise feel themselves obliged to set on foot, [for] in regard [*sic*] misapplication or concealment of monies by Mr Prettejohn"—— A bill of enquiry would not suit him I know.

I take the liberty to enclose y[e] Letter from M[r] Erskine ab[t] the living. W[m] Scotts[5] opinion I have not yet been able to find. Your Lordship will have the goodness to send it to M[r] Bicknell;[6] it will save me some postage.

Petworth House Archives MS. No address or postmark.

NOTES

1. This fragmented letter has an explanatory note by William Tyler on its cover sheet: "Smith's Trusteeship/ 5. April 1801/ M[rs] Smith to Lord Egremont, in consequence of M[r] Rob[t] Berney's application to his Lordship's Letter (Introductory part not deliverd)." Thus the letter begins in mid-sentence, its front page missing.

2. Edmund Boehm, husband of Richard Smith's granddaughter, Dorothy Elizabeth Berney (see CS to John Robinson, 19 Sept. 1785, n. 5, and Genealogical Chart).

3. Robert Berney, grandson of Richard Smith and first child and only son of William and Mary Smith Berney. (See Genealogical Chart.) Boehm was his brother-in-law.

4. John Robinson and Anthony Parkin, trustees to the Smith estate since 2 July 1784 and 31 July 1788, respectively. Egremont and Nicholas Turner assumed the task in 1799.

5. It is not clear what opinion CS sought of the eminent barrister William Scott, Lord Stowell (1745–1836), who practiced in the admiralty and ecclesiastical courts.

6. Charles Bicknell was CS's own particular lawyer; the lawyer Thomas Erskine also interceded for her (see CS to BS, 19 Feb. 1790, n. 4).

To Joseph Cooper Walker

Tunbridge Wells. April 14th 1801

When I look, Dear Sir, on the date of your last Letter and see that almost twelve months have pass'd since that proof of your friendly recollection was received, I cannot but fear that you must long since have ceased to think with your former kindness of one who appears so ungrateful & so insensible of the obligations she owes you. As the suspicion of ingratitude—however I may seem to have deserved it—is what I most deprecate, do not think me tedious if I enter into an history of myself for this last Year—— I received your most kind Letter in June last at Hastings where I was slowly recovering from the effect which London, I know not why, always has on me: Or perhaps I ought rather to say that it is the vexation I generally suffer there that invariably makes me ill. My poor Lucy & her two infant children were there with me, but her husband, chusing to behave extremely ill to me, sent for her away in July (on purpose to pique me),[1] and as soon afterwards as I could, I came hither because this place was nearer London, & I was obligd to go thither to meet a Gentleman engag'd in our affairs who was just arrived from Barbados. Having perform'd this warm service in the dreadful hot weather of the beginning of August and convinced myself the terms we had received for the purchase of the plantation in Barbados were by all means to be accepted,[2] I return'd hither soon after which Charles & his eldest Sister (who had for some time resided with him at Berwick) came to me, their assistance being necessary in settling this important agreement, My eldest daughter having the most considerable claims on her Grandfathers assets——

Charles a few days after his arrival re[ceive]d Lttrs from Lionel from Holly<ard?> to say he was going at the especial desire of the Duke of Kent to take charge of six hundred Maroons who were to be conducted to Sierra Leone. This perilous voyage he undertook with only forty Soldiers & one other subaltern, & I was wretched in hearing of it tho I said but little; it seem'd however to be bitterness enough for one six months. Charles left me to go to Petworth to Lord Egremont our Trustee about the Affairs, & scarce had he been gone a week before I received a Letter overland from My eldest Son at Bengal, who in April 1799 had taken his youngest Sister Harriet over with him, to inform me that she had been seized with a most dangerous fever which threatend her life, & it had return'd from time to time to such a degree that if her life was preserved, her intellects would be lost, as it affected her head more & more on every attack & reduced her to a state of such weakness that the medical Men had assured him all hope of her recovery in that Country would be vain, in consequence of which he had taken her passage on board the Lord Hawksbury India ship, and she was then on her way to England. He desir'd her family would be ready to meet her at Portsmouth.

This intelligence reach'd me in the last days of August, and I could think of nothing better than going with my eldest daughter to My Sisters house at Bignor Park in Sussex which is only thirty miles from Portsmouth and there waiting the arrival of the Fleet. During our stay there of six weeks, Genl Dalrymple who met Charles at Lord Egremonts gave him the Paymastership of the 47th Regiment station'd at Bermuda, & as the receipt & final arrangement of so considerable a Sum as the Estate will be sold for demanded the interposition of one of the family, Lord E. thought Charles ought to proceed first to Barbados & then join his regiment at Bermuda. He therefore resign'd his town adjutancy and Lieutenancy of Invalids at Berwick.

In the mean time the East India fleet arriv'd and was driven so rapidly thro the Channel that our intention of meeting poor Harriet at Portsmouth was frustrated. She landed at Deal & her sister, who is my greatest assistance in such cases, met her in Town, & as I meant to reside here for some time, I cross'd the Country and they met me here the middle of October. Harriet had recoverd from the time of her landing at St Helena & was a great deal better than I expected to have seen her tho alarms for her health had not then nor indeed have they ever subsided. Thus (with some little episodes of ill treatment from M[r] Smith in refusing me money from the interest of part of my own fortune lately fallen to me & M[r] Newhouse's quarrel with the whole family) pass'd my time till October.

I had hardly ever the pen out of my hand when I was able to hold it, for amidst all this, I was compelld to finish the three volumes of "Letters of a Solitary Wanderer," which I had been two years about, & I do assure you that there were times when the anxiety of my mind & the labor I was notwithstanding oblig'd to go thro so entirely overcame me that I thought I must have given all up & desisted from so vain & hopeless an attempt as resisting any longer so overwhelming a destiny.

Charles saild for Barbados early in December. At Christmas Lionel had assur'd us he should be at home. Alas, Christmas came & he came not. I had made myself in the interim but too well acquainted with the dangers he was incurring and every hour as it pass'd added to my dread, while I found that the Officers of the 24th Reg[t], who have an almost general affection & attachment to my Son, were extremely uneasy and apprehensive of the event. In this painful solicitude, with accumulations of uneasiness on account of Lucy's sad situation, pass'd the months of January and February. Still no news of Lionel—& I found he was suppos'd to be lost. At that time, poor Lucy's affairs became so unfortunately critical that I felt it absolutely necessary to go to town tho I was so miserable on account of her Brother that I was hardly able to undertake even so short a journey—— I will not, since the poor Man is no more, relate what I had to endure from Her husband.

All the evils however appeard light when suddenly my long lost Lionel appeard at my lodgings, a few moments after I had seen in the paper that the Asia ship was arrived & was considering of the means of getting news of him that night. His sight was indeed a cordial to me, and it seem'd like a resurrection from the dead. God knows what would have become of me without him: Lucy, unable to stay with M[r] Newhouse who treated her with extreme harshness, was come down to my temporary house here, leaving me to settle with that unhappy Man what was to be done ab[t] hers and her children's support. But I was afraid that Lionel would resent the conduct he had observed & was afraid of their meeting. However Lionel who is really an extraordinary young Man was so rational & so cool that I consented to his seeing M[r] Newhouse. He found him ill in bed with a fever caught in his attendance (as studying Physician at the Hospital). All resentment was of course at an end, & we thought only of procuring this luckless Man such comforts as his condition required. I was however so very ill myself that I was under the necessity of coming home. Lionel came down with me and return'd immediately with Lucy to attend her sick husband. He became daily worse, his own relations who are Chicester people were sent for, but his Mother came too late to see him alive; he died on Saturday the 28th of last Month & has left my unfortunate Daughter absolutely destitute (for they have had considerably more than the interest of her Grandfather's legacy), and she has two children to provide for—One only two years old, another one year, and in August next, a third is likely to encrease this desolate little group.[3] From his family who are person's with whom it was once very unlikely any of mine should be connected, she has nothing to expect, and it is with great difficulty the means were found to perform the last sad Offices to this unfortunate Man, & not without an heavy tax on the small & inadequate payment Lionel had received of part of his expences incurred at Sierra Leone. Lucy and her children are at present with me. What is to become of them hereafter when I may no longer exist, or indeed how they are to be supported now, I have yet no idea.

My own situation never was much more distressing, for tho by Lord Egremonts kindness my family's property is out of the hands which so inhumanly robbed us, Mr Smiths conduct towards me counteracts, as far as relates to me, all the advantages which ought to accrue from it. He positively refuses to let me have even the small share of interest from my fortune which he formerly allow'd me, & because in consequence of my Mother-in-law's death there is more to have, he will let me have none. It does not appear that there is any way of compelling him, as his residence in Scotland puts him out of the reach of the Courts here without a long process which he may easily evade, and I own my courage in continuing my literary labour is almost exhausted.

However a Mother who, after fearing for his life, has such a Son as Lionel restored to her ought not to complain of pecuniary inconvenience. I am now anxious for his obtaining the promotion he so well deserves (I wish I had an opportunity of sending you the testimonials of his merit as an Officer). But without money to purchase, a Young Man, whatever may be his merit, is I fear but too likely to be overlookd. The D of Kent is much his friend, but it is beleived the Royal Military Brothers do not agree.[4] Lionel proposes to do himself the pleasure of writing to you, but I would no longer delay telling you, Dear Sir, that nothing but a sort of procession of troubles prevented my writing to you for some months, & afterwards when I became doubtful of Lionels safety, I had not the courage to write to you, since I know the kind recollection you have of him, & hardly daring to look steadily at my fears, I could not bear to put them upon paper——

I will not add another word in the way of excuse but talk of other matters. You have long since heard of poor Mr Hayley's loss & probably received his last poem of which he just recollected enough of our former friendship to send me a Copy from Cadells;[5] I wrote to thank him in the usual course, but afterwards tho I was for many weeks within a few miles of him and in correspondence with some of his friends who resided at Bognor near his Marine Villa, he never gave me the pleasure of a single line from him or express'd a wish to see me. I, who have sufferd & must for ever suffer under a loss cruel as that which he has sustain'd, am well aware how much such a blow prevents or annihilates every other feeling but of anguish, & to that I imputed what I could not otherwise have consider'd as an unkind dereliction of an old friendship: But I learned from many persons who had an opportunity of seeing him that he was tolerably chearful & resign'd & did not shun, even so much as was his custom, the intercourse of society. It is now many months since I have heard of Mr Hayley otherwise than by common report, which says that he is going to be married to a Mrs Chetwynd,[6] the widow of a Gentleman who was killed in Ireland in the rebellion & who has five children, none of them quite children.

Mr H. was in Town when I was there but I did not see him. I will not pretend to say that I am not mortified by the total cessation of a literary commerce from which, for so many years of life, I derived so much pleasure and advantage, & I have sometimes feard I must have been myself to blame tho I declare I know not how.[7] Tout finit hormis mes malheurs,[8] however, & I must submit to that deprivation as I have done to others.

I fear the death of my publisher Mr Low prevented you havg my last work sent you from the Author, as on enquiring what number of copies were remaining of mine I am sure he could not have fufilld my directions. A copy remains for you if you will do me the honor to accept it. Mrs Piozzi's book I have not seen, but I understand it is very little liked.[9] I fear our friend Hayley has not been very successful in his last work, but the subject is cold & hard, & I think he has not given it the spirit that it might have been releived with. Yet in such a state of miserable anxiety, it is wonderful that he even compos'd it at all. May I hope, tho I acknowledge I do not deserve, that you will let me hear from you soon? I shall be here at least 6 weeks; I then shall go only two miles farther to a village in Sussex to which this is the post town. Is there any hope of seeing you in England? Beleive, Dear Sir, that nothing would give more pleasure to yr ever oblig'd & faithful humble Sert, Charlotte Smith——

Will you give me leave to ask when we may expect the Essay on the revival of the Drama in Italy? I never received the Memoir on Italian Tragedy[10] which I wish much to see. I do not know Mrs West at all. Her poems I thought better than her Novels. I am no great admirer of Books written to please particular people or parties, but I beleive she is a woman of talents.[11] I have been so bewilderd by domestic miseries that I have had no intercourse with the Lees for a great while. Of the Canterbury tales, I think Harriet Lees far the best.[12] These are woeful times for Authors!

Huntington MS (HM10829). Address: Josepth Cooper Walker Esqre/ St Valori. No postmark.

NOTES

1. See CS to Walker, 18 May 1800, from Hastings, in which CS describes the circumstances of Lucy and her husband more fully.

2. Early in Aug. 1800, CS met John Forster Alleyne of Barbados twice in London about the trust's selling Gay's plantation to William Prescod. See CS to Egremont, 9 and 18 July and 4 and 9 Aug. 1800.

3. For details about Lucy's first two children, Thomas Henry and William Charles Newhouse, see CS to Walker, 9 Jan. 1799, n. 5, and 18 May 1800, n. 2. Lucy's third child, Charlotte Susan Newhouse, was overdue in October of this year. Her place of birth is not known. By the time she was four she was said to be CS's favorite grandchild (BS to Egremont, 25 Feb. 1805, unpub. letter in PHA #0.11).

4. The sons of George III had military training and careers in varying degrees. Edward, duke of Kent (1767–1820), the happiest at soldiering and known as the "simple soldier," served in Canada from 1792 to 1802 during Lionel's posting there and did much to advance Lionel's career.

5. Hayley's son, Thomas Alphonso, died the previous year on 2 May, one week after Hayley's friend Cowper. The work was *An Essay on Sculpture: In a Series of Epistles to John Flaxman, Esq., R.A.* (1800).

6. Penelope Carleton Chetwynd, daughter of John Carleton of Woodside, Co. Cork, whom Hayley did not, in fact, marry. William Chetwynd (1754–1798), grandson of the third Viscount Chetwynd, was killed in action with the Irish rebels near Saintfield, Co. Down, 11 June 1798. Hayley's first wife Eliza Ball died in 1800; he remarried in 1809.

7. Several events may have contributed to Hayley's withdrawal from CS's literary affairs. In 1793, he was acutely embarrassed when CS took a £50 advance from Thomas Cadell, Sr., without warning him; Hayley felt obliged to defend her but uncomfortable at having to do so (Hayley to Thomas Cadell, Sr., 12 Apr. 1793, Cowper and Newton Museum). In the meantime, he continued old friendships with Anna Seward, who derided all works by CS, and William Cowper and embarked on his new friendship with William Blake.

8. Everything ends except my misfortunes.

9. Hester Thrale Piozzi's innovative and ambitious book *Retrospection; or a Review of the Most Striking and Important Events, Characters, Situations, and Their Consequences Which the Last Eighteen Hundred Years Have Presented to the View of Mankind* (1801) had already been unfavorably reviewed by the *Antijacobin* (8 [1801]: 241–56) and *European Magazine* (39 [1801]: 188–93) when Smith wrote this letter. Only 516 sets of 750 printed were sold, in part because typographical errors led some prospective buyers to wait for a second edition. When the *Critical Review* panned it in May (32 [1801]: 28–29), it had little chance for revival (Clifford, *Hector Lynch Piozzi,* pp. 403, 405).

10. Walker's *An Historical and Critical Essay on the Revival of the Drama in Italy* was

not published until 1805; his *Historical Memoir on Italian Tragedy* had been published in 1799 (see CS to Walker, 23 June 1799 and n. 7).

11. For Jane West's novels, see CS to Walker, 23 June 1799, n. 10. Like CS's career, West's began with poetry: *Miscellaneous Poems* (1780), *Miscellaneous Poetry* (1786), *The Humours of Brighthelmstone* (1788), *Miscellaneous Poems, and a Tragedy* (1791), *An Elegy on the Death of the Right Honourable Edmund Burke* (1797), and *Poems and Plays* (1799–1805). Politically a Tory, she wrote one expressly anti-Jacobin novel, *A Tale of the Times* (1799), to which CS refers here.

12. On this work by the Lee sisters, see CS to Walker, 23 June 1799, n. 8.

To William Davies

[London, 21 April 1801]
Sir,

I have by no means forgotten that I am your debtor, but such have been the difficulties I have been under from Mr Smiths conduct towards me & almost continual ill health that, when I have been in town which has only been once this twelve month, it has not been in my power to acquit myself ——— I was very sorry you were troubled with my Letters being left at your house and did all I could to prevent it, but my Son Nicholas at Bombay is very likely still to direct thither—I therefore send to enquire if you have any Letters for me, & if I can find a moment from the disagreeable business which brought me to town, I will call at your house before I return to Tunbridge. My Son Lionel is very desirous of knowing whether you were so obliging as to comply with his request in regard to sending a set of Sonnets to Governor Wentworth at Halifax[1]——I am, Sir,

your oblig'd hble Ser^t^,
Charlotte Smith

April 21st 1801

Osborn Collection MS, Yale University. Address: Mr Davis / Messrs Cadell & Davis / Opposite the end of/ Catherine Street/ Strand. No postmark.

NOTE

1. Sir John Wentworth (1737–1820), formerly governor of New Hampshire (1766–76), retained his earlier title when he was appointed lieutenant governor of Nova Scotia; he lived in Halifax.

To the earl of Egremont

[Frant, 24 July 1801]
My Lord,

I have this morn^{g} re^{d} the enclos'd from Mr Bicknell. Your Lordships appointing a Gentleman to attend on your part when M^{r} B Smith's Trustee, Mr Tayler,[1] attends Mr Mitford[2] on his, to receive this money 2000£ St^{g}[3] & I beleive 8 dividends ~~on his~~, & letting me know when y^{r} Lordship gives this direction will much oblige, My Lord,

your ever grateful Ser^{t},
Charlotte Smith

July 24th 1801

Petworth House Archives MS. No address or postmark.

NOTES

1. From London, BS wrote to Egremont on 6 July, that he was "compel'd My Lord from necessity to come to London to obtain my pecuniary rights, which have been withheld from me, and reduced me to the most painful situation." There he requested an interview and asked that notice be sent a day or two in advance to "Robt Tayler Esqr Merct Broad Street" (for Tayler, see Biographical Notes). On 22 July, he wrote that he was "extremely mortified" to have missed the long-sought interview because a clerk had misplaced Egremont's note (unpub. letters in PHA #0.11). In an uncannily similar request, CS asks in a 31 July letter to Egremont for two days' notice for an appointment for herself.

On 17 Aug. BS complains that if Egremont has seen CS, he should see him, according to "the Maxim Audi alteram partem" ("Hear the other side," a phrase from St. Augustine), which suggests at least a passing familiarity with popular Latin phrases if not some formal schooling in the language. BS continues, "I have friends of integrity, who are ready to vouch that since our unhappy schism, my general conduct has been such, as to make me deserving of very different letters than those Mrs Smith has thought fit to address to me, and those I have seen of hers to others, yet I have not deign'd to retaliate, though invidiously, and undeservedly attack'd and at a period, when I am under the most severe pressure of circumstances, and need of pecuniary aid, occasion'd by my property being withheld from me" (unpub. letter in PHA #0.11). Whatever BS said to his estranged wife or about her in private, he was indeed circumspect not to deride her in letters in the early years of Egremont's trusteeship, although he did decry her opinions and her actions.

2. Mitford, a lawyer long involved in the trust, is not well identified in the letters. At times he lent CS money.

3. The £2,000 marriage settlement came to CS on the death of her stepmother, Mrs. Henrietta Meriton Turner Chafys.

To the earl of Egremont

[Frant, 31 July 1801]
My Lord,

I have received a Letter from Mr Mitford of which I enclose a copy.

Your Lordship will, I am sure, in the present state of the business, forgive me if I beg leave to solicit your kindness in directing that when it is convenient to <u>you to make the appointment</u>, I may be inform'd of <u>it two days before</u>, As the circumstances I am under, as well in regard to myself as to the two younger children of this worthless & unfeeling Man, will no longer allow me to hesitate how to act. His youngest Son is so situated as to make it impossible for me to delay any longer forcing his father to assist in providing for him——

I have done everything that might prevail upon Mr Benjn Smith to hear reason & not outrage every honest & honourable feeling. He resists every thing & must take the consequence.

I took the liberty with which I hope your Lordship was not offended to ask whether there would be anything improper in asking Genl Dalrymple[1] to give George an Ensigncy in the 47th where, by the Army list, there appears to be three or four vacancies. I have had a Letter from Lord Clanricarde[2] who, tho—from some political difference of opinion which prevents his asking any thing now—he cannot at this moment do what I requested for George, yet assures me that he will seize the first moment in his power to oblige me & that, if in the mean time I can procure an Ensigncy, he will in future assist my boy with all his interest, & I have great reason to beleive his Lordship will befriend me whenever & in whatever way he can. If therefore I could obtain a pair of Colours for George, I should not be without hope of getting him on by means of Lord Clanricarde & another General with whom I beleive I have some little interest tho he has not now a Regiment.

Be assured, my Lord, that when you condescended to give your opinion that the Army would not be a good line for this boy to pursue, I should have attended to that opinion with all the deference I owe, as well to your judgement as your kindness. But after trying the possibility of getting him out to India and failing & casting about on every side, I saw not the least chance of providing for him in any other Way, & I know the ruin that attends his being at home and feel my incapacity to support him——

I hoped the June West India (Leeward Island) fleet was arrived, but since it was slightly mention'd as being off Cape Clear, there has been no account of its getting into Port.

If it should be come, I shall be a good deal distress'd to know how to pay the Duties on the Madeira & some more trifling things which Charles has (I suppose) sent, As Messrs Daniel[3] refuse to pay them as is usual.

It is I hope needless to say how greatly concernd I am at the necessity of so often troubling y^r Lordship on my wretched business—Or that I am most gratefully, My Lord,

your obliged humble Ser^t,
Charlotte Smith

Frant, Tunbridge Wells
July 31, 1801

Petworth House Archives MS. No address or postmark.

NOTES

1. General William Dalrymple (Col. Dalrymple of Charles's regiment, the 47th, from 1794 until his promotion to general of the army on 1 Jan. 1798) had once obtained Charles an appointment through the earl of Egremont's interest (CS to Egremont, 25 Jan. 1804). Dalrymple was less helpful with George, but Egremont or Tyler perhaps failed to pass on CS's note requesting help (see CS to Egremont and CS to Dalrymple, 10 Feb. 1803; and CS to Egremont, after 10 Feb. and before 2 Mar. 1803).

2. See CS to Cadell and Davies [Mar. 1798], and n. 3. The earl of Clanricarde had previously aided both Charles and Lionel. CS was long acquainted with both earls of Clanricarde—Henry, who died in Dec. 1797, and his brother and successor John Thomas, who was created earl in Dec. 1800. When she and BS were still living together (before 1787), they were invited to dinner on at least one occasion (CS to Egremont, 25 Jan. 1804).

3. Thomas Daniel and Sons, merchants, of Mincing Lane.

To William Tyler[1]

Frant. Tunbridge Wells
Aug^st 9th 1801
Sir,

Believing it certain that Lord Egremont is at Lewes or Brighthelmstone this week & will be next, on account of the races which I think his Lordship usually attends, & recollecting it is a time of the year when there is generally a good deal of company at Petworth House, it may perhaps be more proper to address to you a Letter on the affairs of the Smith Trust which you can communicate to his Lordship when it may be least troublesome to him to give me his commands——

With this is a copy of a Letter received from Mr Charles Smith by a Liverpool Ship in less than 2 months from Barbados. Lord Egremont will perceive that he has come to an arrangement with Prettejohn & (perhaps wisely) taken what ballance could be had and given him a discharge. I know not that, considering the delays & expence of Chancery in Barbados, it is not better thus than to have pursued him thro the doubles he would have made in which he is well experienced & have risk'd losing it all by the death of the Wretch who is very old and infirm.[2] I hope Lord Egremont will approve of what Charles has done——

I submit it to his Lordships consideration whether it would not be proper to take some measures in regard to Mr Boehm by fyling a bill of discovery against him & the other parties who (as entitled to the Money due from Richd Smith's estate to the estate of William Berney[3]) have most undoubtedly been paid a very considerable Sum above the debt and interest. From the knowledge I had of the affairs, I was very sure there was iniquity going on between the old Trustees & Prettejohn in regard to the payment of these debts to the Berneys. I was call'd upon time after time to sign, as Attorney to M^r^ B Smith & as Executrix to the elder Mr Smith, accounts which were laid before me in three great folio's, & which I had neither time nor opportunity to understand, & I was very well convinced that Steeles, Tyrells & the remains of Millingtons Debts[4] were more than the Berney debt could possibly amount to. Mr Boehms conduct was always mark'd with something that was not the plain & open countenance of conscious integrity, nor could there be any good reason for the continual evasions that were used to escape shewing me, otherwise than in these great folio's, the accounts.

So long ago as 1791, Mr Harding[5] demanded them on my behalf, & they were then said to be lost or mislaid. A very strange excuse for a Merchant to give! In 1792, however, they were found again, for I was then made to sign them for the last time when a ballance of thirteen pounds was paid to Mr Boehm, & that was stated to be in full of all demands—tho it happen'd a little unluckily that After this, Mr Berney received 600£ of the crops of 1793 of which, when I ask'd an account of Mr Boehm, he said, that if I would apply to Mr Berney as a Gentleman he would give me an answer. I replied that, not considering him as one, because no Man is a Gentleman who is not an honest Man, I could not as such apply to Mr Robt Berney—Which gave great offence to Mess^r^ Boehm & his Lady & Co—— The fact I take to be that Boehm has never had the money himself, but he knew that Berney had, & on making up the account he saw that too much had been received which, as Berney could not refund, he must in case of enquiry. Now as he really had lent money at times to the estate (I believe about 350£ which Robinson promis'd to pay but never did); as he had had all the law expences thrown upon him for the Berney family which I have heard amounted to 1000£; & as Berney had play'd the Devil with the Estate in which he had a third share & run him into debt & taken his money in Barbados; & as he had besides, Berney, his wife, & five or six children of his to keep for he was entirely ruin'd, M[r] Boehm set all these losses against his conscience and thought it was, on striking a ballance, as well to let this little affair of 2000 or 3000£ rest as it was; when We had lost thirty thousand pounds, he supposed that three or four one way or the other made no great difference—— & then he quieted his said conscience (which in a Merchant is seldom very troublesome) by doing little acts of kindness to M[r] Benj[n] Smith & on one or two occasions to his family.

I am very certain that M[r] Robert Tayler knows very well that this transaction cannot bear investigation, for I have more than once spoken my opinion very plainly, & he did not deny, he only evaded, the assertions I made— We certainly cannot afford to make the Sieurs[6] Boehem & Berney a present of even half what Charles says they have had beyond their due, & I apprehend that, even if the Legatees in the first instance were all paid, The residuary legatees (whoever they shall appear to be) would think it proper to try to recover this debt. I beg leave therefore to ask Lord Egremont whether it is his Lordships opinion that a bill of enquiry should be fyled, the expence of which will not, as I believe, be very great, or whether he thinks it would be better to write to M[r] Boehm, which I have abstain'd from doing, till I had his Lordships commands.

I imagine that Lord Egremont will have the goodness to give some directions relative to a supply of money for Miss Smith, who is a good deal distress'd and detain'd at Lymington for want of it.[7] It seems to be out of doubt that a remittance will speedily arrive, & I hope & believe that besides pay[g] what may appear due to M[r] Benj[n] Smith as arrears & one year to me, there will be enough from said remittances to pay (I speak not of M[r] Daniels debt) all the interest & some of the Lawyers (I am anxious that M[r] Bicknell should be paid) & that I may have a part of what is due to me to pay the debts I have unavoidably incurred & assist George with what is necessary for his going out as an Ensign should I be so fortunate as to obtain an Ensigncy for him.

In regard to the debt stated to be due from Gays to Mapps estate the property of M[r] Rich[d] Smith and M[r] Allen, I cannot think with Charles that it is due. When I know that every year that infamous old Scoundrel Prettejohn kept back half the income of the Estate to pay its expences, when I have Notes of what M[r] John Forster Alleyne told me as to what was due, & his & M[r] Bremes accounts on their receiving the Estate in which no mention is made of any such debt, I cannot possibly consent to allow that any such debt is likely to exist. But if it did, I much doubt whether the mutual release given by both parties by the advice of M[r] Hollist does not put an end to any claim on behalf of Mess[r] R Smith & Allen. Charles was not apprized of or had forgotten this circumstance.

I learn from a Letter received to day from Mr Bicknell that Mr Benjn Smith has been with him (but I beleive it will be best to send a copy of it). Mr Mitford being now in possession of the dividends for which I have with my children so much occasion, I hope Lord Egremont, on whom is my greatest dependance, will let me know as soon as his Lordship conveniently can what I can most properly do to come to some immediate & final arrangement with Mr Benjn Smith, & I also request his Lordship to let me know whether, on the arrival of the Fleet which will hardly be later than between the 15th & 20th ins^{t}, It would not be saving troublesome law expences & commissions if I were to go for a week to Town to act (under his Lordships orders however) in what will I apprehend be necessary as to an arrangement of the claims, of which perhaps some interest will then be paid. In short to act merely as agent to the Trustees instead of having Mr Daniels charges added of 5 pC^{t} for paying & receiving. I should charge the Estate only half of any expences that may occur (& they w^{d} be the most moderate possible) because I must at the same time get thro the business of my own settlement being secured by a new trust, which I see will not be done unless I attend it myself, for Mr Bicknell, with the kindest heart & best meaning, is so fully occupied & has in the instance of our affairs been hitherto so ill paid that I really have not the conscience to hunt him with frequent applications for dispatch tho it is certain that this business should not on many accounts be delay'd. At present, notwithstanding what Mr Bicknell says, I beleive & am told by other Solicitors that the affairs, for want of a regular appointment of Lord Egremont to the Trust of the 7000£ belonging to me, might in the event of my death be left in a state of which ~~their father~~ Mr Smith would take advantage. I believe that, by means of my friend Bishop[8] and in consequence of other circumstances, it might now be possible to bind Mr Smith to settle the income of my fortune on a more equal footing ~~now~~ at present &, if I should die, to bind him to make an allowance to my unprovided for Children during his life out of the whole near 400£ a year, which would then be his from my fortune: if he is not compell'd to do this, they will never have a shilling to support them.[9] I am sure Lord Egremont will see the propriety and justice of this, and I therefore cannot doubt that generous concurrence and assistance from his Lordship to which I am indebted for my very existence & that of my family.

I beg the favor of you, as you will see the occasion there is for dispatch, to take the earliest opportunity that without my being too troublesome may occur, in laying these circumstances before his Lordship. And with apologies for the trouble I give you, I am, Sir,

Your most obedient Scr^{r}, Charlotte Smith

Petworth House Archives MS. Address: Mr Tyler./ On affairs of the Smith Trust. No postmark.

NOTES

1. This detailed letter to William Tyler, Egremont's steward and solicitor at Petworth, is typical of CS's correspondence with him. Most of her rambling, repetitive business letters to Tyler are not reproduced here; this one introduces several ongoing issues in settling the trust, reviews trust history, and openly disparages persons CS did not trust. Later letters are more hostile, as Tyler earned a place on her list of those she could not trust.

2. William Prettyjohn died on 29 June 1803 (PHA #8010).

3. William Berney, of Barbados, married Mary Smith, Richard Smith's third child. He died before Nov. 1768, at which time she married Thomas Dyer. The three Berney children (Robert, Dorothy Elizabeth afterward Boehm, and Mary Eleanor afterward Henchman) and the five Dyer children (Richard, Thomas, John, Edward, and Maria Elizabeth Charlotte) were to have received smaller portions of the estate than BS and CS's children. But Richard died in 1794. (See Genealogical Chart.)

The debt to the Berneys had been overpaid by as much as £2,000, and that issue remained unsettled throughout CS's lifetime. CS chiefly blamed Robert Berney, William's eldest child and only son, for failing to settle the overpayment, because he was the senior member of the family. How the younger Berney came to his ruin is not known.

4. That is, more than £2,000. None of the three is further identified in surviving financial records in PHA, but Steele, Tyrrell, and Millington were common family names in Barbados.

5. From 1790 to 1792, George Hardinge, justice and member of Parliament, sometimes helped CS financially (see CS to Cadell, Sr., 8 Sept. 1790 and n. 5).

6. CS elsewhere uses "Sieurs" sarcastically and here invites a mocking mispronunciation of Boehm as "Bo-hem" instead of the usual "Beam."

7. Charlotte Mary's cousin, Mary Gibbes Smith Allen, lived at the Grove, Lymington, Hants. (See Genealogical Chart.) She and her husband, Capt. Robert Allen, along with her brother, Richard Smith, had a long-contested claim against the estate. CS refers to it later in this letter.

8. There were two Bishops, the Honorable William Bishop (named in CS to Egremont, 4 Aug. 1800, as one who could accept the title deeds in Barbados for the sale of Gay's to Prescod) and Henry Bishop, Esq., of Spring Hall in Barbados. How CS came to call either of these men her "friend" is not clear. Of the solicitors involved with John Forster Alleyne in the sale of Gay's—Bishop, Breme, Phillips—Breme was to have been in England on 20 Aug. 1800 (see CS to Egremont, 9 July 1800).

9. Meanwhile, on 20 Aug. BS writes in his own defense to Egremont that he requested an interview "for the purpose to conciliate matters, not to inflame them[.]" He also complains that CS "violently attacks me on every side, vilifies my character, even to a valuable friend, & to everyone she thinks partial to me[.]" He proposes that if her claims are proved in arbitration, he will assist his two youngest children "in the manner he shall judge most for their interest." At the same time, he must have money now "to discharge debts contracted by a detention of his property" in Scotland (unpub. letter in PHA #0.11).

To the earl of Egremont

{?London, received ca. 30 September 1801}
My Lord,

I am extremely unwilling to harrass y^{r} Lordship with farther applications on the business, & as I understand to day from an enquiry George has made in Grosvenor place that you are not expected in town, I have determind, unless I have yr Lordship's commands to the contrary, to go down to Bignor on Thursday when I hope & beleive the matter in agitation may be settled without farther trouble. I should be much oblig'd to y^{r} Lordship to direct by Thursdays post the Messrs Pybus's[1] to give me a memorandum of the date & amount of the bills of Mr Gibbons[2] yet due, as I think it will be necessary to know, & I have forgotten——My Brother w^{d} forward the order if I apply perhaps without your Lordships authority————————————

. . . Gentlemen[3] may think it impertinent. I beleive nothing can be done about investing my 3000£[4] till the 21st of October arrives, & before that I can take information what is to be done, which Mr Bicknell does not seem to know & which may as well be done in Sussex as here. I have the honor to be,

My Lord, your most oblig'd Ser^{t},
Charlotte Smith

Petworth House Archives MS. No address or postmark.

NOTES

1. Egremont's bankers, the firm of Pybus, Call, Grant, and Hale, 148 Old Bond Street, handled much of the money that Egremont, as trustee, allowed CS to have.

2. Probably Robert Gibbons of Barbados (d. 1805), youngest brother of Sir William Gibbons, acting as his agent. By 14 Aug. 1806, he had made payments totaling £3,985, money owed on a portion of Gay's plantation, which Prescod had purchased.

3. A page between "authority" and "Gentlemen" is lost.

4. On 21 Apr. 1802, in an action related to Prescod's purchase of Gay's, an old indenture from 2 July 1784 was brought to the attention of the new trustees. They "expressly directed" that the £3,000 settlement made on CS and BS's marriage, on 22 Feb. 1765, be set apart from Prescod's purchase money and invested in the trust (PHA #7371).

To the earl of Egremont

Bignor Park. Octr 6th 1801
My Lord,

I have a favor to request of your Lordship which is to lend me Hume's history of England, 1st volume (if it is not so finely bound as to be injur'd by being sent) and Mrs Macaulay's, should it be in the library at Petworth.[1] I am at work on a compilation for a bookseller & have no time to lose, having already faild of fulfilling my agreement by being constantly oblig'd to attend to My family's affairs & to go to town which must be my excuse for taking this liberty——

I beg leave to request of your Lordship to give orders when you go to Town that Mr Benjn Smith may have 200£[2] which is nearly what is due to him as arrears and that Miss Smith may have an hundred, as she is very much distress'd. I am unwilling to speak of myself who am unfortunately too often the subject of complaint ~~& rage~~. But it is absolutely necessary for me to represent that I borrow'd 40£ to enable me to go to Town, which I solemnly engaged to repay in a month & that my stay in Town, ~~tho I had nothing but absolute necessaries, & hardly that,~~ cost me every shilling of the 55£ I received from M^{r} B Smith as part of the accumulated dividend, which would otherwise have paid my bills at home.

As all this expence was incurred by Mr Smith's absurdity & I have already sufferd so much from the same cause, I hope & beleive your Lordship will see the hardship of my suffering in this instance, for not only I am deprived of the money I have so long waited for but prevented from earning any & am therefore doubly a loser. I venture therefore to beg I may have liberty to take 200£ on my own account; the expences I have been at (which must fall on the residue) I will make out; & the Sum above named will not do more than cover my account against the estate. There is an arrear of 70£ & 35£ due to me for interest which must go to the interest account——

It appears to me that the way to save your Lordship from any unnecessary trouble in future will be for you to direct me to lay the accounts of what is due to the legatees before some person authorised by your Lordship who understands these sort of things & who shall be competent to decide if the calculate is made right & then to settle the proportions to be paid to the various claimants & how the present payments are to be made. Mr Tyler is probably too much engaged at this time; otherwise if it were judged proper by your Lordship to order it so, I would go to Petworth at any time this were most convenient to him, & I am persuaded that in an hour the business might be put in a way of going on without giving your Lordship any trouble hereafter, & I should suppose that then, acting under your orders & your Lordship still having the goodness to see there was no misapplication of the Sum saved out of the fire, I might as Executrix do all that remains to be done.

In this I have no meaning or wish but that while M^{r} B Smiths family so materially benefit by your goodness towards them, Your Lordship may no longer be subject to applications or trouble of any kind, otherwise than to direct the payment of the money at stated periods as it falls in———

I could under Your Lordships orders, proceed as Executrix, to bring M[r] Berney to account; In regard to M[r] Richard Smiths & M[r] Allens claims,[3] if they are substantiated (which is in my opinion far from being the case at present), there will be money enough in Barbados to pay them there. I cannot imagine they ought to be paid from the installments, but at all events Charles' accounts must be waited for.

I have the honor to be y[r] Lordships most oblig'd Ser[t],

Charlotte Smith

Petworth House Archives MS. No address or postmark.

NOTES

1. David Hume's *History of England,* 8 vols. (1754–63) and Catharine Macauley's *History of England,* 8 vols. (1763–83). On 18 Feb. 1802, CS returned a copy of the Hume to William Davies, apparently having been unable to borrow it from Egremont.

2. On 14 Oct., BS wrote to Egremont that it didn't matter whether he received £300 or 200 now and the remainder upon settlement. He also tried to correct Egremont's misunderstanding: BS had "no intention of departing from the amicable adjustment made by my friend Mr Robert Tayler & my son Lionel" (unpub. letter in PHA #0.11).

3. On 14 May 1803, a bill for Smith and Allen's claim was filed in Chancery (PHA #8010). Richard Smith and Mary Gibbes Smith Allen were the children of BS's elder brother, the Reverend Richard Smith, who held the living at Islington. It is odd that they should have any claims, for at their father's death on 15 Feb. 1772, he still owed their grandfather £4,380.5.10 and £400 interest (PHA #7371).

To Joseph Cooper Walker

[Bignor Park, 7 October 1801]

Dear Sir,

An opportunity offering of sending a Letter to Dublin by means of a Young Lady of this Neighbourhood[1] who is going to Ireland, I cannot help enquiring after you; It is very long since I have had the pleasure of hearing from you. Yet I think I have acknowledged your last Letter—— I should be very sorry to think you had forgotten me, still more to beleive I had done any thing to forfeit the friendly interest with which you have so long honour'd me & which I trust I know how to value.

Of literary news I have none to tell you, for I have been so circumstanced lately, as to have been deprived of all intercourse with those whose society is best worth having, & I hardly ever see any new books. My whole time has been occupied in attending to the affairs of my family, on which I begin to think a spell certainly rests which will for the small remainder of my life render my endeavours after peace & competence as fruitless as those attempts have been in which I have consumed the best of my days.

You probably correspond with our old friend Mr Hayley and know the Lady of your County[2] with whom he is as I understand soon to be united. I never hear from him now, but I shall ever retain the lively recollection of his former friendship and kindness. Of Mr Godwin whom you name in your last Letter, I have seen but little lately,[3] for my health has made it necessary for me to remain almost entirely in the Country—— Poor Lucy, who is now a Widow with two children & a third expected immediately, has taken up a great deal of my time & attention, & I am hardly ever able to see any of those friends whose pursuits & ideas are so unlike those with which I am surrounded that they have but little pleasure in seeking me——— I sometimes think that I should be happier & be able to live in a manner better suited to my taste if I were to go to the Continent. The excessive price of every article necessary to life in the Country, which even Peace will not diminish, & my predilection for France would decide me now to go thither were not my health so much injured that it appears hardly worth the trouble of going to another Country only to die.

I fear that, by the death of Low my Publisher, you did not receive my last volumes. The two last of that work the Solitary Wanderer are now ready for the press, and I hope to have the pleasure of sending you a complete set of five volumes.[4] I was highly flatterd by your approbation of the former three.

I write this at Bignor Park, my old paternal house, but my present residence is at Frant near Tunbridge Wells, whither I shall return in about a fortnight & where it will give me great satisfaction to hear from you, as I am, Dear Sir,

with the sincerest gratitude & regard,
your oblig'd Ser^t^,
Charlotte Smith

Bignor, Octr 7th 1801

Haverford College Library MS. No address or postmark.

NOTES

1. Not identified.

2. Penelope Carleton Chetwynd; see CS to Walker, 14 Apr. 1801, n. 6. They did not, in fact, marry.

3. William Godwin recorded CS's applause for *St. Leon* in 1799, and CS had written the prologue to Godwin's ill-fated play *Antonio, a Tragedy,* which barely survived its opening night on 13 Dec. 1800. His second wife, Mary Jane Godwin, visited CS in the country.

4. Vols. 4 and 5 of CS's last prose work for adults, *Letters of a Solitary Wanderer,* were published by T. N. Longman and O. Rees in 1802. They purchased a projected sixth volume that was never finished. CS was very dissatisfied with the quality of their paper and printing (see CS to Walker, [late Mar.–early Apr. 1802]).

To William Tyler

[Bignor Park] Oct[r] 13th 1801
Sir,

Before I leave Petworth, I must trouble you to obtain for me change of the note for 100 G[s] which Lord Egremont has sign'd on Pybus & Co on account of arrears, as I have not any money whatever for my journey.

As I greatly fear his Lordship will have more trouble than it is reasonable he should take on the unhappy affairs of my family, & as there seems no other way of his being exonnerated from it, I have ventured to propose to resume my charge of Executrix to Richard Smith, which I have never resign'd & which I am qualified by an oath of administration taken in 1791 to act in, notwithstanding M[r] Smith[1] is still living. By this means there would be an end of all the trouble Lord Egremont may have; My gratitude to his Lordship would be in no degree lessen'd, and I trust I should so act as to shew myself not unworthy of the charge given me by the Testator nor of the efforts of unexampled generousity & goodness which his Lordship has made to releive one from the unjust persecution I had fallen under & from as much of my misfortunes as have been attending on pecuniary distress. I am, Sir,

y[r] oblig'd & obed[t] Ser[t],
Ch Smith

———All the parties concern'd would give Lord Egremont discharges for monies, &c, to this time & would assent to my acting as Executrix. Surely it would be the shortest way. M[r] B Smith would soon be quiet when he found there was no hope by applying & menacing which I have always in my own hands the means to convince him of——

If some decision is not come to to day on the division of the money, I cannot return to my distressd & afflicted family——

Petworth House Archives MS. No address or postmark.

NOTE

1. That is, Benjamin Smith.

To William Tyler

[Bignor, 20 October 1801]
Sir,

In addition to the almost insupportable calamities I have had to encounter since I left home by Lord Egremonts order, My Son Lionel[1] is now gone off to Portsmouth to embark with his company for the West Indies. I have taken leave of him this evening, well persuaded that it is for ever, for if he escapes the Grave his unfortunate brother has found in that accursed climate,[2] I cannot hope to live till his return, overwhelmed as I am with every misery that can be inflicted.

When Lord Egremont was so good as to say that, if I stay'd here 'till his Lordships return from Brighthelmston, something might finally be settled, I endeavord to submit as well as I could to the many, very many inconveniencies that such a continuance here and absence from My daughters at this period inevitably occasion'd me. But now that his Lordship is gone to London & has not as I understand left any orders for my government, I have determin'd to go immediately to London. A farther residence here is particularly disagreeable & inconvenient at this time, even if I had not such real occasion to be in London on account of the investiture of the 3000£, which must be done on the 21st, & the fitting out of My youngest Son who is order'd to the Isle of Wight immediately.[3] I had hoped my representation of these pressing circumstances would have induced Lord Egremont to shorten what ever difficulties yet may appear to remain, as most undoubtedly Messr Smiths & Allens demand will not nor cannot be allow'd without an investigation which cannot be given now, & I will not imagine Lord Egremont will suffer the whole family to be ruin'd at last by waiting for this developement. At all events when I am in London I can see (if I have strength to undertake it) Mr Foster Alleyne and Mr Phillips Solicitor from Barbados, to whom my poor Charles repeatedly referred me but who, when I was in Town last, was still at Liverpool. I must therefore on every account go to Town & from thence home—— I have supplied my Son Lionel with thirty pounds, all ~~I had~~ I had reserved of the 100£ after sendg what was absolutely necessary to Tunbridge, I must therefore request the favor of you to supply me with 10£ to bear my expences to Town, for which I will give you an acknowledgement to be repaid by so much left in Pybus's hands when the money is paid to me, & with this assistance, I shall be able to get to London on Wednesday morning,[4] & I hope be able to put an end in some way or other to suspence, which the present circumstances of my family, renders most needful. Your early answer & compliance, as I will if possible begin my journey this evening & go as far as Godalming, will oblige, Sir,

your most obed Sert,
Charlotte Smith

Bigner, Octr 20th 1801

Petworth House Archives MS. No address or postmark.

NOTES

1. Still a lieutenant in the 24th (Warwickshire) Regiment.

2. The first mention of Charles's death in Barbados. The exact date is unknown, but in CS to Tyler, 9 Aug. 1801, CS refers to Charles's last letter, written 18 June. Though the exact disease is not described, it was almost certainly yellow fever, contracted during the summer months.

3. George Frederick Smith enlisted as ensign on 27 Sept. 1801 in his brother Charles's regiment, the 47th, presumably an appointment available because of his brother's death. "Investiture" is archaic for "investment."

4. The next day, 21 Oct.

To William Tyler

[Bignor, 20 October 1801]
Sir,

I acknowledge to have receivd of you the loan of a Bank note value 10£ which I will settle to repay before I leave Petworth. I propose being at the Half Moon tomorrow evening & beg the favour of you to oblige me with a few moments of y[r] time that every thing necessary may be canvass'd before I trouble Lord Egremont on the following morning—at which time I hope we may agree on some final procedure. I am, Sir,

y[r] oblig'd hble Ser[t],
Charlotte Smith

Oct[r] 20th 1801

Petworth House Archives MS. Address: M[r] Tyler. No postmark.

To William Tyler

[?Bignor, received 21 October 1801]
Sir,

I have had the comfort of finding that the information in the papers was unfounded & that Capt[n] Smith need not have hurried away to Portsmouth as he did, as the detachment of the 85th which he belongs to are neither embarked or embarking for the W Indies or any other place at this time.

Lionel sent his Servant over last night to appease my alarm, which was indeed dreadful, & to return the money. A part of it I have however sent back to him that he may be repaid the expences of going to Town &c on his fathers nonsensical account, which must fall finally on the residue, for neither myself nor Captain Smith can afford these expences, & it is fit that he who is the occasion of them should eventually suffer.

I enclose with many thanks the bank note for 10£ with which you were so very obliging as to supply me on my representation of the situation I should have been in. I hope & beleive Lord Egremont will have the goodness to see me tomorrow, & I beleive I can convince his Lordship that it is equally my wish and my Duty to settle on the strictest principle of justice all the will entrust [*sic*] me with. I never yet have wilfully misrepresented any one circumstance, & I certainly, after having worked like a copying clerk for fourteen years for Mr B Smiths family, shall not injure them at last. Their Grandfather in making me his Executrix, tho I was but a young Woman (not seven & twenty) when he died, beleived I should do justice to his intentions—— I hope I have done so as far as has depended on me, & certainly I can have now no motive to act on any other view—~~xxxx~~—— I shall be happy in every opportunity of evincing my sense of the trouble I have given you individually, & of your obliging attention to my request, & Am, Sir,

yr most obedt Sert,
Charlotte Smith

Petworth House Archives MS. No address or postmark.

To the earl of Egremont

[?Bignor, 21 October 1801]

Mrs Smith[1] proposes that Lord Egremont shall give her and Mr Lionel Smith an order to receive of Messrs Pybus & Co. the Sums now in their hands—to be divided according to the several claims as shall appear due——& the acquittances for such sums to be immediately obtain'd from Miss Smith on behalf of herself, Mr William Towers Smith, and her deceas'd Brother Charles. Mr Duncan[2] will be in Town on the 25th & will give acquittances for Mrs L. Newhouse and has already directed Mrs C. Smith to leave in the hands of Lord Egremonts Banker whatever may belong to Mrs Newhouse, till he, Mr Duncan, can dispose of it for her.

Mr Turner will give an acquittance for Mr Nicholas Hankey Smith — — & there can be no difficulty in the matter ~~on~~ as Mrs C. S. hopes any hazard to Lord Egremont—should his Lordship approve of this mode which she would take care—shall be perfectly regular.

It is proposed to pay Mr Bicknell, Mr Wightman, & Mr Dayrell's[3] which will clear the estate from Any law claims if this measure is approved of by Lord Egremont.

Mrs Smith has been so much harrassd & destroyed in consequence of her recent loss, of the apprehension of her Son Lionel's going to the W Indies,

& of pecuniary difficulties & the melancholy Letters she receives from home that it is with the utmost effort she is able to support herself, & she is persuaded that Lord Egremont, who has done so much for her hitherto, will releive her from her present wretched suspence as soon as possible.

The fund from which George must be supplied is his Bro^{r} Nicholas's Money, which Mrs Smith has full authority from him to take. The expences Mrs Smith has been at for the Estate in Journies, &c, have totally deprived her of all she has received, except ab^{t} 10£, & if she is not repaid, then she cannot return to her daughters. Mrs Newhouse is without resource—— She wishes to reach London to night.

Petworth House Archives MS. No address or postmark.

NOTES

1. CS had written three desperate letters to Tyler in twenty-four hours before penning this very formal, third-person request to Egremont.

2. John Shute Duncan, No. 16 Lincoln's Inn, Old Square, Thomas Newhouse's friend and attorney, had witnessed the Newhouse marriage.

3. Charles Bicknell and Edmund Dayrell were lawyers. Wightman's role in trust business was fleeting, as this is the only reference to him.

To the earl of Egremont

[London, 26 October 1801]
My Lord,

In obedience to your Lordships commands, I beg leave to inform you that I am at No. 35 in Rathbone Place, not being able on arriving in Town to procure my former lodgings.

I went on Saturday to Messrs Pybus's and have taken the money for George & 100£ for the Lawyers of which I presented 50£ to Mr Dayrells who appear'd to be satisfied & ready to undertake what is immediately requisite in regard to the 3000£ belonging to me; & in order to avoid any farther loss from the probable rise of the funds, he has agreed to make application to Mr Prescod to invest the money to day in yr Lordships name and his Mr Prescods own which will be an accommodation to me & be equally secure to him till the necessary forms are gone thro. Some delay it appears is likely to be occasion'd by the uncertainty of which of the Original Trustees was the survivor, William Nash or William Towers.[1] My Uncle died in August 74. As Mr Nash was an Alderman of London, his decease may easily be ascertain'd. I am persuaded he died many years before. If so, the late Captain Towers[2] was the representative of the surviving Trustee, & the Trust I imagine devolves in that case to my Brother who is, I suppose, his heir at Law. I am waiting for Miss Smiths broker, Mr Josepth Smith, a distant relation,[3] who is entrusted by her & to whom I shall make over hers & Mr William Smith's money, & direct him to invest My lamented Charles's share in the 3 pC^{ts} in my Lordships name. I saw Mr Duncan on Saturday who was that instant returning to Oxford. He desird me to put what money belongs to Mrs Newhouse into the Stocks in the joint names of John Shute Duncan & John Newhouse; I mention'd that I had directions to obtain from the parties the stamped receipts for Legacies, but he seem'd desirous of avoiding the expence which is 20^{s} for every 100£, & he said his receipt & the certificate of the broker would answer the same purpose. In this however, as in all other transactions relative to this business, I shall observe as nearly as possible your Lordships orders. I have the honor to be y^{r} most oblig'd Ser^{t},

Ch Smith

35 Rathbone Place
Octr 26th 1801

Petworth House Archives MS. No address or postmark.

NOTES

1. Rev. Richard Smith (BS's older brother), William Nash, and William Towers (CS's maternal uncle) signed the marriage settlement of 22 Feb. 1765 and were its original trustees (PHA #7371).

2. "The late Captain Towers" would have been CS's cousin, a son of William Towers (CS to Cadell and Davies, 19 Dec. 1799, may describe his death). Her brother Nicholas Turner did inherit that trust.

3. A stockbroker and accountant of Hatton Garden who acted in Charlotte Mary's financial interest, Smith was a moneyed man. I have not traced the exact family connection, but Charlotte Mary often stayed with his family in London.

To the earl of Egremont

[London] 4th Novr 1801
My Lord,

I ought to beg yr pardon for not explaining myself & giving y^{r} Lordship needless trouble. My reason for applying as I did was not to have the money remain in a Banker's hands, but merely to get it paid at Pybus's in y^{r} Lordships name—to remain only a day or two till stocks are <lowering> which I am assured they will be with directions to Mr Hipuff,[1] Mr Pybus's broker, to invest it the first fair opportunity under 68, which is very likely to happen, & will be a considerable difference to me.

But Mr Dayrell faild to make himself master of the subject as he promis'd, & I have now waited many days in hopes of getting it done before I go out of town because I know very well when term begins that Lawyers will do nothing for me & stocks will rise, by which I shall lose. Mr ~~B Smith~~, however, after having agreed to let his son have 20£ which I proposed to him if I got advanced the third hundred, has received the Sum of 70£ (& 10 I shall keep for expences) & has let George have the 20£, is to give a receipt for 100£ & is gone in the diligence to Scotland.[2] I imagine yr Lordship will direct therefore that one of the 100£s retaind for him (to be paid in 3 months of which two months are expired) shall be paid by Mr Pybus &c to me, as I took this 100£ I have so advanced to Mr B Smith (for the sake of getting a present for George) from that, which I am to account for on behalf of my son Nicholas, one hundred being applied to Georges use before of Nicholas's money—& I have been put by being kept in Town to great expence & have great expence to expect at home. I shall therefore be much oblig'd by this order, at yr <leisure> however. Mr B Smith will then have had 300£ of the four agreed upon——

Mr Tayler, whom I saw to day, seems to think he Mr Smith is quite incapable of governing or acting for himself. However I went with a design to get his signature to the trust proposed & as he is gone, Mr Dayrell says he thinks I may act under the power of Attorney & sign for him & myself. My request to your Lordship is that you will permit the 3000£ to be deposited in yr name at Pybus's till the forms can be gone thro—— if I can prevail on Prescod to pay it.

I had rather better accounts of Mrs Newhouse to day, but Miss Smith is so ill that I must return tomorrow. I have no excuse to offer for being so indistinct, but the fatigue of mind I go thro. I am yr Lordships

most oblig'd Sert, Charlotte Smith

I beg the favor of a frank for the enclosed to Mr Duncan; it contains the brokers certificate for the Stock bought for Mrs Newhouse.

I will not trouble yr Lordship about the receipts, but send them altogether with my accounts & vouchers to Mr Tyler.

Petworth House Archives MS. No address or postmark.

NOTES

1. Charles Hippuff, 12 Birchin Lane.

2. BS had been in London since early July, writing letters on his own behalf on trust matters to Egremont. His last letter from London was written on 14 Oct.

CS's run-on sentence is hard to follow, but it is typical of this letter in which she later complains of fatigue of mind. Here, she crossed out "B Smith" without replacing it, and loses track of her relative and subordinate clauses. Several sentences later she inserted "Mr Smith" but forgot to cross out "he." A *diligence* is a public stagecoach, a term more used in France than England.

To the earl of Egremont

[Frant, 3 December 1801]
My Lord,

I have the mortification of learning that, contrary to my just expectations & contrary to common sense Mr Dayrell has so contrived, that I have no chance at present of getting the 3000£ (which ought to have been paid on the 21st of Oct^r^) settled in the New Trust,[1] & I shall lose the dividend for which the 5 pC^t^ Mr Prescod offers to pay will be no compensation, for the dividend would have been 75£. Mr Dayrell writes to Mr Turner exactly the reverse of what he says to me—— I have a Letter also from Mr Mitford so very puzzling that I cannot even guess what he means, & I very much doubt if he knows himself. It seems to me that Mr Bicknell & he have been perplexing each other about nothing. I must not, indeed I ought not, to offend either of these Gentlemen on my Brothers account, but I cannot be passive while they are bewildering a very simple affair, as they seem disposed to do—— I am extremely unlucky in almost every thing, save in the fortunate circumstance of having permission to hope for your Lordship's continued goodness & that, when I <u>can</u> get this money collected, it will be in your trust & I shall then & not till then, be easy about it. I must attend on the 10th the meeting of My Brother C^rs^[2]——

My eldest daughter is in such a state of health that it is absolutely necessary for her to have advice. We are in hourly expectation of the October fleet from Barbados in some vessel of which My dear Charles's Servant & the papers so necessary to us, yet now so disturbing, will certainly arrive. My daughter therefore must be in Town, & I have determin'd for all these & other reasons, with which it is not requisite to trouble your Lordship, to go to Town <u>on Sunday</u> & put myself into the cheapest lodging I can find till I can get thro these affairs. I hope I may solicit the honor of seeing your Lordship. I will take the liberty to inform you where I fix by a note to Grosvenor place[3] & when I have the favor of seeing you will give you an account of the mission you trusted me with & the acquittances.

I have the honor to be y^r^ Lordships ever oblig'd Ser^t^,
Charlotte Smith

Frant, Decr 3rd 1801

Petworth House Archives MS. No address or postmark.

NOTES

1. See CS to Egremont, ca. 30 Sept. 1801, n. 4. CS expected to receive from her marriage settlement a dividend of £75, half of what it would earn invested at 5 percent, the other half going to BS. Exactly what sum Prescod would pay her 5 percent of is not

clear. His own payment, one-third of the remainder owed on his purchase of Gay's, was £3,331.

2. Creditors. Turner's financial difficulties are first mentioned in CS to Egremont, 18 July 1800, when their sister Catherine Dorset refused to lend him £100.

3. Egremont's town residence.

To Robert Southey[1]

Frant, Tunbridge Wells
Decr 3rd 1801
Sir,

I know not whether I am authorized by what my friend Miss Barker[2] says to take the liberty of addressing myself to you. But as she is going to Ealing & cannot receive my answer in time, I venture to introduce myself. Miss Barker says, "There is an house in Buckingham Street which would suit, I think, yours & Mr Southey's families; The whole is five G^{s} which, if divided, would make it come easy to both. Mrs Southey has not yet seen it, but I am sure will not dislike it"——

Should this be so, I shall be extremely glad to take a part of this house and to pay in proportion to the part, as I think Miss Barkers proposal hardly reasonable that you should pay two guineas & I three because the room I want is so much more than, as I apprehend, you would occupy, & therefore I ought to pay three and an half should the scheme be approv'd. In such a matter of fact Letter, I will forbear to say much on a matter of fact of another description. I mean the rare and very great pleasure it will afford me to become acquainted with a Gentleman whose talents are as far above my praise as they are above those of almost if not absolutely, all (as perhaps I ought to say) who for many years, very many indeed, have been call'd Poets in this Country——

May I beg the favor of you to let me know by a line, directed to be left at Charles Bicknell, Esqre, Norfolk Street, Strand, whether Mrs Southey, to whom I shall be happy to be known, approves of this proposal. I forget Buckingham Street but can trust to Miss Barkers judgement. If fortunately you decide on it, I beg leave to request that the necessary orders for beer & coals may be given for me, as I purpose being in London on Sunday evening & shall call at Mr Bicknells to know. I write in the dark & will therefore only add that I am, with great esteem,

Sir, your most obed^{t} Ser^{t}, Charlotte Smith

Huntington MS (HM10830). No address or postmark.

NOTES

1. When CS wrote this letter, Southey was 27; he had published his first book, *Poems,* with his friend Robert Lovell in 1795. An enlarged version containing only Southey's poems appeared in 1797, and vol. 2 appeared in 1799. His *Thalaba,* published in 1801, surely added to Smith's eagerness to meet him. He had married Edith Fricker in 1795.

Whether CS shared a house with him is not clear. On 6 Feb. 1802, Southey wrote to John Rickman from the Strand; CS was in London from 22 Jan. onward but gave no street address. Without question, the two met; in the winter of 1802, Southey wrote to Rickman, ". . . I am increasing my knowledge of the Living Remarkables, and added to my list—Charlotte Smith, a woman of genius, good sense, and pleasant manners." In the same letter, Southey writes of meeting Elizabeth Inchbald, Isaac D'Israeli, Sharon Turner, Agnes and Mary Berry, Anne Seymour Damer, Sir Thomas Lawrence, and John Hoppner—an assortment of writers and artists (Southey, *New Letters,* pp. 269–70).

2. Mary Barker (d. 1851), a lifelong friend of the Southeys and correspondent of Robert, who wrote many of his best letters to her (Southey, *New Letters,* p. 262, n. 4).

1802
"Petty duns & continual want"

— 14 March 1802

Charlotte Smith's career as a writer hit rock bottom in a year filled with poor health, increasing debt, and decreasing effectiveness as a representative of her children's trust business. The fourth and fifth volumes of Letters of a Solitary Wanderer *were published by Longman's, who had bought out Sampson Low's estate. They were cheaply printed and poorly bound. Smith was working unhappily on her history of England for girls, undertaken two years earlier for Richard Phillips, who nagged her to finish it and threatened reprisals if she did not.*

But she was devoting most of her time to trust business and felt herself "doubly a loser," for the time she would have spent writing for money was spent on the trust, and she could not bring it to an end working alone. Smith's relationship with Egremont deteriorated, as he took offense at all her efforts to further trust business and turned most trust matters over to his steward, William Tyler. Exactly what precipitated Egremont's displeasure is not clear, but this year's letters afford several clues. Egremont or Tyler or both took exception to her determination to award some portion of Augusta's inheritance to her French son-in-law. Egremont was offended by her complaints about her brother, Turner, now also a trustee. And both Egremont and Tyler objected to her initiative in consulting with lawyers about the trust business, especially when her lawyers questioned a course of action they had planned.

Under these stressful conditions, Smith's ever-precarious health worsened, aggravated by her residence in London. After years of crippling rheumatoid arthritis, she had episodes of pleurisy. Even so, she supplied George and Lionel with money to advance their military careers. Lucy's family depended on her, and Nicholas, unaware of the gravity of his mother's condition, sent his very young daughter Luzena to live with her grandmother. Harriet suffered a severe and costly return of her malarial fevers. By August, Charlotte Smith was living in fear of being arrested for debt and placed in the county jail. Instead, she suffered a concussion in a carriage accident, and her house was robbed of what modest possessions she had. Faced with starvation, she began to look for a buyer for her library, a collection of almost a thousand fine volumes.

To the earl of Egremont

[London, 12 January 1802]
My Lord,

As I cannot rest while this business of my very dear Lionel is uncertain, I have been Considering how, in case y^{r} Ldships most kind & friendly interposition should succeed, the money for a Majority in an old Regiment might be rais'd. By my marriage articles on which I have lately had counsels Opinion, I find that the whole 7000£—vis. 2000£ paid at my Fathers death, 3000£ paid on my marriage & now to be invested, & 2000£ re^{d} from Mrs Chafy[1]—is all subject to the Will of the survivor ~~of the~~ Unless by a joint deed we give it away before our decease.

It is but just that the Bulk of this sh^{d} go to the Children who do not share in the money y^{r} Lordships noble humanity has rescued for them from the wreck of Richard Smiths property. We <u>have</u> so given 2000£ by an irrevocable deed of 1788 sign'd by us both. B Smith <u>says</u> he has also so dispos'd of the rest—& given Lionel, Harriet & George each a third of the remainder—which is above 2000£ in all to each.[2] I know he will make this irrevocable by a joint deed as far as relates to Lionel, & the moment he does, it will, as my Counsel informs me, become <u>vested</u> property in Lionel. As such is capable of being sold in the way of Post Obit, The life of a Man of Sixty & a Woman of fifty one & upwards is easily valued, & if the money by discounting the Bill might be tried (partly from Nicholas's share & partly borrow'd), it might by the means above stated be <u>replaced</u>. I understand it is necessary the D[uke]. of Y[ork]. should know ~~understand~~ that the money would be forthcoming,[3] which made <turn> this in my mind with so much anxiety—

<u>Could</u> it be obtaind, this desirable delay, it would save more than my life by rendering its poor remains more comfortable. I cannot endure his going & had rather die at once than live in the horrors I shall have to suffer.

I heard from Mr Bicknell last night. There are <u>hopes</u> of Mrs Bicknell's life, but she is so delirious that there is more fear than hope. I have got the deed & shall send George with it to Ottershaw.[4]

I am y^{r} Lordships
most truly obligd Ser^{t},
Charlotte Smith

7 o clock
Jany 12th 1802

Petworth House Archives MS. No address or postmark.

NOTES

1. Mrs. Henrietta Meriton Turner Chafys, CS's stepmother.

2. Lionel, Harriet, and George were born after Richard Smith died in 1776, and so were not named in his will. One of CS's most pressing concerns was to obtain BS's agreement to make them equal beneficiaries to the three different settlements—worth £7,000—made upon her marriage. In 1803, when BS was at "the acme of my distress" (BS to Egremont, 6 May) for need of money, he complained of a letter CS had written to his friend Tayler: "The letter as usual is full of invective, and menace, in regard to myself but she insists upon her right to dispose of what she calls her fortune, share, & share alike, to the three younger children (tho I have Deeds which give me full power over it)" (BS to Egremont, 7 May). But then he agrees—"if she wo^{d} but be quiet—to do as she wishes on the £5000, the £2000 having been made over irrevocably years earlier" (unpub. letters in PHA #0.11).

The entire £7,000 that CS called her fortune were her marriage settlements. They had not, however, been properly secured to her use, and her leaving BS without a separation agreement binding them to her further reduced her claim to them. She considered it a just claim if he would only act by the three younger children as an honorable man.

3. CS is trying to ensure Lionel a majority, worth about £900, under Frederick, duke of York, second son of George III. Since 1795, after failing to distinguish himself in the field, the duke had been commander in chief of the army in Great Britain. He embarked on a program of reform, especially in the appointment of officers, that improved the army.

4. That is, to Edmund Boehm, of Ottershaw Park, Chertsey, Surrey, husband of Dorothy Elizabeth Berney, one of the cousins in the trust. (See Genealogical Chart.) Boehm managed to maintain a cordial relationship with CS's children and usually with CS.

To the earl of Egremont

9 Buckingham Street [London]
Jany 17th 1802
My Lord,

I have the honor to inform your Lordship that I have received the Deed back from Ottershaw sign'd by Mr Boehm, & I now understand that nothing remains to impede the receipt of the 3000£ of mine from Mr Prescod, but the want of the Bond given by Mr Prescod to my deceased Son. There are yet none of the Leeward Island fleet arrived at the port of London—notwithstanding the Convoy has been here ever since the 8th Instant—— Mr Daniel however says there are no apprehensions entertain'd for their safety, nor would it occasion any alarm were they not to arrive for a fortnight. Since he said this on friday, the wind is changed, and a few hours may bring them into the Channel.

Mr Dayrell notwithstanding advises my applying to your Lordship to propose your giving Mr Prescod an assurance that the bond shall be deliverd up as soon as it comes into your possession, which assurance will he says satisfy Mr Prescod without waiting any longer, & that he will then pay the money & agree to Mr Daniels accepting the last bill which is at present without their acceptance. Should therefore your Lordship be in Town, I beg the favor of you to honor me with your commands which I will send to Mr Dayrell and endeavour to get thro the business if possible this week, as the expence of being in Town with all my family falls very heavily upon me and will prolong any distress which Mr Benjn Smith seems little disposed to share; having written to Mr Tayler[1] not to pay me half the dividend on the 3333£ bought for 2000£ in the 3pC^ts^ & standing in yr Lordships name and Mr Robt Taylers—& that Gentleman sent me by George a very rude message, "that he should not receive the dividend (about 50£ I beleive) nor trouble his head about it unless Mr Smith and I could agree"—I shall not put the name of this Man into the trust of the 3000£ now to be paid, as I am not obliged to do it & he is sometimes taken with fits of sullen impertinence which I do not understand—oweing him no sort of obligation & beleiving that he has sometimes encouraged Mr Smiths unreasonable & unnatural conduct towards me and his children.

Mr Josepth Smith, a distant relation of the family's, a very respectable Man of business, has inform'd my daughter that he knows a proper person who will now immediately discount the Bill for 3737£ if he could see it.[2] Of course your Lordship will not put the Trustees endorsement to it, or part with it, till the money is ready, but as Mr Dayrell advises as a Lawyer that it should be discounted & Mr Josepth Smith thinks it would be particularly advantageous to Miss Smith and the other legatees to have it done before the month of February, I am persuaded your Lordship, who appeard to think its being discounted perfectly right, would give directions to have a copy made of the bill which is perhaps at Mr Pybus's—in order that Mr Josepth Smith may shew such copy to his friend, & as there can be no doubt of his finding it as good as the bank, a day may then be named for the money being paid into the hands of your Lordships Banker—& I will submit to you a proposal for its diversion among the legatees, which My daughter, the principal person to be consulted, approves of for herself and her Brothers should it meet your Lordships approbation. I would then give notice to Mr Duncan, Mrs Newhouses Trustee, and take for the Trust acquittances for this division as well as what has already been paid in the manner which Mr Dayrell says will be proper for the security of the Trustees.

My fortunate Lionel, for so I must consider him whom your Lordship has so interposed for his detention & promotion, writes in high Spirits from Portsmouth where he thinks his actual duty will yet detain him a week or ten days longer. He says that success in his present pursuit will make him a made Man in his profession. His gratitude is equalled only by that of Your Lordships . . .[3]

I have omitted to say that we have made every possible enquiry about M[r] Strahan:[4] Charlotte has seen two or three of her former acquaintance at Islington, but could only learn that M[r] Strahan had been for some time at his Essex living & they did not know that his health was otherwise than usual.

Petworth House Archives MS. No address or postmark.

NOTES

1. Robert Tayler, a trustee to both of CS's £2,000 marriage settlements (CS to William Tyler, unpub., 13 Feb. 1802) and to the £3,000 settlement (CS to Egremont, 20 Feb. 1802).

2. None of the surviving accounts list this sum. Prescod finally invested the £3,000 in consolidated bank annuities at 3 percent on 4 Feb. 1802, almost four months late. At the same time, he signed over £4,371 to the trustees, Egremont and Rev. Nicholas Turner, at 3 percent.

3. The rest of this line, including CS's complimentary close and signature, is cut away. The truncated sentence does not make sense; perhaps she compared her son's gratitude to "your Lordship's generosity."

4. The incumbent of the living of Islington that Richard Smith intended for one of CS's sons; see CS to Joseph Cooper Walker, 9 Oct. 1793, n. 3.

To the earl of Egremont

8 o clock
[London] Jan[y] 22nd 1802
My Lord,

Lionel not being arrived, I take it for granted the 85th c[d] not embark on account of the weather. I wrote to him yesterday to say that y[r] Ldship had had the goodness to call here, that you were going out of town this morning, & I thought he had better make Petworth in his way to Town, & have the honor of waiting on y[r] Lordship there.

I am ashamed to trouble you, my Lord, ab[t] trifles at any time & more particularly now, but I know not how to avoid it. I have injurd M[r] Tayler; he was kind enough to call here last night & said he had sent me he beleived a peevish answer by George, but he is labouring under the severest of all the afflictions that can befall a good father[1] & suffering so dreadfully, he says he cannot be teized with M[r] Benj[n] Smith who has broken his word with him & torments him with Letters to receive the dividend on the 2000£ (3333 nominal) & send it all to him—which he, M[r] Tayler will not do. He has to day written to him to say he will not, as it is contrary to his solemn promise, & he is disgusted with his attempt to get back the 20£ he gave George, &

Mr Tayler declares he will throw up the business if Mr Smith persists in this abominable conduct.

My situation is in the mean time very distressing. I cannot stir till the business of the 3000£ is got thro (M^r^ B Smith says it is all nonsense & that the impediments to its being paid are raised by me). Nor could I, even when yr Lordships infinite goodness has enabled me to conquer these difficulties which I hope may be done to day or tomorrow, leave Charlotte to go thro the other painful business till Lionel can certainly be with her[2]—& There is great reason to fear, as I learned yesterday from Mr Daniel that the only London Ship expected in which it is probable poor Charles's servant & the papers were sent is lost. Great apprehensions are entertaind for it. It is very distressing & a great addition to our troubles.

In the mean time, I pay weekly here for every thing. In the uncertainty I was under about Lionels going, I laid out about 30£ in medicines & cotton shirts for him & some other things which w^d^ have been necessary to his health & comfort, had I been as wretched as to have seen him embark. I am therefore (not being able to write) quite upon the pavée[3] & compelled to ask y^r^ Lordship to Send me a credit on Messrs Pybus for 50£ which, when I get the dividend, I will replace with them or make up in the money that is yet due to me. Pray forgive my being so very troublesome, & allow me to repeat that no words can express my gratitude. I am y^r^ Lordships most oblig'd Ser^t^,

Charlotte Smith

Petworth House Archives MS. No address or postmark.

NOTES

1. Tayler continued to be harassed by his worthless son (CS to William Tyler, ?1 Nov. 1802).

2. Charlotte Mary as sole executrix proved Charles Smith's will in London on 8 Apr. 1802 (PRO). Christened Charles Dyer Smith, Charles appears to have dropped his middle name to protest his namesake Thomas Dyer's handling of the trust.

3. Alluding, incorrectly, to *être sur le pavé:* that is, to be without home or employment.

To the earl of Egremont

[London] Feby 15th 1802

My Lord,

I am afraid I made some mistake in my expressions by leaving out a word or otherwise writing obscurely, as it is too certain no Letters or papers are arrived or have we any intelligence from Barbados or from the Servant——

Had we received any accounts or information whatsoever, I should not have faild to have forwarded these accounts to your Lordship—— I was about to name to you that Mr Phillips of Barbados, Partner and Uncle to Mr Went (from whom we received the only account we ever have had of poor Charles's death), is now in England for his health, but proposes to return to Barbados with the Spring fleet.[1] He is a Man of character & appears to have taken great interest in my unfortunate Charles & to understand the affairs his sad fate compelld him after all his exertions to leave unfinishd. Mr Dayrell proposed to me to engage him, Mr Phillips, if your Lordship approved of it in collecting the monies & securities which were to have been sent to England or taken by bond at 12 months had my Son's life been spared. For this purpose, I imagine new powers must be given both to receive & sue for money and sell land. These will be attended with considerable expence, but as there is either about eight, or thirteen hundred pounds to collect besides a piece of land unsold which is worth something, It would probably be worth while to take some early measures to secure it. Yet on the other hand Mr Phillips is quite a Barbadian, at least in his manner. He will not speak out even against Prettejohn, and being an Attorney, he may however good his character be too politic to exert himself for those ~~against his~~ he knows little of, & who reside in England, against his clients & old connections in his own Island—— Mr Dayrell's advice is to engage him, but I am decided not to speak to him till I have your Lordships opinion & directions —— This may perhaps be our best resource, for I see not what else can be done, & it may answer no purpose whatever——

I understand that in regard to the bill for 3737£, it would be discounted by the bank if your Lordship thought proper to allow my asking it of the directors, as their own bank notes are not better, & they accommodate even before they are bound to do so persons applying from Gentlemen or Merchants of consequence. If, as Mr Hippuff the stock Broker[2] seems to think, Stocks will be from 75 to 80, it would be well worth while to get it done in order to invest the money before so considerable a rise. As for the interest on the various Sums, which is of course going on—& of which half a year is now due since the accounts were made up on 2nd July 1801—I own I wish that & the present exigencies might be supplied by getting the bill of Mr Gibbons[3] discounted which is due on the 2nd Octr next—for (I think) between five and six hundred pounds—& Accepted by Daniels for as the installment to be paid for Gays cover the legacies yet due, leaving a ballance of about an hundred pounds. I wish to make as few deductions as possible in order that there may be a certainty of the legacies being paid by Gays installments, setting aside all other contingencies, & it is Mr Dayrells opinion that all expences incurred for the estate & all contingent expenses should fall upon the residue & would be orderd so to fall by the Chancellor; He says Mr Benjn Smith has not at present a right to any thing. And as he has wasted so much of his Fathers property[4] & what has been saved has been saved entirely by y^r^ Lordships goodness, no court in the World would direct that his childrens rescued provision should be diminish'd.

If we could get the next Gibbons's bill discounted, it would releive us from the pressure of very great inconvenience. I see much to do before I can leave Town, yet the expence runs so high & I am so entirely without resource that I am half distracted. Mr Smith must, whether he likes it or no, take in some way or other his share of these expenses & the support of his family.

I will not add to my Letter, & were I to say half I feel on your Lordship's unequalled goodness to my Son & to all of us, it would be long indeed!

I am y^r^ Lordships
ever obligd Ser^t^,
Charlotte Smith

All Mr Dayrell meant by the Letter he propos'd writing to me was to prove as a Lawyer, & even from Mr Hollists[5] own opinion, that Messrs Smith & Allen must go to Prettejohn & make him prove the facts before they can make any legal demands on Gays. "The Man (meaning Mr Allen) is a fool, Madam," says Mr Dayrell, "& has over reached himself"——

Petworth House Archives MS. No address or postmark.

NOTES

1. Phillips had been an agent of Alleyne's in the sale of Gay's plantation. Phillips's nephew and partner Thomas Went, Esq., sent CS an account of Charles's death in 1801. By 1804 CS suspected Went of dirty tricks with regard to Charles's effects and perhaps even his death.

2. Charles Hippuff, Pybus's broker (see CS to Egremont, 4 Nov. 1801 and n. 1).

3. See CS to Egremont, ca. 30 Sept. 1801 and n. 2.

4. On 20 July 1803, BS defended himself to Egremont against the charges that sent him to jail: "The Devastavit proved against me by Dyer [in 1783], was not on account of Waste but for having paid simple contract debts, previous to the Bond debts, my Accounts will set aside all the Allegations respecting the heavy charges which have been made against me" (unpub. letter in PHA #0.11).

5. Richard Hollist, lawyer and family advisor (see CS to Egremont, 18 July 1800, n. 2).

To William Davies

[London, 18 February 1802]
Sir,

I beg leave to return with many thanks the volume of Hume's history which you were kind enough to lend me. I borrow'd it in the intention of referring to it in an abridged history[1] I am writing, but it is such a nice book & belongs to so high priced a set that I have not ventured to use it with pen & ink about me, & in a lodging, least it should be damaged. I am not however the less ~~obliged~~ indebted to you for your obliging readiness to assist me when I am not writing for you. I made an attempt to thank you in person to day, but the Streets are so dirty that I am unequal to the walk, having been ill almost ever since I have been in Town. Disappointment in regard to money matters has not a little contributed to distress me by keeping my mind in a state of anxiety and suspence, for it happens from some cause which it is impossible to understand that none of the papers of my deceased Son are received from Barbados, neither his Will, or accounts, or the remittances which after having sent the installments for the Estate remaind. On these the family & myself depended for our current expences, but where they are, or why they are not come, I have no means of knowing. A Servant who at his poor Master's desire was to be sent back to England is not come, nor the 14 years accounts on which depended the final settlement of the affairs, for which I came to Town—— I mention this to inform you why I have been compelled to delay payment of your long due account in which I think myself particularly unfortunate—

I mention'd in a former note, that I wish'd to know the state of the present edition of Emmeline, The copy right being mine, & I cannot help repeating my wish that it were worth your while to reprint Ethelinde.[2] I assure you that I have within these three or four years had above twenty applications for a new edition & some of them from Strangers in remote parts of the Country—— But you are undoubtedly the best judges—— There has also been many applications to me to write another School book, & if I could make an engagement with an house of respectability, I should very readily set about one which I have thought of long since & had some part of the materials collected[3]———By the persuasions of a friend and the incessant application of Mr Philips,[4] I was induced on the death of Low to undertake an abridgement of English History for the use of Young Ladies—— I have done a great deal of it, but to say the truth, I do not, on knowing more of the person I have engaged with, feel at all satisfied, nor is the price by any means adequate to the labour it has cost me; I know that it is very well done & that I have taken such pains with it as I ought to do to preserve my own credit with the public. As you have done me the justice to say I have always been punctual, I do not mean to lose that part of my good name, but I had a thousand times rather settle in any other way with Mr Phillips than complete an engagement tho it is more than half done, which I have reason to think will finally give me no satisfaction, Even if he is induced to enlarge the proffits. I could finish the book in six weeks after I return to my House in the Country; It need not therefore obstruct my other plans.

From long habit & I may say from general success, tho under very great disadvantages, I am never so well pleased as when I have a good deal of work to do, & my greatest vexation is that the affairs of my family require so much of my attention that I cannot work at my literary business & at that only. Lord Egremont is their Trustee & mine, but I cannot suffer his Lordship to take any of the trouble or at least more than I ~~could~~ can avoid, & my Sons are all in active life & placed where they cannot undertake these affairs. If under these circumstances you were disposed to engage with me, I flatter myself that, as you have not hitherto, you would <u>not</u> have reason to repent it in a pecuniary light—— I have been very ingenuous with you, relying on our former long connection that you will not name to the trade my dissatisfaction with Mr Phillips. I know these matters are sometimes discussed among the Booksellers, but I do not wish to consider you as merely such & trust that with you I shall not rank on a footing with Dr Mavor[5] & such sort of book makers.

I address myself particularly to Mr Davies, having had the pleasure of knowing him so many years, but it will of course be understood that I mean the respectable firm of T Cadell & W Davies.

I am interrupted—but will send this evening for an an^{r}.

I am, Gent^{n},
y^{r} oblig'd Ser^{t},
Charlotte Smith

Feby 18th 1802

Osborn Collection MS, Yale University. No address or postmark.

NOTES

1. Described more fully later in the following paragraph. CS had tried to borrow the Hume from Egremont (CS to Egremont, 6 Oct. 1801).

2. CS received no further remuneration from her first two novels. She argued in several letters that the copyright of *Emmeline* was hers (CS to Cadell and Davies, 16 Dec. 1802, and 2 Sept. and 20 Oct. 1805), but apparently to no avail. *Emmeline* was reprinted in Belfast in 1799 by Doherty and Sims, and in America in 1802 by J. Conrad and Co., Philadelphia; M. and J. Conrad & Co., Baltimore; and H. Maxwell, Washington. These printings did not benefit her. *Ethelinde* was reprinted for Minerva Press in 1814.

3. Probably the book that was to become *Conversations Introducing Poetry: Chiefly on*

Subjects of Natural History. For the Use of Children and Young Persons, published by Joseph Johnson in 1804. Another schoolbook, her *Natural History of Birds,* was published in 1807.

4. The publisher Richard Phillips (see Biographical Notes).

5. William Fordyce Mavor (1758–1837); after years as tutor to the duke of Marlborough's children, he was given a vicarage by the duke and an L.L.D. by the University of Aberdeen. He compiled numerous educational books for children, perhaps the best known being *The English Spelling Book,* first published in 1801. He also invented a universal shorthand (*Universal Stenography,* 1779) and published a book of poetry in 1793.

To the earl of Egremont

[London, 20 February 1802]
My Lord,

Yesterday my daughters servant, who is a native of the same Country as Benjn Maule, the Lad who attended our poor Charles to Barbados, received an answer to a Letter of enquiry she had written by my daughter's desire to the Brother of Benjn Maule, the writer:[1]

"We received a Letter from Benjamin on the 6th of January in which he inform'd us of the death of his worthy Master, who had left him 50£ Sterling for his good behavior and services; he has had the fever five times & been given over, but was in good health when he wrote & was going to remain in Barbados to learn to be a planter under a Mr Hollingsworth. We direct to him to the care of Thos Went, Esqre Barbados"——

Your Lordship was right in your conjecture that this Boy staid in Barbados, but the certainty of it makes the detention of the papers, accounts, & effects still more extraordinary. My lamented Charles had personal effects which his Sister, as having been his,[2] is very desirous of having sent to her. We have caused enquiry to be made at Bristol in The Warehouses & custom houses, ~~and custom houses~~ but to no purpose, & I own for myself I cannot help beleiving there is some intentional mischief in such an otherwise unaccountable delay. It has distressd us more than I can describe, & unless we can obtain a supply of money for our immediate purposes, I really cannot tell what can be done. I took the liberty of asking your Lordships permission to get one of Gibbons's Bills discounted which might perhaps be done as a matter of favor.

I went yesterday to the Bank to see what investment Mr Prescod had made. I find the 3000 St^{g} bo[ugh]^{t} in at 68 and a fraction produced 4587.0.5$^{d.}$ in the 3 pC^{ts} Consols, which Sum stands in the names of the Earl of Egremont & Nich^{s} Turner. I heartily wish this, & the other 4000£ belonging to my family of mine, & which has bo^{t} in all 7000£ more in the 3 pC[ts] more, all included in one trust under y[r] Lordship As now it seems to me to be likely to be more troublesome & less secure than I should think it then. M[r] Tayler seems to have a great inclination to resign his part & declares he will if M[r] Smith acts as he does———M[r] Tayler however will not pay one half the dividend on ½ years interest for 3000£, & I am consequently without a guinea—— There is money to receive of M[r] Prescod as interest, but I know not when he will pay it, nor can I guess what I am to do to pay my unavoidable expences here; I cannot get away.

I do not send the box of seeds, as y[r] Lordship was pleased to say you would send for it.

I have the honor to be
Your Lordships most obliged
and obed Ser[t],
Charlotte Smith

No 9 Buckingham S[t] [London]
Feb[y] 20th 1802

Petworth House Archives MS. No address or postmark.

NOTES

1. Not identified.

2. That is, Charles left personal effects that Charlotte Mary wanted because they had been his.

To Thomas Cadell, Jr., and William Davies

[London, 23 February 1802]
Sirs,

I shall be much oblig'd to you for an answer to my Letter of three days since—— I had in the course of yesterday an offer of literary engagement which I shall not attend to till I know whether there is any probability of your renewing a connection that I trust you have had no reason to regret having formed some years since.

I am, Gent[n],
your obed[t] & oblig'd Ser[t],
Charlotte Smith

Feb[y] 23rd 1802

Osborn Collection MS, Yale University. Address: Mess[rs] Cadell & Davies/ Private). No postmark.

To the earl of Egremont

[London, 1 March 1802]
My Lord,

I have at length met with a person of credit[1] who will discount both the Bills I named to y[r] Lordship: Vis. that for 3737£ from M[r] Prescod due the 7th July 1802, & that for ———— (I am not quite sure of the Sum) (ab[t] 500£ I beleive) from M[r] Gibbons[2] due the 2nd Oct[r] 1802. This will make so considerable a division & shorten so much the trouble yr Lordship has had the goodness to take that I have no doubt of your approbation, and therefore venture to request the favor of you to order the bills to be sent down for your Lordships and M[r] Turners signature, & should ~~yr Lor~~ you not be in Town, it will I beleive be safest to direct M[r] Pybus to receive them back & the money, when ready, which may then remain to be divided as y[r] Lordship on a statement of the claims shall be pleased to approve—

The probability of a great fluctuation in the stocks & other very powerful reasons persuade me of the necessity of losing no time in this matter, & I beg leave to request that you will give immediate orders if you approve of the proposal for the closing the business ~~by~~.

I have the honor to be, with the greatest gratitude & respect,

y[r] Lordships most oblig'd Ser[t],
Charlotte Smith

It is greatly to be lamented by us that, Sir W[m] Meadows having named Capt[n] Beckwith to the Majority,[3] Lionel is not likely to succeed Unless, which I have hardly any hope of, interest can be made with his RH the Commander in Cheif[4] to direct that Captain Smith should be allowd to make the purchase. It will I fear be long before another will offer on such advantageous terms so old a Regiment. One disappointment does not lessen our very great obligation to your Lordship.
March 1st 1802
9 Buckingham Street

Petworth House Archives MS. No address or postmark.

NOTES

1. Probably William Fauntleroy, Esq., of 6 Berners Street, a London merchant who discounted bills and lent CS money during this period of increasingly perilous finances. On 14 Mar., it appears that Tyler has recommended that Mr. Mitford, rather than Fauntleroy, discount the bill.

2. The £500 was owed on Gay's plantation and was being settled as part of the sale to Prescod.

3. General Meadows (1738–1813) had served in Germany, America, and India and had been governor of the Isle of Wight before briefly succeeding Cornwallis as com-

mander in chief of Ireland. Thomas Sidney Beckwith was named major in the army on 11 Mar. 1802 and in the regiment on 28 Apr. 1802. Lionel's appointments came only a little later: he was named major in the army on 22 Apr. 1802 and in the 16th Regiment on 24 June 1802.

4. That is, His Royal Highness, Frederick, duke of York.

To William Tyler

[London, 9 March 1802]
Sir,

I have received to day a Letter from the friend in the City who thought it probable, indeed almost certain, that he should get the Bill for £3737.10s discounted. He says the extreme uncertainty in which monied Men are and the vague situation of public affairs make it less likely than it was when I wrote to Lord E — — —— I am, as is Miss Smith, inconceivably distress'd at this—— I am press'd for money by the people where I lodge, & there are a few debts for her deceased Brother which Charlotte has repeatedly promisd to pay, not doubting but that she should have had the means of doing it before now, but oweing to the want of the Codicil, she cannot administer nor take for this purpose the 150£ in the funds belonging to her Brother standing in Lord E—s & Mr Turners names in the 3 pC^ts^.

For my own part, I am quite worn down with vexation, & the complaint which I have long had hanging about me & which My Medical friend seems decidedly to think is Water on the chest or about the heart is rapidly encreasing, & they say I must go out of town.

That I cannot do circumstanced as I am now. If Lord Egremont w^d^ only be so good as to send me or rather Miss Smith a credit on Messrs Pybus & Co for 200£, It would be replaced by Gibbons's Bill which I have no doubt of getting discounted — — & I am persuaded Messrs Pybus would advance it without hesitation. Nothing should make me give Lord Egremont such trouble but the state in which I find myself. I wrote to Mr Baxter, Attorney[1] to Mr Prescod, to beg he would pay me only a part of the interest money if he had doubts of the propriety of paying the whole, but he has not condescended to answer my Letter, and I cannot tell what to do thus situated, nor have I resolution to struggle against it.

I am unwilling to trouble Lord E. with another application. May I therefore earnestly entreat you to try what can be done for me before friday,[2] or the distress and convenience I shall suffer, I cannot encounter.

I am, Sir, y^r^ oblig'd hble Ser^t^,
Charlotte Smith

March 9th 1802

Petworth House Archives MS. No address or postmark.

NOTES

1. Of John Dayrell Martin, Squire Stafford Baxter, and Robert Baxter, 4 Furnival's Inn.

2. Friday, 12 Mar. The letter was written on Tuesday.

To William Tyler

[London] March 11th 1802
Sir,

By the message brought by Captain Smiths Servant Yesterday, I rather expected to have had the pleasure of an opportunity of speaking to you to day—— My situation becom[es] extremely distressing, and really I beleive I shall be in some danger of being arrested on friday,[1] & tho I cannot perhaps go to a prison, I shall be subject to distress such as I have no strength to encounter. I am very sorry to give you trouble, but if you could in any way assist me before friday with 60 or 70£, it would prevent my enduring very great and serious evils As there are bills now in Pybus's house to the amount of 120.00£.[2] I am sure My children (even tho I should have no right myself) will not wish me to suffer so much calamity for expences incurred solely for their affairs. I write in considerable pain & still greater uneasiness, and am, Sir,

Yr oblig'd & obedt Sert,
Charlotte Smith

Petworth House Archives MS. No address or postmark.

NOTES

1. That is, the following day, 12 Mar.

2. The original reads "12000£," but CS clearly means the smaller amount, 120.00£.

To William Tyler

[London] 12th March 1802
Sir,

To my great mortification, I have not received the Order on Mr Prescod or his Solicitor. If it has reached you, I beg the favor of you to send it that I may appease some part of the clamors which now drive me to distraction. I see only encrease of expence by remaining in Town, yet I cannot escape from it. I see nothing but continued distress for me while I am obliged to keep house for Mr Smiths family and to be the responsible person while he denies me every share of what belongs to me. Far far rather had I retire to some very humble & obscure place where I could have time to write for my own bread, for that I might still earn. But how can I abandon those who cannot do without me? I really know not what to do or which way to disengage myself from what I feel it to be every day more impossible for me to support.

Not doubting but that I should get the Bills discounted or receive money & be able to settle my business by Teusday next, I gave the people here (who began to be extremely impatient & impertinent a fortnight ago) notice that I should quit their house on Teusday next, & they have let it. If I cannot pay them between this & then, I see nothing that can happen but my leaving it for a Sheriffs Officers house, for as to their being told I am a married Woman or any thing being represented of that sort, they will not care at all, but go strait to the obtaining their money.

I shall be oblig'd to you to signify to Messrs Pybus's that the 500£ bill (Gibbon's) may be deliverd to me or Captain Smith & Miss Smith if I sh^d obtain discount for it which I have some hopes of on more reasonable terms than I named in my last. If the order for the Money due from Prescod is not come (as Lord Egremont is probably much engagd), will you be so good as to lend me on your own account 10£, as I am really distressd beyond all description, & I will return it with thanks.

C S.

Petworth House Archives MS. No address or postmark.

To William Tyler

[London, received 14 March 1802]
Sir,

I am much oblig'd to you for the information you sent me last night which has releived me from the very awkard and distressing situation I was in—— I am indeed very glad Mr Mitford is so friendly as discount<ing> the Bill & gives us some hopes of befriending us in regard to the greater Bill. In order to make it impossible that any difficulty should hereafter arise as to any money I may have had, I will as soon as I have time make out some accounts & send you for Lord Egremonts inspection at his leisure.

The first shall state from the documents in my hands all the monies I have had from the Estate beyond my actual right for interest, or what has been allowed me by my Sons, & is placed to their accounts.

The 2nd shall state the expences I have been at for the Estate: such as money actually paid, postage, journies, & many &c&c a—s Not agency, for were I to charge only six pence an hour for the business I have done, & which it happend that nobody could do but me, & which therefore must have remain'd undone had I not undertaken it, it would come to a Sum which it would impoverishd the Legatees to pay. I am however doubly a loser because the same time, & less pains, applied to literary labour would have ensured me an independance in a way of life certainly more agreeable to me——

Thirdly, I will state what the Legatees owe me for maintenance. This as none of them are particularly desirous & some of them cannot pay, I shall not insist upon having fully discharged, but I own I do wish to have a distinction made in their minds & that they may know I might take as a right what their father has taken before, & indeed that worthy Gentleman, in a late Letter to his daughter, refers me to that as a support. He says— "Your Mother has money due to her for your Aliment & also other resources; why then should she expect me to give up any part of the interest Money which all belongs to me?"

Whether I or his children have aliment or no is a matter of perfect indifference, but he will find something more goes to this business than this wise & honest way of settling it.

If however it appears that something is yet fairly & legally due to me, It is not for myself I want it. Could I be disengaged from Petty duns & continual want of the actual means of feeding clothing & sheltering those who are still dependant upon me, I could, unless my health continues to fail as it has done lately, always assist in my own support, but I should very earnestly desire leave to borrow on my future claim One hundred & fifty pounds, for which I might now purchase An Lieutenants commission in the 47th for My Son George[1] which would be one & a very material step in providing for him in his profession. I would pay 5 pCt for it & repay it when ever, as the installments come in, the Legatees pay me. Perhaps I might borrow such a sum for such a purpose, as Genl Dalrymple has signified to day that the Commission must be immediately filled up. This poor boy, who has never known a fathers care or received above 20£ of him in his life (which he now wants to take back), is particularly thrown on my exertions. They cannot long be made, & therefore they must be earnest — — I have none so wholly relying upon me, & I feel myself called upon to fulfil what may be consider'd as the last of my duties for my Sons.

I enclose for Lord Egremonts Trust in the 3000£ a paper sent to me to day from Mr Prescod. By this it appears that the clerk of the Bank mistated the Sum to me, which he said & I wrote so to Lord Egremont, had for 3000£

St^{g} purchased——4587.5. Whereas it appears by this paper that it bo^{t} only <u>4371.11.8</u>. 3 pC^{t} Consels.[2] I rather think the mistake arose from the Clerks reckoning both the Sums that stand in the names of Lord Egremont & Nich^{s} Turner, the first of which is the division paid on account of my deceased Son, Charles, which his Sister cannot receive till the Codicil to the will comes. On the back is a calculate of the interest for which Mr Prescodd desires an acquittal (together with my receipt) from Lord E. & Mr T. I am, with many thanks for the trouble you have taken, Sir,

your obed^{t} humble Ser^{t},
Charlotte Smith

Petworth House Archives MS. Address: To Mr Tyler. No postmark.

NOTES

1. This attempt to purchase a promotion for George probably did not succeed. George was enlisted as George Frederick Smith, and no lieutenant's appointment can be found under this name. However, George's memorial plaque at Stoke Church, Guildford, gives his full name as George Frederick Augustus Smith, and his will has George Augustus Frederick Smith. Thus, he may have been the George Augustus Smith who was promoted to lieutenant on 9 July 1803 (*Army List* [1805], p. 290).

2. That is, consols, or consolidated annuities.

To William Tyler

[London, received 19 March 1802]
Sir,

I enclose a statement of one years interest to the Legatees, up to July 1802—made up by Mr Josepth Smith, Stockbroker and accomptant[1]—

As I do not recollect any objection having been made to the account I gave in last year, in which the interest was consolidated to July 2nd 1801 & interest charged on the Sum so consolidated, & as Mr Dayrell has seen the account & thought it right, I might perhaps be authorised in carrying it on in the same manner, but as it is not absolutely ascertain'd that this is one of the cases wherein compound interest is allowed, the equity would certainly decide so (because no interest, God knows, could make the Legatees amends for so many years of poverty & distress occasion'd by the mismanagement of their Father & the wickedness of the old Trustees). Yet <u>we</u> wish (I speak for Miss Smith, as acting for three parties, and Mr Duncan for Mrs Newhouse) to confine the present payment to one years interest on the <u>principal</u> sums of the Legacies. And in doing so, I beleive no error can arise or blame be imputed to the present Trustees. If however Lord Egremont thinks otherwise,

I shall submit to his Lordships opinion with the deference due to him from me and mine. It is however proper to add that such a division would be at this time particularly useful, & I trust nothing wrong would be found in it———————————

I must also beg your patience, while I state that some doubts having been suggested whether the Representative[2] of my deceased daughter Anna Augusta Smith was entitled to anything whatsoever, I have taken measures to have those doubts cleared up. Whatever I may have sufferd from the little tenderness shewn to me by attempts to deprive one (who deserved better of the little due to him on account of her who was dearer to me than any other human being, and whose memory ought on my account, if not on her own, to have been held sacred) with her Brothers & Sisters, yet I would by no means desire that any thing should be done contrary to the Letter of the Will of Richard Smith. That Letter however can in the present instance be complied with only by allowing to Mr De Foville for life the interest of the two Sums of 166.3.4 and 166.3.4 being the shares of 1000£ & 1000£ given to Benjn & Brathwaite Smith[3] deceased & which were undoubtedly vested property in my deceased daughter on the day of marriage, according to the Will in which she is expressly named, as being to share in whatever legacies might fall on the death of any of the other parties on attaining the age of 21, or day of marriage which should first happen. Now so far Should, in my opinion, the legatees be from complaining of this trifling deduction that they ought to recollect, first that but for me (there are times when it is not arrogant to speak of oneself) they would none of them have had an hundred pounds, & therefore even if I was wrong, I ought in such a mere trifle to be indulged, & secondly, that if I had not had made certain articles of marriage previous to that of my daughter, her husband would have been entitled, not for life only, but to the absolute possession of whatever legacies were vested property in his Wife at her decease, & tho Mr De Foville has never made any claim or given any trouble because he knew the excessive pain I felt in agitating the subject, yet he might have given a great deal since it is not at all clear that My second daughter was not entitled to 1000£ as well as the rest.

On this he has never insisted, but leaving the matter entirely to me & there being not the least doubt of his claims as above stated, I sent the Statement to Mr Hippuff, desiring him to value those claims with the interest that had accrued for the life of an healthy Man aged 36. He did so, & informs me Mr De Fovilles interest in R Ss[4] estate might be sold on the Exchange of London for 165£ (exclusive of this years interest) & that Sum, 165£, Mr Benjn Smiths family have agreed to give, & Mr De Foville is to give them a discharge for all & every [*sic*] his claims against the estate of Richard Smith.

This appears so equitable & just that I hope and beleive Lord Egremont will approve of it, & My family will spare me any farther discussion of a subject that, by recalling to my memory more forcibly the heaviest misfortune Of my unhappy life, tears my heart to pieces. Till this 165£ is paid, the interest goes on, the same as on the other Sums to the other legatees. I hope I have made myself understood, but it is a business on which (tho seven wretched years have since passed) I cannot write without suffering. I should however add that I have shewn Mr Dayrell the passages of the Will, & he authorised me to say what I have done, I hope for the last time because it kills me.

I would, on receiving your Letter this morning, have sent to Mr Dayrell for the deeds & documents Entrusted to me by Lord Egremont & for the form of the receipts which all the parties are willing to sign for the monies paid to them, which <u>form</u> Mr Dayrell promisd to send me. But he is gone on the Circuit, & his chambers are shut. I was surprised at his going with^t^ letting me know it, as I had business before him. As soon as he returns, Lord Egremont shall assuredly receive all the papers, & before that the <bill and?> form of receipt according to what Mr Dayrell told me was legal, together with my account. My health is such that tho I know it is an additional reason for leaving nothing undone, I am not always able to do all I wish—— It is useless to complain, but I feel it to be impossible to contend much longer with the fatigue of mind I am oblig'd to undergo & the cares & anxiety which Mr Smiths barbarous & unnatural conduct towards his children obliges me to sustain, & from which the generous & unexapled kindness of some such friends, as nothing I could do deserves, cannot I beleive much longer save me, nor do I wish it but On account of the Persons who yet depend on me.

Mr Mitford had <u>not</u> yesterday call'd On Messrs Pybus to discount the bill. I gave him notice last night that Lord Egremonts order to deliver it to him had been received & that it waited his disposal, so I trust he will be kind enough to do it to day & that I shall receive or rather Miss Smith the order for the disposal of the money, should Lord E. be satisfied of its propriety, as soon as may be convenient to his Lordship because of the expence of staying in town which falls very heavily upon me As well as my wretched state of health & medicine ruins my pocket without doing me any permanent good.

I always end with a representation of the sad circumstances of our having no news from Barbados tho two Leeward Island Packets have come in. I have seen Mr Phillips, uncle to & partner with Mr Went, & to speak plainly, I do not like his <u>manner</u> well enough to trust him willingly with a new power of Attorney.[5] He now says Mr Went has been very ill & makes some very miserable excuses for the effects & Papers left by poor Charles not having been sent, but I have more than ever reason to fear the real reason rises from dishonesty & the embezzlement of the property. How to act I am utterly at a loss, yet I wish to do something before I leave London — — I saw Mr Dunn with Mr Winterbottom[6] the day before yesterday, & he shewed me the accounts which, in a Letter from Mrs Allen to Miss Smith, she stated to be a full explanation of the particulars of Messrs Allen & R Smiths claims. But they are directly the reverse, containing only the same account as sent to Lord Egremont of two articles without one particular on which to ground even that vague & loose document. This is a little unfortunate because Mr Allen says positively in one of his Letters that debts due from Gays were paid off by these loans from Mapps—— debts bearing interest at 6 pCt——

Now if it were so, Mr Dayrell very justly observes that it would be the simplest thing imaginable for Messrs Allen & Smith to get at & produce the copies of receipts of these creditors of Gays so paid by Money taken from Mapps. If John Such a one was paid an hundred or two hundred pounds & Thomas Such a one three or four hundred pounds, is it possible their receipts should not be taken? I never will consent to the payment of one shilling till I have proof that the money was actually applied as they affirm, & it is their affair not ours to prove it. Mr Dunn, I think, is not extremely sanguine himself tho he puts as good a face as he can on the matter.

I am, Sir,
your obedt & oblig'd Sert,
Charlotte Smith

Petworth House Archives MS. Address: Mr Tyler. No postmark.

NOTES

1. CS and her children covered by Richard Smith's will received semiannual payments from the interest accumulating on trust moneys. CS and BS divided a dividend payment that dwindled from £70 to about £60 as the trust lost value. Surviving accounts (PHA #8232) show that the children were allowed to draw against the trust for cash, much as one would draw on a modern checking account, or to receive payment from it for services rendered.

2. Alexander de Foville, Augusta's husband, a French émigré. CS was doubly fond of de Foville for his consideration of her and his love of her deceased daughter. Her insistence that he receive a proper legacy, though entirely legal, was not well received by Egremont or Turner; it probably was the final straw in the collapse of her relationship with them.

3. On Benjamin Berney Smith and Brathwaite Smith, see Biographical Notes.

4. Richard Smith's.

5. Phillips was a solicitor from Barbados, who had been acting as an agent to John Forster Alleyne in the sale of Gay's. In an unpublished letter to Tyler of 15 Feb. 1802, CS states that he was also a partner and uncle of Thomas Went, who was inexplicably

withholding an account of Charles's death. At that time, she thought he was a man of character and reported that Dayrell advised them to engage him. Meeting him clearly changed her mind.

6. Ralph Dunn, 32 Threadneedle Street, London, and his partner Abraham Winterbottom were solicitors for Robert Allen and Richard Smith, the younger, who were threatening a Chancery suit (CS to Tyler, unpub., 13 Feb. 1802).

To Joseph Cooper Walker

[London, late March–early April 1802][1]

. . . I had the faculty he[2] appears so eminently to possess of finding new friends at a late period of life who may more than supply the place of the old. He has a succession house[3] to raise them in I beleive, & I heartily hope he will find the fruits of a second marriage less bitter than were those of the first. He certainly takes a considerable time to meditate on this important step—more than many more prudent Men than he has hitherto shewn himself would think it wise to spare from wedded felicity at the respectable epocha of fifty & six. But perhaps he may still fear that he shall have time enough to be as weary of his wife, as he generally has continued to be of his friends.

I fear that, from the death & previous illness of Mr Low my former printer, you never received according to my order the three first volumes of "the Letters of a Solitary Wanderer," for my orders in regard to the copies for my friends were entirely neglected. The two other volumes have just been sent from the press of the people who bought them of Mr Low's executors in a most disgraceful state being worse printed than an half penny ballad & on paper the very coarsest I ever saw. I consider myself as having been extremely ill used by Messrs Longman & Rees. Such however as the books are, I wait only to hear from you, Dear Sir, whether you ever received the former three that, if you did not, I may forward them altogether & if you have those already, the two last, that you may have the five if you are so good as to accept them, unworthy as they are. At all events I will leave them at Cadell & Davies's where perhaps you may direct some friend to call for them.

My present work is a short history of England for the use of Young Women which I am very ill paid for & find extremely labourious.[4] I have had no time to read lately & think, from what I hear from those who have, that there never were fewer books of entertainment merely less worth reading. Miss Edgeworths Novel[5] is not much liked—the machinery of a cancer & a Cockatoo, disgusts, but there is strong character in it & some knowledge of life tho the harshness & rude manner of the execution is unpleasing. Mrs Ratcliffe[6] is restraind by the authority of her husband from calling any more "spirits from the vasty deep"[7] of her imagination, the Lees seem to have laid by the pen for some time, & of greater & more important books, the failure of M[r] Hayley's Essay on Sculpture & M[rs] Piozzi's Retrospection[8]—which neither of them sold so as to pay the printing—has made the Booksellers more grave than ever & lament in more pathetic terms the uncertainty of genius & the certain price of paper.

Miss Baillies second volume of plays[9] however are likely to be (and deservedly) as popular as the first. By this time I dare say you have read them. She is a woman of very extraordinary talents.

To hear from you very soon & to be assured of a continuance of your friendship will give me very great pleasure. Above all, I trust you will lose no time in giving me the satisfaction of hearing you have regained your health,[10] nor would it be otherwise than a great addition to that satisfaction to know you had thoughts of visiting England.

I will write in a few days to M[r] Caldwell[11]—— I wish he was to revisit this Country, and my usual abode within a mile of Tunbridge Wells is not so remote as to deprive me of the probability of seeing my friends. To that cottage, where Lucy & her children at present are, I shall return in a few days Where to receive an early Letter from you soon is sincerely desired by, Dear Sir,

your oblig'd & obed[t] Ser[t],
Charlotte Smith

My address all the Summer if I so long live will be Frant near Tunbridge Wells.

Huntington MS (HM10831). Address: Josepth Cooper Walker Esq[re]/ Eccles Street./ Dublin. No postmark.

NOTES

1. This letter appears to have been written on two sheets. The outside sheet, and thus the date and at least the first page, did not survive.

Forced to remain in London on trust business since winter, CS probably wrote this undated letter in late March or early April of 1802. At the end of it, she plans to "return in a few days" to Frant where her daughter Lucy and grandchildren are living in her house. So this letter would have been written before CS's first letter from Frant to William Tyler on 16 Apr. 1802. She was still in London when she wrote to Egremont on 7 Apr.; at that time her daughter Harriet had contracted a sore throat, no doubt delaying her return to Frant a few more days.

2. William Hayley, who CS thought was about to marry an Irishwoman, Penelope Carleton Chetwynd (CS to Walker, 14 Apr. 1801 and n. 6); but this marriage did not take place. Hayley's first marriage was unhappy, and he thought his wife was mentally ill.

3. One of a series of greenhouses with different temperatures to which plants are moved in succession.

4. CS's research on the *History of England . . . to a young lady at school* dragged on for years before Richard Phillips published it in 1806.

5. The plot of Maria Edgeworth's *Belinda* (1801) is advanced by a macaw (not a cockatoo), a large dog, and Lady Delacour's feigned cancer. CS's judgment of the machinery seems rather harsh, given some of her own; perhaps, as her mistake about the bird suggests, she had not read the novel carefully.

6. Ann Radcliffe, the most popular novelist of the time, stopped publishing after the great successes of *The Mysteries of Udolpho* (1794) and *The Italian* (1797), but she continued to write. In 1802, she was working on *Gaston de Blondeville,* which was published posthumously in 1826, along with a metrical romance. Having encouraged her to start writing, her husband was thought to have asked her to stop.

7. *Henry IV, Part I,* 3.1.52.

8. On Hayley's *Essay on Sculpture,* see CS to Walker, 14 Apr. 1801, n. 5. In that letter CS also mentions that she had not yet seen Piozzi's *Retrospection* (see n. 9).

9. Joanna Baillie's *A Series of Plays: In Which It Is Attempted to Delineate the Stronger Passions of the Mind,* vol. 2—usually called *Plays on the Passions*—was published in 1802; the first volume appeared in 1798.

10. Walker was asthmatic.

11. Andrew Caldwell, an Irish solicitor; see CS to Walker, 23 June 1799, n. 5. Writing to Bishop Percy on 4 Mar. 1807, Caldwell confirms that he had met CS in England in 1799 and that she wrote him several letters, which have not been found (Nichols, *Literary History,* vol. 7).

To William Tyler

[London] April 7th 1802

Sir,

I am very sorry for Mr Smiths having been again troublesome; I cannot help it, & there is no other way for Lord Egremont to avoid such applications from a Man who knows not what he is about, but never to notice them—— I have sent for The Attorney & shall probably find means to put an end to any present trouble from that quarter.

I beg to assure Lord Egremont that nothing can be farther from my intentions than harrassing him, but his Lordships candour will lead him to consider that, if there is business to be done which cannot be done without the Trustees, I must either apply to him or it must go undone, & then the money & time it has cost me, as well as all his past goodness, would be thrown away. The unfortunate death of my Son involves the affairs & makes new powers of Attorney necessary. It is my misfortune—not my fault—Had I not been unfortunate, I should never have needed the generous trouble Lord Egremont has condescended to take. Had I not struggled myself against my misfortunes, I should not have deserved it, as he has sometimes been pleased to say I did——

I came not, Sir, to Town for my own pleasure but because it was absolutely necessary. I have sufferd in my health, in my peace, in my purse by endeavoring to settle these affairs. And am I, who Lord E. so very kindly has meant to serve, to be the sole person who is to have no benefit? You say it is doubtful whether I have any claims for remuneration for my expences? By whom is it doubted?—— I go to a Counsel (whether as my friend or as being feed[1] is not material), & he tells me I have claims—— If I have not, however, I give the matter up; But here I am in London and unable to leave it. Let then what I now ask for be placed to the legatees, to my elder Sons, to any source you may point out; but let me entreat you to obtain of Lord E. an order for one hundred pounds out of what remains in Mr Pybus's hands (which is three hundred & seventeen) so as that I may on Friday pay the people here & not be as I am now, a prisoner in fact for debt, & suffering anguish both of body & mind, such as I am sure Lord Egremonts justice and humanity would not desire me to endure. Messrs Tourle, Palmer, & Pugh[2] have prepared the power of Attorney which I shall send down tomorrow. I regret that the affairs harrass Lord E, & rather than they should continue to do so, I would let Chancery take its course with them. The Legatees will be paid so soon that I should hope our only friend will not till then give us up, but we have no right to expect he will do more if he is fatigued with our unhappy business. I beseech you, Sir, not to delay your answer & the order beyond friday, & it shall go to the account in any way agreeable to Lord Egremont.

I am Sir y^r^ obed Ser^t^ Charlotte Smith

I have only to remark that, upon looking on the books, you will see that act for stamps for receipts does not affect legacies left 20 years ago—— but if it must be so, it must. M^r^ De Fovilles business I leave to Mr Palmer who will see the necessary papers. I wish I was dead rather than go thro all this———

Petworth House Archives MS. Address: Mr Tyler. No postmark.

NOTES

1. That is, whether she consults an attorney as a friend or as a paid professional.

2. Of the law firm of Thomas Tourle, George Palmer and Benjamin Pugh, 9 Bartlett Buildings, Holborn (see CS to Egremont, 7 Apr. 1802, n. 2); Palmer is mentioned in the postscript.

To the earl of Egremont

Wednesday night
{London} April 7th 1802
My Lord,

I know not whether Mr Tyler understands the requisite forms of a power of Attorney to go to the West Indies, but least needless expence should be incurred, I have sent down a rough copy of that which I have orderd to be drawn up in the hope of recovering some part of what the unhappy death of my Son seems likely to deprive his family of. I am truly sorry, my Lord, for this & all the rest of the trouble it has been my wretched lot to give you. I regret that the goodness of your heart should have let you into more difficulties than you ever intended to have engaged in, & I now humbly & earnestly request that, for the business that remains to be done, you would please to Appoint at our expence some Solicitor in Town in whom you can confide, who shall understand~~s~~ the trust affairs with whom I may communicate without troubling your Lordship than which nothing is farther from my thoughts ~~or~~ wishes.

Very fain would I withdraw from the misery & expence I am involved in. But If I were to do so, the affairs must be wholly neglected or the trouble I give encreased. Sickness & sorrow are overwhelming me, & I dare not even complain. I have no brother—— & now I have no friend tho I know not what I have done to offend yr Lordship.

Any expence incurred by law the Estate must pay. I thought it safer to act with Mr Dayrells advice, & When he shewed me by the act of Parliament abt stamped receipts for Legacies that Mr Tyler was wrong, & that the act affected only legacies left since it was enacted and did not affect legacies left four & twenty years ago, I really thought it better not to throw away four or five guineas, merely for a form which Mr Dayrell said might as well be done otherwise.

In regard to the claims of my second daughter for as such I consider those of her representative,[1] I did hope I should have been spared the discussion & that not only all my own right to repayment wd not have been disputed, but that this at least would be allowed when all the parties are willing it should be so. But I am now to have deeds & papers recurred to which I am not possess'd of at an expence of almost half as much as the Sum for which these claims are offerd to be compounded. If your Lordship were to order me to undergo a painful death, I would not complain. I never could be otherwise than grateful, but indeed the anguish I have endured these last few weeks is not to be described. I am sure you could not mean it, but death would be infinitely preferable to what I suffer. I must leave the matter relative to Mr De Foville to Messrs Tourle, Palmer, and Pugh.[2]

Allow me to hope, My Lord, that you will not refuse me an order for money to releive me from the situation I am now in. My sanguin hope about Lionel & my anxiety to get the business settled have kept me here. Sickness has fallen heavily upon me, & now my daughter is ill of a sore throat!—— I am y^r Lordships

most oblig'd Ser^t, Charlotte Smith

Petworth House Archives MS. No address or postmark.

NOTES

1. Augusta's surviving husband, Alexandre de Foville.

2. The law firm of Tourle, Palmer, and Pugh was involved in the trust only to the extent of advising on de Foville's claim and drawing up powers of attorney for someone in Barbados. One surviving document (PHA #8220) shows Thomas Tourle and Thomas Croswellen of Gray's Inn witnessing a power of attorney from Egremont and Turner to Matthew Coulthurst and Henry Bishop, 6 Apr. 1806.

To William Tyler

Frant
Friday
April 16th
1802
Sir,

In compliance as far as in my power with the requisition you thought proper to make, I enclose a copy of that part of the marriage articles of my late daughter wh^ch will perhaps convince you (since it has convinced others) and the deed was drawn up by a Lawyer grown grey in his profession & what is better, grown rich so that probably he knows his business.[1] After the very unpleasant & distressing hour I pass'd in October last in going over with you the various & distracting clauses of Mr Richard Smiths will, & satisfying you as I supposed of the grounds on which all the legatees claim under that will (against which there are now no other claims), I did hope that I might have been spared any farther discussion, and that on small matters, no difficulties would have been rais'd when there are none of the parties interested at all disposed to dispute or cavil at the regulation, in regard to the representative of my late second daughter, which I took great pains to put on a fair & just footing. The testator, when I was yet a young Woman, thought proper to entrust me as an Executrix, & I might have had in my trust a property of 50,000£. Now at the Age of fifty two, after having passed so many labourious & miserable years because I would not abandon this family, After having by the assistance of Lord Egremont snatch'd near 20,000£ out of the fire for them, & supported them by my own Earnings to the amount of 5,000£ while I was making this struggle, I cannot but feel that it [is] hard to have no voice, no opinion & to have doubts raised on a point which is really comparatively a trifle——

But to Lord Egremont, I owe more than my existence. I owe him gratitude beyond what I shall ever have words to express. If this poor little pittance which I conceive to be absolutely the due of Mr De Foville (& which on being paid will exonerate the Estate from all future demands) is, after the perusal of this document & recourse being had to the Will, doubted by his Lordship, I will go to any Counsel his Lordship shall direct at my own expence (or some friend will assist me)—— Or I will appeal to Mr Dayrell tho I understand Lord Egremont thinks I have done wrong in applying to him. I also heard his Lordship was displeasd at my having left Mr Bicknell.[2] Mr Bicknell could not do the business & desired to be released when I paid him in October last, & if Lord Egremont Will recall the confused state in which he himself saw our papers lay (which his Lordship observed to me Were very likely to be taken by the Housemaid to light fires), & if he remembers the many instances of mistake & neglect which happen'd while he acted as our Solicitor, I trust his Ldship will acquit me of caprice or ingratitude towards Mr Bicknell who is a very worthy excellent honest man, but neither fit for the business which yet remains or desirous of engaging in it. He was paid in October. I went by chance to his house in February to enquire after his sick family, & he then put into my hands the original copy of Richard Smiths will with all the Codicils correct & other papers & deeds or copies of them relative to other part of the business, which he has twenty times declared to me he never saw, & many of which I have been at a great expence otherwise to obtain & have been tormented to death by the want of them. If Lord Egremont considers this, he will, I think, not blame me for going to another solicitor & one on whom I imagine, as they are your Agents, there is no objection to——

I had very good reason for what I said about Mr Turner. He may not have interfered lately, but, as I never forget any thing, I know what he did do. I know not by what sophistry the rights of the dead are to be overlooked or annihilated, or why Mr Turner should shew so little regard to the memory of one of whom he once seem'd so extremely fond ~~of~~.[3] But he is my Brother—— & I will forbear to express what however I cannot but feel.

If you still wish, Sir, to be farther satisfied on the subject of my late daughters rights, I must trouble you to state your doubts that I may put them before Council. I am extremely sorry to have disgusted (as appears by your Letter) Lord Egremont by frequently writing on the general business, but besides that I remain'd in Town purposely to get thro it, I really do not see how I could avoid writing about the power of Attorney & other things which I could not do without the Trustees & which it was surely necessary to do. Setting aside the impolicy and impertinence of needlessly tiezing Lord Egremont, none will beleive, I hope, that I write officious & trifling Letters by way of shewing my knowledge in the affairs when I sacrifice my own bread by the continual attention I must give them & would relinquish all I have a right to tomorrow, could I without ruin to the family get away to some other Country where I might never hear the hateful name of the Smith trust again.

I see you have, among other notes to the rough draft of the power of Attorney, made a query, whether it will be of any use?—— I submitted the measure some weeks since to Lord Egremont who bade me do as I thought best. It is however not easy to answer y^{r} Query. All I can do is to act as my knowledge of the people there makes me <think it> right & take measures by which if probable ~~that~~ I may hear of the 1200 or 1500£ which ought to be forthcoming. I am, Sir,

Your obed^{t} humble Ser^{t},
Charlotte Smith

Petworth House Archives MS. No address or postmark.

NOTES

1. Augusta and de Foville's marriage articles were drawn up on 1 Aug. 1792 [*sic*] by Jonathan Morgan, Lincoln's Inn (PHA #8222; the year 1792 is probably a copying error for 1793). In the second half of 1802, Morgan acted on several occasions for BS. In an unpublished letter to Tyler on 27 Sept. 1802, CS complained that Morgan "is old and twaddles."

2. Despite this claim of his release, Charles Bicknell, CS's solicitor since at least 1790, clearly continued to handle trust business and, with a younger partner Anthony Spedding, concluded it.

3. That is, the rights of Augusta's surviving husband and Turner's memory of her.

To the earl of Egremont

[Frant, 1 June 1802]
My Lord,

Not hearing from your Lordship & being driven to the last extremity for money, I have ventured to draw on Messrs Pybus & Co. at 14 days for 20£, & I humbly and earnestly entreat that your Lordship will have the goodness to allow them to pay it when due, otherwise my distress & inconveniences will be extreme, as it is with the utmost difficulty I have gone on till now. The money is useless where it now is; to me it is impossible to do without a supply as I must keep house, & my expences must go on. As it is, I am myself destitute of every thing. I proposed being at Bignor on thursday sennight the 10th of June, but as Mrs Dorset has or is likely to have company whom I shall not meet, I shall stay only a day or two & wish your Lordship would have the goodness to inform me whether I may hope you will allow me to see you for a few moments, & If that time is not likely to suit you, I would make it any other, being very desirous for the twelvemonth which yet remains to have the unhappy business just upon such a footing as to include the necessity of my being so troublesome as to give your Lordship cause for complaint—— Being ever with unabated gratitude, your Lordships

ever oblig'd humble Sert,
Charlotte Smith

Frant
June 1st 1802
The money in Mr Pybus's hands is 152 & 165 which I hoped might have been paid to Mr De Foville, making together 317£. I ask at present only for 50£.

Petworth House Archives MS. No address or postmark.

To the earl of Egremont

{Frant, 6 June 1802}
My Lord,

Beleiving your Lordships goodness & humanity too great to suffer me, after all you have already done, to undergo such distress as must follow my not having a small present supply of money, I have drawn for 50£ & do humbly & earnestly implore your Lordship not to refuse giving Messrs Pybus directions to honor my draft. I almost despair of every thing, & nothing but the necessity of my going thro my miserable task for the sake of others would prevent my raising what money I can directly by the sale of a few books & some furniture & going abroad. I am threatend with arrests for actual necessaries for George, due these two years.[1] I have directed the persons who threaten me to apply to Mr B Smith, but I expect again to see bailiffs at my door, & surely all this is not my fault. If I had thrown away money or acted as I might have done, this cup of bitterness, never long removed, might have been justly my portion, but, as it is, I think I have not deserved so to suffer, & in that confidence, I appeal to your Lordships justice & mercy.

I am ever, My Lord,
your grateful &
oblig'd Ser[t],
Charlotte Smith

Frant, Tunbridge Wells
June 6th 1802
M[r] Tyler has not sent the receipts. I wish I could know at once your Lordships orders ab[t] them that such orders might be obey'd.

Petworth House Archives MS. No address or postmark.

NOTE

1. John Simpson, draper, had hired a lawyer to pursue his claim.

Madam
I am desired by M[r] Simpson (of Welbeck Street Cavendish Sq[re] Linnen Draper) to apply to you for payment of £16.18.9 being the amount of a Bill due from you to him for goods sold & delivered: And unless the same is immediately remitted to me, I have his positive directions, to send down a Writt for arresting you, without further Notice.

I am Madam
Y[r] ob[t] hble Serv[t]
John Richards
N[o] 9 Inner Temple
Lane Fleet St.

5th June 1802

To William Tyler

[Frant] June 13th 1802
Sir,

I send you, as beleiving it to be Lord Egremonts desire, the account of the money accruing to M[r] Benjamin Smith, and what he has really had. I know not how far the estate ought to make up to him the failure of the interest, oweing to the difficulties that arose as to investing the principal money. It is not a very great object. But you will allow me to state that the Trustees cannot, as you seem to think, be made to pay over again what they paid to me, or allowed M[r] Prescod to pay, inasmuch as by M[r] Smiths own agreement with the former Trustees, I was always to have a share of that money, & as such I am ready to give my receipt for it.

Lord Egremont, if I understand aright, wishes to know on what account Mr B Smith has had the advances made which you perceive amount to 620£? Except 10£ sent by me & 10£ by Miss Smith to enable him to go to Berwick to sign in his own name the agreement with Mr Gibbons, & powers of Attorney which he could not do at Hamilton where he pass'd as Mr Bryan Simmonds,[1] I really am unable to say to what account this 600£ is to be put, But perhaps Chancery may order it to go to the same account as the 16, or 17,000 which he sunk of his Fathers property while he was Executor. At present all that can be said is that—as his consent and signature was supposed to be requisite & he refused to give that signature, tho so greatly to the advantage of his children and his own—the family thought it better to let him have this money at different periods than have the business of the Trust stand still.

The transactions with Mr B Smith in 1798 when Mr Graham[2] gave his opinion & what afterwards pass'd between him & his deceased Son are evidences of his conduct in these affairs. In regard to the last money, the agreement for which Mr Taylor was Guarantee & which was only verbal, was that, on condition of dividing with Mrs C Smith the income arising from five thousand pounds Stg, now invested in the funds (3 pCt), he Mr B Smith should receive 400£ at two payments. Of this 300£ was paid, & the other 100£ was left to be paid, but Mrs Smith having had all the expence & trouble of journies to do all the business requisite, and being obliged to go to town to get a settlement with Mr Prescod, & having no support for herself & family, this last 100£[3] was paid to her because, as Mr B S. refused to fulfill the agreement made with Mr Tayler by allowing Mrs Smith & his children half the interest money, the agreement with him is void—at least until Mr Smith does so. I comply. I think last Autumn Mr B Smith laid claim to about 6000£, including certain articles which he call'd unpaid <short>: what that meant I have no guess.

I thank you for the copy of the very proper & I think unanswerable Letter you wrote in reply to Mr Benjn Follets Epistle[4] of the 2nd June. I am persuaded from long & sad experience that nothing short of ruining his family will satisfy Mr Benjamin Smith and that he will do so if he is not prevented by strong and decisive measures. It was only the high rank, fortune, & character of Lord Egremont that could have protected them in the part they have already received & in security for the rest, for any person in inferior life would have found it impossible to contend with the folly, falsehood, & dishonesty of Mr Benjn Smith; Against all he can do, Lord Egremont must be invulnerable; & if his Lordship would only determine to pay him no regard & let him fyle a bill or do any other senseless thing without deigning to notice it otherwise than by an official answer (if it should go to that), I dare venture to assert that he would very soon be sick of his plan.

What! fyle a Bill against Lord Egremont, for having paid for his family what is adequate to 6000£? for having taken from the purest motives of humanity such a charge upon himself & rescued them from persons who robbed them every year & who in another year would have had the Estate seized for debt? The idea is so ridiculous that it could enter no other head but that of a Madman & a fool——

Lord Egremont however is certainly authorised to say how far he will submit to the impertinence & stupidity of this unfortunate person, or some Attorney who supposes he can make money by him. None can be more sensible than I am of Lord Egremonts goodness; none feel more gratefully how much we owe him; nor how improper it is & how foreign from my meaning ~~it is~~ that Lord Egremont should be tiezed in this manner. But if his Lordship *now* gives the trust up, there will not be enough to pay the legatees. It is now only twelve months before it must end of itself. The Legatees will then be paid, & I hope the rest *will* be left to Chancery. I intend it shall if I have any influence——

The only part of your Letter to Mr Follet that I cannot think quite correct is where you say *that all parties are discontent with Lord Egremonts Trusteeship*. I must beg leave in the most positive terms to *deny* that I or my children are discontent—— I certainly do wish Mr De Foville's claim was settled on the easy & amicable footing I proposed because I have pledged myself that it should be so & know it to be just. I also do think I have a right to be allowed my expences for journies, postage, coach hire, & money actually advanced for the Estate. I am told by counsel I have such right; I know Chancery always allows it, & how & where am I to find the means of existence if it is denied me. On *me* the burthen & heat of the day has fallen. I have labourd in this work & neglected that by which I could have been independent, & now, because Mr Benjamin Smith demands that which he has *no* right to, I am to be literally starved, for I assure you I have no means of living, & after all Lord Egremont has done for me, I must be reduced to the hard necessity of giving up my house & selling every thing for want of 50£ which is all I solicited. I was told before Mr Smith came that I could not have it tho no reason was then assigned. I must submit & suffer. There seems no redress for me against Mr B Smith, & if Lord Egremont finds it necessary for his security, I must want bread——

But I know his Lordship intends right, & I must not ask him to risk any thing for me. His Lordship told Major Smith I must send all my debts to Mr B Smith. True, I may do so, of any debts save the current expence of my house. But can I send my *butcher, Miller, Grocer* & *Milkman* to Mr Benjn Smith, or can I expect them, knowing my situation, to trust me? And where am I to get money for the petty expences that daily occur? I have now not a shilling, & it is no small inconvenience to dread from day [*sic*] the refusal of

Tradesmen to supply my house. Two mournings[5] & heavy expences for George as well as in London swallowed up 80£ of my own, that I earned in the course of last year. My journies have devoured every thing else. All this I cannot say to Lord Egremont. It is not easy to convey an idea of the hardship of my situation. If his Lordship will not consider it, I have but one part to take. I sent you, Sir, some accounts which I wish you would be kind enough to refer to. Mr Dayrell assured me every expence would be allowed, & Mr Benjamin Smith (whose usefulness in adjusting the affairs is so very remarkable) lays claim to his journies! of course he cannot dispute mine.

But I beleive I have said all this over & over again. Since I am upon the subject however & know Lord Egremont is too candid & generous to dislike my speaking plainly, I will say that the only requests in regard to the affairs I have ever made have been refused. I entreated M^r^ De Foville might have the money agreed upon by compromise, even if I gave up my share of my late daughters maintenance; that was refused. I then begged he might at least have the 165£ put into the stocks that some interest may arise from it. That has not been done tho I think you will not deny but that to that interest, he has as good a right as any of the other legatees to their money—— I requested, very earnestly requested, that the terms might be complied with on which Messrs Daniel will accept the last bill, & I am very sure there is no risk in it to Lord Egremont, while I think the hazard of omitting it are to us, considerable. But this I cannot obtain. If having made these requests, which I think I have a sort of right to hope Lord E. would indulge me in, & feeling distress'd by refusal is discontent, I must so far plead guilty to the charge contained in your Letter to Mr Follet. But it by no means follows that I am for a moment insensible of the great obligations I owe to Lord Egremont, or for a moment doubt that in all he orders he consults what appears best for the Trust without too much committing himself. I must become as weak and wicked as poor Mr Smith before I could cease to consider Lord Egremonts goodness to me & my family as claiming all our gratitude to the last day of our lives.

Now Sir, I am to speak on the subject of the receipts. You sent the forms for me to fill up. I did so, naming the Sum's & returned the forms almost a month since. You said that, rather than have any dispute, Lord E. would be at the expence of the receipts. I desired they might be charged to the estate, & I imagined that your meaning was to fill them up & send them on the proper stamps. Now you write that you have never received the forms back, yet they reach me returned from you by the same post. There appears to be a mistake somewhere in this matter. However to give no more trouble, I would have sent ~~down~~ yesterday for five stamps at one guinea each to Tunbridge Town where alone they can be purchased, but I had not the 5 G^s^ to send, having only two Guineas in the house which I have paid away to day. I therefore sent to my Solicitor Mr Henry Fry[6] to desire him to get them for me, but he was gone to London. Had I had the money & means to send to Tunbridge Town (7 miles), Miss Smith would have returnd three of them to you by this post. Mr Duncan is I know not where; as soon as I know, I will send for his name. Mr Turner you will please to speak to <For> Nicholas. I hope you will explain to Lord Egremont why I do not return the receipts & assure his Lordship I will obey him the moment I have the power.

If I can borrow or procure any money, I hope to be at Bignor next week, having business to do of my own, & also in regard to Mrs Newhouse's cottage, & I hope Lord E. will allow me the honor of speaking to him. I am, Sir,

your obedt obligd hble Sert, Charlotte Smith

Petworth House Archives MS. No address or postmark.

NOTES

1. BS's earliest use of this alias is found in BS to William Tyler, 27 Feb. 1799 (unpub. letter in PHA #0.11). "Brian Simmonds Esqr/ Hamilton" is not in his handwriting, perhaps to further protect his identity from creditors and the law. The alias also survives in CS's important letter to Egremont, 14 and 15 Oct. 1803. Hamilton, Scotland, near Glasgow, was BS's home in exile for many years. In Berwick, across the border in England, he could sign his legal name.

2. The lawyer Robert Graham (see CS to Cadell and Davies, 22 June 1797, n. 1).

3. A note in another hand observes: "It was only 96£ received by Mrs Smith; which Messrs Pybus said was left, but as she has not seen the account she does not know what occasiond the difference—"

4. Benjamin Follet, a King's Bench lawyer of 2 Paper Buildings, Inner Temple, acted for BS until late 1803. CS saw Follet as the most grasping of her husband's legal counsel.

5. For Charles, who died in the summer of 1801, and CS's son-in-law Thomas Newhouse, Lucy's husband, who died in Mar. 1801.

6. Of Tunbridge Wells. Fry was also associated with Richard Cumberland, who described him as "a most sincere and honorable friend . . . with great legal ability" (*Memoirs,* 2:341).

To William Tyler

Half Moon, Petworth
July 2nd 1802
Sir,

As to day was the day I had fix'd upon to come hither, I did not postpone my journey again because the extraordinary circumstance I ~~lay~~ am under admits of no hesitation. Your opinion as to the allowance to be made to me for expences, a regular account of which I have kept, is exactly the reverse of Mr Grahams, now a Judge and who helped me to arrange the Trust, of Mr Harding, a Welsh Judge, of Mr Dayrell & Mr Morgan,[1] & it very unfortunately happens that whatever I desire or think ought to be done is always diametrically opposite to your opinion. Lord Egremont would have had much less reason to complain of trouble if he had had the goodness, as he formerly did, to give me his confidence or to give it to those who are acquainted with my conduct for the fifteen years that I have supported the family. I shall not put the charges for money advanced to me to the legatees accounts, but leave it to Chancery to decide Since Lord Egremont, after having saved us so far, has been prevail'd upon to give us up and throw us into a worse situation than we were before he so generously took us up.

I would willingly ask you to what Account Mr Benjn Smiths 6 hundred pounds is to be placed—He, who has never laid out a shilling. But it is I it seems who are to suffer & to be denied repayments of money advanced out of my pocket without which the affairs could not have gone on at all.

I beg your pardon for giving you so much trouble & do it the more unwillingly because I perceive you have not time to form any other than a very hasty judgement. It can hardly happen that I am <u>always</u> in the wrong. I <u>beleive</u> it is a rule with Chancery that Trustees are not to let money lie dead. Yet (except the 60£ lately so hardly begged—& so insufficient) there is a sum now laying utterly useless in Mr Pybus's hands, & I am denied wherewithal to answer the bills drawn on me from Barbados for the Expences of illness & the funeral of my unfortunate Charles, The victim of these accursed affairs. I should say of any other person than Lord Egremont that this is cruel.

I shall give no ~~xxxx~~ orders to Mr Morgan because I do not know what is meant or why Lord Egremont takes one trust for 2000£ & not that for £3000 & because I will not be at any more expence. I am desperate & care not what is done since I shall be oblig'd to sell my books, furniture, & every thing to subsist. Lord Egremont, who has on so many occasions been so generous, could never reduce me to this, if my situation was fairly before him.

I shall be at Bignor about a fortnight.

I am, Sir, y^r^ humble Ser^t^,
Ch Smith

Petworth House Archives MS. Address: M^r^ <u>Tyler</u>/Petworth.

NOTE

1. CS's obvious frustration with Tyler's position on expenses is heightened by the

fact that three of the four lawyers she names had been involved in trust affairs longer than Tyler—Sir Robert Graham since the trust was established in 1776; George Hardinge since at least 1791; and Jonathan Morgan, Lincoln's Inn, since 1793 when he finalized marriage articles for Augusta and de Foville (PHA #8222). In 1794, Morgan still held a copy of a deed of 1784 (see CS to Mr. Fordyce, 27 Dec. 1794).

To William Tyler

[Bignor, 13 July 1802]
Sir,

I was yesterday nearly concluding all the accounts in a way that would I trust put an end to all difficulties & doubts & was about to write to you to name a day for y^r coming. But an express arrived this morning from Tunbridge to inform me my youngest daughter is so dangerously ill[1] that my return is necessary instantly. I do not expect to find her alive. I have exhausted the little I had in an useless & fatiguing journey & now return perhaps to a dying child, not knowing where to obtain money for the purposes that may be required——— It is too much——

I am, Sir,
y^r humble Ser^t,
Charlotte Smith

Bignor 2 oclock
Teusday 13th July [1802]

Petworth House Archives MS. No address or postmark.

NOTE

1. A return of the malarial fever Harriet contracted while in India (1799–1801).

To William Tyler

Frant
July 18th 1802
Sir,

Mrs Dorset forwarded y^r Letter to me In answer to which I can at present only say that, as nobody thought of the necessity of making out the accounts at all till I mention'd it, I imagine there is no such very urgent occasion to hasten them that I need be compelled to attend to them at this time when my daughters dangerous state demands every moment of my time, when I have been in bed only one night out of five & am under the greatest anxiety as to the event—An anxiety not a little aggravated by the cruelty with which I am deprived of the means of providing for the additional expence this heavy affliction necessarily involves me in. I think myself treated with ~~xxxxxxxxxxxxxxxx~~ a degree of rigour which I little expected—— & have sufferd more than if I had never been flatterd by a more favourable termination of the affairs of this ill fated family.

It is I suppose useless to name to you that I have received the most satisfactory answer from Barbados from Mr Adams,[1] a Man of large independent fortune & a Gentleman, who willingly undertakes to do every thing to recover the money from Griffith[2] (500£ St^g^ I beleive) & every other outstanding debt—— If I ~~am~~ was properly authorised, I would get thro this, but under the present confused & unsettled state of the Trust, which may cease before Mr Adams can act under the power sent out, it is folly for me to give any more time to it———

I am really sorry for Mr Turner, & I hope for <u>his own</u> sake he will recollect himself in time to preclude the necessity of my explaining at length to Lord Egremont <u>why</u> I did not <u>chuse</u> to ~~give~~ leave to Mr Turner the application of the money.[3] It is very immaterial whether he signs the receipts or no. I will sign Any acknowledgement for the present, & I expect ~~by~~ to receive from Mr N. H. Smith a full power for me to act with his Sister in his Affairs, & ~~not to~~ preclude the necessity of troubling Mr Turner at all, & when such power arrives, She or I will sign the receipt. I every day expect a child of Mr N. H. Smiths[4] by the David Scott, India ship, & I must take care of the little property he has here for her & the rest of his children. I shall be ready to finish & send the accounts as soon as I am releived from my present distressing state of solicitude which is all I can say. I am, Sir, y^r^ obed^t^ Ser^t^,

Charlotte Smith

Petworth House Archives MS. Addressed first to Sussex then to London: Mr Tyler/ The Earl of Egremont/ N° 5. Grosvenor place/ {Petworth}/ London/ {Sussex}. Postmarked first: JUL 19? 1802/ TUNB-WELLS 36. And: D JUL21 1802/ PETWORTH 37.

NOTES

1. Thomas Maxwell Adams, son of a Thomas Adams of Barbados who had matriculated at Lincoln's Inn in 1762, was 33 at the time he became involved in trust matters in Barbados. He was one of the few Barbadians whom CS continued to view as trustworthy during a long relationship.

2. James Griffith (d. winter 1803–1804) of Barbados. CS considered him "that rogue Griffith" (see CS to Egremont, 23 or 24 Mar. 1803). Charles Smith's fatal trip to the West Indies in 1801 was made in part to collect that debt.

3. During his tenure as a civil servant in India, Nicholas Hankey Smith left a power of attorney with the uncle for whom he was named, Nicholas Turner. Because Turner had been involved in lawsuits over his own debts, CS no longer trusted her brother to handle her son's finances. Charlotte Mary, who had a great deal of experience in trust matters, was granted power of attorney for Nicholas Smith on 8 July 1804.

4. Luzena, Nicholas's daughter by his first wife or consort who may have been Persian or Indian (see Nicholas Hankey Smith in Biographical Notes). Although supported by remittances from her father and a small trust, Luzena meant additional financial burdens for her grandmother, particularly when remittances arrived late. Nevertheless, the 5-year-old brought CS much pleasure and joy, for she felt Luzena was "*tout a moi*"—"all mine." The child arrived without a command of English, and CS tailored her next children's book, *Conversations Introducing Poetry,* to help Luzena learn the language. George was especially fond of his little niece: his will leaves all property to "my dear sister Luzena, daughter of my dear brother Nicholas Smith." The will, which Charlotte Mary unaccountably left unadministered, was settled on 3 Jan. 1862 with everything granted to Lucena [*sic*] Smith Spinster (PRO).

To the earl of Egremont

Frant. Augst 11th 1802
My Lord,

Self vindication I owe to myself, how ever humbled & sunk I may be by undeserved misery. I never was, I never will be ungrateful to your Lordship. But whatever may be the triumph of those from whose oppression your Goodness rescued me (& they will triumph), whatever I may suffer from deprivations of every sort, & however I may be accused of what I never was guilty of in regard to misrepresentations & falsehood, I shall still say that your Lordships goodness to me has been unexampled & beleive that it would not at last have deserted me, but from the predominance of that miserable destiny which converts even my virtues & sufferings to my destruction. I have nothing left to wish for but death & shall importune you no more. The accounts so imperiously demanded by Mr Tyler when it was impossible for me to finish them, I will collect & send in a few days—— Your Lordships Letter has actually disabled me from working at them or any other business to day. I am not conscious of hav^g said any thing rude or abusive of Mr Tyler. I respect any person you are pleasd to entrust as your Agent, but when I receive directions absolutely contradictory & from Mr Tyler en chef at least in tone, I must feel that I was once treated with more humanity & consideration, nor could I obey what I did not understand.

As to Mr Turner, I have avoided as much as possible naming him, & whenever I have done so, I think I have always palliated his faults. Except in the single instance when I beleived the vulgar national prejudice of a coarse mind & other less defensible motives had made him interfere about the rights of my deceasd daughter,[1] I surely have never found any fault with him to y^r Lordship. I have lived longer in the World than you have my Lord, & tho without your power to confer benefits, I too have drank deeply of the bitter cup of ingratitude & cannot blame your suspicions that all are alike ungrateful. Mr Turner shall not provoke me, however, to be more explicit in regard to him,[2] & if I am violent, there is at least some merit in checking the ebullition of that temper on some occasions which might justify violence. Mr Morgan wrote to me a few days ago to propose another attempt at accommodation or rather hinted that it might be brought about. I an[swere][d] him on Sunday, that I would acquiese in any thing tho I beleive this is the first instance of its being left to arbitration whether a Man shall support his Wife & children. I am now very indifferent about all but preventing y^r Lordship from thinking worse of me than you do——

A long and ineffectual struggle with calamity, which encreases in proportion as I resist it, ends in the humble project of selling my books & what little furniture I have, & trying if I can go out of England to die. I had agreed for a small house at Elsted near Godalming because Mr Cumberland has taken this for his daughter,[3] & my time in it is out. My Son Nicholas having sent over his little Girl born of a Georgian Woman and meaning to make a yearly remittance & to give me his dividend here for her support, I thought I might with the assistance of my eldest daughter & some allowance at least out of my own fortune have existed the little time I have to live. But it is hardly worth while to try again, & I shall write to Mr Peacock & give it (the house) up. My youngest daughter is still very weak, for I cannot change the air for her for want of money. I sent her father the Apothecaries bill of 13.8.0, but he refuses to pay it, & As I owe a bill myself of 20£, I cannot now obtain bark[4] for her Since there is no likelihood of My pay^g for it. Her illness has cost above 50£

I am, my Lord, your ever grateful Ser^t,
<CS>

Petworth House Archives MS. No address or postmark.

NOTES

1. Turner's interference in the onetime payment of Augusta's legacy to de Foville showed his prejudice against the French and possibly his lingering pique at CS for not continuing to lend him money.

2. CS does, however, in her own defense finally elaborate on Turner's troubles and misconduct (CS to Egremont, 7 and 13 Feb. 1803).

3. Sophia Badcock, second daughter of the playwright Richard Cumberland of Tunbridge Wells.

4. That is, quinine, a powder ground from the bark of the cinchona tree and taken to reduce fever.

To William Hayley[1]

[Frant, 16 August 1802]
Dear Sir,

I have deliberated some time whether or no I should take the liberty of intruding upon you, & were it on a subject merely relating to myself, I should have decided against giving you the trouble of reading a letter which is to make a request.

It is painful to me to recall the past days of a life which has been a series of, I trust, underserved misfortunes. That which is the heaviest & most severely felt even at this distance of time is the loss of her among my children who was to me the only being on Earth I ever passionately loved. And since that miserable day, now more than seven years, My only consolation has been attempting to fulfil her wishes in serving the unfortunate Man who was a sincere sharer of my sorrow & whose conduct has never disgraced her attachment to him. The other parts of my family have made this a very distressing attempt by their rudeness & injustice to M^r^ De Foville, and ~~I xxxxx~~ and I have suffer'd more than I would, if I could help it, recollect.

That however is over; M^r^ De Foville, who found resources in his own talents and industry for some years & supported himself with universal respect, is now returnd to France, & M^r^ B Smith's family are never likely to be call'd upon again to forbear insulting in his person the memory of my lost & deplored Augusta ——— But I feel it incumbent on me to do in regard to pecuniary affairs that justice to him which would have been <u>demanded</u> by any man less disinterested, circumstanced and treated as he has been ——

Without entering into any unpleasant detail, let it suffice to say that Lord Egremont, usually so generous & liberal-minded, has always resisted (and I think with unnecessary unkindness & asperity) any claim of M^r^ De Foville on the assets of Richard Smith, the Grandfather of this family, & refused every thing I have asked. At length, however, his Lordship has been pleas'd to acknowledge by his Steward that M^r^ De Foville <u>has</u> a right to the interest for his life of 333£ (there being a flaw in the Will, by which her G[ran]dfather meant to give my second daughter the same Sum as he did all those born before his decease). This, with the interest accruing upon it, made a Sum of about 500£.

I had a valuation made of M^r^ De Foville's interest in this Sum by a person whose business it is to make such calculations, & it was found to amount to 165£ present money. A Sum which, as he wish'd to return to France & to put an end to all conversation on this subject with persons who had so little consideration for him or for me, he agreed to take. And, upon my making a division of the last installment paid for the Estate in March last, I left this money in the hands of Lord Egremont's Banker to be paid to M^r^ De Foville as soon as his discharge could be drawn up. The other legatees consented to this; Lord Egremont himself appeard to think it would be advisable, & I was particularly anxious that it might be done as well to accommodate M^r^ De Foville on his return to France, as to prevent the necessity of my giving you any trouble whatsoever—— Lord Egremont however, whose decisions I must respect & submit to, whatever they may be, has since been advised and discoverd that he <u>cannot</u> do this and that he must pay the Sum of which M^r^ De Foville is to have the interest for his life into the funds in the name of one or both the Trustees namd in the marriage articles between him and my deceased daughter.

I am not more happy in one of my <u>collateral</u> relations than in that miserable connection to which I was sold in my early youth, & it is with extreme reluctance I ask Mr Turner[2] to take this trust upon him, as his coarse mind makes him consider a Man of another nation as out[3] of the Laws of this or, I believe, of Justice. To you I appeal also with great unwillingness. Certainly not for that same reason, but because, when I presumed to put your name into the Trust of my poor Girl's little fortune, I thought there was very little probability of my ever giving you the slightest trouble about it, tho at that time, I flatterd myself, that our long friendship would in duration and equality have made such an act of kindness to one I loved, not very burthensome or disagreeable to you. The change that has in every respect occurred during the laspse [*sic*] of more than eight years, has made me regret extremely having thus attempted to tax your kindness. The time however is come, when Mr Benjn Smith's conduct—in depriving me of all the income of my own little fortune[4] and leaving me absolutely destitute with his two younger children, whose support still rests in a great measure on me—obliges me to make a last effort to settle the affairs of the Grandfather, which with infinite pains & labour & Lord Egremont's assistance are nearly brought to a conclusion, before I seek some means of subsistence such as my advanced time of life & shatterd health will allow me to hope I may yet obtain. But which will be incompatible with the constant attention I have given to the arrangement of these affairs—attention that has been necessarily redoubled by the unhappy death of my poor invalid Son Charles in Barbados, & by the cruel & frantic conduct of M^r^ B Smith, which has provoked Lord Egremont to say, that unless every thing is immediately agreed upon & settled so as that his Lordship shall no more be troubled, he will throw the property into Chancery.

In consequence of this & of his directing me to get the accounts & receipts &c all ready, I have given up the time which would otherwise have been employ'd in earning my humble bread to this irksome & perhaps useless task; and one of the most painful duties it imposes upon me is that of asking you if you will condescend so far to act as Trustee to my late daughter's representative, as to suffer the sum of 333£, or whatever the interest may make it, to stand in your name in the Stocks & to appoint some person to receive the half yearly dividends which will amount to scarce 20£ a year to be paid to M[r] Boyn, whom M[r] De Foville has appointed his Attorney, every expence incidental to this being deducted & paid by him. Or, in case you will not do this, will you have the goodness to inform me (for I can get no answer to the question) from your own Solicitor or Councel how you can be divested of this trust, so as to put M[r] Boyn in a situation to execute it & releive you from all farther trouble.

As I wait only till these things are done before I quit this place (and if I can, this Kingdom altogether), I venture to entreat you will oblige me with as early an answer as may be convenient and that I may hear you forgive my importunity in consideration of its being altogether involuntary, & of my assurance that it shall be the last I [*sic*] time I will ever take such a liberty——

I have the honor to be,
Dear Sir,
your oblig'd & obed humble Ser[t],
Charlotte Smith

Frant near Tunbridge Wells
Aug[st] 16th 1802

I understand by a letter from M[r] Tyler, Lord Egremont's Steward, that if the Trustees who are named in the deed of the 3rd Aug[st] 1793 signifying that one or both will consent to the money's being placed in their names, Lord E. would then let a part be so deposited, which—contrary I think to justice—now remains unapropriated at the Bankers & the interest lost to M[r] de Foville.

J. Pierpont Morgan MS. No address or postmark.

NOTES

1. Hayley and Nicholas Turner are named as trustees to the marriage settlement for Augusta and de Foville, dated 1 Aug. 1792 [*sic*] (PHA #7371). There is no record of Hayley's involvement at this later date.

2. CS's growing alienation from her brother is described elsewhere (see CS to Egremont, 9 July 1800, n. 7; 7 Apr. and 11 Aug. 1802, n. 1; and 7 Feb. 1803, n. 1).

3. That is, outside.

4. It was probably not hers, in law. See CS to Egremont, 12 Jan. 1802, n. 2.

To William Tyler

[Frant, 23 August 1802]
Sir,

It is with extreme reluctance I write again to you, & the more so, as having heard nothing from Mr Morgan, I have great reason to beleive he cannot bring Mr Benjn Smith to bind himself to abide by the purposed agreement in such a way as to make the referrence propos'd of any use. In the mean time, my large family—from the support of which I can neither escape nor provide for it—occasions my being in the most distressing and uneasy of all situations. My youngest daughter's illness has added <u>above fifty pounds</u> to my expence to which M^r^ B Smith, to whom I sent some of the bills, refuses to contribute a shilling. Mrs Newhouse & her three children with a servant and my Son George who came home for two months in order to save his pay & enable him to meet the Regiment when it comes home—all are depending at this moment on the home they have hitherto found, & I am now deeply in debt for the actual necessaries of life without knowing where to get a guinea. My credit will not last another week. I have hoped that Lord Egremont, who has so long preserved me from the extremity of (surely undeserved) distress, would not suffer me now to sink under it, especially as I did not ask any farther advance <u>on my own account</u>, but merely entreated he would let Miss Smith & her two elder brothers have 150£ (50£ cash) with which I might have been assisted at this moment.

But his Lordship seems to determine against me, & notwithstanding all I had reason to hope, from his former kindness, he thought in my favor, I am now left to my fate. When I read over the numerous and most friendly Letters he has written to me, on the affairs while they were intricate & almost hopeless as well as observe his generous solicitude about the living of Islington, I cannot conceive <u>what</u> I have done that now, when his benevolent intentions are within a few months of answering their end, he should thus repel my humble application for bread till that period arrives—— He was pleased to say, even when I had last the honor of seeing him, that he hoped I should survive M^r^ B Smith, & on my life depends more than merely my own wretched existence, but the shocks & perpetual distresses I am exposed to must shorten, indeed soon end my life, as no fortitude of mind or strength of body <u>can</u> endure <u>what</u> I suffer.

I must remove from hence the first week in September, as the house is let to another person who has agreed to let me remain a week longer, but my time is up on the 1st when I must pay my rent. How to move or how to stay, I know not! If it had been profitable for me escaped [*sic*] from the miseries I am chaind to, I would have gone abroad never to return, but I promis'd Lord Egremont when first he had the goodness to accept the Trust that I would do every thing to assist in getting thro it, nor could I go abroad without some income. I therefore decided on taking the House near Godalming, which is cheaper than this; It is now ready for me, & had I the means of paying my bills here I would immediately go thither for the present, & sell every thing I can spare.

When there, if you would take the trouble to come thither, the whole of these accounts might be gone over & the mistakes, which on a minute investigation of them I have detected, rectified, & then whatever Lord Egremont determines to do, no farther difficulty as far as relates to his Lordships trust can arise, for you will see that I have had no more advanced to me, than my absolute expences justify.

I did not understand some part of Mr Daniels accounts that related to my deceased Son; I therefore wrote to them last week for an explanation & find that, besides 50£ not placed to his account by me last year, there was a farther ballance of 93£ paid by the Trustees for his private account, & other of the Legatees have had more than those accounts contain'd (for which omission I beleive I accounted in a former Letter).

I am now by the assistance of a writing master[1] & accountant (for I cannot do it myself) making out anew the whole accounts down to July 2nd 1802: for I suppose that, while interest is deducted <u>on one side</u> for money received <u>by the legatees</u>, Interest at 4 pC^t^ must still go on on that part of the principal that remains unpaid—— If <u>I am wrong, you will do me a kindness in letting me know</u>—— I shall proceed to make out all these accounts that they may be ready for Mr Morgan if the referrence takes place Or for Chancery should it be finally Lord Egremonts resolution to threw the affairs into that Court where I understand they will in all probability remain five years to the certain destruction of the residue—— if not of the Legatees interest.

In the mean time, let me entreat you Sir to lay before Lord Egremont, who is I apprehend at a distance, the present state of distress & threatend want I am in, & how vain my attempts of every sort must be unless his Lordship condescends to allow my family (which is all I ask) the means of assisting me. Or If you could <u>otherwise</u> procure the money, 150£ as a loan to Miss Smith, she would give security & pay 5 pC^t^ ~~xx~~ or draw a bill on the Trust at 6 months which I could get discounted by Mr Fauntleroy,[2] & by that time I trust the next division of the estate will be made, & my Sons would not suffer me to want thus & would do all that depended on them to mitigate to me the cruelty & injustice of Mr Benjn Smith.

Lord Egremont told me I ought to send my bills to him M^r^ B Smith, but my butcher & baker, I cannot send; nor my Grocer, brewer & chandler, & how little efficacy I have attempted to do so with other bills, the enclosed Letter will shew you. I expect to see the Bailiff for the County of Sussex enter my doors every hour & imagine one of them has already been in the village making enquiries, for this morning before I had left my bed, two of the tradesmen who supply my house sent to ask money of me in a way they never did before which I can no otherwise account for—— Money I have not, & if Mr Richards puts his threat in execution, I must go to the County jail,[3] & my distress must terminate that way—

If I had, either by extravagance or neglect of the few powers I have left, brought this upon myself, there would be some very good reason for my being left thus destitute & impoverished, but I have not only denied myself everything, given up vanity,[4] & gone almost without the decencies of life but exerted myself beyond my strength to earn money. This bill is for linnen for my youngest Son & myself & not for any luxuries or indulgencies.

It is very dreadful at my time of life to be thus situated. If I could escape from it even to servit[ude, I] would do it, but I am chained to it & canno[t] shake it off—— If I am sometimes driven to despair & almost to frenzy, none surely can wonder at it. Lord Egremont however says I misrepresent. I may have done so, but certainly not designedly, for I have seen too many instances of the impolicy of falsehood to be wilfully guilty of it even if I had from principle no attachment to truth. I hope his Lordship will think better of me. Ungrateful I never was; I should detest myself if I were capable of ingratitude, but after all it is the consciousness of his own benevolent actions, & not any thing I can say, that must gratify his Lordships feelings.

I had yesterday another long Letter by the Packet from Mr Adams in Barbados who waits only to hear from me to recover the monies which poor Charles considerd as good debts to the amount of near or quite 1000£ Sterling. I have likewise seen a Gentleman just come from Barbados after a passage of two months[5] who has given me considerable information on the remaining affairs, but in truth I have no heart to sit down & do what is required when I think that, from the affairs being thrown into Chancery, the Trustees powers of Attorney will be <superceded?>[6]— and whatever is obtaind wasted in Law; or, if Lord Egremont is so good as to forbear doing this, that I am not to be allowed my expences ~~xxxx~~ of postage & stationary & am giving up my time for the benefit of a Man of whom Lord E. very justly said that he did not consider him as so honest a Man as an highwayman!

Let me entreat, Sir, some answer by the return of the post that I may know whether there is any hope of my being deliverd from this state of unmerited suffering & whether I may give the tradesmen hope of being paid in a week or ten days. I am, Sir, y^{r} obed^{t} humble Ser^{t}, Charlotte Smith

Petworth House Archives MS. Address: The Earl of Egremon——/ Petworth/ Sussex/ By London Tunbridge Augst 23rd/ 1802. Postmark: FREE/ AUG 24/ 1802. TUNB-WELLS/ 26.

NOTES

1. Probably Davey Stidolph (see CS to Tyler, 13 Sept. 1802, n. 5).

2. William Fauntleroy readily discounted bills for CS over the next two years until finally he denied her a "trifle" she owed to Pybus's, and he is mentioned no more.

3. On 11 Aug. 1802, John Simpson, draper, renewed his two-month-old threat through his solicitor (see CS to Egremont, 6 June 1802, n. 1). This time, John Richards wrote in a manner not likely to incite CS to repay this old debt quickly:

> Madam, You should have heard from me long since in Answer to your's on the subject of Mr Simpson's Claim, but nearly the whole of my time has been occupied in preparing or the Assizes which is now at an end with me—I have only to observe that Mr Simpson has nothing to do with Mr Smith; to you only he look's for the payment of the Debt you contracted with him, & I have no hesitation in saying that in my opinion, the Law will compel you to pay it—— I am therefore instructed to Sue out a Writ against you, which I shall do, in the course of a few days, in the mean time, you will have an opportunity of Judging whether it will be most prudent in you to remit to me the amount of the Money without the interference of Law.

4. Could be read as "sanity," but "vanity" seems more likely in context.

5. This person is never named.

6. This awkwardly written word could be a misspelling for "suspended."

To William Tyler[1]

Frant Augst 26th
1802
Sir,

As I am unwilling to go thro all the trouble of making out the Legatees accounts again, I think it best to enclose to you a sheet containing that of Mr William Towers Smith That you may see if it is done right or that you may make any corrections for my government in this & the others, which I propose making up with interest to the 2nd July last; but knowing as I do that Mr Ben^{n} Smith will take every advantage of any mistake & is ashamed of no baseness that may enable him to injure and rob his own children, I do not chuse to commit myself by sending them to Mr Morgan till they are adjudged to be right by those who arc empowerd to act for Lord Egremont.

I likewise send you a copy of Mr Benjamin Smiths agrement with the former Trustees after I seperated myself from him.[2] My Son Nicholas was provided for (not by his father) on the 17th February 1790.[3] My Son Charles had a commission (a fatal commission) in May 1793.[4] My Son Lionel not till 1795.[5] And to both the latter, I advanced considerable Sums for many years afterwards. I had then M^r^ B Smiths remaining family of four daughters and his younger Son to support: nevertheless in the Spring at 1795 when I was in peculiar distress and anguish of mind from the long and fatal illness of my most beloved daughter, Mr Benjamin Smith took <u>that</u> opportunity of <u>trying</u> to take from me this 70£ a year & wrote to Mr Robinson, who sent me the paragraph (mark'd no. 2)[6] & declared at the same time that <u>he could not consent, as a Trustee</u>, to withdraw from me the 70£, according to the request so made to him by Mr Benjn Smith. Even Robinsons long harden'd heart & his aversion to me because I knew what he was & dared to tell him so[7] were not equal to the barbarous injustice then intended by M^r^ B Smith. My daughter died! My distress was dreadful, & I wrote to him a remonstrance on his intention of taking away from me & his and his [*sic*] remaining children the pittance of 70£ a year. I enclose a copy of his answer. No. 3—— wherein he <u>positively denies</u> ever having had such a thought tho Mr Robinson had <u>actually sent me a copy of his Application</u>. I wish to know when you have read these whether you think the Trustees have not sufficient authority for continuing to pay me half the interest of 3000£ now in the 3 pC^ts^ in the names of Lord Egremont & Mr Turner.

I shall send in a few days an account of all the money I have received as interest or otherwise & the items of my charges for Postage, Stationary, Coach hire, & journies (with the orders I received for these journies) and also money advanced by me not otherwise charged. And this I should have done together with copies of Mr Daniels sales & invoices before, but on minute investigation, I found some errors in the accounts as heretofore received, particularly in that of my deceased Son, which I could not understand. I therefore wrote to Messrs Daniel & received their explanation only yesterday when I could make no progress in this or any other business, my house having been broke open on Teusday night & of the little merely useful & necessary plate I had, more than <u>half</u> was taken to the amount of about fifteen pounds—— I have no means of replacing it and must submit among others to this deprivation also. Your early answer to this & to my former Letter will oblige, Sir, your obed^t^ humble Ser^t^,

Charlotte Smith

Petworth House Archives MS. No address or postmark.

NOTES

1. A barely legible note by Tyler in the upper margin of the first page seems to say that Egremont did not intend to intercede in CS's trust, but that the trustees themselves, during the authorized period, agreed to present the matter of the trusteeship into Chancery.

2. On 15 Apr. 1787. The agreement has not survived.

3. The meaning of "provided for" is not exactly clear, and no will, deed, or provision from Feb. 1790 has been found. Nicholas had obtained the rank of writer in 1788 and arrived in India in Sept. 1790. As one of the grandchildren born before Richard Smith died, Nicholas had always been provided for in his grandfather's will.

4. The *Army List* gives the date of Charles's commission as 10 Apr. 1793.

5. The *Army List* shows Lionel Smith as lieutenant as of 28 Oct. 1795.

6. The paragraph marked no. 2 and the two other letters mentioned do not survive.

7. We have little record of what CS said to John Robinson, since only two of her letters to him survive (of 19 Sept. 1785 and before 29 July 1797), but what she said about him was severe. She blamed him for impoverishing her family by mismanaging the trust. In a letter to an unknown recipient (8 Dec. 1791), she wrote that she had "but little delight in exposing myself to the supercilious and purse proud insolence of Robinson." In prefaces to various works, she accuses the trustees of delaying settlement to her children's disadvantage, but she does not go so far as to name Robinson.

To William Davies

[Frant, 30 August 1802]
Sir,

The obliging note which accompanied Mr Hayleys Letter received yesterday demands my earliest acknowledgement. As I know Mr Hayleys dislike to business of the nature with which it <u>was</u> my fault & is <u>now</u> my misfortune that I am in some measure under the necessity of troubling him, I take the liberty of writing to you. M^r^ De Foville has taken with him to France the deed made on his marriage with my deceased daughter.[1] There were only two parts as I recollect, & the other is in the hands of a Gentleman who holds other papers of mine.[2] I will write to him by tomorrows post & enquire whether there is any power inserted to transfer the Trust.

In the mean time, I imagine I may say to Lord Egremont that the objection started by his Steward of by I know not whom, against investing the money which for his life does undoubtedly belong to M^r^ De Foville—i e <u>that</u> neither of the Trustees named in the settlement had signified their assent to having that money placed in their name—is done away by Mr Hayleys consent to let it for the present or till another is named Trustee stand in his—— Whatever may be the event, I am much oblig'd to Mr Hayley & to you.

I will not intrude upon him with another Letter nor trouble him with a refutation of the idea he has received of my actual situation since it is no longer in the power of friendship itself to change or mitigate the sufferings I am condemned to, & I have now lived long enough to know that there is a degree, & a continuance of ill fortune, which wearies or blunts the most real & acute sensibility——

To quit a subject equally painful & useless, I beg the favor of you to allow me to send to you to be transmitted to Mr Hayley two Letters from your most excellent & illustrious friend Mr Cowper. I am greatly flatterd by Mr Hayleys recollection that I ever was honord by this mark of esteem from such a Man. The Letter of October 1793 which I beleive came under cover from Mr Hayley, he had probably forgotten tho I value it even more than the other. He will make whatever extracts from it he thinks proper, <or> perhaps he might chuse to publish it all;[3] & I cannot but be honor'd by the insertion of either or both of them in Mr Hayleys work——— As he names it as being soon to appear & that no time is be [*sic*] lost, I venture to transmit these Letters immediately—— Some months since, Mr Walker,[4] who has never entirely ceased to favor me with his Correspondence, enquired of me whether I had not a Letter from Mr Cowper in answer to the dedication of my humble and unsuccessful attempt in blank verse—advising me if I did possess such a Letter to send it to Mr Hayley; I did not however do so, being unwilling on any occasion to intrude myself in his recollection and beleiving that, if he had thought any thing relating to me of importance enough to appear in the Life of Cowper, he would have signified as much to me, either by Letter or by Messrs Cadell & Davies, who generally know where I am to be found. Instead of copying the Letters, which I observe Mr Hayley requests, I send the originals, being indeed too much indisposed & harrass'd to be well able to write what I must of necessity try to do to send to London, on business, the most irksome & hopeless—— This must serve for my excuse to you for writing so ill. Allow me to assure you that I am, with gratitude and esteem,

Sir your most oblig'd & obed Ser^t^,
Charlotte Smith

Frant near Tunbridge Wells
Aug^st^ 30th 1802

Osborn Collection MS, Yale University. No address or postmark.

NOTES

1. According to a deposition taken in the Chancery case (PHA #8010, p. 29), de Foville lived in England as an emigrant from 1791 to 1802. On 24 July 1802, he left

for France, returning to England on 24 Nov. 1802, and going back to France on 22 June 1803. There were other trips back and forth in other years. CS describes his life as a French tutor and drawing master in England in a letter to the duchess of Devonshire (23 Nov. 1800).

2. Possibly Jonathan Morgan, BS's lawyer, who signed the marriage agreement between Augusta and de Foville.

3. These two letters survive at the British Library and Cowper and Newton Museum and are reprinted in collections of Cowper's letters, including those edited by King and Ryskamp.

4. Joseph Cooper Walker, CS's literary friend in Dublin.

To the earl of Egremont

[Frant, September 1802]

My Lord,

In pursuance of your Lordships directions, I send up two books of Accounts.[1]

The first contains the Legatees Claims in account with their Grandfathers Estate.

On this I have only to remark that if my deceas'd daughter has no claim to any thing under her Grandfathers will Save a remote residue, then, instead of the other legatees having a sixth share in the Sums of 1000£ & 1000£ from the death of my eldest & third Sons, ~~then~~ the surviving Legatees will have each a fifth & ~~at~~ a sixth of those Sums.

And I apprehend that I must then lose the 70£.9s which I paid on account to her representative Unsolicited by him, but because it seem'd to be my duty that as such, he should not be wholly overlook'd. I am persuaded in my own mind & am much deceived if the Will [which Mr Bicknell has not yet sent][2] does not express that, if any die, their shares to go among the surviving Sons & their two eldest Sisters. I submit this however to your Lordships consideration or any opinion you may be pleased to have taken on the Will in that instance——I trust that your Lordship will not think I am very unreasonable in my charges. I have carefully deducted for any thing I recollect to have received, & I am very sure I have never supported any of Mr B Smiths Children for 40£ a year. I have been at very great expence for Charles on many occasions & have supplied him while he was soliciting his Commission & at other times with pocket money & support not any of which I have charged. My poor Nicholas cost me in cloathes only in one year more by ten pounds than his Grandfathers allowance. But he has more than repaid me, & I shall submit this account agst him to his option.

It is to be remarked that Lucy's debt is more than the rest because she was always with me till she married two months after my charge ends. I have deducted for one years absence tho her clothes, pocket money, & journies ~~have~~ then come to as much as if she had remain'd at home.

I have deducted more <largely> for Miss Smith because she was oftener absent. But it may not be improper to remark that, as I was (& indeed am now) oblig'd to have a larger house & more servants than if I had not had these young persons with me, that expence always went on whether they were or were not with me. When the Miss Berneys & the present Mrs Allen lived with the Widow of Richd Smith,[3] they paid her 50 Guineas a year (without their working), & if they were absent twelve months, it made no difference. She was still paid——

I mention this to shew that a charge of 40£ a year, for which I have supplied them with everything, could not be unreasonable had I not made these deductions.

Mr Benjamin Smith in his account deliverd to the Trustees in 178<4> lumps his charge for his children in two articles——of which this is a copy.

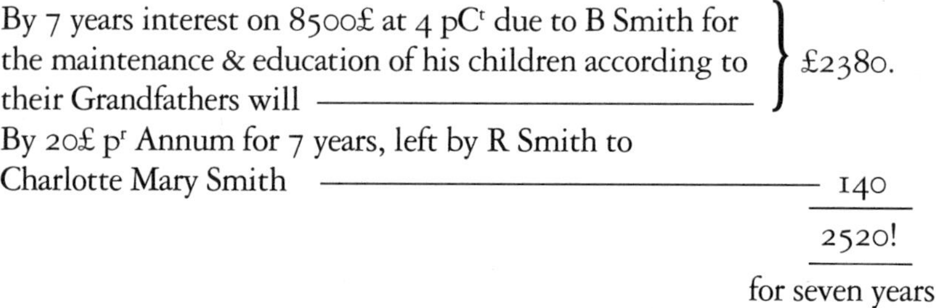

By 7 years interest on 8500£ at 4 pC^{t} due to B Smith for the maintenance & education of his children according to their Grandfathers will ———	£2380.
By 20£ p^{r} Annum for 7 years, left by R Smith to Charlotte Mary Smith ———	140
	2520!
	for seven years.

This last iniquitous charge of the poor Girls pocket money, which she never had, I have taken out & allowed her for the whole in her account, & Smith must dispute it when the residue comes to be settled if he is wretched enough. Your Lordship will remark that I charge from the 15th April 1787, the day when I quitted Mr Smith to avoid personal ill treatment on one hand & an execution from Mr Silver on the other which would have stripped my family of the very beds they slept on.[4] My eldest Son went to India the winter of the preceeding year 1786,[5] and my third Son Brathwaite died on the June following, 1786.[6] I had then these Children wholly dependent on me: Charlotte, Augusta, Lucy, & Harriet, Nicholas, Charles, Lionel, & George—to not one of whom their father has ever given one single shilling. I have earned for them very near 5000£ besides many Sums lent & given me by my friends.

I flatter myself on considering this matter your Lordship will permit me to hope for the present relief so absolutely necessary to my subsistence & my younger childrens, & that when there shall be time to investigate the accounts you will give orders that I may be paid in such way as shall be least injurious to the Estate. If I have not this payment made, which I cannot help thinking yr Lordship will allow to be just, there will be just so much the more for M[r] Benjamin Smith to take for himself, for as to residue, there is no trust appointed to that, & if once it gets into his hands, it will never produce a shilling to his family.

In anxious expectation of hearing from your Lordship, I have the honor to be, My Lord,

your ever oblig'd Ser[t],
Charlotte Smith

I have not time, harrass'd as I have been been to day, to assign reasons for all the dates on their accounts, but I do assure y[r] Lordship they are perfectly right.

Petworth House Archives MS. No address or postmark.

NOTES

1. Several ledgers survive among papers in the Petworth House Archives, including one (#8232) that covers a period from Aug. 1797 to June 1802. It records many, usually small, sums paid to CS, BS, and their children on the trust account held by Daniel.

2. CS's brackets.

3. Richard Smith had four granddaughters by his two other children: Dorothy Elizabeth Berney, Mary Eleanor Berney, and Maria Elizabeth Charlotte Dyer, daughters of Mary Smith Berney Dyer, and Mary Gibbes Smith, daughter of Rev. Richard Smith. (See Genealogical Chart.) By 1802, Dorothy was married to Edmund Boehm, Mary Eleanor to Thomas Henchman, and Mary Gibbes Smith to Capt. Robert Allen. CS's aunt and mother-in-law, Lucy Towers Smith, was Richard Smith's widow.

4. John Silver, mercer and draper, of Winchester, where the older sons were enrolled. In an unpublished letter to William Tyler written between 10 and 14 July 1804, CS elaborated on how Silver's threat contributed to her leaving BS: "I went with five of his children that I might have an home for them, & his three other children then at School & not be liable to have their beds taken in execution, as they would have been at the suit of Silver of Winchester."

5. Official records conflict with this date. William received his letter of appointment for Bengal on 20 Jan. 1784 (IRO Personal Records Ref. No. 0/6/5, 13:699), but first arrived in India 7 Aug. 1788 and was appointed second assistant to the collector of Ramghyr on 3 Sept. 1788 (Dodwell and Miles, *Bengal Civil Servants,* pp. 464–65).

6. 18 June 1786.

To Samuel Rose[1]

[Frant, 9 September 1802]
Sir,

Some days since, I beleive more than a week, I sent up to Mr Phillips, Bookseller in St Paul's Church yard, a Letter addressed to you enclosing two Letters of Mr Cowpers which he honord me with some years since. I have since had a Letter from Mr Phillips, my present task master, urging me to exertion (in a work which necessity only compelled me to undertake) & mingled with some reproaches for my want of punctuality, but he makes no mention of having received the pacquet I sent to him, or of having forwarded the Letters which by that opportunity I sent to London, and, as I have not heard from you or from two other friends to whom I likewise sent Letters, I fear the MMS Letters &c may never have reachd Mr Phillips, to whom I would have written to enquire, but he informd me he was going on a journey, & he is generally so full of other business & of himself, that it is not easy to get a direct answer from him.

I therefore take the liberty of asking whether you received those Letters which I should be much concern'd to lose. And at the same time I wish to assure you how very sensible I am of the obliging & friendly manner in which you are pleas'd to offer your endeavours in the business which induced me, with whatever reluctance, to intrude myself on Mr Hayley——

In consequence perhaps of having formerly listen'd with too much avidity, to the flattering opinion of my <u>then</u> friends, I foolishly fancied that good meaning and slender talents would counteract the strange & unfortunate destiny I was in early youth condemned to, and that I might by some sacrifices preserve my family. The death of her amongst them whom I most fondly loved Deprived me for some time of all courage & hope till I rememberd that my affection for my lost child would be shown, not by unavailing tears but by doing what I knew were her last wishes in regard to her unhappy husband, a Man who adord her with affection equal to mine & who, during their short marriage of only twenty months, had loved her with encreasing attachment. I will pass over the uneasiness I underwent from certain other persons of my family because I would not abandon one whom my Augusta had preferred. As I then subsisted on the fruit of my own industry, I had a right to share it with whom I pleased, & I never relax'd in my exertions for all those who look'd up to me either for immediate support or future assistance——

In 1797, Lord Egremont most generously releas'd the Estate that belong'd to my childrens' Grandfather from claims amounting to above 7000£; I was lucky enough the following year to obtain the restoration of near 4000£ from a debt supposed to be worth nothing, and in consequence of Lord Egremont's making himself Trustee, there was every prospect that all these unhappy & complicated affairs would be settld so as that every one of the legatees would receive the principal and interest with a considerable surplus left. But, to forbear troubling you with an history of all I have sufferd since I venturd to form this hope, I will only say that my wounded Son, poor Charles, went at Lord Egremonts desire to Barbados where, in consequence of an agreement previously set on foot here by me, he sold the Estate for 16,000£ &, Collecting many debts before considerd as desperate, paid off all incumbrances and was proceeding to recover other debts to the amount of two or three thousand pounds more when he most unfortunately took the fatal fever of the Climate & died to my inexpressible sorrow——

One would have imagined that M^r^ B Smith his father would, after such a sacrifice, & after the years of toil of solicitude & deprivation which I had undergone, have felt it to be his duty to do everything that rested with him to promote the interest of his remaining children, to which the life of this excellent young Man had been devoted; instead of doing so, he has not only before this cruel event, but ever since, so harrass'd Lord Egremont with demands for money & with threats of proceeding against him in Chancery that Lord Egremonts naturally generous & humane temper is sourd by such folly & ingratitude.

His Lordship has divided two of the four installments paid for the estate out of which (tho he had not the least right to it, M^r^ B Smith has had a Sum of money). Now he insists on having refunded to him all the money, which during his Trust Lord Egremont has paid me as interest of a part of my own fortune lent on the estate & which, by agreement with M^r^ B Smith, the former Trustees always paid, & he is at this moment at Petworth with a relation he has there, waiting Lord Egremonts return from a tour into Scotland to beseige him with this & I know not what other wild & unreasonable demands.

I had for some months been trying by every means in my power to prevail on Lord Egremont only to retain the trust he had so generously undertaken till July 1803 When the last installment for the estate becomes due and the legatees would be paid,[2] & I had even thought of conquering the reluctance I had to trouble Mr Hayley with business and asking him to use his interest with Lord Egremont on my behalf, or rather that of my children, who will lose above a thousand pounds by the affairs being now thrown into Chancery, besides the delay, as I am assured of four or five years before they will receive the remainder or Legacies, for which they have already waited five and twenty years. But this last step of Mr Smiths deprives me of every hope in regard to Lord Egremonts relenting, & since the affairs must at last go into Chancery, The small claim of M^r^ De Foville, which it was my earnest wish to have compromisd for 160£ ready money as much more advantageous to him, & which is desird by the rest of the Legatees, must now remain to be decided upon with the rest. I have done everything possible to acquit myself of what I thought a sacred duty with which I must endeavour to console myself, & indeed the reflection of having pass'd my life in attempting to fulfill all the duties imposed upon me must now support my last years under all the humiliations of poverty.

In consequence of the death of my fathers widow two years ago, my little fortune received an encrease, & I thought M[r] B Smith would encrease my small income by at least part of the interest arising from it. Instead of which, he not only refuses to allow me a shilling from thence but insists on having a right to withdraw the 70£ a year from the interest of another part which he has hitherto allowd to be paid by agreement with the former Trustees, & it seems that he is advised he has a right to do this, & is not oblig'd to allow me any maintenance whatsoever. My younger children I have supported for many years, & for the Youngest of my Sons I last year obtain'd an Ensigns commission & fitted him out for his profession to which his father, on being applied to, contributed 20£ (which he has since insisted on having Returned to him), for this young Man whom till last year he never saw since he was three years old, he refuses any allowance, and as he was born after his Grandfathers death, he has no claim on the estate. It is impossible he can live on an Ensigns pay, and I am no longer able to work for him as I have hitherto done.

My youngest daughter returned from India in a deplorable state of health. She apparently recoverd here, but in July last was seized again with a return of the same dreadful malady; I was then in the West of Sussex trying to interest Lord Egremont once more in favor of the unhappy persons suffering from such a father, but I was sent for away Express to attend this poor Girl & at Horsham met with an accident in the post chaise from the carelessness of the driver, which stunned me for some hours & of which tho it is now two months ago, I still feel the effects so much as to make me beleive there is some internal injury in the head; and by this together with health before greatly injur'd & exhausted hope, I find myself utterly disabled from the attempt to live as I have hitherto done on the produce of my own industry, & I am still less able to support my children.

It is my death M[r] B Smith seeks, as he would then be possess'd of near 400£ a year of mine with[t] any claim of mine upon it & be able to dispose of it to which of my children he pleases of 5000£ of my fortune tho his contract in the marriage articles, he has never fulfilld, & I am told I might have redress by an application to Chancery. But I am weary of contending & sick of an existence which depends on such a being. Instead therefore of troubling my friends, of whom some are still good enough to be willing to exert themselves for me, I have determind to give up keeping house and retire to the humblest obscurity. I would go to Service if I were not too far advanced in life and too much shook in constitution. Perhaps I may still obtain just enough to exist the little while I shall live, & I have determind, in order to acquit myself as far as I can towards those to whom I am unavoidably indebted for the support of my family these last months, to sell my books & such furniture as I had collected—except some which I must give to my widow'd daughter who is left with three infant children (one born after the fathers death) & who on her own little income—all of which she will not receive now that the affairs go into Chancery—is going to reside at a cottage at North Chapel near Petworth——

I had myself taken a Cottage at Elsted between Liphook and Godalming where I hoped I might be able to remain the few years I can expect to live, & I thought I should there be conveniently situated to transact with Lord Egremonts agent, the remaining business of the estate, all of which has always fallen upon me—— But Lord E. will not hear now of affording me even temporary assistance & doubts whether he has been authorised in allowing me the expences of postage, stationary, journies, & extra residence, which I have been at during fifteen or sixteen years & by which means only the estate was saved—— M^r^ B Smiths importunity, & I must call it wickedness, has disgusted & offended Lord E. so much that he said before he went to Scotland he would not hear of any of the name mention'd, & thus repulsed & deprived of all I could call my own, hopeless & heartless, it were folly for me to tire my few remaining friends by asking their interposition & very bootless to make any farther struggle; I have therefore agreed to give up the Cottage at Elsted to Mr Johnstone, Member for Hindon,[3] who saw it by chance & was so pleased with it that he offerd me double the rent I had agreed to give or any terms I would put upon it, but I cannot think of making any advantage of it & give it up in the same term as I took it) very reluctantly I own, for it would have suited me exactly could I have lived any where, in an house I might call my own——

The only favor that under such circumstances I can think of asking either of you or My once good friend Mr Hayley is perhaps one that you may both think impertinent & improper; it is that you would interest yourselves in the disposal of my books, which some time since I wrote to Cadell & Davis about to offer them to Mr White in Fleet Street. There is nothing among them particularly valuable. But they are a tolerable collection of about 800 volumes of the best French & English Authors. Some are valuable to me as being the gifts of particular friends, & I once thought that some might acquire a trifling additional value as having belongd to me, but I am cured now of such vanity & see that the ci devant celebrated Charlotte Smith may as quietly sink into the gulph of oblivion, as if she had only been Shakespeares matron & had suckled fools & chronicled small beer[4] without having ever done any thing else. Such is the effect of ill fortune when youth & years are flown. There is something petrifying in its influence, & it even throws a degree of opprobrium on the patient which justifies the dereliction of happier persons——

Knowing this fact, you may think it strange that, since I hardly dare boast the advantage of knowing you personally, Sir, I should presume to solicit your kindness on such an occasion, but had Mr Rose been only a character respectable for professional talents, I had not ventured it; I rely on the virtues of your heart, if not to serve me in it, to forgive whatever impropriety there may be in the request. I wrote to Messrs Cadell & Davies ~~xxxxxxxxxxxxxxxx~~ as soon indeed as I found I must submit, to this last deprivation—— But I have not had any answer. They do not themselves deal in second hand books, but they are connected with Mr White who does, & I thought, foolishly perhaps thought, that as they have acknowledged I was heretofore a rather profitable connection they might have undertaken to assist me in this matter the more willingly—— Perhaps they are out of town perhaps they are offended at my request.

But time presses. My stay here every day lessens the little I shall have from this source to send my poor George back to the depot in the isle of Wight (his regiment ye 47th is not in England) to discharge my old servants, who have lived with me six, eight, & one four & twenty years, and to pay my bills here—— Therefore I hazard a step which I feel to be presumptuous, least the end of my taking it & parting with my tools should be baffled. Should you be in Town, I know you are so good that you would speak to Mr White.[5]

I had once, I own, in my cruel reluctance to give up my books & furniture, intended to have asked you if you thought Mr Hayley wd try to soften Lord Egremont in my favor or if you had interest with his Lordship yourself, but his heart seems quite hardend against me, & tho I shall ever be most grateful for all his unmerited kindness, I am too much hurt by his late repulses & too conscious of the trouble I have given him to ask him again. I will not lengthen by further apologies a Letter already too long, but entreat you to beleive, that I am with great esteem,

Sir, your most oblig'd humble Sert,
Charlotte Smith

Perhaps I have written nonsense, for my head has for some days given me so much pain that I have been oblig'd to have leaches & to be blistered last night & to day. If I have done any thing very foolish therefore in this writing, burn my Letter & think no more about it. Only let me know if Mr Cowpers came safety to hand.
Frant near Tunbridge Wells
Sept 9th 1802

McMaster University Library MS. No address or postmark.

NOTES

1. Samuel Rose last appeared in the letters in 1796, in a note regarding the copyright terms for *Elegiac Sonnets ii* (see CS to Cadell and Davies, 13 Dec. 1796, n. 1). He was important to CS in two ways: in 1803, he arbitrated the dispute between CS and BS over their rightful share of interest and other trust income; and by 1804, his wife Sarah had become CS's correspondent and confidante.

2. William Prescod's purchase of Gay's plantation in Barbados settled the estate's outstanding business. After a large down payment, he owed £3,331 payable in July of 1801, 1802, and 1803.

3. In an unpublished letter to William Tyler, 8 Sept. 1802, CS wrote that she had "agreed to give up the beautiful little cottage at Elsted" to George Johnstone (1764–1813) of Hanover Square, London. He was member of Parliament not for Hindon, as she thought, but for Hedon Borough, Yorkshire, from 5 July 1802 to 20 Nov. 1813. He had retired from service in the East India Company in 1797.

4. *Othello* 2.1.160, spoken by Iago, in a list of paradoxes about women.

5. Rose's prompt, courteous response, dated 11 Sept., survives in the PHA (#7866). He discovered that White was in the country and both Cadell and Davies were out of town, but believed that Cadell had received her note. He continues:

> I regret that the Intelligence I communicate should be so unsatisfactory, and I still more regret the cruel Necessity, which compels you to adopt so painful a Measure as the parting with your Library. The love I have always had for Books sufficiently informs me what your feelings must be on this Occasion.

He also believed that interfering with Lord Egremont on her behalf "without benefiting you, would injure me justly in his Lordship's Opinion." CS had sent Rose's letter to Tyler with a note that she sent it "merely to prove, that I do not misrepresent & that a temporary aid was all I meant to solicit—& for the last time."

To William Tyler

[Frant, 13 September 1802]
Sir,

Had Lord Egremont condescended with his former generous consideration to my request, I would, however unable to bear the fatigue of another journey at this time, have set out tomorrow or Thursday with my daughter Mrs Newhouse, whose helpless situation with three young infants in a cross country road, short days, & the chance of waiting for Horses at those posts where she must cross the Brighthelmstone road, would have induced me to have encountered some fatigue to have assisted her, and I hoped to have had the accounts done by that day—Thursday. I would have remain'd at the Inn at Petworth till you had inspected the whole, for Mrs Dorset is at Pashley,[1] & I have no Brother——

However, his Lordships displeasure & refusal deprives me of the power of doing this and gives me up to the desperate condition, which, conscious of not having brought it upon myself, I will endeavour to support with patience. If I had acted as Mr B Smith has done, I could not be treated more harshly. It is in vain to attempt to represent to Lord Egremont a situation which his rank of life prevents his having any idea of. And let me suffer what I will, I shall never be otherwise than grateful for his Lordships goodness tho the effect he intended is baffled and I am in every respect worse off now than when in 1791 or 1792 his generous compassion was first excited in my favor. I have devoted myself for years in vain. The fruit of my labour does not benefit my surviving children. (Two have lost their lives in this cruel contest[2]——) But Mr Benjn Smith, useless worthless brutal as he is, is to benefit not only from the residue, but he is to take my fortune also!—— & because I cannot exist without some support & keep his children still dependant upon me, I have had the misfortune to offend Lord Egremont! & he abandons me to actual want—after years of misery which he seemd to pity—when I am hopeless & heartless, when I can no longer assist myself and tho I ask neither present money or advance nor any thing on my own account ———

I merely wish'd assistance 'till I can sell my books & furniture. I cannot raise immediate money upon such articles, & more than half my plate is stolen. I have done all I could to dispose of the little I have saleable, as the enclosed Letter will shew. Beleiving Mr Rose had some acquaintance with Lord Egremont, I mention'd to him a bare possibility that the interference in my favor of some friend might soften Lord Egremonts resolution, yet I knew this was a mere Chance & troubled Mr Rose principally to see Mr White, that from a Man of his character I might get some money advanced on my little collection of books which I must now part with & see how I can live on Charity till my Son Nicholas can releive me. I shall apply to the literary fund[3] & endeavour to be received, with my Nicholas' little Girl Luzena, into some School where what I can teach may assist to pay for my board till then. It is hard at my time of life—but inevitable——

You requested items of my charges. I have therefore made out a pretty exact account of stationary & postage, partly from accounts kept & partly from the immense number of Letters on the affairs which I have by me, & if there are errors in the charges, they are [ag]ainst myself. I wish however to know whether these amounts will or [wi]ll not be allowed or whether all the expences as well as all the toil is to [be] thrown on me by law; Tho still in the apprehension that it will be so, I shall follow this account (No. 1) with my charges for journies & coach hire & for money advanced out of my pocket to Mr B Smith himself, to his Son Charles when he attended him at Hamilton, to Mr Turner for <xxxxxxx> the affairs, & to My Son when he waited on Lord Egremont two years ago. The whole of this latter charge, amounting to near another hundred pounds, I beg leave to ask if on these charges no interest is to be allowd & may surely add that, if any one but me had done what I have done for the family, they would have been allowed for their time & trouble

—— There are people who think I should be, were the question ever fairly brought forward, & I should not be sorry to see it at issue.

I beg leave to remark that Mr Benjn Smith charges 700 for the expences of his exorship for seven years; therefore I do not see that that worthy wight cannot well object to my absolute expences. His exorship consisted of dissipating about 16000£ sixteen thousand[4]—— and entangling the affairs; How I have acted I might leave to the candour & discernment of Lord Egremont if I could hope that his Lordship had not determind to hear nothing that I can say. I will not importune him but remain his grateful, tho very unfortunate hble Ser^t^,

Charlotte Smith

Tomorrow is the day for writing to Barbados. While M^r^ B Smith is trying to rob & ruin his unhappy children here, there the price of his Sons blood is escaping him. I shall write to thank Mr Adams, but this thankless hopeless task I will not any more pursue. Unless Lord E. says I ought to do it——

I will send another account tomorrow if I can, but Lord E. sh^d^ recollect that I am sick & poor & have a large family to provide for daily in some sort of labour. I am a wretched slave———

Mr Stidolph[5] has just sent to say the legatees accounts, made up as you last mention'd to Octr 2nd 1802, will be done tomorrow night.

His charges are a guinea for the book. But I cannot do fractions of interest, did my life depend upon it.

Petworth House Archives MS. No address or postmark.

NOTES

1. Not identified.

2. That is, Augusta died for lack of money to send her to a warm climate, and Charles died while in Barbados specially on trust business.

3. Rev. David Williams established the Literary Fund, a charitable organization for needy authors and their families, in 1788. Samuel Taylor Coleridge and William Cowper were among its early beneficiaries, but not CS—although a woman of the same name did apply in the 1860s. Now the Royal Literary Fund, it continues to support authors today.

4. Elsewhere CS puts this figure at £17,000 (see CS to Egremont, [?Dec. 1802]).

5. Davey Stidolph, writing master and accountant at Tunbridge Wells, worked on the accounts from 8 Sept. to 4 Oct. He was a self-styled "professor of Writing in Public Seminaries, and Private Tutor to Ladies and Gentlemen." His only book, *The Penman's Delight* (?1795), printed by Sampson Low, shows alphabets in different engraved hands, elegant pensmanship, curious flourishes, and ornately designed capitals.

To William Tyler

{Frant, received 16 September 1802}

Sir,

I now enclose to you an account of money actually paid out of my pocket in furtherance of the settlement of the affairs Which I hope will not be denied me even by the strictest Court of equity———(I might add 20£ I gave Mr Turner when I paid him the 30£, as he was then extremely ill & in distress & unable from sickness to attend the business without such assistance, but if I were to enumerate the aid I have from time to time lent him, it would be a long account indeed. And as he has so far forgotten it as to quarrel with me because I cannot do what is neither honest on my part or what I could answer to my conscience, I will endeavour to forget it too.

I know the pressure of necessity & how often it compels persons not otherwise unprincipled to act with too little regard to strict rectitude. I may perhaps have done so myself, as Lord Egremont accuses me of misrepresentation, & I trust I shall never harden my heart against others & less than any one against my brother, tho I can now do him no more good, & am destitute myself even of the necessaries of life!)

When Lord Egremont considers—if indeed he condescends to give still a thought to so unhappy a subject—that I only wish to save the Legatees as much as I can, & particularly Mrs Newhouse, who were I to take all I might charge for her would be literally starved. When his Lordship considers that I do not live, that I have not toild for myself, but for these poor young people abandond & robbed by their unnatural father, that for his younger children I could not charge anything against the estate of R. S. because they were not legatees, & that when I sent Mr B Smith an account of half their maintenance only as a charge against him, he return'd the account (in a double cover to put Me to expence). Surely his Lordship must be not merely convinced who has the best claim to his protection & good offices, but it is I think impossible that his Lordship will ~~xxxxxxxx~~ listen to a Man who violates every duty and every principle & then threatens with law the persons who have saved his children from the parish——

As I shall certainly sue him in Chancery to compel him to make good my settlement, I wish to know whether Lord Egremont & Mr Turner are or are not to be considerd as Trustees to the 3000£ & his Lordship to my settlement in general; I reckon this quite a distinct thing from Richard Smiths affairs, & it is Mr Palmer,[1] of whom I have a very high opinion, whom I shall intrust with it. The measure was recommended to me many years ago by Mr Bettesworth of Portsdown & Bishops Waltham in Hampshire.[2]

As Lord E. was pleased to say he thought there was a chance yet left of Mr Morgans[3] obtaining a settlement between Mr B Smith & his family, I ought in vindication of myself to state how that matter rests—— In answer to Mr

Morgans Letter demanding immediate accounts of money in the stocks & God knows what with which surely M[r] B. Smith has nothing to do, I answerd that, as soon as Lord Egremonts proposal was complied with, i.e. that M[r] Benj[n] Smith should bind himself to abide by the award & not fly off as he did last year—that then, & not till then, every account that I could furnish with which M[r] B Smith could have anything to do should be produced & that I would go to London myself with them & meet you there if Lord E. should be pleased to think proper & go over the accounts——

I knew that when M[r] B.S. was calld upon to bind himself, he would fly off, & so I suppose it has proved, for since that, M[r] Morgans Letters talk of nothing but my unconditional submission to let the money belonging to me be divided thus: to

M[r] B Smith	200.0.0 p[r] An
Miss H Smith ———	50.0.0
M[rs] C Smith ———	0.0.0—

& he says M[r] B.S. may do this—— Now if he may, I am sure he will, & my consent & agreement cannot be required, any more than it was to the Housebreaker who robbed me a short time since because he found he might open the closet door & steal my spoons. Lord E. has decided that M[r] B.S. is no better than an highwayman: for my part, I think him not so good, & when he frisks about to Petworth & exhibits his amiable person & just cause to a wondering World, I am always in hopes that by his taking rope enough, he will do that for himself which only those who might be disgraced by it can help wishing Was done for him——

If Lord Egremont would only allow me to be releived from my present embarrassment, I would never trouble him again, but the extremity of my present distress is most dreadful. If I could borrow the money till I could sell my books, I should be releived. I cannot hear from M[r] White & have no answer to my application!

I shall continue to send the accounts as fast as they can be written out. You will be pleased to recollect that Coach hire, journies, & extra residence in town ~~is an~~ are accounts yet to follow, & Lord Egremont I trust will not find I have had so much more than I could claim, as his Lordship seems to apprehend.

I am very very unwell & scarce able to write
but remain, Sir,
your oblig'd hble Ser[t],
Charlotte Smith

Petworth House Archives MS. No address or postmark.

NOTES

1. Of Tourle, Palmer, and Pugh, Bartlett's Buildings, Holborn.

2. The Smiths lived at Lys Farm in Hampshire from 1774 until BS was imprisoned for debt in Dec. 1783; CS would have consulted William Augustus Bettesworth (d. after 1804), attorney, of Portsdown and Bishop Waltham, Hampshire, when BS entangled the affairs after his father died in Oct. 1776.

3. Jonathan Morgan of Lincoln's Inn, BS's lawyer.

To William Tyler

[Frant] 17th Sept^r^
1802
Sir,

I was in hopes to have sent you the Legatees accounts to day, but Mr Stidolph has not yet finish'd them, & when he has, I shall be much at loss how to pay him being absolutely without a guinea. A thousand circumstances combine to render my present situation particularly dreadful, & my difficulties daily encrease without my being able either to mitigate or escape from them. I live on from week to week, encreasing my debt without seeing any prospect of repaying those I contract it with. Mr White is not yet come to town, & I cannot sell my furniture till I know whither to go. Mrs Newhouse was setting out for Mr Turners yesterday morning, & the chaise was at the door when she found herself so very ill & so unable to undertake so fatigueing a journey with three young children that I prevaild upon her (tho it is very inconvenient to me) to remain here till she can have an answer to the Letter which I enclose & which, if it be not too much trouble, I shall be extremely obliged to you if you could forward for me to Luggershall so that I might have an answer by Teusdays post. I know Lord Egremont would not be offended if I ask'd him to allow one of his people to go over with it, as an early answer is <u>particularly material</u> to me and to Mrs Newhouse, & I know Mr Turner does not regularly get his Letters.

I should have sent you the remainder of <u>my</u> account, particularized to day, but yesterday I was so interrupted that I had no time to write at all, & to day I am oblig'd as soon as I have done this to begin my Letters to Bengal & Bombay, which will weary me God knows dreadfully, but they must be in town tomorrow or I shall lose the opportunity. I did not write to Barbados by the packet of last Wednesday, as I should have done had Lord Egremont been so good as to have told me whether his opinion was that I ought to do it. I request the favor of you to obtain an answer for me & also to tell me whether Mr Boehms[1] accounts of the Berney debt were ever deliver'd as he states. I can do nothing till I know, but wherefore should I do any thing for M^r^ B Smith—

Would to God that the Earth would open & swallow me—![2]

Oh none know what I endure!

[Unsigned]

I was so harrass'd just as I was finishing this that I would not send it if my hands were not too tired to suffer me to write it over again—— Would Lord Egremont could form any idea of what I go thro & from which I might be released (at least till I can help myself) for seventy pounds which I would repay as soon as I can sell my books. Madness I think will ensue if this lasts much longer.[3]

Petworth House Archives MS. No address or postmark. Photograph by Michael Moore, by permission of the Right Honorable the Lord Egremont, Petworth House Archives, West Sussex Record Office.

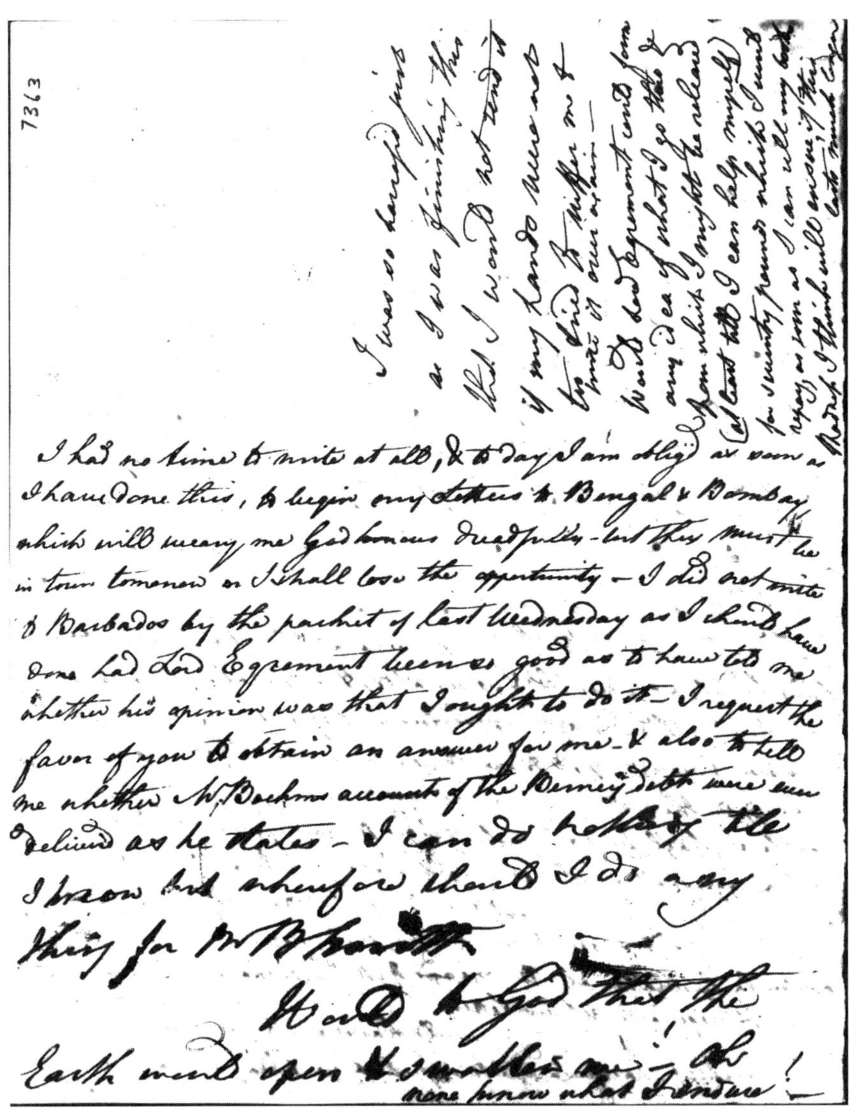

7363

I was so harrass'd just as I was finishing this that I would not send it if my hands were not too tired to suffer me to write it over again— Would Lord Egremont could form any idea of what I go thro & from which I might be released (at least till I can help myself) for seventy pounds which I would repay as soon as I can sell my books. Madness I think will ensue if this lasts much longer.

I had no time to write at all, & to day I am oblig'd as soon as I have done this, to begin my letters to Bengal & Bombay which will weary me God knows dreadfully - but they must be in town tomorrow or I shall lose the opportunity - I did not write to Barbados by the packet of last Wednesday as I should have done had Lord Egremont been so good as to have told me whether his opinion was that I ought to do it - I request the favor of you to obtain an answer for me - & also to tell me whether Mr Bockms accounts of the Berney debts were ever delivered as he states - I can do nothing [illegible] I know but wherefore should I do any thing for Mr B[illegible]

Would to God that the Earth would open & swallow me! - Oh none know what I endure! —

Figure 4. Letter to William Tyler, 19 Sept. 1802.

NOTES

1. Edmund Boehm was married to Richard Smith's granddaughter, Dorothy Elizabeth Berney; her brother was Robert Berney.

2. Here CS's normally regular handwriting is large and erratic, and the ink is smeared in this and the preceding sentences, especially in naming BS.

3. Written vertically in the top margin of this page.

To William Tyler

[Frant, 19 September 1802]
Sir,

With an hopeless heart, I once more entreat you to lay my situation before Lord Egremont or inform me where I may address myself to his Lordship. There are a gang of Ruffians in this Country who, tho the inhabitants of the village were alarmed, had the audacity to come into my Garden last night & attempt the place by which they robbed me before. I am without arms, or persons to use them, except George & a lad who would be little defence, & tho God knows nobody can be much poorer than I am & therefore have only my life to lose, which is a miserable life, yet this terror, added to the anguish of mind I daily & hourly suffer from the wretched state of my affairs, is absolutely killing me by the most dreadful & cruel death.

Represent, Sir, I beseech you to Lord Egremont that, if his Lordship will only enable me to subsist till I can sell what little I have left, that I will repay it & never trouble him more; I should not have struggled thus long if he had not encouraged me by his goodness to hope that so assisted I might save my family, for as to myself, if I had thought only of myself some years ago, I should not now have implored in vain for Mercy Or suffer what I do. Lord Egremont would I think be unwilling to inflict on any one, even the greatest delinquent, such misery as I at this moment undergo. I have no hope, no expectation but from death. Surely his Lordship who has done so many benevolent actions will not now condemn me to such calamity as guilt could hardly deserve—when I ask only what would be replaced;[1] those who ought to protect & befriend me, M^r B Smith & the Brother I once had, are my cruellest enemies!———

The Legatees accounts are done, & copying on seperate sheets out of the book, Mr Stidolph has made them out in, & I shall send them sheet by sheet. My head is so much affected, & I am so overcome with the fatigue and terror I have undergone last night that I scarce know what I do or say. For God sake, let me hear if I may expect any relief. I am, Sir, y^r Obligd hble Ser^t,

Charlotte Smith

I hope you will be so good as to write at least where Lord Egremont is to be address'd. A few days longer pass'd thus & it will be too late: (19th) Septr 19th 1802.

Petworth House Archives MS. Address: The Earl of Egremont/ Petworth/ Sussex/ Septr 19th 1802. Postmark: TUNB-WELLS/ 36. FREE/ SEP 20/ 1802.

NOTE

1. That is, I ask only for a loan which I would repay.

To the earl of Egremont

Frant Septr 26th——
1802
My Lord,

No harshness which I may receive from your Lordship,[1] shall compel me to utter what may be construed into ingratitude; It shall not be even in your power to cancel the kindness you have shewn me—— I took over to Petworth when I waited on your Lordship several books of accounts, Mr Daniels accounts & those documents from which I had hastily sketched, the paper I sent up to Grosvenor place when My Son Lionel informed me that you insisted upon having these accounts & was going to France the next day, so that I had no time to do it more correctly. Mr Tyler returnd it, pointing out many errors, & some founded & other unfounded objections. I then hastend to Bignor in hopes of seeing you before you went to the Continent (as Lionel said you desired I would see you, & indeed a Letter of your own was to the same purpose). When y^{r} Lordship had not time to look at those books & papers, & when as you informed me Mr Tyler was not at liberty, I returnd to Bignor & set about correcting the errors in the accounts & making out the items demanded of money I had expended; I found that certain Sums had been omitted, particularly an account of my poor Charles's which I did not understand; nevertheless I should have met Mr Tyler the following Teusday to have cleared up the general account as far as I could, but I was sent for away by an express, & for near a month after my return, Harriets condition was such as made it impracticable for me to attend to any thing. As soon as I could, I wrote to Mr Daniel for an explanation of Charles's account, & when I got it, I gave as much time as I could to the affairs, but My Lord I have many long Letters to write, besides those with which it is my ill fortune to have troubled your Lordship, & a great deal of other writing to do.

But is it not likely I can convey to you, My Lord, an idea of the difficulties & distresses of poverty, nor the fatigue I have to encounter, who have a large family to supply without any income, and yet cannot disperse them. To represent my situation is disgusting & offensive; I will therefore only say that, being no accomptant myself, I tried to get the village Schoolmaster[2] to make out the accounts down to Octr 2nd 1802 but, after wasting a week, found he was not versed in such sort of reckoning, & therefore I sent the Legatees accounts to the Schoolmaster at Tunbridge Wells who finish'd two of them on Friday, which I immediately sent off. The others are not yet come; as soon as they do come, I will forward them &, as soon as I can, what Mr Tyler demands in his last Letter, i.e. A dated account of the Sums passing thro my hands on account of the legatees. It is hardly possible for me to do this, as I paid or was allowd ten pounds at one time & twenty at another from Willm & Nicholas, but as far as I can do it, I will. Thus much it is necessary for me to say in answer to the bitter charges with which it is your Lordships pleasure to load me, & I beg leave to state farther that, being absolutely destitute of money, I could not go as I intended to a furnish'd Cottage I had agreed for at Elsted; meaning [as I am oblig'd to quit this house, & only have it now from week to week,][3] to have given my daughter Newhouse, furniture enough to make her little hut at NorthChapel habitable, as she cannot afford to buy; & to have sold my books & the rest, & Then, As I informed Mr Tyler, I would have met him at Godalming, for as I have no longer a Brother, & Mrs Dorset is absent, I had no place to go to in the neighbourhood of Petworth.

But without a Guinea in the World, & distressd even for money to pay the postage of my Letters, I am chaind here, my chains strengthening every day by getting more deeply in debt. I have done every thing in my power; but what your Lordship formerly praisd as activity, you now appear to consider as impertinence or deception, & certainly after having snatched us from the waves, you are at liberty to throw us back again, if you apprehend that persevering in your benevolent intentions is too burthensome to yourself.

I can only say farther that I had last night prepard two accounts, such as I am able myself to make out, & that Mrs Newhouse puts off her journey till Wednesday,[4] because if your Lordship will afford me (on any account you please either the legatees or otherwise) money, not to leave my family here destitute & supply my journey, I will go with her to Petworth & stay there till all the accounts demanded of me are adjusted to y^{r} Lordships orders, & in my last Letter to Mr Tyler, I enquired whether I could have a lodging there for a few days. More I cannot say than to assure your Lordship I will after this never trouble you more but remain still

y^{r} Grateful Ser^{t}, Charlotte Smith

Petworth House Archives MS. No address or postmark.

NOTES

1. Several things may have conspired to bring on Egremont's unexpected harshness. While he was on the Continent, CS had written several letters to him and William Tyler lambasting BS: He was "ashamed of no baseness that may enable him to injure and rob his own children" (to Tyler, 26 Aug. 1802). He subjected her to "personal ill treatment" just before she left him in 1787 (to Egremont, Sept.). He was "useless worthless brutal." He was responsible for "dissipating about 16000£ . . . and entangling the affairs" of the estate. While he "is trying to rob & ruin his unhappy children here, there [in Barbados] the price of his Sons blood is escaping him" (to Tyler, 13 Sept.).

Meanwhile, Egremont returned from his travels to a 17 Sept. letter in which BS calmly writes of his "earnest desire to make one effort more to obtain an amicable adjustment of my affairs." Nor, he continues, "shall the cruel, and nefarious endeavours of M[rs] Smiths, to carry her point by starving me into compliance, of her unjustifiable demands, in which your Lordship seems to aid her, have any avail" (unpub. letter in PHA #0.11).

On 24 Sept., BS complains that Egremont's last letter didn't answer his request, then calls "upon your humanity, and as a Gentleman, to notice it. If I had adhered to the maxim—Principiis obsta, sero medicina parator, I sho[d] have saved myself much anxiety, and your Lordship some trouble" (unpub. letter in PHA #0.11). The Latin is the first line of a couplet from Ovid (*Remedia Amoris* 91–92): "Resist the beginnings: the medicine is prepared too late [when the ills have grown strong through long delays]."

2. Not identified. The writing master at Tunbridge Wells was Davey Stidolph.

3. CS's brackets.

4. According to CS to Egremont, 1 Oct., Lucy finally left on that day, a Friday.

To the earl of Egremont

[Frant, received ca. 29 September 1802]

Tho I have reason to beleive your Lordship will not read any thing I write, I must beg the favor of you to tell me which of the enclosed Letters I am to beleive—& what it is that is expected of me—— for in truth I neither know that, or why, I am so suddenly deprived of that good opinion of your Lordship[1] which w[d] I hoped have prevented my being (after your long kindness) deprived of the necessaries of life when I can least endure its hardships.

The unmerited harshness with which I am treated, I must endure without complaint. Sufferings like mine cannot last long. It was your Lordships pleasure to raise me from despondence & misery. You even condescended to interpose with Parkin & others[2] & to raise up for me other friends. Now, because I cannot do what would puzzle an able accomptant (especially when he[3] is dead who alone could explain some of the articles that puzzle & distract me), because, instead of a competency of my own, I am deprived of every thing that ought to be mine, because I cannot live on air or on those illusive talents which did for a while buoy me up, I am left to perish, & my last resource, my last comfort, my books go to the brokers—for 60£, for I askd no more!—— I am saying however more than I intended—— All I mean is to ask your Lordship to tell me, with your own hand, whether I am to beleive Mr Morgan or Mr Bicknell[4]—& to add that, as to meeting Mr Tyler in London whither he summons's me, I can not, for I have not one shilling upon earth, nor will I again put myself in the way of meeting M[r] Benjamin Smith.[5] I offerd to take a lodging at Petworth, but M[r] Tyler informs me there are none tho my intentions were very humble. However to reach Petworth, or London, is equally impossible to one who is as destitute as I am, & if such a journey is necessary to the estate, the estate must pay it, for I cannot.

If I could know what is expected of me, I should I trust find courage enough (if I have bodily strength enough) to do what ever is required of me, except going to London, & that I will not do. I think My Lord your humanity & your sense of justice & of mercy will equally induce you to give me an early & explicit answer, in which hope I have the honor to be, with that consciousness of former favours which nothing will eradicate but death, y[r] Lordships

obed[t] & very unfortunate Ser[t],
Charlotte Smith

I desire nothing more than to be deliverd from my present most dreadful situation & to get rid of the trouble I am now condemn'd to, & upon my word upon my Soul—Your Lordship shall never hear my name again.

I desir'd M[r] Palmer to call on M[r] Morgan for a copy of my marriage articles. It is very strange that I cannot prevail upon any one to seperate that in their minds from the affairs of Richard Smith? Good God Almighty! what has my seeking redress against a flaw in my marriage articles to do with the assets of Richard Smith Or why must they be confounded?[6]

Petworth House Archives MS. No address or postmark.

NOTES

1. In a letter at the end of Sept. or early Oct., BS complained again to Egremont that he was "suffering M[rs] Smith to bias you." In Feb. 1802, £4,371.11.8 were placed in the stocks, with Egremont and Turner having agreed with BS's lawyer Benjamin Follet that the interest on that money should go to BS. Then Egremont went abroad, "knowing at the same time how distress'd I was for money to support myself, and suffer'd the matter to lay dormant without feeling for me, or acting consistent with your duty as a Trustee, or consonant with your own words, which I quote from two letters of your Lordships." BS requests payment of the £300 dividend now due him; otherwise he will take legal action that will implicate "your honor, your humanity & your conduct as a Nobleman, & as a Gentleman." He continues that "I am asking but for my own" but is resolved "to take every step to procure the redress I am entitled to."

On 2 Oct., BS has heard from Jonathan Morgan that Egremont has executed a power of attorney that will enable Robert Tayler to receive the dividend for BS (who presumably cannot do so himself without risk of discovery by creditors). On 4 Oct., he thanks Egremont for the power: "I beg to make you my best acknowledgment for the favor done me." But, he reminds Egremont, there are further arrears on the estate due to him, and he complains of being detained "most unpleasantly, & expensively five Months in London" (unpub. letters in PHA #0.11).

2. Anthony Parkin and John Robinson, trustees to the Smith estate before Egremont and Turner.

3. Presumably CS's father-in-law, Richard Smith, author of the will that CS and everyone else found puzzling, even contradictory.

4. Charles Bicknell, CS's lawyer.

5. At Egremont's insistence, CS was forced to meet BS in London in the autumn of 1801. She found the experience "disagreeable" and "mortifying" (see CS to Egremont, 10 Feb. 1803).

6. Indeed the marriage articles consisted of three separate, unrelated settlements, and had no legal connection to Richard Smith's estate. The source of confusion may simply have been that several of the same people, including Egremont and Turner, were trustees to more than one of them. Furthermore, CS asked for special consideration in the handling of interest money from both the marriage articles and the estate. Finally, marriage articles generally were designed to benefit the wife after the *death* of the spouse; CS wanted special consideration during the separation, which was never legalized.

To William Tyler

[Frant, received 30 September 1802]

Sir,

I have received from Lord Egremont a letter of so harsh a description, and his Lordship seems so determind to Urge on my utter destruction, from whence he once took so much pains to rescue me, that I find it will be a very hopeless attempt to solicit his Lordships farther compassion. I am now in a situation infinitely worse than that from which he deign'd five years since to rescue me, & I know not <u>what</u> I have done to deserve that I should thus suffer———

When Lord E. thus generously interposed on my behalf he knew my situation; he knew that with a very large family of Children, I had been left to struggle against a combination of interested persons who delighted to oppress & harrass me, and that the great origin of all the evils I had to encounter was Mr B Smith whose allowance to me was only 70£, a part of my own fortune, I having been oblig'd to sink for my life (unless the legatees should ever enable me to repurchase it) the 110£ a year which belong'd exclusively to me in the 3 pCts,[1] & which <u>you</u> now have, as I imagine, with Mr

Tripps[2] representatives. All this Lord Egremont knew & other than from such a distress'd condition arising from no fault of my own, I could [have]—I had no claim, no pretence whatsoever on Lord Egremonts bounty or friendly assistance.

When from Lord Egremonts interposition the property of Rich[d] Smith first became available, surely there was nothing either unjust or strange that I should expect not only my expences to be paid & allowed for, but that I should from time to time have money for the support of my family[3] & not be subjected to the hardships & difficulties & toils I had undergone for so many years. Yet having considerd myself as entitled by all the laws of equity & reason to this remuneration, & having acted upon it (tho by no means to the extent that Lord E. seems to apprehend), appears now to his Lordship such a crime that he casts me off indignantly & angrily at the very moment when his perseverance for a few months would complete his generous & noble task of saving an unhappy family. At the very moment when———his dereliction of the business counteracts and destroys the effect of his benevolence for so many years. His Lordship with great reason apprehends trouble & complains of my writing long Letters? But he has often orderd me to write & to explain this or that thing. He has often said, no one understood the business but me & as often commended my activity. He once in 1800 said of M[r] Turner: "If he had half your activity & perseverance, there would be yet some chance of saving him from ruin." And is this activity & perseverance now become a crime? When I was naturally encouraged to it not only by his Lordships repeated approbation, but by the hope that it must soon end.

As to M[r] B Smiths giving trouble, I cannot help that it is my curse, my misery that the children have so worthless a father & that I was consigned in my infancy[4] to a wretch who does not blush to rob & ruin his own children. It is in itself a dreadful punishment, a dreadful degradation, and surely Lord E is too just & humane to inflict an heavier punishment for that?—— I have said over & over again, & I now repeat, that M[r] Benjamin Smith dares not execute his nonsensical threat & had no other meaning in it than to extort money from his children or from any body else, & had not Lord E. ever listend to him, if he had shut his doors upon him & M[r] Follett, it would have died away. But with all the contempt that M[r] B Smith must excite in every body, he was heard. The promises of M[r] Tayler to me vanishd into air, & I am now left utterly destitute of the means of existence with my family, who I am no more able to disperse now, than when they were infants, while time & sorrow, the loss of those I best loved, of my friends & my fortune disable me from assisting myself, & I find myself not only a beggar, but blamed for being so!— —

Complaint however makes the matter worse, but the misery I have undergone since the receipt of Lord Egremonts last letter and since every thing, every resource is gone, & I am compelled to sell the little I have for a return to Mr Fauntleroy, for the 50£ I have overdrawn him (which must now be done in a few days), the misery of my mind in being exposed to such humiliation, such actual distress, will probably shorten my Sufferings. In the grave there is rest!—— My daughter Mrs Newhouse goes tomorrow; as to my meeting you in town, it is <u>impossible</u>, as I am without the means of moving till these things are sold, not having literally one shilling in the World of my own, nor knowing where to apply. I have lived & paid my last journey into West Sussex with what I obtained with the utmost difficulty of a bookseller So that I have no farther resource there, but if I had, I must otherwise apply it, & not expend for the estate what there is any doubt of my being allowed.[5]

I must also add that it is <u>impossible</u> for me to give the dates of the two Sums of 213£ on account of M^r^ W T Smith & 213 on that of M^r^ N H Smith because I know not when the Sums that they either allow'd me, or that I expended for them, were disbursd to or by me, but when the Sums had were adjusted to the respective persons by my poor lost Charles, it was agreed that the Sum of 213£ should be put to the account of M^r^ W T Smith & 213£ to Nicholas's. These could not be charged 'till the estate became available, which was not till Septr 1799 or the preceding July, & surely it can make no great difference to any body, & there can be no occasion to be thus minute. If there be, let 50£ & the odd money to make the 13 be charged half yearly; it can never signify, & give me leave to say it would be more materially serving the interest of the estate, if you would have the goodness to obtain of Lord Egremont an answer as to the proceedings to be observed in recovering the debts of which I send you a list. Mr Adams informs me he is likely almost immediately to succeed in getting in the principal debt due from Griffith but could <u>not close</u> the business till he hears from me again. If Lord E. puts the matter into Chancery, my writing to him to pursue it will merely be giving him trouble, & I have no right to take such a liberty with him. I entreat Lord Es [i.e., E's] commands one way or the other that I may not be ungrateful to Mr Adams to whom I am much oblig'd; How welcome would a small part only of this Sum be to me—this Sum which no one thinks it worth while even to write about!

I suppose when all the accounts come to be made out, I shall be found to have had between two & three hundred pounds <u>more</u> than the interest due to me from Jany 1797. The Legatees must be charged with it if it proves so; the expences &c (which I am willing to appeal to any Chancery Lawyer upon) & the money given me or paid by me on account of M^r^ W T Smith &

My Son Nicholas, I am willing to refer to any two Lawyers of reputation whether I had <u>not</u> a right to the interest, & whether Lord E was not fully justified in paying it, for the pretence infamously set up by M^r B Smith is that he only allowed it while his sons Nicholas Charles & Lionel were to be maintain'd by it: the former Trustees not only continued to pay it till July 1796 above a year after the youngest of those Sons had left England, but repelled an attempt of M^r B Smiths to possess himself of it, As the copies of Letters sent would surely convince Lord E. if he would have the goodness to attend to them for one moment. On this however you have never as I requested given me your opinion. It is the opinion of persons in whose knowledge & integrity I have a just confidence that M^r B Smith will be <u>compelld</u> to allow for the maintenance of his younger children. None can therefore suppose that on <u>my own account</u> I would shrink from the investigation, or the decision of Chancery.

My conduct towards the family has not only been right, but I venture to say <u>exemplary</u>. It is not therefore for myself I fear——for admitting I had had more money than the precise Letter of the Law would allow me [which however I do not beleive will appear to be the case],[6] the Court of Equity would take into consideration the manner in which I have expended it—that it was for food & shelter for the family who would otherwise have been destitute. Not for myself who have always been the only person of the house, who has gone without if not the necessaries, the decencies of life——Who ever saw me at a public place or heard of my taking even a day's relaxation? While others have some respite, some enjoyment, <u>my</u> life has been a series of care & trouble, of toil for the booksellers or attention to irksome business in which I never get any forwarder & at last——here I am!——worn down with anxiety & misery, forgotten by all my friends because I could not afford to associate with them, ill treated by my <u>nearest relations</u> because I cannot do what appears to me not to be just, & discarded by Lord Egremont whose discountenance will be followed by that of all on whom I might perhaps have some claim to be heard, & who will say——"Why this Woman must have been guilty of something very wrong, or Lord Egremont would not give her up to such distress after all he has done for her." I shall not attempt to vindicate myself, & thus I must drink to the dregs the bitter cup of poverty, humiliation & disappointment.

Lord Egremont, however, shall never have just reason to say I am ungrateful. His Lordships present unkindness, for which no doubt he thinks he has good reason, shall never make me forget all he has done & the greater kindness still he intended. My health is so very bad at this moment that it is impossible for me to go to London, nor have I, I repeat the means; Where I shall be, or what I shall do, I know not. All my hopes & all my intentions are baffled by Lord Egremonts total refusal to hear & assist me or to let the affairs go on. Driven about by poverty, stripped of all the few comforts I had collected, I have no place wherein to lay my head—— This old house was taken by M[r] Cumberland for M[rs] Badcock,[7] but she first hesitated whether to come to it because her dear Husband was buried here in the church in March last, & while her father was debating the point with her, she put an end to the dispute by marrying her Welsh footman of twenty one.

So I go on in the house from week to week at one guinea a week, but it is so miserably out of repair that it neither keeps out wind or wanderers, & not thinking I should stay, I neither laid in coals or took precautions to have a supply of water by repairing the Well, & thus I am like an excomunicated being, without fire or water. I cannot pay my servants to the three of whom I owe about five & thirty pounds—— I cannot by going to another house spare some furniture I have here to M[rs] Newhouse for hers, & I cannot, if I had health for it, obey Lord Egremonts commands by appointing a place at present to meet you & settle the accounts—— My nerves are shook to death, & had they been made of iron, they must have been worn out by all I have gone thro. I have no hope Sir that any thing I can now say will move Lord Egremont in my favor. I see that the more I attempt it the more hopeless it is, but I owe it to myself to vindicate my conduct from the charge of malversation of the effects, from that of imposing on Lord Egremonts goodness, or of ingratitude & misrepresentation. I will send the accounts No. 5 & 6 by my daughter M[rs] Newhouse & some others if I can, & wish I could receive his Lordships commands about the ~~enclosed by~~ account on the other side before next Teusday when the packets are made up for Barbados. I am, Sir, with thanks for the trouble you take in the affairs, y[r] obligd & obed[t] Ser[t],

Charlotte Smith

List of Money due in Barbados to the proprietors of the plantation calld Gay when taken by M[r] Prescod:

From John Sober	2.3.1½
Cumberbatch Sober	1.2.6
Philip Crick	12
William Firebrace	254.2.11
Will[m] Redman	11
Abraham Cumberbatch	1.17.6
Josepth Terrill	2.9.0
Walker plantation	3.4.0
Morgan Lewes	1.5.7½
John Edwards	2.13.9

John Bovell	130.5.
Josth Jordan	5.12.
Late Seaman Gibbon	18.12.8
	423.2.5

423.2.5 Barbados Currency—I beleive, but I am distracted by noise & bustle.

Mr Griffith (which there are hopes of being immediately received) upwards of 500£ St^{g} & this makes together the 800£ or thereabouts which poor Charles expected to collect & send over when his death put an end to his generous exertions for his family & to all the little comfort we might now have enjoy'd.

Pray let me if possible hear time enough to write, if I am to write, by Teusdays packet.

Petworth House Archives MS. No address or postmark.

NOTES

1. The £70 yearly income was interest from one of CS's two £2,000 marriage settlements; the £110 yearly income, which she had forfeited to her husband to enable him to buy land in Hampshire (CS to Egremont, 3 Dec. 1802), was from the £3,000 marriage settlement.

2. James Upton Tripp (d. 21 Sept. 1801), Tyler's predecessor.

3. The phrase "but that I should from time to time have money for the support of my family" is underlined, probably by Tyler, who also wrote between the lines: "The Trustees had no power to <dispose> of <this> Property thus."

4. Legal term for minority: an *infant* is under age, a minor.

5. Reimbursed.

6. CS's brackets.

7. See CS to Egremont, 11 Aug. 1802. Sophia Badcock's husband, William, Esq., "died a victim to excess in the prime of life, before he had attained the age of thirty." Richard Cumberland buried his son-in-law at Frant and was awarded the care of his five children by Chancery. Cumberland's memoirs do not mention Sophia's second ill-conceived marriage (Cumberland, *Memoirs,* 2:339).

To the earl of Egremont

[Frant] Octr 1st 1802

In pursuance of your Lordships orders, I beg leave to reply to your favor receivd this morning that I can have no objection to meeting Mr Tyler any where but in London, which I wish to avoid, not only because I am invariably ill there before I have been in the town four & twenty hours, but because I can <u>not</u> put myself in the way of Mr Benjamin Smith. If it be convenient to your Lordship to let Mr Tyler come hither, It will be equally convenient to me, or more so, than going elsewhere. Indeed I could not go at present being destitute of the means. My intention in naming Petworth was to have accompanied poor Lucy, to whom a cross country journey with three young & helpless children[1] & only a girl of fifteen with her, who never was from this village before, is rather a tremendous undertaking. By going with her, I should have saved her a part of the expence, & it would have been a satisfaction to me to have seen her safe with Mr Turner. After which, <if> I had gone over the accounts with Mr Tyler, I intended to have gone to Elsted to have seen what of my little furniture & books I could send thither whether I give up the Cottage or no, entirely.

At present, I have told Mr Tayler of Liphook (who Mr Johnstone left on his going to France to treat with me for it) that I would let him have it for six months on the same terms I took it upon (tho he offerd me any advance I pleas'd to put upon it) on condition only of his paying for the carriage of such articles as I should send for the better furnishing the house. To this he readily agreed & circumstanced as I find myself, I thought it would be the means of my saving for my future use the few comforts of furniture &c I possess without being at the expence of the carriage, & that after six months, I might perhaps be able to live at Elsted if I live any where. This proposed removal is not from any restlessness of disposition tho I have reason enough to be restless, but because this house is so old & out of repair that it is impossible for me to pass a winter in it, & I wishd to end my days nearer the few relations I have (for I shall probably end them soon) & to be buried at Stoke with my Mother——

Such was my intention & to have pass'd the winter, while Mr Johnstone inhabited this covetted cottage, at the cheapest bathing place I could find on this coast for the benefit of an hot sea bath, which has been long accounted necessary for me, & which for cold baths is [a] very desirable plan on account of Luzena my little Indian Girl, who is not very well. But my Lord without meaning to trouble you with all that I hoped to do, I need now only say that, in consequence of my being deprived of every resource by Mr Benjn Smith & by the resolution your Lordship has taken to let the affairs end in Chancery (where Mr Morgan says they will remain <six>[2] years), I have relinquishd every hope of being able to live any where as I thought I had a right to do, & my endeavours now go no farther than to raise enough to pay my bills here & replace what I have borrowd for the actual subsistence of my family from Mr Fauntleroy. And to this end, I must sacrifice not only the few conveniencies I have, but my working tools—for I cannot write without books, & my resources in my own industry & perseverance must then end——

To this however I have made up my mind to submit. Lucy & her children are gone to day. George will join his regiment if it comes home, or if not, go to the depot as soon as his pay, which he has overdrawn, is again productive, for I have no money to assist him with. And then M^r B Smith must allow me something for his youngest daughter if I am to have her with me[3]——I must discharge my servants & board somewhere with my Sons child till I am released from my weary pilgrimage. The sooner it is convenient for Mr Tyler to come, the more convenient it will be to me———

I have got all Mr Daniels accounts down to the present time, which I had not when I made out the hasty sketch (partly from memory which I sent up in consequence of what Major Smith said of your Lordships desire to have it directly) And as to the Bankers books, Mr Tyler sent me some time ago a very correct statement of the account of the Trust with Messrs Pybus & Co. since which no alterations have, I beleive, taken place so that on those accounts, there will be no necessity perhaps for Mr Tylers going to London ——I beg leave to say that I never stated it to be difficult to make out the account otherwise than as it was impossible for me to recollect the exact times when I either received the 70£ a year for interest, or what was advanced <u>to</u> me, or paid <u>by</u> me on account of M^r W T Smith & M^r N H Smith. Nor can I do the latter now.

Another subject of some difficulty is poor Charles's account of the whole from which I took that I sent in 1801 made out in a very hasty way & without dates which on comparing with Mr Daniels do not tally. He states a receipt at 83, which Mr Daniel makes 93, & I now beleive it is charged wrong in the account made out lately by Stidolph & forwarded on Wednesday[4] to Mr Tyler, & that there is one sum too much placed, to his, Charles's account & another of 70£ omitted. Were it not for these & some other points which he appears to have been mistaken in & some errors of my own, the thing is simple enough if I can make what has pass'd thro my hands for legatees tally with what they have actually received as given in their accounts, but now it looks as if <u>I</u> had had about 3000£ to my own use—— & to pick out & date every article is not easy——

In regard to poor Lucy, I must <u>lose</u>, or she must starve. She has not now fifteen pounds to furnish her house & support her & her children till the January dividend. In regard to furniture, if I could have removed as I intended, I should have given her almost enough to have made her small Cottage habitable, & if Your Lordships goodness & patience had not been worn out & you would have allowed Prescods next bill (which has not now more than three months & five days to run) to have been discounted <u>at the expence of the Legatees</u>, then she would have had a dividend in January that would have help'd her on, & in the present low & fluctuating state of the stocks, the money would be laid out to great advantage for these unfortunate young people whose interest & <u>not my own advantage or gratification</u> I have considerd throughout.

Assuredly, My Lord, I had no right to indulge even a laudable desire at your expence, nor was it ever my intention. In protecting them as far as I was able from the unnatural rapacity of their worthless & wicked father, I had no right to presume too much on your great generousity, & if it be found that in supporting them (For I have done nothing else with the money), I have had more than your Lordship is justified in advancing, they must among them make it up. I may have erred in judgement, but I trust I shall not at this late period belie the uniform tenor of my life & that your Lordship will not find me deficient either in honor or honesty. In gratitude, I am sure you will not, as whatever may happen or whatever I may suffer, I shall ever feel the great obligation conferred by

Your Lordship on your most obed^t & obligd Ser^t,
Charlotte Smith

I continue to send the accounts to Mr Tyler as fast as I receive them or can make them up. He has now got No. 1, 2, 3, & 4 of the Legatees accounts, & I shall send away 5 & 6 to day—— I meant to have sent them by Lucy, but they did not come till half an hour ago, & she set out at 7 this morning.

If your Lordship will have the goodness to let a servant put this enclosure in the two penny post, it will save me the postage which I must pay as I am oblig'd again to solicit Mr Simpsons forbearance, who has been long threatening to arrest me for a bill for linnen for George.[5] God help me!

As I cannot too soon know what can become of me for the winter, I shall be glad to have a notice of Mr Tyler's coming as soon as it may be convenient. A change of weather will bring on Winter rapidly, & I cannot stay here, yet have no place to go to——

May I request to hear whether M^r B Smith has received from y^r Lordship or Mr Turner the 70£ which remain'd in the Bank as dividend for ½ a year on the 3000£? I wish, if it be still your Lordships intention so far to befriend me as to be Trustee for this & the other 4000£ that you would give Mr Tyler orders (at the expence of the property) to have Mr Palmer make a regular & proper deed of Trust for that purpose. In case of my death, it is now very vague & unsettled—— & with all the regard I have, as a brother, for Mr Turner, I <u>cannot consent</u> to have all [that] my children are sure of, of mine so stand, as to be liable to ~~the~~ any act <u>of his, his heirs & assigns</u>. He is very angry with me & tells me I have acted <u>infamously</u> towards him. Rather an harsh expression, but I forgive him & wish I could still serve him without injuring those who have a still superior claim on me.[6]

Petworth House Archives MS. Address: The Earl of Egremont/ Petworth/ <u>Sussex</u>/ {Grosvenor Place}/ {London}. Postmark: TUNB-WELLS/ 36; FREE/ OCT ?/ 1802; R/ OC/ 2/ 1802; MAYFAIR.

NOTES

1. Lucy's children were ages 1, 2, and 3.

2. "Six" appears to be written over "five," or "five" over "six."

3. BS seems to have allowed CS's proposal for a division of the interest on £3,000, allowing CS and Harriet £100 a year and himself £50. It is not clear when or if she received this money. She would have used it all right away to pay her current debts.

4. Two days earlier, on 29 Sept.

5. Past pleas to delay John Simpson, linen draper, must have been successful: his solicitor John Richards first threatened CS with arrest "without further Notice" on 5 June 1802 (see CS to Egremont, 6 June 1802, n. 1, and to William Tyler, 23 Aug. 1802, n. 3).

6. The notes following the signature were sent as a separate page across which CS has written lengthwise.

To William Tyler

[Frant, 4 October 1802]

Sir,

I was not able to send the accounts I now enclose by Mrs Newhouse, as Mr Stidolph did not send them till after she went on friday morning[1]—— On the evening of that day, I was a good deal shook & terrified by an accident with Gunpowder which happen'd in the house, & tho it proved of no other consequence than burning Georges face a good deal, the fear I sufferd for some time least his eyes should have been put out made me, who am not able to bear such frequent alarms, so ill that I was really unfit to attend to any thing for some time & am even to day in a state of suffering which might well excuse me from entering on business tho I exerted myself yesterday to write to Mr Tayler[2] & make one more effort to engage M^r^ B Smith to come to some agreement, Seperating however ~~any of~~ that part of the question which relates to my interest money from that which relates to his fathers effects———

It would be better for his children to <u>give</u> him a Sum of money than to be compelled by his folly to see the little saved for them wasted in Chancery. But I know not <u>what</u> to do. Fetterd as I am in every respect without the means of living from day to day, Not knowing how either to support or disperse my family, & my health hourly declining, my situation is more dreadful than Can be conceived, and it would be charity in any one to put an end to my life. Lord Egremont observes in the Letter with which he last honourd me that, if the accounts are difficult to settle now, they will be much more so two or three years hence, but his Lordship perhaps did not at that moment recollect that if he has the goodness to continue the generous, the unpleasant task he has undertaken, it must end in July 1803. When, the last installment being paid, the whole of the Legatees claims will be paid, and my intention (if I so long live) was to petition Chancery myself as Executrix to take charge of whatever residue may remain to the uses of the Will, thus releasing (as I apprehend) Lord E. from any farther trouble. Even admitting that it shall appear that I have receivd for the support of the family more than my expences [which I am very sure will be allowed],[3] I should suppose that on enquiry how such sum had been appropriated, & on proof being given that it had been absolutely necessary for the maintenance of the Testators family, & that their Mother had no other means of providing them with the necessaries of life, that circumstance would be considerd as sufficiently authorising what had been done——

I am so unwilling to annoy Lord Egremont with all that may be said on this irksome subject that I forbear to urge it, yet before you take the trouble his Lordship directs in coming hither, I wish you to turn in your mind every subject that can come under examination. I wish you to enquire (if you are not already informed on the subject) whether my late Son would not be allowed for his trouble in selling the Estate &c. Mr Trotman, the Manager who took possession of it from Mr Walker, charged 5 pC^t^ on the 10,700£ it was valued at & had it. When the Trust was created in 1784, it was Messrs Robinsons &c pleasure to remove Mr Trotman & put Mr Prettejohn in his place, & for this transfer from one Manager to another, a second charge was made & allowed.[4] Whoever goes over to the West Indies to collect debts is always considerd as being entitled to 5 pC^t^ for paying & receiving. This will be a question necessary on every account to be resolved. My unfortunate Charles certainly had 208£ of Mr Daniel on his departure (out of the 600£ Gibbon's bill, discounted by them), & you see that, if this charge is not allowed, it will make a great difference in his Account which is otherwise more intricate than the others, & I cannot now have an explanation!

Mr Turner tells me that the reason Lord Egremont is so offended is because I gave him trouble about M^r^ De Foville & that is the cause of his Ldships declining the Trust.[5] In the first place, I did only what I knew to be my duty & ask'd nothing but what the will directs & what the other parties concernd would gladly agree to. M^r^ De Foville himself was so far from meaning to give trouble that, when he found a Mr Dore,[6] a Lawyer recommended to him by Mr Boyn,[7] had—instead of drawing up a plain power of Attorney to enable Mr Boyn to sign for him (as his name has always been demanded)—written to the Trustees & taken other measures to make a job of it; he withdrew his orders from Mr Dore & wrote to me to say he would leave the whole to me & authorise me to sign or do any thing required of him & that it never was his intention that Mr Dore should do as he had done. I did not know it till M^r De Foville was gone to France, where he has been now near three months & settled with his Sister at Rouen. Mr Turners assertion is merely ridiculous. Would to God none of mine or of Mr Smiths family were more disposed to take advantage or give trouble than M^r De Foville has been, & if they had all been as observant of my peace, I should not now be circumstanced as I am.

I write in pain & have only ~~time~~ to say that My daughter Lucy's situation as well as my own are such as makes every delay of the most serious consequence. I am, Sir, lamenting that I am obligd thus often to trouble you, your obligd hble Ser^t,

Charlotte Smith

I wish to God Lord Egremont would consider that I could not trespass in asking for 70£ on Miss Smiths & Nicholas's account & that I literally am destitute of the means of living—it is terrible![8]

It may also I beleive be made a question whether I should not be allowed interest on the money advanced or expended in journies or otherwise, & if a charge might not be made for my time & trouble. I will venture to assert that no human being but myself would have taken the trouble that I have had for any pay^t that could have been made to them. Surely considering that I could have earned my subsistence if not employ'd in these affairs, I might charge 20£ a year at least for my time which would amount to 300£ in 15 years during the greater part of which I could have earnd 400£ a year & did do it some years.[9] Advice might be had on this with^t Chancery.[10]
Octr 4th 1802[11]

Petworth House Archives MS. No address or postmark.

NOTES

1. Three days earlier, on 1 Oct.

2. BS refused to accept her letter delivered to him by Tayler on 7 Oct. 1802: "I positively declined receiving it, as I never will have any communication with her, after her unprincipled, unjustifiable, and fallacious conduct towards me." He reported that Tayler, too, refused to correspond with "this intemperate Lady. . . . She is endeavouring to procrastinate the settlement of my affairs, & speaks of Referees, & Tautological Chicane." Then he threatened Chancery (BS to Egremont, 11 Oct. 1802, unpub. letter in PHA #0.11).

3. CS's brackets.

4. These statements are confusing. John Newton first owned Gay's and sold it to George Walker. In 1781, while still executor to his father's estate, BS purchased Gay's from the representatives of George Walker, who was then dead. Trotman managed the estate for BS, but in 1784 the newly created trustees replaced Trotman with Prettyjohn when BS was dismissed for general mismanagement of the estate.

5. An important clue to the now rapidly deteriorating relationship between CS and Egremont.

6. William Dore, 8 Berkeley Street, Clerkenwell.

7. The attorney appointed by de Foville (see CS to William Hayley, 16 Aug. 1802).

8. By the letter of the law, which Egremont and Tyler seem bent on enforcing, CS had no right to money on any of her children's accounts.

9. CS earned at least £470 in 1789 and £420 in 1794. In 1787 she earned at least £330 and in 1798 £315 (see Stanton, "Charlotte Smith's 'Literary Business'").

10. Written vertically in the margin at the top of the second page of this four-page letter.

11. CS wrote the date at the top of the third page instead of at the end of the letter as she usually did.

To the earl of Egremont

[Frant] Oct[r] 5th 1802
My Lord,

Being extremely fatigued to day by the necessity I felt myself under to write by this packet to Barbados, where I consider my poor Charles yet remains unburied till his debts & funeral is paid——I am really disqualified from writing to M[r] Tyler—who (if his Letter is not a mistake) seems to suppose these accounts will take up a week to investigate since he talks of coming on friday next & returning by the 16th——

I have only a certain portion of strength either of mind or body, & God knows how cruelly both have been tried. M[r] Tyler now writes as if he expected me to send him receipts for every hackney coach I have paid. Or what is meant? I do not know—— but I had rather go into an alms house than suffer what I do now & have long done——

I put off once more parting with my books in hopes your Lordship w[d] have compassion on me & not suffer me to be driven to this extremity so as not to have money even to pay the postman or the most trifling things & to live in dread—— Will your Lordship condescend to let Miss Smith have (not me) the odd 57£ which remains in Pybus's hands. There will still be enough to pay M[r] Mitford as there is 257 there, & the 157 Advanced to a legatee can surely not hurt any one while it will save me from breaking my word to a Man who has hitherto prevented my wanting daily food,[1] & enable me to go thro the misery I am condemned to which can be exceeded only by that I sufferd while I had a beloved child lay dying & was refused the means of obtaining her assistance[2]—— That now I should so endure could not indeed have been calculated upon—— If M[r] Tyler puts off his journey (and I see no use in the journey if I am to send all the accounts ~~thro~~ to him). I only beg to know what I am to do, for God is my witness that I have not with my family the necessary subsistence from day to day nor any means of raising it or any friend to whom I can apply—— I had better far better have perish'd at once than be reduced to this. I am however y[r] Lordships still grateful servant, honoring your natural goodness & remembering all owed you,

you[r] obligd Ser[t], Charlotte Smith

Petworth House Archives MS. No address or postmark.

NOTES

1. William Fauntleroy discounted bills for CS under £100 without a charge, even though they had never met. At this time she owed him at least £50 borrowed during Harriet's illness. Apparently CS was unable to pay him back until Mar. On 9 Sept. 1804 (CS to William Tyler, unpub. letter), he refused her a small loan.

2. Augusta was very ill after giving birth to a child (who died shortly thereafter), and died nine months later, in Apr. 1795. CS always blamed the trustees for not allowing her enough money to provide Augusta with the best medical treatment.

To the earl of Egremont

[Frant, 8 October 1802]

I do not know what I write or what I do, having been harrass'd all day not only by the necessity of writing these Letters to Barbados, but by petty duns of seven or eight shillings which I cannot pay. My servants are discontented & desirous of being discharged; I have no winter stock of any thing laid in, every discomfort is surrounding me, I am forced to buy the very water used in the house & have no means of escape from inconveniencies that y[r] Lordship can form no idea of, & ~~therefore~~ I wish madness or death to end all this. I cannot bear it. Beleive me, My Lord, if I had any means of relieving myself I would not, after being so Repulsed, trouble you so often.

I care not how soon M[r] Tayler [*sic*] comes. I have no accounts but M[r] Daniels as vouchers, & I only desire to be relieved from this & not blamed for what I cannot help. I have sent him the Legatees accounts. I sent my own accounts. Here are M[r] Daniels Accounts, & I will send them if they are required. If I know precisely what is demanded of me, I will do it, but the ground is often changed, & to my questions of real importance, I get no answer! I submit myself however to your Lordships candour & humanity.[1]

[Unsigned]

Petworth House Archives MS. Address: The Earl of Egremont/ No. 5 Grosvenor Place/ ~~Petworth~~/ London/ ~~Sussex~~ Postmark: TUNB-WELLS/ 36; FREE/ OCT?/ 1802; PETWORTH/ 57; FREE/ OCT 8/ 1802.

NOTE

1. The second paragraph of this unsigned fragment was written upside down at the top of this page and continued on the reverse side of the sheet.

To William Davies

[Frant, 14 October 1802]
Sir,

The kindness and attention I have during many years experienced from you make me beleive you will have the goodness to assist me in the last trouble I shall probably ever have occasion to give you—— It is perhaps needless to relate at length the circumstances that, having wearied out the kindness & forbearance of Lord Egremont after he had saved about 20,000£[1] for my family, & have determind him to throw the affairs into Chancery the ensuing term by which a great part of the Sum so saved will be wasted in Law. Suffice it to say that instead of the death of my fathers widow (by which I had an encrease of fortune also) having releived me from the difficulties I so long labourd under, M[r] B Smith has taken not only the interest of that, but all he before allowed me So that I have now no income whatsoever either for myself or younger children & find myself, after many unsuccessful efforts to escape it, under the necessity of selling my small collection of books. I named it to you sometime since writing for your interposition with M[r] White and am unwilling to apply to common dealers. But I had no answer & understood from M[r] Rose you were out of town.

Circumstances have very lately occurred which make this painful measure inevitable. M[r] Rose is, as M[r] Bicknell tells me, now absent. May I therefore again solicit you to ask M[r] White whether he will purchase my small library without reserve, & whether I may send him up a Catalogue? or if it would answer as well to sell them here. I should think not. My situation admits of no delay: I trust therefore you will favor me with an early answer, If possible by the posts' return, & with many apologies for this liberty, I am, Sir,

your oblig'd & obed Ser[t],
Charlotte Smith

Frant near Tunbridge Wells
Oct[r] 14th 1802

General Manuscripts, Manuscripts Division, Rare Books and Special Collections, Princeton University Library. Address: M[r] Davis. / Mess[rs] Cadell & Davis./ Strand/ London/ Post paid. Postmark: TUNB-WELLS/36; F/PAID/OCT15/1802.

NOTE

1. This figure is oddly written as "2,0,000£," but the larger sum was intended, not 2,000£ as might appear at a glance.

To William Tyler

[Frant, 25 October 1802]
Sir,

I am so little able in my present dejected state to speak on my present situation that I write the better to make myself understood before I see you—— The long & unsuccessful struggle I have made I now give up. One of the trouble's I shall give you on going to town will be to take a list of my books, which I have been making out to day, to Cadell & Davies who have undertaken to get a purchaser for them—— These—which I had hoped to have kept to have assisted me in earning my bread & the little furniture I have—are the last sacrifices I can make. I already owe to my servants & to persons in this neighbourhood for the common necessaries of life nearly as much as these will bring (as I shall be forced to sell them at disadvantage), & when that is gone, nothing but immediate poverty must be my portion if death does not releive me——

I owe M[r] Fauntleroy 50£ which I am above all other things desirous of paying him——& the sooner I could releive myself from expences here, the better, both for me [and] those to whom I am indebted. My Servants are two of them married & want to be discharged. I have no hope of Lord Egremonts assisting me; despair on every hand encompasses me—— I only trouble you to know if there is any probability of my raising immediately two hundred pounds on such security as these effects may give me, or if you beleive Lord Egremont—as the last trouble I shall ever give his Lordship—would allow M[r] Mitford to lend it me not to save me <u>from</u> this sacrifice, for books are now of no use to me. I shall never again have heart to write. But merely to enable me to put an end to present expence, to pay my servants, & remove, before cold weather sets in, to London—to die———for I cannot live there—— <Here> I have no coals or any provision for winter. The tradespeople are anxious for pay[t], & I shall have no credit after this week— —I have no right or claim to solicit Lord Egremont; I only wish to have enough for the above purposes. All I have, I dispose of not being immediately productive.

I am unable to add more than that I wish you to consider what chance there is of my being thus releived just for the present, before you call this evening. The pain I suffer must be my excuse for incoherence. I am, Sir,

y[r] obed[t] & oblig'd Ser[t],
Charlotte Smith

Monday ev[g], 25 Oct 1802
I have to day changed my last pound note & that was borrow'd. M[r] B Smith will carry his point & destroy me. I cannot endure misery any longer!—

Petworth House Archives MS. Address: M[r] Tyler. No postmark.

To William Davies

[Frant, 25 October 1802]
Sir,

I am much oblig'd to you for your Letter. I waited only for a private hand to send the enclosed Catalogue which is not quite complete, as I am too unwell to make it out, but it contains the greater part of my poor little Library. The generality of them are in very good condition, & all here named are complete. I part with them with infinite reluctance & regret, but My present situation together with the reflection that in the event of my death, these also ~~that~~ would belong to M^{r} B Smith (as well as every thing else & all he has already taken, being all my fortune at 7000£ for his life) has determined me to conquer my repugnance. I will mark y^{r} books that I had of you & wch are not yet paid for, either to be return'd to you or their value paid to you——

I am, Sir,
your oblig'd hble Ser^{t},
Charlotte Smith

Frant
Octr 25th
1802

Yale University MS. Address: Mr Davies. No postmark.

To William Tyler

Frant Octr 31st 1802
Sir,

I had on friday a Letter from Mr Bicknell who has seen Mr Mitford & from that Gentleman acquaints me that he, Mr Mitford, is by no means impatient for the pay^{t} of the 200£ which you have put down as part of my debit to the Trustees & is willing the moment Lord Egremont <&> Mr Turner will endorse the Bill due on the 7th of Jany next to discount that bill. I understand that Lord Egremont is still in Yorkshire. My distress encreases every day & is arrived at a point which Lord Egremont would not in common humanity desire me to suffer. I have not the means of supporting my family or of paying my servants. Yesterday I had a bill of 7£ from the Miller with notice that he could no longer supply me—— I have not been able to obtain a supply of coals & look forward with horror to the cold weather, crippled as I am already with the Rhumatism & dragging on a miserable &

hopeless existence from which I vainly endeavour to escape, & my power of assisting myself by writing is totally at an end——

Good God, what have I done to be reduced to such a dreadful situation! —Friends that I formerly had now stand aloof, fearing to involve themselves by attempting to assist me whose evil destiny seems to baffle even the most powerful assistance! & concluding that if Lord Egremonts interposition, so strenuously exerted & so long continued, leaves me at last in a situation so deplorable that I can not be effectually releived & perhaps deserve to suffer. On the 6th of November, I must pay taxes to the amount of 8£. If I do not, the consequence is evident, & what figure shall I make in such a village as this!——I have also 8 Gs to pay in Town for which I am extremely pressed, & these things are all for absolute necessaries & consequent to the necessity of keeping an house for Mr B. Smiths children.

I enclose you a proposal given by that wretched Man at a meeting with Mr Palmer & Mr Fry, with him and Mr Follet his Attorney.[1] I have positively refused to accede to it & have instructed Mr Fry to say that, on condition of Mr B Smiths dividing the income with me, I will exonnerate him from all future trouble or expence about his younger children & sign a deed of seperation, & this is exactly what he himself proposes in a Letter of which I beleive I sent you a copy, but he says that, "By G—he cannot & will not live on less than 200 a year," & that I had no business to sell my 100£ a year, tho the infamous Monster knows that I did it in the hope of supporting for a time those children whom he had so wickedly abandon'd & particularly to fit & send poor Charles to Oxford whither, if he had gone, the living would have been saved[2] and my Son now probably alive.

It was not my fault that he did not go. It is cruel to have this made a reason for this Man's brutal conduct now. How was it possible for me to support a family of eight persons on an hundred & eighty pounds a year, all I had then for every purpose whatever, & was it not natural for me to hope & beleive that, if I sacrificed my own little income then, I should have it repurchased for me when, as I was yearly promisd, the affairs would be settled & the will fulfilled?—— Mr B Smith, when asked how if he cannot live on less than 200£ a year, I can live on nothing, replies that I can write & get money that way, as if I was compelled to do it or could always command those powers of mind which I have so long & so fruitlessly exerted for his family—— You will have the goodness to observe that even the pittance this unnatural father offers to give his youngest daughter is to be withdrawn if from any other source she has as much given to her, so if her Brother continues to her the interest of what he has in the stocks, this is to cease——

If Lord Egremont would in mercy extend to me the means of releiving myself from my present very cruel & humiliating situation, I would engage in the most solemn manner never to trouble his Lordship again. I will give up housekeeping, sell every thing I have & find some means of support, a plan for which I have sent up to my friends. If Lord Egremont would let the bill be discounted & another division made among the Legatees, the greatest part of ~~my~~ these difficulties might be obviated, & M[rs] Newhouse would have a subsistence which at present she will not have. In a word their salvation seems to depend upon it. Lord Egremonts trouble would undoubtedly end so much the sooner without the interposition of that Chancery which will devour the whole. When the Legatees are paid which the next dividend will almost do, M[r] B Smith must learn from Chancery the purport of his fathers will, & it never was Lord Eg[t] intention to be plagued with him & his residue, which You see he very modestly expects. But it is I think very clear from this curious proposal that the worthless ideot has done with his stupid menaces of a bill against the Trustees & confines his present views to the plunder of my income according to Law—— If Lord Egremont has not so entirely given up his benevolent intentions towards me & his once favourable opinion of me that he will not now desert me & will suffer this bill to be discounted (the discount to be allowed by the Legatees), & the money invested, I shall find the means to bring M[r] B Smith to reason if it be reason that he should live upon my property without having made me any return by settlement.

When M[r] Palmer, at the meeting I have mentiond above, said that it was my intention to fyle a bill for securing the 3000£ which in the marriage settlement it is specified to belong to me, interest for my life & remainder to the children, The answer from M[r] Smith was, "Oh! Damn their Chancery, I care not a farthing for their threats,"[3] & M[r] Follet said very cavalierly, "Why the money is spent & gone, & there is an end of it. M[r] B Smith cannot ~~xxx gi~~ secure what he has not." Is this, can this Law [*sic*] & is there no redress?—— Of what use are settlements if they can be so easily evaded?—— & is it possible that equity will not in such a case interfere?——— I do not enclose M[r] Adams's Letter because I must answer it, but will send it next week———

In the mean time as the very existence of this family depends on Lord Egremonts consent to discount the bill, let me entreat you, Sir, to lay the circumstance before his Lordship—— What I <u>shall</u> do God only knows, till his Compassion can be moved in my favor. I wish to die rather than suffer from day to day the wretchedness I am exposd to, the intolerable sufferings both of mind & body. If you could point out any temporary means of releif only for the ensuing week, it would alleviate my extreme distress—To be compelled to solicit my servants to stay—help me 'till I can pay them—to be humbled in the dust before tax gatherers, butchers & Millers!—— & forced to go on because I can not escape!—— I am, Sir,

y[r] obed[t] & oblig'd Ser[t], Charlotte Smith

Do you think Lord Egremont would give me an hare & a brace of pheasant or a piece of venison in the season to send from Petworth to a Gentleman in Town to whom I am very greatly oblig'd & towards whom I have now no possible way of expressing my sense of obligation.[4] There was a time when he would willingly have shewn me a much greater kindness, how importunate soever this request may seem now.

Petworth House Archives MS. Address: The Earl of Egremont/ Petworth/ Sussex/ Oct[r] 31st/ 1802. Postmark: TUNB-WELLS/ 36; FREE/ ?/ 1802.

NOTES

1. On Saturday, 21 Oct. 1802, a meeting was held at Gray's Inn concerning the £400 interest owed to BS. George Palmer was Tyler's and thus Egremont's agent; Henry Fry of Frant was CS's solicitor; and Benjamin Follet represented BS. On 31 Oct., BS wrote to Egremont, insisting that the disputed interest was a matter "anterior" to his taking up the trusteeship. BS has received only £270, and of that he gave £20 to his youngest son George. Moreover, CS "has had some Thousands for herself and the Children's use, to my few Hundreds."

BS does not say when he received the £270 or how he disposed of it, but his present situation "is the most distressing, and painful. . . . I must be very shortly on the Kings Bench, & have my little property in Scotland taken from me" (unpub. letters in PHA #0.11).

2. That is, the perpetual advowson of Islington, a living held by the family (see CS to Joseph Cooper Walker, 9 Oct. 1793, n. 3).

3. BS was not above threatening Chancery to his own ends, as for example he did to Egremont on 11 Oct. 1802. He planned to make an issue of "the large debt due to me on my Executorship account part of my claims, and instead of having a few Hundreds to pay, you may believe me, there will be Thousands." He considers himself to have been "most cruelly trifled with by M[rs] Smith." But on 10 Dec. he denies wanting the Chancery suit (unpub. letters in PHA #0.11).

4. Probably William Fauntleroy (see CS to Egremont, 5 Oct. 1802, n. 1).

To William Tyler

[Frant, ?1 November 1802]
Sir,

Apprehensive as I am of again offending Lord Egremont by my importunity yet feeling the utter impossibility of continuing in my present uncertain & unhappy situation, I am driven to hazard that misfortune, great as I feel it to be——— Give me leave to request of you a positive answer as to what his Lordship intends to do & whether, as I understand from Mr Fry, you have said to Mr Palmer that a bill against all the parties for the dismission of the Trustees is absolutely decided upon. As whatever may be the event, it cannot be otherwise than fatal to the competence I hoped some part of my family would at length possess, and as my indigence is certain, the sooner I can apply myself to obtain some means of subsistence for the little time I have to live, the more likely I shall be to obtain it—— If after so many & so bitter disappointments I can acquire courage enough to undertake any thing.

Every day that I remain uncertain how to act encreases my expence & diminishes my hope of escaping from it. I cannot discharge my servants, two of whom—the lad who has lived with me five years & a female servant who is cook & waits on me & who has lived with me above seven years—are married & have due to them both from me about two & thirty pounds with which they must try to get into some way of living unless I could get them into some good place. The Young Man is of the most irreproachable honesty, but he has not strong health & therefore is not fit for every service. The Woman is so good a cook that she might serve an Archbishop tho it is a talent of no great use to me. But the difficulty of getting places for married servants, and the few lines of business ~~in~~ which those who have been brought up in servitude are capable of undertaking make me very sorry for these foolish people who have undone themselves by marrying & very unwilling to turn them out without trying to befriend them. At all events, I cannot discharge them till I can pay them. They are as much attach'd to me as servants ever are & unwilling enough to leave me. But I can now keep only one servant & must go into a lodging as soon as I am able to pay what I owe here——

I have at last received the anr I have so long expected from Mr Davies, & I enclose it. The utmost money offerd is not on an average 2s a volume—As I have upwards of 1000 books. . . . & I had much rather die than live without the resource they afford me. Notwithstanding this & the extreme hardship it is after all I have done to be reduced to this expedient and still to be burthen'd with Mr B. Smiths children for whom he will allow nothing, yet as I neither desire nor ought to be burthensome to Lord Egremont & shall by this bill in Chancery be deprived of the resource I might have had in my Son Nicholas's affection to me, I must accept of these hard conditions, & when that resource is exhausted (as it will be by paying what I owe here, particularly to the Apothecary), I shall literaly be penniless & a beggar. I request however the favor of you to let me know very soon what is decided upon, for my strength is rapidly declining——

I really have hardly resolution enough to remind you that you told me Mr Tayler[1] had done an illegal thing in receiving the dividend on the 2000£ before he was appointed Trustee legally. He is a well meaning Man, I suppose, but so harrassd by his own affairs from the conduct of a worthless Son & is of so wavering & imbecile a disposition that I have no reliance even on integrity that seems the sport of accident, & for that & still stronger reasons, I am very desirous of having a trust properly created for that & the 3000£. I do not know to this hour whether Lord E. will decide on taking this trust. I fear to ask him, least it should be troublesome & offend him. But every day & every hour convince me more & more of the necessity of it & increases my wish that his Ldship would condescend to take it.

I am sitting this cold day with all the windows of my book room open because, with a north wind, the smoke stifles me. Yet I have no remedy: & here I must remain during the severity of Winter, tho a cripple with the Rhumatism. Where great evils exist, petty miseries are sometimes not felt, but those that I am condemned to suffer are precisely of that sort which prevent my warding off the greater evils & annihilate my faculties and destroy my resolution—— & all this after fifteen years of constant toil & unremitting anxiety for the children of Mr Benjn Smith!——

I beg your pardon for giving you so much trouble, but I trust that you will see the necessity of my knowing Lord Egremonts Determination. I am, Sir,

y^r^ obed^t^ & obligd Ser^t^,
Charlotte Smith

I direct this to Town, because I think you mentiond your being there the beginning of term.[2] Mr Turner talk'd (& ought to do it) of fyling a bill ag^st^ M^r^ B Smith to compel him to fulfill his agreement in ~~regard to~~ the marriage Articles. I know this might be done, & who but my Brother is there to defend me from the injustice I sustain? Would to God I had been the Brother. I think no Sister of mine should have been oppress'd as I have been by such a biped as that wretched Madman. You desird I remember a receipt for the money I had paid Mr B Smith. On what account he received it, I know not, nor does it signify much to enquire. I will send you all the receipts I have—— One of them is a curious specimen of the mind of the Man who is by law empowerd to starve me & his own children! Almighty God! what a destiny is mine!——

Petworth House Archives MS. No address or postmark.

NOTES

1. Robert Tayler was trustee to each of CS's three marriage settlements.

2. Michaelmas term, during which the high courts—King's Bench, Exchequer, and Common Pleas—sat, began in November.

To the earl of Egremont

[Frant] Nov[r] 5th 1802

My Lord,

By yesterdays post, I acknowledged the receipt of a Bank bill of 50£ which your Lordship had the goodness to send for a present supply, but which I am by no means desirous of finally intruding for on your Lordships bounty. It is not reasonable that I should always beg of you. I would, my Lord, if I knew how, answer your Q[uer][y] to your satisfaction & without that diffuse declamation of which you complain with reason perhaps as a matter of general disgust. It is however hard for a sufferer such as I have been and am, not to utter some murmurs against a destiny as severe as it is undeserved.[1]

Yr Ldship appears (if I understand you aright) to think that, if I And my children lived with M[r] B Smith, the income among us all would be sufficient. This idea I could easily convince you is erroneous, but it would be by an history of the former life and conduct of M[r] B Smith which would be too long for you to read—— If continual & unmeaning waste of money which he refusd to the absolute support of his children, if the most brutish & unmanly personal insults towards me so that my life was often in danger, if the most gross violations of decency and morality before his daughters, & if the entire annihilation of my faculties by terror of his frantic & furious passions on one hand, and on the other of Bailiffs that beseiged the doors, if all these circumstances would contribute to make the income do, then it might be a matter of prudence, but I am sure your Lordship must see that the Man who is the horror of all his family, whose whole life has been a tissue of folly varied only by wickedness & without one virtue to redeem his bad qualities, who, whether as a Son, a brother, husband, father, or Guardian has invariably undone every one with whom he was connected as far as was in his power, & who now avails himself even of his vices to deprive his children of their support arising from my fortune after having spent all his own, & even that which ought to have been settled on me according to those very articles of which he now takes advantage:[2] Your Lordship is too correct a judge of human nature not to be convinced that no good could possibly arise from my living with him. Of his amendment, there can be no hope. Vicious animals always become worse as they grow older: "If these things were done in the green leaf, what shall be done in the dry?"[3]—— There is not one of his children, not even his dear daughter, Harriet, who would live with him a week——

As to myself, my life will be, I beleive, not long, but there is no condition of life, which, while it does last, I would not prefer to living with that mean destroyer of his children, "who is worse than an highwayman"[4]——Yr Ldshp says that we none of us seem dispos'd to submit to our circumstances. Pardon me if I reply that I have submitted not only to give up my situation in society, but to actual & very humiliating deprivations & personal hardship, as well as continual labour greatly above my strength. Never do I expend a superflous shilling, never am I known to enjoy a day's relaxation. I have hardly a change of cloathes even to wear at home, & none fit to appear in were I to go out. "But you have had, say those who enquire, a great deal of money." Very true, & I have had a great many children to provide for for fifteen years & to buy every thing at the worst hand—— It will be found that on an average I have not had 200£ a year, & unless I had worked for these children, what would have become of them? I do not know what it is to submit to circumstances if this was not, & is not, doing it.

I can bring persons who will prove that My leaving M^r^ B Smith was absolutely necessary, That he bade me "go to hell with my children," that I had for years before that time endured at times the most unworthy treatment —— If I were to sue him in the ecclesiastical court as I ought to do if I had the means, I could bring these facts forward however late——but I shall not live to contend with him. I fear yr Ldshp may say, "What is all this to the purpose?" I can no otherwise attempt to do away from your mind the impression it seems lately to have receiv'd that I do not acquiese with calmness in my destiny & trouble others, that I may escape from it. Oh! no my Lord, it is too late for me to make any such efforts now. Indeed I am perfectly resigned to die in poverty, but not to live either as I have done lately or with Mr Benjn Smith.

In answer to the kind interest you are pleased to take about Mrs Newhouses situation, which God knows is pitiable enough, I beg leave to answer that I have done every thing in my power for Mrs Newhouse & have given up above 200£ (which I might claim very reasonably) because she has so little. If I could have gone to the Cottage I had taken at Elsted by Godalming, I should have given her furniture for her Cottage at North Chapel because I could have spared it then very well. To enable her to save money for her removal, I took her and her three children & a servant from March last till Oct^r^—an additional expence which I could very ill afford & of which I am now paying the penalty by being in debt more than I have the least prospect of discharging. Nor was that all. The distraction of three children—two of whom are just old enough to be very noisy & mischeivous & who are spoild by their Mother—entirely prevented my writing. Yr Lordship has little idea how inconvenient these interruptions are or to how many disagreeable endurances a small house so filled exposes any person of my age, but more particularly one whose health & habits alike require some repose. I can not undertake it & can do much more to assist My daughter in another house than if I lived in the same. An old Woman of the village may comb these Children's heads & wash their faces; My time may be better employ'd in earning money to help their Mother feed them, which in the same house is impossible. I confess, my Lord, I have no great delight in La Grande Maternité to Mr Newhouse's children.

The little Girl sent to me by my Son Nicholas is tout a moi.[5] I can do as I please with her, & I have pleasure in teaching her. I owe to her father, who dotes upon her little dark face, a return of that affection he has always shewn me & that support which I have owed lately wholly to him, but If I could have gone to Elsted, I should have been near enough to have assisted poor Lucy from time to time in many things & occasionally to have taken one of her children, but I am very sure a menage altogether would kill me in half a year. Where would the money be found to pay for an house big enough for eight people besides servants?—— If I could have got two cottages very near each other, I would have taken them & made them habitable—one for her & one for myself—but I have now neither money nor courage for any arrangement. I am extremely sorry to differ from y^r^ Ldship, but I really do not see which of her Brothers or Sisters can help Lucy ~~but~~ except Charlotte, who has done so much for Lionel that to do more for any one would quite impoverish her, & it is hardly fair to expect that, because Lucy has married so ill, Charlotte is to give up her little independance & become a nursery maid. I have always thought her fate hard enough without her making this sacrifice which would indeed an^r^ no purpose.

It is at present my intention with her assistance to undertake the care of three or four little Girls from five years old, the age of Luzena, to nine & to take a French Woman into the house as a sort of superior servant. By this means, I may encrease or rather make something like an income (in addition to what my Son will send me for my Indian Girl) & be better enabled to educate her. This is however visionary at the present moment, for I could not execute it in this house, which is tumbling about my ears & in which, if I outlive the winter, I shall lose the use of my limbs from its bleak situation & ruinous state. If I can sell my poor books to pay what I owe, I must go for the present into some very obscure lodging in London. I have my servants to pay & Mr Fauntleroys advance to make up. George, who has been two months at home, will want assistance when he joins his regiment. His cruel father tears every thing from me, & I am actually a beggar with all this load upon me—with a constitution breaking every day & having tired out all my friends!——

Your Lordship says it is of no use to talk of what ought to be, but to consider what is. This then is my situation. I will do what I can to get out of it.

But my mental & bodily distresses give me no prospect but of a Grave. There I shall be at peace, & M^r^ B Smith will triumph & enjoy his Geneva potations & solace himself with Mrs Millar & refuse my children bread

———————————

Your Lordship seems to think I have been misled by Mr Dayrell & others & say that I have misrepresented what they told me in vague conversation. I really do not know in what instance; Mr Dayrell is no particular friend or favourite of mine. He is Mr Turners friend, but I always thought from your Lordships Letters that you approved of him. I have neither seen nor corresponded with him these eight months. If my Lord I have been diffuse, it is because I knew not how to ans^r^ y^r^ Lordship more briefly, & I would very fain exculpate myself from those charges which seem to have arisen against me & to have deprived me of a great part of that favourable opinion, I so highly valued & know not how I have forfeited. I know that nothing will ever make me otherwise than grateful for all that is past, ~~whatever~~ However you may think proper to decide in future. Allow me to repeat how much poor Lucy's being able to live this year depends upon the bills being discounted <u>before the books are shut</u>. I am ever y^r^ Ldships oblig'd & gratefull Ser^t^,

Charlotte Smith

Petworth House Archives MS. No address or postmark.

NOTES

1. A disappointing note from her solicitor, Henry Fry, spurred CS to make the detailed personal revelations in this letter. Fry and Palmer, working in her behalf, contacted BS and his lawyer, Follet, and were told that "M^r^ S— will not consent to deprive himself of half of his income, and rejects your proposal" (PHA #7366). Even so, BS was no longer to receive the stock dividends, and a Chancery bill was being considered.

2. This unusually long sentence, even for CS, is incomplete. After beginning the second half, "but I am sure your Lordship must see that the Man who is the horror . . . ," she becomes lost in the half dozen relative clauses detailing BS's many failings. These are her most explicit, provocative accusations against his character and behavior during marriage.

3. Luke 23.31: "For if they do these things in a green tree, what shall be done in the dry?"

4. So Egremont said of BS, but CS reminded the earl of his hasty characterization perhaps too often (see CS to William Tyler, 23 Aug. and 16 Sept. 1802).

5. All mine. Later, CS calls Luzena "my Indian Girl." Nicholas had sent the child to her from East India.

To the earl of Egremont

[Frant, 18 November 1802]

My Lord,

I thank your Lordship for the information you have been pleas'd to give me. I am unable this morning to answer the whole, as I cannot think it in my power to decide on any thing but what relates to my own money which appears to have been unfortunately confounded with Mr Richard Smiths and to have furnish'd a two edged sword that will compel me to submit to very great hardship myself or, by refusing, to bring inevitable delay & expence on those whose interest I have always consulted more than my own.[1] I do not know what Mr Turner can or will do——I only know what he ought to do & know that, if he had acted differently, Mr Benjn Smith would not have dared to have acted as he has done. This yr Lordship will call a digression, & I know no means of keeping to the points but to answer them on the opposite side of the paper which I will do tomorrow; being excessively sick this morning, I am only able to say that beyond paying the Legatees I never meant to trouble you, nor could I imagine yr Lordship intended when you were pleased to undertake the trust, to enter into a ~~xxxx~~ disposal of the residue——

How to ascertain the amount of that, I certainly know not. But I beleive Mr Berney, were the ballance fairly struck, would have a considerable Sum to pay & refund. The account I have lately obtain'd from Mr Winterbottom & Dun of money paid to him by Prettejohn confirms this.[2] It was to be clear in some matters respecting this that I wrote to Mr Boehm to allow me to have copies of the accounts of Sums he had received from persons of the names of Millington & <Tirrell> as well as Steele (whose debt alone nearly coverd that due to the Berneys from BS).[3] I had the honor to say to your Lordship that Mr Boehm answerd he had sent you those accounts. I know it was not true—But had no authority to say so till Mr Tyler assured me no such accounts had ever been sent. Had I been sooner authoris'd, I should have written again to Mr Boehm, & I should willingly have done what my poor Charles so earnestly urged in one of his last Letters. But I have no encouragement now to do what appears to your Lordship troublesome & officious & may not benefit any one for whom I am interested.

I enclose the last Letter I had from Mr Adams which I answerd by the last packet. He talks of Mrs Smith as if I was the person acting because he undertook it at my request. I name this merely that your Lordship may not think I arrogated to myself what I have in fact no business with. I beleive the money altogether outstanding in Barbados is abt 800£ Sterling. I enclose the last letter I had from Messrs Winterbottom & Dunn, which makes me beleive Mr B Smiths representation not correct as to an accommodation.

I could give no answer till I had heard from Mr Dayrell who was last winter extremely earnest in advising my family by no means to pay the Allens. I wrote to know if he would undertake the business for us if we are compelled to defend ourselves; I say we merely habitually, for I am nothing & shall petition to be dismissed from the bill if it is fyled. It is hard indeed that I am to have more trouble & expence who have no power whatever, even to save myself from actual beggary. If I answer unlike what yr Lordship directs, excuse me I beseech you. I will reply to every particular plainly with Miss Smiths assistance tomorrow if I am able, or if not, on Sunday.

I Am, My Lord,
ever your most obed Ser^t,
Charlotte Smith

On looking at the account sent me by Messrs Winterbottom and Dun which, tho it is the account of expenditure on Gay's plantation, we never could get & which now has only reach'd us by the Allens Solicitor & is witnessd by James Mapp Allen, Mr Allens brother who went to Barbados in Octr or Novr last year. I detect at once a falsehood; they said the money taken from Mapps was to pay off debts which were running on at interest. Mr Dayrells remark was: "Well then let them produce the receipts of the Creditors so paid." Now what is the fact. Here is the statement:

Decr 31st 1791.	By amount taken this year from Mapps for the use of Gay's plantation ————	626.8.2½
Decr 30 1797.	By amount taken this year from Mapps plantation for the use of Gays plantation —	686.19.11½
		1313.8 9

On reflection, I keep Messrs Winterbottoms & Dunns Letter till I have answerd it.

My principal reason for so earnestly desiring to have Mr Mitford's friendly offer accepted as to discounting the bill, was, first, on account of the low price of stocks compared to what they were last winter; 2^ndly, that Mrs Newhouse might have a dividend on what would in that case be invested in the stocks before the books are shut;[4] 4^thly, to shorten your Lordships trouble; & 5^thly, to have a dividend on what will belong to Mr Nicholas Smith (which I shall put into the funds) for the use of his daughter.

But as the books are shut 6 weeks before the dividends, it will soon be too late.

Petworth House Archives MS. Address: The Earl of Egremont/ Grosvenor Place/ London. Postmark: TUNB-WELLS/ 36; FREE/ NOV 19/ 1802.

NOTES

1. CS's "own money," her three marriage settlements, were entirely separate from the Smith trust, but trustees and lawyers familiar with both sometimes spoke of them as if they were all one legal entity.

2. Abraham Winterbottom and Ralph Dunn were acting for Richard Smith and Robert Allen in the case they brought against the Smith trust in Chancery on 14 May 1803.

3. There is no mention elsewhere that either BS or the estate owed money to Robert Berney; on the contrary, CS held out till the bitter end that Berney had been overpaid by at least £2,000 (see CS to Egremont, 14 Aug. 1806; see also unpub. letters of CS to William Tyler, 23 Aug. 1801, 8 Sept. 1802, and 12 Oct. 1803).

4. CS did not list a third point.

To the earl of Egremont

[Frant, 19 November 1802]
My Lord,

Supposing it to be your Lordships meaning that I should send to you my answer to Mr Benj Smiths Conditions, I have taken the liberty to enclose the four paragraphs copied from his Letter to your Lordship & answerd with as little verbiage as I well could—— You must be convinced my Lord that I have no power to agree that he shall have 400£[1] & that it is absurd to make it a condition when I cannot assent to it for want of a voice in the affair. Your Lordship shall have answers <also> to the points you wish to have referred, & as far as depends on me, I can have no objection to any referrence or any thing your Lordship shall prescribe as the means of sparing you trouble during the short remainder of your Trust which I never did wish you to continue beyond the pay^t^ of the Legatees: They will all then give your Lordship a discharge (Mrs Newhouse is only ignorant but I have the means of making her do right), & from whence can come any farther trouble when M^r^ B Smith must abide by the Will? I am a Martyr to the Rhumatism, & in such pain that I repeat with difficulty my hope of being allow'd to remain Y^r^ Lordships,

most oblig'd ser^t^,
Charlotte Smith

Petworth House Archives MS. Address: The Earl of Egremont/ Petworth/ {Grosvenn Place} / Sussex {London}. Postmark: TUNB-WELLS/36; FREE/ NOV20/ 1802. And: Mayfair; FREE/ NOV20/ 1802.

NOTE

1. On 10 Dec., BS is going home to Scotland, hoping Egremont will speedily settle this long-disputed amount—"otherwise I must be compleatly ruined" (unpub. letter in PHA #0.11).

In 1803, he was awarded £500 by arbitration.

To the earl of Egremont

Frant, Novr 24th
1802
My Lord,

In consequence of having been oblig'd to put leaches on my temples for pains in my head, I have brought on such an inflammation or swelling throughout my face & eyes that I was blind for two days & still suffer considerably & am only able to say, that in regard to the questions your Lordship appears to think proper to be submitted to Chancery Lawyers, I trust, if you still continue to require it, I may be permitted to desire that <u>Mr Leach</u>[1] <u>or M^r^</u> <u>Rose</u> may be the Gentleman referred to——Unless the question is referred to some Gentleman acquainted with the affairs—at least so far as to know the parties & have some idea of what I have done & endured; with what difficulties I have contended; how much my family have owed to my own exertions & to the friends those exertions procured for them—it is impossible a fair judgement can be formed of what my claims are to the poor & inadequate remuneration which, after all, leaves me destitute & sick & miserable to contend still with the horrors of poverty & neglect.

Stocks continue to fall, & on every account, it is desirable to have the bill discounted that there may be a January dividend on what shall be invested. To some of my family, it is <u>more material than I can give an idea of unless I enterd into a detail which would be disagreable to your Lordship</u>. Could it be done, <u>I</u> could perhaps save my books & be enabled still to earn a part of my subsistence. Otherwise I must let them go. I am, with the utmost gratitude & respect, yr Lordships oblig'd Ser^t^,

Charlotte Smith

Petworth House Archives MS. No address or postmark.

NOTE

1. Possibly John Leach, equity draftsman, 10 Lincoln's Inn, New Square. But neither Leach nor Rose represented CS in the Chancery suit.

To the earl of Egremont

[London, ?December 1802]
My Lord,

I am greatly oblig'd to you for your favor of Yesterday's date. I beleive I can explain the claims (which however I have only partially made) in a manner that would satisfy your lordship as to the legality as well as the reasonableness of my having at least some assistance while I am engaged in a task so little suited either to my powers or my inclination as wading thro these affairs.

Mr Benjamin Smith not only charges his children 2700£ & upwards for seven years maintenance, but he charges 700£ for the business done as Executor to his father tho that business consisted in taking about seventeen thousand pounds more than could possibly belong to him. These accounts, or what he was pleased to call so, were however sufferd to pass & accepted, such as they were, by Mr Phipps the Commissioner directed by the award of Court to settle the terms on which Mr Benjamin Smith should be releas'd from the Prison where his collateral relations had put him.[1] Not that under such circumstances he could have supported these charges, but the alternative would have been that the Chancery Court would have laid hold on Mr Benjn Smith, & he would have been imprisond for life for the great devastavit he had made, had the accounts, garbled and falsified as they were, been examin'd by a Master.[2] As far as the maintenance of the children went, at 4 pC^{t} on the legacies left them by their Grandfather because it is by his Will directed to be so, he had an acknowledged right to charge——————

I have been so far from taking the advantages this wretched man did—& I trust my conduct has been so very opposite to his—that I will make no comparisons. I have had a very large and expensive family to bring up not only without any assistance from their father, but while he was tearing from them & me every thing he could & by his extreme folly & obstinacy undid and overset every exertion of mine, While he was only the stalking horse[3] of Robinson & Parkin. All that, however, is over. My earnings to the amount of 5000£,[4] Gifts & loans from my friends to the amount of above two more, & the Sum of 70£ a year, my little allowance, have at length carried me on till all my family are grown up. I have obtain'd an Ensigncy for the youngest thro your Lordships favor & interest, Money of his Brother Nicholas fitted him out, Harriet has an allowance directed by her Brother William, & If I could be freed from some debts unavoidably contracted & which harrass me dreadfully, I might hope to be allowed to die in quiet which is all I expect——————————

Mr Dayrell is positive, & There is I beleive no doubt but that the sum of 40£ p^r^ Annum for each of the children might be charged as legally by me as by Mr Benjn Smith for all the Legatees while they were with me, as well before as after they came of age, but this I never meant to press against Mrs Newhouse—— not because Her merit is greater but that her situation disarms me. I am so far from having taken, or meaning to take, any thing from her that I am at this time dunned & tormented almost to distraction for trifling debts left unpaid in 1800 when almost all I could get from my Bookseller, or otherwise received, I was oblig'd to lend her in five & ten guineas at a time to save her from actual want. On what she owes me, I shall never reckon; for what I give her, I shall never be thanked.[5] N'importe![6]

But I dare venture to beleive that Your Lordship on reflection & enquiry (if you think it necessary) will be convinced that for my actual expences I have a right to be repaid. I do not insist upon it as an Agent tho I may without arrogance say that nobody but me would have the patience & perseverance I have had, & that a Lawyer, tho he had been paid half of all he got in, could not have done it—— On that, however, I lay no stress & make no merit because, had my assiduity & attention been ten times greater than they were, they could not have avail'd me, unless I had met with the unusual & invaluable advantage of such a friend as your Lordship——

I will send down a statement of what I have had from the Estate & why, & if I have had any thing which cannot legally be allowed, I will most readily deduct it from what my children are still willing to allow—that is, Miss Smith, for herself & her deceasd Brother (Against my eldest Son, I never had or pretended to have any demand as he went to India in 1786).[7] My Nicholas gives me all, if I chuse to take it, & to him I can make up what I do take because, if I live, I shall have over his female Children by a Georgian Woman whom he is desirous of sending me to take care of & educate as well as I can, for he has been invariably kind & grateful to me, & I should delight in any creature that belong'd to him. However I shall not take any more of his money than as much as—if there is any difficulty as to allowing my claims—would prevent what I w^d^ not for the World incur, the hazard of y^r^ Lordships committing yourself in any way—— My Nicholas thinks nothing too much for his mother, & I have lately got him such Letters of recommendation as he wrote to me for, & as well I trust do all he wants done in the way of preferment. I have no scruple therefore in taking an hundred & fifty pounds of his if I want it for myself, Or for his Brother Lionel a larger Sum. All however I wish at present is an order on Messrs Pybus for 150£ to be replaced from any source y^r^ Lordship pleases among the legatees when the Monies for the Bills are received. If I could have made a bargain with Cadell & Davies, I should have been able to have commanded a great part of this money, which is at least 70£ of it, absolutely necessary for me on the 5th to pay the people of the house, or I shall suffer dreadfully—— more so than I can easily explain to y[r] Lordship, and God knows I came not to London for pleasure, nor have I myself expended half a crown except in Medicines, having been sick the greater part of the time & last night so ill with a nervous cough as to be forced to send for the first medical Man I could hear of, as I was everything but choaked.

God knows when my sufferings will end. I plunge into difficulties myself to save & serve M[r] B Smiths family. They may leave me there, if they will, perhaps, but I am sure they would soon discover how little they could do without me——

But this I know: that If I chose to abandon their interest, I could still support myself by writing & should be far richer than I am now & certainly much happier, but can I do so, or after having been so infinitely oblig'd to y[r] Lordship, leave to you all the trouble that must yet be taken? I should be unnatural in one case & ungrateful in the other——If however I have not a credit for money against friday, the day when the Man here says he must have it, I know not what I can do but send down & sell my books, the only things I have of my own, to raise money to pay for this campaign till I can take or be paid some—On y[r] Lordships mercy & consideration, I depend solely, & am y[r]

most grateful Ser[t],
Charlotte Smith

Petworth House Archives MS. No address or postmark.

NOTES

1. Collateral relations share the same ancestors, but are descended from a different line. (See Genealogical Chart.) CS, however, mistakenly uses the term to refer to her in-law Thomas Dyer, second husband of Mary Smith Berney (Richard Smith's daughter). Dyer brought the devastavit against BS and had him arrested (PHA #8202, a copy of Richard Smith's will in CS's handwriting, with interpretive notes by CS and William Tyler, includes this point).

2. BS claimed that the devastavit wronged him (see CS to Egremont, 15 Feb. 1802, n. 4).

3. Decoy. That is, Robinson and Parkin were only using him to conceal their own ends.

4. A more exact accounting, using information from the letters, confirms that CS earned at least £4,160 (Stanton, "Charlotte Smith's 'Literary Business,'" pp. 391–92).

5. Relations between CS and her daughter Lucy, whose marriage CS had opposed, must have continued to be strained.

6. No matter.

7. On this date, see CS to Egremont, [Sept. 1802], n. 5.

To the earl of Egremont

{Frant} Dec[r] 3rd 1802
My Lord,

I acknowledge with sincere gratitude the pains yr Lordship condescends to take & the patience you have in enduring the ingratitude & impertinence of M[r] B Smith. I never did or could think that you sided with such a Man; I must have been as mad & worthless as he is if I had. I have thought & still think that if no attention had been given to him at first & if M[r] Morgan had not encouraged his wicked attempts to rob me & his children, he would have been quieted sooner. Such is this man that, if he cannot have all he wants, he had <u>rather</u> see his own children ruind than not. Notwithstanding his defiance at this moment, I am well persuaded that his cowardice is equal to his senseless bravado: I have seen during the course of my miserable life repeated instances of this, for his folly has been in a regular gradation till now when I think it has nearly reached its climax. In regard to Mess[rs] Allen & R. Smiths claims, I still beleive they will find it more difficult than they are willing to own to bring them to an issue in Chancery; I am almost sure of it from what M[r] Hollist[1] has said of his inclination to an amicable settlement, which he would hardly have felt if he had not known it was a matter very doubtful. I apprehend some of the parties to be subpeon'd are not in the Kingdom & that at all events it will be a very tedious & uncertain suit——& inevitably entangled with the claims of Rich[d] Smith's estate against Berney, As I think I could convince y[r] Lordship's solicitor.

But my Lord all this in writing <u>cannot</u> be explained, or have I bodily strength to undertake it if I could. It would be an endless & unreasonable tax on your Lordships time, & I might only weary or perhaps offend you tho I am sure I shall never feel any thing but gratitude be the event what it may. Upon my word, My Lord, <u>I know not what to do or say</u>. Were I able to go to Town I would try to prevail by every means ~~of~~ which yet appear feasible to stop the evil which must accrue from the wickedness of this unnatural & inhuman wretch. It was long ago M[r] Boehms opinion, & it was that of his Son, that he should be deprived of the power of doing mischief, & yr Lordship, in saying that I ought to send my creditors to him, appeard to be of the same opinion. But I am every way disabled from acting by the want of the means of subsistence for myself & my family, & by the ruin of my health brought on by anxiety. I cannot tell what to do, nor what is to become of us all!

If M[r] Winterbottom & Dunn fyle an injunction, it will stop every dividend & every pay[t] of the Assets which are immediately coming to hand & perhaps prevent Mess[rs] Daniel from accepting the last bill. These were (among other reasons equally strong) those which most forcibly urged me to implore your Lordship to suffer the next bill to be discounted, and the last Bill accepted—— Would to God it could be done even now. In regard to the marriage articles, I entirely approve of their being laid before some Equity Lawyer. I imagine that as it never can be certain till I am actually dead that I shall not survive Mr B Smith, the Court would compel him to fulfil as far as can now be done his part of the contract, at least such was the opinion of Mr Bettesworth ~~who~~, Voluntarily, on seeing the marriage articles when Mr B. Smith made a purchase with my money of a certain piece of Woodland from Sir James Lake (which money was afterwards repaid & invested in the 3 pCts), he, Mr Bettesworth, desired me in private to fyle an amicable bill against Mr B Smith to secure the 3000£ so settled, for said he, "I fear he is going on very imprudently. You have a large family & may have more. Marriage is a valuable consideration, & Chancery would take care to put it out of your husbands power to leave you burthend with children so much worse than he found you"—— I told Mr Bettesworth I dared not. I was then a young Woman & thought not of consequences so much as of the present certainty that I should have been worse used than I was if I had attempted what he advised—— But I rather beleive he was reckon'd in Hampshire a very good Lawyer & was much trusted as a Man of integrity & abilities, & his advice I am sure was perfectly disinterested & founded on his opinion of Mr B Smiths weak & extravagant conduct, of which he exhibited specimens enough where ever he went. Not to trouble your Lordship too much, I enclose a few lines to Mr Tyler on this & other matters.

I employ'd a friend to enquire for cheap lodgings for me on the outskirts of London, who wrote to me on Wednesday that he had found such, but I must give my answer on Monday. My time in this house is expired. Lucy wants some of the furniture I have in use in it to enable her to remove to Northchapel, & I am uneasy at her being so long with Mr Turner, knowing he cannot afford it & that it distresses him. It is in the neighbourhood of London only that I can give that attention to the affairs that whatever turn they may take I must give. I therefore solicited such assistance as yr Lordships humanity might think reasonable to enable me to remove, & I can only say that it is far from my wish to do this on my own account, preferring rather to subsist if I could by my own labour than to be harrass'd & worn to death as I now am, but I see no other means but personal interviews with Messrs Winterbottom & Dunn & other parties to ward off the utter ruin of my family. God knows while I propose this whether I shall be able to execute it, my personal sufferings being great. But yr Lordship forbids complaint. Accept of my assurances of respect & Gratitude. I have the honor to be yr Lordships oblig'd Sert,

Charlotte Smith

Petworth House Archives MS. No address or postmark.

NOTE

1. Richard Hollist, lawyer and family advisor (see CS to Egremont, 18 July 1800, n. 2).

To William Tyler

[Frant, received 5 December 1802]
Sir,

I wish (as I have to day had the honor to say to Lord Egremont) that the Marriage articles may be laid before some eminent Lawyer in equity; if you think it necessary to draw up a state of the case, I shall be obliged to you to send me a copy of it.

You desired when you were here to have receipts for the money I had paid M^r^ B Smith. I was really ashamed on account of its extreme absurdity & unheard of folly to give you one for 200£ which I now enclose. The receipt for 20£ consists in Mr Taylers acknowledgement of having received my draft for that Sum which I will take another opportunity of sending. This paper was cut as it is to make it less heavy when I sent it from Bignor where I was (extremely ill) when I received it to Scotland to my poor Charles & Miss Smith.[1] I know not what excited his[2] rage but my writing to him twice for a receipt for the 200£ which was sent to him on the 5th of September preceding per <u>post</u>. Surely no person can wonder that I considerd with scorn & contempt every attempt of such a Man to injure his children farther than he had done & thought that such folly would defeat itself. Now however this unhappy Man, who is drunk with Gin half his time & sleeps most of the rest, will in despite of all I have sufferd & done & even of Lord Egremonts unexampled goodness ruin his surviving children——

Will you take the trouble to ans^r^ one question on which I am totally ignorant. Is a father obliged to maintain his daughter after she becomes of age?—— Harriet will complete her 21st year in a few weeks, & if her wretched father is not compelled to support her <u>then</u>, it is probably one part of his politics to trifle & cavil till after that period, & then say she is of age & must provide for herself, for there is nothing wicked or dishonest of which he is not capable.[3]

I beleive still that, notwithstanding M^r^ B Smith is so very fierce just now, he would be again alarmed when subpeona's are deliverd to him. Mr Turner advisd Miss Smiths fyling a bill against him to demand the residue, & since he desires Chancery,[4] I would advise his having enough of it.

If I understood you right, you told me Mr Tayler was not warranted in having paid M^r^ B Smith the interest on the 2000£. Ought I not therefore to prevent his paying him the next dividend of 50£—— Be so obliging as to return the Letter I sent you from Cadell & Davies, as I must endeavour to raise some present money & know not how else to do it. If I were on the spot, I might perhaps get thro some of these difficulties. I entirely agree with you that nothing can be more unfortunate than Mr B Smiths conduct in regard to Messrs Allen & Smith, for I am persuaded & have been so from the first that the business should be settled by amicable referrence——

You will be so good as to keep this senseless letter only if it is necessary as a receipt——I really beleive I have other Letters from the same unhappy person which would prove him a Mad Man if such evidence is ever admitted.

I am, Sir,
your obedt & obligd Sert,
Charlotte Smith

I shall be oblig'd to you to let me know what Counsel ~~xxx~~ Lord Egremont directs to be employ'd in Giving his opinion on the marriage articles.

What Mr B S. means by a second generation was (my having long before this heard) that he had made proposals of marriage to a Miss Gordon & that they had been accepted. I cared not if he had married all the fishwomen at Aberdeen, & certainly, in my Letters asking for a proper receipt, I never named any such stupid folly—— As to Rum & Sugar, I never had any of the first in my life, & of the latter four casks have since come of which he has had two. Nothing can be done with Mr B Smith but by absolute compulsion. I have seen a thousand proofs of it.

Petworth House Archives MS. No address or postmark.

NOTES

1. It is not clear when or why Charles and Charlotte Mary were in Scotland. Up to Aug. 1800, Charlotte Mary had lived for some time with Charles at Berwick-upon-Tweed, where he was stationed (see CS to Joseph Cooper Walker, 14 Apr. 1801). Berwick is in Northumberland, in extreme northeastern England. Charles and Charlotte Mary may have visited BS at his home in Hamilton, Scotland, which is not far from Berwick. BS's one surviving letter to Charlotte Mary (PHA #7364) is written in terms that suggest she was not altogether alienated from him.

2. That is, BS's rage.

3. On leaving London, BS writes to Egremont that CS and Harriet will get £100 a year from him "and more I cannot do." It is not clear whether CS's suspicions were justified (unpub. letter in PHA #0.11).

4. Although he threatens a Chancery suit in an 11 Oct. letter to Egremont, he denies that he wants one on 10 Dec. (unpub. letters in PHA #0.11).

To Thomas Cadell, Jr., and William Davies

Frant Tunbridge Wells
Decr 16th 1802
Sirs,

I received so long since as the 9th Novr the valuation of my small library which you were so obliging as to obtain for me——I felt sufficiently reluctant before to part with books which are not only my greatest resource but have enabled me to counteract at a former period the misfortunes brought upon me wholly by the cruelty & misconduct of others. Yet that reluctance is considerably encreased by the low price offerd tho I am persuaded you did your utmost in the troublesome commission you were so very obliging as to undertake.

I delay'd from time to time coming to any resolution about them in the hope, I own, that Lord Egremont would be prevaild upon to allow a considerable bill due the 7th of Jany 1803 to be discounted; in which case I should receive a Sum of Money wch would preclude the necessity of my making this dreaded sacrifice, & I hoped I had prevaild on his Ldship either to do that, or at least to agree paying the money (3430£) among my children, legatees to their Grandfather, when it actually becomes due wch will now happen in the course of three weeks. But such has been the perverseness & unaccountable infatuation of M^r B Smith that, because Lord Egremont cannot comply with his demands (which are illegal & would make his Lordship liable to future litigation), he has written to him to desire that he would put the affairs into Chancery which will prevent for five or six years the payment of what remains due to his <u>own</u> children of money which I have with great difficulty preserved for them by Lord Egremonts interposition. His Lordship is justly incensed at such conduct, and tho it is indeed very hard that this person should have a second or third time the power to undo the children whom he has from their infancy abandond, yet I fear Lord Egremont will no longer render himself liable to the improper & importunate Applications of such a Man, but will divest himself of the whole business by Chancery.

M^r B Smith has possess'd himself of the whole income of my fortune from which he refuses to let me & his younger children (who were unprovided for by his father having been born after his death) Have any assistance whatsoever & he has withdraw [*sic*] the small share of it which he used to allow me. I have taken every method in my power to prevail on him to be just to <u>them</u> if not to me, but as fast as any agreement is nearly made, he flies off & insists upon money from the Trustees which it is not in their power to grant him. I am weary of the attempt and have wearied Mr Bicknell & all my friends in this most irksome & hopeless negociation. Lord Egremont talks of causing a bill to be fyled against him to compel him to fulfil his part of the settlement made on my marriage, but before it can be brought to an issue, three terms, if not many more must elapse, and I shall want bread——

It is under these humiliating circumstances, and at a time of year when money is particularly wanted, that I find it absolutely necessary to take some resolution. My engagement with M[r] Phillips is nearly completed; it consisted of an abridged history of [Engla]nd for the use principally of young persons, in [which every] thing is omitted that is either unnecessary [for their] information or improper for their reading aloud to their Masters.[1] I have found the work most tedious & disagreeable & long to releive my mind by some pleasanter undertaking of which I have two in hand that I have lain by while this went on & while I was so perplexd by the unfortunate situation of my affairs. One of them is a School book of Poetry[2] to exercise the memories of Children between the ages of five & nine years old to which I meant to have added plates of the subjects from my own drawings, which, as they are cheifly on natural history, I can do with some precision & perhaps taste. If, induced by the recollection of a former connection, not I trust wholly unprofitable, you should feel disposed to become proprietors of such a work, which I think might be ready for publication in June & would make me an advance not exceeding 40£ by a bill at four or five months (which M[r] Fauntleroy would discount for me), I should then be able to reserve the most useful part of my books & releived from my present most unpleasant situation. But I beg of you to bear in mind that I would add to the agreement a stipulation that, in case of my death before the accomplishment of it, your advance or any loss that might accrue from it should be repaid by my Son Nicholas Hankey Smith who empowers me to receive any money payable to him here from his Grandfathers estate. The Copy right of Emmeline is you may recollect mine; Can you allow me nothing for that? In a word, can you assist me consistently with your own safety & profit which is all I desire? M[r] Hayley informd my daughter some time since that he would order his last publication about animals (the title I forget)[3] to be left at Y[r] Shop for her perusal to be returnd for the profit of the person who made the drawings. If it is there, be so good as to let me know. I am, Gent[n], y[r] obligd humble Ser[t], Charlotte Smith

I trust that you will not mention to any other of the profession the purport of this Letter, as such communications give great advantage over luckless Authors who are obliged to subsist by their writing. I consider you as friendly to me, even tho you may decline my proposal & as such I have been very explicit.[4]

Yale University MS. Address: Mess[rs] Cadell & Davies/ Strand/ London/ Single—/ Post-paid. Postmark: TUNB-WELLS/ 36; F/ PAID/ DEC17/ 1802.

NOTES

1. See CS to Joseph Cooper Walker, late Mar.–early Apr. 1802. The history for Phillips was not published until 1806. Words are supplied in this sentence where the seal was torn away.

2. *Conversations Introducing Poetry* (London: Joseph Johnson, 1804), first described to Davies earlier in the year (see CS to Davies, 18 Feb. 1802 and n. 3). The second project "in hand" (not named) was either *Natural History of Birds* or her next volume of poetry, *Beachy Head,* both published posthumously by Johnson.

3. In 1802 Hayley first published *A Series of Ballads,* nos. 1–4, with engravings by William Blake. In 1805, fourteen ballads, with additional plates by Blake, were published as *Ballads . . . founded on Anecdotes Relating to Animals, with Prints . . . by William Blake* (London: R. Phillips).

4. A note in another hand reads: "(declined Dec[r] 20)."

1803
"AN HOUSELESS BEGGAR"

—31 JANUARY 1803

In February 1803, Charlotte Smith's worst fears of destitution and abandonment came true. With no income from writing, her books unsold, all interest payments from her marriage articles going to Benjamin Smith, and child support from the trust blocked by Egremont and Tyler, she was evicted from modest lodgings in Frant and forced to seek an even poorer place to live. Her quarrel with her brother, Nicholas Turner, the other trustee to the estate, deepened as he joined Egremont and Tyler in objecting to any and all suggestions she made to settle the trust. She was incredulous when Samuel Rose's arbitration of trust moneys awarded Benjamin Smith more than she thought his right. Benjamin, in London for that settlement, was outraged that she got more and he got less than he expected. Along with gout, rheumatism, and pleurisy, her illnesses now included terrifying heart palpitations that led to seizures during which she could not breathe. Stripped of hope and dignity, she continued to write letters seeking justice. This year's letters show the depth of her mental anguish, her anger at years of unrewarded labor, and her fear that somehow she might have deserved her miseries, as those around her seemed to think.

In a valiant effort to recover her independence, she proposed a new children's book about poetry to Cadell and Davies, but they rejected it. Moreover, it was September before she could work actively again in settling the trust. Her labors and distresses left her unable to walk, but not unable to challenge Egremont's accusations, and the year ended with her sending the earl remarkably bitter letters.

To Michael Bowman[1]

Frant n^r Tunbridge Wells
Jany 5th 1803
Dear Sir,

I should have answerd your Letter immediately on receiving it, but I was that day extremely ill, & since, I have been extremely alarmed by the news from Bombay that I employed what strength I had in writing Letters of enquiry on the subject. The Papers of to day have somewhat mitigated but by no means appeased my uneasiness. My second Son, Garrison Paymaster at Bombay, was personally acquainted with the Ambassador sent from Persia & was, at the Ambassadors desire, appointed to go with him to Bengal. His knowledge of the Persian language & his friendship for the Ambassador, as well as his desire to see his elder Brother at Calcutta, had determined him to undertake this engagement, & he expected to go about the middle of July. His last Letter to me dated the 1st July, being, he said, the last he should write till he got to Bengal. The death therefore of this Persian (with whom I know my Son constantly was) by assassination naturally gave me the severest alarms for his safety——As it was hardly possible to suppose that the Europeans about him were not implicated in his danger.[2] My Son sent me over his little Girl of five years old in the course of last Summer, & on this dear child's account, as well as on my own & his Sisters, I suffer inexpressibly from the uncertainty I am still in as to this very unfortunate affair.

To recur to others of an unfortunate complexion also, I beg leave to state to you that ever since I encreased my personal & pecuniary obligations to you last Winter in London, I have been contending with the most cruel oppression on the part of Mr Benjn Smith, who Came to town early in the Spring[3] & has possess'd himself of all the income of my fortune under the auspices of a Mr Follet of the Temple. I own I did not imagine he would have found any Lawyer who would have assisted him, but it seems that my marriage articles give him every thing & that I have no remedy but in the Commons. Not content with having so far robbed me & having left his younger Children & me absolutely destitute, he has so harrassed Lord Egremont with threats of making him account in Chancery & other most absurd & impertinent applications that his Lordship has repeatedly declared his resolution of getting rid of such importunity entirely by throwing the whole business into that Court.

In a word, there is no describing all I have endured, & it has thrown me into a state of health from which I am convinced I shall never recover. I have lately had such attacks of that palpitation of the heart, for which you was so good as to give me medicine & advice last winter that I was desired about three weeks since to call in a Physician. But I am convinced, & I beleive Dr Sutterby[4] thinks so too, that it is a disease originating in an over wearied mind & corrosive uneasiness. I have several times been oblig'd to get up in the night & call my family, for, as my pulse was so quick it could not be counted & I could not breathe, I beleived myself dying, and indeed I am now persuaded I shall expire in one of these seizures. Mr B Smith professes a desire that I should die. My situation therefore is rather a motive for his perseverence in the conduct he now holds.

I wish'd a medical friend to represent my state of health to Lord Egremont, but his Ldp is now in the West, & I obtain but little attention to any thing I can say. Within this week however, I had a Letter from him from Bath in which he says he beleives he shall determine to divide the next installment, due now in a few days. I have written to entreat of him to do so because then I shall have some money lent me by my children. But I have no answer & think it but too probable that he may not come to town, or if he does that he may alter his mind should Mr B Smith again irritate him. Miss Smith will be in Town if Lord E. determines to pay the money, & I do assure you my first purpose is to acquit myself, if not entirely, yet as far as I may have at that time the power of my obligation to you— —

In July last, I went over to Petworth by Lord Egremonts directions to settle some accounts in hopes of obtaining a general arra[ngem]ent previous to the general settlement, which I thought might have [bee]n brought about to the advantage & quiet of all parties. Lord E. however went away to France & left the business with his Steward, & while I waited at my Sisters house at Bignor Park, his leisure to go over the accounts, I was sent for express by Miss Smith, Harriet having been seized with a violent fever &, as it was feared, being then at the point of death. On my return (in doing which I received from an accident in the post chaise a violent blow on the head which I have ever since felt & which stunned me for a considerable time), I found Harriet delirious, convulsed & with such other complaints as made her case appear desperate. She remaind long in a most dreadful state, the delerium continuing long after the fever was subdued. As my medical friends here had had an infinite deal of trouble, coming twice & three times a day & one of them sitting up three nights when the fever was at its height to watch the symptoms, I wish'd as immediately as I could to settle their account & make them some Compliment.

I therefore sent the former to Mr B Smith who had affected extreme anxiety ~~about~~ on account of his daughter & to cry to his friends about his poor dear Harriet. He had just received 100£ of mine, when I requested on such an occasion the payment of 13£, but he sent me the bill back again, as he does all the applications I make to him, sometimes in a double cover to put me to more expence,[5] & said he had already disposed of his money & could pay no such bill, nor has he ever sent me or his children one shilling, tho the expences of Harriets illness alone were 50£ which has considerably added to my distress.

Lord Egremont has repeatedly desired me to send my Creditors to him, but his Lordship does not consider, that I cannot do this with my butcher &

baker, & as to superior demands, how can I trouble those who have so kindly trusted me on my own credit with the irksome operation of trying to recover their money from a Man who shrinks from all that is honest or honourable by concealing his abode? The person thro whom I used to write to him[6] now pretends that he knows not where he is, & I have no means of applying to him but thro this Mr Benjamin Follet, his Attorney in the Temple, who advises him to set me & all who apply to him on my behalf at defiance. I most heartily wish he could be made to know that he cannot with impunity continue to receive my income & leave me & his family absolutely destitute. He now waits in town to receive the dividends due this month of which he will not let me have a penny tho they arise from my fortune. I have been tedious in this explanation, but it is not meant by it to excuse myself from what I feel due in every way to you. I have long had it in contemplation to sell my books, the only things I can raise any money upon, but for 1000 volumes of the best Authors in French & English & in very good condition, I am offer'd only 100£ which, deducting the carriage, is not 1^{s} 6^{d} a volume. To this sacrifice, however, I must submit if Lord Egremont does go to Chancery. I am, Dear Sir, y^{r} obligd Ser^{t},

Charlotte Smith

Huntington MS (HM10832). Address: Mr Bowman/ Harley Street/ Cavendish Square/ London. Postmark: TUNB-WELLS/ 36.

NOTES

1. An apothecary and surgeon; see Biographical Notes.

2. Nicholas was in greater danger than CS realized, greater after than during the assassination. He had been selected to accompany the Persian ambassador to Bengal in June 1802, but the assassination took place at the ambassador's house in July before their scheduled departure. Edward Strachy, the mehmendar, appointed Nicholas mehmendar in his absence, while he traveled to Bengal with the news. Staying behind, Nicholas had a central role in conciliating the Persians and was praised for his "zealous service" and the "benefits derived from his intercourse at the Embassy" (IRO Personal Records, Ref #0/6/3, 3:607–608). Strachy's letter of 26 July 1802 justifies appointing Nicholas in terms of highest praise (corroborating CS's high regard for this son):

> his house has been a constant place of resort to them [the Persians]: and there are I am confident but few of the party, who have not benefited in some way or other by his hospitality or his humanity. His great knowledge of the familiar part of their language, and of their names and character; his happy disposition and many of his habits make him an excellent companion for them. (IRO Personal Records Ref # 0/6/9, 9:256)

3. No letters to Egremont and Tyler survived from the spring of 1802 to suggest exactly when BS arrived.

4. Not identified.

5. The double cover was probably to protect his identity from creditors.

6. BS's friend the merchant Robert Tayler, who received BS's mail from Egremont as well.

To the earl of Egremont

Frant. Jany 7th 1803
My Lord,

I beg leave to remind your Lordship that this day the bill for 3412£ 10s becomes payable & will be paid when presented at Mr Daniels.[1] I trust My last Letter convinced you that I am not so wrong, so impracticable as you seem to have beleived. Subdued by sickness & oppression, prevented by the burthens I am forced to sustain from earning my own independance, & every way condemned to unmerited suffering, I am so far from having any courage to oppose what ever is intended that I desire only to have as much as may at present release me from actual want. All voice, all opinion is taken from me, but it does not appear that, however I may submit, I can regain the confidence yr Lordship formerly honourd me with. I beg your pardon if I am impatient, but this state of continual suspence & anxiety is more than I am able to endure. Nor have I the means of subsisting Mr Smiths family.

My Lord, the unfortunate Young Man who lost his life in Barbados when occupied in the laudable hope of benefitting his Sisters & his family is, as if yet unburied, his Sister having had no means of paying the expences of his cruel illness and funeral, till this last due bill is paid from which she means to apply a Sum for that purpose & has solemnly promisd to do so, to the persons to whom the money is oweing in the course of this month. I did hope I should not have been under the painful necessity of reminding your Lordship of this circumstance which has long distress'd my feelings & Charlottes. I named it to your Lordship when I had the honor of seeing you at Petworth. But my hope of being heard as you once heard me, either relative to the living or the dead, becomes daily fainter—— I cannot be silent, yet hardly dare to trouble you!——— If Mr Benjn Smith could be either compelled or persuaded to agree to a general & final settlement & all the other parties acquiesed, would your Lordship approve of having the last (& I am sorry to call it the unaccepted bill due July 7th discounted, & the whole matter so decided upon and ended as to finish Your trouble entirely? I know it might be done, & when I recollect the infinite trouble you have had & how much with reason your Lordship complains of what remains, I most earnestly wish it that I may no longer lament the painful circumstance of hazarding the entire loss of your Lordships friendship and good opinion by the weight of those disagreeable affairs which those flattering & generous sentiments first induced you to undertake.

Miss Smith joins with me in entreating yr Lordships early decision, as she must be in town in two or three days.

I have the honor to be Y^{r} Lordships obligd & obed^{t} Ser^{t},
Charlotte Smith

Petworth House Archives MS. No address or postmark.

NOTE

1. Thomas Daniel, a merchant, had handled money for CS and the trust as early as 1797.

To the earl of Egremont

[Frant] Jany 9th 1803
My Lord,

The lines on the preceding pages I wrote on the 7th but on reflection did not send them, hardly allowing myself to doubt y^{r} Lordships goodness in attending to the pay^{t} of the Bill when due, after what I had before taken the liberty to trouble you with, but not having heard & now despairing of your thinking of it, Pressed beyond endurance with accumulated sufferings, & literally without a shilling for the immediate purposes of my familys expence so that I am in danger of wanting bread & [am] exposed to insults from every quarter more dreadful to endure than every thing else. Imperious necessity, my Lord, forces me to remind you of my situation & that of my family and to observe to you that it is hard so much money should lie useless, benefitting nobody but Messrs Pybus,[1] while those to whom it belongs want the actual necessaries of life.

It is trite & useless to say that the best Men in exalted situations cannot judge of the condition of the less fortunate, but indeed, my Lord, if your Lordship could know a twentieth part of what I have undergone these last eight or ten months, I cannot but think you would be sorry for me & would not prolong my misery when it is in y^{r} power to releive it—— My poor George is now order'd to join the 47th, which is arrived at Portsmouth, but has no money for the expence of his March from thence to the quarters assigned to the Reg^{t}. He says in a Letter I re^{d} from him yesterday, "I would not ask you, knowing yr distress, but I have no money at the Agents, & what can I do? Gordons father has sent him 30£, & I beleive he would share it with me, but I am afraid of borrowing least I should not have it to repay, & generally Gordon is as poor as myself, only he has a father, & I have worse than none"——

Is then this wretched, this worthless, this infamous brute to ruin utterly My unhappy children! Is he to reduce me to beggary in the streets? And have I no remedy? I enclose yr Lordship ~~the copy of~~ a Letter from Mr Boehm[2] which, if you will take the trouble to read, you will see he does not think me so wrong.

It would be a mercy were my life to be immediately ended rather than to die in these lingering tortures. My Lord, I once more call upon your humanity, your justice, & your former assurances of friendship on which I relied to relieve me from the misery inflicted on me & Am

yr obedt oblig'd Sert,
Charlotte Smith

It is too late now to save for me any part of my half years income. That voracious unfeeling Monster to whom possession of it is given has no doubt seized it—Good God what am I to do? What is to become of me!———

Petworth House Archives MS. No address or postmark.

NOTES

1. Pybus, Call, Grant, and Hale, Egremont's bankers.
2. Edmund Boehm, who married Richard Smith's granddaughter, Dorothy Elizabeth Berney (see CS to John Robinson, 19 Sept. 1785, n. 5, and Genealogical Chart).

To the earl of Egremont

Frant
Jany 13th
1803
My Lord,

I am much oblig'd to your Lordship for your last Letter from Bath. My daughter will be in Town on Monday & wd have set out the end of this week but was oblig'd to wait 'till her friend Mr Josepth Smith[1] lent her some money on her dividend and procur'd her a place to be in, for, having her unhappy business in Barbados to settle, she must stay some days.

If I knew to what sums your Lordship objects as doubtful, I should better know how to make out the distribution. As I do not wish to contradict or raise any difficulties, I merely wish the Will to be completed as far as it can be done & submit to yr Lordship whether the claims, however small, which are establish'd by it, can be wholly overlook'd. In regard to Miss Smiths demand on account of her poor Brother or any other doubtful point, she is well content to let them stand over till your Lordship obtains such advice as you wish to have on their propriety & to settle them by the last bill———

I cannot imagine that Mr Turner will finally raise any difficulty in regard to the manner in which I wish to dispose of My Son Nicholas's money, As he has directed in a Letter I lately had from him that what I do not want at present should be put into the stocks for his child's use, & as, in case of my death which is a very probable event, My eldest daughter has by his direction the care & management of the little Girl, surely My daughter is the properest person to receive the dividends. Mr Turner is not perhaps aware that for persons in the East Indies, dividends cannot be received by power of Attorney but must be received in person by those in whose name it stands jointly with the proprietor. For example, If your Lordship was to put in money in the name of any person in India & your own, you could not authorise your Banker to receive the dividend but must appear personally. Now this could not fail to be the case were Mr Turner to put Mr N. H. Smith's money in in his name, & it must put him to great inconvenience & useless expence Merely for a matter of etiquette. Another still stronger objection is that, if once so placed, a new bank power of Attorney must be sent to India & return'd before it can be removed into the hands of those to whom it is his intention to leave the disposal of it, for the use of his Children. For I am very sure that Nicholas will comply with my wishes & send over a power to me & his Sister exclusively, & he would doubtless have done it before now, but he could not imagine his Uncle would dream of opposing his desires & my wishes, & indeed I did not expect from my own brother any opposition to my wishes for my own children & Grand children, and it is no small addition to my many vexations that he should combine to add to them. Poor Man—My heart is heavy for him however I may feel that he is unkind; his Wife is I fear dying, & he will be desolate & miserable without her. Very far should I be from adding to his troubles.

I have had a most kind Letter from the Dts of Devonshire.[2] Indeed it would have given me great concern to have offended her Grace to whom I was so very much oblig'd, & I am releived from great uneasiness to find she still honors me with her Good opinion. I am in some hopes poor Mr Smith may be brought to some final & reasonable settlement. In which case it might perhaps be possible to make such a general arrangement of the Affairs altogether as might releive your Lordship from the burthensome & unwelcome task you so generously undertook, & me from the pain of fearing I shall entirely forfeit your kindness by what I cannot help.

The extreme cold I undergo in this old house has so nearly deprived me the use of my limbs that I cannot write legibly. Forgive that & all the other errors of Your Lordships

most grateful Ser^r^, Charlotte Smith

Having had a Letter from Mr Halliday[3] about M^r^ B Smith & his complaints of cruelty from his family, I have answerd that I will leave the matters in debate between him & me to any two friends of his own. To Mr Boehm & Mr Halliday himself or any two persons they shall appoint for him. What can I say more fair or reasonable?

If I might hope for an answer by the post of Sunday, I would regulate as far as I could the distribution to send up by Miss Smith on Monday, but I am afraid of proposing any thing which y^r^ Lordship may think wrong.

Petworth House Archives MS. No address or postmark.

NOTES

1. A "distant relation": see CS to Egremont, 26 Oct. 1801, and n. 3.

2. The duchess would not have helped much other than to reassure CS of her good opinion. Her health was deteriorating, and her own finances were straitened.

3. In a letter of 6 May 1803 to the earl of Egremont (unpub. letter in PHA #0.11), BS cites two passages from a letter by CS to Halliday, almost certainly the one mentioned here. In the first passage, BS is so desperate for money that he cites CS's argument to support his request:

> I have told Lord E (and he is not pleased at my doing so) that I think this hardly right, because he consented to the agreement made by poor Charles with M^r^ B Smith and Lord Egremont himself gave the drafts and all partys consented . . .

The second passage is her proposal to BS through Halliday for outside arbitration:

> I beg Sir the favor of you to say to M^r^ B Smith that the only probability there is of his obtaining what he wants wo^d^ be to write to Lord Egremont to say he is willing to enter into terms for the final close of the Trust with his family, that he will agree to let the business go on without interruption, and the residue be placed in the funds and to divide with me and his Children the whole income and that two friends of his own shall be Named as receivers of his money and guardians of all his rights while I shall be allow'd so far as to act as Executrix as to be impowerd without any participation or interference to recover the outstanding debts. I mean to take on all the trouble But not for me to touch the money but his friends to receive that as residue when I get it and lastly that he shall make a provision for his unprovided for Children out of my fortune in case I die before him while he lives and divide equally my property among them under such restrictions as shall be for their certain benefit. On Mr Smiths agreeing positively to these terms I think I co^d^ prevail for him to have the £400 on Miss Smiths consenting.

Simon Halliday, whom CS elsewhere calls BS's "soi-disant friend" (CS to William Tyler, unpub., 16 Jan. 1803), had become BS's ally and advocate in the hope of collecting a £2000 debt the estate owed to his father, Simon H. Halliday (see CS to Egremont, 14 and 15 Oct. 1803). CS and the younger Halliday exchanged several letters in 1803 (see CS to Charlotte Mary Smith, 2 Feb.; CS to Samuel Rose, 7 Apr.; CS to Tyler, 15 Apr.; and CS to Egremont, 14 and 15 Oct.). Of that correspondence, only one letter by him (PHA #7364) and the above passages by her survive. Halliday's daughter Jane married into the Dyer family (see Genealogical Chart).

To the earl of Egremont

[Frant, 15 January 1803]
My Lord,

Inconsistent I may be, for I really am more harrass'd than I have strength either of body or mind to bear. I perfectly know the reason of Mr Turners opposition, & if I must, I will say what those reason's are, but I had rather your Lordship w^{d} for once give me credit for knowing what I say to be true, & beleive me, I beseech you, My Lord, when I assure you I say nothing off hand, or do I quoffle[1] & falsify. I have Mr Turner's own Letters in which he tells me he will have so & so done with Nicholas's money. Good God! that my own relation should combine with Mr Benjn Smith to throw impediments in the way of this little pittance's (secured with so much trouble and purchased by the life of poor Charles) being placed as I desire & as the proprietor himself directs.

What is it to Mr Turner, & why does he trouble himself only about that? Will he compel me to give your Lordship the detail of all that has pass'd about it? I will not by him be trifled with & made more wretched than I am already. It was not for this his Nephew entrusted him,[2] Nor I desired him to be Trustee. Does he act like a brother? I said, My Lord, & I say still that it is extremely hard that on me is to be thrown the trouble of writing & engaging my friends in Barbados to take such unpleasant affairs in hand, when doubts were started whether I was entitled to the expences even of postage—When all my former trouble has ended in my being told I must be treated like a child, that I knew nothing of the matter & was to have no voice even in things which are absolutely a part of the Will. I must, my Lord, say, tho perhaps at the risk of offending you, that half the trouble your Lordship has had, would have ended the matter if you had deignd to have lent me that confidence which in the beginning of the business you honor'd me with, If you had deignd to hear what I had to say with your former candour & to have retain'd so much of your once good opinion of me, as I beleive, that I should neither injure these young people to whom my youth

& maturity has been dedicated at the age of near fifty three; nor, when I am more likely than ever to understand business & to feel the extent of my obligation to your Lordship, should so act as to involve you, my greatest benefactor, either in trouble or pecuniary lost [*sic*]. Yet for nothing of all this do you now give me credit. I repeat that, if you will listen to me, I know the whole may be settled & got thro. M^r^ B Smith will be brought to terms which are more reasonable than those he offers, & the Allens business compromisd without a Law suit.

Pray, My Lord allow me to try this—— Give me a carte blanche only thus far—— Say that after the present money is divided, you will have a general statement made of the remainder, the last bill accepted & agree to such an arrangement as Mr Benjn Smith & his children & M^r^ & Mrs Allen &c[3] can make in Regard to the whole & to put a final close to the business. Only say positively my Lord that you will do this, & if in the next three months, you are not exonnerated from every trouble & have nothing more to do than to receive the thanks of all parties, then I shall have had some more trouble & mortification, but no evil can result to you. Whereas continual difficulties started & shifting the ground so often—now Mr Smith threatening & now Mr Turner objecting & now the Allens advancing & retreating—there never can be an end to it, & my children, who have now waited seven & twenty years for their legacies, may all be dead before the last division is paid them.

I am helpless, My Lord; being without money to pay my bills here, I cannot go to London, & being so lately dangerously ill, I know not how to encounter the extreme severity of the weather, but I cannot starve & something I must do. Miss Smith had already made every appointment, and I hoped y^r^ Lordship might have been spared the trouble of attending yrself, as Mr Tyler was to be in town & Mr Turner shall have nothing to do with it. But however, Miss Smith will be in Town on Sunday evening, & I hope no further delay will encrease y^r^ Lordships trouble.

Supposing Mr Tyler in town, I have written to him not to trouble y^r^ Lordship with one of my long letters.

I am ever
your Lordships grateful Ser^t^,
Charlotte Smith

[Frant] 15th Jany 1803

Petworth House Archives MS. No address or postmark.

NOTES

1. Not in the *OED*.

2. Turner held a power of attorney for Nicholas Smith in India, and consistently refused to use it to benefit CS. She felt this refusal violated her son's obvious intention of

aiding her in any way that he could, for he had sent her money yearly since the early 1790s.

3. That is, the Smith and Allen claim. Richard Smith and Mary Gibbes Smith Allen were children of BS's older brother, Richard Smith. (See Genealogical Chart.) They threatened to turn the case over to Chancery, and did so on 14 May 1803 (PHA #8010).

To the earl of Egremont

Frant. Jan[y] 31st
1803
My Lord,

In pursuance of Miss Smiths order from y[r] Lordship, I send up the bill of Mess[rs] Green & Ward.[1] I am sorry it is not to be paid out of the Estate immediately, as I have the order under yr Lordships hand & Mr Turners. I am still more sorry that Chancery is again talk'd of as a reason why this cannot be done. I have been harrass'd with that menace the whole Summer, & as ~~xxxxx~~ all that I was orderd to do, I have done; as I am now wholly divested of every power, of every voice, & of every shilling, I had in the World; As I am an houseless beggar & likely to die in an hospital, I hoped there would be an end at least of all talk of Chancery. I have been made to look like a fool, if not a swindler, to M[r] Green and Ward, but that is nothing to the purpose.

I do not know why I should care tho what is done Since I cannot be worse than I am.

I wish (as I am not able to write ~~a~~ long Letters any more) to have it understood by the parties that if your Lordship is so good as to be Trustee or if you decline it, I in either case am determind that no new appointment of mine shall ever make the Revd Nicholas Turner my Trustee & certainly not Mr Tayler.[2] I am too ill & too much oppress'd by the horrors of poverty, which I have so long endeavourd to ward off from others but which now crush me myself to the Earth, to be able to say more than to express my concern at & thanks for all the trouble I have given your Lordship. I have desired Miss Smith to communicate what I wrote on the matter of my own Trust of the 7000£ to day. I have never the good fortune to be understood, write on what I will, And therefore it is better wholly to desist.

I have the honor to be
gratefully & truly
y[r] Lordships obed[t] Ser[t],
Charlotte Smith

I would humbly propose, with all due deference to M[r] Trustee Turner that you w[d] be pleas'd to let the 800£ now payable On account of M[r] Nicholas Hankey Smith in the 4 pC[ts] instead of the 3pC[ts] because then the little there will be for the support of his poor little Girl will be payable four times a year instead of ~~four~~ twice (& I should be glad you would order y[r] Banker & not M[r] Turner to receive the dividends).

I offer this suggestion in great humility. Perhaps M[r] Turner may know of some better security & more punctual & certain payment, Or I may be told that it is impossible, and all nonsense—— Most unlucky I am in every thing I propose. I will send up the papers (not accounts for they are refused

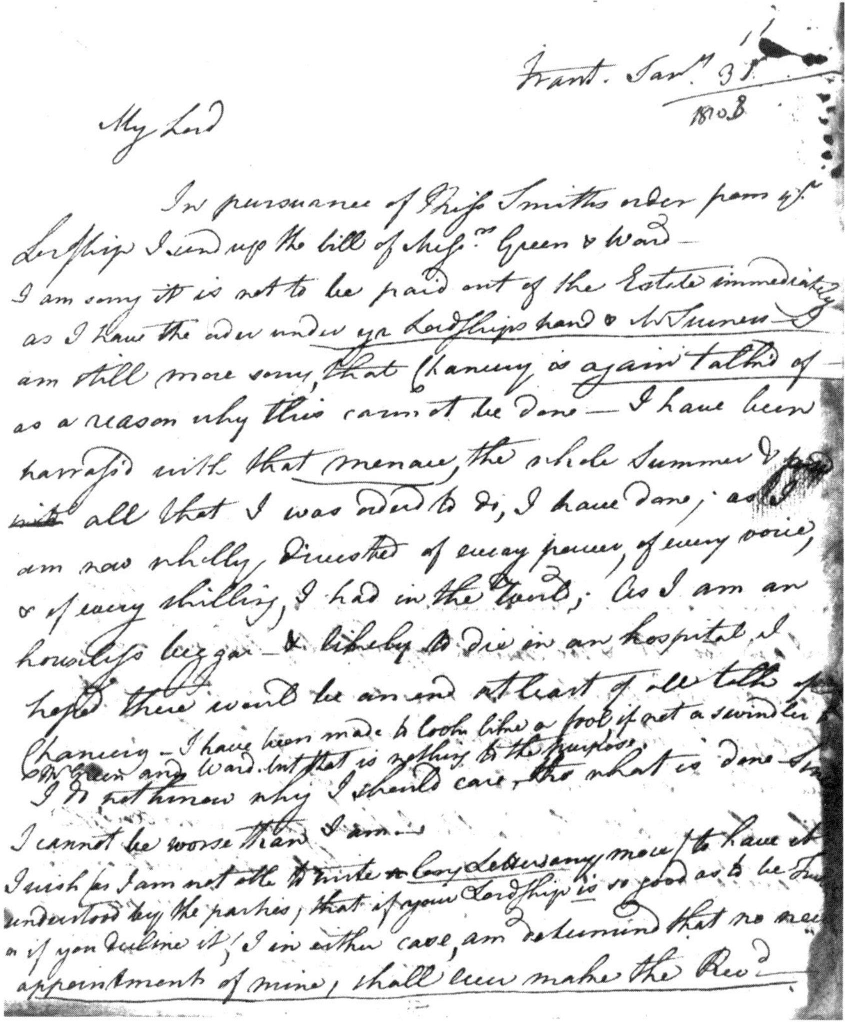

Frant. Jan[y] 31
1803

My Lord

In pursuance of Miss Smiths order pr. my y[r]
Lordship I send up the bill of Mess[rs] Green & Ward—
I am sorry it is not to be paid out of the Estate immediately
as I have the order under y[r] Lordships hand & M[r] Turners—I
am still more sorry, that Chancery is again talkd of—
as a reason why this cannot be done— I have been
harrass'd with that menace, the whole Summer & [illegible]
~~with~~ all that I was order'd to do, I have done; as I
am now wholly divested of every power, of every voice,
& of every shilling, I had in the World; As I am an
houseless beggar—& likely to die in an hospital, I
hoped there would be an end at least of all talk of
Chancery—I have been made to look like a fool if not a swindler
M[r] Green and Ward. but that is nothing to the purpose.
I do not know why I should care tho what is done
I cannot be worse than I am—
I wish for I am not able to write or copy Letters any more, to have it
understood by the parties, that if your Lordship is so good as to be Trus[tee]
or if you decline it, I in either case, am determind that no mee[ting]
appointment of mine, shall ever make the Rec[d]

Figure 5. Letter to the earl of Egremont, 31 Jan. 1803.

& fifty lies told ab[t] them by M[r] Tayler) relative to the Berney business,[3] but I see it will be useless & merely giving y[r] Lordship trouble, for, if I think it right, it will be declared wrong.

In no one instance for these last twenty months, has any one thing I have named been complied with, or one word of kindness or friendship mitigated the harshness of continual contradiction & refusal. I cannot impute this to your Lordship. It must be that I am grown a fool from excess of misery, & deserve what I undergo———

Petworth House Archives MS. No address or postmark. Photograph by Michael Moore, by permission of the Right Honorable the Lord Egremont, Petworth House Archives, West Sussex Record Office.

NOTES

1. Not identified.

2. Robert Tayler, BS's ally in London and at one time trustee to all three of CS's marriage settlements.

3. That is, the claim of Robert Berney, grandson of Richard Smith.

To Charlotte Mary Smith[1]

[Frant, 2 February 1803]
My Dear Charlotte,
2nd Feb[y]
1803

Sleep has been so much a stranger to me that, quite wearied out, I desir'd Betty last night not to call me this morning when the postman came if I happen'd not to ring before, & fortunately for me but unfortunately for my business, I slept till past ten o'clock. Harriet, you know, when well, is not matinal, & now she is ill, with this erysipelas,[2] she sleeps somewhat more. My days are so very wretched that it is something to be able to shorten them. How long is it to last? I have had no answer about my books & know not if that resource is still left me. I thought to have heard to day but had no Letter but yours.

In looking back while I have been sorting papers on the last sixteen years of my miserable life, I cannot but marvel at the singularity of my destiny: The hard struggles I have had to support M[r] Benj[n] Smiths children, at first eight in number; the amazing quantity of writing I have executed, whether for the press or to ward off poverty & oppression they were threatend with & sufferd under; and the various efforts I made to obtain friends for them, all ending in my being deprived at last, & that thro my best friend, Lord

Egremont & my Brother of even the scanty allowance of 70£ a year which even Robinson[3] defended for me & preserved to me, & with which I cannot imagine that the present Trustees have any thing to do, but to pay, while they retain any power over the 3000£, the 70£ a year, as did the former Trustees. You say Mr Tayler assured you he should not have broken his word with me & have paid Mr B Smith the 100£ had not Lord Egremont ~~and Mr Turner~~ orderd him to do it. ~~What had they, at least Mr Turner to do with it~~ & why, Good God, would Lord Egremont thus lend his assistance to take from me the little I might have had, & reduce me literally to want bread? ill & reduced health as I am. After his Lordships having said to me at Petworth that he was very glad to hear from me that Mr Tayler would not pay the money to Mr B Smith, it is altogether inexplicable, but it will altogether kill me, & then an explanation signifies not.

I shall endeavour to send up to day, or if I cannot do it to day tomorrow, some of the papers relative to the over payment of Mr Berney. It is as clear as the light that tho only 13£. 7s. 4d was due to the Boehm & Berney debt in 1792, yet in 1793 (after that great Sum of 13£.7s.4d was paid here), all the money Mr Prettejohn[4] received was paid over to Mr Berney, & it so happen'd that, in that year 1793, an estimate was sent over of the Sugars made & making, which (that estimate being sent as so many pots) I, being anxious for releif, got Messrs Blackman to estimate for me in hogsheads, & the estimate was 9000£ Stg. Now this said year, according to Mr Parkins[5] acknowledgement & according to the accounts, only 9 hgds came which netted at 30£ a hgs, 270£, & was applied 165£ to yr Grandmothers use,[6] & the rest to pay the interest on the 3000£. Robinson himself making up the deficiency. Now this appears incontrovertibly, & Mr Berney had the difference between 9000£ & 270£. Mr Tayler nor Mr Boehm have ever attempted to controvert it. They only evade & shuffle. Let them only prove it not to be so, let them meet this charge fairly, & then we will talk of the rest.

But if Mr Tyler is determin'd to beleive Mr Tayler rather than attend to my evidence or the facts I have stated & can produce; if I am to take all this trouble only to be told, as I have of late invariably been in every thing, that I know nothing of the matter & that a point of law is against me; If Mr Tyler, who whatever may be his knowledge in other respects, can know nothing of these transactions, nor of the affairs & debts in Barbados is to be arbiter & Mr Tayler can so escape from any farther investigation; Why should I take even the trouble it will cost me to explain & to send copies of such papers as I do not chuse to part with? It will be mere labour in vain, or worse, as every thing has yet or at least lately been that I have done. Your poor Brother's word[7] goes no farther than mine. But surely it is very strange that Mr Boehms Agent, Mr Tayler, so obstinately resists and, at the expence of his veracity, sending me or the Trustees (if they rather chuse it) extracts of the Sums received from Millington, Tyrrell, and Steele?[8] Is it possible that this can be so labourious or so difficult of execution as to make it worth good Mr Taylers while to tell so many lies about it? first, that ~~they~~ these accounts had been deliverd to me; then, that Charles had them immediately before his departure (which you know is not true); then, that they had been sent to Lord Egremont another direct lie.

Yet Mr Tyler goes & hears Mr Tayler talk & delivers it as his opinion that all the Sums received by Mr Berney are accounted for. Where? & how, in half an hours conversation, can he know this? Does he know the names even of the debtors to R S.s estate? He must be omniscient indeed, if he knows better in so short a space of time than I do who have served an apprenticeship to these accursed affairs ever since I was sixteen. I suppose matters of fact must be as evident to any one as to a Lawyer. But the first impression or the impression which any person is determind to receive is in these cases every thing, & all the trouble I shall now take will end only in Lord Egremonts complaining of the torment of the trust & the unending plague it gives— —So that I own I am entirely discouraged. Yet when there is talk of paying Mr Berney 600£ tho I know he has had at least three times as much, & when I find that every deduction is made from my children to throw into a residue which is to be scrambled for by those Smiths & this Berney, & that it is finally for them, I have so long labourd & sufferd, all the little strength I have left would be roused if I did not see a resolution taken that it shall avail nothing. I have not yet heard from Mr Halliday so conclude he has not had an answer from Mr Benjn S. Therefore the Gentn does not chuse to agree to Mr Hallidays proposal, or he is sick, or Maistress Mellar[9] is considering whether she sal leet be. And here am I not, "in my old brown sattin," for I have not even that, Surrounded by [the] inhospitalities of Frant. Clamourous tradesmen & Servants 2 who will only do what they please— —God help me! I must add a commission for the fair Miss Ann.

[Unsigned]

Miss H S. is desird by Miss Ann Eydes[10] to desire you to buy for her a pair of patent net gloves, very nice & fine, for which she will pay Harriet. She is suppos'd to have a Son of Melchisedec in view who is to be netted at Ashburnham. Here is my commission: you may execute it or let it be. I have not yet been without aether, but my credit has long since evaporated![11]

I can not send up the papers to day. I am tormented more than I am able to bear, & what I am to say to King, Page, Holmwood, & friend[12]—who all depended on being paid—I know not. My hands ache, & I can write no more.[13]

Petworth House Archives MS. Address: Miss Smith/ Hatton Street/ No 8. London. Postmark: TUNB-WELLS/ 36; F/ FEB 3/ 1803.

NOTES

1. CS must have written many letters to her children; however, this letter to her eldest daughter is the only one to survive. It gives an important recounting of early trust history. Hatton Street was the home of a relative, Joseph Smith, a financially well-off broker and accountant who was Charlotte Mary's friend and advisor. He was not involved in the trust.

2. Popularly known as St. Anthony's fire, or the rose, erysipelas is a streptococcal infection causing fever, swelling, and extreme redness of the skin. It was not related to Harriet's malaria.

3. On John Robinson, trustee to the Smith estate between 1784 and 1799, see Biographical Notes.

4. An agent for Gay's and for Mapp's plantations in Barbados.

5. Anthony Parkin was a trustee from 1788 to 1799; George Blackman, Esq., and Co. had been dealing with the estate since 1795.

6. That is, Lucy Towers Smith, also Charlotte Mary's great-aunt.

7. Charles's report of the affairs in Barbados before he died.

8. Millington, Tyrrell, and Steele were Barbadian debtors to the estate.

9. Mrs. Miller, BS's housekeeper and mistress in Scotland.

10. Harriet Smith's friend, Miss Eydes, is not identified. Melchisedec, who appears in the Old and New Testaments as a priest, is seen in the latter as a type of Christ because he has no beginning and no end, coming from no parents. CS could simply mean a priest, or she might mean for the allusion to be teasing or even sarcastic: Miss Eydes would be going to Ashburnham, a parish in the diocese of Chichester, to set a snare for a young man of uncertain parentage, with no pedigree.

11. Written upside down across the margin at the top of the first page of the letter.

12. CS owed money to each of these local tradesmen. In CS to William Tyler, undated and unpublished, 1802, she said that she couldn't pay King, the grocer and chandler. She owed George Page £20 or would get "no more credit for dinner" (CS to Tyler, unpub., 16 Jan. 1803). To Holmwood she owed £42 for coal, wood, malt, hops, and wine (CS to Egremont, 15 Feb. 1803). George Paige is identified as a local butcher in Frant in 1807, and in 1830 a Mr. Homewood was landlord for the Abergavenny estates (Eeles, *Frant,* pp. 228, 238).

13. This second postscript is squeezed vertically into the remaining space at the beginning of the first page.

To the earl of Egremont

[Frant] 4th Feby 1803
My Lord——

When I wrote to your Lordships Steward yesterday, I did not know what I am inform'd of by to days post: that A Ship is on the point of sailing for

Bombay. And by it I must inform my Son of the disposition of the little property he has here which I trust you will have the goodness to direct Mr Tyler [to] enable me to do. I cannot help my Lord remarking that it was of little use my making out a disposal & division of what I supposed still due to the Legatees if Mr Tyler knew he should set the whole aside. It was like laying in wait to find matter of dispute & blame. I must also remark, my Lord, that the impertinent interference of Mr Turner, who never thought proper to interfere before (& now did it from motives of which he ought to be ashamed & of which I will make him repent), has given me another motive for wishing, most earnestly, that Your Lordship would condescend to listen to the means I would very humbly propose for putting an end to the Trust, which has been the unhappy occasion of my losing what I most highly valued, your Lordships good opinion & kindness, as well as of depriving me of my poor subsistence & placing me in a situation where I must beg or starve, for to that I am literally reduced——

If your Lordship is weary (as indeed well you may) of these concerns in which I never dreamed of your taking the trouble of any contention with any party, if you shudder at the name of Smith and have an horrow [*sic*] of the whole business, Why should not immediate measures be taken for your Lordships release & Mr Turners? I suppose no Trust is immo[r]tal nor need they (when there is no Lawyers pocket to fill) all expire in the honourable Court of Chancery—— Whatever Man has done, Man can undo I imagine & that a Trust is not like marriage or death. Mr Robinson & Sir John Dyer and Mr Parkin & Mr Boehm all gave up the Trust, & when your Lordship has fulfilled the purpose for which you so very generously undertook it, there is no reason why you should be harrass'd by Messrs Allen & Richd Smith & Robt Berney & all the rump of the accursed affairs which Mr Prettejohn has left as last pickings for the Lawyers?

My Lord, I am a poor old Woman, but I beleive still equal to understanding affairs in which, thanks to my favourable stars, I have had the honor of being scribe, ever since my father & my Aunt (peace to their ashes!) thought it a prodigious stroke of domestic policy to sell me like a Southdown sheep to the West India shambles not far from Smithfield (& they would have done me a greater kindness if they had shot me at once). I verily think that, tho in this weary pilgrimage, this worse than African bondage, I have lost all that made life worth having & am now reduced to sell the last property I have or can trust to for future subsistence—my books & a few articles of furniture (for 150£ refused me by my own Brother tho orderd by my own Son)[1]—I do nevertheless beleive I could execute what remains to be done almost as well as I could when Mr Richard Smith trusted me as Executrix. Mr Tylers opinion that this & that & the other is impossible is I own not satisfactory to me. We may go on so for these twenty years if every thing I ask, every thing I propose, is negatived at once without any reason, & I am at a time of life when it becomes absolutely necessary I should have a less precarious subsistance & that I may know the fate of those I am likely soon to leave to the mercy (if I do not take measures to secure them) of Messrs Benjn Smith & Nicholas Turner, who have both proved themselves unworthy of any power or Trust whatever—& shall hold none that I can prevent———

Now my Lord, if your Lordship would only consent to let the whole business, as it now is, be laid before any Counseller of eminence, I care not who; & if you would condescend to enquire (such detail on the affairs being given) whether your Lordship could give up the Trust, all parties consenting and giving you a discharge including Mr Benjn Smith, I am persuaded that a great deal of trouble (quite unreasonable to ask of you) may be saved to you—— And the business be closed except only that of the dispute with the Allens which, if it be not settled by compromise, must be settled in Barbados & not here. Y^r Lordship has repeatedly said you had nothing, would have nothing, to do with it——

My Lord, it is not merely the concerns of Old Smith which I wish now to have finally closed (& surely it is time), but I am very desirous that the 7000£ belonging to me[2] may be secured in trust properly, which it is not now. And it has been hinted to me that in case of my death My family might find a good deal of trouble. On that settlement alone can depend Lionels repayment to your Lordship for your late kindness to him,[3] which he is, as well as I, most desirous of securing. Were your Lordship really, & by a proper deed, a Trustee to this money, I should be easier than I am, but such has been the change which seems to have taken place in your Lordships sentiments of me that I have ceased to hope for an honor & friendship, the exercise of which has cost you so much perplexity already & destroy'd that good opinion of me which first induced you to engage in it.

Your Lordship will perhaps call this de[c]lamation or nonsense; I feel however that it is necessary to speak plainly, & I will not beleive that, whenever I am allowed to appeal directly to your Lordship['s] own generous disposition,[4] you will not hear with that candour, which first encouraged me so far to intrude & has in all events made me, whatever may happen in future, most gratefully sensible of your repeated goodness past, to——

My Lord
Your oblig'd & faithful Ser^t,
Charlotte Smith

I wish I knew what I have done that has so changed your opinion of me between the dates of one of the Letters I enclose copy of & the other. Either your first idea was wrong of me, or I have done something to destroy it, & surely in the latter case, I cannot help being very solicitous to know what.

It is a remark of Fieldings & a very just one that great Men should very cautiously throw off their dependants because it ruins their prospects in every other attempt to live: the World inevitably blames & condemns them. If this be true of the generality of noble & powerful Men & those who look up to them, how much more is it true of one of your Lordships eminent and acknowledged generousity. And what must be the opinion of the World of me, thus decidedly abandon'd to distress after all you have done. It will decide that I have deserved it & deserved my general fate.[5]

Your Lordship must not be angry (if, in reading two letters of tendency so very different, In one of which your high opinion of my consequence goes as far beyond my vainest idea, as the last seems short of the justice I hoped for). I cannot help entreating you to tell me what I have done & when that has work'd so unfortunate a change & whether in candour, you can blame me for thinking that some other cause than any misconduct of mine, some other influence on your opinions, must have made this immeasurable difference —— In other former Letters of your Lordships, there are equally strong expressions of confidence & kindness. But lately, I am accused of ingratitude of folly, of impractibility, of falsehood, of getting opinions from Lawyers by misrepresentation & declamation (which I do not know that I ever did get). Now if this change has happend because I appeard in Septr 1797 a person worthy of your generous interposition on my behalf & that in 1803, you are convinced I am a lyar, a misrepresenter, or a fool——Then, My Lord, I cannot be worthy of your farther regard or trouble and deserve to be consignd to the Brotherly kindness of Mr Turner & to be deprived by the forensic scruples of Mr Tylers doubts of the scanty bread I till now had to eat & which even Robinson, who hated me with the most acrimonious abhorrence, never did attempt to give up to M^{r} B Smith, but positively refused to hear of his touching it.

Perhaps my Lord I shall by being thus explicit incur your farther displeasure. But I cannot suffer in any way more than I have done & do at this moment. My conscience tells me I have not deserved it, & my reason that, for your Lordships releif as well as on every other account, it will be better you should not be longer made liable to be troubled about such a person as I now appear to you.

Petworth House Archives MS. No address or postmark.

NOTES

1. Nicholas had asked that his mother be given his interest money, but Turner used the power of attorney he held for his nephew to keep it from her.

2. That is, her marriage settlements. In law, they were not properly settled to her benefit at the time of her marriage. Nor were proper steps taken to secure their interest money to her and the children after she left BS in 1787 without a separation agreement.

3. Egremont might have lent Lionel money to advance in rank from captain to major. CS had been trying to obtain Lionel's majority through the duke of York (CS to Egremont, 1 Mar. 1802). The *Army List* shows Lionel's actual appointment to major on 22 Apr. 1802 in the army and on 24 June 1802 in the 16th Regiment.

4. Implicit here is a complaint against not being allowed to write directly to Egremont; instead, CS was expected to conduct trust business through his agent William Tyler. Smith long suspected Tyler of purposefully setting out to destroy her (CS to Egremont, 8 Sept. 1804, and to Tyler, 15 Sept. 1804).

5. CS enclosed extracts of two letters from Egremont, one written before and one after she fell out of favor with him, and continued her earnest but unwise appeal:

> Copy of a Letter from Lord Egremont to M^{rs} C Smith dated Septr 19th 1797.
>
> Madam—
> I am very happy to receive from Miss Smith, a good account of your health; not only on your own account; which is a sufficiently strong reason to all your friends; but because I consider your health as absolutely necessary to the protection of your family, and particularly at this juncture, so much so, that I must beg of you, whatever you may think of yourself, that you will dissemble, and carry the appearance of returning health and vigour, as much as possible, at least till the present negociation is settled one way or the other; & I think the report of your ill health, has been sufficiently public, to make it probable that the Trustees may have heard of it, and that you had better take some steps, to make them beleive, that you are quite recoverd, & upon the point of setting out to prosecute the business with your usual activity—for if they conceive hopes of your exertions being suspended by illness, they will certainly protract & evade, well knowing that without your exertions, nothing effectual will ever be done—(Then follow some directions & observations ab^{t} Mr Turner & Mr Bicknell & the conclusion)
>
> I have not leisure to say more, except, that yr uneasiness was perfectly groundless, & that I remain in the same wish of serving you and y^{r} family as strongly as ever—Signd—
>
> Egremont

> Copy of part of a Letter from Lord E. to Miss Smith. Novr 3rd 1802.
>
> I beg to have a plain & rational answer to my last Letter. I have reason to complain of y^{r} Mother's misrepresentations, (which I dare say are not intentional) but she makes her Dayrell & other Lawyers, give opinions which are absolute nonsense & which when I enquire, they absolutely disown—I

These I suppose, are only opinions in conversation which they give without any grounds to form an opinion of the real state of the facts

Signd—Egremont

To the earl of Egremont

Frant. Feby 7th 1803

My Lord. It is only because you order me to do it that I trouble you again & because I really have not deserved to be calld Lyar & to be told that I have within these three months done every thing to ruin my family, & you do not beleive a word I say—— If however your Lordship neither can nor will read my nonsense, it is surely very bootless for me to write it. I have never yet lost sight of the respect I owe you, but there is also some respect due from me, to myself, & with generous minds such as your Lordship always appeard to possess, there is respect due to misfortune which has not been incurred by vice or even misconduct. Your Lordships former manner of conferring the greatest obligations redoubled their value. You are now pleased to tell me that you retain the same desire to serve my family & me, yet that I have within these three months ceased to deserve any consideration whatever! You complain in the strongest, & to my feelings the most humiliating terms, of the trouble of this Trust; yet when I, at whose request you were pleased to condescend to undertake it, ask you to take such measures as you have yourself proposd to put an immediate end to it, you repel me with scorn & indignation.

You are pleasd also ~~so~~ to say that, if I am as destitute as I represent (which however you hope to avert), I must impute it only to my own conduct. To what part of my conduct? Without income for twelvemonths and burthend with such a family, Sinking under disease, the effect of anguish of mind, Suffering actual poverty; unable for want of the means to discharge my servants or pay the Tradesmen, What misconduct have I been guilty of? My Lord, you may cease to befriend me, but you must give me leave to say that you ought not in candour or humanity to say all this of me. And to accuse me of things I never thought of while you tell me you are determind not to hear my defence or to read any nonsence I may write——

Sir, it was from remains of regard to the Man who was once my Brother that I forbore to tell your Lordship the true cause of his late refusal to let me have 100£ of Money belonging to my Son Nicholas. About two years ago, you were as much displeased with Mr Turner as you now are with me, & when I was at Hastings & afterwards in the winter of 1800, wrote to me about him in terms that made me extremely unhappy on his account, as I thought your favor, his sole dependance, was entirely lost. Distress obliged me to say to your Lordship at that time that he had had money of me. You expressd your displeasure in such strong terms that I have ever since avoided reverting to the topic at all, for with all his faults I loved him and would have sacrificed any comfort of my own to contribute to his. I beleive your Lordship may recollect that both in my Letters & in conversation, I have always palliated his failings & endeavourd to serve him.

My Lord, last year when 600£ was paid to My Son Nicholas, Mr Dayrell (my Dayrell) was engaged by Mr Turner to ask me to lend him 300£ or 400£ of that Money—Alledging that his Law suits, & particularly that depending with Mrs Dorset, had reduced him to the greatest exigencies.[1] Mr Tyler perhaps may remember my speaking to him on this subject in Buckingham Street, & I was, I own, much releived by hearing that his distress was not in Mr Tyler's opinion so great as I apprehended; Your Lordship confirm'd this by saying that, for his Lawsuit with his parishioners, you had supplied the money. I had said to Mr Dayrell that whatever was in my power I would do, but Mrs Dorset compromising her dispute & having paid a Sum of money (I know not what) & hearing no more from Mr Dayrell, I was persuaded the urgent necessity was over & was very glad on all accounts to think so because I really did not think it handsome or consistent with integrity that my relations should take My Son's money, on any terms, & the security offer'd—That of the income of the living of Cotes, I did think one of Mr Turners wild & vague plans. Hearing nothing more of his going to Jail, I put the money into the 3 pCts in My Son's & Miss Smiths name—that she might receive the dividends which he had given by letter to me with any part of the principal I chose to have——

But about the Month of June or end of May after I left London, I receivd a most lamentable Letter from young Mr Turner, expressing extreme uneasiness at his fathers situation & his surprize at my having so long delay'd to let him have the money I had promis'd. I told him, & truly, that had I any thing of my own, Mr Turner should share it as he had always done to the last shilling, but that, of my Sons little pittance (of which necessity had already compelld me to take too much for his brothers & sisters), I had no rights to dispose; that I then expected his child, to whose support & education his interest money must be appropriated; that I could not depend either on such security as the living of Cotes or on punctuality of payment of the interest; & that the money was now placed in Nicholas Smiths name & his Sisters and could not be removed. Mr Turner, the elder, was thereupon exceeding wrath—told me I had treated him infamously like a theif, That he never would forgive it and moreover, he swore in his wrath, that he would take Nicholas' next share (On what terms he did not say), but that I should have what I wanted for myself & his, Nicholas's Girl. Then My Lord there were no scruples, no hesitation, No doubts of his safety. To these extraordinary notices (for I have two of them), I answerd that he should not have the money, & that if he attempted it, I would relate to your Lordship the truth of the business, & I knew you would not let it be, & I thought w^{d} be much displeas'd, for which reason, I hoped he would not put me to the disagreeable necessity of informing you. If there is another Man in the World as obstinate & as wrong headed as Mr Benjn Smith, it is the Revd Nich^{s} Turner. The pigheaded Man persisted, & I then desird that if the money cd not be in Miss Smiths & the proprietors own name's, it might be in your Lordships. When therefore he found he could not get it on loan for himself, he said unto himself, "if I am not to have it, she shall not. I will raise scruples & difficulties, & she will not have a shilling to help herself, & so shall I at least be revenged"—— So much for a Christian divine! Now, my Lord, if you do not beleive a word I say, I will produce the Revd Mr Turners own hand writing. I might have told y^{r} Lordship all this at first, but I was unwilling, very unwilling to injure him. He was my Brother still——a Brother to whom I had made thro life many sacrifices.

My Lord, your Lordship will surely not think me so much to blame to refuse security I did not think adequate, but if it had been so as to principal, what chance had I of ever seeing the interest When Mr Turner has never accounted for the difference between 105£ & 110£ 18S[2] which he receives of the 2000£ to which he is Trustee & of which, my necessities (when I had seven children to keep on 70£ a year) compelled me to sell the interest to Messrs Tripp[3] & Tyler or rather to transfer it to them in 1793—15£ 18S[4] a year for ten years comes to some money and would have often been very welcome to me, who have often wanted a guinea, but I have never seen a shilling of it besides which I have given or lent Mr Turner at times considerably upwards of 50£ more, some even so late as last Winter. He says he has paid money for me, & there might be some expences incurred in the transfer, but then he should have stated them. He says however, now, that the ballance is in his favor. I received 10£ of him in 1801, but that was I thought in repayment of what I let him have the preceding Autumn to get in his Harvest———

My Lord, it is extremely painful to me to relate all this, & I evaded it, even when my distress on receiving Charlottes intelligence amounted even to agony. But your Lordship's last harsh Letter & Mr Turners obstinate & ungrateful conduct make it a matter of self defence. Never again shall I consider him as my brother, & if I live thro my present distresses & sufferings both of mind & body (which I do not expect to do), I will go to die as far as possible from people who have abused my affection for them & repaid all I have done with the most unfeeling ingratitude. At present, I must, if I live long enough, go to the Cottage at Elsted which M[r] Johnstone returns upon my hands because it will at least be a shelter for three or four months.[5] Everything here I must sell, & it must all fall very short of what I owe tho I shall be indeed destitute. I enclose your Ldship a copy of a Letter from M[r] N. H. S. received on Saturday over land & a Letter from M[r] B Smith which y[r] Lordship must direct me how to ans[r] I have nothing to do but to obey, & perish. I have the honor to be y[r] most oblig'd hble Ser[t],

Charlotte Smith

Petworth House Archives MS. No address or postmark.

NOTES

1. Turner's lawsuits against his sister and against his parishioners at Fittleworth are discussed in CS to Egremont, 9 July 1800, n. 7. His suit against Catherine Dorset had been settled in his favor in Jan., but he was not awarded costs (PHA #202).

2. Corrected above her figures in another hand to "£109 18 sh," suggesting that their haggling had become petty and acrimonious.

3. James Upton Tripp, steward to the earl of Egremont before William Tyler.

4. Also corrected in another hand to "?16 sh."

5. On George Johnstone and the cottage at Elsted, see CS to Samuel Rose, 9 Sept. 1802, n. 3.

To the earl of Egremont

[Frant, ca. 8 February 1803]

I was perfectly aware that the int[ere]st of money in the 4 pC[ts] was payable in Oct[r] & April, & it was for that very reason I desird my Son Nicholas's money might be put into it that my child[1] might have something for her little wants four times a year instead of twice.

What harm there was in this to provoke y[r] Lordship I own I cannot understand.

M[r] B Smith is remarkably generous: he takes 400£ & 50£ in M[r] Taylers hands, & 16£, the remainder of what he says is in M[r] Pybus's, making 466£ & I am to have 50£.

George is orderd to recruit at Manchester. If I dared ask a favor if it w[d] be that he might not go on Service [in][2] which he will be utterly ruin'd. He now wants money [thi]s March, & I have not one guinea to send him—[in]volves my family, but not from my conduct "these [last thre]e Months surely—

[Unsigned]

Petworth House Archives MS. Address: The Earl of Egre[mont]/ G[rosvenor Place]. Postmark: TUNB-WELLS/ 36.

NOTES

1. That is, CS's granddaughter Luzena, Nicholas's daughter.

2. The blanks in the rest of this letter are where the left lower corner of the page was torn away.

To Samuel Rose

Frant near Tunbridge Wells
Feby 9th [1803]
Dear Sir,

Allow me to thank you for the friendly alacrity with which you have had the goodness to attend to my troublesome request. Miss Smith inform'd me that you had done her the favor to call on her at her dismal lodging and had promised to write to Lord Egremont relative to the money his Lordship has at length, after so much cavilling, deigned to direct might be put into the stocks for the representative[1] of my lost and lamented Augusta—— There is nearly two years interest due while his Lordship has been debating whether any thing should be paid at all & I dare not complain; I will check myself if possible, but I own I have sufferd more from the dispute he & his steward have held about this trifling matter than I do from my present distressd & destitute state, which is occasiond entirely by his Ldps unaccountable & unsettled conduct. He totally forgets or overlooks objects of the greatest importance to wrangle about trifles & raise difficulties where none ever existed before. His Letters to me accuse me of folly & even falsehood in terms so little consistent with his former conduct that I own I feel myself extremely mortified. I was about to say humiliated. Yet nothing ought really to humble a person but the consciousness of having deserved contempt.

However I cannot help considering myself as singularly unfortunate & doubting whether there is not something in my destiny which changes the nature of all those with whom I happen to be concern'd. Between Lord E. & Mr Tyler, I am deprived now even of the little income I used to have, The product of a part of my marriage portion, to all of which it seems M^{r} B Smith has according to them a right, & which he takes or threatens to take so that it is retain'd by the Trustees. He however has wasted the 3000£ which in that deed he covenants to settle on me as a compensation for 5000£ given me then (2000£ more I had afterwards),[2] & I have been advised that I could obtain some redress for what is evidently so glaring an injustice, especially as I have entirely supported his children for many years & have now his youngest daughter & Son to support without possessing or being allow'd one shilling myself———

Lord Egremont took up this matter very warmly some time since, but asking his Chancellor Mr Tyler's advice, he was I suppose discouraged from pursuing it. And now his Lordship informs me that, within these three months, I have so acted as to ruin my family. What I have done I have no guess, for—seeing that he was in a humour to contradict everything I asserted & deny everything I asked, & anxious that nothing might irritate this humour & give Tyler an excuse which he eagerly lay in wait for to throw the affairs into Chancery—I have evaded even giving an opinion for a much longer time than six months, & during the last three, I have more than once thought myself at the point of death, having had such violent palpitations of the heart, during the night principally, that I had not the least expectation of living till morning, & being a great deal too ill to execute any thing that could ruin my family, even if it were likely I should try now to do what I have been so many years endeavoring to avert.

Charges so harsh and so unfounded and deliverd without hesitation by a Man who has been so long known as the friend I most relied upon & have been the most obliged to can hardly fail of being very injurious to me. I therefore ventured very respectfully to represent to Lord E. the injustice he did me by such declarations. I sent him copies of two of his own Letters[3] —— The first was in a strain of panegyric infinitely beyond my deserts. He exhorted me to live (for he had heard I was then very ill) for my family & my friends, & really I was amazed at the energy of his kindness——— In the second—Oh sad reverse—He accuses me of going invidiously to cheat Lawyers into ill founded opinions—— That I misrepres<ent> in short he, & you would imagine I had been guilty of some terrible crime to deserve such a Letter.

I ventured therefore to ask what I had done to occasion this very great change of opinion, & I beleive I have by this hardihood made him more angry than ever. He assures me that there is nothing inconsistent in his conduct——that he will still serve my family, but that I have ruind them & that is all the answer I can obtain, save that I am a fool & write nothing but nonsense. I really found myself compelled to ask whether his Ldp would resign the trust under the direction of any Lawyer of eminence rather than thus allow it to torment him & reduce me to seek an asylum in an Hospital. But I shall probably have only some cruel answer. I should not however trouble you with all this, did I not beleive it very likely that if your kindness to me should induce you to see or write to Ld E. he may make such an impression on you by such direct assertions as may deprive me of what I very highly value—the good opinion {which} I trust you now have of me—— The rest of my paper shall be devoted to a less unpleasant topic—— —

I am afraid of addressing myself to Mr Hayley now on any subject whatever. I have not been favord with any answer to the Letter I took the liberty to address to him under cover to you which related to information my daughter desird me to obtain of Mr Harman[4] relative to the means of sending over a small marble tablet or urn to Barbados inscribed to the memory of my unfortunate Charles. Perhaps however he has been so good as to send an answer to Miss Smith. My present purpose is to enquire whether there is not an ingenious Engraver who executed certain plates for a small work of Mr Hayley's relating to Animals.[5] I know not what it is as I have never seen it.

Now I am going to tell a story all about myself. I have a little Girl of five years old, the daughter of my second son, sent over to my care from India. She is not what is usually call'd an half-cast, her Mother being a Georgian Woman, & her darkness (for perhaps you saw her little face when you calld on Charlotte) she derives from her father who is I understand quite black.[6] Of this little creature, I am become passionately fond & fancy that she has a very uncommon understanding, & I have written some little pieces of poetry to exercise her memory. While they may peradventure replenish my pocket & finish my Parnassian tour in the respectable character of an affectionate Grandmother, I am advised to add plates to those namby pambyisms and print them on my own account. The subjects are entirely from natural history, & some of the drawing I could make myself if I had not the Rhumatism so dreadfully as often to lose the use of my own hands. I imagine however the drawings w[d] not be very expensive, & if M[r] Hayley could, to use a French phrase, indicate to me an artist not above engaging in such a work, I should consider myself under a great obligation to him tho I fear to be troublesome unless you will prefer my request.[7]

Allow me also to beg (for the same reason) that you will make known to M[r] Hayley my gratitude for the work I so earnestly wish'd to see and which arrived here on Teusday. I have only had time to read the dedication & some pages of the first volume. My spirits I hope will serve me to go thro it in the course of the next three or four days. Yet it is not a book (or relating as it does to one such a person) which can be read—at least I cannot read it—without a variety of sensations that no other book in the world can excite.[8] Alas! for the friends I have lost—for the days that are gone!—— I am, Dear Sir,

your most oblig'd & obed[t] Ser[t], Charlotte Smith

I have told M[r] De Foville, who is in Eng[d] for a short time, that I thought he might take the liberty of calling on you.

I can write better sometimes, but I have only for a few minutes at a time the use of my hand. The pen of the once ready writer is often suspended by her aching fingers. Do you ever hear from my frie[nds] the Miss Lees?[9]

McMaster University Library MS. Address: Sam[l] Rose Esq[re]/ Chancery Lane/ London. Postmark: TUNB-WELL/ 36/ FEB 10/ 1803.

NOTES

1. That is, Alexandre de Foville, Augusta's widower.

2. There were two deeds from 1 Feb. 1765 settling £3,000 and £2,000 on CS and a third deed of 9 Aug. 1772 settling another £2,000 on her (CS to William Tyler, unpub., mid-July 1804).

3. See CS to Egremont, 4 Feb. 1803 and n. 5.

4. Not identified.

5. CS had recently asked Cadell and Davies to send her Hayley's ballads of animals, three of which were published in 1802 with plates (see CS to Cadell and Davies, 16 Dec. 1802, and n. 3). The "ingenious Engraver" is William Blake.

6. Presumably, Luzena had her father's dark complexion. CS hastens to assure Rose that Luzena was not the child of an Indian woman, but of a woman from the area of Georgia in eastern Europe. (See Biographical Notes for the family story of Nicholas's possible marriage to her.) In any event, his only recorded marriage was to Annie Petruse in Calcutta on 13 Aug. 1806, where he was named as a bachelor.

7. This work became *Conversations Introducing Poetry,* but it was not illustrated. Rose, whom she knew through Hayley and Cowper, had helped her negotiate the price on *Elegiac Sonnets ii,* with Cadell and Davies (see CS to Cadell and Davies, 13 Dec. 1796, n. 1).

8. Vols. 1 and 2 of Hayley's *Life and Posthumous Writings of William Cowper* (1803) are probably the subject of her remarks to Rose, who also knew Cowper and would understand her reference to "the variety of sensations that no other book in the world can excite."

9. On Sophia and Harriet Lee, see CS to Cadell and Davies, 1 May 1796, n. 4.

To the earl of Egremont

[Frant] 10th Feby 1803
My Lord,

I have no wish more ardent than to obey yr Lordship when you are so good as to interest yrself in my unfortunate business, but in spite of all I can do to simplify my answers or addresses I have lately been always misunderstood—— What yr Lordship in your Letter of yesterdays date directs, I did—— I wrote to Mr B Smith to say that I had forwarded his Letter & request to Your Ldship and would let him know the result but I did not think that, however disposed your Lordship might be, it was in your power to advance 400£. That however I never had opposd, or should oppose it, if you chose to do it. This was precisely the purport of my answer to him in the first instance, & it was not I who put an end to the treaty, if a treaty it can be called, when a Man acts so contrary to common sense, common decency, & common honesty & must be treated with not to starve his family.

I am very sorry to dissent from your opinion in any instance, & especially now, when your last Letter seems written less in anger than these I have lately received, but allow me to ask you to reconsider whether it would be well to engage M[r] B Smith in a treaty on grounds which are not finally meant to be stood upon? & were he to be invited to come up, would he not have reason to complain that he was deceiv'd & to demand his expences? Would he not get again into the clutches of M[r] Follet, who seems to have discover'd that he can make nothing of him & has therefore ceased to interfere? but the moment money was in Question, & M[r] B Smith here, the Attorney would put in his paw (for no Attorney can help it). His family like him a great deal better at a distance & would there be more disposed to let him have any thing that depends on them than they are when he is harrassing them here.

As to myself, any meeting between us is for ever out of the question—— I met him in the Autumn of 1801 when your Lordship orderd me to go to London to make some arrangement with him, & it was so very disagreeable to me, so mortifying (I wish not to explain myself farther or to declaim), but I am perfectly convinced (setting every other consideration aside) that he will be dealt with much better in Scotland than in England.

As to the representation he makes of his distress, I do not beleive it. I lived with him when, tho his father was living, he had an income of near two thousand a year, his children were infants, & the whole expence of his house (as I never went out or kept any company at that time) never exceeded nine hundred, & yet he generally sent me once a quarter to the old Man for money to extricate him from his difficulties & distresses, & I usually succeeded at the expence of my veracity, for old Smith loved me so much that if I had been artful, I might have got all he left for myself & my children.

But I was too young then to know what I was about & have always been a fool— —M[r] B Smith laid out about a thousand pounds a month, in Hampshire; he was then to be extricated again. When he lived in Scotland on 80£ a year and some small addition given him by M[r] Boehm, he was compelled to make it do. Now he is got into Embarrassment again tho he has had 918£ since Sept[r] 1799 (exclusive of 20£ he gave George, 10£ I made him pay Lionel, & one whole pound he gave his daughter Harriet).

Neither M[r] Boehm nor M[r] Tayler beleive a word of his embarrassment &, I am sure, were I to ask them, they would both be decidedly against his coming to London. M[r] Boehm took every pains such a man will take about any thing to keep him away last time. At all events, he will not trust his invaluable life & most precious person while the weather is cold. Nor will he hazard the vernal equinox. He will only venture his butterfly form when the Sun is in Taurus—or Gemini. In my opinion, therefore, the negociation might be carried on more effectually by Letter & more quickly——

In my own mind, I am persuaded, & I have told Miss Smith so, that if his family could buy him quite off—engage him to make such a will in case of surviving me as justice demands & to make an irrevocable disposition of the residue, be it more or less; in short never to interfere again in the affairs, but to sit quietly & take his annual income, which might then be a very decent one—I say I am persuaded it would be the best thing they could do for all their interests and cheap at 400£. But I do not know that they could do it if they would. All negociation or representation will be useless when he has not an immediate prospect of money. Lost to every other feeling but a selfish desire to get all he can from his children & me, he is invulnerable on every quarter. I will write to him a temperate Letter & send a copy of it to yr Lordship.[1]

Allow me once more my Lord to represent to you my own very deplorable situation—To recall to your mind that I have had no income since last March & have had very severe illness both of my own & Harriets to contend with. I am now a prisoner for debt for such I must consider myself & have this day two houses on my hands without being able to live in either. My books & some articles of furniture which I wish'd to reserve, I would have sacrificed long ago, but any attempt to remove them for sale will so alarm the people I cannot pay that I should be denied the little I am now supplied with. As it is, I am without coals & have only been able to obtain some logs of green wood which will not burn, & my sufferings from cold are dreadful in this cold house, & I have nearly lost the use of my limbs by the Rhumatism.

Ought I, my Lord, to be reduced to such distress, & what have I done to deserve such misery? All I askd was that your Lordship would be so good as to allow me to borrow 200£ (to pay these debts) of Mr Mitford[2] who would have lent it me on your saying he might (without interest) till July when the legatees will pay it because Miss Smith will give her security for herself & her Brother, not doubting Nicholas's sendg me assistance & consent long before that time. It is not for myself I have run in debt, but for the actual necessaries of life for Mr B S's children. I ask nothing that wd involve yr Lordship, but surely after all that you have done, & I have sufferd, it is sad to perish at last which I must do if I wait for Mr B Smith & his fifty pounds.

I shall be infinitely oblig'd to your Lordship to let Miss Smith have wherewithal to pay the duties on the Schawl my Son has sent me on my account. It will be lost if the duties are not paid, & from the high price those India articles bear at present, to send to Paris, I am persuaded I can sell it, if it is what he describes, for from 50 to 70£, & I would repay what is borrow'd for the Duties wth a thousand thanks. I have two works in hand,[3] which will produce me at least 250£ if I can sit down to them, but, harrass'd as I now am, I can do nothing & must be starved. Let me entreat y^{r} Lordships consideration to y^{r} obligd & Obed^{t} Ser^{t},

Charlotte Smith

I have taken the liberty to enclose a note unseal'd to Genl Dalrymple,[4] reminding him of a promise he made in regard to my Son, for whom I am distressd beyond measure. Yet I dare not ask any alteration in orders given ab^{t} Recruiting. It is a favor I have no right to suppose can be granted, but I dread the consequence & have no money to supply the unavoidable expence.

Will y^{r} Lordship condescend to forward the note?

I think your Ldship will allow, ~~that~~ from the beginning of this Letter, which relates to the new power I askd him so urgently to send, that there is some reason to be confident that I shall have it. I added the (extraparochial) sentence about the Schawl because he sent me 10£ to clear the duties upon it, which, being much distress'd for that Sum to pay my last quarters house-rent, my landlady being a poor Woman in Maidstone Jail, I took, depending in Octr last when I received the first intelligence of this schawls & <y^{e}> 10£, that I should not want ten pounds when the ship Scaleby Castle was cleared. But now, thanks to my good Brother, I must sell the schawl for the duties tho, if I could clear it, I suppose it would fetch 50 G^{s} at least, if it passes better than the 5 yard Shawl I sent to the Dss. This is very hard!——[5]

Petworth House Archives MS. No address or postmark.

NOTES

1. Perhaps by the time she got to this letter she was no longer temperate. On 25 Feb. 1803, BS responds harshly to a letter—which does not survive—that she evidently wrote on the 16th (see CS to Egremont, ca. 26 Feb. 1803 [first letter] and n. 1).

2. A lawyer long involved in the trust.

3. Certainly, CS had *Conversations Introducing Poetry* (London: J. Johnson, 1804) well under way at this time. She was also working on another children's book, *A Natural History of Birds,* ultimately published posthumously by Joseph Johnson. On 16 Dec. 1802, she wrote to Cadell and Davies that she had nearly completed her history of England for young ladies, but Richard Phillips did not publish it until 1806.

4. See her note which follows, asking Dalrymple to honor his promise to write a letter of introduction for George. As the original note is still in the archives, it apparently was never sent.

5. A postscript containing a copy of the note to General Dalrymple was added to this letter on a half sheet of paper.

This note is immediately followed by an extract from a letter by Nicholas from Bombay:

Copy of part of a Letter from Nich[s] H Smith—

Bombay 31st Aug[st]
1802

My dearest Mother, I rec[d] Yesterday by the Sir E[d] Hughs y[r] Letters of Feb[y] last, with the inclosures from Sir John Macpherson. An overland dispatch being now sealing up, I have only time to say, that I will attend to your wishes in every respect and forward all you desire me to do, by an early ship, when I will write at length. You probably thought me by this time at Calcutta, & nothing but the tragical death of ~~xxxxxxxxxxxxxxxxx~~ the Persian Embassador has put an end for the present to that long desired journey—I have received the thanks of Government for my conduct at that unfortunate time, & the superintendance of the Persons belonging to, & the affairs of the Embassy, are now left to me—

I have sent you a schawl, which I think you will find more beautiful & valuable than that you admird so much—& will send Lucena hers, by a private hand. I have received Charlottes Letter &c &c &c—

To General Dalrymple

[Frant, 10 February 1803]

M[rs] Charlotte Smith begs leave to intrude once more on Gen[l] Dalrymple's kindness[1] & to remind him of the Letter of introduction he was so very obliging as to promise On her former application. As she understands from the public Prints that Col[l] Backhouse[2] is at length arrived, & the Generals condescending to give to Ensign G Smith such a mark of his notice and protection will be of the most important service to the young Man for whom his Mothers anxieties must plead her excuse for her presumption.

Frant. Feb[y] 10th 1803

Petworth House Archives MS. Address: Gen[l] Dalrymple. No postmark.

NOTES

1. See CS to Egremont, 31 July 1801.
2. Lieutenant Colonel Thomas Joseph Backhouse of the 47th (Lancashire) Regiment.

To the earl of Egremont

Frant. Feb[y] 11th
1803

My Lord,

Your Lordships commands I obey as soon as I receive them; I own it is with reluctance at this time, as I never meant to have done any thing that look'd like malice against Mr Turner, to whom I would much rather do good than harm. Nor should I have been piqued as I was if he had not behaved with so much rudeness, & I must say brutishness, towards Miss Smith & my little Georgian Girl, & if yr Lordship had not told me you did not beleive a word I said about it—which I did think hard because I never yet have told yr Ldship a falsehood, Having an utter comtempt for the figure call'd Lying.

It is my unhappy lot (& a most bitter one) to find in the husband & Brother who ought to protect & support me ~~are~~ exactly those who have made me a slave the greatest part of my life to leave me at the end of it to contend with poverty & anguish.

I enclose the account upon which I acted in regard to Mr De Foville. It is the same as was deliver'd to Mr Tyler in July 1801, and if it was not right, it was then I ought to have been told so. If my daughter had lived, there is one point among all those on which Chancery has been talk'd of that I would have referred to that Court which was whether she was not entitled to as much as the rest. Knowing as I do better than any body the testators intentions, I would have tried that question had she or her child been spared to me. As they are lost, I submitted to let the matter pass, & as to Foville himself, he and My Second Son Nichs are the only persons with whom I have had any concern in the affairs of Richd Smith as claimants that have not treated me at times with ingratitude & mistrust. He has never ask'd me for any thing but wishd me rather to take whatever was coming than pay it to him if it distress'd me.

A great many invidious & some impertinent things were said on his continuing to reside in my house for two years, but during that time, he taught George French & accounts & would have given him more instruction than I could any other way have purchasd for him if the chimera of the living of Islington[1] had not induced me to seek other instruction for him which he never would acquire & which, if he had, would have been now of no use to him. Mr De Foville, for some years before he went to France, earned a very competent income & often assisted me—— But before, As the greater part of the money I had then was of my own earning and as Mr Turner is not Trustee to my feelings nor Gauger of my sorrows, I should not think any vindication of my conduct or eulogy on Mr De Fovilles necessary if I had not known & heard too much malice & illiberality on this subject—A subject so very painful to me (who never did love any other being so well as my Augusta) that I some times wonderd your Lordship did not spare me more than you have appeard willing to do. But you seem'd to think that, because my daughter was dead, I was to feel nothing for those who shared my misery in losing her.

If indeed he had been such an husband as was that wretched Man Newhouse, I should have most willingly have dropped the connection, but there was as much difference in their conduct as in their birth & prospects. Yet for the Son of the old Petworth Attorney, I advanced more money & put myself to greater inconvenience than for any body, & now his friend M[r] Duncan[2] is pleased to grumble that I have given M[rs] Newhouse only 200£ of what she owed me when I meant, if I could, to have given her 400£. Your Lordship desires me to keep my temper. Indeed my Lord, it is tried on all hands too severely.

You are so good as to say that (my temper being kept) a negociation may be open'd with M[r] B Smith. Yes! a negociation, which after six or eight weeks will end in my having 50£ & his daughter to keep & his youngest Son to supply. What good will that do me?

In the mean time, I literally perish. There is no describing the personal hardships I go thro in this cold wretched house where I have waited so long that I have no credit for actual necessaries. If I had had any choice, I might be blamed for living beyond what I had reason to expect, but I have none. I must keep house for M[r] B S family. I cannot turn his youngest daughter out into the street. I could not help her having a return of the frenzy fever she had in India & its costing me (besides the Apothecary) more than 50£!

My Lord, I can bear this misery no longer. I ought not to do it. Will you allow me to borrow 200£ for which I will make over my furniture & books and the 50£ I shall have from M[r] B. S. as security. My books are valued at 105£ by a bookseller to sell again, but that is hardly 18[d] a volume. (I was offerd 16 G[s] last year for one set, & another is worth 20£). They therefore are undervalued & must be security for 200£ with 50£ & my furniture, & I will, (not willingly) but as a matter of irresistable necessity, give them all up for the supply I now want (& which I have been imploring for, ever since last March in vain) to prevent my perishing here. As soon as I can set down to finish the literary work that I am about, which is impossible, worried & frozen as I am now, I will release every body from any farther trouble about me & go to another country which I have always wish'd & am now determind to do. I repeat that this torture I can not bear. My gratitude to y[r] Lordship is however unchanged. I am, My Lord,

Y[r] oblig'd Ser[t], Charlotte Smith

I beseech you, My Lord—without adverting to any expectations from M[r] Benj[n] Smith which you may be assured if he has not the 400£ will come to nothing—to answer me whether you will let me apply to those who I know will lend it me for 200£. If I apply without your leave, the answer, "I cannot do it unless Lord Egremont will say he allows of it however good the security you may have to offer."

If I would sell the little I have directly (cruel—cruel necessity), I should give such an alarm that I should want food as well as firing. God of Heaven! What have I done to suffer thus!

Petworth House Archives MS. No address or postmark.

NOTES

1. That is, the perpetual advowson of Islington, a living held by the family. In his will, Richard Smith had conferred this living on any one of CS's sons who obtained a university education (see CS to Joseph Cooper Walker, 9 Oct. 1793, n. 3).

2. John Shute Duncan, the friend and attorney of Lucy's husband, Thomas Newhouse. It is difficult to tell whether the amount CS gave Lucy was £200 or £220, as she wrote over the second digit of the number.

To the earl of Egremont

[Frant, 13 February 1803]

Your Lordship will observe that these letters (& I think one other which I rather beleive I have burnt) came under cover from M[rs] Newhouse. She informd me that M[r] Turner had sent her those papers to copy, but to me (as she is no scribe) she did not take the trouble to do that but sent them as they were. I do not know the dates.

I beg leave to say that where I have markd in red No. 1 never was before fully explaind to me, but if it had been so, I should not have thought myself authorised to lend my Sons money in this manner. How would it have been when the interest was to have been paid? Why, he would have been in distress, & I should not have had the heart, to have taken it.

But surely I had no occasion to assign any other reason than that I did not chuse to lend Nicholas's[1] money on any but Government security. If he[2] was not angry with me for this, what was he so angry for, that he deignd not to answer my Letters tho I wrote three or four to him, shewing every disposition to be on friendly terms with him. And I declare to God that had I now the means I would assist him if he wanted it tho I sufferd myself. My heart aches for him, & I see him again reduced perhaps, if your Lordship should withdraw your favor, to the dreadful situation he was in when you took him from the extreme indigence he was reduced to by his own weakness & Dorsets artful & wicked conduct, for such I must ever think it.

I beseech you, my Lord, discard him not. His Wife is dying & he is a very unhappy Man & an object of compassion. He is more weak than any thing else.

"I am tired to the top of my bent"[3]——

Would to God the Earth would open & swallow me.[4]

[Unsigned]

I am not sure I have numberd the papers in the order they were received.[5]

I have found another scrap of that Paper which I thought I had thrown into the fire with M[rs] Newhouses Letter. Not imagining Any of these things w[d] be call'd for, I tore this with some other papers; the advice M[r] Turner gives, however well meant, is never consistent, has always misled, & seldom of the same tenor two months together.[6]

Petworth House Archives MS. No address or postmark.

NOTES

1. Her son Nicholas's money.

2. That is, Nicholas Turner, CS's brother, not her son Nicholas Smith. Turner was angry because CS refused to lend him his nephew's interest money.

3. *Hamlet* 3.2.384. But the original line is "They fool me to the top of my bent."

4. The handwriting in this letter is light and irregular, as if she could not afford a decent quill or was too distressed to sharpen it.

5. Written upside down in the top margin of the first page.

6. Written upside down in the top margin of the second page.

To the earl of Egremont

[Frant, 14 February 1803]
My Lord,

Having some business with M[rs] Newhouse & never willingly putting her to expence on my account (tho at this time my paying the postage w[d] be an object to me), I take the liberty of asking the favor of y[r] Lordship to free this enclosure if you will take the trouble.

On looking over the account y[r] Ldship was pleas'd to forward to me, I find I understand it better than I did at first; indeed it is clear enough, but I ~~should~~ do somewhat marvel at the doubts that have been rais'd on claims of Miss Smiths Which the former Trustees never thought of raising,[1] & I wish your Lordship had condescended to ask for the evidence I have of the justice of these claims before the account had been so made out as will give M[r] Benj[n] Smith a handle for dispute he himself has never started. I repeat that, if it be decided, as it seems to be, that I am to die in want & misery, my resistance is wholly useless. It is certain that, as to Mr Berney,[2] you order'd me to send what papers I had, or I should not have sent even the small extracts I did send, for I am very far from desiring M[r] Tyler to trouble himself about it, & however offensive it may be, I assure y[r] Lordship that he knows nothing of the matter. I never said it was p[d] to Boehm & enterd in his account, but I say that Mr Berney had the money, & what is there surprising in it when he also took his Sisters money & never accounted for it, for which, Mr Henchman, who married the youngest, was long at variance with him, but if Mr Tyler knows all these transactions better than I do as well as the meaning of Old Mr Smiths will & Mrs Lucy Smiths, there is no use at all in my writing or troubling myself about it. I care no longer what is done if I am not harrass'd so.

I thought that the proposed settlement by a Chancery Lawyer would die away, as other things have done, & therefore I wrote, not as a new thought, but to press the execution of any resolution yr Lordship may please to take to deliver me from the tortures of your displeasure & Letters of anger & contempt, & the indigence & the want, reduced to, now expose me to, & I repeat that it is out of my power to bear it tho I am, for yr long exerted kindness formerly, yr Lordships

most obligd Sert,
Charlotte Smith

I have heard from Barbados that Prettejohn is dead. There is another scoundrel less in the World, but I fear it will do us more harm than good. I dont know tho why I should care about it.

I send one of the many Letters I have in which you express your opinion of Mr Turner who you say, either in this or some other Letters, is unfit to manage his own affairs. Yet when, after repeated proofs of this, fatal proofs, & when his behaviour to me is so cruel & so unbrotherly, yes, & ungrateful, Your Lordship tells me I am violent & virulent in desiring he may have nothing more to do with my affairs. He settle with Mr Smith!—— My contempt for them both is equal, but I dare not now speak my opinion of my own relations![3]

Petworth House Archives MS. Address: The Earl of Egremont/ Grosvenor Place/ London. Postmark: TUNB-WELLS/36; FREE/ FEB15/ 1803.

NOTES

1. Richard Smith's will clearly settles a larger share of the estate on his eldest granddaughter than on her siblings, and more on them than on their cousins.

2. Robert Berney, son of William and Mary Smith Berney (later Dyer); he was one of the grandchildren who were legatees. His sisters were Dorothy Elizabeth Berney Boehm and Mary Eleanor Berney Henchman. (See Genealogical Chart.)

3. Written vertically in the top margin of the first page. All of CS's letters to Egremont in this month are poorly written with postscripts added in all directions and a large, loopy handwriting, lacking her usual precision and form and making plain her desolation and despair.

To the earl of Egremont

Frant. Feb[y] 15th 1803
My Lord,

Yesterday after I had written to y[r] Ldp taking the liberty to ask a frank for M[rs] Newhouse, I was applied to by Holmwood, a Man to whom I owe 42£ (for Coals Wood, Malt, hops, & wine) for half a year;[1] he inform'd me that he could not supply me with wood or coal any more so that I am now sitting without fire, & that he expected a person from London tomorrow who came to receive a Sum he had to make up to a considerable amount, & therefore he must have what I owe him paid tomorrow. Intimating at the same time that if it was not he should take measures to compel payment.

To pay him or the Butcher his father (who is equally pressing) is at this moment utterly impossible; from your Ldships last Letter, I have no hope You will consent to my having any, notwithstanding Miss Smith offerd to give security for 200£ which surely she was competent to answer & which must have taken off every possibility of risk to your Lordship. You did not however honor her with an answer. The little I have to part with here will not sell for above 30£ except my books, & I cannot well dispose of the bed I sleep on (or might sleep on, if I kept not the vigil of misery) till I can go. Your Lordship can have no idea of what it is to suffer in this manner. I have now taken every means in my power: I have exerted my strength to the utmost. I have been guilty neither of extravagance nor indolence. Yet I am allowed to perish.

Holmwood is a tenant of Lord Abergavennys. His Lordships servants have lately frequented the house (a public house) & been questioning my Servant & talked openly of a Smith's having done such extraordinary things. All this and my evident want of money for the common purposes of my house & not being able to pay my servants—In a word, every thing has combined to alarm these people to whom I am indebted. They know it is my intention to leave the place & that they can expect no farther proffit from me; their sole purpose therefore is to force payment. I have told them that I have no means of paying them, having depended on money that I am not allowed to receive. But this to them is no answer at all. If therefore your Lordship, in whose power I am, continues to refuse me the assistance I have so long implored, I must submit to arrest & will go to Horsham jail— — You were pleased to say you would avert my distress, but what is already overwhelming me cannot be averted.

I have nothing to support my spirits but the consciousness of not having deserved this cruel destiny. My personal strength however fails; I Am a cripple in my limbs & cannot move without help. I retain nothing of all I once possessed but a keen sense of the bitterness of my fate.

Did I thus act towards Mr Turner? Thank God, I did not. Nor would I have to reproach myself with inflicting on the most obnoxious creature in the World that distress which is this moment inflicted on me. All this however I have said before, & your Lordship has call'd it nonsense and declamation & resolutely refused to save me from what is now come upon me at the risk only of 70£, for, had I had that Sum when I ask'd for it, I should have gone peaceably away & have set down to work— —Now it is too late—

I enclose a Letter I have received to day from Mr Halliday.[2] He was one of Mr Benjn Smiths allies & advocates, but as soon as he gave himself time to hear the truth, he saw where the right lay. He propos'd (or rather acquiesed in the propriety of my proposal) to leave every matter in dispute to two Gentlemen whom Mr B Smith himself should name, & to that purpose, he wrote to him. By his Letter to day, it appears evident that M^r^ B Smith, having no excuse whatever to offer for not acceding to a proposal so evidently reasonable, has not answerd him at all &, instead of doing so, made another attempt to get 400£ and 65£ of mine, graciously allowing me 50£—— Your Lordship, with the best intentions I have no doubt, has armed this Man, & now he will try to use those arms. If you had not listend to him—If (as Robinson did) you had turnd a deaf ear to every attempt of his to talk of rights which he had forfeited, you would not have had any of this trouble, & I should have had wherewithal to keep me from cold, & hunger & insult——

I beleive it too late for me now to escape the toils that surround me—— But with all the faults & follies that your Lordship has lately had pointed out to you or discoverd in me & notwithstanding all my understanding is turned into foolishness & my deserts into deserving to suffer, Tho you determine not to beleive a word I say unless I send you proof in black & white (& not always then), I do venture to assert that, if I was let alone, I could bring Mr B Smith into much better terms for me his family & even himself than will be done by any other means—— I would offer, by getting Prescods next bill discounted, certain ready money terms to which Miss Smith, the only legatee specifically interested, would agree on condition of his releasing the trustees, giving up all future power or interference, & contenting himself with receiving half the income both of the residue & my 5,000£. If your Lordship is on all hands released & your troublesome undertaking ended, I am sure you would not object to any plan that might answer this end, as you say you w^d^ interfere in no arrangement we might make among ourselves. Would there in this case be any occasion for Lawyers? I should think not. Be assured that M^r^ B Smith might be brought to this—

present money & present gratification being all he cares for—— Where would be the necessity of starting doubts about so many points as Mr Tyler has made out, if M^{r} B Smith is induced to take a present sum & waive all that. It cannot signify to any human <being>. I could deal with Mr Berney had I the power, & Mr Boehm knows I can. If nothing but dragging on five months more & going to a Chancery Lawyer at last will do, I entreat & implore that the Lawyer may be named, & I will not trouble myself about it at all but go to France as soon as I am releas'd from Jail. I cannot stay in this Country in disgrace & poverty. I am y^{r} Ldships

most Obed^{t} & obligd Ser^{t}, C T Smith

Petworth House Archives MS. No address or postmark.

NOTES

1. On moneys owed to local tradesmen, see CS to Charlotte Mary Smith, 2 Feb. 1803, n. 12.

2. The letter alluded to here is probably one from S. H. Halliday to CS, dated 13 Feb. 1803 from Grove, Camberwell. It suggests that they exchanged several letters, including letters he acknowledged receiving from her on 18 Jan. and 4 Feb. that have not survived. Halliday is clearly writing as a liaison between BS and CS. His short letter concludes:

> What you notice on this head, I should think would be acceptable to him, & have some tendency towards influencing him to meet matters according to the plan you have proposed, but I can see no reasonable ground of objection, when I consider your letters on why he should want any stimulus to do what is his, as much as your own Interest to expedite. If I can spare a little time tomorrow, I will write him again, and state your remarks concerning the Dividends and recommend once more his settling in the way proposed. When I receive his letter you may be assured, I will lose no time in communicating its contents to you[.] (PHA #7364)

To the earl of Egremont

[Frant] 17th Feby 1803
My Lord,

Your Ldsps cover enclosing Mr Turners brotherly and honourable testimonials reach'd me to day. I hope you are convinced that in this instance at least I have not deserved the imputation of a Lyar. Indeed my Lord I wish you would condescend to tell me what I have done to deserve the very harsh treatment & bitter sufferings I have endured & am still to endure! In looking over y^{r} Ldp's letters, I perceive that till within two years they breathed only humanity & benevolence: a constant desire to releive me from undesserved distress & to obtain justice for my unfortunate children. What have I done since that you now seem not only to Abandon me to the miseries of poverty but to embitter it by reproach—— And can you wonder or ought you to be angry when, astonishd at an alteration so strange & unmerited, I cannot but think that some influence, some opinions very unlike those your own heart would dictate, have thus ruind all my hopes of your friendship?

I beg your pardon if I offend. But it is my reverence for your character & conviction of your real goodness of heart that makes me think thus.

My Lord, to avoid the humiliation of insult from the Man of whom I wrote to you yesterday,[1] I was obligd yesterday (as he brought a London Rider with him who supplies him with some of the various articles in which he deals) to give a draft at a fortnight, for 20£ on the trust. To day, I have seen a person who says he will give me 105£ here for my books[2] which will be better than sending them to London. Therefore if your Lordship will only be merciful enough to let Messrs Pybus accept this draft so that it may not be return'd & my distress renew'd——I will immediately, on receiving the money for the books, replace it. Alas! how little I thought I should be reduced to this!

I have had a Letter from M^{r} B Smith dated 11th Feby. He continues to evade my proposal of appointing two Gentlemen Friends of his own to settle his difference with me & insists on having 400£ immediately, which he says I can get for him if I please & that your Lordships had positively agreed to it.

I have sent the Letter to Miss Smith who will send it to yr Ldshp if necessary. I inform'd him of the attempt made by Mr Morris to cheat his Son Willm as a reason why Harriet was more than before dependent on me—— He (being a Man of great reticence of manners & regularity of conduct)[3] is much hurt at this attempt—so contrary to integrity.

Mr Morris on one hand (tho he has luckily fail'd), Mr Turner on the other, & Mr Benjn Smith to make up the respectable trio—have all contributed to shew what is to be done or attempted & to convince me that there is something in old Smiths Money that acts on such characters as Rhodium does on Rats.[4]

While my miseries are accumulated till like the fabled snakes on the head of Medusa, they turn the hearts of those who were most disposed to serve me to Marble—— Y^{r} Lordships directing me an an^{r} ab^{t} Y^{e} 20£ will greatly oblige y^{r}

Most humble & unfortunate Ser^{t},
Charlotte Smith

Petworth House Archives MS. No address or postmark.

NOTES

1. Holmwood, to whom she owed £42.

2. Henry Fry of Tunbridge Wells, her sometime solicitor.

3. A sarcastic and bitter reference to BS. William Towers Smith, who had taken Harriet to India in 1799, married Catherine Maria Morris on 15 Mar. 1800, and he shipped Harriet home about that time seriously ill with malaria. The Mr. Morris named here might have been William's new bride's father ("son" being used for "son-in-law" at the time). But who tried to cheat William and how that made Harriet more dependent on CS is never made clear.

4. Oil of rhodium, from rosewood trees, was used to entice rats.

To Samuel Rose

Frant near Tunbridge Wells
Feby 19th 1803
Dear Sir,

I consider myself as particularly oblig'd to you for the trouble you have so kindly and so effectually taken in a matter which I consider it my duty to have settled & which is (not only on that account, but from every motive of affection towards the darling child so cruelly torn from me) particularly near my heart—— If Mr Tyler had condescended to tell me, either when I wrote so frequently on this subject or when he was here, what was <u>really</u> meant by saying that Mr Hayley had never accepted the Trust, nothing would have been more easy than for me to have obviated that difficulty. But instead of doing so, he affected to be satisfied with the paragraph which I shew'd him in Mr Hayleys letter & never named the <u>omission</u> of his signature to the Articles—— This must have been done only to give trouble & to compel me either to desist from my application on this matter or, by persevering, to irritate Lord Egremont, His Lordship having declared that if <u>he</u> could help it, he never would invest <u>any thing at all</u> in M^r De Fovilles right. <u>Why</u> he took this resolution, I know not. But my having combated it upon the ground of justice & equity & represented that his Lordship had <u>no right</u> to set aside the Will & that the duty of a Trustee was to fulfill it has been one cause of his Lordships fits of displeasure against me. But as these fits came on occasionally on other subjects & disappeard without any ill effects, I was not to be driven back from a purpose which I knew to be right——

Lord Egremont, with all those good qualities which none can be more sensible of than I am, is really the most difficult Man in the World to act with in business since he never takes time to investigate any subject but takes up at an hazard, or perhaps as Tyler chuses to shew it, any matter wch comes before him, & in three days he looks at it under some other aspect &

either forgets or denies every thing he had before declared himself determin'd upon—— This has now happen'd so often—and the consequences to me individually and to the affairs of my family have been already so injurious & are likely to be so much more hurtful—that I own my first wish now is for Lord Egremont to resign a Trust of which he complains so heavily, but in which I must say the greater part of the trouble has arisen from his own undecided conduct & the impertinence of Tyler. That Man is a violent coxcomb in his way & fancies that he is equal to the Chancellor or the Cheif Justice, & by way of convincing Lord Egremont of his abilities & zeal, he has exercised himself in raising difficulties and objections that he may descant upon them with that wide mouth'd eloquence which few people have spirits to contend with.

When Lord E. sent for me over to Petworth house a few days only after I had received the account of my poor Charles's death in Barbados & set this wrangling Attorney to make me give an account of the dates of my childrens death & other particulars which would have shook my spirits dreadfully at any time but which I was very ill able to bear then; When, after having submitted to this & to a long & painful discussion of two days, he went away to Brighthelmstone & left the business undone & undecided for which he had given me all this trouble & torture & kept me waiting in the neighbourhood of Petworth almost a fortnight longer; I own I saw such a want of feeling or of meaning or Both that I found my dream of protection & safety in Lord Egremonts friendship fading fast away.[1]

I was still however willing to beleive he would finally act as he had so repeatedly declared was his intention, but since that time & more especially since last Winter (when he volunteerd a most kind & generous action & then repented of it,[2] & tho it had gone so far that he could not recede, yet he embitterd his generosity by something very like direct insult to those in whose favor he had offerd it); Since he never seems to know for a week together what his purpose is & imputes purposes & plans to me which I never thought of & will not hear a word I have to say; when (tho not legally authorised as Trustee to my marriage articles) he has taken upon him to stop all the income arising from my fortune, to replace money advanced from Rich[d] Smiths estate by Lord Es own direction & consent by that means depriving me of every resource, & irritating to no manner of purpose the Man into whose power this conduct throws me more than before, nothing seems to be now left for me to wish, or to do, but to endeavour to prevail on Lord Egremont to put an end to the trouble, of which he complains. I have told him so & said, "I did not think I should lose the friend in the Trustee, but since from some strange fatality they seem'd to be incompatible, I entreated him to remain my friend & cease to be annoy'd by the Trust"—— His ans[r] to this is at once vague & angry, but I understand that he has now taken up an idea that he cannot resign the trust but under an order of the Court of Chancery or by appeal to a Chancery Lawyer. With the first, I was threatend during the whole Summer, & Tyler said to his agents in Town & to others that he would have Chancery. Lord E. however paid (as Mr Tyler decided) the last installment but one, & Chancery for the present is not talked of. But this Chancery Lawyer is installed on state in his imagination, & he accuses me of being unwilling to agree to it, or if I am, that I insist upon Mr Leach,[3] as I beleive I named before to you. It is in vain I have assured him that I never saw Mr Leach & care not who is engaged if it be a Man of character unprejudiced on any side. He will beleive nothing I say. The truth is that, tho I am willing to do this rather than let the trust remain in such a troublesome & confus'd state as it is now in & without any hope of my ever seeing an end to it, Yet I had much rather his Lordship should resign it to two persons not Lawyers but merely Men of business who shall act as merely the holders of the residue against Mr Smith & pay him the interest of the residue for his life, leaving me to resume my right of Executrx & to act in getting in the remaining debts which amount to upwards of 1000£ the greater part or all of which will be lost—because Mr Tyler knows nothing at all of the business & will fancy that he does——

I should now, thro the very great kindness & attention of a friend of mine in Barbados,[4] have got in 500£ Stg of this, but Mr Tyler could not be prevaild upon to send me a paper that my friend required, & of this such advantage has been taken that the Money now will not be forthcoming these twelvemonths. Two or three times in the course of these ill fated transactions, there have arisen questions on which I have wishd to have legal advice & Lord E. has then said, "It is of no use, for any person may have just what opinion they please of a Counsel. They always say what they know is expected of them." That assertion with all possible defference to his Lordship is certainly not correct, but this I am sure of: that no Counsel upon Earth Can give his opinion or award as the subject demands if the case is drawn up (as it will be) by Tyler. I shall not submit to his statement and we shall have occasion of dissent & altercation on the threshold, & all the business to prose over, & squabble over again. One would be tempted to think that Lord Egremont, having been so active in making experiments on Turnips & Teggs,[5] Ploughs and potatoes, is now trying how much misery and deprivation an old Woman can bear without dying under it, or he never would keep me destitute as he does of the actual necessaries of existence & suffering all the inconveniencies of actual poverty when he could so easily releive me from oppression and himself from the trouble he complains of & entitle himself to the everlasting gratitude of my family——— ——

Will you, Dear Sir, at your leisure, only tell me whether Lord Egremont & Mr Turner <u>cannot with perfect safety resign</u> the Trust, as they took it? That is, if <u>Mr B Smith</u> and <u>all</u> the persons interested agree to release them? To the Original Trust in 1784, there were four Trustees. Every one of whom resignd one after another under the authority of a Clause for that purpose which clause equally exists in the transfer[red] trust. Why then should there be legal interference call'd for, when it is very certain that no Chancery Lawyer can give any award without having the whole of the case before him, which includes a period of six and twenty years & such a Chaos of folly in the maker of the Will & roguery, waste, & ideotism in the persons who have had the (<u>mis</u>)management of the effects since, that it is I am very sure a brouillerie[6] that nobody can disentangle—& which is not worth it now if they could——

If I could prevail on Lord E. to let it be left to two persons (& they shall be chosen by M^r B Smith himself, so little do I apprehend <u>his</u> meeting with any support even from his own connections in this respect), I do assert that in three months there would be an end of the business. Whereas with Mr Tylers offensive impertinence & his influence on Lord E, I know that it never will end while I can drag on life—— I do not mean to presume on any information you may give me to make use of your name. All I would know is if I may not say to Lord E. that it is possible for him to give up the trust with safety, if all parties agree to his doing so, Then perhaps when he is no longer plagued with these chimera's raisd by the Sieur Tyler, only to shew his skill in fighting with them, Lord E may resume towards me that humanity & consideration wch of late he has wholly forgotten, but which is all I ask of him——

I have been very diffuse & am conscious how much I presume on your goodness & intrude on your time, but I find myself so liable to the imputation of ingratitude when I am compelld to say I wish Lord E's Trust at an end that I am driven to an explanation of my motives. I own I <u>do</u> feel it to be extremely cruel that—because he will not beleive my Son Nicholas's intentions tho I have the strongest assurances of what they are under his own hand & that a week or a month may bring over the power of Attorney I expect from him—Lord E. should refuse me so small an assistance as 79£ (belonging to my Son) & thereby compel me to the hard & dreadful necessity of selling not only what little furniture I have, but my books without which I have represented to his Lordship that I cannot live, for without books I cannot write & even were those efforts out of the question, I have no other resource but books, cut off as I am from society & having indeed lost all relish for it. A greater act of cruelty therefore can hardly be exercised, & I really do not know that I <u>can</u> live without them. I am sure it is inhuman to put me to the trial for so small a consideration. But I have implored as for an alms in vain!

Mr De Foville has the deed in question. I have no copy of it myself. I will write to him by the post that carries this to London, & if he has not already waited on you with it, he will do so I am sure immediately, with the most grateful Sense of yours & of Mr Hayleys kindness—

I have the honor to be
Dear Sir your most obliged &
obed Sert
Charlotte Smith

McMaster University Library MS. No address or postmark.

NOTES

1. This torturous sentence and the one that follows it do not admit of any shortening. In the first, two long dependent clauses beginning with *when* precede the independent clause, "I own I saw . . ." Similarly, in next paragraph, three dependent clauses, with dependent clauses, parenthetical phrases, and modifiers attached to them, precede the independent clause, "nothing seems to be now left . . ." I have left CS's semicolons to show the boundaries of each dependent clause.

2. Evidently, Egremont recommended Lionel to the duke of York for advancement to major but did not supply the £900 requisite for purchasing the commission. In her zeal to supply the funds, CS may have overstepped her bounds—not with the patron but with the trustee (see CS to Egremont, 12 Jan. 1802 and n. 3, 17 Jan., 22 Jan., and 1 Mar. 1802). Whatever Egremont had done, and whatever CS had asked of him, the tide had turned by Apr. (see CS to Rose, 7 Apr. 1803). She may have mixed too many requests in with her hopes for Lionel, and Egremont may well have insulted someone.

3. John Leach, equity draftsman. Along with Samuel Rose, CS wanted the Chancery case referred to "some Gentleman acquainted with the affairs" (see CS to Egremont, 24 Nov. 1802). But this is the last we hear of Leach.

4. Thomas Maxwell Adams began working on trust matters in Barbados in Apr. 1802; CS admired him, but nowhere else mentions him as a friend.

5. Yearling sheep before their first clipping. Egremont embarked on a variety of agricultural experiments at Petworth.

6. Misunderstanding or disagreement, with confusion.

To the earl of Egremont

[Frant, 24 February 1803]
My Lord,

There has I imagine been more than time enough for Mr B Smiths answer, but I have received none & am almost sure that when it does come it will be to no other purpose than to require a repetition on my part of entreaties or treaties which I feel it more & more impossible for me to undertake. Your Lordship being decided against beleiving any thing I say, it is of no avail for me to represent that I am now so very ill & so nearly depriv'd of the use of my limbs that I am quite disabled from the fatigue of moving & shall probably remain to die here. Common humanity would, one should have thought, have induced Mr Turner to compassionate me & not to have exposed me to the distress of mind & personal inconvenience that I have undergone— —To be doom'd to a lingering death in this manner, after having so long hoped for competence & peace & earned it, as I thought, so hardly! I trust & hope Such a fate as mine is single in the annals of human misery. It is now too late for a remedy. There is nothing but death for me to expect————I only beg to know whether y^{r} Ldship will allow the 20£ I have drawn for to be paid at Mess^{r} Pybus's. How humiliating to be reduced to beg as for alms!——

Your Lordships
most humble & oblig'd Ser^{t},
Charlotte Smith

Frant. Feby 24th 1803

Petworth House Archives MSS. No address or postmark.

To the earl of Egremont

[Frant, ca. 26 February 1803]
My Lord,

I enclose a Letter which I received on Saturday from Mr Benjn Smith.[1] Your Lordship will perhaps be convinced that I was right in my conjectures that nothing would be done with this unhappy wretch. I & his very unfortunate children are his victims. Little did I think when I was taking so much pains to release these wretched affairs from the hands of Robinson & Prettejohn & Parkin that, at the end of seven years when all I attempted was completed (tho death & misery have been the price), that I should myself be reduced to a <u>state of beggary</u>.

I have now sold my few effects & books & must remove to an Inn at Tunbridge Wells, there to stay till I get the money paid for which I have sold them & till I know whether Y^{r} Lordship will listen to my earnest entreaties to be allow'd 20£ which I drew for, for I cannot go till then. Staying at an Inn is very expensive, but I have no remedy As I could not well sleep here when my bed &c was removed.

An answer my Lord is hoped for even by the most abject petitioner. I have already lost the use of my limbs by remaining in so cold a situation during the winter & probably shall never be able to walk again. I am now writing with blisters on my breast for spasms which reduce me to extreme weakness by pain & want of sleep.

I should hope that M[r] Turners vengeance is nearly satisfied & that my offences whatever they have been are sufficiently punishd!

I must entreat Your Lordship to direct that M[r] Benj[n] Smith may be undeceived in regard to y[r] intentions. As you see, he persists in asserting that I & my eldest daughter prevent his having 400£. It is utterly impossible that he can legally have it. But so far am I from desiring to have any thing to do with the settlement of these affairs that I desire only to have a certainty of a maintenance from my own money, & he & his affairs may go—to the valley of Jehosephat. But My children are old enough & have known enough of their dear good Papa to take care that he shall not strip them more than he has done.

If I should ever get to Elsted, which at present I doubt, would your Lordship so far condescend to recollect your former kindness as to allow me to have now & then books of referrence that I may want from Petworth. Assuring y[r] Lordship that I shall have a conveyance provided to prevent any injury to them.

I have sold my own & cannot write without them. I am y[r] Lordships most oblig'd & ob[t] Ser[t],

Charlotte Smith

Petworth House Archives MS. No address or postmark.

NOTES

1. In a letter to Egremont on 10 Feb., CS agreed to write a "temperate" letter to her estranged husband. It does not survive, but BS sent a firm and angry response on 25 Feb. 1803:

> Madam
>
> Your false, contumelious, malignant, and incongruous letter of the 16th Ins[t], I shall make a very short reply to.
>
> "You bite against a file: Cease.
>
> You say you will pay the Four Hundred pounds due to me, on condition of transfering the completion of the Trust, to yourself, and your amiable Daughter Charlotte, this, after your repeated breach's of faith, I positively refuse to do, and as the late Lord Onslow used to say, I wo[d] not trust either of you, with a hair of my Horses tail, and wo[d] starve first, which I sho[d] be made to do by such an act. If it is your Ultimatum, let it remain so and now I will tell you, what shall be mine——
>
> The Four Hundred pounds I will have voluntarily, or compulsively, if the first as a preliminary step, I will as M[r] Boehm has advised it, leave all other points to be arbitrated by two persons (and a third as usual on these

> occasions call'd in if they disagree)——Lord Egremont, & your self to Nominate one, and me another. If you choose to close with this, I will sign any paper fairly drawn up, and approved by my Solicitor to carry such reference into effect. I am Madam
>
> Your Hum[ble] Serv[t]
> B Smith

Edmund Boehm, writing to Charlotte Mary, cites letters that BS wrote to him on 23 Feb. and 1 Mar., to warn of BS's determination and lack of concern for CS's troubles and the difficulties that extend to their children:

> Nothing shall persuade him to agree to any terms Short of the payment of the arrears due to him. In one [letter] he charges Mrs. Smith and you with procrastinating the payments that Lord Egremont had agreed You might settle with him, and he goes on to say, "I have made up my mind, as firm as a rock, that till they are paid, the family shall share nothing with me, therefore this must be the preliminary step to a peaceable arrangement of the affairs—This being paid I leave every other point to be settled by arbitration—with these Sentiments I remain Invincible."——(Edmund Boehm to Charlotte Mary Smith, unpub., 21 Mar. 1803, PHA #7364)

To the earl of Egremont

[Frant, ca. 26 February 1803]
My Lord,

I enclose your Lordship a second Letter from M[r] Benj[n] Smith.

My proposal was not as he states—or anything like it. If it had, I should be as fit for bedlam as he undoubtedly is.

I could not offer to pay him 400£ on certain conditions, simply because I have no more power over it than over the money in the exchanges.

I said, that if he would cease to torment all the parties & more particularly your Lordship with such applications & to raise such everlasting impediments to the final settlement of the whole business— if he would leave what remain'd to be done, the troublesome part to be settled by me, under the check and direction of two friends of his own, which two friends, when the whole of the residue was collected, should receive & invested for his own use—that then I would endeavour to prevail on the Persons interested which are in fact all the Mans children (& one of them is not yet of age) to consent to the alienation of 400£ more.

This I did, not because I desire to have any thing to do with the accursed affairs; I'd rather sweep a crossing & depend on the charity of the passengers then have any more plague with them. Far be it from me to grind any longer in this Molina Assiranum[1]—— I was desirous of relieving your Lordship &

restoring, as far as I can, that apparent wish to befriend me which you formerly expressed & I was sorry, that after my unhappy Charles's life had been so sacrificed, the seven or eight hundred pounds in Barbados should be lost.

But since this most wretched compound of every bad quality that can disgrace the creature in the human form will neither lead nor drive—Since I have now made the last & only sacrifice I have to make & have parted with my books & furniture for less than half their value to support his children with one of whom I am still entirely & with the other in a great measure burthen'd—Since I dare not now offer to your Lordship any opinion & can give no assistance in the affairs, I request & wish (& believe Miss Smith is of the same opinion) that you immediately take any measure which may secure the residue to the uses of the Will & put it equally out of M[r] B Smiths power to injure those to whom it belongs; or to give you any further trouble, for y[r] wish to serve them.

I cannot nor did I ever comprehend that the money given to me in marriage had any thing in the world to do with Richard Smiths affairs. It never was his; and & now there is no regular Trust for it. That there should be one is a very important point, and I have laboured it in vain. Let me, my Lord, the treatment I receive so undeservedly & the severe and unheard of shocks I every day receive are shortening my life, let me once more call upon your Lordships humanity & entreat that you will suffer me decidedly to have indeed drawn up legally constituting you Trustee, with some other Gentlemen of character (I will have nothing to do with the Rev[d] Nicholas Turner & have desired him to understand that I will not). Or if you foresee trouble in it, which you no longer wish to take for me, I will (at least I will try) to fix on some other friend, whose generosity I have not put to so severe a proof as it has been my misfortune to do your Lordships—— To me, & to the very unfortunate Children of that wretched Lunatic, I feel this to be of the utmost importance.

In consequence of having to day sold & sent away my books & a part of my furniture, I am surrounded by clamours for every shilling I owe, & am exactly as if I was surrounded by Wolves. I find that after all these sad sacrifices, I shall not have enough by above 50£ even if you are so good as to allow me to have 20£ paid by Mess[rs] —— I most humbly my Lord solicit of you a loan of fifty pounds—I shall have the means of repaying it I trust in July, I hope it is probable before, for I think that my Son Nicholas will not let me long remain in my present state, & there is 79£ still due to him.

As I cannot go from hence till I can pay every body and shall be forced to live at a very expensive Inn till then, I hope your Lordships generous consideration will not allow you to keep me in suspense. More I cannot do than I have now done to convince you that I may be poor & reduced by the cruelty injustice & ingratitude of those who ought to have shielded me from every evil; but that I am not abject, tho my dreadful & humiliating situation has made me sometimes humble myself too much where I have brought myself into contempt. But nothing is really degrading but crime & I have been guilty of none. Your Lordships answer to the last request I shall ever make will greatly oblige

Your most humble
& very grateful Ser^{t}
Charlotte ~~Smith~~

Petworth House Archives MS. No address or postmark.

NOTE

1. Mill of asses.

To the earl of Egremont

[Frant, 28 February 1803]

— —I trust your Lordship will have the goodness to Consider & let me know what are your intentions as to M^{r} B Smith. It is hard to be reduced at my time of life to these cruel exigencies & driven about the World—the sport of the unfeeling & the contempt of the more fortunate. And all because I have made s[ome] exertions for the children of a M[an] always hateful to me, as few Women would have done for those of a Man they had loved, & fewer still could have done. I consider myself as barbarously treated particularly by Mr Turner. The tender mercies of Robinson & Co. are exceeded by those I owe to my own brother. I entreat you, my Lord, to let me hear before I am confin'd for debt at an Inn. Be good enough to direct to the care of Mr Sprange,[1] Tunbridge Wells.

If going to town would be of any use, I would as soon as I am releasd here & can get into a chaise go thither, but I can enter into no expence—that will not certainly answer.

God knows what will become of me.

Your Ldship will have the goodness to let the enclosed Go to the Penny post.[2]

Petworth House Archives MS. Address: Earl of Egremont/ Grosvenor Place/ London. Postmark: TUNB-WELLS/ 36; FREE/ FEB28/ 1803.

NOTES

1. Jasper Sprange (1746–1823), printer, bookseller, and author of *The Tunbridge Wells Guide: or an Account of the Ancient and Present State of That Place* (1797).

2. Written on the address page of this single sheet.

To the earl of Egremont

[Frant, after 10 February and before 2 March 1803]

Gen[l] Dalrymple notices not my application, either for a Letter to Col[l] Backhouse Or the more material request I made to him.[1] Every hope, every assistance seems to fail me when I most want them—for others—for as to myself, I shall not long want them. These last cruel disappointments can<u>not</u> be withstood I beseech your Lordship if the bill is not to be divided to direct that I may be informed so at once— —No, there is no describing what I am condemned to endure—— I have now no longer credit wth the Apothecary of the only medicine that releives my Spasms. <Altho> I could not pay him at Christmas & now must perish unassisted—What <u>have</u> I done to deserve this long course of anguish both of body & mind!

[Unsigned]

Petworth House Archives MS. Address: The Earl of Egremont/ Grosvenor Place/ London. Postmark: TUNB-WELLS/ 36; {franked, place illegible}.

NOTE

1. That is, for a letter of introduction for George; see CS to General Dalrymple, 10 Feb. 1803.

To the earl of Egremont

[Frant, 1 March 1803]

I understand from M[r] Bicknell that <u>he did not</u> tell your Lordship of M[r] Will[m] Smiths abortive & nonsensical attempt to give away his money. And therefore it must have come from M[r] Turner, who heard it from Newhouse.[1] Another proof of their gratitude to me, their discretion, & their Reverence for Truth—— I cannot too soon be at a distance from people capable of so acting towards me, & if I had the power instead of going to the Cottage at Elsted, I would go instantly <u>where I might never hear of them more</u>. I hope your Lordship will not refuse to adopt some means (I am now become indifferent what) to release me from any farther <u>exertions</u> ~~at least~~ before the 7th July. If I am not only useless but ruinous to M[r] B Smiths family, I may at least be allowed the privelege of being starved where I please.

Petworth House Archives MS. Address: Earl of Egremont/ Grosvenor Place/ London—. Postmark: TUNB-WELLS/ 36; FREE/ MAR 1/ 1803.

NOTE

1. Nothing further is said about William's attempt to give away money. If Turner

heard about it from Thomas Newhouse, it quite likely happened when William returned to England in 1798–99; this might be connected with his bond for £3,000 made out to Thomas Henchman and Edmund Boehm (IRO Ref. #200). Charles Bicknell was CS's solicitor.

To Benjamin Smith[1]

Frant 1st March 1803
Sir,

I have only to repeat in answer to your second lunatic Letter re[ceive]d to day, that if you will have the £400 & know how to get it, there is no occasion for me to enter with you into any treaty about it. It is Lord Egremont to whom you must apply, & if his Lordship chuses to let you have it, it is nothing to me. I never said, Mr Benjn Smith, that I would pay you the 400£ on such & such conditions, for it is not and never could be mine to pay, nor have I the least power over it. I said that if you would suffer the business to go on to a conclusion under the direction of <u>two friends of your own</u>, without tormenting Lord Egremont any more, I would then exert myself to get in the rest of the Debts due in Barbadoes, & take that trouble for want of which they will be lost, & I said that these two friends should be put in possession of the residue on your account, of course I could not well starve you as you now do me and my poor unhappy children. Your cause must indeed be a wretched one that you dare not leave to two friends of your own. But I shall canvass nothing with you, wretched compound of folly and wickedness——The Curse of your whole family——a being who disgraces the name of Man and the object at once of abhorrence and contempt.

There are means to <u>make</u> you do your Duty, and to those, they who depend on you must be compelled to have recourse.

For my own part, I will answer no more of your Letters nor trouble myself any more about you. The very sight of your sprawling hand is hateful to my Eyes, and the evident proof you give of your insanity, which is of a species not to excite pity but horror, humbles me so much that I sicken to think I have given birth to creatures who may partake and I fear will of your diabolical disposition. Unnatural, barbarous, selfish, hateful in the sight of Heaven and a Burthen to the Earth.

Do what you will with your nonsense & your <u>ultimatum.</u> Go to Law; get into Chancery. Take Rope enough & hang yourself. I shall not cut you down. I have written to Lord Egremont & desired him to go directly to Chancery. I really do not care one farthing what you do.

I leave this place this Evening with your unhappy Harriett, dearer to you than "the ruddy drops that visit your <u>bad</u> heart,"[2] but you should have written bilious and poisonous for ruddy, for not one drop of human blood have you in that piece of putrid flesh which you wear quasi heart.[3] Not one sensation that belongs to a Man or a Gentleman.

Eight and thirty years have you now been my tormentor. Here it ends ——for you shall not have the power of worrying me any more.

If Lord Egremont chuses it, he may pay you the £400, but I cannot advise it as I know it is his own wish.

I cannot sign a name I detest.

I shall certainly advise Miss Smith and the Legatees, & all your Children who are all interested, not to consent to giving you £400. If you are in Debt, you ought not to be, and you have robbed them too much already.

But what need this if you can get the money by force.

I shall leave Orders with the Postmaster here to return any Letters that may come after I am gone with the Hamilton Postmark.

Petworth House Archives MS. No address or postmark.

NOTES

1. Copy of CS's letter in a clerk's hand. On the back, a note in another hand reads, "copy of a scurrilous letter from Mrs Smith to Mr B. Smith." The term "scurrilous" clung to CS's efforts to work for her children's rights. In a lengthy letter to the earl of Egremont a year and a half later (8 Sept. 1804), she seems astonished and hurt that he considers her "scurrilous, abusive, virulent, querulous" and has evidently accused her of "misrepresentation, scurrility." On 10 Sept. 1804, CS wrote to Sarah Rose, "M[r] Benj[n] Smiths visit to Petworth seem'd to change the noble Lords very variable mind, & he began pelting me again with the charges of virulence, violence, & scurrility, & gross misrepresentation." A few days later, CS complained to William Tyler, ". . . Letters as M[r] B-- Smiths to me are to be approved of by Lord Egremont while mine (on a plain matter of business & with as little bitterness as it was possible on such an occasion towards such a Man to use) was condemned as scurrilous . . ." (15 Sept. 1804).

2. From the discussion of wifehood in *Julius Caesar* 2.1.287–89.

3. The copyist or CS herself omitted words needed here for good sense. The phrase should probably read "in that piece of putrid flesh [in] which you wear [your] quasi heart." *Quasi*, meaning "similar to" or "almost," was in current usage and is, of course, insulting.

To the earl of Egremont

[Frant, 2 March 1803]
My Lord,

Having occasion to write to M[r] Bicknell, I take the liberty of requesting y[r] Lordship to allow a servant to put that & the other Letter into the 2[d] post, as I must otherwise pay the postage which is an object. Suffer me, my Lord, as it is not likely I shall now give yr Lordship much more trouble, to request that you would be pleased to inform me as soon as you can what steps you chuse to take. I want only to be at a certainty & not to have the blame for what I cannot help. To be accused of being the Author of my own misery, & death, & all within three months!——

My Lord, if I have been so unfortunate as to have incurred your everlasting displeasure precisely when I most attempted to avoid it, You are surely too candid & too humane not to see that it is not just I should be deprived of the regard & assistance of the rest of my friends (for I may still have some) by the idea they will naturally take up that your Lordship, after a series of unremitting and extraordinary kindness for fourteen or fifteen years, would never so entirely change your conduct & opinion & suffer me rather than run a very trifling & almost imaginary risk of less than 100£ to be exposed to the severest mortifications, the cruellest indigence unless I had deserved to suffer: & In consequence of the trust to my marriage articles, which y^{r} Lordship is not yet legally invested with (at least such was Mr Tylers opinion when he was here) you put it into M^{r} B Smiths power to starve me & his unhappy children. Such has been the effect of giving him ~~power~~ right over the income, & such will be the effect of every thing that gives him any ground to resist the laws of honor, honesty, & humanity— —

For my own part, my Lord, I do assure you I am so very weary of all I have gone thro to so little purpose, It is so hateful to me to be in the power or to have any communication with M^{r} B Smith; I should be so much easier for the poor remnant of my miserable life, had I never any intercourse with that Lunatic that, if I knew how to support Harriet & assist poor George, I had rather trust to my own industry, feeble & cripple as I am, & go where I may never see or hear again of M^{r} B Smith, leaving him to do as he will or as he can, & let him—since it is Law (against me tho in no other instance that ever I heard of)—take all that belongs to me. It w^{d} be something to be allowed to die at a distance & released from him & to be removed from certain other of my relations whom I never wish to see again.

I have now sold every thing & made every sacrifice. Most unjust it is that I should be compelled to do it. I only ask of y^{r} Lordship to do me the justice to say that I have committed no crime to deserve your dereliction.

I take the liberty of sending under another cover Copies of two letters[1] of y^{r} Lordships In one of which you approve in the strongest terms of Mr Dayrell,[2] Yet when any thing in my favor is given in opinion by that very Mr Dayrell, it is not beleived.

Can y^{r} Lordship therefore be surprised at my reluctance to abide by the decision of Counsel (admitting I had ever shewn such) if the case is to be laid before Counsel under these decided impressions against me. Every thing, every point in dispute is stated against me & doubts raisd where none ever were started before If I complain you are offended![3]

As I am sorting my papers & packing up for my removal tomorrow to Wightons at Tunbridge Wells till I can get money to release myself, Therefore I trouble you now for the last time & I beg your answer. I really want a little quiet after this last sad sacrifice & wish to know the worst—if worse can be. Your Lordship will excuse my writing so ill, but I am personally suffering & can do no better. I am your most oblig'd ser^{t},

Charlotte Smith[4]

Petworth House Archives MS. No address or postmark.

NOTES

1. These letters, dated Petworth, 16 Mar. 1802, and Tuesday, [Jan.] 1798, follow this letter in PHA #7364.
2. Edmund Dayrell, a lawyer often consulted by CS as well as by Egremont and Tyler.
3. Written vertically across the top half of the page.
4. Written upside down in the upper left corner of the page.

To the earl of Egremont

Wightons, Tunbridge Wells
March 3rd 1803
My Lord,

Mr Boehm is, as I understand from My daughter, again attempting to see what he can do with M^{r} B S. From him that wretched being has always extorted money, But now he is weary of it.

"Quoth Gilpin, so am I"[1]

Having dared to make the last sacrifice—the last after my fortune, my health, my labour, my repose, my taste, my talents (as to my youth that would have gone of course, but it might have been passt more pleasantly); After I have been degraded by belonging to such a monster——— I who might & who ought to have been very (Oh! how) differently situated; I feel that except my life, which is of no value, I have nothing more to lose.

"The already plunder'd, need no robber fear"[2]

I am therefore determin'd to get the matter settled, & if, as appears probable at present, I cannot live in dear England, I will go somewhere else. But Mr Benjn Smith shall not rob me more than I can help or those unhappy creatures who bear his name—— Would to God none of them partook of his nature—— It is always a comfort to know the worst & At the ne plus ultra is now, I think, the celebrated Charlotte Smith.[3]

May I hope that Your Lordship will have the goodness to let a Servant take this to M[r] Boehms house in Spring Garden, Ste 4, or if he is not there, to free it to

Ed[md] Boehm
Ottershaw Park
Chertsey. Surrey

If any museum should ever be erected of Human phenomena, I hope places will be found for Benj[n] Smith Esq[re] & the Rev[d] Nicholas Turner.

I have sold my books which were valued at £105 (& very much undervalued as Cadell & Davies allowd) for less than 70£.

The poorest labourer is protected in his working materials, But mine are torn from me without remorse!

Fearful of overweight, I have enclosed the Letter in another cover.[4]

Petworth House Archives MS. No address or postmark.

NOTES

1. From William Cowper's comic ballad "The Diverting History of John Gilpin," first published anonymously in the *Public Advertiser* (1782). Gilpin on horseback was following his wife and her party in a carriage to Edmonton, where they are to renew their wedding vows. The horse runs away with him, and when he arrives, exhausted from the wild ride, they all call out to him:

> Stop, stop John Gilpin!—Here's the house—
> They all at once did cry,
> The dinner waits and we are tir'd,
> Said Gilpin—so am I. (ll. 145–48)

But the horse takes off and runs another ten miles back home. It is an apt quotation for CS's endless traversal of ground already trod with respect to her unmanageable husband.

2. Lady Mary Wortley Montagu, "An Answer to a Love Letter in Verse" (1750), l. 18.

3. The letter, which has many short postscripts, is unsigned unless CS considered this ironic outcry to stand for her signature.

4. Written on the last page where the address would be.

To the earl of Egremont

[Elsted, 10 March 1803]

My Lord,

By the sacrifice of every thing I most wish'd to have preserved, By borrowing of my daughter a considerable Sum, & obtaining time of some of the persons to whom I owed money, particularly the Apothecary, I at length was releas'd from the seven months misery that has been inflicted on me, but I was three days on the road, from illness & am now merely alive. Yet a little & I shall trouble nobody, but Your Lordship certainly cannot intend to destroy a person who has never intentionally offended you But has always done justice to your goodness & generousity. It is in your Lordships power to let my very few remaining days pass without more personal distress or to send me to the grave in misery—

I wish to have the power of paying Mrs Dorset a small Sum she lent me some months ago; it is necessary for me to buy a Cow, as I have a field here & no other means of obtaining Milk for my family, & I would fain be able to pay for what I have. Suffer me therefore, my Lord, to ask what resolution it is your pleasure to take, & whether no means can be thought of that may allow me to have the part of the money—ab^t^ 125£—now lying useless from the last dividend on y^r^ 500£ or whether by some method I may not be afforded wherewithal to exist which never was so totally denied me as now— — Whatever may be your Lordships determination, I do most earnestly entreat that I may no longer be kept in suspence. You have now had Mr Benjn Smiths letters before you for some time, & I should hope have come to some decision. Suspense is what I am unable any longer to endure.

What have I done, Good God! to suffer thus?—— I am y^r^

Lordships most humble
and obligd Ser^t^,
Charlotte Smith

Elstead, March 10th 1803

Petworth House Archives MS. No address or postmark.

To the earl of Egremont

Elsted March 20th
1803
My Lord,

Not having been till of late accustomed to the contemptuous treatment I am now compelled to undergo—that of having no answer to any application whatsoever that I make—I am sometimes tempted to beleive y^r^ Lordship either does not receive my Letters or will not take the trouble to read them.

Either your Ldship is or is not Trustee to my Marriage articles. If you are, it is absolutely necessary that a regular & proper Trust deed should be executed; if you are not, give me leave to say that the totally withholding the income—which you empowerd Mr Smith to receive but which [n]ow benefits nobody—is a measure very injurious to me who am absolutely destitute, & I think cannot be legal, as you consented to & sign'd the advances to him, & they cannot be taken back out of my money. If Mr Turners brotherly desire to injure me is satisfied, I trust, my Lord, you will at least have as much recollection of your former goodness as to signify to me what your intentions are. Your Lordship has most undoubtedly a right to get this troublesome business off your hands in any way that you may chuse. But there I apprehend the matter should end, & that y^{r} Lordship has as little right, as I am still willing to hope you have inclination, to perpetuate by suspence & anxiety the misery of one whom you were pleased to undertake to serve & benefit.

An an^{r} therefore, My Lord, which you would not refuse to the petition of one of the humblest of your domestics, you will not I trust Much longer deny to

Y^{r} Lordships most Obed Ser^{t},
Charlotte Smi[th]

Petworth House Archives MS. No address or postmark.

To the earl of Egremont

[Elsted, 23 or 24 March 1803]
My Lord,

Your Lordship having taken out of my hands all management or interference in the affairs, & as I am denied now even an answer, I have only to enclose two Letters I have received to day—One from Mr Boehm, by which it appears that M^{r} B Smith is as firm as a rock[1] in not agreeing to any thing till his arrears are paid (New found arrears I suppose amounting to 400£). His firmness will remain unshaken by any attempt of mine, & I prepare myself for a short sojourn in the County jail, for which I am liable by the refusal of your Lordship to let me have only 20£ as a loan or in any way & returning the draft I was compelled to draw. Be it so—— There is a fatality which cannot be resisted——

By Mr Adams's Letter, it appears that he has not yet been able to obtain a sight of the Deed transferring the trust of 1784 to y^{r} Lordship & the Revd Mr Turner & therefore cannot compel that rogue Griffith[2] to give him security. The Sum is above 500£ St^{g}. Mr Adams is about to sell his property & quit the Island, & the Estate of Richard Smith will lose the Money, as nobody else will take any trouble about it—— From this wretched cause, the want of this paper, my unfortunate Son Charles was detain'd in that accursed Island & lost his life. But such is the manner in which business is done. Mr Turner undertook to be the man of business, & he has done it as he has done his own. From your Lordship, I neither asked nor expected attention to these things, but if a Trust is undertaken, it ought in some way or other to be executed. Perhaps you will deign to give orders to your Solicitor to take information of Messrs Baxter & Martin[3] about this deed—that if Mr Prescod[4] has not taken it with him, an authenticated copy may be obtain'd & sent out. Otherwise the money from Griffith will be lost. If I could have got any information about it, I would have taken the necessary measures long ago. But whatever I have ask'd has been repelled & calld nonsense; Mr Tyler knows so much better than I do what should be done in the West India affairs that it is fit I should retire from ~~any~~ trouble so useless & which only brings upon me expence & treatment such as I never expected to have been exposed to.

I enclose the copy of a charge for sending out a power of Attorney last year. I have paid it to Mr Henry Fry at Tunbridge Wells, to whom on coming away I was forced to sell my books for about two thirds of their value that I might pay him for his applications & meetings with Mr Benjn Smith, & Mr Fauntleroy[5] 50£ which he lent me last Summer, when Harriet's dreadful illness & your Lordships absolute refusal of assistance, compelled me to borrow it or suffer her to want as well as the rest of my family.

Never sure was an human being condemn'd to suffer what I do. As there is now 30£ trust money in Mr Pybus's hands, I hope yr Lordship will be pleased to order me immediate payment of this trifling Sum—to me a matter of importance, and I hope Mr Turner will hereafter allow me to receive the 5.18s. a year which he has taken since 1793. I am in extreme want of the sum which is (I think) due to me on this account, but I have no chance of getting it.

Your Lordship, whether you vouchsafe to answer me or no, will have the goodness to return the Letters enclosed As well as those admirable production's of Mr Benjn Smith which I took the liberty to enclose to yr Lordship—from

Your most obedt humble Sert,
Charlotte ~~Smith~~[6]

Petworth House Archives MS. No address or postmark.

NOTES

1. BS had written to Edmund Boehm on 23 Feb. and 1 Mar.: "I have made up my mind, as firm as a rock, that till they are paid, the family shall share nothing with me . . ." (see Edmund Boehm to Charlotte Mary Smith, 21 Mar. 1803. Petworth MS. Address: Miss Charlotte Smith/ Elsted/ near Godalmin/ Surrey. Postmark: CHERTSEY/ 19; A/ MAR 23/1803).

2. James Griffith of Barbados (see CS to William Tyler, 18 July 1802, n. 2).

3. Prescod's attorneys in London, John Dayrell Martin, Squire Stafford Baxter, and Robert Baxter of 4 Furnival's Inn (see CS to William Tyler, 9 Mar. 1802).

4. William Prescod, who purchased from the estate Gay's plantation in Barbados (see CS to Egremont, 9 July 1800, and nn. 1, 8).

5. William Fauntleroy of London, who often discounted bills for CS during this period.

6. In this and other letters after this date, CS crossed out her husband's hated surname.

To the Reverend Nicholas Turner

[Elsted, ca. 24 March 1803]

If you would be so good as to apply to Lord Egremont only for the eight pounds I have for the Estate—which surely ought to be returnd to me—& if Mr Tyler w^{d} be pleasd to pay me the 2£ 5S or whatever it is—miserable ballance of the annuity I sacrificed to the maintenance of M^{r} B Smiths family, I should be releived from the excessive torture of my servants knowing I have not a sixpence in my pocket, & surely there is neither justice nor humanity in keeping this from me.

It is impossible to describe what I suffer!—it is impossible to bear it.

[Unsigned]

Petworth House Archives MS. Address: Revd Mr Turner/ ~~Mrs Dorset~~/ Luggersale/ ~~Bignor Park~~/ ~~Petworth~~/ n^{r} Petworth. Postmark: GODALMIN/ 34; {date illegible}.

To Thomas Cadell, Jr., and William Davies

[Elsted, 24 March 1803]

Gentlemen,

By the assistance of my Sister Mrs Dorset of Bignor Park, I have nearly completed the little book of Poetry intended for children between the ages of six and twelve years. Part of it, but a small part only, will be compilation, the rest original by her or by me & chiefly on the subjects of natural history with plain explanatory notes where they may be requisite. I namd this to you some time ago, but you declined the purchase; I do not therefore trouble you on that subject now, but merely mean to enquire whether you would be so obliging as to become the publishers if I print it as my own account.[1] I have at length entirely closed my engagement with Mr Phillips, & we part good friends,[2] but reasons not necessary to state will make it, I know, disagreeable to M[rs] Dorset to have the little work in which she has assisted me in his hands, and I am also certain that she will be better pleased could it be publish'd by you. I thought of having plates, but now doubt whether that would answer. Your advice in respect to that & answer whether you would publish it would very greatly oblige me——

I Am in daily expectation of Letters of the greatest importance from Bombay. As my Son Nicholas, tho I have inform'd him I have no longer any pretence to trouble you, sometimes directs his Letters to your care, I trouble you to inform you that my residence for some time to come will be at this place & that, should a packet come which I expect, I shall be greatly oblig'd to you to forward it hither as early as possible. I am, Gent[n],

Your oblig'd & obed Ser[t],
Charlotte Smith

Elsted near Godalming
Surrey
March 24th
1803

General Manuscripts, Manuscripts Division, Rare Books and Special Collections, Princeton University Library. No address or postmark.

NOTES

1. A note at the top of the page in another hand reads: "Ans[d], declining the Publication, March 26th, 1803." This book was *Conversations Introducing Poetry;* see CS to Samuel Rose, 7 Apr. 1803, n. 2.

2. They did not remain friends. Yet by 1806, Phillips had somehow renewed their agreement for *The History of England . . . for a young lady at school,* and began to press CS to complete an additional volume. She was physically unable to comply.

To Samuel Rose

[Elsted, 7 April 1803]
Dear Sir,

After having written in vain about seven Letters (& some of them on business relative to property which required immediate attention), I have obtaind no answer from Lord Egremont, & to day I hear from a M[r] Halliday, who has been trying to get a settlement agreed to by M[r] Smith, that he is come again from Scotland with a resolution to persecute & torment me & his children Unless we comply with what is absolutely no more in my power than it is to take 400£ from the fortune of any stranger. There is nothing of which this wretched Man is not capable. He may very probably come hither & drive me from the house. At all events, he seems determind to starve me & his children.[1] I had just set down to a work which will bring me 2 or 3 hundred pounds & have finish'd a lesser one which I hope will obtain for me 50£.[2] But thus harrass'd, every thing must be at an end. I beg your pardon that, with so little pretensions on your time or your kindness, I thus intrude upon you, but I know not what to do. Misery of so long endurance & so utterly hopeless surely never was sustain'd. Above 16 years, I have now supported this family, but Mr Smith is it seems going to Law with me, & I am very sorry to say that Lord Egremont encourages him in this & has written him a Letter <u>full of abuse of me</u>—— My poor shatterd nerves are so overcome by the return of this vulture & by Lord Egremonts injustice & caprice that I hardly know what I write or why: forgive me if I appear needlessly troublesome. If you knew half or indeed a twentieth part of what is inflicted upon me, you would I am sure forgive me. Lord E is at Petworth, & I fear your kind intentions of speaking to him will be frustrated. Allow me however to ask whether you have had any conversation with him since Mr Bicknell told me you had <u>not</u>. I dare not ask you what you would advise me to do—for I think my case utterly hopeless & know how sickening & disgusting it must be to hear of incurable & non descript miseries—

I hope poor Fovilles business may now be settled but doubt it; if Lord E can help it, I know if he can he will still delay. I wish Foville was {out} of the infection of my wretchedness. I was about to write Mr Hayley a letter of thanks merely, but my spirits are too much agitated & I am unable.

Might I, dear Sir, hope for one line from you by Sunday's post & to be allowed still to remain

y^r^ most oblig'd & grateful Ser^t^,
Charlotte Smith

Elsted, April 7th 1803
Excuse ruld paper; I have no other at hand.

Osborn Collection MS, Yale University. Address: Ap^l^ 7 8th—/ Saml Rose Esqre———/ Chancery Lane. Postmark: {London}; 7 o'clock/ 8.AP/ 1802. N^t^; Two Penny/ Post/ NW Oxford St.

NOTES

1. BS blames her equally for his problems, although his tone is milder. Claiming "heavy charges brought upon me by the procrastination Mrs Smiths conduct imposes upon me," he promises to abide with Egremont's opinion if it is that CS should have an equal share (see BS to Egremont, 11 Apr. 1803, unpub. letter in PHA #0.11).

2. Probably here CS refers to *Beachy Head,* which eventually brought her £235 but was published posthumously, and *Conversations Introducing Poetry,* a draft of which she had just completed with her sister Catherine Dorset's help. First offered to Johnson by Rose for £50, *Conversations* finally went to two volumes and earned her £125 (CS to Sarah Rose, 10 Sept. 1804).

To William Tyler

[Elsted] April 15th 1803
To Mr Tyler.
Sir,

I have received the enclosed from Mr Halliday.[1] I really think it hard that I am to be compelled by want to say what I feel to be wrong—to recommend a thing I know to be illegal, and to be thus liable to Lord Egremonts anger because I will not recommend his paying what is not due. 600£ was ~~before~~ extorted before Mr B S would consent to the transfer of the Trust. Now 400£ more and expenses are demanded. Will you as a Lawyer say it is right? As to arrears, it is nonsense. They have been stated at 6000£, at 600, at 400£.

The fact is there is nothing due to Mr Smith.

If Lord E chuses to give Mr Smith 400£ from the residue, I shall not oppose it, but I cannot recommend it, nor will I undertake to sign my discharge hereafter for that Sum. If Mr Smith were less determined to rob his children at all events, he might persuade them to some adjustment, but I can recommend none (let me suffer what I will) that does not go to a final as well as an immediate close of all the affairs. I am, Sir,

yr hble Sert Charlotte Smith

Petworth House Archives MS. No address or postmark.

NOTE

1. The letter CS mentions is not in the packet, although two earlier ones to CS from Halliday, dated 19 Jan. and 13 Feb. 1803, survive. In the latter (PHA #7366), Halliday says that he has just written to BS on these matters and not received a reply.

To the earl of Egremont

[Elsted, mid- to late April 1803][1]

Allow me, my Lord, to solicit very earnestly your Lordships order on Messrs Pybus for this trifle.[2] About its being due to me there can be no doubt, & such a small matter I cannot submit to Mr Rose; it would look like asking him to enter too minutely into a matter so very immaterial. But to me it is no trifle, for your Lordship must think that I find it very difficult indeed to go on from day to day, having nothing allowed me from any quarter. Let me not again beg for this trifle in vain. It will pay my coal bill, & why should I be distress'd for it?

It is pity that Mr Tyler, since he was paid for one copy that got thither unhappily too late, did not think proper to send the other (for which no doubt he also charges) till that also is too late; he pertinaciously insisted there was no occasion for it, as Mr Prescod had it, but it appears that Mr Prescod will not produce it, & Mr Adams has left the Island so that Griffiths's 500£[3] will I fear be lost. If Mr Tyler undertakes business, this is not the way he ought to do it in———

[Unsigned]

Decr 18th 1802	£. S. d
Letter from Mr Adams ———	2.6
Writing to Do———postage paid ———	3.1
pr Packet	
Letter from Mr Winterbottom & Dun[4] ———	7
Jany 9th	
Letter from Mr Adams ———	3.1
Anr do paid packet ———	3.1
Parcel pr Coach from Winterbottom & Dun ———	1.8
Letter from Do ———	7
Letter from Mr Adams ———	2.6
Jany 20th—Writing to Mr Prescod ———	7
Letter from Mrs Prescod ———	7
he being gone to Barbados.	
Letter from Mr Adams ———	2.5
Stationary ———	3—
2 Letters since from Mr Adams ———	5.8
Mr Frys bill for power of Attorney paid out of the money for which I sold my poor Books! ———	4.2.0
	5.10.10
Mr Tylers charges for the deed ———	2.0.0
	7.10.10
For giving his advice on the manner of the Trustees proceeding which I had not an idea of asking but was desired to do so by Mr Turner—till when viz in Septr 1799 at Bignor I never that I knew had seen Mr Tyler he charges ———	10.6
But Mr Turner puts this whole payt at 2.14	8.0.4
	8.1.4

Petworth House Archives MS. No address or postmark.

NOTES

1. This letter appears in PHA #7364 with other undated letters written in Feb. and Mar. The only clues for dating it are CS's mention of having sold her books, which was done by mid-Mar., and her note about the purchase of a power of attorney from Mr. Fry for £4.2, also mentioned in CS to Egremont, 23 or 24 Mar. 1803. Her remark in the first paragraph about needing money for coal argues slightly for an earlier date, before she had been thrown out of the house at Frant and was still complaining about the cold.

2. Egremont was besieged on both sides for what must have seemed trifles to him. On 28 Apr. 1803, BS complains of further delays and procrastination adding to the expense of living in London. While CS was trying to live on a guinea a week, it costs him two guineas a week for lodging and board plus other expenses, and he is "in danger of an arrest." There is as well "the most unfortunate predicament at home" in Scotland, where he needs to dispose of his property to pay creditors. Then he threatens: "if I am compell'd to this step, I will never attempt another amicable adjustment with my family again." Egremont has not answered his letter by 6 May 1803, even though he has let him stay at Petworth House. BS is "at the acme of my distress" (unpub. letters in PHA #0.11).

3. On James Griffith's debt, see CS to William Tyler, 18 July 1802 and n. 2.

4. Abraham Winterbottom and Ralph Dunn were solicitors to Robert Allen and Richard Smith.

To William Tyler

[Petworth, 7 May 1803]
Sir,

Having business with Mrs Newhouse & my Sister, I came hither as well to meet the latter as to desire you will please to inform me when I can see Lord Egremont or obtain an ans[we]^{r} from his Lordship, it being impossible for me to wait any longer in this state of suspence and inconvenience. Y^{r} an[swe]^{r} will be desirable to, Sir,

y^{r} hble Ser^{t},
Ch Smith[1]

Swan
Petworth, May 7th 1803[2]

Petworth House Archives MS. No address or postmark.

NOTES

1. Written in a large, shaky scrawl.

2. On this date, BS complains to Egremont of a letter from CS that "as usual is full of invective, and menace, in regard to myself, but she still insists upon her right to dispose of what she calls her fortune, share, and share alike, to the Three Younger Children (tho' I have Deeds which give me full power over it)." If she "wo^{d} but be quiet," he writes that he will do as she wishes by the remaining £5,000 of her marriage settlements,

having previously complied about £2,000. He will also bind himself to make allowances to George and Harriet, but at his discretion. She would have scoffed at this proposal as giving him a way out. BS asks for £100 (unpub. letter in PHA #0.11).

On 13 May 1803, BS acknowledges that Egremont informed him of CS's Petworth visit on 11 May and her plan to visit him in London. BS hopes Egremont will use this time to show her his recent letters and come to a speedy settlement. On 14 May, BS calls on Egremont at Grosvenor Place, hoping for an interview himself and leaving a note that his future welfare depended on a favorable answer (unpub. letters in PHA #0.11).

On 18 May, BS complains of having had no answers to his letters of 30 Apr. and 6, 7, 12, 13, and 14 May, but he plans to call on Egremont the following day. "Mrs Smith chooses to remain inflexible," and BS needs £100 "to extricate me out of my present difficulties, and to save me from destruction." As there are no further letters until July, Egremont may have advanced him the money (unpub. letter in PHA #0.11).

To William Tyler

[Elsted, 23 May 1803]
Sir,

In a very clear & correct account made out after some months of recollection by the person who was once my Brother, it is stated that he has paid you 2.14.0 on my account. I did not know that I was (individually) in your debt, and as it is a piece of good fortune for which I know not how to account and know not how much farther it may go at some future period, you will give me leave to put a <u>Query</u> to you who are so remarkable, alert, and correct in accounts of all sorts & to ask you (if it may be done without offence) how I came into your books—as stated by the Revd Mr Turner in his account transmitted at last by the great condescension of Lord Egremont to, Sir,

your most humble Ser^t^
Charlotte Smith[1]

May 23rd 1803

Petworth House Archives MS. Address: Mr Wm Tyler/ Petworth/ Sussex—. Postmark: GODALMIN/ {date illegible}.

NOTE

1. This unusually sarcastic note, which stands out from all the letters to Tyler, including those omitted from this collection, shows how far she had abandoned hope of working with him to any resolution.

573 ❦ 1803

To the earl of Egremont

[Elsted, 21 July 1803]
My Lord,

As well as my feeble state[1] will allow, I have—in consequence of yr Lordships Letter which I had the honor of receiving this morng—read over the rough draft of the Bill in Chancery sent me by Mr Bicknell. I suppose falsehoods of every description are usually stated in such bills; this is full of them & of false statements ~~of~~ as to matters of fact, which it is not my business to put them right in. The Letters yr Ldship is so good as to mention My daughter left with Mr Bicknell. Some other documents, which are I beleive important to the answer, I have here, & I think (but perhaps my judgement is now good for nothing) that Mr Parkyn ought to be applied to for evidence which I know he can give that no mention was ever made to him & the late Mr Robinson,[2] the then Trustees, of any such debt incurred in the years there named. On the contrary, that there was money in the year 1793 kept back & applied to other purposes which, if there had been a necessity for payg these demands agst Gays such as they state, should & must have been paid to those debts— —

So far were they, the late Trustees, from being aware of the existence of these debts that they never could by any application (made at my pressing instance to Prettejohn)[3] obtain any yearly accounts at all. During the space of 14 years, not _one_ regular account or any account was ever renderd, & these which are now calld so were garbled & made up by Prettyjohn ~~when~~ under the threats of My Son Charles, who could not obtain them till he used the most compulsatory means. As to Prettyjohns affadavit, his oath wd be impeached in any court, & I am persuaded that a very substantial defence might be made if the cheif points are properly understood & stated. I fear I am not competent in my present state of health to write all this matter requires to Mr Bicknell, nor are letters ever half read or attended to. Mr Dayrell does understand the business, and it is my opinion that his assistance would be of the greatest use in framing the answer tho he is not a Chancery Lawyer, but a proper compliment should be made to him for the trouble he would have, & no offence would thereby be given to Mr Bicknell who avows his incapability of framing the anr without instructions which I beleive nobody understands how to give so well as Mr Dayrell, who knows the circumstances thoroughly, & the people as well as the necessary steps to be taken in Barbadoes.

It does indeed seem strange even on a cursory view of the matter that, if the accounts had been regularly & fairly renderd from year to year, there shd have been any occasion for an Affadavit because the facts wd have been establishd & admitted, & if an affadavit of this sort is evidence at the end of so many years, any Man may be sworn out of his estate on garbled & false accounts. It is asserted I see in the bill that this money was so taken to pay off debts pressing on the Estate. Why then did not Prettejohn state those debts to the Trustees as they arose? Why, without ever naming them, suffer them to run on at Interest? My Son paid considerable Sums away for ~~those~~ arrears against the estate particularly to Messrs Cumberbatch. One of these Mr Cumberbatchs's was present when Mr Straker, Mr Allens Agent,[4] wished Mr Prescod joy of his purchase. Mr Cumberbatch said <u>his</u> debt ag^st^ the estate had been paid; Mr Straker never utterd a syllable as to any debt to us from it to his principals, Messrs R^d^ Smith & Rob Allen.

If your Lordship pleases, I will, as well as I am able under my present bodily sufferings & extreme weakness, do any thing I can to collect the articles of defence, & write to Mr Dayrell, and get the letters y^r^ Lordship names from Mr Bicknell & forward them to your Lordship, And as far as my power goes, will communicate with any person your Lordship thinks proper to entrust with your commands, having no other meaning or wish than to obey your ~~directions~~ directions, Or I will forward what papers I can collect, with remarks, to Petworth. Awaiting your Lordships commands, I have the honor to be

your most obed^t^ Ser^t^,
Charlotte Smith

Elsted July 21st
1803

Petworth House Archives MS. No address or postmark.

NOTES

1. The handwriting of this letter is indeed blunt, shaken, and clumsy, suggesting weakness, for CS's usual lettering is small and precise. CS seems to have suffered a collapse in June and July after the miseries of the spring of 1803. No letters of hers have survived for the two months following 23 May 1803. She may have been too ill to write, as her own words later in the letter suggest: "present bodily sufferings & extreme weakness."

While CS languishes, BS is still in London—or back in London. On 7 July 1803 he writes to Egremont questioning whether interest money on £3,331.5.0 is lost. On 20 July he writes about selling the living at Islington to Mr. Dawes and accuses CS of forgetting or lying about her knowledge of that deed. Meanwhile, he is still "embarrassed": the previous Saturday, his tailor "took out a Writ against me, which fortunately hearing of, I escaped being served upon me, & paid the debt" with help from his friend Tayler. BS is anxious to pay more than £40 he owes his landlord in London for board and lodging "as I have been treated with great Kindness, & Hospitality." He notes that it would cost him £12 to return to Scotland "as I cannot go by Sea without the hazard of being taken," that is, arrested. Egremont recommends that he wait for Samuel Rose's settlement, expected in Sept. or Oct.

On 5 Sept., BS encloses a letter from Andrew Thomson, his landlord in Scotland, demanding payment ten days from the 30 Aug. date of the letter. Receiving no answer, BS pens a brief, desperate note to Egremont the next day:

> 6th Septr 1803
> My Lord
> That which I have most dreaded, seems now to await me, and the Die will be cast, as your Lordship will observe by the enclosed letter, unless prevented by your kind assistance. I am My Lord
>
> your Lordships
> most obed^t hum^ble Servt
> Benjn Smith

As BS makes no further requests, it is likely that Egremont came to his aid (unpub. letters in PHA #0.11).

2. Anthony Parkin was still living; John Robinson died 23 Dec. 1802.

3. Over the years CS spelled this man's name Prettejohn and Prettyjohn indiscriminately.

4. John Straker, Esq., of St. Thomas's Parish, Robert Allen's agent in Barbados. Two men named Cumberbatch are in a list CS sent to Tyler (unpub., 30 Sept. 1803): Cumberbatch Sober and Abraham Cumberbatch. But their debts to Gay's are quite small (£1.2.6 and £1.17.6).

To the earl of Egremont

[Elsted, 11 September 1803]
My Lord,

As few occurrences have given me so much concern as the displeasure which it appeard your Ldp had entertaind against me, I cannot but feel gratified in receiving your obliging permission to meet Mr Rose (during the referrence)[1] at Petworth house—a permission I should most willingly take advantage of because, in the various points which I have submitted to Mr Rose's decision (points of the greatest future importance to my children), it is almost impossible that I can explain some without a personal conference—which I did not however venture to solicit, least it should be said that I desired to take any undue advantage. I lament therefore on every account that the sad state of my health is such as renders my getting into one of Mr Moons chaises, & I fear into any other I c^d procure, almost impossible, as I have lost the use of my legs, and it is now between four & five months since I have been out of the house except when supported by a servant for a few paces into the little space before my cottage to sit half an hour in the air. Disabled from going up stairs, I have been oblig'd to have a bed put up in one of my parlours, & in such circumstances, I should be even for a few hours a most unpleasant intruder on y^r^ Lordships hospitality. If I could get into a carriage, I might at another time have gone to Bignor, but the absence of my Sister & the arrangement immediately to take place there puts it out of the question; otherwise I should, while it was yet possible, have tried what change of air w^d^ have done which was the only thing (especially had it been Sea air) that Mr Newland[2] thought likely to prevent the encrease of that weakness & debility which is now such that I have very little hope of ever regaining the power of walking. Indeed I have but small hope of living many months— —

I will take the liberty of addressing a packet to Mr Rose while he is at Petworth, & if it be possible for Miss Smith to see him, or could I hope to do it, & if I could clear up many things in which I have been totally misunderstood, it would I own give me great satisfaction. Indeed I am much at a loss to know what I ought or she ought to do about Mr Allen & Smiths bill in Chancery which I find from Mr Bicknell presses, & that an attachment ag^st^ us will be the consequence of ~~my~~ our not putting in our answers, tho whatever the merit of the case may be, it is impossible in my present state of health that I can give any instructions, nor w^d^ they avail, unless consonant to the answers given by the other parties of which & of their intentions I am totally ignorant. I cannot help being uneasy to learn that nothing is yet heard of Mr Prescod, & Mr Adams too is silent. If these sums—3333£ & 500£[3]— are lost or contended for, the referrence as far as relates to the residue will avail my luckless children but little, however Mr Rose may decide— —

I have the honor to be Your Lordships
much obliged & most humble ser^t^,
Charlotte Smith

Elsted, Septr 11th 1803

Petworth House Archives MS. Address: The Earl of Egremont/ Petworth. No postmark.

NOTES

1. Samuel Rose had been appointed to arbitrate a permanent settlement between CS and BS over the disposition of all interest money since Egremont and Turner became trustees. All parties signed the arbitration bond on 18 June 1803 (PHA #8223), and Rose's decision was final on 27 Sept. 1803 (PHA #8224). CS to Egremont, 12 Oct. 1803, n. 1, gives the results.

2. William Newland (1750–after 1800), a local surgeon of Messrs. Newland and Co., surgeons, Guildford, Surrey.

3. The £3,333 (actually £3,331) was Prescod's final payment on Gay's plantation; the £500 was owed by Gibbons. Rose's arbitration does not involve these sums, but rather only about £400 of interest.

To Samuel Rose

[Elsted] Sunday, Sept[r] 11th 1803
Dear Sir,

After all that has pass'd, it would be difficult for me to find words to express my surprize at a Letter I have re[ceive][d] to day from Lord Egremont, saying that you had accepted his Ldps invitation to Petworth house & that as I or my family might like, or might find it necessary, to see you on the affairs of the arbitration, he should be very happy if all or any of us would at any time meet you at his house where he would accommodate us all while the referrence was going on———

I am certainly very glad to find that the extreme & as I think groundless ire of Lord E. against me is on the decline, which surely such a Letter indicates, for few among the many mortifications I have experienced have given me more pain than to have been thought of by Lord E. as he appeard to think of me when he accused me of deception, hypocrisy, falsehood, & misrepresentation—things so remote from my character that I have been thought to injure myself by conduct exactly the reverse. I am so very glad to know that the business may thus be gone thro with less inconvenience to you than must occur at this Season by y[r] longer detention in London, & as I am in other respects glad of the apparent change. Yet wishing as I most truly do to have an opportunity of explaining to you <vis a vous?>[1] many things, which, tedious as my Letters too generally are, it is almost impossible to do in writing, & anxious as I am to have every point of future interest to My eldest daughter, & indeed to all my children, settled & put out of M[r] Benj[n] Smiths power, such is my misfortune that I cannot avail myself of his Lordships renew'd kindness because, tho I have not indeed tried, I am almost sure it would be impossible for me to get into a chaise, at least an hack chaise, & I have no other means of moving.

It is now between four & five months since the attacks of what is supposed to be an hereditary gout (which my constitution has never had strength to throw out) have so weakened me, because attended by other debilitating symptoms, that tho without much pain I have lost the use of my legs, & for near three months, I have been obliged to give up one of my two sitting rooms in this Cottage & make it my bed room, being unable to get up the stairs, nor have I in all that time been farther from my door than three or four yards, led by a servant & seated in a chair that I might breathe the air, tho exercise is now for ever out of my power, One of my legs being I am very well aware irrecoverably crippled. When this addition to my other sufferings first threatend me, I was advised by the medical friend[2] I consulted to make every effort to go to the Sea, but it was at that time impossible. I represented my situation to Lord Egremont, who, either by allowing me a portion of the money he appropriated to Mr B Smith or by letting me have what my Son Nicholas had directed for me of his share, might have enabled me to try if the remedy advised would save me from so heavy a calamity as the loss of limbs—or imbecility equally distressing. But his Lordship did then, & has even since refused, to lend the least attention to any thing that was urged on this subject—tho at the very moment when he was repeating this refusal in the harshest terms & declaring my distresses as all my own fault because I would not agree to Mr B Smiths reasonable proposals (i e to give him 400£ over which I had not could not have the smallest power & which there was no fund to furnish if I had) his Ldp took the trouble to call at the cottage of my widow'd daughter[3] on the road near Petworth to make the most kind enquiries after my health & express his concern at my illness!!——

This appearance of returning humanity, I impute entirely to your interposition, & there are fifty reasons why, if Mr Benj Smith is not there (for I never will meet him any where or on any terms), I shd be particularly desirous of having, with Miss Smith, the advantage of a few hours conversation with you. But I fear it is absolutely impossible. In such an house, a wretched invalid wd be une de trop[4] even for a day, nor could I get up stairs since I am a spectacle of misery. If Bignor was open to me & I could get to Petworth, I might find a gite[5] there, but My Sister is going to London on Monday with her daughter to prepare for the almost immediate marriage of the young Lady, & when they return, I cannot intrude on the wedding festivities[6] so that my ci devant paternal house (which is to be rented by the new married couple) is not at my command. I do indeed feel every hour the necessity of some decisive measures being adopted, & I am utterly at a loss how to act.

This Chancery suit presses,[7] & it seems to be against me & my eldest daughter that the weight of it is to be driven. I would willingly know as what I am subpoena'd who have no interest in Richd Smiths effects & am debarred from acting as Executrix; why My eldest daughter is thus calld upon I cannot imagine when I do not believe that Mr Benjn Smith, the person undoubtedly the most responsible, has even been subpoena'd. It seems probable at present that there will be nothing to ans[wer] this or any other demand, however establish'd, for strange to tell, I have learned from Messrs Daniels, the Merchants, who were to pay the last bill of 3331£ for the estate & who by the advice of their own Counsel Mr Dayrell had agreed to pay it when due 9th July, as their Letter to me (which I sent to Ld E) proves beyond a doubt. I have a Letter from them to say that Ld E. got the advice of another Counsel, a Mr Neyles or Heyles, against Mr Daniels payg it tho surely all his Ldp's business was to get the money according to the agreement, & it was not his affair if the Merchants did wrong. They were of course glad enough to keep such a sum longer in their hands at this time, & I shall be rejoiced to find myself mistaken in thinking that there will now be very great difficulties in getting it at all. Pardon, dear Sir, so many last words from y[r] most oblig'd & grateful Ser[t],

Charlotte Smith

Huntington MS (HM 10833). Address: Samuel Rose Esqre/ Chancery Lane/ London. {Postmark: GODALMIN; G/SEP 12/ 1803}

NOTES

1. To your face; face to face. *Vis-à-vis* is the more usual expression.
2. Newland.
3. Lucy Newhouse, who lived at North Chapel on the Petworth road.
4. One too many.
5. The *OED* defines *gite* as "a stopping place, lodging." It also cites CS's use of the word in *The Young Philosopher* (1798), 4:37: "Would I had any pretension to so happy a *gite!*"
6. Lucy Smith Dorset (christened 21 Sept. 1780) was the only surviving child of Michael and Catherine Turner Dorset. (Lucy was obviously named after Lucy Towers Smith, the maternal aunt who raised Charlotte, Catherine, and Nicholas Turner.) Young Lucy married Charles Henry Fraser, Orchard Street, Portman Square, Middlesex, after 18 Oct. 1803, the date of their marriage settlement. Later on, CS found the couple objectionable (see CS to Sarah Rose, 10 Sept. 1805).
7. The Chancery suit by Richard Smith, grandson of Richard Smith the elder, and Robert Allen and Mary Gibbes Smith Allen, one of the granddaughters.

To the earl of Egremont

{Elsted, 13 September 1803}
My Lord,

In consequence of the Letter I had the honor of receiving from y[r] Ldsp this morning, I have determined to use every effort to attend on the business together with my eldest daughter, & trust that we shall not trespass on y[r] Lordships ~~obliging~~ obliging intention above a day, or at most two; tho I am not able to set out early, yet the distance being only 17 miles, we may reach Petworth by a morning hour, & wait M[r] Rose's time. I am considerably better to day but still a wretched cripple & shall probably long remain so. I beg leave before I enter on any conversation on this business to declare with the utmost sincerity that had I the power to make "the worser seem the better reason"—which I am far from pretending to possess & which I know if I did possess it w[d] avail nothing ag[st] M[r] Rose's integrity

& impartiality—the last thing I should try at w^{d} be to injure or oppress M^{r} B Smith or to try to deprive his old age of a support. Give me credit, my Lord, for this, & for the never failing grateful sentiments with which I have always been

y^{r} Lordships oblig'd ser^{t},
Charlotte Smith

Teusday, Septr 13th

Petworth House Archives MS. No address or postmark.

To the earl of Egremont

Elsted 25th Sept^{r}
<u>1803</u>
My Lord,

I have to day undertaken the woeful task of looking over some Boxes of old papers & venture to send y^{r} Ldship three packets.[1] In No. 1, you will find copies of a Letter from Prettejohn dated in 1793, wherein no mention is made or hint given of any necessity existing or having existed at the close of that year for the measure he since pretends to have adopted of <taking> money from [Gays] Mapps, & in No. 2, you will find that Messrs Robinson & Parkin <u>had</u> (being a little worried I confess by Mrs Charlotte Smith who did not sit quietly while her family were ruining a second time) written frequently to him, at last in very peremptory terms, for the annual accounts which he never did send during the many years he held the estate, but which there could be no other possible reason for his withholding than a consciousness of iniquity too great & too impudent to venture to disclose it or hazard its being disclosed to the two veterans Robinson & Parkin.

No. 3 contains a Bill of the notorious Mr Richmans.[2] Y^{r} Lordship will see a statement of Some of the papers relative to Gays being among those which I took to town in July 1783 (as I had the honor to state to y^{r} Lordship) & may <u>perhaps</u> be the means of tracing the missing papers of conveyance—or something from John Newton to Geo Walker.

Were I authoris'd, without troubling y^{r} Lordship on every occasion, to apply to Mr Rose as our Counsel & director (in the hope that the affairs will allow of a proper remuneration being made for such farther trouble to that Gentleman), I am convinced that much difficulty & writing might be saved to me & trouble to your Lordship, & we may then I trust put an end to the hearing more of these irksome affairs—of which I confess myself so weary that, was I able, I had rather earn my bread in servitude than grind in this mill another year, & my daughter is of the same mind.

We are both, with every sentiment of gratitude towards y^{r} Lordship, your most oblig'd ser^{t}, Charlotte Smith &c———

Petworth House Archives MS. Address: Earl of Egremont/ Petworth/ Sussex/ No. 1. Postmark: Godalmin/ <*3*>.

NOTES

1. The material in the three packets does not appear to have survived.

2. The attorney Gawler Griffith Rickman (see CS to John Robinson, 19 Sept. 1785, n. 2). John Newton owned Gay's plantation and sold it to BS. The papers of conveyance transferred management of Gay's to George Walker.

To the earl of Egremont

[Elsted, 25 September 1803]

Among many kindnesses for which our thanks are due to yr Lordship, I was much flatterd by y^{r} obliging solicitude for Lucy's sick children. We found the most alarming symptoms abated, & I trust they will not have the fever tho neither of them are well. My little Indian Girl has had the same symptoms—& tho not alarmingly ill is not well.

Allow us to present our Comp^{ts} to Miss Wyndham[1] to whose politeness I feel much oblig'd.

[Unsigned]

I have other papers to send, bearing on the two Questions of the Allens claim & the Berneys overpay^{t} but feared sending too many at once.

Petworth House Archives MS. Address: The Earl of Egremont/ Petworth/ Sussex/ No. 2. Postmark: GODALMIN/ [no date].

NOTE

1. Egremont's eldest daughter, later Lady Burrell, by his longtime mistress Elizabeth Iliffe (whom he married on 16 July 1801).

To the earl of Egremont

[Elsted, received 12 October 1803]

My Lord,

When I sign'd the Arbitration bond,[1] I did it, and told Mr Rose I did it, in <u>the firm beleif & intention</u> that it should put an end to your Lordships trouble in a Trust which, while it has been a source of so much complaint, has utterly ruin'd me & left me in declining life & ruin'd health to the most abject poverty. That this is not ended, I see more & more cause to lament.

Why your Lordship should aggravate the evils of want & sickness by telling me it is my fault, I cannot imagine. Your Lordship—after keeping back, as y[r] Letters say, my poor little income for a year because Mr Benj Smith had been paid too much—was pleas'd while you paid him that, to order me to consent to his having more: 400£ & his expences. I certainly should have resisted this, had I any power, even on yr Lordships own opinion that he was no better than an highwayman and had no right to what had been paid him before, but, as I had no power, as the money was neither mine nor in my power to grant, I answerd that if it was legal the trustees were at liberty to do it, but that I could not consent to what I had no power over whatever. I offerd at the same time to leave every thing in dispute to two Gentlemen both to be chosen by Mr Benjn Smith, yet, tho I repeatedly gave this an[r], y[r] Lordship adhered to your first idea that I was wrong, & you chose that an arbitration sh[d] be applied to which I hoped w[d] at least have released you from all farther trouble & put the question of my childrens future provision out of the doubt it is now in.

But nothing of all this has happen'd, & besides an additional expence from my impoverishd children's little & 500£ given to the wretch who has ruin'd them—to say nothing of an expensive journey to Petworth to be dragg'd at the chariot Wheels of M[r] B S. and that he might triumph over the miserable victim of his cruelty & wickedness (for certainly had I known I was to be exposed to meeting that wretch, I would not have troubled y[r] Lordship)—After all this—while one 5th of what is given to him would have saved me from the pain & anguish I now undergo by enabling me to change the air & recover the use of my limbs, now irrecoverable—my misery is added to by hearing from your Lordship that it is my own fault. Surely I cannot have deserved this, and it would once have seem'd incredible.

My Son, the poor boy abandon'd from three years old by his brutal father, has at length obtain'd a Lieutenants commission as I hear to day.[2] For the trouble y[r] Lordship has deign'd to take, I thank you very sincerely, begging you will allow me to correct one mistake as to his failure in his duty. The fact is he was very ill while he was at home with me & was oblig'd to have medical assistance. A Letter from Col[l] Backhouse made him determine to set out for his Reg[t] during that very hot weather when he was in a very unfit state for a journey of near 100 miles, & the consequence was his falling into an intermitting fever which, as I have since heard from others (for he said little about it himself), had nearly proved fatal. A poor lad of eighteen, friendless but for his helpless & oppressed Mother, & pennyless, left to shift as he can by his unnatural & selfish father, might I hoped have made some interest in an humane and generous breast. He is now orderd ahead, without a sixpence on earth, nor can I find for him even the small supply he has the most pressing occasion for. I am likewise with Harriet destitute of the means of present existence & have written to day to Mr Fauntleroy to desire he would advance a years income That I may give this last assistance to my poor George & pay as far as the rest will go what I can here which, if I can do, I will go into a garret in London or any where, where I can live or rather drag on so wretched a being as mine, after all my exertions, is at length reduced to.

As to the suit in Chancery, when y[our] Lordship orderd Mr Benjn Smith to recall what he had written to Mr Bicknell and orderd My daughter to write an official letter to the Trustees expressing her desire to have it carried on, I really did hope & suppose that y^{r} Lordship intended to act in concert with me & the legatees in defending the suit, & all I meant by applying to you was to know if I should be authoris'd by your Lordships order to consult Mr Rose or some Counsel upon it, & upon the grounds of defence which I think I possess. Mr Bicknell is an honest, humane, conscientious & good Man, & it is perhaps those very qualities which render him as an Attorney unfit for the defence of a cause where there has already been great dishonesty & prevarication & falsehood on the part of the assailants. My meaning was to go upon sure ground as much as I could to lay my proofs before some unprejudiced Counsel, & see whether it would be wise to enter into expence, & this it was my object to do without troubling yr Lordship save by y^{r} authority. I have told Mr Bicknell my mind, but after reading y^{r} Letter of to day, I have nothing more to do than to desire him to apply to the court to dismiss me who have nothing at all to do with it; not a shilling of the interest of the residue is secured to me tho, but for me, not a shilling would be forthcoming for Mr Benjn Smiths gluttenous & selfish indulgences! Why therefore should I be harrass'd with it & waste more of that time which, when pain & bodily sufferings allow me to write, I must apply to earn my bitter bread—— My daughter will be obligd to y^{r} Lordship to order that the Letters I sent lately to you upon this subject may be forthwith return'd. As to my being committed, I am very easy about it. I shall, I have no doubt now, end my days in a prison, & it will at least afford me a lodging, which I am not likely otherwise to have.

I do assure y^{r} Lordship that it is with the utmost reluctance I write to give you any trouble. Every thing I do seems to have an effect exactly contrary to my hopes, & I cannot but wonder that any award can authorise a Trust to pay a Man—already acknowledged & known to be a defaulter & plunderer of his own children—a Sum to which he has not the shadow of pretence before the legatees are paid, & when from the doubts of Mr Prescods conduct, there is not a certainty of there being enough to pay them at all. I shall tell M[r] Rose the opinion I can not help entertaining of such an award so far as relates to M[r] B S because it has not in regard to my children an[swere][d] the cheif purpose for which I w[d] willingly have sacrificed myself while I and those who depend upon me starve, that sacrifice notwithstanding!——

Good God—what a destiny—I know complaint is fruitless, & worse than fruitless—& that my misery is a matter of triumph to M[r] B Smith & of sport to others. I have the honor to be

y[r] Lordships most humble Ser[t],
Charlotte Smith

I shall write to M[r] Turner but suppose it is settled to be refused me.

Petworth House Archives MS. No address or postmark.

NOTES

1. The arbitration bond was signed on 18 June 1803. Rose had decided the award on 27 Sept. 1803, and CS considered his decision to be disastrous. He awarded BS the entire £500 in question as well as £230 of the previous year's income. CS was not without remuneration, however. The remaining settlement granted much that she had long fought for: half the dividends to BS and half to CS; a £60-a-year settlement on Harriet and George after CS's death until Harriet would marry and George would be provided for in the military; £736.13.3 to CS for her expenses related to the Trust; £100 to Charlotte Mary as executor to her grandmother's will; £283.11.8 to Charlotte Mary as part of her legacy from her grandfather; 350 Gs. to cover Charles's expenses in going to Barbados; BS to pay any further dividends he receives against debts that he had taken out against Turner; and, finally, £373.8.8 to Egremont (PHA #8224).

BS, too, considered the decision disastrous. In spite of an initial expression of gratitude to Egremont, he was deeply disillusioned with Samuel Rose:

> I should not be reconciled to myself, and it would be diametrically opposite to my disposition, if I did not make your Lordship the most grateful acknowledgment for the kindness, and civility, you have honor'd me with and I shall ever have a pleasure in recollecting your Lordships munificence to me . . . but when I reflect on the small sum I have for my future subsistence, I am chagrin'd, and my spirits very much oppress'd. I am sorry to say I have put the most implicit confidence in a Man very unworthy of it. He has more then done justice to my opponents[.] (BS to Egremont, 8 Oct. 1803, unpub. letter in PHA #0.11)

Still furious a few days later, he breaks down and abuses Rose and, for the first time in his surviving letters, his estranged wife. He cannot believe that Rose "would make so improper a use of the power I gave him, & that it would so far militate against me; that Nefarious steps should be taken, by falsehood, and calumny, to do away with M[rs] Smiths Elopement, in order to entitle the Old Mouser to Alimony." He objects that Rose gives "to the Gremalkin half my Income, without specifying that part of it, was for my dear Harriots uses" (BS to Egremont, 11 Oct. 1803, unpub. letter in PHA #0.11). By *elopement,* BS refers to CS's leaving him on 15 Apr. 1787. Legally, her departure constituted desertion and therefore an abandonment of any right to alimony.

2. The *Army List* gives 9 July 1803 as the date of George Augustus Smith's appointment as lieutenant in the army, but 12 Oct. 1804 as his appointment in his regiment. George was born in Feb. 1785, and CS separated from BS on 15 Apr. 1787 when George was only 2.

To the earl of Egremont

[Elsted, 14 and 15 October 1803]
My Lord,

I this morning rec^d the enclosures of my poor Charles's Letters relative to the Berney debt &c, but There is one other Letter which I suppose will be necessary. It is a copy of a Letter or Letters or rather extracts of Letters from Prettejohn to Robinson & Parkin—relative to his, Prettejohns conduct in 1793 & markd with my notes in red ink. This I thought I had in a drawer where I put the papers on these endless & hopeless concerns, but my daughter says I sent it to Petworth <u>the day after my return from thence</u>. It may be so, but I confess I have no recollection of it, & I am willing, tho sorry to own, my memory & powers of attending to business are not what they once were. I have undergone fatigue that w^d have tried two dozen of Lawyers clerks, & I have the shell while the Sieur Thaumeturgos[1] has the Oyster. I am distress'd for the means of paying for his family's food while he cocks his hat on one side, looks knowing & buckish & struts off with more than is left to any one of his younger children for his "dear Mrs Miller (who had 300£ to her fortune & saved his life <u>once</u>." Vide his pretty Letters)———

I smile, My Lord, with anguish at my heart; The Man is so absurd & such a plain fool (to use an Irish expression) that I am as much asham'd as I am vexd to find myself, after a life spent as his disgraced victim, Quite reduced to poverty by such a Man.

For what so deeply wounds the generous heart
As when a blockhead's insult wings the dart[2]

If I <u>did</u> send such a Letter, have the goodness to direct that it may be sent me back, & unless wanted, by the <u>Coach on Teusday next</u>, I will obey your Lordships orders & send <u>your</u> Letters—i e all that relate to Mr Benjn Smiths offers as to a division & my answers whether to y^r Lordship, or Mr Halliday —who, being a creditor (in right of his father Simon Halliday on B S. for 2000£), had, I cannot but think, a <u>motive</u> beyond what he express'd in listening to the poor unhappy wretches complaints & misrepresentations. The senseless old Man told him & [brot] what he calld accounts—& of which Halliday knew nothing—to prove that his, B S.s Father's estate, owed him 10,000£. Oh ho! thought young Simon. If I can by Mr Follet or Mr any body get but half this, if I can get only half or even a fourth paid to Mr B S., I shall smite him for the arrear due to my Father or at least a part of it. It will answer my purpose. Mr Robt Tayler, who is a very very weak Man & somewhat given to the manouvre calld shuffling, is tenant to Mr Halliday, & thus a kind of league is formd to side with Mr B S on any thing but disinterested or honest principles.

Your Lordship I never for a moment could doubt was actuated by motives the most opposite to those of these people; Nor could I, nor did I, ever for a single moment suppose that any thing but a wish to do justice without committing yrself (& in that you were perfectly right) could for a moment weigh with you. All that grieved me & that I thought hard was that without my knowing my offence yr Ldship seem'd so very angry with me, & to have taken up opinions of me so unlike those which alone could originally have induced a Nobleman in yr Lordships rank of life to have engaged wh so much generous zeal in irksome & troublesome affairs complicated in their nature, & which to yr Ldship must appear contemptible in value, As the whole ~~amount~~ value before it was divided among ten people hardly amounted to a fourth of your yearly income. A thousand times I have wonderd at your patience & a thousand times express'd my consciousness that we were unworthy the trouble you took. I considerd your interposition in payg off Dyer as something approaching to a miracle in my childrens favor, & when I look over all your Letters, not less in number than between sixty & seventy, I am astonish'd at the pains & perseverance shewn by yr Lordship, but I confess I am also mortified at the very different tone of the later ones from those which, at the commencement & even before the Trust, encouraged my often fainting courage to persevere in trying to obtain justice.

By Teusday's conveyance, I will send some other papers which may give some information to yr Lordships solicitor in preparing the anre from the Trustees wch anr it seems to me necessary that I should see, but in this I may perhaps be mistaken. I mean only that ours ought to coincide.

I enclose a Letter I received from Mr Bicknell this morng: I am sorry he seems piqued, but it is better to speak plain on every occasion. Mr Benn Thaumeturgos is waddled off I [*sic*] to Hamilton with his 500£ where he will in the character of Mr Bryan Simmonds[3] exhibit his consequence & begin some new scheme or suggest some unthought of method for paying off the national debt, but he will evade, if he can, answering the bill in Chancery. Mr

Bicknell I think will not undertake it for him, & why should he?—— My reason for wishing to have Mr Roses direction was these: That I know Mr Bicknell with all possible good qualities of honesty and good meaning *does* make blunders & is very apt to yield too soon where there is any doubt. We certainly made some great & *fatal* mistakes in regard to papers that ought to have gone out to the West Indies. Mr Rose is very clear in general (tho I think *he* has been greatly mistaken in making the award, & I, alas! am again the sufferer!). But I have nevertheless an high opinion of him, & his intimacy with Mr Bicknell would I thought make them go on <chearily> together. I could *not* however engage Mr Rose witht your Lordships acquiescence for this simple reason: that I could not anr for the payment & the Trust alone could do that. I send yr Ldp his Letter to me of which I before sent only an extract, & I think he therein moves to acquiesce in my wish if yr Lordp agreed to it.

The time is so short that *I must know as soon as possible*. I *do* think it hard that I am thus made a principal figure in a matter where no benefit can accrue to me, & what makes it still more so is that I have such constant & painful complaints in my stomach that stooping to write, especially after I eat any thing, gives me extreme torture, & I am unable to do as much writing as would (if I cd execute the mechanical part of it) contribute to my support. In all probability I shall not live thro the Winter, for after such a summer as I have passed, I may well say: "If these things were so in the green leaf, what shall be done in the dry?"[4] It is not perhaps so material to me what is to happen hereafter with my miserable little income as to know how I am to exist at present. If Mr B S. was at a loss to exist after he had received 230£ or thereabouts *till* the award (as is stated in your Lordships Letter to Mrs Dorset in July last when he could not many days have received that money), how am I & my children to subsist, who have had, & are to have nothing, either before the award or after it? God knows what I shall do (unless yr Ldship will let me have at least Nicholas's interest money) even for the ensueing week.

My very soul is sick of the perpetual pecuniary misery I suffer from which there seems no escape; I would have obeyd yr Lordships commands to night however as to sending the letters, but it so happens that I cannot send them to Milford tomorrow to the stage if I could have lookd them out, & I have been half dead all day wth this depressing pain (Gout perhaps) in my stomach. I certainly *did* think yr Lordships last letter rather harsh, as it declared, "all the Expence of the award & the additional 100£ to have been lost by *my fault* for not consenting before to let Mr B S. have 400£," when I had *no power*—& one of yr Letters *acknowledges that* I had none—& you say that perhaps Georges promotion has been delay'd by his havg done very little duty. I therefore thought it necessary to state to yr Lordship that my poor boy had been very sick. He is now under orders to be at a moments notice ready to March. The Officers think on a foreign expedition, & he is going to send his heavy baggage to me (which will cost me God knows what), but I hope his movements will be no farther than the coast or to Ireland. Where ever he goes, he goes pennyless & has asked a small supply of me which I have not to send him—the last of my poor earnings of 50 G^s for my verses for Children being gone—& Miss Smiths pocket as empty as mine! It <u>is</u> very hard, & I own I never thought my fate so bitter as now.

If M^r B S. can take advantage of Mr Turners having no power over the 2000£ he most assuredly will. My proportion for myself & my children will then be 70£ On which it is true I did once try to keep eight of that brutes children, but I was then sixteen years younger than I am now. I had not seen my best hopes perish, & my best friends forsake me. La mort vien tout finir,[5] says a French Author, & that is the only finish that <u>can</u> now happen to me. What will become of Lucy & her children I cannot guess. Her barbarous father with 500£ in his pocket pass'd her poor Cottage in a post chaise & pulld up the glass the moment he saw her who accidentally stood at the gate with those helpless Orphans.

I will send proof with the other papers that, when that wretch, that Monster was I thought in distress at Aberdeen, I sent him near 60£ of <u>money I had earned by writing</u> which he said he laid out in furniture. At that very time, the mean spirited dirty animal wrote to his Nieces, Mrs Boehm & Mrs Henchman, to lament his want even of a <u>bed to</u> sleep upon & entreating they would send him <u>any old bed</u> (as if such a thing was worth sending to Scotland). They were shocked at his meanness, yet unwilling wholly to refuse him, they sent him a bank note of 10£ which was what he wanted.

This is only one of an hundred degrading & infamous projects to extort money. It is too late now, but if your Lordship would have lent me a patient hearing, you w^d have seen how worse than useless it is to give this Man his childrens money. Almighty God, what had I done that before I was sixteen I was consigned to a fate so very dreadful![6] I have heard tho that he has told y^r Lordship I <u>was in love with him</u>! I think You could not listen to the paltry coxcomb—Indeed, indeed, I feel the shame of ever having belong'd to such a stupid & vicious wretch, even more disgraceful And harder to bear than the poverty, the actual want he has involved me in.

I sent y^r Lordships last Letter for which you enquire to Mr Rose, wishing to go on sure grounds ab^t the advice I ask of him, but I will write for & send it. Miss Smith has ~~xxxx~~ destroy'd some to her, but I have all those to me. If I had strength & money to go to town for a few days, I c^d give directions about the bill & might do some good in seeing these Barbados people, M^{rs}

Prettejohn & her Son, as Mr Adams recommends, who seems to think they w^d^ be willing rather to make some compromise than have old P exposed as he must be. But this is perhaps visionary, & I have neither bodily strength nor pecuniary means to try the experiment. I write by fits & in pain but am always with great respect your Lordships most oblig'd ser^t^,

Charlotte Smith

Elsted, Octr 14th & 15th 1803

Petworth House Archives MS. No address or postmark.

NOTES

1. Miracle worker, magician.

2. CS had a prodigious memory even as a child. This couplet, loosely rendered from Samuel Johnson's *London* (1738), ll. 168–69, shows how far she trusted to memory; the original reads:

> Fate never wounds more deep the gen'rous heart,
> Than when a blockhead's insult points the dart.

3. BS's alias is first seen in a 1799 address (BS to William Tyler, 27 Feb. 1799, unpub. letter in PHA #0.11). There, it is not in his hand, presumably to further mislead any creditors.

4. Luke 23.31.

5. Death comes to end all. The "French Author" is Louis Racine (1692–1763); CS is quoting canto 2 of his poem *Religion* (1742).

6. Charlotte Turner was not yet 16 when she married BS in Feb. 1765.

To the earl of Egremont

[Elsted, 14 or 15 October 1803]

There is a young Gentleman in this village, unfortunately a cripple who, disabled by this accident for active life, has attached himself to Botanical studies. He is the Son of an old Navy Captain of the name of Geary.[1] He heard us speak in raptures of the Datura Arborea[2] in y^r^ Ldships conservatory & wishes, if it should still be in flower, he might be permitted to see it. I ventured to say I was sure yr Lordship would not only permit him, but give orders for his reception should he ride to Petworth (as he can mount an horse) with your usual noble hospitality. He is to us rather more interesting than a mere acquaintance from some slight resemblance in person, & more from his misfortune, to our lamented Charles.

[Unsigned]

I shall send a large parcel on Teusday—among other things the proof I mentiond of money being kept back in 1792 from Gays <inself> to answer its expences.

Petworth House Archives MS. Address: Earl of Egremont/ Petworth. Postmark: GODALMIN/ —; {no date.}

NOTES

1. For William Geary, see Harriet Amelia Smith Geary in Biographical Notes. In a letter to Egremont, 25 Jan. 1804, CS mentions that Harriet had an opportunity to marry "not disadvantageously," probably referring to Geary.

2. A beautiful tropical plant that is a member of the nightshade family. It is remarkable that CS should attempt to maintain normal relations with Egremont in her friends' and family's names when she herself was on such strained terms with him.

To the earl of Egremont

[Elsted, 15 October 1803]
My Lord,

The Butcher, Mr Andrews, has this evening informd me of his resolution not to trust me next week unless I pay his bill. I have not my Lord a Shilling. My situation is very dreadful. If y^r Lordship has not mercy on me, What can I do?—— As there is a small ballance due to me awarded for money laid out for the estate & Nicholas's interest is 15£ which Mr Turner says I shall have if Miss Smith will give him a bond of indemnity which she is ready to do—let me implore y^r Lordship to let Mr Tyler pay twenty five pounds on my acc^t into the hands of Mr Fauntleroy Berners Street, on whom I will draw at 8 days in fav^r of Andrews whose bill is 10£ for two Months, & I shall not be disgraced & starved.

I write while the Man waits & in misery that none can tell but they who are doom'd to feel what I do——

Y^r Lordships most unfortunate Ser^t,
Ch Smith

Octr 15th [1803]

Petworth House Archives MS. No address or postmark.

To the earl of Egremont

[Elsted, 21 October 1803]
My Lord,

I take the liberty of informing you that I received a Letter from my Son Nicholas accompanying two Bank powers of Attorney to My eldest daughter to receive dividends or sell or otherwise transact any money matters in the public funds. In the present state of funds, I shall not avail myself of this to sell out any of his money, but rather wish to have the power to add to it; The transfer of the stock therefore from your Lordship & Mr Turners names to Miss Smith may be delay'd 'till January, but I flatter myself your Lordship will no longer refuse to let me have the small pittance due from the dividend received in July last, as I have the most pressing occasion for it, small as it is, Not knowing how to exist & being every way distress'd.

My son has also sent over a copy of his Will providing for his Persian children & their Mother which is a great relief to my mind, as I dreaded the rapacity of the brutal Man[1] who would have profitted at the expence of these innocents, had any thing unfortunately happen'd to my Son. I hope your Lordship will now be convinced I have not deceived you in this instance, as you express A suspicion of in y^r Letter to Mrs Dorset—— In hopes of an early answer, every day increasing my inconvenience, I have the honor to be

Your Lordships most oblig'd Ser^t,
Charlotte Smith

Elsted, Octr 21st 1803

I trust I shall be allowed information about Mr Prescod—— relative to which I am extremely uneasy; The fatality seems to be such against these unfortunate young people.[2]

I will verify the powers to any person your Ldship chuses to appoint Mrs Dorset leaves this at Petworth.

Petworth House Archives MS. No address or postmark.

NOTES

1. BS, who could have claimed Nicholas's estate in the absence of such a will.

2. This oddly worded paragraph shows CS's distress. Her children are "these unfortunate young people."

To the earl of Egremont

[Elsted] Octr 23rd 1803
My Lord,

If your Lordship deigns to recollect that, in one of your many letters on the subject of a referrence or an agreement, you are pleased to use these words, "I must be an absolute Madman to trust to any agreement among yourselves"; & if you are so good as just to carry your mind back to the circumstance of Mr Benjn Smiths having once made a verbal agreement guaranteed on the faith of his friend Mr Rob Tayler—which agreement was that I should have half the income on condition of his then receiving 400£, of which he received three & then refused to comply with this convention, instead of which he sent your Lordship threats & insolent Letters from an Attorney—I think you will acquit me of the present charge, that of having purchased by a referrence a worse arrangement than was offerd to me without it when y^{r} Lordship w^{d} not have agreed to such, & which, if you had, would not have been binding on that infamous & unprincipled monster——— Why your Lordship paid him the whole years income after having determined to the contrary; why I was left totally destitute with his children to keep & thus deprived of my income & involved in inextricable difficulties & distress; Why your Lordship chose to encourage & countenance this person by keeping him a month at your house & sending for him a second time without giving me a choice whether I would meet him or no, thus exposing me to very unpleasant circumstances & to the laughter & ridicule of Servants and others who thought it an excellent joke, which I own I did not; & why your Lordship ~~who~~ without any possible risk now refuses me only 15£ of my Sons interest money, tho I am reduced to the most cruel exigence, & have told you so, so as to be denied credit even for food & firing; Why you should deal so very hardly with me, not in one instance or two, but in every thing I ask; it is now as vain as useless to conjecture.[1] It is so strange that it baffles all calculate. I can as little tell why you now wish to throw on me the blame of the award,[2] which has answerd no one purpose to me but has completed the measure of my distress & which has faild in two points most material: having a new trust properly created for all the 7000£ & settling a Sum on Major Smith & George out of it, especially to enable Major Smith to acquit himself towards yr Lordship. I only know that—had I been the worst & most blameable of human beings instead of one of whom y^{r} Lordship deign'd to express so high an opinion & for whose misfortunes you have appeard interested so many years—I could not have been treated with more cruelty, more contempt or have been sunk into a deeper abyss of underserved Misery.

Of 50 Gs gain'd by writing which Mr Rose obtain'd for me of Johnson, I have now eighteen pence in my pocket. I have a bill to pay to Moon[3] who presses for the money, for I have been oblig'd during my illness to have wine for medicine. I have no credit with the Butcher or Miller. I have two bills hangg over me for which I expect to be arrested before term begins. I have nothing more to sell (havg parted with the bulk of my books) but abt 20£ worth of such as I hoped might have been spared me, & these Mr Rose is going to sell for me. With all this I am a cripple, a misery which might have been averted if your Lordship had mercifully listened to my humble & earnest entreaties for a small advance from my Sons money to enable me to go to the Sea. Now the disease is incurable (wch renders me dependant even to move from one room to the other on Servants whom I cannot pay)——

My Lord, if I had not trusted most implicitly to your kindness & condescending friendship, I should not have been thus circumstanced for the old Trustees never allowed me to be thus totally left withr a shilling of the 70£ then Appropriated to me—— My health is so much amended since the short change of air in going to Petworth & since a medicine Mr Newland has given me that, except being incurably lame, I might recover strength enough to work for my subsistence & assist my poor unfortunate Lucy, but under the pressure of present want, dreading every ring at the door, & fearing applications even from my own Servants, there is no strength of mind, no fortitude can struggle under such wretchedness—

Good God, when I think that the 500£ was so instantly paid to that unnatural brute (that very 500£ I obtain'd with so much trouble), that it was illegally paid before the Legatees were satisfied, for no referrence could make that legal which was against the direct tenor of the Will, & when I find myself without a shilling to pay even for my Letters!—& do think my treatment most hard & very unlike what I expected[4]— —My Lord, will you let me have my Son Nicholas's interest & suffer me to have one year in advance on my miserable pittance, & will you give me an immediate answer? I have a servant to discharge on Thursday & must sell my cow. My Son will most likely by the next Ships send the general power of attorney by these he has by mistake sent duplicates of the Bank power—one of which he meant doubtless to have reserved for the next conveyance. I send one of these powers to your Steward[5] hoping it may be found sufficient to enable me to receive the dividend. He will probably send me remittances for his child by the next ships, but he thought I had all I wanted from his share here, little suspecting the possibility of my suffering such treatment from Mr Turner!

I entreat your Lordships early & positive anr. If you will say I shall have a years income ~~130~~ 115£, Mr Fauntleroy without interest will ~~discount~~ advance it for me. Harden not your heart my Lord against my distress. Do not needlessly expose me to suffer more than I have done already. Do not drive me in want to the Grave. I declare to you I can bear my present situation no longer. I will send y^r^ Lordship all your Letters that you may see whether I have overlooked that you wishd to see. There is no occasion to trouble yrself to return them.

I have the honor to be y^r^ Lordships
most humble ser^t^, Charlotte Smith

I shall be oblig'd to yr Lordship to let the within go to Mr Turner; if I send it in the common course of the post, it will not reach him before friday, & my situation admits not of a moments delay. Every moment encreasing distress I have contended with, first on this hope & then on that, till I cannot attempt to stem the torrent any more.

After so much spontaneous kindness as I formerly experienced from yr Lordship, to be denied & put off from time to time such a trifle as would have saved me!—tho I ask nothing that could put you in risk—does seem a degree of extreme calamity—

Petworth House Archives MS. Address: Earl of Egremont/ Petworth/ Sussex. Postmark: GODALMIN; {No date}.

NOTES

1. Unbeknownst to CS, BS had ingratiated himself with Egremont and Tyler with his much calmer, and shorter, letters, even when he was desperate to evade creditors himself. When BS writes to Tyler that he cannot, "consistent with my feelings, comply with His [Egremont's] request" to see Rose, there are no reprisals (15 Oct. 1803, unpub. letter in PHA #0.11).

On 31 Oct. 1803, BS wrote a very courteous letter to Tyler, after having stopped by his office to thank him. In BS's final letter of this year (5 Nov. 1803), he says, again calmly, that he has learned that CS is dissatisfied with Rose's award. BS too is willing to set it aside: "I am not more enamoured with Mr Roses decision then is Mrs Smith" (unpub. letters in PHA #0.11). But the award stood.

2. Rose's arbitration award, which gave BS outright the £500 recovered from Gibbon's debt on Gay's and a year's interest income, £230 (see CS to Egremont, 12 Oct. 1803, n. 1).

3. Not identified.

4. BS felt just as strongly that CS got the better bargain. On 19 Jan. 1804, he wrote to Egremont: "I never supposed Mrs Smith would annul the award, as She has had everything her own way, and more than she was entitled" (unpub. letter in PHA #0.11).

CS's awkward sentence consists of two dependent clauses starting with *when,* and an error in the independent clause: CS wrote an ampersand for *I* after "Letters!"

5. William Tyler.

To the earl of Egremont

[Elsted, 3 December 1803]
My Lord,

My draft on Mr Fauntleroy being return'd in consequence of which I am without either money or credit & reduced to a situation worse than any I have yet known, I have only to beg of y^r Lordship to be pleased to inform me whether you will or will not transfer My Son Nicholas's money to Miss Smith when Mr Turner has received the bond of indemnity which only to day arrived from Mr Bicknell who had it seems forgotten it—of so little consequence is it, whether I perish thro anguish of mind or not!—— If to destroy me has been the purpose of the party which has been made against me, they surely may be satisfied as such a life as I have been condemned to for these last two years is infinitely worse than death—— Surely there never was such another instance!—— I hope not for the sake of human nature—

Your Lordships heart is shut against every appeal I can make, or I should not have been left thus to drain to the dregs the bitter cup of poverty sickness & sorrow. But that it should be closed also against the distresses, the ruin of the young & innocent, I do think more extraordinary. My poor George who is now at Woodbridge in Suffolk is under orders for Ireland; he will want money which I have not for him—— Let me implore you my Lord by common humanity to answer me as to the transfer that Miss Smith (tho she must go to town on purpose) may obtain from Nicholas's money some immediate assistance for him & for your Lordships most distressed & most injured humble ser^t,

Charlotte Smith

A relapse into as much illness as I have ever had, has prevented my being able to help myself. Mr Benjn Smiths obligations will soon be encreased by my death. No human strength can stand it.

I hear from Mr Bicknell that the 3331£ is vested in the 4 names mentiond in Mr Tylers letter——I wish to learn whether it the interest is meant to be divided according to the Sums due to the Legatees not yet paid & to Miss Smith—— As to the deed, it will never be found. Good God, what will become of poor Lucy & her children?

I suppose I have a right to ask these questions but with little hope of an answer.

I entreat however to hear ab^t Nich^s Money, as I have now no other resources upon Earth. Barbarously indeed I have been treated—& to gratify whom?

Elsted, Decr 3rd 1803

Petworth House Archives MS. No address or postmark.

To William Tyler

[Elsted] Decr 7th 1803
Sir,

When a person is injured as I am, it is natural to complain in an high tone; I shall not apologize for it to you. As you act as Solicitor to the Trust & are paid for it & no doubt will take care to be sufficiently paid, it does not appear necessary for me to humble myself before you. I wish the exertions you made to obtain the investment of the money two days after the books were shut for dividends could have been made two days sooner. But you will allow me Sir to remind you that if, when in May last, you had not taken it into your head so peremptorily to assert that it was the deed transferring the Trust to Lord Egremont & Mr Turner that was wanting by Mr Prescod & named in the bill, and no other, there would have been time to have obviated the objections before the bill became due, & much might have been done before now to prevent all the evils that are now to follow—— It is quite a new idea that the Trustees cannot part with the money pending the suit of the Allens & Smith: I thought however that this would happen. It is really a pity that it did not before they paid the 500£ to Mr Benjn Smith contrary to the spirit of their Trust & contrary I am very sure to what is or can be made legal by all the awards in the World. I think that, as under that award, there is a very considerable Sum due to Miss Smith & that M^{r} B Smith had not a right to a shilling, the Trustees would find themselves in the wrong to have applied any money till the Legatees were paid.

But it is very easy to see how all this is to go—Next to having driven me to the most cruel exigencies & reduced me to actual beggary after I have been driven to the selling my books & every thing valuable that I had. Next to the satisfaction all this must have given is that of depriving my daughter of what belongs to her or deferring the payment (as you chose to do her Brothers transfer in 1802) till it is useless to her——

Be pleased, Sir, to forward to me the copy of the deed of transfer which you informd me was ready. I am to send it to Mr Coulthurst in Barbados.[1] I wish to know if every expence attending this is to be charged to me. The rigour of the present Trustees infinitely exceeds that I was treated with by the Sieurs Robinson & Parkin &c &c—— They, the present Trustees, contend inch by inch against every thing I ask & shew no other solicitude than to distress me as much as they possibly can!

If Dyer or any of his Gang ever had the deed, it must have been in possession of the Attorney Rickman. It is singular that the principal, Mr Benjn Smith, is neither call'd upon on this occasion or to give his an^{r} to the Bill in

Chancery.[2] He sneaks off like an infamous coward as he is—with his pocket full of money! & I & my children!—— We—perish!———

[Unsigned]

Petworth House Archives MS. Address: Mr Tyler. No postmark.

NOTES

1. Matthew Coulthurst, of Bedford Row and Barbados. CS considered him to be "a man of the first character and ability" (CS to Tyler, unpub., 9 Nov. 1803). He worked with Adams on trust business in Barbados. The deed of transfer in question is the transfer of Gay's from BS, CS, and Lucy Towers Smith to the new executors to the estate (Sir John Swinnerton Dyer, John Robinson, Edmund Boehm, and Richard Atkinson) on 2 July 1784, the day BS was released from prison. A copy of this release had just been verified against the original on 21 Sept. 1803 by Challen and Sharp, attorneys (PHA #8207).

2. Now that the Smiths and Allens had embarked on the Chancery suit, CS's lawyer Charles Bicknell was attempting to subpoena BS. Remarkably, Egremont advised BS to avoid the subpoena (BS to Tyler, 15 Oct. 1803, unpub. letter in PHA #0.11).

1804
"THE BEST OF THE BUNCH"

—5 MARCH 1804

July 1804 saw the publication of Charlotte Smith's children's book Conversations Introducing Poetry, *the last significant work published before her death. It earned Smith £125 from Joseph Johnson. With that money and Nicholas's remittances she began to pay off debts of the last two years while living modestly in the village of Elsted near Godalming.*

The trust business was still far from decided, and Egremont continued to treat Smith in ways that humiliated and embittered her. Benjamin returned to England several times this year and was as troublesome as ever. After meeting with him, Egremont expressed his disgust with the entire family by calling Benjamin "the best of the bunch." Charlotte Smith almost succeeded in getting her estranged husband to settle the small fortune from her marriage articles on the three youngest children born too late to be included in Richard Smith's will.

Smith resumed working in earnest in order to supply her children's needs and to defend their right to support from the trust. Lionel, refused a substantial payment required to advance in rank, had to take a post in the West Indies. She feared for his life and worried for his wife and new child. George, now a lieutenant, was repeatedly refused money for equipment and supplies needed in his new position. Lucy and her children required support, while Charlotte Mary and Harriet lived with their mother during much of the year, visiting friends when possible. Harriet's health remained unstable.

The successes of Smith's sons had long been the one solace of her life. This year brought a new solace: the friendly correspondence of Sarah Rose, wife of the lawyer who had decided the arbitration award. Although sometimes filled with bitter accounts of trust business or of her life with Benjamin, Smith's letters to this new ally reveal that years of adversity had not altogether dampened the spirits of this cheerful and witty observer of the literary scene.

To Joseph Cooper Walker

[?Ested, January 1804]

. . . somewhat[1] weary of me & my endless troubles. I have heard once or twice from Mr Hayley, but in a way which entirely discourages any approaches to that friendly intercourse that once subsisted between us—— You have undoubtedly seen long since, his celebrated life of Cowper.[2] Another Volume consisting I beleive entirely of Letters is in the press. Our friend seems to have lost none of the amiable feelings of his heart, but his style I think does not improve. It is so emcumberd with certain favourite words that it is almost cant. I wish he had said less about affectionate, worthy, amiable & marvellous, Of admirable divines, & excellent kinsmen, for it makes people laugh. All those good souls could not be such marvellous beings, & I am sure those who knew some of them, if they dared to say as they think, would describe them very differently. But this is of course said to you only——

Godwins life of Chaucer[3] is well spoken of, but the prejudice against him is so strong that it will not be candidly read. I have never seen it. Of lighter reading there has long been a plentiful lack, at lea[st of] any of merit. But the Muse of Poetry, always partial to your Island, seems to have a very animated & eloquent votary in Lord Strangford whose little book I have read with peculiar pleasure.[4] I seem to be no longer in the literary World, and my Pegasus is as much a cripple as I am. Indeed I retain little of all I once poss-ess'd, but an heart still too sensibly alive to misery, for it ought long since to have been callous—— It is however alive also to the remembrance of the few friends whom calamity has not yet quite frighten'd away, & the recollection of their kindness is almost all I have left to support me thro the last sad scene that is fast approaching & which ought not to be unwelcome if to be released from oppression & many cureless woes is desirable. To have a few lines from you, Dear Sir, should you see my boy & comply with my request to notice him on my account, will be most satisfactory to, Dear Sir, your most obliged humble Ser^t,

Charlotte Smith

Huntington MS (HM10827). Address: Josepth Cooper Walker Esqre/ St Vallory, near, or/ Eccles Street, in/ Dublin. No postmark.

NOTES

1. The first and second pages of this letter are missing. Dates of works CS mentions establish this fragment as having been written no earlier than 1804.

2. Hayley's *Life and Posthumous Writings of William Cowper, Esqr.*, 3 vols. (1803–1804) contained primarily letters, interspersed with biographical passages.

3. William Godwin's *Life of Geoffrey Chaucer, the Early English Poet,* 2 vols. (1803).

4. Percy Clinton Sydney Smythe, Viscount Strangford's *Poems, from the Portuguese of Luis de Camoens* (1804).

To the earl of Egremont and the Reverend Nicholas Turner

To the Earl of Egremont & the Revd Nicholas Turner

Elsted, Jany 13th
1804

My Lord & Sir,

Accompanying this is the purport & extract of Letters received from Mr Adams.[1] If you will be so good as to give immediately such orders as it appears from these Letters (& not from any misrepresentation of mine surely) are absolutely requisite, if the money is to be recover'd, it would be advisable to send them out, & I should think with an attested copy under the City seal of the deed of transfer by an early packet, as Mr Adams is likely to return to England with the first Convoy in the spring, & if he does come leaving this unfinishd, the money never will be recover'd at all. I need not say that it is to me a matter of perfect indifference, and therefore I hope ye will not call my application troublesome. I cannot help Mr Adams's addressing himself to me. But I have now inform'd him that I have not the least power—either in the recovery or disposition of the money—and that I have no wish about it.

Major Smith is now embarked at Cork for Barbados, & with his usual desire to do all he could for his family, he offerd to undertake any business that remain'd to be settled. But there is such a fatality attending the accursed money belonging to Richard Smith that, as he never has been or is likely to be one shilling the better for it, I have desired him not to add to his professional fatigues that of engaging in affairs that occasiond the death of his Brother & which, like the fruits of Pandemonium, turn even in the possession to bitter ashes.

In an^{r} to the very harsh & undeserved epithets re^{d} in Miss Smiths Letters from Lord Egremont, I shall only say that I am conscious I never merited them & firmly beleive that on a cooller consideration his Lordship will alter his present opinion as to many atrocious facts which he now seems to think I have committed. I beleive Mr Rose will clear me from the imputation I am now loaded with in regard to Mr Newhouse,[2] & I am sure Mr Turner ought to do it. After a long life entirely dedicated to the thankless office of saving a family whom their father has studied only how to ruin & after having sufferd so many deprivations & miseries, it is hard to be accused as I am now. From Lord Egremonts justice, I expected a conclusion very different: But subdued as I am by personal suffering, pecuniary deprivations, and anxiety of mind on account of Lionel whose destination has so long and justly been the object of my dread, [and] having undergone also great misery on account of my poor George who narrowly escaped a fate which I fear a great part of the 47th Reg^{t} have experienced, I really am equally unable & unwilling to wage a paper war with Lord Egremont of whom I never did either speak or write or intend to speak or write but with respect & gratitude.

In regard to others to whom I am under no obligations & of whom I cannot speak what I do not think—particularly in regard to Mr Benjn Smith, a person whose character for folly & wickedness it is hardly possible & certainly unnecessary to blacken—I hold myself at liberty to say in any manner & at any time the truth & all the truth. If I violate truth, the blame will follow that I shall deserve.[3]

It is impossible for a Mother not to regret that money has been paid to him—744£[4] in six months for which she & her children are now suffering every distress & likely to suffer more. It is impossible for her not to lament in bitterness of heart that the Sum paid to this unnatural father [would] have purchased, with what Mr Gallway[5] would have done for him, a Lieutenant Colonels commission for my deserving Son Lionel—which would have enabled him to have paid all his obligations & have saved him from the dreadful voyage he is now embark'd for!——

But complaint is useless, & regret vain. I have the honor to be,

My Lord & Sir,
your most obed^{t} ser^{t},
Charlotte ~~Smith~~

Jany 13th 1804

Petworth House Archives MS. No address or postmark.

NOTES

1. Thomas Maxwell Adams of Barbados, whom CS found reliable in trust matters.

2. This imputation is not mentioned elsewhere; CS was against Lucy's marriage to Thomas Postlewaite Newhouse from the beginning on grounds of "unconquerable objections" to his family (see CS to Sarah Rose, 14 Feb. 1805). As Newhouse died 28 Mar. 1801, the present imputation may have come from his family. His father, John Newhouse, was an attorney in Petworth.

3. BS, generally restrained up till his disillusionment with Rose's award, had similarly harsh words for CS: "I am very sorry she has treated your Lordship, with so much ingratitude, but what can be expected from a Calumniator, and a perfect Tisiphone" (BS to Egremont, 19 Jan. 1804, unpub. letter in PHA #0.11).

4. BS received £500 through Samuel Rose's arbitration award on 27 Sept. 1803. The remaining money consisted of dividends owed him from other sources. On 19 Jan. 1804, he asks Egremont to send him the money in a bank note cut in half. His "borrowed name"—the alias Brian Simmonds he uses to conceal his presence in England—

prevents him from drawing directly on Pybus, Egremont's banker (unpub. letter in PHA #0.11).

5. Thomas Galway, of Killery, Kerry, Ireland, Lionel's father-in-law. Lionel's promotion to lieutenant colonel was delayed for lack of funds until 6 June 1805. His "dreadful voyage" was first to Barbados and then to Surinam, climates CS feared with good reason.

To Sarah Rose

Elsted, Jany 16th
1804
My dear Madam,

———I should before now have taken the liberty of troubling you, but I have undergone great fatigue in being obligd to write Letters lately to the East & West Indies, the latter on most unpleasant business which Lord Egremont throws entirely on me & then quarrels with me when I have done, but the anxiety of my mind is still greater than the weariness, for my Son Major Smith is at length saild to Barbados with his Reg^{t}.[1] And such is my dread of that climate that I have the most terrible apprehensions of the event, & had I no other cause of anxiety, this alone would embitter ever [*sic*] hour of my life.

I am afraid I have given you a great deal of trouble in Mr Roses absence. But in consequence of Lord Egremonts refusing me every thing I ask'd, even my Son's interest money, & trying every means in his power to throw me into the greatest pecuniary distress, I had no resource but my little India bill & the Tradesmen who complain, and I beleive justly, of unusual poverty and distress were so clamourous for the money due to them that I could not put them off an hour. A bill for 15£ for Coals being paid to John Bridger, little will remain, & that little I am indebted to Mr Rose—— I should have between sixty & seventy pounds now payable at Pybus's in consequence of the award, but I <u>beleive</u> Lord Egremont has taken measures to prevent my receiving it, for I have written twice to Messrs Pybus to know whether they would pay it to my order, but they give me no answer, & the Letters I have, or rather my eldest daughter has received, from the noble Lord in consequence of my having sent him a bill of 100£ from Barbados (of which he knew nothing & which I might have kept if I would) Are really of so extraordinary a nature that I am afraid of applying to him on any subject however necessary.

After reviling me to my daughter in the grossest terms & saying that I have calld both himself & Mr Rose <u>Villains</u>, That I <u>ought to break my heart</u> to think of the trouble I gave a <u>poor innocent Man like him</u> who suffers so much that he is unable to bear it, After saying that I am the cause of the Chancery suit & have ruind by my <u>Violence</u> my daughter Lucy in <u>making</u> her speak to Mr Rose against M^{r} B Smith (Mr Rose knows best whether this is true) and that I am a fury, There is nothing surely that I may not apprehend from the wild caprice of such a Man. Most earnestly do I wish it were possible to get out of his power, for my strength of mind fails under this treatment after a life passd in the exercise of the most painful duties. And as Lord Egremont says he will give 1000£ to be released from me & I shall lose my life or my reason if I am not released from him, one purpose of my going to Town if I should be able to get thither would be to try whether legal means may not be found with his consent but without his 1000£ to dissolve this trust & put the remaining Affairs into Chancery. I wish therefore to know, & I am sure you will have the goodness to tell me, whether Mr Rose is returnd to town and at what time it is probable he will be most at leisure to oblige me with a conference.

A second purpose of my intended journey would be to see Dr Reynolds[2] to enquire what chance he thinks there is of my ever recovering the power of walking by Buxton or warm sea bathing, & if he does not encourage me to try either I shall return quietly to my prison from which, except my reluctant journey to the melancholy magnificence of Petworth house, I have never moved for ten months, & above eight of those months I have not been even round my little Garden. I talk however somewhat at large of going to the Sea or to Buxton, for I do not beleive the noble Earl will let me have any money he can possibly keep from me, & tho my India goods are landed and safe in the Company's Warehouse, the duties will run so high that, unless the noble Lords asperity towards me should be mitigated, I shall hardly find means to pay them. I find his Lordship advises Mr Turner never to let me have either the interest or principal of my Son's money while he can keep it from me! It is impossible to guess what purpose such a Man has to answer in thus oppressing me. I fear there is but one way of accounting for it, but whatever is the cause, the effect to me is very terrible.

One of the most agreeable purposes of my visiting London would be, Dear Madam, to avail myself of the flattering permission you have given me of thanking you personally for your repeated kindness and the interest you are so good as to take in my unexampled misfortunes. To acquire such a friend is in every way consoling, & I shall greatly envy Charlotte who will in a few days have an opportunity of waiting on you, as she proposes being in Town about Sunday next, while my hopes of becoming known to you must at least be doubtful, cripple as I am & without the certainty that the noble Lord with 52,000£ a year will let me have 62£ that belongs to me & about 32£ he holds as interest of my Sons!

Forgive me, Dear Madam, for all the trouble I must have occasiond to you, and for this querulous Letter. If Mr Rose is in town, pray assure him of our best respects, & beleive me most truly your oblig'd Ser^t,

Charlotte Smith

Henry W. and Albert A. Berg Collection of English and American Literature, The New

York Public Library, Astor, Lenox and Tilden Foundations MS. Address: Mrs Rose/ Chancery Lane/ London. Postmark: Godalmin: G/ JAN 16/ 1804.

NOTES

1. Lionel had been a major in the 16th Regiment since 24 June 1802.
2. Henry Revell Reynolds, M.D. (see CS to Cadell and Davies, 19 July 1799, n. 1).

To the earl of Egremont

[Elsted, 25 January 1804]

My Lord,

I should not trouble yr Ldsp, but beleive it to be necessary to forward to you the within Letter and to ask yr Lordsps orders as to the paper in Question which cannot too soon be sign'd & return'd to Barbados. I have to day a Letter from Mr Bicknell desiring directions about the copy of the Transfer deed, which I will give as well as I can, for with such a Man as Griffith to deal with, it is better, if any thing is to be recoverd, to leave him as little pretence as possible for evasion. My poor Son in one of his last Letters states Griffiths's debt at 800£ (I suppose currency) and many years interest, & he had obtain'd from Charles a respite of twelvemonths on condition of giving a bond—& judgement. Of His death, the wretch took advantage, & such is my opinion from long & fatal experience of the people in Barbados that I should not be surprised if his death had been hasten'd.[1] Mr Wents conduct since & the mystery there has been about the papers he left; dirty tricks play'd by those Wents about his effects; the boy he took with him not being sufferd to return but hired at an enormous expence to remain there; have all given me additional pain when ever I have reflected on his loss, & tho I do not say it was so & the Climate is quite enough to account for the sudden illness & death of an healthier Man than was my unfortunate Charles, yet the advantage taken immediately of that cruel event & the triumph the people evidently feel whose interest was so deeply involved in the event of his activity have from the very first made me speak with asperity which I could hardly command tho even to myself I did not assign this doubt as its cause.

But where is the spirit that would, ~~not have sunk~~ under such woes as have been accumulated on me, [not] have sunk into imbecility or been irritated into phrenzy? That your Lordship should so utterly misunderstand those expressions as to suppose that I was senseless or ungrateful enough to impute to your Lordships approving of his going the misfortune of his death, when he himself, poor fellow, always spoke & wrote of you as his best friend & munificent benefactor & when I know that to go (contrary always to my wishes because I knew him to be unfit for it) was his own desire and intention long before he had the appointt from Genl Dalrymple thro yr

Lordships interest, which made it the more desirable to him. That your Lordship should so misinterpret my expressions and accuse me of such a degree of ideotism or wickedness can arise only from one or other of the following causes: either your Lordships more important engagements have not allow'd [you] to read what I wrote, or I have express'd myself like a fool & was not to be understood, or lastly, your Lordships mind has received some impressions in my disfavour which appear to be deep and harsh in proportion as those you formerly were pleased to entertain were kind and favourable even beyond any desert I pretend ever to have had.

Lionel has inform'd me of your Lordships last Letter to him of wch he sent me a copy. He is now or was on the 16th ins^{t} detain'd by contrary winds on board the Aurora Transport in Cork Harbour. His going is on all accounts inevitable, but it was I who encouraged rather his Wife[2] than himself to hope not so much to engage your Lordships or any other interest to get him recalld on promotion as to obtain that promotion by purchase at the regulation price of 950£ of which his father in Law Mr Gallway is ready and desirous ~~of advancing~~ to advance a part & of which the remainder might be rais'd without difficulty if Mr Benjn Smith would only make an irrevocable deed, as he ought in honor & in conscience to do.[3] The debt to your Lordship which Lionel always did &, I am sure, always will consider as having the first claim On his honor & gratitude, & of which Mr Gallway is perfectly aware, would be far from being postponed by this arrangement. It would put him in a way to pay it tho his sense of your kindness will never be diminish'd. His meaning however in his letter was to ask yr Lordships influence with Mr Benjn Smith to get this irrevocable deed done & not to tax your friendship in regard to his R H, the Commander in cheif,[4] being well aware that you must have many other & more immediate claims on your influence with his R H with which my Son never meant nor could dream of interfering, & he seems mortified that your Ldp should think he meant so to presume———

Allow me my Lord—as indeed I am not able if I were desirous of troubling you with long letters often—Allow me earnestly to beg and entreat your attention, while I state what M^{r} B Smith I beleive does not or will not understand but which certainly is so, & I beg leave to appeal to the Marriage Articles of 1765 (fatal epoch to me!) whether what I say is not true——

It is therein specified that the money belonging to me shall be divided in such share's as the survivor, M^{r} B S. or myself, shall by will direct among all the children of the marriage, but I am told that this implies that a due proportion shall be observed & that it is not in Mr B Smith's power nor mine to omit any one of them nor to cut one off with ten or twenty pounds & give an undue share to another. Now my meaning and wish is that 6000£ be divided among the three unprovided for children: that is, 2000£ each, & the remaining 1000£ among the other four, in which case, I have reason to beleive that The two young Men in the East Indies[5] would give their shares up to Lucy, & together with her own would make between seven & eight hundred pounds for her. I have written to them both about it, & I am sure Nicholas will do it at least. Now, my Lord, I surely may venture to appeal to your justice & consideration & to ask whether this is not a fair & reasonable proposal? It cannot injure Mr B Smiths present enjoyments.[6] It cannot prevent his doing as he pleases with the residue, such as it may be, which he still will have to give to his children by his present or any other wife without any restriction as to proportion of the division. It cannot prevent (as he complains the award has done) his providing for Mrs Millar because it is impossible he could provide for her out of my property were I to die tomorrow—not even if he gave her the name & station as his Spouse, which I have always been so ready to resign—nor could he, had no award ever ~~have~~ been made, have given her after his death any of his fathers property tho he may to Any children he may chuse to call his, born after a second marriage. How then can he be injured or his future progeny by doing justice to my children out of what was mine? Every motive of honor, of decency, of honesty, demand it of him. His refusal can arise only from the worst motives—To gratify a revenge against me—Against me who have been his victim from my early youth, & must be so till the grave hides me from the poverty & anxiety which now are drinking my life blood.

Your Lordship said to Miss Smith that it was Mr B Smiths intention to do all that was right by Major Smith. Why then will he not do it when it might save his Son from a premature death? when it would ensure the thanks of a young Man who never in his life offended him, & preserve to me for the little while I have to live one of the few, very few comforts my miserable destiny has left me? If Harriet is his object, she may still have all of his fathers that he has to give, & with 2000£ of mine, it will make her more than equal to the rest tho no reason upon Earth exists why she should be more than equal. Nor is it likely he really cares for her when he has refused her a few guineas while she lay dying of a fever & has never given her but two pound notes during about sixteen or seventeen years. I can tell him that, had she a certain & settled proportion out of what belongs to me, she might now perhaps be married not disadvantageously, but the uncertainty is an insuperable barrier to a young Man,[7] himself dependent upon the future will of others. I am not at liberty to say more on this subject, but surely it ought to be a motive to him to make the deed I request. Yet were I to urge it to him, he would for that reason only determine not to do it. Yet in desiring him to do what is right by her Brothers, I do not wish or mean to injure her—very very far otherwise!——

As to Mrs Newhouse, I will not defend myself against a charge[8] which yr Lordship I am sure on reflection will be too candid & too generous not to own was unfounded. Beleive me, My Lord, I knew nothing of Mr Roses intention to call upon her or any one till the hour it was done, Or I would have taken very different & far more decided measures.[9] There was a lady not six miles off, no friend of mine neither, who would have said that once in his Coach going to dine at Lord Clanricardes he threw a large bunch of keys at me & hurt me on the breast without any provocation but my saying we should make Lady C. wait & put her out of humour. I could have brought another person, a relation of mine, who would have taken the most solemn oath that she has seen him strike & kick me &, once at table, throw a quartern loaf at my head without provocation at all but the phrenzy, for so it seemd at the moment. But all this it is plain I forgave, & he forgot when years after I left him (in consequence of still worse treatment), he condescended to return to me repeatedly to let me pay his debts & send him money at the very time he was actually negociating a marriage with a Miss Gordon—On whom he passd himself for a single Man, a person of fortune, under a temporary cloud. To this Woman, he actually lent my books, saying I was a relation of his familys!—& things went so far that the wedding presents were bought. I know two people who are now in England who will swear that they know these facts to be true. I care not a straw if he had as many wives as the great ~~xxxx~~ Mogul, but what figure would a Man make in Doctors commons had he been put upon his defence there, who has thus acted.

My Lord, Lionels situation & Georges are of the greatest importance to me: On the first depends more than my life, for misery will be mine beyond all calculation should he do ill, & it will then be too late for regret. Forgive me, I beseech you then, for imploring this once your attention to what I ask & y^r^ assistance with Mr Smith. Mr Tayler seems to think he has now no interest with him & tells me that he not [*sic*] live at Camberwell[10] & that all the time he was at Petworth he never heard from him. I have therefore no means of getting him to attend to the just claims of my Son unless your Lordship, who must have weight with him, will generously interpose & add this attempt to the many obligations which, however y^r^ Lordship may have thought of me, I shall never cease to acknowledge. I have the honor to be

y^r^ Lordships obligd Ser^t^,
Charlotte Smith

Elsted, Jany 25th 1804

Can you think, my Lord, that M^r^ B S. w^d^ ever have done any thing voluntarily for Mrs Newhouse when he refused long before the last offence even to see her when your Lordship was so considerate as to offer him a conveyance; W^d^ a Man with human feelings have gone by his daughters door with money in his pocket & never think of her distress but to insult her?

My Lord, to your Lordship who are so affectionate a father, surely I may appeal whether this Man's conduct towards any of his children is what it ought to be?[11]

Forgive me for writing in all respects very ill. I am sick in body & mind—[12]

Petworth House Archives MS. No address or postmark.

NOTES

1. The only indication that CS suspected foul play in Charles's death. Went's troubling and suspicious conduct, however, resulted from mental derangement (CS to Egremont, [?April 1804]). The boy who attended Charles during his illness, Benjamin Maule, himself had the fever five times, but stayed on in Barbados to learn to be a planter from Mr. Hollingsworth (CS to Egremont, unpub., 20 Feb. 1802).

2. Lionel's first wife, Ellen Marianne Galway.

3. CS wanted BS to agree to assign her marriage settlements to be distributed among their children born too late to be included in Richard Smith's will; BS refused. After BS died, CS was able to do this for Lionel, Harriet, and George.

4. His Royal Highness, Frederick, duke of York.

5. William and Nicholas, at 36 and 33, were no longer young.

6. BS is in dire straits himself: "My income has been most ungenerously, and unjustly reduced to one half; my arrears not amply paid, and my Executorship accounts, totally annihilated" (BS to Egremont, 25 Jan. 1804, unpub. letter in PHA #0.11). A week earlier, he actually asked Egremont to "procure some situation for me, to augment my small income, which cannot otherwise support me . . ." (BS to Egremont, 19 Jan. 1804, unpub. letter in PHA #0.11). Egremont had mentioned this alternative to him previously, BS reminds him.

7. William Geary, whom Harriet was able to marry only after CS's death left them an income.

8. That is, that she ruined Lucy and made her speak to Rose; see CS to Sarah Rose, 16 Jan. 1804.

9. What follows is the most detailed account of BS's violence; it also shows a continuing relationship with the earls of Clanricarde (see CS to Cadell and Davies, [Mar. 1798], n. 3).

10. BS's onetime friend and advisor Simon Halliday did, however, live at Camberwell and wrote to CS, and so may have been the source of this confusion (see CS to Egremont, 13 Jan. 1803, n. 2, and 15 Feb. 1803, n. 2). His daughter had married into the Dyer family (see Genealogical Chart).

11. A tactless or at best awkward question for CS to ask of Egremont in this ill-advised lengthy letter. Egremont had three sons and three daughters by his mistress, Elizabeth Iliffe of Petworth. Although he married her on 16 July 1801 and their children prospered, those children were never legitimized. Upon his death, the estate passed to a collateral branch of the family, though portions of it were eventually returned to his two eldest sons.

12. Written vertically across the top half of the last page.

To William Tyler

[Elsted, 25 January 1804]

To Mr Tyler

Sir,

If you have not sent the trifle coming to me otherwise, be pleasd to pay it to Mrs Newhouse. I have bo[ugh]^{t} a pig of her which Mrs Dorset gave her of the wild <herd>,[1] & the money will now be very useful to her.

Ill health & fatigue prevent my troubling you at present with a question occasioned by a reperusal of ye Letters from Charles about Mr Prescods last bill, which makes the whole to me quite uncomprehensible, but I am not able to write upon it now.

I am, Sir,
y^{r} hble Ser^{t},
Charlotte Smith

Be so good as to return this letter when done with & three or four others which I beleive you have one of them from Mr Rose. Elsted 25th Jan^{y}

Petworth House Archives MS. Address: Earl of Egremont/ Petworth/ Sussex. Postmark: GODALMIN/ 51; {no date}.

NOTE

1. Or perhaps "breed."

To Sarah Rose

Elsted, March 5th
1804

My Dear Madam,

I am I fear liable to be thought a most importunate intruder, but you must remember how much encouragement you have given me. And I really have refraind as long as possible from troubling you, partly because I was conscious of my intrusion and partly because I was not quite without hope of seeing you in town. Of that, however, there is now but little probability; Dr Reynolds did not seem to encourage it & thought no advantage to my health would be derived from it, and I am not in circumstances to make the journey merely for pleasure. Nor indeed is it likely I shall now ever be able to do more than vegetate, for my few remaining years or months in this or some other solitude. It is literally vegetating, for I have very little locomotive powers beyond those that appertain to a cauliflower. The Sea, the good

Doctor recommended in April, but I shall not be able to reach any place but Bognor, and for that I have so decided a dislike that I know not whether the certainty of recovering the use of my limbs would engage me to go thither.

But I do not intend to talk any more of myself but of more interesting matters. Mr Rose is I hope quite well and your four delightful boys of whom my Misses[1] speak in raptures. I am solicitous to hear that Mr Rose has forgiven me for the trouble I so unintentionally gave him ab^t^ the 100£ India Bill which however I certainly should not have done had he not forgotten to send me directions how to draw for it when he went out of town, but I assure you I was very much vexd to find that it had been troublesome to him, & I am afraid now that I am in his debt, but I cannot think, hurried with business as I know he is, of troubling him about it. Might I write to the Bankers? or will you have the goodness at any time to make the enquiry for me?—— I should be vexd to have trespass'd upon as well as troubled him——

Do you happen to know whether Mr Johnson[2] is confined by sickness, or to what cause I am to assign it that I can obtain no answer to my Letters of which I have written three. I am quite <u>put down</u> and discouraged at not hearing from him. Under the following circumstances I assured myself I should—— You know, Mr Rose, before my ill fated journey to Petworth, was so obliging as to dispose of my little book of early Poetry for 50 G^s^ to Johnson, who however express'd doubts of the possibility of making a saleable book of so small a quantity; I afterwards sent him up three other short pieces, but he still thought the quantity too little & wrote to me to say that if I would send him up <u>half as much again</u>, that is about 40 pages more, he would make the Sum half as much again, or 25 G^s^ more. To this which I considerd as a very liberal offer, I assented, but Poetry of whatever description, if it be tolerably good (& if it be not it is the <u>most</u> intolerable of all things), <u>will not</u> be written at the moment it is wanted. I found it by no means easy to write 40 pages of Poetry, & I proposed a plan which would give room for a great deal of other information & serve as a vehicle for the Poetry which however I would also enlarge. To this he acquiesed, & since his having done so, I have sent up near or quite <u>200</u> pages instead of the 100 he required, & I have near 40 more including new poems now quite ready for the press. I had however sent him up so much that I wishd he would oblige me by beginning to print, as what remains & the preface I can return with the first proof.

I certainly have <u>more</u> than fulfilled my agreement, indeed nearly or quite doubled what he stipulated, leaving it wholly to him to judge of the worth of the whole, as I know I may depend on his liberality. Of course I cannot have done wrong in that respect, as I have never mentiond any encrease of price. But to three Letters requesting the loan of some books & on other business to which his answer would have been highly gratifying, I have never obtaind any answer whatsoever, tho the last was to request his attention to a matter of business which it is material to me to get thru. Perhaps he is ill and is unable to hear of business at all. I am vexd at it on more accounts than one. I wishd for many reasons to have had the book out early in the Spring. I wish to have it wholly off my mind & the correcting it over that what little strength of body and intellect I can, amid frequent sufferings, command I may apply to some other work in the hope of adding a little to the miserable pittance I am reduced to after all my exertions. But I do not love to tieze Mr Johnson & cannot help persuading myself he is ill. I as little like to tieze Mr Rose. And so you see, I tieze you. My Sister, whose talents are much greater than any one suspects & who has given me some of the best pieces for this book, would call on Johnson, but she went on a <Acton> A few days ago, & I am sure cannot now return, & she does not know him, but she is impatient for some progress. Can you, my Dear Madam, tell me whether Mr Johnson is disabled by illness from answering with his usual kindness & politeness? Mr Rose perhaps knows, & Can you & will you forgive my being thus unreasonable?

I heard with pleasure that Mrs Lee was soon to give the World another Novel. I have not yet seen it advertised.[3] If she & her Sisters are still in Town, recall Me to their recollection. They are among those by whom it wd grieve me to be forgotten Tho I surely cannot deserve to be remember'd & indeed ought with my family to be driven from society & even from the World if it be true, as the noble peer express'd himself not long ago, at his own table, less elegantly than decidedly, "That Mr Benjn Smith was the best of the bunch." If it be indeed so, my Dear Madam, As this British legislator opines, I must have undergone some dreadful metamorphosis unknown to myself & must have been touchd by some Circean wand which has transformed me into a creature compounded of Hyena, Sow, & Wolf. You must be frightend at such a correspondent if you beleive half of such a description. Be assured however that at present I feel myself

yr obligd & faithful Sert, CS—

May I flatter myself that I shall hear from you in a post or two?—I wishd to borrow of Mr Johnson—Miss Sewards life of Dr Darwin,[4] & some other books. Tis misery past compute as Mr Cumberland says, to hear of books, & hunger & thirst after them without being able to get them——My daughters beg their Compts to you & Mr Rose.[5]

Huntington MS (HM10835). Address: Mrs Rose/ Chancery Lane/ London—. Postmark: GODALMIN; G/ MAR 6/ 1804.

NOTES

1. Charlotte Mary had visited Sarah Rose, probably with Luzena, whom she sometimes kept for her mother.

2. Joseph Johnson, who was about to publish *Conversations Introducing Poetry* (the "little book of early Poetry").

3. Sophia Lee's *The Life of a Lover,* an epistolary novel in 6 vols. (1804). CS later ridiculed it (letter to Sarah Rose, 30 July 1804).

4. Anna Seward's *Memoirs of the Life of Dr. Darwin* (London: J. Johnson, 1804). Dr. Erasmus Darwin's *The Botanic Garden* was a great favorite of Smith's, but Seward's *Memoirs* was not (CS to Sarah Rose, 30 July 1804).

5. Written upside down on the page that contains the address.

To the earl of Egremont

[Elsted, 20 March 1804]
My Lord,

It is most unfortunate for me that I fail in every instance either to be approved or understood. I did not expect or suppose that (thinking of me as your Lordship has long thought) you would condescend to trouble yourself about any thing that related to me or the poor pittance allotted me; My Lord, I applied to you as Lionels Creditor and only requested you to be so good as to tell me whether—in the event of my obtaining (it matters not how) of Mr Benjn Smith the irrevocable deed[1] I have so long implored & if, in consequence of having so obtain'd it, the money to make up the Sum for the purchase of a Lieutenant Colonels commission can be raisd by Mr Galways assistance—Your Lordship will consent to its being so applied. My Son, giving you such security for the final discharge of his pecuniary obligation to yr Lordship as you may be pleased to point out——

When, in my anxiety to get him promoted and recalled, I proposed this plan of raising the money if a deed could be obtain'd, he replied that desirous as he was of it and advantageous as it must be to him, he must entreat that I would do nothing in it without having it positively ascertain'd that the transaction had your Lordships acquiesence & approbation & that in acting otherwise, I might commit him in y^{r} Lordships opinion and embitter every satisfaction he should otherwise derive from it.

Do not therefore, My Lord, be offended or surprised at my addressing you. On one side is the prospect, the dreadful prospect of hazard daily and hourly arising to a life so precious to me & his family, besides the confusion that will & must ensue if Mr Benjn Smith surviving me makes a Will which is contrary to the meaning of the Marriage articles. On the other, I have the hope of seeing Lionels return & promotion to the highest professional rank he can for many years obtain. Of having my George provided for & Harriet secure of a certain portion of what belongs to me, with a security also in regard to the other four, two of whom will probably assist Lucy with their shares, & it will also ascertain hers. Forget my Lord all the causes of complaint I have unhappily given you, & at present vouchsafe, my Lord, to oblige me by letting me know whether your Lordship accedes to my plan. After I hear that, I will not lose an hour in trying what can be done. The regulation price is 950£; Mr Galway will assist, but to what extent I know not.

Waving at present every other subject on which I am unlucky enough to be greatly misunderstood, I will only earnestly entreat a decisive ansr & have the honor to be y^r^ Lordships most obed^t^ Ser^t^,

Charlotte Smith

Elsted, March 20th
1804

Will y^r^ Lordship take the trouble to free or, if in London, to send the within to Mr Tayler, as it saves me 1^s^—

Petworth House Archives MS. No address or postmark.

NOTE

1. On 25 Jan. 1804 BS writes to Egremont that he has "agreed to execute an irrevocable deed in favor of some of my Children; and it is so settled, that I am to have the One Hundred pounds as first proposed." He even offers a bill from his eldest son to secure it. Without the £100, BS will "soon be in want of the common necessaries of life" (unpub. letter in PHA #0.11). But he did not execute the deed at this time.

To Sarah Rose

[Elsted, 21 March 1804]
My Dear Madam,

I most sincerely thank you for your kind & obliging Letter as well as your ready interposition with Mr Johnson. No effect however has arisen from that or any subsequent application that I have made to Mr Johnson. On Saturday he must have receivd another MMS, as I sent it by a private hand, & I know it was safely deliver'd because I have heard from a friend to whom by the same conveyance I also sent a pacquet. C'est egal! Mr Johnson is I am convinced determin'd not to write to me, & I cease now to expect it, but after working as hard as I have done & I thought with some success, it is extremely mortifying neither to know that my work is gone to press (for it was material to me to have it publish'd early) or that he thinks his money likely to be well bestow'd. I should fear that somehow or other I had given him offense if he had not with infinite good nature sent a friend of his to Mr Fauntleroys to value my books by which means (having absolutely decided to part with them) I have got about 50£ more than I should otherwise have done. I have written to thank him for this act of kindness. C'est toujours egal,[1] he takes no notice of me or any thanks—— Well, he must take his own way.

Material as it is to me, another object still more important occupies my thoughts. I know you have so much goodness & sensibility of heart that I scruple not to say to you that this is to get M[r] Benj[n] Smith to make the settlement on my three younger children, which it has long been the purpose of my life to effectuate. M[r] Galway, whose daughter Lionel has married, has written to him[2] by my desire, & after a long suspence, I have re[d] a copy of his answer. Her worthy father will, he says, agree to what I ask if I will give up 30£ a year out of my poor pittance of 114£ of my own fortune during my life to him and Harriet 30£ out of the 60£ awarded to her in case of my death. Then he says he will make the irrevocable deed. On it depends whether I shall raise the money to purchase a Lieu[t] Colonels Commiss[n] & get Lionel from the West Indies & a Company for George, & I will do it & have written him word that I will do this After I had applied to Lord Egremont for his consent, who has written as I expected a rude & brutish answer!——

My dear Madam, I am much hurried & have only a moment to say that, as M[r] Rose has seen & is well apprised of the purport of those unfortunate & wretched marriage articles (made when I was not fifteen), I wish I could know his idea of the method in which I ought to set about this, for while I deliberate and hesitate my Son may be lost—& such a Son! I will only say he is the positive opposite to the wretch whom I cannot bear to call his father. A prospect being once open'd to do this, I will give up my plan of going to Southampton to try the hot sea bath and will go to London cripple as I am & devote my powers, such as they are, to the accomplishment of a point dearer to me a thousand times than my existence, but that is not saying much——

What prejudice Lord Egremont has taken against me it is impossible to tell. He accuses me of having ruin'd Lucy (who ruind herself when contrary to my consent & wish she married a Man who in addition to involving her in poverty used her like a bear) and now of having brought upon the noble Lord the Chancery suit which he himself insisted on the familys defending, tho I assure you—& M[r] Rose I am sure knows—that I could be no party in it. But thus it is that the noble Lord like the Wolf in the fable, not being able to fix on me any real cause of complain, blushes not to violate truth & to utter the most palpable falsehoods rather than not have some cause to find faults with me & some excuse for his capricious cruelty. I take refuge against vexation in contempt, for what else can conduct so unmanly and ungenerous inspire—— ——

I was in hopes M[r] Johnson w[d] have given me an opportunity for some literary gossip, but I see no books, & if it was not for my Persian Child[3] should almost forget the use of my tongue. You say you do not think me troublesome. Will you then, my dear Mad^{m}, have the goodness to <order> for me the ~~three~~ Edinburgh Reviews following the 3rd. I have the three first numbers. I have since seen the Imperial Review publish'd by Cadell & Davies.[4] But if the Edinburgh is a caustic, that is a mere milk and water composition, and something like ~~mistress~~ Mrs Quickly, who doth think well of All the worthy gentlemen but speciously on Fenton[5] if he publishes at Cadell & Davies's. The boy waits for my letter, & I have hardly time to say, pray <let me> hear from you & believe me ever, my Dear Mad^{m}—

y^{r} most oblig'd Ser^{t},
Charlotte Smith

21st March 1804

Cowper and Newton Museum MS. Address: M^{rs}: Rose/ Chancery Lane/ London. Postmark: GODALMIN 34; G/ MAR22/ 1804.

NOTES

1. It doesn't matter anyway.

2. That is, has written to BS. In the next sentence, "Her worthy father" is also BS, not Galway.

3. That is, Nicholas's daughter Luzena.

4. *The Imperial Review; or London and Dublin Literary Journal* was published by Cadell and Davies, with publishers from Dublin, Cork, Limerick, and Belfast joining in the effort. It was short-lived, running only from 1804 to 1805, and lacked the point of view and thus the bite of many more political journals of its day, such as the *Edinburgh Review.*

5. *The Merry Wives of Windsor* 3.4.108–109. "Speciously" is a malapropism for "especially."

To the earl of Egremont

[Elsted, 7 April 1804]
My Lord,

On applying to Mr Rose for his friendly opinion as to the measures I sh^{d} pursue to accomplish the objects I have so near my heart in regard to Lionel & George when M^{r} B Smith can be prevaild upon to do what he says he will do (on certain conditions to which conditions I have positively agreed), I have the mortification to learn that Mr Rose has forgotten entirely the substance of the marriage articles which were, as I imagine, laid before him long before the award, & being in a very ill state of health, he cannot recall the business to his mind, or give me any advice about it: I must therefore apply to some other friend.

My Lord, were the object of less importance to those whose service is the sole purpose of my life, and whose safety (as far as can be foreseen) & prosperity in their profession is the only satisfaction I can ever know, I should strictly adhere to the order your Ldship has given me not to trouble you. But such have been my habits & such are my feelings that I cannot, however hopeless it may be, leave any thing undone which may make up to my unfortunate family the disadvantage of having so unfeeling, so unnatural a father. When I reflect that while no one would suffer from the completion of what I ask—tho if any ill befalls my Son, so much misery will be inflicted—While I think that either the interposition of generous friendship towards rising merit or the pecuniary help which might thus be obtain'd by an act of justice on the part of M[r] B Smith, would releive so many persons from the most miserable solicitude, & perhaps save a valuable life, I cannot determine to await the possible evil without making every effort to avert it. If any disaster should happen, I could not exist an hour under the idea that I had left any thing undone, & tho I do not think I should survive it (but none knows as I have experienced before what degree of wretchedness they can bear), I should at least die in the conviction that all my feeble struggles had been made & that the last months of my life were devoted, tho in vain, to rescue my Son from that destiny into which his fathers cruelty had plunged him.

My Lord, this is meant only to account to y[r] Lordship for my presumption in requesting to know whether you will have the goodness to allow me to have, in case it should be necessary, that copy of the marriage articles between M[r] B Smith & me which belongs to your Lordship, as I cannot get at any other. I write now that time may not be lost in writing hereafter if a rational answer can at last be obtaind from this father who studies only how to distress and harass me, even at the expence of destroying his own children. Allow me to hope your Lordship will, with the considerate goodness I had so long occasion to acknowledge, favor me with y[r] an[r] I have the honor to be,

My Lord,
your most obed[t] & oblig'd Ser[t],
Charlotte Smith

Elsted, April 7th 1804

Petworth House Archives MS. No address or postmark.

617 ❦ 1804

To Sarah Rose

Elsted April 18th 1804
My Dear Madam,

As I have an opportunity of writing by a Lady[1] who goes from this village tomorrow, I cannot forbear once more troubling you with a Letter of enquiry & very sincerely hope I shall hear a better account of you than you last gave me. As I have never heard a word from M^{r} B Smith since I implicitly agreed to relinquish a part of the little left me, it is of less importance that Mr Rose cannot recall the circumstances of the marriage articles. I can get nothing done for want of this answer & am oblig'd to relinquish the hopes nearest my heart. As to the objection ab^{t} Harriet, it w^{d} not have existed, as she is in her twenty third year. I am indeed most completely unfortunate. This, of obtaining a division of my fortune among the children was one great inducement to me to have an arbitration. My own deprivations I have learned to bear, but where the very existence & lives of those dearest to me are in question, to be baffled thus—& by M^{r} B Smith, who has already in every other respect ruin'd them & me—is almost too much to be endured. I am very sure that such a destiny as mine never before fell on any one.

I live, however, tho in encreasing infirmity. M^{r} B S. himself could hardly wish me in a fairer way of releasing him. Unable to walk or to afford a conveyance, yet desirous of feeling the breath of Heaven, I sat down on a chair in my garden & my feet on a footstool for a few moments about three weeks ago. In consequence of which I have been labouring ever since under an inflammation on my lungs & a cough. That I have starved away in some degree, but it has left an intermitting fever, which attacks my head with excruciating pain at nine o clock every day & keeps me in agonies till five. I have taken all the bark I had & am now deep with the Apothecary, but it is obstinate. Had it not been so, I should have endeavoured to have got to London & had even fix'd on Thursday to try if I can make any interest for Lionel as 18 Lieut Colonels commissions are to be given away, & he is so well in fav^{r} with the D of York that if he were only properly named, he would succeed to one. Lord Egremont might do it by a single word, but he will not. Yet if I have offended him, my Son has not, and one would think he w^{d} have pleasure in doing a good natured action. But no, he will not. He w^{d} be pleased to see me more miserable than I am——

Mr Johnson, who is a most excellent & worthy Man, has been all that is kind & good tho a little tardy, but he is so really benevolent & liberal with so little parade that I never was so well pleased with a bookseller. The little work is at length in the press,[2] & ill as I have been & am, I have contrived to add to it, for it is become my <hobby poney> if those words do not mean the same thing.

I look out with some impatience for "the life of a Lover"[3] & hope no camphorated ideas will strike the Reviewers from the similarity of names. I look out also over the dull expanse of a newsless newspaper for the Advertisement of M[r] Hayleys third Volume of Cowper[4]—Or for the second edition of his own happiness in the holy estate of Wedlock, for I am told that he has found in the Levant (like a true Hali from whom you know he is said to be descended)[5] a Pool of Bethseda[6] which will, like the fabled Lethe, make him forget all former evils, as he has done all former friends—— L'eau de jouvence and d'obli[7] must be extremely refreshing. If I could obtain a little of it, I should be able to go on with a Novel, which I have begun since 1802, but which personal sickness or anxiety for those better worth being anxious about than myself have continually compelled me to lay aside.[8] Well, no good old body of an Authoress need fear being accused of twaddling I trow, if Miss Seward escapes. I never read so very absurd a book.[9] Had she no friend in the World to tell her how she was exposing herself?

The blisters I have about me prevent my filling my paper tho pain is at the moment suspended.[10] The Edinburgh Review I cannot get. M[r] Johnson however was very good to send me a supply of books, but my insatiable thirst is only irritated by indulgence. Adieu, Dear Madam. Pray tell me soon you are well, & do not forget your most oblig'd & faithful Ser[t],

Charlotte ~~Smith~~

Haverford College Library MS. No address or postmark.

NOTES

1. Not identified.
2. *Conversations Introducing Poetry.*
3. By Sophia Lee.
4. See CS to Joseph Cooper Walker, [Jan. 1804], n. 2.
5. The paragraph that follows is unusually allusive for CS and suggests her relish at having a well-read, sophisticated new friend. Levant is a parish in the county next to Sussex, but it also refers to the countries bordering on the eastern Mediterranean. Hayley claimed to have a Turkish namesake, Hali, the son-in-law of Mahomet. Moreover, Hayley's ancestor William Hayley, dean of Chichester, had spent the early part of his career as domestic chaplain to Sir William Trumbal, British ambassador in Constantinople (Bishop, *Blake's Hayley,* p. 24).
6. Bethesda was a pool near the Sheep Gate of Jerusalem that was reputed to have healing properties (John 5.2–4).
7. The waters of youth and forgetfulness. All this would enable the older Hayley to forget the miseries of his marriage to Eliza Ball in 1769; in 1786 Eliza suffered a mental breakdown, in 1789 she and Hayley separated, and in 1800 she died.
8. Not mentioned again, this novel was probably not finished and has probably not survived.
9. Anna Seward's *Memoirs of the Life of Dr. Darwin* (1804). CS elaborates on her disgust with this work in her letter to Sarah Rose, 30 July 1804.

10. Blisters are anything used to irritate or scarify the skin, here probably achieved by cupping with a heated cupping glass either to create an irritation or to draw blood. It is not clear which procedure CS underwent. She mentions being "blistered" as early as 1802 (see CS to Samuel Rose, 9 Sept. 1802).

To the earl of Egremont

[Elsted, ?April 1804]
My Lord,

The reluctance with which I now always remind y^r^ Lordship of the concerns of the Smith Trust gives way only to the necessity there appears to be to request you w^d^ be so good as to give proper orders in consequence of the information I have to day received from Mr Adams & Major Smith, Of whose Letters I enclose copies, or say extracts, of such parts of them as relate to the business remaining to be done.[1]

My Son arrived on the 21st March after a passage of seven weeks—— His Spirits were a good deal affected by being quarter'd at the Hotel where his poor Brother died & by the enquiries he made. Charles wanted for no care and attention that strangers could administer, but his exertions of body and mind were such as left him no strength, weaken'd as he before was by his wound, to struggle with disease. Poor young Man—he little imagined to how little purpose he was sacrificing his life & that three years after his death, his Sister Charlotte for whom he was chiefly anxious should still remain unpaid & uncertain of payment.

The extraordinary behavior & apparently unhandsome, evasive, & contradictory conduct as to his effects and papers which we experienced from Mr Thomas Went[2] is now accounted for—The poor Man was labouring under occasional fits of mental derangement, which at length have encreased so much that he is confined. But Mr Adams thinks he has now settled with his Brother so as to prevent any farther ill consequences from the Bills which (tho repeatedly told, I had nothing to do with them) he persisted to draw on me, & which made, as Mr Adams apprehended, both me & Miss Smith liable to arrest or suit at law. They are still wandering ab^t^ tho the money has long been deposited in Mr Blackmans hands to pay them.[3]

<u>I</u> am <u>used</u> to dissapointment & humiliation & mortification. But I own that none has more sensibly affected me than that I have experienced in not being able to obtain either answer from Mr Benjn Smith or any other hope that relates to my Son Lionels return or promotion, which purchase w^d^ certainly, & interest might, most probably have obtain'd for him.

He was likely to be only a few days at Barbados where however the troops rendesvous—— The 16th was going against Surinam—Sad waste of life & money for possessions we do not want and cannot keep. If any evil befalls Lionel,[4] I cannot answer for the measures I may keep with M[r] Benjamin Smith.

I have the honor to be, My Lord,
Your Lordships most humble
& obed[t] Ser[t],
Charlotte ~~Smith~~

As I have not time to copy what Major Smith says before the last part of the week goes out, I send at present M[r] Adams's only because not a moment should be lost, Ships going out every day, & it is pity to lose the money which Major Smith says is 1500£ at least.[5]

Petworth House Archives MS. No address or postmark.

NOTES

1. Thomas Maxwell Adams of Barbados had handled trust business related to Gay's plantation; Lionel had just arrived in Barbados on his way to a posting in Surinam. An extract from Adams's letter to Charlotte Mary is below. In it Adams explains that Griffith, who had a debt against Gay's, had died. His estate was being handled by Hugh Williams, guardian for his surviving son, Christopher Wren Griffith. The father had built houses on Gay's plantation that rented for £400 a year, and Williams planned to apply all of the rent toward liquidating the debt.

Extract of a Letter from M[r] Adams Barbados

March 21st 1804

To Miss Smith

And now for Griffith——In a former Letter I beleive I inform'd you of that Man's death——I now find that his Son is a Minor but the Executor a Man of the name of Hugh Williams, has faithfully promis'd me, that he will see M[rs] Smiths claim properly attended to—(the claim is not M[rs] Smiths but no one in Barbados very willingly names M[r] Benj[n] Smith or can allow that he ought to be attended to in any transaction of Business) The rent of the houses which Griffith built on this land, amounts to four hundred a year, and Williams has declared that every shilling of such rent shall go to the liquidation of the debt. I strongly recommend however, that the bill of sale which Griffith had thought proper to demand should be immediately sent out——The sale must now be made to the Minor Christopher Wren Griffith or to Hugh Williams the Guardian and exor as your Lawyer shall advise (I should think to both w[d] be the safest) The Transfer deed under the proper seal is of the most material consequence in this business. You had better desire that these papers may be sent by a Merchant Vessel addressing a Letter by the packet, to My Friend Matthew Coulthurst Esq[re], explaining on board what Vessel they are put, and when they are likely to leave England———

I have very little fear about the debt from Ashfords plantation—M[r] Pindar is very much interested for M[rs] Smith—poor M[rs] Smith! and we are only waiting for a power of Attorney from the representatives of James Butler Harris to place this affair in proper train, & this power Dr Hamilton expects every day & has assurd me that every attention shall be given to it—Of the validity of this claim however there can be no doubt.

2. CS suspected Went of deliberately interfering with the return of Charles's servant, Benjamin Maule, to England with papers that Charles had secured before he died. See CS to Egremont, 25 Jan. 1804 and n. 1.

3. George Blackman, Esq., and Co. had been dealing with the estate since 1795.

4. In Surinam, a South American country between Guyana and French Guiana, the likelihood of fatal illness was high.

5. CS's copy of Lionel's letter was sent in her next letter to Egremont (CS to Egremont, June 1804, n. 1).

To the earl of Egremont

[Elsted, June 1804]
My Lord,

Your Lordship will observe, should you condescend to cast your eye over the enclosed extract of a Letter from my Son Lionel,[1] that tho he landed only on the 21st (and the weight of Military business lay cheifly on him), he lost no time in obeying yr Lordships commands which I communicated to him before his departure from Cork. The affairs being in such hands as those of Mr Adams, it would only be injurious to withdraw them or make any change even if Major Smith had any time to give them. This I took the liberty of representing to your Lordship, & I seem'd to have given you thereby some offence, but I trust that, if it be now reflected upon, your Lordship will see I was not so wrong as you then seem'd to consider me——

As the Sum yet recoverable in the West Indies is considerable, I trust——— (little as it will avail me who with my younger children am condemned to indigence however Mr Benjn Smith may benefit), I trust y^{r} Lordship will deign to give such orders as may now close the business wth Griffiths's Executor by directing that the sale may be made out & <u>dispatched immediately</u> as advised in Mr Adams's Letter, of which I had the honor to send y^{r} Lordship an extract by the last post. Mr Tyler I beleive has the bill of sale sent from Griffith.

I have always supposed and still think that the impediment to the complete investiture of the last installment from Gays plantation was by no means founded in reason & rather a job of the Lawyers than any thing else, & I think so from Mr Martins affecting to know nothing about it when I applied to him before the bill became due & afterwards equivocating & evading as he did. If our good friends—the collateral & worthy relations of Mr Benjamin Smith who so handsomely pursue <u>me</u> & my injur'd family—<u>should</u>

have their rapacity gratified by succeeding in their iniquitous suit (a suit your Lordship once reprobated in the most decisive terms), Yet there will still be more than twice enough to pay the robbery of Mr Prettejohn once over again—— I therefore hope that your Lordship will not as you intimated think it necessary to retain all the Sums that may be available on account of the Trust till the determination of that Suit, & that the legatees will be fully paid, and particularly that Miss Smith's money awarded to her (after a delay so unjust arising from her unnatural fathers opposition) will be paid her. She has now been denied for seven and twenty years the money given her by her Grandfather While Mr B Smith—the wicked & unfeeling plunderer of his own children, the robber of her whom he ought to support—was instantly paid 500£ awarded (God knows why—or for what) to him.

My Lord, you may be assured that your Lordships reluctance to hear of these affairs cannot be greater than is mine to trouble you upon them & that I have a great dislike to do or say any thing which may perhaps encrease the animosity I am so unhappy as to have excited in yr Lordships mind—— But it is impossible for me to see my children so irretrievably & barbarously injur'd, as Mr B Smith has injurd & does still injure them—— to see that they are every way undone while the Author of their ruin most brutishly triumphs in it without expressing feelings so just and so natural & humbly entreating your Lordship (since unfortunately for your Lordship you have undertaken, & appear to think you cannot be released from, the Trust) that you would deign to protect against farther delay in the receipt of this property A young Woman who has already been irreparable [*sic*] injured by the violation of every principle of her Grandfathers will——

If Mr Benjamin Smith fortifies himself in brutal and unnatural obstinacy against his own children & endeavours to prevent every thing I try to do for them while he will not even give an answer, I shall at length lose every consideration but how to hold up to universal detestation a wretch who is not only worse than an highwayman—but a disgrace to the name of Man. There are injuries so great and dreadful as to obliterate every feeling but the sense of them.

I have the honor to be, My Lord,
Your Lordships most humble & obedt Sert,
Charlotte ~~Smith~~

Petworth House Archives MS. No address or postmark.

NOTE

1. Here is a copy of Lionel's letter that CS mentioned in her late April letter to Egremont.

Extract of a Letter from Major Lionel Smith to his Mother

Bridgetown March 24th 25th 1804—
. . . Last night my dearest Mother, I met Mr Adams at Mr Colthursts about two miles in the Country; Mr Coulthurst is as I understand a Gentleman who has given considerable assistance to Mr Adams in the affairs—— Every thing that remains to be settled is in a fair way of adjustment, waiting only the papers, in proper form from England—— Griffiths's death of which Mr Adams says he inform'd you, is likely rather to benefit than injure, as his Executor is more disposed than he was to pay what he owes————which is stated to be from 500£ to 700£ Sterling with an arrear of interest, amounting as I understand to 1500£ Currency. Mr Adams has now little doubt of recovering this; He desires me to represent the absolute necessity of sending without delay every requisite power. Whether he leaves the Island or not, (for that depends on his health &c) this is equally necessary————With respect to the deed he says he cannot conceive, that it is not to be obtain'd either the Original or copy at the Secretaries Office here—I speak of the Deed between George Walker and John Newton, 1765 [see CS to Egremont, 25 Sept. 1803 and n. 2]—I hope If we do not immediately sail, of which nothing is certainly known at present, to be able, as soon as the first hurry of my own business is over, to pass some days at Adams Castle, from whence I shall be able to write more fully—but Mr Adams who is perfectly a Gentleman as well as very understanding in the business of this Island, assures me, he has every prospect of settling every thing well, for you, before he leaves the Island, if no farther delay arises from the want of proper papers, & probably before he quits the England [*sic*]——. . . .

CS added: "The preceding part, & end of the Letter relates to his own affairs & the [affairs] relative to his lamented brother."

To Thomas Cadell, Jr., and William Davies

[Elsted, 1 June 1804]
Gentlemen,

I did not immediately answer your demand because I imagined business would take me to London, and I wish'd & intended to have call'd upon you & to put whatever debt I have to you in a way of payment, the circumstances of it having by no means escaped my memory—— But not being able to prevail on Mr B Smith to execute the business I wishd to have settled in favor of his children & which would have brought Major Smith home from his perilous duty in the West Indies, I have had neither spirits, nor purpose to answer in going to Town——

As the greater part of my income depends on remittances from India (Mr B Smith having taken every thing else from me but 100£ a year), I am on every account anxious for Letters from Thence. My Son at Bombay[1] hardly ever has faild to send my Summer remittance at this season. But now two ships at least are come in, one strait from Bombay & the other wch has touchd at it. But I have yet received no Letters, which keeps me in the greatest inconvenience & alarm—— It may possibly happen that they may have been left at your house, & in the hurry of business at this season, a matter like this for one who is altogether uninteresting to you may be overlookd by the persons in the Shop. I therefore trouble you merely to beg you will be so obliging as to enquire &, should it have happen'd so, to send them down immediately—— I have written to M^{r} N H Smith, requesting him hereafter to send everything to the care of Mr Marter of the India house who will be so obliging as to receive and pay the charges for me of any packet ~~of the India House~~ that may hereafter come to hand. I mean before my Son can have notice of my wishes in this respect. On the remittances I now & a few months hence expect to have will depend my earlier discharge of your demand than I am otherwise enabled to do.

I pay the postage of this Letter & am, Gent^{n},

your most obed^{t} Ser^{t},
Charlotte Smith

Elsted, June 1st
1804

General Manuscripts, Manuscripts Division, Rare Books and Special Collections, Princeton University Library. Address: Messrs Cadell & Davies/ Strand/ Post paid. London. Postmark: GODALMIN/ 31; G/ PAID/ JUN 2/ 1804.

NOTE

1. That is, Nicholas.

To Sarah Rose

Elsted
June 15th
1804
My Dear Madam,

In consequence of having heard from Mr Bicknell that Mr Rose had been very ill but was recovering fast, I now venture to enquire after you. It will give me very great pleasure to hear you are quite releived from the apprehensions his indisposition must have occasion'd, & I am sure you will gratify me with intelligence which will be so truly welcome as early as you can——

I have been sadly harrass'd lately—— but to every sort of embarrassment and vexation, I ought to accustom myself since my lot seems to be composd of nothing else—— I dont know whether I told you that, as the Award could not go to obtaining the settlement I wanted of my fortune hereafter (tho the hopes of my getting that done was one great inducement to me to consent to it)—& as I most earnestly wish'd to obtain this arrangement in order to raise upon it money to purchase a Lieu^t^ Colonels Commission for Major Smith, and by that means to bring him home, I enterd into a correspondence with the person who barely can be calld human from his form & is certainly in every other respect of the last rank of animals thro Mr Galway[1] whose daughter Lionel married, & who is himself the affectionate friend and father of eleven young people. Tho the monster (whose name it has been so long my misery to bear & to whom I was sold a legal prostitute in my early youth, or what the law calls infancy, & while it admits not a contract for ten pounds) tho this monster could not lose, while his odious existence lasts, one shilling by the act of justice I require & tho it is for the advancement and perhaps to save the life of his own Son, he refused unless I would give up to him 30£ out of about 108£ (for it is not more when the tax is deducted) on which I am to live and keep his daughter & supply his youngest Son——

To this, base & infamous as it was, I consented, for I thought my children would not let me want the 30£ so barbarously extorted from me. I lost not a moment in signifying my unqualified consent & even refraind from making any remark least the wretch should fly off. I heard no more of him for many weeks, & when I press'd for an answer, it at last arrived thro his friend, patron, & protector, the noble Lord of Petworth house, who (while the illustrious blood that circulates in his right honourable veins was revolted at M^r^ B Smiths applying to him & giving him trouble tho he has brought the wretches folly upon himself by his ill natured wish to distract & perplex me)[2] yet did not seem at all revolted by the additional infamy of the monsters asking 40£ instead of thirty & 100£ in ready money, & then he told his Lordship he would make the deed I askd. Mr Galway, to whom he has not been ashamed to make this infamous proposal, desires I would not think of acceding to it, & indeed at present I can not, for my remittance from Bombay which usually arrived at this period is not come, nor have I any Letters from my Son. I conclude they will be here next month, but in the mean time, I have no resource for the pay^t^ of bills now due but to take up before hand the small pittance allotted to me in the 3 pC^s^—— I have gone to the utmost of credit allowed me here after the pains Lord Egremont has so generously taken to deprive me of it by every sarcasm & every brutal expression he c^d^ devise so that, if I cannot do this (get my half year advanced) I must with my family starve. The articles from India which I hoped would prove so valuable have produced nothing yet & are not worth a fiftieth part of what I imagined.

I shall be oblig'd after all to join in the advice of those of her and my friends who insist upon it that Miss Smith ought to fyle a bill in Chancery against Lord Egremont and Mr Turner to compel them to fulfill the award. Their treatment of her is so scandalous that something must be done to obtain justice for her. As to me, they have among them utterly ruin'd me—— They have in the most unmanly & cruel manner destroy'd me under pretence of protection, & such is my desperation at present that I cannot answer for what I may be driven to. I am chain'd to the oar; I am compelled, able or not able, to keep an house & maintain Mr Smiths family while every thing is done to strip me—sick & with an exhausted constitution of the actual necessaries of life—— I have had a nervous cough for above these two months and the violence of it within these last days has so much encreas[d] that I have now a large blister on my breast & write with the greatest pain.

I should not, my dear Madam, trouble you with these querulous but surely not unfounded expressions of suffering beyond all endurance but that I am actually compelled to do it. You were so obliging as to tell me there was yet a small ballance in the bankers hands from the 100£ Bill which Mr Rose was so obliging as to get discounted for me so long since as Jany last, and indeed in looking over the bills I had drawn, I thought it might be so tho I could not ascertain the Sum because I did not know the amount of the discount. If it amounts to as much as 16 shillings, May I venture to send a person for that Sum, as I have an article to purchase in London by order of my medical friend here, which will be to that amount, & I literally have no one now to whom I can apply, my Sister having left Town. I feel that it is taking a very great liberty with you Yet trust you will forgive it.

I hope you have been at leisure to read Mrs Lee's book, which I see has long been advertisd. Pray tell me your opinion of it between ourselves, for I fancy I have no chance of receiving it from the Author. Your judgement in regard to the 3^d^ Vol. of Mr Hayleys Cowper was so exactly mine that I shall perhaps be satisfied without reading the Life of a Lover if I hear from you that it may be dispensed with. Mr Johnson—who was so good as to send me down some books a fortnight ago, together with the 1st Volume of my little work, sewn, for the completion of the notes—contrived to forward it, Heaven knows why, by a Portsmouth Coach instead of the Godalmin tho it comes every day. And the consequence is that it is all lost together & the work stands still again! Ever since Easter has this work, which might have been printed in a month as well as in a year, been in the press. Sometimes I have one proof a week, sometimes two, Sometimes none for a fortnight together. Instead of 75 or 80 pages Letter press for which Mr Johnson offerd 75£, I have furnish'd him with upwards of 300, & I think some Poetry among it, that cannot fail to do me some credit & to compose altogether a saleable book. I do not know, nor know I how without indelicacy to enquire, how much more than the 75£ (which I have had) he will finally give me. Alas! how very cruel is my fate. The labour of the Danaids or of Sysiphus was not surely meant to represent punishment more severe than I endure! for, do what I will, sacrifice what I will, distress and misery tread fast upon me.

Does Mr Rose go the Summer circuit? & is it so held as to afford me any chance of seeing him, as he has often promis'd? Could you give me any hope of seeing you for a little time if my horizon should clear up.[3] I assure you few things would give me more pleasure. Charlotte talks of going to Ireland, & it would be a vast charity from any of my friends, but from you particularly, to look in at my green cottage. Can you forgive me for giving you this trouble? I have never written to thank Mr Hayley for the last volume. I once had such pleasure in writing to him; now it is much otherwise. Adieu, dear Madam,

y^rs^ most truly, C S

I have written this in a manner hardly legible, not being able to stoop to my desk my blister[4] pains me so, & I am so nervous I can hardly hold a pen—

Huntington MS (HM10836). Address: Mrs Rose/Chancery Lane/ London. Postmark: GODALMIN/ 3; {date illegible}.

NOTES

1. See CS to Egremont, 20 Mar. 1804.

2. This representation of Egremont, whose country residence was Petworth House, Petworth, Sussex, is unusually critical of him and unguarded of her.

3. CS asked to meet Sarah Rose several times but never did so. Rose was no doubt occupied with her dying husband and four sons but may also have found CS's compromised station as an estranged wife not respectable enough for actual visits.

4. Probably further treatment of blisters on the breast for the cough and lung inflammation CS described earlier to Sarah Rose (see 18 Apr. 1804 and n. 10). Such blisters, which scarify the skin to act as a counterirritant, are necessarily painful.

To the earl of Egremont

Elsted, June 27th 1804

No, my Lord, I never had the presumption or the folly to suppose you could occupy time which must, & ought, to have so many important claims upon it in entering into a discussion of such matters as M^r^ B Smith has made points of controversy with his family or in any correspondence with him. But since your Lordship alone appeard to have any influence with him & had deigned to interest yourself so far as you did on former occasions, I did entertain an hope that you would—in consideration of the young Man for whom you are now pleased to express a regard[1] & to honor with your good opinion as well as in consideration of George, who is unoffending and promising & of Lucy and her children to whom it is of very serious consequence—I did hope that your Lordship would have express'd to M^r B Smith your opinion that he ought to do nothing contrary to the Letter of the marriage articles. And that as what I solicit is merely justice & what will actually be in my own power if I should survive him which, tho improbable, is not absolutely impossible (as he is eight years older than I am), it ought to be done while it can be of use to those for whom surely he ought to feel the liveliest interest and whose welfare ought to be his first purpose.

My Lord, were not this person a non descript in the history of the human mind, She who now presumes to address you would never have been thrown into the extraordinary situations in which she has found herself. Extraordinary cases demand unusual remedies & excuse otherwise unwarranted attempts. Long, very long had your Lordships benevolence to me & my collateral relations accustomed me to the presumption of applying to you, as having at once the power and the will to befriend me. And your Lordships condescension in accepting a Trust (of the entanglements & distraction of which you had long been inform'd) was a proof that I did not always presume too far in hoping, in despite of your elevated rank, your compassion for the unmerited evils which had befallen a person, in mine. Apprehending as I did, and do, the greatest and most insupportable evil that can now befall me, I ventured (even tho I appeard to have lost your Lordships favourable opinion) to implore your generous assistance to avert the misery I dreaded by signifying to M^r B Smith the only opinion likely to have any weight with him. I am conscious that I do presume, but a Mother—who has sufferd so severely as I have done & who pleads for her Sons life, a life valuable to his family and to his Country as an active and excellent Officer in the bloom of youth—A Mother trusted to the goodness she had so often experienced to be forgiven. My Lord, I have still that reliance; And without for a moment supposing your Lordships thoughts or time should be occupied in so very unpleasant a way as a correspondence on any subject with Mr Benjn Smith, Allow me to implore your interposition, signified only in two lines, that what I ask ought to be done. I have taken the liberty to state what that is for fear of any misapprehension on his part, either real or affected, for the purpose of evasion and cavil—and refusal.

Oh! God, how depressing to all my faculties is the reflection from which I cannot for a moment escape that, while I am deprecating the most intollerable and irreperable of all misfortunes, it may already have fallen upon me. The Country where Lionel is has been (as I see on referring to books) designated like Batavia As "the Land that kills." But there,[2] where even a Dutchman cannot live, he seems to suppose he must remain. And he tries with the fortitude of a Soldier to reconcile himself to this miserable prospect. He says, "I shall have I beleive about 600£ prise money, with which and perhaps some additional appointment from the favor of General Charles Green[3] I must try first to pay my debts, and then to make some provision for my poor Ellen and my infant, if I am happy enough to hear that they are doing well"——

My Lord, if the dreadful heats of July and August in an half uncleard colony, surrounded by swamps & swarming with pestilent reptiles and insects, do not baffle and destroy for ever one of my few remaining hopes, I may perhaps owe to your Lordships goodness the greatest blessing this world can afford me. If I could but obtain his recall and there is no other way of doing it than by promotion or an appointment on the staff at home, the money 950£ might be found—— Mr Gallway will contribute; Charlotte would assist if she receives any part of what was awarded; Lionel has a certain 500£ under settlement but which he always considerd as a part of his pecuniary Obligation to your Lordship. From these resources however (with your Lordships permission), I should fearlessly attempt borrowing the money against a certain time. But his R[oyal] H[ighness], the Commander in Cheif,[4] must give permission for purchase at the Regulation price; a seller of a Lieutenant Colonelcy must be found; And all this, to a person helpless from sex and situation and disabled by sickness, must be a slow and doubtful undertaking.

I dare not however, my Lord, while I acknowledge that I have already been too presumptuously troublesome—I dare not say that your Lordship (would you condescend to interest yourself for a young Soldier who has not, I will venture to assert will not, discredit the protection you extended to him when he obtain'd his present rank) ~~You~~ Your Lordship might confer on me an obligation greater than all those I owe you, considerable as I shall ever acknowledge them to be; Obviate, if it be not too late, the evils which the loss of time in soliciting that unfeeling Man at Hamilton may occasion and render his act, tho of not less necessity, not so instantly necessary. And in a word, my Lord, make my Son and all those whose happiness or misery are attach'd to his fate the most grateful of all those that owe your Lordship the tribute of gratitude—— If means could but be found to make this promotion immediate, Mr Gallway and my daughter w^d^ bind themselves for the repayment of the money that might be wanting ~~even~~ earlier than it could be rais'd by the act we demand from M^r^ B Smith. And a single word from your Lordship would obtain leave for the purchase. Pardon me, my Lord, Pardon me if once more contrary to your orders, I thus entreat your attention. Were I to be soliciting for my own life, I should not indeed be so importunate. That has long been valueless, but as I could serve my unhappy children—and if any thing happens to Lionel, it will be far more wretched than it has been. I suppose it is with the hope of destroying me by additional anxiety that M^r^ B Smith has held out: "Alas, what needed that." One would think I have drained the cup of misery he has prepared for me. I have the honor to be, My Lord,

your Lordships most oblig'd Ser[t],
Charlotte ~~Smith~~

I must beg leave to defer the statement which I will not trouble yr Lordship with (but will send to y[r] Solicitor to see if it is correct), being too much overcome with writing even this Letter, to be able to do it today———

Petworth House Archives MS. No address or postmark.

NOTES

1. Lionel.
2. That is, Surinam.
3. Major general as of Sept. 1803, stationed in the Leeward Islands in Oct 1804, and attached to the York Light Infantry in 1805 (*Army List* [1804], pp. 41, 144; [1805], p. 331).
4. Frederick, duke of York.

To Sarah Rose

Elsted,
July 4th at
night, 1804
My Dear Madam,

I cannot sufficiently express my gratitude for your kind & immediate attention to my importunate & troublesome application. There are moments when the bitterness of repeated disappointments, the inconveniencies of the present, and dread of the future (not for myself but for others) counteract every resolution I attempt to form to forbear complaint of every sort & not to harrass those who are still so good as to be interested for me, with what my ci devant friend M[r] Hayley would call "querulous egotism." And I know not how wholly to refrain when I do happen to meet, as in you, with one who understands how difficult it is to stifle all complaints even when conscious of its inutility & who has an heart, A thing much rarer and more wonderful than is generally imagined.

I should have told you all this and a great deal more many days since, but I have been prevented by various circumstances. Your Letter was missent, I cannot guess why, to Petersfield and did not reach me 'till two days after it ought to have done. I was oblig'd to write several letters on the business, which certainly resembles the Sysiphean stone more than any thing else & which comes thundering back upon me when I have fancied it near the top of the hill, & in the midst of all this and my solicitude to finish handsomely with Johnson, came an acc[t] of the attack upon, and surrender of, Surinam. It arrived on Friday, & no particulars being given in the papers that bro[t] it, I was under the most agonizing solicitude for my son Lionel. I sent about in vain for a Gazette. It was not publish'd as promis'd. However on Sunday, I receivd, thank God, two Letters from him, written after the affair was over and enclosing very flattering testimonies of the high opinion the Gen[l] Sir Charles Green entertain'd of him, tho it so happend that the 16th Reg[t] had nothing to do in the only part of the business where blood was shed, & that not one Man or Officer in that Reg[t] were either killd or wounded. All this however is hardly an alleviation of my uneasiness. The climate where he appears likely to remain is as unwholesome as Batavia, Notwithstanding the soldier-like resolution with which he endeavours to conceal this from me and to appear calm & unfearing; I know by the manner of his expressing himself and the medicines he has sent for what his apprehensions are. These I have since been busied in forwarding to him, with every agonizing apprehension of their reaching him too late & every dread of effect of disease of anxiety & regret on his constitution—While the idea that the worthless brute, whom I never can call his father, might have prevented all that <u>may</u> happen sometimes throws me into a state of mind that must be incomprehensible to any one who does not know the sources of my misery. All these things, my dear Madam, and some petty grievances about servants withheld those expressions of real gratitude which you ought long since to have heard.

I wish'd to tell you how delighted I was to find that you did not entirely repress my hopes of seeing you here, & now let me assure you that, if the very humble style and way in which we live in a Cottage in a very lonely village does not deter you, there is nothing would give us more pleasure than receiving you & M[r] Rose also in it. But if the latter is a satisfaction I must not hope for, Why may I not ask to see you & your little boy? We are not famous for the number of our bed rooms, but Charlotte may & probably will be absent after the 14th for some time, and Harriet is at present on a visit so that I should be able to accommodate you without any difficulty —— Matrimony, that bane to happiness in humble as well as in upper life, deprived me of the services of a Woman who had lived with me more than nine years, & since I was most unwillingly compelled to part with her, I have been miserably tormented about a cook (every where the most difficult Servant to get) that I really was afraid to ask a friend to share a dinner so very likely not to be eatable. But my heretofore Cook having now weaned her second child & being in the village whither she follow'd me, as her husband who has lived with me from a boy is still in my service, I <u>can</u> now say that I can command the dressing of a joint & a pudding, & I am going forthwith to send a London cook whose <u>avocations</u> are too <u>numerous</u> to suit in such an house as mine back to her Congeners[1] in St Giles's! for from thence I think she must have come tho I had a good character with her. How much are one['s] time and minor comforts in the power of these people!

I am much ashamd, my Dear Madam, to have troubled you about that paltry affair of the small ballance left to me of the India bill, but the truth is I am and must be extremely poor till my remittances come, & my debts so far exceeded all I could command that I was compelled—with inconceivable reluctance—to take up 50£ of my poor little pittance to keep matters even with butcher and baker, brewer and grocer. I shall however do pretty well if my Nicholas does not forget me & I receive the usual supply in the course of this month.

I never had the least suspicion that Johnson would behave otherwise than liberally. He is now in possession of the whole work, & I feel rather awkard in stating that it very much exceeds both in quantity & quality, <u>I hope</u>, my original design or his plan when he wishd that design enlarged. Yet beyond a certain price I suppose a School book will not be allowed to claim, tho the fact is that I have labourd it I think more than I ever did any book, being very anxious to print only tolerable poetry and to shew that it is not <u>absolutely</u> necessary to write flat puerilities on subjects neither <u>Amatory</u>, to use an affected phrase, nor didactic. However we so little kn[ow] ourselves in any thing that when I fancy I have made a very pretty book, it is possible I may have written a very absurd one, and I have not now, as in other days, a friend[2] who certainly could judge better of the works of others than of his own. I remember he once told me (Alas! it was some fourteen or fifteen years ago) that he wish'd I was old and ugly, for <u>then</u> he could shew the <u>very great friendship</u> he felt for me without hazarding many inconveniences that arise from the malignant disposition of the World. I am now as old & as ugly, God wot, as his heart can desire, & I suspect he would <u>mentally</u> (as the cant of novels goes) say, "I liked thee better as thou wert before"—However I have felt very severely in this little work the want of a corrector & a library, & to have outlived <u>both</u> is rather a foolish thing.

Ah! my dear Madam, where was our friend Sophia's Critic & Corrector?[3] Where slept her Sylph & Sylphids—cold and pure guardians of maidenly meditation!—When <u>fancy free</u> was let loose to run riot so deplorably as in "the life of a lover" or rather, as a poor friend of mine calls it, a loveress. Never surely since Congreve drew the picture of Lady Wishfort[4] were such descriptions given of "hand gripings and hearts heavings, the palpitations, & the tumults and the tremblings, the oglings and the sighings, the dyings and faintings!" No, I really do not think such a book so full of all manner of love and made so strong was ever manufactured since the days of Mrs Haywood.[5] I fear she will be terribly beset by the Reviewers & be compared to Astrea, Mrs Behn,[6] I beleive, of the last century "Who fairly puts all characters to bed" for so doth she except the poor old Col^l^ who she so <u>decently</u> kills after such intimations! What must Men, gross as they are, think of <u>her</u> notions! And will not some wicked quoter cry—with that wicked Ariel—— "Live in an honest way the Dame"——— Upon my word, I am concern'd for her—& for the honor of the novel writing Ladies.

Johnson sent me down the books, only I fancy as a loan and not from Robinson,[7] which I shall be glad of, because a present from "the Author" requires thanks and a fine speech ab[t] the charming entertaining work, which it would be a terrible breach of my sincerity to pay. If I had written such a work, I should not sleep for very horror of the next Reviews & should tremble at every book I saw in a blue cover. Even the gentle Imperial will I think unsheaths its velvet paws to give her A scratch— —Will you tell me what Robinson meant by saying he had paid 700£ and but just turn'd the corner; I cannot comprehend it, & the price of books is material.

May I beg the favor of you to pay to Weldon, Chymist of Wigmore street,[8] who will call for it, this amount his bill for 3 bottles of Aether, a quart of tinc Rhubarb, and a phial antimonial wine;[8] I suppose altogether two pounds or thereabouts. Forgive this unconscionable trouble, & let me hear how M[r] Rose does, & what chance there is of my being so happy as to see you before my green leaves are gone. Alas, my roses are vanishing, & all my beauty is already fading. I think I shall try the sea in the Autumn—— if——— —— ———

Adieu, my dear Madam, beleive me, most truly y[rs],

CS

Huntington MS (HM10837). Address: M[rs] Rose/ Chancery Lane/ London. Postmark: GODALMIN; G/ JUL 6/ 1804.

NOTES

1. The *OED* defines *congener* as "A member of the same kind or class with another, or nearly allied to another in character," but cites its first use as a noun referring to people in 1837. CS also used the word in her ode "To My Lyre," l. 23.

2. William Hayley. As seen here, his friendship seems to have had its light, even flirtatious, moments. Her unguarded irony suggests that the loss of his regard still hurt her.

3. That is, to Sophia Lee's *The Life of a Lover* (1804).

4. In *The Way of the World* (1700).

5. Eliza Haywood (1693–1756), a prolific novelist and playwright, whose works contained many amorous excesses.

6. Aphra Behn (?1640–1689), generally thought to be the first professional woman author in England, whose popular plays contained sexual excesses, bawdiness, and innuendo typical of the Restoration stage. Pope criticizes her in his imitation of Horace, *Epistle* 2.1 (1737): "The stage how loosely does Astræa tread, / Who fairly puts all Characters to bed" (ll. 290–91).

7. George and John Robinson published Lee's book.

8. Walter Weldon, apothecary of Wigmore Street, London.

9. Tincture of rhubarb, usually called Turkey or Russian rhubarb at this time, was a purgative and stomach tonic. Antimonial wine was medicinal, usually sherry containing tartar emetic.

To Benjamin Smith

Copy—Letter from Mrs Charlotte Smith to Mr Benjn Smith
Elsted July 5th 1804
Sir,

In consequence of Lord Egremonts last Letter which I forwarded to you I wrote to desire his Ldship's Solicitor would from the Papers which I immagine he has access to, make out for me at my expence copies of such parts as relate to my Property and a Statement of the power you have under those Deeds to dispose of that Property in case of your surviving me—I accounted to his Lordship for presuming to intrude on him in an affair which every Law, whether of convention or of nature—and common sense should induce you to adjust volantarily and immediately—How little influence these motives have hitherto had on you it is needle[ss] now to say.

I now Mr Smith enclose you post paid, the Letter Lord Egremont has been pleased to honor me with—And I once more re-state to you the Marriage Articles—and entreat you to understand that if by a will contrary to their spirit and meaning you give to any one Child an undue proportion, the Law will set it aside. Good God! that there should exist a Man capable of trying to extort money[1] for doing only common Justice to his own Children when it would in no wise injure him. But it is in vain to argue with such an Heart as yours.

Recollect, Sir, once more Mr Bettesworth's[2] Opinion given in the Year 1778—if you persist in refusing to make this arrangement, I must try whether redress cannot be obtaind by application to the Court of Chancery—I am sure there must be some remedy or prevention for the evil you intend, if none against those I have sustain'd by your breach of that contract—If neither common justice towards your Children, nor the opinion of Lord Egremont to whom you are so much oblig'd, nor any feeling of decency and of humanity move you—I must apply to those means that will be found more effectual—

I do not sign a name which you have made hateful to me.

Petworth House Archives MS. No address or postmark.

NOTES

1. CS was furious about his terms: he would sign if she would give him £30 of her annual £114 and Harriet £30 of her £60 (see CS to Sarah Rose, 21 Mar. 1804).

2. William Augustus Bettesworth, an attorney in Hampshire; see CS to William Tyler, 16 Sept. 1802 and n. 2.

To the earl of Egremont

Elsted, July 10th
1804

My Lord, I beg leave to thank yr Lordship for the information you were so obliging as to leave for me at Moons on Saturday.[1] By some oversight, I did not get it till last night at a late hour—— Mr Benjn Smith smells money, & the keenness of his scent for that commodity does not seem to be impair'd by time, which has sufficiently blunted his sense of decency, honor, humanity or parental affection. I have no doubt of what his intentions are and will venture to say that his sojourn in the South[2] will very much exceed a few days & continue while he has any hope of extorting money from any quarter and on any pretence, however mean and unworthy, and while he can spunge on Mr Tayler,[3] or has any chance of being tolerated in better quarters. I feel all the disgrace of being compelled to speak to your Lordship of this unhappy being tho I did not bring it on myself, but allow me to hope you will not think I presume too much on the interest you have the goodness to take in the settlement of the property if I solicit your Lordships attention for one moment to the following Question? Whether it be your opinion that I should require not only a just distribution of the money belonging to me but of that which (unless great losses indeed occur) will remain (after deducting the specific share given by her Grandfather to Miss Smith) of the Residue. It may be 2500£, it may be more.

Now if Mr B Smith determines to give the whole to Harriet, some deduction in favor of the rest ought to be made from the Sum she will have from my property; otherwise she will have twice as much as the rest, & tho I desire her to have as much, I see no reason for such a difference, while I suppose nothing can prevail on Mr B S to give Lucy a shilling more than he is oblig'd to do. In anr however to any application from me on this subject, I am aware that Mr B S may say——"I shall make no settlement of the residue at all, for I intend to survive you. I am young of my years, frisky and smart at sixty two, &

"Have neither Rhumatism or gout"
"Or Phsic or lumbago"
"I'm therefore sure to see you out"
"And shall a Suitor Gay, grow"

Indeed as he attempted this frolic while I was en pleine sante,[4] and had even purchas'd the wedding gifts & exchanged tender tokens of his youthful ardours with Miss Gordon, there is no doubt but that he would take the earliest opportunity of availing himself of his fathers gift of the three fifths of nine eights of three tenths "to His children by his present or any other wife"—— Tho this would be as unjust as all the rest of his proceedings, there is perhaps no remedy, and possibly it may appear to your Lordship that I had better confine myself to that which relates only to my own property——

I have written to M[r] B. Smith to day and desird an answer by Friday as to his meaning. I am afraid it will contain only unreasonable and cruel demands, & if so I shall desire M[r] Gallway[5] to use the power of Attorney (which I hope he has by this time) in raising the money otherwise. I must repeat, my Lord, my dread of all I can do being too late; such are the dreadful accounts I every day hear of the extreme hazard of life at Surinam. If I was once sure of having the money ready, I could solicit with some confidence your Lordships favor to obtain leave to purchase at the regulation price & his recall on promotion.

My family rely on your Lordships justice and rectitude to prevent M[r] Benj[n] Smith from getting at any part of the interest which may be paid by Agreement with M[r] Prescod[6] or from appropriating to himself any more money which belongs to them under any of the various pretences he will make, for this journey from Scotland has some purpose beyond his pretending to listen to overtures of arrangement. That he might have done many months ago before his Sons invaluable life was hazarded and before, by his inhuman refusal, he had render'd me & so many other persons certainly miserable at present and possibly irretrievably wretched.

Pardon me, my Lord, for troubling you so much at length. My whole heart is in the cause, & every gleam of hope or of satisfaction that may chear my few remaining days depend on my seeing Lionel any where but in a Country where destruction is inhaled in every breath he draws.

I have the honor to be
your Lordships most oblig'd
and obed[t] Ser[t],
Charlotte Smith

Petworth House Archives MS. Address: The Earl of Egremont/ Petworth/ Sussex. Postmark: GODALMIN.

NOTES

1. Half Moon Inn was one of two principal inns in Petworth, located in the Market Square.

2. In January, BS was in Bothwell and Berwick. He wrote to William Tyler on 20 March that "I leave this country altogether" in four to five weeks. But four months pass before he writes from London (BS to Egremont, 19 and 25 Jan. 1804, unpub. letters in PHA #0.11).

3. Robert Tayler, a merchant who received BS's mail under cover in London (see Biographical Notes).

4. In good health.

5. Lionel's father-in-law. CS again solicits Egremont's aid in obtaining a promotion which would bring Lionel home from Surinam and its dangers to his health.

6. In addition, William Prescod's final payment on Gay's plantation in Barbados was due and not yet discharged (CS to William Tyler, unpub., 5 July 1804). CS suspects him of intentional dishonesty (CS to Tyler, unpub., 14 July 1804).

To William Tyler

{Elsted, between 10 and 14 July 1804}

~~As~~ The marriage articles of 1765 declare that 3000£ of the money then given to M[rs] Charlotte Smith is to be given to among the children of the marriage in such proportions as the father and mother by a joint deed shall direct or, in default of such deed, by the will of the survivor———

These are not probably the words of that wretchedly drawn up Instrument, but Professional Men have told me that the meaning is, whatever terms are used, that each child shall have a reasonable proportion from the general sum given to M[rs] CS———

In the deed made in 1771 or 1772 settling 2000£ more on M[rs] Smith, I rather think that it is declared to be appropriated share and share alike among the children of the marriage.

This I should be very glad to know, for if it be so, it puts it out of M[r] B Smiths power wholly to cut off M[rs] Newhouse as he most unjustly intends for an offence not only imaginary in itself but which, if it had been real, was altogether unintentional on her part, as I am sure her appearance at Petworth was on mine, who never was more astonish'd in my life than when I found M[r] Turner had propos'd to Mr Rose to bring her forward as a witness of the ill treatment I had received from M[r] B Smith. To say nothing of the impropriety of it, it should have struck M[r] Rose that, as Lucy is still young, as I have left M[r] Smith above eighteen years and these instances of personal ill treatment occurred from the year——— I cannot affix the date, for he always behaved scandalously to me (Alas many years before I left Hampshire) —it was impossible she could be a witness who was then in her infancy being, when I quitted M[r] Smith in 1787, but ten years old. I had long before endeavourd to impress on M[r] Rose the facts I had to produce in justification of the step I took in leaving M[r] Smith: facts which would have vindicated me in a court of Law even if his (M[r] BS's) deigning, worthy soul!, to live repeatedly with me & at my expence & allowing me to pay his debts out of money I earned by my books, had not done away every pretence he had to complain——

I did not go away with any improper person or for any improper purpose.[1] I went with five of his children that I might have an home for them

& his three other children then at School & not be liable to have their beds taken in execution, as they would have been at the suit of Silver of Winchester,[2] while he would himself have been again in the Kings bench from whence (as he has a thousand times acknowledged) my exertions only deliverd him in 1784.

If Mr Tyler has any or can obtain of Mr Turner any copy of the deed of 1771 or 1772, Lord Egremont would do me and my family a most essential service in permitting me to have a statement made officially of what the powers are under those two deeds, viz. 1st that of Feby 1765 relating to the two Sums of 3000£ & 2000£ (the latter of which is already settled by endorsement on the back of the marriage articles in possession of Mr Morgan[3] & is only named here for the sake of perspicuity) and 2nd that of August 9th 1772 as I think settling another 2000£ of which perhaps Mr Turner has now a copy or an original part—& I should think Mr Mitford had.

These powers once known I could now—as Lord Egremont has been pleas'd to say in his last Letters it ought in Justice to be done—state to M^{r} B S what he can do (which I beleive he entirely mistakes) & what he ought to do. It will be of no use for me to do this unless I am authoris'd by some professional Man in the statement I make & the division I require. There can be no doubt of Mr Tylers being authorised in giving me a correct statement of the power vested in M^{r} B S & me as he has a set of the marriage articles among Lord Egremonts Bigenor deeds. ~~and~~ If he will be so good as to enquire for the deed of 1772 & Lord E. will permit me (with due acknowledgement to Mr Tyler on my side for the profession[al] trouble) to have it done, I need not say that expedition is everything & that if I make a wrong statement to M^{r} B S, it will be fatal to my hopes because he wants only excuses to distress & distract me by refusal—

[Unsigned]

Petworth House Archives MS. No address or postmark.

NOTES

1. CS's only mention of such an accusation against her.
2. John Silver, a mercer and draper of Winchester; see CS to Egremont, Sept. 1802, n. 4.
3. Jonathan Morgan, BS's lawyer. Mitford was another lawyer long involved in the trust.

To William Tyler?[1]

[Elsted, 12 July 1804]

I believe Lord Egremont mistook w[hat I] said ab^{t} papers. The paper I mean must [be] forthcoming because Mr Turners affairs could in no case be settled witht referring to it. Oh! when shall I see an end to all this ignominious contention with a father to do justice to his own—his deserving children. Mr Bettesworth is still living and in practice. As I am now well enough to accept an invitation I have received from Lord Clanricarde,[2] I shall have an opportunity of seeing and consulting him at Swanmore.

[unsigned]

Petworth House Archives MS. Address: Mrs Charlotte Smith/ Elsted. No postmark. Original Address:[3] *Bryan Symmonds, Esqre/ at ~~Camberwell~~/ ~~Hamilton~~/ ~~xxxxxxxxxxxxxxx~~/ double North Britain/ Post paid—/ post-Paid 1/10/ ~~xxxxxxxxxxxxxxx~~. Postmark: GODALMIN; JUL/ 1[80]4/ 12. And: HAMILTON; G/ PAID/ ??/ 1804.*

NOTES

1. This hasty note appears to have been written on the back of a sheet that once enclosed a letter to BS. As it mentions both Egremont and BS in the third person, the addressee seems to be Tyler.

2. CS and BS had known Henry de Burgh, earl of Clanricarde, since before they separated on 15 Apr. 1787 and had been assisted by him. After Henry died in 1798, John Thomas de Burgh, his only brother and heir, was created earl in December 1800. He continued to favor CS with his notice. See CS to Cadell and Davies, [Mar. 1798] and n. 3.

3. CS explains the confused state of this address in a letter to Egremont, 13 Aug. 1804, in which she enclosed the note originally sent to BS for him to read.

To the earl of Egremont

Elsted, July 15th 1804
My Lord,

I have had no answer from Mr Benjn Smith and am more than ever convinced that he came up to extort money & not with any intention of acting as he ought to do in regard to the settlement of the property.

I should not trouble your Lordship again, but Miss Smith being in want of the Money due to her as Interest on the Sum awarded, I request as she is about to leave home on friday next that your Lordship will have the goodness to direct that an answer on that head may be <presently> given her. I need not repeat how very hard her situation has been. And how little her Grandfather supposed, when he left her what he hoped would be a competent fortune, that eight and twenty years after his death, she would still be without a considerable part of it.

I am very much oblig'd to your Lordship for your late kind notice & opinion on the business I had so much at heart, but nothing but compulsion ever did, or ever will, make Mr B Smith act with common decency. I have the honor to be yr Lordships most oblig'd Sert, Charlotte Smith

Petworth House Archives MS. No address or postmark.

To Sarah Rose

Elsted, July 16th
1804

It is with great apprehension, my dear Madam, that I continue to reckon the days as they pass without my having the pleasure of hearing from you. Surely I have not been so troublesome as to weary you? Mortifying as such a supposition is, I would rather undergo it than imagine that illness may have deprived me of a gratification on which I depended. For some days, I flatter'd myself that you were disposed to oblige me for a few days with society I should highly value & might perhaps only wait for some arrangements with other friends before you named the day, but these hopes now give way to very unpleasant apprehensions. Pray releive me from them. I have so many very heavy evils incessantly to encounter that I cannot afford to lose one of the adoueissements[1] that I derive from the good opinion and friendship of those few friends worth having which misfortune has either left me, or gain'd for me. You, my dear Madam, I would very fain consider among the latter, and in writing to you, I forget that we have never met.

I will hasten to say what I have to trouble Mr Rose upon; Will you have the goodness to name to him that my poor George is going into Camp on the Curragh of Kildare[2] and is more than usually distress'd for money in consequence of the expences incident to that mode of life while sa pauvre mere depouillee de tout,[3] & not receiving her India remittances, is more than usually unable to supply him. Of my miserable half years interest, I was obliged—— (none but those who have sufferd what I have done can tell how unwillingly) to solicit Messrs Pybus to advance me by accepting a bill at 6 weeks for 50£ to prevent the total loss of the little credit I have, & pay bills due for absolute necessaries, which I depended on my remittances of May (at which time they almost always have come) to discharge. I have not therefore above seven pounds to receive of Messrs Pybus, & out of that, I have the Sieur Tyler to pay six & twenty shillings for some copies he has made of my happy marriage articles & subsequent settlement.

So is my little made less!—— However, if I sell my few remaining books, I must raise 20£ for my young Soldier, who shall not be inconvenienced, while I can make any struggle for him, & if Mr Rose will have the goodness to receive for me, as before, the small half yearly payment on the Chevalier de Fovilles account, & pay it to Mr Fauntleroy in Berner's Street, adding to it any small ballance—tho it can only be very small[4]—which may remain after your having paid for the medicines I have received. Mr Fauntleroy will then take the few pounds that remain at Pybus's, & altogether I hope to muster the Sum requisite to prevent my poor Lieutenant going to Camp with fewer necessaries than a common Soldier. He is a fine young Man & has been much approved by the inspecting General at the late Review of the Troops in the district of Kilkenny for the Soldier like manner in which he has train'd some raw boys in the eighteen manouvres. He piques himself on emulating the conduct of his Brother, & I pique myself on his being so little like his Father that I am unwilling to beleive my own honesty, for there are cases, I really begin to think, in which it is no merit.

All laugh apart however, on this grave matter, I keep an account of the money I receive as loan from De Foville & will give Mr Rose any receipt requisite, while I cannot but regret the trouble that, on so trifling a matter, I am under the cruel necessity of giving Mr Rose. There is nothing could excuse it, but the peculiarity of my situation. I trust it is altogether unique, and that not only within the circle of your acquaintance, but thro the whole extent of civilized life, no other instance will ever arise to make another precedent of an excuse for thus trespassing on friendly good nature. It is common for the vulgar to say of a rarity, "Why there was only one such, came over in three ships!" How many Ships may come loaded with Sugar, Rum, Cotton & Ginger, or have come from Barbaados since the year 1744 when Mr B Smith made—at three years old—part of the cargo of one of them, the custom house books may perhaps ascertain to future generations while I think I could make it very clear that such another importation was never made or ever can be made. Under his picture may be written, "This is the most unnatural Monster in the World except himself."

The wretch—after trying to extort first 30£ & then 40£ pr annum as the price of the deed I desired to have made in favor of his children for an equal and fair division of my fortune—delay'd agreeing to do it (tho I was desirous at any event then of obtaining it) till it was too late to save My Son Lionel from passing the hot months in the West Indies. Mr Gallway, a Man who was left at six & thirty a Widower with five Sons and six daughters, the second of whom Lionel has married, was almost as anxious as I was to obtain this arrangement as a means of his return, but he was shocked at the terms attempted to be made & wrote to me insisting on my not lessening an income already inadequate to the purposes of life. He saw the drift of that worthless & abject being & desired me, as ready money seem'd to be his object, to offer from him, Mr Gallway 100£. This I did, & that Lord Egremont might not accuse me with intemperance towards the best of the bunch, I sent the Letter open to the noble Lord.

No notice however was taken of it for some weeks till, on this day sennight, I received a note from Lord E. from Godalmin informing me Mr Benj

Smith was in town, going by his own name & not his alias, & intimating that as his stay would be but of a few days, [&] therefore his Ldp thought I should lose no time in applying to him for a settlement of the property of which his Ldp is now pleasd to say he perceives the absolute necessity & wishes for as much as I do (not quite so much I think). However, availing myself of this return to something more like humanity than his conduct has of late been towards me, I sent the noble Lord's Letter to Mr Benjn Smith & desir'd his determination whether he would accept Mr Gallways offer. But he has never answer'd my Letter. And I shall apply no more but endeavour to compel him to do as he ought to do—which I was told long since I might do. This settlement I always intended should make part of the award, but it was refused, & I was in every thing baffled. I think it very likely Mr Monstroso may call on Mr Rose, for there is nothing to which his impudent and daring selfishness will not urge him in consequence of the encouragement he received last year. Nor should I be at all surprised if he was again to be invited to Petworth house.[5] After what then happen'd, I shall wonder at nothing. This is indeed the age of wonders—a Katterfelto[6] period.

I don't know exactly why I say all this (for it is a miserable subject) to you, my dear Madam, unless it be to beg of you to inform me if you have seen this Thaumeturgos[7] or rather heard of his being again an annoy to Mr Rose. I shall try other means than what depends on him, certainly for my most beloved Lionel; God grant they may not be too late, but I dread the climate of Surinam & have no quiet while he is exposed to it. Should any evil befall him, I cannot answer for the effect it would have on a mind already irritated beyond all endurance by the injuries this person has inflicted on me, & I think the last act of my life would be endeavouring to shew him as he is, as a beacon to warn all parents from sacrificing their children to fools for that base consideration, which never bestows happiness even where it is not, as in the present case, fallacious—— I was sold for a worthless price, and I am now a beggar.

Pray forgive me. Hatred & love are both garrulous I suppose unless in some instances where the latter takes Mr Fox's motto.[8] I can laugh you see, but indeed it is with an aching heart. If gratified vanity could, as some opine, apply a remedy or at least alleviation to a woman's woes, Mr Johnson might at this time have given me a chance for a cataplasm[9] of that sort by putting out my poor little book for which I expect some applause.

I have done it, & have been expecting the last proofs this week in vain. There is no proof but of my patience. The printers are either sleeping out the heats, or are encreasing them by printing handbills for the Middlesex election, and my birds & fishes & creeping things will not appear till the feast of St Bartholemew. Grizzle herself of forbearing memory[10] would I think have required all the quietism of her character to be exerted if she had been an Authoress & Mr Johnson her publisher. Mr Hayley no doubt found the advantage of the cooling regimen he has adapted when the three quarto's were to be born. But I forgot that they were printed at his "native City"[11] and therefore his philosophy was not put to the test like mine, but he might behold their equal & regular progress with complacency, & instead of fuming as I have done might "Cream and mantle like a standing pool."[12] I am trespassing most abominably.

Once more pardon me I pray, & in token of it, let me very soon hear from you, & beleive me, my Dear Mad^{m}, that it would give me infinite pleasure to tell you personally how truly I am y^{r} most oblig'd & affect^{n} Ser^{t},

Charlotte ~~Smith~~

My eldest daughter will be in Town next week for a few days unless She determines on going to Ireland in which case her stay will be longer.

Houghton Library Autograph file MS, Harvard University. Address: Mrs Rose/ Chancery Lane/ London. Postmark: GODALMIN; G/ JULY 18/ 1804.

NOTES

1. Sweeteners, mollifiers.

2. In Ireland, due west of Dublin.

3. His poor mother is stripped of everything.

4. De Foville was receiving what would have been Augusta's inheritance—interest on an amount much contested, but probably settled at £160. If invested in the 3 percent consols, it would have earned him a scant £4.8 yearly, or £2.4 twice a year.

5. He was already invited, and he planned to visit "his sister"—presumably Catherine Dorset—on his way to Petworth (BS to William Tyler, 15 July 1804, unpub. letter in PHA #0.11).

6. Gustavus Katterfelto (b. 1760), a German mountebank, conjuror, and lecturer. A 1783 cartoon depicts him holding forth against another quack doctor. Katterfelto says in heavily accented English: "Dare you mus see de Vonders of the Vorld, which make de hair stand on tiptoe. . . . O Vonders, Vonders, Vonderfull Powders" (P. J. and R. V. Wallis, *Eighteenth Century Medics,* p. 337 and pl. XIII).

7. Miracle worker, magician.

8. Perhaps CS was thinking of Aesop's fables, many of which involve a fox. Two fables have similar mottoes: "Happy is the man who learns from the misfortune of others" and "He is wise who is warned by the misfortunes of others." She certainly felt her life to have been an admonition to any considering an arranged marriage.

9. Poultice: a warm mass of clay, bread, or other substance applied to relieve an ache or inflammation.

10. Griselda, a folktale character known for her great patience in the face of her husband's cruelty. Well-known treatments appear in Boccaccio's *Decameron* and Chaucer's "Clerk's Tale." The name occurs in the form CS uses here in Thomas Dekker's comedy *Patient Grissil* (1603) as well as in the character Mrs. Grizzle, sister of Gamaliel Pickle, who married Commodore Trunnion in Tobias Smollett's *Peregrine Pickle* (1751).

11. Hayley's most recent work, *The Life and Posthumous Writings of Cowper* (1803–1804), was printed at Chichester.

12. *The Merchant of Venice* 1.1.89.

To Sarah Rose

Elsted n^{r} Godalming 30th July—1804

Yesterday, my dear Madam, while I was [*sic*] dinner—lackadaisycally staring at a fillet of Veal which it was too hot to eat, I was agreeably surprised by your Letter of the 10th (as I see by the London mark) which from your last I had lamented as lost & imagind it would amuse somebody who had no sort of right to such an entertainment. It had however lain very quietly at the post Office at Farnham (having no Post town on the cover), & a Man of this village calling there brought it to me. As I send up tomorrow my last packet to Johnson (So it is not his fault for once that my book is not born), I take occasion to thank you for it, & to express my concern at hearing so very painful an account of you & Mr Rose as the last Letter I had from you brought me. I hope by this time you are easier—Perhaps have already left London, and I have great reliance on Sea air and chearful scenes. Pray let me hear that every benefit I wish may have been derived from them, and that your health and chearfulness is return'd. I would preach a little about philosophy & all that sort of thing which every body recommends and nobody practices, but you would very justly retort & say, "Cure thy self"——

At this moment I have need to exercise every little "bout et miette"[1] of Philosophy that I can possibly raise. I am alone with poor Harriet, who is not well, tho I dont know what is the matter with her, but I dread a return of one of those fevers of which she has now had three dreadful visitations, twice in India & once since her return, which, after reducing her to the brink of the grave for three weeks or more, leave her in a state between Idiotism and frenzy, from whence she very slowly recovers; Her beauty, which was not inconsiderable when she undertook that unfortunate Voyage to Bengal, has been visibly impairing ever since these dreadful fevers have attack'd her; I never saw a <human being> so changed at two and twenty—She is now sometimes so[2] . . .
as to make any one suppose she had a scarlet fever[3] . . .

while sometimes she is interested and agitated about trifles that dont signify a straw. In my own opinion, nothing will be of the least use to her but Sea bathing, & that would they say enable me to walk; but it is not within our reach—at least not within mine——

My poor George demands every thing I can raise beyond the actual & very heavy expence of housekeeping. Lord Egremont and Mr Smith honourably and kindly have done every thing to destroy my credit so that the moment a bill of two pound is due, I am calld upon for it tho my income can come in but twice a year. This keeps me always on the alert & chafes me about trifles, but it is bootless to complain; the noble Lord having discoverd that Mr Prescods retaining 3300£ payt for the estate is my fault, that Mr Allen & Smith sueing their Uncle is my fault, & I dare say Bonapartes making War was my fault, for I had as much to do with one as the other. So however he treats me!—— I have been oblig'd ~~however~~ notwithstanding to re-excite this honourable & manly anger by sending his Ldp a Letter from Mr Adams, who is on his way to England, whereby it plainly appears that if Mr Tyler had sent over to Barbados papers I solicited so long ago as May twelvemonth, Mr Adams would now have brot home 1600£ for the Trust, which he now beleives is lost or will never be recover'd without infinite trouble. While for want of half that Sum, my poor Lionels invaluable life is every day hazarded! I repeat however that it is of no use to complain. Il faut souffrir,[4] & I am used to it, as the Rat catcher said his ferret was when he sew'd up its jaws, "Why Lord bless ye Mum, he's used to't, why a likes it." Charlotte however, who has not been used to it quite so long, ought I think to find a little more human flesh about the right honourable heart of the noble Lord than I can expect to do—— Poor Mrs Hayley[5] . . .

My repellent period is come, but I should think Charlotte, if she did not attract, would still have middle qualities enough to obtain justice but on her applying to know when any part of the principal or even the interest of the Sum awarded to her might be hoped for, his Ldp Ans[were]d, Never, till the two Chancery suits were settled. So I have advised her to begin a third & try this with the princely peer. It is amazingly wearying. I shall leave it among my Aphorisms to my Grandchildren, Never to put their trust in a Lord——

Mr Benjn Smith, worthy old Gent, has been down to pay his respects at Petworth (Venison being rife) & presented a fish of his own catching. If there were any hopes of a miracle, I wd recommend the liver of this fish to be roasted & applied to the Noble Lords Eyes after the manner of Tobits father[6] who found it an admirable Colysium, but I am afraid none are so blind as those who wont see & that Mr Tyler & Mr Benjn Smith will still appear worthy of the protection & favor of the descendant of Charlemagne. While he discovers as to me as Lady MW Montague says Lords are apt to do—that he mistook misfortune for merit[7] (That said Lady was a wonderfully clever woman, but had not much heart I think). I should not have known that my very much honor'd Sposo had been to Petworth if Harriet had not seen him pass as she sat with an acquaintance at Godalming. He stared at her with those amiable goglers of his but did not know her tho she is his darling dear, & to her he intends to leave all he has unless it should so happen that I, who have lived on "Brandy, Aether and Laudanum now for some years, for so he tells," should ~~have~~ take occasion to die & leave him a jolly Widower of sixty three to cock his hat and set his heart on some happy Abishag,[8] & then he can give his Money, or rather his fathers, to some future

Smithkins. Now really (tho I know you think me quite absurd & that this is my mad string), I do nothing but laugh at these plans & so w^d any body who saw this two legged phenomenon.

Basta Basta e troppo[9]—but one must either laugh or cry, & it is better to do the first if one can. Would that I were like unto Miss Seward who describes herself—even at the present period—as having "her sensibilities always flowing, and her energies ever awake." I suppose all her feelings have as many lives as the Cats whose tender Amours she so properly tells of & whose guttural amatory dialogues She has so felicitously imitated.[10]

But that is nothing to the Authoress of the Single life of a Lover.[11] The scene I like best, next to the non consummation of the old Colonel, is that where Lady Something (but I have forgot all the names, Heaven be prais'd already) pins a stocking on to her ancient Husbands night cap when she finds him. Oh! fie upon it! fast asleep by the side of a damsel, who I fear wore black worsted ones. Lady Easy[12] was I suppose the prototype. I am quite sorry this manner of reproof was not reckon'd the thing when M^r B S. used to trespass with Kitchen stuff. (Here he comes again—No he shall not.) (How amazingly Mr Robinson must have wishd he had known his fair Authoress in the days of her fancy & fire.)

But I was going to say that I began a Novel, for so such things must be calld, three years ago & did a great deal of it, but cares encreasing & comforts decreasing in a blessed proportion & being sick both in spirit & in body, I threw it by & said, "it is time to have done—write lullabies for thy Grandchildren but dont twaddle about love with spectacles on thy nose"—rather try, if none of thy literary friends will die, that thou mayst tell how they lived & live thyself like a Chacal[13] on the carcass, for that seems most lucrative & most the rage as witness Miss Seward & all Mr Phillips's late puttings forth.[14]

However now that my lullabies are done—I took out again my old Novel, & really I dont think it very foolish, & it is as little loving as may be, so if I could divest myself of the fear of growing as foolish in my old Age, as some certain good Ladies of more eminent fame, I should even finish it in the hope of getting 400£ by my imaginary hero to help my living Soldiers. Tell me honestly, my dear Madam, if you think I ought to do this, or go on making Childrens books, as Mr Johnson seems to recommend. I will desire him to send you a set of my late employ[men]^t in that line as soon as it comes out, & I assure you yours & Mr Roses' approbation will be among the highest gratifications hoped for by

Your much oblig'd & Affect^n Ser^t,
Charlotte Smith

Pray write to me. I fear I must not hope to remove from hence to the Sea, necessary as I feel it to be, but If possible I shall try & shall, when that point is ascertain'd, hesitate between Margate, Lowestaff, & Cowes. The latter would be cheapest but I fear I c[d] not get into a boat. I detest all the places on this coast.

Charlotte was fearful of calling on you, hearing so sad an account of your health & M[r] Roses—— I do not know whether or not she goes to Ireland. She is at No 41. Hatton Street,[15] but is going I beleive the end of the Week to Trent park in Hertfordshire for a few days.

Huntington MS (HM10838). Address: M[rs] Rose/ Chancery Lane. Postmark: Two-Penny/ POST/ St. Pauls CYd; { } Clock/ {JY}.31./ {18} 04 N.T.

NOTES

1. Bit and piece, crumb and piece.

2. Part of this line is cut away.

3. The rest of this page, about 3 lines, is cut away. Harriet had erysipelas (see CS to Charlotte Mary Smith, 2 Feb. 1803, and n. 2).

4. One must suffer.

5. The rest of this page, about 3 lines, is cut away.

6. In the Apocryphal Book of Tobit, Tobit's blindness is cured by his son Tobias when the angel Raphael instructs him to cover his eyes with fish gall. When the eyes started to burn, white scales would fall away.

7. CS has probably folded lords into "Melancholy experience has convince'd me of the ill Consequence of mistakeing Distress for Merit" (Montagu, *Letters,* 3:116).

8. A beautiful maiden chosen to lie with and arouse the aged King David (1 Kings 1.2).

9. Enough, enough, and too much.

10. In her life of Erasmus Darwin, Anna Seward published a playful, mock-heroic exchange of letters between herself and the doctor in the names of their cats, Miss Po Felina or Miss Pussey (hers) and Persian Snow (his). CS had to be very resentful of Seward's barbs against her or a determined hater of cats not to be charmed by this passage. Descended from Persian kings, Snow urges the value of his address, offering milk, "mice pent up in twenty garrets," and a Norway Rat, just caught. Puss cannot admire his "fierceness" and concludes: "Marry you, Mr. Snow, I cannot; since, though the laws of our community might not oppose our connection, yet those of principle, of delicacy, of duty to my mistress, do very powerfully oppose it" (*Memoirs of the Life of Dr. Darwin,* pp. 135–43).

11. *The Life of a Lover* (1804), by Sophia Lee.

12. A character in Colley Cibber's *The Careless Husband* (1705). Finding Sir Charles Easy without his periwig, Lady Easy takes a Steinkirk off her neck and lays it on his head. When he awakens he realizes that she has long known of his infidelities.

13. An alternate spelling of jackal.

14. CS alludes to Anna Seward's recent life of Erasmus Darwin and to Richard Phillips's *Public Characters,* a series of biographies and memoirs that began publication in 1799, as well as his children's books.

15. Haddon St. was the home of Joseph Smith, a relation and friend of Charlotte Mary.

To Joseph Cooper Walker

Elsted n[r] Godalmin, Surrey
Aug[t] 12th 1804
Dear Sir,

Ever since I was gratified by the favor of your last obliging Letter, I have felt that I could not too soon thank you for such a proof (& perhaps I ought to say, unmerited proof) of your friendly recollection. I do not mean to make any common place excuses for the date of my answer, but to tell you the whole truth, which is that I intended to have written a very long Letter by my daughter,[1] whose wish and purpose it was to have gone to Ireland more than a month ago. The doubts that have been from time to time started as to the safety of a passage by Bristol and Corke determind her to engage me to write to our good friend M[r] Caldwell,[2] of whose being in England your Letter inform'd me, & as Charlotte seem'd to be fortunate enough to partake of the friendly interest with which he honour'd her Mother, I knew he would forgive our importunity and give her the best information she could receive. Unfortunately, M[r] Caldwell was absent from the Admiral's (whither we directed) when my Letter reachd London, & it wander'd after him for near A month. As soon however as he received it, he most obligingly wrote his thoughts, & while he represented the impropriety at this time of a Voyage par Mere,[3] necessarily of some days, & gave her the most cordial and friendly invitation to pass by Dublin, & take up her abode with his Sister while she remain'd there, he did <u>not</u> conceal from her his opinion that the trajet[4] between Dublin and Killarney could not be pronounced safe for a single Woman; I mean for a young Woman quite alone, as she would probably have travelled [alone] or with only our little Persian child Luzena of six years old who is almost always her companion.

In consequence of these discouragements and other accounts from some friends who have often pass'd to your Island, My daughter had taken no resolution when she left me on the 20th July for London; I rather expect her home to day, but I beleive her journey to Ireland is for the present delay'd, and I have some hopes My Sons wife[5] will come over to pass the winter with us; Her anxiety about him, which none can share so sincerely as we do, is more likely to be soothed here than at a greater distance, & it would be a great pleasure (tho not undiminishd by many painful sensations) were I to see his little Girl, born since his departure. The misery I undergo from the continual accounts we have of the unwholesomeness of the W. Indies, and the particularly [*sic*] unhealthiness of Surinam, is not to be described, & it is renderd more insupportable to us all by certain circumstances of cruelty & brutal conduct on the part of the Man who ought to be the protector & friend of his family, but who is their persecutor and destroyer——— Forgive me for touching on so unpleasant and disgusting a subject; I will quit it, least it should betray me into too much warmth when writing to you, who do not know & I am sure cannot imagine, such a being as the worthless & wicked biped whose name I have the misfortune to bear—

I am extremely oblig'd to you for enquiring where my young Soldier[6] is? He merely pass'd thro Dublin after a very narrow escape from Shipwreck in November last & was marchd immediately to Kilkenny where he has been stationd till the 47th made a part of the encampment which has lately been formed on the Curragh of Kildare. I fear that spot is too far from Dublin to allow him to avail himself of your friendly intentions of favouring him with your notice, but should his duty or any other cause carry him to Dublin, it will be a great pleasure to me & an honor to him if he is allowed to pay his respects to you. You will I think find him a well behaved & not uninteresting young Man. Born an exile[7] and brought up under all the disadvantages of never having had a protector in his father & amidst the hard struggles I have made to provide for him even the necessaries of life, he has the manners & what is better the heart of a Gentleman with as little tendency to the vices of youth as can be hoped for, a total exemption I could not expect. George has had excellent examples of military merit in his two brothers, my lamented Charles & my Lionel, & I hear he is a good Officer for his standing (he is but nineteen), yet I wish he could have been brought up in any other way of life. I have had enough & too much of the trade of blood. His address is Lieut George Smith, 1st Battn 47th Regt, which I name, as it is possible that Regt may be removed nearer Dublin before or by the approach of Winter.

I was not without hope that I should see Mr Caldwell, as he does not seem to be soon returning to Ireland, but his Letter gave me no reason to expect so much pleasure. Of literary matters, I hear very little, Mr Hayley being so much absorbed he says by the dead that he withdraws himself almost entirely from the living. This dereliction is not I beleive quite general, & there <u>are</u> still some <u>living objects</u> who have attractions enough to remind him that he is yet an existing Poet & perhaps to teach him not yet to aspire to the amaranthine bowers of poetical paradise. I had a Letter from him for the first time these ten months a day or two ago in answer to my enquiry if he would accept a work too puerile I was afraid to offer him which, after a thousand interruptions from the most tedious printer existing, is about to Issue from the press. He is good natured & pleasant as usual, but all the really friendly interest he used to take in my works & my fate, is, it [. . .] to see gone.

I cannot help wishing to know if you have read our friend Mrs Sophia Lee's "Life of a Lover." I will not say a word about it till I know whether <u>her name</u> has not tempted you to return in that instance at least to Novel reading. The profane are highly amused, & some of her friends wish that, instead of keeping the work by her more than twice as long as Horace prescribes,[8] she had fed other flames with it than those metaphorical ones which they fear it will be thought to encourage—"but I say nothing." Richardsons Letters[9] are special dampers & appear very Appropos, for in my life I never read any thing so dull & twadling as the greater part of them. Lady Bradshaigh & her fid fads & "Lord Sir!!" & folly about not seeing the divine Man I really could not read— —I have been as much delighted by Lady Mary (tho she had not a grain of feeling as wearied by dear Mr Richardson & his bas blue[10] of the last century. As to Godwins life of Chaucer,[11] I have not yet read a line of it, having but just received it. It is une piece de resistance, & I have so much to do and so much to think of that I undertake it with little prospect of getting fairly thro it.

If I am able, I shall go to the Sea for a few weeks in hopes of strengthening the little health I have—I know not how—acquired lately from a state which appeard likely to end in nothing but the final close of my troubles. But till the Bombay ships come in, I am loaded with chains from which I cannot escape & which before they do come may perhaps be so heavy that I shall not be able to obtain a transient Respite at all. My coming book is for the Governesses room, & therefore I do not, dear Sir, presume to send it to you, but if you sh^d^ perchance meet with it, you may find some of the Poetry, for this sort of thing, not amiss. Beleive me, I am with all gratitude, regard, & esteem, Dear Sir,

y^r^ most obligd Ser^t^ Charlotte ~~Smith~~

I wish I had any right to ask, what I earnestly desire, to hear from you. Indeed it will give me great pleasure if you will indulge me. I send this to be frank'd by Lord Clanricarde who is so good as to say he will receive & forward any Irish Letters for me——if directed to him Belmont Alton, Hampshire.

Huntington MS (HM10839). Address: Josepth Cooper Walker Esqre/ Eccles Street/ Dublin. No postmark.

NOTES

1. Charlotte Mary.

2. Andrew Caldwell, Esq., a wealthy Irish solicitor and one of CS's literary friends, whom she first met in 1799 (see CS to Joseph Cooper Walker, 23 June 1799 and n. 5).

3. By sea.

4. Crossing or passage.

5. Ellen, Lionel's wife.

6. George.

7. George was born in Normandy, near Dieppe, where CS had fled in the winter of 1785 with BS to escape creditors.

8. In the *Ars Poetica,* Horace advises the poet to keep any writings in a notebook at home for eight years (ll. 384–90).

9. Anna Barbauld's six-volume edition of *The Correspondence of Samuel Richardson . . . {with} a Biographical Account* came out in 1804. In Oct. 1748, while *Clarissa* was being serialized, Lady Dorothy Bradshaigh began writing to Richardson as Mrs. Belfour after hearing a report that Clarissa would end tragically, an ending she abhorred. Her 10 Nov. letter rewrites the novel's ending. It is hard to discover anything objectionable in this celebrated exchange. On 28 Jan. 1749, she wrote: "Sir, I received your letter of four pages and a half, with a Pish-pugh! is this all?" (4:322). On 9 Feb. 1749, she began a letter: "O Good God, Sir!" On 14 Feb., she revealed herself to Richardson, and they met in Mar. (4:379). Vol. 6, with an engraving of Lady Bradshaigh as its frontispiece, is devoted to letters between her and Richardson, which discuss readings, plots for new novels, Lady Bradshaigh's life in the country, and wives' duties to husbands.

10. "Bas bleu" was the title of a poem by Hannah More (1786) written as a compliment to Elizabeth Vesey, a hostess to Elizabeth Montagu, Hester Chapone, Elizabeth Carter, Mary Delany, and other literary women called Bluestockings in the 1770s and later. These and other women and some men met to talk and to cultivate their minds. Invited to visit with them early in her career, CS wrote to Mary Hays that "the greatest difficulty I had was to resist a violent inclination to yawn" (CS to Hays, 26 July 1800). Here, CS has appropriated the term to describe Samuel Richardson's own circle of admiring literary women. The poet, essayist, and letter writer Lady Mary Wortley Montagu (1689–1762) had mixed feelings about Richardson too. CS was probably looking at James Dallaway's 1803 edition, *The Works of the Right Honourable Lady Mary Wortley Montagu,* which included her correspondence, poems, and essays.

11. Published in 1803.

To the earl of Egremont

Elsted, Aug[st] 13th 1804
My Lord,

Your Lordship has so often accused me within the last two or three years of intemperance towards M[r] B Smith & (to others with whom it was my misfortune to have to contend) ~~with~~, You seem'd not long ago to be so decidedly of opinion that his were the injuries, and mine the blame, when you declared at your own table that he "was the best of the bunch." It has happend that I have received so much injury—& it might have happend, had not my character been pretty well understood, that I might have sustain'd so much more injury—by your Lordships declaring against me, after having so differently thought of me, that it becomes a matter of self defence & self justification to shew your Lordship (unwilling as I am to trouble you even with my name) of what the wretched insane being is capable, whom you have been pleased to countenance & who was sufferd to rob his unhappy family of so large a Sum last year under the Authority of an Arbitration which I never would have submitted to had I not been assured that it would go to secure the settlement I demanded & have concluded the Trust so justly denominated by your Lordship detestable & which, from its having been allowd to include questions between me & that wretched disgrace to his species, has undoubtedly been made every thing that I hoped it would not be——

I cannot imagine, My Lord, that the Trustees have a right to withhold what was given by the award to My daughter while Mr B Smith was instantly paid; Mr Bicknell seems to think it quite irregular that even the interest should still be denied her, & I, my Lord—very weary both on her account & my own of a trust which has already existed seven years & may exist seven more if some decisive steps are not taken—have advised her application to Chancery the beginning of term. If the doubt of there being money enough to pay the Allens (in case of their iniquitous projects succeeding) prevents my daughter being paid, surely it ought to have demanded some pause on the part of the Trustees before they paid, under the same award, Mr Benjn Smith who had not the shadow of right to it & who received it when the same claim of the Allens[1] &c hung over the property & when two of the persons interested in that property, Lionel & George, had not sign'd the Arbitration bond, & those who did do it, did it to their own wrong.

I hope I shall find, that there is some redress for me as to the violation of the principles of the Marriage Articles, & the resolution Mr Benjn Smith has made & avows—that "if his daughter Lucy & her children were starving & perishing for want at his gate he would not give her a farthing to save their lives"—— And is this Man—or rather this brute, tho brutes have far more human feelings—is this Man one who should boast (as he does) of your Lordships countenance?——

My Lord, this Monster (assure yourself I shall never name him to you again, & allow me to give way to the indignation that even contempt for such a dirty wretch cannot stifle)—this Monster never read the Letter, which I now send exactly as it was return'd to me. It enclos'd as you will see a Letter from your Lordship. His femme d'affaire (as it appears by the cover) forwarded it to him from Hamilton, & he received it at Camberwell, from whence he took the pains, not having read it as he says, to take it with him to his new residence at Berwick,[2] & from thence under a double cover to send it back to me to put me to the expence of near three Shillings While the infamous wretch lives on my property, throws his children on me for support, &— ———— Surely your Lordship never could have received this Person under your roof had you known him better!—— Lady Mary Wortley Montague says in some one of the latest of her Letters that persons of rank often meet with ingratitude because they mistake misfortune for merit.[3] Your Lordship has perhaps made that very usual mistake in regard to me, but I really cannot suppose that you could do it in regard to Mr Benjn

Smith. However that may be, I beg leave without any prejudice to the gratitude I owe your Lordship (for much favor indeed, while you condescended to call yourself my friend, & I considerd you as the benefactor & preserver of my family) to state to you that, be the consequence what it may, I shall try in my own person (if those, who, tho not regularly my Trustees, stand as such will not do it) to bring the question of the future disposition of my property before Chancery. If I once get Mr B Smith into a Court & have a Council properly instructed, I have very little doubt of the Event——— Your Lordship will be pleased to return the billet I send you. I was afraid if I sent a copy only which I have taken, it might not be beleived, & this delicate morceau with some others from the same admirable pen I may have occasion for.

The worthy writer has taken a place near Berwick where he is collecting Guinea fowl, peacocks, and other dainty <devices>. It is very fit he should do all that & that I should work for my own bread and that of his younger Son & daughter & very fit Lionel shd remain at Surinam!

I have the honor to be,
My Lord, your most obedt huble Sert,
Charlotte ~~Smith~~

Petworth House Archives MS. No address or postmark.

NOTES

1. Mary Gibbes Smith Allen, a granddaughter of Richard Smith, and her husband, Capt. Robert Allen. (See Genealogical Chart.)

CS and BS nearly agreed on the matter of the Allens' Chancery suit. CS complained of their "iniquitous projects" (see CS to Egremont, 13 Aug. 1804). Now that BS had moved back to London and was living under his own name, he wrote that "I shall be liable to the wild Hostility of Mr Allen" (BS to William Tyler, 15 July 1804, unpub. letter in PHA #0.11), but also said he would cooperate with their solicitor, Dow. December found him hoping for a way to "suppress the atrocious conduct of Mr Dow" and still trying to evade the man: "As Mr Tayler said I was not in England, I have antedated my letter to Mr Allen . . . some finesse is necessary for the present to prevent Dow from finding me out" (BS to Egremont, 19 Dec. 1804, unpub. letter in PHA #0.11).

2. For evidence of BS's change of residence and CS's double expense, see the address at the end of CS to William Tyler?, 12 July 1804. For some years, BS had lived in exile in Hamilton, Scotland, under the name of Bryan or Brian Symmonds or Simmonds. His friend and advisor Simon Halliday lived in Camberwell. BS was to die in the Berwick jail on 26 Feb. 1806, but he was not yet imprisoned.

3. In Montagu's *Letters,* 3:116; see CS to Sarah Rose, 30 July 1804, n. 7.

To the earl of Egremont

[?Elsted, received 8 September 1804]

My Lord,

I am very sensible of your Ldps condescension in giving yrself the trouble to answer Letters on a subject undoubtedly very odious, & from a person so utterly unworthy as I must be in your judgement, if I am degraded in it even below such a character as Mr Benjn Smith. Y^r^ Lordship certainly says in the Letters to which mine was an answer that my note to M^r^ B S. provoked his reply. The note however & cover were never returned, & if your Lordship sent them, they did not reach me (for which perhaps it might not be difficult to account). I have, contrary to my usual custom, a rough copy of that note which accompanied a Letter of y^r^ Lordships that I hoped might have weight with M^r^ B S, & as I am preparing & have nearly completed a brief account of all that has pass'd on this subject for the information of persons at a distance who are the most concern'd & have copied the Letters I wrote and received, I shall be able to make out from my rough draft this offensive one, & I do assure you, my Lord, that, tho misrepresentation is the gentlest word I receive from y^r^ Ldsp and from M^r^ B S. the elegant appellation of a diabolical Lyar, these will be the most indisputable vouchers for the truth of what I shall assert.

It is very sad to have lost all credit with your Lordship, and that by the Extraordinary intervention of M^r^ B S whose total disregard of truth and every other gentleman like quality is and has been notorious to every one who has known him & felt more severely by those who have sufferd from his meanness, dishonesty, and depravity—— He is as Mr Rose said at Petworth house (on the information of those who knew him, & of whom Mr Rose had enquired) "a wretched miscreant." Forty years, Sir, have nearly expired since I was made over an early & unconscious victim to this half Ideot, half Madman. He has receivd with me 7000£. I have earned with my own hands upwards of 4500£ more. I wish not, My Lord, to boast of what I have done, but it is an indisputable & notorious fact, & it would be false modesty & injustice to myself not to assert that, little as I was calculated to be the slave and martyr of a man contemptible in understanding, but detestable for the corruption of his selfish heart, I have borne my fate honourably. It is denied by none who really know me. It has been acknowledged by your Lordship, or wherefore did you ever give yourself any trouble about me?

Yet your Lordship has been pleased within these three years not only to take in every instance a part against me, but to speak of me in terms which, coming from you, have of course weight & induce some persons to beleive that I am to blame, since few will suppose your Lordship to be unjust, & thus I am not only deprived of your kindness, but of that of others, &

why?—What have I done my Lord?—I am apt to write Letters full of asperity?!—— Y^r^ Lordship may perhaps recollect the story of the German who was broke upon the wheel & was desired to behave during the operation with "plus de bien seance."[1] I have been put to every variety of torture & releived from one, only to be tried by another. My best friends, my nearest relations, those in serving whom I have passd my life have been embodied against me—Now, when <the> death of my children & sorrow aggravated by poverty & disease have render'd me helpless! If I write on the affairs I am contradicted by Mr Tyler & calld querulous—that is the civilest term he allows me. When first your Lordship became Trustee, Mr Tyler had nothing to do with the business. But he has been heard to say he hated & wd do me all the injury he could, or words to that effect, & he has, & will keep his word——

Indeed, my Lord, I little thought ever to have been referred to that person who may, for ought I know, be a very able Attorney in this Country, but he knows nothing of Barbados business & has bedevild that he has interfered in by his obstinate adherence to his own opinion. He now says, when I desire to have another Attorney appointed there, that Mr Bishop is sufficient. What does he know of Mr Bishop? The fact is that Mr Bishop is a very young Man, who neither knows nor cares any thing about the business, is as often as he can absent from the Island, & would not take a twentieth part of the trouble Mr Adams has taken to have all the debts himself when they are recover'd. Mr Adams (who is not a fool I assure your Lordship) knows very well that Mr Bishop will do nothing effectual, but as Mr Tyler, in the power sent out in 1802, omitted to insert a clause enabling Mr Adams to appoint another Attorney in case of his absence, he (Mr Adams) had no remedy but to write from Tortola (where at last he received the necessary papers on his way home) to desire Mr Bishop wd do what he could, & he was piqued & surely with reason to find that all the pains he had taken were thrown away because of Mr Tylers pertinacious adherence to his own opinion that there was no occasion to send the deed of transfer under the City seal— —Your Lordship will see, that the 300£ a year wch Griffith offer'd to pay, till his debt was liquidated will be lost. The money likely to be recoverd from Mr Pindar in the matter of Forster Clarke & Butler Harris[2] is more secure, but that is comparitively a trifle.

I beseech you, Sir, to beleive me when I protest that I would not give you the trouble of reading a single line on this or any other subject were only myself in question, for I could apply my time and talents to much more profitable & certainly much more pleasurable purposes than this Sysiphean labour, but when I reflect that one life has been lost in attempting to retrieve this little property, & that another may be, Oh God perhaps is already lost for the want of it!—When my eldest daughter after waiting eight & twenty years has not to this hour received the legacy left her by her Grandfather, nor is likely to have it or even the interest of it & has been insulted for asking for it, When I remember that in the very teeth of a Will, in direct defiance to Mr Grahams opinion,[3] & even to your Lordships former opinion, the wicked selfish & unnatural plunderer of his children has been sufferd repeatedly to rob them as well as me & that my poor George is condemned to struggle wth penury (tho I am deprived even of necessaries to be able to send him small supplies)—My anxiety for these injurd children conquers the loathing & repugnance I feel to write another Word on such hopeless business. And tho your Lordships anger & indignation is the constant Consequence of my attempts to do them justice, I venture to have it. Had I been the worst of human beings, had I disgraced & then abandon'd my children, had I done as many persons would have done, thought only of myself & considerd, that vows made when I was not competent to contract a debt of ten pounds could not be binding in the eye of reason & left Mr Benjamin Smith & his family, to encounter as they could the consequences of his folly, I could not have been treated with more rudeness, contempt, or insult than I have been made to sustain Or have been the butt of ridicule after having been made the object of compassion.

Your Lordship will perhaps say that this is misrepresentation, scurrility, &c &c & nothing to the purpose. Yes, My Lord, it is to the purpose, for my purpose is to take every means in my power to end someway or other the misery I undergo & not to be tortured in this manner. I was grateful, most grateful to yr Lordship for deigning once more to interest yrself in the division of the property; I hoped I saw a revival of the noble, generous, & friendly conduct you once vouchsafed to shew towards me. But no sooner did Mr B Smith make his visit at Petworth than his cause weighd in the ballance, & I & my innocent Children were again in the wrong. My Gallant, my noble hearted Lionel is left to perish in a climate where every breath is disease while that selfish old monster (My Lord, I must be allowed to speak the truth) is holding out obstinately against law & reason till, out of 108£ a year for myself and his two younger children, he can extort 40£, 100£ from a perfect stranger! Good God, Sir, how am I to live on 108£ a year still as on 70£?—& should this man be again paid for what he ought to do & must do?

He says I can write: Well, then I must write & let him take the consequence of the desperation he has driven me to—I Can write, & I can draw. At this time, the Commission of Lieut Colonel in the 47th is to be purchased & purchas'd at the regulation price; Lionel has 600£ of prize money, & Mr Gallway wd give something considerable so that for less than four hundred pounds I might purchase this rank for him & rescue him, if it be not too late, from death. But the prize money is not yet payable, & I am every way helpless & must see my best hopes perish. God Almighty! where is the Mother of such a Son who can look forward to such a prospect & know that the wretch who has embitterd her life (insulted her, robbed her, struck her, attempted in the frantic jealousy of conscious unworthiness to rob her of her character, & is now keeping a Scotch cook on her property) that such a wretch is the cause of her Sons being thus needlessly exposed & not feel as I do? My Lord, poverty is no sweetener of the temper, but it does not harden the heart. I implored your interest for Lionel three years ago (for I repeat that I never thought of y^r giving or lending money), & you voluntarily offerd it to save him then from going to the West Indies. Now—your Lordship will not say to M^r B S. that he ought, nay that he must make the regulation that I ask, for had your Lordship said this, he had not dared to have sneaked of[f] again to Scotland where he is flourishing away at an handsome house & has sent for Guinea fowl, peacocks, & a filtring stone! The nauseous hypocrite!——

Your Lordship says he was not long enough at Petworth to hear what he ought to do!—— He ought not to have been at Petworth at all. Indeed, my Lord, it is a disgrace to associate with such a Man. However I hope there is redress somewhere, & I do mean to try. I am going to obtain Counsels opinion whether there exists any legal trust at present to my marriage articles; no regular appointment has certainly been made. I would fain releive your Lordship from that part of the detestable business that relates to the worst of the bunch for such I must be if M^r B S. is the best, & I am really in some hope that I shall get the best of the bunch into the Court of Chancery where he shall be exhibited, not En buste, or in Kitcat,[4] but at full length. But if my children were not in question, silent contempt & abhorrence would be my part. As it is, I will try to obtain for them that justice which I have been refused.

In regard to Mr Prescod, my Lord, your Lordship will give me leave to observe that your charge of asperity towards him is certainly oweing to some misunderstanding. What was done when difficulties first began (as to the pay^t of the 3000£ of mine) was done in consequence of an interview I had with him when he was very civil & behaved as much like a Gentleman as such a parvenue could be suppos'd to do. He seem'd to hold M^r B S. in the contempt which all Barbados people as well as most others do hold him in, but spoke in terms of the highest respect & praise of my poor Charles & profess'd a desire to settle every thing fairly & amicably, setting himself forever against the Allens & their claims & laughing at their menace to him.

Since that time, I have never had any intercourse with him, nor did a word like asperity ever pass between us. I said that it was likely he would take every advantage because it is his character, as Mr Dayrell & the other Barbados people have told me, and because he certainly jockey'd the Estate out of 219£ (a running account between him and old Mr Smith or Smith and Turner). But I did not say so to him, Nor did I ever write to him, more than a note two or three years ago about some appointment. Why therefore y^r

Lordship shd say that I have done mischief there, God knows, unless it is because you are determind at all events to think & say ill of me. I occasiond the Allens Lawsuit! I ruin'd Lucy! I am scurrilous, abusive, virulent, querulous —A most diabolical personage in truth. I have injurd Mr Turner too, and in short, your Lordships description of me differs so much from that of the generality of those who know me, & so very much from the public opinion, that none would beleive I was the same person—The same person once praisd beyond her desert & now most cruelly & hardly treated.

My Lord, I give up every hope of fair means prevailing on Mr B S. ~~by fair means~~. There are other ways, and they must be tried; I have no longer any terms to keep & surely nothing to fear. In regard to the Barbados affairs, Mr Adams's Letter meant what I said, & nothing else: He thought himself ill used to have so much trouble given him for a person he wishd to serve & to be baffled by Mr Tyler who even to this present moment persists in saying there was no occasion for the City seal. If your Lordship chuses to authorise me to act with Mr Adams & to send out & do what is requisite without Mr Tylers interference & being made liable to his opposition and cavills (which are made on every occasion to shew his consequence and torment me), I will see Mr Adams, & I know the business will be got thro if it is not already desperate, but without this I can do nothing. I cannot contend with Mr Tyler indeed, my Lord. If yr Lordship thought it worth while, you wd find on enquiry that Mr Adams is not only a Gentleman but a Man of fortune & fashion, and it is not surprising he should be a little hurt at the haut en bas[5] way in which he thought himself treated—— Barbadians are always proud. My proposal in regard to Mr Prescod was to get Mr Harris of Alresford,[6] a Barbadian of fortune, & Mr Adams to try what could be done without any menace or threat of Law, but I am so discouraged by the rebuffs I meet with that I had given it up—& besides, if Charlotte and the rest of the legatees, but my eldest daughter in particular is not (as your Lordship is pleas'd in a former Letter to say) to receive a farthing, Why should I take any trouble? Yet, my Lord, I dont beleive that any award in the world can authorise the payments made to Mr B S. before the legatees are paid, & neither Lionel nor George sign'd the ~~award~~ arbitration bond. The latter could not; He is yet a Minor, & none could give away 500£ which was to his wrong. I have shewn the award to a Lawyer who thinks it the most absurd that ever was made, & certainly my Lord it answerd no one purpose for which I consented to it.

My Lord I hope the 500£ to be receivd from Gibbons the 2nd next month will be applied to the payment of the Legatees—& particularly to Miss Smith. Your Lordship cannot think it necessary to keep that back as well as the 3331 & interest for the Allens whose demands if establishd amount to only 1300£. If to tie up all was requisite, why was the 500£ (when the Man laid his ravenous claw on only 400£) So readily given away?[7] My Lord, nothing will ever erase from my mind the obligations I have owed your

Lordship when the sight of your hand writing was a pleasure and an honor. But tho I shall ever remember what was, I cannot but feel what is & desire by every means in my power to release y[r] Lordship from a burthen which seems wholly to have changed your nature towards

Y[r] Lordships ever obed[t] Ser[t],
Charlotte Smith

Miss Smith will write to Mr Prescod if y[r] Lordship does not think as I do the other plan better.

Have the goodness to return Mr Benjamin Smiths last Letter to Mr Gallway as every specimen is necessary.

Petworth House Archives MS. No address or postmark.

NOTES

1. *Plus de bienséance:* more propriety.

2. Francis Foard Pindar of Barbados purchased the Griffith estate that owed money to the Smith trust (CS to William Tyler, unpub., 1 Feb. 1804), and CS trusted him more than other Barbadians to settle his debts. Thomas Maxwell Adams wrote to Charlotte Mary that Pindar was "very much interested for M[rs] Smith—poor M[rs] Smith!" (see CS to Egremont, ?April 1804, n. 1). The same letter identified Harris as James Butler Harris, not to be confused with William Harris (see n. 6, below). A later letter (CS to Egremont and Tyler, 2 Sept. 1805) identifies George Forster Clarke as a debtor to the Barbadian estate.

3. The lawyer Robert Graham was consulted by CS in 1797 (see letter to Cadell and Davies, 22 June 1797 and n. 1).

4. In painting, a bust portrays the head, shoulders, and breast of the subject; a portrait in kitcat shows the top half of the body and includes the hands.

5. Condescending, contemptuous.

6. William Harris of Alresford, Hampshire (b. 1749) had matriculated at Merton College, Oxford, as "Ward": that is, ward of Richard Smith. He had property in Barbados and was related to Sir Phillip Gibbes of Barbados. CS considered him a friend; see her letters to Egremont, 8 Aug. and 13 Sept. 1806, and unpublished letter to CS from Harris (PHA #8236).

7. The £3,331 and interest was the annual payment from Prescod for Gay's. The £500 was the amount BS received as a result of Samuel Rose's arbitration decision in Sept. 1803.

To Sarah Rose

Elsted, Sept[r] 10th 1804

I was very glad, my Dear Madam, to see your handwriting to day; it is a real satisfaction to me to beleive you take an interest in my destiny, but indeed my pleasure was sadly dash'd by the account you give of your various uneasiness since I had last the favor of a letter. I should have written to enquire after you, but between hope and fear, my faculties have been half annihilated. My hopes were of getting something done towards the promotion of my beloved Lionel, but after Lord Egremont had once more interfered with M^r^ B Smith to get a future settlement made of my property (by which only this most desirable object can be obtain'd), Mr Benjn Smiths visit to Petworth seem'd to change the noble Lords very variable mind, & he began pelting me again with the charges of virulence, violence, & scurrility, & gross misrepresentation, While Mr Tyler, of whose notoriety you may perhaps have heard, is allowed to treat me with as little ceremony as his master—to which it is not very easy quietly to submit when the estate to which my children have a future claim after the death of M^r^ B Smith is likely to lose 1500£ by Tylers obstinancy in refusing to send out to Barbadoes papers under the City seal necessary for its recovery till Mr Adams, a Gentleman of independent property & high principle, who had taken an infinite deal of trouble to get this and other debts in, left the Island, & now it will probably be lost.

I sent Mr Adams's letter to Lord Egremont in which he complains of this treatment, laments the mismanagement, and asks whether Lord E. takes him for an Attorney? So this has roused the blood of the illustrious Hotspur (wch heretofore was enchafed, I trust, by far other causes), & I am—No languages can tell what I am (which a right honourable Man can use), But as I am willing to give you a specimen of the Sieur B S—who is surely a being such as Baelzebub must have been in conjunction with the Goddesses Moira & Cloacine[1] to have produced—& as I cannot pollute my paper with the detestable scroul, I send it to you on a detach'd sheet together with the noble Lords approbation of his performance. I should not do this by way of being entertaining, for it is any thing but delightful to see specimens of ideotism and depravity, but as I feel it to be more and more impossible for me to submit to the insults I at present experience and the fear of the confusion that will occur hereafter, I have determind, while strength is yet lent me, to hazard every thing to get the business out of Lord Egremonts hands & throw it rather into Chancery than be thus tormented by him. Miss Smith is positively refused, first on one pretence and then on another, even the interest of the money awarded to her by Mr Rose twelve months since. And Lord Egremonts whole conduct, from the excessive aversion he has from [*sic*] me or from the most marvellous influence of Mr Tyler, goes so evidently to torment me while I live & ruin my family after me that every motive urges me to end it——

I have told the noble Lord my mind in direct but respectful terms, for from his anger I cannot apprehend more than I have already sufferd, & his sport, (turning me into ridicule to amuse the wretched parasytes round his table) which he does not deny, would cancel any obligation tho twenty times greater than any he has conferred—— But I shall never suffer resentment, however keenly I must feel such very unworthy treatment, to obliterate the remembrance of passd kindness. All I desire is that, since his Lordships opinion of me is so totally changed, he will relinquish a trust he took when it was more favorable, and not do me injury if he determines to do me no good. He is surely a most extraordinary being!

I should have endeavour'd to have remov'd myself at least for a time to a distance from this line of Country, & while a cough, which I have now had ever since April & which is more troublesome than ever, adds another reason to the many I before had to go for a short time to the seaside, I had almost as many motives to prefer Margate or rather Ramsgate or Broadstairs to any of the places on this coast: I need not say that to have an opportunity of meeting you was one of the most powerful. But as my E India remittances are not come in (for Bengal ships, tho my eldest Son is there, never bring me even letters) & there is no immediate probability of their coming, yet I am so far from being able to take any journey that I shall be once more reduced to the most humiliating difficulties here & doubt whether I shall have credit even for another week.

Johnson gave me altogether 125 G[s] for my two Volumes with which I am satisfied, & on which and my poor half yearly pittance, I have subsisted. But tho I am satisfied wth the payment, I am not so with his allowance of books for presents, as he has given me only nine sets—not any thing like the number always allowd by Low, & even Cadell & Davies gave me eighteen. Perhaps he does not mean to limit me so much; he should certainly recollect that my own family is large & that I have many friends to oblige. I have not yet had time to write to him. He informs me in the only letter I could extort from him since the publication of the book (tho when that was I know not) that he had sent your copy, but I imagine it has not reachd you. When it does, I shall hope to hear your ingenuous opinion of it And that you will mark the faults of which, now that it is printed, I see many as well as innumerable errors of the press, Errors the more provoking, as in some places they affect the sense, and as I took great pains to have the press corrected & was [*sic*] the expence of having every sheet sent hither. But these are among the minor miseries of Authorship.

I have sent a set of Books to M[r] Hayley, with a long Letter, or at least a longer than I have troubled him with for some years, for his cold & evidently forced letters in answer to those which about twice in the last year I have written to him are so mortifying that it is painful to me to tax him for les bienseances si constipe,[2] as a french woman would say. Peace to his perambulations—whether on Parnassus or about his native City, for he calls me now Dear Grandmamma of Pindus. Before I would venture to send him my little book, I wrote to know if it would be acceptable, for nothwithstanding he has begun a Poetical Buffon himself to assist his worthy friend

Mr Blake,[3] I was afraid mine would be deem'd too puerile. I wishd to have seen that number of his fables—or whatever they are calld which told some extraordinary feats perform'd by a certain Eagle who carried away a child & then served as Monture[4] to the Mamma—because a remark of Mrs Sargents[5] amused me extremely; when having read this fable, she said, "Dear Mr Hayley, how could you think of telling such a thing—really you do love to put Women in the most extraordinary situations!"—— But the thing is nothing unless you knew Mrs Sargents voice and manner. I fancy you do not know her.

I really beleive I should go to Bognor because it is the nearest Sea (tho I detest it), & it would not cost me so much as going any where else & might answer the same purpose of carrying off this worrying cough, but as Mr Hayley lives so near & would either not willingly know I was there (which he should never know from me) or, if he did know it, think some constraind civility necessary, I avoid the place (which I otherwise dislike) still more on that account, & leave him to continue without any interruption from Pindarick Grandmamma's his weekly pools at twodville.[6] In his Letter accepting my books, he names Mr Roses' being ill (as if it was quite new to me) with great concern——

Did you see the Imperial Reviews for the two last months? They seem to me to encrease in stupid & vapid criticism. I positively will pay no more three shillings, But save all my critical money for the Edinburgh. I quite long for the October review—in the miserably monotonous and half animated existence which I drag on here, where torpidity is often courted as the only relief to anguish, something sharp & awakening in the way of reading is as desirable as acid after the bitterness of Quassia or the mawkish alkali of magnesia. I was rather disappointed in "Letters for literary Ladies" which I never happen'd to read till a few days ago.[7] Most of the Edgeworth exhibition is vastly superior. I heard from an Irish literate who is acquainted with her that Miss Edgeworth is writing a Novel calld Griselda on the story perhaps of Patient Grissel, or Grizzle,[8] & if it be so, calculated I hope for Married Ladies, who for the most part have great occasion for a quantity of the virtue practiced by that Heroine of forbearing fame. I did not like Belinda[9] at all as a whole tho parts of it are excellent, but most of what the Edinburgh calls the productions of Edgeworth & Co are full of sense and talent.

I forget that I shall fill my paper and that I have a delectable correspondence to send you. However I shall send my Letter to Lord Clanricarde to frank it, for it certainly will not be worth eight pence. You kindly enquire after Harriet. She is pretty well unless at particular periods when she has all manner of bilious and odd complaints, & I am continually in apprehension of those fearful fevers. She is now going to a friend of mine at Albury, that lovely spot, to join a party who annually at this season dance in a wood &

dine in a barn, so she is amused and all goes well. A part of my amusement must be to look out for another resting place for my weary head, for the good old humourist who built this pretty little cottage[10] unluckily dying last year, his odious squeezy niece wants either to marry and live here herself, or to build and let it for more than 50 G^s^ a year, and as I took it for only two years and an half, she has given me notice to quit in February when my term ends. I cannot think whither I shall go or what I shall do.

I should like to pass the winter in London, but I should not know what to do with my furniture, the few books I have left, and other incumbrances. Nor would a sojourn in London suit with the probably low ebb of my pocket, and what is worse I always am always [*sic*] sick in London, or fancy myself so—— —It will not however be long before the great setler of all grievances will in all probability adjust mine. How do you think that my correspondence will tell if I should be cut up hereafter, when such letters as these subjoin'd make a part of it. Ah! my dear Madam, with what heart, with what courage can I sit down to a work, de longue haleine,[11] with such misery hanging over me, as even such a connection must make me endure. Yet under this yoke have I groaned till I may literally say "Forty years long have I been plagued" with M^r^ B Smith! Of all the birds in the air & fishes in the Sea, could fate find out no other than this strange wretch to try me with?

My Dear Madam, you will notwithstanding think me querulous I fear, but All this I could bear, as I have hitherto borne it, Yet when I think Major Smith is too likely to be the next victim, all my attempts at philosophy vanish. I heard from him dated at Surinam the 11th June; I observed that the letter was very unlike his usual nice manner of writing, & tho he repeated that he was in perfect health, I told Charlotte that I was sure something was the matter. By a letter from Lieu^t^ Gallway[12] to his father we have learned that the yellow fever had broken out at Surinam and carried off a Captain Carleton[13] of the 16th on whom my Gallant boy waited night & day (like a nurse tender was the expression) till the last. Since this letter from Gallway, dated the day after Captn Careltons desease, we have heard nothing, & the anxiety & dread in which I live is not to be described. Where must be the hearts of people who had the power to prevent all this & who could so terminate a correspondence by which I endeavourd to get promotion secur'd to him? tho the Monster might have been better and could not have been worse.

But I shall weary you, dear Madam. Let me hasten then to say how very happy I shall be to hear you have all found benefit by the Sea air. Indeed there are few things out of my own family which would be more satisfactory than to know your long alarms for Mr Rose's health have subsided—— I hope you will bear in mind that it is a real pleasure to me to be rememberd by you and to receive your pleasant letters—pleasant from the heart they contain, tho the very quality that makes them so produces so much anxiety to the writer———You will hardly beleive yet how much a Woman can endure of many many agonizing solicitudes without sinking under them. God forbid, you should ever know more than You now do, & that the rest may be only theory. But when I look back on my life (of which I have often a mind to give a sketch), I wonder where I have found strength of mind and body to resist such a destiny till this late period.

If you hear of or meet with any books worth reading, pray name them to me, for I send in vain to Guilford for any thing rational. And even hunger will not compel me to feed on the puff paste & liquorice lozenges of the Minerva press.[14]

Charlotte desires to add her affectionate Comp[limen]ts to the best wishes of Dear Madam,

your oblig'd & faithful Sert, Charlotte Smith

Dont imagine that I care about franks when there is a chance of hearing from you, but if you will send two sheets under cover to the Earl of Clanricarde, Belmont, Alton, Hampshire, I should be better pleased because yr Letter wd be longer. Remember it will be two days or three later in reaching me, ~~that~~ And therefore you will I trust write another the sooner.

I red yr Letter to day only.

Houghton Library Autograph file MS, Harvard University. No address or postmark.

NOTES

1. Moira was the Greek personification of fate; Cloacina was one of the Roman numina, or lesser spirits; she oversaw sewers.

The "detach'd sheet" did not survive.

2. Proprieties so constraining.

3. Hayley had already published three ballads of tales about animals illustrated by William Blake (see CS to Cadell and Davies, 16 Dec. 1802 and n. 3), and was working on a volume of more ballads.

4. Or *mounture,* a mount or riding animal.

5. John Sargent of Woollavington, a neighbor and author of *The Mine,* and his wife had been friends of CS as early as 1784 (see CS to James Dodsley, 4 May 1784 and n. 4).

6. Possibly, "weekly card games with endless idle chatter." Though the word is clearly spelled "twodville," CS may have intended a nonsense word, *twadville,* based on a favorite cant word of hers, *twaddle.* She elsewhere refers to "being accused of twaddling" and to Hayley's "talents in such twadling" (see CS to Sarah Rose, 18 Apr. 1804 and 1 Jan. 1805).

7. First published by Maria Edgeworth in 1795.

8. *The Modern Griselda* was published in 1805. Two "Irish literates" with whom CS is known to have corresponded are Andrew Caldwell and Joseph Cooper Walker.

9. *Belinda* was published in 1801. See CS's reaction to it in her letter to Joseph Cooper Walker, [late Mar.–early Apr. 1802] and n. 5.

10. The cottage rented by Mr. Johnstone. Its owner is not identified. See CS to Samuel Rose, 9 Sept. 1802 and n. 3.

11. Long and exacting labor.

12. Lieutenant John Galway of the 16th (Buckinghamshire) Regiment, probably Lionel's brother-in-law.

13. Captain Francis Carleton.

14. The press of William Lane, who produced what CS considered "trumpery Novels" (CS to Cadell and Davies, 5 Jan. 1796).

To William Tyler

[?Elsted, received 15 September 1804]
Sir,

The speech you made was reported to me by the late Mr Newhouse, who heard it at Petworth (but I know not from whom) so long since as 1799. I gave no credit to it then tho it was frequently repeated, but your whole conduct & the inveteracy with which I have been pursued ever since leave me little doubt that whether you used precisely those words or no, your meaning was, & is, to do me & my children as much injury as you can. You have oblig'd me, Mr Tyler, to speak plainly by the rudeness and impertinence of your manner as well as by the real injury you have done me. But I should have resented it less if you had not made a point of insulting my daughter.[1] In 1802 when there was a necessity to transfer my Son Charles's money to her, part of which she wanted at a particular period of time to assist her Brother Lionel in his promotion, You chose to raise every possible difficulty & to create every possible delay, & when these delays were complain'd of, you said with great nonchalence that it could not signify when she was to have the money so long as she had the interest, & as that was your opinion, you kept her a month in town at the expence of near 30£.

I might recall many other instances of overbearing & insulting manners, but I have something else to do than to fatigue my spirits by recurring to such humiliating recollections. It is in being thus exposed that the bitterness of Mr B Smiths robbery is the most severely felt. However I must refer to your behavior towards Miss Smith in January last, which was so very rude and impertinent (when you saw her at her lodgings in town) that you was yourself conscious you had gone too far & desired Mr E. Bridger[2] to make your excuses to her. But I, Sir, do not easily forget such an unworthy proof of your unfeeling and ungentleman like conduct, & as I cannot beleive Lord Egremont authorises such behaviour to defenceless Women whom his Lordship generously undertook to protect, I was much disposed to complain of it at the time, but she desired me to let it pass——

If it were worth while, I could bring proof that in no one instance any thing I have desired in the affairs has ever been done, but my asking to have it done was quite sufficient to determine that it should be omitted or executed in some other way. As to M^r B Smith, bad as he has always been and violating every duty towards me and his children, he never so entirely threw off every pretence to common humanity as since the year 1801 when he was told he had a right to take every thing from me, & when you observed that it was his fortune not mine. Since that period, Lord Egremont who took up my cause for no other reason than because he thought me injur'd and oppressd has taken a direct part against me tho I am very sure his Lordship, were he to condescend to go back to what has pass'd, cannot in candour prove that in any one instance, I have done any thing wrong in regard to my children or towards any one, or that cruelly treated & harshly stigmatized as I have been, I have ever for a moment forgotten the respect his rank & still more his former friendship and goodness demand from me & which (treat me as he will) I shall never cease to feel. His goodness & benevolence is all his own—when he lays those qualities aside in regard to me, I impute it to the enmity of others, who have more opportunities than I have of influencing his opinion— —

You are a Lawyer, Mr Tyler, and know how to give whatever colour you please to your assertions &, I dare say, are delighted at having the power to treat me with rudeness and indignity. But I am every way unequal indeed, Good Sir, to having any demele[3] with you. I have not read your Letter thro, for I have other business to do to day, but no doubt you can write me down as you talk me down when there is any question of business. I cannot imagine, Sir, why you should take upon you to remark on what I said alluding to M^r B Smith, that, as he was of opinion I did not want money because I could write, I must avail myself of that talent (as the only support he could not take from me) & shew him that I could write & could draw. This is a boast which is, it seems, most offensive. But no motive less powerful than self defence would have engaged me to say what I have done, or will ever engage me to embitter my mind with the contemplation of a character so disgraceful to his family, as is M^r B Smith.

But if I am not only to be reduced with his children to want, but am to be continually declaim'd against by Lord Egremont who once thought so differently of me and who now, I am sure, cannot say I have deserved such cruel additional mortifications, If such Letters as M^r B— Smiths to me are to be approved of by Lord Egremont while mine (on a plain matter of business & with as little bitterness as it was possible on such an occasion towards such a Man to use) was condemned as scurrilous & as provoking a reply that nothing should have provoked from a Gentleman or a Man towards the lowest of beings—When I know that this Man has been declared in public company to have more merit than I have, & his unoffending unfortunate children, whom he has reduced by folly to that indigence which thus lays us open to the contempt of the affluent—I must be allowed to use such weapons as are left me to do myself Justice and to repel insult.

I am poor, Sir, but not by my own fault, & nothing is really degrading but doing ill. It will not be doing ill to vindicate my own conduct, never calld in question 'till lately but praised and admired even by his Lordship himself. It will not be doing ill to hold up to parents the misery & mischief that may arise from sacrificing their children in early life to false and vain speculations. But Very certainly I shall be very glad to have no occasion to do this tho nobody has any thing to do between me & Mr B S, & I am much better pleas'd to be occupied in the pursuit of objects very different from any that can arise in having the hideous portrait of an unnatural & unfeeling father, or in such a correspondence as this. You will therefore have no more letters to complain of from Sir, ~~Charlotte Smith~~[4]

Petworth House Archives MS. No address or postmark.

NOTES

1. Charlotte Mary.
2. An associate of William Tyler, not identified.
3. Contention, quarrel, or—especially appropriate for this family—litigation.
4. CS wrote two brief letters to Tyler almost two years later dealing tersely with business matters. See CS to Tyler, 18 May and 14 Aug. 1806.

There are two notes at the top of the page. The first, in one hand, says, "Not answered/ E." The second is in Tyler's hand: "(Recvd 15 Sept 1804 from Lord E. to whom it had been enclosed two or three days before (as his Lordship says) but his Lordship had not opened the Letter, with the determination to read no new Letter from Mrs Smith, whilst she remained in so <abusive> a temper)." Tyler has written numerous responses between the lines, but his handwriting is always difficult at best, and these comments cannot be deciphered.

To the earl of Egremont

Bignor Park
Octr 27th 1804
My Lord,

The enclos'd accounts for Mr Adams's long silence. It is to be apprehended that his kind intentions will be frustrated as such an illness threatens the most alarming consequences, tho he is not yet above five and thirty.[1]

I beg leave to submit to y^{r} Ldship whether some measures should not be taken immediately under Mr Adams's direction both with regard to Griffith's & Pindars affairs.[2] As I beleive I may say without arrogance that Mr Tyler cannot possibly understand the concerns so well as I do, who have served a long apprenticeship to these wretched relicts of property in Barbados,

I offer myself under yr Lordships directions to write any letters or do any thing in them that you may think proper to save expence to the Estate & prevent the trouble & [*sic*] inevitably occurs where the business is not distinctly understood. I would suggest some circumstances in regard to the detention of all the property, & the reasons given for that detention, which do not seem to have occurred to you, but I am so unwilling to give any farther offence that I see my family suffer & condemn myself to silence—Hopeless of doing any good when every thing I attempt is misunderstood—— I wish however your Ldship w^d^ allow me an Opportunity of explaining myself. I have the honor to be

My Lord,
your most humble &
obed^t^ Ser^t^,
Charlotte ~~Smith~~

Petworth House Archives MS. No address or postmark.

NOTES

1. CS copied part of a letter from Adams. He had been confined to bed for eleven weeks after a blood vessel burst, and was not yet well enough to conduct business.

All previous correspondence from Adams was from Barbados. It is not clear when, if ever, Adams was at Frant, given on the inside address below. In Oct. 1804, CS was living in Elsted and visited her sister Mrs. Dorset at Bignor Park. "Frant" might be a copying error.

Copy of part of a Ltter from Mr Adams

Frant, Octr 22nd
1804
Dear Madam

When your last letter was put into my hands I was extremely ill in bed, where I had been confined for eleven weeks by the bursting of a blood vessel—I am now thank God, so far recover'd as to be able to come down stairs, but am not permitted to attend to any business—— Yet I can not longer delay acknowledging, however briefly, your last favor

---

I certainly consider myself responsible to Lord Egremont & Mr Turner for the part I have acted under their authority & you will oblige me by saying to his Lordship that I shall most willingly afford the trust any information that may be required ——

---

2. See CS to Egremont, 8 Sept. 1804 and n. 2.

To the earl of Egremont and the Reverend Nicholas Turner

{Bignor Park, 5 November 1804}

To the Earl of Egremont and the Rev[d] Nich[s] Turner

My Lord and Sir,

The discouragement I have constantly receivd from the Trust, however necessary the application, would effectually deter me from repeating it on my own account, but the duty I still owe to the unfortunate young people whose interest was, as I understood, the original object of the Trust urges me not to desist, Notwithstanding the contempt and hard treatment I have of late invariably met with.

My youngest Son[1] has been promoted by the favor of friends he has made to the adjutancy of the 96th Regiment with the rank of Leiutenant which he now holds in the 47th—— A promotion that, while it proves his good conduct & so merit in his profession for so young a Man, is a considerable advantage in regard to pay and will enable him hereafter to support himself without the assistance he has hitherto received from me, Assistance which, tho I have no reason to accuse him of extravagance, has been yearly more than 2/3[rds] of the income of my own fortune, that after M[r] Benj[n] Smiths[2] wicked injustice & my long support of his family is left to me—— It is however necessary at this juncture to supply Lieu[t] George Smith with a sum of money, as the removal to another Reg[t] is always attended with considerable expence, besides which the 96th is under orders of embarkation for the West Indies & may embark from Corke where it is now station'd in a very short time.

It were useless for me to say how painful that destination is to me, but I may remark that it would be still more so if I was oblig'd to see him go without the necessary accommodations for that climate. I have therefore desir'd him to draw upon me ~~xxxxxxxxx~~ at—— at two months, for the Sum requisite which will be 70£, & I have to day heard that he has done so in fav[r] of the paymaster[3] of the 47th Reg[t] who has advanced him the money.

I have no means of providing this Money which is to be paid into the hands of Pybus & Co but by giving up for this purpose the half yearly dividend (as far as it will go) which is payable in January next & supplying the rest as well as I can. This will leave me entirely destitute of support, as the remittances from my Son Nicholas are always uncertain & will probably be later than usual on account of his having gone in his professional capacity to Calcutta where his stay is precarious.

My request therefore to you, My Lord and Sir, is that you will be pleased to guarantee to Mess[rs] Pybus the advanced pay[t] of my dividend for one half year, if I should want it; that is to say, that the dividend due in January may be applied as far as it will go to Georges use & that I may notwithstanding borrow the like amount on the credit of the succeeding half year, i.e. that becoming due in July 1805 should the delay of remittances or any other circumstance reduce me to the necessity of requiring it for my actual support.

I might with justice remark on the unnatural & every way infamous conduct of M[r] B Smith, who (to say nothing of his former long course of direct robbery so well known to M[r] Turner) has had, since the existence of the present trust, at least 1200£ that ought to have belong'd to the residue, & of course in part to this young Man, whom my deprivations, or my labour only, have maintaind from his earliest infancy to the present hour, While his brutal father has refused him the smallest assistance & has escaped from every claim that honesty, honor, or natural affection ought to have had upon him— —There was a time when Lord Egremont & my Brother would have seen this matter in a light when no representation of mine would have been wanting; now, whatever I say will probably be disregarded if not considerd as offensive—God knows why! but conscious that I have in no way deserved the treatment I am subjected to, I have only to Solicit, my Lord & Sir, your early answer, directed to me at Elsted whither I return tomorrow, and leave this in my way thro Petworth.

I am, my Lord and Sir,
your obed[t] humble Ser[t],
Charlotte ~~Smith~~

Bignor Park,
Nov[r] 5th 1804
I should have added that to prevent the Trust from having any apprehension of losing this Sum should I die before July 1805, I will in that case give them or rather they may take security on the money still due from M[r] Nicholas Smith, over which I have unlimited power, but I am extremely unwilling to sell any money out of the stocks, he having already done so much for me & his family & having an encreasing family of his own—— I humbly request an early & decisive answer.

Petworth House Archives MS. Address: To the Earl of Egremont &/ The Rev[d] Nicholas Turner. No postmark.

NOTES

1. George. The *Army List* for 1805 shows George A. Smith to be a lieutenant in the army as of 9 July 1803, and in his regiment as of 12 Oct. 1804. He is also listed as adjutant. His commander was Major General George James Ludlow.

BS was deeply offended by CS's initiative and success; he believed she had made him look the fool (see CS to Sarah Rose, 24 Nov. 1804, n. 5).

2. CS had earlier vowed never to write his name again (see CS to BS, 5 July 1804). Here she has drawn a line through it.

3. Mr. Phillips.

To the earl of Egremont and the Reverend Nicholas Turner

[?Elsted, after 5 November 1804]
My Lord & Sir,

On an occasion when all I ask'd was the assurance that I should have one half year in advance, when I applied the next to the absolute wants of my youngest Son, whom in all probability I shall never see again, I did flatter myself that the enmity you have on other occasions lately shewn towards me would have for once have been suspended & that you would not aggravate distress already so acute, by delay & contempt. My Son has written to me, which letter I received to day to inform me that the ships are now in the Cove of Cork ready to receive them on board for the West Indies & that he is going without many of the necessaries requisite. I have no means on Earth to raise the money, but that I proposed, & that I must do at all events. Yet hard as my situation is & almost insupportable, I should still find more resolution to bear it, were it not embitterd by the excessive cruelty that condemns me to all these sufferings when I expected & was promis'd protection and assistance, while Mr Benjn Smith is sufferd to forget every duty he owes his children & on occasions of the most urgent necessity is never calld upon. Complaint however from me, who resisted the torrent of adversity for so many years only to prolong unheard of tortures to be crushd at last by the hatred of those who offerd their friendship, or from a quarter whence I had a natural right to claim it—Complaint is vain. But an answer, My Lord & Sir, is due in matters of business to the lowest of applicants. I therefore once again humbly request an answer by an early post, as Mr Phillips, paymaster of the 47th who has advanc'd the money on Georges word only, is uneasy at not having heard from me in the due course, as he had a right to expect. To day I must write to him to tell him he shall have my half years dividend, & I must once more trust to chance for bread—— I cannot exert myself with an heart so oppressd. Oh! my children—thus ends all my long long solicitudes for you. I am, My Lord and Sir,

Your humble Ser^t^,
Charlotte Smith

Petworth House Archives MS. Address: Earl of Egremont/ &/ Revd Nich^s^ Turner. No postmark.

To Sarah Rose

Elsted—Novr 24th 1804

My Dear Madam,

If you knew how apprehensive I am that this Letter may find you as uneasy as when you last had the goodness to write to me, you would beleive that only the peculiarity of my situation would induce me to trouble you, unless I were sure that your own anxieties were at an end.[1] Brief let me be—& let me if possible write to you a clearer Letter than I have just done to Mr Johnson. My youngest Son George, who from having been abandon'd by his cruel father in his infancy I have always calld tout a moi[2] (& I beleive loved him better because he had no other dependence) has Within these three weeks exchanged from the 47th Regiment into the 96th for the great advantage of being appointed to the Adjutancy by favor of the Colonel, A circumstance highly honourable to his industry and proficiency at so early an age as 19 in his perilous profession.

Poor fellow! he knew when he did it the Reg^{t} was going to the West Indies, but he knew also the encrease of income which it nearly doubles would releive me from the support I have hitherto most willingly but with great difficulty afforded him—— Nothing of that sort could be half so painful to me as his going to the W. Indies, & suffering as I have done the loss of my unfortunate Charles, & dreading every account from Surinam,[3] this is a stroke of itself heavy enough to overcome my little courage and resolution——

One would therefore have thought that common humanity would have interested Lord Egremont & Mr Turner not to have refused me such alleviations as the trifling favor I ask'd of them would have given me. George has, in consequence of the expences of the Exchange and of the necessaries requir'd for his dreadful destination, occasion for 70£ & has drawn on me for it. I wrote to Lord Egremont, stating my reasons for requesting of the Trustees only to guarantee to Messrs Pybus & Co. an advance of my next dividend to help make up this Sum & that if my second remittances do not come in before, they would authorise Messrs Pybus to let me have on the security of my July dividend as much as will prevent my actually wanting the necessaries of life. Pybus will not do it without such guarantee, least I should die in the mean time when every thing I have falls to [that detested monster] whose name I never willingly write, but the risk to the Trustees is nothing because they have 80£ of Nicholas's with which, if I should die, they might repay themselves; if the brute (as no doubt he would) should refuse to allow this tho for his own child, They could not have lost a sous!——

Yet does [Lord Egremont & Mr Turner]—my noble Maecenas[4] & my Brother—(that Brother who found a friend in me when he had no other)—refuse this?[5] Yes—my anguish at the departure of my son makes no impression on them. They aggravate it by cruelty and leave me to struggle either with poverty or with the misery of knowing he must go unprovided. I embrace the former. But surely, my dear Madam, no destiny ever equalld mine. No cruelty can be compard to theirs!

I have been writing to Mr Johnson for whom I have a work in two volumes so nearly ready,[6] I dare say he will be so good as to afford me some small present assistance in default of the money wch I must appropriate to George, but which w^d^ otherwise have paid bills now nearly due, & my request to you, my dear Madam, is that you will be so good as to say to Mr Rose that Mr Johnson is to receive for me the small modicum[7] paid on account of my unfortunate friend Foville As he, Mr Johnson, will I beleive (at least I have ask'd it of him) pay a bill I have desird my poor boy to draw for immediate necessaries from Corke where he waits under embarkation orders so that I have had no time to lose & was forced to have recourse to any.[8]

Huntington MS (HM10840). No address or postmark.

NOTES

1. Sarah Rose's husband Samuel, grievously ill with consumption, died on 20 Dec. William Hayley described the illness as a "rapid and incurable decay," adding that Rose's "disorder after much lingering pain borne by him with uncommon patience proved fatal" (WSRO add. MS. 2458, p. 8).

2. All mine.

3. Where Lionel was stationed.

4. The aristocratic patron of Horace, Vergil, and Propertius.

5. Perhaps they did. Or perhaps their refusal made her try if moderation would work with BS. In any event trust business went on, and she wrote to BS presumably about the engagement of their youngest daughter Harriet. From Berwick, he wrote to Egremont on 7 Dec. 1804, including a copy of his response to CS:

> Madam
>
> I received your letter of the 29th Novr this Morning, & as it is wrote with temper, & moderation claims my notice. The information it gives me of Harriot being so well settled, makes me very happy, & I will do any thing in my power to contribute towards her welfare. You have been misinform'd, as you have often been, in regard to my objecting to allow her £60 p^r^ ann^m^, it was the mode in which it is done in the award, that I was not pleased with, as this allowance is not in her Name—— I will accede to your proposals, but shall expect Mr Galway will keep his word in regard to the £100, as I am very much involved, & find it utterly impossible to make my small Income (£109) do; & I am therefore determined to give up Housekeeping. I have several Old bills yet to pay in Glasgow, & Hamilton, one of which is for Medicines from Octr 1799 to 17th April 1804 being 4 years & 7 Months, to the amount of £20.1.4 with an addition of Ten Guineas for attendance on my lame Leg, & two severe sickness, & the person is very urgent for payment——

One part of your letter is very ambiguous, & must be explained, you say, "I have lately had the unexpected good fortune to acquire so far as relates to my Sons an Interest with a person who must at some period & that period not very remote have the power to prove his kindness in the most effectual manner, if by these means George is promoted to a Company & Lionels life is spared & by <routine?> or by Interest becomes a Lieu Colonel neither of which are improbable they would not in that Case be under this obligation"——

So that after you have got me to do what you want, it may be said these preferments were acquired by Interest, & the terms of executing the irrevocable Deed annul'd, & myself laugh'd at. I must be fairly dealt by, if I am to gratify you, & my family in your wishes. I hope Georges Exchange from the 47th to the 96 Reg^{t} may be advantageous to him, but in case of peace the Reg^{t} is sure to be broke, & Colonel Dalrymple did assure me, when I ask'd it of him, that he would do every thing in his power for George, & soon after he got his Lieutenancy.

I shall be happy to hear from Harriet, & with love to her I am Madam . . . (unpub. letter in PHA #0.11)

6. As Johnson had published the two-volume *Conversations Introducing Poetry* at a price suggested by Samuel Rose (£125), CS may refer here to her *Natural History of Birds,* published by Johnson after her death.

7. Barely more than £2 (see CS to Sarah Rose, 16 July 1804, n. 4).

8. The rest of the letter, including the signature, is missing, with the third and fourth pages of the usual folded letter torn away.

1805–1806
"A PRISON & A GRAVE"

—18 JUNE 1806

Charlotte Smith's last years were solitary, impoverished, and embattled. Someone else completed the third volume of her History of England . . . to a young lady at school *because of her failing health. Two other works were published posthumously in 1807: her final volume of poetry,* Beachy Head, *and the last children's book,* The Natural History of Birds.

Apart from visiting her sister at the old family seat, Bignor Park, she lived bedridden at home, crippled and beset with rheumatism, dropsy, and probably uterine cancer. In October 1805, she moved one last time, from Elsted to the even poorer town of Tilford near Farnham. In February 1806, Benjamin Smith died in debtors' prison, substantiating her many assertions about his flawed character. Six months later, Charlotte Smith herself died at Tilford. The few months of respite from his claims against her income were not enough to settle the entangled trust. Upon his death, she felt freer to describe his offenses, and so her last letters paint the darkest portrait of all.

Her sons continued much as before: Lionel and George advanced in the military, Nicholas sent payments and grandchildren from India, William had not written since his rift with his mother in 1800. Lucy and her three children were established in a small cottage at North Chapel near Petworth. Charlotte Mary, living with relatives, intervened as best she could in her mother's quarrels with the earl of Egremont. Harriet had fewer and less alarming episodes of illness and became engaged to William Geary, a young man of the neighborhood, whom her mother admired. Lacking prospects, the couple could marry only after Charlotte Smith died, on the strength of settlements she had arranged. But also after her death, tragically in keeping with the family's misfortunes, news came that George had died, as his mother feared, of yellow fever in Surinam.

To an Unnamed Recipient

Elsted. Jany 1st
1805
My Dear Madam,

In Harriet's absence, who is on a visit at some distance, and because the envellope of your Letter was directed to me, I open'd your obliging recollection of her & of me—— I have many apologies to make for not having sooner return'd Sir Wm Jones. Nor should Harriet so long have detain'd those books you were so good as to lend her, but she has not been at home for above a week since you left Surrey, and I have been either absent or sick or so out of heart and hope that I had no courage to set about any thing——

Thank God, I have heard that my Major[1] was safe the 21st of September & had preserved his health till then, & mon tout a moi my youngest Son who had actually embarked for the West Indies, was by a sudden and very extraordinary change, disembarked & the Regiment are gone into Barracks about fourteen miles from Corke, & this, tho I know it to be only a transient reprieve, is a great releif to my spirits. <__________________________>[2] the cruelty and oppression he has suffer'd <_______> & besides the particular attention this has calld forth, he is as fond of his Mother as his Mother of him & is a pretty fellow to look at, which you know always has some influence on Mamma's vanity. He has now obtaind, tho only nineteen, an Adjutancy in the 96th. But all my hope has been to get a company for him, & that, in a Regiment not going to that detestable Country; & this, & some endeavours I have been using to procure Lionel's removal from that hideous Surinam, would have occupied greater powers of application than my wretched health has left me & allowed me hardly any time to think of the pleasurable part of my reduced existence—the friends who honor me with their kind partiality. I shall send my Servant to Guildford in a few days & will take care your books shall be carefully conveyd thither for Albury, for I expect Harriet (who has lockd up some of them) home on Thursday——

I wish I could answer satisfactorily your enquiry about my having found an House. I have hardly made an <acqui>sition lately because the period is arrived when I am in daily expectations of hearing from my Son Nicholas: & on his decision in regard to sending over his family, my movements must depend. I am extremely unwilling to go near London, but I must be where instruction can be had for the children with which I shall probably be instructed.[3] Unless I can hear of a French Woman or a Swiss with whose assistance all I wish to have them learn might be acquired at home. But this is so very difficult that I quite despair of its being atchieved. Here is a vast deal about myself, & it is more than time to say, that I hope you will not again lose sight of me, as you have powers of which my miserable health deprives me— —

It was probable I thought that before this time Harriet's marriage would have taken place, which I confess would have given me great satisfaction.[4] But tho the Shepherd is faithful, there are impediments which I fear will make it much later than I expected.

I hear to day that Miss Edgeworth's new Something, yclept Griselda[5] (for she disclaims the Name of Novel), is advertised. I shall be desirous of seeing it for there is undoubtedly a vein of good writing in the family. But I ~~thought~~ opined that Belinda was a disagreeable book. I thought I had renounced Novel reading as well as Novel writing, but as I had "the nobility of the heart"[6] sent me by the Authoress & had seen it in MMS, I was under a necessity of looking into it. The Lady has not much ability, & the book is like most of those we now see, compounded of many others & patched like the petticoat of Otway's Old Woman.[7] I strongly remonstrated against the slip of Mrs Radcliff's winding sheet, which is without keeping or meaning, but some other of her friends voted for the Ghost. There is a greater fault, which is here & there the total absence of good English. Yet now it is printed, it is really as well as many other books of the sort & nearly as well as "the lake of Killarney"[8] which is also a sort of Salmagundi collected from other books. We shall see soon what Mr Godwin's new production is. Surely Novel writing is not his forte but his foible—— If you are an admirer of Mr Hayley's, if ever he has found favor in your sight, Do not, oh! do not read his "Triumph of Music."[9] I am really vexd with him for frittering away his talents in such twadling, & love him well enough to be sorry he should be laugh'd at for these <lacry>matory epilogues to his voluminous writings. Since he has had so much connection with the folks that destroy'd the peace of poor Cowper's life by their frantic enthusiasm, he certainly has caught the infection.[10]

J. Pierpont Morgan MS. No address or postmark.

NOTES

1. Lionel. George is the youngest son named later in the sentence.

2. This half line and the word below are missing, as if erased.

3. Probably a hasty misspelling for *entrusted.*

4. Harriet was engaged to a neighbor, William Geary, whom she married on 20 Jan. 1807, less than two months after her mother's death. Their union depended on Harriet's inheriting her portion of her mother's marriage settlements. (See Harriet Geary in Biographical Notes.)

5. *The Modern Griselda* (1805).

6. The second novel (1804) by Elizabeth Isabella Spence (1768–1832), also a travel writer. Despite CS's harsh judgment, Spence published five more novels and a title containing two novellas.

7. In Thomas Otway's *The Orphan* (1680), the heroine's brother Chamount tells of meeting an old hag who urges him to hurry to save his sister. In addition to a "tatter'd Remnant" hanging about her shoulders,

> Her lower weeds were all o're coursely patch'd
> With diff'rent colour'd Rags, black, red, white, yellow,
> And seem'd to speak variety of wretchedness. (2.254–56)

8. The fourth novel (1804) by Anna Maria Porter (1780–1832).
9. Hayley's *The Triumph of Music* (1804) was widely ridiculed.
10. The lower half of the second leaf is cut away. There is no handwriting by CS on the back of it but a note in another hand, "The handwriting of Charlotte Smith."

To Sarah Rose

Elsted—Feby 14th
S^t follenternet S^t [1805]
My Dear Madam,

There needed no apology to me for the mention of the business which, tho the Sum is trifling, I feel may be attended with considerable inconvenience to you. I am however utterly ignorant how to proceed, & there is no hope of obtaining any information or direction from M^r De Foville who, poor fellow, dares not I fear write to me if he is at Rouen. I endeavourd to get a Letter conveyed to him many months ago but have reason to beleive it never reach'd him. It is not however more true than strange that I do not know under what power Mr Rose transacted the business for him, & I wish'd to have applied to you to know, but I had not the heart to tieze you about a matter in which I did not know <u>your</u> pecuniary matters were in any degree implicated. In his last Letter to me dated in January 1803, & consequently more than twelve months ago, poor Foville desired me to apply to Mr Rose to request that he would have the goodness to receive <u>again</u> the marriage articles between him & my lost lovely Augusta, which were sent to Mr Tayler,[1] when I hoped to have had the matter adjusted more to the satisfaction of De Foville than it was at last done by the Trustees & much more to the benefit of the estate. But <u>my</u> wishing and proposing it or its being to serve him (De F) were quite reasons sufficient with the noble Lord to decide that it should <u>not</u> be so.

On the same principle, the worthy Trustees have lately lost 1500£ of my poor luckless childrens which my friend Mr Adams would have recoverd while he was in Barbados but, because <u>I</u> desired to have certain papers he had written for sent out under the City seal, & Mr Tyler, Lord Egremonts Steward, thought he knew better than Mr Adams, & because <u>I</u> earnestly pressed it from my knowledge of the parties, it was refused till Mr Adams came home, who would otherwise have brought the money with him, & it is lost as well as 300£ more.[2]

I am wandering, as you will think from the question, but the meaning is that I wish you, my dear Madam, to be assured that whatever depends on me I will instantly do. And as soon as the money can be received, I will pay it to you or to your order. But I am under the necessity of requesting that your Solicitor will tell me how & to whom I am to apply & under what power Mr Rose acted. De Foville inform'd me that Mr Rose had kindly undertaken to receive the trifle half yearly & to pay it to me. I suppose my receipt will be sufficient, but that also, as I have not given it, your Attorney must tell me— —Mr Turner who was my Brother by Birth & by inclination, as long as I had the power to do him service, And Mr Hayley, who was my friend but whose aversion from trouble of any sort is much stronger than any friendship he is now likely to retain for me, are as you know the Trustees. To neither of them would De Foville desire me to put myself under any obligations—No, not even to answer a Letter. Mr Turner, who was born & might have continued an independent Gentleman, is now the humble creature of Lord Egremont, and Mr Hayley seems to me, if a judgement can be form'd by his last Poem, to be sinking into actual mental imbecility.

Every mention of my Augusta, tho almost ten miserable years are gone by since she was torn from me (under circumstances that pour'd vitriol & acquafortis[3] into a wound otherwise incurable), Every mention of my darling child tears my heart to pieces. But to these feeling[s] which few understand & few care for, tho I am sure you are of that few, I must not sacrifice a moment of your time at the present sad crisis. Be therefore, my dear Madam, so good as to get your Solicitor to tell me in as plain a way as he can how the money not received at the Bank but which Mr Rose advanced can now be received, & I will proceed to recover it for you by any means he yr Solicitor shall direct. I was totally ignorant that Mr Rose had not reimbursed himself. Tho in one of his Letters he says I send you the 7£ <adv[ance]>, tho the power is still unaccepted I think is the word but I will look out his Letters, which as they were all on business I never destroyed— —

While that cruel illness lasted which I was unwilling to beleive would terminate at his time of life so fatally, I wrote to beg to know how I could receive the Jany dividend. My poor George, now gone to the West Indies, had always had this little pittance applied to his use (To him on his being order'd to that horrid climate, I was under the necessity of applying all that his inhuman & unnatural father has left me of income, but I wanted 9£ to make up the Sum he had drawn on me for necessaries for his voyage. As the Bill from the paymaster of the 47th lay in Pybus's hands,[4] I ask'd them (since they receive my small dividends) to advance me the 9£ only till Miss Smith could go to Town who was delay'd from day to day by illness in my family—— But tho at that very time & for some months back the Pybus's have had 700£ of Trust money lying in their hands to play with pr Favor of the noble Lord, they refused me & refus'd me with insolence this small favor for my young soldier———

My son Nicholas's journey to Calcutta has delay'd my remittances. I fear I have no Letters by these Ships, & I am utterly on the pavee & have considerably overdrawn Johnson[5] Which however would not have happen'd if I could have finishd another little work I am about. But illness & vexations of many sorts have lately fallen heavily on me. So heavily indeed that I again thought my troubles were reaching their last period, & two days ago I supposed a few more would end them. I now write with two blisters on my breast. My dear Madam, it grieves my very soul that you are suffering so much uneasiness and distress of mind, & on few occasions I have felt more that deprivation which leaves me only words worth nothing to express how truly I feel what you have to undergo.[6] I know nothing from report, for Mr Bicknell[7] only said he hoped you were left in tolerable circumstances, but there was a coldness & strangeness about his manner which I did not like.

As I have been now for many years strugling with adversity in all its forms and know that it is too often the very want of friends that prevents our having them, I was very glad to learn what I thought your former letter intimated—that you had found such. But even if you should meet in that respect with the usual fate of the unfortunate & learn from sad experience that there is little good among Men, still your solicitudes are for the children of a Man you loved, and every exertion of your fortitude will be scanctified & sweeten'd, While I have labourd for the children of one who lived only to disgrace them & insult me, while he render'd those labours abortive & make me every day & every hour ashamed that I had ever been sold the victim of a ~~Man~~ being, human only in form. Nor even now at this late period are my troubles over—rather I think encreasing. Harriet is not married, nor can I get any thing done by Mr Smith which ought to be done before I can propose settlements for her. The more reasons I have for wishing the agreement about future property to be drawn up, the more he holds out against it—unless his Sons will pay him! & ~~such~~ most extraordinary is his present manner of going on, & not abjectly is he begging for that money which he lays out as I have lately learned in a collection of scarce books, a new hobby horse of his, tho he cannot write even his own language.[8] This is too much. His whole life has been passd in the practice of some strange folly or degrading vice, & at 63 he is worse than ever.

Often have I said "Tout finit, permis mes malheurs!"[9] I have now been married 40 years! "Forty years long have I!!" & do not know whether sick & broken as I am in constitution from the pressure of so many years of misery, I may not [*sic*] even now have to look out for the means of subsistence.

My daughter Lucy ~~who~~ married, much against my wishes, a Man (who too soon justified my opinion of him & used her so ill that had he lived I must have taken her home for he turn'd her out of doors), has three children to support on nothing but the interest of the fortune her Grandfather left her which is under 2000£ & much of that was gone, while her husband lived. Of course I cannot see her want while I can supply her by denying myself or by my labour, but there is misery entaild upon that connection (for to the family of the Man I had unconquerable objections) which makes me shudder to look forward tho the eyes that have been open'd five & fifty years wanting some months on this Sun & all its clouds & storms have no business to look forward to any thing.

My dear Mrs Rose, I should detest myself if I did not love you, tho yet we are personally strangers, much better than I did before your cruel loss & if I did not feel every wish to convince you of it, but I have felt in my long & weary pilgrimage that there are occasions when even expressions of regard become something very like insults. Therefore, tremblingly alive as I still am and bleeding at every pore, [I] am afraid of saying how much I sympathise with you. Fastidious refinement has occasiond such an abuse of terms that it is not easy to avoid those that have a thousand times disgusted me by their sounding so like common place cant. When I fell from the situation of high affluence, tho God knows it never gave me one hours true satisfaction, to that of being obliged to wander as I could round the world & on 70£ a year support eight children, I had advice given me by persons who had before fed me only with flattery, and I underwent insult & persecution from the proud & the profligate. The purse proud Tradesman and the rapacious Attorney, The relation of my children who had sneaked for a subsistence into their family, all were like the birds of ill omen that surround a dying animal, ready to pluck me limb from limb. I look back now with wonder & cannot recall to my mind how I found strength to contend with it all. Yet all was as nothing, compared to the misery I was sometimes forced to undergo of visits from Mr Smith—— If comparison ever alleviates evil, I may indeed say that, great & grievous as those are which you are called upon to sustain, they cannot equal mine.

My dear Madam, Charlotte went to town only yesterday. She will most certainly see you if you will admit her. To avoid all farther trouble, I would send you a draft for the overpay[men][t] if I had it, but till Bombay remittances come, I am a bankrupt. I find I must as soon as Harriet is married take to some less expensive mode of life— —I know not how, as I have God knows nothing now but common necessaries.

I send this up to Charlotte to forward to you— —But you will not receive it till Monday I fear. I have written it with a trembling hand and an aching heart. My Apothecary has been talking to me part of the time about nerves and flatulence, & my back & legs ache like those of one of Shakespeares old Nurses.[10]

My Novel finish'd? Oh no—Johnson <throes> some cold water upon it: he thought I might do better.[11] Sickness and sorrow [. . .] more, & the setting sun throws not on my mind such go<lden char>ms as gild those of our friend Sophia.[12] The reason perhaps <is> that her Amatory scenes are all ideal & sylphish, While mine have been restricted to one who contrived to create only abhorrence & disgust— —I am so often ill & so constantly weak that I have no courage to set about a work where so much of imagination is required & where there is so much bodily labour as the act of writing is to me. You will see it is so by this wretched scrabble. I have not written to Mr Hayley (or as he calls himself, the Dear Brother of Parnassus) to thank him for the Copy of the Triumph of Music because it was so repugnant to me to say one civil thing upon it.[13] (It should have been dedicated to Mrs Piozzi—"Poor dear Mr Hayley!" he will fiddle away his fame, what little was left.) But if it is necessary on this subject of business to write to him, I will do it.

God bless you & your children, my dear Madam. Beleive me ever most affect[ionate]^ly^ yours,

CS

Huntington MS (HM10834). Address: Mrs Rose/ Chancery Lane/ {London}. No postmark.

NOTES

1. Robert Tayler, a merchant and friend of BS in London.

2. Exact amounts owed are nowhere specified, but these are likely to be sums owed by Griffith, whose debt of £1,700 had been Thomas Maxwell Adams's object since 8 Sept. 1802, and by Francis Foard Pindar, who bought Griffith's estate (see CS to Egremont, 8 Sept. 1804 and n. 2). Money from William Prescod for the purchase of Gay's plantation was still outstanding, but Adams never handled it.

3. Sulfuric acid and nitric acid.

4. Pybus, Call, Grant, and Hale were Egremont's bankers.

5. CS's publisher Joseph Johnson.

6. Sarah's husband, Samuel, had died on 20 Dec. 1804, leaving her with four young sons to raise alone.

7. Charles Bicknell, CS's attorney.

8. These angry assertions were exaggerated if not outright erroneous. BS's surviving letters in PHA #0.11 show a command of the language, its grammar, and its spelling, and at least a passing knowledge of classical allusions and Latin maxims. He also bested his estranged wife in having far more effective dealings with Egremont, always writing short and more deferential letters than hers and also insisting that he was acting in an honorable and gentlemanly way. But he may well have owned few books.

CS seems to have had little or no knowledge of what was happening in BS's life at this time. From Berwick he wrote Tyler on 3 Jan. 1805: "I am now betwixt Scylla & Charibdes, in danger of being incarcerated by the Chancellors Warrant, or by a Writ of Messrs Roe & Doe." He had "only Six pounds left" and complains that he has been "rob'd of my birthright, as well as of large sums due to me; both of which I attribute to Mrs Smiths conduct." On 9 Jan., facing imprisonment and having written his sons in India for £200, he begs Egremont for money now: "my mind is so exceedingly agitated, that it will be an act of humanity to alleviate it" (unpub. letters in PHA #0.11).

Egremont wrote him on 21 Feb., evidently offended that BS had sent him a letter by CS "by her own particular desire." She was forbidden to write him. Having "but a few shillings left," BS allows himself a fairly rare bitter statement: "Ninety Nine just Men, would have thought differently from Mr Rose; and not have thought M[rs] Smith entitled to Alimony, which was given to her, from the influence of oppression, & the power of perjury, dissimulation, & falsehood." BS was probably right about her alimony, as CS had technically deserted him without a proper separation agreement (unpub. letter in PHA #0.11).

These are the last of his letters to survive. Perhaps he wrote no more because he was in the Berwick jail. He died there in Feb. 1806. It is not clear whether CS knew of his arrest or incarceration at the time; she mentions it only after his death.

9. When all is said and done, allow me my misfortunes.

10. Juliet's nurse complains, "Fie! how my bones ache! what a jaunce have I had!" (*Romeo and Juliet* 2.5.26).

11. No final novel was published.

12. The obscured words in this phrase might be "golden beams." CS mocks Sophia Lee's elaborately metaphorical apology in the preface to her *The Life of a Lover* for bringing forth a work

> planned and written at the early age when imagination takes the lead of reason, and the heart occasionally over-rules both. . . . Yet every season of life has a charm peculiar to itself; and we may modify away that of youth, without supplying its place. It may be with intellect as it is with sunshine—the beauty of the day is past when the beams become powerful enough to warm us. (v)

13. See CS to unnamed recipient, 1 Jan. 1805 and n. 9.

To Sarah Rose

[April 1805][1]

This is all sad Egotism, but I mean to say what Lord Bacon has said much better—"that there is none who knoweth the extent of his own endurance till it be put to the proof." May yours, my dear M[rs] Rose, never be so severely tried— —I have not yet heard as usual from India at which I extremely wonder. But I hope the month of May will bring me Letters, & in the mean time, I do a little for Johnson's pay & am trying at a slight story. That which I had begun so long since was a design for a larger canvas than I think it is probable I shall ever have health to fill. I thought Fleetwood[2] very la la—not to say a disagreeable Novel. The Man is represented hateful, & the Woman inconsistent, for now she is about to drown herself for grief at the death of her Father & family, & now she laughs she dances & sings at Bath as if nothing had happen'd. Men very seldom write pleasing Novels. I liked the letters of Miss Riversdale which is said to be the work of M[rs] Damer[3] tho there was in it some great absurdities. I should fill my paper most willingly, but there is a Gentleman who escaped Shipwreck in the Abergavenny, now again embarking for the East Indies, & I must write by him, as my last

Letters were lost. I shall put this under the same packet as carries my India Letters to his house in Town, which obliges me to bid you, my dear Madam, hastily Adieu, & to assure you with Charlottes compliments of the unfailing regard with which I must ever be

very truly your affect[n] Ser[t], Charlotte Smith

I never had any book of shells but pickd up the little information I had here & there. I will enquire what is best. I find "the Elements of natural History," 2 vol. ovo. Cadell & Davies, extremely useful in regard to Quadrupeds, Birds, Reptiles, & insects, & there is also in it the elements of conchology.[4] I think your Sister w[d] find, in the notices printed of works from whence that was compiled, before the book, information where to find what she wishes. I sh[d] be happy to give her any other information.

If you see M[rs] & Miss H Lee,[5] pray remember me to them with regard.

Huntington MS (HM 10826). No address or postmark.

NOTES

1. This letter, dated 1803 in the Huntington collection, was written sometime after 14 Feb. 1805, the date of the preface to the novel *Fleetwood* (see n. 2).

The letter is on a single large sheet whose top third has been torn away at the crease.

2. *Fleetwood: or, the New Man of Feeling,* by William Godwin (1805).

3. Anne Seymour Conway Damer (1748–1828), an accomplished sculptor and author of the novel *Belmour* (1801), is not elsewhere identified as the author of *Letters of Miss Riversdale* (1803).

4. The second edition of *The Elements of Natural History,* by Comte Antoine François de Fourcroy, was published by G. G. J. and J. Robinson (London, 1788).

5. Harriet Lee (see CS to Cadell and Davies, 1 May 1796, n. 4).

To Sarah Rose

Bignor Park, Petworth
May 14th 1805

Be assur'd, my dear Madam, your wish to hear from me is among those circumstances the most flattering that can now happen to me, but indeed you overrate my pretensions in every way so much that I shall, if ever I should have the happiness of meeting you, fear that you will find how unequal I am to the idea your partial friendship has form'd of me. There cannot be a stronger proof that I am <u>not</u> a person to merit a long friendship than the coldness or total estrangement of some of those who once seem'd to think no eulogies were high enough, no professions of regard strong enough to express their attachment and good opinion. I might instance the extraordinary circumstance of a certain noble Lord who, having volunteer'd in the most unusual way to serve me and mine, now treats me with such rudeness & persecutes me with such absurd and unfounded accusations as would not be beleived were I to relate them.

Those spoiled children, noble Lords of prosperous fortune, have seldom any principal or founded meaning in what they do, & I should not have been surprised at having been set down as I was taken up in the whim of the moment, but when this Patron gravely assures my family that all their misfortunes are oweing to me & that the law suit now impending was brought on by me—tho it is between Mr Smiths Nephew and Niece[1] & their Grandfathers property for depredations made, as they alledge, by the manager of their property ten years ago, sixteen, twenty years ago in Barbados, & in which I never had, or can have, the remotest interest or concern—When he tells them (my children) that my conduct has been imprudent, wicked, horrid, I do really ask myself whether something of which I am not aware has not happend & whether I am not in the dream of a delirious disease?— —In the very same letter in which he says all this to my daughter, very lately he tells her that he intends to try if he cannot serve my two Sons in the Army and now in the W. Indies!! So that he seems to endeavour to impress my family with an idea that I am the great object of his resentment, & that but for me all would be well. Veteran as I am, I cannot help feeling this which I believe is extremely foolish.

But let this instance help to account to you (If what is unaccountable ought to be thought about at all) for the frigidity of a ci-devant friend of a very different description, I mean the Bard——. There is something wrong about me, & I was not lucky enough to die while the new was on. Now, I am not a subject that in any way can contribute to Mr H.s. satisfaction, & he seems to have forgotten in how many ways he might serve me without its costing him sixpence, & without interfering with his Teusdays studies—which I hope & trust will produce in time a new & enlarged edition of his Essay on Old Maids.[2] Seriously, I never write to him (which I avoid as much as possible & never on any thing that can give him any trouble) without feeling a most unpleasant sensation in receiving the answer. For there is nothing like real friendship in such terms as "Dear Sister of Parnassus!" "Dear Muse" & such stuff while there appears an evident apprehension that this Parnassian Sister should borrow an hour of that time he can so much better dispose of. I am however sorry for the illness he has lately labour'd under which obliged him, when I wrote to enquire about a printer at Chichester, to employ in <answer> the hand of his femme d'affaire I imagine, & I saw with pain how ill to such a Man the place was supplied, & that he has no friend who can assist him with their pen.

How good you are, my dear Madam, in taking an interest in what I confess mortifies me sometime the dereliction of this old friend, who, upon the footing our friendship was, would I thought have continued so to the end of my life, & I trust, had it been so I should not have <xxxx> his regard too heavily. Here is abundance of Egotism tho, on an matter which I should not have touchd upon had you not named it with so much of that real feeling, which makes me feel as if we had long been personally acquainted and perfectly understood each other——

Among the various trials of a life, which has been occupied by many severe ones since I was fifteen is that I am to undergo tomorrow when I must take leave for ever of this place[3]—The residence of my family for about 100 years, having become my Grandfathers property in his youth in 1707. Beauty of situation & the remembrance of my first & only happy days have always made it particularly agreeable to me, even when peu a peu, I have seen all the fine estates near it which once belongd to my father vanish. This last became—— somehow—— the property of my Sister's husband, for My Brother did not pay as he ought to have done the fortune left to her by my father——& so——Somehow— —Mr Dorset got it. It was still my Sisters, & I hoped would have remain'd so, but her only daughter marrying <a> Man who cannot exist where two courses a day are not to be found without much trouble, it is to go to the hammer!

Well! local attachments are extremely foolish. Yet a little, & unless I am anxious, like a Woman in this neighbourhood, to be buried in a pleasant Church yard "on account of the prospect," it will matter but very little on what Earth my head is pillow'd.

I have got a house to seek however, my lease at Elsted expiring on the 10th of August, & it is rather annoying to me & will a good deal break in on my time to remove, if indeed my ill health leaves me any time, but too much is taken up in attending to this wretched compound of failing nature. I have got a vile cough & am foolishly low tho my account from the W—Indies are as well as I can expect, so far as they go, but that is Heaven knows only a small abatement of miserable solicitude.

I do not wonder, my dear Madam, at your being proud of your Boys; by all I have heard, they are justly your pride & will be your comfort. Boys I think love their Mother better than Girls. At least one only of my four Girls ever loved me, as I fancy I could have loved a Mother, & she is gone to Heaven, the ideal inhabitants of which she most resembled. But my Boys, when young, were all extremely attach'd to Mamma, & of the four who survive, the eldest only, who once was the most so, seems to have changed his mind. (But he is a Man, & Man is [. . .] able & inconsistent being—) I was going to say, but <self> always crosses the [. . .] that I hope none of your Boys will ever go into the Army. The wretched solicitude that must be the portion of a Mother who sees her Sons in that "terrible metier"—I do hope will never be yours. I am in anxious expectation of hearing from my Nicholas at Bombay, a much longer time than usual having elapsed since his last letter, & I cannot help thinking some letters must have been taken. If I do not soon hear, I shall be every way distressd, but Johnson is all liberality & kindness.

I have just finishd another book on subjects of natural History[4] which will go to press I hope in a fortnight. So it may, if I have a very industrious printer, appear in September which you know is an excellent time for publication. I am glad the Lees succeeded; their name still tells; & our friend of acute sensation has not, as I thought she would, injurd herself by that very extraordinary performance.[5] They are good & friendly and certainly rank high among female writers. Do you know the price Robinson[6] gave? it is not an enquiry of impertinent curiosity, but is of some moment to me, as Johnson does not seem much delighted with the thoughts of a story book from my hand—whether he thinks I have exhausted my imagination or is afraid I may be too loving, too prosing, or too much like my predecessors. I have finish'd one volume, but nobody has seen it & I doubt its merit. Yet I must finish & sell it. I am of your opinion that nothing produces so much money, save travels & plays, but Johnson holds off, & I shall be sorry to go farther with my goods.

Did not Mr Carr[7] formerly employ him as a publisher? I am persuaded that all you say of Mr Carr is true & that with an elegant mind, the integrity of the heart is never affected by professional prejudices. I know many most respectable exceptions to the general opinion of Solicitors. I do not believe an honester Man lives in any line of life than Mr Bicknell, yet much as I esteem & love him, I wish he was not our Solicitor in this Chancery suit that is hanging over us, for he is not equal to the Attorney of our Adversary, who has given us in a very early stage of the business a pretty decisive proof that he will not hesitate at little matters, such as giving his oath that he knew not where to find a person when he knew that very person was at his clients house & had been there for a month at a time.

But to turn from this subject, Godwin got 120£ a volume for Fleetwood! 360£ for three such volumes! it is really marvellous. I was disappointed in Griselda,[8] it was so very slight, but in these light sketches Miss Edgeworth excells. I never could relish Belinda. I have just read the play of the Honeymoon,[9] which goes off very well & must act better than it reads. The only Novel I have read lately with pleasure is that calld the "Letters of Miss Riversdale."[10] It is said to be by Mrs Damer & has been publishd some time tho I never saw it till lately. I still say, "A blessing on the Man who first invented the thing calld "a Novel": it carries one out of oneself. You did not tell me whether you had read "the Triumph of Music." Miss Pool[11] corrected it, & Mr Marsh[12] has set it to Music. But you dont know either, I beleive. I hope it will not be the requiem of our friends fame, for he deserves to be loved & honor'd for a great deal of good, & I think of him with a sort of melancholy regard, tho I must sometimes smile if I loved him fifty times better than I do at his odd misprision of the vrai beau & the dotage of his taste. It is more to the purpose tho to beg I <u>may hear from you wherever you are</u> & that you will allow me to hope you will long think of me as I truly am, my dear Madam, ever most affectionately & truly yours,

Charlotte ~~Smith~~

I am much obliged to M[r] Carr for the trouble he has taken. Pray say so to him. I shall be most anxious to hear your mind is easier, & that all goes well tho I know it must be some time before there can be much progress.

I have written this on greasey paper & with a vile pen, but I had no other and feard to miss you in Town if I delay'd writing; pray let me hear from you soon.

Cowper and Newton Museum MS. Address: M[rs] Rose/ Henrietta Street/ N. 11/ Covent Garden/ London. Postmark: Petworth/ 57 {MAY} 15/ 1805.

NOTES

1. Richard Smith and Mary Gibbes Smith Allen, BS's nephew and niece, along with Mary's husband Capt. Robert Allen, had filed a bill in Chancery against Egremont and the trust on 14 May 1803. From remarks made by both CS and BS, Capt. Allen may have instigated the suit; he certainly pursued it vehemently (see CS to Egremont, 13 Aug. 1804, n. 1).

2. CS is making a joke in suggesting that William Hayley should enlarge *A Philosophical, Historical and Moral Essay on Old Maids. By a Friend to the Sisterhood* (1785). It went through three editions, the last in 1793.

3. Bignor Park; the other family seat, Stoke Manor, was sold in 1761. CS's younger brother, Rev. Nicholas Turner, had a number of financial difficulties involving both his parishioners at Fittleworth and their younger sister, Catherine Ann Dorset. CS was troubled by Lucy Dorset's marriage to Charles Henry Fraser, who was not only financially foolish but also an obese glutton.

4. *The Natural History of Birds, intended chiefly for Young Persons,* 2 vols. Joseph Johnson did not in fact publish it until 1807, after her death.

5. That is, Sophia Lee's *The Life of a Lover* (1804), which was not well received; CS disliked it very much (CS to Sarah Rose, 4 July 1804). Together, Harriet and Sophia Lee wrote *Canterbury Tales,* 5 vols. (1797–1805).

6. The bookseller and publisher George Robinson.

7. Sir John Carr (1772–1832), author of *A Northern Summer.*

8. Maria Edgeworth's *The Modern Griselda* (1805) was 170 pages long. CS read *Belinda* not long after it came out in 1801 (CS to Joseph Cooper Walker, [late Mar.–early Apr. 1802]).

9. A comedy by John Tobin, acted at Drury Lane and published in 1805. An imitation of Beaumont and Fletcher, it was a great success.

10. See CS to Sarah Rose, April 1805 and n. 3.

11. Henrietta Poole (d. 1827), whose name was shortened to Harriet and who was also nicknamed Paulina, met Hayley in Sept. 1794 and settled near Felpham in 1800. A friend and regular guest of Hayley's, she thought his *Triumph of Music* would be a

success. Unlike his other women friends, she never turned on him (Bishop, *Blake's Hayley,* pp. 187, 188, 267, 311, 326).

12. Edward Garrard Marsh (d. 1862) was about 20 when he met Hayley in Sept. 1800; Blake admired his reading of verses, and Hayley his reading of Hayley's new biography of his son. Ordained in 1807, he held several country livings. In 1837, he published a volume of psalms and hymns adapted to seventy tunes (Bishop, *Blake's Hayley,* pp. 290–91).

To Sarah Rose

Elsted, July 2nd 1805

I was so anxious, my dear Madam, to know on what place on the Coast you had determin'd that I was about to write to Johnson to enquire for me; Perhaps by that means I might never have known, for an answer from him is more rare than a comet, but your kind Letter put an end to my suspence, & I sincerely thank you for remembring me. I obey your injunction as to writing tho I am disqualified from giving you the least amusement by illness, anxiety, and vexation. I have often compared my destiny to the fabled punishment of Sysiphus or the Danaids. My whole life is pass'd in baffled toil & unavailing solicitude, & one way or other, I have contrived to get such a severe return of the debilitating complaint which must kill me if it lasts that I am every thing but dead. I not unfrequently think it would be better to be quite so. How good you are to give me information on literary topics which I have no other means of obtaining.

I write & write & I have lately sent 100£s worth as I thought up to Johnson; he accepts my bills but never tells me what he means to give me or how far I am to go. I sent him up 100£ bill that I received from India. He has not even acknowledged the receipt of it tho it is near a month since. In a word, I can get no answer whatever from him, and it almost wears one to death. I write without courage or spirit because I never know whether I write to any purpose or no, & I see every body, merely because they are not fetterd as I am, make money which I toil for in vain. All my last years income & two hundred pounds more that I must now sell out Nicholas's stock to replace went to furnish my poor George with money for the purpose of equipping him to go out as an Adjutant in the 96th, A post he was utterly unfit for, & which placed him in the power of a Tyrant under whom he could not exist.[1] So he exchanged from the 47th which still remains quietly in Ireland, a Regiment into which I had interests for the adjutancy & Lieutenancy of the 96th now sent to the West Indies, and all this money is only gone to place him in an insupportable situation which he has since resign'd.

I own to you my courage fails me under the toil I am thus condemn'd to while Mr B S lives on my property & I am burthen'd with his children &

overwhelm'd so much one way or other that it is impossible I can long contend with it. Oh how I envy those who have leisure to enjoy the only things that give me any satisfaction—books & literary conversation. Cut off from the latter, it might be thought that the other would be allowed me, but I have neither access to books, nor time to read them if I had. Such is the continual burthen of finding ways and means!

Yes, Bignor is sold!—to a Mr Hawkins[2] & for the Sum of 13500£! Thus is gone the last of the property of my family in the Counties of Surrey & Sussex—Where in the first my Grandfather had the beautiful Estates of Stoke and Woodbridge, both within a mile of Guildford, & Another Estate at Farnham, In Sussex, besides Bignor then only a shooting place; he had the farm of Hardham worth near 700£ a year, Of Bigenor, of Devenish's Warren, of Another considerable timber'd Estate in the Weald, Some property at Petworth, and other farms of less value—Altogether not very short of 4000£ a year; & my Brother now is glad of a living in the very worst part of Sussex;[3] I work for my bread; & the last of the property is to centre in Mr Fraser[4] who will put the greatest part of it into that most enormous paunch of his!——I cannot but think it very very sad! Yet a thousand people are more unfortunate perhaps every day, & all this querulous egotism will make you think me very weak!

But indeed, my dear Madam, altogether I feel very often as if I must give up the contest between my fatigued spirits & the demon Poverty which I have made so many efforts to keep at bay. My weary hands & more weary spirits refuse to continue such unremitting & fruitless toil. Amid all this, Johnsons strange neglect mingled with so much bonhommie that I cannot complain, Phillips begins to worry me again about my non performance of my engagement with him which he himself took out of my hands three years ago.[5] He now once in three or four months writes to me in a threatening & very rude manner, & then I hear no more about him for another interval. He now expects me to bring down the history to the Peace of Amiens, tho at the very beginning of our engagement I declared that for many reasons I neither would or could go beyond the end of the reign of George the second. How I shall get out of this Mans power I do not know; I have now no literary or active friend to interpose for me. The part of the work I executed makes a very thick close printed volume. He has paid me 120£, but I could have made a great deal more in any other way. He now expects me for the same money, as he does not mean to make any addition, to produce for him 17 sheets more letter press by abridging Belsham.[6] I niether can nor will do it, but to be insulted in this manner continually is extremely harrassing to me and annihilates the few faculties I have; I know not what to do, for the few literary friends I have are connected with Phillips & cannot contend with him on my behalf without risking their own interest, which of course I have no right to expect— —I have poetry enough to fill a small volume the size of those that have been so successfull;[7] I named it to Johnson & asked whether it would not be better to get Cadell & Davies to come to some agreement for new plates & new decorations with these additions. He promis'd to consider of it, but it is now two months ago, & I have never had one line from him since: thus baffled & my health again failing from vexation, I know not what I can do. I would most willingly go somewhere & die quietly if it might be.

Your solitude, my dear Madam, at the Sea, even at a place so little pleasant at Seaford, would be to me delightful if I had but one such friend with whom to converse, & I should make an effort to get thither, for I am convinced that quiet and sea air would be of more use than the medicines I now take for that weakening complaint which is gradually draining away my life: but all I can muster is too little to provide for the expence I have been put to in paying for the fixtures & furniture which I was oblig'd to take at an house I am going to on being oblig'd to quit this. It is about three miles from hence and is an old fashion'd ugly house, tho situated in a beautiful country, but it has more bed rooms & is in some respects more convenient than this.[8] They say the grass pays the rent, & this was my cheif inducement to take it & because the removal will not be attended with great expence, for as to myself, I care not where I go to die, which seems to be the only thing I have to do. A younger & I hope a more fortunate generation are coming up to "push me from the seat," & I know not why one should cling so abjectly to a life so little worth either to oneself or others as mine is———

In my literary tribulations, I should apply to M[r] Hayley; at least as far as relates to the sale of the Poetry, I may have, but he is so alterd from the friend I once found him, & when ever I have had occasion to apply to him has answered me, tho civilly yet so apprehensively, as if he dreaded trouble that I am unwilling even in any thing to break in on his Teusdays & fridays studies & amusements—— I am vexd for I shall always have a real regard for him to see how he is ridiculed in the Reviews. Some of my acquaintance who say they have great esteem for Hayley have refused to read his last work because they cannot bear to see him in so humiliating a situation as this strange work they hear places him in. I am very sorry, too, to understand from you that his poor Eyes are still so bad & that he is likely long to suffer. There was a time when most certainly, tho with the most platonic attachment, I would have given my own eyes (which he used to tell me were the most indefatigable little eyes that ever pored upon paper) to have saved his from pain, When I would have given up every thing but my duty to my children to be his secretary; I cannot but consider with some degree of wonder the change that twelve years have made & can hardly think he is the same considerate friend, who once was a brother to me. Basta e troppo[9]—of this—

I am delighted, my dear Madam, to hear you found your sweet boys well & are now with them. I know not how the idea was convey'd to me that you were going to your father at Bath, but so strongly this notion impress'd my mind that when Mrs Dorset wrote to me to know if I thought you would allow her to wait upon you there, I answer'd yes and desird her to enquire at the Post Office for a direction. Do you return to Town after you leave the coast? I wish it might so happen that we could meet, for I am not at all of the mind of our friends the Lees on that matter & cannot imagine their reason for it, unless it be that they think I make the best appearance upon paper & would save me the mortification I might feel if you found—as very probably you might—that I am nothing in conversation. It is the more probable because I beleive it may always be true & was perhaps particularly the case when I was at Bath[10] & when my whole soul was absorbed by the loveliest & dearest of the beings that then belongd to me & when I had neither heart nor spirits for general society & still less for that in which it was expected I should talk like an Author.

Besides which, I have never the happy reliance on my own powers or the decided conviction of the merit of my own performances which our friends in an enviable degree possess. I cannot help peeping now and then at a Review & beleive it is good for us to be told of our faults; I know I might have written much better, & I do verily beleive if I had been no more of a Poet than the elder of our friends, I should never have written even an half penny ballad—— I cannot help envying the perfect satisfaction S. L. expresses in her own performances, while in my opinion the two Emilys & the last work are any thing but what they ought to have been. But we are all mightily pleas'd with the last volume of Canterbury tales of H. L., particularly the first and the last.[11] They are well too, without the affectation & quaintness which is sometimes the blemish of her writing. I always thought the superiority of talents hers.

You are so good as to say my letters are entertaining. Surely nothing can be less so than this is. It is nothing but a tissue of grumbling & egotism. I will do better another time if you will have patience with me now. My daughter in Law[12] arrived from Ireland about three weeks ago, & as far as very uncommon personal beauty without the least vanity and great mildness of manners go, I have every reason to be satisfied with Lionels choice. She is not accomplish'd, but accomplishments, generally speaking, are nothing; I would not give a shaw to hear a great noise made, usually calld Music, to the extinction of all conversation, when I can buy better music: nor would I give a pin for Lady like drawings. I wish however she was a reader, but she is a Catholic, & I fear a bigotted Catholic, & they are never sufferd to read. So, whether the World turns round or stands still, she never ventures to enquire & rather thinks it wrong to ask any questions about it. She is unhappy because we have no mass near us; I have been writing to some connections of mine who are connected with Catholics to find a Priest for her for [I am] extremely desirous that every one should be satisfied [in that] business. If I wanted the heroine of a Novel, I should certainly take her person, for it is almost perfect, but she is rather too thin, & some people would opine that she is too tall, as she is considerably taller than my eldest daughter who is you may remember above the middle size. The baby is the sweetest little animal I have seen [in] a great while. La grande maternité, I confess, gives me but little pleasure, but it is the last act of the miserable drame, & I would fain "give a great gulp" & go thro it with a good grace. So I talk of "caudles[13] & confections" & teething & all that like a sage femme.[14] Perhaps a more useful character than a femme sage or madam blue.

I have not yet seen Mr Carrs book[15] & fear I have little chance of doing it. The party are gone out to dinner to day, as I should hardly have had time to write this. I ought to have thankd you for the trouble you have been so good as to take, & I wd thank Mr Carr if I knew how to direct to him in his absence from home. It is time to end an irksome letter, for such I fear you will find it. I have an opportunity of sending it into Hampshire and therefore disobey your injunction, but I beg you will not punish me by forbearing to write to me since I assure you with great sincerity that to hear from you & one or two other friends affords almost the sole pleasure now enjoy'd by, my Dear Madam,

Your affectionate & oblig'd Sert,
Charlotte ~~Smith~~

All my writing is completely at a stand. I have no moment to spare amid this moving, and Johnsons silence is quite discouraging so that I do nothing —Woe is me![16]

Osborn Collection MS, Yale University. Address: Mrs Rose/ Seaford/ Sussex. No postmark.

NOTES

1. Not identified.

2. John Hawkins (?1758–1841) was a fellow of the Royal Society who wrote scientific papers, mostly on the geology of Cornwall, as well as books based on his extensive travels. He used his considerable wealth to purchase Bignor Park, the Turner family seat, and rebuilt it from 1826 to 1830. He furnished it with a valuable collection of art and antiquities.

3. In Lurgashall, near Petworth House.

4. Charles Fraser, Catherine Dorset's son-in-law.

5. CS had completed *History of England . . . to a young lady at school* two years before, writing then that she had "entirely closed my engagement with Mr Phillips" and "we part good friends" (CS to Cadell and Davies, 24 Mar. 1803).

6. William Belsham wrote a number of histories and memoirs, including *History of Great Britain, from the Revolution to the Accession of the House of Hanover,* 2 vols. (1798).

7. *Beachy Head,* published posthumously in 1807 by Johnson, but after much trouble with Cadell and Davies.

8. Tilford was to be CS's last home. Though beautifully situated with a stream through the center of the village and a large green leading up to a small church on a hill, it was a poor and remote site. The church once contained a reredos in her memory, but it was lost when the church was remodeled.

9. Enough and too much.

10. Between March 1794 and June 1795; CS went to Bath for her own health, but during this period Augusta suffered through a difficult pregnancy and died.

11. S. L., Sophia Lee, author of vol. 2 of *Canterbury Tales* (1798). It consisted of one long tale, "The Young Lady's Tale. The Two Emilys." Harriet Lee wrote all the tales in the final volume, vol. 5 (1805).

12. Lionel's wife, Ellen Marianne Galway Smith.

13. A warm drink of thin gruel mixed with wine or ale and eggs, sugar, and spices. It was used for the sick, often for women in childbed.

14. A *sage-femme* is a midwife, and a *femme sage* is a learned lady. *Madam bleu* is probably CS's error for *bas bleu,* or "bluestocking." Perhaps CS feels that she is of more use as a woman knowledgeable about childbearing than as a learned woman and writer.

15. Sir John Carr's *A Northern Summer; or, Travels round the Baltic, through Denmark, Sweden, Russia, Prussia, and Part of Germany, in the Year 1804* (1804). She did finally obtain a copy (see CS to Sarah Rose, 10 Sept. 1805).

16. Written upside down across the top of margin of the first page.

To Thomas Cadell, Jr., and William Davies

[Elsted, 6 July 1805]

Gentlemen,

As I have as I beleive original & unprinted Poems, if not quite sufficient, to make another volume as large as those you purchas'd some years ago, it is my intention to publish them in the course of the next eight or ten months. There will be some awkwardness in having a third volume publish'd as a single one. I mentiond my intention to Mr Johnson some time since, who said he would consider how this might be done to most advantage to me without its making an awkard appearance; I have not however heard from him, and perhaps he is too much occupied by business to attend to my request. As it is not always that my health permits me to apply myself to the preparing any work & more particularly Poetry for the press, I wish to avail myself of an interval of tolerable health to arrange & give the last corrections to this. It may perhaps be agreeable to you to reprint Your two volumes (as I see the plates are worn almost to nothing) and to add the third or to incorporate the third in a new Edition —in which case I could wish to give a general revisal to the two already so popular, & I know that Mr Johnson to whom I have many obligations would, with his usual candour and liberality, allow me to do whatever would be most conducive to my advantage. I beleive however on looking again on My MMS book that the Poems are too long & would make too many additional sheets to add them.

It would give me pleasure to have by this means the power of discharging my debt to you, which the long delays of India remittances & some very heavy expences incurred on account of my youngest Son have hitherto prevented my doing tho I have never been unmindful of it. Your answer (as I remove from hence in the course of ten days, my Landlady desiring to inhabit the house herself) will oblige, Gent[n],

Your obed humble Ser[t],
Charlotte Smith

Elsted, July 6th 1805
I should not expect payment till the Volume was deliverd in MMS.[1]

Yale University MS. Address: Mess[rs] Cadell & Davies/ Strand/ London. Postmark: GODALMIN; G/JUL 6/1805.

NOTE

1. Written on the third page of this four-page letter is a note, apparently a copy of their reply, dated July 8, 1805:

> Madam
> If you will do us the Favour of sending us the new Poems, whenever they may have received your last Revisal, together with the corrected Copy of those already printed, we doubt not that Terms will be agreed upon, to our mutual Satisfaction——
>
> We are, Madam,
> Your very obedient Servants
> C. & D

In fact, CS reached no agreement with Cadell and Davies: Joseph Johnson published the last volume of CS's poems posthumously as *Beachy Head.*

To Thomas Cadell, Jr., and William Davies

Elsted, Godalming
July 26th 1805
Gentlemen,

The Rev[d] M[r] Dunster[1] with whom I beleive you are well acquainted has, in an[r] to the enquiries I took the liberty to make as to some information I wanted, pointed out to me the following books: Horsleys Britanica Romana, Draytons Polyalbion, & Hays History of Chichester where it may be found.[2]

And I wish for Pennants Zoology And the new Poem of the Lay of the last Minstrel.[3] I should not of course have troubled you with the inquiry, whether you c[d] procure me these books, if I had not decided on putting the poems I before named to you into your hands, M[r] Johnson having, with his usual liberality, declared his readiness to relinquish any claim I might suppose he had on my work from my late engagements with him, & I understand he has spoken with you on the subject.

A Poem of considerable length is on a local subject. I have made very great progress in it, having had it in hand some years, but I wish to be very correct & to leave nothing for Criticism to carp at, & therefore it is that I am desirous in a last revisal of going over the books M[r] Dunster has named to me.

Draytons Polyalbion is I beleive a scarce book. I once borrow'd it at Petworth House & perhaps might have it again, but Lord Egremont having found reason to restrain the admission he very generally gave to his collection, I am unwilling to ask an exception in my favor if I can avoid it.

I will return the books carefully as soon as I have taken the passages I may want for notes or otherwise.

Your early answer will much oblige, Gent[n],

Your obed humble Ser[t],
Charlotte Smith

I cannot send you a corrected Copy of the two first Volumes[4] because I have none. The only copy I have is one in which the last Poems are not inserted in the 2nd Volume. I will go over the whole with pleasure & make some alterations of moment.

If any new plates are intended, I think that, if the drawings I saw a few days ago are done by the young Lady who shew'd them to me of the name of Smith,[5] the daughter of an artist, she is capable of seizing my idea's & would make beautiful designs, but I know nothing of her price—or indeed any thing more of her than meeting her at M[r] Townsends where her father is taking the portraits of some family in Crayons. I was extremely struck with two little designs from the Vicar of Wakefield & think them almost too masterly for so young an Artist. In a few days, i. e. about the 30th, I shall be so busy in removing to Tilford near Farnham, Three miles from hence, that I wish to get the books first that, as soon as my removal is over, no more time may be lost.

Yale University MS. Address: Mess[rs] Cadell & Davies/ Strand/ London. Postmark: GODALMIN; G/JUL 27/1805.

NOTES

1. Charles Dunster, scholar and rector of Petworth from 1789 to 1816 (see Biographical Notes).

2. The antiquarian John Horsley's *Britannia Romana; or the Roman Antiquities of*

Britain (1732), Alexander Hay's *History of Chichester* (1804), and Michael Drayton's *Poly-Olbion* (1612).

3. Thomas Pennant's *British Zoology* (1768–70) and Sir Walter Scott's newly published *The Lay of the Last Minstrel* (1805). Scott's poem had received mixed reviews.

4. Of *Elegiac Sonnets.*

5. A very young watercolor painter and illustrator, Emma Smith (b. 1787), daughter of the painter and engraver John Raphael Smith (1752–1812). She painted miniatures and mounted exhibitions at the Royal Academy in 1799 and 1808. CS met her twice at the Townsends' at Busbridge.

To Sarah Rose

Elsted
July 30th
1805[1]

Beleive me, Dear Madam, I have not willingly neglected to write to you. It would be tiresome to tell you why I have been compelled to appear so negligent where I have so much pleasure in the correspondence, But among other causes have been My daughters absence in Town and my depressing complaint for which, having exhausted every other or rather formerly prescribed remedy, I was obligd again to see My Guildford friend who gives me no hope from any thing but cold sea bathing unless Sea air should do witht it, by giving me the strength I want. I cannot however go to the Sea. The expences of my family are so high that they take away every resource for myself, & moving, which compels me to pay all my bills here, & payg for fixtures & furniture will leave me no choice or chance for myself. It is hard, but I must submit—— Mr Johnson has been very good in assisting me to pay for the fixtures &c at Tilford, but he will not an[swe]r my letters or tell me how the account ~~now~~ stands between us. It is now between four & five hundred pounds pr & contra. A friend of mine has remonstrated with him, & he promisd now a week since instantly to write to me, but I have never heard, & I give it up as quite Hopeless. Cadell & Davies buy my new volume of Poetry because Johnson thinks it best, as they are proprietors of the other two.[2] This he settled verbally with my friend.

Thinking the Holydays may be over & that you may have left Seaford for Uckfield, I venture to send this thither, least it should miss you. Forgive me if my direction is awkard. I shall try to get it frank'd, as I am sure it is not worth the postage. Forgive me, too, for havg neglected to send the Sonnets till they will no longer perhaps suit your scenery. I therefore send the composition of last night, a sleepless night. I know not whether it is good for any thing.

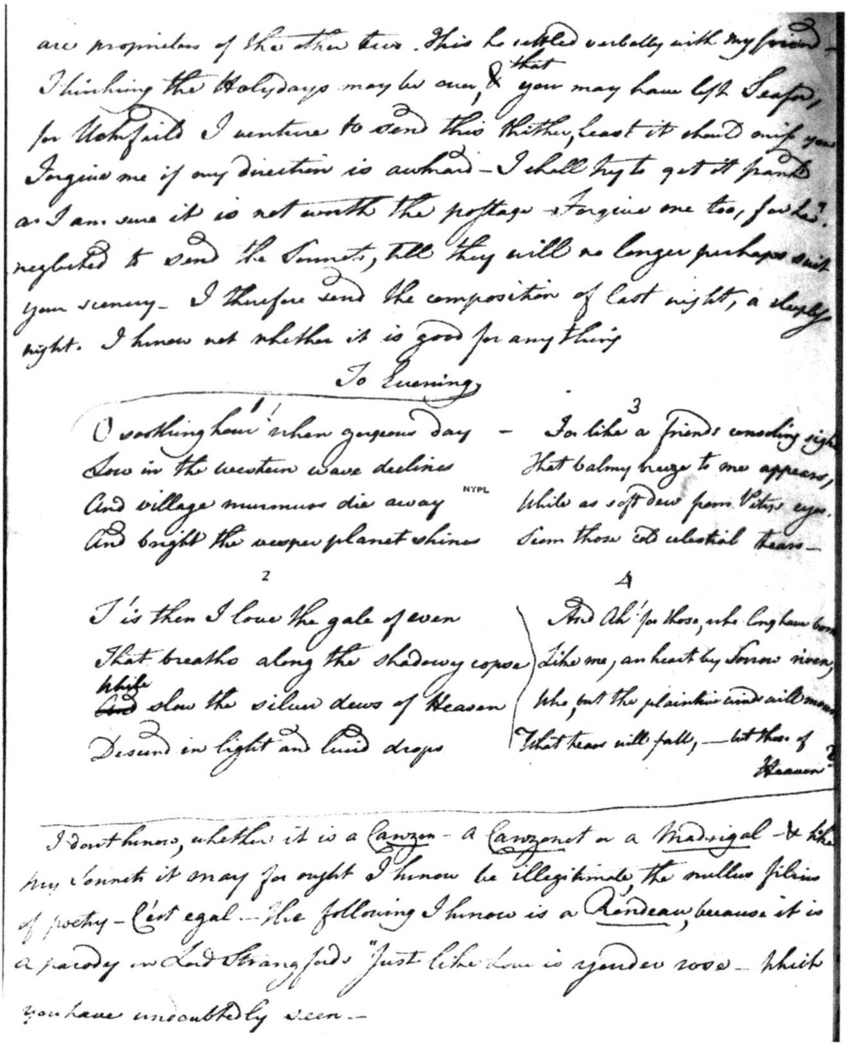

are proprietors of the other two. This he settled verbally with my friend—
Thinking the Holydays may be over, & that you may have left Seaford
for Uckfield I venture to send this thither, least it should miss you
Forgive me if my direction is awkward—I shall try to get it franked
as I am sure it is not worth the postage—Forgive me too, for having
neglected to send the Sonnets, till they will no longer perhaps suit
your scenery—I therefore send the composition of last night, a sleepless
night. I know not whether it is good for any thing

To Evening

1
O soothing hour! when gorgeous day—
Low in the western wave declines
And village murmurs die away
And bright the vesper planet shines

2
'Tis then I love the gale of even
That breaths along the shadowy copse
While ~~And~~ slow the silver dews of Heaven
Descend in light and lucid drops

3
For like a friends consoling sigh
That balmy breeze to me appears,
While as soft dew from Pity's eyes
Seem those celestial tears—

4
And Ah! for those, who long have borne
Like me, an heart by Sorrow riven,
Who, but the plaintive winds will mourn
What tears will fall,—but those of Heaven?

I don't know, whether it is a Canzon—a Canzonet or a Madrigal—& like my Sonnets it may for ought I know be illegitimate, the nullius filius of poetry—C'est egal—The following I know is a Rondeau, because it is a parody on Lord Strangford's "Just like Love is yonder rose—" which you have undoubtedly seen—

Figure 6a. Letter to Sarah Farr Rose, 30 July 1805.

<u>To Evening</u>

1
O soothing hour! when gorgeous day—
Low in the western wave declines
And village murmurs die away
And bright the vesper planet shines

2
'Tis then I love the gale of even
That breaths along the shadowy copse
While ~~And~~ slow the silver dews of Heaven
Descend in light and lucid drops

3
For like a friends consoling sighs
That balmy breeze to me appears,
While as soft dew from Pitys eyes
Seem those cold celestial tears—

4
And Ah! for those, who long have borne
Like me, an heart by Sorrow riven;
Who, but the plaintive winds will mourn?
What tears will fall,—but those of Heaven?

Just like Hope is yonder bow,
That from the center bends so low,
Where bright prismatic colours shew,
How gems of heavenly radience glow;
—Just like Hope!

Yet if, to the illusion new,
The Pilgrim should the arch pursue,
Farther & farther from his view
It flies;—then melts in chilling dew
—Just like hope!

Ye fade celestial hues, for ever!
While cold Reason!—thy endeavour
Soothes not that sad heart, which never,
Glows with Hope!

I dont know what I shall do, should I [continue to] go to the Sea — I detest the
places on this coast —. In some of them, I shall see too continually the
ghost of departed happiness & the image of Ana who, alone of all my children
never gave me pain but when she suffered illness, will be always present to
me — I know not how others feel on this subject, but I cannot bear, what ought
to be like her & is not. & even beauty & sweetness that I do see, only remind me
of what I have lost — Ten years have dragged along, & the image is as new
as ever in my memory & my wound bleeds as painfully as ever; yet I am told
I dare say it is true, that there are a thousand reasons, why I ought to be grateful
My dear Madam this is a dismal theme, but I know you do not dislike [illegible]

Figure 6b. Letter to Sarah Farr Rose, 30 July 1805.

I dont know whether it is a Canzon, a Canzonet, or a Madregal,[3] & like my Sonnets, it may for ought I know be illegitimate, the millus filius of poetry.[4] C'est egal. The following I know is a Rondeau because it is a parody on Lord Strangfords[5] "Just like Love is yonder rose" Which you have undoubtedly seen—

Just like Hope is yonder bow,
That from the center bends so low,
Where bright prismatic colours shew,
How gems of heavenly radience glow;
——Just like Hope!

Yet if, to the illusion new,
The Pilgrim should the arch pursue,
Farther & farther from his view
It flies;——then melts in chilling dew
——Just like hope!

Ye fade celestial hues, for ever!
While cold Reason!,—thy endeavour
Soothes not that sad heart, which never,
Glows with Hope!—

I dont know what I shall do, should I continue to go to the Sea? I detest the places on this coast. In some of them, I shall see too continually the ghost of departed happiness, & the image of One who, alone of all my children, never gave me pain but when she sufferd illness, will be always present to me. I know not how others feel on this subject, but I cannot bear what ought to be like her & is not, & even beauty & sweetness that I do see only remind me of what I have lost. Ten years have dragg'd along, & the image is as new as ever in my memory, & my wound bleeds as painfully as ever; yet I am told & I dare say it is true that there are a thousand reasons why I ought to be grateful. My dear Madam, this is a dismal theme, but I know you do not dislike it. Pray write to me As soon as you have time & tell me where you are likely to be, & I promise not to let any thing but unavoidable evils make me so apparently remiss again. I go to Tilford near Farnham on Saturday.[6] Pray direct thither, & as it is a lone house, [you] may omit the Charlotte pour cause which I will tell you another time.

It is only a place to die at, & therefore I grudge the expence, for as a French Novelist says "il nous faut si peu de chose pour cela!"[7] Mr Hayley expressd some surprize at not having heard from [me]; So I wrote, but I fear something in my letter did not please him, as he has never an[swere][d] it. His friendship for me is transferred—& quite lost. I did not think once that it could be annihilated by si peu de chose,[8] & it is among the losses I regret. I shall feel uncomfortable in going to Bogner, for I should never like to trouble him with a visit & indeed could not because I cannot get in or out of a carriage. So he need not apprehend any visitation. All comfort attend you, dearest Madam. Ever yrs most truly,

CS

Henry W. and Albert A. Berg Collection of English and American Literature, The New York Public Library, Astor, Lenox and Tilden Foundations MS. Address: Mrs Rose. No postmark. Photographs used by permission of the Henry W. and Albert A. Berg Collection of English and American Literature, The New York Public Library, Astor, Lenox and Tilden Foundations.

NOTES

1. Written vertically in upper right-hand corner.
2. In the end, Johnson published *Beachy Head.*
3. CS's uncertainty results from the similarities in her time of these short lyric forms. The canzone consisted of several equal stanzas with a shorter envoy and variable verse form; the canzonet was shorter, but still had more than one movement. The term *madrigal* was used more loosely, but in the Italian, madrigals consisted of 6 to 13 lines with three rhymes. The rondeau was a French set verse form, but it had several variations.
4. It is unclear what word CS had in mind when she wrote *millus,* but her apparent meaning is the "[bastard] son."
5. In Strangford's *Poems, from the Portuguese of Luis de Camoens,* p. 47 (see CS to Joseph Cooper Walker, [?Jan 1804] and n. 4).
6. On 3 Aug.
7. We need so little for that.
8. Such a small thing.

To Sarah Rose

[ca. August 1805][1]

My Dear Madam, I cannot, weary as I am of writing, make up my dispatches for London tomorrow without troubling you with my acknowledgements for the friendly & welcome Letter I received to day. My Sister leaves me tomorrow, a cruel loss to me, & one I shall very severely feel, but in consequence of my illness she has already prolonged her stay to her own inconvenience, & I must submit tho I shall feel the deprivation a very dreadful one & which here cannot be replaced. I rejoice that your fine quartette of Boys are all that you could wish. In them you will find present occupation of the most delightful kind & every future comfort, and to have something to look forward to with hope is one of the greatest blessings if one could but think so— —Sad reality will come at last when hopes are realized ~~and~~ or have lost their charms. I would not be low spirited or thankless but——— What is life worth to me? The flowers are fallen never to reappear; the thorns remain; I try to fancy a sprig or two among them, but it will not do. They are like Autumnal flowers, scentless and pale, Yet I owe so much to friendship that I know I ought to be proud & satisfied, As much pains have been taken, and as much solicitude shown, as if I still was all I was once, or now all I might have been——

My house is indeed triste, & what is worse, I have embarrassed myself in getting into it by paying for fixtures & having furniture still to pay for. But it has always been my lot to be the victim of circumstance; I could not help it. My family is such that a small house will not hold us—nor a small number of servants suffice. And I have the character of being expensive when perhaps no Woman brought up as I was was ever so little expensive. It is not easy to make even our near friends understand the carte du païs, or rather le dessous des cartes.[2] Mr Johnson says in one of his letters (for he often gives me lectures on oeconomy), "if you had not been fosterd in the lap of prosperity, you w^{d} think your income ample." It would indeed be ample for me, tho so much of it (what belongs to me) goes to M^{r} B S. & his bedmaker, but I must keep house & One of my daughters entirely, & of course servants & taxes & ten thousand other expences, besides which my youngest Son has had actually for two years more than my whole regular income comes to. You will think it strange that I should enter into such a vindication to you, but I know the idea of my having no care of money has taken possession of so many people that it has done me a great deal of harm. Mr Hayley among others has said I cannot exclaim, "He talks to me that never had a Son" but I may say "who never had eight children" for whom I was for years to provide & who lookd up to me for an home, for every thing they had early learned to expect, but which only my feeble hands were left to procure for them. I am often half tempted to make a catalogue raisonée of all I have done & sufferd—for yet a little & it will be forgotten. I have been writing to Mr Johnson & have got into a melancholy mood. My Argosies are not arrived, & I rather expect to be in Guildford Bastille N'importe; "Souffrir et meurir est le devoir de l'Homme," & of la femme, I am sure.[3]

You are very good to say you will try to see Mr Johnson. I beleive Charlotte has not yet had time. I wish very much for Cumberlands life and should like Miss Edgeworths forthcoming ~~life~~ book.[4] Mr Johnson seems to think every bodys books better worth printing than mine, for he has had one of mine by him many months[5] & I suspect it has shared the fate of Thaumeturgos[6] in the tale of "Tomorrow." However he has paid me for it, & if he prefers keeping it for cartridges against the landing of the Emperor of the West to the expence of printing it, I must not complain; only it is rather mortifying to be shelfd in Embryo & die before one is born. I suppose he has seen so many instances of twadling "sur leur declin" in Authors that he thought I might have caught the infection & wrote flat & languid fall lalls too—— If you should happen to have any discourse about me, do say (at least if you think you can say it with truth) that my shell, tho the strings are a little rusty, can yet make a tolerable sort of a tune, at least as good as D'Isreali's Jews harp, or M[r] Bowls's viol de gamb, or some of the "broken bellied virginals" whose strumming is in request.[7] I thank the "principal bard"[8] for his kind expression & am persuaded he is as sorry for his "dear Sister of Parnassus" as Pegasus was, when Io miscarried. I was going to quote D[r] Johnsons cow & horse, but that would be too gross for Paulina's Bard.

I never read a line in my life of Miss Cornelia Knight.[9] I dont care for old Roman dresses put upon modern figures, & as to Miss Hamilton,[10] I thought her book all about very little—a sort of verbiage. The Age is an Age of wonders, & therefore it will be none if the next race of refined Ladies are after the model of Romneys divinity, Emma Lady Hamilton.[11] Pray write soon in charity to, my d[r] Mad[m], y[rs] ever, CS

Huntington MS (HM10825). No address or postmark.

NOTES

1. Although the Huntington dates this letter to ca. 1801, it clearly belongs in 1805: CS began to correspond with Sarah Rose only in 1804, and this letter has the more relaxed, familiar tone of those written even later than that. Internal references also support a dating to late summer of 1805: (1) On 14 Feb. 1805, CS wrote to Sarah Rose after her husband's death that her four young sons would be a comfort to her. Here CS repeats that sentiment, but without her earlier expression of sympathy. (2) On 30 July 1805 (to Sarah Rose), CS mentions taking on debt to supply herself with furniture in moving from Elsted to Tilford. Her Elsted lease would expire in August. (3) Johnson had paid CS handsomely for a manuscript (10 Sept.); she mentions it here as already paid for, but not yet printed. (4) Her remark that she had paid more than her whole regular income to support George for the past two years is substantiated in other letters written about this time (CS to Sarah Rose, 2 July 1805, and to Egremont, 13 July 1806). (5) After mentioning Cumberland's life here, CS finally asked Sarah Rose to send it to her on 26 Dec. 1805.

2. Clearly, Sarah Rose knew French, and CS enjoyed displaying her fluency in French in puns like this one: "the customs of the country," or "the other side of the deck," the side other players cannot see.

3. To suffer and die are the duty of man—and woman.

4. The *Memoirs of Richard Cumberland,* 2 vols. (1806-1807). Edgeworth's work published after *The Modern Griselda* (1805) was *Leonora* (1806).

5. Probably CS's *The Natural History of Birds,* published in 1807.

6. A miracle worker or magician—a term CS used elsewhere derisively to refer to BS (CS to Egremont, 14 and 15 Oct. 1803, and to Sarah Rose, 16 July 1804).

7. Isaac D'Israeli (1766-1848), author of *Curiosities of Literature* (1791), was Jewish (his more famous son Benjamin converted before entering society and politics). William Lisle Bowles's poetry is heavy, even lugubrious. In this series of musical comparisons, "broken-bellied virginal" ironically alludes to a virgin who has not had her belly broken—thus, a young, unmarried literary woman, or perhaps, in a further irony, a spinster.

8. "The principle bard" is Hayley; "Paulina" was Henrietta Poole's nickname (see CS to Sarah Rose, 14 May 1805, n. 11). Io, in Greek mythology, was a maiden loved by Zeus; she was turned into a cow. CS may have in mind Samuel Johnson's remark, "A cow is a very good animal in the field; but we turn her out of a garden."

9. E. Cornelia Knight (1758–1837) had most recently produced *A Description of Latium, or La Campagna di Roma* (1805); CS probably remembered *Marcus Flaminius, or A View of the Military, Political, and Social Life of the Romans* (1792), a didactic romance in letters.

10. Elizabeth Hamilton (1758–1816), a Scottish writer of poetry, fiction, satire, and works on education, had recently published *Memoirs of the Life of Agrippina, the Wife of Germanicus* (1804).

11. Emma, Lady Hamilton (?1761–1815), a celebrated beauty of modest background, rose through a number of sexual liaisons to a position of rank. She married Sir William Hamilton in 1791, and then she became the mistress of Lord Nelson in 1798. When she became pregnant by Nelson, he left his wife, and their illegitimate daughter was born in 1801. Before Nelson's death, she was already known for the extravagance that would lead her to die in poverty in 1815. She was indeed beautiful, as Romney's two portraits of her (at the National Portrait Gallery and the Iveagh Bequest, Kenwood House, London) show. CS would have been especially aware of the portraits, for Romney had sketched a portrait of her when she met him at Eartham in 1792. A note at the top of the letter appears to refer to Lady Hamilton.

To Thomas Cadell, Jr., and William Davies

Bignor Park, Aug 18th
1805
Gentn,

If you find any difficulty in procuring Draytons Polyalbion,[1] as I am apprehensive you will, I will endeavour to borrow it here before I go to the Sea or return home, one or other of which I shall do about Saturday next. I am not yet sure which because there were no lodgings to be had at present at Bognor & another place I have written to, & if I do not hear by Teusdays post that such as suit me can be had at one or other of these places, I shall the end of the week return to my new residence at Tilford near Farnham (three miles from the house I have inhabited these last three years). As my Sister is a very good judge of these matters & often of great use in assisting me by criticisms, I wish to have the other books while I am here & shall therefore be oblig'd to you to send them by The first Petworth Coach after the receipt of this, not forgetting the Poem calld the Lay of the last Minstrel. In finishing Poetry on which much of my credit depends, the best Poetry of the day should be read. I will either pay for or return these— —

I am persuaded the Mr Smith you mention is the same Gentleman whom I met at Busbridge where he was accompanied by his daughter[2] while he took the likenesses in small whole length crayons of Mrs Townsend & her two children. I requested Mrs Townsend to send me the address of Miss Smith, but Mrs Townsends severe illness prevented her recollecting it. The young Lady's Christian name I know is Emma, & it would be easy to ascertain whether it is the same. It is not indeed probable that, common as the name of Smith is, there are two Artists of that name, Crayon painters. I hinted to Miss Smith, with whom I dined twice at Busbridge, that if another volume of my Poetry was publishd, I should very much wish to have her designs for the plates, and she appeard to be extremely gratified by the idea. It is most likely she is at present out of Town, as I think I heard she was to be in the north with her father, but if you think it worth while to enter into any treaty with her on this business & will inform me of the extent of your design, I would write to her, settle the designs in a way that would be somewhat better than such things usually are done in. I saw two drawings of hers, mere vignettes, but most elegantly done, for the Poem of the deserted Village,[3] which I doubt not she would be happy to shew you——

I cannot however but wish that, before you take any farther trouble on this matter, ~~that~~ we could come to some understanding on the price of the Volume. The two former volumes were publishd under circumstances so very different that they are no guide in the present instance. To give you some idea of the present volume, This is a table of the propos'd contents:[4]

A rondeau—14 lines
Sonnet from the Italian
Sonnet
Lyrical piece—16 lines
The wood walk—108
The Shepherd of the Hill—25
Sonnet to the River W[yhe]
Piece of—70 lines
St Monica—90
Piece. 64 lines
Do 68 lines
Do From La Fontaines fables. 36

A local Poem—of near 400 lines, which is what I want these books to finish the notes &c, & which is the only part of the work that is not actually ready for the press.[5] You will perceive that the volume will be much larger than the other two. Indeed the last named poem, which embraces a variety of subjects[6] & which if I am not deceived will do me no discredit, is of magnitude to be printed singly in Quarto, but I prefer making it a member of the collection of all I have written, & I confess it is my ambition, as the time cannot be far off when my literary career will close, to make the whole as perfect as it will admit of—As it is on the Poetry I have written that I trust for the little reputation I may hereafter have & know that it is not the <u>least</u> likely among the works of modern Poets to reach another period—if Any judgement can be formed from the success it has had in this; I shall endeavour not to do what I see too frequently done—sacrifice quality to quantity & empty my port folio. And I shall publish nothing that is not allowed by less partial judges than myself to be worth publishing. At the same time, I wish to take out two or three inferior pieces from the two volumes already publish'd & replace them. You will be able to judge what it is worth your while to give, & I think it would be most satisfactory to us both that you should say what you propose on this subject, & in doing so, you will very much oblige, Gent[n], your very obed[t] Ser[t],

Charlotte ~~Smith~~

I wish to hear by the return of the post, my stay being so uncertain.

Yale University MS. Address: Mess[rs] Cadell & Davies/ Strand/ London. Postmark: PETWORTH/ 37; F/ AUG 20/ 180{5}.

NOTES

1. First requested of them on 26 July (see there n. 2).

2. John Raphael Smith and his daughter Emma. See CS to Cadell and Davies, 26 July 1805, n. 5.

3. In *The Poetical Works of Oliver Goldsmith,* ed. John Aikin (London: Cadell and Davies, et al., 1805), two of three plates to "The Deserted Village" are by "A. Smith, A." CS would have found them congenial: one depicts an abandoned woman at a pillar by a door; the other, a ruined family.

4. In the published work, many of these were retitled, and they were printed in a different order. This volume contains fewer sonnets than *Elegiac Sonnets i* and offers longer, more experimental verse forms. The "local Poem—of near 400 lines," "Beachy Head," the title poem, was printed first (pp. 1–51). Its final length was 732 lines.

The rest are "The Truant Dove, from Pilpay. A Fable" (pp. 52–68), "The Lark's Nest. A Fable from Esop" (pp. 69–78), "The Swallow" (pp. 79–83), "Flora" (pp. 84–99), "Studies by the Sea" (pp. 100–109), "The Horologue of the Fields" (pp. 110–16), "Saint Monica" (pp. 117–24), "A Walk in the Shrubbery" (pp. 126–30), "Hope. A Rondeau." (pp. 131–32), "Evening" (pp. 133–34), "Love and Folly, From the Fables of La Fontaine" (pp. 135–38), and "On the Aphorism, 'L'Amitie est l'Amour sans ailes' [Friendship is love without wings]" (pp. 139–40).

Three of these last poems survived as the only holograph poems in the letters. CS sent Sarah Rose "To Evening" and "Hope" on 30 July 1805, and "On the Aphorism, 'L'Amitie est l'Amour sans ailes'" on 26 Apr. 1806. The latter shows that CS continued to add poems once publication was delayed.

5. That is, CS needs the requested books to complete notes for "the local poem of 400 lines." The rest is ready for the press.

6. *Beachy Head* alternates CS's themes of past and present history, city and country,

and wealth and poverty, as well as images of light and dark, morning and night, and coast and heath.

To Sarah Rose

Bignor Park, Augst 21st
1805

I am weary, my dear Madam, of waiting for an address to you for which I took the liberty of applying to Mr Hayley three weeks ago, for circumstances (of very unpleasant varieties) had so long prevented my writing to you that I thought it probable you had left Seaford if not Uckfield. But somehow or other Mr Hayleys transient civilities fade away before I can say they exist; I fear something I said in my plain way about old friends has made him angry— —But I cannot so subdue my feelings as to appear delighted with mere indiscriminate bowing sort of civility, where I expected the solidity of real friendship, which I have never deserved to lose. It is gone however. Peace to its manes.[1] I should not even in the last instance have disturbed the sad remains if I had not been desirous of my letter's reaching you, and happening to know Mr H. was in correspondence with you, I thought myself sure of attaining that end &, as I hoped, without giving him any particular trouble.

I now write at an hazard to Uckfield to say at length I am driven to the Sea Where I should now have been if I could have got any lodging at Bognor likely to suit me, but there were not only none of that description, but none at all, & I was not very sorry, for it is a place I very much dislike & should only have gone thither because the journey thither was less expensive than to some other places. I have now determin'd to conquer the extreme repugnance I have to Brighthelmstone and to go thither as soon as I can hear of a lodging near the Sea, for it is from the Sea Air I am to hope for the benefit I am promis'd—— I have no expectation of it, I confess, but that lingering love of life, an abject love I sometimes think it, induces me to consent to go whithersoever they bid me— —Tho I consented the more readily because I was quite unequal to the bustle of a removal which I was oblig'd to undergo, My Cottage being taken possession of by its owner. I have not gone far afield; an house at Tilford three miles from Elsted now contains my eldest daughter, my Son Lionels beautiful Wife, & her lovely little Girl.

For myself, I am desirous of a few months or say weeks of wandering with only my little Luzena who wants Sea bathing, & her French Governess who can speak very little English & whom I have not yet seen. Now my Dear Madam, is there the smallest probability of my being fortunate enough to see you, & is it quite impossible you could favor me with your company for a week longer, should I go to Brighthelmston Where the lodging I have hopes of would allow me to solicit such a pleasure? Uckfield I think is not very far & on the Lewes road. You would not be far from your Children, & you cannot imagine what sincere pleasure it would bestow on one who has not many pleasures to look forward to & who has a sad certainty of many pains.

My news from India, tho tardy, is satisfactory [. . .][2] gives me some little courage to contend with this [. . .] and singular illness—Now pray ans[r] me [. . .] I have taken the liberty to make by an early p[ost . . .] a favourable answer would determine my wavering resolution—— I write again to Brighton to night, but the idea of [. . .] hours I shall pass there seems to counteract all hop[es?] I am however very sensible of the liberty I take, [. . .] know whether I ought to expect your forgiveness.

M[rs] Dorset expects some London [. . .] strangers to me, & I am oblig'd to finish my letter [. . .] civil & behave very prettily—

I am, my Dear Madam,
most affectionately yours,
Charlotte Smith

Huntington MS (HM10841). Address: ~~M[rs] Rose/ Uckfield/ By London—Sussex~~ M[rs] Rose/ M[r] Pogee's/ New Norfolk Street/ London. Postmark: PETWORTH/ 57; {Aug} 26/ 1805.

NOTES

1. Spirits of the dead.

2. A portion of the third and fourth page, torn away at crease lines, accounts for missing words and phrases in the last two paragraphs.

To the earl of Egremont

[Bignor Park or Brighton, late August 1805][1]
My Lord,

Being orderd to try if change of air & particularly that of the Sea will be of any use in removing the illness & debility I have so long labourd under, I have determind to take the opportunity of my familys removal to make the experiment without much hope of success.

M[rs] Lionel Smith, my daughter & myself, were much oblig'd by Your Lordships information re[ceive][d] this morning. Our anxiety is great to know whether my Son's first promotion has been announced to him & Letters r[eceive][d] today from George encrease our solicitude.[2] I dare not ask yr Lordship whether he will at least, according to such information, be at home before he joins the 16th but yet, should you know, I persuade myself you will do me the Great kindness to inform me.

My state of health is such as renders the anxiety I go thro destructive, but I am not less sensible of the obligation my family owe you. I enclose a receipt from a writing Master here for the money I paid him for copying the papers about the business in Barbados, which I was unable to do myself. Also Mr Daniels an[swe]^r^ to my enquiry whether he had sent in to the Trustees the bill for postage & He has charged it all to me, to which I add what I have paid, & doubt not but that your lordship will direct that I may not be a loser, In my situation every Small Sum being material. I have no correspondence whatever with Messrs Daniels but on account of the Trust.[3]

I have the honor to be
My Lord, your Lordships most obligd
& obed^t^ Ser^t^
Charlotte Smith

Petworth House Archives MS. No address or postmark.

NOTES

1. Three points help in dating this letter. First, Lionel's wife Ellen Marianne Galway Smith had come with her infant daughter to visit CS in June 1805. Second, Lionel had been promoted from major to lieutenant colonel in the 18th Regiment as of 1 Aug. 1805. Third, CS describes her physician's advice for sea bathing in virtually the same words used in a letter to Cadell and Davies (2 Sept. 1805).

It is not clear whether CS wrote this letter from Bignor Park or Brighton. On 21 Aug. she wrote from Bignor that she was planning to visit Bognor, a seaside resort. By 2 Sept. she was at Brighton, her attempts to procure a lodging at Bognor having failed.

2. Both Lionel and George were stationed in the West Indies, Lionel with the 18th Regiment and George with the 16th.

3. Thomas Daniel, a merchant, had handled money for CS and the trust as early as 1797.

To the earl of Egremont and the Reverend Nicholas Turner

[Brighton, 2 September 1805]
My Lord & Sir,

Mr Adams[1] before his departure for the West, in an hopeless illness & under very severe personal suffering as well as Domestic affliction, has taken the trouble to send me the enclos'd opinions as the best proof that his idea of the Justice of the claims of Richard Smiths representatives to the position yet to be had of George Forster Clarkes debt <u>was not chimerical</u>.

I know it is to little purpose that <u>I</u> write on this or any other matter of business. Yet I feel it to be <u>my duty</u> to represent that, while My eldest daughter is without any part even of the interest of money awarded to her two years since, and while the whole family are suffering under a prolongation of that distress, which I have struggled against so many years (till my strength & health fail, & I borrow money to enable me to try the prescription of my Physician as a forlorn hope), it is very mortifying to perceive that every debt due to the estate is by a strange fatality Escaping from the unfortunate claimants——

Perfectly conscious as I am that Lord Egremonts goodness so remarkably exerted in regard to some parts of the family—Goodness which I most sensibly feel—ought not to encourage any unreasonable expectations as to the execution of Affairs which must be so very irksome to him & so entirely improper to trouble him with; I only ask, & never meant to ask more, than that his Lordship would give me such direction to act as he must be aware are necessary to prevent the moneys being lost.

As I cannot afford to remain here, however necessary to my health, longer than a very few days, & indeed am very little able to write more than I am oblig'd to do for my support, I shall be glad that, should any communication be necessary, it may be made to Miss Smith at Tilford near Farnham Who will do whatever she may be directed. I am likely to be absent from thence some weeks, being desired to try change of air, & having already found some little benefit from the change. I am, My Lord & Sir,

your obed^{t} & most hble Ser^{t},
Charlotte Smith

Septr 2nd 1805
I shall be oblig'd to you to let me have Mr Pindars letter sent to Tilford that I may an^{r} it as a matter of civility individually, & I will send it back— —

Petworth House Archives MS. No address or postmark.

NOTE

1. Thomas Maxwell Adams of Barbados had suffered a stroke at the age of 35 (CS to Egremont, 27 Oct. 1804 and n. 1).

To Thomas Cadell, Jr., and William Davies

[Brighton] September 2nd 1805
Gentlemen,

I should sooner have acknowledged the receipt of the books sent to Bignor & of your last letter which preceded them, but being desird by my Physician to try repeated change of Air, & particularly that of the Sea, I came hither for a few days previous to my return into Surrey.

I am much oblig'd to you for your promis'd care of my India Letters, which have for some years given you a great deal of trouble, but hence forward you will be releived from it as My Son Nicholas has at length received my directions to forward them to M[r] Marter of the Accomptants Office by whose hands I have had the very great comfort of receiving most satisfactory accounts after a length of time which gave me the most serious alarm. But his Letters & bills were, as I now find, taken in the Ship Hope and carried into the Isle of France.

The conditions on which the two former Volumes of Sonnets &c were publish'd, were, as I beleive I before observed, so very unlike those in which the projected Vol will appear that I found myself a good deal at a loss to name what should be the price of the Copy right of the last named work. And diffident of my own judgement as well as of the medium thro which I naturally see the matter, I thought it best to consult two of my friends, who, tho persons very differently situated, are both acknowledged judges of literary merit & of the price of Copy right. It was not till Saturday that I received from Bignor Park, whither it had been directed, the Opinion of the last of these my Counsellors, & his opinion coincides with singular exactness with that of the other of my friends, tho they are unacquainted with each other. I laid before each a statement of the particulars of my transactions with the elder M[r] Cadell, & since with your house (from Memorandums taken from his letters, which I happen to have preserved) & in many of which he scruples not to express opinions of my writing which I <u>beleive</u> the event has never proved to be erroneous. And that none of the purchases, either made by him or since by yourselves (tho some must always be less Successful than others) have been among those which you had reason to regret.

Tho I trust I am as little as may be infected with the vanity of an Author And that I know myself tho it is the rarest of all knowledge, Yet I will not affect to say I am <u>not</u> conscious of being some degrees above most of the Lady writers of the day. The writer who could obtain the suffrage of Sir William Jones[1] & the friendship of Cowper to say nothing of the applause of other persons I could enumerate of very great literary celebrity <u>should</u> feel the value of such immortality, & feel, too, that too great care cannot be taken not to fall into the common error of carelessness and, presuming on name only, to sell to the public the emptyings of a port folio. Tho very far removed from the affluence I have a right to because my fortune during his life is possess'd by another, Yet the time is at length come when some parts of my family are enabled to save me from the hardships I have for many years undergone and are willing to shew their gratitude for those long years of toil when <u>they</u> had no other support—— —— ——

All this You will perhaps think a useless & irrelevant string of remarks, but my purpose is to explain that it is not necessity (as you perfectly well know has happen'd) that urges the publication, & that, tho an handsome remuneration is assuredly an object to me, I am not as heretofore under that humiliating necessity, of accepting whatever price is offer'd—for I now know that, while I sold my Novels at 50 G^s^ a volume, very inferior writers obtain'd an hundred, & that the price is now more than double for works which, if they ever entirely get into sale, will never see a second edition—120 Guineas, is now the price of a very mediocre novel of 11 sheets. A book of Travels (which one might write in a good library without stirring from the fire side) is 400 Guineas— —Another more wonderful still is actually sold for 1500£.

To you, Gentlemen, the work I now have in hand is undoubtedly worth more than it can be to any other person, for which reason, as soon as I found I had good poetry enough to make an additional Volume (or should have, as soon as that Poem I have had some years in contemplations was finishd to my mind), I applied to my friend Mr Johnson, who advis'd me by all means to follow what appear'd to me to be the properest mode of proceeding & to offer the Volume to you.[2]

The price I expect for it is 300£ & a discharge of my debt to you, & for this I will agree to receive, on delivery of the Poems fairly written and ready for the press, two bills at six weeks & two months, or at two & three months as you may prefer; I beleive I do not say too much in asserting that I can have this money if not more, but I have never made any enquiry on the subject, save to my two friends,[3] who advised me on a fair view of the whole to name the above as my expectations——

As it is pleasant to know the result of our labour, I shall be oblig'd to you to give me your answer in a few days. But I have so many acquaintance likely to come hither & have not unfrequently experienced a good deal of inconvenience from impertinent curiosity, & I devote myself so entirely to my health & my desk that I wish to be quite unknown here in order to avoid all visits or enquirys. Be so good therefore in y^r^ answer to direct to me thus, omitting my Christian name, Mrs Smith, 26 East Cliff, Brighton. I am, Gent^n^, your most obed humble Ser^t^,

Charlotte Smith

I beleive you recollect that the copyright of Emmeline was never sold, only the third Edition. I have been frequently importuned for the little Book calld "The Romance of real life." Are there any copies to be had?[4] A friend whom I much wish to oblige desir'd me to obtain one for her if possible. I have been very much oblig'd on my Sons account to a certain great Lady,[5] & I wish to show my gratitude. I have an Indian Box coming of fillagreed Ivory of considerable value, the same as I sent one to the Dss of Devonshire. In this box, if it arrives safe by the Worcester & now daily expected, it is my project to put a set of my books of instruction for a child the Lady is fond of. It would therefore extremely oblige me if you would procure a set of "the Conversations" &, with Rural Walks & Rambles farther, have them very elegantly bound in the neatest & most delicate manner against the Arrival of my Casquet & whether our agreement takes place or no, I will thankfully repay you; M[r] Johnson will supply a set of "the Conversations."

Yale University MS. Address: Mess[rs] Cadell & Davies/ Strand/ London. Postmark: BRIGHTON/ 59; A/ SEP 3/ 1805.

NOTES

1. Sir William Jones (1746–1794), a widely known and respected judge, legal writer, and scholar of Oriental studies. Well versed in Latin, Greek, Hebrew, Arabic, Persian, French, German, and Portuguese and familiar with other languages, he translated many important works; he is best known today for hypothesizing that Greek, Sanskrit, and German share a common linguistic ancestor. He was appointed in 1783 to be a judge at Fort William in India at about the same time that he was knighted. CS may have come to his attention through her son William Towers Smith, who was stationed near Calcutta, or through Sir William's friend Sir John Shore, Lord Teignmouth, the governor-general of India from 1793 to 1798, who also befriended her sons (see CS to Cadell and Davies, [Mar. 1798]). *Suffrage* here means "approval."

2. On 4 Sept. Cadell and Davies declined her offer in a short, courteous note that offended her:

> Madam
>
> We esteem ourselves favoured by your Proposal respecting the 3rd Volume of your Poems, which we readily admit is worth more to us than to any other Person, though we cannot also admit that, for that Reason, a higher Demand should be made upon us than upon any other. The Price you have been induced to affix to the Property, is so very far beyond what we conceive the probable Sale of a third Volume, however highly and carefully finished, can justify, that we have no Hesitation in begging your Permission to decline the Purchase——

3. CS was certainly advised by the publisher Joseph Johnson on this offer, but names no other advisor.

4. Though published in Dublin in 1787, Germany in 1789, and Philadelphia and Baltimore in 1799, *The Romance of Real Life* (1787) was not published again in England; thus additional copies may no longer have been available. A very cheap edition was printed in Aberdeen in 1847.

5. Possibly Lady Clanricarde, the only titled woman besides the duchess of Devonshire that CS appears to have known in her later years.

To Sarah Rose

[Brighton, 10 September 1805]

My Dear Madam, I was indeed uneasy at not hearing from you Not however because I doubted your kindness but because I feard you were not well or were engaged painfully by some indisposition among your friends. My Sister forwarded your letter to me to day from Bignor which I left on the 27th of August, yielding at length to her persuasions, & venturing the expence in the hope of acquiring a little strength here. I did not think that any thing could induce me to revisit this place again whither from my earliest recollection I used to come for pleasure & change of scene & where I have been often with "Chariots & with horses & horsemen & footmen," Where I have been a gay dancer at Balls, & a lighthearted Equestrian on the Hills, & afterwards when Matrimony & misery came together, I came hither with sick children who were restored by this air. Then I came—— with ———— Mr B Smith to assist his escape to France when I had deliverd him from an imprisonment of seven months, & when imprisonment again menaced him, Here too I remaind when I was trying to negociate with his Creditors for his return & have watched at the window for Bailiffs while he sat within, uttering curses against me, & while my ten children, one then at the breast, often clung round me in terror as his violence threatend my personal safety—— Lastly, when every hope of his ever behaving with decency was at an end, and when I was turned on the wide world with all these children to provide for, hither I came to write for bread, & here I saw unfolding in beauty & sweetness, her whom I shall behold no more.[1]

Imagine therefore, my dear Madam, all this place recalls, & how little it is calculated to render my spirits better whatever effect the air has on my health. I found it of great use when I first came hither in restoring my appetite which I had nearly lost, and change of air is one of the remedies that has usually been of use to me, but I now sink again & beleive that the money, which will be a grievous consideration before the experiment is finishd, will be thrown away. Nothing surely shews the weakness of human nature more than the pains & trouble we take to retain a life of the misery of which we are always complaining. But as to myself, I can say, I think truly, that it is the act of dying I fear & nothing else, let what will come afterwards, & Tho I ought to have still many comforts, I know, yet they come half cold & half embitterd to an heart which once had so keen a relish for such, as My too vivid fancy imagined, but I shall get into this dreadful croakery, & by way of passing a melancholy Sunday night annoy you with my horrors. It is better to ansr those questions which shew the kind interest you take in my destiny, such as it now is.

I beleive I told you, but perhaps like other old folks I shall run into repetition, that the Sieur Phillips was in a grievous passion & wrote me some very fierce letters;[2] I was advised by one who knows him well to answer him as cavalierly, which I did, & have since heard no more about it: Johnsons good nature and liberality of mind cannot indeed be too highly spoken of. He no sooner Gave himself time to reflect on my letters than he allow'd me most handsomely for the MMS, & as I was distressd for money on account of my removal, and it became every day more & more necessary for me to try the Sea air, he allow'd me, tho considerably in his debt, to draw for 100£ which just as I had done the Belle Packet brought me a supply, but I am still deeply in his debt & trying to write it out.

It was to him I applied when I found I had enough Poetry to make a third Volume, enquiring how I should dispose of it to the best advantage. He advised me by all means to offer it to Cadell & Davies, who said they had no doubt but that if I w[d] send the MMS to them, we should agree. This (after some very mean & shabby tricks they have play'd me, notwithstanding the Sums I have put into their pockets) I did not much delight to do; Some books were necessary to me, & a long poem (long for me), which was to be a member of this Volume, required in polishing it a great deal of application. I thought it better therefore to be at some <u>certainty</u> & named to Johnson the price I intended to ask: 235£. He replied (desiring however that his name should not Appear) that, considering the great Sums which to his certain knowledge the House of Cadell & Davies have gaind by me & the high price of works at this moment, I ought to ask 335£ which I did. But Mess[rs] C. & D. are so far from being of his opinion that they reject my proposal without making any other.[3] It is a sort of <u>damper</u>, I confess, which is not delightful to me; I have written to my good friend Johnson upon it, but it has the effect of suspending my work.

I shall try in a day or two to go on with my story book, but it is my unfortunate destiny never to have any one near me who has the smallest idea of what writing ought to be, & I am always diffident of my own judgement which may be warped or bias'd. Once I had in M[r] Hay[ley] a friend on whose criticism I generally relied & who is perhaps a better critic of the works of others than of his own, but for some reason or for <u>no</u> reason am entirely hors de grace there. I wish I dared to ask you to <u>supply a friendly office</u> which I shall never again solicit him to fill. Indeed when I ventured to hope you could come hither, I was not thinking of that but generally how happy it would have made me.

I have now passd a fortnight most piteously, my only companions being my little Luzena &, since yesterday sennight, the French Woman I have hired for her Governess who has as little information as can well be imagind & I am persuaded has no notion whether the world is round or square. All I expect of her is that she will teach the child French, but I really begin to question whether she can do that. It is a most depressing circumstance, but so it happens that I am doom'd to pass my days without any society that have any ideas in common with me So that in the midst of many I live alone & fly to my desk where only I am occupied. Well, here is egotism enough.

Now it is more than time to tell you that I have read Mr Carrs northern journey with extreme pleasure. The Edinburgh I see sheath the terrors of their Claws for him (they do not even notice a mistake of Goliah for Sampson which in the copy I read seemd to excite the wonder of some Critic in MMS), but how they bedash our poor Hermit of the Tea Tower.[4] I am always vexd when he lays himself open to such attacks, but indeed, my dear Madam, he is hurting himself very much in having recourse to such Critics as Miss Poole & Co.; the other is a Mr Marsh,[5] and between them, what but stagnation can be expected. I wish he knew his real friends. Miss Collins[6] has been lately at Felpham transcribing for him, for I find his eyes are still very weak, but that is not the reason why he has not written to me.

I am very sorry you too have so comfortless a complaint. No, my dear Madam, there is not I beleive the least chance of my ever seeing Bath again tho after finding myself here I must not be positive that I shall never go thither. My poor Sister had soon enough of it. She had you know but one child,[7] a being on which she lavishd as much affection as is usually given to a dozn among them. She could not see a fault while all her perfections were magnified & multiplied.

Alas! at 22, this miracle of wisdom & wit chose to marry a Man who, if he is not old, appears enough so to be her Grandfather. With four children & almost all his property depending on his life which, as he eats & drinks like twenty Aldermen, is supposd not to be worth two years purchase. By this Man who is in character extremely like a large [. . .] put up in a stye, she has had two children within the year. Her beauty is lost in absolute deformity from table indulgences, & her mind so changed that she is quite estrangd from her Mother who has sacrificed every thing to her!—& now poor Bignor is sacrificed because this fat hog did not think the living there good enough!

My Sister return'd from Bath unhappy & in disgust &, I beleive, will pass the greatest part of the winter here, at least the first part & the latter part in London, whither I should go if my finances would admit, but of that I have little hope tho my second Son, whose little boy I expect by this fleet, liberally supplies me.

I am in misery till I hear from Lionel & George, my two poor Soldiers in the W Indies. I did not say, did I, that military lines were to be rejected?[8] I beleive I said that a Mother must suffer more in those than in any other, but it is so difficult to know what to do for or with Boys without a father, & mine have had an enemy in theirs, which is a still greater misfortune. I shall think the worse of the Lees for their notion of <masks>; surely it is very unlike their general manner of thinking. I have obey'd your commands, my dear Madam, & written you a dull letter in hopes you will let me hear from you very very soon, Ever yrs, CS

I wish you would name me to H. & try to discover what is my offence toward him. I should like to know it.[9]

10th Sept 1805

Cowper and Newton Museum MS. Address: M[rs] Rose/ Horndon Street/ Kensington/ No. 2./ by London. Postmark: BRIGHTON/ 59; A/SEP 10/1805; SP40/ 1805.

NOTES

1. Augusta. BS was imprisoned from Dec. 1783 to 2 July 1784, and he escaped to France in Oct. 1784.

2. The bookseller Richard Phillips began to insist that CS owed him the third and final volume of her *History of England . . . to a young lady at school.* See CS to Sarah Rose, 2 July 1805 and n. 5.

3. See CS to Cadell and Davies, 2 Sept. 1805, and their response, n. 2.

4. From his retreat at Eartham, Hayley often signed letters "Hermit."

5. On Henrietta Poole and Edward Marsh, see CS to Sarah Rose, 14 May 1805, nn. 11, 12.

6. Charlotte Collins, of Graffham, Midhurst; she was long a friend of CS and Hayley (see CS to an unnamed recipient, ca. Sept. 1785, n. 1).

7. Lucy Smith Dorset, baptized on 21 Sept. 1780, was Capt. Michael and Catherine Dorset's "only surviving child," according to her marriage settlement (dated 18 Oct. 1803); she married Charles Henry Fraser. The Bignor parish records show a younger brother, Charles Ferguson Dorset, born 24 Oct. and baptized 22 Nov. 1782. His date of death is not known.

8. CS is advising Sarah Rose not to let her sons embark upon military careers (see CS to Sarah Rose, 14 May 1805).

9. A note at the seal of the folded, addressed letter reads: "Brighton Sept[r] 8th. Direct thus Omitting the Charlotte as I wish not to be known. M[rs] Smith. Boeldys [Ship Sh____ Grocer] Brighton"

To Thomas Cadell, Jr., and William Davies

[Tilford, 20 October 1805]

Gent[n], The state of health in which I return'd from Brighton is such—& I find myself so unequal to the attention necessary to finish so long a work as the local poem (which would have made a considerable part of a third Volume) with the care which w[d] be necessary not to commit my reputation—that I have determin'd to lay it by till returning health, if ever it dose return, enables me to finish it as well as I think it is begun. This circumstance induces me to think of disposing otherwise of the Lyrical pieces I have by me of which I beleive I sent you a list, & if, as I understood, it is your purpose to publish a new edition of the two Volumes, it might perhaps answer to you to insert them, In which case you will be so good as to let me know what it would be worth your while to give me, & this I wish to learn with your early convenience that I may decide how to act———

In consequence of what you said relative to prosecuting Mr Capel Lofft if he inserted any of the Poetry your property [*sic*], I thought it highly necessary to inform that Gentleman of your resolution; I told him that, having occasion to write to you about other business,[1] I had named this to you, & that (with abruptness equally bearing on my business & his intentions, for your letter was singularly abrupt & hardly in terms of common civility) you had ans[were][d] my business & announced your resolution to defend your property. I had no other motive than to prevent Mr Loffts getting into the same difficulty that a person I know was likely to do with certain Gentlemen in P[ater] N[oster] Row, for I never saw him in my life or had the least communication with him till this correspondence began. I could not however help noticing the manner in which your reply was couch'd, for, while you refused every offer I made, you told me the work was still no object to you, which seem'd expressly meant to mortify me, because if it was no object, it appear'd strange that you would not part with it as I propos'd.[2]

Of all this however, I said nothing to Mr Lofft, but merely stated your refusal to let him insert any thing of which you were proprietor in his intended collection. He has taken it up very warmly, & much more so than seems worth while, & informs me that after fourteen years, if an Author be living, the property returns to the author, any sale for the intermediate time notwithstanding, & he quotes the act of the 8th year of Q. Anne, Anno 1709, Chapter 19th.[3] Now the first edition of the Sonnets was published in 1784, but only about eighteen were then printed, as I recollect: The book such as it now appears was printed by subscription in 1788 or 1789. And if this doctrine be correct, it is certain that the property of the first Volume of the Sonnets is mine. I am as little disposed as able to enter into any contention; at the same time, I cannot help feeling what I am continually told by others, that considering the great success of that work & the comparatively small expence of printing, I have been less liberally dealt by than might have been expected, considering too the very considerable advantage your house has received from almost every one of the purchases you made of me at very inferior prices[4]—and of which, if I am rightly informed, there are hardly any now to be had.

A person is very apt to fancy their own works bear a greater value than they really do, but I desire only to appeal to facts. I have often named to you that I never parted with the Copy right of Emmeline to the late Mr Cadell, & I have often enquired what number there were left of the last edition, but you never were so obliging as to take the smallest notice of my questions.

At your leisure, I shall be oblig'd to you for a reply to my Letter because, if I do not find a reasonable price likely to be obtaind for my smaller pieces, I shall finish a slight story long by me on purpose to introduce them Unless it be found that, by the property of the first Volume's reverting to me, I may publish a volume on my own account.[5] I am sorry that, from my Son's not sending my last address to Bombay To Messrs Forbes (as he is now at Calcutta himself), the house of Forbes & Co adhered to the old direction & sent the letters to you, thereby occasioning you trouble not intended by, Gent^{n},

Your obed. humble Ser^{t},
Charlotte ~~Smith~~

Tilford near Farnham, Surrey
Octr 20th 1805

Yale University MS. Address: Messrs Cadell & Davies/ Strand/ London. Postmark: GODALMIN; G/ OCT 21/ 180<5?>.

NOTES

1. No correspondence between CS and the barrister, poet, and classical scholar Capell Lofft (1751–1824) has been found, and an intermediate letter from Cadell and Davies appears to be missing. Lofft had written them a "very insolent Letter" because of what CS told him, but they did not respond. CS's advocacy of Lofft's copyright dispute suggests that she still kept in touch with at least some of her pro-revolutionary compatriots from the early 1790s.

2. On 30 Oct., Cadell and Davies answered this and her other charges in this letter at some length. They began on a conciliatory note: "We are exceedingly sorry for the Misconception which has arisen in the later Part of our correspondence, as it has led you to attribute to us a Want of common Civility, as well as to misinterpret our Meaning in other Respects—," conceding that "Our last Letter, written perhaps in Haste, may have been liable to the Charge of Abruptness, but it was far from our Wish or Intention to give you Offence." They continued, "we declined the Purchase, not because it was not an Object to us, but because the Price you mentioned was far beyond what we conceived the Sale to be expected of it would justify our giving." Their reasoning was that as the second volume of *Elegiac Sonnets* had sold less than the first, a third would be even less profitable.

3. This is the letter of the law, but Cadell and Davies doubt the "soundness of his law" and go on to explain their position: "With Regard to the Copyright of your Poems, there cannot be a Doubt that when you disposed of it, you transferred your whole Right—We remember not a single Instance of a Copyright reverting to the Author at the End of 14 Years—— ——."

4. In response, Cadell and Davies agree that the works Cadell, Sr., purchased were profitable, but add that

> on those which we have had the Pleasure of purchaseing, we should have no Difficulty in demonstrating that the aggregate Result has been Loss instead of Profit—yet we do not mention this as a Matter of Complaint—the Booksellers Profits, on new Publications particularly, are in 99 Instances out of 100 most exceedingly over-rated.

5. In response to this and her charge that they had made no counteroffer, Cadell and Davies offered to sponsor a subscription edition.

To Thomas Cadell, Jr., and William Davies

Tilford on Farnham
Novr 3rd 1805
Gent^n^,

The method you propose of a subscription[1] is so entirely out of the question that it is not worth while to say another word on the subject. If a third Volume is worth little or nothing, a republication can be worth still less. But I perfectly comprehend how it might answer, Tho not to me, to do it by subscription if as in former instances I am at the expence of the plates & printing & sell for a trifling consideration the copy right, which might afterwards run thro four or five editions from which I should derive no proffit at all. However as my Sons are in situations[2] which will by no means admit of my humbling myself again to adopt any such expedient, it need not be discuss'd. I did not name the Sum I mention'd without the advice of persons well versed in the business. But their idea of the proffits and your books seem certainly at variance. I happen to know that the purchaser of Marchmont had 70 copies left, had paid every expence, & had then as he told me himself a proffit of 120£. There was no reason why he should deceive me against his own interest which was to depreciate the value of the commodity.

I therefore must be forgiven if I cannot implicitly subscribe to the hint you give that your concern has rather lost than gain'd by your connection with me as an Author.[3] Perhaps upon looking at Rural Walks & its pendant,[4] you may recollect that you cannot have lost by them, & if it be true that, of the greater part of my writings, not a copy remains, & of all, but very few copies, I own it is not easy to comprehend where the loss can have lain or how it has arisen. Mr Bell[5] confessd having cleard 400£ by "the old Manor House." It is singular indeed if, with your characters as Booksellers & all the appliances & means by which you can forward works into notice, You only should have been rather losers than gainers by mine. Mr Cadell the elder, however, once ingenuously told me that Booksellers set the proffits of their successful Authors against Those whose works were shelf'd & by whom the publishers were great losers. Perhaps I am unfortunate enough to have been put, p^r^ Contra, with some very heavy manufacturer whose lead has preponderated, & the average of loss falls on me. But you will suffer me to remark that, if it be so, the sooner you give up a losing concern the better, & therefore I was surpris'd you refus'd to sell the remainder of your interest in the sonnets which appear hardly to be worth another edition even with corrections & additions— —

As to Mr Capel Loffts Law,[6] when a Man refers to the words of an act of Parliament for his Authority, it seems likely that he has some tolerable foundation for his opinion— —The thing either is so or is not so. You never recollect an instance of the Copy right returning to an Author after fourteen years; that may easily be, as the Genus imitabile[7] are not a long-lived race, & poor Authors hardly have a chance of surviving while, to the titled & noble Authors, proffit is no object so that perhaps the question never was at issue. I do not feel dispos'd to be the first to bring it thither, but I cannot help remarking one extraordinary circumstance: You say you cannot think of paying much for a work from the printed Volumes of which Mr Capel Lofft declares he will take as much as he pleases, & he may for aught you know do so by the unprinted one. You must therefore mean to say that I wd have sold to you as original & unprinted works <ms> I was giving to him surreptiously to print at the same time. You not only throw a reflection on me which no part of my conduct authorises, but you forget that, when you (somewhat rudely) refused my terms, the name of Mr Capel Lofft had never been mentiond & of course that your refusal could not be occasion'd by his project. It is usual, where there is a real desire to act with candour & liberality, to name a price which it is worth while to give while that ask'd is rejected. You have purchas'd volumes of Poetry from many different Authors & could tell what this would probably be worth, & with any fair & reasonable proposal, tho it might not meet the sanguine idea's of my friends, I should have closed. But if I am to understand you at all, it is in your opinion worth nothing, & therefore You decline it. Nothing remains therefore but for me to try if it be the opinion of others & if so to throw the poetry into the fire. I am, Gentn,

Yr obed humble Sert,
Charlotte Smith

I have not yet sent back the books, having been very unwell ever since I return'd from Sussex & unable to go out of my drawing room or attend to any thing, but they shall be carefully restord with some that I have to send to Mr Johnson.

Yale University MS. Address: Messrs Cadell & Davies/ Strand/ London. Postmark: FARNHAM/ 41; B/ NOV 5/ 1805.

NOTES

1. They simply offered to assist CS with the subscription edition they proposed and give her a stipulated number of volumes (not named in their letter) on advantageous terms, in return for the copyright of the additional poems (Cadell and Davies to CS, 30 Oct. 1805).

2. William was a judge and magistrate at Allahabad, India; Nicholas was garrison paymaster and secretary and translator to the government in the Offices of Country

Correspondence, as well as mehmendar to the Turkish envoy. But CS was probably more concerned with her younger sons' military careers: Lionel was newly a lieutenant colonel in the 18th Regiment, and George a lieutenant in the 16th Regiment.

3. This continues CS's argument from her previous letter and responds to their answer (see CS to Cadell and Davis, 20 Oct. 1805 and n. 4).

4. Its sequel: i.e., *Rambles Farther.*

5. Joseph Bell (see CS to Joel Barlow, 3 Nov. 1792, n. 7).

6. On the reversion of copyright to the author, see CS to Cadell and Davies, 20 Oct. 1805 and n. 3.

7. Class of imitators.

To Sarah Rose

[Tilford, 26 December 1805]

I am just able, my dear Madam, to say how much I feel your kind solicitude about a poor being so little, so very little, worth it in her own estimation. I am they say out of immediate danger. It may be so. The water is undoubtedly much abated, but I am so weak[1] that, unless the tonic remedies I now am taking have a more immediate and powerful effect than is I beleive likely, it cannot do long, & really circumstanced as I am, I hardly know why I should wish it, for prolong'd life is to me only prolong'd misery. I will try, however, to make the most of this short respite.

I thought & still think Mr Carr p^d^ the last small dividend to Johnson. If not, I request the fav^r^ of him to do so as well as what will become due in January next. My fruitless & ill advis'd journey to Brighthelmston, My removal from Elsted to this melancholy House where I have been now a prisoner in my room since the 5th Oct^r^, & other very untoward circumstances & cruel disappointments have brought me into debt with Johnson & otherwise overwhelmd me, & I am the more in despair about it because he does not seem to think any thing I can now do worth purchasing & has never publishd the last book he purchas'd of me.[2] Are you, my Dear Madam, likely to see him? Perhaps you would ask him to lend me Cumberlands life,[3] or any other book, for I am miserable in having nothing to beguile the heavy & monotonous hours which indeed never were so heavy. I have several books of Mr Johnsons which I will carefully return in a short time— —But most of them I hoped to want as referrences till my hands were palsied and my faculties suspended by this detestable complaint.

I grieve for the Lees, but time is <u>said</u> to heal wounds as deep as that they have received. Farewell, my dear Mad^m^; to hear of your welfare & that of your children will ever afford sincere pleasure to

yours most affectionately,
CS

Charlotte promises herself to see you.
Tilford, Dec 26th
1805

Huntington MS (HM10842). Address: Mrs Rose/ Abingdon Street/ Westminister. Postmark: Two-Penny/ POST/ 46 Strand; 4 oClock/ 3.JA/ 1806 EV.

NOTES

1. CS's handwriting is much lighter than her usual, but not wavering as if she were palsied. Nevertheless, it lacks her usual control; she seemed unable to execute the usual flourishes on her "d's." A note on the address page reads: "How shaken is her hand!"

2. *A Natural History of Birds* (1807).

3. See CS to Sarah Rose, ca. Aug. 1805 and n. 4.

To Sarah Rose

Tilford, March
20th 1806

I should not, my dear Madam, trouble you again so very soon with a Letter[1] (for which I have no means to day of getting a frank And which I am sure will not be worth a penny), did I not feel it to be indispensably necessary to correct as early as possible some error of expression in my last Letter which (if I understand your last favr r[eceive]d to day aright) has led you to beleive I have an intention—in the Poems I talkd of as preparing for the press—of attacking Mr H—! Now Heaven forfend! I have been trying to recollect what I said, & I think I remember the expression—or nearly so. I said I wishd he could recall his two last publications, "the triumph of Music" & "the ballads," & alluding to my own possible, indeed probable failure of powers, I added And perhaps he may wish when he sees it—— I could recall My next publication.

By this I meant to say, tho certainly I have obscurely express'd myself, that if he had any friendship remaining for me, he might in his turn be sorry to see the residuum, the caput mortuum[2] of those feeble powers which his politeness, rather than his partiality, once induced him to rate or to say he rated very highly. But as to any attack on him, on a friend once very dear to me & to whom I have been very much oblig'd, I should be detestable in my own eyes and an object of detestation to others, were I capable of entertaining such a thought. On reperusing your Letter, I am sure my expressions must have been very vague & faulty, or you would not have had this impression. I hope & beleive it has not gone beyond your own bosom, & from thence I hasten my dear Madam to erase it. Do me the justice to beleive that—tho I have sufferd myself in writing confidentially to you to smile at our friend, at his odd weekly tiltups[3] to a female critic (whose remarks certainly have not profitted him much), & at his strange tho benevolent fancy of writing such very sad doggrell, for the purpose of serving a Man,[4] who might be any thing rather than an engraver—Yet I never went beyond such a laugh between ourselves, nor ever wrote a line in my life (& I think I can say never will) with an intention of wounding the bard even if I had the power.

Years have pass'd since we have met, & many more years since the first pleasure of my life was now & then enjoying a day or two of his society at Eartham. I will confess that I have been mortified by his undeserved dereliction of one whose blind partiality to almost all he wrote made her the subject not only of ridicule, but of scandal. It is not however because of that dereliction that I am not now equally blind, but because it is impossible not to see how sadly in those two instances he has lost himself. I know a great many literary folks or soi disant tel,[5] & I have had perpetual attacks from some of the younger candidates for the Bayes on these productions of "my friend Hayley," but I have never to them join'd in the laugh. I am not ashamed of saying that I owe very great obligations to Mr H. & of a nature which it never could be in my power to return. But that I should so far forget them as to meditate an agression towards my former friend is not in my nature; to My Sister and to you only, have I ever sportively spoken of some of his eccentricities or sighd over his fall lalls, & it would vex me to death if I thought he knew I had done even that. So far was I from raising a quill against him that, in my last letter to him written about six weeks since which he has never ~~answered~~ noticed, I thankd him for some Italian extracts he sent me last Summer (~~which~~ I was then too ill to notice the receipt of them) & threw out an hint how much I wanted a friend who could & would correct the work I have now in hand. He has never answer'd my letter and probably would not understand the hint.

I did not know you were acquainted with Mr Cumberland, or I might have spared my pert strictures on him & his book. You mention havg seen in the papers the death of Mr Smith but by a wrong Christian name:[6] will you, my dear Madam, tell me, for it is very material to me to know, whether there was any addition to that circums[tance] & what? & do give me five minutes of your time as soon as you can, for it will be a real charity in the present state of my spirits which nothing cheers like Letters from those I love & esteem. My Sister is so occupied by the long & unexpected stay of Mr & Mrs Charles Fraser[7] that I have quite lost her letters.

You see how feebly I write—without being materially worse. I have certain undescribable sensations that tell me there is something incurably wrong in my frame, & that my days tire vers leurs fin,[8] & this is not low spirits: I accustom myself to look as steadily as possible at an event which must happen & cannot be far distant, & I have now been restord to the power of disposing equitably of my fortune,[9] which I have not lost a moment in doing. I trust my Memory will not disgrace my children, who are all worthy of a better father, particularly Col Smith, who left me yesterday with his beautiful wife & Charlotte for Petworth house where they were to remain last night, and to day they go to Portsmouth & embark for Jamaica! & Charlotte returns home. The parting has almost killed me. Lionel was so dreadfully affected at leaving his little Girl & his poor sick Mother whom there is no chance of his seeing again that it has shook me excessively, & I never miss'd one hour hearing the clock last night so that to day I am half dead & feel as if it were well to be quite so, were it not just for the act of dying which is all I see to dread in it.

I sometimes think that it is better for me that I did not love my husband, for if some of the children of such a Man are so dear to me as to wring my heart with anguish at this late period, what would have become of me if they had been the children of a Man—such as———one might have seen in ones minds eye—at eighteen, & have par ci et par la,[10] had a shadowy resemblance of in the wilderness of the World. I think I am talking a little like our poor friend Sophia. Where are the Sisters?[11] & how are they? I have not yet sent to London for the Supplement, for Col Smiths arrival [&] business I had to do with him & now his departure have wholly occupied me. Do you think it quite impossible that you could deviate a little from your road to London & give me a few days of your company at my hermitage in the course of the Summer, should I so long live? It would be a prodigious good action. M[rs] Dorset, gayer & younger than her daughter, is going as she says into Scotland with Miss Collins.[12] Adieu, my dear Madam—Pray remember I hope to hear from you very very soon. My little Girl & Boy are playing with their balls close to me, & my head is like a smoke jack.[13]

Ever however sincerely y[rs] head & heart, CS.

Huntington MS (HM10843). Address: M[rs] Rose/ at D[r] Farrs/ Bath. Postmark: Farnham 4; {no date}.

NOTES

1. As the most recent surviving letter to Sarah Rose was on 26 Dec. 1805, some of CS's letters to her may be lost; as a rule, the women exchanged letters once or twice a month. But CS had been near death during the winter and thus was probably too ill to write; she reported to Egremont (18 June 1806) that a "violent remedy" had been used on her when she was "given over."

2. Dead head.

3. Not given in the *OED* this early as a noun in its sense here of a contest or tournament.

4. William Blake, whom Hayley first met in 1792, when they began a long friendship.

5. Or formerly such.

6. BS's name and date of death were both points of confusion. Three sources cited in Hilbish (*Charlotte Smith, Poet and Novelist,* pp. 51–52)—a local history of Berwick-upon-Tweed, the *Gentleman's Magazine,* and *Monthly Magazine*—give his name as Thomas Smith. All agree that he died in jail confined for mesne process for debt; that is, he

was in the intermediate stages of a suit against him. Local history gives his date of death as 22 Feb. and *European Magazine* gives it between 22 and 24 Feb., which seems likely. The date of 22 Mar., found in *Gentleman's Magazine,* is obviously too late in light of this letter's date. Accounting documents in PHA #8235 supply 22 Feb. and 26 Feb. as BS's date of death.

7. Catherine Dorset's daughter Lucy and her husband.

8. Draw to an end.

9. BS's death left CS in sole charge of disposing of her marriage settlements, amounting to £7,000. She had long urged him to settle them to the benefit of the youngest children left out of Richard Smith's will, Lionel, Harriet, and George. Now she did so herself.

10. Here and there.

11. That is, Sophia and Harriet Lee.

12. Perhaps Charlotte Collins, of Graffham, Midhurst, a friend of CS and of Hayley.

13. An obsolete term for the head as a seat of confusion; originally an apparatus for turning a roasting spit.

To the earl of Egremont

[Tilford, 11 April 1806]

My Lord.

I ought, since your Lordships letter of the 20th of Septr 1804, to have been perfectly convinced that my asking for any thing of the Trust was quite sufficient to ascertain a refusal & not a refusal only, but a refusal embitterd by every expression that could render it more painfully felt.

I certainly am aware that my income, which ought by settlement to be 500£ pr Annum, is now from 107£ likely to be 214£ or thereabouts.[1] I lose however 18£ a year by the purchase being made just at the peace So that when the income tax comes to be deducted, I shall possess (with his youngest daughter to support and his youngest Son occasionally to assist)[2] the very great Sum of almost an hundred & eighty pounds a year which is a sumptuous provision, for an old & sick woman whose life has already been render'd a burthen to her by the pressure of poverty And disease, for want of having the means of using exercise in the open air which was recommended to me in 1802 as the only thing that could save me from the total decrepitude I have since been reduced to.

But that, & the next year Mr B Smith took all my income—& now my Lord, I am reduced to a state of bodily suffering in which it is more necessary (for the sake of other sufferers) to think of how I am myself to be provided with a grave than to pay for his. I thought decency required my doing as I did, for I never yet considerd another persons acting wrong as an excuse for my doing so. The money I receive (never regularly nor by equal payments) from my second Son is in trust for his three children, two of whom are with me, & a third coming in the Charlton.[3] For <u>them</u>, I have a larger house & more servants than I should otherwise want or could pay for So that individually I neither shall be nor desire to be for the future benefitted by it——

The funeral expences, & Apothecarys and Physicians charges,[4] all of which I thought decency & humanity calld upon somebody to answer for, do not amount altogether to above 18£. I shall be able to borrow it I trust of some one who knows the circumstances I labour under, & now the more publickly they are known the better— —<u>I</u> have nothing to be ashamed of. But how the Trustees could think it right to advance to him at various times such large Sums from his fathers ~~property~~ property yet refuse eighteen or twenty pounds to bury him out of that property when the persons claiming the property desire it, I own I am at a loss to comprehend.

I should not however trouble your Lordship with this nor, in my present weak state of health, put myself in the way of receiving Letters, which would vex me more than they do, <u>were I conscious of deserving them</u>, But that it is necessary to send your Lordship (as I am not to be in Correspondence with the Attorney to the Trust)[5] a Letter I have receivd to day from M[r] Dunn. I have ans[d] it by informing him that in 1790 I <u>did</u> take the Oaths under a Commission sent to the Rev[d]—— Hudson[6] of Brighthelmstone, now I think of Fittleworth under the direction of M[r] James Charles Mitchell of that place: I never acted, nor made any appearance whatever as Executrix because M[r] B. Smith, who had at his own desire given me a full & irrevocable power of Attorney and was desirous of my acting as his fathers Executrix, was persuaded (by persons who then supplied him with money) to withdraw it, & I was by no means equal to contend with the phalanx form'd by the Seiurs Robinson, Parkin,[7] & Co who were worthily united in the honest & manly project of crushing me & reducing me to greater beggary than they had yet done——

I suppose however, tho I confess myself a very ignorant person in such matters, that I need not be at the expence of <u>again administering</u>. But I have no desire nor intention of shrinking from a trust, I have solemnly sworn to discharge— —If your Lordship has any commands on the subject, do me the honor to signify them by an early post, returning the Sieur Dunns billet. As I have committed no waste or devastavit, I am not afraid of meeting these Gents in any Court they can bring me into, but I understood (from your Lordship that ~~Mr Benjn Smith~~ Dunn having by a little matter of an oath ~~in Court~~ (all in the way of business) declared he could <u>not find</u> M[r] B Smith tho <u>I wrote to inform him he was then actually in the house of his Client R Smith)</u>[8]—I understood that the Suit w[d] proceed without any alteration & that the Trustees were representatives of Rich[d] Smith. I have heard various opinions on this matter where it is I apprehend bootless to trouble your Lordship.

I can only say that I should be very glad if my ostensibility could remove from your Lordship a burthen than which nothing was farther from my thoughts and expectations when in 1797 now nine years since your Lordship acceded to a request which I have often wonderd I ever had the audacity to make; But the opinion your Lordship then had of me was so very different from that which you have within these last four or five years seen occasion to adopt that my excuse must be in the encouragement you gave me to beleive your opinion settled & my own consciousness that I should never willingly, or intentionally, do any thing to forfeit it. Whatever I may suffer from the change, it will never make any difference in my gratitude for your unexampled goodness to and most generous protection of those, whose welfare is much more dear to me & of much greater consequence than any thing else—at least than any thing affecting individually, a person likely to be so little a while in want of any thing. Till that last period, I shall ever remain y^{r} Lordships most obed^{t} & obligd Ser^{t},

Charlotte ~~Smith~~

Tilford, April 11th
1806

I have been so very far from tolerably easy for many days past and have so many symptoms of relapse that I write ill because I write in pain & while a person is waiting for my letter so that I cannot do it better.

I might remind y^{r} Lordship that when my poor George was going abroad & I had no other means of helping him, I applied to Y^{r} Ld & the other Trustees, requesting to be allowd to have ye 50£ half years pay^{t} at Pybus's advanced for his use. This was refus'd me!—how am I to take up any Sum now from thence even if I did not want it when due myself? Of the two, the former occasion was far the most pressing, And yet it could not be done!——I askd it, I begged, I implored it—in vain—

Petworth House Archives MS. No address or postmark.

NOTES

1. How CS arrived at these numbers is not clear. If her entire fortune of £7,000 were invested in the 3 percent stocks, it would earn £210 a year. She had also at one time received an allowance of as much as £110 semiannually from the trust to maintain the family, but this was disallowed in 1801, perhaps because any interest from her marriage settlements legally belonged to BS.

2. Harriet was still at home, unable to marry without her competence from her mother's marriage settlements; CS still was sending funds to George, now a lieutenant in the 16th Regiment, as his expenses sometimes exceeded his earnings.

3. Luzena, now about 7 years old, arrived in England in the summer of 1802. She had two younger brothers on whom information has survived: William Hankey, born between 1800 and 1802, and John Hankey, born 11 Mar. 1806, in Calcutta. William was either the one already arrived or coming, but John Hankey was surely too small to

travel. Thus, Nicholas may have had a third child as yet unidentified, born between William and John.

4. All for BS's death on about 22 Feb.

5. Charles Bicknell was attorney to the trust in the Chancery suit brought by Smith and Allen; their attorneys were Abraham Winterbottom and Ralph Dunn.

6. The Reverend Thomas Hudson (ca. 1750–1819), Cambridge, L.L.B., 1792; vicar of Brighton, from 1784 to 1804, and vicar of Fittleworth, from 1804 to 1819. Mitchell is not identified.

7. John Robinson and Anthony Parkin were the trustees before Egremont and Turner.

8. Richard Smith, BS's nephew. The trustees represented Richard Smith the elder, BS's father.

To Sarah Rose

Tilford, April 26th 1806

If my dear Mrs Rose has thought about me at all, she must have thought me most ungrateful in not having sooner acknowleged the kindness of her last letter. But the truth is that, between the care of this poor worthless & withering frame, the necessity of looking forward for ways & means, and the torments of this Scottish business[1] (which more & more torments me), I really have neglected to write to the few correspondents I have & even to my Sister. My life is monotonous. I hardly ever go even from my Sopha to the Window, I see nobody & hear nothing but the Wind—I know not how I creep on from day to day, for it can hardly be calld existing, yet time I have none that I can apply as I please.

I will not pollute my paper by relating the dreadful instances of atrocity & vice, that have (& some of them very lately) come to my knowledge of that wretched being to whom I was so inhumanly sacrificed. They are beyond any thing I could have beleived possible, who had every reason to think as ill as I could well think of any body—— He has endeavourd to entail the most scandalous expences on his family after <leacing>[2] from them every thing he had or fancied he had a right to & had I died, projected & even had promis'd to marry a Girl of 18, the niece of his old Concubine, with both of whom he lived in common!—& by the former, he has left a child which he desires his family to protect & bring up!—— And this Man was sixty three! Almost a monster in his person & worse than a monster in his vices. I am afraid all I have sufferd & all I am still to suffer will make me love my children less than I ought to do. Would to God any one of them were not like him in some way or other. But the only one who had not the remotest resemblance of him, & resembled nothing so much as an Angel, is taken from me. Eleven years on Wednesday[3] have dragg'd their sad length along since that time—yet my misery has never abated.

One lives only to lose. I am glad however that you were undecieved as to some of my losses exciting my resentment. It is rather in sorrow than in Anger[4] that I complain of them & sometimes marvel that, when the pleasures of latter life are so few, any one should throw away an old friend & take up any new one that comes. But then I lose a great part of the regret I might otherwise feel in recollecting that a mind so indiscriminating[5] who is now seized with a rage for a crooked figure-maker & now for an engraver of Ballad pictures (the young Mans tragedy; & the jolly Sailers Farewell to his true love Sally) (I dont mean the Haylayan collection of pretty ballads)—Such a mind can never be really attached or is the attachment it can feel worth having. Who the present most amiable being is, I do not know; I mean as an entremêt, for Miss Poole is like a French family's constant, soup & bouillie, a standing dish, & all correspondence even between me & "The por scrib Peg," who answerd my last letter, is at an end. I ought to write to thank him for the supplement to Cowper, which Johnson sent me, & part of which I read with painful sensations. Every thing that is kind & good I beleive he means, but, as you observe, that eternal & unvaried praise of every body, the affectionate, the good, benevolent, amiable & pure, is absolute ruin to any one he loads with it & is become quite ridiculous.

In the days of our intimate friendship when I was the "dear Muse" & had not stiffend into Sister of Parnassus or sunk into Poor Charlotte, he used to laugh & say if I lived longest I should write his life & if he lived longest he w^{d} write mine. Tho this was mere badinage, I have since thought what work mine would make, for he could not praise me for Unwinian[6] virtues. However I hope he will insert the following ~~Hymn~~ Verses which you will smile at. They were thus occasion'd. The Lady Patronesses of the Charity & Sunday Schools at Brighton applied to me to write an Hymn for the Girls to Scream on some particular day & desired me to ask Mr Hayley for one for the scream of the evening; I wishd to oblige them & wrote three quartrains—such common stuff as one must write. I beleive they were bad, but I protest they were better than the Bards who sung, concerning Charity's varigated plumes—As if Charity was dressd like a <Yuca> Of South America—However the ladys Patronesses opined that these lines were all beautiful. The Lewes Journal printed & praisd them, & the Ladies were at the expence of having an hundred copies struck off for their friends.[7] So we figured like a King & Queen of Brentford,[8] & of course, I sent a printed copy or two to Eartham. The next post bro^{t} me the following which is not quite <gallant?> as his compliments generally are[9] . . .

tho there is no harm in it. It may convince you that the Bard c^{d} be playful and pleasant; tho at times he is now, I understand, si fade,[10] not to say repulsive, that his former friends when they do see him hardly know him.

In regard to my health, my dear Madam, I beleive the matter is utterly hopeless. It is some ~~xxxx disease~~ tho there is nothing ~~<offensive> in the constant <discharge>~~ which is not different from ~~that of a woman of five & twenty in perfect health~~. But I am sure the abdominal bigness I have now & this continual return of such a malady is oweing to some internal enlargement[11]—they say or hint of the ~~. . . .~~, & I have read that it is incurable and kills in a year or two. My adviser here hummeth & haweth & saith that he dont beleive it but I beleive he never saw the disease, & Carlisle,[12] who certainly is an excellent Surgeon & knows more of anatomy than any Man of his standing (as I am told), is an odd creature, & one of his maxims is that when an evil cannot be remedied, the less said about it the better. Vive la insouciance—& vivum dums vivumus[13]

Here are some English verses that came not many mornings since.

On reading the Aphorism, friendship is Love witht his wings:

Friendship as some One says or sings—
Is chasten'd Love deprived of wings
Without or power or wish to wander
Less volatile, tho not less tender
Yet says the Proverb—"Sly &—[14]
"Love creeps, even where he cannot go"
To clip his pinions then is vain;
His old propensities remain;
And whoso, years beyond fifteen,
Has counted Twenty; may have seen
How rarely unplumed Love will stay
He flies not——but he cooly walks away

In my new volume, which would have been out before now if the Frost <Trust> had not struck it in again, Some of these playful trifles will appear.[15] I am tired of Sonnets, & mine you know are almost all illegitimate & must go to the foundling Hospital.

I wish you were here to read over my vorke in Poestry (as the K[ing] of Prussia <valet calld> his Masters)[16] before it goes to the Press. For I have not friend who can tell me this is bad, that but middling. Do, my dear Madm, tell me when you next write when it is probable I may be fortunate enough to see you here. I shall take care no other Engagement shall clash with it, be it when it will, & Charlotte hopes with me that it will be while Summer leaves are green & bright. This Country of Elms is nothing after July. My letter must end. Pray tell me you pardon my not beginning it sooner, & believe me,

My dear Madm, ever truly yrs, Charlotte Smith

Combines Huntington MS (HM10844), no address or postmark, and MS in the Comyn

Collection of Burney Family Papers. Address: Alton April Twenty se venth/ 1806/ Mrs Rose/ Doctor Farr's/ Bath/ Clanricarde. Postmark: ALTON; {the rest illegible}.[17]

NOTES

1. At his death BS, who had lived most of his last nineteen years in Scotland, left CS in charge of his estate and his second family, as she explains in the next paragraph.

2. Probably a misspelling for "leaching" or "leeching." Less likely *leasing,* in the sense of "gleaning."

3. Wednesday, 23 Apr., the eleventh anniversary of Augusta's death.

4. In *Hamlet* 1.2.232, Horatio describes Hamlet's father's ghost as having "A countenance more in sorrow than in anger."

5. That is, William Hayley's. Hayley had first taken up with John Flaxman, a crippled sculptor to whom his dying son was apprenticed, and then with William Blake.

6. Mary Cawthorne Unwin (1724–1796), in William Cowper's inner circle, was seen as a woman of "piety, extensive reading, fine taste, sound judgment" (King, *William Cowper,* p. 61).

7. A three-stanza hymn in quatrains was printed anonymously in the *Sussex Weekly Advertiser, or Lewes Journal* on Monday, 27 Apr. 1789. Its title explains the occasion: "A Hymn, Sung by the Children belonging to the Sunday School at Brighthelmston, on the 23d of April 1789, being the day appointed for the General Thanksgiving, for his Majesty's happy recovery."

I.

On Britain's Sovereign, from the *King of Kings,*
May the pure streams of heavenly joy increase!
May Grace descend, with healing in her wings,
To guard a Monarch's life, an Empire's peace!

CHORUS.

Father of goodness! hear *thy* people's prayer,
Long may *thy* servant reign, and long *thy* blessings share!

II.

So shall a grateful nation *Thee* adore,
Who canst alone all nature's laws command;
While Faith reveres *thy* mercy and *thy* power,
Mighty to punish or to save the land.

CHORUS.

Father of goodness! hear *thy* people's prayer,
Long may *thy* servant reign, and long *thy* blessings share!

III.

On *Him* be shed that wisdom from above,
Whence length of days, whence wealth and glories spring,
May private sympathy and public love,
Reward the virtues of a PATRIOT KING.

CHORUS.

Father of goodness! Hear *thy* people's prayer,
Long may *thy* servant reign, and long *thy* blessings share!

8. A reference to the rival kings in *The Rehearsal* (1672), by George Villiers, duke of Buckingham. Well known from this and other dramas, Brentford on a main road from London to the west was a place for assignations. CS's allusion to it does not quite hit the mark.

9. About one-third of this page and thus the back of it too are cut away, where she quoted Hayley. His entire "compliments" are missing.

10. So tasteless or insipid. But her meaning is not clear.

11. Probably uterine cancer.

12. Anthony Carlisle (1769–1840), surgeon to Westminster Hospital; he was a much-published author of tracts on human and animal anatomy.

13. Long live the carefree, and let us live while we live.

The page is cut away here.

14. As published, the line reads, "Sly and slow."

15. This poem was printed last in her new volume, *Beachy Head,* published in 1807; the book contained no sonnets.

16. That is, my work of poetry. Frederick II (1712–1786), king of Prussia, wrote and published *Ode sur la mort,* translated in England as *An Ode, Written by the King of Prussia Immediately After the Victory Which He Gained over the Combined Armies of France and the Empire at Rosbach* (1758).

17. The two parts of this remarkably revealing letter had long been separated, with the first three-quarters of it at the Huntington, and the rest (beginning with "Here are some English verses") in the Collection of Burney Family Papers. Sarah Rose is identified in the first line of the first portion and in the address on the second portion. That they are the same letter is clear from the date in the inside address of the first part (26 Apr.), and the postmark (27 Apr.) on the second part. CS often posted letters the day after she wrote them.

To Richard Phillips

Tilford, April
29th
1806[1]
Sir,

I now return the last proof which I shall look at,[2] & indeed my looking at this is quite useless, as I have not at present one book to tell me whether the names of persons & places are correct, & throughout the few proofs I have seen par ci et par la[3] (about eighteen perhaps at the utmost), it has appeard to me that Your continuator either, from the printers mistaking the hand or from haste, has committed very great errors, for which I do not intend to hold myself answerable.

You seem to have a very good corrector of the press, & therefore I trust that, as I solemnly protested from the very beginning against having any thing to do with the reign of the present King (& for this my reasons are such as make it absolutely impossible for me to be of any farther use), that you will spare me the needless expence of postage at 3^{s} a week without its either being within the compass of my agreement or of the least use to you. Oblige me therefore with attention to this request, Sir, y^{r} obed humble Ser^{t},

Charlotte Smith

Henry W. and Albert A. Berg Collection of English and American Literature, The New York Public Library, Astor, Lenox and Tilden Foundations MS. No address or postmark.

NOTES

1. Written vertically across upper left corner in CS's hand.

2. Of *History of England . . . to a young lady at school;* Phillips had pressed her into writing a third volume (see CS to Sarah Rose, 2 July 1805 and n. 5, and 10 Sept. 1805).

3. Here and there.

To the earl of Egremont

Tilford, April 29th
1806
My Lord,

Nothing but the painful suspence I remain in, as well as my eldest daughter, would enduce me to trouble your Lordship.

The state of my health and many other considerations relating to others make me extremely desirous of seeing an end to the long depending affairs of my Children's Grandfather, & I most sincerely wish I could release your Lordship from the trouble of a concern, which (God is my witness) I should never have ask'd you to undertake, had there, at the time I took so great liberty, been the least apparent probability of your having been annoyed by it as you have been. I wish to know what I am to do & when to be subpeona'd as representative to R Smith & what Mr Prescod's final resolution is. We may go on in this uncertainty till the event will be useful to nobody. I am very sorry to trouble y^{r} Lordship! but it is not my fault. I have the honor to be,

My Lord,
y^{r} most obed^{t} & oblig'd Ser^{t},
Charlotte Smith

The reply given by Mr Martin[1] As coming from Counsel (M^{r} <Negles> I beleive) alluded only to the pay^{t} ask'd of Messrs Daniels. They could not pay it while Mr Prescod was abroad, but that is not at all the same question as is now ask'd of the principal himself three years after that time, who has changed his ground so often that it is evident he has no good ground.

Petworth House Archives MS. No address or postmark.

NOTE

1. Squire Stafford Baxter, Robert Baxter, and John Dayrell Martin, Furnival's Inn, were attorneys to Prescod. Thomas Daniel, a merchant, had handled money for CS and the trust as early as 1797, and now handled payments on the Prescod account. Negles is not identified.

To William Tyler

[?Tilford, 18 May 1806]

It appears to me that the Case is very properly and clearly stated.

It is I beleive of no importance in point of fact, but it may not be improper (lest any cavil should arise on the part of Mr Prescod) to remark to the Sol^r of The Trust that Richard Smith, the Testator & Mtgagee, died in 1776 and that it was Benjn Smith, his Exor & representative, who in 1781 purchased the Estate of the Assignees & Representatives of George Walker who was then dead.[1]

Benjn Smith purchas'd it in his own name which was the cause of great mistrust & confusion on the part of the Collateral branches of the family who had claims either as C[redito]^rs or as legatees on the Assets of Richd Smith, & they compelled M^r B Smith in the Summer of 1783 to give up the papers, deeds, &c, to their Solicitor Gawler Griffith Rickman who had them long in his possession; afterwards they were given up to the original Trustees ——Robinson, Atkinson, & Boehm—together with those relative to the Advowson of Islington living, Tho Gibbons's, and other securities. They were said to be deposited in a Box at Drummonds at Charing Cross. But M^r B Smith, in consequence of having lent 3000£ of mine on Gays, was put in possession of the title deeds of Gays which he always carried about with him, & as it may be remember'd, that he demanded & was paid a Sum of money for giving them up, when the present Trustees were about selling the Estate. But is it certain <u>none were retain'd</u> either from <u>mistake or otherwise</u>? It is by no means clear to me that the very paper in question is not even now among his, M^r B Smiths, papers which are in a desk in the possession of the Sheriff of Berwick & which (tho I have offerd the value of it) he refuses to give up unless some person appears properly qualified to demand it. I should think the detention illegal, but I cannot help myself.

The declaration of Trust, signd at the same period—as was this missing paper or deed, is I am almost certain among the papers of M^r B S——. He was so little a Man of business & so indolent when no design of obtaining present money occupied him that it is to be lamented his papers cannot be got at.

My state of health is again such as makes me very desirous of leaving as little undecided as I can; I am extremely well satisfied with the Case as now drawn up & have made these remarks only for the notice of the Solicitor to the Trust———May I be allow'd, tho foreign to the present business, to state that I have heard Griffith, the Son of the Man[2] who has acknowledged A considerable debt to the Estate of RS, is in London And that it might be worth while to consider what can be made of an application to him.

Charlotte ~~Smith~~

May 18th 1806

Petworth House Archives MS. No address or postmark.

NOTES

1. This letter provides a fairly complete review of how Gay's plantation came to be an issue in settling the Smith trust. BS, as executor to the estate, bought Gay's from George Walker in 1781 and added it to estate holdings. The "collateral branches" of the family, possibly including Sir John or Thomas Dyer, Robert Berney, and Edmund Boehm, got possession of the deeds through their solicitor Rickman in 1783 when they brought the suit that sent BS to jail for mismanaging the estate. Later, BS lent CS's £3,000 marriage settlement on Gay's, and regained possession of the title deeds. In 1801, when the new trustees, Egremont and Turner, set about selling Gay's to William Prescod, BS extorted money from them for the title deeds. CS suspected that there were still important estate papers among BS's effects held by the sheriff at Berwick.

2. Christopher Wren Griffith was a minor on 21 Mar. 1804 when Thomas Maxwell Adams described him to CS (part of Adams's letter is copied in CS to Egremont, [?Apr. 1804], n. 1).

To the earl of Egremont

Tilford, June 18th 1806

My Lord,

I very unwillingly prevail on myself to intrude once more on your Lordship, but feeling it more & more evident that extreme anxiety and the want of those means which might prolong my life, must in a short time destroy me (& being obligd already to have recourse again to the violent remedy I used, when given over in the winter), It is a duty I owe myself (whom I have hitherto consider'd too little) to address myself once more to yr Lordship, who alone has the power to mitigate the undeserved evils I suffer under.

When the Grandfather of my children made me his Executrix and Trustee, he little imagined that, in consequence of Mr B Smiths folly & the persecution that follow'd from the collateral branches of the family & their associates, I should not only be deprived of all the power he invested me with but should solicit in vain for a few pounds to bury his Son, While his grandchildren should equally in vain implore wherewithal to pay for decent mourning for that Son. Yet to this point are his affairs brought exactly thirty years after his death![1]

On my former application to your Lordship for 20£ to pay for Mr B Smiths funeral (that only being what I undertook to pay), You inform'd me I might pay it out of my own income. That income, instead of being 500£ as it ought by the settlement to have been, is now 206. Mr Smith robbed me of the interest of 3000£. I <sunk> 110£ to feed & clothe his numerous family (to which 70£ a year & the labour I exerted were unequal). Eighteen pounds a year I lose by having the money invested exactly at the peace, and the property tax takes 20£ more. So in age & sickness, with a constitution worn down by many miseries, I am to live if I can on 206£ a year & keep Mr B Smiths youngest daughter who would be settled in marriage if the affairs were once out of litigation. But that is not all. I am to be arrested for Mr B Smiths last expences, while he lived, by the prison keeper at Berwick, & I am to answer for his funeral expences.

I might once, my Lord, have venturd fearlessly to have appeald to your general humanity & to your avowed wish, to befriend me individually; I think I might still appeal to your justice. I might still ask whether with twelve hundred pounds or at least a considerable Sum in the stocks belonging to the property of Richard Smith, it is just that impoverishd and even distressd as I am, I should have these expences thrown on me.

Slowly dying, I am allow'd no prospect of ending my days any where but in the County Jail. No remittances will come from India till the end of August, as they are on board the Charlton, which the Gentn at the India house inform me will not be in earlier. I have exhausted the kindness of my Bookseller, Mr Johnson, who has latterly assisted me, & I am absolutely without resource.

Coll Maclean,[2] who at the request of Coll Smith & myself orderd & paid for Mr B Smiths funeral & a Lawyer who attended him, have [*sic*] written to me to claim payment of these charges & so pressingly that I cannot delay compliance. My dividend which Mr Pybus informs me is 103£ is appropriated, partly to reimburse Mr Johnson & partly for the expences I am daily incurring, so that I shall not have a shilling. What then am I do?—what is to become of me? My eldest daughter who would assist me is refused even a few pounds for her most pressing personal expences. Personal suffering, while I contend with the slow, but certainly fatal, advances of dropsy[3] brought on by a sedentary life renders me incapable of working as I have done; my very soul sickens and recoils, from the perspective of misery, terminating only in a prison & a grave, after all I have endured—after all the struggles I have made. But I recollect the repeated refusals even of the least help for my youngest Son & for myself when I was pennyless & destitute, & Check my complaints. I only desire to know if I may endeavour to raise

100£ on my income beyond what I am to have in July next & if My daughter can borrow 150£ for her own present occasions & mine since the Law suits keep her out of all so justly her due, & of those there is no likelihood of any end. I am very unwilling, injurd as she has already been, that she should sell out the very little she has— —

Let me entreat your answer my Lord. If a suit had been commenced at first against Prescod, it would by this time have been terminated. No doubt your Lordship did what appeard best for the interest of the concern'd, but it was impossible, as I always well knew, that any one of your Lordships rank and honor could be aware of what it is to have to do with Barbados traders —Men who are notorious for their total want of honesty and who do not even affect the semblance of it. M[r] Baxter & Martin are worthy attornies to such Men. The very pretence they formerly made use of—that I had offended them & therefore they prevented Prescods paying the money—was quite enough to have proved what manner of Men they were, for what had any offence of mine (had it been real) to do with the justice due to the Trust and the family for whom that Trust act?—— The very mention of such a species of revenge would hold these Men up to scorn if such Men were capable of feeling shame.

Did I not feel & know myself to be dying, I should propose to your Lordship an appeal to Chancery to know if I could not, now M[r] B Smith is dead, resume those rights which were never legally resign'd because I never possessd them, & my signature to the deed of Trust to Robinson, Atkinson, &c &c, was forced from me by compulsion. I have been assurd since, as I was assurd then, that I might resume it when ever I became femme sole. How gladly if that could be done & I had the health now lost for ever—How gladly should I release your Lordship from trouble I so little thought I should give you when, nine years ago, you condescended to agree to assist me in getting out of the hands of Robinson & Parkin—Trouble that had I ever dreamed would have been imposed upon you, I would have perishd sooner than have ask'd such an improper exertion of that generous kindness to which I [have] no sort of claim & to which I had been so very greatly indebted. Perhaps, my Lord, this may be the last trouble I shall ever give you, for My troubles draw to a close, but surely they ought not now to accumulate! I ought to be sufferd to die in peace in my own house & not be harrassd by Bailiffs. I am Your Lordships most humble & obed[t] Ser[t],

Charlotte Smith

As nobody has administer'd, the effects still remain unsold at Berwick. The mere letters from thence have cost me some pounds! But I am helpless—friendless—and every way reduced to despair.

Petworth House Archives MS. Address: The Earl of Egremont/ Grosvenor Place/ London. Postmark: FARNHAM; FREE/ JUN19/ 1806.

NOTES

1. Richard Smith the elder died on 13 Oct. 1776.

2. Possibly Lt. Col. Archibald Mclean, 79th Regiment of Foot, or Cameron Highlanders.

3. Propriety prevented CS from describing to men the ailment she knew to be fatal. She had recently written to Sarah Rose (26 Apr. 1806) of an "abdominal bigness" with a bloody discharge; it was probably uterine cancer.

To William Davies

[Tilford, 11 July 1806]
Sir,

My good friend Mr Johnson tells me in a letter I have from him by yesterdays post that it is his purpose to talk to you about a MMS now in his hands containing Poetry—Of which he appears to think there is not enough for a volume[1]—& that therefore it Might be offerd to you to enrich, to use his phrase, the two volumes already printed so successfully.

It seems to have escaped Mr Johnsons recollection that when this offer was made to you last Summer, your answer was that the work would not sell at all better for any additions. If such is your opinion, you will Of course give nothing for the MMS which it will answer my purpose to accept.

Mr Johnson seems to suppose there is not enough to make a volume. In this, he is undoubtedly in an error. The Poems (tho not containing all I mean to publish because I had not finishd two of them quite to my own satisfaction) contain 147 pages as they are to be printed, the page quite as full as those of my former poems & in some instances fuller; I beleive the two volumes of the last Edition (which I never can get) do not include above 161 pages in each with the notes. It is therefore clear that This proposd volume must be larger than either of those, yet I never heard any complaint of the quantity, & if the quality had not been tolerably good, I must beleive the sale would not have been what it appears to have been, & the worn condition of the plates evince how much they have been used.

You seem'd so averse to the purchase last year that, when after a long & dangerous illness, I was well enough to revise & complete these pages, I did not again trouble you. I am accountable to you for Draytons Polyalbion which I will send up next week (by a person who will deliver it to you without expence) as also the Lay of the last Minstrel. My wish was to have collected all I have lately written which appears to good judges worth publishing & to have republishd the former volumes, divested of some pieces which I wish to remove entirely. It was for this reason I solicited you to name a price at which you would part with any right you may have in these volumes. But, tho you say it is no sort of object to you, you refused to oblige me by making this arrangement—— —— ——

It may save time to all parties to say to you that, as I know the Poetry is good & the size quite as sufficient as not only my former volumes but as large as Mr Bowles's, Lord Strangfords, &c, & contain half as much more than Mr Crowes recent republication of Lewesdon hill,[2] there seems no reason why I should undersell them merely to incorporate with the former volumes. I will therefore print them on my own account or sell them (as I hope & beleive I can do) to those who imagine they will sell at least as well as such publications as Mrs Opie's[3] & other such publications, as have been [printed] lately into two or three editions tho very little superior to such verses as a Miss at a boarding school might compose & which nothing but fashion or puffing raises into notice.

At all events, Mr Johnson will be my Treasurer, but I will take care your account shall be settled.

I now know that for books for which others have received 100£ a volume, I have had but 50£. But I was distress'd. If I now live another six months, that will be at an end, & I beleive that by printing on my own account, I could obtain more than I have ever yet received—at least, it is worth the trial.

As Miss Smith puts this in the 2^d post, I thought it better to explain my view than to give Mr Johnson needless trouble. The notes & two short poems, a long preface, & the close of the local poem[4] I have not yet sent up. The whole will be 200 pages. I am so disgusted By the miserable plates I every day see to these little books that I wish an Edition of mine could be publishd without

I am, Sir,
your most obed humble Ser^t,
Charlotte Smith

Tilford, Farnham
July 11th 1806

Yale University MS. Address: Mr Davies/ Messrs Cadell & Davies's/ Strand/ Lo[ndon]. Postmark: Penny Post/ Unpaid/ Richmond./ 7 o'Clock/ JY 12/ 1806; NT.

NOTES

1. This disputed manuscript was published by Johnson as *Beachy Head* (1807).

2. CS was arguing for treatment comparable to male poets whose works Cadell and Davies bought or sold. They published William Crowe's *Lewesdon Hill; a Poem* (1786) in a third and expanded edition in 1804. Even then it was only 115 pp., 20 of which were notes. Their 8th, expanded edition of Rev. William Lisle Bowles's *Sonnets, and Other Poems* (1802) was 180 pp. with 21 pp. of notes. Their first edition of his *Poems,* vol. 2 (1801), was 165 pp., plus notes. His *Spirit of Discovery* (1804) was published by Rich-

ard Cruttwell of Bath but sold by Cadell and Davies. Lord Strangford's *Poems, from the Portuguese of Luis de Camoens* (1804) came in at 159 pp. for its publisher, J. Carpenter.

3. Primarily a novelist, Amelia Opie (1769–1853) had published *Poems,* her first volume of poetry, in 1802.

4. CS's long preface was not printed in the final edition. The "local poem" was the title poem, "Beachy Head."

To Joseph Johnson

[Tilford] Saturday, July 12th
1806
Dear Sir,

Your letter to day gave me great satisfaction. If you are satisfied that the verses are worth any thing, I am perfectly convinced that they would make a ~~short~~ small volume and sell to advantage; it seems to me that the volume should be printed uniformly with the other two because the probability is that those who are in possession of the other two Volumes will purchase this, & as, of the latter editions, I have reason to beleive some thousands have been sold,[1] this circumstance only would secure the sale of enough to pay the expence of printing, which, for such volumes as these (without plates) I have been informed is not great. It seems to be the fashion of the day to print the notes at the end; sometimes with a (V. N).[2] In this instance they would be rather numerous because of historical, biographal, & local facts relative to Beechy & the Coast & the extraordinary story of Parson Darby, a Man who, disgusted with the World, lived many years as tradition tells in a cave of the Cliff by Beachy head & was lost in attempting to save some Shipwreck'd Seamen.[3] The poems too which relate to natural history will want notes.

My wish was to have made such a bargain with Cadell & Davies, thro your interposition, as would have put an handsome Sum into your hands in liquidation of my debt, which is my first object, & secondly, to have done what they themselves propos'd or at least Mr Davies during some correspondence on this matter last year—that is, to publish a collection of all the Poems I have written which, on my mature judgement, appear worth retaining (expunging all the adulatory lines particularly—As the only means by which I can testify my regard for having ever written them, & I will give those Authors, who have complimented me & if I chose to do like Miss Seward,[4] I could come prancing with several cantering (and canting) outriders of this sort, among whom is the present most reverend Bishop of Glocester, then indeed only the Revd Mr Huntingford, a third Master at Win Col[5])—I say I will give those Authors who, whether in public or in little elegant effusions have complimented me, leave to blot out, annihilate, expunge, & obliterate every civil thing they ever said. Who ever lived for twenty years without seeing abundant cause to alter their opinions of the charming creatures who seem'd once so very delightful?

Bref [*sic*]: If you will have the goodness to propose this plan to Mr Davies, he might perhaps think it worth while to attend to it, & act upon it in a way that may appear satisfactory. I have written to him & told him that you, who were so good as to be my Treasurer, intended talking to him on this business, but that you doubted there being enough—A doubt however I am clear may be done away, But that if he still thought the purchase of no more value than he seem'd to think it last year, I would print on my own account, & on this experiment, I am not at all afraid of venturing, nor ~~at all~~ doubtful of the success, & Yet for reasons I will not again hint at, it really is of importance to me to have the book come out very soon. I am told that I need only remind certain people of me in this way to obtain a Company for my Youngest Son if his life is spared and that I shall get something done for the very deserving young Man[6] who is engaged to Harriet & who has sufferd by a brother a great loss of fortune. Besides which, it would raise my spirits, often sinking into absolute despondence, when my bays seem blighted & Misses amatory verses seem to put me by.

Will you therefore set on foot this little volume? It should be made as much like the two others as can be because the purchasers of those will in all probability buy this. Messrs Cadell & Davies have I beleive some copies left tho when I have sent strangers there twice to buy sets for me, they have sold the 8th & 9th Edition whereas the 1st volume is in the 10th. By the way, the notes to those want re-writing. They are sad nonsense here & there. No indeed I do not doubt your gallantry, or what is better your benevolence & good nature, but in truth, I did think you treated Ladies literature a little like the late James Dodsley who, when I offerd him my Sonnets in 1783, said, "What I suppose now this is all loving stuff about Shepherds and Shepherdesses, & little lambs, & all that."

Lord Egremont has given no orders ab^{t} my dividend, but the Bankers will condescend to pay 30£. Next month I am entitled to receive 3000£ a part of my own fortune back.[7] It was bought in just at the peace of Amiens, & I lose 18£ a year. I have a great mind to sell it out & place it on Landed security. It is my childrens after my death, but why should I lose 18£ a year which w^{d} almost pay my property tax. I am, Dear Sir,

y^{r} oblig'd & grateful Ser^{t}, Charlotte Smith

I will return the <divds>[8] in the course of the week.

Yale University MS, MS Vault. Address: Mr Johnson/ St Pauls Church yard/ 72. Postmark: no place; 7 o'Clock/ 14.JY/ 1806 Nt; {penny post mark illegible}.

NOTES

1. By 1806, *Elegiac Sonnets i* had gone through nine editions and *Elegiac Sonnets ii* through three. The exact number printed for each edition is not known, but for her fiction 1,000 copies were usual for a first edition and 1,000 for a second, unless a slow sale was expected (as was the case for *The Banished Man*). Moreover, for the fifth edition of vol. 1 there were 817 subscribers; for the first edition of vol. 2, 283 (CS to William Davies, 25 Apr. 1797, n. 1).

2. *Vide notam,* or "see note." V.N. is used liberally in Lord Strangford's *Poems, from the Portuguese,* suggesting CS had the volume in hand when she mentioned it in the previous letter and was quick to pick up on trends in publication.

3. In another version of the story, Rev. Jonathan Darby of East Dean was said to have hewed out this cave in a cliff so that he could escape from his wife's tongue (Fleet, *Glimpses of Our Ancestors in Sussex,* p. 323).

4. Anna Seward, poet, novelist, and a protégée of Hayley, had no kind words for CS's poetry. While conceding that CS was "a fine woman in her person," Seward wrote in 1788 that her sonnets "always appeared to me as a mere flow of melancholy and harmonious numbers, full of notorious plagiarisms, barren of original ideas and poetical imagery" (Seward, *Letters,* 2:162). Later she wrote of "Mrs. C. Smith's everlasting lamentables, which she calls sonnets, made up of hackneyed scraps of dismality, with which her memory furnished her from our various poets" (2:287).

5. The Reverend George Isaac Huntingford (1748–1832) became a fellow at Winchester in 1785, taught at a free school, then was recalled to be warden of Winchester in 1789. He was made bishop of Gloucester in 1802. A Tory, he published political discourses as well as sermons.

6. William Geary.

7. In Aug., BS would have been dead for six months. The fortune had belonged to him during his lifetime. Because he predeceased her, CS was finally able to apportion her three marriage settlements, totaling £7,000, to her three youngest children not covered by Richard Smith's will.

8. Possibly *dividends,* as she owed him money.

To the earl of Egremont

Tilford, July 13th 1806
My Lord,

Tho I am never honor'd by your Lordships obliging notice in ans^r to <u>any</u> application (which I never make but when it appears to me absolutely necessary), I am again under the painful necessity of applying to your Lordship to request that you would be so good as to give directions to Messrs Pybus & Co to pay me my <u>half</u> years income, being with the deduction of the income tax 103£—— Of this, having occasion to pay some money in London, I desird Messrs Pybus would apply a certain Sum to that purpose, but they inform me to day <u>they have never received any authority from your Lordship</u>

and therefore cannot pay to my order more than 50£ till you send them such authority as they can act upon.

The delay is attended with considerable inconvenience to me, as a part of this money must go to take up a bill I accepted for my poor George of 20£ for linnen, an article of the first necessity at A place where the heat is so intolerable as in his present situation, & tho I equipped him at the expence of more than a years income when he went to the West Indies, he lost a great part of his clothes while he was with the 96th, & Col^l Smith[1] assur'd me he had been oblig'd to pay more than double the European price for every thing he had occasion to purchase at Surinam of Dutch dealers & that he was not to blame. To whatever inconvenience I may be myself expos'd (& nothing seems to mitigate inconvenience to me), I cannot suffer this poor young Man to be distress'd. I think it probable that Lionel may have written to your Ldship, but as he might not have time at the moment, I take the liberty of stating to you that he & M^rs L Smith arriv'd at Barbados on the 7th of May after a prosperous passage and at Jamaica on the 18th in perfect health.

His stay at Barbados was too short to enable him to do much in the luckless affairs, wherein he is now principally interested with his younger Sister & Brother, as the residue, had there been any, would have been theirs after Miss Smith was p^d a certain share, but Lionel says that Griffith, taking advantage of the non appearance at first of those papers under the City seal, has so contrived to evade & baffle Mr Coulthurst,[2] who has the papers now properly authenticated, that there are very few hopes of the estate recovering this Sum, & that from Pindar will also be lost!—— I cannot but very acutely feel the hardship of this at a time when Prescod has so shamefully treated my family & is most undoubtedly trying to escape making the last payment at all, & while persecuted by another part of the family, my eldest daughter, in order to have the power of assisting me (who am not in a state to contend with pecuniary wants) & indeed of paying for necessaries for herself, is gone to town in the determination of selling out 200£ from the little stock she has left unless she can borrow that Sum (200£) on giving security. She thought of asking your Lordship to take that security & lend it her out of the Trust money in hand—which surely could injure nobody—but the resolution your Lordship appears to have taken to let us suffer all the bitterness of pecuniary distress, deters her.

For my own part, the slow approaches of death are I own render'd more oppressive to me not only by the want of what would make my latter days more tolerable, but by the apprehension that after I am dead those whom all my endeavours have not saved from distress will be reduced to a still worse condition—— It is dreadful to dwell upon this, but perhaps when I am gone, who have had the misfortune to convert my best friend into my enemy (tho God knows how), Your Lordships former goodness will be exerted towards that part of My family who are now the most distressd, & that your unexampled kindness to Col^{l} Smith may be extended to them at least so far as to prevent their losing all that remains of their Grandfathers property.

Mr Dunn[3] has I understand given some hints that an accommodation is desirable. I beleive they have made nothing of their commission in Barbados. They deny having heard the result, but it is understood there is only one Man to be examin'd—Humbleby,[4] a Clerk to Prettejohn, whose oath I will not consent shall be evidence of fact which nothing but books can ascertain, & I would sooner carry the cause to the Lords than be baffled by so palpably roguish an artifice as taking the oath thirteen & ten years after the transactions of a Clerk brought up in such a School of iniquity as Prettejohns Counting house—

Y^{r} Lordship will, I hope, accept my apology for troubling you with another Letter from, My Lord, your obed^{t} & obligd Ser^{t},

Charlotte ~~Smith~~

Petworth House Archives MS. No address or postmark.

NOTES

1. George was a lieutenant. Lionel, now a lieutenant colonel stationed in Surinam, appears to have been in touch with his younger brother and to have written in his defense. Over the years, Egremont corresponded with Charlotte, Charles, Lionel, and even the hapless Lucy, especially after he refused to read any more letters from CS. A number of letters from them written after her death also survive, scattered throughout the PHA holdings.

2. Matthew Coulthurst, a lawyer of Bedford Row and Barbados.

3. Of Winterbottom and Dunn, attorneys on the Smith and Allen Chancery suit.

4. In June and July 1806, depositions were taken from five men in Barbados on matters bearing on the Chancery suit. John Humbleby, age 32, testified at length on Prettyjohn's exact role as an agent for Gay's and Mapp's plantations. CS's distrust of Humbleby's story was not unjustified. Not only did he not do the actual account, but he was only Prettyjohn's apprentice from 1789 until 1798, at which time he became Prettyjohn's clerk.

To the earl of Egremont

[?Tilford, late July 1806]

My Lord,

In my daughters absence, I take the liberty of answering your Ldships letters which appear to have lain at Godalming since the 15th and which therefore should have had earlier attention.

I am sorry y[r] Lordship should think me unreasonable or wishing to misrepresent the unfortunate circumstance of the want of papers being sent out as required in the business of Griffith, but most undoubtedly the delay has had two very ill effects on the winding up of that Affair, & the state of the case is materially alter'd. In the first place, had they been sent out when first required, M[r] Adams would have received them before he left the Island, & in the next place, the Son of old Griffith, who sets up for a fine Gentleman[1] & is now or was very lately in London, is spending the money, thus rogueishly obtain'd by the Father & every day lessens the probability of my family's recovering at all. It is the more to be lamented because the Sum would have materially have help'd to have made some payment possible to my eldest daughter, who has suffer'd so long and so severely by having nothing yet paid her in consequence of the award now made three years since, & it would have been very consolatory to me to know before I die that there would be some residue to be divided among Lionel, George, and their youngest Sister, whose marriage cannot take place while every thing remains in its present uncertain state.

And for many reasons it is an affair which my peace & health are sacrificed to & which it is most material to me to have concluded who have, God knows, endured more misery than enough. The reason I had to suppose M[r] Dunn thought of an accommodation was that he seem'd, tho not directly, to propose it to M[r] Turner, denying that he had had any information of the result of the Commission of enquiry sent out to Barbados, tho certain it is that a Commission of enquiry might have gone out to the East Indies & been returnd since April 1805—now fifteen Months, & with all this parade there is only a Clerk of Prettejohns to be heard! As if such evidence would be accepted after an interval of thirteen & of ten years to a fact which books ought to ascertain. However I shall make no overtures now of accommodation because I beleive that, after a certain number of Terms elapsed, the defendants may Petition to have the Bill dismiss'd, & I have heard that period is not very remote, but with the usual chicane of the profession where Men of honor are not employ'd, they have got the long vacation before them to try what double they can make. To get rid of the Bill would be indeed most desirable, as I apprehend that alone prevents your Lordship from being releived from a Trust so painful and troublesome, & that I might then unopposed resume the Executorship of Richard Smith which all the parties interested are extremely desirous of my doing— —

While there is proffit for Lawyers, There is little hope of the affairs being sufferd to be concluded—Of which I recollect your Lordship being convinced when you saw the manner in which Parkin had the successful impudence to charge my ill fated family for aiding in their destruction. Mess[rs] Baxter and Martin[2] appear perfectly well versed in their metier; They appear to be admirably well skilled in the glorious art of escape And manly and honourable dealing. For some time, their resentment towards me was assign'd as a reason why they were determind to prevent their Client from paying the last installment. Resigning that plea, which no men who had a particle of honesty about them would have dared to have asserted, they pretended to submit to their clients abiding by an Opinion, & while that opinion was obtaining, he slunk off to Barbados, & they laughd at the trick. And all this, to oppress an helpless family of young people who have they know been robbed of many many thousands, and between their fathers folly & the roguery of their Countrymen, the Barbaadians, have been reduced from Affluence, to poverty, dependance, & its consequent contempt.

I am really myself most unfortunate. Compelled to struggle for many years to support my family, abandon'd by their father, I find that when their property is at length deliverd from most of the impediments that prevented its division, & under your Lordships protection in a fair way of being settled, I give offence to some or other of these Gentlemen, & it is their pleasure to persecute me to the last hour of my life.

I must not pretend perhaps to judge of the meaning of a Law opinion. But as far as my poor comprehension goes (and those I have shewn it to think the same), it seems as if Mr Butlers[3] opinion was positively and decidedly in favor of my family; My daughter[4] is oblig'd to return to London tomorrow on business for my Son Nicholas's children & is to day gone with Mrs Dorset to Farnham, but she desired me to say to your Lordship with her thanks and respects that she hopes such an opinion (in which only an improbable & almost impossible contingence is against them) will induce your Lordship to take immediate measures for compelling payment, which I always beleived (from my knowledge of a similar case) the Court would order. If Prescod should die, it is supposed his property would be contested or so divided as to create interminable confusion, and my family would never see an end to their difficulties.

They will long outlive me & have not been a trifling cause of the state of languor and decline I now suffer under. So many years of poverty ~~and~~ follow'd by as many of suspence would destroy any one. Often I have thought my tempest beaten back in <part>, & often have I been driven back to new toils, new sufferings, & unavailing prayers!——My Lord, my eldest daughter is in extreme want of a small Sum of Money. Mr Bicknell, aware of her situation & hoping much from Your Lordships consideration, undertook to wait on you to solicit this favor, & she agrees to borrow it of the estate and give security & pay interest. If you recollect, my Lord, how often you have said her case was very distressing, & that her whole life has been pass'd in waiting for what her Grandfather design'd she should be paid at an early period, I cannot but hope you will not deny a request which it can hurt nobody to grant.

Mr Geary, to whom Harriet has engag'd herself, is naturally desirous of knowing her prospects. It should seem, by all the advice I have been able to obtain, that Mr Benjn Smith's will disposes of the residue under his fathers will (which allots a position to Charlotte) between Lionel, George, & Harriet. The question therefore to him is interesting: "What is the residue?" If y^{r} Lordship would be so good as to allow me to apply to Messrs Pybus & Co to know the amount of the Money in the Stocks (which they refus'd with^{t} your orders & I suppose properly), I might be enabled to answer this question, allowing for all possibilities & contingent draw backs. It would therefore very much oblige me. I have the honor to be Your Lordships most oblig'd & obed^{t} Ser^{t},

Charlotte ~~Smith~~

Petworth House Archives MS. No address or postmark.[5]

NOTES

1. Christopher Wren Griffith. See CS to William Tyler, 18 May 1806, n. 2.
2. Attorneys for William Prescod.
3. Not identified. The opinion in the Chancery suit was given by John Bell (1764–1836), a noted barrister with an extensive practice in Chancery.
4. Charlotte Mary, who often had the care of Nicholas's children.
5. About an inch of the top margin of the third and fourth page is carefully cut away. It may have held the date.

To the earl of Egremont

[Tilford, 2 August 1806]

My Lord,

The illness under which I have so long sufferd, has lately threatend so heavy a return that, however I may attempt to flatter myself (after once being partially restord) that I may again be releived, I cannot beleive my life will be of <u>many weeks duration</u>. Your Lordships humanity therefore will I hope induce you to pardon my intruding upon you. I think it is <u>my duty</u> to attempt once more to obtain an arrangement of the affairs that so long have hung in suspence, utterly ruinous to my family. My own health, time, fortune, & comfort of every sort have been destroy'd. It <u>is</u> hard that, at the close of a life so devoted & so persecuted, I should be denied the only satisfaction I can now receive, the near prospect of a certain settlement of the Affairs on which the subsistence of my family hereafter must in a great measure depend.

I am now told that, if no motion is made or step taken by the opposite party during a certain number of terms, the defend^{ts} have a right to petition to have the bill <u>dismissd. Mr Bicknell is not certain how many terms have</u>

passd. I am very sure that more than three have been gone since the pllffs {plaintiffs} took any measures ag[st] us. Perhaps y[r] Lordships solicitor may know whether any thing has been done since that. I understood that a considerable charge had been allow'd to be paid M[r] Tyler (whether annual or no I do not know) for his extraordinary trouble. Such being the case there will be surely no harm in my asking for information, both on this business and on that of the accounts, but I am repulsed in a way that compels me either to remain in ignorance or to be under the very painful necessity of addressing myself oftener to your Lordship than you approve or I wish.

I beleive that there must be more money in hand than y[r] Lordship apprehends, as an installment from the Gibbons's (being the last) has been paid since the accounts were made out, & if the interest of the 3333£ invested by M[r] Prescod have been duly placed in the stocks from time to time since the Spring of 1803, & the compound interest upon these Sums placed also, they must, I think, make together a Amount much greater than y[r] Lordship seems to think. It was to avoid troubling you on this subject that, some months since, I addressd myself to Mess[rs] Pybus & Co, requesting to know what money belonging to the trust was funded. But their an[r] (which I beleive I stated to your Lordship) was that it was contrary to the custom of Bankers to give any such information. But if 175.16.8. was invested in Jan[y] 1805, there exists no reason why the same Sum should not have been invested in 1804 & 1806 by half year purchases, & the interest on the Gibbons's last payment must also have accumulated. And I hope has not been remaining dead in the Bankers hands while My daughter has been vainly soliciting to be allowed a very small Sum for her immediate and most pressing occasions.

The less there is, the more important it is to those who have no other dependence. I am urgently calld upon by M[r] Geary to give him some information. As Executrix, it is my duty to answer, and I do not consider myself as exonerated from a charge I solemnly undertook to execute. I beleive that in the estimate of residue, the 600£ should be estimated still due from M[r] Turners Bankruptcy and placed by the award in the hands of the Trust. As to the West India debts from Griffith and Pindar, they must now I suppose be considered as lost. And the greater necessity there is for making the most of the sad wreck that is yet retrievable— —It will be of little use to my daughter to have a payment made ten years hence of money which was directed to be paid so many years ago. Nor can it fail of being distressing to those whose legacies are not yet fully paid & those who have a claim on the residue.

Allow me, My Lord, to request, if M[r] Tyler will not do it, that I may be authorisd to employ somebody who will to collect the accounts & state them. I know it must be irksome to you to be liable to such applications, & I beg you to beleive that it is by no means my inclination ever to give y[r]

Lordship the least trouble or to forget how much you have had or the obligations I owe you on many accounts. But you must forgive me if I cannot allow that, when money is paid for business being done, my family, so greatly sufferers from others & at the end of almost nine years of the Trust, are still to remain thus distressd & without knowing their future prospects because the Solicitor employ'd by the Trustees has taken Offence at my saying what the event has proved too truely: that he did not understand Barbados business. The Trust your Lordship so kindly undertook for me as to the 3000£ terminates this month, as the marriage articles direct that it shall be paid to me six months after the death of Mr Benjn Smith. If it be therefore any annoy to yr Lordship, I am very willing to remove it; if not, I shall be obligd by your continuing it. I am sorry to trouble you with so long a letter &

I have the honor to be
yr Lordships most obligd
& Obedt Sert,
Charlotte ~~Smith~~

Tilford, 2nd August
1806

I have been too ill to attend to it, but I will now write to such West India people as I can recollect to enquire about the heirs of Newton,[1] but I dare say the Man has been dead above seven & thirty years, & I know not who to apply to—as all the parties are dead ages since who were then connected with Mr Smith the elder. Nothing remains but the miserable relicts of his property & his impoverishd Grandchildren whose hard fate it is to struggle for years with every difficulty & wear out their lives in fruitless expectation.

Petworth House Archives MS. No address or postmark.

NOTE

1. John Newton (d. 1786) owned Gay's when it was transferred to George Walker.

To the earl of Egremont

Tilford, Augst 8th 1806
My Lord,

I take the liberty of enclosing to you, the ansr I have receivd[1] to my first enquiry about the heirs of Mr Newton that your Lordship may see there is every prospect of my obtaining such intelligence as may lead to the object recommended by Messrs Baxter and Martin. I should have attended to it before, but was unable for ill health and accumulated personal suffering, but as Mr Harris[1] was the ward for many years of the elder Mr Smith & is a Man of considerable property and connections in Barbados, he is inclined and qualified to lend me the assistance I want on this occasion, and I have only to express my hope that your Lordship will give such directions to your Solicitor both on this business and that which relates to the Allens suit that I may have a prospect before the close of my life of seeing those cruel affairs which have impoverishd & harrassd me for so many years brought to some conclusion—which they never will be unless that conclusion can soon be obtaind, as my complaint (tho not so rapidly as on the first attack) daily gains on my shatterd constitution, & I feel it to be impossible I should live many months.

Let not therefore your Lordship consider it as needless importunity if I again entreat you to direct the accounts to be made out so as that it may be known what are the demands against the remaining property and what the assets (without reckoning any thing as likely to arise from that luckless business of Griffiths's which is I suppose gone!). Your Lordship (tho such trifles as all my familys property can appear but as an atom to you) will I trust recollect that to them it is just the difference between actual distress and very moderate competence. To secure the latter to them, your Lordship had nearly nine years ago the goodness to take the affairs under your protection in the most generous and kind manner. I have since had the misfortune to displease your Lordship very much against my intentions and so much against my wishes that tho I feel it to be my urgent duty since you are Trustee to address you, I execute that duty with reluctance, knowing that I am misunderstood because I am misrepresented——

The hour is fast approaching when all human praise or blame will be to me a matter of indifference, But while I do live, I cannot lose sight of the purpose of so many years of my past life, and I beseech of your Lordship to recollect your former good opinion of me, express'd not only in words but in writing, and to give me credit at least for not having been intentionally guilty of the ingratitude and folly of wilfully offending you.

Y^r Lordship, in a letter now before me, declares that you will give any one 1000£ who will release you from the detestable trust. Without claiming the reward, My Lord, I am told I may now release you &, as Executrix, enter into all the rights over the remaining assets of Richard Smith, which I only temporarily & conditionally renounced while I was under compulsion—And which the Court would restore to me. Ill as I am I have no hesitation in declaring I am willing to do this & desirous of doing it.

The part of my marriage Articles that relates to the 3000£ paid on the sale of Gays plantation into y^r Lordships hands, runs thus:

"And in case the said Charlotte Turner should happen to survive the said Benjn Smith, & she should have any child or children living at the time of his decease, then the heirs, Exors, administrators of the said Benj[n] Smith should pay unto the said Charlotte his intended Wife within six months after his decease the said Sum of 3000£, being her then present fortune." It then goes on to secure to me likewise the other 3000£ covenanted to be settled by M[r] B Smith which he dissipated before the fourth year of this wretched Marriage.

But as it seems by the above quoted paragraph that the 3000£ is now to be paid to me (M[r] B Smith having now been dead six months), I can only repeat that, if it be any releif to your Lordship to have this trust off your hands, I will remove it, tho otherwise I should certainly not desire to do so—unless by selling out at an advantage in case of peace, I could lend the money on good landed security at 5 pC[t] and regain what I have lost of income.

Perhaps however, as the money must be divided at my death, it is hardly worth while to do this in the state of health I am in. But I wait your Lordships commands on this subject as well as on the former relative to the account of monies in actual possession of the Trustees. And I trust you will pardon this intrusion from

My Lord your Lordships
most humble & obed[t] Ser[r],
Charlotte ~~Smith~~

If M[r] Newtons heirs are in Barbados, as is highly probable, there will be another delay, & this it is very likely is known to be the case by Baxter & Martin who thus make another double upon us.

Petworth House Archives MS. No address or postmark.

NOTE

1. Unpublished letter to CS from William Harris of Alresford, 7 Aug. 1806 (PHA #8236). Harris had been a ward of Richard Smith (see CS to Egremont, 8 Sept. 1804, n. 6). Letters from Edward Binfield (9 Sept. 1806, PHA #8237) and Thomas Lane to CS and William Tyler (PHA #8239, 8240, 8241, 8242) also help settle these points.

To the earl of Egremont

Tilford Aug[st] 14th
1806

M[rs] C Smith begs leave to state to Lord Egremont that the installments paid by M[r] Gibbons and amounting in the whole to 3985£ were as follows:

Paid when the agreement was made 1798 ———————— 1000
Sep[r] 1799 ———————————————— 375
D[o] 1800 ———————————————— 362

D° 1801 ————	600
D° 1802 ————	575
	2912

Paid at the time of the award in 1803— —553—& this is stated to have been given to M[r] B Smith or the greatest part of it—
Paid since the last installment. 1804 520—I am not quite sure of the fractions, but I am sure of the Sum in gross & the time when they were payable

2912
553
520
3985

Nothing is clearer then, than that at <u>least 500£ has</u> been paid since that gift to M[r] B Smith of his childrens property. M[rs] C Smith hopes that it has not been left all this time in the Bankers hands unproductive. She has been inform'd, & on <u>pretty good authority on former occasions</u>, that Trustees have no right to keep money in their hands but <u>must</u> invest it as fast as received. Her idea on the matter of M[r] Prescod <u>may</u> be erroneous, but according to her calculate, there ought to be the following Sums at least:
Lord Egremont states the interest for one year only to be 175£——
On that estimate there should be between July 1803, (the money being due in April)—&

July 1804 ————	175
Between July 1804 & July 1805 ————	175
Between July 1805 & July 1806 ————	175
	525

His Lordship says that 200£ is <u>now</u> to be put into the stocks. This is unfortunate as stocks are 8 pC[t] higher than they were some weeks ago.

If M[rs] C Smith is not greatly mistaken in this statement, The whole Sum in hand ought to be:

From Gibbons' (not <u>Dyer</u> as Lord Egremont says in his answer r[d] yesterday) last pay[t]	520
From interest on Prescods payments ————	525
	1045

& on these Sums if immediately invested there ought to be compound interest——

M[rs] Smith, as Executrix to Richard Smith, very earnestly requests Lord Egremont to Order the accounts to be made out, as three years have elapsed since they were renderd, & She never was then allow'd a copy of them. She desires to assure his Lordship that she has not the least wish to importune him with desultory correspondance and is well convinced that her requesting to have any thing done is exactly the reason why it is refused. She neither does nor ever did suppose his Lordship could give his mind to these affairs or know any thing about the accounts. But as she now conceives herself fully empowerd to act as Executrix and is determ[ine]d to use her little remaining time & strength in attempting to settle the remaining affairs of R. Smith, she begs leave to request of his Lordship to let the accounts be made up & the business put into the management of some person with whom she can communicate without being repelld by the rudeness of M[r] Tyler— —

M[rs] C S will remove the Trust of the 3000£ as soon as the forms can be gone thro.

If the idea of petitioning to dismiss the suit is absolute nonsense, it is the absolute nonsense of Mr Bicknell—from whom it came

It was absolute nonsense when eighteen or twenty months since M[rs] C Smith desired to have a bill fyled against M[r] Prescod. Now, after Mess[rs] Baxter and Martin on one hand & M[r] Tyler on the other, have been bowing to each other, M[r] Prescod glides off, & what might have been done so long ago is to begin when that worthy Gentleman chuses to reappear unless some other quirk can be found. It is the fate of M[rs] C S. and her unfortunate family to be saved from Scylla to be engulphed by Charybdis. Lord Egremont rescued them from Parkin & Co. Surely he will not let the poor remains be now wasted in contention. M[rs] C Smith is told that his Lordship w[d] be released from the Trust if he would petition Chancery. His Lordship cannot suppose any one base enough or fool enough to take any advantage of what he said about His release. M[rs] C. Smith and her family desire in the most positive manner to repeat to Lord Egremont that they wish for nothing but an early arrangement & to receive what is due to them without being farther liable to Law charges, which will devour all that remains after a period of thirty years. They wish most particularly to release Lord Egremont from any farther trouble with the Allens Law suit And to have it sent back to be defended by the Executrix which she is told would be effected by a petition. When M[r] Berney gives an account of 2000£ which he is known to have received beyond what he had the least right to (and many months after 13 whole pounds were paid here in full payment of the debt due from R Smiths estate) then, & not till then, will M[rs] C S talk to him of Legacies.

In the mean time she does not imagine it is the affair of the Trustees to put him on the quest; He cannot receive a shilling till all the other Legatees are paid, & M^{rs} C S. has reason to beleive Mr Boehm knows better than to stir the question. It can be no reason for keeping Miss Smith so many years out of what was orderd by the award & even out of the interest. M^{rs} C S hopes to be forgiven for her plain dealing. It is too late now to conceal her real feelings which she knows are right, tho no unkindness or misapprehension will ever make her forget Lord Egremonts former kindness to her and hers.

[Unsigned]

Petworth House Archives MS. No address or postmark.

To William Tyler

[Tilford, 14 August 1806]
Sir,

Determining now to exert myself in the settlement of the affairs of Richd Smith as his Executrix, I have been lately calld upon to enquire for the marriage contract between the Chevalier De Foville & my deceasd Daughter. I am inform'd that it was left with you at the time when I endeavourd to make a compromise which would have put some ready money into the hands of the late M^{r} B Smith. But the Trustees refusing to agree to it, the matter dropped, but this deed was never return'd. As it can be of no use to any other party, I trust you will, if it be among the papers of the Smith trust (as I am inform'd), return it to,

Sir,
y^{r} hble Ser^{t},
Charlotte ~~Smith~~

Tilford, August
14th 1806

Petworth House Archives MS. Address: Mr Tyler. No postmark.

To the earl of Egremont

Tilford, Septr 13th
1806
My Lord,

I r^{d} this morning the enclos'd[1] in a Letter from my friend Mr Harris of Alresford—— As it is probable Mr Prescod will be in England with the Fleet expected early in October, I am anxious to leave nothing undone to get thro every objection how ever unfounded or trifling which He or his

Attornies may start. And as I am also desirous of doing myself what an Attorney must be paid for doing, I have written to Mr King[2] ~~Lane~~ & enclose the Letter, requesting your Lordship to have the goodness to frank it & to allow the anr to be sent under cover to you—for postage falls very heavy on me, & as there is now seven pounds at least due to me from the Estate, which I am never likely to be repaid, I hope you will forgive my taking this liberty.

The slow but certain progress of a disease which I know to be incurable, & which in a great degree disables me from any exertion while I do live, might I hoped have been my excuse with your Lordship for the impatience I cannot help feeling and expressing at the unsettled state of my familys affairs by which I am likely to leave them after so many years of labour and anxiety in poverty and dependance. Lucys situation alone is a sufficient cause for my solicitude, as it is almost impossible for her to live & bring up her children, And her being under the necessity of quitting her house without the means of removing or any place to go to is a great addition to the pain I suffer on other accounts, & to that I cannot help feeling from the apprehension that my poor unfortunate Brother will, after all, end his Life in a prison.

Your Lordship seems so determind to misunderstand what I said about yr resignation of the Trust, & so positively at enmity with me, that any farther attempt on my part will only encrease that enmity. I cannot see that what I said about Mr Berney can be calld malignant or malevolent. It is very natural for me to wish justice to be first done to my own children when I know that Mr Berney has had 2000£ that did not, could not belong to him. It will however be time enough to talk of that when those who have an undoubted preferrence are paid, but I shall never live to see it.

I have done nothing in regard to removing the Trust of the 3000£ belonging to me because as I had no other reason for wishing to do it than to save yr Lordship every trouble abt me & a wish to encrease my poor inadequate income if it could be done safely. I forbore to attempt either while continually menaced with a more rapid encrease of my illness, the termination of which will make both unnecessary.

But if the amount & disposition of the residue could even by a loose calculate have been obtaind, I should have been perhaps enabled, in the disposition I have lately thought it my duty to make, to have done more for Lucy than I have done because, if there is something handsome to be divided between the three youngest children (after Miss Smith is paid), I could have added a few hundreds to Mrs Newhouse's share without injustice to My two Youngest Sons & Harriet.

I wish by saying thus much to explain to yr Lordship why I was desirous of seeing the amount of money in the funds &c, & because indeed some present assistance is an object of great importance to more than one of these unfortunate young people, for I have not the means of keeping or helping them. I have now been above twelvemonths the victim of personal sufferings such as seldom have been of so long duration, & at an expence for advice which would have reduced a much better income than mine to nothing. I beg y^{r} Lordships pardon for troubling you with so much ab^{t} myself and have the hon^{r} to be y^{r} most obed^{t} & obligd Ser^{t},

Charlotte ~~Smith~~

I forwarded y^{r} Ldships Letter to My daughter who is at Southampton with Mrs Dorset, having taken that opportunity to obtain Sea bathing for Lionels little Girl,[3] who has an inflammation at times in one of her eyes for which Sea bathing was orderd for her— —

I heard with very sincere pleasure of the safe return of Captn Wyndham.[4]

It seems very likely that this Mr King may not now be in existence, but it seems the only clue to be obtaind. Mr Harris went to the Commons, but he not knowing the year of Mr Newtons death, they would give him no information by shewing the Will.

Petworth House Archives MS. No address or postmark.

NOTES

1. CS enclosed a letter from Edward Binfield, curate of Spetisbury, to William Harris, 9 Sept. 1806 (PHA #8237) that Harris had forwarded to her. Binfield relates that Newton left Spetisbury "somewhere about the year 1779" and died between 1780 and 1786 at Kings Bromley near Lichfield, Staffordshire.

2. Not identified.

3. Luzena, who is with her aunt Charlotte Mary.

4. The eldest son of Egremont's six natural children, George Wyndham (1787–1869), 19, was made captain in the 72nd Regiment of Foot in 1805. He was later first Baron Leconfield.

To the earl of Egremont

Tilford. Septr 20th 1806

My Lord,

Mrs Smith requests the favor of Lord Egremont to inform her or her daughter (who is not yet return'd) whether the Trust will give directions for the necessary step to be taken in regard to the release for 1000 years (she is not sure she is correct in her impression & is unable at this moment to refer to Mr Butlers opinion, it being in another room & she without power to move): Or whether she is to write to Mr Bicknell to apply to Mr King. She apprehends that Mr Prescod will be at home by the Fleet now said to be daily expected & that no time should be lost in cutting off every avenue of subterfuge and shams which Mr Prescod may still attempt to escape by. M^{r}

Butlers opinion appears so clear & so decided that, if the only immaterial pretense is thus removed, it will be hard for Mr Prescod to escape again. But should he attempt it, Mrs Smith, whose power of Executrix to Richd Smith is not and cannot be done away, and who will again take out Letters to fyle a bill immediately against Mr Prescod that Justice to a family already irreparably injurd may no longer be delay'd——

Mrs Smith thanks Lord Egremont for the sketch of the account his Lordship took the trouble to send. If it be not too much trouble, Mrs Smith w^{d} request to know when Gibbons's last installment due in Octr 1804 was paid and its amount. The installment of 1803 was given to Mr Benjn Smith from his family, tho the award sets out with stating the matter very differently. But that of 1804, which to make up the Sum of 3984£ must have been somewhere about 500£, was surely not so applied——

Mrs Smith requests leave to remind Lord Egremont that there will be about 600£ coming to Richd Smiths estate from the last dividend on Mr Turners Bankruptcy which (unless she again in this instance puts nonsense in poor Mr Bicknells mouth) will eventually, tho God knows when, be productive—as she believes she speaks from some little knowledge of the subject when she says there are assets, even before the City business is finishd, to pay the remaining debt if the houses in Oxenden Street & other property (not chimerical) were to be made available and distributed; which one would think it high time to have done at the end of almost thirty years & which as principal C[redito]^{r} on behalf of Richd Smith M^{rs} CS would long since have pressed but wish'd to delay every measure injurious to the future interest of her Brother.

Lord Egremont again expresses his regret that the Trust (his Lordships motive for undertaking which none can be more sensible of than M^{rs} S) should now be so troublesome & can be concluded only by Death. She desires to recall to Lord Egremonts recollection that there have been all these resignations of the Trust within the time it has existed in consequence of a clause for that purpose: 1. Sir John Dyer in 1789 because he was sick & orderd abroad for his health. Secondly Mr Boehm in 1792 the moment he had got all he claimd on behalf of himself & the Berneys (with about 2000£ more than the amount of their debt, as can indubitably be made appear), and lastly, in 1798, The Sieurs Robinson and Parkin—— All this time there were Law suits pending and adverse parties enough. Yet these Gentlemen escaped by the clause in the Trust deed allowing of their resignation.

Can it be suppos'd that the same priveledge should be refus'd to Lord Egremont? While the above named partis were all interested by relationship or claims, his Lordship must evidently have been activated by no other motive than the purest humanity and compassion for a Woman burthend with a large family, not only abandon'd but oppress'd by him who ought to have been their protector and hers. And because at that time, the Woman in question was fortunate enough to be thought well of by his Lordship. Almost nine years have elapsed since the period of Lord Egremonts undertaking this benevolent but irksome task & Difficulties have arisen unforseen by M[rs] CS which have greatly increas'd the trouble.

On the other hand, circumstances have also occurrd which have renderd the continuance of the Trust less necessary. One great object of it was to guard the remaining property from the rapacity of M[r] B Smith— — who however had various Sums on various pretences to which Lord Egremont seemd afterwards so averse that his Lordship actually directed Mess[rs] Pybus to stop his income arising from M[rs] C Smith's property till these Sums were replaced (this appears by Lord Egremonts Letters still in M[rs] Smiths possession)——

Now that unhappy person M[r] B Smith is remov'd by death. M[rs] C Smith is restor'd to the power of acting as Executrix which was dormant while he lived, and she is desirous of reassuming that right. Her family are equally desirous that she should & that the Trust should be at an end, which they never thought of troubling Lord Egremont with for such a length of time. All the children are now of age, & Lieu[t] George Smith having attain'd in February last the age of Twenty one, has sent over a power of Attorney to his Mother and Sister to act for him in every respect whatsoever. The parties concernd could therefore release Lord Egremont and M[r] Turner immediately, & as to any opposition on the part of Mess[rs] Smith and Allen, M[rs] CS is assured that it w[d] be ineffectual, inasmuch as their remedy would lay against the Assets just as it does now. And she is farther inform'd, that on the present Trustees petitioning Chancery for a dismissal from the Trust it would be granted without any expence but what the Estate must answer.

M[rs] C.S. is very sorry to disobey Lord Egremonts injunction not to write, but having made it the rule of her life to do her duty however painfull that duty may be to execute, she cannot omit what she feels to be her duty where her familys bread depends on the want of these transactions, were she herself less a sufferer than she is.

[Unsigned]

Petworth House Archives MS. No address or postmark.

Epilogue
"nothing but the Wind"

—26 April 1806

Charlotte Smith wrote her final letter to the earl of Egremont only five weeks before she died. This last extant epistle shows a strong hand, a vigorous mind, and a gritty determination never to be silenced. Untreatable uterine or ovarian cancer confers on its victims a painful demise even now, yet the letters of Smith's last year show her composing new poems, sharing a jest with her remaining loyal friend, Sarah Rose, and still fighting for her family's rights.

Even as Smith penned her last complaints to Egremont, her youngest son George had been dead for four days in the West Indies. On 28 October, less than six weeks after George, Charlotte Smith died. From modest lodgings in Elsted, Surrey, her body was carried to Stoke Church, Guildford, and interred next to her mother down a slope from Stoke Manor, where young Charlotte had spent her first years. Monumental stones were placed in the church in her honor, with stones to Charles and George alongside hers.

In 1807, Joseph Johnson published Smith's last volume of poetry, Beachy Head, *and her last work for children,* The Natural History of Birds. *Five years passed before new editions of any works were published, the tenth edition of the first volume of* Elegiac Sonnets *and the fourth edition of the second. Already waning in her later years, the popularity of her works ended with her death.*

Her surviving children had lives of varying happiness and success. Harriet Smith married William Geary on 20 January 1807, freed by her inheritance to do so and no doubt in accordance with her mother's wishes. Having already been advanced as much as half of her inheritance, an impoverished Lucy Smith Newhouse and her three children turned to Egremont over the years for aid for her sons' establishment. Charlotte Mary Smith continued her social rounds, living with relatives and plagued by depression. She planned to edit her mother's letters but never did so.

William Towers Smith, who married Catherine Maria Morris in 1800 and had at least two children by her, advanced to become a senior judge in In-

dia. He returned to England in June 1826 and died on 10 October in London. Nicholas Hankey Smith's promising career as a civil servant was cut short when he involved himself in a local uprising. He was sent home in 1813 despite sheaves of letters attesting to his hospitality, humanity, character, and suitability for his work. Of his three known children, one son, William Hankey, died while a civil servant in India; his daughter Luzena died a spinster at a ripe old age. Nicholas retired to Deerbolts Hall, Suffolk, and died there on 15 December 1837.

After his first wife Ellen Galway died, Lionel Smith married Isabella Curwen Pottinger, having in all one son and seven daughters. His military career took him to Canada, Africa, the West Indies, and even India, and he advanced steadily. In the 1830s, he served as governor and commander in chief of the Windward and Leeward Islands, with appointments on Barbados and Jamaica. There he made himself extremely unpopular by taking a stand against owners' abuses of slaves, a position that surely would have gratified his mother. Knighted near the end of his career, he died on 3 January 1842 at Mauritius, where he was governor. Sir Lionel had created for himself the opportunity that his mother so longed to give all her sons.

Funds from Charlotte Smith's three marriage settlements, worth £7,704, were distributed among her children more than a year after her death, delayed by her brother's refusal to sign. Three-fifths was divided among Lionel, Harriet, and George, the younger children who could not benefit from the larger trust, and the remaining two-fifths divided among William, Charlotte Mary, Nicholas, and Lucy. Lucy's award was disproportionately small.

The hated trust was settled at last in 1813, as the correspondence with the trustees and lawyers was taken over by Charlotte Mary and Lionel after their mother's death. Charles Bicknell and Anthony Spedding, the primary legal counsel, had funds ready for distribution on 22 April 1813, thirty-seven years after Richard Smith's death, too little and too late to avail any of the children of Charlotte and Benjamin Smith. Barely £4,000 remained.

Appendix

To James Upton Tripp

[Wyke, 12 September 1787]
Sir,

Mr Turner has informed me that Lord Egremont has directed 50 G^s to be paid for the Horse which his Lordship had upon trial, and that you wish to know who is to receive the Money. I trouble you therefore with this to request the favour of you to pay it to Mr Collins[1] whose receipt on my behalf will be sufficient, he having very kindly undertaken the trouble of dividing it as far as it will go, among Mr Smiths creditors. I cannot conclude without thanking you for having been so obliging as to interest yourself in the disposal of the Horse. And I am, Sir,

your ob^t & obligd humble Ser^t
Charlotte Smith

Wyke. Septr 12th 1787.

Petworth House Archives MS. No address or postmark.

NOTE

1. Not identified.

To James Upton Tripp

[Wyke, 19 September 1787]
Sir,

I yesterday saw Mr Collins & find him much engaged with company in his house for which reason he begs I will myself receive the money for the

Horse. I shall therefore be oblig'd to you to forward it at your leisure by the post or by any safe private hand in the form of a bank or post bill & you shall immediately receive my receipt. I beg your pardon for giving you this additional trouble. And am, Sir,

your ob^{t} hble Ser^{t}
Charlotte Smith

Wyke
Septr 19th 1787.

Petworth House Archives MS. No address or postmark.

To James Upton Tripp

{Wyke, 21 September 1787}
Sir,

Very particular circumstances which have occurred since I wrote to you oblige me to request a fav^{r} of you on which I should not otherwise have presumed. Which is, that you will immediately send thirty pounds to the Revd Charles Parsons[1] at Midhurst on my account & the rest of the money to me. This request must appear very extraordinary and perhaps very improper. ~~If~~ I know not what I would say, But be assured I should not have taken this liberty with^{t} a very particular exigency. I am (in great haste & some confusion of mind from the distressing account of the death of poor Mrs Williams[2]), Sir,

y^{r} most hble Ser^{t}
Charlotte Smith

Septr 21st 1787.

Petworth House Archives MS. No address or postmark.

NOTES

1. Master of Midhurst Grammar School (1788–1795).
2. Not identified.

To James Upton Tripp

{Wyke, 25 September 1787}
Sir,

I yesterday receiv'd your very obliging Letter enclosing a draft for

Twenty two pounds ten shillings, which together with thirty pounds paid by you on my account to the Rev[d] Charles Parsons makes the Sum of fifty Guineas, being the Sum directed by Lord Egremont to be paid for an Horse purchas'd by his Lordship of M[r] Smith—

I have only to repeat my thanks for your very friendly and polite attention throughout this little transaction—And I am with great esteem, Sir,

your most oblig'd & ob[t] Ser[t]
Charlotte Smith

Sept[r] 25th 1787-

Petworth House Archives MS. No address or postmark.

Biographical Notes

Robin Allen (d. 1815) was the partner of James Lackington (d. 1815) who established the Temple of the Muses, a complex of publishing houses and shops at Finsbury Square (Nichols, *Literary History,* vol. 7). After James retired in 1798, Allen continued until his death as partner with James's nephew, George Lackington (d. 1844).

Joel Barlow (1754–1812), remembered in America as one of the Connecticut wits, author of "The Hasty-Pudding" (1796) and "The Columbiad" (1807), was a man of many careers. Having come to Europe in 1788 to sell land, he was an eyewitness to the beginnings of the French Revolution. From 1790 to 1792, he lived in London and Paris and wrote the two influential tracts CS names in her letter to him (3 Nov. 1792). Through Joseph Johnson, his publisher, he was acquainted with most of the English Jacobins, including William Hayley. He left London for Paris later in November 1792 and was made an honorary citizen of France, where he ran unsuccessfully for public office. In 1811, he was appointed minister of France.

Robert Bliss was a bookseller in Oxford in the 1790s.

Michael Bowman (1770–1830), apothecary and surgeon, Hurley Street, Cavendish Square, London, was a member of the Royal College of Surgeons.

Dr. Charles Burney (1726–1814), composer, music teacher, and author, was already famous for his four-volume *History of Music* (1777, 1782, 1789) when CS wrote to him in 1793. Trained as a musician by his half brother James; by Baker, organist at Chester Cathedral; and by the composer Thomas Arne from 1744 to 1747, Burney went to live in London. There he became known as a music teacher and developed the charming manner that contributed to his social as well as musical success. During the next three years he was an organist and composed music for the theater, but illness forced him to leave London. In 1760, he returned to London and to teaching and composing. While working on the *History of Music,* he traveled in Europe; in 1773, he published a book describing his tour through Germany. By that time, he was friends with such literary leaders as Dr. Samuel Johnson and the Thrales and was a member of the Literary Club. His other works include a dictionary of music and his own memoirs published in part in his daughter's 1832 biography of him. He also composed a variety of musical pieces.

Thomas Cadell, Jr. (1773–1836), bookseller and publisher at 141 Strand, London, took over his father's publishing firm in 1793 and managed it until his death. In his early years with the firm, he left much of its daily management to his partner, William Davies (q.v.), who had managed it for his father. Under the leadership of Cadell, Jr., the firm continued to be known as a very respectable firm, though the works published under Cadell, Sr., were more prestigious. Cadell, Jr., was one of the Court of Assistants for the Company of Stationers.

CS was on uneasy terms at best with the younger Cadell and Davies. Accusations flew between them of unfair dealings on her part and financial losses on theirs. Even so, they published several of her later works. *The Banished Man* (1794) did not sell well and was only grudgingly given a small run for its second edition. *Rural Walks* (1795) and *Rambles Farther* (1796), children's books originally discussed with Cadell, Sr., were well received. Her last novel, *The Young Philosopher* (1798), was not put into a second edition. In spite of quarrels with CS, Cadell and Davies carried all editions of *Elegiac Sonnets i* and *ii* (1797) published during her lifetime.

Thomas Cadell, Sr. (1742–1802), bookseller and publisher at 141 Strand, London, published many of CS's works during the first half of her career. The son of Thomas Cadell, a bookseller in Bristol, he was apprenticed in 1758 to the eminent bookseller Andrew Millar in London; he became a partner in 1765 and owner in 1767. He was one of the coalition of thirty-six leading London booksellers who published the fifty-eight-volume *Works of the English Poets* (1779–80) with Samuel Johnson's biographical prefaces, and the subsequent popular four-volume *Lives* (1781) with the prefaces alone, as well as Edward Gibbon's *Decline and Fall of the Roman Empire* (1776–88) and Sir William Blackstone's *Commentaries* (1765–69). He continued with William Strahan as partner from 1780 to 1784, and Strahan's son Andrew succeeded him. Cadell's business was taken over ultimately by his son Thomas Cadell, Jr. (q.v.), and an associate, William Davies (q.v.). After retiring from publishing in 1793, Cadell was elected alderman of the Ward of Walbrook in 1798. He was a liveryman of the Company of Stationers.

Very much the gentleman that CS wanted in a publisher, the elder Cadell was widely considered to be kind and generous. He published most of her early works, including *Manon Lescaut* (1786, withdrawn from publication), *The Romance of Real Life* (1787), *Emmeline* (1788), *Ethelinde* (1789), *Celestina* (1791), and the poem *The Emigrants* (1793). All but *The Emigrants* went into multiple editions. He and Cadell, Jr., and Davies published all editions of *Elegiac Sonnets* after the fourth edition until her death.

William Davies (d. 1820) was a bookseller at 141 Strand. After a few years of working in the publishing firm of Thomas Cadell, Sr. (q.v.), Davies was selected to shepherd Cadell, Jr. (q.v.), through the early years of conducting the business when the senior Cadell retired in 1793. He carried on much of the daily correspondence with CS. A stockkeeper in the Company of Stationers, he was a liberal.

Anna Augusta Smith de Foville (chr. 18 June 1774–23 Apr. 1795), the eighth child born to CS and BS and her mother's most beloved child, was baptized at All Hallows Church, Tottenham. At the age of 19, the blonde beauty fell in love with a French émigré, le chevalier Alexandre Mark Constant de Foville of Notre Dame Alikermont (variously reported by CS as 26 or 30 years old); he was the son of Marie Charlotte Le Carvier de Foville, who had possession of his estates in Normandy. Augusta and de Foville married in early August 1793; their marriage settlement was dated 1 Aug. 1792 [*sic*]. His escape from France, the prejudices he faced in Europe and England, the young couple's romance, and CS's own admiration for her son-in-law inspired and informed her sixth novel, *The Banished Man* (1794).

Augusta's first pregnancy in 1794 took a tremendous toll on her. The child, a son, was born on 24 July and died in his grandmother's arms on 27 July. Despite expensive medical treatment and trips to spas, Augusta's fragile health steadily declined. She died on 23 Apr. 1795 at Clifton Hot Wells, noted for its treatment of consumptives, and was buried in the Strangers Burial Ground there. Her obituary in the *Bristol Journal* has all the earmarks of her grief-stricken mother's pain and prose:

> Thursday se'ennight died at Clifton, in the 21st year of her age, the Lady of the Chevalier de Foville, second daughter of the celebrated Mrs. Charlotte Smith. The anguish of her husband, her mother, and her family, can only be imagined by those who, having known this young and lovely woman, feel that her personal charms are the least of those perfections which make her early death the subject of such deep regret. (2 May 1795, p. 3)

De Foville lived in England as an emigrant from 1791 until 1802. He returned to France from July through Nov. 1802 and again to Rouen in June 1803. CS last corresponded with him in Jan. 1803. Nicholas Turner, trustee to the Smith estate, objected to the Frenchman and to CS's insistence that her adored son-in-law was owed his wife's modest interest money from the trust. Although like her sisters Augusta evidently served as scribe to her mother, no letters by her survive.

Georgiana Cavendish, duchess of Devonshire (1757–1806), was an author, eldest daughter of the first Earl Spencer, and first wife of William Cavendish, duke of Devonshire. She received fame and some notoriety on a number of fronts, including politics and fashion. A notable beauty, she helped popularize the largest of plumed hats. She was a close friend and advisor to the Prince of Wales until her death, and he was said to be concerned for her health during her 1785 pregnancy. She published two novels, *Emma, or The Unfortunate Attachment* (1773) and *The Sylph* (1779), and one poem, "The Passage of Mount St. Gothard" (1802). An obsessive spender, she ran up a debt of £60,000 in 1790 and in 1804 confessed to her husband a debt of £40,000 (while probably owing more than £100,000). She and the duke lived for many years in a ménage à trois with Lady Elizabeth Foster, whom the duke married after Georgiana died.

Along with other women writers, the duchess patronized CS. In addition to joining the effort to settle the Smith estate in Chancery, she helped gather subscribers and their fees for *Elegiac Sonnets ii;* however, she misplaced both the list and the money. She also permitted CS to dedicate *Rambles Farther* to her elder daughter, Lady Georgiana Cavendish.

James Dodsley (1724–1797), publisher at Pall Mall, London, took over the business when his more famous brother Robert, twenty-two years older than he, gave it up in 1759. A liberal, respected, and learned man in his own right, he published significant works by major writers. He was, with Thomas Cadell, Jr. (q.v), among the group of influential London booksellers who published *Works of the English Poets* with Samuel Johnson's popular biographical prefaces. In 1790, he published Edmund Burke's *Reflections on the Revolution in France.* For CS, he published the first four editions of *Elegiac Sonnets,* the first and second in 1784 and third and fourth in 1786.

The Reverend John Douglass, D.D. (1743–1812), bishop of London, was consecrated in 1790. Quiet and modest but firm in his stands, he would have been known to CS for his work on the 1791 Catholic Relief Act. Educated at Douay from 1764 to 1768, he taught philosophy at Valladolid until 1773, when he was transferred to York.

The Reverend Charles Dunster (1750–1816), dean of West Sussex and rector of Petworth until his death, was a scholar and author. His fifteen titles range from his noted edition of John Milton's *Paradise Regained* (1795) to sacred tracts to a sonnet on the death of George Monck Berkley published in *Gentleman's Magazine.*

The third earl of Egremont (1751–1837), **George O'Brien Wyndham,** of Petworth House, Petworth, Sussex, and Grosvenor Place, Piccadilly. A distinguished, widely respected, and fabulously wealthy aristocrat, Egremont had been educated at Westminster, Eton, and Oxford. Only moderately active in politics, he resumed Tory activities after showing early Whig tendencies. He was best known for his agricultural experiments, racing stables, and generous patronage of artists, of whom CS was only one. The several thousand pounds he seems to have contributed to settling the Smith trust was a mere fraction of the more than a million pounds he ultimately distributed to artists such as J. W. M. Turner and John Flaxman.

CS's unfortunate, ultimately bitter relationship with Egremont shows a side of him not elsewhere revealed. Three things probably contributed to their estrangement. First, CS's brother, Nicholas Turner, co-trustee with Egremont and himself a bankrupt and a bigot, troubled Egremont with his own affairs and complained about CS's defense of her French son-in-law's inheritance. Second, Egremont's steward, William Tyler, took offense at CS's aggressive involvement in legal affairs, which took the form of frequent letters and torturous restating of all the issues in the case. Third, Egremont likely had his own grounds for turning against her. He had lived for years unmarried with his mistress, Elizabeth Iliffe. Their three sons and three daughters were not legitimized when the couple finally married on 16 July 1801, and marriage strained the couple's relationship. Under the circumstances, CS's complaints about BS as an "unnatural" father were hardly tactful. See Appendix for four letters about CS's earliest relationship with Egremont.

Dr. George Fordyce (1736–1802), an eminent physician and noted lecturer on medicine, was a member of the Literary Club and the Royal Society, through which he knew others concerned with CS, including the politician Thomas Erskine and the playwright

Richard Brinsley Sheridan. Brilliant but unrefined, he was known for his belief that man eats far too often. He limited himself to one gargantuan hour-and-a-half-long meal daily at Dolly's chophouse on Paternoster Row.

Harriet Amelia Smith Geary (b. Apr. 1782) was the second-youngest child and the youngest daughter born to CS and BS, and one of the three children left out of her grandfather's will. She lived with her mother except for her year in India, where she had gone with her eldest brother William in the hopes of making a suitable marriage. On 2 Apr. 1799 they sailed with a fleet of East Indiamen on the *William Pitt,* arriving in Calcutta on 5 Sept. 1799. After she contracted malaria, William sent her home as her only chance for recovery. She sailed on 20 Mar. 1800 on the *Lord Hawkesbury.* Its expected Aug. arrival at Portsmouth was delayed by weather. When the ship landed at Deal, Charlotte Mary took Harriet to London and reunited her with CS in mid-Oct. Until CS died, she cared for Harriet during harrowing recurrences of fever, convulsions, and delusions. An allowance from William evidently did not greatly help with CS's expenses during these episodes.

This horrific illness left the young beauty "much alter'd." By Oct. 1803, while living with her mother in Elsted near Godalming, Harriet met a neighbor, a handsome young botanist, William Geary. Even though he was crippled and his brother had lost his family's fortune, CS considered him an advantageous match. But both families made the couple wait until they could afford to set up house. The couple married in Farnham on 20 Jan. 1807, a mere three months after CS's death; Harriet's share of her mother's small fortune was £695.14.4 transferred to her in 28 Nov. 1807 and another £730.16.9 in Apr. 1808. No record of children and no letters by Harriet have been found.

The Reverend Samuel Greatheed (d. 1823), a Dissenting minister of Newport Pagnell, Buckinghamshire, was a neighbor and friend of William Cowper, whom he first met in 1785, and of William Hayley. Married in Sept. 1788, he and his wife subscribed separately to CS's *Elegiac Sonnets ii.* In June 1793, he lent Cowper his copy of the sonnets while Cowper was waiting for his own to arrive.

William Hayley (1745–1820), poet, novelist, and patron of other writers, was CS's first and most effective literary friend and sponsor. Cheerful and well liked, he wrote mediocre verse prolifically and one rather bad epistolary novel, *The Young Widow: or the History of Cornelia Sedley* (1789), an effort that CS attributed to his reading her novels. He turned down an offer of the laureateship when Thomas Warton died in 1790. When CS turned to Hayley for advice on her *Elegiac Sonnets* in 1784, Hayley had recently launched his most successful poem, *The Triumphs of Temper* (1781). A friend of the artist George Romney since 1777, he met and befriended William Cowper in 1792 on discovering that they were both working on a life of Milton. About this time Hayley also met William Blake. He often intervened in his friends' lives in significant ways: he arranged for a pension for Cowper in 1796 and worked with Samuel Rose during Blake's trial for treason in Jan. 1804. The year 1800 was a sorrowful one for Hayley, for his friend Cowper and his beloved illegitimate son, Thomas Alphonso Hayley, died within a week of each other. Tom, a talented sculptor, had suffered the complications of a severe scoliosis for several years before his death.

CS dedicated the first edition of *Elegiac Sonnets* to Hayley, her neighbor at Eartham and a careful, sympathetic reader of many of her early works. In 1794, CS began to write of having lost his friendship, but he continued to help her occasionally by reading her works before publication.

Mary Hays (1760–1843), feminist and radical thinker, was reviled for *Memoirs of Emma Courtney* (1796), a novel that explores the consequences of a woman's pursuing love. In her anonymously published *Appeal to the Men of Great Britain in Behalf of the Women* (1798), she called for education and financial independence of women. Her second novel, *A Victim of Prejudice* (1799), explores the effect of crime on women. She also wrote Dissenting religious tracts and sermons, fiction for children, and biographies of women. Her letters to her tutor Eccles and from her friend Eliza Fenwick have been published.

Joseph Johnson (1738–1809), bookseller and publisher at 2 St. Paul's Churchyard, focused on medical, theological, and liberal political works. He was so admired for his judgment and generosity to needy authors, as well as for his contributions to the book-making industry, that he was known as the "father of the book trade." His authors included Anna Letitia Barbauld, William Cowper, Erasmus Darwin, Mary Wollstonecraft, and Maria Edgeworth. From 1788 to 1799, he published the liberal magazine *Analytical Review.*

Lucy Hill Lowe (1762–1855), eldest daughter and co-heiress of Thomas Hill of Court of Hill, Shropshire, married Thomas Humphrey Lowe and bore him at least two sons, one of whom became dean of Exeter (1839–61). The Lowes also had a London residence, to which CS refers in her letter of 27 Nov. 1791. In writing "Lowes" for "Lowe," CS made a mistake unusual for her. (There was a Thomas Lowes of Ridley Hall [d. 1812] near Nottingham, but I have not found evidence that he was married. On the contrary, his natural daughter was his heiress.)

Barbara Marsden Meyer (1743–1818), daughter of John and Elizabeth Marsden of St. John, Smith Square, Westminster, was a musician and talented artist who earned several prizes from the Society of Arts. When on 6 Mar. 1763 she married Jeremiah Meyer (1735–1789), she brought a respectable fortune to the marriage. It was a happy marriage of like spirits: she was celebrated for virtue, and he for beneficence and loyalty to friends. They had ten children, three boys and seven girls. Jeremiah had come from Germany at the age of 6 (some sources say 14) to England, where he studied under C. F. Zincke in 1757 and 1758. Known for his enamels, he was appointed miniature painter to the queen and then enamel painter to the king in 1764. A founding member of the Royal Academy of Arts, he is remembered for establishing its pension fund.

The couple were friends with Romney and Hayley. In 1797, years after Jeremiah's death, Hayley arranged for a depressed Romney to visit Barbara Meyer, and she cheered him by sketching his portrait. In 1798 and 1799, she corresponded with Hayley's dying son Thomas. In May 1799, there was the prospect of her moving from Kew to Eartham, but this did not come to pass.

Lucy Eleanor Smith Newhouse (chr. 17 April 1776–after 1845), ninth child of CS and BS and third-oldest daughter, was privately baptized at Hinton Ampner. (Lucy's middle name is spelled "Elenore" in the Marylebone marriage register as well as in abstracts of deeds related to the Smith trust. But in two letters to the earl of Egremont, she signs herself Lucy Eleanor Newhouse.) Schooled at home by her mother, Lucy acted as her mother's scribe and copyist when Charlotte Mary was away. In the 1790s she wrote several notes to publishers for her mother. In July 1797, CS returned from London to find Lucy involved in a scandal, possibly an affair. On 12 June 1798, against her mother's wishes, she married the eldest son of John and Susanna Newhouse of Petworth, Thomas Postlewaite Newhouse (chr. 22 Dec. 1763–28 Mar. 1801). He had no profession or means of earning money and was a man not unlike her father—improvident, violent, and abusive. After a stint as tutor to Lord Allen's sons, he attempted medical studies at New College, Oxford, but he caught a violent fever and died, attended by his brother-in-law Lionel.

Lucy and Thomas's first son, Thomas Henry, was born on 25 May 1799, and their second, William Charles, on 29 Apr. 1800. At the time of her husband's death, Lucy was pregnant with her third child, Charlotte Susan, born in mid-Oct. 1801, who became her grandmother's favorite. Lucy lived in poverty at North Chapel, dependent on advances against her small inheritance from her mother's marriage settlements. When that was not enough, her increasingly beleaguered mother found her a few more pounds. She received £231.17.11 from her mother's marriage settlements in Nov. 1807 and £310.5.7 in Apr. 1808, half that of the other beneficiaries. Her dozen letters to Egremont, the last in 1816, suggest that he assisted in her sons' schooling and early advancement; the eldest went to India to work under his uncle William. Lucy was probably the longest lived of all CS's children, still alive at Lymington in 1845.

John Nichols (1745–1826), printer, publisher, and compiler of the lives of literary figures, was best known as editor of and contributor to *Gentleman's Magazine.* As early as 1778, he became involved in managing *Gentleman's Magazine,* and he ran it entirely from 1792 until 1826. From that source and his own wide knowledge of the literary scene of his time, he compiled the nine-volume *Literary Anecdotes of the Eighteenth Century* (1812–15) and the eight-volume *Illustrations of the Literary of the Eighteenth Century* (1817–58), whose final volumes appeared posthumously.

Sir Richard Phillips (1767–1840), author and publisher, knighted in 1808, was perhaps best known for his eighteen-month incarceration in Leicester for selling Thomas Paine's *The Rights of Man* (1791). In addition to establishing the *Monthly Magazine* in 1796, he published cheap books for elementary schools. A contemporary described him as having "four valuable qualities: honesty, zeal, ability, and courage. He applied them all to teaching matters about which he knew nothing, and gained himself an uncomfortable life and a ridiculous memory" (*Biographical Dictionary of Living Authors,* pp. 1096–97).

CS spent the last troubled years of her life completing *The History of England, from the earliest records to the peace of Amiens. In a series of letters to a young lady at school* (1808), a work she contracted to do for him shortly after writing to him on 4 Feb. 1801. Her difficulties with the research for the book as well as with her health and finances created many delays, and she found him to be rudely insistent that she finish.

William Prescod (d. after 1815) was an enormously wealthy landowner in Barbados, with six plantations and £70,000 to £80,000 in securities in England; he was therefore a good prospect to purchase Gay's plantation, which he did in Sept. 1800 (see CS to Egremont, 9 July 1800 and nn. 1, 8). Late in life, when he moved back to London and wrote his will, he still owned Kendalls in St. Johns; Sion Hill, Rock Dundo, Small Hopes, and Carleton in St. Peter; and Searles, Territts, and Dayrells in Christ Church. Whether he had sold Gay's or renamed it Dayrells is not clear (Brandow, *Genealogies of Barbados Families,* p. 601).

George Robinson (1737–1801), bookseller in Addison's Head, Paternoster Row, London, conducted a large wholesale trade from 1764 to 1801. On coming to London from Dalston in Cumberland in 1755, he was apprenticed to John Rivington, then to William Johnston before beginning a business on his own in partnership with J. Roberts, who died in 1776. Thomas Longman lent him money, and his business was a success. From 1784 on, he was in partnership with his son George and brother John. His publications included such important periodicals as *The Critical Review, Town and Country Magazine, The New Annual Register,* and *The Modern Universal History* as well as literature. Called "King of booksellers" by William West, he supported liberal causes. He was fined in 1793 for publishing Paine's *The Rights of Man.*

John Robinson (1727–1802), secretary of the treasury from 1770 to 1782 under Lord North. He declined a peerage in 1784; but from 1787, he was surveyor-general of wood and forests under William Pitt. He was a trustee to the Smith estate, and CS did battle with him (and Thomas Dyer) in letters, meetings, and prefaces to her work. Robinson's involvement with the estate resulted from his marriage to Mary Crow, a daughter of Nathaniel Crow (a wealthy merchant and planter from Barbados) and stepdaughter of Richard Smith. Because his relationship to the estate was only indirect, CS found his obstructions especially embittering.

Samuel Rose (1767–1804), attorney and special pleader, 55 Chancery Lane, London, was a friend of William Cowper, whom he met in 1787, and of William Hayley. After four years at Glasgow University, he attended the courts of law at Edinburgh, where he knew Adam Smith and Henry McKenzie. In 1786, he entered as a student at Lincoln's Inn and read with Sergeant Praed until 1790. In 1790, he married Sarah Farr (q.v. below). In addition to arranging for Cowper's pension and administering that trust, he defended William Blake against a charge of treason in January 1804, fell ill, and never regained his health. He died of consumption on 20 Dec. 1804. He was editor of two legal books and contributed to the *Monthly Review* on legal matters, he collected and published miscellaneous works of Goldsmith, and he may have aided Lord Sheffield in editing Gibbon's miscellaneous and posthumous works. He was greatly respected. In a 15 Feb. 1806 letter to Hayley, William Davies called Rose "our mutual and excellent Friend, who was Kindness itself." Hayley wrote that he died of "a rapid and incurable decay . . . after much lingering pain borne by him with uncommon patience" (WSRO add. MS 2758).

Sarah Farr Rose (ca. 1759–1848), elder daughter of Dr. William Farr, married Samuel Rose in 1790 and had borne him four sons by the time he left her a widow in 1804. Dr. Farr was a student with Goldsmith, and Samuel Rose edited Goldsmith's *Miscellaneous Works* (1801) in addition to his legal work for other literary figures such as William Cowper and William Blake. For CS, isolated from social and literary circles at the end of her life, these associations made Sarah Rose a highly desirable and respectable acquaintance. Rose became a faithful correspondent of CS after helping her with legal matters while Samuel was out of town. Although the two women never met, their epistolary friendship was warm and intimate, and CS wrote to her with more wit and acerbity than to anyone else.

Dr. Thomas Shirley (1729–ca. 1781) was an Islington surgeon.

Benjamin Smith (21 July 1742–26 Feb. 1806), second son of Richard Smith and Elizabeth Crow of Barbados, came to England at the age of three. His father was a successful merchant, Barbadian property owner, and director of the East India Company. Nothing is known of BS's education or experiences as an adolescent or young man, but he was employed as his father's junior partner. On 22 Feb. 1765, at the age of 22, BS married Charlotte Turner, not quite 16, in a match arranged through his father and her father, Nicholas Turner, and her aunt Lucy Towers. The young couple did not suit: her literary interests repelled him, while his absorption in schemes, gambling, and other women and his lack of interest in learning repelled her. But he took advantage of her very good working relationship as his father's clerk to extract more money from the old man, sending her in once a quarter for funds when he had run through their yearly £2,000 allowance.

For a few months after their marriage, the young couple lived with BS's sister, Mary Smith Berney; they then moved to Cheapside, where they lived with his parents. After the couple's first child died in 1767, Richard Smith set them up in a small house in Southgate, a village near London, for CS's health. By 1771, they and their five children moved nearer London to a larger residence in Tottenham. As BS's spending became wilder, Richard Smith intervened again in 1774 and relocated his son's growing family to Lys Farm, a safer, remote location in Hampshire, where they lived for the next nine years. There, in 1781, the unlikely candidate BS was elected sheriff.

Upon Richard Smith's death in 1776, responsibility for the considerable Smith estate worth £36,000 devolved on BS as executor. In December 1783, BS's siblings had him arrested for debt and charged with a devastavit for failure to manage the estate properly. He was released on 2 July 1784. In October, he fled to France to escape creditors, renting on old castle in Dieppe near Normandy, where the last of his twelve children was born. By October 1785, he had returned to England and settled his family at Woolbeding.

On 15 April 1787, BS's wife left him, fearing for her children's safety and for her own life at his hands. The couple never reunited and rarely met facc to face again. See Appendix for four letters about CS and BS's relationship immediately after the separation. For the next nineteen years, BS lived in Hamilton, Scotland, under an alias, Bryan or Brian Symmonds or Simmonds, with his housekeeper and mistress, a Mrs. Miller or Millar. Always under a cloud for debt, he seems to have made numerous sallies into England to claim his wife's interest money and literary earnings. Presumably, his charm cloaked him with safety if not honor. He died while imprisoned for debt in the Berwick jail, and his funeral expenses were sent to his widow. His will had also attempted to foist off on her responsibility for his final and thirteenth known child, born to the niece of his mistress who lived with them.

Benjamin Berney Smith (chr. 30 Apr. 1767–1 June 1777), second son of CS and BS, was christened at Saint Faith under St. Paul's. A brilliant child and a favorite of his mother, he was weak from birth. He died seven months after his grandfather's death, probably of consumption. He was buried at the little country church at Hinton Ampner in Hampshire, where the country air had failed to improve his health.

Brathwaite Smith (chr. 19 July 1770–18 June 1786), third son of CS and BS, was christened at Saint Faith under St. Paul's. Brathwaite was enrolled at Winchester College but left in 1782, almost certainly because of the family's financial difficulties. In June 1786 a malignant fever swept through the household, infecting children and servants; Brathwaite died within two or three days.

Charles Dyer Smith (chr. 27 Feb. 1773–d. after June 1801), the seventh child born to CS and BS and perhaps the most unfortunate, was baptized at All Hallow's Church, Tottenham. Enrolled for a short time at Winchester, he left in 1788 for unspecified reasons; CS was to lament that she never had enough money to enroll him at Oxford and spare him the dangers of a military life. She first describes him as a grown man, waiting idly at home for the trustees to provide him with enough money to join the army. He gained the rank of ensign with the 14th (Bedfordshire) Regiment by April 1793, in time to join the European campaign. He probably stormed Famars in May and participated in other fierce fighting throughout the summer. On 6 Sept., at the Siege of Dunkirk, he was one of fifty-six casualties. Only hours after his right leg was amputated, his regiment risked his life to move him to safety. In Oct. CS sent his younger brother Lionel to bring him back to England. There CS protested the government's failure to provide an adequate income for its wounded heroes. She supported his recuperation and lent him her house at Storrington during his early months as a recruiting officer; they quarreled when his stay cost her money she could ill afford.

By Sept. 1795, Charles had returned to active duty as a lieutenant in the Royal Garrison Battalion under General Thomas Trigge in Gibraltar. In 1798, he served as lieutenant of invalids at Berwick near his father in Hamilton, Scotland. His oldest brother William, home from India, visited him; they put BS to great expense entertaining them and Charles's military friends. In quieter times, Charles's oldest sister, Charlotte Mary, visited him too. In Oct. 1800, he became paymaster of the 47th (Lancashire) Regiment of Foot. The position gave him a chance to sail to Barbados, where he tried to settle some debts on the plantations belonging to his grandfather's estate. Charles wrote several letters to the earl of Egremont—including what was probably his last, from

Bridgetown, Barbados, on 5 June 1801; shortly afterward, he died of yellow fever. He never married and had no children. A rather bad epitaph by William Hayley (in a bound volume of holograph poems, WSRO #2758, p. 100) called Charles his mother's "Favorite by Choice," but she awarded that honor to her youngest son George.

Charlotte Mary Smith (10 Apr. 1769–1842) was the fourth child and oldest daughter of CS and BS. Charlotte Mary often served as her mother's amanuensis, writing out fair copy of her novels and handling some business letters. After her mother's death, Charlotte Mary, along with Lionel, wrote a number of letters concerning the settlement of the Smith estate. Once grown, Charlotte Mary often lived apart from her mother, with relatives in London and in the country. Although she was the grandchild most benefited by Richard Smith's will, she received no money until well past marriageable age and so never married. There are hints that she suffered from bouts of depression. About 30 of her letters to Egremont, Tyler, and Cadell and Davies survive.

George Augustus Frederick Smith (Feb. 1785–16 Sept. 1806), youngest of the twelve children of CS and BS, and one of three left out of his grandfather's will. Born in a cold castle in Normandy, where his parents had fled from creditors, he was torn from his mother's arms by local Catholic priests to be properly baptized. Back in England, CS was always at great expense to provide schooling and then military clothing and advancements for this last son of her heart. She once called him *tout à moi,* all mine, for she had left his father when George was two. Charles Parson's Midhurst Grammar School was his earliest schooling experience; he later went to Hackney School. His brother-in-law Alexandre de Foville also tutored him in French and in drawing. He began his army career in 1801 as a 15-year-old ensign in Charles's old regiment, the 47th, and narrowly escaped shipwreck in Nov. 1803. A year later, he was promoted to the adjutancy of the 96th Regiment, but found himself serving under a tyrant. With difficulty and the loss of the funds needed to purchase his promotion, he returned briefly to the 47th. After transferring to the 16th Regiment, he shipped out to the West Indies. True to his mother's worst fears, he died of yellow fever on 16 Sept. 1806 in the unforgiving tropical climate of Surinam. CS died before news of his death arrived. George left everything to "my dear sister Luzena" (actually his niece), but his will lay unproved until 3 Jan. 1862. He never married and left no letters.

Dr. James Edward Smith (1759–1828) was a botanist and author. After studying medicine and botany at the University of Edinburgh in 1781 under Dr. John Hope, an early proponent of the Linnaean method, Smith studied in London. There he purchased the entire Linnaean collection for £1,088. Consisting of a library, manuscripts, a herbarium, and natural history materials, it became the foundation for his future publications, professional activity, and success as a botanist. Elected to the Royal Society at the age of 26, he toured the Continent the next year, meeting many important people and publishing in 1793 a three-volume *Sketch of a Tour on the Continent.* As president of the Linnaean Society, he convened its first meeting in 1788.

When CS wrote to him in 1797 (see letter of 15 Mar. 1798), she was aiming high for a sanction for her work. She doubtless admired *English Botany,* the beautiful result of Smith's lengthy collaboration with James Sowerby (begun in 1790). Smith's last work, *English Flora* (1821–28), considered by many his best, was published long after CS could have relished it.

Lionel Smith (9 Oct. 1777, chr. 11 Nov. 1777–2 or 3 Jan. 1842), tenth child and seventh son of CS and BS, and one of the three children left out of his grandfather's will, was baptized at Hinton Ampner in Hampshire, five months after the death of his brother Benjamin. He was by any measure their most accomplished child. He showed an early bent for heroic action when he led a schoolboy rebellion at Winchester in 1793 to protest a schoolmate's unjust punishment. He and his cousin Nicholas Turner were sent down for raiding the armory and threatening the masters with muskets. That fall CS entrusted him to travel to Ostend to bring home his wounded brother Charles. From an early age, Lionel actively backed his mother's efforts to settle the trust; in Jan. 1795, he went so far as to issue a challenge to Thomas Dyer over his refusal to disburse £500 among his children and CS's.

Lionel's military career began with an appointment to an ensigncy (rather than a purchase of one) to the 24th Regiment on 28 Oct. 1795. A stint as aide-de-camp for the duke of Kent earned his later support. By 1801 the young lieutenant had served in Canada, Nova Scotia, and Sierra Leone, where he put down an insurrection. From there he advanced rapidly, obtaining a company in 1801 and the rank of major in 1802, aided by the earl of Egremont as well as his father-in-law, Thomas Galway of Kilkerry, Co. Kerry. Lionel served in a number of foreign possessions: the West Indies, Surinam, Essequibo, Berbice, and others. He was briefly a lieutenant colonel in the 18th Regiment, but he transferred to the 65th and was sent to Bombay, where he fought pirates in the Persian Gulf. His twenty years in India included steady advancement through the ranks to colonel and dramatic action as commander of the fourth division that captured Poonah. A severe saber cut to the head during cavalry action at Ashta slowed him only briefly.

Knighted in 1832, he was reassigned to the West Indies in 1833. He spent the remainder of his illustrious career there, first as governor and commander in chief of the Windward and Leeward Islands. In keeping with his mother's idealism, he supported emancipation: in the process of enforcing it and showing sympathy for the freed slaves, he alienated his European constituency. He succeeded the marquis of Sligo as captain general and commander in chief of Jamaica in 1836 and faced even greater opposition when slaves were fully emancipated in 1838. Planters tried to subvert the new freedoms by charging heavy rents, perverting vagrancy laws, and kicking the former slaves off estates. Lionel's efforts to control these abuses failed but made him so unpopular that he was replaced. He spent his last years as governor of Mauritius, although he was perhaps always a better soldier than politician.

He had two daughters by his first wife, Ellen Marianne Galway (d. 1814), and five daughters and a son (Lionel, who succeeded to his baronetcy) by his second wife, Isabella Curwen Pottinger, whom he married 20 Nov. 1819. Isabella died three days after him. His dozen surviving letters include five to Egremont. Two to his mother show his love and respect for her. A warm letter to him from his cousin Nicholas Turner (fellow rebel at Winchester in 1793) suggests that the next generation stayed on better terms than their embattled parents.

Details of his descendants to the present day are given in Burke.

Nicholas Hankey Smith (chr. 4 Nov. 1771–15 Dec. 1837), CS and BS's sixth-born child and second-oldest son to survive into adulthood, was christened at All Hallow's Church, Tottenham. His exemplary career with the East India Company as a civil servant was cut short after he violated company policy and led armed forces against an uprising in Bushire, Persia.

Appointed a writer in 1788, he worked in the Accountants Department on arriving in Bombay in Sept. 1790. From Oct. 1792 to 1798, he served as resident at Bushire. In 1800 he began to serve as garrison paymaster. Because of his excellent Persian, he accompanied the Persian ambassador to Bengal and was present in July 1802 when one ambassador was assassinated. Nicholas was called on to conciliate the other Persians in the party. In 1805, he traveled again with a Turkish envoy from Bombay to Bengal, where he stayed for more than a year. It is tempting to imagine that he and William crossed paths during this time. In Jan. 1807 he accompanied the Persian ambassador back to Bushire and became resident there. He undertook a mission to Sindh in 1808 and successfully concluded a treaty. Some time after his residency was extended to include Muscat, he was dismissed for using armed force against natives and sent home to London. A series of supportive letters by prominent men failed to restore his position. One letter remarks on his "great knowledge" of the Persian and personal acquaintance with the people and their ways. Known for "hospitality" and "humanity," he kept his home as "a constant place of resort to the Persians" (IRO Ref. #0/6/9, vol. 9, p. 256). He returned to England, out of service, in 1813 and lived at Deerbolts Hall, Suffolk.

He married or consorted with a native woman, a Georgian or Persian, in the late 1790s, and had two children by her, Luzena (ca. 1799–1885) and William Hankey (ca. 1800–22 June 1821). Another story has it that he stole his 12-year-old Indian bride and drove her to church in a carriage to be married. His fluency in Persian argues that she was Persian. In the summer of 1802, Nicholas sent his daughter Luzena, then 3, with her 14-month-old brother to live with CS. Their voyage lasted eight months. Luzena sometimes stayed with her grandmother and sometimes with her aunt Charlotte Mary. Luzena was the darling of her uncle George. Her need to learn English provided Smith with the impetus to compose *Conversations Introducing Poetry* (1804). In 1806, CS refers to her "little girl and boy playing." In that same year, Nicholas had a second son, John Hankey (b. 11 Mar. 1806), before he married the child's mother, Annie or Anna Petruse at Fort William, Calcutta, on 13 Aug. 1806. Presumably the Georgian woman had died.

Although Luzena and William were a financial burden to CS in her darkest years, Nicholas was among her most supportive and loving children. In addition to sending her money regularly, he allowed the use of his stocks to support his youngest brother in the military.

William Towers Smith (1768?–10 Oct. 1826) was the third child born to CS and BS and the first to survive to adulthood. A civil servant in Bengal from 1788 to 1826, he progressed steadily through the ranks as a magistrate, justifying his mother's pride in his achievements. He obtained his rank as a writer on 7 Aug. 1783 and arrived in India in 1788, beginning as second assistant to the collector of Ramghyr on 3 Sept. By 1 May 1793 his titles included junior merchant, register, and assistant to the judge, magistrate, and collector of Ramghyr. On 20 Oct. 1794, he was assigned to be commissioner of Cooch Behar.

During these years he often sent money home in amounts ranging from £100 to £300. But when he returned to England in July 1798, his mother found him to be a man of pleasure, too like his father, for he quickly ran through the £2,000 he brought with him. He alienated not only her but also his father in Scotland after BS hosted a costly visit. On 2 Apr. 1799, he sailed back to India, owing £3,000 to his cousins' husbands, Thomas Henchman and Edward Boehm. He also took his youngest sister Harriet under his wing, hoping to help her find a match. On 15 Mar. 1800, he married Catherine Maria Morris, shortly before he sent Harriet back to England suffering from a severe case of malaria.

He and his wife eventually had children: Catherine Augusta, baptized 8 Oct. 1810, and Seton Lionel, born in 1817. William became judge and magistrate of Ramghyr on 30 Oct. 1800 and held that same position at Allahabad from 1803 to 1808. He was appointed to the provincial court of appeals as a second judge at Benares (Varanasi) in 1808 and at Moorsheadabad in 1811, and he became senior judge in 1817. He returned to London in June 1826 and died in October, the rupture with his mother never mended. Apart from the bond on Henchman and Boehm and one letter to his son, none of his letters or papers have been found.

For his descendants, see Lionel Smith-Gordon in Burke; a branch of his family settled in America and another in New Zealand.

Robert Southey (1774–1843), poet, was a prolific writer in many genres. When CS wrote to him (3 Dec. 1801), Southey was 27 and newly embarked on his career and marriage. In 1795, he had published his first book, *Poems: Containing The Retrospect, Odes, Elegies, Sonnets, &c,* with Robert Lovell and had married Edith Fricker. An enlarged version of *Poems,* containing works by him alone, was published in 1797. His *Thalaba,* published in 1801, surely added to CS's eagerness to meet him.

Southey anticipated meeting CS. On 2 Dec. 1801, he wrote that his friend Mary Barker planned to spend the winter with CS in London and he expected "to be pleasantly intimate at that house." By 6 Feb. 1802, he had added to his list of "Living Remarkables . . . Charlotte Smith, a woman of genius, good sense, and pleasant manners" (Southey, *New Letters,* pp. 262, 269).

Robert Tayler, a merchant of Broad Street and friend of BS, was extensively involved in Smith family concerns. He was at one time trustee to each of CS's three marriage settlements. On 2 Feb. 1803 he was acting as agent for Edmund Boehm as well. During BS's many secretive stays in London, Tayler received his mail "under cover" to protect him from discovery by creditors. CS thought Tayler "weak" and "shuffling" (see CS to Egremont, 14 and 15 Oct. 1803).

James Upton Tripp (1749–1801), son of Rev. John Upton Tripp, Rector of Sutton (Sussex), then of Spofforth (Yorkshire), both Wyndham family livings, and Sarah, née Burchill. The Tripps were a Somerset family, whom the Wyndhams patronized. James's father had the two family livings. His brother Charles was given Devon and Somerset livings, while their brother Henry was a barrister at Middle Temple. Henry seems to have acted as legal agent for the Wyndhams, and eventually settled at Orchard Wyndham, their estate in Somerset. James became steward at Petworth c. 1772, until his death in 1801. He married Sarah Edsall, and they had four sons and a daughter. Some correspondence at the Petworth House Archives about their very unhappy marriage suggests that she may have been rather deranged. See Appendix for four letters showing CS's earliest correspondence with Tripp.

The Reverend Nicholas Turner (1750–1819), second child and only son of Nicholas and Anna Towers Turner, was christened at Stoke near Guildford. Around 1762, he was enrolled at Westminster School. In 1773, he was active in London as a merchant, married Sarah, and had one son Nicholas, later a captain in the Royal Artillery Corps of Drivers. In 1789, he was rector of Sutton near Petworth; in the mid-1790s, he served as rector at Storrington and Fittleworth, where he became involved in lawsuits with his parishioners over debts. In 1798, the earl of Egremont became his patron, assigning him first to Coates and then to Lurgasale, "a frontier parish." CS lamented that he was reduced to "a living in the very worst part of Sussex" (letter to Sarah Rose, 2 July 1805).

In 1799, he joined the earl of Egremont as new trustee to the Smith estate. By 1801, he had quarreled with both his older and his younger sister, Catherine Dorset. He held a power of attorney for his namesake, Nicholas Hankey Smith, who was in India. CS was sure that her son intended to support his small children in her care with generous financial supplements, but Turner resisted all of CS's efforts to influence his handling of the power. With his younger sister, he became embroiled in a quarrel over money; the subsequent lawsuit bankrupted him.

William Tyler (1764–1835) was steward to the third earl of Egremont. Tyler became clerk to James Upton Tripp, his predecessor as agent at Petworth, as early as 1787. Tyler lived in the Cook House, East Street, Petworth, and never married, passing the house along to the Goulds, his sister and their descendants. He appears in the *Law Lists* with John Daintrey and Tripp in 1795 and with Daintrey, Percival Hart, and William Johnson in 1802. His charge of the Petworth estate and holdings would have begun by 21 September 1801, when Tripp died, and his earliest surviving letter to CS is dated 2 September 1801.

That Tyler had a critical role in the demise of CS's relationship with Egremont is unquestionable. He was a difficult man of legendary unpopularity. His lowering of estate wages alarmed many. Agricultural workers once made a gibbet and gallows and burned him and his man Goatcher in effigy. At another time, the two were carried about Egdean Fair in effigy, and a tramp was hired to sing songs about him so obscene that ladies could not come to the fair. There is a further tradition, probably not founded in fact, that his enemies among ordinary people filled his grave with cabbage stumps and danced on it. A letter by his nephew, Thomas Gould, defended him, pointing to the "multiplicity of his business, the importance of which keeps his mind constantly employed" (see Jerrome, *Tales of Old Petworth,* p. 44, and *Lightly Tread Here,* pp. 61–64; WSRO Add. Ms. 5770, 1787, and WSRO Oglethorpe and Anderson uncat. box 49).

Many letterbooks of his estate work survive, but his handwriting is almost unreadable.

The Reverend Joseph Cooper Walker (1761–1810), Irish antiquarian, arranged for the sale of some of CS's works to Irish booksellers and maintained a friendly correspondence with her from 1792 to 1804. An original member of the Royal Irish Academy, he had traveled extensively when young. His first two books were on Irish antiquities, while later ones reflected modern interests: *Historical Memoirs of the Irish Bards . . . with Anecdotes . . . on the Music of Ireland {and an} . . . Account of the Musical Instruments of the Ancient Irish* (1786), *An Historical Essay on the Dress of the Ancient and Modern Irish . . . {and} A Memoir on the Armour and Weapons of the Irish* (1788), *Outlines of a Plan for Promoting the Art of Painting in Ireland* (1790), and *Historical Memoir on Italian Tragedy* (1799).

His travels restricted by asthma and failing health, he never met Hayley, who introduced him to CS, or CS herself, who proposed that they meet while he was on a rare visit to England. CS's letters to Walker are among her liveliest and most revealing, covering a range of topics from literary pursuits and ideas to events in her family's life.

The Reverend Joseph Warton, D.D. (1722–1800), critic and educator, was headmaster at Winchester College, where Charles and Lionel were educated. In 1788, Dr. Warton became prebendary at Winchester and obtained the rectory at Upham. He resigned as headmaster in 1795. His term at "Winton" was known for his lax discipline, which resulted in "the rebellion of 1793"; Lionel was one of its student leaders. Even so, Dr. Warton was admired as a learned and benevolent man, as was his younger brother Thomas (1728–1790), a poet, particularly a writer of sonnets, and poet laureate from 1785 until his death.

Works Consulted

This list does not include standard reference works consulted such as Burke's Peerage, County Families, *biographical dictionaries, London and provincial directories, directories to the book trades, atlases and geographical works, concordances and dictionaries, or law, medical, and military lists. The following abbreviations of standard works and archives appear in the annotations to the letters:*

DNB	Dictionary of National Biography
IRO	*India Records Office, London*
OED	Oxford English Dictionary
PHA	*Petworth House Archives, Petworth, Sussex*
PRO	*Public Records Office, London*
SRO	*Surrey Records Office*
WSRO	*West Sussex Record Office, Chichester, Sussex*

Adams, Rev. H. C. *Wykehamica: A History of Winchester College and Commoners, From the Foundation to the Present Day.* Oxford: James Parker, 1878.

Alumni Oxonienses: The Members of the University of Oxford, 1715–1886. 4 vols. Oxford: Parker, 1891.

Ayling, Stanley. *George the Third.* London: Collins, 1972.

Barbeau, Alfred. *Life and Letters at Bath in the Eighteenth Century.* New York: Dodd, Mead, 1904.

Bellenger, Dominic Aidan. *The French Exiled Clergy in the British Isles after 1789: An Historical Introduction and Working List.* Bath: Downside Abbey, 1986.

Berry, Mary, and Agnes Berry. *The Berry Papers: Being the Correspondence, Hitherto Unpublished, of Mary and Agnes Berry, 1763–1852.* Ed. Lewis Melville. London: John Lane, 1914.

Bessborough, Henrietta Frances Spencer Ponsonby, countess of. *Lady Bessborough and Her Family Circle.* Ed. the earl of Bessborough and A. Aspinall. London: John Murray, 1940.

Besterman, Theodore, ed. *The Publishing Firm of Cadell and Davies: Select Correspondence and Accounts, 1793–1836.* London: Oxford University Press, 1938.

Bishop, [Evelyn] Morchard. *Blake's Hayley: The Life, Works, and Friendships of William Hayley.* London: Victor Gollancz, 1951.

Brandow, James C., comp. *Genealogies of Barbados Families: From "Caribbeana" and "The Journal of the Barbados Museum and Historical Society."* Baltimore, Md.: Genealogical Publishing, 1983.

Brooke, John. *King George III*. London: Constable, 1792.

Butler, Maida. "Mrs. Smith and Mr. Cadell." *Sussex County Magazine* 30 (1956): 330–34.

Clifford, James L. *Hester Lynch Piozzi.* 2nd ed. New York: Columbia University Press, 1987.

Cokayne, George Edward. *The Complete Peerage of England, Scotland, Ireland, Great Britain, and the United Kingdom.* Ed. Vickery Gibbs. 13 vols. London: St. Catherine Press, 1910.

Cowper, William. *The Letters and Prose Writings of William Cowper.* Ed. James King and Charles Ryskamp. 5 vols. Oxford: Clarendon, 1979–86.

Cross, Nigel. *The Royal Literary Fund: 1790–1918: An Introduction to the Fund's History and Archives with an Index of Applicants.* London: World Microfilms Publications, 1984.

Cumberland, Richard. *Memoirs of Richard Cumberland. Written by Himself; Containing an Account of His Life and Writings . . .* 2 vols. London: Lackington and Allen, 1807.

Dallaway, James. *History of the Western Division of the County of Sussex, including the Rapes of Chichester, Arundel, and Bramber.* London: T. Bensley and Son, 1819.

Devonshire, Georgiana Spencer Cavendish, duchess of. *Georgiana; Extracts from the Correspondence of Georgiana, Duchess of Devonshire.* Ed. the earl of Bessborough. London: John Murray, 1955.

Dodwell, [Edward], and [James Samuel] Miles. *Alphabetical List of the Honble. East India Company Bengal Civil Servants, from the Year 1780, to the Year 1838.* London: Woking, 1839.

Dorset, Catherine. "Charlotte Smith." In *The Miscellaneous Prose Works of Sir Walter Scott, Bart.,* by Sir Walter Scott, 4:20–58. Edinburgh: Robert Cadell, 1834.

Eeles, Henry S. *Frant: A Parish History.* Tunbridge Wells: Courier, 1947.

The English Novel, 1770–1829: A Bibliographical Survey of Prose Fiction Published in the British Isles. Peter Garside, James Raven, and Rainer Schöwerling, gen. eds., Vol. 1, *1770–1799.* Ed. James Raven and Antonia Forster. Oxford: Oxford University Press, 2000.

Fleet, Charles. *Glimpses of Our Ancestors in Sussex; with Sketches of Sussex Characters, Remarkable Incidents, etc.* 2nd ed. Lewes: Farncombe, 1882.

Fletcher, Loraine. *Charlotte Smith: A Critical Biography.* New York: St. Martin's Press, 1998.

Fry, Carroll. *Charlotte Smith.* New York: Twayne, 1996.

Haller, William. *The Early Life of Robert Southey: 1774–1803.* New York: Columbia University Press, 1917.

Hayley, William. *The Epitaph Book of William Hayley,* ed. Noel H. Osborne. Chichester: Chichester City Council, 1965.

———. *Memoirs of the Life and Writings of William Hayley, Esq., the Friend and Biographer of Cowper, Written by Himself.* Ed. John Johnson. 2 vols. London: Henry Colburn, 1823.

[Hays, Mary]. "Mrs. Charlotte Smith." In *British Public Characters,* ed. Richard Phillips, 3:44–67. London: T. Gillet, 1800–1801.

Hibbert, Christopher. *George IV, Prince of Wales: 1762–1811.* London: Longman, 1972.

Hilbish, Florence May Anna. *Charlotte Smith, Poet and Novelist (1749–1806).* Philadelphia: University of Pennsylvania Press, 1941.

Holgate, Clifford Wyndham. *Winchester Long Rolls, 1723–1812.* Winchester: Wells, 1904.

Jerrome, Peter. *Lightly Tread Here: An Affectionate Look at Petworth's Ancient Streets.* Petworth: Window Press, 1990.

———, ed. *Tales of Old Petworth.* Petworth: Window Press, 1976.

Jones, S. Paul. *A List of French Prose Fiction from 1700 to 1750.* New York: H. W. Wilson, 1939.

King, James. *William Cowper: A Biography.* Durham, N.C.: Duke University Press, 1986.

Kirby, Thomas Frederick. *Winchester Scholars: A List of the Wardens, Fellows, and Scholars of Saint Mary College of Winchester, Commonly Called Winchester College.* London: Henry Frowde, 1888.

Lower, Mark Antony. *The Worthies of Sussex: Biographical Sketches of the Most Eminent Natives or Inhabitants of the County.* Lewes: G. P. Bacon, 1865.

Lucas, E. V. *Highways and Byways in Sussex.* London: Macmillan, 1924.

Maxted, Ian. *The London Book Trades: 1775–1800: A Preliminary Checklist of Members.* Old Woking, Surrey: Gresham Press, 1977.

McKillip, Alan Dugald. "Charlotte Smith's Letters." *Huntington Library Quarterly* 15 (1951–52): 237–55.

Montague, Lady Mary Wortley. *Letters of the Right Honourable Lady M——y W——y M——e: Written, During Her Travels in Europe, Asia, and Africa.* 3 vols. 3rd ed. London: T. Becket and P. A. De Hondt, 1763.

Nichols, John. *Illustrations of the Literary History of the Eighteenth Century, Consisting of Authentic Memoirs and Original Letters of Eminent Persons.* 6 vols. London: Nichols, 1817–31.

O'Donnell, H[enry], Capt. *Historical Records of the Fourteenth Regiment, now the Prince of Wales Own (West Yorkshire Regiment,) from Its Formation, in 1685, to 1892.* Devonport: A. H. Swiss, [1983].

Peach, R. E. *Historic Houses in Bath and Their Associations.* Vol. 2. London: Simpkin, Marshall, 1884.

Price, F. G. Hilton. *A Handbook of London Bankers.* New York: Burt Franklin, 1970.

Reed, Mark L. *Wordsworth: The Chronology of the Early Years, 1770–1799.* Cambridge, Mass.: Harvard University Press, 1967.

The Registers of Marriages of St. Mary le Bone, Middlesex, 1796–1801. Ed. W. Bruce Bannerman. Publications of the Harleian Society, 54. London: Harleian Society, 1924.

Seward, Anna. *Letters of Anna Seward; Written between the Years 1784 and 1807.* London: Longman, Hurst, Rees, 1807.

———. *Memoirs of the Life of Dr. Darwin, Chiefly during His Residence at Lichfield, with Anecdotes of His Friends, and Criticisms on His Writings.* London: J. Johnson, 1804.

Southey, Robert. *New Letters of Robert Southey.* Ed. Kenneth Curry. Vol. 1. New York: Columbia University Press, 1965.

Stanton, Judith. "Charlotte Smith's 'Literary Business': Income, Patronage, and Poverty." *Age of Johnson: A Scholarly Annual* 1 (1987): 375–401.

Sterne, Laurence. *The Life and Opinions of Tristram Shandy, Gentleman.* Vols. 1–3 of *The Florida Edition of the Works of Laurence Sterne.* Ed. Melvyn New and Joan New. [Gainesville]: University Presses of Florida, 1978.

Strangford, Percy Clinton Sidney Smythe, Viscount. *Poems, from the Portuguese of the Luis de Cameons: with Remarks on His Life and Writing.* London: J. Carpenter, 1804.

Tompkins, J. M. S. *The Popular Novel in England, 1770–1800.* London: Constable, 1932. Reprint, Lincoln: University of Nebraska Press, 1961.

Turner, Rufus Paul. "Charlotte Smith (1749–1806): New Light on Her Life and Literary Career." Ph.D. diss., University of Southern California, 1966.

Vere, Foster, ed. *The Two Duchesses; Georgiana, Duchess of Devonshire, Elizabeth, Duchess of Devonshire: Family Correspondence . . . , 1777–1859.* London: Blackie and Son, 1898.

Wallis, P. J., and R. V. Wallis. *Eighteenth Century Medics (Subscriptions, Licenses, Apprenticeships).* 2nd ed. Newcastle upon Tyne: Project for Historical Biobibliography, 1988.

Woodress, James. *A Yankee's Odyssey: The Life of Joel Barlow.* Philadelphia: Lippincott, 1958.

Index

Page numbers in italics refer to illustrations of letters. Page numbers in bold refer to letters. Names in bold are treated in biographical notes.

CHARLOTTE SMITH, English novelist, poet, and translator, was author of the novels *Emmeline, or the Orphan of the Castle* (1788), *Ethelinde* (1789), *Celestina* (1791), *Desmond* (1792), *The Old Manor House* (1793), *The Banished Man* (1794), *Montalbert* (1795), *Marchmont* (1796), *The Young Philosopher* (1798), and *Letters of a Solitary Wanderer* (1800, 1802). Volumes of poetry included *Elegiac Sonnets* (1784 and 1797), *The Emigrants* (1793), and *Beachy Head* (1807). She translated the French novel *Manon Lescaut* (1731) by Abbé Prévost, as well as accounts of several famous trials from *Causes célèbres et intéressantes,* which appeared as *The Romance of Real Life* (1786). She also wrote six educational books for children.

Judith Phillips Stanton has taught courses in women's studies and feminist theory at Clemson University and has published articles on Charlotte Smith and statistical studies of trends in eighteenth-century women's writing. Now an independent scholar, she continues her work on Smith and has published three historical romances.